THE
QUR'AN

THE
QUR'AN

The Eternal Revelation vouchsafed to Muhammad
The Seal of the Prophets

Arabic text with a new translation by
Muhammad Zafrulla Khan

OLIVE
BRANCH
PRESS

An imprint of Interlink Publishing Group, Inc.
NEW YORK

First American paperback edition published 1997 by

Olive Branch Press
An imprint of Interlink Publishing Group, Inc.
99 Seventh Avenue
Brooklyn, New York 11215

Originally published in Great Britain by Curzon Press, Ltd.

Library of Congress Cataloging-in-Publication Data

Koran. English and Arabic
The Quran = [Qur'an majid]: the eternal revelation
vouchsafed to Muhammad, the Seal of the Prophets / Arabic
text with a new translation by Muhammad Zafrulla Khan.
First American paperback edition.
p. cm.
ISBN 1-56656-255-4
I.   Khan, Muhammad Zafrulla, Sir 1893 —. II. Title
III. Title: Qur'an majid.
BP109.K48 1991   90—7180
297'. 122521—dc20   CIP

Printed and bound in Canada
10 9 8 7 6 5 4 3 2 1

CONTENTS

PREFACE

There are several good English translations of the Holy Quran, some of the more recent ones a great improvement on some of the earlier ones. The Quran being the Scripture of one of the great faiths, even non-Muslim scholars who have essayed a translation of its text into English have, with one or two regrettable exceptions in earlier years, approached their task in a spirit of reverence. But Muslims and non-Muslims alike have, with rare exceptions, generally adhered to the Arabic idiom in the English version. The result has been an Arabicised version of the text in English. Where the translation of the text is supplemented with explanatory notes a reader unfamiliar with Arabic is able, with diligence and patience, to spell out the meaning which a too faithful adherence to Arabic idiom may have left obscure in the translation. Where no notes are available and the reader has no access to any other aid in unravelling the meaning of such passages and phrases, he is apt to feel frustrated and to abandon the effort to penetrate to the true meaning of the Quran.

Yet, one appreciates the dilemma of the translator. If the original is not faithfully adhered to, even in the matter of idiom and style, the translator may be charged with taking liberties with the sacred text. Where explanatory notes are furnished the task of the reader is rendered laborious, and if he is unable to spare the time needed for the study of the notes he may feel his effort is tedious and unrewarding.

The Quran has been pronounced untranslatable by one of its best and most reverent translators who is gifted with an exceptional and most delicate faculty of transmuting Arabic and Persian poetry and prose into delightful English. His pronouncement is broadly true; but the effort must nevertheless be made. His own has produced an excellent translation, faithful and literal, which by the adoption of certain simple devices has made it comparatively easy to discover the meaning, so far as a translation is capable of conveying it. He has not given his translation that title but that does not in the least detract from its value.

However careful and meritorious a translation may be, it can only go a certain distance in helping to convey the meaning of a book so many-faceted and rich in meaning as is the Quran. The main burden of the effort needed for the understanding of the Quran must be borne by the reader himself. The translator's part is to make the bearing of that burden easy, attractive and rewarding. There are several ways of doing this. Explanatory notes are perhaps the most helpful way. But in the crowded pattern of today's life, few can afford the time needed to eke out the sense of every unfamiliar phrase through a study of voluminous explanatory notes, however illuminating. One of the urgent, inescapable needs of today is that the Quran be widely read, pondered and accepted as a guide. The values inculcated by it need to be put into effect in our daily lives at every level. This may be neglected only at direst peril. That is no longer hypothetical.

We find ourselves in the midst of the peril which is advancing from many directions at accelerated speed.

This handy volume is a humble and modest effort at making a beginner's study of the Quran a cheering, even an absorbing and profitable experience. The translation is strictly faithful in meaning to the text though it spells out, where it is inescapable, the inherent implications which would be obvious to one familiar with the language of the original and the context of the events referred to, but would escape those who do not possess that advantage. Even the Arabic idiom has been retained except where adherence to it would make the meaning elusive and difficult to discover. An attempt has been made to so arrange the paragraphs as to preserve the underlying continuity of the context.

All this is designed to encourage the reader to try to discover and arrive at the meaning through his own sustained effort. That which he discovers for himself will become a permanent possession, and to the degree to which it is absorbed and acted upon it will help to mould his life into a wholly beneficent pattern.

The Introduction is designed to serve as a key to the study of the Quran and should itself be carefully studied. The reader will find that it does not spell out anything in detail. It operates as a pointer for the reader's mind and beckons it on to an exercise, necessary and essential, for a profitable study of the Quran. By his study of the Introduction the reader will acquire some familiarity with the style, diction, the method of persuasion and the manner of reasoning of the Quran. He will find this helpful when he enters upon a study of the Quran itself.

To some degree the Introduction essays to fill the need that would be filled by explanatory notes. By equipping himself in advance with the help that the Introduction is designed to furnish him, the reader will be in a better position to grasp the meaning of the Quran as he proceeds with his study, than if he were to depend entirely upon a series of explanatory notes. He will already have trained himself to some degree for a meaningful study.

This study must in turn be pursued with the utmost attention and should be constantly repeated. To reap a full measure of benefit from it, the Divine Book must be wooed with the diligence, the devotion, the delicacy, the zeal, the reverence and the assiduity of the lover. The treasures of the Quran are inexhaustible. It endows most generously those who seek them with sincere persistence. An eminent divine and a great lover of the Quran has very truly said:

I compare not this Light with the light of the sun, for I perceive a hundred orbs bright as the sun revolving joyously around it.

It will be noted that every chapter of the Quran, with the sole exception of the ninth, which some commentators have surmised is a continuation of the eighth chapter, opens with the invocation: 'In the name of Allah, Most Gracious, Ever Merciful.' The invocation is part of the revelation and is numbered as the first verse of each chapter, the succeeding verses being numbered accordingly. This is the system followed in the Arabic text and the translation, and the references set out in the Introduction. As some editions and translations do not include the invocation in the numbering, their numbering of the verses, except in the case of the ninth chapter, is generally one short of that followed here. The reader needs to keep this in mind for purposes of comparison.

Some chapters, for instance the second, third, seventh, eleventh to fifteenth, etc. begin with combinations of letters which follow immediately after the invocation. Commentators are not agreed upon their significance. The most acceptable explanation, which is offered on good authority and which has been adopted here, is that these are abbreviations of Divine attributes which are apposite to the subject matter of the chapter.

The Quran is verbal revelation and thus literally the Word of Allah. The reader needs to keep in mind that it is Allah speaking. The pronouns I, We, My, Ours, Ourself, therefore, obviously refer to the Divine; but often He, His, Him are also used to indicate the Divine, and there is constantly a transition from the first person to the third and *vice versa*. The English usage of employing the capital letter for the purpose of indicating that the pronoun has reference to the Divine proves very helpful in this context. Nevertheless, in the beginning the reader needs to keep himself alert in the matter of this frequent transition and interchange between pronouns. Once he becomes familiar with the style of the Quran he will experience no difficulty in this behalf.

The Quran is extremely concise and is a masterpiece of condensation. It leaves a great deal to the intelligence of the reader, urges reflection and appeals constantly to the understanding. In the Introduction an effort has been made to induce in the mind of the reader the attitude that would help him to make the most of the translation. The translation itself is so patterned as to help the reader in his effort to penetrate to the true meaning of the text. It is of the utmost importance that urged on by his own eagerness, he should succeed mainly through his own effort in his quest. Once he is convinced how richly rewarding that quest can be, he will find a vast domain opening out before him for his profitable exploration. He will be taken by the hand, by Divine grace and mercy, and led into a universe of the spirit of unsuspected and exceeding charm and beauty.

For those of us who have been associated together in preparing the translation, it has been a sheer labour of love. We lay no claim to high scholarship or profound thinking. But we have had the good fortune of having access to unexceptionable sources upon which we have based ourselves. Where we have fallen short, the default is ours. We pray Allah for better and clearer guidance and an early opportunity of repairing our defaults. Should our effort prove helpful in leading any of our fellow beings to a better understanding and appreciation of Allah's greatest bounty bestowed upon man, our humble gratitude would be due to Him to Whom all praise is due, the Bestower of all bounties. We offer our sincere prayers in behalf of those upon whose works we have been privileged to draw throughout. May Allah, of His abundant grace, richly reward them. Amen.

Our last word is one of humble praise to Allah, Who nourishes, sustains and leads stage by stage towards perfection all the worlds, and we call down His blessings upon and offer the salutation of peace to His Messenger Muhammad, through whom mankind has been vouchsafed the vast Bounty and Glory, which is the Quran.

THE EDITORS

PREFACE TO THE THIRD EDITION

Translation is a difficult task of great delicacy, especially when the original is as rich and vast in meaning as Arabic. The difficulty is multiplied manifold in the case of a translation of the Quran, which being verbal revelation is the very Word of God, and whose meaning is limitless and inexhaustible (18.110; 31.28).

A translation, not being a commentary, is tied down to one rendering out of several possible ones, and the choice is not always an easy one. The context is very helpful in this behalf, but the reader should bear it constantly in mind that the translator's choice does by no means exclude alternative renderings, some of which might be even more apposite in a certain combination of circumstances, than the one selected by him.

The translation here offered normally adheres to the simple primary connotation of words which is easy of comprehension and is free from commentarial controversies. Yet on occasion, the context compels recourse to the secondary, rather than the primary, connotation of a word or phrase. Sometimes a word or phrase is encountered which conveys opposite meanings at the same time, and the context permits recourse to either. In such case two or more renderings are not only possible but may even be intended. The translator makes a choice, leaving it to the commentator to enlarge upon the different facets. Some illustrations might prove helpful.

The commandment with regard to the obligatory fast of Ramadhan lays down: 'Whoso from among you should be ailing or should be on a journey, shall complete the reckoning by fasting on a corresponding number of other days; for those who find fasting a strain hard to bear is an expiation, the feeding of a poor person, if they can afford it' (2.185).

The expression in the original which has been construed as a strain hard to bear (*yuteequnahu*) also connotes having the capacity for, depending upon whether it has reference to observing the fast or to feeding a poor person. The translation has to a certain degree adopted both, preferring the secondary, but equally valid, connotation to the primary one.

It is said of Abraham's wife that on learning of the doom of Lot's people: 'She too was perturbed, whereupon We conveyed to her the glad tidings of the birth of Isaac, and beyond Isaac of Jacob' (11.72). Here the original which has been construed as was perturbed (*dhahakat*) also connotes smiled, but the context is compulsive that the secondary connotation, namely perturbation, must be preferred and that is the connotation adopted in the translation.

We read: 'So continue to admonish for admonition always helps' (87.10). The verse is equally capable of the construction: 'Continue to admonish where admonition should be helpful', but again the context almost demands the construction which has been adopted in the translation.

A wife and a husband are described as a garment for each other (2.188). It is, however, obvious to an intelligent reader that the expression garment has been used not in its literal sense but in its metaphorical connotation as something which is closest to the person wearing it and affords protection and is a means of adornment.

The Holy Prophet is commanded: 'Purify thy garments' (74.5). The expression for garments (*thayab*) also connotes companions or associates. Being mindful of the context, that is to say of the source of the command and the person commanded, the translation prefers the rendering: 'Purify those around thee'. For the same reason in the succeeding verse the commandment, the primary connotation of which is: 'Discard all impurity', has been rendered: 'Stamp out idolatry', thus preferring the spiritual rather than the material connotation.

There are many instances of an expression having been used in its various connotations in different contexts; for instance, the expression *deen* connotes judgment, judgment day, victory, government, decision, faith, religion, etc., and has been construed in accord with each context in which it has been employed. Similarly the expression *hudan* has been construed as connoting guidance as well as leading to the goal.

The expression which has been construed as: 'Observing prayer', (*yuqeemunas salat*) has several simultaneous connotations; for instance, performing Prayer with full concentration, performing Prayer in congregation, propagating the observance of Prayer among the community, observing Prayer in conformity with all the conditions laid down, safeguarding Prayer against every shortcoming, observing Prayer regularly without interruption, and so on. It is not, however, possible to include more than one rendering in the translation.

The expression *qatl* has also several connotations; for instance, murder, slaying, reducing the severity of something, forming a design to kill, moral ruin, boycotting etc.

In this new edition, the Introduction has been expanded to include three subjects at the end. Certain textual changes have been made in the translation in order to reinforce the meaning.

April, 1981

INTRODUCTION

THE REVELATION OF THE QURAN

The Quran is a record of the verbal revelation vouchsafed to Muhammaa, the Prophet of Islam (on whom be peace) during a period of approximately twenty-two years at Mecca (610—622) and Medina (622—632). The arrangement of the text does not follow the chronological order of the revelation. The very first revelation was verses 2—6 of Chapter 96. The last Chapter revealed was Chapter 110.

When a verse or group of verses was revealed the Prophet announced the text of the revelation and indicated its place in the sequence of the Quran. It was memorised in the order of the sequence and was recited in the Prayer services and otherwise in that order. The Prophet himself was not conversant with reading and writing (29.49) but, when the assistance of those so conversant became available, he selected a half dozen of them as scribes for the revelation. As the revelation came he would send for one of them and dictate the text to him, and also proclaim it, so that it could be memorised forthwith. There were few facilities for recording the text and those available were of a primitive character, but those entrusted with the task managed to transcribe the text as best they could. The principal and the most reliable method of preserving the text was, however, to memorise it. Committing the text of the revelation to memory was considered a most meritorious activity and was obviously beneficial in many ways for the small but growing community of believers. With the increase in its members the number of those who could recite the entire text from memory also went on increasing. Today they are counted in hundreds of thousands, possibly in millions, and the number of those who can recite portions of the Quran from memory certainly exceeds a hundred million.

The memorising of the text of the Quran demands the utmost care and is achieved so painstakingly that strict accuracy is ensured. Once achieved it is preserved and safeguarded by dint of constant recitation.

As facilities for reproducing the text in manuscript, and later in print, became available the fullest advantage was taken of them, but this did not obviate the need of committing the entire text to memory in proper sequence. The easy availability of the text in writing only made it easier to commit it to memory. The accuracy of the written or printed text needs to be attested by at least two persons of good repute who can recite it from memory, and not the other way about.

MEANING OF QURAN

Quran means that which is read, recited, rehearsed. The very first revelation directed the Prophet (on whom be peace): 'Recite in the name of thy Lord Who created everything. He created man from a clot of blood. Recite, for thy Lord is Most Beneficent, Who has taught by the pen, taught man that which he knew not.' (96.2—6). The name Quran was bestowed upon the revelation by Allah (12.3; 43.4).

The very name is a grand prophecy, the continuous fulfilment of which is proof of the Divine authorship of the Book. The name Quran signifies that the Book would be widely read, recited and rehearsed through the ages in ever expanding regions; and thus has it been. It has continued to be read, recited and rehearsed *in the original*, that is to say, in the very words of the revelation, by many times the number of people who could have had access to any other revealed scripture in the original language of that scripture. This could not be achieved through any human contrivance; it could only be brought about by Divine design.

SAFEGUARDING OF THE QURAN

Another more explicit and even more striking prophecy is: 'Surely, We Ourself have sent down this Exhortation, and We will most surely safeguard it.' (15.10). The safeguarding of the Exhortation comprises several aspects, the most important being the preservation of the integrity of the text of the revelation. In this context it must be borne in mind that the Quran was revealed piecemeal in the course of more than twenty years during the greater part of which the Prophet (on whom be peace) and the Muslims enjoyed little peace and tranquillity and were seldom free from anxiety of some kind or another. There was little literacy in Mecca, and only limited though steadily increasing literacy in Medina. The Prophet himself was not literate (29.49). Paper and other facilities for preserving a record with which we are familiar today were normally not available in the Central Arabia of the early seventh century. Nevertheless, the most thorough and critical research carried out by Western orientalists has established that the Quran is, word for word, exactly as Muhammad (on whom be peace) gave it out to the world as the revelation vouchsafed to him.

An equally vital aspect of the safeguarding of the Exhortation is that the language in which it is contained should continue in vigorous currency and should never fall into disuse.

It would not be enough for the text to be preserved intact if the means of access to it were rendered inadequate or obscure. We are familiar with the example of languages which, after having achieved luxuriant flowering and having produced marvellous literary masterpieces fell completely into disuse so that they became subjects of archaeological research and now only limited circles of savants are able to decipher and interpret such rare specimens as diligent search may succeed in rescuing from the ruins of ancient civilizations.

This has resulted from the natural process of evolution which serves to strengthen and to bestow an independent existence on dialects deriving from these languages as, for instance, Italian, French and Spanish, the rich and vigorous daughters of Latin which itself, having passed through a long period of drying up, is now withering like its sister, ancient Greek.

In the case of classical Arabic a totally different pattern is discernible. From the archaeologist's well-known epitaph of the fourth century, the

oldest extant specimen of written Arabic, through the flourishing literary
pre-Islamic period with Imr-ul-Qais, Zuhair ibn Abi Salma, Aws ibn Hajar,
on and on, through the transcendant glory of the Arabic language, the
Exalted Quran, after the phenomenon of explosive domination during the
centuries of the great and vast Islamic Empire until our own era, classical
Arabic has always demonstrated, in its grammar and lexicography, an
astonishing unity and vigour which could not be the result of any human
contrivance.

Even during the deep slumber that oppressed the Islamic world for about
five hundred years until the middle of the nineteenth century, no dialect
or local tongue deriving from Arabic succeeded in developing itself to the
dignity of a rival literary language. During these five centuries classical
Arabic, the language of the Quran, remained aloof and venerated as a privileged repository and source of nourishment of enfeebled Islamic values.
We are now witnessing an amazing process of rejuvenation and vigorous
expansion of Arabic literature in which, far from yielding to some local
dialect, the original, ever alive and now once more completely awake, spirit
of the language which is the proud bearer of the Message of Allah, the
Noble Quran, pours itself forth in literary jewels which are read, understood and appreciated over much larger areas than was the case fourteen
centuries ago. This is part of the fulfilment of the Divine assurance of safeguarding the Exhortation. The avenues of access to it have always been
wide open.

It must be recognized that there is no substantial deviation between the
style and pattern of classical Arabic and those that characterize the living
language that flourishes again in revived Islam, specimens of which may
be enjoyed in the works of a galaxy of such modern writers as, to name only
a few out of a host, Sulaiman-al-Bustani, Wali-ad-Din Yeghen, Jameel-
al-Mudawwar, Aisha-at-Taimuriyya, Jurji Zaidan, Ilia Abu Madi and Ta
Ha Husain.

THE QURAN AND PREVIOUS SCRIPTURES

The Quran affirms the truth of previous revelations. 'Surely, We sent
down the Torah full of guidance and light' (5.45). 'We caused Jesus son of
Mary to follow in their footsteps, fulfilling that which was revealed before
him in the Torah; and We gave him the Gospel which contained guidance
and light, fulfilling that which was revealed before it in the Torah, and
a guidance and an admonition for the righteous.' (5.47) But it points out
that previous revelations have suffered from interpolations and perversions
at the hands of those whose duty it was to safeguard them (2.80, 3.79).

The Quran fulfils that which was revealed before it and also acts as
a guardian over it; pointing out, where necessary, the perversion of its
text or meaning by those who professed to follow it. 'We have revealed
unto thee this Book comprising the truth and fulfilling that which was
revealed before it of the Book, and as a guardian over it.' (5.49) 'People
of the Book, there has come to you Our Messenger who unfolds to you much
of that which you used to hide of the Book and he overlooks many of your
defaults.' (5.16)

For instance, the Quran emphasizes the purity and righteousness of all Prophets, including all those mentioned in the Bible, thus rejecting as perversions and interpolations such passages in the Bible as could be construed as casting reflections on the purity, righteousness, sincerity or singleminded devotion of any of them. Abraham is held up as a model of virtue (16.121) in complete submission to the Lord of the worlds (2.132), a truthful person and a Prophet (19.42). Lot is described as one of the righteous upon whom God had bestowed wisdom and knowledge, and whom He admitted to His mercy (21.75, 76). Moses is declared to have been free from blemish (20.23). Of David it is said: 'He turned constantly to Us' (38.18). 'We bestowed upon him wisdom and decisive judgment' (38.21). He was God's vicegerent in the earth (38.27). Solomon is cleared of all suspicion of having swerved from the worship of the One True God (2.103; 27.45).

Mary, mother of Jesus, is referred to in the Quran with far greater reverence than in the Gospels. 'The angels said to Mary: Allah has exalted thee and purified thee and chosen thee from among all the women of thy time' (3.43). She is cited as an example for the believers in her obedience to Allah (66.13). Jesus was always gentle and dutiful towards her (19.33).

ORIGINAL SIN

The Quran does not countenance the idea of original sin, nor anything to which it has given rise. It stresses as fundamental the purity of 'the nature designed by Allah — the nature according to which He has fashioned mankind. There is no altering the creation of Allah. That is the everlasting religion; but most people know not' (30.31). Thus the function of religion is to assist man in fostering his inherent pure nature with which his Beneficent Creator has endowed him, to guide him along the straight path, to warn him of pitfalls and deviations and, should he slip or go astray, to show him how he may win back to grace.

This is illustrated in that which befell Adam and his wife. 'We commanded: Adam, dwell thou and thy wife in the garden, and eat plentifully therefrom wherever you will, but approach not this one tree, lest you be of the wrongdoers. But Satan caused them both to slip from their stand of obedience by means of that tree and thus drove them out of the state in which they were. Whereupon We decreed: Go forth; some of you are enemies of others, and for you there is in the earth a place of abode and provision for a time. Thereafter Adam learnt certain words of prayer from his Lord, and began to pray as he was taught. So He turned towards him with mercy; surely, He is Oft-returning with compassion towards His creatures and is Ever Merciful. We decreed: Go forth hence, all of you, but remember that if there comes to you guidance from Me, then whoso follows My guidance, on them shall come no fear nor shall they grieve; but such as disbelieve and reject Our Signs as false these shall be the inmates of the Fire; therein shall they abide' (2.36—40). 'They pleaded: Our Lord, we have wronged ourselves; and if Thou forgive us not and have not mercy on us, we shall surely be of the lost' (7.24). 'We indeed laid a commandment on Adam aforetime, but he forgot; yet We did not discover in him any determination to disobey' (20.116). 'Adam thus disobeyed his Lord and fell into error. Then his Lord chose him for His grace, and turned to him with mercy and guided him' (20.122, 123).

ATONEMENT AND REPENTANCE

No one can atone for another. 'Everyone's doings have We fastened firmly to his neck; and on the Day of Judgment We shall place before him a book which he will find wide open, and he will be told: Read thy record, thou art sufficient as a reckoner against thyself this day. He who follows the right way follows it to his own good; and he who goes astray, does it to his own loss. He who carries a responsibility cannot be relieved of it by another' (17.14—16). 'No one can bear the burden of another. If a heavily laden one should call another to carry his load, naught of it shall be carried by the other, even though he be a kinsman' (35.19). The only way is to turn to Allah in sincere repentance. He accepts repentance and forgives sins (40.4). 'He it is Who accepts repentance from His servants and forgives sins, and knows all that you do' (42.26). 'Whatever misfortune befalls you is in consequence of that which you practise. He overlooks many of your defaults' (42.31). 'Convey to them: O My servants who have committed excesses against your own selves, despair not of the mercy of Allah, surely Allah forgives all sins. He is Most Forgiving, Ever Merciful. Turn ye to your Lord and submit yourselves to Him before the punishment overtakes you and no one is able to help you' (39.54, 55).

'When those who believe in Our Signs come to thee, greet them with: Peace unto you. Your Lord has charged Himself with mercy, so that whoso among you does evil, in ignorance, and repents thereafter and amends, then He is Most Forgiving, Ever Merciful' (6.55). 'Surely, thy Lord is Most Forgiving, Ever Merciful towards those who do evil in ignorance and truly repent thereafter and make amends' (16.120).

'Allah would accept the repentance only of those who do evil in ignorance and then are quick to repent. These are they to whom Allah turns with mercy. Allah is All-Knowing, Wise. Repentance is not for those who continue in their evil courses until, when death faces one of them, he exclaims: I do now repent; nor for those who die disbelieving. It is these for whom We have prepared a painful chastisement' (4.18, 19).

Adam erred in ignorance, having been misled by Satan, and as soon as he discovered his error he repented. So his Lord turned to him in mercy and guided him and chose him for His grace (20.123).

ADAM AND SATAN

According to the Quran, Iblis was not an angel who fell from grace because he disobeyed the command of his Lord. Angels are a creation who always carry out the commands of their Lord and never disobey (16.51; 66.7). Iblis was the prototype of fiery-tempered arrogant men, who, because of his pride and arrogance, disobeyed the command of his Lord. His type is encountered in all climes, all ages and all guises. 'Call to mind when We commanded the angels: Fall down prostrate along with Adam. They did so, but Iblis did not. He was one of the fiery-tempered arrogant ones, so he disobeyed the command of his Lord. Will you then take him and his progeny, all of whom are your enemies, for friends instead of Me? Evil is this exchange for the wrongdoers' (18.51).

Adam was not the first man. He was the first whose faculties had been developed to a degree that he could become the recipient of revelation. In that capacity he was appointed God's vicegerent on earth (2.31) and was instructed in elementary social values (20.119, 120). The foundation of human society was thus laid. But pride and arrogance prompted opposition to Adam, God's vicegerent. 'Call to mind when thy Lord apprised the angels: I am about to create man from clay; so when I have brought his faculties to perfection, and have breathed into him of My Spirit, fall ye down in submission to him. The angels submitted, all of them together, but Iblis did not. He behaved arrogantly, and he was of the disbelievers. Allah demanded of him: Iblis, what hindered thee from submitting to one whom I had created of My own power? Art thou too proud, or dost thou fancy thyself as being too exalted? Iblis replied: I am better than he. Me hast Thou created of fire and him hast Thou created of clay' (38.72—77).

MEANING OF JINN

The word jinn has been used in the Quran in diverse connotations. When used in juxtaposition to man, it connotes a class or group who consider themselves distinct from or above the ordinary run of people. The root of the word connotes that which is covered up; hence, those who for any reason, birth, wealth, rank, dignity, office, skill, power, authority, strength or the like would have a tendency to regard themselves as superior to and to withdraw themselves from the society and companionship of their less-favoured fellows. For instance, the aristocracy vis-a-vis the commonalty, the patricians vis-a-vis the plebeians, the rich vis-a-vis the poor, the affluent vis-a-vis the indigent, the skilled vis-a-vis the unskilled. Where this situation continues over a period the favoured class or group develops a sensitiveness concerning that which it regards as its position or its privileges. Any change affecting these is viewed as a threat and is resented. Resentment may flare up and manifest itself in fiery outbursts of temper.

Divine guidance is treated as a challenge by such a class or group which considers itself above such guidance. This sparked Satan's disobedience to the Divine Command to submit to Adam, God's vicegerent (2. 31). He sought to justify it by asserting his superiority over Adam whose nature had been moulded like clay to receive the Divine impress, while Satan and his ilk had cultivated fiery, arrogant tempers and considered submission a humiliation. They were not humble like Adam, but creatures of hot wind (15.27, 28) and fierce blasts (55.15, 16).

The opponents of Prophets are described as Satans from among men and jinn, meaning rebellious ones from among men, high and low (6.113) and the mission of Prophets is directed towards the company of jinn and men meaning men big and small (6.131). If men and jinn (i.e. all men, high and low) combined together to produce the like of this Quran, they would not be able to produce the like thereof, eveu though they all combined in the effort (17.89).

'Of the people, high and low (jinn and men) created to be recipients of Our mercy, many are headed for hell. They have hearts but they do not use them for understanding, they have eyes but they do not use them for seeing, and they have ears but they do not use them for listening. They are like cattle; only more astray. They are utterly heedless' (7.180). 'Allah will say to them: Enter into the Fire along with groups of men high and low (jinn and men) who passed away before you' (7.39). 'The disbelievers will say: Lord, show us those from among the jinn and men who led us astray that we may trample them under foot and reduce them to an abject condition' (41.30).

Solomon's hosts comprised gentiles (jinn), natives (men) and saintly people (birds) formed into companies (27.18). Foreign experts (jinn) who were subject to his authority worked for him and fashioned whatever he desired: palaces, statues, basins as large as reservoirs, huge cauldrons (34.13, 14). A powerful chieftain is called jinn (27.40).

The jinn mentioned in 46.30 and in 72.2 were a party of men who happened to listen on one occasion to the Holy Prophet reciting the Quran one night during his return journey from Taif to Mecca and another party who came and talked to him and reported their impressions to their people when they returned home.

MEANING OF THE FATIHAH

The last word can never be said on the Quran. Like the universe it is limitless. It is rich beyond compare and counting. Take the seven concise verses of the Fatihah alone, which has been called the Quran in Brief. Most eminent and profound students of the Quran have, time after time, declared that every reading of the Fatihah reveals richer and more profound truths. Even a cursory reading of it enriches and uplifts mind and soul and opens the prospect of communion with one's Maker.

The Fatihah illustrates several characteristics of the Quran of which it is a Divine Summary and Foreword. Some concept of its exalted purpose may be formed even in a first reading in translation by a beginner. It begins with the name of Allah. Then follow two of the principal Divine attributes: Rahman and Rahim. Rahman has been translated Most Gracious. Its connotation is that aspect of Divine grace which manifests itself in providing all that may be needed before the need arises and without any action or effort on the part of the beneficiary; for instance, all that sustains, supports, strengthens and enriches life at every stage. The mere mention of the attribute opens up unending vistas of multifarious and limitless Divine bounties which stagger the imagination and fill and overpower the mind with deep and humble gratitude.

Rahim has been translated Ever Merciful. It connotes that aspect of Divine mercy which manifests itself through investing righteous action with beneficent results, far and away beyond the strict scope of the action itself. 'If there be a good deed, He multiplies it and bestows from Himself a great reward' (4.41).

Thus at the very threshold of his study of the Quran the student is ushered into the Presence, as it were, of his Maker, is made aware of His name and is reminded of His boundless grace and mercy. His mind subdued and overflowing with gratitude and adoration, he is eager to proceed. He is now ready to affirm: The plenitude of every type of praise is due to Allah alone, Who is the Rabb of (i.e., has brought into being, nourishes, sustains and leads stage by stage towards perfection) all the worlds, the Rahman, the Rahim, Master of the Day of Judgment. Being now reminded of two more Divine attributes, he begins to feel that he is within the orbit of operation of all those attributes and is encouraged to submit his supplication to the Divine Majesty direct, to the revealed Presence, rather than to the merely believed One.

From the use of the third person he boldly turns to the more familiar second person, for gratitude and adoration have now been transmuted into overpowering love. His devoted homage is rendered: Thee alone do we seek to worship! Having given expression to the yearning that is gripping his soul, he realizes his own emptiness, his inadequacy, his ignorance, his utter helplessness. Where can he find the help, the knowledge, the guidance, the strength needed to enable him to worship the Lord of the worlds? The help must also be sought from Him, for He is the Rahman, the Gracious, the Beneficent. At once then he supplicates: Thee alone do we beseech for help!

He is eager now, as it were, to be taken by the hand and to be led along the path that would lead him to the object of his worship, to the fulfilment of the yearning of his soul. He realizes that the treading on that path is the worship of the Lord of the worlds. 'Worship Me alone, that is the right path' (36.62). As Jesus also taught: 'Verily, Allah is my Lord and your Lord; so worship Him. That is the straight path' (3.52; 19.37; 43.65). So he implores: Guide us along the straight path. He knows that treading along that path would call for effort on his part. He is ready to put it forth relying on the Rahim to bless it and make it fruitful.

He is anxious that at the end of the journey he should find favour with the Master of the Day of Judgment. So he supplicates that the path he treads should prove to be the path trodden by those 'on whom Thou hast bestowed Thy favours, those who have not incurred Thy displeasure, and those who have not gone astray' (1.7).

The Fatihah is the principal prayer offered in each *raka'a* of the five daily Prayer services and in every *raka'a* of the voluntary prayers. It is also recited several times a day on other occasions. Thus during every hour of the day and night this divinely taught hymn of adoration, glorification and supplication rises from millions of humble hearts around the globe to the footstool of Allah, the Lord of the worlds, Most Gracious, Ever Merciful, Master of the Day of Judgment.

SOME CHARACTERISTICS OF THE QURAN

Even with the best translation available a student of the Quran must bring certain qualities to his study if he is to derive real profit from it. The two most important are reverence and humility. The Quran claims to be the Word of God. A non-Muslim reader may not accept this, but he must keep it in mind and must respect it, failing which he will gain nothing by his study except frustration. The Quran reacts towards one who studies it according to his own attitude towards the Quran. If he starts with the assumption that it is a fabrication, his study will avail him nothing except to confirm his preconceived bias. A student must free his mind from all prejudice and be sincerely eager to learn and to appreciate.

A seeker should expect wisdom from Allah and should maintain an attitude of reverence (71.14). The Quran expects understanding and reflection and an open mind from one who seeks to derive benefit from it (47.25). It respects the intelligence of the reader and assumes that he will exercise it. It is full of metaphors, similes and illustrations of various types. It draws attention repeatedly to natural phenomena and argues from the physical and material to the moral and spiritual.

Repeated attention is drawn to this feature of the Quran. 'We have expounded in this Quran every type of illustration for the people' (30.59). 'We have expounded for mankind all things necessary in this Quran but most people adhere obstinately to disbelief' (17.90). 'We have, indeed, expounded all necessary things in diverse ways in this Quran for the benefit of mankind but man is most contentious' (18.55).

It may be helpful to set out a few of these illustrations so that the student may become familiar with this feature of the Quran and may learn to reflect upon and draw full benefit from it.

'The case of those who spend their wealth in the cause of Allah is like that of a grain of corn, which grows seven ears, and in each ear there are a hundred grains. Allah multiplies it even more for whomsoever He pleases. Allah is Lord of vast bounty, All-Knowing' (2.262).

'O ye who believe, render not vain your alms by reproaches and injury, like one who spends his wealth to be seen of people, but believes not in Allah and the Last Day. His case is like that of a smooth rock covered with earth, on which heavy rain falls and washes it clean, leaving it bare and hard. Such people shall not secure for themselves aught of that which they earn. Allah guides not the disbelieving people. The case of those who spend their wealth to seek the pleasure of Allah and to gain inner strength is like that of a garden on elevated ground, on which heavy rain falls so that it brings forth its fruit twofold. Even if heavy rain does not fall on it, a light shower suffices. Allah sees well that which you do' (2.265, 266).

'Would any of you desire that having a garden of date-palms and vines with streams flowing beneath it, which brings forth for him all kinds of fruit, he should be stricken with old age when his children are small, and a fiery whirlwind should sweep through his garden consuming it all? Thus does Allah make His Signs clear to you that you may reflect' (2.267)

'That which they spend in pursuit of the life of this world is like a biting frosty blast which smites the harvest of a people who have wronged themselves and utterly destroys it. Allah does not wrong them; they wrong themselves' (3.118).

'The life of this world is like water that We send down from the clouds, then the vegetation of the earth, of which men and cattle eat, mingles with it and the earth is embellished and looks beautiful, and its owners believe they are its complete masters; then by day or by night Our command comes to it and We convert it into a mown-down field, as if nothing had existed there the day before. Thus do We expound the Signs for a people who reflect' (10.25).

'He alone hears prayer. Those on whom they call beside Him do not respond to them at all. Their case is like that of one who stretches forth his two hands toward water that it may reach his mouth, but it reaches it not. The prayer of the disbelievers is in vain' (13.15).

'We have expounded for mankind everything in this Quran that they may take heed; a Quran expressed in clear language wherein there is no deviation from the truth, that they may become righteous. Allah sets forth the case of a man belonging to several partners who are at odds with one another, and of another who belongs wholly to one man. Are the two in equal case? All praise belongs to Allah, but most of them know not' (39.28—30).

'Allah draws attention to the case of a person who is owned by another and has no power over anything, and the case of one whom We have provided with a fair provision from Ourself, and he spends thereof both secretly and openly. Can they be equal? All praise belongs to Allah, but most of them know not. Allah also calls attention to the case of two men: one of them is dumb, having no capacity to achieve anything, and is a burden on his master; whithersoever he sends him, he brings back no good. Can such a one be the equal of him who enjoins justice and follows the straight path?' (16.76, 77)

'He sends down water from the sky, so that valleys begin to flow according to their capacity and the flood carries swelling foam on its surface. In the same way foam comes up from that which they heat up in the fire for the purpose of making ornaments or articles of domestic use. Thus does Allah illustrate truth and falsehood. The foam passes off like froth, and that which benefits people stays on in the earth'. (13.18)

'The works of those who deny their Lord are like ashes on which the wind blows fiercely on a stormy day. They shall not be able to avail of any portion of that which they seek to earn. That, indeed, is utter ruin' (14.19).

'Listen, O people, carefully to this illustration. Surely, those on whom you call instead of Allah cannot create even a fly, though they should all combine together for the purpose; and if a fly should snatch away anything from them, they cannot recover it therefrom. How helpless is he who calls on them and how helpless are those on whom he calls! They have not a true concept of Allah's attributes. Surely, Allah is Powerful, Mighty' (22.74, 75).

'The case of those who take helpers beside Allah is like the case of the spider who builds itself a house; but the frailest of all structures is the house of the spider, if they but knew. Surely, Allah knows whatever they call upon beside Him. He is the Mighty, the Wise. These are illustrations that We set forth for people, but only those who possess knowledge comprehend them' (29.42—44).

'Allah is the Light of the heavens and of the earth. His light is as if there were a lustrous niche, wherein is a lamp contained in a crystal globe, the globe as bright as a glittering star. The lamp is lit with the oil of a blessed tree, an olive, neither of the east nor of the west. The oil would well-nigh glow forth even though no fire were to touch it. Light upon light! Allah guides to His light whomsoever He wills. Allah sets forth all that is needful for the people. Allah knows all things well' (24.36).

'The deeds of those who disbelieve are like a mirage in a wide plain. A thirsty one imagines it to be water until, when he comes up to it, he finds it to be nothing, and he encounters Allah near him, Who then pays him his account in full. Allah is swift at reckoning. Or their deeds are like thick darkness spread over a vast and deep sea, the surface of which is agitated by waves rolling upon waves, above which are clouds; layers of darkness, one upon another, so thick that when a person holds out his hand he can hardly see it. For him whom Allah grants no light there is no light at all' (24.40, 41).

PIECEMEAL REVELATION OF THE QURAN

The Quran was revealed piecemeal, under Divine design, so as to provide for the needs of each situation as it arose, and yet to prove adequate in all unforeseen contingencies. The first need was to create faith in the Creator, the One, the Supreme, the All-Powerful, the Mighty, the Wise, the Gracious, the Merciful, the All-Knowing, the All-Aware, the Forgiving, the Compassionate. For this purpose the early revelations abound with recitals of Allah's Signs, designed to create and strengthen faith. Yet embedded in them are Signs for later generations in the shape of grand prophecies, many of which have found fulfilment during the course of the centuries; some are in the course of fulfilment in our own age and several are awaiting fulfilment, though indications of their early fulfilment are already being manifested.

Along with all this the values to be established as the basis of the new culture were being attended to, and portions of the law began to be revealed. The individual, the community, and even the State, the last still a subject of prophecy and Divine promise, were being taken care of. All this was proceeding simultaneously, but necessarily piecemeal. The disbelievers taunted and jeered at this which seemed to them a haphazard method. 'The disbelievers object: Why was not the Quran revealed to him all at once? It is revealed progressively that We may strengthen thy heart therewith. We have arranged it in the best form. Whenever they raise an objection, We refute it with a firm argument, and We provide thee with an excellent explanation' (25.33, 34).

After the emigration to Medina a host of new problems arose and detailed commandments and regulations concerning these were revealed. Many of these related to statecraft, administration, intercommunal and international relations and problems. But always beyond the immediate and proximate problem and purpose was the transcendent objective to strengthen faith in and reliance upon Allah, to foster beneficent relations between individuals and groups and to weld mankind into a true brotherhood. Everything else was subordinated to that purpose and contributed to it. In a study of the Quran that purpose must always be kept in view.

INTERPRETATION OF THE QURAN

If that is adhered to, it will be found that the Quran provides its own interpretation and is a sure guide in that as in every other respect. Once a fundamental law is stated, that law will hold (33.63; 35.44; 48.24). Any statement which may appear to be in conflict with it must be subject to explanation or interpretation. For instance: 'There is no altering the creation of Allah' (30.31) is fundamental. Yet we read: 'You have surely known the end of those from amongst you who transgressed in the matter of the Sabbath, in consequence of which We condemned them: Be ye apes, despised' (2.66). Or, 'They are those whom Allah has cast aside and on whom His wrath has fallen and of whom He has made some as apes and swine who worship the Evil One' (5.61). It should be obvious that apes and swine in these verses mean people having their qualities.

Again: 'It is an inviolable law for a township that We have destroyed that they shall not return' (21.96). 'When death comes to one of them, he implores: Lord send me back that I may act righteously in the life that I have departed. Indeed not. Those are but words that he utters. Behind them is a barrier until the day when they shall be raised up again' (23.100, 101). Thus it is a fundamental law that those who depart this life do not come back here. In 2.260, the context makes it clear that Allah caused a man to sleep and in his dream revealed to him events spread over a hundred years. In the verse that follows (2.261), Abraham's request: 'Lord, show me how dost Thou bring the dead to life' has reference to the revival or renaissance of a people spiritually dead and not to the return to this life of those who have departed this life. Whenever coming to life is mentioned it means life Hereafter, or spiritual revival of those who have not yet departed this life. 'O ye who believe, respond to Allah and the Messenger when he calls you that he may bring you to life' (8.25). 'Can he who was as dead and We gave him life and appointed for him a light whereby he walks among people, be like one who is, as it were, in utter darkness whence he can by no means come forth? In like manner have the doings of the disbelievers been made to seem fair to them' (6.123).

Once the fundamental commandments and directions are clearly grasped, there will be little difficulty in discovering the key that would help to unravel that which at first sight might appear to demand an explanation or to need adjustment.

For instance: 'Permission to fight is granted to those against whom war is made, because they have been wronged, and Allah indeed has the power to help them. They are those who have been driven out of their homes unjustly only because they affirmed: Our Lord is Allah. If Allah did not repel the transgression of some people by means of others, cloisters and churches and synagogues and mosques, wherein the name of Allah is oft commemorated, would surely be destroyed. Allah will surely help him who helps His cause. Allah is indeed Powerful, Mighty. If We establish these persecuted ones in the earth, they will observe Prayer and pay the Zakat and enjoin good and forbid evil. With Allah rests the final issue of all affairs' (22.40—42). 'Fight in the cause of Allah against those who fight against you, but transgress not. Surely, Allah loves not the transgressors. But fight them not in the proximity of the Sacred Mosque unless they fight you therein. Should they fight you even there, then fight them. Such is the requital of the disbelievers. Then if they desist surely Allah is Most Forgiving, Ever Merciful. Fight them until all aggression ceases, and religion is professed for the pleasure of Allah alone. If they desist, then be mindful that no retaliation is permissible except against the aggressors' (2.191—

194). If during the progress of hostilities the enemy should show an inclination towards a truce or making peace, 'do thou incline towards it also, and put thy trust in Allah. Surely, it is He Who is All-Hearing, All-Knowing. Should they design to deceive thee, then surely Allah is sufficient for thee as Protector' (8.62, 63).

Here is thus a complete code on war. Fighting is permitted only to repel aggression, more particularly in defence of freedom of conscience. Should the enemy desist, all hostilities must stop. If he should be inclined to make a truce, advantage should be taken of it to put a stop to the fighting. In fact aggressive war is a harmful activity which imposes an obligation to fight in defence. But fighting must be stopped as soon as the enemy affords the opportunity of doing so. 'Whenever they kindle a fire to start a war, Allah puts it out. They strive to create disorder in the land and Allah loves not those who create disorder' (5.65).

There are numerous commandments and regulations concerning war, the due discharge of the obligation to fight when it should arise, precautions relating to security, alertness towards the fifth column, keeping the enemy at arm's length during hostilities, the granting of asylum and a host of connected matters. But they are war regulations and are all subject to the overriding conditions and limitations set out above, which are fundamental and imperative. Any doubt or seeming discrepancy that may arise concerning any of them as, for instance, 'O ye who believe, do not make friends with My enemy and your enemy. You send them messages of affection, while they disbelieve in the truth that has come to you and call out the Messenger and yourselves to battle solely because you believe in Allah, your Lord' (60.2) is resolved by relevant directions like: 'It may be that Allah will bring about amity between you and those of them with whom you are at enmity. Allah has the power; Allah is Most Forgiving, Ever Merciful. Allah does not forbid you to be kind and to act equitably towards those who have not fought you because of your religion and who have not driven you forth from your homes. Surely, Allah loves those who are equitable. Allah only forbids you that you make friends with those who have fought against you because of your religion, and have driven you out of your homes, and have aided others in driving you out. Whoso makes friends with them, those are the transgressors' (60.8—10).

Carrying out of treaty obligations is imperative (2.178; 17.35), even overriding the obligation to go to the help of those persecuted on account of their faith (8.73). Should it be established that the other party to a treaty is bent upon treachery, the treaty may be repudiated on terms of equality which occasion no prejudice to the other side (8.59).

SEQUENCE OF THE QURAN

The Quran is most concise and also multi-faceted, and makes a constant demand for intelligent reflection (4.83; 38.30). Failure to exercise that faculty has sometimes led to the hasty but utterly erroneous conclusion that there is little order in the sequence of the Quran. In fact those who reflect upon and seek to discover an order in the sequence of the Quran are richly rewarded and discover not one order but a multiplicity of satisfying and revealing orders in the sequence and juxtaposition of its verses and chapters, depending upon the character of the quest on which they are embarked. In this regard also the Quran is like the universe. To the roving eyes of a casual thoughtless observer, a landscape he traverses may present a succession of glimpses of natural beauty, but he may fail to discover any order in them. To the trained and practised eyes of a geologist, a botanist, a herbalist, a soil expert, a painter, the same landscape would present a galaxy of diverse and yet co-ordinated orders. There is perfect harmony in the universe, there is neither incongruity nor discord (67.4, 5). The same is the case with the Quran. There is no incongruity or discord.

The Fatihah is an excellent example of orderly sequence.

In the name of Allah, Most Gracious, Ever Merciful.

All types of perfect praise are due to Allah alone, the Lord of all the worlds;
The Rahman;
The Rahim;
Master of the Day of Judgment;

Thee alone do we worship;

Thee alone do we implore for help;
Guide us along the straight path;
The path of those on whom Thou hast bestowed Thy favours, those who have not incurred Thy displeasure, and those who have not gone astray.

That is the supplication: Guide us along the straight path. The opening verses of the next chapter furnish the response: 'This is the Perfect Book: in that there is no doubt; it is a guidance for the righteous, who believe in the unseen, observe Prayer, and spend out of whatsoever We have bestowed upon them; and who believe in that which has been revealed to thee, and in that which was revealed before thee, and have firm faith in that which has been foretold and is yet to come. It is these who are firmly grounded in the guidance that has come from their Lord, and it is these who shall prosper' (2.2—6).

PURPOSE OF THE QURAN

The purpose of the Quran is to furnish guidance to mankind so that they may be led along the path that would bring them to their Maker in a state of complete submission to Him, thus fulfilling the purpose of their own creation. 'This is a Book that We have revealed to thee that thou mayest bring mankind out of every kind of darkness into the light, by the command of their Lord, to the path of the Mighty, the Praiseworthy Allah, to Whom belongs whatsoever is in the heavens and whatsoever is in the earth' (14.2, 3). For that purpose it draws attention to every type of phenomenon and thereby reveals vast treasures of profound truths, but all this is in pursuit of its appointed purpose, and must be viewed and appreciated in that context.

For instance, the Quran makes numerous statements based on historical fact to emphasize different aspects of the guidance it sets forth, but it is not a book of history. It draws attention to stages of creation of the universe

(21.31) and of man (71.15; 32.8; 40.68) but it is not a treatise on cosmology or on the origin of species. 'He is the One Who created the night and the day, and the sun and the moon, each gliding along its orbit' (21.34). 'He has constrained to your service the sun and the moon, both carrying out their functions incessantly' (14.34). 'He created the sun and the moon and the stars, all made subservient to man by His command. Hearken, His is the creation and its regulation. Blessed is Allah, the Lord of the worlds' (7.55). 'He has constrained to your service the night and the day and the sun and the moon; and the stars too have been constrained to your service by His command. Surely, in all this there are Signs for a people who make use of their understanding' (16.13). Yet the Quran is not a primer on astronomy. It makes reference to the operation of the law which revives the dry earth through rain (7.58) and to the wonderful system through which the supply of sweet and salt water is maintained in rivers and oceans (25.54; 35.13) but it is not a manual of meteorology or hydraulics.

'He it is Who has constrained the sea to your service that you may eat fresh sea-food therefrom, and may take out therefrom articles that you wear as ornaments. Thou seest the vessels ploughing through it that you may voyage across the oceans seeking His bounty and that you may be grateful' (16.15). Yet it is not a volume of oceanography, nor a guidebook on pearl fishing or deep-sea fishing.

'We created man from an extract of clay; then We placed him as a drop of sperm in a safe depository; then We fashioned the sperm into a clot; then We fashioned the clot into a shapeless lump; then out of this shapeless lump We fashioned bones; then We clothed the bones with flesh; then We developed it into a new creation. So blessed be Allah the Best of Creators' (23.13—15). This was revealed close upon fourteen centuries ago, and yet the Quran is not a work on obstetrics.

It mentions that David and Solomon were taught the process of smelting iron and copper (34.11—14), and this has recently been confirmed by the discovery of the site of the furnaces and the system employed for the purpose, but the Quran does not treat of metallurgy. It warns that flourishing ancient civilizations, very much more advanced than that of Central Arabia of the early seventh century of the Christian era, were destroyed in consequence of the disobedience and wrongdoing of the people (30.10) and the discovery of their remains in different parts of Arabia and of the rest of the earth has supplied confirmatory proof, but the Quran is no archaeological tome. It states that when the Pharoah who pursued Moses and the Israelites was about to be overwhelmed by the rising tide and beseeched God for mercy, he was told his last-minute repentance could not avail him, but that: 'We will grant thee a measure of deliverance by preserving thy body this day that thou mayest serve as a Sign for those who come after thee' (10.93). This was confirmed by the discovery of his body in 1909. But the Quran is not concerned with Egyptology. The prophecies contained in the Quran continue to be fulfilled in every age. All this is in support of the purpose of the Quran set out above.

REQUISITES FOR STUDY OF THE QURAN

The Quran, being the Word of Allah, is all purity, and demands from those who would seek to penetrate to its deeper meaning purity of thought, action, motive and design (56.80). The greater the purity of a student of the Quran, the deeper and clearer will be his grasp and understanding of its meaning. This too is proof of its Divine authorship. Purity of thought, action and motive is not a prerequisite for full understanding and appreciation of any work on, or of, any branch of art or science. But it is a prerequisite of a wholly profitable study of the Quran, for the portals that guard its inner meaning and significance will suffer and yield only to the purest approach and touch. This is no mystery; its truth has been attested numberless times down the corridor of the centuries.

An indispensable requisite for a profitable study of the Quran is prayer. He who seeks to discover the true meaning and purport of the guidance contained in the Quran cannot afford to neglect supplicating its All-Knowing Author for enlightenment (40.61; 29.70).

METHOD OF PERSUASION OF THE QURAN

The Quran adopts the most persuasive way of leading people, step by step, towards the highest grades of virtue and beneficence. The method adopted by it fills the heart with a deep appreciation of the concern of the Creator for His creatures, and predisposes one to respond with eager devotion and deep love.

'The recompense of an injury is a penalty in proportion thereto, but whoso forgives and effects a reform thereby, his reward is with Allah. Surely, He loves not the wrongdoers. No blame attaches to those who exact due retribution when they are wronged; blame attaches only to those who wrong others and transgress in the earth without justification. They will have a painful chastisement. But the wronged one who endures with fortitude and forgives, achieves a matter of high resolve' (42.41—44).

'You will surely be tried in respect of your possessions and your persons and you will surely hear many hurtful things from those who were given the Book before you and from those who set up partners with Allah; but if you endure with fortitude and restrain yourselves, that indeed is a matter of strong determination' (3.187).

'If you desire to exact retribution, then adjust the penalty to the wrong you have suffered; but if you endure with fortitude, that surely is best for the steadfast. Do thou endure with fortitude and thou canst do so only with the help of Allah; and grieve not for them, nor feel distressed because of their plottings. Surely Allah is with those who restrain themselves and those who are benevolent' (16.127—129).

'Those who spend in prosperity and adversity, who control their tempers when they are roused and who overlook people's faults (and Allah loves the benevolent) and those who, when they commit an indecency or wrong themselves, call Allah to mind and implore forgiveness for their sins (and who can forgive sins except Allah?) and do not persist knowingly in that of which they have been guilty shall have as their reward forgiveness from their Lord, and gardens beneath which rivers flow, wherein they shall abide. Excellent is the reward of those who work righteousness' (3.135—137).

To forgive, when in anger, is a positive virtue (42.38); and so is the overlooking of a default or injury. 'Whether you make public a good deed or perform it secretly, or pardon a wrong, Allah is surely very Forgiving and determines the measure of everything' (4.150). 'If you forbear and forgive and pardon, then surely, Allah is Most Forgiving, Ever Merciful' (64.15). To withhold beneficence in consequence of some default of the beneficiary may in turn disentitle the withholding benefactor from becoming the recipient of Divine grace and mercy. 'Let not those who are possessed of means and plenty resolve to withhold their bounty from the kindred and the needy and those who have migrated from their homes in the cause of Allah, because of some default on the part of the recipient. Let them forgive and forbear. Do you not desire that Allah should forgive you? Allah is Most Forgiving, Ever Merciful' (24.23).

When a loan is taken the date of repayment should be agreed upon. If on the due date 'the debtor be in straitened circumstances, then grant him respite in respect of the repayment of the capital sum, till a time of ease. But if, in such a case, you remit the capital sum also as charity, it will be the better for you, if you only knew. Be ever mindful of the day when you shall be made to return to Allah; when every one shall be paid in full that which he has earned, and they shall not be wronged' (2.281, 282).

Prisoners of war are to be released as a favour or in return for ransom (47.5). Those who desire to pay off their ransom from their earnings may be given a writing to that effect, and they should be helped to secure their freedom 'with a portion of the wealth of Allah which He has bestowed upon you' (24.34).

GRADATION OF MORAL VALUES

Indeed a perfect gradation of moral values has been prescribed. 'Allah enjoins justice and benevolence, and graciousness as between kindred; and forbids evil designs, ill behaviour and transgression. He admonishes you that you may take heed' (16.91). On the negative side, not only must every kind of trespass against person, property and honour be eschewed; but unmannerly behaviour and evil thoughts and designs must also be guarded against. On the positive side, it is not enough to be just; that is, to return good for good and to exact only proportionate retribution for a wrong suffered. He who seeks the pleasure of Allah must be benevolent; that is, he must render good without any thought of return, and forgive wrongs and injuries till beneficence towards fellow beings becomes part of his nature and flows out of him as naturally as affection for close kindred. A brief admonition comprising a whole philosophy of conduct !

REASONING OF THE QURAN

For every commandment and every prohibition, in support of every claim and every refutation the Quran furnishes reasons that satisfy the intellect, enlighten the mind, strengthen faith and generate the motive power for action in conformity to its teachings. The Quran is guidance for mankind, comprising clear proofs of guidance and discriminating between truth and falsehood (2.186).

It affirms: Allah is the Creator of all things; and follows up the affirmation immediately with the proof: He is the One, and the whole of creation is under His complete control. Are there any partners of Allah who have created the like of His creation so that the two creations appear alike? (13.17)

The disbelievers called the Holy Prophet a madman. The Quran affirmed: By the grace of thy Lord, thou art not a madman; and set forth the proof:

(a) The pen and the inkstand and whatever is written therewith will affirm the wisdom of that which is being revealed to thee. How could such consummate wisdom be revealed to a madman?

(b) A madman's actions are arbitrary and futile. Thy efforts shall lead to the spiritual rebirth of mankind, and thou shalt have an unending reward here and Hereafter. Witness, for instance, that in response to the Divine command (33.57) millions of people call down upon the Holy Prophet, several times in the course of each day, Allah's blessings and offer him the salutation of peace.

(c) A madman's conduct is erratic and is not regulated by any set of values. In contrast, thou dost illustrate in thy conduct high moral excellences.

(d) Events will soon show which of you, thou or thy opponents, are afflicted with madness.

All this is very succinctly but very clearly set out (68.2 – 7).

'They allege Allah has taken unto Himself a son. Holy is He! On the contrary, to Him belongs all that is in the heavens and in the earth; to Him are all obedient. Originator of the heavens and the earth, when He determines the coming into being of a thing, He says concerning it: Be! and it is' (2.117, 118).

What need has Allah of a son? He is Holy and free from all weakness and defects, including the contingency of death. He needs not a son to take His place. Everyone and everything belongs to Him and is obedient to Him and under His control. That which belongs to Him cannot be His equal. That which is obedient to Him and is under His control cannot rebel against His authority. No one can, therefore, aspire to equality with Him, nor would He need a helper to subdue such an aspirant. He is the Originator of the heavens and the earth; the sole Creator of the universe. He needed not a son to assist Him in the creation of the universe. Whatever He decrees is carried into effect. He needs no son to assist Him in the governance of the universe.

'They say: Allah has taken unto Himself a son. Holy is He. He is Self-Sufficient. To Him belongs whatsoever is in the heavens and whatsoever is in the earth. You have no authority in support of that which you allege. Do you, then, say that concerning Allah of which you have no knowledge?' (10.69) Being Self-Sufficient Allah needs no son as helper. Those who assert Allah has taken unto Himself a son can cite no reason or argument in support of their assertion. Some of them may be misled by expressions like 'son of God' in earlier scriptures, but as those scriptures clearly affirm the unity of God they should realize that such expressions are used metaphorically. Their failure to realize this is evidence of their lack of knowledge.

To insist upon Allah having a son in any but a purely spiritual or metaphorical sense, is to insist upon an utter incongruity and impossibility. 'They have appointed partners of Allah, out of the jinn, whereas He has created them; and they falsely attribute to Him sons and daughters without any knowledge. Holy is He and exalted far above that which they attribute to Him. Originator of the heavens and the earth! How can He have a son when He has no consort, and He has created everything and has full knowledge of all things. That is Allah, your Lord; there is no god but He, the Creator of all things; so worship Him alone. He is Guardian over everything. Eyes cannot reach Him, but He manifests Himself before the eyes. He is the Imperceptible, the All-Aware' (6.101—104). 'Proclaim: He is Allah, the Single; Allah, the Self-Existing and Besought of all. He begets not, nor is He begotten; nor is there anyone like unto Him or His equal' (112.2—5).

PROHIBITIONS

Extravagance and miserliness are both condemned and the harmfulness of both is set out. The true servants of the Gracious One 'are neither extravagant nor niggardly in spending, but keep a balance between the two' (25.68). 'Give the kinsman his due, and the needy and the wayfarer, but squander not thy substance extravagantly, for the extravagant fall into evil company, and misuse the bounties of their Lord. On occasions when thou must turn away from any of those who are the objects of thy benevolence, while seeking thy Lord's mercy for which thou art eager, speak kindly to them. Do not hold back altogether out of miserliness and render thyself blameworthy, nor spend without restraint and exhaust thy means, thus becoming thyself an object of charity. Thy Lord enlarges His provision for whom He pleases, and straitens it for whom He pleases. He is well-aware of all that relates to His servants and sees it all' (17.27—31). 'Hearken, you are those who are called upon to spend in the cause of Allah; then of you there are some who hold back, and whoso holds back, does so only against himself. Allah is Self-Sufficient; it is you who are needy. If you turn away, He will bring in your stead another people, who will not be such laggards as you' (47.39).

Similarly, concerning liquor and gambling the evil involved is clearly pointed out. 'O ye who believe, liquor, gambling, idols and divining arrows are but abomination and Satanic devices. So turn wholly away from each one of them that you may prosper. Satan desires only to create enmity and hatred between you by means of liquor and gambling and to keep you back from the remembrance of Allah and from Prayer. Will you, then, desist? Obey Allah and obey the Messenger and be ever on your guard; but if you turn away, then remember that the duty of Our Messenger is only to convey Our Message clearly. There shall be no sin on those who believe and act righteously, in respect of that which they eat of things lawful and wholesome if they are mindful of their duty to Allah and hold firmly to the faith and act in conformity thereto, and keep marching forward in righteousness and in firmness of faith, and then go forward in righteousness and perform their duty to the uttermost. Allah loves those who perform their duty to the uttermost' (5.91—94).

Thus liquor has been prohibited as its use undermines the principal faculties: the intellect, physical health and strength, the moral sense and the spiritual sense. Of the eatables also those are prohibited which would affect deleteriously any one or more of these. 'Eat of the lawful and wholesome things that Allah has provided for you; and be grateful for the bounty of Allah, if it is Him you worship. He has forbidden you only the flesh of dead animals, blood, the flesh of swine and that on which the name of any other than Allah has been invoked' (16.115, 116). The first two are principally injurious to physical and mental health; the last two destroy or damage principally the moral and spiritual senses.

COMMANDMENTS: PRAYER

As with prohibitions so with commandments. The five daily Prayer services *(Salat)* have been prescribed (4.104; 17.79; 11.115) and there are exhortations towards voluntary Prayers (17.80; 76.27). One of the numerous benefits of *Salat* is that it safeguards the true and sincere participant against all manner of evils and indecencies (29.46). Prayer is the most potent means of establishing and strengthening one's communion with one's Maker and of drawing near to Him (96.20). 'When My servants enquire from thee concerning Me, O Prophet, tell them I am close. I respond to the call of the supplicant when he calls on Me. So should they respond to Me and have firm faith in Me, that they may be rightly guided' (2.187).

ZAKAT

The capital levy prescribed denotes its purpose and its object by its very name *Zakat*. The word means that which purifies and fosters. By subtracting from all wealth the share of the community the rest is purified for those entitled to make use of it, and by the application of the proceeds to the service of the community, the welfare of the community is fostered. 'Whatever you remit as *Zakat* seeking the pleasure of Allah, that is multiplied manifold' (30.40).

FASTING

Fasting during the month of Ramadhan is prescribed as a discipline which promotes righteousness and makes it easier for a seeker to scale the spiritual heights and to appreciate Divine bounties and to employ them beneficently (2.184—186).

PILGRIMAGE

Upon those who can afford it, Pilgrimage to the House of Allah, the *Ka'aba* at Mecca, is prescribed (2.197; 3.98). This, if properly observed by those upon whom it is obligatory, would constitute the Annual World Assembly of Islam in spiritual fellowship. This too is a great discipline and is a tremendous emotional and cleansing experience (2.198; 22.27—30).

Honouring that which has been hallowed is acceptable to Allah (2.159; 22l3l). Among the rites of the Pilgrimage is the sacrifice of an animal (22. 35—37). It is stressed that it is not the flesh of these animals or their blood that reaches Allah, but the spirit of righteousness that inspires the pilgrim which finds favour with Allah (22.38).

CONCISENESS

The Quran furnishes many striking illustrations of condensation and economy of expression. It packs volumes of meaning within the briefest compass. 'We directed the mother of Moses: Suckle him; and when thou fearest for his life, cast him afloat into the river and fear not nor grieve; for We shall restore him to thee, and shall make him a Messenger' (28.8).

'Has the account of Moses reached thee, when His Lord called him in the sacred valley of Tuwa, and directed him: Go thou to Pharoah, he is in rebellion; and say to him: Wouldst thou be purified, and shall I guide thee to thy Lord so that thou mayest fear Him? Then Moses showed him the great Sign. But he rejected him and was disobedient. Then he turned away and busied himself with devising his scheme. He gathered his people and proclaimed: I am your most high lord. So Allah seized him for the chastisement of this world and the Hereafter. In this surely is a lesson for him who fears Allah' (79.16—27).

Perhaps the most characteristic example of economy of expression is: 'They also ask thee what shall they spend? Tell them: Whatever is spare. Thus does Allah make his commandments clear to you that you may reflect upon this world and the next' (2.220). Here just one word *ala'fv* has been employed to convey the basic economic concept, which is that absolute ownership of everything belongs to Allah. Man has limited control over that which he acquires through legitimate means. Subject to the payment of *Zakat* and other charges leviable upon it, the owner may put it to any permissible use, but again subject to a heavy moral obligation not to be wasteful and 'to render to the kinsman his due and to the needy and the wayfarer' (17.27) and generally to keep spending in the way of Allah. Here the answer to the question: What and how much shall we spend in the way of Allah? is: Whatever is spare! Once legitimate needs have been filled at a modest scale (no extravagance is permitted) the rest is spare. Reflect then, ye who are gifted with understanding.

With its brevity the Quran is often dramatic. An account of Noah, the deluge and the Ark concludes: 'Thereafter, the command went forth: Swallow up thy water, O earth; and O sky: Desist. The water subsided and the affair was closed. The Ark came to rest on Judi and the decree went forth: Ruined are the wrongdoers !' (11.45)

FREEDOM OF CONSCIENCE

The Quran is most emphatic on freedom of conscience. Faith is a matter of conscience and conscience cannot be compelled. A person may be forced or coerced into saying he believes or disbelieves, but he cannot be forced to believe or disbelieve. Such an effort is futile and self-defeating. 'There shall be no compulsion in religion, for guidance and error have been clearly distinguished (2.257).

'Proclaim: This is the truth from your Lord; then let him who will, believe, and let him who will, disbelieve' (18.30).

'If thy Lord had enforced His will, surely all those on the earth would have believed, without exception. Will thou, then, take it upon thyself to force people to become believers? Except by Allah's leave no one can believe' (10.100, 101).

On the other hand the Prophet was charged, and so are we all, to convey the truth to all and to proclaim it widely. 'O Messenger, proclaim widely that which has been sent down to thee from thy Lord; for if thou do it not, thou wilt not have conveyed His Message at all. Allah will safeguard thee against harm by people' (5.68). The method of conveying Allah's Message has been set forth. 'Call unto the way of thy Lord with wisdom and goodly exhortation, and reason with them on the basis of that which is best. Thy Lord knows best those who have strayed away from His way; and He knows best those who are rightly guided' (16.126). 'Contend not with the People of the Book except on the basis of that which is best but contend not at all with such of them as are unjust. Tell them: We believe in that which has been revealed to us, and in that which has been revealed to you; our God and your God is One; and to Him we submit' (29.47).

'Say to the People of the Book: You have nothing to stand on until you carry out the commandments of the Torah and the Gospel and of that which has now been sent down to you from your Lord. That which has been sent down to thee from thy Lord will most surely cause many of them to grow firmer in rebellion and disbelief; so grieve not over such disbelieving people. Surely, of those who have believed, and the Jews and the Sabians and the Christians, whoso truly believes in Allah and the Last Day and acts righteously, shall have no fear nor shall they grieve' (5.69, 70).

'If the People of the Book had believed and been mindful of their duty to Allah, We would surely have removed from them their ills and We would surely have admitted them into Gardens of Bliss. If they had carried out the commandments of the Torah and the Gospel and of that which has now been sent down to them from their Lord, they would surely have partaken of spiritual as well as of material bounties. Of them there is a section which is moderate, but evil indeed is that which most of them do' (5.66, 67).

'Say to the People of the Book: Let us agree upon one matter which is the same for you and for us, namely, that we worship none but Allah, and that we associate no partner with Him, and that some of us take not others for lords beside Allah. Then if they turn away say to them: Bear ye witness that we have submitted to Allah' (3.65).

The Quran is uncompromising on the Unity of God and brooks not anything that may savour of ascribing partners to Him. Yet it makes allowance for the sensitiveness of those who are in error, for to them that to which they hold seems fair. 'Revile ye not those whom they call upon beside Allah, lest they, out of spite, should revile Allah in their ignorance. Thus have We caused their conduct to seem fair to every people. Then unto their Lord is their return; and He will inform them of that which they used to do' (6.109).

METHOD OF PROPAGATION

In conveying Allah's Message regard must be had to every factor that may influence the attitude of the person concerned. It should be remembered that the object is that he should appreciate and respond to the Divine call. This is part of the wisdom to be exercised in pursuance of the direction set out in 16.126. It is well illustrated in the directions given to Moses and Aaron concerning the manner in which Pharaoh was to be approached and admonished.

'Go, thou and thy brother, with My Signs, and be diligent in remembering Me. Go, both of you, to Pharaoh, for he has transgressed grievously; but speak gently to him, perchance he may take heed or be humble. They urged: Lord, we fear lest he commit some excess against us or press us hard. Allah reassured them: Fear not at all; for I am with you both, hearing and seeing. So go ye both to him and say: We are the Messengers of thy Lord, so let the children of Israel go with us, and oppress them not. We have indeed brought thee a Sign from thy Lord. Allah's Peace shall be on him who follows the guidance brought by us; and, it has been revealed to us, that punishment shall overtake him who rejects it and turns away from it' (20.43—49).

Finally: 'Who speaks better than one who invites people to Allah and acts righteously and says: Of a surety, I am of those who submit wholly to Allah? Good and evil are not alike. Repel evil with that which is best; and lo, he between whom and thyself was enmity is as though he were a warm friend. But none attains to this save those who are steadfast, and none attains to this save those who are granted a large share of good' (41.34—36).

FAITH IN PROPHETS

The Quran affirms that Allah has sent guidance to every people; it thus affirms the truth and righteousness of every Prophet. 'We did raise among every people a Messenger' (16.37). 'We have sent thee with enduring truth, as a bearer of glad tidings and as a Warner. There is no people to whom a Warner has not been sent' (35.25).

What could be more explicit than the following? 'They invite you: Be ye Jews; or Be ye Christians; that you may be rightly guided. Tell them: Nay, not so; let us agree to follow the religion of Abraham, who was ever inclined towards Allah and was not one of those who set up partners with Him. Affirm: We believe in Allah and in that which has been sent down to us, and that which was sent down to Abraham and Ishmael, and Isaac and Jacob and his children, and that which was given to Moses and Jesus, and that which was given to all other Prophets from their Lord. We make no distinction between any of them. To Him do we wholly submit ourselves. Then, if they believe as you have believed, they are rightly guided, but if they turn back, then know that they are determined to create a schism. In that event Allah will surely guard thee against their mischief. He is the All-Hearing, the All-Knowing' (2.136—138).

Or, again: Abraham announced: 'I have single-mindedly devoted the whole of my attention toward Him Who created the heavens and the earth, and I am not of those who associate partners with Allah. His people sought to contend with him. He admonished them: Do you contend with me concerning Allah Who has guided me aright? I fear not that which you associate with Him; I fear only that which my Lord may determine. My Lord comprehends all within His Knowledge; will you not then take heed? How should I be afraid of that which you associate with Allah, when you are not afraid to associate with Allah that concerning which He has sent down to you no authority? Which, then, of the two parties has better right to security, if indeed you know? Those who believe and debase not their belief with injustice, for them is peace, and they are rightly guided' (6.80—83).

'That was Our argument that We furnished to Abraham against his people. We exalt in rank whomsoever We please. Thy Lord is indeed Wise, All Knowing. We bestowed upon him Isaac and Jacob; each did We guide aright, and Noah did We guide aright aforetime, and of Abraham's progeny did We guide aright David and Solomon and Job and Joseph and Moses and Aaron. Thus do We reward those who do good. We also guided Zachariah and John and Jesus and Elias; each one was of the righteous. We also guided Ishmael and Isaiah and Jonah and Lot; each one did We exalt above the people, and of their fathers and their children and their brethren; We chose them and We guided them along the straight path. That is the guidance of Allah, whereby He guides those of His servants whom He pleases. Had they associated aught with Allah, all that they did would have been of no avail to them. It is these to whom We gave the Book, the faculty of judgment and Prophethood. Then if these people disbelieve in Prophethood, We have now committed it to a people who do not disbelieve in it. Those are the ones whom Allah guided aright, so do thou follow their guidance. Say to these people: I ask not of you any recompense for it. It is but an admonition for all mankind' (6.84—91).

REVERENCE FOR ALLAH

It will have been appreciated that the Quran is most mindful of all that is due to everyone and sets forth everything with dignity and due courtesy, not neglecting that which is due to the Divine Author Himself.

One of the two delegations who came secretly to discover something about Islam and heard portions of the Quran being recited, reported their experience to their people and in the course of their recital stated: We know not whether 'misfortune is designed for those who are in the earth, or whether their Lord designs to guide them aright' (72.11). Good and ill are both determined by Divine decree. Here, however, the ill that may be decreed is not attributed by the narrator of the experience, out of a sense of reverence and veneration, to the Divine. Any such reference is obviated by the adoption of the passive form: 'We know not whether misfortune is designed for those in the earth'. The good that may be decreed is attributed to Allah: 'Or whether their Lord designs to guide them aright.'

MAN'S RESPONSIBILITY

Within the sphere of his responsibility man has been given a choice, to follow one course or another. His choice, according to Divine law, would result in good or harm. In that sense, it is Divine law that determines the consequences of all action. The wrong action, or default, may not have been deliberate, or of purpose, and may be followed by repentance. The decree of the All-Knowing, All-Hearing, Most Forgiving, Ever Merciful will take everything into account. 'I inflict My punishment on whom I so determine; but My mercy encompasses all things' (7.157). 'Your Lord has charged Himself with mercy, so that whoso among you does evil, in ignorance, and repents thereafter and amends, then He is Most Forgiving, Ever Merciful' (6.55). 'He it is Who accepts repentance from His servants, and forgives sins, and knows all that you do' (42.26). 'Whatever misfortune befalls you is in consequence of that which you practise. He overlooks many of your defaults' (42.31).

Thus Allah having created man in the best mould (95.5), having perfected his faculties (75.39), having invested him with the sense of right and wrong (91.8, 9), having guided him through revelation (32.10), whatever good befalls man is from Allah. If nevertheless he chooses error, then the ill encountered by him through the operation of Divine law is from himself. 'If some good befalls them, they say: This is from Allah; and if ill befalls them, they say: This is from thee. Tell them: All is from Allah. What ails these people that they do not even approach the grasping of a reality? Whatever of good comes to thee is from Allah; and whatever of ill befalls thee is from thyself' (4.79, 80).

COURTESY TOWARDS OPPONENTS

Again, the Quran is mindful of the sensitiveness even of those who reject it. 'Tell them: of the two, you and us, one is rightly guided and the other is in manifest error. You will not be called to account for our sins and we shall not be called to account for that which you do' (34.25, 26).

Indeed it is most careful in stressing all obligations, even when they are owed to those who are at most serious variance with one in matters of faith. 'We have enjoined on man concerning his parents: Be grateful to Me and to thy parents. Unto Me is the final return. His mother bears him in travail after travail, and his weaning takes two years. Should they contend with thee to associate with Me that of which thou hast no knowledge, obey them not in that, but keep up thy kindly co-operation with them in worldly matters and follow the way of him who turns to Me in humility. Then unto Me will be your return and I shall inform you of that which you used to do' (31.15, 16).

DUTY OWED TO PARENTS

'We have enjoined on man to act benevolently towards his parents. His mother bears him in pain and brings him forth in pain, and the bearing of him and his weaning extends over thirty months. When he attains his full maturity at forty years, he prays: Lord, grant me the favour that I may be grateful to Thee for the bounty that Thou hast bestowed upon me and upon my parents, and that I may act righteously so as to please Thee; and make my progeny righteous also. I do turn to Thee; and truly I am of Thy obedient servants. Of these We shall accept the best of their works, and We shall overlook their defaults. They shall be among the inmates of the Garden. That is a true promise that is held out to them.

'Then there is he who upbraids his parents: Fie on you! Do you threaten me that I shall be brought forth again, when generations have already passed on before me and not one of them has come back? They beseech Allah for help and adjure him: Woe unto thee, believe, for Allah's promise is true. But he shrugs it off with: These are but old wives' tales! These are those concerning whom the sentence of punishment was executed from among communities of jinn and men that had passed on before. They were indeed the losers. They shall all be requited fully according to the quality of their conduct; and they shall not be wronged' (46.16—20).

As an example of parental admonition attention may be drawn to Luqman's exhortation addressed to his son. 'We bestowed wisdom upon Luqman and enjoined on him: Be grateful to Allah. Whoso is grateful, is grateful to the good of his ownself; and whoso is ungrateful should know that Allah is Self-Sufficient, Praiseworthy. Call to mind when Luqman exhorted his son: Dear son, associate not partners with Allah. Surely, associating partners with Allah is a grievous wrong' (31.13, 14). 'Dear son, Allah will surely bring forth the slightest action, even if it be of no greater weight than a grain of mustard seed, and may be hidden behind a rock, or anywhere in the heavens or in the earth. Verily Allah is the Knower of the most secret matters, All-Aware. Dear son, observe Prayer, and enjoin good and forbid evil, and endure steadfastly whatever may befall thee. That is indeed a matter of high resolve. Do not puff up thy cheeks with pride before people nor tread haughtily upon the earth. Surely, Allah loves not any arrogant boaster. Walk at a moderate pace and restrain thy voice; verily, the most disagreeable sound is the bray of a donkey' (31.17—20).

The duty owed to one's parents and others including oneself is persuasively set out: 'Thy Lord has commanded that ye worship none but Him, and has enjoined benevolence towards parents. Should either or both of them attain old age in thy lifetime, never say: Ugh! to them, nor chide them, but always speak gently to them. Be always tender towards them and pray: Lord, have mercy on them, even as they nurtured me when I was little. Your Lord knows best that which is in your minds; if you will be righteous, then surely, He is Most Forgiving towards those who turn constantly to Him. Render to the kinsman his due and the needy and the wayfarer, and squander not thy substance extravagantly, for the extravagant fall into evil company and misuse the bounties of their Lord. On occasions when thou must turn away from any of those who are the objects of thy benevolence while seeking thy Lord's mercy for which thou art eager, speak kindly to them. Do not hold back altogether out of miserliness and render thyself blameworthy nor spend without restraint and exhaust thy means thus becoming thyself an object of charity. Thy Lord enlarges His provision for whom He pleases, and straitens it for whom He pleases. He is well-aware of all that relates to His servants and sees it all' (17.24—31).

SPECIFIC MORAL INJUNCTIONS

This is followed by a summary of the principal injunctions:
'Do not destroy your offspring, for fear of poverty; it is We Who provide for them and for you; surely, destroying them is a great sin;
Do not even approach adultery; surely, it is a foul thing and an evil way;
Do not destroy the life that Allah has made sacred, save for just cause;
The heir of one who is killed wrongfully has Our authority to demand retribution, but let him not transgress the prescribed limits in exacting retribution, for within the limits he is upheld by law;
Do not approach the property of the orphan during his minority, except for the most beneficent purpose, and fulfil every covenant; for you shall be called to account for it;
Give full measure when you measure out, and weigh out with a true balance; that is best and most commendable in the end;
Do not follow that of which thou hast no knowledge; for the ear and the eye and the heart shall all be called to account;
Do not tread haughtily upon the earth, for thou canst not thereby reach its confines nor outstrip those who occupy the highest rank;
The evil of all this is hateful in the sight of thy Lord. This is part of the wisdom that thy Lord has revealed to thee' (17.32—40).
'Come, let me rehearse to you that which your Lord has enjoined:
— that you associate not anything as partner with Him;
— that you behave benevolently towards your parents;
— that you destroy not your offspring for fear of poverty, it is We Who provide for you and for them;
— that you approach not evil of anykind, whether manifest or hidden; and that you destroy not the life that Allah has made sacred, except for just cause. That is what He has enjoined upon you that you may understand; and further
— that you approach not the property of the orphan during his minority, except for the most beneficent purpose;
— that you give full measure and weight with justice; We require not of anyone that which is beyond his capacity;
— that when you speak, you hold the scales even though the person concerned be a kinsman; and
— that you fulfil the covenant of Allah. That is what He has enjoined upon you that you may take heed, and that:
This is My straight path; so follow it. Follow not diverse ways, lest they lead you away from His way. That is what He has enjoined upon you, that you may become righteous' (6.152—154).
'Righteousness is not that you turn your faces to the East or the West; but truly righteous are those who believe in Allah and the Last Day and the angels and the Book and the Prophets, and spend their wealth, for love of Him, on the kindred and the orphans and the needy and the wayfarer and those who ask, and for procuring the freedom of captives; and who observe Prayer and pay the *Zakat;* and whenever they make a promise carry it out, and are steadfast in adversity, and under affliction, and in battle. It is these who have proved faithful and it is these who are righteous' (2.178).

CHARACTERISTICS OF SERVANTS OF ALLAH

Man has been created that he may become a true servant of Allah, that is to say, a manifestation of Divine attributes (51.57). The Prophet was directed to express that ideal thus: 'Affirm: My Lord has guided me unto the straight path, the perfect religion, the religion of Abraham, the upright, who was not of those who associate partners with Allah. My Prayer, by which I hope to win through to everlasting life, and my sacrifices, which entail a type of death upon me, are all for Allah, the Lord of the worlds. He has no partner. Thus am I commanded, and I am the foremost of those who submit wholly to Allah' (6.162—164).

Some of the characteristics of the true servants of Allah are set out thus: 'The true servants of the Gracious One are those
— who walk upon the earth with humility, and when they are accosted by the ignorant ones their response is: Peace;
— who pass the hours of the night in prostration and standing before their Lord;
— who entreat: Lord, avert from us the punishment of hell, for it is a heavy torment; it is indeed an evil resort and dwelling-place;
— who are neither extravagant nor niggardly in spending and keep a balance between the two;
— who call not on any god beside Allah, nor destroy a life that Allah has declared sacred, except for just cause, and commit not adultery; for whoso does that shall meet with the punishment of his sin and his punishment will be intensified on the Day of Judgment and he will abide therein disgraced, except for those who repent, and believe and work righteousness; Allah will convert their evil deeds into good ones, Allah being Most Forgiving, Ever Merciful (and he who repents and works righteousness indeed turns to Allah with true repentance)
— who bear not false witness, and when they come upon anything vain, they pass on with dignity;
— who, when they are reminded of the Signs of their Lord, do not contemplate them like one without hearing and sight;
— and who implore: Lord, grant us of our spouses and our offspring the delight of our eyes, and make us a model for the righteous.
These are the ones who will be rewarded with lofty mansions in Paradise because they were steadfast, and they will be welcomed thereunto with greetings and salutations of peace, abiding therein. Excellent it is as a resort and dwelling place' (25.64—77).

PROPHECIES

Many of the earliest revealed chapters of the Quran cite various phenomena as evidence in support of the cardinal doctrines and teachings of the Quran. Some of these citations constitute prophecies, the fulfilment of which has been witnessed in the course of the centuries, or is being witnessed in the present age. Often the fulfilment is of the literal meaning, sometimes it is of the metaphorical connotation, or it may be of both. That this feature should be so prominent in the earliest revelations makes it even more striking. This offers a rich and rewarding field for the student's exploration.

Man is accountable for whatever he does; he should, therefore, be heedful. He shall one day be brought to Judgment. The proof of this has been planted in his very nature. He has been equipped with the faculty of distinguishing between right and wrong; and so long as he does not blunt it altogether by the persistent rejection or neglect of its signals, it keeps on warning him (91.8—11). The *raison d'être* of man's being equipped with this faculty is his ultimate accountability. 'I call to witness the Judgment Day; and in support thereof I call to witness the self-accusing faculty' (75.2, 3).

Allah is Master of the Day of Judgment (1.4). His attributes are constantly in operation. Judgment takes place continuously, here and Hereafter. One may be confronted with *a* judgment at any time, before being confronted with *the* Judgment. The present age appears to be approaching a tremendous judgment. 'Watch for the time when the heaven is cleft asunder, and those conversant with it give ear to their Lord, though this was incumbent upon them anyhow; and when the earth is stretched forth, and pours out its contents and seems to become empty, and those conversant with it give ear to their Lord, though this was incumbent upon them anyhow; thou, O man, having striven hard towards thy Lord shalt face Him. Then he who is handed his statement of account in his right hand, will soon have an easy reckoning, and will return to his people rejoicing; but he to whom his statement of account is passed on behind his back, will soon cry ruin, and will enter a blazing fire. He was joyful among his people and fancied that his condition would never change. But surely his Lord observed everything concerning him' (84.2—16).

The Divine Call to the Holy Prophet was the break of spiritual dawn for mankind. For three years the Prophet and the few Muslims were ridiculed and jeered at, but there was little active persecution. Then finding that his message was beginning to be listened to, and to receive a response, the *Quraish* (the principal tribe in Mecca) embarked upon a course of bitter and cruel persecution which persisted for ten long years. Life having been made impossible for them in Mecca, the Prophet told the Muslims to migrate to Medina where their fellow-Muslims were willing to receive them. Finally, under Divine Command, the Prophet himself slipped out of Mecca one night in the company of Abu Bakr, and the two took shelter in a cave above Mecca, infested with reptiles and all manner of crawling, creeping creatures. A party of the Quraish, led by a tracker, pursued them next morning to the very entrance of the cave. Perceiving them Abu Bakr became anxious. The Prophet reassured him: 'Be not apprehensive. Allah is with us' (9.40); and added: Abu Bakr, what thinkest thou of the two, with whom Allah is the third ! The Quraish, being assured by the tracker that the tracks went no further and thinking that no one in his senses would take shelter in the cave, returned to Mecca foiled. The next day the Prophet and his companion started on their journey to Medina. A year later the Quraish having led a strong force in the direction of Medina, were met a third of the way out of Medina by the Prophet and his hastily assembled ill-equipped small company at Badr. Battle was joined and the Quraish were beaten with great loss. This was by no means the end of the struggle; but the long night of oppression was at its end. All this had been set forth in one of the earliest revelations. 'We call to witness the Dawn, and the Ten Nights, and the Even and the Odd, and the Night when it is on the move. Is there not in all this strong evidence for one gifted with understanding?' (89.2—6).

In Chapter 81 we come upon a description of some of the salient features of an age that we cannot fail to recognise as our own, depicted in a few broad strokes of the Divine Master's brush. 'When the sun is veiled, and the stars are dimmed, and the mountains are made to move and the ten-month pregnant she-camels are discarded as a means of transportation, and the beasts are gathered together, and the rivers are diverted, and people are brought together, and the female infant buried alive is questioned about: For what crime was she killed? and when books are spread abroad, and when the heaven is laid bare, and when hell is stoked up, and when paradise is brought nigh, then everyone will know that which he has wrought. I call to witness the planets that recede and advance, and seem to disappear, and the night when it sneaks away and the dawn when its breath blows away the darkness, that the Quran is the word revealed to a noble Messenger, mighty and established in the presence of the Lord of the Throne, entitled to obedience and faithful to his trust. Your companion is not mad. Indeed he saw Him on the clear horizon, and he is not niggardly in disclosing that which he has been vouchsafed of the unseen. This is not the word of Satan the rejected. Then, whither are you bent? This is but a Reminder unto all the worlds, unto such of you as desire to go straight, but you can desire nothing except that Allah, the Lord of the worlds, should desire it' (81. 2—30).

The Quran abounds in prophecies. As already explained, the very name of the Book is a grand prophecy, the fulfilment of which has been witnessed through the ages. The very first revelation announced the advent of the age of learning through the extensive use of the pen (96.4—6). What a tremendous upsurge it proved to be! It rescued from oblivion a large part of that which had gone before and wrenched open the gates of learning, science, knowledge and philosophy in all of the then known parts of the world, thus releasing currents which centuries later furnished the impulse that stirred up the Renaissance and ushered in the modern age. The reader will, by this time, have appreciated the constant urging of the Quran towards reflection, and the use of reason and understanding. 'Keep in mind the favour that Allah has bestowed upon you, and that which He has sent down to you of the Book and Wisdom whereby He exhorts you' (2.232). 'He grants wisdom to whom He pleases, and whoever is granted wisdom has indeed been granted abundant good' (2.270).

Attention may be drawn to some of the more specific prophecies which have been fulfilled, or which are in the course of fulfilment. The Prophet had been commanded: 'O Messenger, proclaim widely that which has been sent down to thee from thy Lord, for if thou do it not, thou wilt not have conveyed His Message at all'. This was accompanied by the assurance: 'Allah will safeguard thee against harm by people' (5.68). The Prophet had to face every kind of peril and to run every type of hazard in the carrying out of the mission with which he was charged. In Medina he was not only faced with the hostility of the idolatrous Arabs and of the Jews, but was also exposed to the devices adopted by the hypocrites. He was very easily accessible. In the field of battle he was the principal target of the enemy, Yet the Divine assurance was completely fulfilled.

He was deeply attached to Mecca, where he had been born and nurtured, where he had married, and where his children had been born and reared, where he had received the Divine Call, and at the centre of which was situated the *Ka'aba*, the House of Allah, 'abounding in blessings and a means of guidance for all peoples' (3.97). When the hostile Quraish made life impossible for him and his in Mecca he counselled the Muslims to find means of migrating to Medina. Finally, on the very night when the Quraish had determined to do away with him, he too, under Divine Command, but with a heavy heart, slipped out of Mecca, in the company of Abu Bakr. During the course of the long and hazardous journey he received the comforting Divine assurance: 'He Who has made the teachings of the Quran obligatory on thee will most surely bring thee back to this place of resort' (28.86). Within less than eight years, that which his enemies must have accounted an utter impossibility and an empty boast was gloriously achieved. In the meantime, not long after the Prophet had been established in Medina, further confirmation of the Divine promise was received in the command that the Muslims should in the Prayer services face henceforth towards the Sacred Mosque *(the Ka'aba)* and not towards the Distant Mosque (the site of the Temple in Jerusalem) as they had hitherto done (2.145, 151). This was a clear indication that the *Ka'aba* would be cleared of idols, a consummation that predicated the fall of Mecca.

Within a year of the Prophet's migration to Medina the Quraish led a well-armed force, a thousand strong, against him. He marched out of Medina with a motley company of 313 young and old, ill-clad, ill-armed and ill-nourished, but utterly devoted followers, and offered battle at Badr, against heavy odds. After drawing them up in battle order and giving necessary directions he drew apart and prostrated himself in a paroxysm of prayer and supplication. In a short while Abu Bakr approached and laying his hand gently on the Prophet's shoulder said: Messenger of Allah, you have been praying long enough. The Prophet raised his head and said that the verse: 'The hosts shall soon be routed and will turn their backs in flight', had just been revealed to him over again. It was part of a revelation vouchsafed to him several years earlier in Mecca. 'To the people of Pharoah also came Warners. They rejected all Our Signs; so We seized them, with the seizure of One Mighty, Omnipotent. Are your disbelievers, then, better than those; or have you been granted an exemption in the Scriptures? Or do they boast: We are a strong host, well succoured? The hosts shall soon be routed and will turn their backs in flight. Aye, the Hour is their appointed time; and the Hour will be most grievous, and most bitter' (54.42—47). So it proved. Battle was joined and soon the flower of Quraish chivalry and valour sprawled bedraggled in the mud. The rest sought security in flight.

The Victory had also been foretold in another striking revelation of the early Meccan period. The two great Empires of the time, the Byzantine and the Iranian, were pitted against each other in a struggle for supremacy and survival. The Quraish considered that the sympathies of the Muslims were with Byzantium. The armies of the latter suffered a heavy defeat at the hands of the Iranians in Asia Minor, and this furnished the Quraish with an excuse for rejoicing, as they treated the event as an augury of their own triumph over the Muslims. The Muslims were reassured by the revelation: 'The Byzantines have been defeated in the land nearby, but after their defeat they will be victorious within a few years; Allah's is the supreme authority before and after; and the believers will rejoice on that day, with the help of Allah. He helps whom He pleases; He is the Mighty, the Ever Merciful. This is Allah's promise. Allah goes not back on His promise; but most people know it not' (30.3—7). The revelation announced the victory of the Byzantines over the Iranians within a few years (the Arabic term employed signifies a period not longer than nine years) and also that on the day of the Byzantine victory the Muslims would have cause to rejoice over an event signalised by Allah's special help. Within the period indicated the Byzantines scored a triumph over the Iranians and on the same day the might of the Quraish was broken and their pride and arrogance were humbled on the field of Badr by a very much inferior company of Muslims, solely through Divine help.

Another prophecy of the early Meccan period was fulfilled in the fourth year after the Migration to Medina. 'A host from among the confederates shall be routed here' (38.12). The earlier efforts of the Meccans to crush the Muslims by force having been foiled at Badr and Uhud and in other encounters, they resolved to make one supreme effort in conjunction with tribes who were in alliance or in sympathy with them. They succeeded in getting together a large force of well-armed, well-mounted men and marched against Medina, determined upon its sack and ruin and the wiping out of Islam and the Muslims. Arrived in front of Medina they found their way barred by a moat, which had been hastily dug by the Muslims under the Prophet's directions, who had adopted a suggestion made by Salman Farisi to that effect. Nothing daunted, the confederate forces invested Medina, in the expectation of subduing the Muslims through starvation and mounting repeated assaults across the moat. The Muslims were sore pressed. Their condition was described in a later revelation: 'When they came upon you from above you, and from below you, your eyes became distracted and your hearts rose up to your throats and some of you began to think unworthy thoughts about Allah. Then were the believers sorely tried and were violently shaken. The hypocrites and those whose minds were diseased exclaimed: Allah and His Messenger have merely deluded us. A party of them went so far as to urge: O people of Yathrib, you have now no way of deliverance left, so turn back from your faith. A section of them asked leave of the Prophet, pleading: Our houses are exposed. Their houses were not exposed. They only sought a way of escape' (33.11—14). But when the true believers saw the confederate hosts, it only added to their faith and devotion, and they affirmed: 'Here is what Allah and His Messenger had promised us. Allah and His Messenger have been proved right' (33.23). When the situation became desperate, 'We sent against them a wind and hosts that you saw not' (33.10) and they were routed in much confusion and disorder.

'He has created horses, mules and donkeys that you may ride them and also for display; and He will create for that purpose other means of which you do not yet know' (16.9); and 'It is a Sign for them that We carry their offspring in crowded vessels; and We have created for them other like means of transportation whereon they ride' (36.42, 43); and 'His are the vessels with lofty sails raised high on the ocean like mountains' (55.25); and when the she-camels are discarded as a means of transportation (81.5); all predict rapid means of transportation. When people are brought into intimate contact with one another (81.8) also indicates the same.

He has put the two oceans in motion; they will meet; just now they are divided by a barrier; Pearls and coral come out of them (55.20, 21, 23); is a prediction concerning oceans being joined together by canals.

'When the rivers are diverted' (82.4), predicts the development of irrigation systems. 'When the graves are laid open' (82.5), clearly points to archaeological excavations of ancient tombs.

'When the mountains are blown away' (77.11) has been fulfilled literally, and also metaphorically as indicating the toppling of Kingdoms and the deposition of monarchs.

Infanticide has been proscribed; books, periodicals and journals are widely published, the heavens are being probed and sinfulness abounds (81.9—13).

Pillars of the Church are proclaiming: There is no god outside of our being: the centre of our being is the only god. We should discard the word god from our vocabulary. God is dead. But we have been forewarned of all this. 'Man, what has emboldened thee against thy Gracious Lord, Who created thee, then perfected thee, then proportioned thee aright? He fashioned thee in whatever form He pleased. In effect, you deny the Judgment. But there are guardians over you, honoured recorders, who know all that you do' (82.7—13).

Because of such widespread denial of God to-day, more even by conduct than by proclaimed word, we have at the very end of the Quran been exhorted to pray: 'I seek protection of the Lord of mankind, the King of mankind, the God of mankind, from the mischief of every sneaking whisperer, who whispers into the minds of people, whether he be hidden from sight or be one of the common people' (114.2—7).

The breath of dawn, the revelation vouchsafed to His noble Messenger by the Lord of the Throne, is beginning to drive away the darkness of the night (81.16—22).

To-day we need to ponder gravely over warnings such as the following: 'We call to witness this perspicuous Book. We revealed it in a blessed Night — We have ever been warning — in which all matters of wisdom are determined by Our command. We have ever sent Messengers, as a mercy from thy Lord. He is the All-Hearing, the All-Knowing, the Lord of the heavens and the earth and all that is between them, if you would only have faith. There is no god but He. He gives life and He causes death. He is your Lord and the Lord of your forefathers. Yet they play about in doubt.Then watch for the day when a pall of smoke will appear in the sky and envelop the people. That will be a painful torment. The cry will go up: Lord, remove from us the torment; we do believe. How will they be admonished, seeing that there came to them a Messenger, expounding matters clearly, and they turned away from him declaring: He has been coached, he is a man possessed. Yet, We shall remove the torment for a while, but you will certainly revert to your misdeeds. Be warned, however, that on the day We seize you with the great seizure, We will certainly exact retribution' (44.3—17).

'An enquirer enquires concerning the torment that will afflict the disbelievers, which none can repel, from Allah, Lord of great ascents. The angels and the Spirit ascend to Him in a day the measure of which is fifty thousand years. So continue steadfast in a becoming manner. They imagine it to be far off, but We see it nigh. On that day the heaven will be like molten copper, and the mountains will be like flakes of wool, and a friend will not enquire after a friend, for they will be within sight of one another. A guilty one would fain ransom himself from the torment of that day by offering his children, and his wife and his brother, and his kinsfolk who gave him shelter, and all those who are on the earth, if only thus he might save himself. All in vain. It will be a fierce blaze, stripping off the skin to the scalp. It will encompass him who turns his back on it and retreats, and who hoarded wealth and withheld it' (70.2—19).

Mankind will become divided into two main groups. These are warned: Soon shall We attend to you two mighty ones. O company of jinn and men, if you have the capacity to penetrate beyond the confines of the heavens and the earth, by all means do so; but you cannot do so except with authority. You will be afflicted with smokeless fire, and with smoke without flame and you will not be able to help yourselves' (55.32—34, 36).

Armageddon is described thus: 'When that day comes We shall let some of them surge against others like the waves of the ocean, and the trumpet will be blown and We shall gather them all together. On that day We shall present hell, face to face, to the disbelievers, whose eyes were veiled against My Reminder (the Quran) so that they heeded it not, and who could not even afford to listen' (18.100—102).

CREATION OF UNIVERSE AND MAN

The Quran is explicit on the creation of the universe and of man. Both have been created with a purpose.

'Allah is the Creator of all things and He is Guardian over all. To Him belong the keys of the heavens and the earth' (39.63, 64). To Him 'belongs the Kingdom of the heavens and the earth. He has taken unto Himself no son, and has no partner in the Kingdom. He has created everything and has determined its measure' (25.3).

'Originator of the heavens and the earth, when He determines the coming into being of a thing, He says concerning it: Be! and it is' (2.118). The process of creation is continuous. 'He originates the creation, then He repeats it' (10.5). 'Ask them: Is there any of your associate-gods who originates creation and then repeats it? Tell them: It is Allah alone Who originates creation and then repeats it. Then whither are you turned away?' (10.35). 'Who originates creation and then repeats it, and Who provides for you from the heaven and the earth? Then is there a god beside Allah? Ask them: Bring forward your proofs, if you are telling the truth' (27.65). 'Be mindful of the day when We shall roll up the heavens like the rolling up of the scrolls by a scribe. As We began the first creation, so shall We repeat it. This is Our promise; We shall certainly perform it' (21.105). 'Know they not how Allah originates creation, then repeats it? That indeed is easy for Allah. Tell them: Travel in the earth, and observe how Allah originated the creation, then will He provide the second creation. Surely, Allah has power to do all that He wills' (29.20, 21).

But the process is gradual and proceeds by stages. All perfect praise belongs to Allah, Who nourishes, sustains and leads stage by stage towards perfection all the worlds (1.2).

'Do not the disbelievers realise that the heavens and the earth were a closed-up mass, then We split them asunder and We made from water every living thing? Will they not then believe? We have placed in the earth firm mountains, lest it should roll beneath them; and We have made wide pathways therein, that they may thereby journey from place to place. We have made the heaven a guarded and protecting roof; yet they turn away from its Signs. He it is Who created the night and the day, and the sun and the moon, each gliding freely in its orbit' (21.31—34).

The universe was brought into being in six periods. 'We created the heavens and the earth and all that is between them in six periods, and We suffered no weariness' (50.39). 'Your Lord is Allah Who created the heavens and the earth in six periods; then He settled Himself on the Throne. He makes the night cover the day, pursuing it swiftly. He has created the sun and the moon and the stars, all made subservient to His command. Hearken: His is the creation and its regulation. Blessed is Allah the Lord of the worlds' (7.55). 'Whatever is in the heavens and the earth glorifies Allah. He is the Mighty, the Wise. His is the Kingdom of the heavens and the earth; He bestows life and He causes death; and He has power to do all that He wills. He is the First and the Last, the Manifest and the Hidden, and He has full knowledge of all things. He it is Who created the heavens and the earth in six periods, then He settled Himself on the Throne. He knows that which enters the earth and that which comes out of it, and that which comes down from heaven and that which goes up into it. He is with you wheresoever you may be. Allah sees all that you do. His is the Kingdom of the heavens and the earth; to Allah are all affairs returned for final determination. He causes the night to pass into the day, and causes the day to pass into the night. He has full knowledge of all that passes through people's minds' (57.2—7).

All life began in water (21.31). Man began to take shape in clay. 'Allah is He Who has created the heavens and the earth, and that which is between the two, in six periods; then He settled Himself on the Throne. You have no helper or intercessor beside Him. Will you not, then, take heed? He will establish His command from the heaven to the earth according to His plan, then it will ascend to Him during a period, which, according to your reckoning, will extend to a thousand years. Such is the Knower of the unseen and the seen, the Mighty, the Ever Merciful, Who has created everything in the best condition and Who began the creation of man from clay' (32.5—8). Then a stage came when the human species began to be procreated through the union of the male and female. 'Then He made his progeny from an extract of an insignificant fluid. Then He perfected his faculties and breathed into him of His spirit. He has bestowed upon you hearing and sight and understanding; but little thanks do you give' (32.9, 10). 'His companion admonished him: Dost thou deny Him Who created thee from dust, then from a sperm-drop, then fashioned thee into a whole man?' (18.38) 'Has not man passed through a space of time when he was not anything made mention of? We created man from a sperm-drop comprising diverse qualities, that We might try him; so We made him hearing and seeing; and We showed him the way. He is either appreciative and follows it, or is ungrateful and rejects it' (76.2—4).

LIFE AFTER DEATH

The Quran insists upon belief in the life after death (5.70). On the other hand, man has ever been reluctant to accept and face that contingency. He is apt to say: 'There is no life other than our present life; we were without life and now we live, but we shall not be raised up again' (23.38). 'Man will ever ask: When I am dead shall I be brought forth alive? Does not man remember that We created him before, when he was nought?' (19.67, 68) 'They ask: When we shall have become bones and broken particles shall we indeed be raised up as a new creation? Tell them: Aye, even if you become stones or iron or any other form of creation that you deem hardest of all, you shall be raised up. Then will they ask: Who is it that shall restore us to life? Answer them: He Who created you the first time' (17.50—52).

The continuation of life after death does not involve the assembly of a dead body's bones and particles, so as to reconstitute the body. The body which is fashioned and developed for terrestrial existence, is suited only to the conditions of this life. Its decomposition and disintegration is wholly irrelevant to the possibility of life after death.

The Quran invites attention to physical birth into this life for the purpose of illustrating the process of rebirth through which the soul passes after death. 'Does not man know that We have created him from a mere sperm-drop? Then he becomes a persistent disputer; he forgets the process of his own creation but coins a lot of theories concerning Us! He asks: Who will quicken the bones when they are decayed? Tell them: He Who created them the first time will quicken them. He knows well every type of creation; the One Who produces fire for you out of the green tree, which you kindle. Has not He Who created the heavens and the earth power to create the like of them? Yea, and He is indeed the Supreme Creator, the All-Knowing' (36.78—82).

'Ruin seize man! How ungrateful he is! Let him reflect out of what did He create him? Out of a sperm-drop! He created him and set a measure for him; then He made the way easy for him, then He causes him to die and assigns a grave to him. Then, when He pleases, He will raise him up again' (80.18—23).

In connection with man's being 'raised up again', attention is repeatedly drawn to the process of man's creation for the purpose of his terrestrial existence. The flesh, the bones, the blood, the muscle, the brain, and indeed all the faculties and the whole complicated and yet wonderfully co-ordinated mechanism of the human body constituting a complete microcosm are all potentially contained in less than a minute fraction of a drop of fluid. In accord with the manifold provisions made by a Wise Creator, the drop of fluid in due course experiences a new creation (23.15) at birth and matures into an intelligent human being, capable of the highest attainment in every field of life. The centre of the whole process is the soul. The body is an essential part, as the means of expression for the soul. It is attuned and adjusted to the conditions of this life. Up to a point the soul and the body together constitute a unit and are indissoluble; then dissolution comes and that is the end of life upon earth, but that is not the end of life itself. At death the functions of the body come to an end, and but for considerations of decency and respect for the dead, it is of no consequence how the body may be disposed of.

The soul then enters upon a process of rebirth, during the course of which it develops a new shell, and the result is another organism suited and adjusted to the conditions of the new life. Thus 'the bones are quickened', but they are quickened out of the soul itself. 'He knows every kind of creation well' clearly indicates that this 'quickening of the bones' will be a new kind of creation, just as the quickening of the embryo in the mother's womb signified its development 'into another creation' (23.15).

At death, with reference to the fuller life awaiting it, the soul is, so to speak, in the stage of the sperm-drop in the mother's womb, when it develops the faculties needed in and appropriate to the conditions of the Hereafter. Its birth into a new life, after passing through this process, is the resurrection. 'Does man think that he is to be left purposeless? Was he not a drop of fluid emitted forth? Then he became a clot, then Allah shaped and proportioned him, and He made of him a pair, male and female. Has He not the power to bring the dead to life'? (75.37—41)

Those who reject the life after death do so because they are too arrogant to admit the possibility of even the Creator having power over them to call them to account for that which they do in this life. 'The minds of those who do not believe in the Hereafter are strangers to reality, and they are arrogant. Of a surety, Allah knows that which they conceal and that which they disclose. Surely, He loves not the arrogant. When it is said to them: How glorious is that which your Lord has sent down! they retort: Old wives' tales!' (16.23—25).

The conditions of the life after death, compared with those of this life are purely spiritual, yet they will be felt, experienced and realised with far greater intensity than are the conditions of this life in the course of existence here. It is not, however, possible to realise here, through our present faculties, the true nature of the conditions of the life hereafter. 'No one knows what bliss is kept hidden for them as a reward for what they used to do' (32.18).

Each human being by his or her conduct in this life develops certain qualities or defects in the soul which render it capable of the appreciation and enjoyment of the conditions of the life hereafter, or which would cause it to react painfully to those conditions; just as a healthy organism reacts agreeably to the conditions of this life and finds joy and happiness in them, while a defective or diseased organism reacts painfully to them. 'We call to witness the soul and its perfect proportioning (He revealed to it the right and wrong of everything), he indeed prospers who purifies it, and he is ruined who corrupts it' (91.8—11). 'The truth is that the portion of him who comes to his Lord a sinner is hell; he shall neither die therein nor live. But he who comes to Him a believer, having acted righteously, for such are the highest ranks in Gardens of Eternity, beneath which rivers flow; they will abide therein for ever. That is the recompense of those who keep themselves pure' (20.75—77).

'He who continues blind in this life will be blind in the Hereafter and even more astray from the right path' (17.73). 'Have they not travelled in the earth that they may have hearts wherewith to understand, and ears wherewith to hear? For the truth is that it is not the eyes that are blind, but blinded are the hearts that are in the breasts' (22.47). This means that the failure to observe, to ponder, and to take heed gradually deprives a person of spiritual insight. He becomes spiritually blind. Such persons, when brought face to face with the consequences of their neglect or indifference, will exclaim: 'Had we but listened and exercised our judgment we would not have been among the inmates of the Blaze' (67.11).

He who develops the faculty of observation and reflects over that which he observes and draws the right conclusions therefrom, has his spiritual insight sharpened and will enter upon the life to come in a state capable of experiencing the utmost delight in reaction to the conditions of that life. In the same way, whoever turns away from Divine guidance and closes his eyes to it is bound to lose his spiritual sight. 'Whoso will turn away from My Reminder, his will be a strait life, and on the Day of Judgment We shall raise him up blind. He will plead: Lord, why hast Thou raised me up blind, while I had good sight before? Allah will say: Thus it is. Our Signs came to thee and thou didst disregard them; in like manner wilt thou be disregarded this day of the manifestation of My mercy' (20.125—127).

All human action leaves an impress upon the soul and the soul carries the sum total of this impress with it and reacts correspondingly in the life to come. 'Every person's doings have We fastened firmly to his neck; and on the Day of Judgment We shall place before him a book which he will find wide open, and he will be told: Read thy record, thou art sufficient as a reckoner against thyself this day. He who follows the right way follows it to his own good; and he who goes astray, does it to his own loss. He who carries a responsibility cannot be relieved of it by another' (17.14—16).

When they face the torment 'their ears, and their eyes, and their skins will bear witness against them concerning that which they used to do. They will enquire from their skins: Why bear ye witness against us? These will make answer: Allah Who has made everything else to speak has made us to speak also. He it is Who created you the first time, and unto Him have you been brought back. You did not apprehend that your ears and your eyes and your skins would bear witness against you; nay, you imagined that even Allah did not know much of that which you did. That notion of yours, which you entertained concerning your Lord, has been your ruin, and you became losers' (41.21—24).

Those who live their lives in the full consciousness of being in the sight of Allah every moment shall enter upon the new life in perfect spiritual health and all their reactions will be joyful. 'Those who were mindful of their duty to their Lord will be conducted to the Garden in groups. When they approach it, and its gates are thrown open, its keepers will greet them with: Peace be upon you; you have attained to the state of bliss, so enter it, abiding therein. They will respond: All praise belongs to Allah, Who has fulfilled His promise to us, and has bestowed upon us this vast region as an inheritance to make our abode in the Garden wherever we please. How excellent, then, is the reward of the righteous workers' (39.74, 75).

CONCEPT OF HEAVEN AND HELL

Heaven and hell are not separate, defined and divided regions, but exist, as it were, coextensively. The Quran says the extent of heaven is like the whole extent of the heavens and the earth (57.22). Someone asked the Holy Prophet: If heaven occupies the whole extent of the heavens and the earth, then where is hell? He replied with another question: When there is day, where is night? Night is the absence of light; hell is the absence of spiritual health.

The phraseology employed, no doubt, constantly creates physical images in the mind, but in the conditions of human existence in this life that is inescapable. The only language that man can understand is the language to which he is accustomed. It is only through explanation and paraphrase that the human mind can be brought closer to some understanding of the conditions the reality of which is beyond its ken.

The conditions of the life to come will be symbolic representations of a person's thoughts, designs and actions in this life, and will be the consequences or fruits thereof. 'Give glad tidings to those who believe and act righteously, that for them there are Gardens beneath which rivers flow. Whenever they are provided with fruit therefrom they will exclaim: This is what was given us before; and similar gifts will be bestowed upon them' (2.26). This means that in the fruits of the Garden the righteous will perceive a resemblance to the spiritual joys experienced by them in this life.

The similitude of the Garden promised to the righteous is: 'Therein are rivers of water that corrupts not; and rivers of milk of which the taste changes not; and rivers of wine, a delight for those who drink; and rivers of pure honey. In it will they have all kinds of fruit, and forgiveness from their Lord' (47.16). This similitude, interpreted according to the science of the interpretation of dreams would mean that the righteous would be in the midst of plenty of every description (water), would acquire increasing knowledge and understanding of Divine attributes (milk), would be filled with the love of Allah (wine), and would be enveloped in the grace and mercy of Allah (honey). The quality of the 'wine' is described as 'sparkling white, delicious to the taste, wherein there will be neither intoxication nor heaviness' (37.47, 48). 'Out of a flowing spring, neither causing headache nor inebriating' (56.19, 20).

The torments of the wicked are summed up as: 'Allah's kindled fire which rises over the hearts' (104.7, 8). There will be seven approaches to it (15.45). These might be the seven senses: sight, hearing, smell, taste, touch, sensitivity to heat and cold, and the muscular sense, that is the sense of fatigue. When the transgressors see the torment they will realise that all power belongs to Allah and that Allah's punishment is severe indeed (2.166). They shall hear its raging and roaring from afar (25.13). They shall drink boiling water; they will sip it and will not be able to swallow it easily (14.17, 18). Their drink will be either boiling or intensely cold, both difficult to swallow, and they shall endure various kinds of other torments of a similar nature (38.58, 59). They shall taste neither coolness nor pleasant drink save boiling water and a fluid that stinks (78.25, 26). Their food will be dry, bitter, thorny herbage; it will neither nourish nor satisfy hunger (88.7, 8). Hell will be their bed as well as their covering (7.42). They will be thrown into a confined space chained together, and will wish for death, but death will not come to them (25.14). They will be closely confined in chains and iron collars (76.5). Their faces will be downcast, lined, weary (88.3, 4). But the greatest torment will be that Allah will not speak to them, nor look at them, nor purify them (2.175; 3.78). Then will they realise how completely have they placed themselves at the pole opposite to the purpose of their creation (14.4; 34.9, 53).

The faces of the righteous will be bright, laughing, joyous (80.39, 40) and will reflect happiness; they will be well pleased with the results of their labour (88.9, 10). They will experience mounting bliss and enjoy a vast kingdom (76.21). They will hear no idle talk, nor any falsehood (78.36), nor anything vain, but only: Peace (19.63; 56.26, 27). They will not feel the unpleasant effects of heat or cold (76.14). Their faces will exhibit the freshness of bliss, and they will be given to drink of a pure beverage, sealed with musk (83.25, 27). They will dwell among gardens and springs (15.46), and will not be affected by fatigue and lassitude (15.49). They will enjoy perfect comfort and the fragrance of happiness (56.90), and will ever be in rapture (76.12). The supreme triumph, however, will be the realisation of having won the pleasure of Allah (3.16; 57.21). 'Their Lord gives them glad tidings of mercy from Him and of His pleasure' (9.21). 'Allah has promised the believers, men and women, Gardens beneath which rivers flow, wherein they will abide, and delightful dwelling-places in Gardens of Eternity, and the pleasure of Allah, which is the greatest of all. That is the supreme triumph' (9.72). 'Allah is well pleased with them and they are well pleased with Him' (9.100).

The Quran teaches that the rewards and joys of the life to come will be everlasting and will be ever intensified, but that the pains and torments will come to an end and that all mankind will ultimately find admission to the grace and mercy of Allah. As man has been created for the purpose of becoming a manifestation of Divine attributes (51.57), that purpose must be fulfilled in respect of everyone. 'I inflict My punishment on whom I so determine; but My mercy encompasses all things' (7.157). Allah has charged Himself with mercy (6.13, 55); mankind has been created for the fulfilment of His mercy (11.120). When pain, punishment and torment will have achieved their curative purpose, which is in itself a manifestation of Divine mercy, each human being will then be capable of reacting joyfully to the conditions of the life hereafter.

The Prophet has said a time will come when hell will be empty and the cool breezes of Divine mercy will blow through it. The concept and quality of time in the Hereafter is within God's knowledge alone and He alone determines and knows how long any particular condition will last. But it is a common experience that periods of joy and happiness seem to race by, while moments of pain and anxiety appear unending. Pain and torment will appear long, for torment suffered under the operation of Divine law will be severely felt, and no alleviation of it may be in sight. But eternity is infinite, and in each case a stage will be reached when torment will cease, pain will disappear and all will be joy. The Quran states that the punishment of evildoers will appear to be unending, but will be terminated when God so wills (11.108). The duration of the joys of the life hereafter is also subject to God's will, but in respect of these the Divine will has determined that 'this is a bounty which shall never be cut off' (11.109). For the righteous there is 'an unending reward' (95.7). The righteous will be greeted by their Lord with: 'O soul at rest, return to thy Lord; thou well-pleased with Him and He well-pleased with thee. So enter among My chosen servants and enter My Garden' (89.28—31).

There will be continuous progress for all in the life to come. Those under sentence will work out their sentence, not merely as an affliction, but as a curative process designed to heal the soul of the defects and disorders accumulated in its life upon earth and to restore it to a state of health and purity which would enable it to react with joy and pleasure to the conditions of the after life. The righteous will be continuously praying for, and seeking, the perfection of their light (66.9). Divine attributes being without limit, the quest of the righteous for greater and greater knowledge thereof, so that they may become perfect manifestations of them, will also be unending.

It is the progressive realisation of the nature and operation of Divine attributes that fills the mind with awe of Divine Majesty and constitutes the most effective deterrent against wrong-doing and furnishes the most potent incentive towards righteous action. The Quran is unique in that it supplies a wealth of knowledge concerning Divine attributes and their operation. 'Had We sent down this Quran on a mountain, thou wouldst certainly have seen it bend down in humility and rent asunder in awe of Allah's Majesty. These are illustrations that We set forth for mankind that they may reflect. Allah is He beside Whom there is no god, Knower of the unseen and the seen. He is the Most Gracious, the Ever Merciful. Allah is He beside Whom there is no god, the Sovereign, the Most Holy, the Source of Peace, the Bestower of Security, the Protector, the Mighty, the Subduer, the Exalted. Holy is Allah far above that which they associate with Him. He is Allah, the Creator, the Maker, the Fashioner. His are the most beautiful names. All that is in the heavens and the earth glorifies Him. He is the Mighty, the Wise' (59.22—25).

UNIVERSAL, COMPREHENSIVE, DYNAMIC TEACHING OF THE QURAN

Human life and society are dynamic. New problems entailing new approaches, broader outlooks and fresh philosophic concepts continue to arise. The Quran claims that the guidance set forth in it would prove adequate at all times and in all contingencies. In this context the unique characteristic of the Quran, that its entire text is verbal revelation and that thus it is literally the Word of God, has supreme significance and relevance. Like the universe the Quran is alive. It is like a good tree, which is firmly rooted and whose branches reach into heaven. It brings forth its fruit at all times by the command of its Lord (14.25, 26). Whenever, in view of any approaching contingency, the need of fresh interpretation has arisen, Divine grace has inspired and illumined the mind of some devoted righteous servant of His to set it forth clearly for the instruction and benefit of mankind. This has been the case, as foretold by the Holy Prophet (on whom be peace) in each century of Islam, and has furnished a continuous manifestation of the Divine assurance that the Exhortation would be fully safeguarded through the ages.

The first half of the twentieth century witnessed an unprecedented intellectual, scientific and technological upsurge, which has ushered in a new era in these domains, and appears to have added, as it were, a new dimension to human life. In consequence, all values, including moral and spiritual ones, which are the peculiar concern of religion, have been put on trial. In pursuance of the Divine assurance the guidance needed by mankind in the era that is now unfolding itself was set forth and expounded in advance, from the Quran, during the latter part of the nineteenth and the early years of the twentieth century by a divinely inspired teacher and guide who had been designated a witness to the truth of the Holy Prophet (11.18) and in whose person the prophecy (62.4) concerning the second advent of the Holy Prophet (on whom be peace) was fulfilled.

Thus the Quran is a universal and perpetual fountain of comprehensive guidance. It seeks to convince through reason and persuasion and not merely on the basis of authority (12.109). 'We have expounded everything in this Quran that they may take heed; a Quran expressed in clear language. wherein there is no deviation from the truth, that they may become righteous' (39.28, 29). That for close upon fourteen centuries the Quran has steadily kept well ahead of man's need for guidance in every sphere and has never fallen behind is not only an impressive tribute to its consummate wisdom (54.6) but is proof beyond doubt or cavil of its having come down from the Wise, All-Knowing One (27.7). Neither history, nor archaeology, nor any discovery about or research into the past; nor any advance of science or technology, or any research into or well-founded speculation concerning that which lies ahead will furnish contradiction of the truth contained in the Quran. 'Truly, it is a mighty Book. Falsehood cannot approach it from fore or aft, for it is a revelation from the Wise, the Praiseworthy' (41.42, 43). 'This Quran is a revelation from the Most Gracious, the Ever Merciful; a Book whose commandments have been expounded in detail, which will be repeatedly read, couched in clear, eloquent language, for the benefit of people who possess knowledge; bearer of glad tidings and a warner' (41.3—5). 'The Spirit of Holiness has brought it down from thy Lord in accordance with the requirements of truth and wisdom, that He may strengthen those who believe, and also as a guidance and good tidings for those who submit' (16.103).

The Quran is called an Exhortation (15.10), a blessed Reminder (21.51), a wise Reminder (3.59), a Book 'which makes provision for your uplift' (21.11). 'It is a Light from Allah and a clear Book, whereby does Allah guide those who seek His pleasure along the paths of peace, and leads them out of every kind of darkness into the light by His will, and guides them to the right path' (5.16, 17). 'Surely this Quran guides to the way which is most firm and right; and gives to the believers who act righteously the glad tidings that they shall have a great reward' (17.10). 'O mankind, there has indeed come to you a Book from your Lord which is full of admonition and a healing for all the ills of the spirit, and a guidance and a mercy for the believers' (10.58).

The guidance contained in the Quran is inexhaustible. 'Tell them: If the ocean became ink for inscribing the words of my Lord, the ocean would be exhausted before the words of my Lord came to an end, even though We augmented it with the like quantity' (18.110). 'If all the trees in the earth became pens, and the ocean, reinforced by seven oceans, became ink for transcribing the words of Allah, these would not be exhausted. Surely, Allah is Mighty, Wise' (31.28).

That which was fundamental in previous revelations is comprised in the Quran (98.3, 4). That which was of purely local or temporary character has been omitted or abrogated; that which was still needed but had been forgotten has been revived; and that which was to be needed henceforth has been supplied. 'Those from among the People of the Book and from among those who associate partners with Allah, who have disbelieved, desire not that any good may be sent down to you from your Lord. They forget that Allah chooses as the recipients of His mercy whomsoever He pleases. Allah is Lord of exceeding bounty. Whatever previous commandment We abrogate or cause to be forgotten, We reveal in this Quran one better or the like thereof. Knowest thou not that Allah has full power to do all that He wills?' (2.106, 107).

Such and vastly more is the Quran: guidance, light, healing, wisdom. Therein would distracted mankind find an adequate remedy for the ills from which it suffers today and which threaten to overwhelm it tomorrow. It is a revelation from Him Who created the earth and the high heavens (20.5), the Lord of the worlds (26.193; 32.3; 56.81; 69.44), the Mighty, the Ever Merciful (36.6), the Mighty, the Wise (39.2; 45.3; 46.3), the Mighty, the All-Knowing (40.3), the Most Gracious, the Ever Merciful (41.3), the One Wise, Praiseworthy (41.43).

Mankind stands poised on the brink of a limitless pit of raging fire. The only means of security is to take fast hold of Allah's rope. 'O ye who believe, be mindful of your duty to Allah in all respects, every moment of your lives, so that death whenever it overtakes you, should find you in a state of complete submission to Him. Take fast hold, all together, of the rope of Allah, and be not divided. Call to mind the favour of Allah which He bestowed upon you when you were at enmity with each other and He united your hearts in love, so that by His grace you became as brethren. You were on the brink of a pit of fire and He delivered you from it. Thus does Allah explain to you His commandments that you may be guided. Let there be from among you a party whose business it should be to invite to goodness, to enjoin equity and to forbid evil. It is they who shall prosper' (3.103—105).

Today, careful, diligent and repeated study of the Quran is an indispensable imperative for Muslim and non-Muslim alike. As has been pointed out, it may be neglected only at serious risk of direst peril to man's future, here and Hereafter. To make available to those who have no ready means of access to them even a fraction of the vast and limitless treasures of wisdom and guidance comprised in the Quran is to fill man's greatest need at this fateful juncture in his fortunes.

HARMONY IN THE UNIVERSE

There is complete harmony in the universe; there is no incongruity and no discord. 'Blessed is He in Whose hand is the kingdom and He has the power to do all that He wills, Who has created death and life that He might try you which of you is best in conduct. He is the Mighty, the Most Forgiving, Who has created the seven heavens in order, one above the other. Thou canst not discover a flaw in the creation of the Gracious One. Then look again: Seest thou any disparity? Look again and yet again, thy sight will return to thee frustrated and fatigued' (67.2—5).

It is Allah who maintains harmony between different parts of the universe and thus safeguards it against ruin. 'Allah holds the heavens and the earth, lest they should deviate from their places. Were they to deviate none could keep them from destruction thereafter except Him. Surely, He is Forbearing, Most Forgiving' (35.42).

Attention is drawn to different aspects of this harmony as divine Signs. For instance: 'The night is also a Sign for them. We strip off the day from it, and they are left in darkness. The sun is moving towards an appointed goal. That is the decree of the Almighty the All-Knowing. We have appointed stages for the moon, till it wanes into the shape of an old dry branch of a palm-tree. It is not permissible for the sun to approach the moon, nor may the night outstrip the day. All glide along in an orbit' (36.38—41).

Allah has established a Balance which must be respected so that it may continue to yield the beneficence which it is designed to generate. 'Allah it is Who has sent down the Book with truth and also the Balance' (42.18). 'He has raised the heaven high and set up the measure, that you may not transgress the measure' (55.8, 9).

It is part of this Balance that an alternation is maintained between the day and the night, which makes human life possible on earth and whence flow untold streams of beneficence for mankind. In the creation of the heavens and the earth and in the alternation of the night and the day there are indeed Signs for people of understanding, who remember Allah standing, sitting and lying on their sides, and ponder over the creation of the heavens and the earth, which impels them to supplicate: Lord, Thou hast not created all this without purpose' (3.191, 192).

We are reminded that the system of the universe is so arranged that the faculties with which man is endowed should be able to function at their highest: 'Have We not made the earth a bed and driven in the mountains as stakes? We have created you in pairs, and made your sleep a source of rest and made the night a covering, and made the day for the activities of life. We have built above you seven heavens and made the sun a brightly burning lamp. We send down from the dripping clouds water pouring forth abundantly, that We may bring forth thereby grain and vegetation, and luxuriant gardens' (78.7—17).

Man takes all this for granted and pays little heed to the wisdom and beneficence that established this harmonious system. A sharp reminder is administered: 'Ask them: Tell me, if Allah were to extend the night over you till the Day of Judgment, what god is there beside Allah who could bring you light? Will you not then hearken? Ask them also: Tell me, if Allah were to extend the day over you till the Day of Judgment, what god is there beside Allah who could bring you night wherein you could rest? Will you not then see? Of His mercy He made for you the night and the day, that you may rest therein and that you may seek of His bounty, and that you may be grateful' (28.72, 74).

Allah is the source of all beneficence which is limitless, but He determines the measure of everything. 'There is not a thing but We have unbounded stores thereof, and We send it down in regulated quantities' (15.22). As an illustration, consider the supply of water for the earth. 'We put in motion winds carrying moisture, then We send down fresh water from the clouds, wherewith We provide you with drink. You could not have stored it up for yourselves' (15.23). A moment's reflection would bring to mind how wonderful is this system of storing up water for the earth and its creatures. The oceans are of course the major reservoirs. Through the action of the sun vapours are lifted into the air and the moist winds carry the vapours in the form of clouds to regions where rain is needed.

'Verily, in the heavens and the earth are Signs for those who believe. Likewise in your own creation, and in that of all the creatures that He spreads out in the earth are Signs for a people who possess firm faith. Also in the alternation of the night and the day, and in the provision that Allah sends down from the sky, whereby He quickens the earth after its death, and in the courses of the winds, are Signs for a people who use their understanding' (45.3—6). 'Allah is He Who sends the winds, so that they raise the vapours in the form of clouds which He spreads in the sky as He pleases, layer upon layer, and thou seest the rain issuing forth from their midst. When He causes it to fall on whom He pleases of His servants, they rejoice thereat; though before its coming down they were in despair. Observe, then, the token of Allah's mercy; how He revives the earth after its death' (30.49—51).

Fresh rain water comes down from the clouds and is not only supplied direct to the dry and parched earth where it provides irrigation for the crops, trees and shrubs and renews the subsoil reservoirs but it is also stored up in huge quantities in the form of snow on the mountains and higher plateaus and glaciers which form a permanent reservoir of fresh water and reinforce the supply for the earth as it is needed. 'Seest thou not that Allah wafts the clouds gently, then joins them together, then piles them up so that thou seest the rain issue forth from the midst thereof? He sends down from the clouds volumes of matter, part of it in the form of hail and He causes it to fall on whom He pleases and turns it away from whom He pleases' (24.44).

He has so ordained this system that one part of it reinforces the other, thus forming a cycle, the oceans reinforcing the supply of fresh water through rain, hail, snow, etc., and fresh water reinforcing the oceans through streams, rivers and the lava that is thrown up by volcanic eruption: 'Of stones there are some out of which gush forth streams, and there are some that cleave asunder and water flows out from them' (2.75). This cycle is so arranged as to ensure a balance between the supply of fresh water and the maintenance of the needed supply in the oceans. 'He it is Who has caused the two waters to flow, one of the rivers and springs, sweet and palatable, and the other of the oceans, salt and bitter; and between them he has placed as a barrier a system that keeps them apart' (25.54). 'The two waters are not alike; the one of the rivers and springs sweet, palatable and pleasant to drink and the other of the sea, salt and bitter. From each you eat fresh meat and fish out articles that you wear as ornaments. Thou seest the vessels ploughing through each so that you may be grateful' (35.13). He Who has instituted this system and brought it into operation has complete power over it and He alone can repair any default or deficiency that may manifest itself. 'Ask them: Tell me, if all your water were to disappear in the earth, then who will bring you clear flowing water' (67.31)?

Any serious interference with the cycle that has been established in nature, whether deliberate or accidental, conscious or unconscious, is bound to entail prejudicial consequences. History furnishes many instances of it. In the present age with the tremendous advance of science and technology the risk of interference or interruption of a natural cycle has been tremendously augmented and consequently there is much greater need of study, research and caution in this sphere, reinforced by the revival and strengthening of moral and spiritual values so that man's own efforts may be blessed and strengthened by divine grace, which may be sought and won through communion with Him. We are directed: 'Supplicate: Oh Allah, Lord of sovereignty, Thou bestowest sovereignty upon whomsoever Thou pleasest, and Thou takest away sovereignty from whomsoever Thou pleasest, Thou exaltest whomsoever Thou pleasest, and Thou abasest whomsoever Thou pleasest, in Thy hand is all good. Thou surely hast power to do all that Thou dost will. Thou makest the night pass into day and makest the day pass into night; Thou bringest forth the living from the dead and bringest forth the dead from the living. Thou bestowest upon whomsoever Thou pleasest without measure' (3.27, 28).

The cycle described in bringing forth the living from the dead and bringing forth the dead from the living must be maintained and strengthened in efficient operation so as to obviate any imbalance that might threaten the upholding of material, moral and spiritual values.

WARNINGS

The Quran contains a continuous series of alternating 'glad tidings' and 'warnings'. The fundamental is that if man seeks for guidance and adheres to the 'straight path' (1.6), his life will be one continuous course of progress in every respect, here and Hereafter. If he neglects seeking guidance, or, being invited to it, rejects it and turns his back on it, or having recognized it persists in ignoring or defying it, he must take the consequences of his neglect or default of which he is continuously and repeatedly warned. Attention may be drawn, as illustration, to some of these warnings.

The earth is mankind's habitat and is invested with capacities which, properly exploited, would yield continuous and increasing beneficence. Abuse or misuse of these capacities would spell ruin. One of the forms of abuse may be over-exploitation, against which also there are warnings. For instance:

'When the earth is shaken violently and brings forth its burdens, and man cries out: What is the matter with it? On that day it will narrate its account, for thy Lord has so directed it. On that day people will come forth in diverse groups that they may be shown the consequences of their actions. Then whoso will have done the smallest particle of good will see it, and whoso will have done the smallest particle of ill will also see it' (99.2—9).

It is pointed out that the beneficent exploitation of the earth's capacities and resources will be a source of delight but that if the exploitation is not beneficent the ultimate result will be ruin. 'We have made all that is on the earth an ornament for it, that We may try the dwellers thereof which of them is best in conduct. The time will come when We shall turn all that is on it into a barren waste' (18.8, 9).

It needs to be stressed that non-beneficent exploitation does not comprise only harmful methods of say cultivation, mining, forestry, cattle breeding, horticulture and all the other multifarious ways of direct exploitation of the capacities and resources of the earth. It also includes the non-beneficent character of the uses to which the fruits of the earth may be put and all the consequences that might flow therefrom. For instance: 'There is a lesson for you in the cattle. We provide you with a drink out of that which is in their bellies; that is, from betwixt the faeces and the blood We provide milk pure and pleasant for those who drink it. Of the fruits of date-palms and the grapes you obtain intoxicating drinks, and also pure and wholesome food. Surely, in that is a Sign for a people who make use of their understanding' (16.67, 68).

Part of the warning is more specifically spelled out: 'Oh ye who believe, liquor, gambling, idols and divining arrows are but abominations and Satanic devices. So turn wholly away from each of them that you may prosper. Satan desires only to create enmity and hatred between you by means of liquor and gambling and to keep you back from the remembrance of Allah and from Prayer. Will you, then, desist?' (5.91, 92). There is of course also the peril that over-exploitation may become non-beneficent and confront man-kind with a crisis. Attention is drawn to this: 'When the earth is stretched forth and pours out its contents and becomes empty' (84.4, 5).

MEANING OF ISTIGHFAR

The root of the word *istighfar* is *ghafar*, which means to cover up, protect or suppress. The primary connotation of istighfar is to supplicate for the suppression of the human tendency to fall into error so as to be safeguarded against error or sin. Its secondary connotation is to supplicate for the suppression of the consequences of error or sin so as to be safeguarded against the harm or suffering that might ensue therefrom. Istighfar might seek protection for oneself or for others. It might seek protection against one's own tendency towards error or sin, or against the consequences of such error or sin; or it might seek protection for others against their tendency towards error or sin, or the consequences of their errors or sins; or for one's own protection against the consequences of the errors and sins of others. Thus ghafar might connote suppression of a person's tendency towards falling into error or sin; or his protection against the consequences of such error or sin, or of the errors and sins of others.

A righteous person is diligent in istighfar in all its connotations. This does not mean that such a one has necessarily been guilty of error or sin. Indeed, the purer a person is the more eager and diligent he is in istighfar as a means of approach and nearness to the Divine.

God has warned: 'If you will use My bounties beneficently, I will surely multiply them unto you, but if you misuse them, My punishment is severe indeed' (14.8). Every divine bounty, therefore, impels a righteous person towards istighfar, thereby seeking protection against neglect or slighting of the bounty, by himself or by others. Thus the Holy Prophet (on whom be peace) was exhorted to istighfar on a large accession of people to the faith (110.4), that is to say, to supplicate for protection against neglect or slackness on the part of Muslims in consequence of such accession.

Neglect, slackness, omission or a tendency towards these or towards disobedience is comprised within the connotation of *dhanb*. A Prophet is safeguarded against all sin, disobedience, neglect, omission or the eruption into action of the human tendency towards any of them and is, therefore, constant and diligent in istighfar against such eruption on his own part as well as on the part of others. The Truce of Hudaibiyyah is named a clear victory in the Holy Quran and God also announced that it imported the safe-guarding by God of the Holy Prophet in the past as well as in the future against neglect, omission, slackness or any tendency towards them (48.2—3). He was also assured of the continuation of effective divine help.

PUBLISHER'S NOTE

In the following .free-flowing English version the numbered paragraphs incorporate several verses. This is essential to the concept of the translation. Every effort has therefore been made to relate the English to the Arabic without disturbing the presentation of the translation

THE QURAN

CONTENTS

AL-FĀTIḤAH
(Revealed before Hijra)

In the name of Allah, Most Gracious, Ever Merciful. (1)

بِسْمِ اللهِ الرَّحْمٰنِ الرَّحِيْمِ ۚ ①

All types of perfect praise belong to Allah alone,

اَلْحَمْدُ لِلّٰهِ رَبِّ الْعٰلَمِيْنَ ۚ ②

the Lord of all the worlds,
Most Gracious,
Ever Merciful,
Master of the Day of Judgment. (2—4)

الرَّحْمٰنِ الرَّحِيْمِ ۚ ③

مٰلِكِ يَوْمِ الدِّيْنِ ۚ ④

Thee alone do we worship and Thee alone do we implore for help.

اِيَّاكَ نَعْبُدُ وَاِيَّاكَ نَسْتَعِيْنُ ۚ ⑤

Guide us along the straight path —
the path of those on whom Thou hast bestowed Thy favours,

اِهْدِنَا الصِّرَاطَ الْمُسْتَقِيْمَ ۙ ⑥

those who have not incurred Thy displeasure, and

صِرَاطَ الَّذِيْنَ اَنْعَمْتَ عَلَيْهِمْ ۙ غَيْرِ الْمَغْضُوْبِ

those who have not gone astray. (5—7)

عَلَيْهِمْ وَلَا الضَّآلِّيْنَ ۚ ⑦

سُوْرَةُ الْبَقَرَةِ مَدَنِيَّتٌ

AL-BAQARAH
(Revealed after Hijra)

In the name of Allah, Most Gracious, Ever Merciful. (1)

بِسْمِ اللهِ الرَّحْمٰنِ الرَّحِيْمِ ۞

I AM ALLAH, THE ALL-KNOWING.

الۤمّۤ ۞

This is the Perfect Book, free from all doubt; it is a guidance for the righteous, who believe in the unseen, observe Prayer, and spend out of whatsoever We have bestowed upon them; and who believe in that which has been revealed to thee, and in that which was revealed before thee, and have firm faith in that which has been foretold and is yet to come. It is these who are firmly grounded in the guidance that has come from their Lord, and it is these who shall prosper. Those who have disbelieved so that it is the same whether thou warn them or warn them not, will not believe. Allah has set a seal on their hearts and their ears, and over their eyes there is a covering. For them there is a great punishment. (2—8)

ذٰلِكَ الْكِتٰبُ لَا رَيْبَ فِيْهِ هُدًى لِّلْمُتَّقِيْنَ ۞ الَّذِيْنَ يُؤْمِنُوْنَ بِالْغَيْبِ وَيُقِيْمُوْنَ الصَّلٰوةَ وَمِمَّا رَزَقْنٰهُمْ يُنْفِقُوْنَ ۞ وَالَّذِيْنَ يُؤْمِنُوْنَ بِمَا أُنْزِلَ إِلَيْكَ وَمَا أُنْزِلَ مِنْ قَبْلِكَ وَبِالْاٰخِرَةِ هُمْ يُوْقِنُوْنَ ۞ أُولٰٓئِكَ عَلٰى هُدًى مِّنْ رَّبِّهِمْ وَأُولٰٓئِكَ هُمُ الْمُفْلِحُوْنَ ۞ إِنَّ الَّذِيْنَ كَفَرُوْا سَوَآءٌ عَلَيْهِمْ ءَأَنْذَرْتَهُمْ أَمْ لَمْ تُنْذِرْهُمْ لَا يُؤْمِنُوْنَ ۞ خَتَمَ اللهُ عَلٰى قُلُوْبِهِمْ وَعَلٰى سَمْعِهِمْ وَعَلٰى أَبْصَارِهِمْ غِشَاوَةٌ وَّلَهُمْ عَذَابٌ عَظِيْمٌ ۞

Of the people there are some who say: We believe in Allah and the Last Day; yet they do not believe at all. They seek to deceive Allah and those who believe, but in truth they deceive none save themselves; only they perceive it not. In their minds is a disease; Allah through the continuous manifestation of His Signs causes their disease to grow worse. For them there is a painful punishment because of their lying. (9—11)

وَمِنَ النَّاسِ مَنْ يَّقُوْلُ اٰمَنَّا بِاللهِ وَبِالْيَوْمِ الْاٰخِرِ وَمَا هُمْ بِمُؤْمِنِيْنَ ۞ يُخٰدِعُوْنَ اللهَ وَالَّذِيْنَ اٰمَنُوْا وَمَا يَخْدَعُوْنَ إِلَّا أَنْفُسَهُمْ وَمَا يَشْعُرُوْنَ ۞ فِيْ قُلُوْبِهِمْ مَّرَضٌ فَزَادَهُمُ اللهُ مَرَضًا وَّلَهُمْ عَذَابٌ أَلِيْمٌ بِمَا كَانُوْا يَكْذِبُوْنَ ۞

6

When it is said to them: Create not dis-order in the land; they retort: We are only seeking to promote peace. Take note: Most certainly it is they who create disorder, but they realise it not. When it is said to them: Believe ye as other people have be-lieved; they exclaim: Shall we also believe as the foolish ones have believed? Take note: Most certainly it is they who are foolish but they know it not. When they meet those who believe, they assert: We believe; but when they are in the company of their ringleaders they assure them: We are certainly with you, we were only mock-ing these believers. Allah will punish them for their mockery and will leave them to flounder on in their transgression. These are they who have rejected guidance and chosen error, but their traffic has brought them no gain, nor are they rightly guided. (12—17)

وَإِذَا قِيلَ لَهُمْ لَا تُفْسِدُوا فِي الْأَرْضِ قَالُوا إِنَّمَا نَحْنُ مُصْلِحُونَ ۞

أَلَا إِنَّهُمْ هُمُ الْمُفْسِدُونَ وَلَٰكِن لَّا يَشْعُرُونَ ۞

وَإِذَا قِيلَ لَهُمْ آمِنُوا كَمَا آمَنَ النَّاسُ قَالُوا أَنُؤْمِنُ كَمَا آمَنَ السُّفَهَاءُ أَلَا إِنَّهُمْ هُمُ السُّفَهَاءُ وَلَٰكِن لَّا يَعْلَمُونَ ۞

وَإِذَا لَقُوا الَّذِينَ آمَنُوا قَالُوا آمَنَّا وَإِذَا خَلَوْا إِلَىٰ شَيَاطِينِهِمْ قَالُوا إِنَّا مَعَكُمْ إِنَّمَا نَحْنُ مُسْتَهْزِئُونَ ۞

اللَّهُ يَسْتَهْزِئُ بِهِمْ وَيَمُدُّهُمْ فِي طُغْيَانِهِمْ يَعْمَهُونَ ۞

أُولَٰئِكَ الَّذِينَ اشْتَرَوُا الضَّلَالَةَ بِالْهُدَىٰ فَمَا رَبِحَت تِّجَارَتُهُمْ وَمَا كَانُوا مُهْتَدِينَ ۞

Their case is like that of a person who kindles a fire, and when it lights up all around him, Allah takes away their light and leaves them in manifold darknesses out of which they can see no way of deliver-ance. They are deaf, dumb and blind and cannot find their way back. Or, their case is like that of heavy rain pouring down from thick clouds, wherein there are manifold darknesses and thunder and lightning; they thrust their fingers into their ears to keep out the sound of the thunder-claps, being fearful of death, while Allah is sure to compass the ruin of the disbelievers. The lightning flash might well-nigh strike them blind; whenever it flashes they walk in its light, and when it is dark they stand still. If Allah so willed, He could destroy their hearing and their sight; surely Allah has the power to carry out all that He wills. (18—21)

مَثَلُهُمْ كَمَثَلِ الَّذِي اسْتَوْقَدَ نَارًا فَلَمَّا أَضَاءَتْ مَا حَوْلَهُ ذَهَبَ اللَّهُ بِنُورِهِمْ وَتَرَكَهُمْ فِي ظُلُمَاتٍ لَّا يُبْصِرُونَ ۞

صُمٌّ بُكْمٌ عُمْيٌ فَهُمْ لَا يَرْجِعُونَ ۞

أَوْ كَصَيِّبٍ مِّنَ السَّمَاءِ فِيهِ ظُلُمَاتٌ وَرَعْدٌ وَبَرْقٌ يَجْعَلُونَ أَصَابِعَهُمْ فِي آذَانِهِم مِّنَ الصَّوَاعِقِ حَذَرَ الْمَوْتِ وَاللَّهُ مُحِيطٌ بِالْكَافِرِينَ ۞

يَكَادُ الْبَرْقُ يَخْطَفُ أَبْصَارَهُمْ كُلَّمَا أَضَاءَ لَهُم مَّشَوْا فِيهِ وَإِذَا أَظْلَمَ عَلَيْهِمْ قَامُوا وَلَوْ شَاءَ اللَّهُ لَذَهَبَ بِسَمْعِهِمْ وَأَبْصَارِهِمْ إِنَّ اللَّهَ عَلَىٰ كُلِّ شَيْءٍ قَدِيرٌ ۞

7

R. 3.

O mankind, worship your Lord Who has created you and created those who were before you, that you may be shielded against all ill; Who has spread out the earth like a bed for you and has made the heaven like a canopy, and has caused water to come down from the clouds and has therewith brought forth provision for you in the shape of fruits. Do not, therefore, deliberately set up equals with Allah. If you are in doubt concerning that which We have sent down to Our servant, then produce a chapter like it and call upon your helpers beside Allah to help you out, if you are truthful. But if you do it not, and never shall you be able to do it, then guard against the Fire, whose fuel are men and stones, which is prepared for the disbelievers. (22—25)

Give glad tidings to those who believe and work righteousness, that for them there are Gardens beneath which rivers flow. Whenever they are provided with fruit therefrom, they will exclaim: This is what was given us before; and similar gifts will be bestowed upon them. They will have therein mates most pure, and therein will they abide. (26)

Allah disdains not the recital of anything, even as small as a gnat or smaller. Those who believe recognise it as truth from their Lord; while those who disbelieve mutter: What does Allah mean by such a recital? The truth is that many does Allah adjudge to be in error and many does He guide by means of the Quran, and none does He adjudge thereby to be erring save the disobedient ones, who break the covenant of Allah after having affirmed it, and cut asunder that which Allah has bidden to be joined, and create disorder in the land; it is these that are the losers. (27—28)

8

How can you disbelieve in Allah? You were without life and He gave you life, then He will cause you to die, then He will restore you to life and then to Him will you be made to return. He it is Who has created for your benefit all that is in the earth; then He turned towards the heavens and perfected them seven heavens. He has full knowledge of all things. (29—30)

في الْاَرْضِ اُولٰٓئِكَ هُمُ الْخٰسِرُوْنَ ۲۸

كَيْفَ تَكْفُرُوْنَ بِاللّٰهِ وَكُنْتُمْ اَمْوَاتًا فَاَحْيَاكُمْ ثُمَّ يُمِيْتُكُمْ ثُمَّ يُحْيِيْكُمْ ثُمَّ اِلَيْهِ تُرْجَعُوْنَ ۲۹

هُوَ الَّذِيْ خَلَقَ لَكُمْ مَّا فِي الْاَرْضِ جَمِيْعًا ثُمَّ اسْتَوٰٓى اِلَى السَّمَاءِ فَسَوّٰىهُنَّ سَبْعَ سَمٰوٰتٍ وَهُوَ بِكُلِّ شَيْءٍ عَلِيْمٌ ۳۰

Call to mind, when thy Lord announced to the angels: I am about to place a vicegerent in the earth. They said: Wilt Thou then place there also such as will create disorder therein and shed blood, while we glorify Thee with Thy praise and extol Thy Holiness? Whereupon He admonished them: I know that which you know not. He taught Adam the names of all His attributes, then He presented the manifestations of those attributes to the angels and asked them: Tell Me the names of these, if you are right. They answered: Holy art Thou! No knowledge have we save that which Thou hast taught us. Thou alone art the All-Knowing, the Possessor of Wisdom. He turned to Adam and commanded him: Adam, do thou inform them of the names of these. When Adam had told them the names, Allah said to the angels: Did I not say to you: I know the secrets of the heavens and of the earth, and I know all that you disclose and all that you conceal? (31—34)

وَاِذْ قَالَ رَبُّكَ لِلْمَلٰٓئِكَةِ اِنِّيْ جَاعِلٌ فِي الْاَرْضِ خَلِيْفَةً قَالُوْا اَتَجْعَلُ فِيْهَا مَنْ يُّفْسِدُ فِيْهَا وَيَسْفِكُ الدِّمَاءَ وَنَحْنُ نُسَبِّحُ بِحَمْدِكَ وَنُقَدِّسُ لَكَ قَالَ اِنِّيْ اَعْلَمُ مَا لَا تَعْلَمُوْنَ ۳۱

وَعَلَّمَ اٰدَمَ الْاَسْمَاءَ كُلَّهَا ثُمَّ عَرَضَهُمْ عَلَى الْمَلٰٓئِكَةِ فَقَالَ اَنْبِئُوْنِيْ بِاَسْمَاءِ هٰٓؤُلَاءِ اِنْ كُنْتُمْ صٰدِقِيْنَ ۳۲

قَالُوْا سُبْحٰنَكَ لَا عِلْمَ لَنَا اِلَّا مَا عَلَّمْتَنَا اِنَّكَ اَنْتَ الْعَلِيْمُ الْحَكِيْمُ ۳۳

قَالَ يٰٓاٰدَمُ اَنْبِئْهُمْ بِاَسْمَائِهِمْ فَلَمَّا اَنْبَاَهُمْ بِاَسْمَائِهِمْ قَالَ اَلَمْ اَقُلْ لَّكُمْ اِنِّيْ اَعْلَمُ غَيْبَ السَّمٰوٰتِ وَالْاَرْضِ وَاَعْلَمُ مَا تُبْدُوْنَ وَمَا كُنْتُمْ تَكْتُمُوْنَ ۳۴

Call to mind, when We commanded the angels: Submit to Adam; they all submitted, but Iblis did not; he refused and was arrogant, being already one of the disbelievers. We commanded Adam: Dwell thou and thy wife in the garden, and eat plentifully therefrom wherever you will, but approach not this one tree, lest you be of the wrongdoers.

وَاِذْ قُلْنَا لِلْمَلٰٓئِكَةِ اسْجُدُوْا لِاٰدَمَ فَسَجَدُوْا اِلَّا اِبْلِيْسَ اَبٰى وَاسْتَكْبَرَ وَكَانَ مِنَ الْكٰفِرِيْنَ ۳۵

وَقُلْنَا يٰٓاٰدَمُ اسْكُنْ اَنْتَ وَزَوْجُكَ الْجَنَّةَ وَكُلَا مِنْهَا رَغَدًا حَيْثُ شِئْتُمَا وَلَا تَقْرَبَا هٰذِهِ الشَّجَرَةَ فَتَكُوْنَا مِنَ الظّٰلِمِيْنَ ۳۶

9

But Satan caused them both to slip from
their stand of obedience by means of that
tree, and thus drove them out of the state
in which they were. Whereupon We
decreed: Go forth, some of you are enemies
of others, and for you there is in the earth
a place of abode and provision for a time.
Thereafter Adam learnt certain words of
prayer from his Lord, and began to pray
as he was taught. So He turned towards
him with mercy; surely He is Oft-returning
with compassion towards His creatures
and is Ever Merciful. We decreed: Go
forth hence, all of you, but remember
that if there comes to you guidance from
Me, then whoso follows My guidance, on
them shall come no fear, nor shall they
grieve; but such as shall disbelieve and
reject Our Signs as false, these shall be the
inmates of the Fire; therein shall they
abide. (35—40)

فَأَزَلَّهُمَا الشَّيْطٰنُ عَنْهَا فَأَخْرَجَهُمَا مِمَّا كَانَا فِيْهِ ۖ
وَقُلْنَا اهْبِطُوْا بَعْضُكُمْ لِبَعْضٍ عَدُوٌّ ۚ وَ لَكُمْ فِي
الْأَرْضِ مُسْتَقَرٌّ وَّ مَتَاعٌ اِلٰى حِيْنٍ ۝

فَتَلَقّٰى اٰدَمُ مِنْ رَّبِّهٖ كَلِمٰتٍ فَتَابَ عَلَيْهِ ۚ اِنَّهٗ هُوَ
التَّوَّابُ الرَّحِيْمُ ۝

قُلْنَا اهْبِطُوْا مِنْهَا جَمِيْعًا ۚ فَاِمَّا يَأْتِيَنَّكُمْ مِّنِّيْ هُدًى
فَمَنْ تَبِعَ هُدَايَ فَلَا خَوْفٌ عَلَيْهِمْ وَلَا هُمْ يَحْزَنُوْنَ ۝
وَالَّذِيْنَ كَفَرُوْا وَ كَذَّبُوْا بِاٰيٰتِنَا أُولٰٓئِكَ أَصْحٰبُ النَّارِ ۚ
هُمْ فِيْهَا خٰلِدُوْنَ ۝

يٰبَنِيْ اِسْرَآءِيْلَ اذْكُرُوْا نِعْمَتِيَ الَّتِيْ أَنْعَمْتُ عَلَيْكُمْ
وَأَوْفُوْا بِعَهْدِيْ أُوْفِ بِعَهْدِكُمْ ۚ وَاِيَّايَ فَارْهَبُوْنِ ۝
وَاٰمِنُوْا بِمَا أَنْزَلْتُ مُصَدِّقًا لِّمَا مَعَكُمْ وَلَا تَكُوْنُوْا
أَوَّلَ كَافِرٍ بِهٖ ۖ وَلَا تَشْتَرُوْا بِاٰيٰتِيْ ثَمَنًا قَلِيْلًا ۚ وَاِيَّايَ
فَاتَّقُوْنِ ۝
وَ لَا تَلْبِسُوا الْحَقَّ بِالْبَاطِلِ وَ تَكْتُمُوا الْحَقَّ وَأَنْتُمْ
تَعْلَمُوْنَ ۝
وَأَقِيْمُوا الصَّلٰوةَ وَاٰتُوا الزَّكٰوةَ وَارْكَعُوْا مَعَ الرّٰكِعِيْنَ ۝
أَتَأْمُرُوْنَ النَّاسَ بِالْبِرِّ وَ تَنْسَوْنَ أَنْفُسَكُمْ وَأَنْتُمْ
تَتْلُوْنَ الْكِتٰبَ ۚ أَفَلَا تَعْقِلُوْنَ ۝
وَاسْتَعِيْنُوْا بِالصَّبْرِ وَالصَّلٰوةِ ۚ وَ اِنَّهَا لَكَبِيْرَةٌ اِلَّا عَلَى
الْخٰشِعِيْنَ ۝
الَّذِيْنَ يَظُنُّوْنَ أَنَّهُمْ مُّلٰقُوْا رَبِّهِمْ وَأَنَّهُمْ اِلَيْهِ

Children of Israel, call to mind My
favour which I bestowed upon you, and
fulfil the covenant that you made with
Me, I shall fulfil the covenant I made with
you, and fear Me alone, I repeat, fear Me
alone. Believe in the revelation that I have
now sent down which fulfils the revelation
that was sent down to you, and be not the
first to disbelieve therein, and barter not
My Signs for a paltry price, and seek protection with Me alone, I repeat, seek protection with Me alone. Confound not
truth with falsehood nor hide the truth
deliberately; and observe Prayer and pay
the Zakat, and worship Allah whole heart-
edly, along with those who worship Him
whole-heartedly. Do you, then, admonish
others to do good and forget your own
selves, while you read the Book — the
Torah. Will you not then understand?
Seek Allah's help with steadfastness and
Prayer; and this indeed is hard, except
for the humble in spirit, who know for
certain that they will meet their Lord, and
that to Him will they return. (41—47)

10

Children of Israel, call to mind My favour which I bestowed upon you and that I exalted you above the peoples of the time; and be mindful of the day when no one shall serve as a substitute for another at all, nor shall any intercession be accepted on his behalf, nor shall ransom be taken from him, nor shall they be helped. Call to mind when We delivered you from Pharaoh's people, who subjected you to grievous torment, slaying your male children and sparing your female children; and in that there was a great trial for you from your Lord. Call to mind also when We held back the sea for you and delivered you and drowned Pharaoh's people, while you looked on. Call to mind also when We made Moses a promise extending over forty nights; then you took the calf for worship, wrongfully, in his absence. Even then We forgave you thereafter, that you might be grateful. Call to mind also when We gave Moses the Book, the Torah, and the Signs discriminating between truth and falsehood, that you might be rightly guided. (48—54)

Call to mind when Moses said to his people: O my people you have indeed wronged your souls by taking the calf for worship; so turn to your Maker and let each one of you slay the evil propensities of his mind; that course is best for you in the sight of your Maker. Then He turned towards you with compassion. Surely, He is Oft-returning with compassion and is Merciful. Call to mind also, when you said: Moses, we shall by no means put faith in what thou sayest until we see Allah face to face; then a grievous chastisement overtook you and you were witnesses thereof. Then after your downfall We raised you up again by strengthening your faith and multiplying your numbers, that you might be grateful. (55—57)

رٰجِعُوۡنَ ۞

يٰبَنِىۡۤ اِسۡرَآءِیۡلَ اذۡکُرُوۡا نِعۡمَتِیَ الَّتِیۡۤ اَنۡعَمۡتُ عَلَیۡکُمۡ وَاَنِّیۡ فَضَّلۡتُکُمۡ عَلَی الۡعٰلَمِیۡنَ ۞

وَاتَّقُوۡا یَوۡمًا لَّا تَجۡزِیۡ نَفۡسٌ عَنۡ نَّفۡسٍ شَیۡئًا وَّلَا یُقۡبَلُ مِنۡهَا شَفَاعَۃٌ وَّلَا یُؤۡخَذُ مِنۡهَا عَدۡلٌ وَّلَا هُمۡ یُنۡصَرُوۡنَ ۞

وَاِذۡ نَجَّیۡنٰکُمۡ مِّنۡ اٰلِ فِرۡعَوۡنَ یَسُوۡمُوۡنَکُمۡ سُوۡٓءَ الۡعَذَابِ یُذَبِّحُوۡنَ اَبۡنَآءَکُمۡ وَیَسۡتَحۡیُوۡنَ نِسَآءَکُمۡ وَفِیۡ ذٰلِکُمۡ بَلَآءٌ مِّنۡ رَّبِّکُمۡ عَظِیۡمٌ ۞

وَاِذۡ فَرَقۡنَا بِکُمُ الۡبَحۡرَ فَاَنۡجَیۡنٰکُمۡ وَاَغۡرَقۡنَاۤ اٰلَ فِرۡعَوۡنَ وَاَنۡتُمۡ تَنۡظُرُوۡنَ ۞

وَاِذۡ وٰعَدۡنَا مُوۡسٰۤی اَرۡبَعِیۡنَ لَیۡلَۃً ثُمَّ اتَّخَذۡتُمُ الۡعِجۡلَ مِنۡۢ بَعۡدِہٖ وَاَنۡتُمۡ ظٰلِمُوۡنَ ۞

ثُمَّ عَفَوۡنَا عَنۡکُمۡ مِّنۡۢ بَعۡدِ ذٰلِکَ لَعَلَّکُمۡ تَشۡکُرُوۡنَ ۞

وَاِذۡ اٰتَیۡنَا مُوۡسَی الۡکِتٰبَ وَالۡفُرۡقَانَ لَعَلَّکُمۡ تَهۡتَدُوۡنَ ۞

وَاِذۡ قَالَ مُوۡسٰی لِقَوۡمِہٖ یٰقَوۡمِ اِنَّکُمۡ ظَلَمۡتُمۡ اَنۡفُسَکُمۡ بِاتِّخَاذِکُمُ الۡعِجۡلَ فَتُوۡبُوۡۤا اِلٰی بَارِئِکُمۡ فَاقۡتُلُوۡۤا اَنۡفُسَکُمۡ ذٰلِکُمۡ خَیۡرٌ لَّکُمۡ عِنۡدَ بَارِئِکُمۡ فَتَابَ عَلَیۡکُمۡ اِنَّہٗ هُوَ التَّوَّابُ الرَّحِیۡمُ ۞

وَاِذۡ قُلۡتُمۡ یٰمُوۡسٰی لَنۡ نُّؤۡمِنَ لَکَ حَتّٰی نَرَی اللّٰهَ جَهۡرَۃً فَاَخَذَتۡکُمُ الصّٰعِقَۃُ وَاَنۡتُمۡ تَنۡظُرُوۡنَ ۞

ثُمَّ بَعَثۡنٰکُمۡ مِّنۡۢ بَعۡدِ مَوۡتِکُمۡ لَعَلَّکُمۡ تَشۡکُرُوۡنَ ۞

11

Then We caused the clouds to provide shade for you and sent down for you Manna and Salwa and announced: Eat of the good things We have provided for you. They wronged Us not by their disobedience; it was themselves that they wronged. Call to mind also, when We said: Enter ye this township and eat therefrom, wherever you will, freely; and enter its gate in submission, saying: We pray for the lightening of our burdens. We shall forgive you your sins and We shall bestow increase upon those who do good. Then out of a spirit of mischief the transgressors substituted something else in place of that which was told them; whereupon, We sent down upon the transgressors a punishment from heaven, because of their disobedience. (58—60)

Call to mind also when Moses prayed for water for his people, and We directed him: Strike that rock with your rod; and there gushed forth from it twelve springs, so that every tribe knew its drinking place. They were told: Eat and drink of what Allah has provided, and do not go about in the land creating disorder. Call to mind also when you said to Moses: We cannot restrict ourselves to one kind of food; pray, then, to thy Lord for us that He bring forth for us of what the earth grows, of its herbs, cucumbers, wheat, lentils and onions. Allah rebuked them: Would you change that which is better for that which is worse? If that is what you desire, go down into any town and there you will find what you demand. Thus were they smitten with abasement and penury, and they incurred the wrath of Allah because they rejected the Signs of Allah and would slay the Prophets unjustly, and this had resulted from their persisting in rebellion and transgression. (61—62)

وَظَلَّلْنَا عَلَيْكُمُ الْغَمَامَ وَاَنْزَلْنَا عَلَيْكُمُ الْمَنَّ وَ السَّلْوٰى كُلُوْا مِنْ طَيِّبٰتِ مَا رَزَقْنٰكُمْ وَمَا ظَلَمُوْنَا وَ لٰكِنْ كَانُوْا اَنْفُسَهُمْ يَظْلِمُوْنَ ۞

وَاِذْ قُلْنَا ادْخُلُوْا هٰذِهِ الْقَرْيَةَ فَكُلُوْا مِنْهَا حَيْثُ شِئْتُمْ رَغَدًا وَّادْخُلُوا الْبَابَ سُجَّدًا وَّقُوْلُوْا حِطَّةٌ نَّغْفِرْ لَكُمْ خَطٰيٰكُمْ وَسَنَزِيْدُ الْمُحْسِنِيْنَ ۞

فَبَدَّلَ الَّذِيْنَ ظَلَمُوْا قَوْلًا غَيْرَ الَّذِيْ قِيْلَ لَهُمْ فَاَنْزَلْنَا عَلَى الَّذِيْنَ ظَلَمُوْا رِجْزًا مِّنَ السَّمَاءِ بِمَا كَانُوْا يَفْسُقُوْنَ ۞

وَاِذِ اسْتَسْقٰى مُوْسٰى لِقَوْمِهٖ فَقُلْنَا اضْرِبْ بِّعَصَاكَ الْحَجَرَ فَانْفَجَرَتْ مِنْهُ اثْنَتَا عَشْرَةَ عَيْنًا قَدْ عَلِمَ كُلُّ اُنَاسٍ مَّشْرَبَهُمْ كُلُوْا وَاشْرَبُوْا مِنْ رِّزْقِ اللّٰهِ وَلَا تَعْثَوْا فِى الْاَرْضِ مُفْسِدِيْنَ ۞

وَاِذْ قُلْتُمْ يٰمُوْسٰى لَنْ نَّصْبِرَ عَلٰى طَعَامٍ وَّاحِدٍ فَادْعُ لَنَا رَبَّكَ يُخْرِجْ لَنَا مِمَّا تُنْۢبِتُ الْاَرْضُ مِنْ بَقْلِهَا وَ قِثَّآئِهَا وَفُوْمِهَا وَعَدَسِهَا وَبَصَلِهَا قَالَ اَتَسْتَبْدِلُوْنَ الَّذِيْ هُوَ اَدْنٰى بِالَّذِيْ هُوَ خَيْرٌ اِهْبِطُوْا مِصْرًا فَاِنَّ لَكُمْ مَّا سَاَلْتُمْ وَضُرِبَتْ عَلَيْهِمُ الذِّلَّةُ وَالْمَسْكَنَةُ وَبَآءُوْ بِغَضَبٍ مِّنَ اللّٰهِ ذٰلِكَ بِاَنَّهُمْ كَانُوْا يَكْفُرُوْنَ بِاٰيٰتِ اللّٰهِ وَيَقْتُلُوْنَ النَّبِيّٖنَ بِغَيْرِ الْحَقِّ ذٰلِكَ بِمَا عَصَوْا وَّكَانُوْا يَعْتَدُوْنَ ۞

اِنَّ الَّذِيْنَ اٰمَنُوْا وَالَّذِيْنَ هَادُوْا وَالنَّصٰرٰى وَ

12

Surely, of the Believers, the Jews, the Christians and the Sabians, those who truly believe in Allah and the Last Day and act righteously, shall have their reward with their Lord, and no fear shall come upon them nor shall they grieve. (63)

Call to mind, children of Israel, when We took a covenant from you and raised the Mount high above you, and said: Hold fast that which We have given you and bear its contents in mind that you may attain to righteousness. Yet you turned back thereafter; and had it not been for Allah's grace upon you and His mercy, you would surely have been of the losers. You have surely known the end of those from amongst you who transgressed in the matter of the Sabbath, in consequence of which We condemned them: Be ye like apes, despised. Thus We made this event a lesson for their contemporaries and for those who came after and an admonition for the God-fearing. (64—67)

Call to mind also, when Moses said to his people: Allah commands you to slaughter a cow; and they exclaimed: Dost thou make a mockery of us? to which Moses retorted: I seek the protection of Allah that I should behave foolishly. Whereupon, they temporised: Pray for us to thy Lord that He may make plain to us what sort of a cow it is. Moses told them: He says, it is a cow neither old nor young, full grown, of middle age. Now do what you are told. They came back with: Pray again for us to thy Lord that He explain to us what colour she is. Moses said: He says: It is a cow of dun colour, pure and rich in tone, which delights the beholders. But they persisted: Pray once more for us to thy Lord to make plain to us what she is, for all such cows appear to us alike; and if Allah please we shall indeed be guided. Moses answered: He says: It is a cow not broken in to plough the earth or water the tilth; one without blemish; of uniform colour. They said: Now have you given us correct particulars. Then they slaughtered her, though they would rather not have done it. (68—72)

13

Call to mind also when you claimed to have brought about the death of a Personage and then differed among yourselves concerning it, and Allah would bring to light that which you concealed. So We said: Test the crucial question by putting together other incidents relating to the affair and you will arrive at the truth. Thus does Allah plan to preserve alive those considered dead and shows you His Signs that you may understand. Thereafter your hearts became hardened and became like stones or even harder, for of stones there are some out of which gush forth streams, and there are some that cleave asunder and water flows out from them. Of the hearts also there are some that humble themselves before Allah for fear of Him. Allah is not at all unmindful of that which you do. (73—75)

Do you expect that the children of Israel will put faith in you, when a party of them are such that they hear the word of Allah, then pervert it after they have understood it, well knowing the consequences of their enormity? When they meet those who believe they say: We believe; and when they meet one another in private, they upbraid one another: You communicate to the believers that which Allah has unfolded to you. Do you not realise that they may thereby contend against you before your Lord? Are they not aware that Allah knows all that they conceal and that they disclose? Some of them are illiterate; they know not the Book, treating their own false notions as such, and follow only conjecture. Painful is the chastisement awaiting those who write the Book with their own hands, and then say: This is from Allah; to gain therewith a paltry sum; so for them is a painful chastisement for that which they write and a painful chastisement for that which they earn. (76—80)

14

They boast: The Fire shall not touch us except for a limited number of days. Ask them: Have you then taken a promise from Allah, in which case Allah will not go back on His promise, or, do you allege concerning Allah that of which you have no knowledge? Verily, those who do evil and are encompassed by their misdeeds, are the inmates of the Fire, therein shall they abide; but those who believe and act righteously are the dwellers of the Garden, therein shall they abide. (81—83)

Call to mind when We took a covenant from the children of Israel: You shall worship none save Allah, and shall behave kindly towards parents, and kindred and the orphans and the needy, and speak graciously to people and observe Prayer and pay the Zakat. Then you turned away in aversion except a small number of you. Call to mind also when We took a covenant from you: You shall not shed each other's blood, nor turn your people out of their homes; thus did you affirm and you have throughout borne witness to it. Yet you are a people who slay one another and turn out a section of your people from their homes, backing up their enemies against them, committing sin and transgression. Thereafter if they come to you as captives seeking your help you deem it meritorious to ransom them, while their turning out in the first place was unlawful for you. Do you, then, believe in a part of the Book and disbelieve in a part of it? For those of you, therefore, who do this, the penalty in this life is humiliation, and on the Day of Judgment they shall be driven to a most severe chastisement.

لَهُمۡ مِّمَّا كَتَبَتۡ اَيۡدِيۡهِمۡ وَوَيۡلٌ لَّهُمۡ مِّمَّا يَكۡسِبُوۡنَ ۞

وَقَالُوۡا لَنۡ تَمَسَّنَا النَّارُ اِلَّاۤ اَيَّامًا مَّعۡدُوۡدَةً ؕ قُلۡ اَتَّخَذۡتُمۡ عِنۡدَ اللّٰهِ عَهۡدًا فَلَنۡ يُّخۡلِفَ اللّٰهُ عَهۡدَهٗۤ اَمۡ تَقُوۡلُوۡنَ عَلَى اللّٰهِ مَا لَا تَعۡلَمُوۡنَ ۞

بَلٰى مَنۡ كَسَبَ سَيِّئَةً وَّاَحَاطَتۡ بِهٖ خَطِيۡٓئَتُهٗ فَاُولٰٓئِكَ اَصۡحٰبُ النَّارِ ۚ هُمۡ فِيۡهَا خٰلِدُوۡنَ ۞

وَالَّذِيۡنَ اٰمَنُوۡا وَعَمِلُوا الصّٰلِحٰتِ اُولٰٓئِكَ اَصۡحٰبُ الۡجَنَّةِ ۚ هُمۡ فِيۡهَا خٰلِدُوۡنَ ۞

وَاِذۡ اَخَذۡنَا مِيۡثَاقَ بَنِىۡۤ اِسۡرَآءِيۡلَ لَا تَعۡبُدُوۡنَ اِلَّا اللّٰهَ ۟ وَبِالۡوَالِدَيۡنِ اِحۡسَانًا وَّذِى الۡقُرۡبٰى وَالۡيَتٰمٰى وَالۡمَسٰكِيۡنِ وَقُوۡلُوۡا لِلنَّاسِ حُسۡنًا وَّاَقِيۡمُوا الصَّلٰوةَ وَاٰتُوا الزَّكٰوةَ ؕ ثُمَّ تَوَلَّيۡتُمۡ اِلَّا قَلِيۡلًا مِّنۡكُمۡ وَاَنۡتُمۡ مُّعۡرِضُوۡنَ ۞

وَاِذۡ اَخَذۡنَا مِيۡثَاقَكُمۡ لَا تَسۡفِكُوۡنَ دِمَآءَكُمۡ وَلَا تُخۡرِجُوۡنَ اَنۡفُسَكُمۡ مِّنۡ دِيَارِكُمۡ ثُمَّ اَقۡرَرۡتُمۡ وَاَنۡتُمۡ تَشۡهَدُوۡنَ ۞

ثُمَّ اَنۡتُمۡ هٰٓؤُلَآءِ تَقۡتُلُوۡنَ اَنۡفُسَكُمۡ وَتُخۡرِجُوۡنَ فَرِيۡقًا مِّنۡكُمۡ مِّنۡ دِيَارِهِمۡ ۫ تَظٰهَرُوۡنَ عَلَيۡهِمۡ بِالۡاِثۡمِ وَالۡعُدۡوَانِ ؕ وَاِنۡ يَّاۡتُوۡكُمۡ اُسٰرٰى تُفٰدُوۡهُمۡ وَهُوَ مُحَرَّمٌ عَلَيۡكُمۡ اِخۡرَاجُهُمۡ ؕ اَفَتُؤۡمِنُوۡنَ بِبَعۡضِ الۡكِتٰبِ وَتَكۡفُرُوۡنَ بِبَعۡضٍ ۚ فَمَا جَزَآءُ مَنۡ يَّفۡعَلُ ذٰلِكَ مِنۡكُمۡ اِلَّا خِزۡيٌ فِى الۡحَيٰوةِ الدُّنۡيَا ۚ وَيَوۡمَ الۡقِيٰمَةِ

Surely, Allah is not unmindful of that which you do. These are they who have chosen the hither life in preference to the Hereafter. Their punishment shall not therefore be lightened, nor shall they be helped in any other way. (84—87)

يُرَدُّوْنَ اِلٰٓى اَشَدِّ الْعَذَابِ ۗ وَ مَا اللّٰهُ بِغَافِلٍ عَمَّا تَعْمَلُوْنَ ۝

اُولٰٓئِكَ الَّذِيْنَ اشْتَرَوُا الْحَيٰوةَ الدُّنْيَا بِالْاٰخِرَةِ ۫ فَلَا يُخَفَّفُ عَنْهُمُ الْعَذَابُ وَ لَا هُمْ يُنْصَرُوْنَ ۝

Indeed We gave Moses the Book and caused a number of Messengers to follow after him; and to Jesus son of Mary, We gave manifest Signs and strengthened him with the Spirit of holiness. But as for you, was it not that whenever there came to you a Messenger with that which you desired not you behaved arrogantly and some you called liars and some you were after slaying? They have also said: Our hearts are wrapped up in covers. That is not so, but Allah has condemned them for their rebellion; thus little it is that they believe. So that when there came to them a Book from Allah fulfilling the prophecies contained in the Book which is with them — and they used before that to pray to Allah for victory over the disbelievers — yet when there came to them that which they recognised, they rejected it. Such disbelievers are under Allah's curse. Evil is that for which they have sold their souls, namely, that they should reject that which Allah has revealed, out of grudge that Allah should send down His grace on whomsoever of His servants He pleases. Thus they incurred wrath upon wrath, and for such disbelievers there is humiliating chastisement. When it is said to them: Believe ye in that which Allah has sent down; they retort: We do believe in that which has been sent down to us; and saying this they reject that which has been sent down after that; yet it has been proved to be the truth by fulfilling that which is with them. Ask them: If you did truly believe, why were you after slaying the Prophets of Allah before this? Moses

وَ لَقَدْ اٰتَيْنَا مُوْسَى الْكِتٰبَ وَ قَفَّيْنَا مِنْ بَعْدِهٖ بِالرُّسُلِ ۫ وَ اٰتَيْنَا عِيْسَى ابْنَ مَرْيَمَ الْبَيِّنٰتِ وَ اَيَّدْنٰهُ بِرُوْحِ الْقُدُسِ ۗ اَفَكُلَّمَا جَآءَكُمْ رَسُوْلٌۢ بِمَا لَا تَهْوٰٓى اَنْفُسُكُمُ اسْتَكْبَرْتُمْ ۚ فَفَرِيْقًا كَذَّبْتُمْ ۫ وَ فَرِيْقًا تَقْتُلُوْنَ ۝

وَ قَالُوْا قُلُوْبُنَا غُلْفٌ ۗ بَلْ لَّعَنَهُمُ اللّٰهُ بِكُفْرِهِمْ فَقَلِيْلًا مَّا يُؤْمِنُوْنَ ۝

وَ لَمَّا جَآءَهُمْ كِتٰبٌ مِّنْ عِنْدِ اللّٰهِ مُصَدِّقٌ لِّمَا مَعَهُمْ ۙ وَ كَانُوْا مِنْ قَبْلُ يَسْتَفْتِحُوْنَ عَلَى الَّذِيْنَ كَفَرُوْا ۚ فَلَمَّا جَآءَهُمْ مَّا عَرَفُوْا كَفَرُوْا بِهٖ ۫ فَلَعْنَةُ اللّٰهِ عَلَى الْكٰفِرِيْنَ ۝

بِئْسَمَا اشْتَرَوْا بِهٖۤ اَنْفُسَهُمْ اَنْ يَّكْفُرُوْا بِمَاۤ اَنْزَلَ اللّٰهُ بَغْيًا اَنْ يُّنَزِّلَ اللّٰهُ مِنْ فَضْلِهٖ عَلٰى مَنْ يَّشَآءُ مِنْ عِبَادِهٖ ۚ فَبَآءُوْ بِغَضَبٍ عَلٰى غَضَبٍ ۫ وَ لِلْكٰفِرِيْنَ عَذَابٌ مُّهِيْنٌ ۝

وَ اِذَا قِيْلَ لَهُمْ اٰمِنُوْا بِمَاۤ اَنْزَلَ اللّٰهُ قَالُوْا نُؤْمِنُ بِمَاۤ اُنْزِلَ عَلَيْنَا وَ يَكْفُرُوْنَ بِمَا وَرَآءَهٗ وَ هُوَ الْحَقُّ مُصَدِّقًا لِّمَا مَعَهُمْ ۗ قُلْ فَلِمَ تَقْتُلُوْنَ اَنْۢبِيَآءَ اللّٰهِ مِنْ قَبْلُ اِنْ كُنْتُمْ مُّؤْمِنِيْنَ ۝

16

came to you with manifest Signs, yet you took the calf for worship in his absence, because you were transgressors. (88—93)

Call to mind when We took a covenant from you and raised the Mount high above you and admonished you: Hold fast that which We have given you and obey; but those admonished said: We have heard but we shall not obey; and because of their disbelief their hearts were filled with love of the calf. Say to them: If you are believers, evil is indeed that which your faith enjoins on you. Say to them: If the abode of the Hereafter has been adjudged by Allah to be solely for you to the exclusion of all other people, then call for death upon whichever party of us adheres to falsehood, if you are truthful in your assertion. But never will they pray for death in such terms, because of that which their own hands have wrought; and Allah knows the wrongdoers well. Thou shalt surely find them and some of those who set up partners with Allah, the most covetous of life, of all people. Every one of them desires that he may be granted a span extending over a thousand years, but his being granted a long life will not rescue him from his doom; Allah sees all that they do. (94—97)

Announce, O Prophet: Whoso bears enmity towards Gabriel — because of his having caused to descend upon thy heart, by the command of Allah, this Book which fulfils that which precedes it and contains guidance and glad tidings for the believers — whoso bears enmity towards Allah, His angels, His Messengers, Gabriel and Michael, then surely, Allah too is the enemy of such disbelievers. Indeed We have sent down to thee manifest Signs, and no one disbelieves in them but the disobedient. (98—100)

وَلَقَدْ جَآءَكُمْ مُّوْسٰى بِالْبَيِّنٰتِ ثُمَّ اتَّخَذْتُمُ الْعِجْلَ مِنْ بَعْدِهٖ وَأَنْتُمْ ظٰلِمُوْنَ ۝

وَإِذْ أَخَذْنَا مِيْثَاقَكُمْ وَرَفَعْنَا فَوْقَكُمُ الطُّوْرَ خُذُوْا مَآ اٰتَيْنٰكُمْ بِقُوَّةٍ وَّاسْمَعُوْا قَالُوْا سَمِعْنَا وَعَصَيْنَا وَأُشْرِبُوْا فِيْ قُلُوْبِهِمُ الْعِجْلَ بِكُفْرِهِمْ قُلْ بِئْسَمَا يَأْمُرُكُمْ بِهٖ إِيْمَانُكُمْ إِنْ كُنْتُمْ مُّؤْمِنِيْنَ ۝

قُلْ إِنْ كَانَتْ لَكُمُ الدَّارُ الْاٰخِرَةُ عِنْدَ اللّٰهِ خَالِصَةً مِّنْ دُوْنِ النَّاسِ فَتَمَنَّوُا الْمَوْتَ إِنْ كُنْتُمْ صٰدِقِيْنَ ۝

وَلَنْ يَّتَمَنَّوْهُ أَبَدًۢا بِمَا قَدَّمَتْ أَيْدِيْهِمْ وَاللّٰهُ عَلِيْمٌۢ بِالظّٰلِمِيْنَ ۝

وَلَتَجِدَنَّهُمْ أَحْرَصَ النَّاسِ عَلٰى حَيٰوةٍ وَّمِنَ الَّذِيْنَ أَشْرَكُوْا يَوَدُّ أَحَدُهُمْ لَوْ يُعَمَّرُ أَلْفَ سَنَةٍ وَّمَا هُوَ بِمُزَحْزِحِهٖ مِنَ الْعَذَابِ أَنْ يُّعَمَّرَ وَاللّٰهُ بَصِيْرٌۢ بِمَا يَعْمَلُوْنَ ۝

قُلْ مَنْ كَانَ عَدُوًّا لِّجِبْرِيْلَ فَإِنَّهٗ نَزَّلَهٗ عَلٰى قَلْبِكَ بِإِذْنِ اللّٰهِ مُصَدِّقًا لِّمَا بَيْنَ يَدَيْهِ وَهُدًى وَّبُشْرٰى لِلْمُؤْمِنِيْنَ ۝

مَنْ كَانَ عَدُوًّا لِّلّٰهِ وَمَلٰٓئِكَتِهٖ وَرُسُلِهٖ وَجِبْرِيْلَ وَمِيْكَالَ فَإِنَّ اللّٰهَ عَدُوٌّ لِّلْكٰفِرِيْنَ ۝

وَلَقَدْ أَنْزَلْنَآ إِلَيْكَ اٰيٰتٍۢ بَيِّنٰتٍ وَّمَا يَكْفُرُ بِهَآ إِلَّا الْفٰسِقُوْنَ ۝

أَوَكُلَّمَا عٰهَدُوْا عَهْدًا نَّبَذَهٗ فَرِيْقٌ مِّنْهُمْ بَلْ

Has it not been that every time they make a covenant, a party of them throws it aside? In truth most of them have no faith. Now when there has come to them a Messenger from Allah, fulfilling the Book which is with them, a party of people to whom the Book was given have thrown this Book of Allah behind their backs, as if they knew it not. They pursue the course which the rebellious ones followed in the reign of Solomon. It was not Solomon who disbelieved; it was the rebellious ones who disbelieved, teaching people falsehood and deception. They claim also to pursue that which was revealed to the two saintly ones in Babylon, Harut and Marut. But these two taught no one till they had warned: We are surely a trial from Allah, therefore, do not reject that which we set forth. So people learnt from them that by which they brought about discrimination between a man and his wife, but they harmed no one thereby except by the command of Allah. But these are seeking to learn that which shall do them harm and shall do them no good, and they have certainly known that he who traffics therein, for him there is no share of good in the Hereafter. Surely, evil is that for which they have sold their souls; if they but knew. If they had believed and acted righteously, they would have found that Allah's recompense is best, had they but known. (101—104)

O ye who believe, say not to the Prophet *ra'ina* but say *unzurna*, and listen to him with attention. For the disbelievers there is a painful punishment. (105)

Those ones from among the People of the Book and from among those who associate partners with Allah, who have disbelieved, desire not that any good may be sent down to you from your Lord. They forget that Allah chooses as the recipients of His mercy whomsoever He pleases. Allah is Lord of exceeding bounty. Whatever previous commandment We abrogate or cause to be forgotten, We reveal in this Quran one better or the like thereof:

اَكْثَرُهُمْ لَا يُؤْمِنُوْنَ ۞

وَلَمَّا جَآءَهُمْ رَسُوْلٌ مِّنْ عِنْدِ اللّٰهِ مُصَدِّقٌ لِّمَا مَعَهُمْ نَبَذَ فَرِيْقٌ مِّنَ الَّذِيْنَ اُوْتُوا الْكِتٰبَ ۟ كِتٰبَ اللّٰهِ وَرَآءَ ظُهُوْرِهِمْ كَاَنَّهُمْ لَا يَعْلَمُوْنَ ۞

وَاتَّبَعُوْا مَا تَتْلُوا الشَّيٰطِيْنُ عَلٰى مُلْكِ سُلَيْمٰنَ ۚ وَ مَا كَفَرَ سُلَيْمٰنُ وَلٰكِنَّ الشَّيٰطِيْنَ كَفَرُوْا يُعَلِّمُوْنَ النَّاسَ السِّحْرَ ۟ وَمَآ اُنْزِلَ عَلَى الْمَلَكَيْنِ بِبَابِلَ هَارُوْتَ وَمَارُوْتَ ۚ وَمَا يُعَلِّمٰنِ مِنْ اَحَدٍ حَتّٰى يَقُوْلَآ اِنَّمَا نَحْنُ فِتْنَةٌ فَلَا تَكْفُرْ ۚ فَيَتَعَلَّمُوْنَ مِنْهُمَا مَا يُفَرِّقُوْنَ بِهٖ بَيْنَ الْمَرْءِ وَزَوْجِهٖ ۚ وَمَا هُمْ بِضَآرِّيْنَ بِهٖ مِنْ اَحَدٍ اِلَّا بِاِذْنِ اللّٰهِ ۚ وَيَتَعَلَّمُوْنَ مَا يَضُرُّهُمْ وَلَا يَنْفَعُهُمْ ۚ وَلَقَدْ عَلِمُوْا لَمَنِ اشْتَرٰىهُ مَا لَهٗ فِى الْاٰخِرَةِ مِنْ خَلَاقٍ ۟ وَلَبِئْسَ مَا شَرَوْا بِهٖۤ اَنْفُسَهُمْ ۚ لَوْ كَانُوْا يَعْلَمُوْنَ ۞

وَلَوْ اَنَّهُمْ اٰمَنُوْا وَاتَّقَوْا لَمَثُوْبَةٌ مِّنْ عِنْدِ اللّٰهِ خَيْرٌ ۚ لَوْ كَانُوْا يَعْلَمُوْنَ ۞

يٰۤاَيُّهَا الَّذِيْنَ اٰمَنُوْا لَا تَقُوْلُوْا رَاعِنَا وَقُوْلُوا انْظُرْنَا وَاسْمَعُوْا ۚ وَلِلْكٰفِرِيْنَ عَذَابٌ اَلِيْمٌ ۞

مَا يَوَدُّ الَّذِيْنَ كَفَرُوْا مِنْ اَهْلِ الْكِتٰبِ وَلَا الْمُشْرِكِيْنَ اَنْ يُّنَزَّلَ عَلَيْكُمْ مِّنْ خَيْرٍ مِّنْ رَّبِّكُمْ ۚ وَاللّٰهُ يَخْتَصُّ بِرَحْمَتِهٖ مَنْ يَّشَآءُ ۚ وَاللّٰهُ ذُو الْفَضْلِ الْعَظِيْمِ ۞

مَا نَنْسَخْ مِنْ اٰيَةٍ اَوْ نُنْسِهَا نَأْتِ بِخَيْرٍ مِّنْهَآ اَوْ

18

Knowest thou not that Allah has full power to do all that He wills? Knowest thou not that to Allah belongs the Kingdom of the heavens and the earth, and that for you beside Allah there is no helper or protector? (106—108)

مِثْلِهَا ۚ اَلَمْ تَعْلَمْ اَنَّ اللّٰهَ عَلٰى كُلِّ شَيْءٍ قَدِيْرٌ ۞ اَلَمْ تَعْلَمْ اَنَّ اللّٰهَ لَهٗ مُلْكُ السَّمٰوٰتِ وَالْاَرْضِ ۚ وَ مَا لَكُمْ مِّنْ دُوْنِ اللّٰهِ مِنْ وَّلِيٍّ وَّ لَا نَصِيْرٍ ۞

Would you question the Messenger sent to you as Moses was questioned before, forgetting that whoever takes disbelief in exchange for belief has undoubtedly gone astray from the right path? (109)

اَمْ تُرِيْدُوْنَ اَنْ تَسْئَلُوْا رَسُوْلَكُمْ كَمَا سُئِلَ مُوْسٰى مِنْ قَبْلُ ۚ وَ مَنْ يَّتَبَدَّلِ الْكُفْرَ بِالْاِيْمَانِ فَقَدْ ضَلَّ سَوَآءَ السَّبِيْلِ ۞

Many of the People of the Book, after the truth has become manifest to them, would desire out of sheer envy generated by their minds that, after you have believed, they could turn you into disbelievers. But do you forgive them and forbear, till Allah sends down His decree. Surely, Allah has full power to do all that He wills. Observe Prayer, and pay the Zakat, therefore, for whatever good you send on before you for yourselves, you shall find it with Allah. Surely Allah sees all that you do. (110—111)

وَدَّ كَثِيْرٌ مِّنْ اَهْلِ الْكِتٰبِ لَوْ يَرُدُّوْنَكُمْ مِّنْ بَعْدِ اِيْمَانِكُمْ كُفَّارًا ۖ حَسَدًا مِّنْ عِنْدِ اَنْفُسِهِمْ مِّنْ بَعْدِ مَا تَبَيَّنَ لَهُمُ الْحَقُّ ۚ فَاعْفُوْا وَاصْفَحُوْا حَتّٰى يَاْتِيَ اللّٰهُ بِاَمْرِهٖ ۗ اِنَّ اللّٰهَ عَلٰى كُلِّ شَيْءٍ قَدِيْرٌ ۞ وَاَقِيْمُوا الصَّلٰوةَ وَاٰتُوا الزَّكٰوةَ ۚ وَمَا تُقَدِّمُوْا لِاَنْفُسِكُمْ مِّنْ خَيْرٍ تَجِدُوْهُ عِنْدَ اللّٰهِ ۗ اِنَّ اللّٰهَ بِمَا تَعْمَلُوْنَ بَصِيْرٌ ۞

They claim that no one shall enter Paradise unless he is a Jew or a Christian. These are their vain desires. Ask them: Produce your proof, if you are truthful. The truth is that whoever submits himself completely to the will of Allah and acts righteously, shall have his reward with his Lord. No fear shall come upon such, nor shall they grieve. The Jews say the Christians base themselves on no firm truth, and the Christians say the Jews base themselves on no firm truth, yet both read the same Book. In like manner did those who had no knowledge say that which these say. Allah shall judge between them on the Day of Judgment concerning that wherein they disagree. (112—114)

وَقَالُوْا لَنْ يَّدْخُلَ الْجَنَّةَ اِلَّا مَنْ كَانَ هُوْدًا اَوْ نَصٰرٰى ۗ تِلْكَ اَمَانِيُّهُمْ ۗ قُلْ هَاتُوْا بُرْهَانَكُمْ اِنْ كُنْتُمْ صٰدِقِيْنَ ۞ بَلٰى مَنْ اَسْلَمَ وَجْهَهٗ لِلّٰهِ وَهُوَ مُحْسِنٌ فَلَهٗٓ اَجْرُهٗ عِنْدَ رَبِّهٖ ۪ وَلَا خَوْفٌ عَلَيْهِمْ وَلَا هُمْ يَحْزَنُوْنَ ۞ وَقَالَتِ الْيَهُوْدُ لَيْسَتِ النَّصٰرٰى عَلٰى شَيْءٍ ۖ وَّقَالَتِ النَّصٰرٰى لَيْسَتِ الْيَهُوْدُ عَلٰى شَيْءٍ ۙ وَّهُمْ يَتْلُوْنَ الْكِتٰبَ ۗ كَذٰلِكَ قَالَ الَّذِيْنَ لَا يَعْلَمُوْنَ مِثْلَ قَوْلِهِمْ ۚ فَاللّٰهُ يَحْكُمُ بَيْنَهُمْ يَوْمَ الْقِيٰمَةِ فِيْمَا كَانُوْا فِيْهِ يَخْتَلِفُوْنَ ۞

19

Who can be guilty of a greater wrong than one who forbids Allah's name being glorified in His mosques and seeks to bring about their ruin? It behoves not such to enter therein except in fear of Allah. For them is disgrace in this world and a great chastisement in the next. To Allah belong the East and the West; so whithersoever you turn, there is the countenance of Allah. Surely Allah is vastly Bountiful, All-Knowing. (115—116)

They allege Allah has taken unto Himself a son. Holy is He! On the contrary, to Him belongs all that is in the heavens and the earth; to Him are all obedient. Originator of the heavens and the earth, when He determines the coming into being of a thing, He says concerning it: Be! and it is. (117—118)

Those who have no knowledge of Allah's purpose ask: Why does Allah not speak to us direct, or a Sign not come to us? Likewise said those before them, similar to their saying; their hearts are alike. Indeed have We made all varieties of Signs plain to the people who believe. (119)

Most surely have We sent thee with the Truth, a bearer of glad tidings and a warner; nor art thou answerable for the inmates of the Fire. The Jews will by no means be pleased with thee, nor the Christians, unless thou conform to their creed. Proclaim, therefore: Surely Allah's guidance is the only true guidance. If thou follow their evil desires after the knowledge that has come to thee, thou shalt have neither friend nor helper from Allah. Those whom We have given this Book follow it as it should be followed; it is these who have firm faith therein. Whoso believes not therein, these are they who are the losers. (120—122)

20

Children of Israel, call to mind My favour which I bestowed upon you and that I exalted you above the peoples of the time; and fear the day when no one shall serve as a substitute for another at all, nor shall any ransom be accepted from him, nor any intercession avail him, nor shall they be helped. (123—124)

Call to mind also, when his Lord tried Abraham with certain commands which he fulfilled, and his Lord said: I shall make thee a leader of men. Abraham asked: And from among my offspring also? to which his Lord replied: Indeed, but My covenant will not embrace the transgressors. Call to mind also, when We made the House a resort for mankind and a place of security, and commanded: Take ye the station of Abraham as a place for Prayer. We laid a strict command upon Abraham and Ishmael: Purify My House for those who perform the circuits and those who go into retreat and those who bow down and fall prostrate in Prayer. Call to mind also, when Abraham prayed: My Lord, make this city inviolate, and provide such of its dwellers as believe in Allah and the Last Day with all varieties of fruit. His Lord responded: So shall it be, and on him too who believes not I shall bestow benefits for a short while; then will I drive him to the punishment of the Fire, and an evil destination it is. Call to mind also when Abraham raised the foundations of the House and also Ishmael, and they prayed: Our Lord, accept this offering from us, it is Thou Who art All-Hearing, All-Knowing. Our Lord, make us submissive to Thy will and pleasure and make of our offspring a people submissive to Thee. Teach us our appropriate ways of worship, and turn to us in mercy; for Thou art Oft-Returning with compassion and Ever Merciful. Our Lord, raise up from among them a Messenger who may recite to them Thy Signs and teach them the Book and Wisdom and may purify them. Surely, Thou art the Mighty, the Wise. (125—130)

وَاَنِّیْ فَضَّلْتُکُمْ عَلَی الْعٰلَمِیْنَ ۱۲۳

وَاتَّقُوْا یَوْمًا لَّا تَجْزِیْ نَفْسٌ عَنْ نَّفْسٍ شَیْئًا وَّ لَا یُقْبَلُ مِنْھَا عَدْلٌ وَّلَا تَنْفَعُھَا شَفَاعَةٌ وَّلَاھُمْ یُنْصَرُوْنَ ۱۲۴

وَاِذِ ابْتَلٰۤی اِبْرٰھٖمَ رَبُّہٗ بِکَلِمٰتٍ فَاَتَمَّھُنَّ ۭ قَالَ اِنِّیْ جَاعِلُکَ لِلنَّاسِ اِمَامًا ۭ قَالَ وَ مِنْ ذُرِّیَّتِیْ ۭ قَالَ لَا یَنَالُ عَھْدِی الظّٰلِمِیْنَ ۱۲۵

وَاِذْ جَعَلْنَا الْبَیْتَ مَثَابَةً لِّلنَّاسِ وَاَمْنًا ۭ وَاتَّخِذُوْا مِنْ مَّقَامِ اِبْرٰھٖمَ مُصَلًّی ۭ وَعَھِدْنَاۤ اِلٰۤی اِبْرٰھٖمَ وَاِسْمٰعِیْلَ اَنْ طَھِّرَا بَیْتِیَ لِلطَّآئِفِیْنَ وَالْعٰکِفِیْنَ وَالرُّکَّعِ السُّجُوْدِ ۱۲۶

وَاِذْ قَالَ اِبْرٰھٖمُ رَبِّ اجْعَلْ ھٰذَا بَلَدًا اٰمِنًا وَّارْزُقْ اَھْلَهٗ مِنَ الثَّمَرٰتِ مَنْ اٰمَنَ مِنْھُمْ بِاللّٰهِ وَالْیَوْمِ الْاٰخِرِ ۭ قَالَ وَمَنْ کَفَرَ فَاُمَتِّعُهٗ قَلِیْلًا ثُمَّ اَضْطَرُّهٗۤ اِلٰی عَذَابِ النَّارِ ۭ وَبِئْسَ الْمَصِیْرُ ۱۲۷

وَاِذْ یَرْفَعُ اِبْرٰھٖمُ الْقَوَاعِدَ مِنَ الْبَیْتِ وَاِسْمٰعِیْلُ ۭ رَبَّنَا تَقَبَّلْ مِنَّا ۭ اِنَّکَ اَنْتَ السَّمِیْعُ الْعَلِیْمُ ۱۲۸

رَبَّنَا وَاجْعَلْنَا مُسْلِمَیْنِ لَکَ وَ مِنْ ذُرِّیَّتِنَاۤ اُمَّةً مُّسْلِمَةً لَّکَ وَاَرِنَا مَنَاسِکَنَا وَتُبْ عَلَیْنَا ۭ اِنَّکَ اَنْتَ التَّوَّابُ الرَّحِیْمُ ۱۲۹

رَبَّنَا وَابْعَثْ فِیْھِمْ رَسُوْلًا مِّنْھُمْ یَتْلُوْا عَلَیْھِمْ اٰیٰتِکَ وَیُعَلِّمُھُمُ الْکِتٰبَ وَالْحِکْمَةَ وَیُزَکِّیْھِمْ

Thus who will turn away from the religion of Abraham but he who has ruined his soul? Of a surety, We exalted him in this world, and in the next also he will be among the righteous. When his Lord commanded him: Do thou submit thyself to Me, he responded: I submit myself to the Lord of the worlds. The same did Abraham enjoin upon his sons and also Jacob: Sons of mine, truly Allah has chosen this religion for you, so live every moment in submission to Allah, so that death whenever it comes should find you in a state of submission to Him. Were you present when Jacob faced the hour of death and he asked his sons: Who will you worship after I am gone? They answered: We will worship thy God and the God of thy fathers Abraham and Ishmael and Isaac, the One God, and to Him have we submitted ourselves. Those were a people that have passed away; for them was what they earned and for you is what you earn. You will not be answerable for what they did. (131—135)

The Jews and the Christians invite you: Be ye Jews, or be ye Christians, that you may be rightly guided. Tell them: Nay, not so, let us agree to follow the religion of Abraham, who was ever inclined towards Allah and was not one of those who set up partners with Him. Affirm, We believe in Allah and in that which has been sent down to us and that which was sent down to Abraham and Ishmael and Isaac and Jacob and his children and that which was given to Moses and Jesus, and that which was given to all other Prophets from their Lord. We make no distinction between any of them and to Him do we wholly submit ourselves. Then, if they believe as you have believed, they are rightly guided, but if they turn back, then know that they are determined to create a schism. In that event Allah will surely guard thee against their mischief. He is the All-Hearing, the All-Knowing. (136—138)

Proclaim: We adopt the Faith revealed by Allah, and who is better than Allah in teaching the Faith? Him alone do we worship. Ask them: Do you dispute with us concerning Allah, when He is our Lord and also your Lord? We are responsible for that which we do and you are responsible for that which you do. To Him alone are we devoted. (139—140)

People of the Book, do you say that Abraham and Ishmael and Isaac and Jacob and his children were Jews, or, that they were Christians? Do you know better or Allah? Who can be more unjust than one who conceals such testimony as he has from Allah? Allah is not unaware of that which you do. Those were a people that have passed away; for them was what they earned and for you is what you earn. You will not be answerable for what they did. (141—142)

Foolish people will say: What has caused the Muslims to turn away from the Qibla towards which they faced when in Prayer? Tell them: To Allah belong the East and the West. He guides whom He pleases to the right path. By guiding you along the right path have We made you an exalted people, that you may be guardians over mankind and the Messenger may be a guardian over you. We did not appoint the Qibla which thou didst follow, except that We might distinguish him who follows the Messenger from him who turns away upon his heels, though this is indeed hard, save for those whom Allah has guided. Allah is not the One to let your faith go in vain; surely, Allah is Compassionate and Merciful towards the people. Surely, We see thy mind turning frequently to heaven; We shall, therefore, certainly make thee turn to the Qibla thou likest.

So, turn thy face now towards the Sacred
Mosque; and wheresoever you be, turn
your faces towards it. They to whom the
Book has been given know that this is the
truth from their Lord. Surely, Allah is not
unmindful of that which they do. Even if
thou shouldst produce every kind of Sign
before those who have been given the
Book, they would never follow thy Qibla,
nor canst thou follow their Qibla; nor
would some of them follow the Qibla of
the others. If thou shouldst follow their
desires after the knowledge that has been
vouchsafed to thee, then thou shalt surely
be of the transgressors. Those to whom
We have given the Book recognise the
truth of this even as they recognise their
sons, but surely some of them conceal the
truth deliberately. This truth is from thy
Lord; be not, therefore, of those who
doubt. (143—148)

Everyone has a goal which dominates
him; do you, then, vie with one another
in good works. Wherever you be, Allah
will bring you all together. Surely, Allah
has the power to do all that He wills.
(149)

From wheresoever thou comest forth
turn thy attention towards the Sacred
Mosque; for that, indeed, is the truth
from thy Lord. Allah is not unmindful of
what you do. From wheresoever thou
comest forth, turn thy attention towards
the Sacred Mosque; and wheresoever you
be, turn your full attention. towards it, so
that excepting such of your enemies who
are bent upon transgression against you,
the rest of the people be left with no valid
cause of contention against you in this
respect. So fear not the transgressors, but
fear only Me. I have ordained this that
I may perfect My favour unto you; and
that you may be rightly guided.

Even as We have sent to you a Messenger from among yourselves who recites Our Signs to you, and purifies you, and teaches you the Book and Wisdom, and teaches you that which you did not know. Keep Me, therefore, constantly in mind, I shall keep you in mind, and be grateful to Me and be not unmindful of the bounties that I have bestowed upon you. O ye who believe, seek the help of Allah through steadfastness and Prayer; surely Allah is with the steadfast. Say not of those who are killed in the cause of Allah that they are dead; they are not dead but alive; only you perceive it not. We will surely try you with somewhat of fear and hunger, and loss of wealth and lives and fruits; then give glad tidings to the steadfast, who, when a misfortune overtakes them do not lose heart, but say: Surely, to Allah we belong and to Him shall we return. It is these on whom are blessings from their Lord and mercy, and it is these who are rightly guided. (150—158)

Surely, Safa and Marwa are among the Signs of Allah; it is no sin for him who is on Pilgrimage to the House or performs 'Umra to ambulate between the two. Whoso does good voluntarily, beyond that which is prescribed, should know that Allah is Appreciating, All-Knowing. (159)

Those who conceal that which We have sent down comprising Signs and guidance after We have made it clear for the people in the Book, it is these who are cursed by Allah and by those who curse; but those who repent and amend and openly declare that which Allah has revealed, to them I turn with forgiveness, for I am Oft-Returning with compassion and Ever Merciful. (160—161)

25

As for those who have disbelieved and die
while they are disbelievers, on them shall
be the curse of Allah and of angels and of
men all together; they shall continue under
it. Their punishment shall not be lightened
nor shall they be granted respite. Your
God is One God; there is no god but He
Ever Gracious, Most Merciful. (162—164)

In the creation of the heavens and the
earth and in the alternation of the night
and the day, and in the vessels that sail
in the sea carrying that which profits
people, and in the water that Allah sends
down from the clouds and quickens therewith the earth after its death and scatters
therein all kinds of beasts, and in the
courses of the winds, and the clouds pressed into service between the heaven and
the earth, are indeed Signs for a people
who understand. (165)

Some people adopt objects of worship
other than Allah and love them as they
should love Allah, but those who believe
love Allah most. Those who are guilty of
such transgression, if they could perceive
now the hour when they shall find themselves face to face with the punishment,
they would realise that all power belongs
to Allah and that Allah is severe in punishment; in the hour in which they shall witness that, those who were followed shall
disown their followers in the face of the
punishment and all their avenues of escape
shall be cut off. At that hour, those who
followed will say: If we could only return
to the world, we would disown them as
they have disowned us. Thus will Allah
apprise them that the end of all their
striving is only a bundle of regrets and
that they will not find a way of deliverance
from the Fire. (166—168)

O mankind, eat of that which is lawful
and wholesome in the earth; and do not
follow in the footsteps of Satan; surely,
he is your declared enemy. (169)

اِنَّ الَّذِیْنَ کَفَرُوْا وَ مَاتُوْا وَ ہُمْ کُفَّارٌ اُولٰٓئِکَ عَلَیْہِمْ لَعْنَۃُ اللہِ وَالْمَلٰٓئِکَۃِ وَالنَّاسِ اَجْمَعِیْنَ ۞

خٰلِدِیْنَ فِیْہَا ۚ لَا یُخَفَّفُ عَنْہُمُ الْعَذَابُ وَلَا ہُمْ یُنْظَرُوْنَ ۞

وَ اِلٰہُکُمْ اِلٰہٌ وَّاحِدٌ ۚ لَآ اِلٰہَ اِلَّا ہُوَ الرَّحْمٰنُ الرَّحِیْمُ ۞

اِنَّ فِیْ خَلْقِ السَّمٰوٰتِ وَالْاَرْضِ وَاخْتِلَافِ الَّیْلِ وَ النَّہَارِ وَالْفُلْکِ الَّتِیْ تَجْرِیْ فِی الْبَحْرِ بِمَا یَنْفَعُ النَّاسَ وَمَآ اَنْزَلَ اللہُ مِنَ السَّمَآءِ مِنْ مَّآءٍ فَاَحْیَا بِہِ الْاَرْضَ بَعْدَ مَوْتِہَا وَبَثَّ فِیْہَا مِنْ کُلِّ دَآبَّۃٍ ۪ وَّ تَصْرِیْفِ الرِّیٰحِ وَالسَّحَابِ الْمُسَخَّرِ بَیْنَ السَّمَآءِ وَالْاَرْضِ لَاٰیٰتٍ لِّقَوْمٍ یَّعْقِلُوْنَ ۞

وَ مِنَ النَّاسِ مَنْ یَّتَّخِذُ مِنْ دُوْنِ اللہِ اَنْدَادًا یُّحِبُّوْنَہُمْ کَحُبِّ اللہِ ۚ وَالَّذِیْنَ اٰمَنُوْا اَشَدُّ حُبًّا لِّلہِ ۙ وَلَوْ یَرَی الَّذِیْنَ ظَلَمُوْٓا اِذْ یَرَوْنَ الْعَذَابَ ۙ اَنَّ الْقُوَّۃَ لِلہِ جَمِیْعًا ۙ وَّ اَنَّ اللہَ شَدِیْدُ الْعَذَابِ ۞

اِذْ تَبَرَّاَ الَّذِیْنَ اتُّبِعُوْا مِنَ الَّذِیْنَ اتَّبَعُوْا وَرَاَوُا الْعَذَابَ وَتَقَطَّعَتْ بِہِمُ الْاَسْبَابُ ۞

وَقَالَ الَّذِیْنَ اتَّبَعُوْا لَوْ اَنَّ لَنَا کَرَّۃً فَنَتَبَرَّاَ مِنْہُمْ کَمَا تَبَرَّءُوْا مِنَّا ۭ کَذٰلِکَ یُرِیْہِمُ اللہُ اَعْمَالَہُمْ حَسَرٰتٍ عَلَیْہِمْ ۭ وَمَا ہُمْ بِخٰرِجِیْنَ مِنَ النَّارِ ۞

یٰٓاَیُّہَا النَّاسُ کُلُوْا مِمَّا فِی الْاَرْضِ حَلٰلًا طَیِّبًا ۫ وَّلَا تَتَّبِعُوْا خُطُوٰتِ الشَّیْطٰنِ ۭ اِنَّہُ لَکُمْ عَدُوٌّ مُّبِیْنٌ ۞

He enjoins upon you only that which is
vicious and foul and that you should say
concerning Allah falsely that which you
know not. When it is said to them: Follow
that which Allah has sent down; their
response is: Indeed not. We shall follow
in the way of our fathers. But what if their
fathers had no sense and followed not the
right path? The case of those who disbelieve is like that of one who calls out to
an animal which pays heed only to the
sound of the voice, without comprehending
its import. They are deaf, dumb and blind
and are not able to understand. (170—
172)

O ye who believe, eat of the lawful and
wholesome things We have provided for
you, and render thanks to Allah, if truly
it is He Whom you worship. He has made
unlawful for you only that which has died,
and blood and the flesh of swine, and that
on which the name of any other than
Allah has been invoked. But he who is
driven by extreme need to partake of any
of them, not being defiant of the law nor
exceeding the limit of his need, it shall be
no sin for him. Surely, Allah is most Forgiving, Merciful. Those who conceal that
which Allah has sent down of the Book
and take in exchange for it a paltry price,
only fill their bellies with fire. Allah
will not speak to them on the Day of
Judgment, nor will He purify them; and
for them is a grievous punishment. These
are they who have chosen error rather
than guidance and punishment rather than
forgiveness. How great is their endurance
of the Fire! They will find themselves in
this predicament because Allah has sent
down the Book comprising the Truth; and
those who disagree concerning the Book
are, surely, far gone in enmity. (173—177)

27

Righteousness is not that you turn your faces to the East or the West; but truly righteous are those who believe in Allah and the Last Day and the angels and the Book and the Prophets, and spend their wealth, for love of Him, on the kindred and the orphans and the needy and the wayfarer and those who ask, and for procuring the freedom of captives; and who observe Prayer and pay the Zakat; and whenever they make a promise carry it out, and are steadfast in adversity and under affliction and in battle. It is these who have proved faithful and it is these who are righteous. (178)

O ye who believe, equitable retribution in the matter of the slain is prescribed for you: exact it from the freeman if he is the offender, from the slave if he is the offender, from the woman if she is the offender. If the offender is granted some remission by the heir of the slain person, the agreed penalty should be equitably exacted and should be handsomely discharged. This is an alleviation from your Lord and a mercy. Whoso transgresses thereafter, for him there is a grievous chastisement. There is safeguarding of life for you in the law of retribution, O men of understanding, that you may have security. (179—180)

When death approaches any of you who is a person of substance it is incumbent on him, as an obligation laid on those who fear Allah, that he should leave directions for his parents and near relations to act with fairness. Those who vary these directions after having heard them, the sin thereof shall surely lie on such. Allah is All-Hearing, All-Knowing. But whoso apprehends partiality or wrong in consequence of such directions of the deceased it shall be no sin on him to bring about reconciliation between the parties affected thereby. Surely, Allah is Most Forgiving, Ever Merciful. (181—183)

O ye who believe, fasting is prescribed for you during a fixed number of days, as it was prescribed for those before you, so that you may safeguard yourselves against moral and spiritual ills. But whoso from among you should be ailing, not being permanently incapacitated, or should be on a journey, shall complete the reckoning by fasting on a corresponding number of other days; and for those who find fasting a strain hard to bear is an expiation, the feeding of a poor person, if they can afford it. Whoso carries through a good work with eager obedience, it is the better for him. If you had knowledge you would realise that it is better for you that you should fast. The month of Ramadhan is the month in which the Quran began to be revealed, the Book which comprises guidance for mankind and clear proofs of guidance and divine Signs which discriminate between truth and falsehood. Therefore, he who witnesses this month, being stationary and in health, should fast through it. But whoso is ailing, not being permanently incapacitated, or is on a journey, should complete the reckoning by fasting on a corresponding number of other days. Allah desires ease for you and desires not hardship for you; He has granted you this facility so that you should encounter no hardship in completing the reckoning, and that you may exalt Allah for His having guided you and that you may be grateful to Him. (184—186)

When My servants enquire from thee concerning Me, O Prophet, tell them I am close. I respond to the call of the supplicant when he calls on Me. So should they respond to Me and have firm faith in Me, that they may be rightly guided. (187)

It is made lawful for you to consort with your wives during the nights of the fast. They are as a garment for you and you are as a garment for them. Allah knows that you were being unjust to yourselves, wherefore He has turned to you with mercy and has corrected your error. So consort with them now without compunction and seek that which Allah has ordained for you, and eat and drink till the break of dawn begins to manifest itself. From then on, complete the fast till nightfall. But do not consort with your wives during the period when you are in retreat in the

عَلَى الَّذِيْنَ مِنْ قَبْلِكُمْ لَعَلَّكُمْ تَتَّقُوْنَ ۞

اَيَّامًا مَّعْدُوْدٰتٍ ۖ فَمَنْ كَانَ مِنْكُمْ مَّرِيْضًا اَوْ عَلٰى

سَفَرٍ فَعِدَّةٌ مِّنْ اَيَّامٍ اُخَرَ ۚ وَعَلَى الَّذِيْنَ يُطِيْقُوْنَهٗ

فِدْيَةٌ طَعَامُ مِسْكِيْنٍ ۖ فَمَنْ تَطَوَّعَ خَيْرًا فَهُوَ خَيْرٌ

لَّهٗ ۚ وَاَنْ تَصُوْمُوْا خَيْرٌ لَّكُمْ اِنْ كُنْتُمْ تَعْلَمُوْنَ ۞

شَهْرُ رَمَضَانَ الَّذِيْٓ اُنْزِلَ فِيْهِ الْقُرْاٰنُ هُدًى

لِّلنَّاسِ وَبَيِّنٰتٍ مِّنَ الْهُدٰى وَالْفُرْقَانِ ۚ فَمَنْ شَهِدَ

مِنْكُمُ الشَّهْرَ فَلْيَصُمْهُ ۖ وَمَنْ كَانَ مَرِيْضًا اَوْ عَلٰى

سَفَرٍ فَعِدَّةٌ مِّنْ اَيَّامٍ اُخَرَ ۗ يُرِيْدُ اللّٰهُ بِكُمُ

الْيُسْرَ وَلَا يُرِيْدُ بِكُمُ الْعُسْرَ ۖ وَلِتُكْمِلُوا الْعِدَّةَ

وَلِتُكَبِّرُوا اللّٰهَ عَلٰى مَا هَدٰىكُمْ وَلَعَلَّكُمْ تَشْكُرُوْنَ ۞

وَاِذَا سَاَلَكَ عِبَادِيْ عَنِّيْ فَاِنِّيْ قَرِيْبٌ ۖ اُجِيْبُ دَعْوَةَ

الدَّاعِ اِذَا دَعَانِ ۙ فَلْيَسْتَجِيْبُوْا لِيْ وَلْيُؤْمِنُوْا بِيْ لَعَلَّهُمْ

يَرْشُدُوْنَ ۞

اُحِلَّ لَكُمْ لَيْلَةَ الصِّيَامِ الرَّفَثُ اِلٰى نِسَآئِكُمْ ۚ هُنَّ

لِبَاسٌ لَّكُمْ وَاَنْتُمْ لِبَاسٌ لَّهُنَّ ۗ عَلِمَ اللّٰهُ اَنَّكُمْ

كُنْتُمْ تَخْتَانُوْنَ اَنْفُسَكُمْ فَتَابَ عَلَيْكُمْ وَعَفَا

عَنْكُمْ ۖ فَالْـٰٔنَ بَاشِرُوْهُنَّ وَابْتَغُوْا مَا كَتَبَ اللّٰهُ لَكُمْ ۖ

وَكُلُوْا وَاشْرَبُوْا حَتّٰى يَتَبَيَّنَ لَكُمُ الْخَيْطُ الْاَبْيَضُ

مِنَ الْخَيْطِ الْاَسْوَدِ مِنَ الْفَجْرِ ۖ ثُمَّ اَتِمُّوا الصِّيَامَ

اِلَى الَّيْلِ ۚ وَلَا تُبَاشِرُوْهُنَّ وَاَنْتُمْ عٰكِفُوْنَ فِى الْمَسٰجِدِ ۗ

تِلْكَ حُدُوْدُ اللّٰهِ فَلَا تَقْرَبُوْهَا ۗ كَذٰلِكَ يُبَيِّنُ اللّٰهُ

mosques. These are the limits prescribed by Allah, so approach them not. Thus does Allah expound His commandments to the people, so that they may safeguard themselves against evil. (188)

Do not devour each other's wealth among yourselves through deceit and falsehood, nor offer your wealth as a bribe to the authorities that you may deliberately devour a part of other people's wealth through injustice. (189)

They ask thee, O Prophet, concerning the phases of the moon. Tell them: These alternations are a means of determining time for regulation of people's affairs and for the Pilgrimage. Once you set forth for the Pilgrimage and then have occasion to revisit your homes, it is no part of righteousness that you should enter them from the backs thereof; indeed truly righteous is he who guards himself against evil out of fear of Allah. Enter your houses by the doors thereof, and be mindful of your duty to Allah that you may prosper. (190)

Fight in the cause of Allah against those who fight against you, but transgress not. Surely, Allah loves not the transgressors. Once they start the fighting, kill them wherever you meet them, and drive them out from where they have driven you out; for aggression is more heinous than killing. But fight them not in the proximity of the Sacred Mosque unless they fight you therein; should they fight you even there, then fight them: such is the requital of these disbelievers. Then if they desist, surely Allah is Most Forgiving, Ever Merciful. Fight them until all aggression ceases and religion is professed for the pleasure of Allah alone. If they desist, then be mindful that no retaliation is permissible except against the aggressors. (191—194)

The violation of a sacred month may be retaliated in a sacred month, for the law of retaliation applies in respect of all sacred things. Thus whoso transgresses against you, you may exact retribution from him in proportion to his transgression and be mindful of your obligations to Allah, and remember that Allah is with those who are mindful of their obligations to Him. (195)

Spend yourselves and your belongings in the cause of Allah and do not push yourselves into ruin with your own hands, and be benevolent, surely Allah loves the benevolent. (196)

Perform the Hajj and the Umra for winning the pleasure of Allah: but if you are hindered from doing so, then make whatever offering is easily available and do not shave your heads until the offering reaches its appointed place. If any of you should have to shave his head before that time because of illness or of some ailment of the head, he should make an expiation by way of fasting or almsgiving or a sacrifice. When there is no longer any hindrance, then he who would avail himself of the Umra together with the Hajj should make whatever offering is easily available. Such of you whose families do not reside near the Sacred Mosque, and who cannot find an offering should fast three days during the Pilgrimage, and seven days when they return home; thus completing ten. Fear Allah and be mindful that Allah's chastisement is severe. The months of Hajj are well known. For him who determines to perform the Pilgrimage therein, there is to be no loose talk, nor any transgression nor any contention during the Pilgrimage. Whatever of good you do, Allah will recognise its value. Furnish yourselves with necessary provisions; surely, the best provision is righteousness. Be ever mindful of your obligations to Me, O ye who possess understanding. It is no sin for you to seek any of the bounties of your Lord during the days of the Pilgrimage. When you return from Arafat, remember Allah at Mash'ar-al-Haram, and remember Him as He has guided you. Before this you were surely misguided. Thereafter, proceed as people have been proceeding, and seek forgiveness from Allah; surely Allah is Most Forgiving, Ever Merciful. On completing the acts of worship prescribed for you, celebrate the praises of Allah as eagerly as

وَ اَتِمُّوا الْحَجَّ وَ الْعُمْرَةَ لِلّٰهِ ۚ فَاِنْ اُحْصِرْتُمْ فَمَا اسْتَيْسَرَ مِنَ الْهَدْيِ ۚ وَ لَا تَحْلِقُوْا رُءُوْسَكُمْ حَتّٰى يَبْلُغَ الْهَدْيُ مَحِلَّهٗ ۚ فَمَنْ كَانَ مِنْكُمْ مَّرِيْضًا اَوْ بِهٖۤ اَذًى مِّنْ رَّأْسِهٖ فَفِدْيَةٌ مِّنْ صِيَامٍ اَوْ صَدَقَةٍ اَوْ نُسُكٍ ۚ فَاِذَاۤ اَمِنْتُمْ ۚ فَمَنْ تَمَتَّعَ بِالْعُمْرَةِ اِلَى الْحَجِّ فَمَا اسْتَيْسَرَ مِنَ الْهَدْيِ ۚ فَمَنْ لَّمْ يَجِدْ فَصِيَامُ ثَلٰثَةِ اَيَّامٍ فِى الْحَجِّ وَ سَبْعَةٍ اِذَا رَجَعْتُمْ ۗ تِلْكَ عَشَرَةٌ كَامِلَةٌ ۗ ذٰلِكَ لِمَنْ لَّمْ يَكُنْ اَهْلُهٗ حَاضِرِى الْمَسْجِدِ الْحَرَامِ ۚ وَ اتَّقُوا اللّٰهَ وَ اعْلَمُوْۤا اَنَّ اللّٰهَ شَدِيْدُ الْعِقَابِ ۝

اَلْحَجُّ اَشْهُرٌ مَّعْلُوْمٰتٌ ۚ فَمَنْ فَرَضَ فِيْهِنَّ الْحَجَّ فَلَا رَفَثَ وَ لَا فُسُوْقَ ۙ وَ لَا جِدَالَ فِى الْحَجِّ ۗ وَ مَا تَفْعَلُوْا مِنْ خَيْرٍ يَّعْلَمْهُ اللّٰهُ ۗ وَ تَزَوَّدُوْا فَاِنَّ خَيْرَ الزَّادِ التَّقْوٰى ۫ وَ اتَّقُوْنِ يٰۤاُولِى الْاَلْبَابِ ۝

لَيْسَ عَلَيْكُمْ جُنَاحٌ اَنْ تَبْتَغُوْا فَضْلًا مِّنْ رَّبِّكُمْ ۗ فَاِذَاۤ اَفَضْتُمْ مِّنْ عَرَفٰتٍ فَاذْكُرُوا اللّٰهَ عِنْدَ الْمَشْعَرِ الْحَرَامِ ۪ وَ اذْكُرُوْهُ كَمَا هَدٰىكُمْ ۚ وَ اِنْ كُنْتُمْ مِّنْ قَبْلِهٖ لَمِنَ الضَّآلِّيْنَ ۝

ثُمَّ اَفِيْضُوْا مِنْ حَيْثُ اَفَاضَ النَّاسُ وَ اسْتَغْفِرُوا اللّٰهَ ۚ اِنَّ اللّٰهَ غَفُوْرٌ رَّحِيْمٌ ۝

فَاِذَا قَضَيْتُمْ مَّنَاسِكَكُمْ فَاذْكُرُوا اللّٰهَ كَذِكْرِكُمْ اٰبَآءَكُمْ اَوْ اَشَدَّ ذِكْرًا ۗ فَمِنَ النَّاسِ مَنْ يَّقُوْلُ رَبَّنَاۤ اٰتِنَا فِى الدُّنْيَا وَ مَا لَهٗ فِى الْاٰخِرَةِ مِنْ خَلَاقٍ ۝

you used to celebrate the praises of your forefathers, or even with greater eagerness. There are some who keep supplicating: Lord, grant us of the bounties of this world; these have no portion in the Hereafter. (197—201)

There are others who pray: Lord, grant us the best in this world as well as the best in the world to come and safeguard us against the torment of the Fire. It is these for whom there will be a goodly recompense because of that which they have earned. Allah is Swift at reckoning. Remember Allah during the appointed number of days; but if any should be pressed and leave in two days' time it shall be no sin for him, and if any should linger it shall be no sin for him, so long as each is inspired by the spirit of righteousness. So be mindful of your obligations to Allah, and know that you shall all be brought together before Him. (202—204)

Of the people there are some whose talk on the affairs of this life would please thee, and who would call Allah to witness as to the sincerity of that which is in their minds, yet they are the most cantankerous contenders. When they attain to authority, they run about in the land to create disorder and destroy the tilth and the young; and Allah loves not disorder. When it is said to them: Be mindful of your duty to Allah; self esteem incites them to further misconduct. For such as these hell is a sufficiency, and an evil resting place it is. Also of the people there are those who dedicate themselves to seeking the pleasure of Allah; and Allah is Most Compassionate towards such devoted servants. O ye who believe, enter wholly into submission and follow not in the footsteps of Satan; surely, he is your declared enemy. But, if, despite the clear Signs that have come to you, you were to slip, then know that Allah is Mighty, Wise. Those others, what do they wait for? That Allah should come to them in the coverings of the clouds and the angels also, and that the affair be settled out of hand? To Allah are all affairs returned. (205—211)

32

Enquire from the children of Israel how many a clear Sign did We give them? Then whoso exchanges the bounty of Allah, after having received it and recognised its value, for something inferior, must realise that the chastisement of Allah is severe. The hither life is made to appear attractive to those who are disdainful of the bounties of Allah: they scoff at those who believe. But those who are mindful of their duty to Allah shall be superior in rank to them on the Day of Judgment. Allah bestows His bounties on whomsoever He pleases without measure. (212—213)

Mankind were of one persuasion, then they developed differences, so Allah raised Prophets as bearers of good tidings and as warners, and sent down with them the Book comprising the Truth, that He might judge between the people on that wherein they differed. Then those very people to whom it was given differed about the Book, after clear Signs had come to them, out of insolence and envy of one another. Whereupon, Allah guided by His command those who believed to the Truth in regard to which the others had differed. Allah guides whomsoever He pleases to the right path. (214)

Do you reckon that you will enter Paradise while you have not yet been subjected to the like of that to which those were subjected who have passed away before you? They were afflicted with indigence and adversity and were sorely tried, so that the Messenger sent to them and those who believed along with him should beseech: When will succour arrive from Allah? Yea, surely, at such times the succour of Allah is nigh. (215)

They ask thee what shall they spend? Tell them: Of pure and abundant wealth that which you spend is, in the first instance, for parents, near relations, orphans, the needy and the wayfarer. Whatever good you do, surely Allah knows it well. (216)

Fighting is ordained for you, while it is repugnant to you. It may be that you dislike a thing which is good for you, and it

33

may also be that you prefer a thing and it may be the worse for you. Allah knows all and you know not. They enquire from thee about fighting in the Sacred Month. Say to them: Fighting in it is a great evil; but to hinder people from the way of Allah and to deny Him and to profane the sanctity of the Sacred Mosque, and to turn out its people therefrom is a much greater evil in the sight of Allah; and disorder is a worse evil than killing. They will not stop fighting you until they turn you back from your Faith, if they can. The works of those from among you who turn back from their Faith and die in a state of disbelief shall be vain in this world and the next. These are the inmates of the Fire, therein shall they abide. Those who have believed and have emigrated, and have striven hard in the cause of Allah, are those who hope for Allah's mercy. Allah is Most Forgiving, Ever Merciful. (217—219)

They ask thee concerning liquor and gambling. Tell them: There is great harm in both and also some benefit for people, but their harm is greater than their benefit. They also ask thee what shall they spend. Tell them: Whatever is spare. Thus does Allah make His commandments clear to you that you may reflect upon this world and the next. (220)

They ask thee concerning orphans. Tell them: The promotion of their welfare is very meritorious. There is no harm in your living together with them, for they are your brethren, and Allah well knows him who seeks to promote their welfare and also him who seeks to do them harm. If Allah had so willed, He would have put you to hardship. Surely, Allah is Mighty, Wise. (221)

Marry not idolatrous women till after they have believed; surely a believing bondwoman would make a better wife than an idolatress, however pleasing she may appear to you. Nor give believing women in marriage to idolaters till after they have believed; surely a believing bondman would make a better husband

34

than an idolater, however pleasing he may appear to you. These invite to the Fire and Allah invites to Paradise and forgiveness by His command. He makes His Signs clear to the people that they may take heed. (222)

They enquire from thee as to consorting with their wives during their monthly courses. Tell them: It is harmful, so keep away from women during their monthly courses and do not consort with them until they are clean. But when they have washed themselves clean, consort with them as Allah has commanded you. Indeed Allah loves those who turn to Him often, and Allah loves those who are clean and pure. Your wives are as a tilth for you, so approach your tilth as you like and lay up a store of good for yourselves. Be mindful of your duty to Allah, and be sure you shall meet Him. Give glad tidings concerning that day to the believers. (223—224)

Use not Allah's name for your vain oaths, making them an excuse for refraining from doing good and working righteousness and promoting public welfare. Allah is All-Hearing, All-Knowing. Allah will not call you to account for such of your oaths as are vain, but will call you to account for the evil you have deliberately assented to. Allah is Most Forgiving, Forbearing. For those who vow abstinence from their wives, the maximum period for making up their minds is four months; then, if they revert towards conciliation, surely, Allah is Most Forgiving, Ever Merciful; and if they decide upon divorce, Allah is All-Hearing, All-Knowing. (225—228)

Divorced women shall wait, concerning themselves, for the space of three courses. It is not lawful for them to conceal what Allah may have created in their wombs, if they believe in Allah and the Last Day. If their husbands should desire reconciliation during this period, they would have the stronger right to the continuation of the marriage than that it should be irrevocably dissolved. In such

حَتّٰى يُؤْمِنُوْا ۚ وَلَعَبْدٌ مُّؤْمِنٌ خَيْرٌ مِّنْ مُّشْرِكٍ وَّ لَوْ اَعْجَبَكُمْ ۗ اُولٰٓئِكَ يَدْعُوْنَ اِلَى النَّارِ ۖ وَاللّٰهُ يَدْعُوْٓا اِلَى الْجَنَّةِ وَالْمَغْفِرَةِ بِاِذْنِهٖ ۚ وَيُبَيِّنُ اٰيٰتِهٖ لِلنَّاسِ لَعَلَّهُمْ يَتَذَكَّرُوْنَ ۞

وَيَسْـَٔلُوْنَكَ عَنِ الْمَحِيْضِ ۖ قُلْ هُوَ اَذًى ۙ فَاعْتَزِلُوا النِّسَآءَ فِى الْمَحِيْضِ ۙ وَلَا تَقْرَبُوْهُنَّ حَتّٰى يَطْهُرْنَ ۚ فَاِذَا تَطَهَّرْنَ فَأْتُوْهُنَّ مِنْ حَيْثُ اَمَرَكُمُ اللّٰهُ ۚ اِنَّ اللّٰهَ يُحِبُّ التَّوَّابِيْنَ وَيُحِبُّ الْمُتَطَهِّرِيْنَ ۞

نِسَآؤُكُمْ حَرْثٌ لَّكُمْ ۖ فَأْتُوْا حَرْثَكُمْ اَنّٰى شِئْتُمْ ۖ وَقَدِّمُوْا لِاَنْفُسِكُمْ ۗ وَاتَّقُوا اللّٰهَ وَاعْلَمُوْٓا اَنَّكُمْ مُّلٰقُوْهُ ۗ وَبَشِّرِ الْمُؤْمِنِيْنَ ۞

وَلَا تَجْعَلُوا اللّٰهَ عُرْضَةً لِّاَيْمَانِكُمْ اَنْ تَبَرُّوْا وَتَتَّقُوْا وَتُصْلِحُوْا بَيْنَ النَّاسِ ۗ وَاللّٰهُ سَمِيْعٌ عَلِيْمٌ ۞

لَا يُؤَاخِذُكُمُ اللّٰهُ بِاللَّغْوِ فِيْٓ اَيْمَانِكُمْ وَلٰكِنْ يُؤَاخِذُكُمْ بِمَا كَسَبَتْ قُلُوْبُكُمْ ۗ وَاللّٰهُ غَفُوْرٌ حَلِيْمٌ ۞

لِلَّذِيْنَ يُؤْلُوْنَ مِنْ نِّسَآئِهِمْ تَرَبُّصُ اَرْبَعَةِ اَشْهُرٍ ۖ فَاِنْ فَآءُوْ فَاِنَّ اللّٰهَ غَفُوْرٌ رَّحِيْمٌ ۞

وَاِنْ عَزَمُوا الطَّلَاقَ فَاِنَّ اللّٰهَ سَمِيْعٌ عَلِيْمٌ ۞

وَالْمُطَلَّقٰتُ يَتَرَبَّصْنَ بِاَنْفُسِهِنَّ ثَلٰثَةَ قُرُوْٓءٍ ۚ وَلَا يَحِلُّ لَهُنَّ اَنْ يَّكْتُمْنَ مَا خَلَقَ اللّٰهُ فِيْٓ اَرْحَامِهِنَّ اِنْ كُنَّ يُؤْمِنَّ بِاللّٰهِ وَالْيَوْمِ الْاٰخِرِ ۚ وَبُعُوْلَتُهُنَّ اَحَقُّ بِرَدِّهِنَّ فِيْ ذٰلِكَ اِنْ اَرَادُوْٓا اِصْلَاحًا ۚ وَلَهُنَّ مِثْلُ

case the wives have rights corresponding to those which the husbands have, in equitable reciprocity, though, in certain situations men would have the final word and would thus enjoy a preference. Allah is Mighty, Wise. (229)

Revocable divorce can only be pronounced twice; whereafter there should be reconciliation in approved form or final separation with beneficence. It is not lawful for you to take away anything of that which you have given your wives, unless the husband and wife should be afraid that they would not be able to observe the limits prescribed by Allah. In such case there will be no sin on either of them in respect of that which the wife may surrender by way of compromise. These are the limits prescribed by Allah, so transgress them not; whoso transgresses the limits prescribed by Allah, it is they that are the wrongdoers. Should the husband divorce the wife a third time, then she would not be lawful for him thereafter, except in case she should marry another husband and he too should divorce her. Should this happen, it would be no sin for them to return to each other, provided they are sure they would be able to observe the limits prescribed by Allah. These are the limits prescribed by Allah which He makes clear to the people who possess knowledge. In the case of a revocable divorce, when the end of the appointed period of waiting approaches, there should be reconciliation in approved form or final separation in approved form but do not hold back such women to impose hardship upon them. Whoso does that, surely wrongs his own self. Do not bring the commandments of Allah into contempt and keep in mind the favour that Allah has bestowed upon you and that which He has sent down to you of the Book and Wisdom, whereby He exhorts you. Be mindful of your duty to Allah and be sure that Allah knows all things well. When you divorce your wives and they reach the end of their waiting period and the divorce becomes

الَّذِىْ عَلَيْهِنَّ بِالْمَعْرُوْفِ وَ لِلرِّجَالِ عَلَيْهِنَّ دَرَجَةٌ وَ اللّٰهُ عَزِيْزٌ حَكِيْمٌ ۞

اَلطَّلَاقُ مَرَّتٰنِ فَاِمْسَاكٌ بِمَعْرُوْفٍ اَوْ تَسْرِيْحٌ بِاِحْسَانٍ وَ لَا يَحِلُّ لَكُمْ اَنْ تَأْخُذُوْا مِمَّا اٰتَيْتُمُوْهُنَّ شَيْئًا اِلَّا اَنْ يَّخَافَا اَلَّا يُقِيْمَا حُدُوْدَ اللّٰهِ فَاِنْ خِفْتُمْ اَلَّا يُقِيْمَا حُدُوْدَ اللّٰهِ فَلَا جُنَاحَ عَلَيْهِمَا فِيْمَا افْتَدَتْ بِهٖ تِلْكَ حُدُوْدُ اللّٰهِ فَلَا تَعْتَدُوْهَا وَ مَنْ يَّتَعَدَّ حُدُوْدَ اللّٰهِ فَاُولٰٓئِكَ هُمُ الظّٰلِمُوْنَ ۞

فَاِنْ طَلَّقَهَا فَلَا تَحِلُّ لَهٗ مِنْ بَعْدُ حَتّٰى تَنْكِحَ زَوْجًا غَيْرَهٗ فَاِنْ طَلَّقَهَا فَلَا جُنَاحَ عَلَيْهِمَا اَنْ يَّتَرَاجَعَا اِنْ ظَنَّا اَنْ يُّقِيْمَا حُدُوْدَ اللّٰهِ وَ تِلْكَ حُدُوْدُ اللّٰهِ يُبَيِّنُهَا لِقَوْمٍ يَّعْلَمُوْنَ ۞

وَ اِذَا طَلَّقْتُمُ النِّسَاءَ فَبَلَغْنَ اَجَلَهُنَّ فَاَمْسِكُوْهُنَّ بِمَعْرُوْفٍ اَوْ سَرِّحُوْهُنَّ بِمَعْرُوْفٍ وَ لَا تُمْسِكُوْهُنَّ ضِرَارًا لِّتَعْتَدُوْا وَ مَنْ يَّفْعَلْ ذٰلِكَ فَقَدْ ظَلَمَ نَفْسَهٗ وَ لَا تَتَّخِذُوْۤا اٰيٰتِ اللّٰهِ هُزُوًا وَّ اذْكُرُوْا نِعْمَتَ اللّٰهِ عَلَيْكُمْ وَ مَاۤ اَنْزَلَ عَلَيْكُمْ مِّنَ الْكِتٰبِ وَ الْحِكْمَةِ يَعِظُكُمْ بِهٖ وَ اتَّقُوا اللّٰهَ وَ اعْلَمُوْۤا اَنَّ اللّٰهَ بِكُلِّ شَيْءٍ عَلِيْمٌ ۞

وَ اِذَا طَلَّقْتُمُ النِّسَاءَ فَبَلَغْنَ اَجَلَهُنَّ فَلَا تَعْضُلُوْهُنَّ اَنْ يَّنْكِحْنَ اَزْوَاجَهُنَّ اِذَا تَرَاضَوْا بَيْنَهُمْ بِالْمَعْرُوْفِ ذٰلِكَ يُوْعَظُ بِهٖ مَنْ كَانَ مِنْكُمْ يُؤْمِنُ بِاللّٰهِ وَ الْيَوْمِ الْاٰخِرِ ذٰلِكُمْ اَزْكٰى لَكُمْ وَ اَطْهَرُ وَ اللّٰهُ يَعْلَمُ وَ اَنْتُمْ

36

irrevocable, do not hinder them from marrying their chosen husbands, if they agree between themselves in an approved manner. This is an admonition for everyone of you who believes in Allah and the Last Day: it is most blessed for you and purest. Allah knows and you know not. (230—233)

In cases of divorce, mothers shall give suck to their children for two whole years, where it is desired to complete the suckling, and the father of the child shall be responsible for the maintenance of the mother during that period, according to usage. No one shall be burdened beyond his capacity. No mother shall be made to suffer on account of her child, and no father shall be made to suffer on account of his child, and the same is the obligation of the heir. If both should agree by mutual consultation and consent upon weaning the child, there shall be no blame on them. Should you desire to engage a wet-nurse for your children, there shall be no blame on you, provided you hand over what you have agreed to pay, in a fair manner. Be mindful of your duty to Allah and be sure that Allah sees what you do. (234)

Women who survive their husbands shall wait concerning themselves for four months and ten days, and when they arrive at the end of that period there shall be no sin for you in anything that they do with regard to themselves according to what is fair. Allah is aware of what you do. There shall be no blame on you in hinting at a proposal of marriage to divorced or widowed women or in contemplating the possibility in your minds. Allah knows that you will think of them in that connection; but do not enter into any secret engagement with them, beyond conveying some indication to them of your inclination. Do not, however, resolve on the marriage tie until after the expiry of the period of waiting. Be sure Allah knows what is in your minds, so beware of it. Know also that Allah is Most Forgiving, Forbearing. (235—236)

لَا تَعْلَمُونَ ۞

وَالْوَالِدَاتُ يُرْضِعْنَ أَوْلَادَهُنَّ حَوْلَيْنِ كَامِلَيْنِ لِمَنْ أَرَادَ أَنْ يُّتِمَّ الرَّضَاعَةَ ۚ وَعَلَى الْمَوْلُودِ لَهُ رِزْقُهُنَّ وَكِسْوَتُهُنَّ بِالْمَعْرُوفِ ۚ لَا تُكَلَّفُ نَفْسٌ إِلَّا وُسْعَهَا ۚ لَا تُضَآرَّ وَالِدَةٌ بِوَلَدِهَا وَلَا مَوْلُودٌ لَهُ بِوَلَدِهِ ۚ وَعَلَى الْوَارِثِ مِثْلُ ذٰلِكَ ۚ فَإِنْ أَرَادَا فِصَالًا عَنْ تَرَاضٍ مِّنْهُمَا وَتَشَاوُرٍ فَلَا جُنَاحَ عَلَيْهِمَا ۚ وَإِنْ أَرَدْتُّمْ أَنْ تَسْتَرْضِعُوا أَوْلَادَكُمْ فَلَا جُنَاحَ عَلَيْكُمْ إِذَا سَلَّمْتُمْ مَّآ أَتَيْتُمْ بِالْمَعْرُوفِ ۚ وَاتَّقُوا اللّٰهَ وَاعْلَمُوا أَنَّ اللّٰهَ بِمَا تَعْمَلُونَ بَصِيرٌ ۞

وَالَّذِينَ يُتَوَفَّوْنَ مِنْكُمْ وَيَذَرُونَ أَزْوَاجًا يَّتَرَبَّصْنَ بِأَنْفُسِهِنَّ أَرْبَعَةَ أَشْهُرٍ وَّعَشْرًا ۚ فَإِذَا بَلَغْنَ أَجَلَهُنَّ فَلَا جُنَاحَ عَلَيْكُمْ فِيمَا فَعَلْنَ فِيۤ أَنْفُسِهِنَّ بِالْمَعْرُوفِ ۗ وَاللّٰهُ بِمَا تَعْمَلُونَ خَبِيرٌ ۞

وَلَا جُنَاحَ عَلَيْكُمْ فِيمَا عَرَّضْتُمْ بِهِ مِنْ خِطْبَةِ النِّسَآءِ أَوْ أَكْنَنْتُمْ فِيۤ أَنْفُسِكُمْ ۚ عَلِمَ اللّٰهُ أَنَّكُمْ سَتَذْكُرُونَهُنَّ وَلٰكِنْ لَّا تُوَاعِدُوهُنَّ سِرًّا إِلَّاۤ أَنْ تَقُولُوا قَوْلًا مَّعْرُوفًا ۚ وَلَا تَعْزِمُوا عُقْدَةَ النِّكَاحِ حَتّٰى يَبْلُغَ الْكِتَابُ أَجَلَهُ ۚ وَاعْلَمُوا أَنَّ اللّٰهَ يَعْلَمُ مَا فِيۤ أَنْفُسِكُمْ فَاحْذَرُوهُ ۚ وَاعْلَمُوا أَنَّ اللّٰهَ غَفُورٌ حَلِيمٌ ۞

لَا جُنَاحَ عَلَيْكُمْ إِنْ طَلَّقْتُمُ النِّسَآءَ مَا لَمْ تَمَسُّوهُنَّ أَوْ تَفْرِضُوا لَهُنَّ فَرِيضَةً ۚ وَمَتِّعُوهُنَّ ۚ عَلَى الْمُوسِعِ

It will be no sin for you, if need arises, to divorce women whom you have not even touched, or for whom no definite dower has been fixed. In such case, make provision for them — the rich man according to his means and the poor man according to his means — a provision in a becoming manner. This is an obligation binding upon the virtuous. If you divorce them before you have touched them, but you have fixed a dower for them, then make over to them half of that which you have fixed, unless they should remit it or the guardian for the marriage should remit it, or unless the husband should voluntarily decide to pay a sum in excess of the half. That you should remit or should pay a larger sum, as the case may be, would be closer to righteousness. Do not neglect any chance of behaving benevolently towards each other. Surely, Allah sees what you do. (237—238)

Be watchful over Prayers, particularly over the Prayer the hour of which approaches when you are pre-occupied, and stand before Allah in submissive devotion. Should you be in a state of fear, then observe Prayer on foot or riding, as the case may be; then when you feel secure, remember Allah as He has taught you that which you knew not. (239—240)

Those of you who die leaving them surviving widows shall bequeath to their widows provision for a year, without being turned out. Should they depart on their own, after the expiry of the period of waiting, there shall be no blame upon you in regard to any proper thing which they do concerning themselves. Allah is Mighty, Wise. For divorced women also there shall be provision according to what is fair. This is an obligation binding on the righteous. Thus does Allah make His commandments clear to you that you may understand. (241—243)

Knowest thou not of those who went forth from their homes in their thousands, fearing death? Allah said to them: Be you as the dead. Thereafter He bestowed life upon them. Surely, Allah is Bountiful

قَدَرُهُ وَعَلَى الْمُقْتِرِ قَدَرُهُ مَتَاعًا بِالْمَعْرُوفِ حَقًّا عَلَى الْمُحْسِنِينَ ﴿٢٣٦﴾

وَإِنْ طَلَّقْتُمُوهُنَّ مِنْ قَبْلِ أَنْ تَمَسُّوهُنَّ وَقَدْ فَرَضْتُمْ لَهُنَّ فَرِيضَةً فَنِصْفُ مَا فَرَضْتُمْ إِلَّا أَنْ يَعْفُونَ أَوْ يَعْفُوَ الَّذِي بِيَدِهِ عُقْدَةُ النِّكَاحِ وَأَنْ تَعْفُوا أَقْرَبُ لِلتَّقْوَى وَلَا تَنْسَوُا الْفَضْلَ بَيْنَكُمْ إِنَّ اللَّهَ بِمَا تَعْمَلُونَ بَصِيرٌ ﴿٢٣٧﴾

حَافِظُوا عَلَى الصَّلَوَاتِ وَالصَّلَاةِ الْوُسْطَى وَقُومُوا لِلَّهِ قَانِتِينَ ﴿٢٣٨﴾

فَإِنْ خِفْتُمْ فَرِجَالًا أَوْ رُكْبَانًا فَإِذَا أَمِنْتُمْ فَاذْكُرُوا اللَّهَ كَمَا عَلَّمَكُمْ مَا لَمْ تَكُونُوا تَعْلَمُونَ ﴿٢٣٩﴾

وَالَّذِينَ يُتَوَفَّوْنَ مِنْكُمْ وَيَذَرُونَ أَزْوَاجًا وَصِيَّةً لِأَزْوَاجِهِمْ مَتَاعًا إِلَى الْحَوْلِ غَيْرَ إِخْرَاجٍ فَإِنْ خَرَجْنَ فَلَا جُنَاحَ عَلَيْكُمْ فِي مَا فَعَلْنَ فِي أَنْفُسِهِنَّ مِنْ مَعْرُوفٍ وَاللَّهُ عَزِيزٌ حَكِيمٌ ﴿٢٤٠﴾

وَلِلْمُطَلَّقَاتِ مَتَاعٌ بِالْمَعْرُوفِ حَقًّا عَلَى الْمُتَّقِينَ ﴿٢٤١﴾

كَذَلِكَ يُبَيِّنُ اللَّهُ لَكُمْ آيَاتِهِ لَعَلَّكُمْ تَعْقِلُونَ ﴿٢٤٢﴾

أَلَمْ تَرَ إِلَى الَّذِينَ خَرَجُوا مِنْ دِيَارِهِمْ وَهُمْ أُلُوفٌ حَذَرَ الْمَوْتِ فَقَالَ لَهُمُ اللَّهُ مُوتُوا ثُمَّ أَحْيَاهُمْ إِنَّ اللَّهَ لَذُو فَضْلٍ عَلَى النَّاسِ وَلَكِنَّ أَكْثَرَ النَّاسِ لَا يَشْكُرُونَ ﴿٢٤٣﴾

وَقَاتِلُوا فِي سَبِيلِ اللَّهِ وَاعْلَمُوا أَنَّ اللَّهَ سَمِيعٌ

towards people, but most people are not grateful. (244)

Fight in the cause of Allah and know that Allah is All-Hearing, All-Knowing. Is there any who would set aside a goodly portion of his wealth for Allah that He may multiply it for him manifold? Allah does, indeed, receive of the wealth of His servants and multiply it and to Him shall you be made to return. (245—246)

Knowest thou not of the chiefs of the children of Israel, who came after Moses, when they said to a Prophet of theirs: Appoint for us a king that we may fight in the cause of Allah, under his command. He said to them: Perchance you may not fight, if fighting is prescribed for you. They said: Wherefore would we hold back from fighting in the cause of Allah, when we have been driven forth from our homes and our children? But when fighting was prescribed for them, they turned back, except a small number of them. Allah knows the wrongdoers well. Their Prophet said to them: Allah has appointed for you Talut as a king. They demurred, saying: How can he have sovereignty over us while we are better entitled to sovereignty than he, and he has not even been granted abundance of wealth? He answered: Surely Allah has granted him superiority over you and has given him a large portion of knowledge and strength. Allah bestows sovereignty upon whom He pleases; Allah is Lord of vast bounty, All-Knowing. Their Prophet added: Another proof of his sovereignty is that there shall come to you the casket borne by angels wherein there will be tranquillity from your Lord and a legacy of that which was left by the family of Moses and the family of Aaron. Surely, in this there is a Sign for you if you are believers. (247—249)

عَلِيمٌ ۝

مَنْ ذَا الَّذِيْ يُقْرِضُ اللهَ قَرْضًا حَسَنًا فَيُضٰعِفَهٗ لَهٗٓ اَضْعَافًا كَثِيْرَةً ۗ وَاللهُ يَقْبِضُ وَيَبْصُطُ ۠ وَ اِلَيْهِ تُرْجَعُوْنَ ۝

اَلَمْ تَرَ اِلَى الْمَلَاِ مِنْۢ بَنِيْٓ اِسْرَآءِيْلَ مِنْۢ بَعْدِ مُوْسٰى ۘ اِذْ قَالُوْا لِنَبِيٍّ لَّهُمُ ابْعَثْ لَنَا مَلِكًا نُّقَاتِلْ فِيْ سَبِيْلِ اللهِ ۗ قَالَ هَلْ عَسَيْتُمْ اِنْ كُتِبَ عَلَيْكُمُ الْقِتَالُ اَلَّا تُقَاتِلُوْا ۗ قَالُوْا وَمَا لَنَآ اَلَّا نُقَاتِلَ فِيْ سَبِيْلِ اللهِ وَقَدْ اُخْرِجْنَا مِنْ دِيَارِنَا وَاَبْنَآئِنَا ۗ فَلَمَّا كُتِبَ عَلَيْهِمُ الْقِتَالُ تَوَلَّوْا اِلَّا قَلِيْلًا مِّنْهُمْ ۗ وَاللهُ عَلِيْمٌۢ بِالظّٰلِمِيْنَ ۝

وَقَالَ لَهُمْ نَبِيُّهُمْ اِنَّ اللهَ قَدْ بَعَثَ لَكُمْ طَالُوْتَ مَلِكًا ۗ قَالُوْٓا اَنّٰى يَكُوْنُ لَهُ الْمُلْكُ عَلَيْنَا وَنَحْنُ اَحَقُّ بِالْمُلْكِ مِنْهُ وَلَمْ يُؤْتَ سَعَةً مِّنَ الْمَالِ ۗ قَالَ اِنَّ اللهَ اصْطَفٰىهُ عَلَيْكُمْ وَزَادَهٗ بَسْطَةً فِى الْعِلْمِ وَالْجِسْمِ ۗ وَاللهُ يُؤْتِيْ مُلْكَهٗ مَنْ يَّشَآءُ ۗ وَاللهُ وَاسِعٌ عَلِيْمٌ ۝

وَقَالَ لَهُمْ نَبِيُّهُمْ اِنَّ اٰيَةَ مُلْكِهٖٓ اَنْ يَّأْتِيَكُمُ التَّابُوْتُ فِيْهِ سَكِيْنَةٌ مِّنْ رَّبِّكُمْ وَبَقِيَّةٌ مِّمَّا تَرَكَ اٰلُ مُوْسٰى وَاٰلُ هٰرُوْنَ تَحْمِلُهُ الْمَلٰٓئِكَةُ ۗ اِنَّ فِيْ ذٰلِكَ لَاٰيَةً لَّكُمْ اِنْ كُنْتُمْ مُّؤْمِنِيْنَ ۝

فَلَمَّا فَصَلَ طَالُوْتُ بِالْجُنُوْدِ ۙ قَالَ اِنَّ اللهَ مُبْتَلِيْكُمْ

When Talut set out with his forces, he announced: Surely, Allah will put you to the test in respect of a river; he who drinks his fill therefrom will not remain with me; and he who tastes it not will of a surety continue with me. There will, however, be no blame upon him who sips only a handful from it. But, except a few of them, they all drank of it. When he and those who believed along with him had crossed it, they said: We have no strength today to oppose Jalut and his forces. Those who were certain that they would one day meet Allah said: Many a small party has triumphed over a large party by Allah's command; Allah is indeed with the steadfast. When they issued forth to encounter Jalut and his forces, they prayed: Lord grant us stead-fastness and make our steps firm in the battlefield and help us against the dis-believing people. The issue was joined and they routed the enemy by the command of Allah. (250—251)

When his time came David slew the Jalut of his time, and Allah bestowed upon him sovereignty and wisdom and taught him of what He pleased. If Allah were not to repel a section of mankind by another, the earth would be filled with disorder; but Allah is full of bounty towards all peoples. (252)

These are Signs of Allah; We recite them unto thee with truth. Surely, thou art one of the Messengers. Of these Messengers some have We exalted above others; among them there are those to whom Allah spoke and revealed to them a Law; and some of them He only exalted in rank. We gave Jesus son of Mary clear proofs and strengthened him with the Spirit of holiness. Had Allah so willed, those who came after them would not have fought with one another after clear Signs had come to them, but they dis-agreed nevertheless. Some of them believed and some of them disbelieved. Had Allah so willed, they would not have fought with one another; but Allah does what He wills. (253—254)

40

O ye who believe, spend out of whatever We have bestowed on you before the day comes wherein there will be no buying and selling, nor friendship, nor intercession. Those who reject this admonition are the ones who wrong themselves. (255)

Allah is He save Whom none is worthy of worship, the Ever-Living, the Self-Subsisting and All-Sustaining. Slumber seizes Him not, nor sleep. To Him belongs whatsoever is in the heavens and whatsoever is in the earth. Who is he that dare intercede with Him, except by His permission? He knows all that is before them and all that is behind them, and they cannot compass aught of His knowledge, except that which He pleases. His knowledge extends over the heavens and the earth, and the care of them wearies Him not. He is the Most High, the Most Great. (256)

There shall be no compulsion in religion, for guidance and error have been clearly distinguished; then whoso rejects those who hinder people from following the right path and believes in Allah, has surely taken hold of a strong and dependable support which will never break. Allah is All-Hearing, All-Knowing. (257)

Allah is the Friend of those who believe: He brings them out of every kind of darkness into light. Those who disbelieve, their friends are those who hinder people from following the right path; they bring them out of light into every kind of darkness. These are the inmates of the Fire; therein shall they abide. (258)

Knowest thou not of him who, because Allah had bestowed sovereignty upon him, began to dispute with Abraham concerning his Lord. When Abraham said to him: My Lord is He who bestows life and causes death; he countered with: I too grant life and inflict death. Said Abraham: Well, then, Allah causes the sun to rise in the East, do thou cause it to rise in the West. Thus the infidel was confounded. Indeed Allah guides not the unjust to success. (259)

وَلٰكِنَّ اللّٰهَ يَفْعَلُ مَا يُرِيْدُ ۟

يٰۤاَيُّهَا الَّذِيْنَ اٰمَنُوۤا اَنْفِقُوْا مِمَّا رَزَقْنٰكُمْ مِّنْ قَبْلِ اَنْ يَّاْتِيَ يَوْمٌ لَّا بَيْعٌ فِيْهِ وَلَا خُلَّةٌ وَّلَا شَفَاعَةٌ ۟ وَالْكٰفِرُوْنَ هُمُ الظّٰلِمُوْنَ ۟

اَللّٰهُ لَاۤ اِلٰهَ اِلَّا هُوَ ۚ اَلْحَيُّ الْقَيُّوْمُ ۚ لَا تَاْخُذُهٗ سِنَةٌ وَّلَا نَوْمٌ ۚ لَهٗ مَا فِي السَّمٰوٰتِ وَمَا فِي الْاَرْضِ ۗ مَنْ ذَا الَّذِيْ يَشْفَعُ عِنْدَهٗۤ اِلَّا بِاِذْنِهٖ ۚ يَعْلَمُ مَا بَيْنَ اَيْدِيْهِمْ وَمَا خَلْفَهُمْ ۚ وَلَا يُحِيْطُوْنَ بِشَيْءٍ مِّنْ عِلْمِهٖۤ اِلَّا بِمَا شَآءَ ۚ وَسِعَ كُرْسِيُّهُ السَّمٰوٰتِ وَالْاَرْضَ ۚ وَلَا يَـُٔوْدُهٗ حِفْظُهُمَا ۚ وَهُوَ الْعَلِيُّ الْعَظِيْمُ ۟

لَاۤ اِكْرَاهَ فِي الدِّيْنِ ۟ قَدْ تَّبَيَّنَ الرُّشْدُ مِنَ الْغَيِّ ۚ فَمَنْ يَّكْفُرْ بِالطَّاغُوْتِ وَيُؤْمِنْ بِاللّٰهِ فَقَدِ اسْتَمْسَكَ بِالْعُرْوَةِ الْوُثْقٰى ۙ لَا انْفِصَامَ لَهَا ۗ وَاللّٰهُ سَمِيْعٌ عَلِيْمٌ ۟

اَللّٰهُ وَلِيُّ الَّذِيْنَ اٰمَنُوْا ۙ يُخْرِجُهُمْ مِّنَ الظُّلُمٰتِ اِلَى النُّوْرِ ۚ وَالَّذِيْنَ كَفَرُوْۤا اَوْلِيٰٓـُٔهُمُ الطَّاغُوْتُ ۙ يُخْرِجُوْنَهُمْ مِّنَ النُّوْرِ اِلَى الظُّلُمٰتِ ۗ اُولٰٓئِكَ اَصْحٰبُ النَّارِ ۚ هُمْ فِيْهَا خٰلِدُوْنَ ۟

اَلَمْ تَرَ اِلَى الَّذِيْ حَآجَّ اِبْرٰهٖمَ فِيْ رَبِّهٖۤ اَنْ اٰتٰىهُ اللّٰهُ الْمُلْكَ ۘ اِذْ قَالَ اِبْرٰهٖمُ رَبِّيَ الَّذِيْ يُحْيٖ وَيُمِيْتُ ۙ قَالَ اَنَا اُحْيٖ وَاُمِيْتُ ۗ قَالَ اِبْرٰهٖمُ فَاِنَّ اللّٰهَ يَاْتِيْ بِالشَّمْسِ مِنَ الْمَشْرِقِ فَاْتِ بِهَا مِنَ الْمَغْرِبِ

Or knowest thou one like him who passed by a town which was in ruin, its roofs all fallen down? Whereupon he exclaimed: When will Allah restore it after its ruin? Thereupon Allah caused him to sleep and to dream that he had died and risen after a hundred years. When he woke up, Allah asked him: How long hast thou passed in that state? He answered: I remained thus for a day or part of a day. Allah said: That is so, but thou hast witnessed developments over a hundred years. Now look at thy provision for food and for drink, they have not deteriorated, and look at thy donkey likewise. We have made thee a Sign unto people. Observe how We adjust and set the bones and then clothe them with flesh. When all became clear to him, he said: I know that Allah has the power to do all that He wills. (260)

Call to mind when Abraham supplicated: Lord, show me how dost Thou bring the dead to life. Allah said: Hast thou not believed? Said Abraham; Indeed, I have believed; but I have asked this question that my mind may be comforted. Said Allah: Well, then, take four birds and train them to be attached to thee. Thereafter put each one of them on a hillock. Then call them; they will hasten towards thee. Know then that Allah is Mighty, Wise. (261)

The case of those who spend their wealth in the cause of Allah is like that of a grain of corn, which grows seven ears, and in each ear there are a hundred grains. Allah multiplies it even more for whomsoever He pleases. Allah is Lord of vast bounty, All-Knowing. Those who spend their wealth in the cause of Allah, then follow not up that which they have spent with reproaches or injury, have their reward with their Lord. They shall have no fear, nor shall they grieve. A kind word and forgiveness are better than charity followed by injury. Allah is Self-Sufficient, Forbearing. (262—264)

فَبُهِتَ الَّذِى كَفَرَ وَاللّٰهُ لَا يَهۡدِى الۡقَوۡمَ الظّٰلِمِيۡنَ ۞

اَوۡ كَالَّذِىۡ مَرَّ عَلٰى قَرۡيَةٍ وَّهِىَ خَاوِيَةٌ عَلٰى عُرُوۡشِهَا ۚ قَالَ اَنّٰى يُحۡىٖ هٰذِهِ اللّٰهُ بَعۡدَ مَوۡتِهَا ۚ فَاَمَاتَهُ اللّٰهُ مِائَةَ عَامٍ ثُمَّ بَعَثَهٗ ؕ قَالَ كَمۡ لَبِثۡتَ ؕ قَالَ لَبِثۡتُ يَوۡمًا اَوۡ بَعۡضَ يَوۡمٍ ؕ قَالَ بَلۡ لَبِثۡتَ مِائَةَ عَامٍ فَانۡظُرۡ اِلٰى طَعَامِكَ وَشَرَابِكَ لَمۡ يَتَسَنَّهۡ ۚ وَانۡظُرۡ اِلٰى حِمَارِكَ وَلِنَجۡعَلَكَ اٰيَةً لِّلنَّاسِ وَانۡظُرۡ اِلَى الۡعِظَامِ كَيۡفَ نُنۡشِزُهَا ثُمَّ نَكۡسُوۡهَا لَحۡمًا ؕ فَلَمَّا تَبَيَّنَ لَهٗ ۙ قَالَ اَعۡلَمُ اَنَّ اللّٰهَ عَلٰى كُلِّ شَىۡءٍ قَدِيۡرٌ ۞

وَاِذۡ قَالَ اِبۡرٰهٖمُ رَبِّ اَرِنِىۡ كَيۡفَ تُحۡىِ الۡمَوۡتٰى ؕ قَالَ اَوَلَمۡ تُؤۡمِنۡ ؕ قَالَ بَلٰى وَلٰكِنۡ لِّيَطۡمَئِنَّ قَلۡبِىۡ ؕ قَالَ فَخُذۡ اَرۡبَعَةً مِّنَ الطَّيۡرِ فَصُرۡهُنَّ اِلَيۡكَ ثُمَّ اجۡعَلۡ عَلٰى كُلِّ جَبَلٍ مِّنۡهُنَّ جُزۡءًا ثُمَّ ادۡعُهُنَّ يَاۡتِيۡنَكَ سَعۡيًا ؕ وَاعۡلَمۡ اَنَّ اللّٰهَ عَزِيۡزٌ حَكِيۡمٌ ۞

مَثَلُ الَّذِيۡنَ يُنۡفِقُوۡنَ اَمۡوَالَهُمۡ فِىۡ سَبِيۡلِ اللّٰهِ كَمَثَلِ حَبَّةٍ اَنۡۢبَتَتۡ سَبۡعَ سَنَابِلَ فِىۡ كُلِّ سُنۡۢبُلَةٍ مِّائَةُ حَبَّةٍ ؕ وَاللّٰهُ يُضٰعِفُ لِمَنۡ يَّشَاءُ ؕ وَاللّٰهُ وَاسِعٌ عَلِيۡمٌ ۞

اَلَّذِيۡنَ يُنۡفِقُوۡنَ اَمۡوَالَهُمۡ فِىۡ سَبِيۡلِ اللّٰهِ ثُمَّ لَا يُتۡبِعُوۡنَ مَاۤ اَنۡفَقُوۡا مَنًّا وَّلَاۤ اَذًى ۙ لَّهُمۡ اَجۡرُهُمۡ عِنۡدَ رَبِّهِمۡ ۚ وَلَا خَوۡفٌ عَلَيۡهِمۡ وَلَا هُمۡ يَحۡزَنُوۡنَ ۞

قَوۡلٌ مَّعۡرُوۡفٌ وَّمَغۡفِرَةٌ خَيۡرٌ مِّنۡ صَدَقَةٍ يَّتۡبَعُهَاۤ اَذًى ؕ وَاللّٰهُ غَنِىٌّ حَلِيۡمٌ ۞

O ye who believe, render not vain your alms by reproaches or injury, like one who spends his wealth to be seen of people and believes not in Allah and the Last Day. His case is like that of a smooth rock covered with earth, on which heavy rain falls and washes it clean, leaving it bare and hard. Such people shall not secure for themselves aught of that which they earn. Allah guides not the disbelieving people. The case of those who spend their wealth to seek the pleasure of Allah and to gain inner strength is like that of a garden on elevated ground, on which heavy rain falls, so that it brings forth its fruit twofold. Even if heavy rain does not fall on it, a light shower suffices. Allah sees well that which you do. Would any of you desire that having a garden of date-palms and vines with streams flowing beneath it, which brings forth for him all kinds of fruits, he should be stricken with old age while his children are small, and a fiery whirlwind should sweep through his garden consuming it all? Thus does Allah make His Signs clear to you that you may reflect. (265—267)

O ye who believe, spend of the good things that you have earned, and of that which We produce for you from the earth; and do not select out of it for charity that which is useless, when you would not yourselves accept the like of it, save with reluctance. Know that Allah is Self-Sufficient, Worthy of Highest Praise. Satan threatens you with poverty and enjoins upon you that which is indecent, whereas Allah promises you forgiveness from Himself and bounty. Allah is the Lord of vast bounty, All-Knowing. He grants wisdom to whom He pleases, and whoever is granted wisdom has indeed been granted abundant good, and none takes heed except those endowed with understanding. (268—270)

يَاۤيُّهَا الَّذِيْنَ اٰمَنُوْا لَا تُبْطِلُوْا صَدَقٰتِكُمْ بِالْمَنِّ وَالْاَذٰىۙ كَالَّذِيْ يُنْفِقُ مَالَهٗ رِئَآءَ النَّاسِ وَلَا يُؤْمِنُ بِاللّٰهِ وَالْيَوْمِ الْاٰخِرِ فَمَثَلُهٗ كَمَثَلِ صَفْوَانٍ عَلَيْهِ تُرَابٌ فَاَصَابَهٗ وَابِلٌ فَتَرَكَهٗ صَلْدًاؕ لَا يَقْدِرُوْنَ عَلٰى شَيْءٍ مِّمَّا كَسَبُوْاؕ وَاللّٰهُ لَا يَهْدِى الْقَوْمَ الْكٰفِرِيْنَ ۝

وَمَثَلُ الَّذِيْنَ يُنْفِقُوْنَ اَمْوَالَهُمُ ابْتِغَآءَ مَرْضَاتِ اللّٰهِ وَتَثْبِيْتًا مِّنْ اَنْفُسِهِمْ كَمَثَلِ جَنَّةٍ بِرَبْوَةٍ اَصَابَهَا وَابِلٌ فَاٰتَتْ اُكُلَهَا ضِعْفَيْنِۚ فَاِنْ لَّمْ يُصِبْهَا وَابِلٌ فَطَلٌّؕ وَاللّٰهُ بِمَا تَعْمَلُوْنَ بَصِيْرٌ ۝

اَيَوَدُّ اَحَدُكُمْ اَنْ تَكُوْنَ لَهٗ جَنَّةٌ مِّنْ نَّخِيْلٍ وَّاَعْنَابٍ تَجْرِيْ مِنْ تَحْتِهَا الْاَنْهٰرُۙ لَهٗ فِيْهَا مِنْ كُلِّ الثَّمَرٰتِۙ وَاَصَابَهُ الْكِبَرُ وَلَهٗ ذُرِّيَّةٌ ضُعَفَآءُۖ فَاَصَابَهَاۤ اِعْصَارٌ فِيْهِ نَارٌ فَاحْتَرَقَتْؕ كَذٰلِكَ يُبَيِّنُ اللّٰهُ لَكُمُ الْاٰيٰتِ لَعَلَّكُمْ تَتَفَكَّرُوْنَ ۝

يَاۤيُّهَا الَّذِيْنَ اٰمَنُوۤا اَنْفِقُوْا مِنْ طَيِّبٰتِ مَا كَسَبْتُمْ وَمِمَّاۤ اَخْرَجْنَا لَكُمْ مِّنَ الْاَرْضِۖ وَلَا تَيَمَّمُوا الْخَبِيْثَ مِنْهُ تُنْفِقُوْنَ وَلَسْتُمْ بِاٰخِذِيْهِ اِلَّاۤ اَنْ تُغْمِضُوْا فِيْهِؕ وَاعْلَمُوۤا اَنَّ اللّٰهَ غَنِيٌّ حَمِيْدٌ ۝

اَلشَّيْطٰنُ يَعِدُكُمُ الْفَقْرَ وَيَاْمُرُكُمْ بِالْفَحْشَآءِۚ وَاللّٰهُ يَعِدُكُمْ مَّغْفِرَةً مِّنْهُ وَفَضْلًاؕ وَاللّٰهُ وَاسِعٌ عَلِيْمٌ ۝

يُؤْتِى الْحِكْمَةَ مَنْ يَّشَآءُۚ وَمَنْ يُّؤْتَ الْحِكْمَةَ فَقَدْ

Whatsoever you spend in the cause of Allah or vow as an offering, surely Allah knows it well, but the wrongdoers shall have no helpers. If you give alms openly that is indeed good, but if you give them secretly to the poor, it is even better for your own selves; thereby will He remove from you many of your ills. Allah is aware of what you do. (271—272)

Thou art not charged with guiding them to the right path; it is Allah Who guides whomsoever He pleases. Whatever of your pure wealth you spend in the cause of Allah, and undoubtedly you spend it to seek the favour of Allah, its benefit accrues to yourselves. Whatever of your pure wealth you spend, it shall be paid back to you in full and you shall not be wronged. These alms are for the deserving poor who are detained in the cause of Allah and are unable to move about in the land. Those who lack knowledge of their circumstances consider them to be free from want because of their abstaining from soliciting alms. They can be known from their appearance. They do not importune people. Whatever of your pure wealth you spend, Allah has full knowledge thereof. Those who spend their wealth in the cause of Allah by night and day, secretly and openly, have their reward with their Lord; on them shall come no fear, nor shall they grieve. (273—275)

Those who devour interest stand like one whom Satan has smitten with insanity. That is so because they keep saying: The business of buying and selling is also like lending money on interest; whereas Allah has made buying and selling lawful and has made the taking of interest unlawful. Remember, therefore, that he who desists because of the admonition that has come to him from his Lord, may retain what he has received in the past; and his affair is committed to Allah. But those who revert to the practice, they are the inmates of the Fire; therein shall they abide. (276)

Allah will wipe out interest and will foster charity. Allah loves not confirmed disbelievers and arch-sinners. Those who believe and act righteously and observe Prayer and pay the Zakat, shall have their reward with their Lord. No fear shall come on them, nor shall they grieve. O Ye who believe, be mindful of your duty to Allah and relinquish your claim to what remains of interest, if you are truly believers. But if you do it not, then beware of war from the side of Allah and His Messenger. If, however, you desist you will still have your capital sums; thus you will commit no wrong, nor suffer any wrong yourselves. Should a debtor be in straitened circumstances, then grant him respite, in respect of the repayment of the capital sum, till a time of ease. But if, in such a case, you remit the capital sum also as charity, it will be the better for you, if you only knew. Be ever mindful of the day when you shall be made to return to Allah; when every one shall be paid in full that which he has earned and they shall not be wronged. (277—282)

O ye who believe, when you take a loan, one from another, for a term, reduce the transaction to writing; and let a scribe record it in your presence faithfully. No scribe should refuse to set it down in writing, because Allah has taught him, so he should write. Let him who undertakes the liability dictate the terms of the contract, and in so doing let him be mindful of his duty to Allah, his Lord, and not keep back anything therefrom. If he who undertakes the liability should be of defective intelligence, or a minor, or unable to dictate, then let his guardian dictate faithfully. Procure two witnesses from among your men; and if two men be not available, then one man and two women, of such as you like as witnesses, so that if either of the two women should be in danger of forgetting, the other may refresh her memory.

45

The witnesses should not refuse to testify when they are called upon to do so. Whether the transaction be large or small do not be disinclined to write it down, together with the appointed time of payment. This is more equitable in the sight of Allah, makes testimony surer and is more likely to exclude doubts. In case of ready transactions when goods and money pass from hand to hand, it shall be no sin for you not to reduce them to writing. Have witnesses when you buy or sell. Let no harm befall a scribe or a witness, and if you do such a thing it shall certainly be disobedience on your part. Be ever mindful of your duty to Allah. Allah grants you knowledge and Allah knows all things well. Should you be on a journey and not find a scribe, the alternative is a pledge with possession. When one of you entrusts something to another, then let him who is entrusted render back his trust when he is called upon to do so, and let him be mindful of his duty to Allah, his Lord. Conceal not testimony; whoever conceals it is one whose heart is certainly sinful. Remember Allah knows well all that you do. (283—284)

To Allah belongs whatever is in the heavens and whatever is in the earth. Whether you disclose that which is in your minds or keep it hidden, Allah will call you to account for it; then will He forgive whomsoever He wills and punish whomsoever He wills. Allah has the power to do all that He wills. The Messenger has full faith in that which has been sent down to him from his Lord and so have the believers: all of them believe in Allah, and in His angels, and in His Books and in His Messengers, affirming: We make no distinction between any of His Messengers; we have heard Allah's command and we have submitted ourselves wholly to Him. They supplicate: We implore Thy forgiveness, Lord, and to Thee is our return.

فَاِنْ لَّمْ يَكُوْنَا رَجُلَيْنِ فَرَجُلٌ وَّامْرَاَتٰنِ مِمَّنْ تَرْضَوْنَ مِنَ الشُّهَدَآءِ اَنْ تَضِلَّ اِحْدٰىهُمَا فَتُذَكِّرَ اِحْدٰىهُمَا الْاُخْرٰى ۚ وَلَا يَاْبَ الشُّهَدَآءُ اِذَا مَا دُعُوْا ۚ وَلَا تَسْـَٔمُوْٓا اَنْ تَكْتُبُوْهُ صَغِيْرًا اَوْ كَبِيْرًا اِلٰٓى اَجَلِهٖ ۚ ذٰلِكُمْ اَقْسَطُ عِنْدَ اللّٰهِ وَاَقْوَمُ لِلشَّهَادَةِ وَاَدْنٰٓى اَلَّا تَرْتَابُوْٓا اِلَّا اَنْ تَكُوْنَ تِجَارَةً حَاضِرَةً تُدِيْرُوْنَهَا بَيْنَكُمْ فَلَيْسَ عَلَيْكُمْ جُنَاحٌ اَلَّا تَكْتُبُوْهَا ۚ وَاَشْهِدُوْٓا اِذَا تَبَايَعْتُمْ ۚ وَلَا يُضَآرَّ كَاتِبٌ وَّلَا شَهِيْدٌ ۚ وَاِنْ تَفْعَلُوْا فَاِنَّهٗ فُسُوْقٌ بِكُمْ ۚ وَاتَّقُوا اللّٰهَ ۚ وَيُعَلِّمُكُمُ اللّٰهُ ۚ وَاللّٰهُ بِكُلِّ شَيْءٍ عَلِيْمٌ ۞

وَاِنْ كُنْتُمْ عَلٰى سَفَرٍ وَّلَمْ تَجِدُوْا كَاتِبًا فَرِهٰنٌ مَّقْبُوْضَةٌ ۚ فَاِنْ اَمِنَ بَعْضُكُمْ بَعْضًا فَلْيُؤَدِّ الَّذِى اؤْتُمِنَ اَمَانَتَهٗ وَلْيَتَّقِ اللّٰهَ رَبَّهٗ ۚ وَلَا تَكْتُمُوا الشَّهَادَةَ ۚ وَمَنْ يَّكْتُمْهَا فَاِنَّهٗٓ اٰثِمٌ قَلْبُهٗ ۚ وَاللّٰهُ بِمَا تَعْمَلُوْنَ عَلِيْمٌ ۞

لِلّٰهِ مَا فِى السَّمٰوٰتِ وَمَا فِى الْاَرْضِ ۚ وَاِنْ تُبْدُوْا مَا فِىٓ اَنْفُسِكُمْ اَوْ تُخْفُوْهُ يُحَاسِبْكُمْ بِهِ اللّٰهُ ۚ فَيَغْفِرُ لِمَنْ يَّشَآءُ وَيُعَذِّبُ مَنْ يَّشَآءُ ۚ وَاللّٰهُ عَلٰى كُلِّ شَيْءٍ قَدِيْرٌ ۞

اٰمَنَ الرَّسُوْلُ بِمَآ اُنْزِلَ اِلَيْهِ مِنْ رَّبِّهٖ وَالْمُؤْمِنُوْنَ ۚ كُلٌّ اٰمَنَ بِاللّٰهِ وَمَلٰٓئِكَتِهٖ وَكُتُبِهٖ وَرُسُلِهٖ لَا نُفَرِّقُ بَيْنَ اَحَدٍ مِّنْ رُّسُلِهٖ ۚ وَقَالُوْا سَمِعْنَا وَاَطَعْنَا غُفْرَانَكَ

Allah requires not of any one that which is beyond his capacity; each shall have the benefit of the good he does and shall suffer the consequences of the ill he works. Supplicate, therefore: Lord, take us not to task if we forget or fall into error; Lord, place us not under responsibility in the manner of those whom Thou didst place under responsibility before us; Lord, burden us not with that which we have not the strength to bear; overlook our defaults and grant us forgiveness and have mercy on us; Thou art our Master, so grant us succour against those who reject Thee. (285—287)

رَبَّنَا وَاِلَيْكَ الْمَصِيْرُ ۝

لَا يُكَلِّفُ اللّٰهُ نَفْسًا اِلَّا وُسْعَهَا لَهَا مَا كَسَبَتْ وَعَلَيْهَا مَا اكْتَسَبَتْ رَبَّنَا لَا تُؤَاخِذْنَا اِنْ نَسِيْنَا اَوْ اَخْطَاْنَا رَبَّنَا وَلَا تَحْمِلْ عَلَيْنَا اِصْرًا كَمَا حَمَلْتَهٗ عَلَى الَّذِيْنَ مِنْ قَبْلِنَا رَبَّنَا وَلَا تُحَمِّلْنَا مَا لَا طَاقَةَ لَنَا بِهٖ وَاعْفُ عَنَّا وَاغْفِرْ لَنَا وَارْحَمْنَا اَنْتَ مَوْلٰىنَا فَانْصُرْنَا عَلَى الْقَوْمِ الْكٰفِرِيْنَ ۝

سُوْرَةُ اٰلِ عِمْرٰنَ مَدَنِيَّةٌ

ĀL-'IMRĀN

(Revealed after Hijra)

بِسْمِ اللهِ الرَّحْمٰنِ الرَّحِيْمِ ۝

In the Name of Allah, Most Gracious, Ever Merciful. (1)

الۗمّۗ ۝

I AM ALLAH, THE ALL-KNOWING. (2)

اللهُ لَا اِلٰهَ اِلَّا هُوَ الْحَيُّ الْقَيُّوْمُ ۝

Allah is He beside Whom there is none worthy of worship, the Living, the Self-Subsisting, All-Sustaining. (3)

نَزَّلَ عَلَيْكَ الْكِتٰبَ بِالْحَقِّ مُصَدِّقًا لِّمَا بَيْنَ يَدَيْهِ وَاَنْزَلَ التَّوْرٰىةَ وَالْاِنْجِيْلَ ۝

He has sent down to thee the Book, comprising the truth, which fulfils the revelation that preceded it; and He sent down the Torah and the Gospel before this as a guidance for the people; and He has sent down the Criterion. Those who have rejected the Signs of Allah shall certainly receive a severe punishment. Allah is Mighty, Possessor of the power to requite. Nothing is hidden from Allah, in the earth or in the heaven. He it is Who fashions you in the wombs as He wills; there is none worthy of worship beside Him, the Mighty, the Wise. (4—7)

مِنْ قَبْلُ هُدًى لِّلنَّاسِ وَاَنْزَلَ الْفُرْقَانَ ۚ اِنَّ الَّذِيْنَ كَفَرُوْا بِاٰيٰتِ اللهِ لَهُمْ عَذَابٌ شَدِيْدٌ وَاللهُ عَزِيْزٌ ذُو انْتِقَامٍ ۝ اِنَّ اللهَ لَا يَخْفٰى عَلَيْهِ شَيْءٌ فِى الْاَرْضِ وَلَا فِى السَّمَاءِ ۝

هُوَ الَّذِيْ يُصَوِّرُكُمْ فِى الْاَرْحَامِ كَيْفَ يَشَاءُ ۚ لَا اِلٰهَ اِلَّا هُوَ الْعَزِيْزُ الْحَكِيْمُ ۝

He it is Who has sent down to thee the Book; in it there are verses that are fundamental — they are the basis of the Book — and there are others which are allegoric. Wherefore, those in whose hearts is perversity pursue such thereof as are allegoric seeking to create confusion and to pervert their meaning, and none knows the meaning thereof except Allah and those who are firmly grounded in knowledge; these last affirm: We believe in it, all of it is from our Lord (and, indeed, none takes heed except those gifted with understanding); Lord, let not our hearts become perverse after Thou hast guided us; and bestow upon us mercy from Thyself, surely Thou art the Great Bestower.

هُوَ الَّذِيْٓ اَنْزَلَ عَلَيْكَ الْكِتٰبَ مِنْهُ اٰيٰتٌ مُّحْكَمٰتٌ هُنَّ اُمُّ الْكِتٰبِ وَاُخَرُ مُتَشٰبِهٰتٌ ۚ فَاَمَّا الَّذِيْنَ فِيْ قُلُوْبِهِمْ زَيْغٌ فَيَتَّبِعُوْنَ مَا تَشَابَهَ مِنْهُ ابْتِغَاءَ الْفِتْنَةِ وَابْتِغَاءَ تَأْوِيْلِهٖ ۚ وَمَا يَعْلَمُ تَأْوِيْلَهٗٓ اِلَّا اللهُ ۘ وَالرّٰسِخُوْنَ فِى الْعِلْمِ يَقُوْلُوْنَ اٰمَنَّا بِهٖ ۙ كُلٌّ مِّنْ عِنْدِ رَبِّنَا ۚ وَمَا يَذَّكَّرُ اِلَّآ اُولُوا الْاَلْبَابِ ۝

رَبَّنَا لَا تُزِغْ قُلُوْبَنَا بَعْدَ اِذْ هَدَيْتَنَا وَهَبْ لَنَا مِنْ

Our Lord, Thou wilt certainly assemble mankind together on the Day concerning which there is no doubt. Surely, Allah does not contravene His promise. (8—10)

لَدُنْكَ رَحْمَةً ۚ إِنَّكَ أَنْتَ الْوَهَّابُ ۞

رَبَّنَآ إِنَّكَ جَامِعُ النَّاسِ لِيَوْمٍ لَّا رَيْبَ فِيْهِ ۚ إِنَّ اللَّهَ لَا يُخْلِفُ الْمِيْعَادَ ۞

The possessions and the children of those who disbelieve shall not avail them at all against Allah; it is they that are the fuel of the Fire. Their case is like that of the people of Pharaoh and those before them; they rejected Our Signs; so Allah seized them because of their sins. Allah's chastisement is severe. Warn those who disbelieve: You shall surely be vanquished and gathered unto hell; and an evil place of rest it is. (11—13)

إِنَّ الَّذِيْنَ كَفَرُوْا لَنْ تُغْنِيَ عَنْهُمْ أَمْوَالُهُمْ وَلَا أَوْلَادُهُمْ مِّنَ اللَّهِ شَيْئًا ۚ وَأُولٰٓئِكَ هُمْ وَقُوْدُ النَّارِ ۞

كَدَأْبِ آلِ فِرْعَوْنَ ۙ وَالَّذِيْنَ مِنْ قَبْلِهِمْ ۚ كَذَّبُوْا بِاٰيٰتِنَا ۚ فَأَخَذَهُمُ اللَّهُ بِذُنُوْبِهِمْ ۗ وَاللَّهُ شَدِيْدُ الْعِقَابِ ۞

قُلْ لِّلَّذِيْنَ كَفَرُوْا سَتُغْلَبُوْنَ وَتُحْشَرُوْنَ إِلٰى جَهَنَّمَ ۚ وَبِئْسَ الْمِهَادُ ۞

Certainly there was for you a Sign in the two parties that encountered each other, one party fighting in the cause of Allah and the other disbelieving, whom they saw with their eyes to be twice as many as themselves. Allah strengthens with His aid whomsoever He pleases. In that surely is a lesson for those who have eyes. (14)

قَدْ كَانَ لَكُمْ اٰيَةٌ فِيْ فِئَتَيْنِ الْتَقَتَا ۚ فِئَةٌ تُقَاتِلُ فِيْ سَبِيْلِ اللَّهِ وَأُخْرٰى كَافِرَةٌ يَّرَوْنَهُمْ مِّثْلَيْهِمْ رَأْيَ الْعَيْنِ ۚ وَاللَّهُ يُؤَيِّدُ بِنَصْرِهٖ مَنْ يَّشَآءُ ۗ إِنَّ فِيْ ذٰلِكَ لَعِبْرَةً لِّأُولِى الْأَبْصَارِ ۞

The love of desired objects, like women and children and stored-up reserves of gold and silver, and pastured horses and cattle and crops, appears attractive to people. All this is the provision of the hither life; and it is Allah with Whom is an excellent abode. Ask them: Shall I apprise you of something which is better than all this? For those who are constantly mindful of their duty to Allah, there are Gardens with their Lord beneath which rivers flow, wherein they shall abide, and pure spouses. They shall also enjoy the pleasure of Allah.

زُيِّنَ لِلنَّاسِ حُبُّ الشَّهَوَاتِ مِنَ النِّسَآءِ وَالْبَنِيْنَ وَالْقَنَاطِيْرِ الْمُقَنْطَرَةِ مِنَ الذَّهَبِ وَالْفِضَّةِ وَالْخَيْلِ الْمُسَوَّمَةِ وَالْأَنْعَامِ وَالْحَرْثِ ۗ ذٰلِكَ مَتَاعُ الْحَيٰوةِ الدُّنْيَا ۚ وَاللَّهُ عِنْدَهٗ حُسْنُ الْمَاٰبِ ۞

قُلْ أَؤُنَبِّئُكُمْ بِخَيْرٍ مِّنْ ذٰلِكُمْ ۚ لِلَّذِيْنَ اتَّقَوْا عِنْدَ رَبِّهِمْ جَنَّاتٌ تَجْرِيْ مِنْ تَحْتِهَا الْأَنْهَارُ خَالِدِيْنَ فِيْهَا وَأَزْوَاجٌ مُّطَهَّرَةٌ ۚ وَرِضْوَانٌ مِّنَ اللَّهِ ۗ وَاللَّهُ بَصِيْرٌ بِالْعِبَادِ ۞

Allah is Mindful of His servants who supplicate: Lord, surely we have believed; forgive
us, therefore, our sins and shield us from the
torment of the Fire. They are the steadfast,
the faithful, the humble, those who spend in
the cause of Allah and those who seek forgiveness in the small hours of the morning.
(15—18)

Allah bears witness that there is none
worthy of worship beside Him, and so do
the angels and those who possess knowledge; Maintainer of justice; there is none
worthy of worship beside Him, the
Mighty, the Wise. (19)

Surely the true religion in the estimation of Allah is Islam, that is, complete
submission to Him, and those who were
given the Book disagreed only, out of
mutual envy, after knowledge had come
to them. Whoso rejects the Signs of Allah
should remember that Allah is Swift at
reckoning. (20)

Now if they should dispute with thee,
say to them: I have submitted myself
wholly to Allah, and also those who follow
me. Say to those who have been given the
Book and to those to whom no revelation
has been vouchsafed: Do you submit
yourselves to Allah also? If they submit
they will surely be guided; but if they
turn away, thy duty is only to convey
the message. Allah is Watchful of His
servants. (21)

To those who reject the Signs of Allah
and seek to kill the Prophets and those
from among the people who enjoin equity,
without just cause, announce thou a painful chastisement. These are they whose
works shall come to naught in this world
and the next, and they shall have no
helpers. (22—23)

Knowest thou not that of those who
have been given their portion of the Book,
when they are called to the Book of Allah
that it may judge between them, a party
turn away in aversion? (24)

That is because they claim: The Fire shall not touch us except for a limited number of days; and that which they concoct has become a snare for them in the matter of their religion. How will it be with them when We shall gather them together on the Day concerning which there is no doubt, when every one shall be paid in full that which he has earned, and they shall not be wronged? (25—26)

Supplicate: O Allah, Lord of sovereignty, Thou bestowest sovereignty upon whomsoever Thou pleasest, and Thou takest away sovereignty from whomsoever Thou pleasest, Thou exaltest whomsoever Thou pleasest, and Thou abasest whomsoever Thou pleasest; in Thy hand is all good. Thou surely hast power to do all that Thou dost will. Thou makest the night pass into day and makest the day pass into night; Thou bringest forth the living from the dead and bringest forth the dead from the living. Thou bestowest upon whomsoever Thou pleasest without measure. (27—28)

Let not the believers take the disbelievers for intimate friends in preference to believers; whoever does that has no connection with Allah. Your only course is to keep away from them altogether. Allah warns you against His chastisement; and to Allah is your return. Warn them: Whether you keep hidden that which is in your minds, or disclose it, Allah knows it; and He knows whatever is in the heavens and whatever is in the earth. Allah has full power over all things. Beware of the day when everyone shall find confronting him all the good he has done and all the evil he has done. He will wish there were a great distance between him and the evil. Allah warns you against His chastisement; Allah is Most Compassionate towards His servants. (29—31)

ذٰلِكَ بِأَنَّهُمْ قَالُوْا لَنْ تَمَسَّنَا النَّارُ اِلَّا اَيَّامًا مَّعْدُوْدٰتٍ ۪ وَّغَرَّهُمْ فِيْ دِيْنِهِمْ مَّا كَانُوْا يَفْتَرُوْنَ ۝

فَكَيْفَ اِذَا جَمَعْنٰهُمْ لِيَوْمٍ لَّا رَيْبَ فِيْهِ ۪ وَوُفِّيَتْ كُلُّ نَفْسٍ مَّا كَسَبَتْ وَهُمْ لَا يُظْلَمُوْنَ ۝

قُلِ اللّٰهُمَّ مٰلِكَ الْمُلْكِ تُؤْتِي الْمُلْكَ مَنْ تَشَآءُ وَتَنْزِعُ الْمُلْكَ مِمَّنْ تَشَآءُ ۪ وَتُعِزُّ مَنْ تَشَآءُ وَتُذِلُّ مَنْ تَشَآءُ ۪ بِيَدِكَ الْخَيْرُ ۪ اِنَّكَ عَلٰى كُلِّ شَيْءٍ قَدِيْرٌ ۝

تُوْلِجُ الَّيْلَ فِي النَّهَارِ وَتُوْلِجُ النَّهَارَ فِي الَّيْلِ ۪ وَتُخْرِجُ الْحَيَّ مِنَ الْمَيِّتِ وَتُخْرِجُ الْمَيِّتَ مِنَ الْحَيِّ ۪ وَتَرْزُقُ مَنْ تَشَآءُ بِغَيْرِ حِسَابٍ ۝

لَا يَتَّخِذِ الْمُؤْمِنُوْنَ الْكٰفِرِيْنَ اَوْلِيَآءَ مِنْ دُوْنِ الْمُؤْمِنِيْنَ ۪ وَمَنْ يَّفْعَلْ ذٰلِكَ فَلَيْسَ مِنَ اللّٰهِ فِيْ شَيْءٍ اِلَّا اَنْ تَتَّقُوْا مِنْهُمْ تُقٰةً ۪ وَيُحَذِّرُكُمُ اللّٰهُ نَفْسَهُ ۪ وَاِلَى اللّٰهِ الْمَصِيْرُ ۝

قُلْ اِنْ تُخْفُوْا مَا فِيْ صُدُوْرِكُمْ اَوْ تُبْدُوْهُ يَعْلَمْهُ اللّٰهُ ۪ وَيَعْلَمُ مَا فِي السَّمٰوٰتِ وَمَا فِي الْاَرْضِ ۪ وَاللّٰهُ عَلٰى كُلِّ شَيْءٍ قَدِيْرٌ ۝

يَوْمَ تَجِدُ كُلُّ نَفْسٍ مَّا عَمِلَتْ مِنْ خَيْرٍ مُّحْضَرًا ۛۚ وَّمَا عَمِلَتْ مِنْ سُوْءٍ ۛۚ تَوَدُّ لَوْ اَنَّ بَيْنَهَا وَبَيْنَهٗ اَمَدًۢا بَعِيْدًا ۪ وَيُحَذِّرُكُمُ اللّٰهُ نَفْسَهُ ۪ وَاللّٰهُ رَءُوْفٌۢ بِالْعِبَادِ ۝

قُلْ اِنْ كُنْتُمْ تُحِبُّوْنَ اللّٰهَ فَاتَّبِعُوْنِيْ يُحْبِبْكُمُ

51

Announce: If you love Allah, then follow
me, Allah will then love you and forgive
you your faults. Allah is Most Forgiving,
Ever Merciful. Call on them: Obey Allah
and the Messenger. Then if they turn away,
let them remember that Allah loves not
the disbelievers. (32—33)

Allah did exalt Adam and Noah and the
family of Abraham and the family of
Imran above all the people of their times
— a group spiritually akin one to another.
Allah is All-Hearing, All-Knowing. (34—
35)

Call to mind when the woman of Imran
offered: Lord, I have dedicated to Thy
service that which is in my womb free
from all other obligations; so do accept it
of me. Thou alone art the All-Hearing,
the All-Knowing. (36)

When she was delivered of it she supplicated: Lord, I am delivered of a female
child, and I have named her Mary, and
I commit her and her offspring to Thy protection against the mischief of Satan, the
rejected. Allah knew best what she had
brought forth and the male child of her
fancy was not like the female child she
brought forth. So her Lord accepted her
with a gracious acceptance and caused her
to grow up an excellent growing up.
Zachariah became her guardian. Whenever Zachariah entered her chamber, he
found some provision with her. One day
he said to her: Mary, whence hast thou
this? She answered: It is from Allah;
surely, Allah bestows upon whomsoever
He pleases without measure. (37—38)

Thereupon Zachariah prayed to his Lord:
Lord, grant me from Thyself pure offspring, surely Thou art the Hearer of
prayer. The angels called to him as he
stood praying in the chamber: Allah gives
thee glad tidings of Yahya, who shall fulfil a word of Allah; he will be noble, chaste
and a Prophet from among the righteous.

Zachariah submitted: Lord, how shall I have a youth as my son when I am already of advanced age and moreover my wife is barren. He responded: Such is the power of Allah, He does what He pleases. Zachariah beseeched: My Lord, lay upon me a special commandment. He replied: The commandment for thee is that thou shalt not communicate with people for three days except by signs, and shalt remember thy Lord much and shalt glorify Him night and morn. (39—42)

Call to mind when the angels said to Mary: Allah has exalted thee and purified thee and chosen thee from among all the women of thy time. Mary, be obedient to thy Lord and prostrate thyself before Him and worship Him alone with single-minded devotion along with those who worship. (43—44)

This is of the tidings of the unseen that We reveal to thee: Thou wast not with them when they cast their arrows to determine which of them should take care of Mary, nor wast thou with them when they disputed with one another. (45)

Call to mind when the angels said to Mary: Allah, through His word, gives thee glad tidings of a son named the Messiah, Jesus son of Mary, honoured in this world and the next, and of those who are granted nearness to Allah. He shall admonish people in his early years and also in his ripe years, and he shall be of the righteous. Mary said: Lord, how shall I have a son, when no man has touched me? He answered: Such is the power of Allah, He creates what He pleases. When He decrees a thing, He says to it: Be; and it is. He will teach him the Book and the Wisdom and the Torah and the Gospel and will make him a Messenger to the children of Israel, bearing the message: I have come to you with a Sign from your Lord, that for your benefit, in the manner of a bird, I shall fashion, from among persons who are capable of receiving an impress, shapes and shall breathe into them a new spirit, then they will begin to soar like birds by the command of Allah; and I shall declare clean the blind and the leprous and shall bestow life on the spiritually dead, by the command of Allah; and shall announce to you what you will eat and what you will store up in your houses. In all this there is a Sign for you, if you will believe. I fulfil that which has been sent down before me, namely the Torah, and shall make lawful for you some of that which was forbidden you. I come to you with a Sign from your Lord; so be mindful of your duty to Allah and obey me. Verily, Allah is my Lord and your Lord; so worship Him. That is the straight path. (46—52)

When Jesus perceived their disbelief, he asked: Who will be my helpers in the cause of Allah? The disciples answered: We are helpers in the cause of Allah. We have believed in Allah, and bear thou witness we are obedient to Allah. They affirmed: Our Lord we have believed in that whch Thou hast sent down and we have become the followers of this Messenger, so write us down among the witnesses. (53—54)

The enemies of Jesus devised their plans and Allah devised His plan; Allah is the best of planners. Allah reassured Jesus: I shall cause thee to die a natural death, and shall exalt thee to Myself, and shall clear thee from the calumnies of those who disbelieve, and shall place those who follow thee above those who disbelieve, until the Day of Judgment; then to Me shall be your return and I will judge between you concerning that wherein you differ. As for those who disbelieve, I will punish

مِنْ رَّبِّكُمْ ۙ اَنِّیْۤ اَخْلُقُ لَكُمْ مِّنَ الطِّیْنِ كَهَیْئَةِ الطَّیْرِ فَاَنْفُخُ فِیْهِ فَیَكُوْنُ طَیْرًۢا بِاِذْنِ اللّٰهِ ۚ وَ اُبْرِئُ الْاَكْمَهَ وَ الْاَبْرَصَ وَ اُحْیِ الْمَوْتٰی بِاِذْنِ اللّٰهِ ۚ وَ اُنَبِّئُكُمْ بِمَا تَاْكُلُوْنَ وَ مَا تَدَّخِرُوْنَ ۙ فِیْ بُیُوْتِكُمْ ؕ اِنَّ فِیْ ذٰلِكَ لَاٰیَةً لَّكُمْ اِنْ كُنْتُمْ مُّؤْمِنِیْنَ ۟

وَ مُصَدِّقًا لِّمَا بَیْنَ یَدَیَّ مِنَ التَّوْرٰىةِ وَ لِاُحِلَّ لَكُمْ بَعْضَ الَّذِیْ حُرِّمَ عَلَیْكُمْ وَ جِئْتُكُمْ بِاٰیَةٍ مِّنْ رَّبِّكُمْ ۫ فَاتَّقُوا اللّٰهَ وَ اَطِیْعُوْنِ ۟

اِنَّ اللّٰهَ رَبِّیْ وَ رَبُّكُمْ فَاعْبُدُوْهُ ؕ هٰذَا صِرَاطٌ مُّسْتَقِیْمٌ ۟

فَلَمَّاۤ اَحَسَّ عِیْسٰی مِنْهُمُ الْكُفْرَ قَالَ مَنْ اَنْصَارِیْۤ اِلَی اللّٰهِ ؕ قَالَ الْحَوَارِیُّوْنَ نَحْنُ اَنْصَارُ اللّٰهِ ۚ اٰمَنَّا بِاللّٰهِ ۚ وَ اشْهَدْ بِاَنَّا مُسْلِمُوْنَ ۟

رَبَّنَاۤ اٰمَنَّا بِمَاۤ اَنْزَلْتَ وَ اتَّبَعْنَا الرَّسُوْلَ فَاكْتُبْنَا مَعَ الشّٰهِدِیْنَ ۟

وَ مَكَرُوْا وَ مَكَرَ اللّٰهُ ؕ وَ اللّٰهُ خَیْرُ الْمٰكِرِیْنَ ۟

اِذْ قَالَ اللّٰهُ یٰعِیْسٰۤی اِنِّیْ مُتَوَفِّیْكَ وَ رَافِعُكَ اِلَیَّ وَ مُطَهِّرُكَ مِنَ الَّذِیْنَ كَفَرُوْا وَ جَاعِلُ الَّذِیْنَ اتَّبَعُوْكَ فَوْقَ الَّذِیْنَ كَفَرُوْۤا اِلٰی یَوْمِ الْقِیٰمَةِ ۚ ثُمَّ اِلَیَّ مَرْجِعُكُمْ فَاَحْكُمُ بَیْنَكُمْ فِیْمَا كُنْتُمْ فِیْهِ تَخْتَلِفُوْنَ ۟

فَاَمَّا الَّذِیْنَ كَفَرُوْا فَاُعَذِّبُهُمْ عَذَابًا شَدِیْدًا فِی

them with a severe punishment in this world and in the next, and they shall have no helpers; and as for those who believe and work righteousness, Allah will pay them their full deserts. Allah loves not the wrongdoers. That is what We recite unto thee of the Signs and the Wise Instructions. (55—59)

The case of Jesus in the sight of Allah is like unto the case of Adam. He created him out of dust. He said concerning him: Be; and he began to be. This is the truth from thy Lord, so be thou not of those who doubt. Then whoso should dispute with thee concerning it, after that which has come to thee of divinely revealed knowledge, say to them: Come, let us call our sons and you call your sons, and let us call our women and you call your women, and let us call our people and you call your people, then let us pray fervently for the triumph of the truth and invoke the curse of Allah on those who lie. Most certainly this is the true account. There is none worthy of worship save Allah; and surely, it is Allah Who is the Mighty, the Wise. Then if they turn away, let them remember that Allah knows well those who create mischief. (60—64)

Say to the People of the Book: Let us agree upon one matter which is the same for you and for us, namely, that we worship none but Allah, and that we associate no partner with Him, and that some of us take not others for lords beside Allah. Then, if they turn away, say to them: Bear ye witness that we have submitted to Allah. (65)

People of the Book, why do you dispute concerning Abraham, whereas the Torah and Gospel were surely not sent down till after him? Will you not then understand? Hearken, you are those who have disputed about that whereof you had some knowledge; why do you now dispute about that whereof you have no knowledge at all? Allah knows and you know not.

الدُّنْيَا وَالْاٰخِرَةِ وَمَا لَهُمْ مِّنْ نّٰصِرِيْنَ ۞

وَأَمَّا الَّذِيْنَ اٰمَنُوْا وَعَمِلُوا الصّٰلِحٰتِ فَيُوَفِّيْهِمْ اُجُوْرَهُمْ وَاللّٰهُ لَا يُحِبُّ الظّٰلِمِيْنَ ۞

ذٰلِكَ نَتْلُوْهُ عَلَيْكَ مِنَ الْاٰيٰتِ وَالذِّكْرِ الْحَكِيْمِ ۞

اِنَّ مَثَلَ عِيْسٰى عِنْدَ اللّٰهِ كَمَثَلِ اٰدَمَ ۘ خَلَقَهُ مِنْ تُرَابٍ ثُمَّ قَالَ لَهُ كُنْ فَيَكُوْنُ ۞

اَلْحَقُّ مِنْ رَّبِّكَ فَلَا تَكُنْ مِّنَ الْمُمْتَرِيْنَ ۞

فَمَنْ حَاجَّكَ فِيْهِ مِنْ بَعْدِ مَا جَاۤءَكَ مِنَ الْعِلْمِ فَقُلْ تَعَالَوْا نَدْعُ اَبْنَاۤءَنَا وَاَبْنَاۤءَكُمْ وَنِسَاۤءَنَا وَنِسَاۤءَكُمْ وَاَنْفُسَنَا وَاَنْفُسَكُمْ ثُمَّ نَبْتَهِلْ فَنَجْعَلْ لَّعْنَتَ اللّٰهِ عَلَى الْكٰذِبِيْنَ ۞

اِنَّ هٰذَا لَهُوَ الْقَصَصُ الْحَقُّ ۚ وَمَا مِنْ اِلٰهٍ اِلَّا اللّٰهُ ۗ وَاِنَّ اللّٰهَ لَهُوَ الْعَزِيْزُ الْحَكِيْمُ ۞

فَاِنْ تَوَلَّوْا فَاِنَّ اللّٰهَ عَلِيْمٌۢ بِالْمُفْسِدِيْنَ ۞

قُلْ يٰٓاَهْلَ الْكِتٰبِ تَعَالَوْا اِلٰى كَلِمَةٍ سَوَاۤءٍۢ بَيْنَنَا وَبَيْنَكُمْ اَلَّا نَعْبُدَ اِلَّا اللّٰهَ وَلَا نُشْرِكَ بِهٖ شَيْئًا وَّلَا يَتَّخِذَ بَعْضُنَا بَعْضًا اَرْبَابًا مِّنْ دُوْنِ اللّٰهِ ۚ فَاِنْ تَوَلَّوْا فَقُوْلُوا اشْهَدُوْا بِاَنَّا مُسْلِمُوْنَ ۞

يٰٓاَهْلَ الْكِتٰبِ لِمَ تُحَاۤجُّوْنَ فِيْٓ اِبْرٰهِيْمَ وَمَآ اُنْزِلَتِ التَّوْرٰىةُ وَالْاِنْجِيْلُ اِلَّا مِنْۢ بَعْدِهٖ ۗ اَفَلَا تَعْقِلُوْنَ ۞

هٰٓاَنْتُمْ هٰٓؤُلَاۤءِ حَاجَجْتُمْ فِيْمَا لَكُمْ بِهٖ عِلْمٌ فَلِمَ تُحَاۤجُّوْنَ فِيْمَا لَيْسَ لَكُمْ بِهٖ عِلْمٌ ۚ وَاللّٰهُ يَعْلَمُ وَ

Abraham was neither a Jew nor a Christian; he was ever inclined to Allah and obedient to Him, and he was not of those who associate partners with Allah. Surely, the people closest to Abraham are those who followed him, and this Prophet and those who believe in him. Allah is the Friend of believers. (66—69)

A section of the People of the Book would fain lead you astray, but they only lead themselves astray, only they perceive it not. People of the Book, why do you reject the Signs of Allah, having been witnesses thereof? People of the Book, why do you confound truth with falsehood and hide the truth deliberately? (70—72)

A section of the People of the Book urge some from among themselves: Why not affirm, in the early part of the day, belief in that which has been revealed unto the believers and repudiate it in the latter part thereof, perchance they may return? But put no faith in any save him who follows your religion. Say to them: Surely, the true guidance is the guidance of Allah — that one may be given the like of that which has been given to you — or else that they should contend against you before your Lord. Say to them also: All bounty is in the hand of Allah, He bestows it upon whomsoever He pleases. Allah is Lord of vast bounty, All-Knowing. He singles out for His mercy whomsoever He pleases. Allah is the Lord of exceeding bounty. (73—75)

Among the People of the Book there are those who, if thou trust them with a treasure, will return it to thee faithfully; and among them are those who, if thou trust them with a single dinar, will not return it to thee, unless thou keep dunning them. That is because they say: We owe no obligation in respect of the unenlightened. They utter a lie against Allah and they know it. The truth is that whoso fulfils his pledge and is mindful of his duty to Allah is righteous, and Allah loves the righteous. (76—77)

Those who take a paltry price in exchange for their covenant with Allah and their oaths, shall have no portion in the life to come. Allah will not speak to them nor cast a look upon them on the Day of Judgment, nor will He purify them. For them shall be a grievous punishment. There surely is a section of them who twist their tongues as if they were reciting the Book, that you may take that which they are reciting to be part of the Book, while it is not part of the Book. They say: It is from Allah; while it is not from Allah. They utter a lie against Allah and they know it. (78—79)

It would not behove a righteous person that Allah should give him the Book and dominion and Prophethood, and yet he should say to people: Worship me instead of Allah. Such a one could only say: Be solely devoted to the Lord because you teach the Book and because you study it attentively. Nor would he bid you take the angels and the Prophets for lords. Would he teach you to disbelieve after you had submitted to Allah? (80—81)

Call to mind when Allah took from their people, through the Prophets, a firm covenant: Whatever I give you of the Book and Wisdom and then there comes to you a Messenger, fulfilling that which is with you, you shall most surely believe in him and help him. Do you then promise and

إِلَيْكَ إِلَّا مَا دُمْتَ عَلَيْهِ قَآئِمًا ذٰلِكَ بِأَنَّهُمْ قَالُوْا لَيْسَ عَلَيْنَا فِي الْأُمِّيِّنَ سَبِيْلٌ وَيَقُوْلُوْنَ عَلَى اللّٰهِ الْكَذِبَ وَهُمْ يَعْلَمُوْنَ ۞

بَلٰى مَنْ أَوْفٰى بِعَهْدِهِ وَاتَّقٰى فَإِنَّ اللّٰهَ يُحِبُّ الْمُتَّقِيْنَ ۞

إِنَّ الَّذِيْنَ يَشْتَرُوْنَ بِعَهْدِ اللّٰهِ وَأَيْمَانِهِمْ ثَمَنًا قَلِيْلًا أُولٰٓئِكَ لَا خَلَاقَ لَهُمْ فِي الْآخِرَةِ وَلَا يُكَلِّمُهُمُ اللّٰهُ وَلَا يَنْظُرُ إِلَيْهِمْ يَوْمَ الْقِيٰمَةِ وَلَا يُزَكِّيْهِمْ وَلَهُمْ عَذَابٌ أَلِيْمٌ ۞

وَإِنَّ مِنْهُمْ لَفَرِيْقًا يَّلْوُوْنَ أَلْسِنَتَهُمْ بِالْكِتٰبِ لِتَحْسَبُوْهُ مِنَ الْكِتٰبِ وَمَا هُوَ مِنَ الْكِتٰبِ وَيَقُوْلُوْنَ هُوَ مِنْ عِنْدِ اللّٰهِ وَمَا هُوَ مِنْ عِنْدِ اللّٰهِ وَيَقُوْلُوْنَ عَلَى اللّٰهِ الْكَذِبَ وَهُمْ يَعْلَمُوْنَ ۞

مَا كَانَ لِبَشَرٍ أَنْ يُّؤْتِيَهُ اللّٰهُ الْكِتٰبَ وَالْحُكْمَ وَالنُّبُوَّةَ ثُمَّ يَقُوْلَ لِلنَّاسِ كُوْنُوْا عِبَادًا لِّيْ مِنْ دُوْنِ اللّٰهِ وَلٰكِنْ كُوْنُوْا رَبَّانِيِّيْنَ بِمَا كُنْتُمْ تُعَلِّمُوْنَ الْكِتٰبَ وَبِمَا كُنْتُمْ تَدْرُسُوْنَ ۞

وَلَا يَأْمُرَكُمْ أَنْ تَتَّخِذُوا الْمَلٰٓئِكَةَ وَالنَّبِيِّيْنَ أَرْبَابًا أَيَأْمُرُكُمْ بِالْكُفْرِ بَعْدَ إِذْ أَنْتُمْ مُّسْلِمُوْنَ ۞

وَإِذْ أَخَذَ اللّٰهُ مِيْثَاقَ النَّبِيِّيْنَ لَمَآ آتَيْتُكُمْ مِّنْ كِتٰبٍ وَّحِكْمَةٍ ثُمَّ جَآءَكُمْ رَسُوْلٌ مُّصَدِّقٌ لِّمَا مَعَكُمْ لَتُؤْمِنُنَّ بِهِ وَلَتَنْصُرُنَّهُ قَالَ ءَأَقْرَرْتُمْ

accept the obligation I lay upon you in this
respect? They affirmed: We promise. Allah
said: Then bear witness and I am also a
witness along with you. Now whoso turns
away after this, those surely are transgressors. (82—83)

Then do they seek a religion other than
Allah's while to Him submits whosoever
is in the heavens and the earth, willingly
or unwillingly, and to Him shall they be
returned? Proclaim: We believe in Allah
and in that which has been revealed to us,
and that which was revealed to Abraham
and Ishmael and Isaac and Jacob and the
Tribes, and that which was given to Moses
and Jesus and other Prophets from their
Lord. We make no distinction between
any of them and to Him we submit. Whoso seeks a religion other than Islam, it
shall not be accepted from him, and in the
life to come he shall be among the losers.
(84—86)

How shall Allah guide a people who have
disbelieved after having believed and who
had borne witness that the Messenger is
true and to whom clear proofs had come?
Allah guides not the wrongdoers. Of such
the punishment is that on them shall be
the curse of Allah and of angels and of
men, all together; thereunder shall they
abide. Their punishment shall not be
lightened nor shall they be granted respite;
except in the case of those who repent
thereafter and amend. Surely, Allah is
Most Forgiving, Ever Merciful. Those who
disbelieve after having believed, and then
continue to advance in disbelief, their
repentance shall not be accepted. Those
are they who have gone utterly astray.
(87—91)

وَ اَخَذْتُمْ عَلٰى ذٰلِكُمْ اِصْرِىْ ۗ قَالُوْٓا اَقْرَرْنَا ۗ قَالَ
فَاشْهَدُوْا وَاَنَا مَعَكُمْ مِّنَ الشّٰهِدِيْنَ ۝

فَمَنْ تَوَلّٰى بَعْدَ ذٰلِكَ فَاُولٰٓئِكَ هُمُ الْفٰسِقُوْنَ ۝

اَفَغَيْرَ دِيْنِ اللّٰهِ يَبْغُوْنَ وَلَهٗٓ اَسْلَمَ مَنْ فِى السَّمٰوٰتِ
وَالْاَرْضِ طَوْعًا وَّكَرْهًا وَّاِلَيْهِ يُرْجَعُوْنَ ۝

قُلْ اٰمَنَّا بِاللّٰهِ وَمَآ اُنْزِلَ عَلَيْنَا وَمَآ اُنْزِلَ عَلٰٓى اِبْرٰهِيْمَ
وَاِسْمٰعِيْلَ وَاِسْحٰقَ وَيَعْقُوْبَ وَالْاَسْبَاطِ وَمَآ
اُوْتِيَ مُوْسٰى وَعِيْسٰى وَالنَّبِيُّوْنَ مِنْ رَّبِّهِمْ ۖ لَا نُفَرِّقُ
بَيْنَ اَحَدٍ مِّنْهُمْ ۖ وَنَحْنُ لَهٗ مُسْلِمُوْنَ ۝

وَمَنْ يَّبْتَغِ غَيْرَ الْاِسْلَامِ دِيْنًا فَلَنْ يُّقْبَلَ مِنْهُ ۚ
وَهُوَ فِى الْاٰخِرَةِ مِنَ الْخٰسِرِيْنَ ۝

كَيْفَ يَهْدِى اللّٰهُ قَوْمًا كَفَرُوْا بَعْدَ اِيْمَانِهِمْ وَ
شَهِدُوْٓا اَنَّ الرَّسُوْلَ حَقٌّ وَّجَآءَهُمُ الْبَيِّنٰتُ ۗ وَاللّٰهُ
لَا يَهْدِى الْقَوْمَ الظّٰلِمِيْنَ ۝

اُولٰٓئِكَ جَزَآؤُهُمْ اَنَّ عَلَيْهِمْ لَعْنَةَ اللّٰهِ وَالْمَلٰٓئِكَةِ
وَالنَّاسِ اَجْمَعِيْنَ ۝

خٰلِدِيْنَ فِيْهَا ۚ لَا يُخَفَّفُ عَنْهُمُ الْعَذَابُ وَ
لَا هُمْ يُنْظَرُوْنَ ۝

اِلَّا الَّذِيْنَ تَابُوْا مِنْ بَعْدِ ذٰلِكَ وَاَصْلَحُوْا ۖ فَاِنَّ
اللّٰهَ غَفُوْرٌ رَّحِيْمٌ ۝

اِنَّ الَّذِيْنَ كَفَرُوْا بَعْدَ اِيْمَانِهِمْ ثُمَّ ازْدَادُوْا كُفْرًا
لَّنْ تُقْبَلَ تَوْبَتُهُمْ ۚ وَاُولٰٓئِكَ هُمُ الضَّآلُّوْنَ ۝

From any one of those who have disbelieved, and die while they are disbelievers, there shall not be accepted even an earthful of gold, though he offer it in ransom. For those there shall be a grievous punishment, and they shall have no helpers. (92)

Never will you attain to the highest degree of virtue unless you spend in the cause of Allah out of that which you love; and whatever you spend, Allah surely knows it well. (93)

All food was lawful for the children of Israel, except that which Israel had forbidden himself before the Torah was sent down. Say to them: Bring then the Torah and read it, if you are truthful. Whoso, therefore, fabricates a lie against Allah after this, it is these who are the wrong-doers. Affirm: Allah has spoken the truth; follow, therefore, the religion of Abraham, who was ever inclined to Allah and was not of those who associate partners with Him. (94—96)

Surely, the first House established for the benefit of all mankind is the one at Mecca, abounding in blessings and a means of guidance for all peoples. In it are manifest Signs: in it is the station of Abraham; and whoso enters it is secure. Pilgrimage to the House is a duty laid upon people which they owe to Allah, those of them who can afford the journey thither. Those who repudiate it should remember that Allah is Independent of all creatures. (97—98)

Say to them: People of the Book, why do you reject the Signs of Allah, while Allah is Watchful of that which you do? Ask them: People of the Book, why do you hinder those who believe, from the path of Allah, seeking to make it appear crooked while you are witnesses thereof? Allah is not unmindful of that which you do. (99—100)

O ye who believe, if you obey any party of those who have been given the Book, they will turn you again into disbelievers after you have believed. How would you disbelieve, while you are the people to whom the Signs of Allah are rehearsed and among whom the Messenger of Allah is present? He who holds fast to Allah is indeed guided to the right path. (101—102)

O ye who believe, be mindful of your duty to Allah in all respects, every moment of your lives, so that death, whenever it overtakes you, should find you in a state of complete submission to Him. Take fast hold, all together, of the rope of Allah, and be not divided. Call to mind the favour of Allah which He bestowed upon you when you were at enmity with each other and He united your hearts in love so that by His grace you became as brethren. You were on the brink of a pit of fire and He rescued you from it. Thus does Allah explain to you His commandments that you may be guided. Let there be from among you a party whose business it should be to invite to goodness, to enjoin equity and to forbid evil. It is they who shall prosper. (103—105)

Be not like those who became divided and created dissensions after clear proofs had come to them. It is they for whom there will be a great punishment, on the Day when some faces will be bright and some faces will be gloomy. Those whose faces will be gloomy will be questioned: Did you, then, disbelieve after having believed? Then suffer the torment because you disbelieved. Those whose faces will be bright will rejoice in the mercy of Allah; therein will they abide. (106—108)

يَاۤاَيُّهَا الَّذِيۡنَ اٰمَنُوۡۤا اِنۡ تُطِيۡعُوۡا فَرِيۡقًا مِّنَ الَّذِيۡنَ اُوۡتُوا الۡكِتٰبَ يَرُدُّوۡكُمۡ بَعۡدَ اِيۡمَانِكُمۡ كٰفِرِيۡنَ ۞

وَكَيۡفَ تَكۡفُرُوۡنَ وَاَنۡتُمۡ تُتۡلٰى عَلَيۡكُمۡ اٰيٰتُ اللّٰهِ وَفِيۡكُمۡ رَسُوۡلُهٗ ؕ وَمَنۡ يَّعۡتَصِمۡ بِاللّٰهِ فَقَدۡ هُدِىَ اِلٰى صِرَاطٍ مُّسۡتَقِيۡمٍ ۞

يَاۤاَيُّهَا الَّذِيۡنَ اٰمَنُوا اتَّقُوا اللّٰهَ حَقَّ تُقٰتِهٖ وَلَا تَمُوۡتُنَّ اِلَّا وَاَنۡتُمۡ مُّسۡلِمُوۡنَ ۞

وَاعۡتَصِمُوۡا بِحَبۡلِ اللّٰهِ جَمِيۡعًا وَّلَا تَفَرَّقُوۡا ۪ وَاذۡكُرُوۡا نِعۡمَتَ اللّٰهِ عَلَيۡكُمۡ اِذۡ كُنۡتُمۡ اَعۡدَآءً فَاَلَّفَ بَيۡنَ قُلُوۡبِكُمۡ فَاَصۡبَحۡتُمۡ بِنِعۡمَتِهٖۤ اِخۡوَانًا ۚ وَكُنۡتُمۡ عَلٰى شَفَا حُفۡرَةٍ مِّنَ النَّارِ فَاَنۡقَذَكُمۡ مِّنۡهَا ؕ كَذٰلِكَ يُبَيِّنُ اللّٰهُ لَكُمۡ اٰيٰتِهٖ لَعَلَّكُمۡ تَهۡتَدُوۡنَ ۞

وَلۡتَكُنۡ مِّنۡكُمۡ اُمَّةٌ يَّدۡعُوۡنَ اِلَى الۡخَيۡرِ وَيَأۡمُرُوۡنَ بِالۡمَعۡرُوۡفِ وَيَنۡهَوۡنَ عَنِ الۡمُنۡكَرِ ؕ وَاُولٰٓئِكَ هُمُ الۡمُفۡلِحُوۡنَ ۞

وَلَا تَكُوۡنُوۡا كَالَّذِيۡنَ تَفَرَّقُوۡا وَاخۡتَلَفُوۡا مِنۡ بَعۡدِ مَا جَآءَهُمُ الۡبَيِّنٰتُ ؕ وَاُولٰٓئِكَ لَهُمۡ عَذَابٌ عَظِيۡمٌ ۞

يَّوۡمَ تَبۡيَضُّ وُجُوۡهٌ وَّتَسۡوَدُّ وُجُوۡهٌ ۚ فَاَمَّا الَّذِيۡنَ اسۡوَدَّتۡ وُجُوۡهُهُمۡ ؕ اَكَفَرۡتُمۡ بَعۡدَ اِيۡمَانِكُمۡ فَذُوۡقُوا الۡعَذَابَ بِمَا كُنۡتُمۡ تَكۡفُرُوۡنَ ۞

These are the Signs of Allah, comprising the truth, that We recite to thee. Allah wills not any wrong to His creatures. To Allah belongs whatever is in the heavens and whatever is in the earth; and to Allah shall all affairs be returned. (109—110)

وَاَمَّا الَّذِيْنَ ابْيَضَّتْ وُجُوْهُهُمْ فَفِيْ رَحْمَةِ اللهِ هُمْ فِيْهَا خٰلِدُوْنَ ۩

تِلْكَ اٰيٰتُ اللهِ نَتْلُوْهَا عَلَيْكَ بِالْحَقِّ وَمَا اللهُ يُرِيْدُ ظُلْمًا لِّلْعٰلَمِيْنَ ۩

وَ لِلّٰهِ مَا فِى السَّمٰوٰتِ وَمَا فِى الْاَرْضِ وَاِلَى اللهِ تُرْجَعُ الْاُمُوْرُ ۩

You are the best people for you have been raised for the benefit of mankind; you enjoin good, forbid evil and believe in Allah. If the People of the Book had believed, it would surely have been the better for them. Some of them have believed, but most of them are disobedient. They cannot harm you beyond causing you some slight injury; and if they fight you, they will turn their backs upon you. They will receive no help from any quarter. They will be humiliated wherever they are found, unless they are protected under a covenant with Allah, or a covenant with another people. They have incurred Allah's wrath and they have been afflicted with misery. That is because they continuously rejected the Signs of Allah and were after slaying the Prophets without just cause, and this resulted from their disobedience and their habit of transgression. (111—113)

كُنْتُمْ خَيْرَ اُمَّةٍ اُخْرِجَتْ لِلنَّاسِ تَأْمُرُوْنَ بِالْمَعْرُوْفِ وَتَنْهَوْنَ عَنِ الْمُنْكَرِ وَتُؤْمِنُوْنَ بِاللهِ وَلَوْ اٰمَنَ اَهْلُ الْكِتٰبِ لَكَانَ خَيْرًا لَّهُمْ مِنْهُمُ الْمُؤْمِنُوْنَ وَ اَكْثَرُهُمُ الْفٰسِقُوْنَ ۩

لَنْ يَّضُرُّوْكُمْ اِلَّا اَذًى وَاِنْ يُّقَاتِلُوْكُمْ يُوَلُّوْكُمُ الْاَدْبَارَ ثُمَّ لَا يُنْصَرُوْنَ ۩

ضُرِبَتْ عَلَيْهِمُ الذِّلَّةُ اَيْنَ مَا ثُقِفُوْا اِلَّا بِحَبْلٍ مِّنَ اللهِ وَحَبْلٍ مِّنَ النَّاسِ وَبَآءُوْ بِغَضَبٍ مِّنَ اللهِ وَضُرِبَتْ عَلَيْهِمُ الْمَسْكَنَةُ ذٰلِكَ بِاَنَّهُمْ كَانُوْا يَكْفُرُوْنَ بِاٰيٰتِ اللهِ وَيَقْتُلُوْنَ الْاَنْبِيَآءَ بِغَيْرِ حَقٍّ ذٰلِكَ بِمَا عَصَوْا وَّكَانُوْا يَعْتَدُوْنَ ۩

They are not all alike. Of the People of the Book there is a party who stand by their covenant; they recite the Word of Allah in the hours of night and prostrate themselves before Him. They believe in Allah and the Last Day, enjoin good, forbid evil, and hasten to outdo each other in benevolence. These are among the righteous. Whatever good they do will not be ignored. Allah knows well those who are mindful of their duty to Him. (114—116)

لَيْسُوْا سَوَآءً مِنْ اَهْلِ الْكِتٰبِ اُمَّةٌ قَآئِمَةٌ يَّتْلُوْنَ اٰيٰتِ اللهِ اٰنَآءَ الَّيْلِ وَهُمْ يَسْجُدُوْنَ ۩

يُؤْمِنُوْنَ بِاللهِ وَالْيَوْمِ الْاٰخِرِ وَيَأْمُرُوْنَ بِالْمَعْرُوْفِ وَيَنْهَوْنَ عَنِ الْمُنْكَرِ وَيُسَارِعُوْنَ فِى الْخَيْرٰتِ وَاُولٰٓئِكَ مِنَ الصّٰلِحِيْنَ ۩

وَمَا يَفْعَلُوْا مِنْ خَيْرٍ فَلَنْ يُّكْفَرُوْهُ وَاللهُ عَلِيْمٌ

Those who disbelieve will find that their possessions and their children shall not avail them aught against Allah. They are the inmates of the Fire; therein shall they abide. That which they spend in pursuit of the life of this world is like a biting frosty blast which smites the harvest of a people who have wronged themselves, and utterly destroys it. Allah does not wrong them; they wrong themselves. (117—118)

بِالْمُتَّقِيْنَ ۝

اِنَّ الَّذِيْنَ كَفَرُوْا لَنْ تُغْنِيَ عَنْهُمْ اَمْوَالُهُمْ وَ لَاۤ اَوْلَادُهُمْ مِّنَ اللّٰهِ شَيْئًا ۭ وَ اُولٰٓئِكَ اَصْحٰبُ النَّارِ ۚ هُمْ فِيْهَا خٰلِدُوْنَ ۝

مَثَلُ مَا يُنْفِقُوْنَ فِيْ هٰذِهِ الْحَيٰوةِ الدُّنْيَا كَمَثَلِ رِيْحٍ فِيْهَا صِرٌّ اَصَابَتْ حَرْثَ قَوْمٍ ظَلَمُوْا اَنْفُسَهُمْ فَاَهْلَكَتْهُ ۭ وَمَا ظَلَمَهُمُ اللّٰهُ وَلٰكِنْ اَنْفُسَهُمْ يَظْلِمُوْنَ ۝

يٰۤاَيُّهَا الَّذِيْنَ اٰمَنُوْا لَا تَتَّخِذُوْا بِطَانَةً مِّنْ دُوْنِكُمْ لَا يَاْلُوْنَكُمْ خَبَالًا ۭ وَدُّوْا مَا عَنِتُّمْ ۚ قَدْ بَدَتِ الْبَغْضَآءُ مِنْ اَفْوَاهِهِمْ ۖۚ وَمَا تُخْفِيْ صُدُوْرُهُمْ اَكْبَرُ ۭ قَدْ بَيَّنَّا لَكُمُ الْاٰيٰتِ اِنْ كُنْتُمْ تَعْقِلُوْنَ ۝

O ye who believe, do not take outsiders as your intimate friends, they will not fail to cause you injury. They love to see you in trouble. Their hatred has been expressed in words, and that which they design is even more virulent. We have made Our commandments clear to you, if you will understand. Hearken, you are the ones who love them, but they love you not. You believe in all the Book, but they only pretend to do so. When they are with you they say: We believe; but, when they part from you, they bite their fingertips with rage against you. Say to them: Perish in your rage. Surely Allah knows well your designs. Your success grieves them and your being involved in trouble gladdens their hearts. But if you are steadfast and mindful of your duty to Allah, their designs will not harm you at all. Surely, Allah will demolish all that they do. (119—121)

هٰۤاَنْتُمْ اُولَآءِ تُحِبُّوْنَهُمْ وَلَا يُحِبُّوْنَكُمْ وَتُؤْمِنُوْنَ بِالْكِتٰبِ كُلِّهٖ ۚ وَاِذَا لَقُوْكُمْ قَالُوْۤا اٰمَنَّا ۖۚ وَاِذَا خَلَوْا عَضُّوْا عَلَيْكُمُ الْاَنَامِلَ مِنَ الْغَيْظِ ۭ قُلْ مُوْتُوْا بِغَيْظِكُمْ ۭ اِنَّ اللّٰهَ عَلِيْمٌۢ بِذَاتِ الصُّدُوْرِ ۝

اِنْ تَمْسَسْكُمْ حَسَنَةٌ تَسُؤْهُمْ ۖ وَاِنْ تُصِبْكُمْ سَيِّئَةٌ يَّفْرَحُوْا بِهَا ۭ وَاِنْ تَصْبِرُوْا وَتَتَّقُوْا لَا يَضُرُّكُمْ كَيْدُهُمْ شَيْئًا ۭ اِنَّ اللّٰهَ بِمَا يَعْمَلُوْنَ مُحِيْطٌ ۝

وَاِذْ غَدَوْتَ مِنْ اَهْلِكَ تُبَوِّئُ الْمُؤْمِنِيْنَ مَقَاعِدَ

Call to mind, when thou didst go forth early from thy household, on the day of Uhud, to assign to the believers their positions for battle; and Allah is All-Hearing, All-Knowing. (122)

Call to mind also, when two of your groups meditated cowardice, while Allah was their friend; and upon Allah should the believers rely. Allah had already helped you in the battle of Badr, when you were inconsiderable. So be mindful of your duty to Allah that you may be grateful. (123—124)

Call to mind also, when thou didst say to the believers: Will it not suffice you that your Lord should help you with three thousand angels sent down from on high? Indeed, if you are steadfast and mindful of your duty to Allah and the enemy should come upon you without respite, your Lord will help you with five thousand angels attacking vehemently. Allah has designed this as glad tidings for you and that your hearts may be comforted thereby, and that He may cut off a portion of the disbelievers or abase them so that they might go back frustrated. All help comes from Allah alone, the Mighty, the Wise. Thou art not concerned in the matter; their end is in Allah's hands; He may turn to them in mercy, or punish them; for, surely, they are wrongdoers. To Allah belongs whatever is in the heavens and whatever is in the earth. He forgives whomsoever He pleases and punishes whomsoever He pleases. Allah is Most Forgiving, Ever Merciful. (125—130)

O ye who believe, devour not interest, for it goes on multiplying itself; and be mindful of your obligation to Allah that you may prosper; and safeguard yourselves against the Fire which is prepared for the disbelievers. Obey Allah and the Messenger that you may be shown mercy;

لِلْقِتَالِ ۗ وَاللهُ سَمِيعٌ عَلِيمٌ ۝

اِذْ هَمَّتْ طَّآئِفَتٰنِ مِنْكُمْ اَنْ تَفْشَلَا ۙ وَاللهُ وَلِيُّهُمَا ۗ وَعَلَى اللهِ فَلْيَتَوَكَّلِ الْمُؤْمِنُوْنَ ۝

وَلَقَدْ نَصَرَكُمُ اللهُ بِبَدْرٍ وَّاَنْتُمْ اَذِلَّةٌ ۚ فَاتَّقُوا اللهَ لَعَلَّكُمْ تَشْكُرُوْنَ ۝

اِذْ تَقُوْلُ لِلْمُؤْمِنِيْنَ اَلَنْ يَّكْفِيَكُمْ اَنْ يُّمِدَّكُمْ رَبُّكُمْ بِثَلٰثَةِ اٰلَافٍ مِّنَ الْمَلٰٓئِكَةِ مُنْزَلِيْنَ ۝

بَلٰى ۙ اِنْ تَصْبِرُوْا وَتَتَّقُوْا وَيَأْتُوْكُمْ مِّنْ فَوْرِهِمْ هٰذَا يُمْدِدْكُمْ رَبُّكُمْ بِخَمْسَةِ اٰلَافٍ مِّنَ الْمَلٰٓئِكَةِ مُسَوِّمِيْنَ ۝

وَمَا جَعَلَهُ اللهُ اِلَّا بُشْرٰى لَكُمْ وَلِتَطْمَئِنَّ قُلُوْبُكُمْ بِهٖ ۗ وَمَا النَّصْرُ اِلَّا مِنْ عِنْدِ اللهِ الْعَزِيْزِ الْحَكِيْمِ ۝

لِيَقْطَعَ طَرَفًا مِّنَ الَّذِيْنَ كَفَرُوْۤا اَوْ يَكْبِتَهُمْ فَيَنْقَلِبُوْا خَآئِبِيْنَ ۝

لَيْسَ لَكَ مِنَ الْاَمْرِ شَيْءٌ اَوْ يَتُوْبَ عَلَيْهِمْ اَوْ يُعَذِّبَهُمْ فَاِنَّهُمْ ظٰلِمُوْنَ ۝

وَلِلّٰهِ مَا فِى السَّمٰوٰتِ وَمَا فِى الْاَرْضِ ۗ يَغْفِرُ لِمَنْ يَّشَآءُ وَيُعَذِّبُ مَنْ يَّشَآءُ ۗ وَاللهُ غَفُوْرٌ رَّحِيْمٌ ۝

يٰۤاَيُّهَا الَّذِيْنَ اٰمَنُوْا لَا تَأْكُلُوا الرِّبٰۤوا اَضْعَافًا مُّضٰعَفَةً ۖ وَاتَّقُوا اللهَ لَعَلَّكُمْ تُفْلِحُوْنَ ۝

وَاتَّقُوا النَّارَ الَّتِيْۤ اُعِدَّتْ لِلْكٰفِرِيْنَ ۝

وَاَطِيْعُوا اللهَ وَالرَّسُوْلَ لَعَلَّكُمْ تُرْحَمُوْنَ ۝

and advance towards forgiveness from
your Lord and a Paradise whose price is
the heavens and the earth, prepared for
the righteous — those who spend in
prosperity and adversity, who control
their tempers when they are roused and
who overlook people's faults (and Allah
loves the benevolent) and those who,
when they commit an indecency or wrong
themselves, call Allah to mind and implore forgiveness for their sins (and who
can forgive sins except Allah?) and do not
persist knowingly in that of which they
have been guilty. It is these whose reward
is forgiveness from their Lord and Gardens beneath which rivers flow, wherein
they shall abide. Excellent is the reward
of those who work righteousness. Surely,
there have been many dispensations before you, then go about in the earth and
observe how evil was the end of those who
rejected them. This Quran is an exposition
for the people and a guidance and admonition for the God-fearing. (131—139)

Do not slacken, therefore, nor grieve;
you will have the upper hand, if you continue firm in the faith. If you should
receive an injury, they will have received
a like injury; and We cause these days,
with their ups and downs, to alternate
between the people that they may be
admonished, and that Allah may cause
to be known those who believe and may
make some of you martyrs, and that Allah
may purify those who believe and may
utterly destroy the disbelievers. Allah loves
not the unjust. Do you reckon that you
will enter Paradise while Allah has not
yet caused to be known those of you that
strive hard in the cause of Allah and has
not yet caused to be known the steadfast?

You used to wish for this type of death before you met it; now that you have encountered it in all its aspects, there is no cause for any of you to hold back. (140—144)

Muhammad is but a Messenger; of a surety, all Messengers before him have passed away. If then, he die or be slain, will you turn back on your heels? He who turns back on his heels shall not harm Allah a whit. Allah will certainly reward the grateful. No one can die except by Allah's leave, that is a decree with a fixed term. Whoever desires the reward of this world, We will give him thereof; and whoever desires the reward of the Hereafter We will give him thereof, and We will surely reward the grateful richly. (145—146)

Many Prophets have there been along with whom large numbers of their followers went into battle. They slackened not for aught that befell them in the way of Allah, nor did they weaken or humiliate themselves before the enemy. Allah loves the steadfast. They uttered no word except the prayer: Lord, forgive us our sins and our excesses in our affairs, and make firm our steps and help us against the disbelieving people. So Allah bestowed upon them the reward of this world, as also the best reward of the Hereafter. Allah loves those who do their duty to the utmost. (147—149)

O ye who believe, if you obey those who have disbelieved, they will cause you to revert to disbelief and you will become losers. Indeed, Allah is your Protector and He is the Best of helpers. We shall strike terror into the hearts of those who have disbelieved because they associate partners with Allah, for which He has sent down no authority. Their abode is the Fire, and evil is the habitation of the wrongdoers. (150—152)

وَلَقَدْ كُنْتُمْ تَمَنَّوْنَ الْمَوْتَ مِنْ قَبْلِ اَنْ تَلْقَوْهُ

فَقَدْ رَاَيْتُمُوْهُ وَاَنْتُمْ تَنْظُرُوْنَ ۝

وَمَا مُحَمَّدٌ اِلَّا رَسُوْلٌ قَدْ خَلَتْ مِنْ قَبْلِهِ الرُّسُلُ

اَفَاۡئِنْ مَّاتَ اَوْ قُتِلَ انْقَلَبْتُمْ عَلٰۤى اَعْقَابِكُمْ وَمَنْ

يَّنْقَلِبْ عَلٰى عَقِبَيْهِ فَلَنْ يَّضُرَّ اللّٰهَ شَيْئًا وَسَيَجْزِى

اللّٰهُ الشّٰكِرِيْنَ ۝

وَمَا كَانَ لِنَفْسٍ اَنْ تَمُوْتَ اِلَّا بِاِذْنِ اللّٰهِ كِتٰبًا

مُّؤَجَّلًا وَمَنْ يُّرِدْ ثَوَابَ الدُّنْيَا نُؤْتِهٖ مِنْهَا

وَمَنْ يُّرِدْ ثَوَابَ الْاٰخِرَةِ نُؤْتِهٖ مِنْهَا وَسَنَجْزِى

الشّٰكِرِيْنَ ۝

وَكَاَيِّنْ مِّنْ نَّبِيٍّ قَاتَلَ مَعَهٗ رِبِّيُّوْنَ كَثِيْرٌ فَمَا

وَهَنُوْا لِمَاۤ اَصَابَهُمْ فِيْ سَبِيْلِ اللّٰهِ وَمَا ضَعُفُوْا

وَمَا اسْتَكَانُوْا وَاللّٰهُ يُحِبُّ الصّٰبِرِيْنَ ۝

وَمَا كَانَ قَوْلَهُمْ اِلَّاۤ اَنْ قَالُوْا رَبَّنَا اغْفِرْ لَنَا ذُنُوْبَنَا

وَاِسْرَافَنَا فِيْۤ اَمْرِنَا وَثَبِّتْ اَقْدَامَنَا وَانْصُرْنَا عَلَى

الْقَوْمِ الْكٰفِرِيْنَ ۝

فَاٰتٰىهُمُ اللّٰهُ ثَوَابَ الدُّنْيَا وَحُسْنَ ثَوَابِ الْاٰخِرَةِ

وَاللّٰهُ يُحِبُّ الْمُحْسِنِيْنَ ۝

يٰۤاَيُّهَا الَّذِيْنَ اٰمَنُوْۤا اِنْ تُطِيْعُوا الَّذِيْنَ كَفَرُوْا

يَرُدُّوْكُمْ عَلٰۤى اَعْقَابِكُمْ فَتَنْقَلِبُوْا خٰسِرِيْنَ ۝

بَلِ اللّٰهُ مَوْلٰىكُمْ وَهُوَ خَيْرُ النّٰصِرِيْنَ ۝

سَنُلْقِيْ فِيْ قُلُوْبِ الَّذِيْنَ كَفَرُوا الرُّعْبَ بِمَاۤ اَشْرَكُوْا

Allah surely made good to you His promise on the day of Uhud when you were slaying and destroying them by His leave. Then, when, after He had shown you what you desired and victory was within your grasp, you became lax and disagreed among yourselves concerning the Prophet's direction and disobeyed it, He withdrew His support from you. Some of you desired the goods of this world and some of you desired the Hereafter. Then He safeguarded you against the attack of the enemy that He might try you, having pardoned you, and Allah is Gracious to the believers. You were running away and looked not back at anyone, while the Messenger called to you from the rear. Then He inflicted upon you the sorrow of defeat as an expiation to lighten the burden of your sorrow over having disobeyed the Prophet's order, that you might not grieve over that which you had missed nor over what had befallen you. Allah is well aware of what you do. (153—154)

Then, after the sorrow, He sent down peace of mind upon you in the shape of a slumber that overcame a party of you. But there was another party who were anxious only concerning their own selves, they entertained false notions concerning Allah like the notions of the days of Ignorance. They muttered: Have we any say in matters of administration? Tell them: All government belongs to Allah. They conceal that in their minds which they disclose not to thee. They say: Had we any say in matters of administration, we would not have been slaughtered here. Say to them: Had you remained in your homes, surely those on whom fighting had been enjoined would have issued forth to the stations where they were to die. Thus would Allah's decree have been carried out. Allah desired to test your secret thoughts and to purge that which was in your minds. Allah knows well that which passes through your minds. (155)

بِاللّٰهِ مَا لَمْ يُنَزِّلْ بِهٖ سُلْطٰنًا ۚ وَمَأْوٰىهُمُ النَّارُ ۚ وَبِئْسَ مَثْوَى الظّٰلِمِيْنَ ۝

وَلَقَدْ صَدَقَكُمُ اللّٰهُ وَعْدَهٗٓ اِذْ تَحُسُّوْنَهُمْ بِاِذْنِهٖ ۚ حَتّٰٓى اِذَا فَشِلْتُمْ وَتَنَازَعْتُمْ فِى الْاَمْرِ وَعَصَيْتُمْ مِّنْ بَعْدِ مَآ اَرٰىكُمْ مَّا تُحِبُّوْنَ ۚ مِنْكُمْ مَّنْ يُّرِيْدُ الدُّنْيَا وَمِنْكُمْ مَّنْ يُّرِيْدُ الْاٰخِرَةَ ۚ ثُمَّ صَرَفَكُمْ عَنْهُمْ لِيَبْتَلِيَكُمْ ۚ وَلَقَدْ عَفَا عَنْكُمْ ۚ وَاللّٰهُ ذُوْ فَضْلٍ عَلَى الْمُؤْمِنِيْنَ ۝

اِذْ تُصْعِدُوْنَ وَلَا تَلْوٗنَ عَلٰٓى اَحَدٍ وَّالرَّسُوْلُ يَدْعُوْكُمْ فِيْٓ اُخْرٰىكُمْ فَاَثَابَكُمْ غَمًّا بِغَمٍّ لِّكَيْلَا تَحْزَنُوْا عَلٰى مَا فَاتَكُمْ وَلَا مَآ اَصَابَكُمْ ۚ وَاللّٰهُ خَبِيْرٌ بِمَا تَعْمَلُوْنَ ۝

ثُمَّ اَنْزَلَ عَلَيْكُمْ مِّنْ بَعْدِ الْغَمِّ اَمَنَةً نُّعَاسًا يَّغْشٰى طَآئِفَةً مِّنْكُمْ ۚ وَطَآئِفَةٌ قَدْ اَهَمَّتْهُمْ اَنْفُسُهُمْ يَظُنُّوْنَ بِاللّٰهِ غَيْرَ الْحَقِّ ظَنَّ الْجَاهِلِيَّةِ ۚ يَقُوْلُوْنَ هَلْ لَّنَا مِنَ الْاَمْرِ مِنْ شَيْءٍ ۚ قُلْ اِنَّ الْاَمْرَ كُلَّهٗ لِلّٰهِ ۚ يُخْفُوْنَ فِىٓ اَنْفُسِهِمْ مَّا لَا يُبْدُوْنَ لَكَ ۚ يَقُوْلُوْنَ لَوْ كَانَ لَنَا مِنَ الْاَمْرِ شَيْءٌ مَّا قُتِلْنَا هٰهُنَا ۚ قُلْ لَّوْ كُنْتُمْ فِىْ بُيُوْتِكُمْ لَبَرَزَ الَّذِيْنَ كُتِبَ عَلَيْهِمُ الْقَتْلُ اِلٰى مَضَاجِعِهِمْ ۚ وَلِيَبْتَلِىَ اللّٰهُ مَا فِىْ صُدُوْرِكُمْ وَلِيُمَحِّصَ مَا فِىْ قُلُوْبِكُمْ ۚ وَاللّٰهُ عَلِيْمٌ بِذَاتِ الصُّدُوْرِ ۝

Those of you who turned their backs on the day when the two hosts met at Uhud, were sought to be made to slip by Satan, in consequence of some of their doings. Allah has, however, granted them pardon. Verily, Allah is Most Forgiving, Forbearing. (156)

O ye who believe, be not like those who have disbelieved and who say of their brethren, when they go about in the land or go forth to war, in the cause of Allah: Had they bided with us they would not have died or been slain. Allah will make this a cause of regret in their hearts. It is Allah who gives life and causes death. Allah sees well what you do. If you are slain or you die in the cause of Allah, surely Allah's forgiveness and mercy are far better than that which they hoard. If you die or be slain surely it is Allah unto Whom you shall be gathered together. (157—159)

It is by the great mercy of Allah that thou art gentle with them, for if thou hadst been rough and hard-hearted they would surely have dispersed from around thee. So bear with them and pray for forgiveness for them and take counsel with them in matters of administration. Then when thou hast made up thy mind concerning a matter, put thy trust in Allah. Surely Allah loves those who put their trust in Him. If Allah help you, none shall prevail against you; but if He forsake you, then who is it that can help you beside Him? It is in Allah that the believers should put their trust. (160—161)

It behoves not a Prophet to act dishonestly, and whoever acts dishonestly shall disclose that concerning which he shall have been dishonest on the Day of Judgment. Then shall every one be paid in full that which he has earned; and they shall not be wronged. Can he who follows the pleasure of Allah, be like him who draws on himself the wrath of Allah, and whose abode is hell? An evil retreat it is!

Each of them has his standing in the sight of Allah, and Allah sees well what they do. (162—164)

Indeed, Allah has conferred a great favour on the believers by raising among them a Messenger from among themselves, who recites to them His Signs, and purifies them and teaches them the Book and Wisdom. Before that they were surely in manifest error. (165)

Is it not that whenever a misfortune befalls you, though you may have inflicted upon the enemy twice as much, you say: Whence is this? Say to them: It is from your own selves. Surely, Allah has power over all things. That which befell you, on the day when the two hosts met at Uhud, was by Allah's command, that He might distinguish between the believers and the hypocrites. It was said to the hypocrites: Come, fight in the cause of Allah and repel the enemy. They countered: If we knew how to fight, we would surely go forth with you. They were that day nearer to disbelief than to belief. They utter through their mouths that which is not in their hearts. Allah knows well that which they conceal. These are those who said of their brethren, while they themselves remained behind: Had they listened to us, they would not have been slain. Say to them: Then avert death from your own selves; if you are truthful. (166—169)

Do not account those who are slain in the cause of Allah, as dead. Indeed, they are living in the presence of their Lord and are provided for. They are jubilant over that which Allah has bestowed upon them of His bounty, and rejoice for those who have not yet joined them out of such as they left behind, because on them shall come no fear, nor shall they grieve. They rejoice at the favour of Allah and His bounty, and at the realisation that Allah suffers not the reward of the faithful to be lost. (170—172)

لَمْ يَلْحَقُوْا بِهِمْ مِّنْ خَلْفِهِمْ ۙ اَلَّا خَوْفٌ عَلَيْهِمْ وَلَا هُمْ يَحْزَنُوْنَ ۞

يَسْتَبْشِرُوْنَ بِنِعْمَةٍ مِّنَ اللّٰهِ وَ فَضْلٍ ۙ وَّاَنَّ اللّٰهَ لَا يُضِيْعُ اَجْرَ الْمُؤْمِنِيْنَ ۞

Those who responded to the call of Allah and the Messenger despite their having received an injury, for such of them as perform their duty in all respects and act righteously there is a great reward; those who were told: People have mustered against you, so fear them; but this only added to their faith and they affirmed: Sufficient for us is Allah, and an excellent Guardian is He. So they returned with a mighty favour from Allah and a great bounty, having suffered no harm; they followed the pleasure of Allah, and Allah is the Lord of great bounty. It is Satan who seeks to frighten his friends; so fear them not and fear Me, if you are believers (173—176)

اَلَّذِيْنَ اسْتَجَابُوْا لِلّٰهِ وَالرَّسُوْلِ مِنْۢ بَعْدِ مَاۤ اَصَابَهُمُ الْقَرْحُ ۛ لِلَّذِيْنَ اَحْسَنُوْا مِنْهُمْ وَاتَّقَوْا اَجْرٌ عَظِيْمٌ ۚ۞

اَلَّذِيْنَ قَالَ لَهُمُ النَّاسُ اِنَّ النَّاسَ قَدْ جَمَعُوْا لَكُمْ فَاخْشَوْهُمْ فَزَادَهُمْ اِيْمَانًا ۖ وَّقَالُوْا حَسْبُنَا اللّٰهُ وَ نِعْمَ الْوَكِيْلُ ۞

فَانْقَلَبُوْا بِنِعْمَةٍ مِّنَ اللّٰهِ وَ فَضْلٍ لَّمْ يَمْسَسْهُمْ سُوْٓءٌ ۙ وَّاتَّبَعُوْا رِضْوَانَ اللّٰهِ ۗ وَ اللّٰهُ ذُوْ فَضْلٍ عَظِيْمٍ ۞

اِنَّمَا ذٰلِكُمُ الشَّيْطٰنُ يُخَوِّفُ اَوْلِيَآءَهٗ ۖ فَلَا تَخَافُوْهُمْ وَخَافُوْنِ اِنْ كُنْتُمْ مُّؤْمِنِيْنَ ۞

Let not those who advance rapidly into disbelief cause thee concern; surely they cannot harm Allah in any way. Allah designs to assign them no portion in the Hereafter; and for them there is a severe chastisement. Those who have chosen disbelief in place of belief cannot harm Allah at all; for them is a grievous punishment. Let not the disbelievers imagine that Our granting them respite is good for them; Our granting them respite will only cause them to increase in disobedience, and for them is an humiliating punishment. (177—179)

وَ لَا يَحْزُنْكَ الَّذِيْنَ يُسَارِعُوْنَ فِى الْكُفْرِ ۚ اِنَّهُمْ لَنْ يَّضُرُّوا اللّٰهَ شَيْئًا ۗ يُرِيْدُ اللّٰهُ اَلَّا يَجْعَلَ لَهُمْ حَظًّا فِى الْاٰخِرَةِ ۚ وَلَهُمْ عَذَابٌ عَظِيْمٌ ۞

اِنَّ الَّذِيْنَ اشْتَرَوُا الْكُفْرَ بِالْاِيْمَانِ لَنْ يَّضُرُّوا اللّٰهَ شَيْئًا ۚ وَلَهُمْ عَذَابٌ اَلِيْمٌ ۞

وَلَا يَحْسَبَنَّ الَّذِيْنَ كَفَرُوْۤا اَنَّمَا نُمْلِيْ لَهُمْ خَيْرٌ لِّاَنْفُسِهِمْ ۚ اِنَّمَا نُمْلِيْ لَهُمْ لِيَزْدَادُوْۤا اِثْمًا ۚ وَ لَهُمْ عَذَابٌ مُّهِيْنٌ ۞

مَا كَانَ اللّٰهُ لِيَذَرَ الْمُؤْمِنِيْنَ عَلٰى مَاۤ اَنْتُمْ عَلَيْهِ

Allah would not leave the believers in the state in which you are at present, until He separates the wicked from the good. Nor would Allah reveal to you the unseen. But Allah chooses of His Messengers whom He pleases and vouchsafes to them the knowledge of the unseen. Believe, therefore, in Allah and His Messengers. If you believe and are righteous, you shall have a great reward. (180)

Let not those who are niggardly of that which Allah has bestowed upon them of His bounty imagine that it is good for them. Indeed, it is evil for them. That of which they are niggardly shall be twisted as a collar round their necks on the Day of Judgment. To Allah belongs the heritage of the heavens and the earth. Allah is well aware of that which you do. Surely, Allah has heard the utterance of those who have said: Allah is needy and we are rich. We shall record what they have said and also their seeking to kill the Prophets without just cause, and We shall say to them: Suffer the torment of burning. This is the recompense of that which you have wrought. The truth is that Allah does not wrong His servants. (181—183)

To those who say: Allah has charged us not to believe in any Messenger unless he enjoins a burnt offering; do thou make answer: There have already come to you Messengers before me with clear Signs, and with that which you speak of, then why did you seek to kill them, if you are truthful? Then, if they call thee false, even so were called false Messengers before thee who came with clear Signs, Scriptures and shining commandments. (184—185)

Every one shall suffer death, and you shall be paid your full recompense on the Day of Judgment. He who is kept away from the Fire and is admitted to Paradise, has indeed attained felicity. The life of this world is but an illusory enjoyment. (186)

70

You will surely be tried in respect of your possessions and your persons and you shall surely hear many hurtful things from those who were given the Book before you and from those who set up partners with Allah, but if you show fortitude and restrain yourselves, that indeed is a matter of strong determination. (187)

Call to mind when Allah took a covenant from those who were given the Book: You shall make it known to the people and shall not conceal it; yet they threw it away behind their backs, and bartered it for a paltry price. Evil is that which they have taken in exchange for it. Imagine not that those who exult in their deeds, and love to be eulogised for that which they have not done, that they are secure from punishment. They shall suffer a grievous chastisement. To Allah belongs the kingdom of the heavens and the earth; and Allah has power over all things. (188—190)

In the creation of the heavens and the earth and in the alternation of the night and the day there are indeed Signs for people of understanding, who remember Allah standing, sitting and lying on their sides and ponder over the creation of the heavens and the earth, which impels them to supplicate: Lord, Thou hast not created all this without purpose, Holy art Thou; shield us then from the torment of the Fire. Lord, him whom Thou dost condemn to enter the Fire hast Thou surely humiliated, and for the transgressors there is no helper. Lord, we have heard a Caller calling unto faith: Believe ye in your Lord; and we have believed. Lord, forgive us, therefore, our errors and remove from us our ills, and in death number us with the righteous.

لَتُبْلَوُنَّ فِىۡۤ اَمۡوَالِكُمۡ وَاَنۡفُسِكُمۡ وَلَتَسۡمَعُنَّ مِنَ الَّذِيۡنَ اُوۡتُوا الۡكِتٰبَ مِنۡ قَبۡلِكُمۡ وَمِنَ الَّذِيۡنَ اَشۡرَكُوۡۤا اَذًى كَثِيۡرًا ؕ وَاِنۡ تَصۡبِرُوۡا وَتَتَّقُوۡا فَاِنَّ ذٰلِكَ مِنۡ عَزۡمِ الۡاُمُوۡرِ ۝

وَاِذۡ اَخَذَ اللّٰهُ مِيۡثَاقَ الَّذِيۡنَ اُوۡتُوا الۡكِتٰبَ لَتُبَيِّنُنَّهٗ لِلنَّاسِ وَلَا تَكۡتُمُوۡنَهٗ ۫ فَنَبَذُوۡهُ وَرَآءَ ظُهُوۡرِهِمۡ وَاشۡتَرَوۡا بِهٖ ثَمَنًا قَلِيۡلًا ؕ فَبِئۡسَ مَا يَشۡتَرُوۡنَ ۝ لَا تَحۡسَبَنَّ الَّذِيۡنَ يَفۡرَحُوۡنَ بِمَاۤ اَتَوۡا وَّيُحِبُّوۡنَ اَنۡ يُّحۡمَدُوۡا بِمَا لَمۡ يَفۡعَلُوۡا فَلَا تَحۡسَبَنَّهُمۡ بِمَفَازَةٍ مِّنَ الۡعَذَابِ ۚ وَلَهُمۡ عَذَابٌ اَلِيۡمٌ ۝ وَلِلّٰهِ مُلۡكُ السَّمٰوٰتِ وَالۡاَرۡضِ ؕ وَاللّٰهُ عَلٰى كُلِّ شَىۡءٍ قَدِيۡرٌ ۝

اِنَّ فِىۡ خَلۡقِ السَّمٰوٰتِ وَالۡاَرۡضِ وَاخۡتِلَافِ الَّيۡلِ وَالنَّهَارِ لَاٰيٰتٍ لِّاُولِى الۡاَلۡبَابِ ۝ الَّذِيۡنَ يَذۡكُرُوۡنَ اللّٰهَ قِيٰمًا وَّقُعُوۡدًا وَّعَلٰى جُنُوۡبِهِمۡ وَيَتَفَكَّرُوۡنَ فِىۡ خَلۡقِ السَّمٰوٰتِ وَالۡاَرۡضِ ۚ رَبَّنَا مَا خَلَقۡتَ هٰذَا بَاطِلًا ۚ سُبۡحٰنَكَ فَقِنَا عَذَابَ النَّارِ ۝ رَبَّنَاۤ اِنَّكَ مَنۡ تُدۡخِلِ النَّارَ فَقَدۡ اَخۡزَيۡتَهٗ ؕ وَمَا لِلظّٰلِمِيۡنَ مِنۡ اَنۡصَارٍ ۝ رَبَّنَاۤ اِنَّنَا سَمِعۡنَا مُنَادِيًا يُّنَادِىۡ لِلۡاِيۡمَانِ اَنۡ اٰمِنُوۡا بِرَبِّكُمۡ فَاٰمَنَّا ۖ رَبَّنَا فَاغۡفِرۡ لَنَا ذُنُوۡبَنَا وَكَفِّرۡ عَنَّا سَيِّاٰتِنَا وَتَوَفَّنَا مَعَ الۡاَبۡرَارِ ۝

Lord, grant us that which Thou hast promised us through Thy Messengers and humiliate us not on the Day of Judgment, surely Thou doest not contrary to Thy promise. Their Lord would answer their supplication: I will not suffer the labour of any labourer from among you, male or female, to perish. You are spiritually akin one to another. Those, therefore, who have emigrated and have been driven forth from their homes and have been persecuted in My cause, and have fought and have been slain, from them will I surely remove their ills and I will admit them to Gardens through which rivers flow — a reward from Allah, and with Allah is the best reward. (191—196)

Let not the going about of the disbelievers in the land mislead thee. A brief respite, and then hell shall be their abode. What an evil resting place! (197—198)

But those who make their Lord their shield shall have Gardens through which rivers flow; therein shall they abide — an entertainment from Allah. That which is with Allah is even better for the righteous. (199)

Among the People of the Book are some who believe in Allah and in that which has been sent down to you and in that which was sent down to them, humbling themselves before Allah. They barter not the Signs of Allah for a paltry price. It is these who shall have their reward with Allah. Surely, Allah is Swift at reckoning. (200)

O ye who believe, be steadfast and strive to excel in steadfastness and be on your guard and be mindful of your duty to Allah that you may prosper. (201)

رَبَّنَا وَ اٰتِنَا مَا وَعَدْتَّنَا عَلٰى رُسُلِكَ وَلَا تُخْزِنَا يَوْمَ الْقِيٰمَةِ ؕ اِنَّكَ لَا تُخْلِفُ الْمِيْعَادَ ۝

فَاسْتَجَابَ لَهُمْ رَبُّهُمْ اَنِّیْ لَاۤ اُضِیْعُ عَمَلَ عَامِلٍ مِّنْكُمْ مِّنْ ذَكَرٍ اَوْ اُنْثٰی ۚ بَعْضُكُمْ مِّنْ بَعْضٍ ۚ فَالَّذِیْنَ هَاجَرُوْا وَ اُخْرِجُوْا مِنْ دِیَارِهِمْ وَ اُوْذُوْا فِیْ سَبِیْلِیْ وَ قٰتَلُوْا وَ قُتِلُوْا لَاُكَفِّرَنَّ عَنْهُمْ سَیِّاٰتِهِمْ وَلَاُدْخِلَنَّهُمْ جَنّٰتٍ تَجْرِیْ مِنْ تَحْتِهَا الْاَنْهٰرُ ۚ ثَوَابًا مِّنْ عِنْدِ اللّٰهِ ؕ وَ اللّٰهُ عِنْدَهٗ حُسْنُ الثَّوَابِ ۝

لَا یَغُرَّنَّكَ تَقَلُّبُ الَّذِیْنَ كَفَرُوْا فِی الْبِلَادِ ۝

مَتَاعٌ قَلِیْلٌ ۟ ثُمَّ مَاْوٰىهُمْ جَهَنَّمُ ؕ وَ بِئْسَ الْمِهَادُ ۝

لٰكِنِ الَّذِیْنَ اتَّقَوْا رَبَّهُمْ لَهُمْ جَنّٰتٌ تَجْرِیْ مِنْ تَحْتِهَا الْاَنْهٰرُ خٰلِدِیْنَ فِیْهَا نُزُلًا مِّنْ عِنْدِ اللّٰهِ ؕ وَمَا عِنْدَ اللّٰهِ خَیْرٌ لِّلْاَبْرَارِ ۝

وَ اِنَّ مِنْ اَهْلِ الْكِتٰبِ لَمَنْ یُّؤْمِنُ بِاللّٰهِ وَ مَاۤ اُنْزِلَ اِلَیْكُمْ وَ مَاۤ اُنْزِلَ اِلَیْهِمْ خٰشِعِیْنَ لِلّٰهِ ۙ لَا یَشْتَرُوْنَ بِاٰیٰتِ اللّٰهِ ثَمَنًا قَلِیْلًا ؕ اُولٰٓئِكَ لَهُمْ اَجْرُهُمْ عِنْدَ رَبِّهِمْ ؕ اِنَّ اللّٰهَ سَرِیْعُ الْحِسَابِ ۝

یٰۤاَیُّهَا الَّذِیْنَ اٰمَنُوا اصْبِرُوْا وَ صَابِرُوْا وَ رَابِطُوْا ۟ وَ اتَّقُوا اللّٰهَ لَعَلَّكُمْ تُفْلِحُوْنَ ۝

سُوْرَةُ النِّسَآءِ مَدَنِيَّةٌ

AL-NISĀ

(Revealed after Hijra)

In the name of Allah, Most Gracious, Ever Merciful. (1)

O mankind, be mindful of your duty to your Lord, Who created you from a single soul and from it created its mate and from the two created and spread many men and women; and be mindful of your duty to Allah in Whose name you appeal to one another, and of your obligations in respect of ties of kinship. Verily, Allah watches over you. (2)

Hand over their property to the orphans and do not exchange the bad for the good, and do not devour their property mixing it with your own. Surely, that is a great sin. (3)

Should you apprehend that you will not be able to deal fairly with orphans, then marry of other women as may be agreeable to you, two or three, or four; but if you feel you will not deal justly between them, then marry only one, or, out of those over whom you have authority. That is the best way for you to obviate injustice. Hand over to the women their dowers freely; but if they, of their own pleasure, should remit to you a part thereof, then enjoy it as a thing agreeable and wholesome. (4—5)

Hand not over to those of immature mind your property which Allah has made a means of support for you; but make provision for them out of it and give them good advice. Check up on the orphans till they attain the age of marriage; then if you find them sensible hand over their property to them, and consume it not in

بِسْمِ اللهِ الرَّحْمٰنِ الرَّحِيْمِ ۝

يٰۤاَيُّهَا النَّاسُ اتَّقُوْا رَبَّكُمُ الَّذِيْ خَلَقَكُمْ مِّنْ نَّفْسٍ وَّاحِدَةٍ وَّخَلَقَ مِنْهَا زَوْجَهَا وَبَثَّ مِنْهُمَا رِجَالًا كَثِيْرًا وَّنِسَآءً ۚ وَاتَّقُوا اللهَ الَّذِيْ تَسَآءَلُوْنَ بِهٖ وَالْاَرْحَامَ ۚ اِنَّ اللهَ كَانَ عَلَيْكُمْ رَقِيْبًا ۝

وَاٰتُوا الْيَتٰمٰۤى اَمْوَالَهُمْ وَلَا تَتَبَدَّلُوا الْخَبِيْثَ بِالطَّيِّبِ ۪ وَلَا تَأْكُلُوْۤا اَمْوَالَهُمْ اِلٰۤى اَمْوَالِكُمْ ۚ اِنَّهٗ كَانَ حُوْبًا كَبِيْرًا ۝

وَاِنْ خِفْتُمْ اَلَّا تُقْسِطُوْا فِى الْيَتٰمٰى فَانْكِحُوْا مَا طَابَ لَكُمْ مِّنَ النِّسَآءِ مَثْنٰى وَثُلٰثَ وَرُبٰعَ ۚ فَاِنْ خِفْتُمْ اَلَّا تَعْدِلُوْا فَوَاحِدَةً اَوْ مَا مَلَكَتْ اَيْمَانُكُمْ ۚ ذٰلِكَ اَدْنٰۤى اَلَّا تَعُوْلُوْا ۝

وَاٰتُوا النِّسَآءَ صَدُقٰتِهِنَّ نِحْلَةً ۚ فَاِنْ طِبْنَ لَكُمْ عَنْ شَيْءٍ مِّنْهُ نَفْسًا فَكُلُوْهُ هَنِيْئًا مَّرِيْئًا ۝

وَلَا تُؤْتُوا السُّفَهَآءَ اَمْوَالَكُمُ الَّتِيْ جَعَلَ اللهُ لَكُمْ قِيٰمًا وَّارْزُقُوْهُمْ فِيْهَا وَاكْسُوْهُمْ وَقُوْلُوْا لَهُمْ قَوْلًا مَّعْرُوْفًا ۝

وَابْتَلُوا الْيَتٰمٰى حَتّٰۤى اِذَا بَلَغُوا النِّكَاحَ ۚ فَاِنْ اٰنَسْتُمْ مِّنْهُمْ رُشْدًا فَادْفَعُوْۤا اِلَيْهِمْ اَمْوَالَهُمْ ۚ وَلَا تَأْكُلُوْهَاۤ

73

extravagance and haste against their growing up. Whoso is rich let him abstain altogether; and whoso is poor, let him make use of as much as is fair. When you hand over their property to them, call witnesses in their presence. Allah is Sufficient as a Reckoner. (6—7)

For men, as well as for women, there is a share in that which parents and near relations leave, whether it be little or much, a share which has been determined by Allah. At the time of the division of the inheritance, if there are present other relations and orphans and the needy, give them also something out of it and speak to them graciously. Those who would be anxious if they should leave behind them helpless offspring, should be mindful of their obligation to Allah in respect of orphans and should speak and act in a straightforward manner. Surely, those who eat up the property of orphans unjustly, only swallow fire into their bellies and shall enter a blazing fire. (8—11)

Allah commands you concerning your children as follows: the share of a male is as much as the share of two females: but if there are only females, two or more, they shall have two-thirds of what the deceased should leave and if there is only one she shall have one half. His parents shall have, each of them, a sixth of the inheritance, if he have a child; but if he have no child and his parents be his heirs, then his mother shall have a third; but if he have brothers and sisters then his mother shall have a sixth. All this is subject to the payment of any bequests made by him and his debts. You know not whether your parents or your children are nearer to you in conferring benefits upon you. These shares are fixed by Allah. Surely, Allah is All-Knowing, Wise. You shall have half of that which your wives leave, if they have no child; but if they have a child, then you shall have a fourth of that which they leave, after the payment of any bequests made by them and their debts. They shall have a fourth of that which you leave, if you have no child; but if you have a child, then they shall have an eighth of that which you leave, after the payment of any bequests made by you and your debts. If there be a man or a woman leaving property to be inherited, and there is no parent or child, but there is a uterine brother or uterine sister, then each of them shall have a sixth; but if they be more than that, then they shall be equal sharers in one third, after the payment of bequests and debts, without prejudice. This is an injunction from Allah, and Allah is All-Knowing, Forbearing. (12—13)

These are the limits set by Allah. Those who obey Allah and His Messenger, will He admit to Gardens through which rivers flow; therein shall they abide. That is the great triumph. Those who disobey Allah and His Messenger and transgress the limits set by Him, will He cause to enter a fire wherein they shall abide, and they shall have an humiliating punishment. (14—15)

Confront those of your women who are guilty of unbecoming conduct with four witnesses. If they bear witness, then confine the women to their houses till death overtakes them or Allah opens a way for them. Punish such of your men who are guilty of unbecoming conduct, but if they should repent and amend, then leave them alone. Surely, Allah is Oft-Returning with compassion and is Ever Merciful. Allah would accept the repentance of those who do evil in ignorance and then are quick to repent. These are they to whom Allah turns with mercy. Allah is All-Knowing, Wise.

مِنْۢ بَعْدِ وَصِيَّةٍ يُّوْصِيْنَ بِهَآ اَوْ دَيْنٍ ۭ وَلَهُنَّ الرُّبُعُ مِمَّا تَرَكْتُمْ اِنْ لَّمْ يَكُنْ لَّكُمْ وَلَدٌ ۚ فَاِنْ كَانَ لَكُمْ وَلَدٌ فَلَهُنَّ الثُّمُنُ مِمَّا تَرَكْتُمْ مِّنْۢ بَعْدِ وَصِيَّةٍ تُوْصُوْنَ بِهَآ اَوْ دَيْنٍ ۭ وَاِنْ كَانَ رَجُلٌ يُّوْرَثُ كَلٰلَةً اَوِ امْرَاَةٌ وَّلَهٗٓ اَخٌ اَوْ اُخْتٌ فَلِكُلِّ وَاحِدٍ مِّنْهُمَا السُّدُسُ ۚ فَاِنْ كَانُوْٓا اَكْثَرَ مِنْ ذٰلِكَ فَهُمْ شُرَكَآءُ فِى الثُّلُثِ مِنْۢ بَعْدِ وَصِيَّةٍ يُّوْصٰى بِهَآ اَوْ دَيْنٍ ۙ غَيْرَ مُضَآرٍّ ۚ وَصِيَّةً مِّنَ اللّٰهِ ۭ وَاللّٰهُ عَلِيْمٌ حَلِيْمٌ ۝

تِلْكَ حُدُوْدُ اللّٰهِ ۭ وَمَنْ يُّطِعِ اللّٰهَ وَرَسُوْلَهٗ يُدْخِلْهُ جَنّٰتٍ تَجْرِيْ مِنْ تَحْتِهَا الْاَنْهٰرُ خٰلِدِيْنَ فِيْهَا ۭ وَ ذٰلِكَ الْفَوْزُ الْعَظِيْمُ ۝

وَمَنْ يَّعْصِ اللّٰهَ وَرَسُوْلَهٗ وَيَتَعَدَّ حُدُوْدَهٗ يُدْخِلْهُ نَارًا خَالِدًا فِيْهَا ۠ وَلَهٗ عَذَابٌ مُّهِيْنٌ ۝

وَالّٰتِيْ يَاْتِيْنَ الْفَاحِشَةَ مِنْ نِّسَآئِكُمْ فَاسْتَشْهِدُوْا عَلَيْهِنَّ اَرْبَعَةً مِّنْكُمْ ۚ فَاِنْ شَهِدُوْا فَاَمْسِكُوْهُنَّ فِى الْبُيُوْتِ حَتّٰى يَتَوَفّٰىهُنَّ الْمَوْتُ اَوْ يَجْعَلَ اللّٰهُ لَهُنَّ سَبِيْلًا ۝

وَالَّذٰنِ يَاْتِيٰنِهَا مِنْكُمْ فَاٰذُوْهُمَا ۚ فَاِنْ تَابَا وَاَصْلَحَا فَاَعْرِضُوْا عَنْهُمَا ۭ اِنَّ اللّٰهَ كَانَ تَوَّابًا رَّحِيْمًا ۝

اِنَّمَا التَّوْبَةُ عَلَى اللّٰهِ لِلَّذِيْنَ يَعْمَلُوْنَ السُّوْٓءَ بِجَهَالَةٍ ثُمَّ يَتُوْبُوْنَ مِنْ قَرِيْبٍ فَاُولٰٓئِكَ يَتُوْبُ اللّٰهُ عَلَيْهِمْ ۭ وَكَانَ اللّٰهُ عَلِيْمًا حَكِيْمًا ۝

Repentance is not for those who continue in their evil courses until, when death faces one of them, he exclaims: I do now repent; nor for those who die disbelieving. It is these for whom We have prepared a painful chastisement. (16—19)

O ye who believe, it is not lawful for you to inherit from women against their will, nor should you hold them back wrongfully that you may take away from them part of that which you may have given them; their being confined to their houses for unbecoming conduct is a matter apart. Consort with them in kindness. If you dislike them, it may be that you dislike something in which Allah has placed much good. (20)

If you desire to take a wife in place of another and you have given one of them a treasure, take not back aught therefrom. Will you take it by calumny and manifest sin? How can you take it when you have consorted together and they have taken from you a strong covenant? (21—22)

Marry not women whom your fathers had married. What has passed has passed. It was a foul and hateful practice and an evil way. (23)

Forbidden to you are your mothers, and your daughters and your sisters, and your fathers' sisters and your mothers' sisters, and the daughters of your brothers and the daughters of your sisters, and your foster-mothers and your foster-sisters, and the mothers of your wives, and your step-daughters who are your wards by your wives with whom you have consorted, but if you have consorted not with them, it will be no sin upon you, and the wives of your sons from your loins. It is also forbidden to you to have two sisters together in marriage, but what has passed has passed. Surely Allah is Most Forgiving, Ever Merciful. (24)

76

Forbidden to you also are married women, except those who have passed into your hands as prisoners. This is the commandment of Allah for you. Lawful for you are those outside these categories, that you seek them in marriage, by means of your properties, not committing fornication. For the benefit that you receive from them pay them their dowers as fixed, and there will be no sin upon you in respect of anything that you mutually agree upon after the fixing of the dower. Surely, Allah is All-Knowing, Wise. (25)

Whoso of you cannot afford to marry from among free, believing women, let him marry out of those believing women who have passed into your hands as prisoners. Allah knows your faith best; you are spiritually akin one to another. You may marry them with the leave of their masters and pay them their dowers according to what is fair, they being chaste, not committing fornication, nor taking secret paramours. If they are guilty of unbecoming conduct after marriage, their punishment will be half of that prescribed for free women. This facility is for him among you who fears lest he should fall into sin, but that you should restrain yourselves is better for you. Allah is Most Forgiving, Ever Merciful. (26)

Allah desires to make clear to you, and guide you to, the ways of those before you, and to turn to you in mercy. Allah is All-Knowing, Wise. Allah desires to turn to you in mercy, but those who pursue evil courses, desire that you should incline wholly towards evil. Allah desires to lighten your burden, for man has been created weak (27—29)

O ye who believe, consume not your property between yourselves unlawfully; it being lawful to acquire property through trade with mutual consent; and destroy not yourselves. Surely, Allah is Ever Merciful to you. Whoever seeks to acquire property by way of transgression and injustice, We shall cast him into the Fire; and that is easy for Allah. If you keep away from the more grievous of the things that are forbidden you, We will remove from you your faults and will admit you to a place of honour. (30—32)

Covet not that whereby Allah has made some of you excel others. Men shall have a share of that which they earn, and women shall have a share of that which they earn. Ask Allah alone of His bounty. Surely, Allah has perfect knowledge of all things. For everyone leaving an inheritance we have appointed heirs, parents and near relations, and also husbands and wives with whom you have made firm covenants. So give all of them their appointed shares. Surely, Allah watches over all things. (33—34)

Men are appointed guardians over women, because of that in respect of which Allah has made some of them excel others, and because the men spend of their wealth. So virtuous women are obedient and safeguard, with Allah's help, matters the knowledge of which is shared by them with their husbands. Admonish those of them on whose part you apprehend disobedience, and leave them alone in their beds and chastise them. Then if they obey you, seek no pretext against them. Surely, Allah is High, Great. (35)

If you apprehend a breach between husband and wife, then appoint an arbiter from among his people and an arbiter from among her people. If they desire reconciliation, Allah will bring about accord between husband and wife. Surely, Allah is All-Knowing, All-Aware. (36)

78

Worship Allah and associate naught with Him, and be benevolent towards parents, and kindred, and orphans, and the needy, and the neighbour who is a kinsman, and the neighbour who is not related to you, and your associates and the wayfarer, and those who are under your control. Surely, Allah loves not the proud and boastful, who are niggardly and enjoin people to be niggardly, and conceal that which Allah has given them of His bounty. We have prepared for the disbelievers an humiliating chastisement, and for those who spend their wealth to be seen of people and believe not in Allah nor in the Last Day. Whoso has Satan for his companion should remember that he is an evil companion. (37—39)

What harm would befall them, if they were to believe in Allah and the Last Day and to spend out of that which Allah has given them? Allah knows them well. Allah wrongs not any one even by the weight of the smallest particle; and if there be a good deed, He multiplies it and bestows from Himself a great reward, (40—41)

How will it be when We shall bring a witness from every people, and shall bring thee as a witness against these? On that day those who have disbelieved and disobeyed the Messenger will wish they were buried in the ground and the earth were made level above them, and they shall not be able to conceal anything from Allah. (42—43)

O ye who believe, approach not Prayer when you are not in full possession of your faculties, until you realise the true import of your supplications, nor when you have consorted with your wives, except during the course of a journey, until you have washed. Should you be ill or on a journey,

اللهَ بَيْنَهُمَا إِنَّ اللهَ كَانَ عَلِيْمًا خَبِيْرًا ۞

وَاعْبُدُوا اللهَ وَلَا تُشْرِكُوْا بِهِ شَيْئًا وَّ بِالْوَالِدَيْنِ اِحْسَانًا وَّبِذِى الْقُرْبٰى وَالْيَتٰمٰى وَالْمَسٰكِيْنِ وَالْجَارِ ذِى الْقُرْبٰى وَالْجَارِ الْجُنُبِ وَّ الصَّاحِبِ بِالْجَنْبِ وَ ابْنِ السَّبِيْلِ وَمَا مَلَكَتْ اَيْمَانُكُمْ إِنَّ اللهَ لَا يُحِبُّ مَنْ كَانَ مُخْتَالًا فَخُوْرَا ۞

الَّذِيْنَ يَبْخَلُوْنَ وَ يَأْمُرُوْنَ النَّاسَ بِالْبُخْلِ وَيَكْتُمُوْنَ مَا اٰتٰهُمُ اللهُ مِنْ فَضْلِهِ وَ اَعْتَدْنَا لِلْكٰفِرِيْنَ عَذَابًا مُّهِيْنًا ۞

وَالَّذِيْنَ يُنْفِقُوْنَ اَمْوَالَهُمْ رِئَاءَ النَّاسِ وَلَا يُؤْمِنُوْنَ بِاللهِ وَ لَا بِالْيَوْمِ الْاٰخِرِ وَمَنْ يَّكُنِ الشَّيْطٰنُ لَهُ قَرِيْنًا فَسَاءَ قَرِيْنًا ۞

وَمَاذَا عَلَيْهِمْ لَوْ اٰمَنُوْا بِاللهِ وَالْيَوْمِ الْاٰخِرِ وَاَنْفَقُوْا مِمَّا رَزَقَهُمُ اللهُ ۖ وَكَانَ اللهُ بِهِمْ عَلِيْمًا ۞

إِنَّ اللهَ لَا يَظْلِمُ مِثْقَالَ ذَرَّةٍ وَاِنْ تَكُ حَسَنَةً يُّضٰعِفْهَا وَيُؤْتِ مِنْ لَّدُنْهُ اَجْرًا عَظِيْمًا ۞

فَكَيْفَ اِذَا جِئْنَا مِنْ كُلِّ اُمَّةٍ بِشَهِيْدٍ وَّ جِئْنَا بِكَ عَلٰى هٰؤُلَاءِ شَهِيْدًا ۞

يَوْمَئِذٍ يَّوَدُّ الَّذِيْنَ كَفَرُوْا وَعَصَوُا الرَّسُوْلَ لَوْ تُسَوّٰى بِهِمُ الْاَرْضُ وَلَا يَكْتُمُوْنَ اللهَ حَدِيْثًا ۞

يٰاَيُّهَا الَّذِيْنَ اٰمَنُوْا لَا تَقْرَبُوا الصَّلٰوةَ وَ اَنْتُمْ سُكٰرٰى حَتّٰى تَعْلَمُوْا مَا تَقُوْلُوْنَ وَ لَا جُنُبًا اِلَّا عَابِرِيْ سَبِيْلٍ

or if one of you comes from the privy, or you have consorted with your wives and you find no water, then betake yourselves to clean dust and wipe therewith your faces and your hands. Surely, Allah is Most Indulgent, Most Forgiving. (44)

حَتّٰى تَغْتَسِلُوْا وَ اِنْ كُنْتُمْ مَّرْضٰى اَوْ عَلٰى سَفَرٍ اَوْ جَآءَ اَحَدٌ مِّنْكُمْ مِّنَ الْغَآئِطِ اَوْ لٰمَسْتُمُ النِّسَآءَ فَلَمْ تَجِدُوْا مَآءً فَتَيَمَّمُوْا صَعِيْدًا طَيِّبًا فَامْسَحُوْا بِوُجُوْهِكُمْ وَ اَيْدِيْكُمْ اِنَّ اللّٰهَ كَانَ عَفُوًّا غَفُوْرًا ۝

Knowest thou not of those who were given a portion of the Book, who deliberately choose error and desire that you too may lose the way? Allah knows your enemies better than you do; and sufficient is Allah as a Friend, and sufficient is Allah as a Helper. (45—46)

اَلَمْ تَرَ اِلَى الَّذِيْنَ اُوْتُوْا نَصِيْبًا مِّنَ الْكِتٰبِ يَشْتَرُوْنَ الضَّلٰلَةَ وَ يُرِيْدُوْنَ اَنْ تَضِلُّوا السَّبِيْلَ ۝ وَ اللّٰهُ اَعْلَمُ بِاَعْدَآئِكُمْ وَ كَفٰى بِاللّٰهِ وَلِيًّا ۙ وَ كَفٰى بِاللّٰهِ نَصِيْرًا ۝

Of the Jews there are some who pervert Allah's words from their places. They say: We have heard, yet we disobey; or, Hear thou, may thou never hear Allah's word; or, Show favour to us; lying with their tongues and seeking to ridicule the faith. Had they said: We hear and we obey; and: Listen to us and look at us with kindness; it would have been the better for them and more upright. But Allah has cast them aside for their disbelief; so little it is that they believe. O ye who have been given the Book, believe in that which We have now sent down, fulfilling that which is with you, before We destroy your leaders and turn them on their backs or cast them aside as We cast aside the people of the Sabbath. The decree of Allah is bound to be carried out. (47—48)

مِنَ الَّذِيْنَ هَادُوْا يُحَرِّفُوْنَ الْكَلِمَ عَنْ مَّوَاضِعِهٖ وَ يَقُوْلُوْنَ سَمِعْنَا وَ عَصَيْنَا وَ اسْمَعْ غَيْرَ مُسْمَعٍ وَّ رَاعِنَا لَيًّا بِاَلْسِنَتِهِمْ وَ طَعْنًا فِى الدِّيْنِ وَ لَوْ اَنَّهُمْ قَالُوْا سَمِعْنَا وَ اَطَعْنَا وَ اسْمَعْ وَ انْظُرْنَا لَكَانَ خَيْرًا لَّهُمْ وَ اَقْوَمَ ۙ وَ لٰكِنْ لَّعَنَهُمُ اللّٰهُ بِكُفْرِهِمْ فَلَا يُؤْمِنُوْنَ اِلَّا قَلِيْلًا ۝ يٰۤاَيُّهَا الَّذِيْنَ اُوْتُوا الْكِتٰبَ اٰمِنُوْا بِمَا نَزَّلْنَا مُصَدِّقًا لِّمَا مَعَكُمْ مِّنْ قَبْلِ اَنْ نَّطْمِسَ وُجُوْهًا فَنَرُدَّهَا عَلٰۤى اَدْبَارِهَآ اَوْ نَلْعَنَهُمْ كَمَا لَعَنَّآ اَصْحٰبَ السَّبْتِ ۚ وَ كَانَ اَمْرُ اللّٰهِ مَفْعُوْلًا ۝

Surely, Allah will not forgive that any partner be associated with Him, but will forgive anything short of that to whomsoever He pleases. Whoso associates partners with Allah has indeed devised enormous evil. (49)

اِنَّ اللّٰهَ لَا يَغْفِرُ اَنْ يُّشْرَكَ بِهٖ وَ يَغْفِرُ مَا دُوْنَ ذٰلِكَ لِمَنْ يَّشَآءُ ۚ وَ مَنْ يُّشْرِكْ بِاللّٰهِ فَقَدِ افْتَرٰۤى اِثْمًا عَظِيْمًا ۝ اَلَمْ تَرَ اِلَى الَّذِيْنَ يُزَكُّوْنَ اَنْفُسَهُمْ ۚ بَلِ اللّٰهُ يُزَكِّى

Knowest thou not of those who account themselves pure? Surely, it is Allah Who purifies whomsoever He pleases, and they will not be wronged a whit. Behold, how they fabricate a lie against Allah and sufficient is that as a manifest sin. (50—51)

Knowest thou not of those who were given a portion of the Book, who put their faith in vain things and in those who transgress, and they say of the disbelievers: These are better guided in religion than those who believe. These it is whom Allah has cast aside; and thou shalt not find anyone helping him whom Allah has cast aside. Have they a share in the kingdom? In that case they would not give the people even as little as the hollow in a date stone. Or, do they envy people that which Allah has given them out of His bounty? Surely, We gave the children of Abraham the Book and Wisdom, and We also gave them a great kingdom. Of them were some who believed in it, and of them were some who held back from it; their portion is hell and it is exceedingly hot. (52—56)

We shall soon cause those who disbelieve in Our Signs to enter the Fire. As often as their hides are burnt up, We shall give them in exchange other hides that they may feel the torment keenly. Surely, Allah is Mighty, Wise. (57)

We shall admit those who have believed and have worked righteousness into Gardens through which rivers flow, abiding therein for ever. Therein shall they have pure spouses, and We shall admit them into pleasant and plenteous shade. (58)

81

Allah commands you to make over the trusts to those best fitted to discharge them and that when you judge between the people, you do it with justice. Excellent indeed is that with which Allah admonishes you. Allah is All-Hearing, All-Seeing. O ye who believe, obey Allah and obey His Messenger and those who are in authority among you. Then if you differ in anything refer it to Allah and His Messenger if you are believers in Allah and the Last Day. That is the best and most commendable in the end. (59—60)

Knowest thou not of those who pretend that they believe in that which has been sent down to thee and that which has been sent down before thee, and yet they desire to seek judgment from the rebellious ones though they had been commanded not to obey them? Satan desires to lead them astray grievously. When it is said to them: Come ye to that which Allah has sent down to the Messenger; thou seest the hypocrites turn completely away from thee. Then how is it that when an affliction befalls them because of their conduct, they come to thee swearing by Allah: We meant nothing but benevolence and conciliation? These are people whose designs Allah knows well. So forbear and admonish them and talk to them effectively concerning their own selves. (61—64)

We have sent no Messenger but that he should be obeyed by the command of Allah. If, when they had wronged their souls, they had come to thee and asked forgiveness of Allah and the Messenger also had asked forgiveness for them, they would have surely found Allah Oft-Returning with compassion, Ever Merciful. (65)

By thy Lord, they will not truly believe until they make thee judge in all that is in dispute between them and then find not in their hearts any demur concerning that which thou decidest and submit with full submission. (66)

If We had commanded them: Kill yourselves in striving for the cause of Allah or go forth from your homes for the same purpose: they would not have done it except a few of them; yet if they had done what they are exhorted to do, it would surely have been the better for them and conducive to greater firmness and strength. We would then bestow upon them a great reward from Ourself, and We would surely guide them along the straight path. Whoso obeys Allah and the Messenger shall be among those upon whom Allah has bestowed His favours — the Prophets, the Faithful ones, the Martyrs and the Righteous; and excellent companions these are. This is Allah's grace and Allah is All-Comprehending. (67—71)

O ye who believe, take due precautions for your security and then go forth in separate parties or go forth all together. Of a surety there are those among you who will tarry behind. If a misfortune befalls you such a one says: Allah has surely been gracious to me, since I was not present with them. But if some good fortune should come to you from Allah, he says, as if there were no amity between him and you: Would that I had been with them, then should I have achieved a great success. Let those then fight in the cause of Allah who would exchange the present life with the Hereafter. Whoso fights in the cause of Allah, be he slain or be he victorious, We shall soon give him a great reward. (72—75)

83

What keeps you from fighting in the cause of Allah and of the weak from among men, women and children who supplicate: Lord, deliver us from this town whose people are oppressors, and appoint for us from Thyself some friend and appoint for us from Thyself some helper? Those who believe fight in the cause of Allah, and those who disbelieve fight in the cause of the Evil One. Fight ye then against the friends of Satan; surely Satan's strategy is weak. (76—77)

مِنَ الرِّجَالِ وَ النِّسَآءِ وَ الْوِلْدَانِ الَّذِيْنَ يَقُوْلُوْنَ رَبَّنَآ اَخْرِجْنَا مِنْ هٰذِهِ الْقَرْيَةِ الظَّالِمِ اَهْلُهَا وَ اجْعَلْ لَّنَا مِنْ لَّدُنْكَ وَلِيًّا ۙ وَّ اجْعَلْ لَّنَا مِنْ لَّدُنْكَ نَصِيْرًا ۞

اَلَّذِيْنَ اٰمَنُوْا يُقَاتِلُوْنَ فِيْ سَبِيْلِ اللّٰهِ ۖ وَ الَّذِيْنَ كَفَرُوْا يُقَاتِلُوْنَ فِيْ سَبِيْلِ الطَّاغُوْتِ فَقَاتِلُوْٓا اَوْلِيَآءَ الشَّيْطٰنِ ۖ اِنَّ كَيْدَ الشَّيْطٰنِ كَانَ ضَعِيْفًا ۟

اَلَمْ تَرَ اِلَى الَّذِيْنَ قِيْلَ لَهُمْ كُفُّوْٓا اَيْدِيَكُمْ وَ اَقِيْمُوا الصَّلٰوةَ وَ اٰتُوا الزَّكٰوةَ ۚ فَلَمَّا كُتِبَ عَلَيْهِمُ الْقِتَالُ

Knowest thou not of those who were told: Restrain your hands, observe Prayer and pay the Zakat; but they were eager to fight? Yet, now that fighting has been prescribed for them, suddenly a section of them have begun to fear people as they should fear Allah or even more, and they say: Lord, why hast Thou prescribed fighting for us? Wouldst Thou not grant us respite yet awhile? Tell them: The enjoyment of this life is a trifle and the Hereafter is better for those who are mindful of their duty to Allah; and you shall not be wronged a whit. Wheresoever you may be, death will overtake you, even if you be in strongly built towers. If some good befalls them, they say: This is from Allah; and if ill befalls them, they say: This is from thee. Tell them: All is from Allah. What ails these people that they do not even approach the grasping of a reality? Whatever of good comes to thee is from Allah: and whatever of ill befalls thee is from thyself. We have sent thee as a Messenger to mankind. Sufficient is Allah as a Witness. (78—80)

اِذَا فَرِيْقٌ مِّنْهُمْ يَخْشَوْنَ النَّاسَ كَخَشْيَةِ اللّٰهِ اَوْ اَشَدَّ خَشْيَةً ۚ وَ قَالُوْا رَبَّنَا لِمَ كَتَبْتَ عَلَيْنَا الْقِتَالَ ۚ لَوْ لَآ اَخَّرْتَنَآ اِلَى اَجَلٍ قَرِيْبٍ ۗ قُلْ مَتَاعُ الدُّنْيَا قَلِيْلٌ ۚ وَ الْاٰخِرَةُ خَيْرٌ لِّمَنِ اتَّقٰى ۚ وَ لَا تُظْلَمُوْنَ فَتِيْلًا ۞

اَيْنَمَا تَكُوْنُوْا يُدْرِكْكُّمُ الْمَوْتُ وَ لَوْ كُنْتُمْ فِيْ بُرُوْجٍ مُّشَيَّدَةٍ ۗ وَ اِنْ تُصِبْهُمْ حَسَنَةٌ يَّقُوْلُوْا هٰذِهٖ مِنْ عِنْدِ اللّٰهِ ۚ وَ اِنْ تُصِبْهُمْ سَيِّئَةٌ يَّقُوْلُوْا هٰذِهٖ مِنْ عِنْدِكَ ۚ قُلْ كُلٌّ مِّنْ عِنْدِ اللّٰهِ ۖ فَمَالِ هٰٓؤُلَآءِ الْقَوْمِ لَا يَكَادُوْنَ يَفْقَهُوْنَ حَدِيْثًا ۞

مَآ اَصَابَكَ مِنْ حَسَنَةٍ فَمِنَ اللّٰهِ ۖ وَ مَآ اَصَابَكَ مِنْ سَيِّئَةٍ فَمِنْ نَّفْسِكَ ۚ وَ اَرْسَلْنٰكَ لِلنَّاسِ رَسُوْلًا ۚ وَ كَفٰى بِاللّٰهِ شَهِيْدًا ۞

Whoso obeys the Messenger has indeed obeyed Allah; and whoso turns away, then We have not sent thee as a keeper over them. They assert: Ours is but to obey; but when they depart from thee, a section of them spends the night scheming against that which thou sayest. Allah records their schemes. So turn away from them and put thy trust in Allah. Sufficient is Allah as a Guardian. (81—82)

Will they not, then, meditate upon the Quran? Had it been from any one other than Allah they would surely have found therein much contradiction. (83)

When there comes to them any tidings bearing upon security or causing fear they bruit it about; whereas if they were to refer it to the Messenger and to those in authority among them, surely those of them who are adept at discovering the truth, would assess it at its true value. Had it not been for the grace of Allah upon you and His mercy, you would have followed Satan, save a few. (84)

Fight, therefore, in the cause of Allah; thou art not responsible for any except thy own self, and urge on the believers. It may be that Allah will restrain the might of the disbelievers. Allah is Strong in might and is Strong in chastisement. (85)

Whoso makes a righteous intercession shall share in the good that ensues therefrom, and whoso makes an evil intercession shall share in the evil that ensues in consequence thereof. Allah has full power over all things. (86)

When you are greeted with a salutation greet with a better salutation, or return the same. Surely, Allah takes account of all things. (87)

Allah is He beside Whom there is none worthy of worship. He will certainly continue to gather you together till the Day of Judgment, about which there is no doubt. Who can be more truthful in his word than Allah? (88)

How is it that you are divided into two parties regarding the hypocrites? Allah has overthrown them because of what they did. Would you guide him whom Allah has caused to perish? For him whom Allah causes to perish thou shalt not find a way. They wish that you would disbelieve as they have disbelieved, so that you may become all alike. Make not, therefore, friends with any of them, until they emigrate in the way of Allah. If they turn away, then seize them and kill them wherever you find them; and take no friend or helper from among them except such of them as are connected with a people between whom and you there is a pact, or such as come to you, while their hearts shrink from fighting you or fighting their own people. If Allah had so pleased, He would have given them power over you, then they would surely have fought you. Now, if they leave you alone and do not fight you, and offer you peace, in that case Allah has left you no cause of grievance against them. You will find others of them, the hypocrites, who desire to be secure from you and to be secure from their own people also. Whenever they find an opportunity of hostility, they fall headlong into it. Therefore, if they do not leave you alone and offer you peace and restrain their hands, seize them and kill them wherever you find them. Against these We have given you clear authority. (89—92)

It behoves not a believer to kill a believer unless it be by mistake. He who kills a believer by mistake shall free, or procure the freedom of, a believing slave, and provide blood-money to be handed over to the heirs of the person slain, unless they remit it as charity. If the person slain be of people hostile to you, though himself a believer, the offender shall free, or procure the freedom of, a believing slave. If he be of a people between whom

86

and you is a pact, then blood-money payable to his heirs and the freedom of a believing slave shall both be due. Whoso finds not a slave to set free shall fast for two consecutive months. This concession is a mercy from Allah. Allah is All-Knowing, Wise. (93)

Whoso kills a believer deliberately, his reward shall be hell, wherein he shall abide, and Allah will be wroth with him and will cast him away and will prepare for him a great punishment. (94)

O ye who believe, when you go forth in the cause of Allah make due investigation, and say not to him who offers you the greeting of peace: Thou art not a believer. You seek the goods of this life, and Allah has good things in plenty. You too were like this before, but Allah conferred His special favour on you; so do make due investigation. Allah is well aware of what you do. (95)

Those of the believers who remain at home, except those who are disabled, and those who strive in the cause of Allah with their belongings and their persons, are not equal. Allah has exalted in rank those who strive with their belongings and their persons above those who remain at home. To all Allah has promised good. Allah has exalted those who strive above those who remain at ·home with the promise of a great reward, in the shape of degrees of excellence to be bestowed by Him, and forgiveness and mercy. Allah is Most Forgiving, Ever Merciful. (96—97)

When the angels cause those who wrong their souls to die, they will question them: What were you after? They will answer: We were accounted weak in the land. The angels will retort: Was not Allah's earth vast enough for you to emigrate therein? It is these whose abode shall be hell, and an evil destination it is; except such weak

ones from among men, women and children, as are incapable of devising any plan
or of finding any way. In their case Allah
would be inclined towards forgiveness; for
Allah overlooks shortcomings and is Most
Forgiving. (98—100)

إِلَّا الْمُسْتَضْعَفِيْنَ مِنَ الرِّجَالِ وَالنِّسَآءِ وَالْوِلْدَانِ لَا
يَسْتَطِيْعُوْنَ حِيْلَةً وَّلَا يَهْتَدُوْنَ سَبِيْلًا ۞

فَأُولٰٓئِكَ عَسَى اللّٰهُ أَنْ يَّعْفُوَ عَنْهُمْ وَكَانَ اللّٰهُ عَفُوًّا
غَفُوْرًا ۞

Whoso emigrates in the cause of Allah
will find many places of refuge in the
earth and plentiful provision. Whoso goes
forth from his home, emigrating in the
cause of Allah and His Messenger, and
death overtakes him, his reward is due
from Allah. Allah is Most Forgiving, Ever
Merciful. (101)

وَمَنْ يُّهَاجِرْ فِيْ سَبِيْلِ اللّٰهِ يَجِدْ فِى الْأَرْضِ مُرَاغَمًا
كَثِيْرًا وَّسَعَةً وَمَنْ يَّخْرُجْ مِنْ بَيْتِهٖ مُهَاجِرًا إِلَى
اللّٰهِ وَرَسُوْلِهٖ ثُمَّ يُدْرِكْهُ الْمَوْتُ فَقَدْ وَقَعَ أَجْرُهٗ
عَلَى اللّٰهِ وَكَانَ اللّٰهُ غَفُوْرًا رَّحِيْمًا ۞

When you journey in the land, it will
be no sin on you to shorten the Prayer,
if you are afraid that those who disbelieve
may put you to trouble. The disbelievers
are your declared enemies. If in such case
thou art among them and leadest them
in Prayer, let a party of them stand with
thee and let them take their arms. When
they have performed their prostrations,
let them go to your rear to stand guard,
and let another party, who have not yet
prayed come forward and pray with thee,
and let them also take their precautions
for defence and their arms. The disbelievers wish that you be neglectful of your
arms and your baggage that they may
fall upon you suddenly. It shall be no sin
on you, if you are inconvenienced by rain
or you are sick, that you lay aside your
arms; but always take your precautions
for defence. Surely, Allah has prepared an
humiliating chastisement for the disbelievers. When you have finished the
Prayer, remember Allah standing, and
sitting, and lying on your sides. When you
feel secure, observe Prayer in the prescribed form: Prayer is an obligation on
the believers to be observed at its appointed time. (102—104)

وَإِذَا ضَرَبْتُمْ فِى الْأَرْضِ فَلَيْسَ عَلَيْكُمْ جُنَاحٌ أَنْ
تَقْصُرُوْا مِنَ الصَّلٰوةِ ۖ إِنْ خِفْتُمْ أَنْ يَّفْتِنَكُمُ
الَّذِيْنَ كَفَرُوْا ۚ إِنَّ الْكٰفِرِيْنَ كَانُوْا لَكُمْ عَدُوًّا مُّبِيْنًا ۞
وَإِذَا كُنْتَ فِيْهِمْ فَأَقَمْتَ لَهُمُ الصَّلٰوةَ فَلْتَقُمْ طَآئِفَةٌ
مِّنْهُمْ مَّعَكَ وَلْيَأْخُذُوْا أَسْلِحَتَهُمْ ۚ فَإِذَا سَجَدُوْا
فَلْيَكُوْنُوْا مِنْ وَّرَآئِكُمْ ۚ وَلْتَأْتِ طَآئِفَةٌ أُخْرٰى لَمْ
يُصَلُّوْا فَلْيُصَلُّوْا مَعَكَ وَلْيَأْخُذُوْا حِذْرَهُمْ وَأَسْلِحَتَهُمْ ۚ
وَدَّ الَّذِيْنَ كَفَرُوْا لَوْ تَغْفُلُوْنَ عَنْ أَسْلِحَتِكُمْ وَأَمْتِعَتِكُمْ
فَيَمِيْلُوْنَ عَلَيْكُمْ مَّيْلَةً وَّاحِدَةً ۚ وَلَا جُنَاحَ عَلَيْكُمْ
إِنْ كَانَ بِكُمْ أَذًى مِّنْ مَّطَرٍ أَوْ كُنْتُمْ مَّرْضٰى أَنْ تَضَعُوْا
أَسْلِحَتَكُمْ ۚ وَخُذُوْا حِذْرَكُمْ ۗ إِنَّ اللّٰهَ أَعَدَّ لِلْكٰفِرِيْنَ
عَذَابًا مُّهِيْنًا ۞

فَإِذَا قَضَيْتُمُ الصَّلٰوةَ فَاذْكُرُوا اللّٰهَ قِيَامًا وَّقُعُوْدًا وَّعَلٰى
جُنُوْبِكُمْ ۚ فَإِذَا اطْمَأْنَنْتُمْ فَأَقِيْمُوا الصَّلٰوةَ ۚ إِنَّ

Slacken not in seeking the enemy. If you suffer in the process, they too suffer even as you suffer; but you hope for from Allah what they do not. Allah is All-Knowing, Wise. (105)

الصَّلٰوةَ كَانَتْ عَلَى الْمُؤْمِنِيْنَ كِتٰبًا مَّوْقُوْتًا ۝

وَلَا تَهِنُوْا فِي ابْتِغَاءِ الْقَوْمِ ۗ اِنْ تَكُوْنُوْا تَأْلَمُوْنَ

فَاِنَّهُمْ يَأْلَمُوْنَ كَمَا تَأْلَمُوْنَ ۚ وَتَرْجُوْنَ مِنَ اللهِ مَا

لَا يَرْجُوْنَ ۗ وَكَانَ اللهُ عَلِيْمًا حَكِيْمًا ۝

We have sent down to thee this Book comprising the truth, that thou mayest judge between the people by that which Allah has shown thee. Be not thou a contender on behalf of the treacherous ones and ask forgiveness of Allah; surely, Allah is Most Forgiving, Ever Merciful. Plead not on behalf of those who are unfaithful to themselves. Surely Allah loves not those who are perfidious and persistent sinners. They seek to hide from people but cannot hide from Allah. He is with them when they plot at night that which He does not approve of. Allah will bring to naught that which they do. (106—109)

اِنَّا اَنْزَلْنَا اِلَيْكَ الْكِتٰبَ بِالْحَقِّ لِتَحْكُمَ بَيْنَ النَّاسِ

بِمَا اَرٰىكَ اللهُ ۗ وَلَا تَكُنْ لِّلْخَائِنِيْنَ خَصِيْمًا ۝

وَّاسْتَغْفِرِ اللهَ ۗ اِنَّ اللهَ كَانَ غَفُوْرًا رَّحِيْمًا ۝

وَلَا تُجَادِلْ عَنِ الَّذِيْنَ يَخْتَانُوْنَ اَنْفُسَهُمْ ۗ اِنَّ اللهَ

لَا يُحِبُّ مَنْ كَانَ خَوَّانًا اَثِيْمًا ۝

يَّسْتَخْفُوْنَ مِنَ النَّاسِ وَلَا يَسْتَخْفُوْنَ مِنَ اللهِ

وَهُوَ مَعَهُمْ اِذْ يُبَيِّتُوْنَ مَا لَا يَرْضٰى مِنَ الْقَوْلِ ۗ

وَكَانَ اللهُ بِمَا يَعْمَلُوْنَ مُحِيْطًا ۝

هٰاَنْتُمْ هٰؤُلَاءِ جَادَلْتُمْ عَنْهُمْ فِي الْحَيٰوةِ الدُّنْيَا ۖ

Hearken, you are those who have pleaded for them in this life; but who will plead for them with Allah on the Day of Judgment, or who will be their guardian? (110)

فَمَنْ يُّجَادِلُ اللهَ عَنْهُمْ يَوْمَ الْقِيٰمَةِ اَمْ مَّنْ يَّكُوْنُ

عَلَيْهِمْ وَكِيْلًا ۝

وَمَنْ يَّعْمَلْ سُوْءًا اَوْ يَظْلِمْ نَفْسَهُ ثُمَّ يَسْتَغْفِرِ اللهَ

يَجِدِ اللهَ غَفُوْرًا رَّحِيْمًا ۝

Whoso does evil or wrongs his soul, and then asks forgiveness of Allah, will find Allah Most Forgiving, Ever Merciful. Whoso does evil only burdens his own soul. Allah is All-Knowing, Wise. Whoso commits a fault or a sin, then charges an innocent person with it, takes on the burden of a calumny and a manifest sin. (111—113)

وَمَنْ يَّكْسِبْ اِثْمًا فَاِنَّمَا يَكْسِبُهُ عَلٰى نَفْسِهِ ۗ وَكَانَ

اللهُ عَلِيْمًا حَكِيْمًا ۝

وَمَنْ يَّكْسِبْ خَطِيْئَةً اَوْ اِثْمًا ثُمَّ يَرْمِ بِهٖ بَرِيْئًا

فَقَدِ احْتَمَلَ بُهْتَانًا وَّاِثْمًا مُّبِيْنًا ۝

وَلَوْلَا فَضْلُ اللهِ عَلَيْكَ وَرَحْمَتُهُ لَهَمَّتْ طَائِفَةٌ

But for the grace of Allah upon thee and His mercy, a party of them, who had resolved to bring about thy ruin, would have succeeded in their design. They ruin none save themselves and they cannot harm thee. Allah has sent down to thee the Book and Wisdom and has taught thee that which thou knewest not, and great is Allah's grace on thee. (114)

مِّنْهُمْ اَنْ يُّضِلُّوْكَ وَمَا يُضِلُّوْنَ اِلَّا اَنْفُسَهُمْ وَمَا يَضُرُّوْنَكَ مِنْ شَيْءٍ وَاَنْزَلَ اللهُ عَلَيْكَ الْكِتٰبَ وَ الْحِكْمَةَ وَعَلَّمَكَ مَا لَمْ تَكُنْ تَعْلَمُ وَكَانَ فَضْلُ اللهِ عَلَيْكَ عَظِيْمًا ۝

لَا خَيْرَ فِيْ كَثِيْرٍ مِّنْ نَّجْوٰىهُمْ اِلَّا مَنْ اَمَرَ بِصَدَقَةٍ اَوْ مَعْرُوْفٍ اَوْ اِصْلَاحٍۭ بَيْنَ النَّاسِ وَمَنْ يَّفْعَلْ

Most of their conferrings together are devoid of good, except such as enjoin charity, or the promotion of public welfare or of public peace; and on him who strives after these, seeking the pleasure of Allah, shall We soon bestow a great reward. We shall let him who persists in his opposition to the Messenger after guidance has become clear and follows a way other than that of the believers, pursue the bent of his inclination and shall cast him into hell; and an evil destination it is. (115—116)

ذٰلِكَ ابْتِغَآءَ مَرْضَاتِ اللهِ فَسَوْفَ نُؤْتِيْهِ اَجْرًا عَظِيْمًا ۝

وَمَنْ يُّشَاقِقِ الرَّسُوْلَ مِنْ بَعْدِ مَا تَبَيَّنَ لَهُ الْهُدٰى وَيَتَّبِعْ غَيْرَ سَبِيْلِ الْمُؤْمِنِيْنَ نُوَلِّهِ مَا تَوَلّٰى وَنُصْلِهِ جَهَنَّمَ وَسَآءَتْ مَصِيْرًا ۝

اِنَّ اللهَ لَا يَغْفِرُ اَنْ يُّشْرَكَ بِهِ وَيَغْفِرُ مَا دُوْنَ

Allah will not forgive anything being associated with Him as partner, but will forgive anything short of that to whomsoever He pleases. Whoso associates anything with Allah as His partner, has indeed strayed far away. They invoke beside Him none but lifeless objects; and they invoke none but Satan, the rebellious one, whom Allah has cast away. He said to Allah: I will assuredly beguile a fixed portion from Thy servants, and will lead them astray, and will excite in them vain desires, and will incite them to cut off the ears of cattle and to alter Allah's creation. Thus whoso takes Satan for a friend beside Allah has certainly suffered a manifest loss. He makes promises to them and excites vain desires in them.

ذٰلِكَ لِمَنْ يَّشَآءُ وَمَنْ يُّشْرِكْ بِاللهِ فَقَدْ ضَلَّ ضَلٰلًۢا بَعِيْدًا ۝

اِنْ يَّدْعُوْنَ مِنْ دُوْنِهٖ اِلَّا اِنَاثًا وَاِنْ يَّدْعُوْنَ اِلَّا شَيْطٰنًا مَّرِيْدًا ۝ لَّعَنَهُ اللهُ وَقَالَ لَاَتَّخِذَنَّ مِنْ عِبَادِكَ نَصِيْبًا مَّفْرُوْضًا ۝

وَّلَاُضِلَّنَّهُمْ وَلَاُمَنِّيَنَّهُمْ وَلَاٰمُرَنَّهُمْ فَلَيُبَتِّكُنَّ اٰذَانَ الْاَنْعَامِ وَلَاٰمُرَنَّهُمْ فَلَيُغَيِّرُنَّ خَلْقَ اللهِ وَمَنْ يَّتَّخِذِ الشَّيْطٰنَ وَلِيًّا مِّنْ دُوْنِ اللهِ فَقَدْ خَسِرَ خُسْرَانًا مُّبِيْنًا ۝

يَعِدُهُمْ وَيُمَنِّيْهِمْ وَمَا يَعِدُهُمُ الشَّيْطٰنُ اِلَّا

Satan promises them nothing but vain things. These are they whose abode shall be hell and they shall find no way of escape from it. (117—122)

We shall admit those who have believed and have worked righteousness, to Gardens beneath which rivers flow, abiding therein for ever. This is Allah's promise which is bound to be fulfilled, for who can be more truthful than Allah in what He says? It is not your desires, nor the desires of the people of the Book that shall prevail. Whoso does evil shall be requited for it, and he shall not find for himself any friend or helper beside Allah. Whoso does good, whether male or female, and is a believer, shall enter Paradise and they shall not be wronged a whit. (123—125)

Who is better in faith than one who submits himself wholly to Allah acting righteously, and follows the religion of Abraham, the upright? Allah did take Abraham for a special friend. To Allah belongs all that is in the heavens and all that is in the earth; and Allah encompasses all things. (126—127)

They seek directions from thee in the matter of marrying more women than one. Say to them: Allah has given you directions concerning them. The commandment given to you elsewhere in the Book has reference to orphan girls whom you give not what is prescribed for them and yet whom you desire to marry, and to unprotected female children. You have also been commanded to deal equitably with orphans. Whatever good you do, Allah knows it well. (128)

Should a woman apprehend ill-treatment or indifference on the part of her husband, it shall be no sin on them that they be suitably reconciled to each other, for reconciliation is best. People are prone to covetousness. If you are benevolent towards each other and are mindful of your duty to Allah, surely Allah is Well Aware of what you do. (129)

You cannot keep perfect balance emotionally between your wives, however much you may desire it, but incline not wholly towards one, leaving the other in suspense. If you will maintain accord and are mindful of your duty to Allah, surely Allah is Most Forgiving, Ever Merciful. Should they, in such a case, decide to separate, Allah will make both independent out of His abundance; Allah is Bountiful, Wise. (130—131)

To Allah belongs whatever is in the heavens and whatever is in the earth. We assuredly laid a strict commandment on those who were given the Book before you and on you also; Be mindful of your duty to Allah. Now if you reject Our commandment, then remember, to Allah belongs whatever is in the heavens and whatever is in the earth, and Allah is Self-sufficient, Praiseworthy. To Allah belongs whatever is in the heavens and whatever is in the earth, and sufficient is Allah as a Guardian. If He please, He could destroy you, O people, and bring others in your place; Allah has full power to do that. Whoso desires the reward of this world should remember that with Allah is the reward of this world and the next; and Allah is All-Hearing, All-Seeing. (132—135)

O ye who believe, be strict in observing justice and bear witness only for the sake of Allah, even if it be against your own selves or against parents or kindred.

عَلِيمًا ۝

وَإِنِ امْرَأَةٌ خَافَتْ مِنْ بَعْلِهَا نُشُوزًا أَوْ إِعْرَاضًا فَلَا جُنَاحَ عَلَيْهِمَا أَنْ يُصْلِحَا بَيْنَهُمَا صُلْحًا ۚ وَالصُّلْحُ خَيْرٌ ۗ وَأُحْضِرَتِ الْأَنْفُسُ الشُّحَّ ۚ وَإِنْ تُحْسِنُوا وَتَتَّقُوا فَإِنَّ اللّٰهَ كَانَ بِمَا تَعْمَلُوْنَ خَبِيرًا ۝

وَلَنْ تَسْتَطِيعُوٓا أَنْ تَعْدِلُوا بَيْنَ النِّسَآءِ وَلَوْ حَرَصْتُمْ فَلَا تَمِيلُوا كُلَّ الْمَيْلِ فَتَذَرُوهَا كَالْمُعَلَّقَةِ ۚ وَإِنْ تُصْلِحُوا وَتَتَّقُوا فَإِنَّ اللّٰهَ كَانَ غَفُورًا رَّحِيمًا ۝

وَإِنْ يَّتَفَرَّقَا يُغْنِ اللّٰهُ كُلًّا مِّنْ سَعَتِهِ ۚ وَكَانَ اللّٰهُ وَاسِعًا حَكِيمًا ۝

وَلِلّٰهِ مَا فِي السَّمٰوٰتِ وَمَا فِي الْأَرْضِ ۗ وَلَقَدْ وَصَّيْنَا الَّذِيْنَ أُوْتُوا الْكِتٰبَ مِنْ قَبْلِكُمْ وَإِيَّاكُمْ أَنِ اتَّقُوا اللّٰهَ ۚ وَإِنْ تَكْفُرُوْا فَإِنَّ لِلّٰهِ مَا فِي السَّمٰوٰتِ وَمَا فِي الْأَرْضِ ۚ وَكَانَ اللّٰهُ غَنِيًّا حَمِيدًا ۝

وَلِلّٰهِ مَا فِي السَّمٰوٰتِ وَمَا فِي الْأَرْضِ ۚ وَكَفٰى بِاللّٰهِ وَكِيلًا ۝

إِنْ يَّشَأْ يُذْهِبْكُمْ أَيُّهَا النَّاسُ وَيَأْتِ بِآخَرِيْنَ ۚ وَكَانَ اللّٰهُ عَلٰى ذٰلِكَ قَدِيرًا ۝

مَنْ كَانَ يُرِيدُ ثَوَابَ الدُّنْيَا فَعِنْدَ اللّٰهِ ثَوَابُ الدُّنْيَا وَالْآخِرَةِ ۚ وَكَانَ اللّٰهُ سَمِيعًا بَصِيرًا ۝

يٰأَيُّهَا الَّذِيْنَ آمَنُوا كُوْنُوا قَوَّامِيْنَ بِالْقِسْطِ شُهَدَآءَ لِلّٰهِ وَلَوْ عَلٰى أَنْفُسِكُمْ أَوِ الْوَالِدَيْنِ وَالْأَقْرَبِيْنَ ۚ إِنْ

Whether the person be rich or poor, in either case, Allah is more regardful of him than you could be. Therefore, follow not vain desires so that you may act equitably. If you conceal the truth or evade it, then remember that Allah is well aware of that which you do. (136)

O you who believe, have firm faith in Allah and His Messenger, and in the Book which He has revealed to His Messenger, and the Book which He revealed before it. Whoso disbelieves in Allah, and His angels, and His Books, and His Messengers, and the Last Day, has surely strayed far away. Those who believe, then disbelieve, then again believe, then disbelieve and thereafter go on increasing in disbelief, Allah will never forgive them, nor guide them to any way of deliverance. (137—138)

Convey to the hypocrites, those who make friends with disbelievers rather than with believers, the tidings that for them is a grievous chastisement. Do they seek honour in their company? All honour belongs to Allah. (139—140)

He has laid upon you a commandment in the Book that when you hear the Signs of Allah being denied and mocked at, do not continue in that company, until they engage in some other discourse; otherwise you would be like them. Surely, Allah will assemble the hypocrites and the disbelievers in hell, all together. They are those who watch for news of you. If you are granted a victory from Allah, they say to you: Were we not with you? If the disbelievers have a portion of luck, they say to them: Did we not get the better of you on a previous occasion and protect you against the believers? Allah will judge between you on the Day of Judgment, and Allah will never grant the disbelievers a way to prevail against the believers. (141—142)

يَكُنْ غَنِيًّا اَوْ فَقِيْرًا فَاللّٰهُ اَوْلٰى بِهِمَا ۗ فَلَا تَتَّبِعُوا الْهَوٰى اَنْ تَعْدِلُوْا ۚ وَاِنْ تَلْوٗٓا اَوْ تُعْرِضُوْا فَاِنَّ اللّٰهَ كَانَ بِمَا تَعْمَلُوْنَ خَبِيْرًا ۝

يٰٓاَيُّهَا الَّذِيْنَ اٰمَنُوْٓا اٰمِنُوْا بِاللّٰهِ وَرَسُوْلِهٖ وَالْكِتٰبِ الَّذِيْ نَزَّلَ عَلٰى رَسُوْلِهٖ وَالْكِتٰبِ الَّذِيْٓ اَنْزَلَ مِنْ قَبْلُ ۚ وَمَنْ يَّكْفُرْ بِاللّٰهِ وَمَلٰٓئِكَتِهٖ وَكُتُبِهٖ وَرُسُلِهٖ وَالْيَوْمِ الْاٰخِرِ فَقَدْ ضَلَّ ضَلٰلًا بَعِيْدًا ۝

اِنَّ الَّذِيْنَ اٰمَنُوْا ثُمَّ كَفَرُوْا ثُمَّ اٰمَنُوْا ثُمَّ كَفَرُوْا ثُمَّ ازْدَادُوْا كُفْرًا لَّمْ يَكُنِ اللّٰهُ لِيَغْفِرَ لَهُمْ وَلَا لِيَهْدِيَهُمْ سَبِيْلًا ۝

بَشِّرِ الْمُنٰفِقِيْنَ بِاَنَّ لَهُمْ عَذَابًا اَلِيْمًا ۝

اَلَّذِيْنَ يَتَّخِذُوْنَ الْكٰفِرِيْنَ اَوْلِيَآءَ مِنْ دُوْنِ الْمُؤْمِنِيْنَ ۚ اَيَبْتَغُوْنَ عِنْدَهُمُ الْعِزَّةَ فَاِنَّ الْعِزَّةَ لِلّٰهِ جَمِيْعًا ۝

وَقَدْ نَزَّلَ عَلَيْكُمْ فِى الْكِتٰبِ اَنْ اِذَا سَمِعْتُمْ اٰيٰتِ اللّٰهِ يُكْفَرُ بِهَا وَيُسْتَهْزَاُ بِهَا فَلَا تَقْعُدُوْا مَعَهُمْ حَتّٰى يَخُوْضُوْا فِيْ حَدِيْثٍ غَيْرِهٖ ۖ اِنَّكُمْ اِذًا مِّثْلُهُمْ ۗ اِنَّ اللّٰهَ جَامِعُ الْمُنٰفِقِيْنَ وَالْكٰفِرِيْنَ فِيْ جَهَنَّمَ جَمِيْعًا ۝

اَلَّذِيْنَ يَتَرَبَّصُوْنَ بِكُمْ ۚ فَاِنْ كَانَ لَكُمْ فَتْحٌ مِّنَ اللّٰهِ قَالُوْٓا اَلَمْ نَكُنْ مَّعَكُمْ ۖ وَاِنْ كَانَ لِلْكٰفِرِيْنَ نَصِيْبٌ قَالُوْٓا اَلَمْ نَسْتَحْوِذْ عَلَيْكُمْ وَنَمْنَعْكُمْ مِّنَ الْمُؤْمِنِيْنَ ۗ فَاللّٰهُ يَحْكُمُ بَيْنَكُمْ يَوْمَ الْقِيٰمَةِ ۗ وَلَنْ يَّجْعَلَ اللّٰهُ

The hypocrites seek to deceive Allah and He will chastise them for their attempt at deception. When they stand in Prayer they are slack; they join the Prayer only for show, and they remember Allah but little. Wavering from side to side, they belong neither to one side nor to the other. For him whom Allah causes to perish, thou shalt not find a way of deliverance. (143—144)

إِلْكُفِرِينَ عَلَى الْمُؤْمِنِينَ سَبِيلًا ۝

إِنَّ الْمُنْفِقِينَ يُخْدِعُونَ اللهَ وَهُوَخَادِعُهُمْ وَإِذَا

قَامُوَا إِلَى الصَّلٰوةِ قَامُوْا كُسَالٰى يُرَاءُوْنَ النَّاسَ

وَلَا يَذْكُرُوْنَ اللهَ إِلَّا قَلِيْلًا ۝

مُّذَبْذَبِيْنَ بَيْنَ ذٰلِكَ ۚ لَا آ إِلٰى هٰؤُلَاءِ وَلَا آ إِلٰى هٰؤُلَاءِ

وَمَنْ يُّضْلِلِ اللهُ فَلَنْ تَجِدَ لَهُ سَبِيْلًا ۝

O you who believe, make not intimate friends with disbelievers in preference to believers. Do you wish to give Allah a manifest proof against yourselves? The hypocrites shall surely be in the lowest depth of the Fire; and thou shalt not find that they have any helper, except such of them as repent and amend and hold fast to Allah for protection and are sincere in their worship of Allah. These are among the believers; and Allah will soon bestow a great reward upon the believers. Wherefore should Allah punish you, if you will be grateful and believe? Allah is Appreciating, All-Knowing. (145—148)

يٰاَيُّهَا الَّذِيْنَ اٰمَنُوْا لَا تَتَّخِذُوا الْكٰفِرِيْنَ اَوْلِيَآءَ مِنْ

دُوْنِ الْمُؤْمِنِيْنَ ؕ اَتُرِيْدُوْنَ اَنْ تَجْعَلُوْا للهِ عَلَيْكُمْ

سُلْطٰنًا مُّبِيْنًا ۝

إِنَّ الْمُنْفِقِيْنَ فِى الدَّرْكِ الْاَسْفَلِ مِنَ النَّارِ ۚ وَلَنْ

تَجِدَ لَهُمْ نَصِيْرًا ۝

إِلَّا الَّذِيْنَ تَابُوْا وَاَصْلَحُوْا وَاعْتَصَمُوْا بِاللهِ وَاَخْلَصُوْا

دِيْنَهُمْ للهِ فَاُولٰٓئِكَ مَعَ الْمُؤْمِنِيْنَ ؕ وَسَوْفَ يُؤْتِ

اللهُ الْمُؤْمِنِيْنَ اَجْرًا عَظِيْمًا ۝

Allah likes not the public avowal of evil, except on the part of one who is wronged. Allah is All-Hearing, All-Knowing. Whether you make public a good deed or perform it secretly, or pardon a wrong, Allah is surely very Forgiving, and determines the measure of everything. (149—150)

مَا يَفْعَلُ اللهُ بِعَذَابِكُمْ اِنْ شَكَرْتُمْ وَاٰمَنْتُمْ ؕ وَ

كَانَ اللهُ شَاكِرًا عَلِيْمًا ۝

لَا يُحِبُّ اللهُ الْجَهْرَ بِالسُّوْٓءِ مِنَ الْقَوْلِ إِلَّا

مَنْ ظُلِمَ ؕ وَكَانَ اللهُ سَمِيْعًا عَلِيْمًا ۝

اِنْ تُبْدُوْا خَيْرًا اَوْ تُخْفُوْهُ اَوْ تَعْفُوْا عَنْ سُوْٓءٍ

فَاِنَّ اللهَ كَانَ عَفُوًّا قَدِيْرًا ۝

Those who disbelieve in Allah and His Messengers and seek to make a distinction between Allah and His Messengers and say: We believe in some Messengers and disbelieve in others; and desire to adopt

اِنَّ الَّذِيْنَ يَكْفُرُوْنَ بِاللهِ وَرُسُلِهٖ وَيُرِيْدُوْنَ اَنْ

يُّفَرِّقُوْا بَيْنَ اللهِ وَرُسُلِهٖ وَيَقُوْلُوْنَ نُؤْمِنُ بِبَعْضٍ

a position in between, these indeed are disbelievers beyond doubt, and We have prepared for the disbelievers an humiliating chastisement. Those who believe in Allah and in all of His Messengers and make no distinction between any of them, these are they whom He will soon give their rewards. Allah is Most Forgiving, Ever Merciful. (151—153)

The People of the Book demand that thou cause a Book to descend on them from heaven. They had made an even more preposterous demand from Moses. They demanded: Show us Allah visibly. Because of their presumption they were afflicted with a destructive chastisement. Then, after clear Signs had come to them, they took to worshipping the calf, but We pardoned even that and We bestowed manifest authority upon Moses. We raised high above them the Mount whilst making a covenant with them, and We commanded them: Enter the gate submissively; and We also commanded them: Transgress not in the matter of the Sabbath. We took from them a firm covenant. (154—155)

Then, because of their breaking of their covenant; and their rejection of the Signs of Allah; and their seeking to slay the Prophets without cause; and their saying: Our hearts are wrapped up in covers; whereas Allah has sealed them up because of their disbelief, so that they believe but little; and their disbelief; and their uttering against Mary a grievous calumny;

and their saying: We did kill the Messiah, Jesus son of Mary, the Messenger of Allah; whereas they slew him not, nor did they compass his death upon the cross, but he was made to appear to them like one crucified to death; and those who have differed in the matter of his having been taken down alive from the cross are certainly in a state of doubt concerning it, they have no definite knowledge about it, but only follow a conjecture; they certainly did not compass his death in the manner they allege; indeed, Allah exalted him to Himself; Allah is Mighty, Wise, and there is none among the People of the Book but will continue to believe till his death that Jesus died on the cross, and on the Day of Judgment Jesus shall bear witness against them; and their taking interest, though they had been forbidden it; and their devouring people's wealth wrongfully; because of all the transgressions of the Jews, and their hindering many from Allah's way, We barred them from the enjoyment of Our spiritual favours which had been allowed to them, and We have prepared for those of them who disbelieve a painful torment. (156—162)

But those among them who are firmly grounded in knowledge, and the believers, have firm faith in that which has been sent down to thee and that which was sent down before thee. To those who observe Prayer and pay the Zakat and believe sincerely in Allah and the Last Day, will We surely give a great reward. (163)

We have sent revelation to thee, as We sent revelation to Noah and the Prophets after him. We sent revelation to Abraham and Ishmael and Isaac and Jacob and his children and to Jesus and Job and Jonah and Aaron and Solomon, and We gave David a Book. (164)

We sent Messengers whose names We have mentioned to thee and Messengers whose names We have not mentioned to thee, and Allah spoke to Moses at length. We sent these Messengers as bearers of glad tidings and as warners, that people may have no plea against Allah after the coming of the Messengers. Allah is Mighty, Wise. Allah bears witness by means of the revelation that He has sent down to thee that He has sent it down charged with His knowledge; and the angels also bear witness; but Allah is Sufficient as a Witness. (165—167)

Those who disbelieve and hinder others from the way of Allah, have certainly strayed far away. Those who have disbelieved and have acted unjustly, Allah will by no means forgive them, nor will He show them any way, except the way of hell, wherein they shall abide for a prolonged period, and that is easy for Allah. (168—170)

O mankind, the Messenger has indeed come to you with Truth from your Lord; believe, therefore, it will be the better for you. But if you disbelieve, then remember to Allah belongs whatsoever is in the heavens and in the earth. Allah is All-Knowing, Wise. (171)

People of the Book! Exceed not the limits in the matter of your religion, and say not of Allah anything but the truth. Indeed, the Messiah, Jesus son of Mary, was but a Messenger of Allah and the fulfilment of glad tidings which He conveyed to Mary and a mercy from Him. So believe in Allah and His Messengers and say not: There are three gods. Desist, it will be the better for you. Indeed, Allah is the only One God. His Holiness brooks not that He should have a son. To Him belongs whatever is in the heavens and whatever is in the earth. Sufficient is Allah as a Guardian. (172)

97

Surely, the Messiah would never disdain to be accounted a servant of Allah, nor would even those angels who are close to Allah. Those who disdain to worship Him and consider themselves above it, will He gather all together before Himself. He will give those who believed and worked righteousness their rewards in full, and will bestow upon them more out of His bounty. He will punish those who disdained and were proud with a painful punishment, and they shall find, beside Allah, no friend or helper for themselves. (173—174)

O mankind, there has come to you a manifest proof from your Lord, and We have sent down to you a clear Light. Those who believe in Allah and hold fast to Him for protection, will He surely admit to His mercy and grace and guide to a straight path leading to Himself. (175—176)

They ask thee for directions concerning the inheritance of a Kalala. Say to them: Allah gives you His directions concerning the inheritance of such a one. If a man dies leaving no child and he has a consanguine sister, she shall have half of what he leaves; and he shall inherit her if she leaves no child. But if there be two or more sisters, consanguine, or consanguine and uterine, they shall have two thirds of what he leaves. If the heirs be brothers and sisters, the male shall have as much as the portion of two females. Allah explains matters to you lest you go astray, and Allah knows all things well. (177)

سُوْرَةُ الْمَائِدَةِ مَدَنِيَّةٌ ۵

AL-MĀ'IDAH

(Revealed after Hijra)

In the name of Allah, Most Gracious,
Ever Merciful. (1)

O ye who believe, fulfil your compacts.
Made lawful for you are quadrupeds of
the class of cattle, other than those which
may be expressly forbidden, provided
that game is not lawful for you while
you are in the course of Pilgrimage. Allah
decrees what He wills. (2)

O ye who believe, profane not the Signs
of Allah, nor the Sacred Month, nor the
animals brought to the Sanctuary as
offering, nor the animals wearing collars
indicating they are to be sacrified, nor
those repairing to the Sacred House,
seeking grace from their Lord and His
pleasure. When on completion of the
Pilgrimage you put off the pilgrim's garb,
you may hunt. Let not the enmity of a
people in that they hindered you from the
Sacred Mosque, incite you to transgress.
Assist one another in piety and rectitude,
and assist not one another in sin and
transgression; and be mindful of your
duty to Allah; surely, Allah's punishment
is severe. (3)

Forbidden to you is the flesh of a dead
animal, and blood, and the flesh of
swine; and that on which the name of
one other than Allah is invoked; and the
flesh of an animal that has been strangled,
or is beaten to death, or is killed by a
fall, or is gored to death; and of which
a wild animal has eaten, unless you have
slaughtered it properly before its death;
and that which has been slaughtered at
an altar. But whoso is driven by necessity
to eat any of these, without being wilfully
inclined to sin, in such a case, surely,
Allah is Most Forgiving, Ever Merciful.
It is also forbidden that you should seek
to draw lots by means of divining arrows.
That is an act of disobedience. This day

بِسْمِ اللهِ الرَّحْمٰنِ الرَّحِيْمِ ۝

يٰٓاَيُّهَا الَّذِيْنَ اٰمَنُوْٓا اَوْفُوْا بِالْعُقُوْدِ ۗ اُحِلَّتْ لَكُمْ بَهِيْمَةُ الْاَنْعَامِ اِلَّا مَا يُتْلٰى عَلَيْكُمْ غَيْرَ مُحِلِّى الصَّيْدِ وَاَنْتُمْ حُرُمٌ ۗ اِنَّ اللهَ يَحْكُمُ مَا يُرِيْدُ ۝

يٰٓاَيُّهَا الَّذِيْنَ اٰمَنُوْا لَا تُحِلُّوْا شَعَآئِرَ اللهِ وَلَا الشَّهْرَ الْحَرَامَ وَلَا الْهَدْىَ وَلَا الْقَلَآئِدَ وَلَآ اٰمِّيْنَ الْبَيْتَ الْحَرَامَ يَبْتَغُوْنَ فَضْلًا مِّنْ رَّبِّهِمْ وَرِضْوَانًا ۗ وَاِذَا حَلَلْتُمْ فَاصْطَادُوْا ۗ وَلَا يَجْرِمَنَّكُمْ شَنَاٰنُ قَوْمٍ اَنْ صَدُّوْكُمْ عَنِ الْمَسْجِدِ الْحَرَامِ اَنْ تَعْتَدُوْا ۘ وَتَعَاوَنُوْا عَلَى الْبِرِّ وَالتَّقْوٰى ۖ وَلَا تَعَاوَنُوْا عَلَى الْاِثْمِ وَالْعُدْوَانِ ۖ وَاتَّقُوا اللهَ ۗ اِنَّ اللهَ شَدِيْدُ الْعِقَابِ ۝

حُرِّمَتْ عَلَيْكُمُ الْمَيْتَةُ وَالدَّمُ وَلَحْمُ الْخِنْزِيْرِ وَمَآ اُهِلَّ لِغَيْرِ اللهِ بِهِ وَالْمُنْخَنِقَةُ وَالْمَوْقُوْذَةُ وَالْمُتَرَدِّيَةُ وَالنَّطِيْحَةُ وَمَآ اَكَلَ السَّبُعُ اِلَّا مَا ذَكَّيْتُمْ ۗ وَمَا ذُبِحَ عَلَى النُّصُبِ وَاَنْ تَسْتَقْسِمُوْا بِالْاَزْلَامِ ۗ ذٰلِكُمْ فِسْقٌ ۗ اَلْيَوْمَ يَئِسَ الَّذِيْنَ كَفَرُوْا مِنْ دِيْنِكُمْ فَلَا تَخْشَوْهُمْ وَاخْشَوْنِ ۗ اَلْيَوْمَ اَكْمَلْتُ لَكُمْ دِيْنَكُمْ وَاَتْمَمْتُ عَلَيْكُمْ نِعْمَتِى وَرَضِيْتُ لَكُمُ الْاِسْلَامَ دِيْنًا ۗ فَمَنِ اضْطُرَّ فِى مَخْمَصَةٍ غَيْرَ مُتَجَانِفٍ لِّاِثْمٍ ۙ فَاِنَّ اللهَ غَفُوْرٌ رَّحِيْمٌ ۝

99

have those who disbelieve despaired of causing harm to your religion; so fear them not, but fear Me alone. This day have I perfected your religion for your benefit, and have completed My favour unto you, and have chosen for you Islam as your faith. (4)

They ask thee what is declared lawful for them. Tell them: all good things are declared lawful for you; and that which you teach hunting animals to catch for you, training them for the hunt and teaching them of that which Allah has taught you. So eat of that which they catch for you, and pronounce thereon the name of Allah. Be mindful of your duty to Allah; surely, Allah is Swift at reckoning. This day all good things are declared lawful for you; the food of the People of the Book is lawful for you and your food is lawful for them. Lawful for you are chaste believing women and chaste women from among those who were given the Book before you, when you give them their dowers, contracting valid marriages, not committing fornication nor taking secret paramours. Whoever disbelieves, having believed, his work has doubtless come to naught, and in the Hereafter he will be among the losers. (5—6)

O ye who believe, when you make ready for Prayer, wash your faces and your hands up to the elbows, and pass your wet hands over your heads, and wash your feet up to the ankles. Should you have consorted with your spouses, purify yourselves by bathing. Should you be ill or on a journey, or one of you comes from the privy, or you have consorted with your spouses and you find not water, then have recourse to pure dust and having placed your hands on it pass them over your faces and forearms. Allah desires not to put you in a difficulty, but desires to purify you and to complete His favour unto you that you may be grateful. Call to mind Allah's favour upon you and the covenant whereby He bound you, when you said: We have heard and we shall obey. Be mindful of your duty to Allah;

يَسْـَٔلُوْنَكَ مَاذَآ اُحِلَّ لَهُمْ ۚ قُلْ اُحِلَّ لَكُمُ الطَّيِّبٰتُ ۙ وَمَا عَلَّمْتُمْ مِّنَ الْجَوَارِحِ مُكَلِّبِيْنَ تُعَلِّمُوْنَهُنَّ مِمَّا عَلَّمَكُمُ اللّٰهُ فَكُلُوْا مِمَّآ اَمْسَكْنَ عَلَيْكُمْ وَاذْكُرُوا اسْمَ اللّٰهِ عَلَيْهِ ۖ وَاتَّقُوا اللّٰهَ ۗ اِنَّ اللّٰهَ سَرِيْعُ الْحِسَابِ ۞ اَلْيَوْمَ اُحِلَّ لَكُمُ الطَّيِّبٰتُ ۗ وَطَعَامُ الَّذِيْنَ اُوْتُوا الْكِتٰبَ حِلٌّ لَّكُمْ ۖ وَطَعَامُكُمْ حِلٌّ لَّهُمْ ۖ وَالْمُحْصَنٰتُ مِنَ الْمُؤْمِنٰتِ وَالْمُحْصَنٰتُ مِنَ الَّذِيْنَ اُوْتُوا الْكِتٰبَ مِنْ قَبْلِكُمْ اِذَآ اٰتَيْتُمُوْهُنَّ اُجُوْرَهُنَّ مُحْصِنِيْنَ غَيْرَ مُسٰفِحِيْنَ وَلَا مُتَّخِذِيْۤ اَخْدَانٍ ۗ وَمَنْ يَّكْفُرْ بِالْاِيْمَانِ فَقَدْ حَبِطَ عَمَلُهٗ ۖ وَهُوَ فِي الْاٰخِرَةِ مِنَ الْخٰسِرِيْنَ ۞

يٰۤاَيُّهَا الَّذِيْنَ اٰمَنُوْۤا اِذَا قُمْتُمْ اِلَى الصَّلٰوةِ فَاغْسِلُوْا وُجُوْهَكُمْ وَاَيْدِيَكُمْ اِلَى الْمَرَافِقِ وَامْسَحُوْا بِرُءُوْسِكُمْ وَاَرْجُلَكُمْ اِلَى الْكَعْبَيْنِ ۚ وَاِنْ كُنْتُمْ جُنُبًا فَاطَّهَّرُوْا ۗ وَاِنْ كُنْتُمْ مَّرْضٰٓى اَوْ عَلٰى سَفَرٍ اَوْ جَآءَ اَحَدٌ مِّنْكُمْ مِّنَ الْغَآئِطِ اَوْ لٰمَسْتُمُ النِّسَآءَ فَلَمْ تَجِدُوْا مَآءً فَتَيَمَّمُوْا صَعِيْدًا طَيِّبًا فَامْسَحُوْا بِوُجُوْهِكُمْ وَاَيْدِيْكُمْ مِّنْهُ ۗ مَا يُرِيْدُ اللّٰهُ لِيَجْعَلَ عَلَيْكُمْ مِّنْ حَرَجٍ وَّلٰكِنْ يُّرِيْدُ لِيُطَهِّرَكُمْ وَلِيُتِمَّ نِعْمَتَهٗ عَلَيْكُمْ لَعَلَّكُمْ تَشْكُرُوْنَ ۞ وَاذْكُرُوْا نِعْمَةَ اللّٰهِ عَلَيْكُمْ وَمِيْثَاقَهُ الَّذِيْ وَاثَقَكُمْ بِهٖۤ ۙ اِذْ قُلْتُمْ سَمِعْنَا وَاَطَعْنَا ۖ وَاتَّقُوا اللّٰهَ ۗ اِنَّ اللّٰهَ عَلِيْمٌۢ بِذَاتِ الصُّدُوْرِ ۞

surely, Allah knows all that is in your minds. (7—8)

O ye who believe, be steadfast in the cause of Allah, bearing witness in equity. Let not a people's enmity towards you incite you to act contrary to justice; be always just, that is closest to righteousness. Be mindful of your duty to Allah; surely, Allah is aware of all that you do. Allah has promised those who believe and act righteously that they shall have forgiveness and a great reward. Those who disbelieve and reject Our Signs, they are the people of hell. O ye who believe, call to mind Allah's favour upon you when a people designed to stretch forth its hands against you, but He restrained their hands and thus safeguarded you. Be mindful of your duty to Allah; and on Allah should the believers rely. (9—12)

Indeed did Allah take a firm covenant from the children of Israel; and We raised among them twelve leaders. Allah announced: Surely, I am with you. If you observe Prayer, and pay the Zakat, and believe in My Messengers and support them in every way, and place at Allah's disposal a goodly portion of your properties, I will remove from you your ills and will admit you to Gardens beneath which rivers flow. But whoso from among you disbelieves thereafter has indeed strayed away from the right path. So, because of their breaking of their covenant, We cast them away, and have hardened their hearts. They pervert the words of the Book from their proper places and have forgotten a portion of that with which they were exhorted. Thou wilt constantly discover treachery on their part, except on the part of a few of them. So, pardon them and overlook their defaults. Surely, Allah loves the benevolent. From those who say: We are Christians; We also took

101

a covenant, but they too have forgotten a portion of that with which they were exhorted. So, We have put enmity and hatred between them till the day of Judgment; and soon will Allah let them know what they have been doing. (13—15)

People of the Book, there has come to you Our Messenger who unfolds to you much of that which you used to hide of the Book, and passes over much. There has come to you indeed from Allah a Light and a clear Book. Thereby does Allah guide those who seek His pleasure along the paths of peace, and leads them out of every kind of darkness into the light by His will, and guides them to the right path. (16—17)

They are indeed disbelievers who say: Allah is the Messiah son of Mary. Say to them: Who can have any power against Allah, if He should desire to bring to naught the Messiah son of Mary, and his mother and all those that are in the earth? To Allah belongs the kingdom of the heavens and the earth and of all that which is between them. He creates what He pleases. Allah has full power over all things. The Jews and the Christians say: We are the sons of Allah and His loved ones. Ask them: Why then does He punish you for your sins? Indeed, you are but human beings among those He has created. He forgives whom He pleases and punishes whom He pleases. To Allah belongs the kingdom of the heavens and the earth and of all that which is between them, and to Him shall be the return. (18—19)

People of the Book, there has come to you Our Messenger who makes things clear to you after a break in the succession of Prophets, lest you should say: There has come to us no bearer of glad tidings and no warner. Now there has come to you a bearer of glad tidings and a warner. Allah has full power over all things. (20)

Call to mind when Moses said to his people: O my people, recall the favour that Allah bestowed upon you when He appointed Prophets among you and made you Kings, and gave you that which He had not given to any other of the peoples. O my people, enter the Holy Land which Allah has ordained for you, and do not turn back, for in that case you will turn back losers. They said: Moses, there is in that land a powerful people, and we shall certainly not enter it until they go forth from it. When they go forth from it, we shall enter forthwith. Thereupon two men from among those who feared Allah, on whom Allah had bestowed His favour, said: Mount an assault upon the gate; once you have entered it, you will surely be victorious. Put your trust in Allah, if you are believers. They protested: Moses, we most certainly will not enter it so long as they remain in it. Therefore, go thou and thy Lord and fight them. Here we sit. Moses supplicated: Lord, I have power over none but myself and my brother; therefore, make Thou a distinction between us and this rebellious people. Allah said: The land shall be forbidden them for forty years; in distraction shall they wander through the countryside. Grieve not, therefore, over the rebellious people. (21—27)

Relate to them, O Prophet, the true story of the two sons of Adam, when each of them made an offering, and it was accepted from one of them and was not accepted from the other. The latter said to the former: I will surely kill thee. He replied: Allah accepts only from the righteous. If thou stretchest forth thy hand against me to kill me, I will not, in my defence, use such force as to kill thee.

وَاِذْ قَالَ مُوسٰی لِقَوْمِهٖ یٰقَوْمِ اذْکُرُوْا نِعْمَۃَ اللّٰهِ
عَلَیْکُمْ اِذْ جَعَلَ فِیْکُمْ اَنْبِیَآءَ وَ جَعَلَکُمْ مُّلُوْکًا ٭
وَّ اٰتٰکُمْ مَّا لَمْ یُؤْتِ اَحَدًا مِّنَ الْعٰلَمِیْنَ ۞

یٰقَوْمِ ادْخُلُوا الْاَرْضَ الْمُقَدَّسَۃَ الَّتِیْ کَتَبَ اللّٰهُ لَکُمْ
وَلَا تَرْتَدُّوْا عَلٰۤی اَدْبَارِکُمْ فَتَنْقَلِبُوْا خٰسِرِیْنَ ۞

قَالُوْا یٰمُوْسٰۤی اِنَّ فِیْهَا قَوْمًا جَبَّارِیْنَ ۙ۬ وَاِنَّا لَنْ
نَّدْخُلَهَا حَتّٰی یَخْرُجُوْا مِنْهَا ۚ فَاِنْ یَّخْرُجُوْا مِنْهَا
فَاِنَّا دٰخِلُوْنَ ۞

قَالَ رَجُلٰنِ مِنَ الَّذِیْنَ یَخَافُوْنَ اَنْعَمَ اللّٰهُ عَلَیْهِمَا
ادْخُلُوْا عَلَیْهِمُ الْبَابَ ۚ فَاِذَا دَخَلْتُمُوْهُ فَاِنَّکُمْ غٰلِبُوْنَ ۚ۬
وَعَلَی اللّٰهِ فَتَوَکَّلُوْۤا اِنْ کُنْتُمْ مُّؤْمِنِیْنَ ۞

قَالُوْا یٰمُوْسٰۤی اِنَّا لَنْ نَّدْخُلَهَاۤ اَبَدًا مَّا دَامُوْا فِیْهَا
فَاذْهَبْ اَنْتَ وَرَبُّکَ فَقَاتِلَاۤ اِنَّا هٰهُنَا قٰعِدُوْنَ ۞

قَالَ رَبِّ اِنِّیْ لَاۤ اَمْلِکُ اِلَّا نَفْسِیْ وَاَخِیْ فَافْرُقْ بَیْنَنَا
وَبَیْنَ الْقَوْمِ الْفٰسِقِیْنَ ۞

قَالَ فَاِنَّهَا مُحَرَّمَۃٌ عَلَیْهِمْ اَرْبَعِیْنَ سَنَۃً ۚ یَتِیْهُوْنَ
فِی الْاَرْضِ ۟ فَلَا تَاْسَ عَلَی الْقَوْمِ الْفٰسِقِیْنَ ۞

وَاتْلُ عَلَیْهِمْ نَبَاَ ابْنَیْ اٰدَمَ بِالْحَقِّ ۘ اِذْ قَرَّبَا قُرْبَانًا
فَتُقُبِّلَ مِنْ اَحَدِهِمَا وَلَمْ یُتَقَبَّلْ مِنَ الْاٰخَرِ ۚ قَالَ
لَاَقْتُلَنَّکَ ۚ قَالَ اِنَّمَا یَتَقَبَّلُ اللّٰهُ مِنَ الْمُتَّقِیْنَ ۞

لَئِنْۢ بَسَطْتَّ اِلَیَّ یَدَکَ لِتَقْتُلَنِیْ مَاۤ اَنَا بِبَاسِطٍ یَّدِیَ
اِلَیْکَ لِاَقْتُلَکَ ۚ اِنِّیْۤ اَخَافُ اللّٰهَ رَبَّ الْعٰلَمِیْنَ ۞

103

I do fear Allah, the Lord of the universe. I shall restrain myself as I desire that the responsibility for my sin and thy own sin should rest on thee, with the result that thou wilt be among the inmates of the Fire, and that is the reward of the wrong-doers. The mind of the brother who was chagrined became reconciled to the killing of his brother, and so he killed him and thus became one of the losers. Then Allah sent a raven which scratched the earth that He might show him how to hide the corpse of his brother. Seeing this he exclaimed: Woe is me. Have I fallen so far that I am not able to be even like this raven so that I may hide the corpse of my brother? On this he became penitent. (28—32)

On account of this we prescribed for the children of Israel that whoso kills a person, except for killing another or for creating disorder in the land, it shall be as if he had killed all mankind; and whoso helps one to live, it shall be as if he had given life to all mankind. Our Messengers came to them with clear Signs, yet many of them continue to commit excesses in the land. (33)

The appropriate penalty for those who wage war against Allah and His Messenger and run about in the land creating disorder is that they be slain or crucified or their hands and their feet be cut off on alternate sides, or they be expelled from the land. That would be a disgrace for them in this world, and in the Hereafter they shall have a great punishment; except in the case of those who repent before you obtain power over them. Take note that Allah is Most Forgiving, Ever Merciful. (34—35)

O ye who believe, be mindful of your duty to Allah and seek out ways of approach unto Him and strive in His way that you may prosper. (36)

104

If those who disbelieve had all that is in the earth and as much over again, to ransom themselves therewith from the punishment of the Day of Judgment, it would not be accepted from them. They shall have a painful punishment. They will wish to come out of the Fire, but they will not be able to come out of it by any effort of their own. They shall have a lasting punishment. (37—38)

Cut off the hands of the man who steals and of the woman who steals in retribution of their offence as an exemplary punishment from Allah. Allah is Mighty, Wise. But Allah will surely turn in mercy to him who repents after his transgression and amends. Surely, Allah is Most Forgiving, Ever Merciful. Knowest thou not that Allah is He to whom belongs the Kingdom of the heavens and the earth? He punishes whom He pleases and forgives whom He pleases. Allah has full power to do all that He wills. (39—41)

O Messenger, grieve not on account of those who rush into disbelief from among those who say with their tongues: We believe; but their hearts believe not. From among the Jews also there are those who listen eagerly to any lie. They listen to them for conveying them to another people who have not come to thee. They pervert the words of the Quran after their being put in their right places. They say: If you are commanded thus and thus, then accept it, but if you are not commanded thus and thus, then beware. Him whom Allah desires to try, thou shalt not avail aught against Allah. These are they whose hearts Allah has not desired to purify. For them is humiliation in this world, and in the Hereafter they shall have a severe punishment. They listen eagerly to falsehood, and

اِنَّ الَّذِيۡنَ كَفَرُوۡا لَوۡ اَنَّ لَهُمۡ مَّا فِى الۡاَرۡضِ جَمِيۡعًا وَّمِثۡلَهٗ مَعَهٗ لِيَفۡتَدُوۡا بِهٖ مِنۡ عَذَابِ يَوۡمِ الۡقِيٰمَةِ مَا تُقُبِّلَ مِنۡهُمۡ ۚ وَلَهُمۡ عَذَابٌ اَلِيۡمٌ ۝

يُرِيۡدُوۡنَ اَنۡ يَّخۡرُجُوۡا مِنَ النَّارِ وَمَا هُمۡ بِخٰرِجِيۡنَ مِنۡهَا ۚ وَلَهُمۡ عَذَابٌ مُّقِيۡمٌ ۝

وَالسَّارِقُ وَالسَّارِقَةُ فَاقۡطَعُوۡۤا اَيۡدِيَهُمَا جَزَآءً بِمَا كَسَبَا نَكَالًا مِّنَ اللّٰهِ ۚ وَاللّٰهُ عَزِيۡزٌ حَكِيۡمٌ ۝

فَمَنۡ تَابَ مِنۡۢ بَعۡدِ ظُلۡمِهٖ وَاَصۡلَحَ فَاِنَّ اللّٰهَ يَتُوۡبُ عَلَيۡهِ ؕ اِنَّ اللّٰهَ غَفُوۡرٌ رَّحِيۡمٌ ۝

اَلَمۡ تَعۡلَمۡ اَنَّ اللّٰهَ لَهٗ مُلۡكُ السَّمٰوٰتِ وَالۡاَرۡضِ ؕ يُعَذِّبُ مَنۡ يَّشَآءُ وَيَغۡفِرُ لِمَنۡ يَّشَآءُ ؕ وَاللّٰهُ عَلٰى كُلِّ شَىۡءٍ قَدِيۡرٌ ۝

يٰۤاَيُّهَا الرَّسُوۡلُ لَا يَحۡزُنۡكَ الَّذِيۡنَ يُسَارِعُوۡنَ فِى الۡكُفۡرِ مِنَ الَّذِيۡنَ قَالُوۡۤا اٰمَنَّا بِاَفۡوَاهِهِمۡ وَلَمۡ تُؤۡمِنۡ قُلُوۡبُهُمۡ ۛۚ وَمِنَ الَّذِيۡنَ هَادُوۡا ۛۚ سَمّٰعُوۡنَ لِلۡكَذِبِ سَمّٰعُوۡنَ لِقَوۡمٍ اٰخَرِيۡنَ ۙ لَمۡ يَأۡتُوۡكَ ؕ يُحَرِّفُوۡنَ الۡكَلِمَ مِنۡۢ بَعۡدِ مَوَاضِعِهٖ ۚ يَقُوۡلُوۡنَ اِنۡ اُوۡتِيۡتُمۡ هٰذَا فَخُذُوۡهُ وَاِنۡ لَّمۡ تُؤۡتَوۡهُ فَاحۡذَرُوۡا ؕ وَمَنۡ يُّرِدِ اللّٰهُ فِتۡنَتَهٗ فَلَنۡ تَمۡلِكَ لَهٗ مِنَ اللّٰهِ شَيۡـًٔا ؕ اُولٰٓئِكَ الَّذِيۡنَ لَمۡ يُرِدِ اللّٰهُ اَنۡ يُّطَهِّرَ قُلُوۡبَهُمۡ ؕ لَهُمۡ فِى الدُّنۡيَا خِزۡيٌ ۖ وَّلَهُمۡ فِى الۡاٰخِرَةِ عَذَابٌ عَظِيۡمٌ ۝

سَمّٰعُوۡنَ لِلۡكَذِبِ اَكّٰلُوۡنَ لِلسُّحۡتِ ؕ فَاِنۡ جَآءُوۡكَ

devour forbidden things voraciously. Should they come to thee seeking judgment in a dispute, then judge between them or keep away from them. If thou keepest away from them, they cannot harm thee at all. But shouldst thou decide to judge, then judge between them with justice. Surely, Allah loves the just. How will they make thee their judge, when they have the Torah which contains Allah's commandments? Yet, in spite of that they turn their backs; and they certainly do not believe. (42—44)

Surely, We sent down the Torah full of guidance and light. By it did the Prophets, who were obedient to Us, judge for the Jews and so did the divines and the jurists, for they were required to safeguard the Book of Allah, and because they were guardians over it. Therefore, fear not people but fear only Me; and barter not My Signs for a paltry price. Whoso judges not by that which Allah has sent down, these it is who are the disbelievers. In the Torah We had prescribed for them: A life for a life and an eye for an eye, and a nose for a nose, and an ear for an ear, and a tooth for a tooth, and equitable retaliation for other injuries. Whoso waives his right thereto, it shall be an expiation for his sins, and whoso judges not by that which Allah has sent down, these it is who are the wrongdoers. (45—46)

We caused Jesus son of Mary to follow in their footsteps, fulfilling that which was revealed before him in the Torah. We gave him the Gospel which contained guidance and light, fulfilling that which was revealed before it in the Torah, and a guidance and an admonition for the righteous. Let the People of the Gospel judge according to that which Allah has revealed therein, and whoso judges not by that which Allah has revealed, these it is who are the rebellious. (47—48)

فَاحْكُمْ بَيْنَهُمْ اَوْ اَعْرِضْ عَنْهُمْ ۚ وَاِنْ تُعْرِضْ عَنْهُمْ فَلَنْ يَّضُرُّوْكَ شَيْئًا ۚ وَاِنْ حَكَمْتَ فَاحْكُمْ بَيْنَهُمْ بِالْقِسْطِ ۚ اِنَّ اللّٰهَ يُحِبُّ الْمُقْسِطِيْنَ ۝

وَكَيْفَ يُحَكِّمُوْنَكَ وَعِنْدَهُمُ التَّوْرٰىةُ فِيْهَا حُكْمُ اللّٰهِ ثُمَّ يَتَوَلَّوْنَ مِنْ بَعْدِ ذٰلِكَ ۚ وَمَآ اُولٰٓئِكَ بِالْمُؤْمِنِيْنَ ۝

اِنَّآ اَنْزَلْنَا التَّوْرٰىةَ فِيْهَا هُدًى وَّنُوْرٌ ۚ يَحْكُمُ بِهَا النَّبِيُّوْنَ الَّذِيْنَ اَسْلَمُوْا لِلَّذِيْنَ هَادُوْا وَالرَّبّٰنِيُّوْنَ وَالْاَحْبَارُ بِمَا اسْتُحْفِظُوْا مِنْ كِتٰبِ اللّٰهِ وَكَانُوْا عَلَيْهِ شُهَدَآءَ ۚ فَلَا تَخْشَوُا النَّاسَ وَاخْشَوْنِ وَلَا تَشْتَرُوْا بِاٰيٰتِيْ ثَمَنًا قَلِيْلًا ۚ وَمَنْ لَّمْ يَحْكُمْ بِمَآ اَنْزَلَ اللّٰهُ فَاُولٰٓئِكَ هُمُ الْكٰفِرُوْنَ ۝

وَكَتَبْنَا عَلَيْهِمْ فِيْهَآ اَنَّ النَّفْسَ بِالنَّفْسِ وَالْعَيْنَ بِالْعَيْنِ وَالْاَنْفَ بِالْاَنْفِ وَالْاُذُنَ بِالْاُذُنِ وَالسِّنَّ بِالسِّنِّ وَالْجُرُوْحَ قِصَاصٌ ۚ فَمَنْ تَصَدَّقَ بِهٖ فَهُوَ كَفَّارَةٌ لَّهٗ ۚ وَمَنْ لَّمْ يَحْكُمْ بِمَآ اَنْزَلَ اللّٰهُ فَاُولٰٓئِكَ هُمُ الظّٰلِمُوْنَ ۝

وَقَفَّيْنَا عَلٰٓى اٰثَارِهِمْ بِعِيْسَى ابْنِ مَرْيَمَ مُصَدِّقًا لِّمَا بَيْنَ يَدَيْهِ مِنَ التَّوْرٰىةِ ۚ وَاٰتَيْنٰهُ الْاِنْجِيْلَ فِيْهِ هُدًى وَّنُوْرٌ ۙ وَّمُصَدِّقًا لِّمَا بَيْنَ يَدَيْهِ مِنَ التَّوْرٰىةِ وَهُدًى وَّمَوْعِظَةً لِّلْمُتَّقِيْنَ ۝

وَلْيَحْكُمْ اَهْلُ الْاِنْجِيْلِ بِمَآ اَنْزَلَ اللّٰهُ فِيْهِ ۚ وَمَنْ لَّمْ

Now We have revealed unto thee this Book comprising the truth, fulfilling that which was revealed before it of the Book, and as a guardian over it. Judge, therefore, between them by that which Allah has revealed, and follow not their vain desires in preference to the truth which has come to thee. For each of you We have prepared, according to the capacity of each, a path or a highway, to enable you to approach the fountain of revealed guidance. Had Allah so willed, He would have made you all one people, but He wishes to try you by that which He has given you. Then try to outstrip each other in the pursuit of good. To Allah shall you all return; then will He enlighten you in respect of all that wherein you differed. Judge between them by that which Allah has sent down, and follow not their vain desires, and be on thy guard against them lest they should involve thee in trouble and lead thee away from part of that which Allah has revealed to thee. If they should turn away, then know that Allah intends to punish them for some of their sins. Indeed a large number of the people are disobedient. Do they seek judgment in accordance with the standards of the days before revelation? Who is better than Allah as a Judge for a people who have firm faith? (49—51)

O ye who believe, take not the Jews and the Christians as your helpers, for they are helpers of one another. Whoso from among you takes them as helpers will indeed be one of them. Verily, Allah guides not the unjust people. Thou wilt see those whose minds are diseased hastening towards them, saying to themselves in justification: We fear lest a misfortune befall us. Maybe, Allah will soon bring about your victory or some other event from Himself favourable to you. Then will they become remorseful of that which they keep hidden in their minds. Those who believe will say concerning them: Are these they who swore the most solemn oaths by Allah that they are entirely with you? Their works are vain and they have

107

become the losers. (52—54)

O ye who believe, whoso from among you turns back from his religion let him remember that in his stead Allah will soon bring a people whom He will love and who will love Him, who will be kind and considerate towards the believers and firm and unyielding towards the disbelievers. They will strive hard in the cause of Allah and will not at all take to heart the reproaches of fault finders. That is Allah's grace; He bestows it upon whosoever He pleases. Allah is the Lord of vast bounty, All-Knowing. (55)

Your helpers are only Allah and His Messenger and the believers who observe Prayer and pay the Zakat and who worship none save Allah alone. Those who take Allah and His Messenger and the believers as their helpers should have firm faith that it is the party of Allah that must triumph. (56—57)

O ye who believe, take not as helpers those who make a jest and sport of your religion from among those who were given the Book before you and the other disbelievers. Be mindful of your duty to Allah, if you are believers. When you call people to Prayer, they take it as jest and sport, because they are a people who lack understanding. (58—59)

Say to them: People of the Book, you persecute us for the only fault that we believe in Allah and in that which has been sent down to us and in that which was sent down before it, and you do that because most of you are disobedient to Allah. Say to them: Shall I apprise you of those whose recompense from Allah is worse than that of those whom you despise? They are those whom Allah has cast aside and on whom His wrath has fallen and of whom He has made some as apes and swine who worship the Evil One. These are in the worst plight and farthest astray from the right path. (60—61)

108

When they come to you they say: We believe; but they come in disbelieving and go out disbelieving and Allah knows best that which they seek to hide. Thou seest many of them hastening towards sin and transgression and running eagerly after that which is forbidden. Evil indeed is that which they practise. Why do not the divines and those learned in the Law restrain them from uttering falsehood and devouring that which is forbidden? Evil indeed is that which they do. (62—64)

The Jews say: Allah's hand is chained up. Their own hands will be chained up and they will be cast aside by Allah because of what they say. His hands are wide open; He spends as He pleases. That which has been sent down to thee from Thy Lord will most surely cause many of them to grow firmer in rebellion and disbelief. We have cast enmity and hatred between them till the Day of Judgment. Whenever they kindle a fire to start a war, Allah puts it out. They strive to create disorder in the land and Allah loves not those who create disorder. (65)

If the People of the Book had believed and been mindful of their duty to Allah, We would surely have removed from them their ills and We would surely have admitted them into Gardens of Bliss. Had they carried out the commandments of the Torah and the Gospel and of that which has now been sent down to them from their Lord, they would surely have partaken of spiritual as well as of material bounties. Of them there is a section which is moderate, but evil indeed is that which most of them do. (66—67)

O Messenger, proclaim widely that which has been sent down to thee from thy Lord; for if thou do it not, thou wilt not have conveyed His Message at all. Allah will safeguard thee against harm by people. Allah guides not the disbelieving people. (68)

Say to the People of the Book: You have nothing to stand on until you carry out the commandments of the Torah and the Gospel and of that which has now been sent down to you from your Lord. That which has been sent down to thee from thy Lord will most surely cause many of them to grow firmer in rebellion and disbelief; so grieve not over such disbelieving people. Surely of those who have believed, and the Jews and the Sabians and the Christians whoso truly believes in Allah and the Last Day and acts righteously, shall have no fear, nor shall they grieve. (69—70)

We took a firm covenant from the children of Israel, and We sent many Messengers to them. Every time there came to them a Messenger with that which their hearts desired not, they treated him as a liar or they sought to slay him. They reckoned their conduct would entail no harm, so they became blind and deaf. But Allah turned to them in mercy; yet again many of them became blind and deaf. Allah watches what they do. (71—72)

Those certainly are disbelievers who say: Allah is none but the Messiah son of Mary; whereas the Messiah himself taught: Children of Israel, worship Allah Who is my Lord and your Lord. Surely, Allah has forbidden Heaven to him who associates partners with Allah, and the Fire will be his resort. The wrongdoers shall have no helpers. Those certainly are disbelievers who say: Allah is the third of three. There is no one worthy of worship but the One God. If they desist not from that which they say, a grievous chastisement shall surely afflict those of them that disbelieve. Will they not then turn to Allah and beg His forgiveness, seeing that Allah is Most Forgiving, Ever Merciful? (73—75)

The Messiah son of Mary was only a Messenger; many Messengers have passed away before him. His mother was a paragon of truth and they both were in need of and ate food. Observe how We explain the Signs for their benefit, then observe how they are led away. Ask them: Do you worship beside Allah that which has no power to do you harm or good? It is Allah Who is All-Hearing, All-Knowing. Admonish them: People of the Book, exceed not the limits in the matter of your religion unjustly, nor follow the vain desires of a people who themselves went astray before and caused many others to go astray, and who strayed away from the right path. (76—78)

Those of the children of Israel who disbelieved were cursed by David, and by Jesus son of Mary. That was because they disobeyed and were given to transgression. They did not try to restrain one another from the iniquity which they committed. Evil indeed was that which they used to do. Thou shalt see many of them taking the disbelievers as their helpers. Evil indeed is that which they have chosen to send on ahead for themselves, which is that Allah is displeased with them and in this torment shall they abide. Had they believed in Allah and this Prophet, and in that which has been sent down to him, they would not have taken the disbelievers as their helpers, but most of them are disobedient. (79—82)

Thou shalt certainly find the bitterest of people in enmity against the believers to be the Jews and the pagans, and thou shalt assuredly find the closest of them in friendship towards the believers to be those who say: We are Christians. That is because some of them are savants and monks and because they are not arrogant. (83)

111

When they hear that which has been sent down to this Messenger, thou seest their eyes overflow with tears, because of that which they have recognised of the Truth. They affirm: Our Lord, we have believed, so write us down among the witnesses. Wherefore should we not believe in Allah and in the truth which has come to us, when we earnestly desire that our Lord should include us among the righteous people? So Allah will reward them, because of that which they affirmed, with Gardens beneath which rivers flow; therein shall they abide. That is the recompense of those who do good. Those who have disbelieved and rejected Our Signs, these are the inmates of hell. (84—87)

O ye who believe, declare not as unlawful the wholesome things Allah has made lawful for you and transgress not the prescribed limits. Allah loves not those who transgress. Eat freely of that which Allah has provided for you of lawful and wholesome things, and be mindful of your duty to Allah in Whom you believe. (88—89)

Allah will not call you to account for your meaningless oaths but will call you to account for breaking your oaths by which you bind yourselves; the expiation of such breach is the feeding of ten poor persons with such average food as you eat yourselves, or providing clothing for them, or procuring the freedom of one held in bondage. Whoso lacks the means shall fast for three days. That is the expiation of your breaking the oaths that you have sworn. Do observe your oaths. Thus does Allah expound to you His commandments that you may be grateful. (90)

O ye who believe, liquor, gambling, idols and divining arrows are but abominations and Satanic devices. So turn wholly away from each one of them that you may prosper. Satan desires only to create enmity and hatred between you by means of liquor and gambling and to keep you back from the remembrance of Allah and from Prayer. Will you, then, desist? Obey

112

Allah and obey the Messenger and be ever on your guard; but if you turn away then remember that the duty of Our Messenger is only to convey Our Message clearly. (91—93)

There shall be no sin on those who believe and act righteously, in respect of that which they eat of things lawful and wholesome if they are mindful of their duty to Allah and hold firmly to the faith and act in conformity thereto, and keep marching forward in righeousness and in firmness of faith, and then go forward in righteousness and perform their duty to the uttermost. Allah loves those who perform their duty to the uttermost. (94)

O ye who believe, Allah will surely try you in respect of a small matter, namely, the game within the reach of your hands and your lances, so that Allah may make known those who fear Him in secret. Whoso, therefore, will transgress thereafter shall suffer a grievous punishment. O ye who believe, kill not game while you are in the course of Pilgrimage. Whoso of you kills it intentionally, the penalty is a quadruped like unto that which he has killed as determined by two of your just men, which must reach the Ka'ba as an offering. If the offender should not find this within his means, the expiation shall be the feeding of a certain number of poor persons, or fasting during a corresponding number of days, so that he should realise the gravity of his offence. Allah forgives that which is past; but whoso reverts to it, Allah will punish him for his offence. Allah is Mighty, Lord of retribution. The game of the sea and eating thereof are made lawful for you as a provision for you and for travellers; but forbidden to you is game of the land as long as you are in the course of Pilgrimage. Be mindful of your duty to Allah to Whom you will be gathered. (95—97)

Allah has made the Ka'ba, the inviolable House, a permanent means of support and uplift for mankind, as also the Sacred month, the offerings and the animals with collars designed for sacrifice. That is so that you may know that Allah has knowledge of whatever is in the heavens and whatever is in the earth and that Allah knows all things well. Remember that Allah is Severe in punishment and that Allah is also Most Forgiving, Ever Merciful. (98—99)

The Messenger's duty is only to convey the Message; and Allah knows your overt actions, as well as your secret designs. Tell them: That which is useless and that which is useful are not alike even though the abundance of that which is useless may appear pleasing to you. So be mindful of your duty to Allah, O ye who possess understanding, that you may prosper. (100—101)

O ye who believe, do not enquire about things which, if they were disclosed to you, would become burdensome for you; though if you enquire about them while the Quran is being sent down, they will be disclosed to you. Allah has left them out on purpose. Allah is Most Forgiving, Forbearing. A people before you enquired about such things, but when they were disclosed to them they refused to carry them out. (102—103)

Allah has ordained no sanctity about animals described as Bahira, or Saiba, or Wasila or Hami; but those who disbelieve fabricate lies against Allah and most of them have no understanding. When it is said to them: Come to that which Allah has sent down, and to the Messenger; they retort: Sufficient for us is that wherein we found our fathers. Would they persist in their attitude even if their fathers knew nothing and had no notion of guidance? O ye who believe, be heedful of your own selves. If you make sure of being rightly guided yourselves, the going astray of another will not harm you. To Allah will you all return; then will He disclose to you that which you used to do. (104—106)

114

O ye who believe, the best way of providing proof, at the time of making a will, when one of you is approaching his end, is that the witnesses should be two just men from among you, but if you should be on a journey when the calamity of death overtakes you and witnesses from among you should not be available, then two just men who are not from among you. You shall detain the two of them after Prayer, and should you doubt their testimony, they shall both swear by Allah and affirm: We shall have no personal interest to serve by our testimony, even if the person affected be a near relation, and we shall not conceal the testimony enjoined by Allah; surely, in that case we shall be guilty of sin. If it be discovered thereafter that the two are guilty of such sin, then two others shall take their place from among those against whom the two had sinfully deposed, and these two shall swear by Allah: Our testimony is truer than the testimony of the first two, and we have not been guilty of any misstatement; for then indeed we would be transgressors. It is more likely that in this way, the first witnesses will adhere to the facts in giving their evidence, being afraid that if they departed therefrom other sworn testimony may be offered to contradict their sworn testimony. Be mindful of your duty to Allah and carry out His commandments fully. Allah guides not the disobedient people. (107—109)

Keep in mind the day when Allah will assemble the Messengers and will ask them: What reply did the people make to you? and they will answer: We have no real knowledge of it, it is only Thou who possessest full knowledge of all that is hidden. Allah will also say to Jesus son of Mary: Call to mind My favour upon thee and thy mother, when I strengthened thee with the Spirit of holiness, so that thou didst talk to people of things divine in thy early and late years; and when I taught thee the Book and Wisdom and the Torah and the Gospel; and when thou didst create from among common men, by My Command, in the manner of a bird, a new creation, into which thou didst breathe a new spirit and it became a soaring being, by My command; and when thou didst declare clean the blind and the leprous by My command; and when thou didst raise the spiritually dead by My command; and when I held back from thee the children of Israel who had designed to put thee to death, when thou didst come to them with clear Signs and those who disbelieved from among them said: This is nothing but clear deception; and when I inspired the disciples: Believe ye, in Me and in My Messenger; and they responded: We believe, and bear Thou witness that we have submitted wholly. (110—112)

Call to mind also when the disciples asked Jesus son of Mary: Has thy Lord power to send down to us from heaven a table spread with food? He rebuked them: Be mindful of Allah's Majesty, if you are true believers. But they persisted: We desire to partake of it that our hearts may be satisfied that our Lord is All-Powerful, and we may realise that thou hast told us the truth, and that we may become witnesses thereof. Thereupon Jesus son of Mary prayed: Allah, our Lord, do Thou send down to us from heaven a table spread with food, that it may be a festival for the first of us and for the last of us, and a Sign from Thee; and do provide for us from Thyself for Thou art the Best Provider. Said Allah: I will certainly send it down to you but whosoever of you is ungrateful thereafter, such as him I will surely punish with torment wherewith I will not punish any other of the peoples. (113—116)

Keep in mind, when Allah will ask Jesus son of Mary: Didst thou say to the people: Take me and my mother for two gods besides Allah? and he will answer: Holy art Thou. It behoves me not to have said that to which I have no right. Had I said it, Thou wouldst surely have known it. Thou knowest what is in my mind, and I know not what is in Thy mind. It is only Thou Who possessest full knowledge of all that is hidden. I said naught to them except that which Thou didst command me, that is: Worship Allah, my Lord and your Lord. I watched over them as long as I was present among them, but since Thou didst cause me to die, Thou hast been the One to watch over them. Indeed Thou dost watch over all things. If Thou decide to punish them, they are Thy servants; and if Thou forgive them, Thou surely art the Mighty, the Wise. Allah will say: This day the truthful shall profit by their truthfulness. For them are Gardens beneath which rivers flow; therein shall they abide for ever. Allah is well pleased with them, and they are well pleased with Him; that indeed is the supreme triumph. To Allah belongs the kingdom of the heavens and the earth and of whatever is in them; and He has full power over all things. (117—121)

تَوَفَّيْتَنِى كُنْتَ أَنْتَ الرَّقِيْبَ عَلَيْهِمْ ۚ وَ أَنْتَ عَلٰى كُلِّ شَىْءٍ شَهِيْدٌ ۝

اِنْ تُعَذِّبْهُمْ فَاِنَّهُمْ عِبَادُكَ ۚ وَ اِنْ تَغْفِرْلَهُمْ فَاِنَّكَ أَنْتَ الْعَزِيْزُ الْحَكِيْمُ ۝

قَالَ اللّٰهُ هٰذَا يَوْمُ يَنْفَعُ الصّٰدِقِيْنَ صِدْقُهُمْ ۚ لَهُمْ جَنّٰتٌ تَجْرِىْ مِنْ تَحْتِهَا الْاَنْهٰرُ خٰلِدِيْنَ فِيْهَا اَبَدًا ۚ رَضِىَ اللّٰهُ عَنْهُمْ وَ رَضُوْا عَنْهُ ۚ ذٰلِكَ الْفَوْزُ الْعَظِيْمُ ۝

لِلّٰهِ مُلْكُ السَّمٰوٰتِ وَالْاَرْضِ وَ مَا فِيْهِنَّ ۚ وَ هُوَ عَلٰى كُلِّ شَىْءٍ قَدِيْرٌ ۝

AL-AN'ĀM

(Revealed before Hijra)

In the name of Allah, Most Gracious, Ever Merciful. (1)

All praise is due to Allah Who created the heavens and the earth and made darknesses and light; yet those who disbelieve set up equals with their Lord. He it is Who created you from clay, and decreed a term for all life, and there is another term fixed for the universe of which He alone has knowledge. Yet you entertain doubt. He alone is Allah, in the heavens and in the earth. He knows your secret thoughts and your overt acts and also knows whatever you acquire. (2—4)

There comes not to the disbelievers any Sign of the Signs of their Lord, but they turn away from it, and thus they have rejected the Truth, the Quran, when it came to them; soon, therefore, shall come to them the tidings of that at which they mocked. Know they not how many a generation have We destroyed before them, whom We had made more powerful in the land than We have made this generation? We had sent clouds over them pouring down abundant rain and had caused streams to flow whose waters they regulated. Then did We destroy them because of their sins and We raised up another generation after them. (5—7)

Even if We had sent down to thee a book inscribed upon parchment, which they could have touched with their hands, the disbelievers would surely have said: This is palpable deception. They say: Why has not an angel been sent down to him? Had We sent an angel, their doom would have been sealed, and they would not have been granted a respite. (8—9)

118

Besides, if We had appointed an angel as Messenger, We would have invested him with the form of a man, and thus We would again have made obscure to them that which they now consider obscure. Before thee also were Messengers mocked at, but then that which they had mocked at encompassed those of them who scoffed. (10—11)

Say to them: Travel through the earth and see what was the end of those who rejected Our Signs. Ask them: To whom does that which is in the heavens and the earth belong? Tell them it belongs to Allah. He has charged Himself with mercy. He will continue to assemble you till the Day of Judgment, in which there is no doubt. Those who have ruined their souls will not believe. To Him belongs all that exists in the night and the day. He is the All-Hearing, the All-Knowing. (12—14)

Ask them: Shall I take as protector someone other than Allah, Creator of the heavens and the earth, Who feeds all and needs not to be fed? Tell them: I have been commanded to render the most perfect obedience. I have also been commanded: Be thou not of those who associate partners with Allah. Tell them also: Assuredly, I fear, if I were to disobey my Lord, the torment of an awful day. He from whom the torment is averted on that day will have been shown mercy by Allah. That indeed is manifest triumph. (15—17)

If Allah were to afflict thee, there is none that can remove the affliction but He, and if He were to bestow upon thee some good, He has power to do all that He wills. He is Supreme over His servants; and He is the Wise, the All-Aware. (18—19)

Ask them: What is weightiest in evidence? and then tell them it is Allah. He is a Witness between you and me. This Quran is revealed to me so that through it I may warn you, and whomsoever it reaches, of that which is impending. Do you really affirm that there are other gods beside Allah?

وَلَوْ جَعَلْنٰهُ مَلَكًا لَّجَعَلْنٰهُ رَجُلًا وَّلَلَبَسْنَا عَلَيْهِمْ مَّا يَلْبِسُوْنَ ۝

وَلَقَدِ اسْتُهْزِئَ بِرُسُلٍ مِّنْ قَبْلِكَ فَحَاقَ بِالَّذِيْنَ سَخِرُوْا مِنْهُمْ مَّا كَانُوْا بِهٖ يَسْتَهْزِئُوْنَ ۝

قُلْ سِيْرُوْا فِى الْاَرْضِ ثُمَّ انْظُرُوْا كَيْفَ كَانَ عَاقِبَةُ الْمُكَذِّبِيْنَ ۝

قُلْ لِّمَنْ مَّا فِى السَّمٰوٰتِ وَالْاَرْضِ قُلْ لِّلّٰهِ كَتَبَ عَلٰى نَفْسِهِ الرَّحْمَةَ لَيَجْمَعَنَّكُمْ اِلٰى يَوْمِ الْقِيٰمَةِ لَا رَيْبَ فِيْهِ اَلَّذِيْنَ خَسِرُوْا اَنْفُسَهُمْ فَهُمْ لَا يُؤْمِنُوْنَ ۝

وَلَهُ مَا سَكَنَ فِى الَّيْلِ وَالنَّهَارِ وَهُوَ السَّمِيْعُ الْعَلِيْمُ ۝

قُلْ اَغَيْرَ اللّٰهِ اَتَّخِذُ وَلِيًّا فَاطِرِ السَّمٰوٰتِ وَالْاَرْضِ وَهُوَ يُطْعِمُ وَلَا يُطْعَمُ قُلْ اِنِّيْ اُمِرْتُ اَنْ اَكُوْنَ اَوَّلَ مَنْ اَسْلَمَ وَلَا تَكُوْنَنَّ مِنَ الْمُشْرِكِيْنَ ۝

قُلْ اِنِّيْ اَخَافُ اِنْ عَصَيْتُ رَبِّيْ عَذَابَ يَوْمٍ عَظِيْمٍ ۝

مَنْ يُّصْرَفْ عَنْهُ يَوْمَئِذٍ فَقَدْ رَحِمَهُ وَذٰلِكَ الْفَوْزُ الْمُبِيْنُ ۝

وَاِنْ يَّمْسَسْكَ اللّٰهُ بِضُرٍّ فَلَا كَاشِفَ لَهُ اِلَّا هُوَ وَاِنْ يَّمْسَسْكَ بِخَيْرٍ فَهُوَ عَلٰى كُلِّ شَيْءٍ قَدِيْرٌ ۝

وَهُوَ الْقَاهِرُ فَوْقَ عِبَادِهٖ وَهُوَ الْحَكِيْمُ الْخَبِيْرُ ۝

قُلْ اَيُّ شَيْءٍ اَكْبَرُ شَهَادَةً قُلِ اللّٰهُ شَهِيْدٌ بَيْنِيْ وَبَيْنَكُمْ وَاُوْحِيَ اِلَيَّ هٰذَا الْقُرْاٰنُ لِاُنْذِرَكُمْ بِهٖ وَمَنْ بَلَغَ اَئِنَّكُمْ لَتَشْهَدُوْنَ اَنَّ مَعَ اللّٰهِ اٰلِهَةً

Tell them: I affirm no such thing. Then do thou affirm: He is the One God and I am most averse to that which you associate with Him. Those to whom We have given the Book recognise Allah as they recognise their sons; but those who have ruined their souls will not believe. (20—21)

Who is guilty of greater injustice than one who fabricates a lie against Allah or rejects His Signs as falsehood? Surely, the wrongdoers shall not prosper. On the day when We shall gather them all together, We shall question those who associate partners with Us: Where are the partners that you used to set up? Their only answer will be: By Allah, our true Lord, We were never guilty of associating partners with Allah. Observe, how they shall lie against their own selves, forgetting all that they used to fabricate. (22—25)

Some of them appear to listen to thee, but because of their misdeeds We have put coverings over their hearts and deafness in their ears which prevent them understanding what thou sayest. Even if they were to witness every kind of Sign, they would not believe therein, so much so, that when they come to thee, disputing with thee, those who disbelieve say: All this is nothing but tales of the ancients. They hinder people from it, and themselves keep away from it, not realising that thereby they only ruin their own selves. (26—27)

If thou couldst see them when they are made to stand before the Fire, when they will lament: Would that we might be sent back: We would not now reject the Signs of our Lord and we would be believers. Thus would that which they used to conceal before become manifest to them. But they would still be lying, for if they were to be sent back, they would surely revert to that which they were forbidden. (28—29)

اُخْرَىٰ ۚ قُلْ لَّآ اَشْهَدُ ۚ قُلْ اِنَّمَا هُوَ اِلٰهٌ وَّاحِدٌ وَّ اِنَّنِىْ بَرِىْٓءٌ مِّمَّا تُشْرِكُوْنَ ۞

اَلَّذِيْنَ اٰتَيْنٰهُمُ الْكِتٰبَ يَعْرِفُوْنَهٗ كَمَا يَعْرِفُوْنَ اَبْنَآءَهُمْ ۘ اَلَّذِيْنَ خَسِرُوْٓا اَنْفُسَهُمْ فَهُمْ لَا يُؤْمِنُوْنَ ۞

وَمَنْ اَظْلَمُ مِمَّنِ افْتَرٰى عَلَى اللهِ كَذِبًا اَوْ كَذَّبَ بِاٰيٰتِهٖ ۚ اِنَّهٗ لَا يُفْلِحُ الظّٰلِمُوْنَ ۞

وَيَوْمَ نَحْشُرُهُمْ جَمِيْعًا ثُمَّ نَقُوْلُ لِلَّذِيْنَ اَشْرَكُوْٓا اَيْنَ شُرَكَآؤُكُمُ الَّذِيْنَ كُنْتُمْ تَزْعُمُوْنَ ۞

ثُمَّ لَمْ تَكُنْ فِتْنَتُهُمْ اِلَّآ اَنْ قَالُوْا وَاللهِ رَبِّنَا مَا كُنَّا مُشْرِكِيْنَ ۞

اُنْظُرْ كَيْفَ كَذَبُوْا عَلٰٓى اَنْفُسِهِمْ وَضَلَّ عَنْهُمْ مَّا كَانُوْا يَفْتَرُوْنَ ۞

وَمِنْهُمْ مَّنْ يَّسْتَمِعُ اِلَيْكَ ۚ وَجَعَلْنَا عَلٰى قُلُوْبِهِمْ اَكِنَّةً اَنْ يَّفْقَهُوْهُ وَفِىْٓ اٰذَانِهِمْ وَقْرًا ۚ وَاِنْ يَّرَوْا كُلَّ اٰيَةٍ لَّا يُؤْمِنُوْا بِهَا ۚ حَتّٰٓى اِذَا جَآءُوْكَ يُجَادِلُوْنَكَ يَقُوْلُ الَّذِيْنَ كَفَرُوْٓا اِنْ هٰذَآ اِلَّآ اَسَاطِيْرُ الْاَوَّلِيْنَ ۞

وَهُمْ يَنْهَوْنَ عَنْهُ وَيَنْئَوْنَ عَنْهُ ۚ وَاِنْ يُّهْلِكُوْنَ اِلَّآ اَنْفُسَهُمْ وَمَا يَشْعُرُوْنَ ۞

وَلَوْ تَرٰٓى اِذْ وُقِفُوْا عَلَى النَّارِ فَقَالُوْا يٰلَيْتَنَا نُرَدُّ وَلَا نُكَذِّبَ بِاٰيٰتِ رَبِّنَا وَنَكُوْنَ مِنَ الْمُؤْمِنِيْنَ ۞

بَلْ بَدَا لَهُمْ مَّا كَانُوْا يُخْفُوْنَ مِنْ قَبْلُ ۚ وَلَوْ رُدُّوْا لَعَادُوْا لِمَا نُهُوْا عَنْهُ وَاِنَّهُمْ لَكٰذِبُوْنَ ۞

They assert: There is nothing beyond our present life and we shall certainly not be raised up again. If thou couldst see them when they are made to stand before their Lord and He would ask them: Is this, your being raised up again, not a reality? They would answer: Indeed yes, by our Lord. He would say: Then suffer the torment because you disbelieved. (30—31)

Those who deny that they are bound to face Allah are indeed the losers, so much so, that when the Hour shall come on them unawares, they will exclaim: Oh, the bitterness of our remorse at neglecting this Hour! They will be carrying their burdens on their backs; and evil burdens will they be. The hither life is but sport and play; and surely the abode of the Hereafter is better for those who are mindful of their duty to Allah. Will you not, then, understand? (32—33)

We know well that what they say grieves thee sorely; for they charge not thee with falsehood, but it is the Signs of Allah that the evil-doers reject. Messengers before thee were also rejected and they continued steadfast, despite rejection and persecution, until Our help came to them. There is none that can change the words of Allah, and surely there have come to thee some of the tidings of past Messengers. Yet, if the turning away of the disbelievers bears hardly upon thee, then if thou art able to seek a passage into the earth or a ladder up to heaven and bring them a Sign, by all means do so. Had Allah enforced His will, He would surely have brought them together into the guidance. So be thou not one of the unenlightened. Only those respond to Allah's call who listen; and Allah will raise those who are dead and to Him shall they be brought back. (34—37)

وَقَالُوْٓا اِنْ هِيَ اِلَّا حَيَاتُنَا الدُّنْيَا وَمَا نَحْنُ بِمَبْعُوْثِيْنَ ۝

وَلَوْ تَرٰٓى اِذْ وُقِفُوْا عَلٰى رَبِّهِمْ ۚ قَالَ اَلَيْسَ هٰذَا بِالْحَقِّ ۚ قَالُوْا بَلٰى وَرَبِّنَا ۚ قَالَ فَذُوْقُوا الْعَذَابَ بِمَا كُنْتُمْ تَكْفُرُوْنَ ۝

قَدْ خَسِرَ الَّذِيْنَ كَذَّبُوْا بِلِقَآءِ اللّٰهِ ۚ حَتّٰۤى اِذَا جَآءَتْهُمُ السَّاعَةُ بَغْتَةً قَالُوْا يٰحَسْرَتَنَا عَلٰى مَا فَرَّطْنَا فِيْهَا ۙ وَهُمْ يَحْمِلُوْنَ اَوْزَارَهُمْ عَلٰى ظُهُوْرِهِمْ ۚ اَلَا سَآءَ مَا يَزِرُوْنَ ۝

وَمَا الْحَيٰوةُ الدُّنْيَآ اِلَّا لَعِبٌ وَّلَهْوٌ ۚ وَلَلدَّارُ الْاٰخِرَةُ خَيْرٌ لِّلَّذِيْنَ يَتَّقُوْنَ ۗ اَفَلَا تَعْقِلُوْنَ ۝

قَدْ نَعْلَمُ اِنَّهٗ لَيَحْزُنُكَ الَّذِيْ يَقُوْلُوْنَ فَاِنَّهُمْ لَا يُكَذِّبُوْنَكَ وَلٰكِنَّ الظّٰلِمِيْنَ بِاٰيٰتِ اللّٰهِ يَجْحَدُوْنَ ۝

وَلَقَدْ كُذِّبَتْ رُسُلٌ مِّنْ قَبْلِكَ فَصَبَرُوْا عَلٰى مَا كُذِّبُوْا وَاُوْذُوْا حَتّٰۤى اَتٰىهُمْ نَصْرُنَا ۚ وَلَا مُبَدِّلَ لِكَلِمٰتِ اللّٰهِ ۚ وَلَقَدْ جَآءَكَ مِنْ نَّبَاِئِ الْمُرْسَلِيْنَ ۝

وَاِنْ كَانَ كَبُرَ عَلَيْكَ اِعْرَاضُهُمْ فَاِنِ اسْتَطَعْتَ اَنْ تَبْتَغِيَ نَفَقًا فِى الْاَرْضِ اَوْ سُلَّمًا فِى السَّمَآءِ فَتَاْتِيَهُمْ بِاٰيَةٍ ۚ وَلَوْ شَآءَ اللّٰهُ لَجَمَعَهُمْ عَلَى الْهُدٰى فَلَا تَكُوْنَنَّ مِنَ الْجٰهِلِيْنَ ۝

اِنَّمَا يَسْتَجِيْبُ الَّذِيْنَ يَسْمَعُوْنَ ۘ وَالْمَوْتٰى يَبْعَثُهُمُ اللّٰهُ ثُمَّ اِلَيْهِ يُرْجَعُوْنَ ۝

وَقَالُوْا لَوْلَا نُزِّلَ عَلَيْهِ اٰيَةٌ مِّنْ رَّبِّهٖ ۚ قُلْ اِنَّ اللّٰهَ

They ask: Why has not a Sign been sent down to him from his Lord? Tell them: Surely, Allah has power to send down a Sign, but most of them know it not. There is not an animal that moves about in the earth, nor a bird that flies on its two wings, but are communities like you. We have not left out anything in the Book. Then to their Lord shall they be gathered together. Those who have rejected Our Signs are deaf and dumb, caught in manifold darknesses. Whom Allah wills He allows to perish, and whom He wills He puts on the right path. (38—40)

قَادِرٌ عَلَى اَنْ يُّنَزِّلَ اٰيَةً وَّلٰكِنَّ اَكْثَرَهُمْ لَا يَعْلَمُوْنَ ۞

وَمَا مِنْ دَآبَّةٍ فِي الْاَرْضِ وَلَا طٰٓئِرٍ يَّطِيْرُ بِجَنَاحَيْهِ اِلَّاۤ اُمَمٌ اَمْثَالُكُمْ مَا فَرَّطْنَا فِي الْكِتٰبِ مِنْ شَيْءٍ ثُمَّ اِلٰى رَبِّهِمْ يُحْشَرُوْنَ ۞

وَالَّذِيْنَ كَذَّبُوْا بِاٰيٰتِنَا صُمٌّ وَّبُكْمٌ فِي الظُّلُمٰتِ ط مَنْ يَّشَاِ اللّٰهُ يُضْلِلْهُ وَمَنْ يَّشَأْ يَجْعَلْهُ عَلٰى صِرَاطٍ مُّسْتَقِيْمٍ ۞

Ask them: Tell me truly, if the punishment of Allah came upon you or the Hour overtook you, would you call upon any other than Allah? Indeed no, in such an event, you will call on Him alone and will forget all that you associate with Him; then will He remove that which you call on Him to remove, if He please. (41—42)

قُلْ اَرَءَيْتَكُمْ اِنْ اَتٰىكُمْ عَذَابُ اللّٰهِ اَوْ اَتَتْكُمُ السَّاعَةُ اَغَيْرَ اللّٰهِ تَدْعُوْنَ اِنْ كُنْتُمْ صٰدِقِيْنَ ۞

بَلْ اِيَّاهُ تَدْعُوْنَ فَيَكْشِفُ مَا تَدْعُوْنَ اِلَيْهِ اِنْ شَآءَ وَتَنْسَوْنَ مَا تُشْرِكُوْنَ ۞

Indeed We sent Messengers to different peoples before thee, then We afflicted the disbelievers with poverty and adversity that they might humble themselves. Why did they not, then, humble themselves when Our punishment came upon them? Instead, their hearts became even more hardened and Satan made all that they did appear attractive to them. Thereafter when they forgot that with which they had been admonished, We bestowed upon them abundance of everything, until when they were in a state of exultation over that which they had been given, We seized them suddenly and they were struck dumb with despair. Thus was cut off the last remnant of the people who did wrong. All praise belongs to Allah, the Lord of all the worlds. (43—46)

وَلَقَدْ اَرْسَلْنَاۤ اِلٰٓى اُمَمٍ مِّنْ قَبْلِكَ فَاَخَذْنٰهُمْ بِالْبَأْسَاءِ وَالضَّرَّآءِ لَعَلَّهُمْ يَتَضَرَّعُوْنَ ۞

فَلَوْلَاۤ اِذْ جَآءَهُمْ بَأْسُنَا تَضَرَّعُوْا وَلٰكِنْ قَسَتْ قُلُوْبُهُمْ وَزَيَّنَ لَهُمُ الشَّيْطٰنُ مَا كَانُوْا يَعْمَلُوْنَ ۞

فَلَمَّا نَسُوْا مَا ذُكِّرُوْا بِهِ فَتَحْنَا عَلَيْهِمْ اَبْوَابَ كُلِّ شَيْءٍ ط حَتّٰٓى اِذَا فَرِحُوْا بِمَاۤ اُوْتُوْا اَخَذْنٰهُمْ بَغْتَةً فَاِذَا هُمْ مُّبْلِسُوْنَ ۞

فَقُطِعَ دَابِرُ الْقَوْمِ الَّذِيْنَ ظَلَمُوْا ط وَالْحَمْدُ لِلّٰهِ رَبِّ الْعٰلَمِيْنَ ۞

قُلْ اَرَءَيْتُمْ اِنْ اَخَذَ اللّٰهُ سَمْعَكُمْ وَاَبْصَارَكُمْ وَخَتَمَ

Ask them: Tell me, if Allah were to take away your hearing and your sight, and to seal up your hearts, who is the god, other than Allah, who could bring them back to you? Observe, how We expound the Signs to them in diverse ways, yet they turn away. Ask them: Tell me, if the punishment of Allah came upon you without presage, or visibly, will any be destroyed except the wrongdoing people? (47—48)

We send the Messengers only as bearers of glad tidings and as warners, then those who believe and work righteousness are subject neither to fear nor to grief; and chastisement befalls those who reject Our Signs because of their disobedience. (49—50)

Tell them: I do not say to you: I possess the treasures of Allah; nor do I know the unseen; nor do I say to you: I am an angel. I but follow that which is revealed to me. Ask them, however: Can the blind and the seeing be alike? Will you not, then, reflect? (51)

Warn by means of the Quran those who fear that they shall be gathered to their Lord when they shall have no friend nor intercessor beside Him, so that they may become righteous; and drive not away those who call upon their Lord morning and evening seeking His countenance. Thou art not at all accountable for them nor are they at all accountable for thee. If thou drive them away thou wilt be of the unjust. (52—53)

Thus We have tried some of them by means of others in this manner that they may ask: Are these lowly ones those whom Allah has singled out for His favours from among us? Quite so; does not Allah know best those who are grateful? When those who believe in Our Signs come to thee, greet them with: Peace unto you. Your Lord has charged Himself with mercy, so that whoso among you does evil in ignorance and repents thereafter and amends, then He is Most Forgiving, Ever Merciful. Thus do We expound the Signs so that truth may be proclaimed and the way of the sinners may become manifest. (54—56)

Proclaim, O Prophet: I am forbidden to worship the false gods on whom you call beside Allah; and say to them: I will not follow your low desires; for if I did, I would be lost and would not be of those rightly guided. Say to them: I take my stand on clear proof from my Lord, and you reject it. That which you desire to be hastened is not within my power; all judgment rests with Allah, He expounds the truth and He is the Best of judges. Say to them: If that which you desire to be hastened were in my power, surely the matter in controversy between you and me would be quickly decided. Allah knows best the unjust. (57—59)

With Him are the keys of the unseen, none knows it but He. He knows whatsoever is in the land and in the sea; not a leaf falls but He knows it. Nor is there a grain in the darknesses of the earth, nor anything green or dry but is under His effective protection. He it is Who takes your souls into custody by night and knows all that you do by day; then He raises you up during the day that a term that has been appointed may be completed. Then to Him is your return and He will inform you of that which you used to do. (60—61)

He is Supreme over His servants and He sends guardians to watch over you, until, when death comes to any one of you, our deputed angels take his soul and they fail not in the discharge of their duty in any respect. Then are they returned to Allah, their true Lord. Hearken, His is the judgment and He is the Swiftest of reckoners. (62—63)

Ask them: Who is it Who delivers you from the calamities of the land and the sea; when you call upon Him in humility and in secret: If He deliver us from this we will surely be among the grateful? Tell them: It is Allah Who delivers you from them and from every other distress, yet you associate partners with Him. Warn them: He has power to afflict you with chastisement from above you or from beneath your feet, or to split you into hostile groups and involve you with each other in violence. Observe, how We expound the Signs in diverse ways that they may understand. (64 – 66)

Thy people have rejected the message We have sent through thee, though it is the Truth. Tell them: I am not a guardian over you. There is a fixed time for every prophecy and soon will you come to know. (67—68)

When thou seest those who are engaged in vain discourse concerning Our Signs, keep away from them until they turn to some other topic. Should Satan cause thee to forget, do not continue to sit with the unjust people after recollection. Those who are righteous are not at all accountable for them, but it is their duty to admonish them, that they may desist. (69—70)

حَتّٰى اِذَا جَآءَ اَحَدَكُمُ الْمَوْتُ تَوَفَّتْهُ رُسُلُنَا وَهُمْ لَا يُفَرِّطُوْنَ ۝

ثُمَّ رُدُّوْۤا اِلَى اللّٰهِ مَوْلٰىهُمُ الْحَقِّ ؕ اَلَا لَهُ الْحُكْمُ ٙ وَهُوَ اَسْرَعُ الْحَاسِبِيْنَ ۝

قُلْ مَنْ يُّنَجِّيْكُمْ مِّنْ ظُلُمٰتِ الْبَرِّ وَالْبَحْرِ تَدْعُوْنَهٗ تَضَرُّعًا وَّخُفْيَةً ۚ لَئِنْ اَنْجٰنَا مِنْ هٰذِهٖ لَنَكُوْنَنَّ مِنَ الشّٰكِرِيْنَ ۝

قُلِ اللّٰهُ يُنَجِّيْكُمْ مِّنْهَا وَمِنْ كُلِّ كَرْبٍ ثُمَّ اَنْتُمْ تُشْرِكُوْنَ ۝

قُلْ هُوَ الْقَادِرُ عَلٰۤى اَنْ يَّبْعَثَ عَلَيْكُمْ عَذَابًا مِّنْ فَوْقِكُمْ اَوْ مِنْ تَحْتِ اَرْجُلِكُمْ اَوْ يَلْبِسَكُمْ شِيَعًا وَّيُذِيْقَ بَعْضَكُمْ بَأْسَ بَعْضٍ ؕ اُنْظُرْ كَيْفَ نُصَرِّفُ الْاٰيٰتِ لَعَلَّهُمْ يَفْقَهُوْنَ ۝

وَكَذَّبَ بِهٖ قَوْمُكَ وَهُوَ الْحَقُّ ؕ قُلْ لَّسْتُ عَلَيْكُمْ بِوَكِيْلٍ ۙ ۝

لِكُلِّ نَبَاٍ مُّسْتَقَرٌّ ٚ وَّسَوْفَ تَعْلَمُوْنَ ۝

وَاِذَا رَاَيْتَ الَّذِيْنَ يَخُوْضُوْنَ فِيْۤ اٰيٰتِنَا فَاَعْرِضْ عَنْهُمْ حَتّٰى يَخُوْضُوْا فِيْ حَدِيْثٍ غَيْرِهٖ ؕ وَاِمَّا يُنْسِيَنَّكَ الشَّيْطٰنُ فَلَا تَقْعُدْ بَعْدَ الذِّكْرٰى مَعَ الْقَوْمِ الظّٰلِمِيْنَ ۝

وَمَا عَلَى الَّذِيْنَ يَتَّقُوْنَ مِنْ حِسَابِهِمْ مِّنْ شَيْءٍ وَّلٰكِنْ ذِكْرٰى لَعَلَّهُمْ يَتَّقُوْنَ ۝

Leave alone those for whom religion is only a sport and pastime and whom wordly life has beguiled; and continue to admonish people by means of the Quran, lest a soul be ruined because of that which it has wrought, having no helper or intercessor beside Allah. If it were to offer every ransom it shall not be accepted from it. These are they who are ruined in consequence of that which they have wrought. Their drink will be boiling water and they will suffer painful torment because they disbelieved. (71)

Ask them: Shall we call, beside Allah, upon that which can neither benefit us nor harm us and be turned back on our heels after Allah has guided us, like one who is enticed away by the rebellious ones and is left bewildered in the land, some of whose companions call him: Come to us that you may be guided? Tell them: Surely, the guidance of Allah is the only true guidance, and we have been commanded to submit to the Lord of all the worlds; and we have been commanded: Observe Prayer and be mindful of your duty to Him. He it is to Whom you shall be gathered. He it is Who created the heavens and the earth in accordance with the requirements of wisdom; the day He says concerning that which He wills: Be; it will be. His word shall be fulfilled. His will be the kingdom on the day when the trumpet will be blown. He has full knowledge of the unseen and the seen; He is the Wise, the All-Aware. (72—74)

Call to mind when Abraham said to his father Aazar: Dost thou take idols for gods? I consider thee and thy people as being in manifest error. We showed Abraham Our kingdom over the heavens and the earth so that his knowledge being perfected he might be of those who have certainty of faith. (75—76)

126

Thus, it happened, that when he was enveloped in the darkness of night, he saw a star, whereupon he exclaimed: Can that be my Lord? and when it set, he muttered: I like not those that set. Then when he saw the moon rising, he said: Can this be my Lord? and when it set he said: Had my Lord not guided me, I would surely have been of those who go astray. Finally, when he saw the sun rising, he said: Can this be my Lord, no doubt this is the biggest? But when that also set, he said to his people: Most certainly, I have no truck with that which you associate with Allah; I have single-mindedly devoted the whole of my attention to Him Who created the heavens and the earth, and I am not of those who associate partners with Allah. (77—80)

His people sought to contend with him. He said: Do you contend with me concerning Allah, Who has guided me aright? I fear not that which you associate with Him; I fear only that which my Lord may determine. My Lord comprehends all within His knowledge; will you not then take heed? How should I be afraid of that which you associate with Allah, when you are not afraid to associate with Allah that concerning which He has sent down to you no authority? Which, then, of the two parties has a better right to security, if indeed you know? Those who believe and debase not their faith with injustice, for them is peace and they are rightly guided. (81—83)

That was Our argument that We furnished to Abraham against his people. We exalt in rank whomso We please. Thy Lord is indeed Wise, All-Knowing. We bestowed upon him Isaac and Jacob; each did We guide aright, and Noah did We guide aright aforetime, and of Abraham's progeny did We guide aright David and Solomon and Job and Joseph and Moses and Aaron. Thus do we reward those who do good. (84—85)

فَلَمَّا اَفَلَ قَالَ لَا اُحِبُّ الْاٰفِلِيْنَ ۞

فَلَمَّا رَاَ الْقَمَرَ بَازِغًا قَالَ هٰذَا رَبِّيْ فَلَمَّا اَفَلَ قَالَ لَئِنْ لَّمْ يَهْدِنِيْ رَبِّيْ لَاَكُوْنَنَّ مِنَ الْقَوْمِ الضَّآلِّيْنَ ۞

فَلَمَّا رَاَ الشَّمْسَ بَازِغَةً قَالَ هٰذَا رَبِّيْ هٰذَآ اَكْبَرُ فَلَمَّآ اَفَلَتْ قَالَ يٰقَوْمِ اِنِّيْ بَرِيْٓءٌ مِّمَّا تُشْرِكُوْنَ ۞

اِنِّيْ وَجَّهْتُ وَجْهِيَ لِلَّذِيْ فَطَرَ السَّمٰوٰتِ وَالْاَرْضَ حَنِيْفًا وَّمَآ اَنَا مِنَ الْمُشْرِكِيْنَ ۞

وَحَآجَّهٗ قَوْمُهٗ قَالَ اَتُحَآجُّوْٓنِّيْ فِي اللّٰهِ وَقَدْ هَدٰنِ وَلَآ اَخَافُ مَا تُشْرِكُوْنَ بِهٖٓ اِلَّآ اَنْ يَّشَآءَ رَبِّيْ شَيْئًا وَسِعَ رَبِّيْ كُلَّ شَيْءٍ عِلْمًا اَفَلَا تَتَذَكَّرُوْنَ ۞

وَكَيْفَ اَخَافُ مَآ اَشْرَكْتُمْ وَلَا تَخَافُوْنَ اَنَّكُمْ اَشْرَكْتُمْ بِاللّٰهِ مَا لَمْ يُنَزِّلْ بِهٖ عَلَيْكُمْ سُلْطٰنًا فَاَيُّ الْفَرِيْقَيْنِ اَحَقُّ بِالْاَمْنِ اِنْ كُنْتُمْ تَعْلَمُوْنَ ۞

اَلَّذِيْنَ اٰمَنُوْا وَلَمْ يَلْبِسُوْٓا اِيْمَانَهُمْ بِظُلْمٍ اُولٰٓئِكَ لَهُمُ الْاَمْنُ وَهُمْ مُّهْتَدُوْنَ ۞

وَتِلْكَ حُجَّتُنَآ اٰتَيْنٰهَآ اِبْرٰهِيْمَ عَلٰى قَوْمِهٖ نَرْفَعُ دَرَجٰتٍ مَّنْ نَّشَآءُ اِنَّ رَبَّكَ حَكِيْمٌ عَلِيْمٌ ۞

وَوَهَبْنَا لَهٗٓ اِسْحٰقَ وَيَعْقُوْبَ كُلًّا هَدَيْنَا وَنُوْحًا هَدَيْنَا مِنْ قَبْلُ وَمِنْ ذُرِّيَّتِهٖ دَاوٗدَ وَسُلَيْمٰنَ وَاَيُّوْبَ وَيُوْسُفَ وَمُوْسٰى وَهٰرُوْنَ وَكَذٰلِكَ نَجْزِى الْمُحْسِنِيْنَ ۞

127

We also guided Zachariah and John and Jesus and Elias, each one of them was of the righteous; and Ishmael and Elisha and Jonas and Lot, each one did We exalt above the people, and of their fathers and their children and their brethren; We chose them and We guided them along the straight path. (86—88)

وَ ذَكَرِيَّا وَ يَحْيٰى وَ عِيْسٰى وَ اِلْيَاسَ كُلٌّ مِّنَ الصّٰلِحِيْنَ ۞

وَ اِسْمٰعِيْلَ وَ الْيَسَعَ وَ يُوْنُسَ وَ لُوْطًا وَ كُلًّا فَضَّلْنَا عَلَى الْعٰلَمِيْنَ ۞

وَ مِنْ اٰبَآئِهِمْ وَ ذُرِّيّٰتِهِمْ وَ اِخْوَانِهِمْ وَ اجْتَبَيْنٰهُمْ وَ هَدَيْنٰهُمْ اِلٰى صِرَاطٍ مُّسْتَقِيْمٍ ۞

That is the guidance of Allah, whereby He guides those of His servants whom He pleases. Had they associated aught with Allah, all that they did would have been of no avail to them. It is these to whom We gave the Book, the faculty of judgment and Prophethood. Then if these people disbelieve in Prophethood, We have now committed it to a people who do not disbelieve in it. These are the ones whom Allah guided aright, so do thou follow their guidance. Say to these people: I ask not of you any recompense for it. It is but an admonition for all mankind. (89—91)

ذٰلِكَ هُدَى اللهِ يَهْدِيْ بِهِ مَنْ يَّشَآءُ مِنْ عِبَادِهِ وَ لَوْ اَشْرَكُوْا لَحَبِطَ عَنْهُمْ مَّا كَانُوْا يَعْمَلُوْنَ ۞

اُولٰٓئِكَ الَّذِيْنَ اٰتَيْنٰهُمُ الْكِتٰبَ وَ الْحُكْمَ وَ النُّبُوَّةَ فَاِنْ يَّكْفُرْ بِهَا هٰٓؤُلَآءِ فَقَدْ وَكَّلْنَا بِهَا قَوْمًا لَّيْسُوْا بِهَا بِكٰفِرِيْنَ ۞

اُولٰٓئِكَ الَّذِيْنَ هَدَى اللهُ فَبِهُدٰىهُمُ اقْتَدِهْ قُلْ لَّاۤ اَسْئَلُكُمْ عَلَيْهِ اَجْرًا اِنْ هُوَ اِلَّا ذِكْرٰى لِلْعٰلَمِيْنَ ۞

Those who say Allah has not revealed anything to any man, do not appreciate Allah's attributes justly. Ask them: Who revealed the Book which Moses brought, a light and guidance for the people? You have reduced it to scraps and bits, some of it you disclose and much of it you conceal; though you have been taught by means of it that which neither you nor your fathers knew. Say to them: It was revealed by Allah; then leave them to disport with their falsehood. (92)

وَ مَا قَدَرُوا اللهَ حَقَّ قَدْرِهٖ اِذْ قَالُوْا مَاۤ اَنْزَلَ اللهُ عَلٰى بَشَرٍ مِّنْ شَيْءٍ قُلْ مَنْ اَنْزَلَ الْكِتٰبَ الَّذِيْ جَآءَ بِهٖ مُوْسٰى نُوْرًا وَّ هُدًى لِّلنَّاسِ تَجْعَلُوْنَهٗ قَرَاطِيْسَ تُبْدُوْنَهَا وَ تُخْفُوْنَ كَثِيْرًا وَ عُلِّمْتُمْ مَّا لَمْ تَعْلَمُوْا اَنْتُمْ وَ لَاۤ اٰبَآؤُكُمْ قُلِ اللهُ ثُمَّ ذَرْهُمْ فِيْ خَوْضِهِمْ يَلْعَبُوْنَ ۞

This Quran is a noble Book that We have revealed, full of blessings, fulfilling that which preceded it, that thou mayest thereby warn the people of Mecca and those around it. Those who believe in that which is yet to come believe therein and they keep a watch over their Prayer. (93)

وَ هٰذَا كِتٰبٌ اَنْزَلْنٰهُ مُبٰرَكٌ مُّصَدِّقُ الَّذِيْ بَيْنَ يَدَيْهِ وَ لِتُنْذِرَ اُمَّ الْقُرٰى وَ مَنْ حَوْلَهَا وَ الَّذِيْنَ يُؤْمِنُوْنَ بِالْاٰخِرَةِ يُؤْمِنُوْنَ بِهٖ وَ هُمْ عَلٰى صَلَاتِهِمْ

Who is more unjust than one who deliberately fabricates a lie against Allah: or says: I am the recipient of revelation, while nothing has been revealed to him; or says: I will surely send down the like of that which Allah has sent down? If thou couldst but see, when the wrongdoers are in the agonies of death, and the angels stretch forth their hands, demanding: Yield up your souls; this day shall you be awarded an humiliating punishment, because of that which you used to speak against Allah falsely and becuase you used to turn away from His Signs with disdain. Allah will say to them: You have now come to Us one by one even as We created you at first, and you have left behind you that which We bestowed upon you as a favour. We see not with you your intercessors, who, according to you, were partners with Allah in ruling over you. Now you have been cut off from one another and that which you asserted has failed you. (94—95)

Surely, it is Allah Who causes the grain and the date-stones to sprout. He brings forth the living from the dead and it is He Who brings forth the dead from the living. That is your Allah; wherefore, then are you turned back? He causes the break of day, and has made the night for rest and the sun and the moon the means for reckoning time. That is the measure determined by the Mighty, the All-Knowing. He it is Who has made for you the stars, that you may follow the right direction in the darkness of the land and sea. We have expounded the Signs in detail for a people who possess knowledge. He it is Who has created you from a single soul and has appointed for you a place of temporary resort and a more permanent abode. We have expounded the Signs in detail for a people who understand. (96—99)

يُحَافِظُونَ ۞

وَمَنْ أَظْلَمُ مِمَّنِ افْتَرَى عَلَى اللهِ كَذِبًا أَوْ قَالَ أُوْحِىَ اِلَىَّ وَلَمْ يُوْحَ اِلَيْهِ شَىْءٌ وَّمَنْ قَالَ سَأُنْزِلُ مِثْلَ مَا أَنْزَلَ اللهُ وَلَوْ تَرَى إِذِ الظَّالِمُوْنَ فِى غَمَرَاتِ الْمَوْتِ وَالْمَلٰئِكَةُ بَاسِطُوْا اَيْدِيْهِمْ أَخْرِجُوْا اَنْفُسَكُمُ الْيَوْمَ تُجْزَوْنَ عَذَابَ الْهُوْنِ بِمَا كُنْتُمْ تَقُوْلُوْنَ عَلَى اللهِ غَيْرَ الْحَقِّ وَكُنْتُمْ عَنْ اٰيٰتِهِ تَسْتَكْبِرُوْنَ ۞

وَلَقَدْ جِئْتُمُوْنَا فُرَادَى كَمَا خَلَقْنٰكُمْ أَوَّلَ مَرَّةٍ وَّتَرَكْتُمْ مَّا خَوَّلْنٰكُمْ وَرَاءَ ظُهُوْرِكُمْ وَمَا نَرٰى مَعَكُمْ شُفَعَاءَكُمُ الَّذِيْنَ زَعَمْتُمْ اَنَّهُمْ فِيْكُمْ شُرَكٰٓؤُا لَقَدْ تَقَطَّعَ بَيْنَكُمْ وَضَلَّ عَنْكُمْ مَّا كُنْتُمْ تَزْعُمُوْنَ ۞

اِنَّ اللهَ فَالِقُ الْحَبِّ وَالنَّوٰى يُخْرِجُ الْحَىَّ مِنَ الْمَيِّتِ وَمُخْرِجُ الْمَيِّتِ مِنَ الْحَىِّ ذٰلِكُمُ اللهُ فَاَنّٰى تُؤْفَكُوْنَ ۞

فَالِقُ الْاِصْبَاحِ وَجَعَلَ الَّيْلَ سَكَنًا وَّالشَّمْسَ وَالْقَمَرَ حُسْبَانًا ذٰلِكَ تَقْدِيْرُ الْعَزِيْزِ الْعَلِيْمِ ۞

وَهُوَ الَّذِىْ جَعَلَ لَكُمُ النُّجُوْمَ لِتَهْتَدُوْا بِهَا فِىْ ظُلُمٰتِ الْبَرِّ وَالْبَحْرِ قَدْ فَصَّلْنَا الْاٰيٰتِ لِقَوْمٍ يَّعْلَمُوْنَ ۞

وَهُوَ الَّذِىْ اَنْشَاَكُمْ مِنْ نَّفْسٍ وَّاحِدَةٍ فَمُسْتَقَرٌّ وَّمُسْتَوْدَعٌ قَدْ فَصَّلْنَا الْاٰيٰتِ لِقَوْمٍ يَّفْقَهُوْنَ ۞

وَهُوَ الَّذِىْ اَنْزَلَ مِنَ السَّمَاءِ مَاءً فَاَخْرَجْنَا بِهٖ

It is He Who sends down water from the sky; and We bring forth therewith every kind of growth and therefrom, out of green foliage, We produce clustered grain; and from the date-palm, out of its sheath, We produce bunches hanging low. We also produce therewith gardens of grapes, and the olive and the pomegranate, some similar and some dissimilar. Observe the fruit of every kind of tree when it bears fruit and the process of its ripening. Surely, in this are Signs for the people who believe. (100)

They have appointed partners of Allah out of the Jinn, whereas He has created them; and they falsely attribute to Him sons and daughters without any knowledge. Holy is He and exalted far above that which they attribute to Him. Originator of the heavens and the earth! How can He have a son when He has no consort, and He has created everything and has full knowledge of all things? That is Allah, your Lord; there is no god but He, the Creator of all things; so worship Him alone. He is Guardian over everything. Eyes cannot reach Him, but He manifests Himself before the eyes. He is the Imperceptible, the All-Aware. (101—104)

Proofs have indeed come to you from your Lord; so he who comprehends, it is for his own benefit, and he who ignores, it is to his own loss. I am not a guardian over you. (105)

Thus do We expound the Signs in diverse ways that they should concede: Thou hast read out to us; and that We may explain them to a people who have knowledge. (106)

Follow that which has been revealed to thee from thy Lord; there is no god but He; and turn aside from those who set up partners with Allah. Had Allah so willed, they would not have set up partners with Him.

نَبَاتَ كُلِّ شَيْءٍ فَاَخْرَجْنَا مِنْهُ خَضِرًا نُّخْرِجُ مِنْهُ حَبًّا مُّتَرَاكِبًا ۚ وَمِنَ النَّخْلِ مِنْ طَلْعِهَا قِنْوَانٌ دَانِيَةٌ وَّجَنّٰتٍ مِّنْ اَعْنَابٍ وَّالزَّيْتُوْنَ وَالرُّمَّانَ مُشْتَبِهًا وَّغَيْرَ مُتَشَابِهٍ ۗ اُنْظُرُوْٓا اِلٰى ثَمَرِهٖٓ اِذَآ اَثْمَرَ وَيَنْعِهٖ ۚ اِنَّ فِيْ ذٰلِكُمْ لَاٰيٰتٍ لِّقَوْمٍ يُّؤْمِنُوْنَ ۞

وَجَعَلُوْا لِلّٰهِ شُرَكَآءَ الْجِنَّ وَخَلَقَهُمْ وَخَرَقُوْا لَهٗ بَنِيْنَ وَبَنٰتٍ بِغَيْرِ عِلْمٍ ۚ سُبْحٰنَهٗ وَتَعٰلٰى عَمَّا يَصِفُوْنَ ۞

بَدِيْعُ السَّمٰوٰتِ وَالْاَرْضِ ۚ اَنّٰى يَكُوْنُ لَهٗ وَلَدٌ وَّلَمْ تَكُنْ لَّهٗ صَاحِبَةٌ ۚ وَخَلَقَ كُلَّ شَيْءٍ ۚ وَهُوَ بِكُلِّ شَيْءٍ عَلِيْمٌ ۞

ذٰلِكُمُ اللّٰهُ رَبُّكُمْ ۚ لَآ اِلٰهَ اِلَّا هُوَ ۚ خَالِقُ كُلِّ شَيْءٍ فَاعْبُدُوْهُ ۚ وَهُوَ عَلٰى كُلِّ شَيْءٍ وَّكِيْلٌ ۞

لَا تُدْرِكُهُ الْاَبْصَارُ ۖ وَهُوَ يُدْرِكُ الْاَبْصَارَ ۚ وَهُوَ اللَّطِيْفُ الْخَبِيْرُ ۞

قَدْ جَآءَكُمْ بَصَآئِرُ مِنْ رَّبِّكُمْ ۚ فَمَنْ اَبْصَرَ فَلِنَفْسِهٖ ۚ وَمَنْ عَمِيَ فَعَلَيْهَا ۚ وَمَآ اَنَا عَلَيْكُمْ بِحَفِيْظٍ ۞

وَكَذٰلِكَ نُصَرِّفُ الْاٰيٰتِ وَلِيَقُوْلُوْا دَرَسْتَ وَلِنُبَيِّنَهٗ لِقَوْمٍ يَّعْلَمُوْنَ ۞

اِتَّبِعْ مَآ اُوْحِيَ اِلَيْكَ مِنْ رَّبِّكَ ۚ لَآ اِلٰهَ اِلَّا هُوَ ۚ وَاَعْرِضْ عَنِ الْمُشْرِكِيْنَ ۞

وَلَوْ شَآءَ اللّٰهُ مَآ اَشْرَكُوْا ۗ وَمَا جَعَلْنٰكَ عَلَيْهِمْ

We have not appointed thee a keeper over them nor art thou their guardian. Revile ye not those whom they call upon beside Allah, lest they, out of spite, should revile Allah in their ignorance. Thus have We caused their conduct to seem fair to every people. Then unto their Lord is their return; and He will inform them of that which they used to do. (107—109)

They swear the strongest oaths by Allah that if there came to them a Sign, they would surely believe therein. Say to them: Surely, Signs are with Allah, and also that which would make you understand that even when the Signs come they will not believe. We shall confound their hearts and their eyes, as they believed not in it in the first instance, and shall leave them in their transgression to wander in distraction. (110—111)

Even if We had sent down angels to them, and the dead had spoken to them, and We had gathered before them all things face to face, they would not have believed, unless Allah had so willed. Most of them behave ignorantly. In like manner have We made for every Prophet enemies, rebellious ones from among men, high and low. They make evil suggestions one to another in flowery language in order to deceive. (If thy Lord had so willed they would not have done so, then leave them alone and that which they fabricate.) This We do, so that the hearts of those who do not believe in the Hereafter may be inclined towards those suggestions and that they may be pleased therewith and that they may experience the consequences of their conduct. (112—114)

Ask them: Shall I seek one other than Allah as Judge, when He it is Who has sent down to you the Book, clearly explained? Those to whom We gave the Book know that it has been sent down by thy Lord with truth; so be thou not of those who doubt. The word of thy Lord shall be fulfilled in truth and justice, none can change His words. He is the All-Hearing; the All-Knowing. (115—116)

حَفِيظًا ۖ وَمَا أَنتَ عَلَيْهِم بِوَكِيلٍ ۝

وَلَا تَسُبُّوا الَّذِينَ يَدْعُونَ مِن دُونِ اللَّهِ فَيَسُبُّوا اللَّهَ عَدْوًا بِغَيْرِ عِلْمٍ ۗ كَذَٰلِكَ زَيَّنَّا لِكُلِّ أُمَّةٍ عَمَلَهُمْ ثُمَّ إِلَىٰ رَبِّهِم مَّرْجِعُهُمْ فَيُنَبِّئُهُم بِمَا كَانُوا يَعْمَلُونَ ۝

وَأَقْسَمُوا بِاللَّهِ جَهْدَ أَيْمَانِهِمْ لَئِن جَاءَتْهُمْ آيَةٌ لَّيُؤْمِنُنَّ بِهَا ۚ قُلْ إِنَّمَا الْآيَاتُ عِندَ اللَّهِ ۖ وَمَا يُشْعِرُكُمْ أَنَّهَا إِذَا جَاءَتْ لَا يُؤْمِنُونَ ۝

وَنُقَلِّبُ أَفْئِدَتَهُمْ وَأَبْصَارَهُمْ كَمَا لَمْ يُؤْمِنُوا بِهِ أَوَّلَ مَرَّةٍ وَنَذَرُهُمْ فِي طُغْيَانِهِمْ يَعْمَهُونَ ۝

وَلَوْ أَنَّنَا نَزَّلْنَا إِلَيْهِمُ الْمَلَائِكَةَ وَكَلَّمَهُمُ الْمَوْتَىٰ وَحَشَرْنَا عَلَيْهِمْ كُلَّ شَيْءٍ قُبُلًا مَّا كَانُوا لِيُؤْمِنُوا إِلَّا أَن يَشَاءَ اللَّهُ وَلَٰكِنَّ أَكْثَرَهُمْ يَجْهَلُونَ ۝

وَكَذَٰلِكَ جَعَلْنَا لِكُلِّ نَبِيٍّ عَدُوًّا شَيَاطِينَ الْإِنسِ وَالْجِنِّ يُوحِي بَعْضُهُمْ إِلَىٰ بَعْضٍ زُخْرُفَ الْقَوْلِ غُرُورًا ۚ وَلَوْ شَاءَ رَبُّكَ مَا فَعَلُوهُ ۖ فَذَرْهُمْ وَمَا يَفْتَرُونَ ۝

وَلِتَصْغَىٰ إِلَيْهِ أَفْئِدَةُ الَّذِينَ لَا يُؤْمِنُونَ بِالْآخِرَةِ وَلِيَرْضَوْهُ وَلِيَقْتَرِفُوا مَا هُم مُّقْتَرِفُونَ ۝

أَفَغَيْرَ اللَّهِ أَبْتَغِي حَكَمًا وَهُوَ الَّذِي أَنزَلَ إِلَيْكُمُ الْكِتَابَ مُفَصَّلًا ۚ وَالَّذِينَ آتَيْنَاهُمُ الْكِتَابَ يَعْلَمُونَ أَنَّهُ مُنَزَّلٌ مِّن رَّبِّكَ بِالْحَقِّ ۖ فَلَا تَكُونَنَّ مِنَ الْمُمْتَرِينَ ۝

وَتَمَّتْ كَلِمَتُ رَبِّكَ صِدْقًا وَعَدْلًا ۚ لَّا مُبَدِّلَ لِ

131

If thou were to obey the majority of those on earth, they would lead thee astray from Allah's way. They follow only conjecture, and they do nothing but guess. Surely, thy Lord knows best those who stray away from His way, and He knows best those who are rightly guided. (117—118)

Eat ye of that over which the name of Allah has been pronounced, if you are believers in His Signs. Why should you not eat of that over which the name of Allah has been pronounced, when He has already explained to you that which He has forbidden unto you, save that to which you are driven by necessity? Surely, many mislead others by following their vain desires through lack of knowledge. Assuredly, thy Lord knows best the transgressors. Eschew both that which is manifestly sinful and that which is sinful in essence though not appearing to be so. Surely, those who commit sin will be requited for that which they do. Eat not that on which the name of Allah has not been pronounced, for that, surely, is disobedience. The rebellious ones keep inciting their friends that they may contend with you. If you obey them you will become of those who associate partners with Allah. (119—122)

Can he who was as dead and We gave him life and appointed for him a light whereby he walks among people, be like one who is, as it were, in utter darkness whence he can by no means come forth? In like manner have the doings of the disbelievers been made to seem fair to them. (123)

لِكَلِمٰتِهٖ وَهُوَ السَّمِيْعُ الْعَلِيْمُ ۞

وَاِنْ تُطِعْ اَكْثَرَ مَنْ فِى الْاَرْضِ يُضِلُّوْكَ عَنْ سَبِيْلِ اللّٰهِ اِنْ يَّتَّبِعُوْنَ اِلَّا الظَّنَّ وَاِنْ هُمْ اِلَّا يَخْرُصُوْنَ ۞

اِنَّ رَبَّكَ هُوَ اَعْلَمُ مَنْ يَّضِلُّ عَنْ سَبِيْلِهٖ وَهُوَ اَعْلَمُ بِالْمُهْتَدِيْنَ ۞

فَكُلُوْا مِمَّا ذُكِرَ اسْمُ اللّٰهِ عَلَيْهِ اِنْ كُنْتُمْ بِاٰيٰتِهٖ مُؤْمِنِيْنَ ۞

وَمَا لَكُمْ اَلَّا تَأْكُلُوْا مِمَّا ذُكِرَ اسْمُ اللّٰهِ عَلَيْهِ وَقَدْ فَصَّلَ لَكُمْ مَّا حَرَّمَ عَلَيْكُمْ اِلَّا مَا اضْطُرِرْتُمْ اِلَيْهِ وَاِنَّ كَثِيْرًا لَّيُضِلُّوْنَ بِاَهْوَآئِهِمْ بِغَيْرِ عِلْمٍ اِنَّ رَبَّكَ هُوَ اَعْلَمُ بِالْمُعْتَدِيْنَ ۞

وَذَرُوْا ظَاهِرَ الْاِثْمِ وَبَاطِنَهٗ اِنَّ الَّذِيْنَ يَكْسِبُوْنَ الْاِثْمَ سَيُجْزَوْنَ بِمَا كَانُوْا يَقْتَرِفُوْنَ ۞

وَلَا تَأْكُلُوْا مِمَّا لَمْ يُذْكَرِ اسْمُ اللّٰهِ عَلَيْهِ وَاِنَّهٗ لَفِسْقٌ وَاِنَّ الشَّيٰطِيْنَ لَيُوْحُوْنَ اِلٰٓى اَوْلِيٰٓئِهِمْ لِيُجَادِلُوْكُمْ وَاِنْ اَطَعْتُمُوْهُمْ اِنَّكُمْ لَمُشْرِكُوْنَ ۞

اَوَمَنْ كَانَ مَيْتًا فَاَحْيَيْنٰهُ وَجَعَلْنَا لَهٗ نُوْرًا يَّمْشِىْ بِهٖ فِى النَّاسِ كَمَنْ مَّثَلُهٗ فِى الظُّلُمٰتِ لَيْسَ بِخَارِجٍ مِّنْهَا كَذٰلِكَ زُيِّنَ لِلْكٰفِرِيْنَ مَا كَانُوْا يَعْمَلُوْنَ ۞

وَكَذٰلِكَ جَعَلْنَا فِىْ كُلِّ قَرْيَةٍ اَكٰبِرَ مُجْرِمِيْهَا لِيَمْكُرُوْا

Thus have We oriented the leading sinners in every town, with the result that they devise plots therein against Allah's Messengers, but in truth they plot only against their own selves and they perceive it not. When a Sign comes to them they say: We will not believe until to us is vouchsafed revelation like that which is vouchsafed to the Messengers of Allah. Allah knows best whom to appoint His Messenger. Humiliation before Allah and severe punishment shall surely overtake the sinners because of their plotting. Whomsoever Allah wills to guide, He opens his mind to the acceptance of Islam; and whomsoever He wills to let go astray, He causes His breast to be constricted and oppressed, as though he was mounting up into the sky. Thus does Allah inflict punishment on those who do not believe. (124—126)

This is the straight path leading to thy Lord. We have explained the Signs in detail for a people who take heed. For them is the abode of peace with their Lord, and He is their Helper because of that which they did. (127—128)

On the day when He will gather them all together, He will say: O company of big ones, you exploited the people. Their supporters from among the common people will say: Our Lord, some of us have benefited from others, but now we have reached the end of our term which Thou didst appoint for us. He will announce: The Fire is your abode, wherein you shall abide, except that which Allah may will. Surely thy Lord is Wise, All-Knowing. In this manner We make the wrongdoers helpers some of the others, because of that which they do. (129—130)

O company of men, big and small, did not Messengers come to you from among yourselves who recited to you My Signs and warned you of your meeting with Me this day? They will say: We bear witness against ourselves to that effect. The life of this world beguiled them with vain hopes, and they will bear witness against themselves that they were disbelievers. Messengers are sent because thy Lord would not destroy the towns unjustly while their people have not been warned. Everyone will rank according to his conduct. Thy Lord is not unmindful of that which they do. (131—133)

Thy Lord is Self-Sufficient, full of mercy. He can do away with you if He please and cause to succeed you whoso He pleases even as He raised you from the off-spring of another people. That which you are promised shall surely come to pass and you cannot frustrate Allah's design. Say to them: O my people, do you pursue your purpose and I shall pursue mine, then soon will you know in whose favour is determined the ultimate issue of this life. Surely, the wrongdoers shall not prosper. (134—136)

They assign to Allah a portion of the crops and cattle which He produces and out of their fancy they say: So much is for Allah and so much is for our idols. Then they claim that the portion which is for their idols does not reach Allah but that the portion which is for Allah reaches their idols. Evil is that which they judge. In like manner have those they associate with Allah made the slaying of their children appear pleasing to many of the idolaters that they may ruin them and make their religion obscure to them. If Allah had so willed, the idolaters would not have done this; so do thou ignore them and that which they fabricate. Of their fancy they assert: Such and such cattle and crops are forbidden.

134

None shall eat thereof save those we designate. They forbid some cattle being ridden or used as beasts of burden. There are some cattle over which they do not pronounce the name of Allah. All this they fabricate as a lie against Allah. Soon will He requite them for that which they fabricate. They also assert: That which is in the wombs of such and such cattle is exclusively for our males and is forbidden to our women; but if it be born dead, they can all share in it. Soon will He requite them for their assertion. Surely, He is Wise, All-Knowing. Losers indeed are they who kill their children foolishly out of ignorance, and make unlawful that which Allah has provided for them, fabricating a lie against Allah. They have gone astray and have not chosen to be rightly guided. (137—141)

He it is Who has produced trellised and untrellised gardens and date-palms and crops, all varying in taste, and the olive and the pomegranate, similar and dissimilar. Eat of the fruit of each when it bears fruit, and pay His due on the day of harvesting, but be not extravagant. Surely, He loves not the extravagant. (142)

Of the cattle there are some for burden and some for slaughter. Eat of that which Allah has provided for you, and follow not in the footsteps of Satan, surely he is your declared enemy. Allah has created in pairs eight animals; of the sheep two and of the goats two. Ask them: Is it the two males He has forbidden or the two females or that which the wombs of the two females contain? Answer me on the basis of knowledge, if you are truthful. Again, of the camels there are two, and of the oxen two. Ask them: Is it the two males He has forbidden, or the two females or that which the wombs of the two females contain? Were you present when Allah enjoined this on you? If not, then who is more unjust than one who fabricates a lie against Allah that he may lead people astray without knowledge? Surely, Allah guides not the unjust people. (143—145)

Tell them: In that which has been revealed to me I do not find aught forbidden to one who wishes to eat, except that which dies of itself, or blood poured forth, or the flesh of swine, all these being unclean; or that which is profane, on which the name of someone other than Allah is invoked. But whoso is driven by necessity, not intending disobedience or exceeding his need, should know that thy Lord is Most Forgiving, Ever Merciful. To the Jews We forbade the flesh of all animals having claws, and the fat of oxen and sheep and goats, save that borne by their backs or intestines or that which adheres to the bones. We prescribed this as a penalty for their rebellion; and most certainly We are Truthful. Should they accuse thee of falsehood, answer them: Your Lord is possessed of all-embracing mercy, but His wrath will not be averted from the guilty people. (146—148)

Those who associate partners with Allah will surely say: If Allah had so willed, neither we nor our fathers would have associated partners with Allah; nor would we have declared anything as unlawful. In like manner did those who were before them reject as false Our commandments, until they experienced Our wrath. Ask them: Have you any sure knowledge that you can put forth to refute us? In fact you follow only conjecture and do nothing but guess. Tell them: Allah's is the argument that carries conviction. Had He so willed, He could surely have guided you all. (149—150)

حَرَّمَ أَمِ الْأُنْثَيَيْنِ أَمَّا اشْتَمَلَتْ عَلَيْهِ أَرْحَامُ الْأُنْثَيَيْنِ أَمْ كُنْتُمْ شُهَدَآءَ إِذْ وَصَّىٰكُمُ اللّٰهُ بِهٰذَا فَمَنْ أَظْلَمُ مِمَّنِ افْتَرٰى عَلَى اللّٰهِ كَذِبًا لِّيُضِلَّ النَّاسَ بِغَيْرِ عِلْمٍ إِنَّ اللّٰهَ لَا يَهْدِى الْقَوْمَ الظّٰلِمِيْنَ ۞

قُلْ لَّا أَجِدُ فِيْ مَا أُوْحِيَ إِلَيَّ مُحَرَّمًا عَلٰى طَاعِمٍ يَّطْعَمُهُ إِلَّا أَنْ يَّكُوْنَ مَيْتَةً أَوْ دَمًا مَّسْفُوْحًا أَوْ لَحْمَ خِنْزِيْرٍ فَإِنَّهُ رِجْسٌ أَوْ فِسْقًا أُهِلَّ لِغَيْرِ اللّٰهِ بِهٖ فَمَنِ اضْطُرَّ غَيْرَ بَاغٍ وَّلَا عَادٍ فَإِنَّ رَبَّكَ غَفُوْرٌ رَّحِيْمٌ ۞

وَعَلَى الَّذِيْنَ هَادُوْا حَرَّمْنَا كُلَّ ذِيْ ظُفُرٍ وَمِنَ الْبَقَرِ وَالْغَنَمِ حَرَّمْنَا عَلَيْهِمْ شُحُوْمَهُمَا إِلَّا مَا حَمَلَتْ ظُهُوْرُهُمَا أَوِ الْحَوَايَا أَوْ مَا اخْتَلَطَ بِعَظْمٍ ذٰلِكَ جَزَيْنٰهُمْ بِبَغْيِهِمْ وَإِنَّا لَصٰدِقُوْنَ ۞

فَإِنْ كَذَّبُوْكَ فَقُلْ رَّبُّكُمْ ذُوْ رَحْمَةٍ وَّاسِعَةٍ وَلَا يُرَدُّ بَأْسُهُ عَنِ الْقَوْمِ الْمُجْرِمِيْنَ ۞

سَيَقُوْلُ الَّذِيْنَ أَشْرَكُوْا لَوْ شَآءَ اللّٰهُ مَا أَشْرَكْنَا وَلَا آبَاؤُنَا وَلَا حَرَّمْنَا مِنْ شَيْءٍ كَذٰلِكَ كَذَّبَ الَّذِيْنَ مِنْ قَبْلِهِمْ حَتّٰى ذَاقُوْا بَأْسَنَا قُلْ هَلْ عِنْدَكُمْ مِّنْ عِلْمٍ فَتُخْرِجُوْهُ لَنَا إِنْ تَتَّبِعُوْنَ إِلَّا الظَّنَّ وَإِنْ أَنْتُمْ إِلَّا تَخْرُصُوْنَ ۞

قُلْ فَلِلّٰهِ الْحُجَّةُ الْبَالِغَةُ فَلَوْ شَآءَ لَهَدٰىكُمْ أَجْمَعِيْنَ ۞

قُلْ هَلُمَّ شُهَدَآءَكُمُ الَّذِيْنَ يَشْهَدُوْنَ أَنَّ اللّٰهَ

Say to them: Call your witnesses who would testify that Allah has forbidden such and such. Then if any should so testify, do not thou testify along with them, nor follow the vain desires of those who have rejected Our Signs as false, and those who do not believe in the Hereafter and who set up equals with their Lord. (151)

Say, O Prophet: Come, let me rehearse to you that which your Lord has enjoined: that you associate not anything as partner with Him; that you behave benevolently towards your parents; that you destroy not your offspring for fear of poverty, it is We Who provide for you and for them; that you approach not evil of any kind whether manifest or hidden; and that you destroy not the life that Allah has declared sacred, except for just cause. That is what He has enjoined upon you, that you may understand. He has also enjoined upon you that you approach not the property of the orphan during his minority, except for the most beneficent purpose and that you give full measure and weight with justice; We require not of any one that which is beyond his capacity; and that when you speak, hold the scales even, though the person concerned be a kinsman; and that you fulfil the covenant of Allah. That is what He has enjoined upon you that you may take heed. He has also enjoined: This is My straight path; so follow it. Follow not diverse ways lest they lead you away from His way. That is what He has enjoined upon you that you may safeguard yourselves. (152—154)

We gave Moses the Book, to complete Our favour unto him who would pursue good, and an explanation of all things needed and a guidance and a mercy, that they might believe in the meeting with their Lord. (155)

This Quran is a Book that We have sent down, full of blessings; so follow it and be mindful of your duty to Allah that you may be shown mercy. We have sent it down lest you should say: The Book was sent down to only two peoples before us and we were not aware of their reading; or lest you should say: Had the Book been sent down to us, we would surely have been better guided than they. There has now come to you clear proof from your Lord and guidance and mercy. Who, then, is more unjust than one who rejects the Signs of Allah as false and turns aside from them? We will requite those who turn aside from our Signs with a dire chastisement because of their turning aside. They are waiting only that angels should come to them, or that thy Lord should come or that some of the Signs of thy Lord should come. The day some of the Signs of thy Lord shall come, it shall not profit any one who had not believed before, nor earned any good by his faith, to believe in them. Say to them: Wait on, we too are waiting. (156—159)

Thou hast no concern at all with those who have split up their religion and have become divided into factions. Their case is with Allah. He will inform them of that which they used to do. Whoso does good shall have ten times as much, and whoso does ill shall be requited with the like thereof; and they shall not be wrong-ed. (160—161)

Affirm: My Lord has guided me unto the straight path, the perfect religion, the religion of Abraham the upright, who was not of those who associate partners with Allah. Say: My Prayer, by which I hope to win through to everlasting life, and my sacrifices, which entail a type of death upon me, are all for Allah, the Lord of the worlds; He has no partner. Thus am I commanded and I am the foremost of those who submit wholly to Allah. (162—164)

Ask them: Shall I seek someone other than Allah as Lord; while He is the Lord of all things? Every one must bear the consequence of that which he does, and no bearer of a burden can bear the burden of another. Then to your Lord will be your return, and He will inform you of that wherein you used to differ. He it is Who has made you take the place of others on the earth, and has exalted some of you over others in rank, that He may try you by that which He has bestowed upon you. Surely, thy Lord's punishment approaches swiftly; and surely He is Most Forgiving, Ever-Merciful. (165—166)

قُلْ اَغَيْرَ اللّٰهِ اَبْغِيْ رَبًّا وَّهُوَ رَبُّ كُلِّ شَيْءٍ ۚ وَلَا تَكْسِبُ

كُلُّ نَفْسٍ اِلَّا عَلَيْهَا ۚ وَلَا تَزِرُ وَازِرَةٌ وِّزْرَ اُخْرٰى ۚ

ثُمَّ اِلٰى رَبِّكُمْ مَّرْجِعُكُمْ فَيُنَبِّئُكُمْ بِمَا كُنْتُمْ فِيْهِ

تَخْتَلِفُوْنَ ۝

وَهُوَ الَّذِيْ جَعَلَكُمْ خَلٰئِفَ الْاَرْضِ وَرَفَعَ بَعْضَكُمْ

فَوْقَ بَعْضٍ دَرَجٰتٍ لِّيَبْلُوَكُمْ فِيْ مَآ اٰتٰىكُمْ ۗ اِنَّ رَبَّكَ

سَرِيْعُ الْعِقَابِ ۖ وَاِنَّهٗ لَغَفُوْرٌ رَّحِيْمٌ ۝

سُوْرَةُ الْاَعْرَافِ مَكِّيَّةٌ

AL-A'RĀF

(Revealed before Hijra)

In the name of Allah, Most Gracious, Ever Merciful. (1)

بِسْمِ اللهِ الرَّحْمٰنِ الرَّحِيْمِ ۟

I AM ALLAH THE ALL-KNOWING, THE TRUTHFUL. (2)

الٓمّٓصۤ ۟

This Quran is a noble Book that is revealed unto thee, so let there be no constraint upon thee on account of it. Its purpose is that thou mayest warn thereby and that it should be a reminder to those who believe: Follow that which has been sent down to you from your Lord and follow not others as protectors beside Him. Little it is that you heed. How many a town have We destroyed! Our punishment came upon their dwellers by night or while they slept at noon. When Our punishment came upon them all they could utter was: We are indeed wrongdoers. We will certainly question those to whom We sent Messengers and We will certainly question the Messengers. Then will We expound to them the true position from Our knowledge, for We were never absent. (3—8)

كِتٰبٌ اُنْزِلَ اِلَيْكَ فَلَا يَكُنْ فِيْ صَدْرِكَ حَرَجٌ مِّنْهُ لِتُنْذِرَ بِهٖ وَذِكْرٰى لِلْمُؤْمِنِيْنَ ۟

اِتَّبِعُوْا مَا اُنْزِلَ اِلَيْكُمْ مِّنْ رَّبِّكُمْ وَلَا تَتَّبِعُوْا مِنْ دُوْنِهٖۤ اَوْلِيَاءَ ۗ قَلِيْلًا مَّا تَذَكَّرُوْنَ ۟

وَكَمْ مِّنْ قَرْيَةٍ اَهْلَكْنٰهَا فَجَاءَهَا بَأْسُنَا بَيَاتًا اَوْ هُمْ قَآئِلُوْنَ ۟

فَمَا كَانَ دَعْوٰىهُمْ اِذْ جَاءَهُمْ بَأْسُنَا اِلَّاۤ اَنْ قَالُوْۤا اِنَّا كُنَّا ظٰلِمِيْنَ ۟

فَلَنَسْئَلَنَّ الَّذِيْنَ اُرْسِلَ اِلَيْهِمْ وَلَنَسْئَلَنَّ الْمُرْسَلِيْنَ ۙ

فَلَنَقُصَّنَّ عَلَيْهِمْ بِعِلْمٍ وَّمَا كُنَّا غَآئِبِيْنَ ۟

The setting up of scales on that day will be a fact. Those will prosper whose scales will be heavy; while those whose scales are light will have ruined their souls because of their having been unjust to Our Signs. We did indeed establish you in the earth and provided for you therein the means of subsistence. But little thanks do you give. (9—11)

وَالْوَزْنُ يَوْمَئِذِ ِالْحَقُّ ۚ فَمَنْ ثَقُلَتْ مَوَازِيْنُهٗ فَاُولٰٓئِكَ هُمُ الْمُفْلِحُوْنَ ۟

وَمَنْ خَفَّتْ مَوَازِيْنُهٗ فَاُولٰٓئِكَ الَّذِيْنَ خَسِرُوْۤا اَنْفُسَهُمْ بِمَا كَانُوْا بِاٰيٰتِنَا يَظْلِمُوْنَ ۟

وَلَقَدْ مَكَّنّٰكُمْ فِي الْاَرْضِ وَجَعَلْنَا لَكُمْ فِيْهَا مَعَايِشَ ۗ قَلِيْلًا مَّا تَشْكُرُوْنَ ۟

We did bring you into being, then We gave you shape, then We commanded the angels: Submit to Adam. The angels submitted, but not Iblis, he was not among those who submitted. (12)

وَلَقَدْ خَلَقْنٰكُمْ ثُمَّ صَوَّرْنٰكُمْ ثُمَّ قُلْنَا لِلْمَلٰٓئِكَةِ اسْجُدُوْا لِاٰدَمَ ۖ فَسَجَدُوْۤا اِلَّاۤ اِبْلِيْسَ ۗ لَمْ يَكُنْ مِّنَ السّٰجِدِيْنَ ۟

Allah questioned him: What prevented thee from submitting when I commanded thee? He retorted: I am better than he. Thou hast created me of fire while him hast Thou created of clay. Allah said: In that case, depart hence. It behoves thee not to be arrogant here. Get out, thou art surely of those abased. Iblis pleaded: Grant me respite till the day when they will be raised up. Allah said: Thou art given respite. Iblis said: Since Thou hast brought about my ruin, I will assuredly lie in wait for them on Thy straight path and will approach them from fore and aft, and from right and left, and Thou wilt not find most of them grateful. Allah said: Get out hence, despised and banished. Whoso of them shall follow thee should know that I will surely fill hell with you all. (13—19)

قَالَ مَا مَنَعَكَ اَلَّا تَسْجُدَ اِذْ اَمَرْتُكَ قَالَ اَنَا خَيْرٌ مِّنْهُ خَلَقْتَنِى مِنْ نَّارٍ وَّخَلَقْتَهُ مِنْ طِيْنٍ ۝

قَالَ فَاهْبِطْ مِنْهَا فَمَا يَكُوْنُ لَكَ اَنْ تَتَكَبَّرَ فِيْهَا فَاخْرُجْ اِنَّكَ مِنَ الصّٰغِرِيْنَ ۝

قَالَ اَنْظِرْنِىْ اِلٰى يَوْمِ يُبْعَثُوْنَ ۝

قَالَ اِنَّكَ مِنَ الْمُنْظَرِيْنَ ۝

قَالَ فَبِمَا اَغْوَيْتَنِىْ لَاَقْعُدَنَّ لَهُمْ صِرَاطَكَ الْمُسْتَقِيْمَ ۙ۝

ثُمَّ لَاٰتِيَنَّهُمْ مِّنْ بَيْنِ اَيْدِيْهِمْ وَمِنْ خَلْفِهِمْ وَعَنْ اَيْمَانِهِمْ وَعَنْ شَمَآئِلِهِمْ ط وَلَا تَجِدُ اَكْثَرَهُمْ شٰكِرِيْنَ ۝

قَالَ اخْرُجْ مِنْهَا مَذْءُوْمًا مَّدْحُوْرًا ط لَمَنْ تَبِعَكَ مِنْهُمْ لَاَمْلَئَنَّ جَهَنَّمَ مِنْكُمْ اَجْمَعِيْنَ ۝

وَيٰٓاٰدَمُ اسْكُنْ اَنْتَ وَزَوْجُكَ الْجَنَّةَ فَكُلَا مِنْ حَيْثُ شِئْتُمَا وَلَا تَقْرَبَا هٰذِهِ الشَّجَرَةَ فَتَكُوْنَا مِنَ الظّٰلِمِيْنَ ۝

Allah said to Adam: Dwell thou and thy wife in the garden and eat and drink therefrom wherever you wish, but approach not this one tree lest you become wrong-doers. But Satan tempted them so that he might make known to them that which was hidden from them of their nakedness, and said to them: Your Lord has forbidden you this tree only lest you should become angels or should live for ever. He assured them with oaths: Surely, I am your sincere counsellor. Thus he brought about their fall by deceit. When they

فَوَسْوَسَ لَهُمَا الشَّيْطٰنُ لِيُبْدِىَ لَهُمَا مَا وُرِىَ عَنْهُمَا مِنْ سَوْاٰتِهِمَا وَقَالَ مَا نَهٰىكُمَا رَبُّكُمَا عَنْ هٰذِهِ الشَّجَرَةِ اِلَّآ اَنْ تَكُوْنَا مَلَكَيْنِ اَوْ تَكُوْنَا مِنَ الْخٰلِدِيْنَ ۝

وَقَاسَمَهُمَآ اِنِّىْ لَكُمَا لَمِنَ النّٰصِحِيْنَ ۙ۝

فَدَلّٰهُمَا بِغُرُوْرٍ ج فَلَمَّا ذَاقَا الشَّجَرَةَ بَدَتْ لَهُمَا

tasted of the tree their nakedness became
manifest to them and they started covering themselves with the embellishments
of the garden. Their Lord called out to
them: Did I not forbid you that tree and
say to you: Satan is surely your declared
enemy? They pleaded: Our Lord we have
wronged ourselves, and if Thou forgive us
not and have not mercy on us, we shall
surely be of the lost. Allah said: Go forth,
some of you will be enemies of others.
There is an abode for you and a provision
for a time on this earth. He told them: Therein shall you live, and therein shall you die,
and therefrom shall you be brought forth.
(20—26)

سَوْاٰتُهُمَا وَطَفِقَا يَخْصِفٰنِ عَلَيْهِمَا مِنْ وَّرَقِ
الْجَنَّةِ ؕ وَنَادٰىهُمَا رَبُّهُمَاۤ اَلَمْ اَنْهَكُمَا عَنْ تِلْكُمَا
الشَّجَرَةِ وَاَقُلْ لَّكُمَاۤ اِنَّ الشَّيْطٰنَ لَكُمَا عَدُوٌّ
مُّبِيْنٌ ۝

قَالَا رَبَّنَا ظَلَمْنَاۤ اَنْفُسَنَا ٚ وَاِنْ لَّمْ تَغْفِرْ لَنَا وَ
تَرْحَمْنَا لَنَكُوْنَنَّ مِنَ الْخٰسِرِيْنَ ۝

قَالَ اهْبِطُوْا بَعْضُكُمْ لِبَعْضٍ عَدُوٌّ ؕ وَلَكُمْ فِى الْاَرْضِ
مُسْتَقَرٌّ وَّمَتَاعٌ اِلٰى حِيْنٍ ۝

قَالَ فِيْهَا تَحْيَوْنَ وَفِيْهَا تَمُوْتُوْنَ وَمِنْهَا
تُخْرَجُوْنَ ۝

يٰبَنِيْۤ اٰدَمَ قَدْ اَنْزَلْنَا عَلَيْكُمْ لِبَاسًا يُّوَارِيْ سَوْاٰتِكُمْ
وَرِيْشًا ؕ وَلِبَاسُ التَّقْوٰى ٚ ذٰلِكَ خَيْرٌ ؕ ذٰلِكَ مِنْ
اٰيٰتِ اللهِ لَعَلَّهُمْ يَذَّكَّرُوْنَ ۝

يٰبَنِيْۤ اٰدَمَ لَا يَفْتِنَنَّكُمُ الشَّيْطٰنُ كَمَاۤ اَخْرَجَ اَبَوَيْكُمْ
مِّنَ الْجَنَّةِ يَنْزِعُ عَنْهُمَا لِبَاسَهُمَا لِيُرِيَهُمَا
سَوْاٰتِهِمَا ؕ اِنَّهٗ يَرٰىكُمْ هُوَ وَقَبِيْلُهٗ مِنْ حَيْثُ لَا
تَرَوْنَهُمْ ؕ اِنَّا جَعَلْنَا الشَّيٰطِيْنَ اَوْلِيَاۤءَ لِلَّذِيْنَ لَا
يُؤْمِنُوْنَ ۝

Children of Adam, We have created for
you raiment which covers your nakedness
and is a source of elegance; but the
raiment of righteousness is the best. That
is one of the Signs of Allah that they
may take heed. Children of Adam, let not
Satan seduce you, even as he turned your
parents out of the garden, stripping them
of their raiment that he might show them
their nakedness. He and his tribe espy you
from where you see them not. Surely We
have made the wicked ones friends of
those who do not believe. When they
commit an evil, they say: We found our
fathers doing it, and Allah has enjoined
it upon us. Say to them: Allah never
enjoins evil. Do you say of Allah that
which you know not? Tell them: My Lord

وَاِذَا فَعَلُوْا فَاحِشَةً قَالُوْا وَجَدْنَا عَلَيْهَاۤ اٰبَاۤءَنَا
وَاللهُ اَمَرَنَا بِهَا ؕ قُلْ اِنَّ اللهَ لَا يَأْمُرُ بِالْفَحْشَاۤءِ ؕ
اَتَقُوْلُوْنَ عَلَى اللهِ مَا لَا تَعْلَمُوْنَ ۝

قُلْ اَمَرَ رَبِّيْ بِالْقِسْطِ ؕ وَاَقِيْمُوْا وُجُوْهَكُمْ عِنْدَ كُلِّ

has enjoined justice and that you fix your attention aright at every time and place of worship and that you call upon Him holding Him alone worthy of worship. As He brought you into being, so shall you return. A portion has He guided, and a portion have earned error as their desert. They have taken evil ones for their friends, leaving aside Allah, and they imagine they are rightly guided. (27—31)

Children of Adam, put your minds and bodies in a state of tidiness at every time and place of worship and eat and drink but be not immoderate; surely He loves not the immoderate. Ask them: Who has forbidden the use of adornment which Allah has produced for His servants and wholesome articles of food? Tell them: These are for the benefit of those who believe, in this life also, and exclusively for them on the Day of Judgment. Thus do We expound the Signs for those who have knowledge. Tell them: My Lord has only forbidden indecencies, overt and hidden, and all manner of sin and wrongful transgression and that you associate with Allah that for which He has sent down no authority, and that you say of Allah that of which you have not knowledge. For every people there is a term, and when their time arrives, they cannot tarry behind a single hour, nor can they get ahead of it. (32—35)

Children of Adam, if Messengers come to you from among yourselves, rehearsing My commandments unto you, then whoso is mindful of his duty to Allah and acts righteously, on such shall come no fear nor shall they grieve. But those who reject Our Signs and turn away from them in disdain, these shall be the inmates of the Fire; therein shall they abide. Who is, then, more unjust than one who fabricates a lie against Allah or rejects His Signs as false? These shall continue to receive their share of the ordained punishment, until when Our messengers shall visit them to take charge of their souls, they shall ask them: Where are those you used to call upon beside Allah? They will answer: They have disappeared; and they will bear witness against themselves that they were disbelievers. Allah will say to them: Enter into the Fire along with groups of men, high and low, who passed away before you. Every time a people enters, it shall curse its sister people, until when they have all arrived in it, the last of them will say of the preceding one: Our Lord, these led us astray, so intensify their punishment in the Fire. He will say: The punishment of each is intensified, but you know it not. Thereupon the preceding one will say to the succeeding one: You have thus no preference over us; suffer, therefore, the punishment for all that you did. (36—40)

For those who reject Our Signs and turn away from them in disdain, the gates of heaven will not be opened, and they will not enter Paradise until their pride and arrogance are so humbled and reduced that they can pass through the eye of a needle. Thus do We requite the guilty ones. Hell will be their bed, and over them will be coverings of the same. Thus do We requite the wrongdoers. Those who believe and work righteousness (We do not require from any soul that which is beyond its capacity) are the inmates of heaven, therein shall they abide. We shall remove all rancour from their hearts. Beneath them shall flow rivers. They will say: All praise belongs to Allah Who has guided us hither; if Allah had not guided us we could not have found the way. The Messengers of our Lord did indeed bring us the truth. It shall be proclaimed unto them: This is the Paradise which has been bestowed upon you because of that which you did. (41—44)

بِاٰيٰتِهٖۤ اُولٰٓئِكَ يَنَالُهُمْ نَصِيْبُهُمْ مِّنَ الْكِتٰبِ ۭ حَتّٰۤى اِذَا جَآءَتْهُمْ رُسُلُنَا يَتَوَفَّوْنَهُمْ ۙ قَالُوْۤا اَيْنَ مَا كُنْتُمْ تَدْعُوْنَ مِنْ دُوْنِ اللّٰهِ ۭ قَالُوْا ضَلُّوْا عَنَّا وَشَهِدُوْا عَلٰۤى اَنْفُسِهِمْ اَنَّهُمْ كَانُوْا كٰفِرِيْنَ ۝

قَالَ ادْخُلُوْا فِيْۤ اُمَمٍ قَدْ خَلَتْ مِنْ قَبْلِكُمْ مِّنَ الْجِنِّ وَالْاِنْسِ فِى النَّارِ ۭ كُلَّمَا دَخَلَتْ اُمَّةٌ لَّعَنَتْ اُخْتَهَا ۭ حَتّٰۤى اِذَا ادَّارَكُوْا فِيْهَا جَمِيْعًا ۙ قَالَتْ اُخْرٰىهُمْ لِاُوْلٰىهُمْ رَبَّنَا هٰۤؤُلَآءِ اَضَلُّوْنَا فَاٰتِهِمْ عَذَابًا ضِعْفًا مِّنَ النَّارِ ۭ قَالَ لِكُلٍّ ضِعْفٌ وَّلٰكِنْ لَّا تَعْلَمُوْنَ ۝

وَقَالَتْ اُوْلٰىهُمْ لِاُخْرٰىهُمْ فَمَا كَانَ لَكُمْ عَلَيْنَا مِنْ فَضْلٍ فَذُوْقُوا الْعَذَابَ بِمَا كُنْتُمْ تَكْسِبُوْنَ ۧ

اِنَّ الَّذِيْنَ كَذَّبُوْا بِاٰيٰتِنَا وَاسْتَكْبَرُوْا عَنْهَا لَا تُفَتَّحُ لَهُمْ اَبْوَابُ السَّمَآءِ وَلَا يَدْخُلُوْنَ الْجَنَّةَ حَتّٰى يَلِجَ الْجَمَلُ فِيْ سَمِّ الْخِيَاطِ ۭ وَكَذٰلِكَ نَجْزِى الْمُجْرِمِيْنَ ۝

لَهُمْ مِّنْ جَهَنَّمَ مِهَادٌ وَّمِنْ فَوْقِهِمْ غَوَاشٍ ۭ وَكَذٰلِكَ نَجْزِى الظّٰلِمِيْنَ ۝

وَالَّذِيْنَ اٰمَنُوْا وَعَمِلُوا الصّٰلِحٰتِ لَا نُكَلِّفُ نَفْسًا اِلَّا وُسْعَهَآ اُولٰٓئِكَ اَصْحٰبُ الْجَنَّةِ ۚ هُمْ فِيْهَا خٰلِدُوْنَ ۝

وَنَزَعْنَا مَا فِيْ صُدُوْرِهِمْ مِّنْ غِلٍّ تَجْرِيْ مِنْ تَحْتِهِمُ الْاَنْهٰرُ ۚ وَقَالُوا الْحَمْدُ لِلّٰهِ الَّذِيْ هَدٰىنَا لِهٰذَا ۣ وَمَا كُنَّا لِنَهْتَدِيَ لَوْلَاۤ اَنْ هَدٰىنَا اللّٰهُ ۚ لَقَدْ جَآءَتْ رُسُلُ رَبِّنَا بِالْحَقِّ ۭ وَنُوْدُوْۤا اَنْ تِلْكُمُ الْجَنَّةُ اُوْرِثْتُمُوْهَا

The inmates of heaven will call out to the inmates of hell: We have indeed found that which our Lord had promised us to be true. Have you too found that which your Lord had promised to be true? Their answer will be: Indeed. Thereupon a crier will call out: The curse of Allah is on those wrongdoers who turned people away from the path of Allah and sought to make it appear crooked and who disbelieved in the life that was to come. Between the two parties there shall be a screen, and on the elevated places there shall be men who will know everyone by their distinguishing marks and they will call out to the people of heaven, who will not yet have entered it but will be hoping to do so: Peace be on you. When the eyes of these are turned towards the people of the Fire, they will supplicate: Our Lord, include us not among the wrongdoing people. (45—48)

The occupants of the elevated places will call out to men whom they will know by their distinguishing marks: Your numbers availed you not, nor your haughty claims. Pointing to the inmates of heaven they will ask: Are these the people about whom you swore that Allah will not extend mercy to them? Allah will say to the people of heaven: Enter Paradise; no fear shall come upon you nor shall you grieve. The inmates of the Fire shall call out to the inmates of heaven: Pour out some water on us, or give us something out of that which Allah has bestowed upon you. They will answer: Allah has forbidden all that to disbelievers, who treated religion as a pastime and a sport and whom the life of the world had beguiled. That day We shall forget them, as they forgot their meeting of that day with Us, and as they persisted in denying Our Signs. (49—52)

145

Surely, We have brought them a great Book which We have expounded with knowledge and which is a guidance and a mercy for a people who believe. Do they wait for the fulfilment of that of which it warns? On the day when that fulfilment comes, those who had neglected it before will say: The Messengers of our Lord did indeed bring the truth. Have we then any intercessors who would intercede for us? Or, could we be sent back that we might act differently from that which we used to do? They have indeed ruined their souls and that which they used to fabricate has failed them. (53—54)

وَ لَقَدْ جِئْنٰهُمْ بِكِتٰبٍ فَصَّلْنٰهُ عَلٰى عِلْمٍ هُدًى وَّ رَحْمَةً لِّقَوْمٍ يُّؤْمِنُوْنَ ۞

هَلْ يَنْظُرُوْنَ اِلَّا تَاْوِيْلَهٗ يَوْمَ يَاْتِىْ تَاْوِيْلُهٗ يَقُوْلُ الَّذِيْنَ نَسُوْهُ مِنْ قَبْلُ قَدْ جَآءَتْ رُسُلُ رَبِّنَا بِالْحَقِّ فَهَلْ لَّنَا مِنْ شُفَعَآءَ فَيَشْفَعُوْا لَنَآ اَوْ نُرَدُّ فَنَعْمَلَ غَيْرَ الَّذِيْ كُنَّا نَعْمَلُ قَدْ خَسِرُوْا اَنْفُسَهُمْ وَ ضَلَّ عَنْهُمْ مَّا كَانُوْا يَفْتَرُوْنَ ۞

Surely, your Lord is Allah, Who created the heavens and the earth in six periods; then He settled Himself on the Throne. He makes the night cover the day, pursuing it swiftly. He has created the sun and the moon and the stars, all made subservient by His command. Hearken, His is the creation and its regulation. Blessed is Allah, the Lord of the worlds. Call upon your Lord in humble entreaty in secret. He loves not those who exceed the limits. Create not disorder in the earth after it has been set in order, and call upon Him in fear and hope. Surely the mercy of Allah is close to those who carry out their duty to the utmost. (55—57)

اِنَّ رَبَّكُمُ اللّٰهُ الَّذِيْ خَلَقَ السَّمٰوٰتِ وَ الْاَرْضَ فِىْ سِتَّةِ اَيَّامٍ ثُمَّ اسْتَوٰى عَلَى الْعَرْشِ يُغْشِى الَّيْلَ النَّهَارَ يَطْلُبُهٗ حَثِيْثًا ۙ وَّ الشَّمْسَ وَ الْقَمَرَ وَ النُّجُوْمَ مُسَخَّرٰتٍ بِاَمْرِهٖ اَلَا لَهُ الْخَلْقُ وَ الْاَمْرُ تَبٰرَكَ اللّٰهُ رَبُّ الْعٰلَمِيْنَ ۞

اُدْعُوْا رَبَّكُمْ تَضَرُّعًا وَّخُفْيَةً اِنَّهٗ لَا يُحِبُّ الْمُعْتَدِيْنَ ۞

وَ لَا تُفْسِدُوْا فِى الْاَرْضِ بَعْدَ اِصْلَاحِهَا وَ ادْعُوْهُ خَوْفًا وَّطَمَعًا اِنَّ رَحْمَتَ اللّٰهِ قَرِيْبٌ مِّنَ الْمُحْسِنِيْنَ ۞

He it is Who sends the winds as glad tidings in advance of His mercy, till when they bear a heavy cloud, We drive it to a dead land, then We send down water therefrom, and We bring forth therewith fruits of every kind. In this manner We bring forth the dead that you may take heed. Good land brings forth its vegetation plentifully by the command of its Lord, and that which is poor brings forth poor crops scantily. Thus do We expound the Signs in diverse ways for a people who are grateful. (58—59)

وَ هُوَ الَّذِيْ يُرْسِلُ الرِّيٰحَ بُشْرًا بَيْنَ يَدَىْ رَحْمَتِهٖ حَتّٰى اِذَآ اَقَلَّتْ سَحَابًا ثِقَالًا سُقْنٰهُ لِبَلَدٍ مَّيِّتٍ فَاَنْزَلْنَا بِهِ الْمَآءَ فَاَخْرَجْنَا بِهٖ مِنْ كُلِّ الثَّمَرٰتِ كَذٰلِكَ نُخْرِجُ الْمَوْتٰى لَعَلَّكُمْ تَذَكَّرُوْنَ ۞

وَ الْبَلَدُ الطَّيِّبُ يَخْرُجُ نَبَاتُهٗ بِاِذْنِ رَبِّهٖ وَ الَّذِيْ خَبُثَ لَا يَخْرُجُ اِلَّا نَكِدًا كَذٰلِكَ نُصَرِّفُ الْاٰيٰتِ

146

We did send Noah to his people and he exhorted them: O my people worship Allah; you have no other god but He. I fear for you the chastisement of a heavy day. The leading men of his people said: Surely, we see that thou art involved in manifest error. Noah remonstrated: O my people I am involved in no error. Indeed I am a Messenger from the Lord of the worlds. I convey to you the messages of my Lord, and give you good advice, and I know from Allah that which you know not. Do you wonder that an exhortation has come to you from your Lord through a man from among yourselves, that he may warn you and that you may become righteous, so that Allah may show you mercy? But they charged him with falsehood. So We delivered him and those who were with him in the Ark, and caused to be drowned those who had rejected Our Signs. They were indeed a blind people. (60—65)

To 'Ad We sent their brother Hud. He exhorted them: O my people worship Allah, you have no other god but He. Will you not, then, be righteous? The leading men of his people who disbelieved said: We surely see that thou art involved in foolishness and we believe that thou art a liar. Hud remonstrated: O my people, I am not involved in any foolishness. Indeed I am a Messenger from the Lord of the worlds. I convey to you the messages of my Lord and I am your sincere and faithful counsellor. Do you wonder that an exhortation has come to you from your Lord through a man from among yourselves that he may warn you?

Call to mind, when He made you successors of the people of Noah and multiplied your numbers. Remember, then, the favours of Allah that you may prosper. They retorted: Hast thou come to us that we should worship Allah as the One God and should forsake that which our fathers used to worship? In that case, bring us that which thou dost threaten us with, if thou art truthful. Hud warned them: Punishment and wrath have befallen on you from your Lord. Do you contend with me about mere names that you and your fathers have devised, for which Allah has sent down no authority? Wait, then, for Allah's judgment; I am with you among those who wait. Then We delivered him and those who were with him, by Our mercy, and We cut off the last remnant of those who rejected Our Signs. They were not believers. (66—73)

To Thamud We sent their brother Saleh. He exhorted them: O my people, worship Allah: You have no other god but He. Truly there has come to you a clear proof from Him. This is a she-camel dedicated to the service of Allah which is a Sign for you. Leave her that she may feed in Allah's earth and do her no harm, lest a painful chastisement afflict you. Call to mind when He made you successors of 'Ad and settled you in the land. You build strongholds in the plains and hew out dwellings in the mountains. Remember, therefore, the favours of Allah and do not go about creating disorder in the land. (74—75)

The leading men of his people who were haughty asked those who were reckoned weak and had believed: Are you sure Saleh is a Messenger from his Lord? They answered: We surely believe in the teaching with which he has been sent. (76)

بَعْدِ قَوْمِ نُوحٍ وَّ زَادَكُمْ فِى الْخَلْقِ بَصْطَةً ۚ فَاذْكُرُوْۤا اٰلَآءَ اللّٰهِ لَعَلَّكُمْ تُفْلِحُوْنَ ۝

قَالُوْۤا اَجِئْتَنَا لِنَعْبُدَ اللّٰهَ وَحْدَهٗ وَنَذَرَ مَا كَانَ يَعْبُدُ اٰبَآؤُنَا ۚ فَأْتِنَا بِمَا تَعِدُنَآ اِنْ كُنْتَ مِنَ الصّٰدِقِيْنَ ۝

قَالَ قَدْ وَقَعَ عَلَيْكُمْ مِّنْ رَّبِّكُمْ رِجْسٌ وَّغَضَبٌ ۗ اَتُجَادِلُوْنَنِيْ فِيْۤ اَسْمَآءٍ سَمَّيْتُمُوْهَآ اَنْتُمْ وَاٰبَآؤُكُمْ مَّا نَزَّلَ اللّٰهُ بِهَا مِنْ سُلْطٰنٍ ۗ فَانْتَظِرُوْۤا اِنِّيْ مَعَكُمْ مِّنَ الْمُنْتَظِرِيْنَ ۝

فَاَنْجَيْنٰهُ وَالَّذِيْنَ مَعَهٗ بِرَحْمَةٍ مِّنَّا وَقَطَعْنَا دَابِرَ الَّذِيْنَ كَذَّبُوْا بِاٰيٰتِنَا وَمَا كَانُوْا مُؤْمِنِيْنَ ۝

وَاِلٰى ثَمُوْدَ اَخَاهُمْ صٰلِحًا ۘ قَالَ يٰقَوْمِ اعْبُدُوا اللّٰهَ مَا لَكُمْ مِّنْ اِلٰهٍ غَيْرُهٗ ۚ قَدْ جَآءَتْكُمْ بَيِّنَةٌ مِّنْ رَّبِّكُمْ ۗ هٰذِهٖ نَاقَةُ اللّٰهِ لَكُمْ اٰيَةً فَذَرُوْهَا تَأْكُلْ فِيْۤ اَرْضِ اللّٰهِ وَلَا تَمَسُّوْهَا بِسُوْٓءٍ فَيَأْخُذَكُمْ عَذَابٌ اَلِيْمٌ ۝

وَاذْكُرُوْۤا اِذْ جَعَلَكُمْ خُلَفَآءَ مِنْ بَعْدِ عَادٍ وَّبَوَّاَكُمْ فِى الْاَرْضِ تَتَّخِذُوْنَ مِنْ سُهُوْلِهَا قُصُوْرًا وَّتَنْحِتُوْنَ الْجِبَالَ بُيُوْتًا ۚ فَاذْكُرُوْۤا اٰلَآءَ اللّٰهِ وَلَا تَعْثَوْا فِى الْاَرْضِ مُفْسِدِيْنَ ۝

قَالَ الْمَلَاُ الَّذِيْنَ اسْتَكْبَرُوْا مِنْ قَوْمِهٖ لِلَّذِيْنَ اسْتُضْعِفُوْا لِمَنْ اٰمَنَ مِنْهُمْ اَتَعْلَمُوْنَ اَنَّ صٰلِحًا مُّرْسَلٌ مِّنْ رَّبِّهٖ ۗ قَالُوْۤا اِنَّا بِمَاۤ اُرْسِلَ بِهٖ مُؤْمِنُوْنَ ۝

The haughty ones said: We definitely disbelieve in that in which you believe. Then they hamstrung the she-camel, and disobeyed the command of their Lord and said to Saleh: Now bring us that with which thou dost threaten us, if thou art truly one of the Messengers. So the earthquake seized them and they lay prone upon the ground in their homes. Saleh then departed communing with himself: O my people, I did convey to you the message of my Lord and gave you good advice, but you love not being advised. (77—80)

قَالَ الَّذِيۡنَ اسۡتَكۡبَرُوۡۤا اِنَّا بِالَّذِيۡۤ اٰمَنۡتُمۡ بِهٖ كٰفِرُوۡنَ ۞

فَعَقَرُوا النَّاقَةَ وَعَتَوۡا عَنۡ اَمۡرِ رَبِّهِمۡ وَقَالُوۡا يٰصٰلِحُ ائۡتِنَا بِمَا تَعِدُنَاۤ اِنۡ كُنۡتَ مِنَ الۡمُرۡسَلِيۡنَ ۞

فَاَخَذَتۡهُمُ الرَّجۡفَةُ فَاَصۡبَحُوۡا فِيۡ دَارِهِمۡ جٰثِمِيۡنَ ۞

فَتَوَلّٰى عَنۡهُمۡ وَقَالَ يٰقَوۡمِ لَقَدۡ اَبۡلَغۡتُكُمۡ رِسَالَةَ رَبِّيۡ وَنَصَحۡتُ لَكُمۡ وَلٰكِنۡ لَّا تُحِبُّوۡنَ النّٰصِحِيۡنَ ۞

وَلُوۡطًا اِذۡ قَالَ لِقَوۡمِهٖۤ اَتَاۡتُوۡنَ الۡفَاحِشَةَ مَا سَبَقَكُمۡ بِهَا مِنۡ اَحَدٍ مِّنَ الۡعٰلَمِيۡنَ ۞

Lot, whom We sent, rebuked his people: Do you realise you practise an abomination of which no people in the world before you has been guilty? You approach men lustfully in place of women. You are a people who exceed all bounds. The only answer of his people was: Turn them out of the town. They like to be accounted pure. We delivered Lot and his family, except his wife, who stayed behind. On them We loosed an avalanche of clay. Observe then, what was the end of the guilty ones. (81—85)

اِنَّكُمۡ لَتَاۡتُوۡنَ الرِّجَالَ شَهۡوَةً مِّنۡ دُوۡنِ النِّسَآءِ ۚ بَلۡ اَنۡتُمۡ قَوۡمٌ مُّسۡرِفُوۡنَ ۞

وَمَا كَانَ جَوَابَ قَوۡمِهٖۤ اِلَّاۤ اَنۡ قَالُوۡۤا اَخۡرِجُوۡهُمۡ مِّنۡ قَرۡيَتِكُمۡ ۚ اِنَّهُمۡ اُنَاسٌ يَّتَطَهَّرُوۡنَ ۞

فَاَنۡجَيۡنٰهُ وَاَهۡلَهٗۤ اِلَّا امۡرَاَتَهٗ ۖ كَانَتۡ مِنَ الۡغٰبِرِيۡنَ ۞

وَاَمۡطَرۡنَا عَلَيۡهِمۡ مَّطَرًا ۚ فَانۡظُرۡ كَيۡفَ كَانَ عَاقِبَةُ الۡمُجۡرِمِيۡنَ ۞

To Midian We sent their brother Shu'aib. He exhorted them: O my people, worship Allah, you have no other god but He. A clear Sign has come to you from your Lord. So give full measure and full weight and do not deliver short, and create not disorder in the earth after it has been set in order. This is the better for you, if you will believe. Do not set pickets along every path seeking to overawe those who would believe in Allah and to turn them away from Allah's path and to make it appear crooked.

وَاِلٰى مَدۡيَنَ اَخَاهُمۡ شُعَيۡبًا ۚ قَالَ يٰقَوۡمِ اعۡبُدُوا اللّٰهَ مَا لَكُمۡ مِّنۡ اِلٰهٍ غَيۡرُهٗ ۚ قَدۡ جَآءَتۡكُمۡ بَيِّنَةٌ مِّنۡ رَّبِّكُمۡ فَاَوۡفُوا الۡكَيۡلَ وَالۡمِيۡزَانَ وَلَا تَبۡخَسُوا النَّاسَ اَشۡيَآءَهُمۡ وَلَا تُفۡسِدُوۡا فِى الۡاَرۡضِ بَعۡدَ اِصۡلَاحِهَا ۚ ذٰلِكُمۡ خَيۡرٌ لَّكُمۡ اِنۡ كُنۡتُمۡ مُّؤۡمِنِيۡنَ ۞

وَلَا تَقۡعُدُوۡا بِكُلِّ صِرَاطٍ تُوۡعِدُوۡنَ وَتَصُدُّوۡنَ عَنۡ سَبِيۡلِ اللّٰهِ مَنۡ اٰمَنَ بِهٖ وَتَبۡغُوۡنَهَا عِوَجًا ۚ

Remember, you were few and He multiplied you, and keep in mind what was the end of those who created disorder. If it is the case that a party among you believes in that with which I have been sent, and a party does not believe, then have patience until Allah judges between us; He is the Best of judges. (86—88)

The leading men of his people, who were haughty, said: Assuredly, we will drive thee out, Shu'aib, and those with thee who have believed, from our town, or else you shall return to our creed. Shu'aib said: What! Even though we should be unwilling? If we were to return to your creed, after Allah has delivered us therefrom, we would be guilty of fabricating a lie against Allah. It behoves us not to return thereto except that Allah, our Lord, should so will. Our Lord has full knowledge of everything. In Allah have we put our trust. Our Lord, judge between us and our people with justice, for Thou art the Best of those who judge. The leading men of his people who disbelieved said: If you follow Shu'aib, you will certainly be the losers. So the earthquake seized them and they lay prone upon the ground in their homes; those who had charged Shu'aib with lying, as if they had never dwelt therein. Those who had charged Shu'aib with lying, it was they who were the losers. Shu'aib then departed, communing with himself: O my people, indeed I conveyed to you the messages of my Lord and gave you good advice. Now, how shall I sorrow after a disbelieving people? (89—94)

Never did We send a Prophet to any town but We afflicted its people with adversity and suffering, that they might become humble. (95)

Then We changed their hardship into ease until when they began to experience affluence and said: Our fathers also had experience of adversity and prosperity; We afflicted them suddenly with chastisement, while they perceived not the cause thereof. If the people of those towns had believed and been righteous, We would surely have bestowed blessings upon them from heaven and earth, but they rejected the Prophets, so We seized them because of that which they did. Do the people of these towns now feel secure against the coming of Our punishment upon them by night while they are asleep? Or, do they feel secure against the coming of Our punishment upon them in the forenoon while they are at play? Do they feel secure against the design of Allah? None feels secure against the design of Allah, except those that are losers. (96—100)

Does it not instruct those who have inherited the earth in succession to its former people that We could punish them for their sins, if We please, and seal up their hearts, so that they would not lend ear to words of guidance? Such were the towns some of whose annals We have recited to thee. Their Messengers did come to them with clear proofs, but they would not believe that which they had rejected initially. In this manner does Allah seal up the hearts of the disbelievers. We did not find most of them true to their covenants, indeed We found most of them to be unfaithful. (101—103)

After them We sent Moses with Our Signs to Pharaoh and his nobles, but they rejected them unjustly. Observe, then, what was the end of those who stirred up mischief. (104)

Moses said to Pharaoh: Truly I am a Messenger from the Lord of the worlds. It is not befitting that I should say aught concerning Allah except the truth. I have come to you with a clear Sign from your Lord, therefore, let the children of Israel go with me. Pharaoh replied: If thou hast indeed come with a Sign, then come out with it, if thou art truthful. Thereupon Moses put down his rod, and suddenly it appeared as a visible serpent; and he drew forth his hand, and it appeared white to the onlookers. Some of the chiefs of Pharaoh's people said: This is most surely a skilful magician who desires to turn you out from your land. Then what do you advise? Others said to Pharaoh: Put off Moses and his brother awhile, and send announcers into the cities, who should bring into thy presence every skilful magician. The magicians came to Pharaoh and asked: Shall we have a reward, if we should prevail? Pharaoh said: Certainly, and you will also become my courtiers. (105—115)

The magicians said to Moses: Will you make your cast or shall we? He answered: You make your cast. When they made their cast, they bewitched the eyes of the people and struck them with awe and perpetrated a mighty illusion. We directed Moses: Cast down thy rod; and lo, it appeared to swallow up all that they had fabricated. So was the truth established, and what they did was proved vain. Thus were they vanquished there and then and retreated in humiliation. (116—120)

وَقَالَ مُوۡسٰى يٰفِرۡعَوۡنُ اِنِّىۡ رَسُوۡلٌ مِّنۡ رَّبِّ الۡعٰلَمِيۡنَ ۙ

حَقِيۡقٌ عَلٰٓى اَنۡ لَّاۤ اَقُوۡلَ عَلَى اللّٰهِ اِلَّا الۡحَقَّ ؕ قَدۡ جِئۡتُكُمۡ بِبَيِّنَةٍ مِّنۡ رَّبِّكُمۡ فَاَرۡسِلۡ مَعِىَ بَنِىۡۤ اِسۡرَآءِيۡلَ ؕ

قَالَ اِنۡ كُنۡتَ جِئۡتَ بِاٰيَةٍ فَاۡتِ بِهَاۤ اِنۡ كُنۡتَ مِنَ الصّٰدِقِيۡنَ ۞

فَاَلۡقٰى عَصَاهُ فَاِذَا هِىَ ثُعۡبَانٌ مُّبِيۡنٌ ۚ

وَّنَزَعَ يَدَهُ فَاِذَا هِىَ بَيۡضَآءُ لِلنّٰظِرِيۡنَ ۧ

قَالَ الۡمَلَاُ مِنۡ قَوۡمِ فِرۡعَوۡنَ اِنَّ هٰذَا لَسٰحِرٌ عَلِيۡمٌ ۙ

يُّرِيۡدُ اَنۡ يُّخۡرِجَكُمۡ مِّنۡ اَرۡضِكُمۡ ۚ فَمَاذَا تَاۡمُرُوۡنَ ۞

قَالُوۡۤا اَرۡجِهۡ وَاَخَاهُ وَاَرۡسِلۡ فِى الۡمَدَآئِنِ حٰشِرِيۡنَ ۙ

يَاۡتُوۡكَ بِكُلِّ سٰحِرٍ عَلِيۡمٍ ۞

وَجَآءَ السَّحَرَةُ فِرۡعَوۡنَ قَالُوۡۤا اِنَّ لَنَا لَاَجۡرًا اِنۡ كُنَّا نَحۡنُ الۡغٰلِبِيۡنَ ۞

قَالَ نَعَمۡ وَاِنَّكُمۡ لَمِنَ الۡمُقَرَّبِيۡنَ ۞

قَالُوۡا يٰمُوۡسٰٓى اِمَّاۤ اَنۡ تُلۡقِىَ وَاِمَّاۤ اَنۡ نَّكُوۡنَ نَحۡنُ الۡمُلۡقِيۡنَ ۞

قَالَ اَلۡقُوۡا ۚ فَلَمَّاۤ اَلۡقَوۡا سَحَرُوۡۤا اَعۡيُنَ النَّاسِ وَاسۡتَرۡهَبُوۡهُمۡ وَجَآءُوۡ بِسِحۡرٍ عَظِيۡمٍ ۞

وَاَوۡحَيۡنَاۤ اِلٰى مُوۡسٰٓى اَنۡ اَلۡقِ عَصَاكَ ۚ فَاِذَا هِىَ تَلۡقَفُ مَا يَاۡفِكُوۡنَ ۚ

فَوَقَعَ الۡحَقُّ وَبَطَلَ مَا كَانُوۡا يَعۡمَلُوۡنَ ۚ

فَغُلِبُوۡا هُنَالِكَ وَانۡقَلَبُوۡا صٰغِرِيۡنَ ۚ

They felt impelled to fall down prostrate in token of submission, and said: We believe in the Lord of the worlds, the Lord of Moses and Aaron. Pharaoh exploded: What! You have believed in him even before I gave you leave! Surely, this is a plot that you have hatched together in the city, that you may turn out there-from its people, but you shall soon know the consequences. Most surely will I cut off your hands and your feet on alternate sides, then will I crucify you all together. They answered: What then? In any case, to our Lord shall we return. Thou art incensed with us only because we have believed in the Signs of our Lord when they came to us. We pray to our Lord: Send down on us steadfastness and cause us to die in a state of submission to Thee. (121—127)

Some of the chiefs of Pharaoh's people said to him: Wilt thou leave Moses and his people to create disorder in the land and forsake thee and thy gods? He answered: We shall certainly slay their male children and spare their female ones. Surely, We dominate them. Moses said to his people: Seek help from Allah and be steadfast. Surely, the earth belongs to Allah; He bestows it as heritage on whomsoever He pleases of His servants, and the pleasing end is that of the righteous. They replied: We were persecuted before thou camest to us and even after thou camest to us. Moses said: Your Lord might soon destroy your enemy and make you His vicegerents in the land, that He may then see how you conduct yourselves. (128—130)

We afflicted the people of Pharaoh with hard times and poor harvests, that they might be admonished. When prosperity came to them, they said: This is our due; but when they were afflicted with hardship they ascribed it as an ill-omen to Moses and those with him. Surely, the cause of their evil fortune was with Allah, though most of them knew not. They said to Moses: Whatever Sign thou mayest bring us to delude us with, we shall not believe in thee. Then We afflicted them with storms, and locusts, and lice, and frogs, and blood, so many distinct Signs, but they remained haughty and became a sinful people. Each time the punishment fell upon them they cried out: Pray for us, Moses, to thy Lord reminding Him of the promises He has made thee; if thou remove from us this torment, we will surely believe in thee and we will surely send with thee the children of Israel. But when We removed from them the torment for a determined term, they at once broke their promise. So We exacted retribution from them and drowned them in the sea, because they rejected Our Signs as false and were heedless of them. (131—137)

We made the people who were esteemed weak and were illtreated, inheritors of the eastern parts and western parts of the land which We had blessed. The gracious promise of thy Lord was thus fulfilled in favour of the children of Israel, because they had been steadfast; and We destroyed all that Pharaoh and his people had built and all that they had raised high. We brought the children of Israel across the sea, and they came upon a people who

الشَّمَرٰتِ لَعَلَّهُمْ يَذَّكَّرُوْنَ ۞

فَاِذَا جَآءَتْهُمُ الْحَسَنَةُ قَالُوْا لَنَا هٰذِهٖ ۚ وَاِنْ تُصِبْهُمْ سَيِّئَةٌ يَّطَّيَّرُوْا بِمُوْسٰى وَمَنْ مَّعَهٗ ؕ اَلَآ اِنَّمَا طٰٓئِرُهُمْ عِنْدَ اللّٰهِ وَلٰكِنَّ اَكْثَرَهُمْ لَا يَعْلَمُوْنَ ۞

وَقَالُوْا مَهْمَا تَأْتِنَا بِهٖ مِنْ اٰيَةٍ لِّتَسْحَرَنَا بِهَا ۙ فَمَا نَحْنُ لَكَ بِمُؤْمِنِيْنَ ۞

فَاَرْسَلْنَا عَلَيْهِمُ الطُّوْفَانَ وَالْجَرَادَ وَالْقُمَّلَ وَالضَّفَادِعَ وَالدَّمَ اٰيٰتٍ مُّفَصَّلٰتٍ ۫ فَاسْتَكْبَرُوْا وَكَانُوْا قَوْمًا مُّجْرِمِيْنَ ۞

وَلَمَّا وَقَعَ عَلَيْهِمُ الرِّجْزُ قَالُوْا يٰمُوْسَى ادْعُ لَنَا رَبَّكَ بِمَا عَهِدَ عِنْدَكَ ۚ لَئِنْ كَشَفْتَ عَنَّا الرِّجْزَ لَنُؤْمِنَنَّ لَكَ وَلَنُرْسِلَنَّ مَعَكَ بَنِيْٓ اِسْرَآءِيْلَ ۞

فَلَمَّا كَشَفْنَا عَنْهُمُ الرِّجْزَ اِلٰٓى اَجَلٍ هُمْ بَالِغُوْهُ اِذَا هُمْ يَنْكُثُوْنَ ۞

فَانْتَقَمْنَا مِنْهُمْ فَاَغْرَقْنٰهُمْ فِى الْيَمِّ بِاَنَّهُمْ كَذَّبُوْا بِاٰيٰتِنَا وَكَانُوْا عَنْهَا غٰفِلِيْنَ ۞

وَاَوْرَثْنَا الْقَوْمَ الَّذِيْنَ كَانُوْا يُسْتَضْعَفُوْنَ مَشَارِقَ الْاَرْضِ وَمَغَارِبَهَا الَّتِيْ بٰرَكْنَا فِيْهَا ؕ وَتَمَّتْ كَلِمَتُ رَبِّكَ الْحُسْنٰى عَلٰى بَنِيْٓ اِسْرَآءِيْلَ ۙ بِمَا صَبَرُوْا ؕ وَدَمَّرْنَا مَا كَانَ يَصْنَعُ فِرْعَوْنُ وَقَوْمُهٗ وَمَا كَانُوْا يَعْرِشُوْنَ ۞

وَجَاوَزْنَا بِبَنِيْٓ اِسْرَآءِيْلَ الْبَحْرَ فَاَتَوْا عَلٰى قَوْمٍ

were assiduous in the worship of their idols. So they said to Moses: Make for us a god like their gods. He rebuked them: You are indeed an ignorant people. Doomed to destruction is that in which they are engaged and vain is all that they do. He added: Shall I seek for you a god other than Allah, while it is He who has exalted you above all peoples? (138—141)

Children of Israel, call to mind when We delivered you from Pharaoh's people who afflicted you with grievous torment, slaying your male children and sparing your female ones; and that was a great trial for you from your Lord. (142)

We made Moses a promise of thirty nights and supplemented it with ten. Thus the period appointed by his Lord was completed, extending over forty nights. Moses said to his brother Aaron: Take my place among my people in my absence and keep their welfare in mind, and follow not the way of the mischief-makers. When Moses arrived at the tryst at Our appointed time and his Lord spoke to him, he supplicated: Lord, show Thyself to me that I may behold Thee. He replied: Thou canst by no means behold Me, but look towards the mountain, if it remains firm in its place, then shalt thou see Me. When his Lord manifested Himself on the mountain, He broke it into bits and Moses fell into a faint. When he recovered, he exclaimed: Holy art Thou, I turn wholly towards Thee, and I am the foremost among those who believe. Allah reassured him: Moses, I have exalted thee above the people of thy time by My messages and My words. So take fast hold of that which I have given thee and be among the grateful. We wrote for him upon some tablets Our commandments comprising admonition of all descriptions and explanation of all things needed, and

يَعْكُفُوْنَ عَلٰۤى اَصْنَامٍ لَّهُمْ ۚ قَالُوْا يٰمُوْسَى اجْعَلْ لَّنَاۤ اِلٰهًا كَمَا لَهُمْ اٰلِهَةٌ ۚ قَالَ اِنَّكُمْ قَوْمٌ تَجْهَلُوْنَ ۝

اِنَّ هٰۤؤُلَآءِ مُتَبَّرٌ مَّا هُمْ فِيْهِ وَ بٰطِلٌ مَّا كَانُوْا يَعْمَلُوْنَ ۝

قَالَ اَغَيْرَ اللّٰهِ اَبْغِيْكُمْ اِلٰهًا وَّ هُوَ فَضَّلَكُمْ عَلَى الْعٰلَمِيْنَ ۝

وَ اِذْ اَنْجَيْنٰكُمْ مِّنْ اٰلِ فِرْعَوْنَ يَسُوْمُوْنَكُمْ سُوْٓءَ الْعَذَابِ ۚ يُقَتِّلُوْنَ اَبْنَآءَكُمْ وَ يَسْتَحْيُوْنَ نِسَآءَكُمْ ۚ وَ فِيْ ذٰلِكُمْ بَلَآءٌ مِّنْ رَّبِّكُمْ عَظِيْمٌ ۝

وَ وٰعَدْنَا مُوْسٰى ثَلٰثِيْنَ لَيْلَةً وَّ اَتْمَمْنٰهَا بِعَشْرٍ فَتَمَّ مِيْقَاتُ رَبِّهٖۤ اَرْبَعِيْنَ لَيْلَةً ۚ وَ قَالَ مُوْسٰى لِاَخِيْهِ هٰرُوْنَ اخْلُفْنِيْ فِيْ قَوْمِيْ وَ اَصْلِحْ وَلَا تَتَّبِعْ سَبِيْلَ الْمُفْسِدِيْنَ ۝

وَ لَمَّا جَآءَ مُوْسٰى لِمِيْقَاتِنَا وَ كَلَّمَهٗ رَبُّهٗ ۙ قَالَ رَبِّ اَرِنِيْۤ اَنْظُرْ اِلَيْكَ ۚ قَالَ لَنْ تَرٰىنِيْ وَلٰكِنِ انْظُرْ اِلَى الْجَبَلِ فَاِنِ اسْتَقَرَّ مَكَانَهٗ فَسَوْفَ تَرٰىنِيْ ۚ فَلَمَّا تَجَلّٰى رَبُّهٗ لِلْجَبَلِ جَعَلَهٗ دَكًّا وَّ خَرَّ مُوْسٰى صَعِقًا ۚ فَلَمَّاۤ اَفَاقَ قَالَ سُبْحٰنَكَ تُبْتُ اِلَيْكَ وَ اَنَا اَوَّلُ الْمُؤْمِنِيْنَ ۝

قَالَ يٰمُوْسٰۤى اِنِّي اصْطَفَيْتُكَ عَلَى النَّاسِ بِرِسٰلٰتِيْ وَ بِكَلَامِيْ ۖ فَخُذْ مَاۤ اٰتَيْتُكَ وَ كُنْ مِّنَ الشّٰكِرِيْنَ ۝

وَ كَتَبْنَا لَهٗ فِي الْاَلْوَاحِ مِنْ كُلِّ شَيْءٍ مَّوْعِظَةً وَّ تَفْصِيْلًا

said to him: Take fast hold of these and bid thy people to hold fast to the best thereof. Soon shall I show you the destination of the transgressors. I shall turn away from My Signs those who behave haughtily in the land in an unjust manner; even if they see every kind of Sign, they will not believe therein. Even if they recognise the right way, they will not follow it; but if they see the way of error they will follow it eagerly. That is because they rejected Our Signs as false and were heedless of them. Those who disbelieve in Our Signs and the meeting of the Hereafter, vain is all they do. They will be requited only according to that which they did. (143—148)

In his absence, the people of Moses took to the worship of a calf, fashioned out of their ornaments, which was a mere lifeless body from which issued a meaningless sound. Did they not consider that it did not speak coherently to them nor indicate to them any way of guidance? They took to worshipping it and became transgressors. When they were afflicted with remorse, and realised that they had indeed gone astray, they said: If our Lord does not have mercy on us, and forgive us, we shall surely be among the losers. When Moses returned to his people, full of indignation and grief, he shouted at them: Evil is that which you did in my place in my absence! Was this an attempt to hasten the command of your Lord? He put down the tablets and catching hold of his brother by the hair of his head started pulling him towards himself. Aaron pleaded: Son of my mother, the people considered me weak, and were about to kill me. Therefore, do not furnish the enemies with cause to rejoice over my discomfiture, and count me not with the unjust people. Thereupon Moses prayed: Lord, forgive me and my brother, and admit us to Thy mercy: Thou art the most Merciful of those

لِكُلِّ شَيْءٍ فَخُذْهَا بِقُوَّةٍ وَّأْمُرْ قَوْمَكَ يَأْخُذُوْا بِأَحْسَنِهَا ۚ سَأُورِيْكُمْ دَارَ الْفٰسِقِيْنَ ۝

سَأَصْرِفُ عَنْ اٰيٰتِيَ الَّذِيْنَ يَتَكَبَّرُوْنَ فِى الْأَرْضِ بِغَيْرِ الْحَقِّ ۚ وَاِنْ يَّرَوْا كُلَّ اٰيَةٍ لَّا يُؤْمِنُوْا بِهَا ۚ وَاِنْ يَّرَوْا سَبِيْلَ الرُّشْدِ لَا يَتَّخِذُوْهُ سَبِيْلًا ۚ وَاِنْ يَّرَوْا سَبِيْلَ الْغَيِّ يَتَّخِذُوْهُ سَبِيْلًا ۚ ذٰلِكَ بِأَنَّهُمْ كَذَّبُوْا بِاٰيٰتِنَا وَكَانُوْا عَنْهَا غٰفِلِيْنَ ۝

وَالَّذِيْنَ كَذَّبُوْا بِاٰيٰتِنَا وَلِقَآءِ الْاٰخِرَةِ حَبِطَتْ أَعْمَالُهُمْ ۚ هَلْ يُجْزَوْنَ اِلَّا مَا كَانُوْا يَعْمَلُوْنَ ۝

وَاتَّخَذَ قَوْمُ مُوْسٰى مِنْ بَعْدِهِ مِنْ حُلِيِّهِمْ عِجْلًا جَسَدًا لَّهُ خُوَارٌ ۚ أَلَمْ يَرَوْا أَنَّهُ لَا يُكَلِّمُهُمْ وَلَا يَهْدِيْهِمْ سَبِيْلًا ۘ اتَّخَذُوْهُ وَكَانُوْا ظٰلِمِيْنَ ۝

وَلَمَّا سُقِطَ فِيْ أَيْدِيْهِمْ وَرَأَوْا أَنَّهُمْ قَدْ ضَلُّوْا ۙ قَالُوْا لَئِنْ لَّمْ يَرْحَمْنَا رَبُّنَا وَيَغْفِرْ لَنَا لَنَكُوْنَنَّ مِنَ الْخٰسِرِيْنَ ۝

وَلَمَّا رَجَعَ مُوْسٰى اِلٰى قَوْمِهِ غَضْبَانَ أَسِفًا ۙ قَالَ بِئْسَمَا خَلَفْتُمُوْنِيْ مِنْ بَعْدِيْ ۚ أَعَجِلْتُمْ أَمْرَ رَبِّكُمْ ۚ وَأَلْقَى الْأَلْوَاحَ وَأَخَذَ بِرَأْسِ أَخِيْهِ يَجُرُّهُ اِلَيْهِ ۚ قَالَ ابْنَ أُمَّ اِنَّ الْقَوْمَ اسْتَضْعَفُوْنِيْ وَكَادُوْا يَقْتُلُوْنَنِيْ ۖ فَلَا تُشْمِتْ بِيَ الْأَعْدَآءَ وَلَا تَجْعَلْنِيْ مَعَ الْقَوْمِ الظّٰلِمِيْنَ ۝

قَالَ رَبِّ اغْفِرْ لِيْ وَلِأَخِيْ وَأَدْخِلْنَا فِيْ رَحْمَتِكَ ۖ

who show mercy. Allah decreed: Those who took the calf for worship will be afflicted with wrath from their Lord and humiliation in the present life. Thus do We requite the impostors. As for those who worked evil and repented thereafter and believed; surely thy Lord is Most Forgiving, Ever Merciful after repentance. (149—154)

When the anger of Moses was somewhat appeased, he took up the tablets again, the text of which comprised guidance and mercy for those who fear their Lord. Moses chose seventy men of his people for Our meeting. When the earthquake overtook them, he supplicated: Lord, if Thou hadst pleased Thou couldst have destroyed them before this and me also. Wilt Thou destroy us for that which the foolish among us have done? This is but a trial from Thee. Thereby dost Thou adjudge as having gone astray those whom Thou willest, and Thou guidest whom Thou willest. Thou art our Protector, forgive us, therefore, and have mercy on us, for Thou art the Best of those who forgive. Ordain for us good in this world and in the next; we have been impelled towards thee. Allah reassured him: I will inflict My chastisement on those concerning whom I so determine; but My mercy encompasses all things; so I will ordain it for those who act righteously and pay the Zakat, and those who believe in Our Signs; and for those who follow the Messenger, the Prophet, the Immaculate one, whom they find mentioned in the Torah and the Gospel which are with them. He enjoins on them good and forbids them evil, declares lawful for them things wholesome and forbids them things harmful, and removes from them their burdens and the shackles that bound them. So those who shall believe in him and honour and support him, and

١٨ ع وَ اَنْتَ اَرْحَمُ الرّٰحِمِيْنَ ۟٥ ۚ

اِنَّ الَّذِيْنَ اتَّخَذُوا الْعِجْلَ سَيَنَالُهُمْ غَضَبٌ مِّنْ رَّبِّهِمْ وَ ذِلَّةٌ فِي الْحَيٰوةِ الدُّنْيَا ۚ وَ كَذٰلِكَ نَجْزِي الْمُفْتَرِيْنَ ۟٥

وَ الَّذِيْنَ عَمِلُوا السَّيِّاٰتِ ثُمَّ تَابُوْا مِنْ بَعْدِهَا وَ اٰمَنُوْۤا ۫ اِنَّ رَبَّكَ مِنْ بَعْدِهَا لَغَفُوْرٌ رَّحِيْمٌ ۟٥

وَ لَمَّا سَكَتَ عَنْ مُّوْسَى الْغَضَبُ اَخَذَ الْاَلْوَاحَ ۖ وَ فِيْ نُسْخَتِهَا هُدًى وَّ رَحْمَةٌ لِّلَّذِيْنَ هُمْ لِرَبِّهِمْ يَرْهَبُوْنَ ۟٥

وَ اخْتَارَ مُوْسٰى قَوْمَهٗ سَبْعِيْنَ رَجُلًا لِّمِيْقَاتِنَا ۚ فَلَمَّاۤ اَخَذَتْهُمُ الرَّجْفَةُ قَالَ رَبِّ لَوْ شِئْتَ اَهْلَكْتَهُمْ مِّنْ قَبْلُ وَ اِيَّايَ ۚ اَتُهْلِكُنَا بِمَا فَعَلَ السُّفَهَآءُ مِنَّا ۚ اِنْ هِيَ اِلَّا فِتْنَتُكَ ۚ تُضِلُّ بِهَا مَنْ تَشَآءُ وَ تَهْدِيْ مَنْ تَشَآءُ ۚ اَنْتَ وَلِيُّنَا فَاغْفِرْ لَنَا وَ ارْحَمْنَا وَ اَنْتَ خَيْرُ الْغَافِرِيْنَ ۟٥

وَ اكْتُبْ لَنَا فِيْ هٰذِهِ الدُّنْيَا حَسَنَةً وَّ فِي الْاٰخِرَةِ اِنَّا هُدْنَاۤ اِلَيْكَ ۚ قَالَ عَذَابِيْۤ اُصِيْبُ بِهٖ مَنْ اَشَآءُ ۚ وَ رَحْمَتِيْ وَسِعَتْ كُلَّ شَيْءٍ ۚ فَسَاَكْتُبُهَا لِلَّذِيْنَ يَتَّقُوْنَ وَ يُؤْتُوْنَ الزَّكٰوةَ وَ الَّذِيْنَ هُمْ بِاٰيٰتِنَا يُؤْمِنُوْنَ ۟٥

اَلَّذِيْنَ يَتَّبِعُوْنَ الرَّسُوْلَ النَّبِيَّ الْاُمِّيَّ الَّذِيْ يَجِدُوْنَهٗ مَكْتُوْبًا عِنْدَهُمْ فِي التَّوْرٰىةِ وَ الْاِنْجِيْلِ ۫ يَأْمُرُهُمْ بِالْمَعْرُوْفِ وَ يَنْهٰىهُمْ عَنِ الْمُنْكَرِ وَ يُحِلُّ لَهُمُ الطَّيِّبٰتِ وَ يُحَرِّمُ عَلَيْهِمُ الْخَبٰٓئِثَ وَ يَضَعُ عَنْهُمْ اِصْرَهُمْ وَ الْاَغْلٰلَ الَّتِيْ كَانَتْ عَلَيْهِمْ ۚ فَالَّذِيْنَ اٰمَنُوْا بِهٖ وَ

help him and follow the light that is sent down with him, they shall prosper. (155—158)

Proclaim, O Prophet: O mankind, verily I am Allah's Messenger to you all. To Him belongs the kingdom of the heavens and the earth. There is no god but He. He bestows life and He causes death. So believe in Allah and His Messenger, the Prophet, the Immaculate one, who believes in Allah and His words, and follow him that you may be rightly guided. (159)

Of the people of Moses there is a party who are guided by the truth and establish justice by means of it. We divided them into twelve tribes, now separate peoples. When his people asked for water We directed Moses: Strike that rock with thy rod; and there gushed forth from it twelve springs. Every tribe did know its drinking place. We caused the clouds to provide shade for them and We sent down for them Manna and Salwa, and exhorted them: Eat of the good things We have provided for you. They wronged us not, but it was themselves that they wronged. It was said to them: Dwell in this town and eat therefrom wherever you will, and say: Allah lighten our burden; and enter the gate in humility, We shall forgive you your sins and shall bestow further favours upon those who render perfect obedience. But the transgressors among them substituted another word in place of the one told them. So We sent upon them chastisement from heaven, because of their wrong-doing. (160—163)

Ask the people of Moses concerning the town situated along the sea, the people of which profaned the Sabbath. Their fish came to them in shoals on the Sabbath day, but did not come at all on non-Sabbath days. Thus did We try them because of their disobedience. When one party of them said to the other: Wherefore do you remonstrate with a people whom Allah is going to destroy or to afflict with a severe punishment? they answered: To acquit ourselves of our duty to your Lord, and that they may become righteous. When they forgot that with which they had been admonished, We delivered those who had admonished them, and We afflicted the transgressors with a grievous chastisement because they were rebellious. When, instead of amending, they became more persistent in the pursuit of that which they were forbidden, We condemned them: Be ye as apes, despised. (164—167)

Call to mind, when thy Lord proclaimed that He would surely set in authority over them, till the Day of Judgment, those who would afflict them with grievous torment. Thy Lord is Swift in exacting retribution, and He is also Most Forgiving, Ever Merciful. We broke them up into separate peoples in the earth. Among them are those that are righteous, and among them are those that are otherwise. We keep trying them with prosperity and adversity that they might turn back. They have been succeeded by others who have inherited the Book, but who occupy themselves in acquiring the goods of this world and keep saying: It will be forgiven us. If there came to them the opportunity of acquiring more of such goods, they would seize it. Was not the covenant taken from them in the Book that they would not say of Allah anything but the truth? They read that which is in the Book, and they know that the abode of the Hereafter is better for the righteous. Will you not, then, understand? (168—170)

سَبْتِهِمْ شُرَّعًا وَّيَوْمَ لَا يَسْبِتُوْنَ لَا تَأْتِيْهِمْ كَذٰلِكَ نَبْلُوْهُمْ بِمَا كَانُوْا يَفْسُقُوْنَ ۝

وَاِذْ قَالَتْ اُمَّةٌ مِّنْهُمْ لِمَ تَعِظُوْنَ قَوْمًا اللّٰهُ مُهْلِكُهُمْ اَوْ مُعَذِّبُهُمْ عَذَابًا شَدِيْدًا قَالُوْا مَعْذِرَةً اِلٰى رَبِّكُمْ وَلَعَلَّهُمْ يَتَّقُوْنَ ۝

فَلَمَّا نَسُوْا مَا ذُكِّرُوْا بِهٖ اَنْجَيْنَا الَّذِيْنَ يَنْهَوْنَ عَنِ السُّوْءِ وَاَخَذْنَا الَّذِيْنَ ظَلَمُوْا بِعَذَابٍ بَئِيْسٍ بِمَا كَانُوْا يَفْسُقُوْنَ ۝

فَلَمَّا عَتَوْا عَنْ مَّا نُهُوْا عَنْهُ قُلْنَا لَهُمْ كُوْنُوْا قِرَدَةً خَاسِئِيْنَ ۝

وَاِذْ تَأَذَّنَ رَبُّكَ لَيَبْعَثَنَّ عَلَيْهِمْ اِلٰى يَوْمِ الْقِيٰمَةِ مَنْ يَّسُوْمُهُمْ سُوْءَ الْعَذَابِ اِنَّ رَبَّكَ لَسَرِيْعُ الْعِقَابِ وَاِنَّهٗ لَغَفُوْرٌ رَّحِيْمٌ ۝

وَقَطَّعْنٰهُمْ فِى الْاَرْضِ اُمَمًا مِّنْهُمُ الصّٰلِحُوْنَ وَمِنْهُمْ دُوْنَ ذٰلِكَ وَبَلَوْنٰهُمْ بِالْحَسَنٰتِ وَالسَّيِّاٰتِ لَعَلَّهُمْ يَرْجِعُوْنَ ۝

فَخَلَفَ مِنْ بَعْدِهِمْ خَلْفٌ وَّرِثُوا الْكِتٰبَ يَأْخُذُوْنَ عَرَضَ هٰذَا الْاَدْنٰى وَيَقُوْلُوْنَ سَيُغْفَرُ لَنَا وَاِنْ يَّأْتِهِمْ عَرَضٌ مِّثْلُهٗ يَأْخُذُوْهُ اَلَمْ يُؤْخَذْ عَلَيْهِمْ مِّيْثَاقُ الْكِتٰبِ اَنْ لَّا يَقُوْلُوْا عَلَى اللّٰهِ اِلَّا الْحَقَّ وَدَرَسُوْا مَا فِيْهِ وَالدَّارُ الْاٰخِرَةُ خَيْرٌ لِّلَّذِيْنَ يَتَّقُوْنَ اَفَلَا تَعْقِلُوْنَ ۝

Those who hold fast by the Book, and observe Prayer, should know that surely We suffer not the reward of such righteous people to perish. When We shook the mountain above them, as if it were a canopy, they imagined it was about to fall on them, and We said to them: Hold fast to that which We have given you and keep in mind that which is in it that you may become righteous. (171—172)

وَالَّذِيْنَ يُمَسِّكُوْنَ بِالْكِتٰبِ وَاَقَامُوا الصَّلٰوةَ اِنَّا لَا نُضِيْعُ اَجْرَ الْمُصْلِحِيْنَ ۞

وَاِذْ نَتَقْنَا الْجَبَلَ فَوْقَهُمْ كَاَنَّهٗ ظُلَّةٌ وَّظَنُّوْا اَنَّهٗ وَاقِعٌ بِهِمْ خُذُوْا مَا اٰتَيْنٰكُمْ بِقُوَّةٍ وَّاذْكُرُوْا مَا فِيْهِ لَعَلَّكُمْ تَتَّقُوْنَ ۞

When thy Lord brought forth offspring from the loins of the sons of Adam, He made them witnesses against their own selves by asking them: Am I not your Lord? and they said: Indeed, we do bear witness to that. This He did lest you should say on the Day of Judgment: We were unaware of this; or you should say: It was our fathers who associated partners with Allah before us, and we were but their offspring following them. Wilt Thou then destroy us because of that which was done by the vain people? Thus do We expound the Signs that they may turn back. (173—175)

وَاِذْ اَخَذَ رَبُّكَ مِنْ بَنِيْ اٰدَمَ مِنْ ظُهُوْرِهِمْ ذُرِّيَّتَهُمْ وَاَشْهَدَهُمْ عَلٰى اَنْفُسِهِمْ اَلَسْتُ بِرَبِّكُمْ قَالُوْا بَلٰى شَهِدْنَا اَنْ تَقُوْلُوْا يَوْمَ الْقِيٰمَةِ اِنَّا كُنَّا عَنْ هٰذَا غٰفِلِيْنَ ۞

اَوْ تَقُوْلُوْا اِنَّمَا اَشْرَكَ اٰبَاؤُنَا مِنْ قَبْلُ وَكُنَّا ذُرِّيَّةً مِّنْ بَعْدِهِمْ اَفَتُهْلِكُنَا بِمَا فَعَلَ الْمُبْطِلُوْنَ ۞

وَكَذٰلِكَ نُفَصِّلُ الْاٰيٰتِ وَلَعَلَّهُمْ يَرْجِعُوْنَ ۞

Recite to them the case of him to whom We gave Our Signs, but he passed them by. Then Satan went after him and he became one of those who had gone astray. Had We so willed We would have exalted him by means of Our Signs, but he leaned towards the earth and followed his vain desires. His case is like that of a thirsty dog, if a stick is raised at it, it lolls out its tongue, and if it is left alone it does the same. Such is the case of the people who reject Our Signs as false. Recite all this to them that they may reflect. Evil is the case of the people who reject Our Signs; they only wrong themselves. Those whom Allah guides are alone on the right path; those whom He adjudges astray are the losers. (176—179)

وَاتْلُ عَلَيْهِمْ نَبَاَ الَّذِيْ اٰتَيْنٰهُ اٰيٰتِنَا فَانْسَلَخَ مِنْهَا فَاَتْبَعَهُ الشَّيْطٰنُ فَكَانَ مِنَ الْغٰوِيْنَ ۞

وَلَوْ شِئْنَا لَرَفَعْنٰهُ بِهَا وَلٰكِنَّهٗ اَخْلَدَ اِلَى الْاَرْضِ وَاتَّبَعَ هَوٰىهُ فَمَثَلُهٗ كَمَثَلِ الْكَلْبِ اِنْ تَحْمِلْ عَلَيْهِ يَلْهَثْ اَوْ تَتْرُكْهُ يَلْهَثْ ذٰلِكَ مَثَلُ الْقَوْمِ الَّذِيْنَ كَذَّبُوْا بِاٰيٰتِنَا فَاقْصُصِ الْقَصَصَ لَعَلَّهُمْ يَتَفَكَّرُوْنَ ۞

سَاءَ مَثَلًا الْقَوْمُ الَّذِيْنَ كَذَّبُوْا بِاٰيٰتِنَا وَاَنْفُسَهُمْ كَانُوْا يَظْلِمُوْنَ ۞

مَنْ يَّهْدِ اللّٰهُ فَهُوَ الْمُهْتَدِيْ وَمَنْ يُّضْلِلْ فَاُولٰئِكَ هُمُ الْخٰسِرُوْنَ ۞

Of the people, high and low, created to be recipients of Our mercy, many are headed for hell. They have hearts but they do not use them for understanding, they have eyes but they do not use them for seeing, and they have ears but they do not use them for listening. They are like cattle; only more astray. They are utterly heedless. To Allah alone belong all perfect attributes; so call on Him by those. Leave alone those who pervert His attributes; they shall be requited for that which they do. Of those We have created there is a party who guide men through truth and who do justice through it. Those who reject Our Signs shall be drawn by Us step by step towards ruin by ways of which they have no concept. I grant them respite; My design is mighty. (180—184)

Do they not consider that their companion is not afflicted with insanity? He is only a plain Warner. Do they not observe the kingdom of the heavens and the earth and whatever Allah has created? Do they not reflect that the time appointed for their destruction may be drawing nigh? Then in what will they believe thereafter? For him whom Allah adjudges astray, there can be no guide. He leaves them in their transgression, wandering in distraction. (185—187)

They ask thee concerning the Hour: When will it come to pass? Say to them: My Lord alone has knowledge of it. None can manifest it at its time but He. It will lie heavy on the heavens and the earth. It will not come upon you but of a sudden. They ask thee as if thou wert well acqaainted with it; Tell them: Allah alone has knowledge of it, but most people do not know this. (188)

161

Tell them: I have no power to benefit or harm myself, save as Allah pleases. If I had knowledge of the unseen, I would have secured abundance of good, and no harm would have befallen me. I am but a Warner and a bearer of glad tidings for a people who believe. (189)

قُلْ لَّا اَمْلِكُ لِنَفْسِيْ نَفْعًا وَّلَا ضَرًّا اِلَّا مَا شَآءَ اللّٰهُ وَلَوْ كُنْتُ اَعْلَمُ الْغَيْبَ لَا سْتَكْثَرْتُ مِنَ الْخَيْرِ وَمَا مَسَّنِيَ السُّوْٓءُ اِنْ اَنَا اِلَّا نَذِيْرٌ وَّبَشِيْرٌ لِّقَوْمٍ يُّؤْمِنُوْنَ ۞

He it is Who has created you from a single soul and made therefrom its mate, that he might incline towards her and find comfort in her. When he consorts with her, she bears a light burden and goes about with it. When she grows heavy, they both pray to Allah, their Lord: If Thou bestow on us a healthy child, we will surely be grateful. When He bestows on them a healthy child, they attribute to Him partners in respect of that which He has bestowed upon them. Exalted is Allah above that which they associate with Him. Do they associate with Him those who create nothing and are themselves created? They can give them no help nor can they help themselves. If you call them to guidance they will not follow you. It will make no difference to you whether you call them or remain silent. Those whom you call on beside Allah are but creatures like you. Then go on calling on them and let them respond to you if you are justified in your claim. Have they any feet with which they can walk, or have they any hands with which they can grasp, or have they any eyes with which they can see, or have they any ears with which they can hear? Say to them: Call upon those you associate with Allah as partners, then contrive all of you against me and give me no respite. My Protector is Allah Who has revealed this Perfect Book and He stands by the right-

هُوَ الَّذِيْ خَلَقَكُمْ مِّنْ نَّفْسٍ وَّاحِدَةٍ وَّجَعَلَ مِنْهَا زَوْجَهَا لِيَسْكُنَ اِلَيْهَا فَلَمَّا تَغَشّٰهَا حَمَلَتْ حَمْلًا خَفِيْفًا فَمَرَّتْ بِهٖ فَلَمَّآ اَثْقَلَتْ دَّعَوَا اللّٰهَ رَبَّهُمَا لَئِنْ اٰتَيْتَنَا صَالِحًا لَّنَكُوْنَنَّ مِنَ الشّٰكِرِيْنَ ۞ فَلَمَّآ اٰتٰهُمَا صَالِحًا جَعَلَا لَهٗ شُرَكَآءَ فِيْمَآ اٰتٰهُمَا فَتَعٰلَى اللّٰهُ عَمَّا يُشْرِكُوْنَ ۞ اَيُشْرِكُوْنَ مَا لَا يَخْلُقُ شَيْئًا وَّهُمْ يُخْلَقُوْنَ ۞ وَلَا يَسْتَطِيْعُوْنَ لَهُمْ نَصْرًا وَّلَا اَنْفُسَهُمْ يَنْصُرُوْنَ ۞ وَاِنْ تَدْعُوْهُمْ اِلَى الْهُدٰى لَا يَتَّبِعُوْكُمْ سَوَآءٌ عَلَيْكُمْ اَدَعَوْتُمُوْهُمْ اَمْ اَنْتُمْ صَامِتُوْنَ ۞ اِنَّ الَّذِيْنَ تَدْعُوْنَ مِنْ دُوْنِ اللّٰهِ عِبَادٌ اَمْثَالُكُمْ فَادْعُوْهُمْ فَلْيَسْتَجِيْبُوْا لَكُمْ اِنْ كُنْتُمْ صٰدِقِيْنَ ۞ اَلَهُمْ اَرْجُلٌ يَّمْشُوْنَ بِهَآ اَمْ لَهُمْ اَيْدٍ يَّبْطِشُوْنَ بِهَآ اَمْ لَهُمْ اَعْيُنٌ يُّبْصِرُوْنَ بِهَآ اَمْ لَهُمْ اٰذَانٌ يَّسْمَعُوْنَ بِهَا قُلِ ادْعُوْا شُرَكَآءَكُمْ ثُمَّ كِيْدُوْنِ فَلَا تُنْظِرُوْنِ ۞ اِنَّ وَلِيِّ اللّٰهُ الَّذِيْ نَزَّلَ الْكِتٰبَ وَهُوَ يَتَوَلَّى الصّٰلِحِيْنَ ۞ وَالَّذِيْنَ تَدْعُوْنَ مِنْ دُوْنِهٖ لَا يَسْتَطِيْعُوْنَ نَصْرَكُمْ

eous. Those whom you call beside Him have no power to help you nor can they help themselves. If thou call them to guidance, they hear not. Thou seest them looking towards thee, but they see not. (190—199)

Make forbearance thy rule, O Prophet, and enjoin equity and turn away from the ignorant. Should thou be distressed by a contrivance of Satan, seek refuge with Allah, He is All-Hearing, All-Knowing. When a suggestion from Satan assails those who are righteous, they are instantly alerted and become watchful. The companions of the disbelievers draw them deeper into error and relax not their efforts. When thou dost not bring them a Sign in quick succession, they say: Wherefore dost thou not contrive one? Tell them: I but follow that which is revealed to me by my Lord. This revelation is replete with clear proofs from your Lord and guidance and mercy for a people who believe. (200—204)

When the Quran is recited, listen carefully to it in silence, that you may become the recipients of mercy. Remember thy Lord in thy mind with humility and fear, silently, morning and evening, and be not neglectful. Those who are near to thy Lord, do not turn away from His worship in haughtiness, but glorify Him and prostrate themselves before Him constantly. (205—207)

وَلَا أَنْفُسَهُمْ يَنْصُرُونَ ۞

وَإِنْ تَدْعُوهُمْ إِلَى الْهُدَى لَا يَسْمَعُوا ۖ وَتَرَاهُمْ يَنْظُرُونَ إِلَيْكَ وَهُمْ لَا يُبْصِرُونَ ۞

خُذِ الْعَفْوَ وَأْمُرْ بِالْعُرْفِ وَأَعْرِضْ عَنِ الْجَاهِلِينَ ۞

وَإِمَّا يَنْزَغَنَّكَ مِنَ الشَّيْطَانِ نَزْغٌ فَاسْتَعِذْ بِاللَّهِ ۚ إِنَّهُ سَمِيعٌ عَلِيمٌ ۞

إِنَّ الَّذِينَ اتَّقَوْا إِذَا مَسَّهُمْ طَائِفٌ مِّنَ الشَّيْطَانِ تَذَكَّرُوا فَإِذَا هُمْ مُّبْصِرُونَ ۞

وَإِخْوَانُهُمْ يَمُدُّونَهُمْ فِي الْغَيِّ ثُمَّ لَا يُقْصِرُونَ ۞

وَإِذَا لَمْ تَأْتِهِمْ بِآيَةٍ قَالُوا لَوْلَا اجْتَبَيْتَهَا ۚ قُلْ إِنَّمَا أَتَّبِعُ مَا يُوحَى إِلَيَّ مِنْ رَّبِّي ۚ هَٰذَا بَصَائِرُ مِنْ رَّبِّكُمْ وَهُدًى وَرَحْمَةٌ لِّقَوْمٍ يُؤْمِنُونَ ۞

وَإِذَا قُرِئَ الْقُرْآنُ فَاسْتَمِعُوا لَهُ وَأَنْصِتُوا لَعَلَّكُمْ تُرْحَمُونَ ۞

وَاذْكُر رَّبَّكَ فِي نَفْسِكَ تَضَرُّعًا وَخِيفَةً وَدُونَ الْجَهْرِ مِنَ الْقَوْلِ بِالْغُدُوِّ وَالْآصَالِ وَلَا تَكُن مِّنَ الْغَافِلِينَ ۞

إِنَّ الَّذِينَ عِنْدَ رَبِّكَ لَا يَسْتَكْبِرُونَ عَنْ عِبَادَتِهِ وَيُسَبِّحُونَهُ وَلَهُ يَسْجُدُونَ ۩

AL-ANFĀL

(Revealed after Hijra)

In the name of Allah, Most Gracious, Ever Merciful. (1)

They seek directions from thee concerning the spoils of war. Tell them: The spoils belong to Allah and the Messenger. So be mindful of your duty to Allah and try to promote accord between yourselves, and obey Allah and His Messenger, if you are believers. Believers are only those whose hearts are smitten with awe when Allah's name is mentioned and whose faith is strengthened when His Signs are recited to them, and who put their trust in their Lord and observe Prayer and spend out of that which We have provided for them. These it is who are true believers. They have high ranks with their Lord and forgiveness and honourable provision, as was the case when thy Lord brought thee forth from thy house to take up arms in a righteous cause at a time when a party of the believers were much averse to it. (2—6)

The hypocrites disputed with thee concerning the right course after it had become manifest, as if they were being driven to death which they could see confronting them. (7)

Call to mind the time when Allah promised that one of the two parties of disbelievers, the lightly armed trade caravan proceeding south to Mecca or the well armed host coming up north from Mecca, should fall into your hands; and you desired that you may be confronted with the one without weapons, but Allah desired to establish the truth by His commandments and to cut off the source of strength of the disbelievers, so that the truth may be firmly established and falsehood be brought to naught though the guilty ones be averse to it. (8—9)

164

Call to mind also when you implored your Lord for help and He responded to you with the assurance: I will help you with a thousand angels, advancing host after host. Allah meant this only as glad tidings and that your hearts might thereby be set at rest. Help comes from Allah alone; surely, Allah is Mighty, Wise. He brought drowsiness upon you as a presage of security and sent down upon you water from the clouds, that He might purify you thereby, and remove from you the fear of Satan, and that He might strengthen your hearts and make your steps firm by settling and making firm therewith the sand under-foot. At the same time thy Lord commanded the angels: I am with you; so make firm the steps of those who believe. I will cast terror into the hearts of those who disbelieve. O ye who believe, strike at their necks and strike at every pore and tip, because they have pitted themselves against Allah and His Messenger. Whoever sets himself up in opposition to Allah and His Messenger must know that Allah is surely Severe in exacting retribution. That is so; then taste ye His chastisement; for such disbelievers there is the torment of the Fire. (10—15)

O ye who believe, when you encounter an hostile force of the disbelievers, turn not your backs on them. Whoso turns his back on them on such an occasion, unless manoeuvring for battle or turning to join another company, shall draw upon himself the wrath of Allah, and hell shall be his abode. An evil resort it is. (16—17)

Thus on the day of Badr it was not you who slew them, but it was Allah Who killed them; and it was not thou who didst throw the handful of gravel at their faces, but it was Allah Who threw it, that He might confer a great favour upon the believers. Surely, Allah is All-Hearing, All-Knowing. That is so; and Allah will surely undermine the design of the disbelievers. (18—19)

O ye who disbelieve, if you sought a judgment, then judgment has indeed come to you. If you will now desist, it will be the better for you; but if you revert to mischief, We will again chastise you; and your party shall be of no avail to you at all, however numerous it be, and be sure Allah is with the believers. (20)

O ye who believe, obey Allah and His Messenger, and do not turn away from him while you hear his directions; and be not like those who say: We hear; but they hear not. Even worse than the beasts, in the sight of Allah, are the spiritually deaf and dumb, who possess no understanding. If Allah had known any good in them He would certainly have made them hear the Quran; but being as they are, even if He makes them hear it, they will turn away in aversion. (21—24)

O ye who believe, respond to Allah and His Messenger when he calls you that he may bring you to life, and know that Allah surely supervenes between a man and his mind and that He it is unto Whom you shall be gathered. Seek to guard yourselves against an affliction that will not smite exlusively the wrongdoers among you. Know that Allah is Severe in exacting retribution. Call to mind the time when you were few in numbers and were accounted weak in the land and were afraid of being despoiled by people, but He provided you with shelter, and supported you with His help and provided you with good things that you may be grateful. (25—27)

O ye who believe, prove not unfaithful to Allah and the Messenger, nor prove unfaithful to your trusts designedly; and know that your belongings and your children are but a trial and that it is Allah with Whom is a great reward. (28—29)

O ye who believe, if you are mindful of your duty to Allah, He will bestow upon you a mark of distinction, and will remove from you your ills, and will forgive you. Allah is Lord of great bounty. (30)

Call to mind the time, when the disbelievers plotted against thee that they might confine thee, or kill thee, or expel thee. They planned and Allah also planned, and Allah is the Best of planners. When Our verses are recited to them they say: Enough! We have heard. If we wished we could certainly compose and recite the like of it. This is nothing but old wives' tales. Call to mind also when they said: O Allah, if this be indeed the truth from Thee, then rain down upon us stones from heaven or bring down upon us a grievous chastisement. Allah would not chastise them while thou wast among them, nor would Allah chastise them if they supplicated for forgiveness. But what would shield them from punishment now, when they hinder people from the Sacred Mosque, and they are not even its true guardians. Its true guardians are only those who are righteous, but most of them know not this. Their prayer at the Sacred House is nothing but whistling and clapping of hands. Suffer, then, the chastisement because you disbelieved. (31—36)

Those who disbelieve spend their wealth to turn people away from Allah's way. They will continue to spend it in this way till in the end this spending will become a source of regret for them, and then they will be vanquished. The disbelievers shall all be gathered unto hell, that Allah may separate the bad from the good, and heap up the different parts of the bad, one upon another, and then cast them all into hell. These indeed are the losers. (37—38)

فُرْقَانًا وَّيُكَفِّرْ عَنْكُمْ سَيِّاٰتِكُمْ وَيَغْفِرْ لَكُمْ وَاللّٰهُ ذُو الْفَضْلِ الْعَظِيْمِ ۞

وَاِذْ يَمْكُرُ بِكَ الَّذِيْنَ كَفَرُوْا لِيُثْبِتُوْكَ اَوْ يَقْتُلُوْكَ اَوْ يُخْرِجُوْكَ وَيَمْكُرُوْنَ وَيَمْكُرُ اللّٰهُ وَاللّٰهُ خَيْرُ الْمَاكِرِيْنَ ۞

وَاِذَا تُتْلٰى عَلَيْهِمْ اٰيٰتُنَا قَالُوْا قَدْ سَمِعْنَا لَوْ نَشَآءُ لَقُلْنَا مِثْلَ هٰذَآ اِنْ هٰذَآ اِلَّآ اَسَاطِيْرُ الْاَوَّلِيْنَ ۞

وَاِذْ قَالُوا اللّٰهُمَّ اِنْ كَانَ هٰذَا هُوَ الْحَقَّ مِنْ عِنْدِكَ فَاَمْطِرْ عَلَيْنَا حِجَارَةً مِّنَ السَّمَآءِ اَوِ ائْتِنَا بِعَذَابٍ اَلِيْمٍ ۞

وَمَا كَانَ اللّٰهُ لِيُعَذِّبَهُمْ وَاَنْتَ فِيْهِمْ وَمَا كَانَ اللّٰهُ مُعَذِّبَهُمْ وَهُمْ يَسْتَغْفِرُوْنَ ۞

وَمَا لَهُمْ اَلَّا يُعَذِّبَهُمُ اللّٰهُ وَهُمْ يَصُدُّوْنَ عَنِ الْمَسْجِدِ الْحَرَامِ وَمَا كَانُوْا اَوْلِيَآءَهُ اِنْ اَوْلِيَآؤُهُ اِلَّا الْمُتَّقُوْنَ وَلٰكِنَّ اَكْثَرَهُمْ لَا يَعْلَمُوْنَ ۞

وَمَا كَانَ صَلَاتُهُمْ عِنْدَ الْبَيْتِ اِلَّا مُكَآءً وَّتَصْدِيَةً فَذُوْقُوا الْعَذَابَ بِمَا كُنْتُمْ تَكْفُرُوْنَ ۞

اِنَّ الَّذِيْنَ كَفَرُوْا يُنْفِقُوْنَ اَمْوَالَهُمْ لِيَصُدُّوْا عَنْ سَبِيْلِ اللّٰهِ فَسَيُنْفِقُوْنَهَا ثُمَّ تَكُوْنُ عَلَيْهِمْ حَسْرَةً ثُمَّ يُغْلَبُوْنَ وَالَّذِيْنَ كَفَرُوْا اِلٰى جَهَنَّمَ يُحْشَرُوْنَ ۞

لِيَمِيْزَ اللّٰهُ الْخَبِيْثَ مِنَ الطَّيِّبِ وَيَجْعَلَ الْخَبِيْثَ بَعْضَهُ عَلٰى بَعْضٍ فَيَرْكُمَهُ جَمِيْعًا فَيَجْعَلَهُ فِيْ جَهَنَّمَ

Say, O Prophet, to those who disbelieve, that if they desist their past misdeeds will be forgiven them, but if they revert to their misdeeds they should learn a lesson from the fate of the people who behaved like this before them. Then fight them, until persecution ceases altogether and religion is held wholly for the sake of Allah. If they desist, then surely Allah is watchful of what they do; and if they turn away, then know that Allah is your Protector; an excellent Protector and an excellent Helper. (39—41)

Take note that whatever you gain as spoils of war, a fifth thereof is for Allah and the Messenger and those close to him and orphans and the needy and the wayfarer, if you believe in Allah and in that which We sent down on Our servant on the Day of Discrimination between falsehood and truth, the day when the two hosts met at Badr. Allah has the power to do all that He wills. On that day you were on the nearer bank of the valley and they were on the farther bank, and the caravan was below you in the direction of the sea. Had you wished to arrange a rendezvous by mutual agreement you would certainly have disagreed on the timing, but the encounter was brought about that Allah might accomplish that which had been decreed; so that he who had already been vanquished through a clear Sign might perish and he who had already come to life through a clear Sign might live. Surely, Allah is All-Hearing, All-Knowing. (42—43)

Call to mind when Allah showed them to thee in thy dream as small in number; and if He had shown them to thee as a large force, you would have faltered and would have disagreed with one another in the matter of giving battle; but Allah saved you from dissension and gave you victory. Surely, Allah knows all hidden thoughts. At the time of your encounter He made them appear weak in your eyes, and made you appear weak in their eyes, that Allah might bring about that which had been decreed. The determination of all affairs is in Allah's hands. (44—45)

O ye who believe, when you encounter an enemy force, remain firm and remember Allah much that you may triumph; and obey Allah and His Messenger, and avoid dissension, lest you falter and your strength depart from you. Be steadfast; surely, Allah is with the steadfast. Be not like those who issued forth from their homes insolently and to be seen of people, and who turn people away from the path of Allah. Allah will bring to naught all that they do. (46—48)

Call to mind when Satan made the conduct of the disbelievers appear fair to them and told them: None of the people shall prevail against you this day and I am your strong supporter. But when the two hosts came in sight of each other, he turned on his heels and announced: I am absolved of all obligation to you; I see that which you see not. Surely, I fear Allah; Allah is Severe in punishing. The hypocrites and those whose hearts are perverted say: Their religion has deluded the believers. The truth is that whoso puts his trust in Allah surely finds that Allah is Mighty, Wise. (49—50)

If thou couldst see the angels taking away the souls of the disbelievers, striking them front and back, saying: Suffer the torment of burning, because of your past conduct, and know that Allah is not in the least unjust towards His creatures. Their case is like that of the people of Pharaoh and those before them; they rejected the Signs of Allah, so Allah requited them for their sins.

Surely, Allah is Powerful, Severe in chastisement. Allah would never withdraw a favour that He has conferred upon a people, until they change their own attitude towards Him. Surely, Allah is All-Hearing, All-Knowing. Their case will be like that of the people of Pharaoh and those before them. They rejected the Signs of their Lord, so We destroyed them for their sins. We drowned the people of Pharaoh. All of them were wrongdoers. (51—55)

Worse than the beasts, in the sight of Allah, are those who have rejected the Signs of Allah and do not believe; those with whom thou makest a covenant, then they break their covenant every time and are not mindful of their obligation to Allah. When thou gainest mastery over them in war, then deal with them in such manner that those making hostile preparations beyond them should abandon their designs and be admonished. Shouldst thou apprehend treachery from a people who have made a pact with thee, terminate the pact in a manner that should occasion no prejudice to either side. Surely, Allah loves not the treacherous. Let not the disbelievers imagine that they will gain any advantage over the believers through their machinations. Surely, they can never reduce the believers to helplessness. (56—60)

Make ready for them whatever you can of armed strength and of mounted pickets at the frontier, whereby you may daunt the enemy of Allah and your enemy and others beyond them whom you know not, but whom Allah knows. Whatever you spend in the way of Allah, it shall be repaid to you in full and you shall not be wronged. Then if they should be inclined to make peace, do thou incline towards it also, and put thy trust in Allah. Surely,

قَوِىٌّ شَدِيدُ الْعِقَابِ ۝

ذٰلِكَ بِاَنَّ اللّٰهَ لَمْ يَكُ مُغَيِّرًا نِّعْمَةً اَنْعَمَهَا عَلٰى قَوْمٍ حَتّٰى يُغَيِّرُوْا مَا بِاَنْفُسِهِمْ وَاَنَّ اللّٰهَ سَمِيعٌ عَلِيْمٌ ۝

كَدَاْبِ اٰلِ فِرْعَوْنَ وَالَّذِيْنَ مِنْ قَبْلِهِمْ كَذَّبُوْا بِاٰيٰتِ رَبِّهِمْ فَاَهْلَكْنٰهُمْ بِذُنُوْبِهِمْ وَاَغْرَقْنَا اٰلَ فِرْعَوْنَ وَكُلٌّ كَانُوْا ظٰلِمِيْنَ ۝

اِنَّ شَرَّ الدَّوَآبِّ عِنْدَ اللّٰهِ الَّذِيْنَ كَفَرُوْا فَهُمْ لَا يُؤْمِنُوْنَ ۝

الَّذِيْنَ عٰهَدْتَّ مِنْهُمْ ثُمَّ يَنْقُضُوْنَ عَهْدَهُمْ فِىْ كُلِّ مَرَّةٍ وَّهُمْ لَا يَتَّقُوْنَ ۝

فَاِمَّا تَثْقَفَنَّهُمْ فِى الْحَرْبِ فَشَرِّدْ بِهِمْ مَّنْ خَلْفَهُمْ لَعَلَّهُمْ يَذَّكَّرُوْنَ ۝

وَاِمَّا تَخَافَنَّ مِنْ قَوْمٍ خِيَانَةً فَانْبِذْ اِلَيْهِمْ عَلٰى سَوَآءٍ ۚ اِنَّ اللّٰهَ لَا يُحِبُّ الْخَآئِنِيْنَ ۝

وَلَا يَحْسَبَنَّ الَّذِيْنَ كَفَرُوْا سَبَقُوْا ۗ اِنَّهُمْ لَا يُعْجِزُوْنَ ۝

وَاَعِدُّوْا لَهُمْ مَّا اسْتَطَعْتُمْ مِّنْ قُوَّةٍ وَّمِنْ رِّبَاطِ الْخَيْلِ تُرْهِبُوْنَ بِهٖ عَدُوَّ اللّٰهِ وَعَدُوَّكُمْ وَاٰخَرِيْنَ مِنْ دُوْنِهِمْ ۚ لَا تَعْلَمُوْنَهُمْ ۚ اَللّٰهُ يَعْلَمُهُمْ ۚ وَمَا تُنْفِقُوْا مِنْ شَيْءٍ فِىْ سَبِيْلِ اللّٰهِ يُوَفَّ اِلَيْكُمْ وَاَنْتُمْ لَا تُظْلَمُوْنَ ۝

وَاِنْ جَنَحُوْا لِلسَّلْمِ فَاجْنَحْ لَهَا وَتَوَكَّلْ عَلَى اللّٰهِ

it is He Who is All-Hearing, All-Knowing. Should they design to deceive thee, then surely Allah is sufficient for thee as Protector. He it is Who has strengthened thee with His help and with the support of the believers, and bound their hearts together in love. If thou hadst spent all that is in the earth, thou couldst not have bound their hearts together, but Allah has bound them together. Surely, He is Mighty, Wise. (61—64)

O Prophet, sufficient for thee are Allah and those believers who follow thee. O Prophet, exhort the believers to fight. If there be of you twenty steadfast ones, they shall overcome two hundred, and if there be a hundred of you, they shall overcome a thousand of those who disbelieve, because they are a people who lack understanding. (65—66)

Allah knows that at present you are weak, so He has lightened your burden. If there be of you a hundred steadfast ones, they shall overcome two hundred; and if there be a thousand of you they shall overcome two thousand, by the command of Allah. Allah is with those who are steadfast. (67)

It behoves not a Prophet to take captives, except in the course of regular fighting. To take captives in the course of skirmishes and small-scale action would mean that you are merely seeking temporal gain, whereas Allah desires for you the Hereafter. Allah is Mighty, Wise. Had there not been an antecedent commandment from Allah, you would have been afflicted with severe chastisement, in respect of the ransom that you took. Enjoy the lawful and good spoils that you win, and be mindful of your duty to Allah. Surely, Allah is Most Forgiving, Ever Merciful. (68—70)

O Prophet, say to the captives who are in your hands: If Allah knows of any good in your hearts, He will bestow on you better than that which has been taken from you, and will forgive you. Allah is Most Forgiving, Ever Merciful. If they design treachery against thee, they have already been guilty of treachery towards Allah, yet He gave thee power over them. Allah is All-Knowing, Wise. (71—72)

Those who have believed and migrated and striven with their belongings and their persons in the cause of Allah, and those who have given them shelter and help, are friends one of another. But you are under no obligation towards those who have believed and have not migrated, until they migrate. Nevertheless, if they seek your help in the matter of religion it is incumbent on you to help them except against a people between whom and yourselves there is a pact. Allah sees what you do. Those who disbelieve are friends one of another. If you do not as you are commanded, there will be great mischief and disorder in the land. Those who have believed and migrated and striven in the cause of Allah, and those who have given them shelter and help, are the true believers. For them is forgiveness and an honourable provision. Those who believe hereafter, and migrate and strive in the cause of Allah along with you, will be counted among you. Of blood relations some are nearer than others in the Book of Allah. Surely, Allah knows all things well. (73—76)

اِنۡ يَّعۡلَمِ اللّٰهُ فِیۡ قُلُوۡبِكُمۡ خَیۡرًا يُّؤۡتِكُمۡ خَیۡرًا مِّمَّاۤ اُخِذَ مِنۡكُمۡ وَيَغۡفِرۡ لَكُمۡ ۚ وَاللّٰهُ غَفُوۡرٌ رَّحِیۡمٌ ۞

وَاِنۡ يُّرِيۡدُوۡا خِیَانَتَكَ فَقَدۡ خَانُوا اللّٰهَ مِنۡ قَبۡلُ فَاَمۡكَنَ مِنۡهُمۡ ۗ وَاللّٰهُ عَلِیۡمٌ حَكِیۡمٌ ۞

اِنَّ الَّذِيۡنَ اٰمَنُوۡا وَهَاجَرُوۡا وَجَاهَدُوۡا بِاَمۡوَالِهِمۡ وَاَنۡفُسِهِمۡ فِیۡ سَبِیۡلِ اللّٰهِ وَالَّذِيۡنَ اٰوَوۡا وَّنَصَرُوۡۤا اُولٰٓئِكَ بَعۡضُهُمۡ اَوۡلِیَآءُ بَعۡضٍ ۚ وَالَّذِيۡنَ اٰمَنُوۡا وَلَمۡ يُهَاجِرُوۡا مَا لَكُمۡ مِّنۡ وَّلَایَتِهِمۡ مِّنۡ شَیۡءٍ حَتّٰی يُهَاجِرُوۡا ۚ وَاِنِ اسۡتَنۡصَرُوۡكُمۡ فِی الدِّيۡنِ فَعَلَیۡكُمُ النَّصۡرُ اِلَّا عَلٰی قَوۡمٍ بَیۡنَكُمۡ وَبَیۡنَهُمۡ مِّیۡثَاقٌ ۗ وَاللّٰهُ بِمَا تَعۡمَلُوۡنَ بَصِیۡرٌ ۞

وَالَّذِيۡنَ كَفَرُوۡا بَعۡضُهُمۡ اَوۡلِیَآءُ بَعۡضٍ ۚ اِلَّا تَفۡعَلُوۡهُ تَكُنۡ فِتۡنَةٌ فِی الۡاَرۡضِ وَفَسَادٌ كَبِیۡرٌ ۞

وَالَّذِيۡنَ اٰمَنُوۡا وَهَاجَرُوۡا وَجَاهَدُوۡا فِیۡ سَبِیۡلِ اللّٰهِ وَالَّذِيۡنَ اٰوَوۡا وَّنَصَرُوۡۤا اُولٰٓئِكَ هُمُ الۡمُؤۡمِنُوۡنَ حَقًّا ۚ لَهُمۡ مَّغۡفِرَةٌ وَّرِزۡقٌ كَرِيۡمٌ ۞

وَالَّذِيۡنَ اٰمَنُوۡا مِنۡ بَعۡدُ وَهَاجَرُوۡا وَجَاهَدُوۡا مَعَكُمۡ فَاُولٰٓئِكَ مِنۡكُمۡ ۚ وَاُولُوا الۡاَرۡحَامِ بَعۡضُهُمۡ اَوۡلٰی بِبَعۡضٍ فِیۡ كِتٰبِ اللّٰهِ ۚ اِنَّ اللّٰهَ بِكُلِّ شَیۡءٍ عَلِیۡمٌ ۞

سُوْرَةُ التَّوْبَةِ مَدَنِيَّةٌ

AL-TAUBA

(Revealed after Hijra)

This is a declaration on the part of
Allah and His Messenger addressed to the
idolaters whom you had promised that
Allah and His Messenger would surely
triumph, that the promise has been fulfilled and that Allah and His Messenger
are absolved of all obligation in that
respect. So go about freely in the land
for four months and satisfy yourselves
that you cannot frustrate the design of
Allah and that Allah will humiliate the
disbelievers. (1—2)

This is a public proclamation on the
part of Allah and His Messenger on the
day of the Great Pilgrimage, that Allah is
free of all obligation to the idolaters, and
so is His Messenger. So now, having witnessed this Sign, if you will repent and
make peace, it will be the better for you;
but if you turn away, then know that
you cannot frustrate Allah's design. Warn
the disbelievers of a painful chastisement,
excepting those of them with whom you
have a pact and who have not defaulted
in any respect, nor supported anyone
against you. Carry out the obligations you
have assumed towards them till the end
of their terms. Surely, Allah loves those
who are mindful of their obligations.
When the period of four months during
which hostilities are suspended expires,
without the idolaters having settled the
terms of peace with you, resume fighting
with them and kill them wherever you find
them and make them prisoners and
beleaguer them, and lie in wait for them
at every place of ambush. Then if they
repent and observe Prayer and pay the
Zakat, leave them alone. Surely, Allah is
Most Forgiving, Ever Merciful. If any one
of the idolaters seeks asylum with thee,
grant him asylum so that he may hear the
Word of Allah; then convey him to a
place of security for him, for they are a
people who lack knowledge (3—6)

بَرَآءَةٌ مِّنَ اللهِ وَرَسُوْلِهٖٓ اِلَى الَّذِيْنَ عٰهَدْتُّمْ مِّنَ الْمُشْرِكِيْنَ ۝

فَسِيْحُوْا فِى الْاَرْضِ اَرْبَعَةَ اَشْهُرٍ وَّاعْلَمُوْٓا اَنَّكُمْ غَيْرُ مُعْجِزِى اللهِ وَاَنَّ اللهَ مُخْزِى الْكٰفِرِيْنَ ۝

وَاَذَانٌ مِّنَ اللهِ وَرَسُوْلِهٖٓ اِلَى النَّاسِ يَوْمَ الْحَجِّ الْاَكْبَرِ اَنَّ اللهَ بَرِيْٓءٌ مِّنَ الْمُشْرِكِيْنَ ۙ وَرَسُوْلُهٗ ۚ فَاِنْ تُبْتُمْ فَهُوَ خَيْرٌ لَّكُمْ ۚ وَاِنْ تَوَلَّيْتُمْ فَاعْلَمُوْٓا اَنَّكُمْ غَيْرُ مُعْجِزِى اللهِ ۗ وَبَشِّرِ الَّذِيْنَ كَفَرُوْا بِعَذَابٍ اَلِيْمٍ ۝

اِلَّا الَّذِيْنَ عٰهَدْتُّمْ مِّنَ الْمُشْرِكِيْنَ ثُمَّ لَمْ يَنْقُصُوْكُمْ شَيْئًا وَّلَمْ يُظَاهِرُوْا عَلَيْكُمْ اَحَدًا فَاَتِمُّوْٓا اِلَيْهِمْ عَهْدَهُمْ اِلٰى مُدَّتِهِمْ ۗ اِنَّ اللهَ يُحِبُّ الْمُتَّقِيْنَ ۝

فَاِذَا انْسَلَخَ الْاَشْهُرُ الْحُرُمُ فَاقْتُلُوا الْمُشْرِكِيْنَ حَيْثُ وَجَدْتُّمُوْهُمْ وَخُذُوْهُمْ وَاحْصُرُوْهُمْ وَاقْعُدُوْا لَهُمْ كُلَّ مَرْصَدٍ ۚ فَاِنْ تَابُوْا وَاَقَامُوا الصَّلٰوةَ وَاٰتَوُا الزَّكٰوةَ فَخَلُّوْا سَبِيْلَهُمْ ۗ اِنَّ اللهَ غَفُوْرٌ رَّحِيْمٌ ۝

وَاِنْ اَحَدٌ مِّنَ الْمُشْرِكِيْنَ اسْتَجَارَكَ فَاَجِرْهُ حَتّٰى يَسْمَعَ كَلٰمَ اللهِ ثُمَّ اَبْلِغْهُ مَأْمَنَهٗ ۗ ذٰلِكَ بِاَنَّهُمْ قَوْمٌ لَّا يَعْلَمُوْنَ ۝

How could there be a guarantee for the idolaters on the part of Allah and His Messenger, except in favour of those with whom you entered into an express treaty at the Sacred Mosque? So long as they carry out their obligations thereunder, you must carry out your obligations. Surely, Allah loves those who are mindful of their obligations. How can there be a guarantee for the others, who, if they were to prevail against you, would have no regard for any tie of kinship or pact in respect of you. They seek to please you with words, while their hearts repudiate them; most of them are perfidious. They have bartered the Signs of Allah for small gains and hindered people from His way. Evil indeed is that which they have done. They show no regard for any tie of kinship or any pact in respect of a believer. It is they who are the transgressors. If they repent and observe Prayer and pay the Zakat, then they are your brethren in faith. We expound Our commandments for a people who know. (7—11)

But if they break faith after pledging it and ridicule your religion, then fight these leaders of disbelief that they may desist, for they have no regard for their pledged word. Will you not fight a people who have violated their oaths, who plotted to turn out the Messenger from his home, and who were the first to start hostilities against you? Do you fear them? It is Allah Who is most worthy that you should fear Him, if you are believers. Fight them: Allah will punish them at your hands, and will humiliate them, and will help you to overcome them, and will relieve the minds of the believers of fear and distress and will remove their feeling of resentment. Allah turns with mercy to whomsoever He pleases. Allah is All-Knowing, Wise. Do you imagine that you

174

would be left alone, while Allah has not yet made known those of you who strive in the cause of Allah and have no secret association with anyone beside Allah and His Messenger and the believers? Allah is Well Aware of that which you do. (12—16)

It is not up to the idolaters, while they assert their disbelief, to service the mosques of Allah. It is they whose works are vain, and in the Fire shall they abide. He alone can service the mosques of Allah who believes in Allah and the Last Day, and observes Prayer, and pays the Zakat, and fears no one but Allah. It is these who are likely to be guided aright. Do you equate the provision of water for the pilgrims and the maintenance of the Sacred Mosque with belief in Allah and the Last Day and striving in the cause of Allah? The two are not at all equal in the sight of Allah. Allah guides not the unjust people. Those who have believed and have migrated and have striven in the cause of Allah with their belongings and their persons have the highest rank in the sight of Allah. It is they who shall triumph. Their Lord gives them glad tidings of mercy from Him, and of His pleasure, and of Gardens wherein there shall be lasting bliss for them, therein will they abide. With Allah there is a great reward. (17—22)

O ye who believe, do not cultivate intimacy with your fathers and your brothers if they love disbelief more than faith. Whoso from among you cultivates intimacy with them, it is they that are the wrongdoers. Say to the believers: If

175

your fathers, and your sons, and your brethren, and your wives, and your kinsfolk, and the wealth you have acquired and the trade the dullness of which you apprehend, and the dwellings that you fancy, are dearer to you than Allah and His Messenger and striving in His cause, then wait until Allah declares His judgment. Allah guides not the disobedient people. (23—24)

Allah has helped you on many a battlefield, especially on the day of Hunain, when your numbers had made you vain, but they availed you naught, and you were sore pressed, and you turned your backs in retreat. Then Allah sent down tranquillity from Himself upon His Messenger and upon the believers and He sent down hosts which you saw not, and He chastised the disbelievers; such is the requital of the disbelievers. Thereafter Allah will turn with compassion to whomsoever He pleases. Allah is Most Forgiving, Ever Merciful. (25—27)

O ye who believe, surely, those who worship idols are unclean. So they shall not approach the Sacred Mosque after this year. If, in consequence of this commandment, you should apprehend poverty, Allah will enrich you out of His bounty, if He please. Surely, Allah is All-Knowing, Wise. (28)

Fight those from among the People of the Book who believe not in Allah, nor in the Last Day, nor hold as unlawful that which Allah and His Messenger have declared to be unlawful nor follow the true religion, and who have not yet made peace with you, until they pay the tax willingly and make their submission. (29)

The Jews say: Uzair is Allah's son; and the Christians say: The Messiah is Allah's son; these are but their verbal assertions, whereby they imitate the sayings of those who disbelieved before them. Allah ruin them, how are they turned away from the truth! They have taken their divines and their monks for lords beside Allah, and also the Messiah son of Mary. They had only been commanded to worship the One God. There is no god but He. Holy is He above that which they associate with Him. They desire to extinguish the light of Allah by blowing through their mouths, but Allah utterly rejects everything except that He will perfect His light, even though the disbelievers may dislike it. He it is Who sent His Messenger with guidance and the Religion of Truth, that He may make it prevail over every other religion, even though those who associate partners with Allah may dislike it. O ye who believe, surely, many of the divines and monks devour people's wealth by false means, and hinder people from the way of Allah. Warn those who hoard up gold and silver and spend it not in the cause of Allah of a painful chastisement on the day when it will be heated up in the fire of hell, and their foreheads and their sides and their backs shall be branded therewith, and they will be told: This is what you treasured up for yourselves, so now suffer the torment in respect of that which you used to treasure up. (30—35)

The number of months with Allah has been twelve months by Allah's ordinance since the day He created the heavens and the earth. Of these, four are known as sacred. That is the correct system. So wrong not yourselves therein by contravening the ordinances relating to them. Fight the idolaters all together, as they fight you all together, and know that Allah is with the righteous. The device of postponement and changing about of sacred months is an innovation of the period of disbelief, whereby those who disbelieve are led astray. They permit it one year and forbid it another year, that they may keep in step with the number of months which Allah has made sacred, and yet may make lawful that which Allah has forbidden. The evil of their conduct is made to seem fair to them. Allah guides not the disbelieving people. (36—37)

O ye who believe, what ails you that, when it is said to you: Go forth, all together, to fight in the cause of Allah; you are held down by your worldly interests? Is it that you prefer the hither life to the Hereafter? If so, you must remember that all this life has to offer is of little value in comparison with the Hereafter. If you go not forth, He will chastise you with a painful chastisement and will replace you with another people, and you shall do Him no harm at all. Allah has full power to do all that He wills. If you help not the Messenger, you should know that he is not dependent upon your help. Allah helped him when the disbelievers drove him forth from his home, one of two, when they were both in the cave and he reassured his companion, saying: Be not concerned; surely, Allah is with us. Then Allah sent down tranquillity on him and strengthened him with hosts which you did not see, and brought low the boast of those who disbelieve. It is the word of Allah which is supreme; Allah is Mighty, Wise. Go forth, without equipment or with equipment, and strive in the cause of Allah with your belongings and your persons. That is the better for you, if only you knew. They would certainly have followed thee if they had seen an immediate advantage and the journey had been short, but the hard journey appeared too long to them. On your return they will swear by Allah: Had we been able we would surely have gone forth with you. They ruin their souls; Allah knows they are liars. (38—42)

Allah has safeguarded thee against the consequences of thy over-leniency towards them and has exalted thee, but why didst thou permit them to stay back, before those who spoke the truth had become known to thee and before thou hadst known the liars? Those who believe in Allah and the Last Day, do not ask to be exempted from striving in the cause of Allah with their belongings and their persons. Allah knows well those who are mindful of their duty to Him. Only those ask thee to be exempted who do not believe in Allah and the Last Day, and whose minds are involved in doubt. Their doubt keeps their minds in agitation. If they had intended to go forth they would surely have made some preparation for it; but Allah disliked their going forth, so He kept them back, and their cronies said to them: Remain at home with those who are staying back. Had they gone forth with you, they would only have proved a source of trouble for you, and would have run back and forth among you, seeking to create discord among you. There are those among you who act as listeners for them. Allah knows well the wrongdoers. They sought to create trouble before also, and devised stratagems against thee till the truth came and Allah's decree became manifest, though they liked it not. (43—48)

There are some among them who say to thee: Permit us to stay back and do not put us to trial. Hearken, they have already fallen into trial, and surely, hell shall encompass such disbelievers. Thy good fortune grieves them, and if a misfortune befalls thee, they say: We had taken our measures in advance; and they turn away rejoicing.

لَوِ اسْتَطَعْنَا لَخَرَجْنَا مَعَكُمْ يُهْلِكُوْنَ اَنْفُسَهُمْ ۚ وَاللّٰهُ يَعْلَمُ اِنَّهُمْ لَكٰذِبُوْنَ ۟

عَفَا اللّٰهُ عَنْكَ ۚ لِمَ اَذِنْتَ لَهُمْ حَتّٰى يَتَبَيَّنَ لَكَ الَّذِيْنَ صَدَقُوْا وَتَعْلَمَ الْكٰذِبِيْنَ ۟

لَا يَسْتَاْذِنُكَ الَّذِيْنَ يُؤْمِنُوْنَ بِاللّٰهِ وَالْيَوْمِ الْاٰخِرِ اَنْ يُّجَاهِدُوْا بِاَمْوَالِهِمْ وَاَنْفُسِهِمْ ۚ وَاللّٰهُ عَلِيْمٌۢ بِالْمُتَّقِيْنَ ۟

اِنَّمَا يَسْتَاْذِنُكَ الَّذِيْنَ لَا يُؤْمِنُوْنَ بِاللّٰهِ وَالْيَوْمِ الْاٰخِرِ وَارْتَابَتْ قُلُوْبُهُمْ فَهُمْ فِيْ رَيْبِهِمْ يَتَرَدَّدُوْنَ ۟

وَلَوْ اَرَادُوا الْخُرُوْجَ لَاَعَدُّوْا لَهٗ عُدَّةً وَّلٰكِنْ كَرِهَ اللّٰهُ انْبِعَاثَهُمْ فَثَبَّطَهُمْ وَقِيْلَ اقْعُدُوْا مَعَ الْقٰعِدِيْنَ ۟

لَوْ خَرَجُوْا فِيْكُمْ مَّا زَادُوْكُمْ اِلَّا خَبَالًا وَّلَاَوْضَعُوْا خِلٰلَكُمْ يَبْغُوْنَكُمُ الْفِتْنَةَ ۚ وَفِيْكُمْ سَمّٰعُوْنَ لَهُمْ ۚ وَاللّٰهُ عَلِيْمٌۢ بِالظّٰلِمِيْنَ ۟

لَقَدِ ابْتَغَوُا الْفِتْنَةَ مِنْ قَبْلُ وَقَلَّبُوْا لَكَ الْاُمُوْرَ حَتّٰى جَآءَ الْحَقُّ وَظَهَرَ اَمْرُ اللّٰهِ وَهُمْ كٰرِهُوْنَ ۟

وَمِنْهُمْ مَّنْ يَّقُوْلُ ائْذَنْ لِّيْ وَلَا تَفْتِنِّيْ ۚ اَلَا فِي الْفِتْنَةِ سَقَطُوْا ۚ وَاِنَّ جَهَنَّمَ لَمُحِيْطَةٌۢ بِالْكٰفِرِيْنَ ۟

اِنْ تُصِبْكَ حَسَنَةٌ تَسُؤْهُمْ ۚ وَاِنْ تُصِبْكَ مُصِيْبَةٌ يَّقُوْلُوْا قَدْ اَخَذْنَا اَمْرَنَا مِنْ قَبْلُ وَيَتَوَلَّوْا وَّهُمْ فَرِحُوْنَ ۟

Tell them: Nothing shall befall us save that which Allah has ordained for us. He is our Protector, and in Allah should the believers put their trust. Tell them: You await for us one of two pieces of good fortune, martyrdom in the cause of Allah or victory; while concerning you we await that Allah will afflict you with chastisement direct or at our hands. So wait on, we too shall wait with you. Tell them: Spend willingly or unwillingly, it shall not find acceptance with Allah. You are indeed a disobedient people. (49—53)

قُلْ لَّنْ يُّصِيْبَنَآ اِلَّا مَا كَتَبَ اللّٰهُ لَنَا ۚ هُوَ مَوْلٰىنَا ۚ وَعَلَى اللّٰهِ فَلْيَتَوَكَّلِ الْمُؤْمِنُوْنَ ۞

قُلْ هَلْ تَرَبَّصُوْنَ بِنَآ اِلَّآ اِحْدَى الْحُسْنَيَيْنِ ۗ وَنَحْنُ نَتَرَبَّصُ بِكُمْ اَنْ يُّصِيْبَكُمُ اللّٰهُ بِعَذَابٍ مِّنْ عِنْدِهٖۤ اَوْ بِاَيْدِيْنَا ۖ فَتَرَبَّصُوْۤا اِنَّا مَعَكُمْ مُّتَرَبِّصُوْنَ ۞

قُلْ اَنْفِقُوْا طَوْعًا اَوْ كَرْهًا لَّنْ يُّتَقَبَّلَ مِنْكُمْ ۚ اِنَّكُمْ كُنْتُمْ قَوْمًا فٰسِقِيْنَ ۞

The only reason that has made their contributions unacceptable to Allah is that they have disbelieved in Allah and His Messenger, and they come not to Prayer but sluggishly and they make not their contributions but reluctantly. So let not their possessions or their children cause thee to wonder. Allah only intends to chastise them therewith in the present life and that their souls may depart while they are disbelievers. They swear by Allah that they are of you, while they are not of you; they are a cowardly people. Could they find a place of refuge, or a cave, or a retreat they would turn away and rush headlong into it. (54—57)

وَمَا مَنَعَهُمْ اَنْ تُقْبَلَ مِنْهُمْ نَفَقٰتُهُمْ اِلَّاۤ اَنَّهُمْ كَفَرُوْا بِاللّٰهِ وَبِرَسُوْلِهٖ وَلَا يَأْتُوْنَ الصَّلٰوةَ اِلَّا وَهُمْ كُسَالٰى وَلَا يُنْفِقُوْنَ اِلَّا وَهُمْ كٰرِهُوْنَ ۞

فَلَا تُعْجِبْكَ اَمْوَالُهُمْ وَلَاۤ اَوْلَادُهُمْ ۚ اِنَّمَا يُرِيْدُ اللّٰهُ لِيُعَذِّبَهُمْ بِهَا فِى الْحَيٰوةِ الدُّنْيَا وَتَزْهَقَ اَنْفُسُهُمْ وَهُمْ كٰفِرُوْنَ ۞

وَيَحْلِفُوْنَ بِاللّٰهِ اِنَّهُمْ لَمِنْكُمْ ۚ وَمَا هُمْ مِّنْكُمْ وَلٰكِنَّهُمْ قَوْمٌ يَّفْرَقُوْنَ ۞

لَوْ يَجِدُوْنَ مَلْجَاً اَوْ مَغٰرٰتٍ اَوْ مُدَّخَلًا لَّوَلَّوْا اِلَيْهِ وَهُمْ يَجْمَحُوْنَ ۞

There are some among them who find fault with thee in the matter of the distribution of alms. If they are given thereof they are pleased, but if they are not given thereof, they are at once put out. Had they been content with that which Allah and His Messenger had given them and said: Sufficient for us is Allah; in case of need Allah will give us of His bounty and so will His Messenger; to Allah do

وَمِنْهُمْ مَّنْ يَّلْمِزُكَ فِى الصَّدَقٰتِ ۚ فَاِنْ اُعْطُوْا مِنْهَا رَضُوْا وَاِنْ لَّمْ يُعْطَوْا مِنْهَاۤ اِذَا هُمْ يَسْخَطُوْنَ ۞

وَلَوْ اَنَّهُمْ رَضُوْا مَاۤ اٰتٰىهُمُ اللّٰهُ وَرَسُوْلُهٗ ۙ وَقَالُوْا حَسْبُنَا اللّٰهُ سَيُؤْتِيْنَا اللّٰهُ مِنْ فَضْلِهٖ وَرَسُوْلُهٗۤ ۙ

we turn in supplication; it would have been the better for them. Alms are only for the poor and the needy, and for those employed in connection with their collection and distribution, and for those whose hearts are to be comforted, and for the freeing of slaves, and for those burdened with debt, and for those striving in the cause of Allah, and for wayfarers. This is an ordinance from Allah. Allah is All-Knowing, Wise. (58—60)

Of them there are some who distress the Prophet by saying: He listens to all and sundry. Tell them: He listens for your good. He believes in Allah and trusts the believers, and is a mercy for those of you who believe. For those who cause distress to the Messenger of Allah is a painful chastisement. They swear by Allah to please you, but Allah is more worthy that they should please Him and also His Messenger, if they are true believers. Have they not known that for him who opposes Allah and His Messenger is the fire of hell, wherein he shall abide? That is the great humiliation. The hypocrites pretend to fear lest a chapter of the Quran should be revealed concerning them, informing them and the believers of that which is in their minds. Say to them: Continue your mockery. Allah will surely bring to light that which you fear. If thou were to question them concerning that which they say, they will most surely answer: We were only talking idly and jesting. Say to them: Was it Allah and His Signs and His Messenger that you mocked at? Now, make no excuses. The truth is you have certainly disbelieved after having believed. If We forgive a party from among you, a party shall We punish, because they were guilty. (61—66)

The hypocrites, men and women, are all connected one with another. They enjoin evil and forbid good and are close-fisted. They forgot Allah, so He has cast them aside.

Surely, it is the hypocrites who are the disobedient ones. Allah has promised the hypocrites, men and women, and the disbelievers, the fire of hell, wherein they shall abide. It shall suffice them. Allah has cast them out, and they shall have a lasting punishment, like those before you. They were mightier than you in power and richer in possessions and offspring. They enjoyed their lot, and you have enjoyed your lot as those before you enjoyed their lot; and you have indulged in idle talk as they indulged in idle talk. Their works shall be vain in this world and the Hereafter, and it is they who are the losers. Has no account reached them of those who were before them — the people of Noah, 'Ad, and Thamud, and the people of Abraham and the dwellers of Midian, and the cities which were overthrown? Their Messengers came to them with clear Signs. So Allah would not wrong them, but they wronged themselves. (67—70)

The believers, men and women, are friends one of another. They enjoin good and forbid evil and observe Prayer and pay the Zakat and obey Allah and His Messenger. It is these on whom Allah will have mercy. Surely, Allah is Mighty, Wise. Allah has promised the believers, men and women, Gardens beneath which rivers flow, wherein they will abide, and delightful dwelling places in Gardens of Eternity, and the pleasure of Allah, which is the greatest of all. That is the supreme triumph. (71—72)

نَسُوا اللّٰهَ فَنَسِيَهُمْ ۚ اِنَّ الْمُنٰفِقِيْنَ هُمُ الْفٰسِقُوْنَ ۞

وَعَدَ اللّٰهُ الْمُنٰفِقِيْنَ وَالْمُنٰفِقٰتِ وَالْكُفَّارَ نَارَ جَهَنَّمَ خٰلِدِيْنَ فِيْهَا ۚ هِيَ حَسْبُهُمْ ۚ وَلَعَنَهُمُ اللّٰهُ ۚ وَلَهُمْ عَذَابٌ مُّقِيْمٌ ۞

كَالَّذِيْنَ مِنْ قَبْلِكُمْ كَانُوْا اَشَدَّ مِنْكُمْ قُوَّةً وَّاَكْثَرَ اَمْوَالًا وَّاَوْلَادًا ۚ فَاسْتَمْتَعُوْا بِخَلَاقِهِمْ فَاسْتَمْتَعْتُمْ بِخَلَاقِكُمْ كَمَا اسْتَمْتَعَ الَّذِيْنَ مِنْ قَبْلِكُمْ بِخَلَاقِهِمْ وَخُضْتُمْ كَالَّذِيْ خَاضُوْا ۚ اُولٰٓئِكَ حَبِطَتْ اَعْمَالُهُمْ فِي الدُّنْيَا وَالْاٰخِرَةِ ۚ وَاُولٰٓئِكَ هُمُ الْخٰسِرُوْنَ ۞

اَلَمْ يَاْتِهِمْ نَبَاُ الَّذِيْنَ مِنْ قَبْلِهِمْ قَوْمِ نُوْحٍ وَّعَادٍ وَّثَمُوْدَ ۙ وَقَوْمِ اِبْرٰهِيْمَ وَاَصْحٰبِ مَدْيَنَ وَالْمُؤْتَفِكٰتِ ۚ اَتَتْهُمْ رُسُلُهُمْ بِالْبَيِّنٰتِ ۚ فَمَا كَانَ اللّٰهُ لِيَظْلِمَهُمْ وَلٰكِنْ كَانُوْا اَنْفُسَهُمْ يَظْلِمُوْنَ ۞

وَالْمُؤْمِنُوْنَ وَالْمُؤْمِنٰتُ بَعْضُهُمْ اَوْلِيَآءُ بَعْضٍ ۚ يَاْمُرُوْنَ بِالْمَعْرُوْفِ وَيَنْهَوْنَ عَنِ الْمُنْكَرِ وَيُقِيْمُوْنَ الصَّلٰوةَ وَيُؤْتُوْنَ الزَّكٰوةَ وَيُطِيْعُوْنَ اللّٰهَ وَرَسُوْلَهٗ ۚ اُولٰٓئِكَ سَيَرْحَمُهُمُ اللّٰهُ ۚ اِنَّ اللّٰهَ عَزِيْزٌ حَكِيْمٌ ۞

وَعَدَ اللّٰهُ الْمُؤْمِنِيْنَ وَالْمُؤْمِنٰتِ جَنّٰتٍ تَجْرِيْ مِنْ تَحْتِهَا الْاَنْهٰرُ خٰلِدِيْنَ فِيْهَا وَمَسٰكِنَ طَيِّبَةً فِيْ جَنّٰتِ عَدْنٍ ۚ وَرِضْوَانٌ مِّنَ اللّٰهِ اَكْبَرُ ۚ ذٰلِكَ هُوَ الْفَوْزُ الْعَظِيْمُ ۞

O Prophet, strive against the disbelievers and the hypocrites and press hard on them. Their abode is hell and an evil destination it is. They swear by Allah they have not said anything derogatory. Most certainly have they blasphemed, and disbelieved after they had professed Islam. They entertained evil designs which they could not carry into effect. They cherish hatred against the believers only because Allah and His Messenger had enriched them out of His bounty. Now if they repent it will be the better for them, but if they turn away, Allah will chastise them with a painful chastisement in this life, and the Hereafter, and they shall have neither friend not helper in the world. Among them are those who vowed: If Allah gives us of His bounty, we would assuredly give alms and be virtuous. But when He gave them of His bounty, they were niggardly of it, and they reverted to their old ways, turning away in aversion from that which was required of them. So He requited them with hypocrisy which shall continue to taint their hearts until the day when they shall meet Him, because they violated their promise to Allah and because they lied. Did they not know that Allah knows their secret counsels as well as their overt discussions, and that Allah has full knowledge of whatever is hidden? It is these hypocrites who find fault with such of the believers as give alms freely and deride those who have nothing to give save that which they earn through their toil. Allah shall requite them for their derision, and for them there is a painful chastisement. Ask thou forgiveness for them or ask thou not, it is the same to them. Even if thou were to ask forgiveness for them seventy times, Allah will never forgive them. That is because they disbelieved in Allah and His Messenger, and Allah guides not the perfidious people. (73—80)

يَاأَيُّهَا النَّبِيُّ جَاهِدِ الْكُفَّارَ وَالْمُنَافِقِينَ وَاغْلُظْ عَلَيْهِمْ وَمَأْوَاهُمْ جَهَنَّمُ وَبِئْسَ الْمَصِيرُ ۝

يَحْلِفُونَ بِاللَّهِ مَا قَالُوا وَلَقَدْ قَالُوا كَلِمَةَ الْكُفْرِ وَكَفَرُوا بَعْدَ إِسْلَامِهِمْ وَهَمُّوا بِمَا لَمْ يَنَالُوا وَمَا نَقَمُوا إِلَّا أَنْ أَغْنَاهُمُ اللَّهُ وَرَسُولُهُ مِنْ فَضْلِهِ فَإِنْ يَتُوبُوا يَكُ خَيْرًا لَهُمْ وَإِنْ يَتَوَلَّوْا يُعَذِّبْهُمُ اللَّهُ عَذَابًا أَلِيمًا فِي الدُّنْيَا وَالْآخِرَةِ وَمَا لَهُمْ فِي الْأَرْضِ مِنْ وَلِيٍّ وَلَا نَصِيرٍ ۝

وَمِنْهُمْ مَنْ عَاهَدَ اللَّهَ لَئِنْ آتَانَا مِنْ فَضْلِهِ لَنَصَّدَّقَنَّ وَلَنَكُونَنَّ مِنَ الصَّالِحِينَ ۝

فَلَمَّا آتَاهُمْ مِنْ فَضْلِهِ بَخِلُوا بِهِ وَتَوَلَّوْا وَهُمْ مُعْرِضُونَ ۝ فَأَعْقَبَهُمْ نِفَاقًا فِي قُلُوبِهِمْ إِلَى يَوْمِ يَلْقَوْنَهُ بِمَا أَخْلَفُوا اللَّهَ مَا وَعَدُوهُ وَبِمَا كَانُوا يَكْذِبُونَ ۝

أَلَمْ يَعْلَمُوا أَنَّ اللَّهَ يَعْلَمُ سِرَّهُمْ وَنَجْوَاهُمْ وَأَنَّ اللَّهَ عَلَّامُ الْغُيُوبِ ۝

الَّذِينَ يَلْمِزُونَ الْمُطَّوِّعِينَ مِنَ الْمُؤْمِنِينَ فِي الصَّدَقَاتِ وَالَّذِينَ لَا يَجِدُونَ إِلَّا جُهْدَهُمْ فَيَسْخَرُونَ مِنْهُمْ سَخِرَ اللَّهُ مِنْهُمْ وَلَهُمْ عَذَابٌ أَلِيمٌ ۝

اسْتَغْفِرْ لَهُمْ أَوْ لَا تَسْتَغْفِرْ لَهُمْ إِنْ تَسْتَغْفِرْ لَهُمْ سَبْعِينَ مَرَّةً فَلَنْ يَغْفِرَ اللَّهُ لَهُمْ ذَلِكَ بِأَنَّهُمْ كَفَرُوا بِاللَّهِ وَرَسُولِهِ وَاللَّهُ لَا يَهْدِي الْقَوْمَ الْفَاسِقِينَ ۝

فَرِحَ الْمُخَلَّفُونَ بِمَقْعَدِهِمْ خِلَافَ رَسُولِ اللَّهِ وَ

Those who continued to be left behind rejoiced at their remaining at home, contrary to the directions of the Messenger of Allah. They were averse to striving in the cause of Allah with their belongings and their persons, and they said, one to another: Go not forth in such heat. Remind them: The fire of hell is fiercer far in heat; did they but understand. So let them rejoice less at the supposed success of their stratagem and weep more at the contemplation of the punishment for their duplicity awaiting them. Should Allah take thee back to a party of them and should they ask of thee leave to go forth with thee, tell them: You shall never go forth with me and shall never fight an enemy along with me. You chose to remain at home the first time, so now continue with those who remain behind. Pray not for any of them who dies, nor stand by his grave asking forgiveness for him; they disbelieved in Allah and His Messenger and died while they were disobedient. Let not their possessions or their children cause thee to wonder. Allah only intends to chastise them therewith in the present life and that their souls may depart while they are disbelievers. (81—85)

When a chapter is revealed enjoining: Believe in Allah and strive in the cause of Allah along with His Messenger; those of them who are affluent start asking thee for exemption, and say: Leave us with those who will be at home. They are content to be with the womenfolk. Their hearts are sealed so they understand not. But the Messenger and those who have believed with him strive in the cause of Allah with their belongings and their persons. It is they who shall have all kinds of good, and it is they who shall prosper.

كَرِهُوْۤا اَنْ يُّجَاهِدُوْا بِاَمْوَالِهِمْ وَاَنْفُسِهِمْ فِيْ سَبِيْلِ اللّٰهِ وَقَالُوْا لَا تَنْفِرُوْا فِي الْحَرِّ قُلْ نَارُ جَهَنَّمَ اَشَدُّ حَرًّا لَّوْ كَانُوْا يَفْقَهُوْنَ ۞

فَلْيَضْحَكُوْا قَلِيْلًا وَّلْيَبْكُوْا كَثِيْرًا جَزَآءًۢ بِمَا كَانُوْا يَكْسِبُوْنَ ۞

فَاِنْ رَّجَعَكَ اللّٰهُ اِلٰى طَآئِفَةٍ مِّنْهُمْ فَاسْتَاْذَنُوْكَ لِلْخُرُوْجِ فَقُلْ لَّنْ تَخْرُجُوْا مَعِيَ اَبَدًا وَّلَنْ تُقَاتِلُوْا مَعِيَ عَدُوًّا اِنَّكُمْ رَضِيْتُمْ بِالْقُعُوْدِ اَوَّلَ مَرَّةٍ فَاقْعُدُوْا مَعَ الْخٰلِفِيْنَ ۞

وَلَا تُصَلِّ عَلٰۤى اَحَدٍ مِّنْهُمْ مَّاتَ اَبَدًا وَّلَا تَقُمْ عَلٰى قَبْرِهٖۤ اِنَّهُمْ كَفَرُوْا بِاللّٰهِ وَرَسُوْلِهٖ وَمَاتُوْا وَهُمْ فٰسِقُوْنَ ۞

وَلَا تُعْجِبْكَ اَمْوَالُهُمْ وَاَوْلَادُهُمْ اِنَّمَا يُرِيْدُ اللّٰهُ اَنْ يُّعَذِّبَهُمْ بِهَا فِي الدُّنْيَا وَتَزْهَقَ اَنْفُسُهُمْ وَهُمْ كٰفِرُوْنَ ۞

وَاِذَاۤ اُنْزِلَتْ سُوْرَةٌ اَنْ اٰمِنُوْا بِاللّٰهِ وَجَاهِدُوْا مَعَ رَسُوْلِهِ اسْتَاْذَنَكَ اُولُوا الطَّوْلِ مِنْهُمْ وَقَالُوْا ذَرْنَا نَكُنْ مَّعَ الْقٰعِدِيْنَ ۞

رَضُوْا بِاَنْ يَّكُوْنُوْا مَعَ الْخَوَالِفِ وَطُبِعَ عَلٰى قُلُوْبِهِمْ فَهُمْ لَا يَفْقَهُوْنَ ۞

لٰكِنِ الرَّسُوْلُ وَالَّذِيْنَ اٰمَنُوْا مَعَهٗ جَاهَدُوْا بِاَمْوَالِهِمْ وَاَنْفُسِهِمْ وَاُولٰٓئِكَ لَهُمُ الْخَيْرٰتُ وَاُولٰٓئِكَ هُمُ

Allah has prepared for them Gardens beneath which rivers flow; therein shall they abide. That is the supreme triumph. (86—89)

Those of the desert Arabs who sought excuses came to beg for exemption, and those who were false to Allah and His Messenger stayed behind anyhow. A painful chastisement shall befall those of them who disbelieve. But no blame attaches to the weak, or the sick, or those who have nothing which they can spend, if they are sincere to Allah and His Messenger. There is no cause of reproach against those who do their best; Allah is Most Forgiving, Ever Merciful. Nor is there any cause of reproach against those who came to thee that thou mayest provide them with mounts and to whom thou didst say: I have nothing on which I can mount you. They went back with streaming eyes, out of grief that they had nothing which they could spend. The blameworthy are those who are affluent and yet ask for exemption. They are content to be with the womenfolk. Allah has set a seal upon their hearts so that they know not. They will put forth explanations to you when you return to them. Tell them: Make no explanations; we will not believe you. Allah has apprised us of your situation. Allah will observe your conduct, and also His Messenger; then will you be brought back to Him Who knows the unseen and the seen, and He will tell you all that you used to do. They will swear to you by Allah, when you return to them, that you may leave them alone.

اَلْمُفْلِحُوْنَ ۞

اَعَدَّ اللّٰهُ لَهُمْ جَنّٰتٍ تَجْرِیْ مِنْ تَحْتِهَا الْاَنْهٰرُ

خٰلِدِیْنَ فِیْهَا ؕ ذٰلِكَ الْفَوْزُ الْعَظِیْمُ ۞

وَ جَآءَ الْمُعَذِّرُوْنَ مِنَ الْاَعْرَابِ لِیُؤْذَنَ لَهُمْ

وَ قَعَدَ الَّذِیْنَ كَذَبُوا اللّٰهَ وَ رَسُوْلَهٗ ؕ سَیُصِیْبُ الَّذِیْنَ

كَفَرُوْا مِنْهُمْ عَذَابٌ اَلِیْمٌ ۞

لَیْسَ عَلَی الضُّعَفَآءِ وَ لَا عَلَی الْمَرْضٰی وَ لَا عَلَی

الَّذِیْنَ لَا یَجِدُوْنَ مَا یُنْفِقُوْنَ حَرَجٌ اِذَا نَصَحُوْا

لِلّٰهِ وَ رَسُوْلِهٖ ؕ مَا عَلَی الْمُحْسِنِیْنَ مِنْ سَبِیْلٍ ؕ وَ

اللّٰهُ غَفُوْرٌ رَّحِیْمٌ ۞

وَّ لَا عَلَی الَّذِیْنَ اِذَا مَآ اَتَوْكَ لِتَحْمِلَهُمْ قُلْتَ لَاۤ

اَجِدُ مَاۤ اَحْمِلُكُمْ عَلَیْهِ ۖ تَوَلَّوْا وَّ اَعْیُنُهُمْ تَفِیْضُ مِنَ

الدَّمْعِ حَزَنًا اَلَّا یَجِدُوْا مَا یُنْفِقُوْنَ ۞

اِنَّمَا السَّبِیْلُ عَلَی الَّذِیْنَ یَسْتَأْذِنُوْنَكَ وَ هُمْ

اَغْنِیَآءُ ۚ رَضُوْا بِاَنْ یَّكُوْنُوْا مَعَ الْخَوَالِفِ ۙ وَ طَبَعَ

اللّٰهُ عَلٰی قُلُوْبِهِمْ فَهُمْ لَا یَعْلَمُوْنَ ۞

یَعْتَذِرُوْنَ اِلَیْكُمْ اِذَا رَجَعْتُمْ اِلَیْهِمْ ؕ قُلْ

لَّا تَعْتَذِرُوْا لَنْ نُّؤْمِنَ لَكُمْ قَدْ نَبَّاَنَا اللّٰهُ مِنْ

اَخْبَارِكُمْ ؕ وَ سَیَرَی اللّٰهُ عَمَلَكُمْ وَ رَسُوْلُهٗ ثُمَّ تُرَدُّوْنَ

اِلٰی عٰلِمِ الْغَیْبِ وَ الشَّهَادَةِ فَیُنَبِّئُكُمْ بِمَا كُنْتُمْ

تَعْمَلُوْنَ ۞

سَیَحْلِفُوْنَ بِاللّٰهِ لَكُمْ اِذَا انْقَلَبْتُمْ اِلَیْهِمْ لِتُعْرِضُوْا

So leave them alone. They are, indeed,
an abomination, and their abode is hell,
a recompense for that which they did.
They will swear to you that you may be
pleased with them, but even if you are
pleased with them, Allah will not be
pleased with the rebellious people. (90—
96)

The Arabs of the desert are the farthest
gone in disbelief and hypocrisy and most
likely to be unaware of the limits prescribed in that which Allah has sent down
to His Messenger. Allah is All-Knowing,
Wise. There are those among them who
regard that which they spend in the cause
of Allah as an exaction and they await
your being afflicted with misfortune. They
themselves will be the subjects of evil
fortune. Allah is All-Hearing, All-Knowing. There are also those among them who
believe in Allah and the Last Day and
regard that which they spend in the cause
of Allah as a means of drawing near to
Allah and of deserving the prayers of the
Messenger. Hearken, this shall certainly
be for them a means of drawing near to
Allah. Allah will surely admit them to
His mercy; Allah is indeed Most Forgiving, Ever Merciful. (97—99)

Allah is well pleased with those who
were foremost among the Emigrants from
Mecca and the Helpers in Medina, and
those who followed them in the best
possible manner, and they are well pleased
with Him. He has prepared for them
Gardens beneath which rivers flow; therein
will they abide for ever. That is the
supreme triumph. (100)

Of the desert Arabs around you some
are hypocrites; and of the people of
Medina also. They are obstinate in their
hypocrisy. Thou knowest them not: but
We know them. We will punish them
twice; then shall they be passed on to
face a great torment. There are others
who have confessed their defaults. They
mixed good deeds with bad.

عَنْهُمْ فَاَعْرِضُوا عَنْهُمْ إِنَّهُمْ رِجْسٌ وَّ مَأْوٰىهُمْ
جَهَنَّمُ جَزَآءً بِمَا كَانُوْا يَكْسِبُوْنَ ٩

يَحْلِفُوْنَ لَكُمْ لِتَرْضَوْا عَنْهُمْ فَاِنْ تَرْضَوْا عَنْهُمْ
فَاِنَّ اللّٰهَ لَا يَرْضٰى عَنِ الْقَوْمِ الْفٰسِقِيْنَ ٩

اَلْاَعْرَابُ اَشَدُّ كُفْرًا وَّ نِفَاقًا وَّ اَجْدَرُ اَلَّا يَعْلَمُوْا
حُدُوْدَ مَآ اَنْزَلَ اللّٰهُ عَلٰى رَسُوْلِهٖ وَاللّٰهُ عَلِيْمٌ حَكِيْمٌ ٩

وَمِنَ الْاَعْرَابِ مَنْ يَّتَّخِذُ مَا يُنْفِقُ مَغْرَمًا وَّيَتَرَبَّصُ
بِكُمُ الدَّوَآئِرَ عَلَيْهِمْ دَآئِرَةُ السَّوْءِ وَاللّٰهُ سَمِيْعٌ
عَلِيْمٌ ٩

وَمِنَ الْاَعْرَابِ مَنْ يُّؤْمِنُ بِاللّٰهِ وَالْيَوْمِ الْاٰخِرِ
وَيَتَّخِذُ مَا يُنْفِقُ قُرُبٰتٍ عِنْدَ اللّٰهِ وَصَلَوٰتِ الرَّسُوْلِ
اَلَا اِنَّهَا قُرْبَةٌ لَّهُمْ سَيُدْخِلُهُمُ اللّٰهُ فِيْ رَحْمَتِهٖ
اِنَّ اللّٰهَ غَفُوْرٌ رَّحِيْمٌ ٩

وَالسّٰبِقُوْنَ الْاَوَّلُوْنَ مِنَ الْمُهٰجِرِيْنَ وَالْاَنْصَارِ
وَالَّذِيْنَ اتَّبَعُوْهُمْ بِاِحْسَانٍ رَّضِيَ اللّٰهُ عَنْهُمْ
وَرَضُوْا عَنْهُ وَاَعَدَّ لَهُمْ جَنّٰتٍ تَجْرِيْ تَحْتَهَا
الْاَنْهٰرُ خٰلِدِيْنَ فِيْهَآ اَبَدًا ذٰلِكَ الْفَوْزُ الْعَظِيْمُ ٠

وَمِمَّنْ حَوْلَكُمْ مِّنَ الْاَعْرَابِ مُنٰفِقُوْنَ وَمِنْ
اَهْلِ الْمَدِيْنَةِ مَرَدُوْا عَلَى النِّفَاقِ لَا تَعْلَمُهُمْ
نَحْنُ نَعْلَمُهُمْ سَنُعَذِّبُهُمْ مَّرَّتَيْنِ ثُمَّ يُرَدُّوْنَ اِلٰى
عَذَابٍ عَظِيْمٍ ٠

وَاٰخَرُوْنَ اعْتَرَفُوْا بِذُنُوْبِهِمْ خَلَطُوْا عَمَلًا صَالِحًا

It is likely that Allah will turn to them with compassion. Surely, Allah is Most Forgiving, Ever Merciful. Take a portion of their wealth as alms, that thou mayest purify them thereby and provide for their uplift and welfare; and pray for them, thy prayer is indeed a source of tranquillity for them. Allah is All-Hearing, All-Knowing. Know they not that it is Allah Who accepts repentance from His servants and takes alms, and that it is Allah Who is Oft-Returning with compassion and is Ever Merciful. Tell them: Carry on. Allah will surely watch your conduct and also His Messenger and the believers; and you shall be brought back to Him Who knows the unseen and the seen; then He will tell you what you used to do. There are others awaiting Allah's decree. He may punish them or He may turn to them with compassion. Allah is All-Knowing, Wise. (101—106)

Then there are those who built a mosque designing injury to the cause of Allah and support for disbelief and division among the believers, and as an ambush for him who had fought against Allah and His Messenger. They will surely swear: We intended nothing but good; but Allah bears witness that they certainly are liars. Never stand therein to lead Prayer. A mosque that was founded upon piety from the very first day is surely more worthy that thou shouldst stand therein to lead Prayer. In it are men who love to be purified and Allah loves those who purify themselves. Is he who lays the foundation of his structure on fear of Allah and His pleasure better off, or he who lays the foundation of his structure on the brink of a tottering hollow bank which tumbles down with it into the fire

وَاٰخَرُوْنَ اعْتَرَفُوْا عَسَى اللّٰهُ اَنْ يَّتُوْبَ عَلَيْهِمْ اِنَّ اللّٰهَ غَفُوْرٌ رَّحِيْمٌ ۞

خُذْ مِنْ اَمْوَالِهِمْ صَدَقَةً تُطَهِّرُهُمْ وَتُزَكِّيْهِمْ بِهَا وَصَلِّ عَلَيْهِمْ اِنَّ صَلٰوتَكَ سَكَنٌ لَّهُمْ وَاللّٰهُ سَمِيْعٌ عَلِيْمٌ ۞

اَلَمْ يَعْلَمُوْٓا اَنَّ اللّٰهَ هُوَ يَقْبَلُ التَّوْبَةَ عَنْ عِبَادِهٖ وَيَاْخُذُ الصَّدَقٰتِ وَاَنَّ اللّٰهَ هُوَ التَّوَّابُ الرَّحِيْمُ ۞

وَقُلِ اعْمَلُوْا فَسَيَرَى اللّٰهُ عَمَلَكُمْ وَرَسُوْلُهٗ وَالْمُؤْمِنُوْنَ وَسَتُرَدُّوْنَ اِلٰى عٰلِمِ الْغَيْبِ وَالشَّهَادَةِ فَيُنَبِّئُكُمْ بِمَا كُنْتُمْ تَعْمَلُوْنَ ۞

وَاٰخَرُوْنَ مُرْجَوْنَ لِاَمْرِ اللّٰهِ اِمَّا يُعَذِّبُهُمْ وَاِمَّا يَتُوْبُ عَلَيْهِمْ وَاللّٰهُ عَلِيْمٌ حَكِيْمٌ ۞

وَالَّذِيْنَ اتَّخَذُوْا مَسْجِدًا ضِرَارًا وَّكُفْرًا وَّتَفْرِيْقًا بَيْنَ الْمُؤْمِنِيْنَ وَاِرْصَادًا لِّمَنْ حَارَبَ اللّٰهَ وَرَسُوْلَهٗ مِنْ قَبْلُ وَلَيَحْلِفُنَّ اِنْ اَرَدْنَآ اِلَّا الْحُسْنٰى وَاللّٰهُ يَشْهَدُ اِنَّهُمْ لَكٰذِبُوْنَ ۞

لَا تَقُمْ فِيْهِ اَبَدًا لَمَسْجِدٌ اُسِّسَ عَلَى التَّقْوٰى مِنْ اَوَّلِ يَوْمٍ اَحَقُّ اَنْ تَقُوْمَ فِيْهِ فِيْهِ رِجَالٌ يُّحِبُّوْنَ اَنْ يَّتَطَهَّرُوْا وَاللّٰهُ يُحِبُّ الْمُطَّهِّرِيْنَ ۞

اَفَمَنْ اَسَّسَ بُنْيَانَهٗ عَلٰى تَقْوٰى مِنَ اللّٰهِ وَرِضْوَانٍ خَيْرٌ اَمْ مَّنْ اَسَّسَ بُنْيَانَهٗ عَلٰى شَفَا جُرُفٍ هَارٍ فَانْهَارَ بِهٖ فِيْ نَارِ جَهَنَّمَ وَاللّٰهُ لَا يَهْدِى الْقَوْمَ

of hell? Allah guides not the wrongdoing people. This structure of theirs, which they have built, will ever continue to be a source of disquiet in their hearts, unless their hearts are cut to pieces and they perish. Allah is All-Knowing, Wise. (107—110)

Allah has purchased of the believers their persons and their belongings in return for the promise that they shall have Paradise, for they fight in the cause of Allah and they slay the enemy or are themselves slain. This is a promise that He has made incumbent upon Himself as set out in the Torah, and the Gospel and the Quran; and who is more faithful to his promise than Allah? Rejoice, then, in the bargain that you have made with Him; that indeed is the supreme triumph. These believers are the ones who turn to Allah in repentance, who worship Him, who praise Him, who go about serving His cause, who bow down to Him, who prostrate themselves before Him, who enjoin good and forbid evil, and who observe the limits set by Allah. Give glad tidings to such believers. (111—112)

It is not for the Prophet and those who believe to ask forgiveness of Allah for the idolaters, even though they may be kinsmen, after it has become plain to them that they are condemned to hell. Abraham's asking forgiveness for his father was only because of a promise he had made to him, but when it became clear to him that he was Allah's enemy, he dissociated himself from him. Surely, Abraham was most tenderhearted, intelligent. (113—114)

It is not consonant with Allah's dignity that He should adjuge a people as having gone astray after He had guided them, until He makes clear to them that which they should guard against. Surely, Allah knows all things well. Surely, it is Allah to Whom belongs the kingdom of the heavens and the earth. He gives life and He causes death. You have no friend nor helper beside Allah. (115—116)

Allah has assuredly turned with mercy to the Prophet and to the Emigrants and the Helpers who stood by him in the hour of distress when the hearts of a party of them had wellnigh swerved, and He has turned with mercy to these last also. Surely, He is Compassionate and Merciful to all of them. He has also turned with mercy to the three whose case was deferred, who were sore distressed and whose lives became a burden to them and who became convinced that there was no refuge against the wrath of Allah save in Himself. He turned to them with mercy that they might turn to Him in repentance. Surely, it is Allah Who is Oft-Returning with Compassion and is Ever Merciful. (117—118)

O ye who believe, be mindful of your duty to Allah and keep company with the righteous. It was not proper for the people of Medina and those around them from among the Arabs of the desert to remain behind, leaving the Messenger of Allah to go forth, or to prefer their own security to his. It is so ordained because they endure no thirst, or fatigue or hunger in the cause of Allah, nor do they tread a track which chagrins the disbelievers, nor do they wrest an advantage from the enemy, but there is written down for them a good deed on account of it. Surely, Allah suffers not the reward of those who carry out their duty in the best manner to be lost. They spend not, in the cause of Allah, any sum, small or big, nor do they traverse a valley, but that it is written down for them, that Allah may bestow upon them the best reward for that which they do. (119—121)

It is not possible for the believers to go forth all together to obtain religious instruction. Why, then, does not a party from every section of them go forth that they may be fully instructed in religion, and that they may warn their people when they return to them, so that they may guard against ignorance? (122)

لَقَدْ تَابَ اللّٰهُ عَلَى النَّبِيِّ وَالْمُهٰجِرِيْنَ وَالْاَنْصَارِ الَّذِيْنَ اتَّبَعُوْهُ فِيْ سَاعَةِ الْعُسْرَةِ مِنْ بَعْدِ مَا كَادَ يَزِيْغُ قُلُوْبُ فَرِيْقٍ مِّنْهُمْ ثُمَّ تَابَ عَلَيْهِمْ اِنَّهٗ بِهِمْ رَءُوْفٌ رَّحِيْمٌ ۟ۙ

وَّعَلَى الثَّلٰثَةِ الَّذِيْنَ خُلِّفُوْا حَتّٰۤى اِذَا ضَاقَتْ عَلَيْهِمُ الْاَرْضُ بِمَا رَحُبَتْ وَضَاقَتْ عَلَيْهِمْ اَنْفُسُهُمْ وَظَنُّوْۤا اَنْ لَّا مَلْجَاَ مِنَ اللّٰهِ اِلَّاۤ اِلَيْهِ ثُمَّ تَابَ عَلَيْهِمْ لِيَتُوْبُوْا اِنَّ اللّٰهَ هُوَ التَّوَّابُ الرَّحِيْمُ ۟ۚ

يٰۤاَيُّهَا الَّذِيْنَ اٰمَنُوا اتَّقُوا اللّٰهَ وَكُوْنُوْا مَعَ الصّٰدِقِيْنَ ۟

مَا كَانَ لِاَهْلِ الْمَدِيْنَةِ وَمَنْ حَوْلَهُمْ مِّنَ الْاَعْرَابِ اَنْ يَّتَخَلَّفُوْا عَنْ رَّسُوْلِ اللّٰهِ وَلَا يَرْغَبُوْا بِاَنْفُسِهِمْ عَنْ نَّفْسِهٖ ذٰلِكَ بِاَنَّهُمْ لَا يُصِيْبُهُمْ ظَمَاٌ وَّلَا نَصَبٌ وَّلَا مَخْمَصَةٌ فِيْ سَبِيْلِ اللّٰهِ وَلَا يَطَؤُوْنَ مَوْطِئًا يَّغِيْظُ الْكُفَّارَ وَلَا يَنَالُوْنَ مِنْ عَدُوٍّ نَّيْلًا اِلَّا كُتِبَ لَهُمْ بِهٖ عَمَلٌ صَالِحٌ اِنَّ اللّٰهَ لَا يُضِيْعُ اَجْرَ الْمُحْسِنِيْنَ ۟

وَلَا يُنْفِقُوْنَ نَفَقَةً صَغِيْرَةً وَّلَا كَبِيْرَةً وَّلَا يَقْطَعُوْنَ وَادِيًا اِلَّا كُتِبَ لَهُمْ لِيَجْزِيَهُمُ اللّٰهُ اَحْسَنَ مَا كَانُوْا يَعْمَلُوْنَ ۟

وَمَا كَانَ الْمُؤْمِنُوْنَ لِيَنْفِرُوْا كَآفَّةً ۗ فَلَوْلَا نَفَرَ مِنْ كُلِّ فِرْقَةٍ مِّنْهُمْ طَآئِفَةٌ لِّيَتَفَقَّهُوْا فِي الدِّيْنِ وَلِيُنْذِرُوْا قَوْمَهُمْ اِذَا رَجَعُوْۤا اِلَيْهِمْ لَعَلَّهُمْ يَحْذَرُوْنَ ۟

O ye who believe, continue your fight against the disbelievers who are adjacent to you, and let them find you unrelenting; and know that Allah is with those who are mindful of their duty to Him. (123)

يَاأَيُّهَا الَّذِينَ اٰمَنُوا قَاتِلُوا الَّذِينَ يَلُوْنَكُمْ مِّنَ الْكُفَّارِ وَلْيَجِدُوا فِيكُمْ غِلْظَةً ۚ وَاعْلَمُوا أَنَّ اللّٰهَ مَعَ الْمُتَّقِينَ ۝

Whenever a chapter is revealed, some of the hypocrites say: Is there any of you to whose faith it has added? It certainly adds to the faith of those who believe and they rejoice over it. But it adds only vileness to the vileness of those whose minds are diseased; they will die while they are disbelievers. Do they not see that they are tried once or twice in every year? Yet they repent not, nor would they be admonished. Whenever a chapter is revealed they look at one another to find out whether they are being watched. Then they turn away. Allah has turned away their hearts for they are a people who do not exercise their understanding. (124—127)

وَإِذَا مَا أُنْزِلَتْ سُورَةٌ فَمِنْهُمْ مَّنْ يَّقُولُ أَيُّكُمْ زَادَتْهُ هٰذِهِ إِيمَانًا ۚ فَأَمَّا الَّذِينَ اٰمَنُوا فَزَادَتْهُمْ إِيمَانًا وَّهُمْ يَسْتَبْشِرُونَ ۝

وَأَمَّا الَّذِينَ فِي قُلُوبِهِمْ مَّرَضٌ فَزَادَتْهُمْ رِجْسًا إِلَى رِجْسِهِمْ وَمَاتُوا وَهُمْ كَافِرُونَ ۝

أَوَلَا يَرَوْنَ أَنَّهُمْ يُفْتَنُونَ فِي كُلِّ عَامٍ مَّرَّةً أَوْ مَرَّتَيْنِ ثُمَّ لَا يَتُوبُونَ وَلَا هُمْ يَذَّكَّرُونَ ۝

وَإِذَا مَا أُنْزِلَتْ سُورَةٌ نَّظَرَ بَعْضُهُمْ إِلَى بَعْضٍ هَلْ يَرَاكُمْ مِّنْ أَحَدٍ ثُمَّ انْصَرَفُوا ۚ صَرَفَ اللّٰهُ قُلُوبَهُمْ بِأَنَّهُمْ قَوْمٌ لَّا يَفْقَهُونَ ۝

Surely, a Messenger has come to you from among yourselves; grievously heavy is it on him that you should fall into trouble, ardently desirous is he of your welfare; compassionate and merciful towards the believers. Yet, if they should turn away, say to them: Sufficient for me is Allah. There is no god but He. In Him do I put my trust. He is the Lord of the Mighty Throne. (128—129)

لَقَدْ جَاءَكُمْ رَسُولٌ مِّنْ أَنْفُسِكُمْ عَزِيزٌ عَلَيْهِ مَا عَنِتُّمْ حَرِيصٌ عَلَيْكُمْ بِالْمُؤْمِنِينَ رَءُوفٌ رَّحِيمٌ ۝

فَإِنْ تَوَلَّوْا فَقُلْ حَسْبِيَ اللّٰهُ ۖ لَا إِلٰهَ إِلَّا هُوَ ۖ عَلَيْهِ تَوَكَّلْتُ وَهُوَ رَبُّ الْعَرْشِ الْعَظِيمِ ۝

سُوْرَة يُوْنُس مَكِّيَّة (١٠)

YŪNUS

(Revealed before Hijra)

In the name of Allah, Most Gracious, Ever Merciful. (1)

I AM ALLAH THE ALL-SEEING.

These are the verses of the Perfect Book that is full of wisdom. (2)

Is it a matter of wonder for people that We have sent revelation to a man from among them, directing him: Warn mankind and give glad tidings to those who believe that they have a perfect rank of honour with their Lord? The disbelievers assert: Surely, this one is a palpable deceiver! Of a surety, your Lord is Allah Who created the heavens and the earth in six periods; then He settled Himself on the Throne. He regulates all. No one may intercede with Him save with His permission. That is Allah, your Lord, so worship Him. Will you not then be admonished? To Him shall you all return. This is the promise of Allah which shall be fulfilled. He originates the creation, then He repeats it, that He may reward fully those who believe and work righteousness. Those who disbelieve shall have a drink of boiling water, and a painful chastisement, because they disbelieved. He it is Who has made the sun a source of light and the moon shedding lustre, and ordained for it stages, that you might learn the method of calculating the years and determining time. Allah has created this system in accordance with truth and wisdom. He expounds the Signs in detail for a people who have knowledge. In the alternation of the night and the day, and in all that Allah has created in the heavens and the earth, there are many Signs for a people who are mindful of their duty to Allah. (3—7)

بِسْمِ اللّٰهِ الرَّحْمٰنِ الرَّحِيْمِ ۞

الٓرٰ ۫ تِلْكَ اٰيٰتُ الْكِتٰبِ الْحَكِيْمِ ۞

اَكَانَ لِلنَّاسِ عَجَبًا اَنْ اَوْحَيْنَآ اِلٰى رَجُلٍ مِّنْهُمْ اَنْ اَنْذِرِ النَّاسَ وَبَشِّرِ الَّذِيْنَ اٰمَنُوْۤا اَنَّ لَهُمْ قَدَمَ صِدْقٍ عِنْدَ رَبِّهِمْ ۦ قَالَ الْكٰفِرُوْنَ اِنَّ هٰذَا لَسٰحِرٌ مُّبِيْنٌ ۞

اِنَّ رَبَّكُمُ اللّٰهُ الَّذِيْ خَلَقَ السَّمٰوٰتِ وَالْاَرْضَ فِيْ سِتَّةِ اَيَّامٍ ثُمَّ اسْتَوٰى عَلَى الْعَرْشِ يُدَبِّرُ الْاَمْرَ ۦ مَا مِنْ شَفِيْعٍ اِلَّا مِنْۢ بَعْدِ اِذْنِهٖ ۦ ذٰلِكُمُ اللّٰهُ رَبُّكُمْ فَاعْبُدُوْهُ ۦ اَفَلَا تَذَكَّرُوْنَ ۞

اِلَيْهِ مَرْجِعُكُمْ جَمِيْعًا ۦ وَعْدَ اللّٰهِ حَقًّا ۦ اِنَّهٗ يَبْدَؤُا الْخَلْقَ ثُمَّ يُعِيْدُهٗ لِيَجْزِيَ الَّذِيْنَ اٰمَنُوْا وَعَمِلُوا الصّٰلِحٰتِ بِالْقِسْطِ ۦ وَالَّذِيْنَ كَفَرُوْا لَهُمْ شَرَابٌ مِّنْ حَمِيْمٍ وَّعَذَابٌ اَلِيْمٌۢ بِمَا كَانُوْا يَكْفُرُوْنَ ۞

هُوَ الَّذِيْ جَعَلَ الشَّمْسَ ضِيَآءً وَّالْقَمَرَ نُوْرًا وَّقَدَّرَهٗ مَنَازِلَ لِتَعْلَمُوْا عَدَدَ السِّنِيْنَ وَالْحِسَابَ ۦ مَا خَلَقَ اللّٰهُ ذٰلِكَ اِلَّا بِالْحَقِّ ۦ يُفَصِّلُ الْاٰيٰتِ لِقَوْمٍ يَّعْلَمُوْنَ ۞

اِنَّ فِيْ اخْتِلَافِ الَّيْلِ وَالنَّهَارِ وَمَا خَلَقَ اللّٰهُ فِي

Those who desire not to meet Us and are content with the hither life and are well pleased with it, and those who are heedless of Our Signs, shall have their abode in the Fire, because of their conduct. Those who believe and work righteousness will be guided by their Lord because of their faith. Rivers shall flow beneath them in the Gardens of Bliss. Their call therein will be: Holy art Thou, O Allah; and their greeting will be: Peace. The end of their prayer will be: All praise belongs to Allah, the Lord of the worlds. (8—11)

السَّمٰوٰتِ وَ الْاَرْضِ لَاٰيٰتٍ لِّقَوْمٍ يَّتَّقُوْنَ ۞

اِنَّ الَّذِيْنَ لَا يَرْجُوْنَ لِقَآءَنَا وَرَضُوْا بِالْحَيٰوةِ الدُّنْيَا وَاطْمَاَنُّوْا بِهَا وَالَّذِيْنَ هُمْ عَنْ اٰيٰتِنَا غٰفِلُوْنَ ۞

اُولٰٓئِكَ مَاْوٰىهُمُ النَّارُ بِمَا كَانُوْا يَكْسِبُوْنَ ۞

اِنَّ الَّذِيْنَ اٰمَنُوْا وَعَمِلُوا الصّٰلِحٰتِ يَهْدِيْهِمْ رَبُّهُمْ بِاِيْمَانِهِمْ ۚ تَجْرِيْ مِنْ تَحْتِهِمُ الْاَنْهٰرُ فِيْ جَنّٰتِ النَّعِيْمِ ۞

دَعْوٰىهُمْ فِيْهَا سُبْحٰنَكَ اللّٰهُمَّ وَتَحِيَّتُهُمْ فِيْهَا سَلٰمٌ ۚ وَاٰخِرُ دَعْوٰىهُمْ اَنِ الْحَمْدُ لِلّٰهِ رَبِّ الْعٰلَمِيْنَ ۞

وَلَوْ يُعَجِّلُ اللّٰهُ لِلنَّاسِ الشَّرَّ اسْتِعْجَالَهُمْ بِالْخَيْرِ لَقُضِيَ اِلَيْهِمْ اَجَلُهُمْ ۚ فَنَذَرُ الَّذِيْنَ لَا يَرْجُوْنَ لِقَآءَنَا فِيْ طُغْيَانِهِمْ يَعْمَهُوْنَ ۞

If Allah had imposed upon people the evil consequences of their conduct as quickly as they desire the acquisition of worldly goods, the end of their term of life would already have been reached. But We leave those who believe not in meeting Us to wander distractedly in their transgression. When trouble befalls a person he calls on Us all the time, lying on his side, sitting and standing; but when We relieve him or remove his trouble, he goes his way unconcernedly as if he had never called on Us for the removal of his trouble. Thus it is that the doings of the transgressors are made to look fair to them. We destroyed generation after generation before you when they did wrong. Their Messengers came to them with clear Signs, but they would not believe. Thus do We requite the guilty people. Then, after them We made you their successors in the earth, that We might see how you would behave. (12—15)

وَاِذَا مَسَّ الْاِنْسَانَ الضُّرُّ دَعَانَا لِجَنْبِهٖٓ اَوْ قَاعِدًا اَوْ قَآئِمًا ۚ فَلَمَّا كَشَفْنَا عَنْهُ ضُرَّهٗ مَرَّ كَاَنْ لَّمْ يَدْعُنَا اِلٰى ضُرٍّ مَّسَّهٗ ۚ كَذٰلِكَ زُيِّنَ لِلْمُسْرِفِيْنَ مَا كَانُوْا يَعْمَلُوْنَ ۞

وَلَقَدْ اَهْلَكْنَا الْقُرُوْنَ مِنْ قَبْلِكُمْ لَمَّا ظَلَمُوْا ۙ وَجَآءَتْهُمْ رُسُلُهُمْ بِالْبَيِّنٰتِ وَمَا كَانُوْا لِيُؤْمِنُوْا ۚ كَذٰلِكَ نَجْزِي الْقَوْمَ الْمُجْرِمِيْنَ ۞

ثُمَّ جَعَلْنٰكُمْ خَلٰٓئِفَ فِى الْاَرْضِ مِنْ بَعْدِهِمْ لِنَنْظُرَ كَيْفَ تَعْمَلُوْنَ ۞

وَاِذَا تُتْلٰى عَلَيْهِمْ اٰيَاتُنَا بَيِّنٰتٍ ۙ قَالَ الَّذِيْنَ لَا يَرْجُوْنَ

When Our clear Signs are recited unto them, those who believe not in Our meeting say to thee: Bring us a Quran other than this one or, at least, modify this one in certain respects. Tell them: It is not for me to modify it on my own. I but follow that which is revealed to me. Were I to disobey my Lord, I would be liable to the chastisement of a terrible day. Tell them: Had Allah so willed, I would not have recited it to you nor would He have made it known to you. I have spent a whole lifetime among you before this. Will you not then understand? Who is, then, more unjust than one who fabricates a lie against Allah, or one who rejects His Signs as false? Surely, the guilty never prosper. (16—18)

They worship, in place of Allah, that which can neither harm them nor benefit them. They say: These are our intercessors with Allah. Ask them: Do you presume to inform Allah of something of the existence of which, in the heavens or the earth, He has no knowledge? Holy is He and exalted far above that which they associate with Him. Mankind were but one community; then they differed among themselves. Had not the promise of mercy made by thy Lord stood in the way, that concerning which they differed would have been decreed long before. They ask: Why has not a Sign been sent down to him from his Lord? Tell them: Allah alone has knowledge of the unseen. So wait on, I too wait along with you. (19—21)

When We bestow mercy upon people after they have suffered from adversity, at once they begin to conspire against Our Signs. Warn them: Allah is swifter in planning. Surely, Our messengers write down all that you plan. He it is Who enables you to journey through land and sea. When you and all the others with you have boarded the vessels and they sail with them with a fair wind and they rejoice at the prospect of a pleasant voyage, the vessels suddenly encounter a fierce gale and wave upon wave comes

upon them from every side, and they
believe they are about to perish, then
they call upon Allah, in utter sincerity
of faith: If Thou deliver us from this, we
will surely be grateful. But when He
delivers them and they imagine themselves secure on land, they revert to
committing excesses in the earth wrongfully. O ye people, your pursuit of the
enjoyment of the hither life will be an
affliction for you. Then to Us will be your
return and We will inform you of that
which you used to do. (22—24)

مَكَانٍ وَظَنُّوۤا اَنَّهُمْ اُحِيطَ بِهِمْ دَعَوُا اللهَ مُخْلِصِينَ
لَهُ الدِّينَ لَئِنْ اَنْجَيْتَنَا مِنْ هٰذِهٖ لَنَكُونَنَّ مِنَ
الشّٰكِرِينَ ۝

فَلَمَّاۤ اَنْجٰهُمْ اِذَا هُمْ يَبْغُونَ فِى الْاَرْضِ بِغَيْرِ الْحَقِّ
يٰۤاَيُّهَا النَّاسُ اِنَّمَا بَغْيُكُمْ عَلٰۤى اَنْفُسِكُمْ مَتَاعَ الْحَيٰوةِ
الدُّنْيَا ثُمَّ اِلَيْنَا مَرْجِعُكُمْ فَنُنَبِّئُكُمْ بِمَا كُنْتُمْ
تَعْمَلُونَ ۝

The life of this world is like water that
We send down from the clouds, then the
vegetation of the earth, of which men
and cattle eat, mingles with it and the
earth is embellished and looks beautiful,
and its owners believe they are its complete masters; then by day or by night,
Our command comes to it and We convert it into a mown-down field, as if
nothing had existed there the day before.
Thus do We expound the Signs for a
people who reflect. (25)

اِنَّمَا مَثَلُ الْحَيٰوةِ الدُّنْيَا كَمَآءٍ اَنْزَلْنٰهُ مِنَ السَّمَآءِ
فَاخْتَلَطَ بِهٖ نَبَاتُ الْاَرْضِ مِمَّا يَأْكُلُ النَّاسُ وَ
الْاَنْعَامُ حَتّٰۤى اِذَاۤ اَخَذَتِ الْاَرْضُ زُخْرُفَهَا وَ
ازَّيَّنَتْ وَظَنَّ اَهْلُهَاۤ اَنَّهُمْ قٰدِرُونَ عَلَيْهَاۤ اَتٰىهَاۤ
اَمْرُنَا لَيْلًا اَوْ نَهَارًا فَجَعَلْنٰهَا حَصِيدًا كَاَنْ لَّمْ تَغْنَ
بِالْاَمْسِ كَذٰلِكَ نُفَصِّلُ الْاٰيٰتِ لِقَوْمٍ يَتَفَكَّرُونَ ۝

وَاللهُ يَدْعُوۤا اِلٰى دَارِ السَّلٰمِ وَيَهْدِى مَنْ يَّشَآءُ
اِلٰى صِرَاطٍ مُّسْتَقِيمٍ ۝

Allah calls to the abode of peace, and
guides whom He pleases to the straight
path. For those who do good, will be a
good recompense and more besides. Neither
gloom nor ignominy shall spread over their
faces. It is these who are the inmates of
heaven; therein shall they abide. For
those who do evil, the penalty shall be in
proportion thereto, and ignominy shall
cover them. There will be none to shield
them from Allah's chastisement. They
shall appear as if their faces had been
covered with dark patches of night. It is
these who are the inmates of the Fire;
therein shall they abide. (26—28)

لِلَّذِينَ اَحْسَنُوا الْحُسْنٰى وَزِيَادَةٌ وَلَا يَرْهَقُ وُجُوهَهُمْ
قَتَرٌ وَّلَا ذِلَّةٌ اُولٰۤئِكَ اَصْحَابُ الْجَنَّةِ هُمْ فِيهَا
خٰلِدُونَ ۝

وَالَّذِينَ كَسَبُوا السَّيِّاٰتِ جَزَآءُ سَيِّئَةٍ بِمِثْلِهَا وَ
تَرْهَقُهُمْ ذِلَّةٌ مَا لَهُمْ مِّنَ اللهِ مِنْ عَاصِمٍ كَاَنَّمَاۤ
اُغْشِيَتْ وُجُوهُهُمْ قِطَعًا مِّنَ الَّيْلِ مُظْلِمًا اُولٰۤئِكَ
اَصْحَابُ النَّارِ هُمْ فِيهَا خٰلِدُونَ ۝

Keep in mind the day when We shall gather them all together and We shall order those who ascribed partners to Allah: Stand back in your places, you and your alleged partners. Then We shall set them apart, one from another, and those they alleged were partners with Allah will say: It was not us that you worshipped. Allah is sufficient as a witness between you and us. We were entirely unaware of your worship. Every one will then realise the worth of his conduct in this life. They shall be brought back to Allah, their true Master, and all that they used to fabricate will be lost to them. (29—31)

Ask them: Who provides sustenance for you from the heaven and the earth? Or, Who is it that controls the ears and the eyes? Who brings forth the living from the dead and brings forth the dead from the living? Who regulates the universe? They will say: It is Allah. Ask them: Will you not then seek His protection? That is Allah, your true Lord. So what is there after discarding the truth but error? How then are you being turned away in all directions! Thus is the judgment of thy Lord proved true concerning those who are disobedient, that they do not believe. (32—34)

Ask them: Is there any of your associate-gods who originates creation and then repeats it? Tell them: It is Allah alone Who originates creation and then repeats it. Then whither are you turned away? Ask them: Is there any of your associate-gods who guides to the truth? Tell them: It is Allah alone Who guides to the truth. Then, is He Who guides to the truth more worthy to be followed or he who finds not the way himself unless he be guided? What does, then, ail you? How ill do you judge! (35—36)

195

Most of them follow nothing but conjecture; and surely, conjecture avails nothing in place of truth. Allah is well aware of what they do. (37)

It would not be possible for this Quran to be devised by any except Allah. It fulfils the revelation which was sent down before it and is an exposition of all that a revealed Book should comprise. There is no doubt about it; it is from the Lord of the worlds. Do they say: He has fabricated it? Say to them: In that case, bring a chapter like unto it, and call for help on all you can besides Allah, if you are truthful. The truth is that they have rejected that the knowledge of which they did not encompass, and the full significance of which they did not realise. In like manner did those before them reject the truth. Observe, then, what was the end of the wrongdoers. Some of them will believe therein, and others of them will not believe therein. Thy Lord knows well those who act corruptly. (38—41)

Should they reject thy message as false, tell them: I will bear the consequences of my actions and you shall bear the consequences of your actions; you will not be held responsible for that which I do and I shall not be held responsible for that which you do. Some of them appear to be listening to thee; but canst thou make the deaf hear, even though they lack understanding? Some of them look fixedly at thee; but canst thou make the blind see, even though they lack insight? Surely, Allah wrongs not people at all, but people wrong themselves. On the day when He will gather them together, they will feel as if they had not tarried in the world longer than an hour out of a day. They will then become aware of the true position of one another.

وَمَا يَتَّبِعُ أَكْثَرُهُمْ إِلَّا ظَنًّا ۚ إِنَّ الظَّنَّ لَا يُغْنِى مِنَ الْحَقِّ شَيْئًا ۚ إِنَّ اللّٰهَ عَلِيمٌ بِمَا يَفْعَلُوْنَ ۞

وَمَا كَانَ هٰذَا الْقُرْاٰنُ أَنْ يُّفْتَرٰى مِنْ دُوْنِ اللّٰهِ وَلٰكِنْ تَصْدِيْقَ الَّذِىْ بَيْنَ يَدَيْهِ وَتَفْصِيْلَ الْكِتٰبِ لَا رَيْبَ فِيْهِ مِنْ رَّبِّ الْعٰلَمِيْنَ ۞

أَمْ يَقُوْلُوْنَ افْتَرَاهُ ۚ قُلْ فَأْتُوْا بِسُوْرَةٍ مِّثْلِهٖ وَادْعُوْا مَنِ اسْتَطَعْتُمْ مِّنْ دُوْنِ اللّٰهِ إِنْ كُنْتُمْ صٰدِقِيْنَ ۞ بَلْ كَذَّبُوْا بِمَا لَمْ يُحِيْطُوْا بِعِلْمِهٖ وَلَمَّا يَأْتِهِمْ تَأْوِيْلُهُ ۚ كَذٰلِكَ كَذَّبَ الَّذِيْنَ مِنْ قَبْلِهِمْ فَانْظُرْ كَيْفَ كَانَ عَاقِبَةُ الظّٰلِمِيْنَ ۞

وَمِنْهُمْ مَّنْ يُّؤْمِنُ بِهٖ وَمِنْهُمْ مَّنْ لَّا يُؤْمِنُ بِهٖ ۚ وَرَبُّكَ أَعْلَمُ بِالْمُفْسِدِيْنَ ۞

وَإِنْ كَذَّبُوْكَ فَقُلْ لِّيْ عَمَلِيْ وَلَكُمْ عَمَلُكُمْ ۚ أَنْتُمْ بَرِيْئُوْنَ مِمَّا أَعْمَلُ وَأَنَا بَرِيْءٌ مِّمَّا تَعْمَلُوْنَ ۞

وَمِنْهُمْ مَّنْ يَّسْتَمِعُوْنَ إِلَيْكَ ۚ أَفَأَنْتَ تُسْمِعُ الصُّمَّ وَلَوْ كَانُوْا لَا يَعْقِلُوْنَ ۞

وَمِنْهُمْ مَّنْ يَّنْظُرُ إِلَيْكَ ۚ أَفَأَنْتَ تَهْدِى الْعُمْىَ وَلَوْ كَانُوْا لَا يُبْصِرُوْنَ ۞

إِنَّ اللّٰهَ لَا يَظْلِمُ النَّاسَ شَيْئًا وَّلٰكِنَّ النَّاسَ أَنْفُسَهُمْ يَظْلِمُوْنَ ۞

وَيَوْمَ يَحْشُرُهُمْ كَأَنْ لَّمْ يَلْبَثُوْا إِلَّا سَاعَةً مِّنَ النَّهَارِ يَتَعَارَفُوْنَ بَيْنَهُمْ ۚ قَدْ خَسِرَ الَّذِيْنَ كَذَّبُوْا

Losers indeed will be those who denied the possibility of the meeting with Allah and would not be guided. The chastisement We have promised them shall overtake them, in thy lifetime or after thy death; and to Us is their return. Allah is Witness to all that they do. (42—47)

For every people there is a Messenger; when their Messenger comes, the issue between them is justly determined and they are not wronged. They enquire: When will this promise be fulfilled, if you are truthful? Tell them: I have no power over any harm or benefit for myself, save as Allah wills. For every guilty people, however, there is an appointed term, by which their iniquity draws upon them Allah's chastisement. When the end of their term arrives, they cannot linger behind a single moment, nor can they outstrip it. Tell me then, if His punishment comes upon you unperceived by night, or visibly by day, how will the guilty escape it? Will you believe in it only after it has befallen you, when you may be met by the retort: What! Do you believe now, and hitherto you had demanded its speedy coming? Then will it be said to those who did wrong: Suffer now the abiding torment; you are not requited save for that which you did. They enquire of thee: Will this really happen? Tell them: Yea, by my Lord. Most certainly it will happen, and you cannot frustrate Allah's purpose. (48—54)

If every wrongdoer possessed all that is in the earth he would seek to ransom himself therewith. When they perceive the torment they will try to cover up their remorse. The issue will be determined with justice and they shall not be wronged. Hearken, to Allah belongs whatever is in the heavens and in the earth; hearken, Allah's promise shall be fulfilled, but most of them know not. He it is Who gives life and causes death, and to Him shall you be brought back. (55—57)

بِلِقَآءِ اللهِ وَمَا كَانُوْا مُهْتَدِيْنَ ۞

وَاِمَّا نُرِيَنَّكَ بَعْضَ الَّذِى نَعِدُهُمْ اَوْ نَتَوَفَّيَنَّكَ فَاِلَيْنَا مَرْجِعُهُمْ ثُمَّ اللهُ شَهِيْدٌ عَلٰى مَا يَفْعَلُوْنَ ۞

وَلِكُلِّ اُمَّةٍ رَّسُوْلٌ ۚ فَاِذَا جَآءَ رَسُوْلُهُمْ قُضِىَ بَيْنَهُمْ بِالْقِسْطِ وَهُمْ لَا يُظْلَمُوْنَ ۞

وَيَقُوْلُوْنَ مَتٰى هٰذَا الْوَعْدُ اِنْ كُنْتُمْ صٰدِقِيْنَ ۞

قُلْ لَّاۤ اَمْلِكُ لِنَفْسِىْ ضَرًّا وَّلَا نَفْعًا اِلَّا مَا شَآءَ اللهُ ۗ لِكُلِّ اُمَّةٍ اَجَلٌ ۚ اِذَا جَآءَ اَجَلُهُمْ فَلَا يَسْتَأْخِرُوْنَ سَاعَةً وَّلَا يَسْتَقْدِمُوْنَ ۞

قُلْ اَرَءَيْتُمْ اِنْ اَتٰىكُمْ عَذَابُهُ بَيَاتًا اَوْ نَهَارًا مَّاذَا يَسْتَعْجِلُ مِنْهُ الْمُجْرِمُوْنَ ۞

اَثُمَّ اِذَا مَا وَقَعَ اٰمَنْتُمْ بِهٖ ۚ آلْـٰٔنَ وَقَدْ كُنْتُمْ بِهٖ تَسْتَعْجِلُوْنَ ۞

ثُمَّ قِيْلَ لِلَّذِيْنَ ظَلَمُوْا ذُوْقُوْا عَذَابَ الْخُلْدِ ۚ هَلْ تُجْزَوْنَ اِلَّا بِمَا كُنْتُمْ تَكْسِبُوْنَ ۞

وَيَسْتَنْبِئُوْنَكَ اَحَقٌّ هُوَ ؕ قُلْ اِىْ وَرَبِّىْۤ اِنَّهٗ لَحَقٌّ ؕۚ وَمَاۤ اَنْتُمْ بِمُعْجِزِيْنَ ۞

وَلَوْ اَنَّ لِكُلِّ نَفْسٍ ظَلَمَتْ مَا فِى الْاَرْضِ لَافْتَدَتْ بِهٖ ؕ وَاَسَرُّوا النَّدَامَةَ لَمَّا رَاَوُا الْعَذَابَ ۚ وَقُضِىَ بَيْنَهُمْ بِالْقِسْطِ وَهُمْ لَا يُظْلَمُوْنَ ۞

اَلَاۤ اِنَّ لِلّٰهِ مَا فِى السَّمٰوٰتِ وَالْاَرْضِ ؕ اَلَاۤ اِنَّ وَعْدَ اللهِ حَقٌّ وَّلٰكِنَّ اَكْثَرَهُمْ لَا يَعْلَمُوْنَ ۞

O mankind, there has indeed come to
you a Book from your Lord which is full
of admonition and a healing for all the
ills of the spirit, and a guidance and a
mercy for the believers. Tell them: All this
is through the grace of Allah and His
mercy. Therein, therefore, let them rejoice. That is better than that which they
hoard. Ask them: Does it not strike you
that Allah has sent down for you provision
of every description, then some of it you
have declared unlawful and some of it
lawful? Has Allah prescribed this for you,
or do you fabricate lies against Allah?
What is the concept of those who fabricate
lies against Allah, concerning the Day of
Judgment? Surely, Allah is most gracious
towards mankind, but most of them are
not grateful. (58—61)

Whatever thou mayest be engaged on,
whether reciting a portion of the Book
from the Quran, or whatever else all of you
may be occupied with, We are witness of
whatever you may be engrossed in. Not
the smallest particle in the earth or
heaven is hidden from thy Lord; and there
is nothing smaller or bigger but is recorded
in a clear Book. (62)

Hearken, the friends of Allah, that is
those who believe and are ever mindful
of their duty to Allah, shall certainly have
no fear nor shall they grieve; for them are
glad tidings in the hither life and also in
the Hereafter; that indeed is the supreme
triumph; there is no changing the words
of Allah. Let not the hostile utterances of
thy opponents distress thee. Surely, all
power belongs to Allah; He is the All-
Hearing, the All-Knowing. (63—66)

Hearken, whoever is in the heavens and whoever is in the earth all belong to Allah. Those who call on others than Allah do not follow any associates of Allah, they only follow conjecture and they do nothing but guess. He it is Who has made the night dark that you may rest therein, and has made the day bright to enable you to go about your business. Surely, in this alternation there are Signs for people who listen to the truth and seek to derive benefit therefrom. (67—68)

They say: Allah has taken unto Himself a son. Holy is He. He is Self-Sufficient. To Him belongs whatsoever is in the heavens and whatsoever is in the earth. You have no authority in support of that which you allege. Do you, then, say that concerning Allah of which you have no knowledge? Tell them: Those who fabricate lies concerning Allah shall not prosper. Their portion is short-lived enjoyment in this world; then to Us is their return. We shall afflict them with severe torment because they continued to disbelieve. (69—71)

Recite unto them the account of Noah, when he said to his people: O people, if the position which Allah has assigned to me and my constantly reminding you of your duty through Allah's Signs have become insupportable for you, then remember that my whole trust is in Allah. Determine your plan on your side, along with your associate-gods, and leave no part of it obscure; then put it into effect against me and grant me no respite. If you turn away, you will do me no harm, for I have not asked of you any reward. My reward is with Allah alone and I have been commanded to submit completely to Him. But they rejected him. So We delivered him and those who were with him in the Ark, and made them successors of those who had passed away, and We drowned those who had rejected Our Signs. Observe then how ended those who had been warned of Our chastisement. (72—74)

Then We followed him up with other Messengers whom We sent to their respective peoples, and they brought them clear proofs. But they would not believe in the truth, because they had disbelieved in it before. Thus do We seal up the hearts of the transgressors. (75)

ثُمَّ بَعَثْنَا مِنْ بَعْدِهٖ رُسُلًا اِلٰى قَوْمِهِمْ فَجَآءُوْهُمْ بِالْبَيِّنٰتِ فَمَا كَانُوْا لِيُؤْمِنُوْا بِمَا كَذَّبُوْا بِهٖ مِنْ قَبْلُ ؕ كَذٰلِكَ نَطْبَعُ عَلٰى قُلُوْبِ الْمُعْتَدِيْنَ ۝

ثُمَّ بَعَثْنَا مِنْ بَعْدِهِمْ مُّوْسٰى وَهٰرُوْنَ اِلٰى فِرْعَوْنَ وَمَلَائِهٖ بِاٰيٰتِنَا فَاسْتَكْبَرُوْا وَكَانُوْا قَوْمًا مُّجْرِمِيْنَ ۝

Then did We send thereafter Moses and Aaron to Pharaoh and his nobles with Our Signs, but they behaved arrogantly, and they were a sinful people. When the truth came to them from Us, they said: This is manifest sorcery. Moses expostulated: Do you say this of the truth when it has come to you? Can this be sorcery? Sorcerers can never triumph. They countered: Hast thou come to us to turn us away from that which we found our fathers following, and that the two of you may be glorified in the land? We will never believe in you. Pharaoh commanded: Summon to my presence every expert magician. When the magicians assembled, Moses said to them: Make your cast. When they had made their cast, Moses said: That which you have cast is sheer sorcery. Allah will stultify it. Surely, Allah does not permit the design of the corrupt to prosper. Allah establishes the truth by His words, however much the sinners may be averse to it. (76—83)

فَلَمَّا جَآءَهُمُ الْحَقُّ مِنْ عِنْدِنَا قَالُوْا اِنَّ هٰذَا لَسِحْرٌ مُّبِيْنٌ ۝

قَالَ مُوْسٰى اَتَقُوْلُوْنَ لِلْحَقِّ لَمَّا جَآءَكُمْ ؕ اَسِحْرٌ هٰذَا ؕ وَلَا يُفْلِحُ السّٰحِرُوْنَ ۝

قَالُوْا اَجِئْتَنَا لِتَلْفِتَنَا عَمَّا وَجَدْنَا عَلَيْهِ اٰبَآءَنَا وَتَكُوْنَ لَكُمَا الْكِبْرِيَآءُ فِى الْاَرْضِ ؕ وَمَا نَحْنُ لَكُمَا بِمُؤْمِنِيْنَ ۝

وَقَالَ فِرْعَوْنُ ائْتُوْنِيْ بِكُلِّ سٰحِرٍ عَلِيْمٍ ۝

فَلَمَّا جَآءَ السَّحَرَةُ قَالَ لَهُمْ مُّوْسٰى اَلْقُوْا مَآ اَنْتُمْ مُّلْقُوْنَ ۝

فَلَمَّآ اَلْقَوْا قَالَ مُوْسٰى مَا جِئْتُمْ بِهِ ۙ السِّحْرُ ؕ اِنَّ اللّٰهَ سَيُبْطِلُهٗ ؕ اِنَّ اللّٰهَ لَا يُصْلِحُ عَمَلَ الْمُفْسِدِيْنَ ۝

وَيُحِقُّ اللّٰهُ الْحَقَّ بِكَلِمٰتِهٖ وَلَوْ كَرِهَ الْمُجْرِمُوْنَ ۝

Only a few youths from his people declared their faith in Moses. The rest held back, along with their leading men, lest Pharaoh should persecute them. Of a truth, Pharaoh was a tyrant in the land and was a transgressor. Moses said to his people: If you have believed in Allah, then in Him put your trust if you are obedient to Him. (84—85)

فَمَآ اٰمَنَ لِمُوْسٰى اِلَّا ذُرِّيَّةٌ مِّنْ قَوْمِهٖ عَلٰى خَوْفٍ مِّنْ فِرْعَوْنَ وَمَلَائِهِمْ اَنْ يَّفْتِنَهُمْ ؕ وَاِنَّ فِرْعَوْنَ لَعَالٍ فِى الْاَرْضِ ۚ وَاِنَّهٗ لَمِنَ الْمُسْرِفِيْنَ ۝

وَقَالَ مُوْسٰى يٰقَوْمِ اِنْ كُنْتُمْ اٰمَنْتُمْ بِاللّٰهِ فَعَلَيْهِ

They said: In Allah do we put our trust.
Our Lord, make us not the subject of persecution at the hands of the oppressors
and deliver us by Thy mercy from the
disbelieving people. (86—87)

تَوَكَّلْنَا ٓ اِنْ كُنْتُمْ مُّسْلِمِيْنَ ۞

فَقَالُوْا عَلَى اللّٰهِ تَوَكَّلْنَا ۚ رَبَّنَا لَا تَجْعَلْنَا فِتْنَةً لِّلْقَوْمِ الظّٰلِمِيْنَ ۞

وَ نَجِّنَا بِرَحْمَتِكَ مِنَ الْقَوْمِ الْكٰفِرِيْنَ ۞

We directed Moses and his brother:
Prepare some dwellings for your people
in the town, and build your houses facing
one another, and observe Prayer and give
glad tidings to the believers. Moses prayed:
Our Lord, Thou hast bestowed upon
Pharaoh and his nobles pomp and wealth
in the present life, whereby they lead
people astray from Thy path. Our Lord,
destroy their riches and afflict their hearts,
so that they shall not believe until they
are faced with grievous chastisement.
Allah responded: Your prayer is granted.
So be ye twain steadfast, and follow not
the way of those who know not. (88—90)

وَ اَوْحَيْنَاۤ اِلٰى مُوْسٰى وَ اَخِيْهِ اَنْ تَبَوَّاٰ لِقَوْمِكُمَا بِمِصْرَ بُيُوْتًا وَّ اجْعَلُوْا بُيُوْتَكُمْ قِبْلَةً وَّ اَقِيْمُوا الصَّلٰوةَ ۚ وَ بَشِّرِ الْمُؤْمِنِيْنَ ۞

وَ قَالَ مُوْسٰى رَبَّنَاۤ اِنَّكَ اٰتَيْتَ فِرْعَوْنَ وَ مَلَاَهٗ زِيْنَةً وَّ اَمْوَالًا فِى الْحَيٰوةِ الدُّنْيَا ۙ رَبَّنَا لِيُضِلُّوْا عَنْ سَبِيْلِكَ ۚ رَبَّنَا اطْمِسْ عَلٰۤى اَمْوَالِهِمْ وَ اشْدُدْ عَلٰى قُلُوْبِهِمْ فَلَا يُؤْمِنُوْا حَتّٰى يَرَوُا الْعَذَابَ الْاَلِيْمَ ۞

قَالَ قَدْ اُجِيْبَتْ دَّعْوَتُكُمَا فَاسْتَقِيْمَا وَلَا تَتَّبِعٰٓنِّ سَبِيْلَ الَّذِيْنَ لَا يَعْلَمُوْنَ ۞

We brought the children of Israel across
the sea; and Pharaoh and his hosts pursued them wrongfully and aggressively.
When Pharaoh perceived he was drowning he faltered: I believe that there is no
god but He in Whom the children of
Israel believe, and I submit to Him. We
passed judgment on him: Believest thou
now, and hitherto wast thou disobedient
and wast of the corrupt! We will grant
thee a measure of deliverance by preserving thy body this day that thou mayest
serve as a Sign for those who come after
thee. Surely, many people are heedless of
Our Signs. We assigned to the children of
Israel a blessed abode, and We provided
them with all manner of good things.
They differed not in anything till true
knowledge came to them. Surely, thy
Lord will judge between them on the Day
of Judgment concerning that in which
they differed. (91—94)

وَ جٰوَزْنَا بِبَنِيْۤ اِسْرَآءِيْلَ الْبَحْرَ فَاَتْبَعَهُمْ فِرْعَوْنُ وَ جُنُوْدُهٗ بَغْيًا وَّ عَدْوًا ۚ حَتّٰۤى اِذَاۤ اَدْرَكَهُ الْغَرَقُ ۙ قَالَ اٰمَنْتُ اَنَّهٗ لَاۤ اِلٰهَ اِلَّا الَّذِيْۤ اٰمَنَتْ بِهٖ بَنُوْۤا اِسْرَآءِيْلَ وَ اَنَا مِنَ الْمُسْلِمِيْنَ ۞

آٰلْـٰٔنَ وَ قَدْ عَصَيْتَ قَبْلُ وَ كُنْتَ مِنَ الْمُفْسِدِيْنَ ۞

فَالْيَوْمَ نُنَجِّيْكَ بِبَدَنِكَ لِتَكُوْنَ لِمَنْ خَلْفَكَ اٰيَةً ۚ وَ اِنَّ كَثِيْرًا مِّنَ النَّاسِ عَنْ اٰيٰتِنَا لَغٰفِلُوْنَ ۞

وَلَقَدْ بَوَّاْنَا بَنِيْۤ اِسْرَآءِيْلَ مُبَوَّاَ صِدْقٍ وَّ رَزَقْنٰهُمْ مِّنَ الطَّيِّبٰتِ ۚ فَمَا اخْتَلَفُوْا حَتّٰى جَآءَهُمُ الْعِلْمُ ۗ اِنَّ

201

If thou art in doubt concerning that which We have sent down to thee, then ask those who have been reading the Book before thee. Thou wilt know then that the truth has indeed come to thee from thy Lord; be not, therefore, of those who doubt, and be not of those who reject the Signs of Allah, for then thou shalt be of the losers. Surely, those against whom the decree of thy Lord has issued will not believe, even if there came to them every Sign, till they are faced with the grievous torment. Why was not there a people, save the people of Jonah, who should have all believed so that their having believed would have profited them. When the people of Jonah believed We granted them reprieve from humiliating punishment in this life, and We granted them every provision for a while. If thy Lord had enforced His will, surely all those on the earth would have believed, without exception. Will thou, then, take it upon thyself to force people to become believers? Except by Allah's leave no one can believe; and He will afflict with His wrath those who will not use their understanding. (95—101)

Say to them: Observe what is happening in the heavens and the earth. But Signs, whether reassuring or warning, avail not a people who will not believe. Do they, then, await a repetition of the treatment that was accorded to those who have passed away before them? Say to them: If so, then wait on, I too am waiting along with you. When such time comes We always deliver Our Messengers and those who believe; thus We have made it incumbent upon Ourselves to save the believers. (102—104)

Proclaim: O ye people, if you are in doubt concerning my religion, then let me make it clear to you, that I worship not those whom you worship beside Allah. I worship Allah alone Who causes you to die, and I have been commanded to be of the believers, and to instruct each one of you: Devote thyself singlemindedly to religion and be not of those who ascribe partners to Allah. Call not beside Allah on anything that can neither profit thee nor harm thee, for if thou dost so thou wouldst certainly be of the wrongdoers. If Allah afflict thee with distress, there is none who can relieve thee of it but He; and if He desire good for thee, there is none who can repel His grace. He bestows it upon whomsoever of His servants He wills. He is the Most Forgiving, Ever Merciful. (105—108)

قُلْ يَا أَيُّهَا النَّاسُ إِنْ كُنْتُمْ فِى شَكٍّ مِّنْ دِينِى فَلَا أَعْبُدُ الَّذِينَ تَعْبُدُونَ مِنْ دُونِ اللهِ وَ لَكِنْ أَعْبُدُ اللهَ الَّذِى يَتَوَفَّاكُمْ وَ أُمِرْتُ أَنْ أَكُوْنَ مِنَ الْمُؤْمِنِينَ ۝

وَأَنْ أَقِمْ وَجْهَكَ لِلدِّينِ حَنِيفًا وَلَا تَكُوْنَنَّ مِنَ الْمُشْرِكِينَ ۝

وَ لَا تَدْعُ مِنْ دُونِ اللهِ مَا لَا يَنْفَعُكَ وَلَا يَضُرُّكَ فَإِنْ فَعَلْتَ فَإِنَّكَ إِذًا مِّنَ الظَّالِمِينَ ۝

وَإِنْ يَمْسَسْكَ اللهُ بِضُرٍّ فَلَا كَاشِفَ لَهُ إِلَّا هُوَ وَ إِنْ يُرِدْكَ بِخَيْرٍ فَلَا رَادَّ لِفَضْلِهِ يُصِيبُ بِهِ مَنْ يَّشَاءُ مِنْ عِبَادِهِ وَهُوَ الْغَفُورُ الرَّحِيمُ ۝

Say: O ye people, the truth has indeed come to you from your Lord. Then whoso follows the guidance, follows it only for the good of his own self, and who-so errs does so only to his own detriment. I am not appointed a keeper over you. Continue to follow that which is revealed to thee, O Prophet, and be steadfast until Allah gives His judgment. He is the Best of judges. (109—110)

قُلْ يَا أَيُّهَا النَّاسُ قَدْ جَاءَكُمُ الْحَقُّ مِنْ رَبِّكُمْ فَمَنِ اهْتَدَى فَإِنَّمَا يَهْتَدِى لِنَفْسِهِ وَمَنْ ضَلَّ فَإِنَّمَا يَضِلُّ عَلَيْهَا وَمَا أَنَا عَلَيْكُمْ بِوَكِيلٍ ۝

وَ اتَّبِعْ مَا يُوحَى إِلَيْكَ وَ اصْبِرْ حَتَّى يَحْكُمَ اللهُ وَهُوَ خَيْرُ الْحَاكِمِينَ ۝

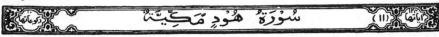

HŪD

(Revealed before Hijra)

In the name of Allah, Most Gracious, Ever Merciful. (1)

I AM ALLAH, THE ALL-SEEING.

This is a Book whose verses have been firmly established and have been expounded in detail It is revealed by One Wise, All-Aware, that you worship none save Allah, seek forgiveness of your Lord and turn to Him in repentance. He will make for you a goodly provision till an appointed term and will grant His grace to every one possessed of merit. But if you turn away, then surely, I would be fearful for you of the chastisement of a dreadful day, for I have been sent to you by Allah as a Warner and a bearer of glad tidings. To Allah is your return; and He has power over all things. (2—5)

Hearken, they fold up their breasts that they may hide their thoughts from Him. Surely, even when they cover themselves up with their garments, He knows what they conceal and what they disclose. Of a surety, He is well aware of that which is in their minds. There is no creature that moves in the earth but it is for Allah to provide it with sustenance and He knows its temporary lodging and its permanent home. All this is recorded in a clear Book. (6—7)

He it is Who created the heavens and the earth in six periods; He originated life from water and exercises His authority through revelation, that He might prove you, to show which of you is best in conduct. If thou were to tell them: You shall surely be raised up after death; those who disbelieve will certainly say: This is manifest deception. (8)

204

If We hold back their punishment for a determined period, they are sure to say: What holds it back? Take note, on the day that it shall come upon them, it shall not be averted from them and that which they used to mock at shall encompass them. (9)

When We bestow upon a person a measure of Our grace, and then take it away from him, verily he is despairing, ungrateful; but if We bestow upon him a bounty after he has experienced some distress, he is sure to say: Gone are all my ills; and he is suddenly exultant, boastful; except those who are steadfast and work righteousness. It is these for whom there is forgiveness and a great reward. (10—12)

Perchance the disbelievers imagine that thou might be prevailed upon to give up a portion of that which has been revealed to thee: or that thou art distressed because they say: Wherefore has not a treasure been sent down to him or an angel come with him? Thou art but a Warner, and Allah is Guardian over all things. Do they say: He has forged it himself? Tell them: In that case, if you are truthful, produce ten chapters like unto it, forged as you allege, and call on whom you can beside Allah, to help you. If they should not respond to you, then know that it has been sent down full of Divine knowledge, and that there is no god but He. Will you then make complete submission? (13—15)

We will fully repay for their works in this life those who desire the provision and pomp of this life and they shall suffer no diminution in respect thereof. Those are they who shall have nothing in the Hereafter save the Fire; that which they do here will be of no avail to them and vain shall be their striving. (16—17)

مُّبِيْنٌ ۞

وَلَئِنْ اَخَّرْنَا عَنْهُمُ الْعَذَابَ اِلٰٓى اُمَّةٍ مَّعْدُوْدَةٍ لَّيَقُوْلُنَّ مَا يَحْبِسُهٗ اَلَا يَوْمَ يَأْتِيْهِمْ لَيْسَ مَصْرُوْفًا عَنْهُمْ وَحَاقَ بِهِمْ مَّا كَانُوْا بِهٖ يَسْتَهْزِءُوْنَ ۞

وَلَئِنْ اَذَقْنَا الْاِنْسَانَ مِنَّا رَحْمَةً ثُمَّ نَزَعْنٰهَا مِنْهُ اِنَّهٗ لَيَئُوْسٌ كَفُوْرٌ ۞

وَلَئِنْ اَذَقْنٰهُ نَعْمَآءَ بَعْدَ ضَرَّآءَ مَسَّتْهُ لَيَقُوْلَنَّ ذَهَبَ السَّيِّاٰتُ عَنِّىْ اِنَّهٗ لَفَرِحٌ فَخُوْرٌ ۞

اِلَّا الَّذِيْنَ صَبَرُوْا وَعَمِلُوا الصّٰلِحٰتِ اُولٰٓئِكَ لَهُمْ مَّغْفِرَةٌ وَّاَجْرٌ كَبِيْرٌ ۞

فَلَعَلَّكَ تَارِكٌ بَعْضَ مَا يُوْحٰٓى اِلَيْكَ وَضَآئِقٌ بِهٖ صَدْرُكَ اَنْ يَّقُوْلُوْا لَوْلَاۤ اُنْزِلَ عَلَيْهِ كَنْزٌ اَوْ جَآءَ مَعَهٗ مَلَكٌ اِنَّمَآ اَنْتَ نَذِيْرٌ وَاللّٰهُ عَلٰى كُلِّ شَيْءٍ وَّكِيْلٌ ۞

اَمْ يَقُوْلُوْنَ افْتَرٰىهُ قُلْ فَأْتُوْا بِعَشْرِ سُوَرٍ مِّثْلِهٖ مُفْتَرَيٰتٍ وَّادْعُوْا مَنِ اسْتَطَعْتُمْ مِّنْ دُوْنِ اللّٰهِ اِنْ كُنْتُمْ صٰدِقِيْنَ ۞

فَاِلَّمْ يَسْتَجِيْبُوْا لَكُمْ فَاعْلَمُوْۤا اَنَّمَاۤ اُنْزِلَ بِعِلْمِ اللّٰهِ وَاَنْ لَّاۤ اِلٰهَ اِلَّا هُوَ فَهَلْ اَنْتُمْ مُّسْلِمُوْنَ ۞

مَنْ كَانَ يُرِيْدُ الْحَيٰوةَ الدُّنْيَا وَزِيْنَتَهَا نُوَفِّ اِلَيْهِمْ اَعْمَالَهُمْ فِيْهَا وَهُمْ فِيْهَا لَا يُبْخَسُوْنَ ۞

اُولٰٓئِكَ الَّذِيْنَ لَيْسَ لَهُمْ فِى الْاٰخِرَةِ اِلَّا النَّارُ

Can there be any doubt concerning him who bases himself on clear proof from his Lord, and will be followed by a witness from Him, and is preceded by the Book of Moses which was a guide and a mercy for people before him? The true followers of Moses will believe in him; but whoever disbelieves in him out of the opposing parties, the Fire shall be his promised resort. So be not thou, O reader, in doubt about it. Surely, it is the truth from thy Lord; but most people do not believe. (18)

وَحِبِطَ مَا صَنَعُوا فِيهَا وَبَطِلَّ مَّا كَانُوا يَعْمَلُونَ ۞

اَفَمَنْ كَانَ عَلٰى بَيِّنَةٍ مِّنْ رَّبِّهٖ وَيَتْلُوهُ شَاهِدٌ مِّنْهُ وَمِنْ قَبْلِهٖ كِتٰبُ مُوسٰى اِمَامًا وَّرَحْمَةً اُولٰٓئِكَ يُؤْمِنُوْنَ بِهٖ وَمَنْ يَّكْفُرْ بِهٖ مِنَ الْاَحْزَابِ فَالنَّارُ مَوْعِدُهٗ فَلَا تَكُ فِيْ مِرْيَةٍ مِّنْهُ اِنَّهُ الْحَقُّ مِنْ رَّبِّكَ وَلٰكِنَّ اَكْثَرَ النَّاسِ لَا يُؤْمِنُوْنَ ۞

Who can be accounted more unjust than one who fabricates a lie against Allah? Such shall be presented before their Lord, and the witnesses shall testify: These are they who lied against their Lord. Take note, the curse of Allah is upon such wrong-doers, who turn people away from the path of Allah and seek to make it appear crooked. These it is who disbelieved in the Hereafter. They can never frustrate Allah's design in the land, nor have they any friends beside Allah. They will be subjected to double punishment, in this life and in the Hereafter. They are unable to hear, nor can they see. It is these who have ruined their souls, and that which they fabricated shall fail them. For sure, it is they who shall be the greatest losers in the Hereafter. (19—23)

وَمَنْ اَظْلَمُ مِمَّنِ افْتَرٰى عَلَى اللّٰهِ كَذِبًا اُولٰٓئِكَ يُعْرَضُوْنَ عَلٰى رَبِّهِمْ وَيَقُوْلُ الْاَشْهَادُ هٰٓؤُلَآءِ الَّذِيْنَ كَذَبُوْا عَلٰى رَبِّهِمْ اَلَا لَعْنَةُ اللّٰهِ عَلَى الظّٰلِمِيْنَ ۞

الَّذِيْنَ يَصُدُّوْنَ عَنْ سَبِيْلِ اللّٰهِ وَيَبْغُوْنَهَا عِوَجًا وَهُمْ بِالْاٰخِرَةِ هُمْ كٰفِرُوْنَ ۞

اُولٰٓئِكَ لَمْ يَكُوْنُوْا مُعْجِزِيْنَ فِى الْاَرْضِ وَمَا كَانَ لَهُمْ مِّنْ دُوْنِ اللّٰهِ مِنْ اَوْلِيَآءَ يُضٰعَفُ لَهُمُ الْعَذَابُ مَا كَانُوْا يَسْتَطِيْعُوْنَ السَّمْعَ وَمَا كَانُوْا يُبْصِرُوْنَ ۞

اُولٰٓئِكَ الَّذِيْنَ خَسِرُوْا اَنْفُسَهُمْ وَضَلَّ عَنْهُمْ مَّا كَانُوْا يَفْتَرُوْنَ ۞

لَا جَرَمَ اَنَّهُمْ فِى الْاٰخِرَةِ هُمُ الْاَخْسَرُوْنَ ۞

Those who have believed and work righteousness, and humble themselves before their Lord are the inmates of heaven; therein shall they abide. The case of the two parties is like that of the blind and the seeing, and of the deaf and the hearing. Can the two be equal? Will you not then understand? (24—25)

اِنَّ الَّذِيْنَ اٰمَنُوْا وَعَمِلُوا الصّٰلِحٰتِ وَاَخْبَتُوٓا اِلٰى رَبِّهِمْ اُولٰٓئِكَ اَصْحٰبُ الْجَنَّةِ هُمْ فِيْهَا خٰلِدُوْنَ ۞

مَثَلُ الْفَرِيْقَيْنِ كَالْاَعْمٰى وَالْاَصَمِّ وَالْبَصِيْرِ وَ

We sent Noah to his people, and he announced to them: I have been sent to you as a plain Warner that you worship none but Allah. Indeed I am fearful for you of the chastisement of a grievous day. The leaders of his people who disbelieved rejoined: Thou art but a man like the rest of us, and we do not find that any but the meanest of us in our estimation have followed thee. We do not consider that you are in any way better than we are; in fact we believe you to be liars. (26—28)

السَّمِيعُ هَلْ يَسْتَوِيٰنِ مَثَلًا ۚ اَفَلَا تَذَكَّرُوۡنَ ۞

وَلَقَدۡ اَرۡسَلۡنَا نُوۡحًا اِلٰى قَوۡمِهٖۤ اِنِّىۡ لَكُمۡ نَذِيۡرٌ مُّبِيۡنٌ ۞

اَنۡ لَّا تَعۡبُدُوۡۤا اِلَّا اللّٰهَ ؕ اِنِّىۡۤ اَخَافُ عَلَيۡكُمۡ عَذَابَ يَوۡمٍ اَلِيۡمٍ ۞

فَقَالَ الۡمَلَاُ الَّذِيۡنَ كَفَرُوۡا مِنۡ قَوۡمِهٖ مَا نَرٰىكَ اِلَّا بَشَرًا مِّثۡلَنَا وَمَا نَرٰىكَ اتَّبَعَكَ اِلَّا الَّذِيۡنَ هُمۡ اَرَاذِلُنَا بَادِىَ الرَّاۡىِ ۚ وَمَا نَرٰى لَكُمۡ عَلَيۡنَا مِنۡ فَضۡلٍ بَلۡ نَظُنُّكُمۡ كٰذِبِيۡنَ ۞

قَالَ يٰقَوۡمِ اَرَءَيۡتُمۡ اِنۡ كُنۡتُ عَلٰى بَيِّنَةٍ مِّنۡ رَّبِّىۡ وَاٰتٰىنِىۡ رَحۡمَةً مِّنۡ عِنۡدِهٖ فَعُمِّيَتۡ عَلَيۡكُمۡ ؕ اَنُلۡزِمُكُمُوۡهَا وَاَنۡتُمۡ لَهَا كٰرِهُوۡنَ ۞

Noah reasoned with them. O my people, tell me: If I base myself upon clear proof from my Lord and He has favoured me with mercy from Himself, which you have been unable to recognise, shall we force it upon you, despite your being averse thereto? I do not demand from you any material recompense in return for it; I look for my recompense to Allah alone. I will by no means drive away those who believe; they shall be honoured by meeting their Lord. Your looking down upon them proves that you are an ignorant lot. If I were to drive them away, tell me, who has the power to shield me against the wrath of Allah? Will you not understand? I do not say to you: I possess the treasures of Allah, nor have I knowledge of the unseen; nor do I say: I am an angel. Nor say I concerning those upon whom you look with contempt: Allah will not bestow any good upon them. Allah knows best what is in their minds. If I were to think of them as you do, I would then certainly be of the unjust. (29—32)

وَيٰقَوۡمِ لَاۤ اَسۡـَٔلُكُمۡ عَلَيۡهِ مَالًا ؕ اِنۡ اَجۡرِىَ اِلَّا عَلَى اللّٰهِ وَمَاۤ اَنَا بِطَارِدِ الَّذِيۡنَ اٰمَنُوۡا ؕ اِنَّهُمۡ مُّلٰقُوۡا رَبِّهِمۡ وَلٰكِنِّىۡۤ اَرٰىكُمۡ قَوۡمًا تَجۡهَلُوۡنَ ۞

وَيٰقَوۡمِ مَنۡ يَّنۡصُرُنِىۡ مِنَ اللّٰهِ اِنۡ طَرَدۡتُّهُمۡ ؕ اَفَلَا تَذَكَّرُوۡنَ ۞

وَلَاۤ اَقُوۡلُ لَكُمۡ عِنۡدِىۡ خَزَآئِنُ اللّٰهِ وَلَاۤ اَعۡلَمُ الۡغَيۡبَ وَلَاۤ اَقُوۡلُ اِنِّىۡ مَلَكٌ وَّلَاۤ اَقُوۡلُ لِلَّذِيۡنَ تَزۡدَرِىۡۤ اَعۡيُنُكُمۡ لَنۡ يُّؤۡتِيَهُمُ اللّٰهُ خَيۡرًا ؕ اَللّٰهُ اَعۡلَمُ بِمَا فِىۡۤ اَنۡفُسِهِمۡ ۚ اِنِّىۡۤ اِذًا لَّمِنَ الظّٰلِمِيۡنَ ۞

قَالُوۡا يٰنُوۡحُ قَدۡ جَادَلۡتَنَا فَاَكۡثَرۡتَ جِدَالَنَا فَاۡتِنَا

They retorted: Noah, thou hast argued with us long and often; so now bring upon us that with which thou dost threaten us, if thou art truthful. To which he replied: Allah alone will bring it upon you, if He please, and you cannot frustrate His purpose. Were I minded to counsel you, my counsel would not profit you, if Allah willed to destroy you. He is your Lord and to Him you shall be made to return. (33—35)

Do they say: He has invented all this about our being punished? Tell them: If I have invented it, the punishment for it will fall on me; you will not be called to account for it, as I will not be called to account for that which you commit. (36)

It was revealed to Noah: No more of thy people will believe than those who have already believed; grieve not, therefore, over that which they have been doing. Build thou the Ark under Our eyes and according to Our directions, and do not supplicate Me concerning the wrongdoers; they are sure to perish by drowning. He occupied himself with building the Ark, and every time the leading men of his people passed by him, they mocked at him. Noah observed: You mock at us now and soon we shall mock at you, even as you mock at us; and you shall then know which party is afflicted with humiliating punishment and is afflicted with lasting torment. (37—40)

When Our decree went forth and the fountains gushed forth, We directed Noah: Embark therein two of every kind of animal, male and female, and thy family, except the one concerning whom Our decree has already gone forth, and those who believe. Only a few had believed in him. When the water swelled, he urged his company: Embark therein. Its course and its mooring will be regulated under the blessing of Allah's name. My Lord is assuredly Most Forgiving, Ever Merciful.

بِمَا تَعِدُنَآ اِنْ كُنْتَ مِنَ الصّٰدِقِيْنَ ۞

قَالَ اِنَّمَا يَاْتِيْكُمْ بِهِ اللّٰهُ اِنْ شَآءَ وَ مَآ اَنْتُمْ بِمُعْجِزِيْنَ ۞

وَلَا يَنْفَعُكُمْ نُصْحِيْٓ اِنْ اَرَدْتُّ اَنْ اَنْصَحَ لَكُمْ اِنْ كَانَ اللّٰهُ يُرِيْدُ اَنْ يُّغْوِيَكُمْ هُوَ رَبُّكُمْ وَاِلَيْهِ تُرْجَعُوْنَ ۞

اَمْ يَقُوْلُوْنَ افْتَرٰىهُ قُلْ اِنِ افْتَرَيْتُهُ فَعَلَيَّ اِجْرَامِيْ وَاَنَا بَرِيْٓءٌ مِّمَّا تُجْرِمُوْنَ ۞

وَاُوْحِيَ اِلٰى نُوْحٍ اَنَّهُ لَنْ يُّؤْمِنَ مِنْ قَوْمِكَ اِلَّا مَنْ قَدْ اٰمَنَ فَلَا تَبْتَئِسْ بِمَا كَانُوْا يَفْعَلُوْنَ ۞

وَاصْنَعِ الْفُلْكَ بِاَعْيُنِنَا وَوَحْيِنَا وَلَا تُخَاطِبْنِيْ فِى الَّذِيْنَ ظَلَمُوْا اِنَّهُمْ مُّغْرَقُوْنَ ۞

وَيَصْنَعُ الْفُلْكَ وَكُلَّمَا مَرَّ عَلَيْهِ مَلَاٌ مِّنْ قَوْمِهٖ سَخِرُوْا مِنْهُ قَالَ اِنْ تَسْخَرُوْا مِنَّا فَاِنَّا نَسْخَرُ مِنْكُمْ كَمَا تَسْخَرُوْنَ ۞

فَسَوْفَ تَعْلَمُوْنَ مَنْ يَّاْتِيْهِ عَذَابٌ يُّخْزِيْهِ وَ يَحِلُّ عَلَيْهِ عَذَابٌ مُّقِيْمٌ ۞

حَتّٰٓى اِذَا جَآءَ اَمْرُنَا وَفَارَ التَّنُّوْرُ قُلْنَا احْمِلْ فِيْهَا مِنْ كُلٍّ زَوْجَيْنِ اثْنَيْنِ وَاَهْلَكَ اِلَّا مَنْ سَبَقَ عَلَيْهِ الْقَوْلُ وَمَنْ اٰمَنَ وَمَآ اٰمَنَ مَعَهٗٓ اِلَّا قَلِيْلٌ ۞

وَقَالَ ارْكَبُوْا فِيْهَا بِسْمِ اللّٰهِ مَجْرٰىهَا وَمُرْسٰىهَا اِنَّ رَبِّيْ لَغَفُوْرٌ رَّحِيْمٌ ۞

The Ark sailed along with them through waves towering like mountains. Noah spotted his son drifting away among the swirling waters and called out to him: My son, embark along with us and be not among the disbelievers. He shouted back: I shall soon gain a footing on some height, where I shall be safe from the water. Noah warned him: There is no safety today for anyone from the decree of Allah, except for those to whom He shows mercy. Thereupon a wave rushed in between the two, and he was drowned. Thereafter, the command went forth: Swallow up thy water, O earth, and O sky: Desist. The water subsided and the affair was closed. The Ark came to rest on Judi and the decree went forth: Ruined are the wrongdoers. (41—45)

Noah supplicated his Lord: My Lord, my son is a part of my family, and surely, Thy promise is true, and Thou art the Most Just of Judges. His Lord responded: He is surely not of thy family, Noah, for he is one of unrighteous conduct. So beseech Me not concerning that of which thou hast no knowledge. I advise thee never to act like the ignorant ones. Noah pleaded: My Lord, I pray Thee safeguard me against asking Thee that of which I have no knowledge; unless Thou forgive me and have mercy on me, I shall be among the losers. He was commanded: Continue with thy mission, O Noah, with peace and all manner of blessings upon thee and upon peoples with thee. There will also be people whom We shall grant provision for a time, then shall a grievous chastisement from Us afflict them. (46—49)

These are grave tidings of the unseen that We reveal to thee, O Prophet, which thou didst not know before, nor did thy people. Do thou continue steadfast, for success is the portion of the righteous. (50)

وَهِىَ تَجْرِىْ بِهِمْ فِىْ مَوْجٍ كَالْجِبَالِ ۗ وَنَادٰى نُوْحُ ابْنَهٗ وَكَانَ فِىْ مَعْزِلٍ يّٰبُنَىَّ ارْكَبْ مَّعَنَا وَلَا تَكُنْ مَّعَ الْكٰفِرِيْنَ ۝

قَالَ سَاٰوِىْۤ اِلٰى جَبَلٍ يَّعْصِمُنِىْ مِنَ الْمَاءِ ۗ قَالَ لَا عَاصِمَ الْيَوْمَ مِنْ اَمْرِ اللّٰهِ اِلَّا مَنْ رَّحِمَ ۚ وَحَالَ بَيْنَهُمَا الْمَوْجُ فَكَانَ مِنَ الْمُغْرَقِيْنَ ۝

وَقِيْلَ يٰٓاَرْضُ ابْلَعِىْ مَاءَكِ وَيٰسَمَاءُ اَقْلِعِىْ وَغِيْضَ الْمَاءُ وَقُضِىَ الْاَمْرُ وَاسْتَوَتْ عَلَى الْجُوْدِىِّ وَقِيْلَ بُعْدًا لِّلْقَوْمِ الظّٰلِمِيْنَ ۝

وَنَادٰى نُوْحٌ رَّبَّهٗ فَقَالَ رَبِّ اِنَّ ابْنِىْ مِنْ اَهْلِىْ وَاِنَّ وَعْدَكَ الْحَقُّ وَاَنْتَ اَحْكَمُ الْحٰكِمِيْنَ ۝

قَالَ يٰنُوْحُ اِنَّهٗ لَيْسَ مِنْ اَهْلِكَ ۚ اِنَّهٗ عَمَلٌ غَيْرُ صَالِحٍ ۖ فَلَا تَسْـَٔلْنِ مَا لَيْسَ لَكَ بِهٖ عِلْمٌ ۗ اِنِّىْۤ اَعِظُكَ اَنْ تَكُوْنَ مِنَ الْجٰهِلِيْنَ ۝

قَالَ رَبِّ اِنِّىْۤ اَعُوْذُ بِكَ اَنْ اَسْـَٔلَكَ مَا لَيْسَ لِىْ بِهٖ عِلْمٌ ۗ وَاِلَّا تَغْفِرْ لِىْ وَتَرْحَمْنِىْۤ اَكُنْ مِّنَ الْخٰسِرِيْنَ ۝

قِيْلَ يٰنُوْحُ اهْبِطْ بِسَلٰمٍ مِّنَّا وَبَرَكٰتٍ عَلَيْكَ وَعَلٰىٓ اُمَمٍ مِّمَّنْ مَّعَكَ ۚ وَاُمَمٌ سَنُمَتِّعُهُمْ ثُمَّ يَمَسُّهُمْ مِّنَّا عَذَابٌ اَلِيْمٌ ۝

تِلْكَ مِنْ اَنْۢبَاءِ الْغَيْبِ نُوْحِيْهَآ اِلَيْكَ ۚ مَا كُنْتَ تَعْلَمُهَآ اَنْتَ وَلَا قَوْمُكَ مِنْ قَبْلِ هٰذَا ۖ فَاصْبِرْ ۖ

To 'Ad We sent their brother Hud. He admonished them: O my people, worship Allah alone; you have no god beside Him. In attributing partners to Him, you do nothing but fabricate lies. I demand from you nothing in return for that with which I admonish you. My recompense is with Him Who has created me. Will you not then understand? O my people, ask forgiveness of your Lord and turn wholly to Him; He will send over you clouds pouring down abundant rain, and will add strength to your strength. Turn not away from Him guiltily. They retorted: Thou hast brought us no clear proof of that which thou dost urge upon us Hud, and we shall not forsake our gods merely because of thy urging, nor shall we believe in thee. All we can say is that some god of ours has afflicted thee with evil. He rejoined: I call Allah to witness, and do you also bear witness, that I reject all that which you associate with Allah beside Him. If you consider I am in error, then devise your plans against me all together, and grant me no respite. I have put my whole trust in Allah, my Lord and your Lord. There is no creature that moves on the earth but He holds it completely in His power. Surely, my Lord stands along the straight path to guide and protect the believers. If now you should turn away, I have conveyed to you that with which I have been sent to you, and my Lord will make another people your successors and you can in no wise do Him any harm. Surely, my Lord is Guardian over all things. (51—58)

When Our decree went forth, We delivered Hud and those who believed with him by Our special mercy, and We saved them from a severe torment. These were 'Ad who denied the Signs of their Lord and disobeyed His Messengers and followed

the bidding of every haughty enemy of
truth. They were pursued by a curse in
this world and shall be so pursued on the
Day of Judgment. Hearken, surely 'Ad
proved ungrateful to their Lord. Hearken,
ruined are 'Ad, the people of Hud. (59—61)

وَاتَّبَعُوۡۤا اَمۡرَ كُلِّ جَبَّارٍ عَنِيۡدٍ ۞

وَاُتۡبِعُوۡا فِىۡ هٰذِهِ الدُّنۡيَا لَعۡنَةً وَّيَوۡمَ الۡقِيٰمَةِ ؕ اَلَاۤ
اِنَّ عَادًا كَفَرُوۡا رَبَّهُمۡ ؕ اَلَا بُعۡدًا لِّعَادٍ قَوۡمِ هُوۡدٍ ۞

To Thamud We sent their brother
Saleh. He admonished them: O my people,
worship Allah alone; you have no god but
Him. He raised you up from the earth,
and settled you therein. Therefore ask forgiveness of Him and turn wholly to Him.
Verily my Lord is nigh, responsive to
prayer. They answered him: Saleh, our
hopes had hitherto centered on thee. Now
dost thou forbid us to worship that which
our fathers worshipped? Truly, we are in
grave doubt concerning that to which
thou callest us. He remonstrated with
them: O my people, tell me, if I base myself on a clear proof from my Lord and He
has bestowed His special mercy upon me,
and yet should I disobey Him, then who
will help me against Allah? You would, in
such case, only augment my ruin. O my
people, this she-camel is dedicated to the
service of Allah, and it is appointed as
a Sign for you. So leave it free to roam
about and find its pasture in Allah's earth,
and do it no harm lest you should be
afflicted with a speedy torment. But they
hamstrung her; whereupon Saleh announced: Enjoy yourselves in your homes for
the space of three days; your doom will
then overtake you and nothing can avert
it. (62—66)

وَاِلٰى ثَمُوۡدَ اَخَاهُمۡ صٰلِحًا ۘ قَالَ يٰقَوۡمِ اعۡبُدُوا اللّٰهَ
مَا لَكُمۡ مِّنۡ اِلٰهٍ غَيۡرُهٗ ؕ هُوَ اَنۡشَاَكُمۡ مِّنَ الۡاَرۡضِ
وَاسۡتَعۡمَرَكُمۡ فِيۡهَا فَاسۡتَغۡفِرُوۡهُ ثُمَّ تُوۡبُوۡۤا اِلَيۡهِ ؕ
اِنَّ رَبِّىۡ قَرِيۡبٌ مُّجِيۡبٌ ۞

قَالُوۡا يٰصٰلِحُ قَدۡ كُنۡتَ فِيۡنَا مَرۡجُوًّا قَبۡلَ هٰذَاۤ اَتَنۡهٰنَاۤ
اَنۡ نَّعۡبُدَ مَا يَعۡبُدُ اٰبَآؤُنَا وَاِنَّنَا لَفِىۡ شَكٍّ مِّمَّا
تَدۡعُوۡنَاۤ اِلَيۡهِ مُرِيۡبٍ ۞

قَالَ يٰقَوۡمِ اَرَءَيۡتُمۡ اِنۡ كُنۡتُ عَلٰى بَيِّنَةٍ مِّنۡ رَّبِّىۡ
وَاٰتٰنِىۡ مِنۡهُ رَحۡمَةً فَمَنۡ يَّنۡصُرُنِىۡ مِنَ اللّٰهِ اِنۡ
عَصَيۡتُهٗ ۖ فَمَا تَزِيۡدُوۡنَنِىۡ غَيۡرَ تَخۡسِيۡرٍ ۞

وَيٰقَوۡمِ هٰذِهٖ نَاقَةُ اللّٰهِ لَكُمۡ اٰيَةً فَذَرُوۡهَا تَاۡكُلۡ
فِىۡۤ اَرۡضِ اللّٰهِ وَلَا تَمَسُّوۡهَا بِسُوۡٓءٍ فَيَاۡخُذَكُمۡ عَذَابٌ
قَرِيۡبٌ ۞

فَعَقَرُوۡهَا فَقَالَ تَمَتَّعُوۡا فِىۡ دَارِكُمۡ ثَلٰثَةَ اَيَّامٍ ؕ
ذٰلِكَ وَعۡدٌ غَيۡرُ مَكۡذُوۡبٍ ۞

So, when Our decree went forth, We
delivered Saleh and those who believed
with him by Our special mercy, and saved
them from the ignominy of that day.
Surely, thy Lord is Powerful, Mighty.

فَلَمَّا جَآءَ اَمۡرُنَا نَجَّيۡنَا صٰلِحًا وَّالَّذِيۡنَ اٰمَنُوۡا مَعَهٗ
بِرَحۡمَةٍ مِّنَّا وَمِنۡ خِزۡىِ يَوۡمِئِذٍ ؕ اِنَّ رَبَّكَ هُوَ
الۡقَوِىُّ الۡعَزِيۡزُ ۞

وَاَخَذَ الَّذِيۡنَ ظَلَمُوا الصَّيۡحَةُ فَاَصۡبَحُوۡا فِىۡ دِيَارِهِمۡ

The wrongdoers were overtaken by a mighty blast and they lay prostrate in their homes, as if they had never dwelt therein. Hearken, Thamud behaved ungratefully to their Lord; hearken, ruined are Thamud. (67—69)

جُثِمِيْنَ ۞

كَاَنْ لَّمْ يَغْنَوْا فِيْهَا ۗ اَلَاۤ اِنَّ ثَمُوْدَا۟ كَفَرُوْا رَبَّهُمْ ۚ اَلَا بُعْدًا لِّثَمُوْدَ ۞

Our messengers came to Abraham with glad tidings and greeted him with: Peace. He responded with: Peace be on you; and hastened to bring a roasted calf. When he perceived that they did not put forth their hands towards it, he was puzzled and conceived a fear of them. They tried to reassure him: Be not afraid, for we have been sent to the people of Lot. His wife was standing by and she too was perturbed, whereupon We conveyed to her the glad tidings of the birth of Isaac, and beyond Isaac of Jacob. She lamented: Ah me! Shall I bear a child in this old age, while my husband here is also old? This is indeed a strange piece of news! The messengers said: Dost thou wonder at the decree of Allah? The mercy of Allah and His blessings are upon you, people of the house. Surely, He is Praiseworthy, Glorious. Thus when Abraham was reassured and was cheered up by the good news, he began to plead with Us on behalf of the people of Lot. Indeed, Abraham was forbearing, tender-hearted and oft-turning to Allah. On this We said to him: Abraham, persist not with thy pleading. The decree of thy Lord has gone forth and they shall be afflicted with a torment that cannot be averted. (70—77)

وَلَقَدْ جَآءَتْ رُسُلُنَاۤ اِبْرٰهِيْمَ بِالْبُشْرٰى قَالُوْا سَلٰمًا ۖ قَالَ سَلٰمٌ فَمَا لَبِثَ اَنْ جَآءَ بِعِجْلٍ حَنِيْذٍ ۞

فَلَمَّا رَاۤ اَيْدِيَهُمْ لَا تَصِلُ اِلَيْهِ نَكِرَهُمْ وَاَوْجَسَ مِنْهُمْ خِيْفَةً ۗ قَالُوْا لَا تَخَفْ اِنَّاۤ اُرْسِلْنَاۤ اِلٰى قَوْمِ لُوْطٍ ۞

وَامْرَاَتُهٗ قَآئِمَةٌ فَضَحِكَتْ فَبَشَّرْنٰهَا بِاِسْحٰقَ ۙ وَمِنْ وَّرَآءِ اِسْحٰقَ يَعْقُوْبَ ۞

قَالَتْ يٰوَيْلَتٰىۤ ءَاَلِدُ وَاَنَا عَجُوْزٌ وَّهٰذَا بَعْلِيْ شَيْخًا ۗ اِنَّ هٰذَا لَشَيْءٌ عَجِيْبٌ ۞

قَالُوْۤا اَتَعْجَبِيْنَ مِنْ اَمْرِ اللّٰهِ رَحْمَتُ اللّٰهِ وَبَرَكٰتُهٗ عَلَيْكُمْ اَهْلَ الْبَيْتِ ۗ اِنَّهٗ حَمِيْدٌ مَّجِيْدٌ ۞

فَلَمَّا ذَهَبَ عَنْ اِبْرٰهِيْمَ الرَّوْعُ وَجَآءَتْهُ الْبُشْرٰى يُجَادِلُنَا فِيْ قَوْمِ لُوْطٍ ۞

اِنَّ اِبْرٰهِيْمَ لَحَلِيْمٌ اَوَّاهٌ مُّنِيْبٌ ۞

يٰۤاِبْرٰهِيْمُ اَعْرِضْ عَنْ هٰذَا ۚ اِنَّهٗ قَدْ جَآءَ اَمْرُ رَبِّكَ ۚ وَاِنَّهُمْ اٰتِيْهِمْ عَذَابٌ غَيْرُ مَرْدُوْدٍ ۞

When Our messengers came to Lot, He was grieved and felt constrained on their account and said: This looks like being a distressing day. His people hurried to him wild with indignation, and before this

وَلَمَّا جَآءَتْ رُسُلُنَا لُوْطًا سِيْٓءَ بِهِمْ وَضَاقَ بِهِمْ ذَرْعًا وَّقَالَ هٰذَا يَوْمٌ عَصِيْبٌ ۞

وَجَآءَهٗ قَوْمُهٗ يُهْرَعُوْنَ اِلَيْهِ ۗ وَمِنْ قَبْلُ كَانُوْا

also they were given to all manner of ill-behaviour. Lot remonstrated with them: O my people, my daughters who are married among you, are well disposed towards you and are a sufficient guarantee for you that no harm shall come to you through my guests. So fear Allah and do not humiliate me in the presence of my guests. Is there not among you one man of good sense? They rejoined: Thou knowest we have no claim against thy daughters, and thou well knowest what it is that we desire; meaning that Lot should send away his guests. Lot expostulated: Would that I had the power to oppose you! Failing that I can only turn to a Mighty Support. The messengers reassured him: Lot, we are the messengers of thy Lord. Thy enemies shall never be able to lay hands upon thee, for they are doomed. So depart quickly with thy family during the night, and let none of you look back; thus will you be safe, except thy wife. That which is going to befall them shall surely befall her also. Their appointed time is the morning, and the morning is now not far off. So when Our decree went forth, We turned the city upside down, and We rained upon it stones of clay, layer upon layer, marked for them in the decree of thy Lord. Such chastisement is not far from the wrongdoers of any age. (78—84)

To Midian We sent their brother Shu'aib. He admonished them: O my people, worship Allah alone, you have no god other than Him. Give not short measure or short weight. You are today in a state of prosperity, but I am fearful for you of the chastisement of a ruinous day. O my people, give full measure and full weight with justice, and do not defraud people by making short delivery; nor commit iniquity in the land thereby creating disorder. If you are believers you should realise that the gains that Allah permits you to retain lawfully are the best for you. I am but a counsellor for you and have not been appointed a keeper over you. (85—87)

213

They retorted: Shu'aib, does thy Prayer bid thee that we should forsake that which our fathers worshipped or that we should stop disposing of our belongings as we please? Thou must fancy thyself very intelligent and discerning! He reasoned with them: O my people tell me, if I base myself on clear proof from my Lord, and He has furnished me with a handsome provision from Himself, then what answer will you make to Him? I do not desire to act contrary to that with which I admonish you; all I desire is rectitude as far as it is within my power to bring it about. I can accomplish nothing save through Allah. In Him I put my trust, and to Him I turn. O my people, let not your hostility towards me lead you on to a position in which the like of that should befall you which befell the people of Noah, or the people of Hud, or the people of Saleh, and the people of Lot dwelt not far from you. Seek forgiveness of your Lord and turn wholly to Him; verily my Lord is Ever Merciful, Most Loving. (88—91)

They replied to him: Shu'aib, we do not understand much of that which thou sayest. We consider thee a weak individual among us, and were it not for thy family, we would surely stone thee. Thou dost not even occupy a position of respect among us. He admonished them: O my people, is my family then worthy of greater respect in your eyes than Allah, Whom you have cast behind your backs as of no account? Surely, my Lord encompasses all that you do. O my people, carry on, then, on your side as you consider best, and I shall carry on on my side. Soon shall you know who is afflicted with humiliating chastisement and who is a liar. Wait on; I shall wait on with you.

So, when Our decree went forth, We saved Shu'aib and those who had believed with him, by Our special mercy; and a fierce blast overtook those who did wrong, so that they lay prostrate in their homes, as though they had never dwelt therein. Hearken, ruined was Midian, as were ruined Thamud (92—96)

وَلَمَّا جَآءَ اَمْرُنَا نَجَّيْنَا شُعَيْبًا وَّالَّذِيْنَ اٰمَنُوْا مَعَهٗ بِرَحْمَةٍ مِّنَّا وَاَخَذَتِ الَّذِيْنَ ظَلَمُوا الصَّيْحَةُ فَاَصْبَحُوْا فِيْ دِيَارِهِمْ جٰثِمِيْنَ ۞

كَاَنْ لَّمْ يَغْنَوْا فِيْهَا ۚ اَلَا بُعْدًا لِّمَدْيَنَ كَمَا بَعِدَتْ ثَمُوْدُ ۞

وَلَقَدْ اَرْسَلْنَا مُوْسٰى بِاٰيٰتِنَا وَسُلْطٰنٍ مُّبِيْنٍ ۞

We did indeed send Moses with Our Signs and with manifest authority to Pharaoh and his nobles; but they obeyed the command of Pharaoh, and Pharaoh's command was not at all well directed. He will precede his people on the Day of Judgment and will lead them into the Fire. Evil is the place they shall arrive at. A curse pursued them in this life and it shall pursue them on the Day of Judgment. Evil is the gift bestowed upon them. (97—100)

اِلٰى فِرْعَوْنَ وَمَلَإِيْهٖ فَاتَّبَعُوْا اَمْرَ فِرْعَوْنَ ۚ وَمَآ اَمْرُ فِرْعَوْنَ بِرَشِيْدٍ ۞

يَقْدُمُ قَوْمَهٗ يَوْمَ الْقِيٰمَةِ فَاَوْرَدَهُمُ النَّارَ ۚ وَبِئْسَ الْوِرْدُ الْمَوْرُوْدُ ۞

وَاُتْبِعُوْا فِيْ هٰذِهٖ لَعْنَةً وَّيَوْمَ الْقِيٰمَةِ ۚ بِئْسَ الرِّفْدُ الْمَرْفُوْدُ ۞

ذٰلِكَ مِنْ اَنْبَآءِ الْقُرٰى نَقُصُّهٗ عَلَيْكَ مِنْهَا قَآئِمٌ وَّحَصِيْدٌ ۞

That is of the tidings of the ruined cities that We relate to thee; the ruins of some are visible and others have been obliterated altogether. We did not wrong them, but they wronged themselves; and their gods on whom they called beside Allah, availed them naught when the decree of thy Lord went forth; they only augmented their ruin. Such is the chastisement of thy Lord which He inflicts upon corrupt cities. Surely, His chastisement is grievously painful. In that is a Sign for him who fears the chastisement of the Hereafter. That is a day for which mankind shall be gathered together, a day which shall be witnessed by all. We hold it back for a computed term. (101—105)

وَمَا ظَلَمْنٰهُمْ وَلٰكِنْ ظَلَمُوْا اَنْفُسَهُمْ فَمَآ اَغْنَتْ عَنْهُمْ اٰلِهَتُهُمُ الَّتِيْ يَدْعُوْنَ مِنْ دُوْنِ اللّٰهِ مِنْ شَيْءٍ لَّمَّا جَآءَ اَمْرُ رَبِّكَ ۚ وَمَا زَادُوْهُمْ غَيْرَ تَتْبِيْبٍ ۞

وَكَذٰلِكَ اَخْذُ رَبِّكَ اِذَآ اَخَذَ الْقُرٰى وَهِيَ ظَالِمَةٌ ۚ اِنَّ اَخْذَهٗ اَلِيْمٌ شَدِيْدٌ ۞

اِنَّ فِيْ ذٰلِكَ لَاٰيَةً لِّمَنْ خَافَ عَذَابَ الْاٰخِرَةِ ۚ ذٰلِكَ يَوْمٌ مَّجْمُوْعٌ لَّهُ النَّاسُ وَذٰلِكَ يَوْمٌ مَّشْهُوْدٌ ۞

وَمَا نُؤَخِّرُهٗ اِلَّا لِاَجَلٍ مَّعْدُوْدٍ ۞

215

When it arrives, no one shall speak except by Allah's leave; then some of them will prove unfortunate and others fortunate. Those who prove unfortunate shall be in the Fire, given to sighing and sobbing, abiding therein so long as the heavens and the earth endure, excepting that which thy Lord may will. Thy Lord does whatever He pleases. Those who prove fortunate shall be in Paradise; abiding therein so long as the heavens and the earth endure, excepting that which thy Lord may will. This is a bounty which shall never be cut off. So doubt not the futility of that which these people worship. They worship only as their fathers worshipped before them, and We shall surely pay out to them their portion in full, undiminished. (106—110)

We gave Moses the Book to settle differences, but his people differed about the Book also; and had it not been for the antecedent promise of mercy of thy Lord, the issue would have been settled between them long before. Now these people are in grave doubt concerning the Book. Thy Lord will surely requite them in full for that which they do; He is Well-Aware of all their doings. (111—112)

So do thou continue to stand upright, as thou hast been commanded, along with those who have turned wholly to Allah with thee. Exceed ye not the bounds, O Muslims, surely Allah sees what you do, and incline not towards those who do wrong lest the Fire should afflict you, and then you will have no friend beside Allah, nor shall you be helped. (113—114)

Observe Prayer at the two ends of the day, and in the hours of the night in the proximity of the day. Surely good does away with evil. This is a reminder for those who would remember. Be steadfast; for surely, Allah suffers not the reward of the righteous to perish. (115—116)

Why were there not, out of the generations that passed away before you persons possessed of understanding who would have forbidden corruption in the earth, except the few whom We saved from among them because of their doing it? The wrongdoers in each generation preferred ease and comfort and thus became offenders. Thy Lord would not destroy communities unjustly while the people thereof were righteous. Had thy Lord enforced His will, He would surely have made mankind one people; as it is, they will not cease to differ, save those on whom thy Lord has had mercy, and for this had He created them. But the word of Thy Lord shall be fulfilled: Verily, I will fill hell with men, high and low, all together, who persist in differing. (117—120)

We relate unto thee all of the tidings of the Messengers whereby We make thy heart firm; and herein have come to thee the truth and wisdom, and an exhortation and a reminder for the believers. Tell those who believe not: Continue to act on your side as you think best; we shall continue to act as we are admonished; and wait on, we too shall wait. The knowledge of the secret of the heavens and the earth belongs to Allah alone, and to Him shall all affairs be returned. So worship Him and put thy trust in Him alone. Thy Lord is not unmindful of that which you do. (121—124)

الْحَسَنٰتِ يُذْهِبْنَ السَّيِّاٰتِ ۚ ذٰلِكَ ذِكْرٰى لِلذّٰكِرِيْنَ ۝

وَاصْبِرْ فَاِنَّ اللّٰهَ لَا يُضِيْعُ اَجْرَ الْمُحْسِنِيْنَ ۝

فَلَوْ لَا كَانَ مِنَ الْقُرُوْنِ مِنْ قَبْلِكُمْ اُولُوْا بَقِيَّةٍ يَّنْهَوْنَ عَنِ الْفَسَادِ فِى الْاَرْضِ اِلَّا قَلِيْلًا مِّمَّنْ اَنْجَيْنَا مِنْهُمْ ۚ وَاتَّبَعَ الَّذِيْنَ ظَلَمُوْا مَا اُتْرِفُوْا فِيْهِ وَكَانُوْا مُجْرِمِيْنَ ۝

وَمَا كَانَ رَبُّكَ لِيُهْلِكَ الْقُرٰى بِظُلْمٍ وَّ اَهْلُهَا مُصْلِحُوْنَ ۝

وَلَوْ شَآءَ رَبُّكَ لَجَعَلَ النَّاسَ اُمَّةً وَّاحِدَةً وَّلَا يَزَالُوْنَ مُخْتَلِفِيْنَ ۙ۝

اِلَّا مَنْ رَّحِمَ رَبُّكَ ۚ وَلِذٰلِكَ خَلَقَهُمْ ۚ وَتَمَّتْ كَلِمَةُ رَبِّكَ لَاَمْلَئَنَّ جَهَنَّمَ مِنَ الْجِنَّةِ وَالنَّاسِ اَجْمَعِيْنَ ۝

وَكُلًّا نَّقُصُّ عَلَيْكَ مِنْ اَنْبَآءِ الرُّسُلِ مَا نُثَبِّتُ بِهٖ فُؤَادَكَ ۚ وَجَآءَكَ فِىْ هٰذِهِ الْحَقُّ وَمَوْعِظَةٌ وَّذِكْرٰى لِلْمُؤْمِنِيْنَ ۝

وَقُلْ لِّلَّذِيْنَ لَا يُؤْمِنُوْنَ اعْمَلُوْا عَلٰى مَكَانَتِكُمْ اِنَّا عٰمِلُوْنَ ۝

وَانْتَظِرُوْا ۚ اِنَّا مُنْتَظِرُوْنَ ۝

وَلِلّٰهِ غَيْبُ السَّمٰوٰتِ وَالْاَرْضِ وَاِلَيْهِ يُرْجَعُ الْاَمْرُ كُلُّهٗ فَاعْبُدْهُ وَتَوَكَّلْ عَلَيْهِ ۚ وَمَا رَبُّكَ بِغَافِلٍ عَمَّا تَعْمَلُوْنَ ۝

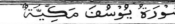

Chapter 12

YŪSUF

(Revealed before Hijra)

In the name of Allah Most Gracious, Ever Merciful. (1)

I AM ALLAH, THE ALL SEEING.

These are verses of the Book which sets forth clearly the truth. We have revealed the Quran which expounds its meaning plainly, so that you may ponder over it with wisdom. We relate everything to thee in the best manner, for We have revealed this Quran to thee comprising the truth. Before this thou wast one of those not aware of the truth. (2—4)

Call to mind when Joseph said to his father: Believe me, father, I have seen eleven stars and the sun and the moon in my dream, and the wonder is that I saw them making obeisance to me. His father said to him: Dear son, do not relate thy dream to thy brethren, lest they should contrive some stratagem against thee. Satan is, indeed, man's declared enemy. Thus will thy Lord, as thou hast seen, make thee His chosen one, and teach thee the meaning of things divine, and perfect His favour unto thee, and unto the true descendants of Jacob, as He perfected it of yore unto thy two forefathers, Abraham and Isaac. Truly thy Lord is All-Knowing, Wise. (5—7)

Surely, in the affair of Joseph and his brethren there are many Signs for seekers after truth, when they conferred together and said: Joseph and his brother are dearer to our father than we are, though we are a strong party. In this matter our father is surely in manifest error. Therefore, let us put Joseph to death or cast him out to some distant land so that we may enjoy our father's favour exclusively, and we can thereafter become a righteous band. (8—10)

218

One of them said: Do not put Joseph to
death, but if you must do something, cast
him into the bottom of a deep well, some
of the travellers will pick him up and you
will achieve your purpose. (11)

So they went to their father and said:
Father, what do you apprehend from us
concerning Joseph that you do not trust
him with us, while we truly wish him well?
Now, send him with us tomorrow, he will
play about and enjoy himself and we shall
take good care of him. He replied: Your
taking him away with you would surely
distress me; besides, I would be afraid
lest, while you are otherwise occupied,
a wolf may approach and rend him and
devour him. They said: Should a wolf
devour him, despite our being a strong
party, what sorry losers we would be!
(12—15)

So, when they took him along and having agreed to cast him into the bottom
of a deep well, they carried out their
design, We comforted him with Our revelation: You will surely tell them one day of
this affair. But they knew naught of this.
They came to their father in the evening
weeping and said: Father, we started
playing and went racing with one another,
leaving Joseph with our things, and a wolf
did rend and devour him, though we know
you will not believe us, however truthful we may be. In support of their tale they
produced Joseph's shirt smeared with
false blood. Seeing this, their father said:
It is not as you say; in truth your minds
have presented to you in an agreeable
shape the evil thing that you have compassed. It now behoves me to be steadfast. It is Allah alone Whose help can avail
against that which you assert, and Him
I shall beseech for help. (16—19)

Presently there arrived a caravan of
travellers and they sent their water-
drawer to draw water from the well. He let
down his bucket into the well and perceiving a youth at the bottom he cried out:
This is a piece of good luck. I have found
a youth. They concealed him as part of
their merchandise, and Allah knew well

قَالَ قَآئِلٌ مِّنْهُمْ لَا تَقْتُلُوْا يُوْسُفَ وَاَلْقُوْهُ فِيْ
غَيٰبَتِ الْجُبِّ يَلْتَقِطْهُ بَعْضُ السَّيَّارَةِ اِنْ كُنْتُمْ
فٰعِلِيْنَ ۱۱

قَالُوْا يٰٓاَبَانَا مَالَكَ لَا تَأْمَنَّا عَلٰى يُوْسُفَ وَاِنَّا
لَهٗ لَنٰصِحُوْنَ ۱۲

اَرْسِلْهُ مَعَنَا غَدًا يَّرْتَعْ وَيَلْعَبْ وَاِنَّا لَهٗ لَحٰفِظُوْنَ ۱۳
قَالَ اِنِّىْ لَيَحْزُنُنِىْٓ اَنْ تَذْهَبُوْا بِهٖ وَاَخَافُ اَنْ
يَّأْكُلَهُ الذِّئْبُ وَاَنْتُمْ عَنْهُ غٰفِلُوْنَ ۱۴

قَالُوْا لَئِنْ اَكَلَهُ الذِّئْبُ وَنَحْنُ عُصْبَةٌ اِنَّآ اِذًا
لَّخٰسِرُوْنَ ۱۵

فَلَمَّا ذَهَبُوْا بِهٖ وَاَجْمَعُوْٓا اَنْ يَّجْعَلُوْهُ فِيْ غَيٰبَتِ الْجُبِّ
وَاَوْحَيْنَآ اِلَيْهِ لَتُنَبِّئَنَّهُمْ بِاَمْرِهِمْ هٰذَا وَهُمْ
لَا يَشْعُرُوْنَ ۱۶

وَجَآءُوْٓ اَبَاهُمْ عِشَآءً يَّبْكُوْنَ ۱۷

قَالُوْا يٰٓاَبَانَآ اِنَّا ذَهَبْنَا نَسْتَبِقُ وَتَرَكْنَا يُوْسُفَ
عِنْدَ مَتَاعِنَا فَاَكَلَهُ الذِّئْبُ وَمَآ اَنْتَ بِمُؤْمِنٍ لَّنَا
وَلَوْ كُنَّا صٰدِقِيْنَ ۱۸

وَجَآءُوْ عَلٰى قَمِيْصِهٖ بِدَمٍ كَذِبٍ قَالَ بَلْ سَوَّلَتْ
لَكُمْ اَنْفُسُكُمْ اَمْرًا فَصَبْرٌ جَمِيْلٌ وَاللّٰهُ الْمُسْتَعَانُ
عَلٰى مَا تَصِفُوْنَ ۱۹

وَجَآءَتْ سَيَّارَةٌ فَاَرْسَلُوْا وَارِدَهُمْ فَاَدْلٰى دَلْوَهُ
قَالَ يٰبُشْرٰى هٰذَا غُلٰمٌ وَاَسَرُّوْهُ بِضَاعَةً وَاللّٰهُ

what they did. Later they sold him for a paltry sum, a few dirhems, not being keen in the matter of the price. The man of Egypt who bought him said to his wife: Lodge him honourably, he may prove of benefit to us, or we may even adopt him as our son. Thus did We establish Joseph honourably in the land so that We may also teach him the meaning of things divine. Allah has full power to carry out His design, but most people do not realise this. (20—22)

عَلِيمٌۢ بِمَا يَعۡمَلُوۡنَ ۞

وَشَرَوۡهُ بِثَمَنٍۭ بَخۡسٍ دَرَاهِمَ مَعۡدُوۡدَةٍ ۚ وَكَانُوۡا فِيۡهِ مِنَ الزَّاهِدِيۡنَ ۞

وَقَالَ الَّذِى اشۡتَرٰىهُ مِنۡ مِّصۡرَ لِامۡرَاَتِهٖۤ اَكۡرِمِىۡ مَثۡوٰىهُ عَسٰۤى اَنۡ يَّنۡفَعَنَاۤ اَوۡ نَتَّخِذَهٗ وَلَدًا ؕ وَكَذٰلِكَ مَكَّنَّا لِيُوۡسُفَ فِى الۡاَرۡضِ ۫ وَلِنُعَلِّمَهٗ مِنۡ تَاۡوِيۡلِ الۡاَحَادِيۡثِ ؕ وَاللّٰهُ غَالِبٌ عَلٰٓى اَمۡرِهٖ وَلٰكِنَّ اَكۡثَرَ النَّاسِ لَا يَعۡلَمُوۡنَ ۞

When Joseph attained his age of full maturity, We granted him judgment and learning; thus do We reward the doers of good. The woman in whose house he was sought to seduce him against his will. She bolted the doors of the house and said: Now come along. He protested: I seek refuge with Allah against any such thing. He is my Lord. He has made honourable provision for me. In truth the wrongdoers never prosper. She made up her mind to have her wish of him, and he made up his mind to stand firm, which he could not have done had he not seen a manifest Sign of his Lord. Thus it was that We might turn away from him all evil and indecency. He was truly of Our chosen servants. (23—25)

وَلَمَّا بَلَغَ اَشُدَّهٗۤ اٰتَيۡنٰهُ حُكۡمًا وَّعِلۡمًا ؕ وَكَذٰلِكَ نَجۡزِى الۡمُحۡسِنِيۡنَ ۞

وَرَاوَدَتۡهُ الَّتِىۡ هُوَ فِىۡ بَيۡتِهَا عَنۡ نَّفۡسِهٖ وَغَلَّقَتِ الۡاَبۡوَابَ وَقَالَتۡ هَيۡتَ لَكَ ؕ قَالَ مَعَاذَ اللّٰهِ اِنَّهٗ رَبِّىۡۤ اَحۡسَنَ مَثۡوَاىَ ؕ اِنَّهٗ لَا يُفۡلِحُ الظّٰلِمُوۡنَ ۞

وَلَقَدۡ هَمَّتۡ بِهٖ ۚ وَهَمَّ بِهَا لَوۡلَاۤ اَنۡ رَّاٰ بُرۡهَانَ رَبِّهٖ ؕ كَذٰلِكَ لِنَصۡرِفَ عَنۡهُ السُّوۡٓءَ وَالۡفَحۡشَآءَ ؕ اِنَّهٗ مِنۡ عِبَادِنَا الۡمُخۡلَصِيۡنَ ۞

They both ran to the door and in the struggle she tore his shirt at the back. They found her husband at the door whereupon she exclaimed: The recompense of one who planned evil towards thy wife can only be that he should be put in prison or be grievously chastised! Joseph said: It was she who sought to seduce me against my will! One of her household testified: If his shirt is rent at the front then she has spoken truth, and he is lying,

وَاسۡتَبَقَا الۡبَابَ وَقَدَّتۡ قَمِيۡصَهٗ مِنۡ دُبُرٍ وَّاَلۡفَيَا سَيِّدَهَا لَدَا الۡبَابِ ؕ قَالَتۡ مَا جَزَآءُ مَنۡ اَرَادَ بِاَهۡلِكَ سُوۡٓءًا اِلَّاۤ اَنۡ يُّسۡجَنَ اَوۡ عَذَابٌ اَلِيۡمٌ ۞

قَالَ هِىَ رَاوَدَتۡنِىۡ عَنۡ نَّفۡسِىۡ وَشَهِدَ شَاهِدٌ مِّنۡ اَهۡلِهَا ۚ اِنۡ كَانَ قَمِيۡصُهٗ قُدَّ مِنۡ قُبُلٍ فَصَدَقَتۡ وَهُوَ مِنَ الۡكٰذِبِيۡنَ ۞

but if his shirt is rent at the back then she has lied and he speaks truth. When her husband saw that Joseph's shirt was rent at the back, he said to his wife: Of a surety, this situation has ensued in consequence of some stratagem devised by you women, you are adept at devising stratagems. Joseph, do thou forbear and, woman, do thou ask forgiveness for thy sin, for undoubtedly thou wert in error. (26—30)

وَ اِنْ كَانَ قَمِيْصُهٗ قُدَّ مِنْ دُبُرٍ فَكَذَبَتْ وَ هُوَ مِنَ الصّٰدِقِيْنَ ۞

فَلَمَّا رَاٰ قَمِيْصَهٗ قُدَّ مِنْ دُبُرٍ قَالَ اِنَّهٗ مِنْ كَيْدِكُنَّ اِنَّ كَيْدَكُنَّ عَظِيْمٌ ۞

يُوْسُفُ اَعْرِضْ عَنْ هٰذَا وَ اسْتَغْفِرِىْ لِذَنْۢبِكِ اِنَّكِ كُنْتِ مِنَ الْخٰطِئِيْنَ ۞

Some of the women in the town began to gossip: The wife of the Aziz seeks to seduce her slave boy. She must be infatuated with him. We consider this great folly on her part. When the gossip reached her ears she invited them to a banquet and prepared seats for them and provided each of them with a knife and then asked Joseph to appear before them. When they beheld him they esteemed him highly and in wonderment pressed their fingers between their teeth and exclaimed: He has resisted evil for fear of Allah: He is superhuman, he must be a noble angel. (31—32)

وَ قَالَ نِسْوَةٌ فِى الْمَدِيْنَةِ امْرَاَتُ الْعَزِيْزِ تُرَاوِدُ فَتٰىهَا عَنْ نَّفْسِهٖ قَدْ شَغَفَهَا حُبًّا اِنَّا لَنَرٰىهَا فِىْ ضَلٰلٍ مُّبِيْنٍ ۞

فَلَمَّا سَمِعَتْ بِمَكْرِهِنَّ اَرْسَلَتْ اِلَيْهِنَّ وَ اَعْتَدَتْ لَهُنَّ مُتَّكَاً وَّ اٰتَتْ كُلَّ وَاحِدَةٍ مِّنْهُنَّ سِكِّيْنًا وَّ قَالَتِ اخْرُجْ عَلَيْهِنَّ فَلَمَّا رَاَيْنَهٗ اَكْبَرْنَهٗ وَ قَطَّعْنَ اَيْدِيَهُنَّ وَ قُلْنَ حَاشَ لِلّٰهِ مَا هٰذَا بَشَرًا اِنْ هٰذَا اِلَّا مَلَكٌ كَرِيْمٌ ۞

She said: Well now, this is the one concerning whom you have been finding fault with me. I did indeed seek to seduce him against his will, but he safeguarded himself. If he will not bend himself to my will he shall certainly be put in prison and be humiliated. Whereupon Joseph prayed: My Lord, prison is more agreeable to me than that to which these women invite me, and unless Thou turn away their guile from me I may incline towards them and behave like a fool. So his Lord heard his prayer and turned away their guile from him. It is He alone who oft hears prayer and knows all about everything. (33—35)

قَالَتْ فَذٰلِكُنَّ الَّذِىْ لُمْتُنَّنِىْ فِيْهِ وَ لَقَدْ رَاوَدْتُّهٗ عَنْ نَّفْسِهٖ فَاسْتَعْصَمَ وَ لَئِنْ لَّمْ يَفْعَلْ مَاۤ اٰمُرُهٗ لَيُسْجَنَنَّ وَ لَيَكُوْنًا مِّنَ الصّٰغِرِيْنَ ۞

قَالَ رَبِّ السِّجْنُ اَحَبُّ اِلَىَّ مِمَّا يَدْعُوْنَنِىْ اِلَيْهِ وَ اِلَّا تَصْرِفْ عَنِّىْ كَيْدَهُنَّ اَصْبُ اِلَيْهِنَّ وَ اَكُنْ مِّنَ الْجٰهِلِيْنَ ۞

فَاسْتَجَابَ لَهٗ رَبُّهٗ فَصَرَفَ عَنْهُ كَيْدَهُنَّ اِنَّهٗ هُوَ السَّمِيْعُ الْعَلِيْمُ ۞

Then it appeared seemly to them, after
they had perceived certain indications,
that he be put in prison for a while. Two
young men entered the prison along with
him. One of them said to Joseph: I have
seen in my dream that I am pressing wine;
and the other said: I have seen that I am
carrying bread upon my head on which
birds are feeding. Interpret these dreams
for us, for we consider thee a righteous
person. Joseph said to them: I shall inform you of the interpretation of your
dreams before your meal is brought to you.
I am able to do this as my Lord has bestowed knowledge upon me. I have shunned the creed of a people who do not believe
in Allah and who reject the Hereafter,
and I have adhered to the faith of my
fathers, Abraham and Isaac and Jacob.
It is not for us to associate anything with
Allah as a partner. This is of Allah's grace
upon us and upon the people, but most
people are not grateful. O my two prison
companions, are diverse lords better or
Allah, the One the Most Supreme? That
which you worship beside Allah is nothing
but idle names which you and your
fathers have devised. Allah has sent down
no authority concerning them. All judgment rests with Allah; He has commanded
that you worship none save only Him.
That is the true faith, but most men know
not. (36—41)

ثُمَّ بَدَا لَهُمْ مِّنْ بَعْدِ مَا رَأَوُا الْاٰيٰتِ لَيَسْجُنُنَّهٗ حَتّٰى حِيْنٍ ۝

وَدَخَلَ مَعَهُ السِّجْنَ فَتَيٰنِ ؕ قَالَ اَحَدُهُمَاۤ اِنِّیْۤ اَرٰىنِیْۤ اَعْصِرُ خَمْرًا ۚ وَقَالَ الْاٰخَرُ اِنِّیْۤ اَرٰىنِیْۤ اَحْمِلُ فَوْقَ رَاْسِیْ خُبْزًا تَاْكُلُ الطَّیْرُ مِنْهُ ؕ نَبِّئْنَا بِتَاْوِیْلِهٖ ۚ اِنَّا نَرٰىكَ مِنَ الْمُحْسِنِیْنَ ۝

قَالَ لَا یَاْتِیْكُمَا طَعَامٌ تُرْزَقٰنِهٖۤ اِلَّا نَبَّاْتُكُمَا بِتَاْوِیْلِهٖ قَبْلَ اَنْ یَّاْتِیَكُمَا ؕ ذٰلِكُمَا مِمَّا عَلَّمَنِیْ رَبِّیْ ؕ اِنِّیْ تَرَكْتُ مِلَّةَ قَوْمٍ لَّا یُؤْمِنُوْنَ بِاللّٰهِ وَهُمْ بِالْاٰخِرَةِ هُمْ كٰفِرُوْنَ ۝

وَاتَّبَعْتُ مِلَّةَ اٰبَآءِیْۤ اِبْرٰهِیْمَ وَاِسْحٰقَ وَیَعْقُوْبَ ؕ مَا كَانَ لَنَاۤ اَنْ نُّشْرِكَ بِاللّٰهِ مِنْ شَیْءٍ ؕ ذٰلِكَ مِنْ فَضْلِ اللّٰهِ عَلَیْنَا وَعَلَى النَّاسِ وَلٰكِنَّ اَكْثَرَ النَّاسِ لَا یَشْكُرُوْنَ ۝

یٰصَاحِبَیِ السِّجْنِ ءَاَرْبَابٌ مُّتَفَرِّقُوْنَ خَیْرٌ اَمِ اللّٰهُ الْوَاحِدُ الْقَهَّارُ ۝

مَا تَعْبُدُوْنَ مِنْ دُوْنِهٖۤ اِلَّاۤ اَسْمَآءً سَمَّیْتُمُوْهَاۤ اَنْتُمْ وَاٰبَآؤُكُمْ مَّاۤ اَنْزَلَ اللّٰهُ بِهَا مِنْ سُلْطٰنٍ ؕ اِنِ الْحُكْمُ اِلَّا لِلّٰهِ ؕ اَمَرَ اَلَّا تَعْبُدُوْۤا اِلَّاۤ اِیَّاهُ ؕ ذٰلِكَ الدِّیْنُ الْقَیِّمُ وَلٰكِنَّ اَكْثَرَ النَّاسِ لَا یَعْلَمُوْنَ ۝

یٰصَاحِبَیِ السِّجْنِ اَمَّاۤ اَحَدُكُمَا فَیَسْقِیْ رَبَّهٗ خَمْرًا ۚ وَاَمَّا الْاٰخَرُ فَیُصْلَبُ فَتَاْكُلُ الطَّیْرُ مِنْ رَّاْسِهٖ ؕ

O my two prison companions, the interpretation of your dreams is this: As for
one of you, he will pour out wine for his
lord to drink; and as for the other, he will
be crucified and birds will feed off his
head. The matter concerning which you
desired to know has been so decreed. To

the one who he believed would be set free, Joseph said: Make mention of me to thy lord. But Satan caused him to forget mentioning this to his lord, so that Joseph bided his time in prison for some years. (42—43)

Some time, thereafter, the King announced to his courtiers: I have seen in my dream seven fat kine being devoured by seven lean ones, and seven fresh green ears of corn and seven others dry and withered. Now ye nobles, expound to me the meaning of my dreams, if you are versed in the interpretation of dreams. They made answer: These are confused dreams, and we know not the meaning of such. Then he of the two companions of Joseph who had been set free, and who now remembered, after the lapse of a period, that which had passed between Joseph and him, exclaimed: I shall let you know the interpretation of the dream, only send me to find out. He hurried to Joseph and implored him: Joseph, thou righteous one, do expound to us the meaning of a dream in which seven fat kine are devoured by seven lean ones, and there are seven green ears of corn and seven others which are dry, that I may return to the people and they may know the interpretation. (44—47)

Joseph explained: You shall work diligently and continuously at cultivation for seven years, but leave what you reap in the ear, except the little that you consume. Then there will follow seven years of great hardship which will eat up all that you will have laid by in advance for them, except the little that you may set aside. After this will come a year in which the people will be relieved and there will be rejoicing and exchange of gifts. (48—50)

When the King heard all this, he said: Bring him to me. When the King's messenger came to Joseph, he said: Go back to thy lord and ask him how fare the women who had gnawed at their fingers? My Lord

قُضِيَ الْاَمْرُ الَّذِيْ فِيْهِ تَسْتَفْتِيٰنِ ۟

وَقَالَ لِلَّذِيْ ظَنَّ اَنَّهٗ نَاجٍ مِّنْهُمَا اذْكُرْنِيْ عِنْدَ رَبِّكَ فَاَنْسٰىهُ الشَّيْطٰنُ ذِكْرَ رَبِّهٖ فَلَبِثَ فِى السِّجْنِ بِضْعَ سِنِيْنَ ۟

وَقَالَ الْمَلِكُ اِنِّيْۤ اَرٰى سَبْعَ بَقَرٰتٍ سِمَانٍ يَّاْكُلُهُنَّ سَبْعٌ عِجَافٌ وَّسَبْعَ سُنْۢبُلٰتٍ خُضْرٍ وَّاُخَرَ يٰبِسٰتٍ ۚ يٰۤاَيُّهَا الْمَلَاُ اَفْتُوْنِيْ فِيْ رُءْيَايَ اِنْ كُنْتُمْ لِلرُّءْيَا تَعْبُرُوْنَ ۟

قَالُوْۤا اَضْغَاثُ اَحْلَامٍ ۚ وَمَا نَحْنُ بِتَاْوِيْلِ الْاَحْلَامِ بِعٰلِمِيْنَ ۟

وَقَالَ الَّذِيْ نَجَا مِنْهُمَا وَادَّكَرَ بَعْدَ اُمَّةٍ اَنَا اُنَبِّئُكُمْ بِتَاْوِيْلِهٖ فَاَرْسِلُوْنِ ۟

يُوْسُفُ اَيُّهَا الصِّدِّيْقُ اَفْتِنَا فِيْ سَبْعِ بَقَرٰتٍ سِمَانٍ يَّاْكُلُهُنَّ سَبْعٌ عِجَافٌ وَّسَبْعِ سُنْۢبُلٰتٍ خُضْرٍ وَّاُخَرَ يٰبِسٰتٍ ۙ لَّعَلِّيْۤ اَرْجِعُ اِلَى النَّاسِ لَعَلَّهُمْ يَعْلَمُوْنَ ۟

قَالَ تَزْرَعُوْنَ سَبْعَ سِنِيْنَ دَاَبًا ۚ فَمَا حَصَدْتُّمْ فَذَرُوْهُ فِيْ سُنْۢبُلِهٖۤ اِلَّا قَلِيْلًا مِّمَّا تَاْكُلُوْنَ ۟

ثُمَّ يَاْتِيْ مِنْۢ بَعْدِ ذٰلِكَ سَبْعٌ شِدَادٌ يَّاْكُلْنَ مَا قَدَّمْتُمْ لَهُنَّ اِلَّا قَلِيْلًا مِّمَّا تُحْصِنُوْنَ ۟

ثُمَّ يَاْتِيْ مِنْۢ بَعْدِ ذٰلِكَ عَامٌ فِيْهِ يُغَاثُ النَّاسُ وَفِيْهِ يَعْصِرُوْنَ ۟

وَقَالَ الْمَلِكُ ائْتُوْنِيْ بِهٖ ۚ فَلَمَّا جَآءَهُ الرَّسُوْلُ قَالَ ارْجِعْ اِلٰى رَبِّكَ فَسْـَٔلْهُ مَا بَالُ النِّسْوَةِ الّٰتِيْ قَطَّعْنَ

knows well their design. The King enquired of the women: What was the truth of the affair in which you sought to seduce Joseph against his will? They answered: He eschewed vice for fear of Allah; we have not known any evil against him. Whereupon the wife of the Aziz exclaimed: The truth has now come to light. It was I who sought to seduce him against his will, he is surely one of the righteous. (51—52)

Joseph declared: I had asked for this enquiry to be made so that the Aziz should know that I had not been disloyal to him in his absence and that I believe that Allah suffers not the design of the unfaithful to prosper. On the other hand, I do not claim infallibility for myself, for the mind of man (except for him upon whom my Lord has mercy) is ever ready to incite to evil. Surely my Lord is Most Forbearing, Ever Merciful. (53—54)

The King commanded: Bring him to me that I may assign him to my special projects. After he had talked to Joseph he told him: From now on you will be a man of established position and trust with us. Said Joseph: Then grant me authority over the resources of the earth for I shall conserve them well and would know how to exploit them. Thus did We bring about the assignment of Joseph to a position of authority in the land. He could dwell therein wherever he pleased. We bestow Our mercy on whomsoever We please in this very life, and We suffer not the reward of the righteous to perish, and of a surety, the reward of the Hereafter is even better for those who believe and are righteous. (55—58)

During the period of famine the brethren of Joseph also came to the country and presented themselves before him. He recognised them as soon as he saw them, but they knew him not. When he had made provision for them he told them: Next time bring with you your brother on the father's side. See you not that I give full measure and am the best of hosts? But if you bring him not to me, you

اَیْدِیَهُنَّ اِنَّ رَبِّیْ بِکَیْدِهِنَّ عَلِیْمٌ ۝

قَالَ مَا خَطْبُکُنَّ اِذْ رَاوَدْتُّنَّ یُوْسُفَ عَنْ نَّفْسِهٖ ؕ

قُلْنَ حَاشَ لِلّٰهِ مَا عَلِمْنَا عَلَیْهِ مِنْ سُوْٓءٍ ؕ قَالَتِ امْرَاَتُ

الْعَزِیْزِ الْـٰٔنَ حَصْحَصَ الْحَقُّ ۫ اَنَا رَاوَدْتُّهٗ عَنْ نَّفْسِهٖ

وَ اِنَّهٗ لَمِنَ الصّٰدِقِیْنَ ۝

ذٰلِکَ لِیَعْلَمَ اَنِّیْ لَمْ اَخُنْهُ بِالْغَیْبِ وَاَنَّ اللّٰهَ لَا یَهْدِیْ

کَیْدَ الْخَآئِنِیْنَ ۝

وَمَآ اُبَرِّئُ نَفْسِیْ ۚ اِنَّ النَّفْسَ لَاَمَّارَةٌ بِالسُّوْٓءِ

اِلَّا مَا رَحِمَ رَبِّیْ ؕ اِنَّ رَبِّیْ غَفُوْرٌ رَّحِیْمٌ ۝

وَ قَالَ الْمَلِکُ ائْتُوْنِیْ بِهٖ اَسْتَخْلِصْهُ لِنَفْسِیْ ۚ فَلَمَّا

کَلَّمَهٗ قَالَ اِنَّکَ الْیَوْمَ لَدَیْنَا مَکِیْنٌ اَمِیْنٌ ۝

قَالَ اجْعَلْنِیْ عَلٰی خَزَآئِنِ الْاَرْضِ ۚ اِنِّیْ حَفِیْظٌ عَلِیْمٌ ۝

وَ کَذٰلِکَ مَکَّنَّا لِیُوْسُفَ فِی الْاَرْضِ ۚ یَتَبَوَّاُ مِنْهَا حَیْثُ

یَشَآءُ ؕ نُصِیْبُ بِرَحْمَتِنَا مَنْ نَّشَآءُ وَلَا نُضِیْعُ اَجْرَ الْمُحْسِنِیْنَ ۝

وَلَاَجْرُ الْاٰخِرَةِ خَیْرٌ لِّلَّذِیْنَ اٰمَنُوْا وَکَانُوْا یَتَّقُوْنَ ۝

وَ جَآءَ اِخْوَةُ یُوْسُفَ فَدَخَلُوْا عَلَیْهِ فَعَرَفَهُمْ وَهُمْ

لَهٗ مُنْکِرُوْنَ ۝

وَ لَمَّا جَهَّزَهُمْ بِجَهَازِهِمْ قَالَ ائْتُوْنِیْ بِاَخٍ لَّکُمْ

مِّنْ اَبِیْکُمْ ۚ اَلَا تَرَوْنَ اَنِّیْ اُوْفِی الْکَیْلَ وَاَنَا خَیْرُ

الْمُنْزِلِیْنَ ۝

فَاِنْ لَّمْ تَاْتُوْنِیْ بِهٖ فَلَا کَیْلَ لَکُمْ عِنْدِیْ وَلَا

تَقْرَبُوْنِ ۝

will get no measure from me and so come not near me. They said: We shall try to induce his father to part with him and we are sure to succeed. Joseph said to those who worked for him: Put their money back into their sacks so that they may call it to mind when they have rejoined their families. Haply they may come back. (59—63)

When they returned home they said to their father: Father, we have been denied further supplies unless you send our brother with us, in which case we shall obtain supplies and we shall certainly take care of him. Their father said: How can I trust you with him expecting anything different from that which befell when I trusted you with his brother aforetime? You may take him with you, but I put my trust in Allah alone Who is the best Protector and the Most Merciful of all. (64—65)

When they unpacked their things they found their money had been returned to them, whereupon they cried: Father what more can we wish for? Here is our money returned to us! This time if we take our brother with us, we shall bring provision for our families, we shall guard our brother, and we shall secure an additional camel-load of grain. That will be a great bounty! Their father said: I will certainly not send him with you until you make me a solemn promise, in the name of Allah, that you will surely bring him back to me, unless you are encompassed yourselves. When they gave him their solemn promise, he said: Allah watches over what we have said. (66—67)

When they were about to set out, their father enjoined them: My sons, do not enter the city all by one gate, but enter it separately by different gates. I can avail you nothing against Allah's decree. All judgment rests with Allah. In Him I put my trust, and in Him should trust all those who trust. When they entered the city in the manner their father had commanded them, his purpose was fulfilled, yet he had no power to guard them against

قَالُوْا سَنُرَاوِدُ عَنْهُ اَبَاهُ وَاِنَّا لَفٰعِلُوْنَ ۝

وَقَالَ لِفِتْيٰنِهِ اجْعَلُوْا بِضَاعَتَهُمْ فِيْ رِحَالِهِمْ لَعَلَّهُمْ يَعْرِفُوْنَهَاۤ اِذَا انْقَلَبُوْاۤ اِلٰۤى اَهْلِهِمْ لَعَلَّهُمْ يَرْجِعُوْنَ ۝

فَلَمَّا رَجَعُوْاۤ اِلٰۤى اَبِيْهِمْ قَالُوْا يٰۤاَبَانَا مُنِعَ مِنَّا الْكَيْلُ فَاَرْسِلْ مَعَنَاۤ اَخَانَا نَكْتَلْ وَاِنَّا لَهٗ لَحٰفِظُوْنَ ۝

قَالَ هَلْ اٰمَنُكُمْ عَلَيْهِ اِلَّا كَمَاۤ اَمِنْتُكُمْ عَلٰۤى اَخِيْهِ مِنْ قَبْلُ ۫ فَاللّٰهُ خَيْرٌ حٰفِظًا ۪ وَّهُوَ اَرْحَمُ الرّٰحِمِيْنَ ۝

وَلَمَّا فَتَحُوْا مَتَاعَهُمْ وَجَدُوْا بِضَاعَتَهُمْ رُدَّتْ اِلَيْهِمْ ؕ قَالُوْا يٰۤاَبَانَا مَا نَبْغِيْ ؕ هٰذِهٖ بِضَاعَتُنَا رُدَّتْ اِلَيْنَا ۚ وَنَمِيْرُ اَهْلَنَا وَنَحْفَظُ اَخَانَا وَنَزْدَادُ كَيْلَ بَعِيْرٍ ؕ ذٰلِكَ كَيْلٌ يَّسِيْرٌ ۝

قَالَ لَنْ اُرْسِلَهٗ مَعَكُمْ حَتّٰى تُؤْتُوْنِ مَوْثِقًا مِّنَ اللّٰهِ لَتَأْتُنَّنِيْ بِهٖۤ اِلَّاۤ اَنْ يُّحَاطَ بِكُمْ ۚ فَلَمَّاۤ اٰتَوْهُ مَوْثِقَهُمْ قَالَ اللّٰهُ عَلٰى مَا نَقُوْلُ وَكِيْلٌ ۝

وَقَالَ يٰبَنِيَّ لَا تَدْخُلُوْا مِنْۢ بَابٍ وَّاحِدٍ وَّادْخُلُوْا مِنْ اَبْوَابٍ مُّتَفَرِّقَةٍ ؕ وَمَاۤ اُغْنِيْ عَنْكُمْ مِّنَ اللّٰهِ مِنْ شَيْءٍ ؕ اِنِ الْحُكْمُ اِلَّا لِلّٰهِ ؕ عَلَيْهِ تَوَكَّلْتُ ۚ وَعَلَيْهِ فَلْيَتَوَكَّلِ الْمُتَوَكِّلُوْنَ ۝

وَلَمَّا دَخَلُوْا مِنْ حَيْثُ اَمَرَهُمْ اَبُوْهُمْ ؕ مَا كَانَ يُغْنِيْ عَنْهُمْ مِّنَ اللّٰهِ مِنْ شَيْءٍ اِلَّا حَاجَةً فِيْ نَفْسِ يَعْقُوْبَ قَضٰىهَا ؕ وَاِنَّهٗ لَذُوْ عِلْمٍ لِّمَا عَلَّمْنٰهُ وَلٰكِنَّ اَكْثَرَ

Allah's decree. He succeeded only in fulfilling a desire he had in his mind. Jacob was a man of great knowledge because of that which We had taught him, but most people know not. When they presented themselves before Joseph, he placed his own brother close to himself, and reassured him saying: I am indeed thy brother who was lost, so grieve no more at what they have been doing. (68—70)

When Joseph had provided for them and they were preparing to depart, he inadvertently placed the drinking cup from which he had just drunk water in his brother's sack. When all was ready, a royal herald announced: Men of the caravan! You have committed theft. They all turned round and asked: What is it that you miss? The answer was: We miss one of the royal measuring cups. Whoso is able to restore it shall have a camel-load of grain and I stand surety for it. They retorted: By Allah, you know well we have not come here to cause disturbance in the land, nor are we thieves. What, then, shall be the penalty, if you are proved wrong? The penalty? He in whose sack it is found shall himself be the penalty for it. Thus do we punish the wrongdoers. Thereupon the herald began to search their sacks before searching the sack of Joseph's brother. In the end, he found the cup in the sack of Joseph's brother, and took it out therefrom. Thus did We devise a plan on behalf of Joseph. He could not have held back his brother under the king's law, except for Allah's plan. We exalt whomsoever We please, and above every possessor of knowledge is One possessing greater knowledge. His brothers said: If this one has stolen, no wonder; for a brother of his had also committed theft aforetime. Joseph concealed his chagrin and did not give expression to it in their presence. He only said to himself: You are a sorry lot, but Allah knows well what you allege. (71—78)

فِ النَّاسِ لَا يَعْلَمُوْنَ ۞

وَلَمَّا دَخَلُوْا عَلٰى يُوْسُفَ اٰوٰى اِلَيْهِ اَخَاهُ قَالَ اِنِّيْ اَنَا اَخُوْكَ فَلَا تَبْتَئِسْ بِمَا كَانُوْا يَعْمَلُوْنَ ۞

فَلَمَّا جَهَّزَهُمْ بِجَهَازِهِمْ جَعَلَ السِّقَايَةَ فِيْ رَحْلِ اَخِيْهِ ثُمَّ اَذَّنَ مُؤَذِّنٌ اَيَّتُهَا الْعِيْرُ اِنَّكُمْ لَسٰرِقُوْنَ ۞

قَالُوْا وَاَقْبَلُوْا عَلَيْهِمْ مَّاذَا تَفْقِدُوْنَ ۞

قَالُوْا نَفْقِدُ صُوَاعَ الْمَلِكِ وَلِمَنْ جَآءَ بِهٖ حِمْلُ بَعِيْرٍ وَّاَنَا بِهٖ زَعِيْمٌ ۞

قَالُوْا تَاللّٰهِ لَقَدْ عَلِمْتُمْ مَّا جِئْنَا لِنُفْسِدَ فِي الْاَرْضِ وَمَا كُنَّا سٰرِقِيْنَ ۞

قَالُوْا فَمَا جَزَآؤُهٗ اِنْ كُنْتُمْ كٰذِبِيْنَ ۞

قَالُوْا جَزَآؤُهٗ مَنْ وُّجِدَ فِيْ رَحْلِهٖ فَهُوَ جَزَآؤُهٗ كَذٰلِكَ نَجْزِي الظّٰلِمِيْنَ ۞

فَبَدَاَ بِاَوْعِيَتِهِمْ قَبْلَ وِعَآءِ اَخِيْهِ ثُمَّ اسْتَخْرَجَهَا مِنْ وِعَآءِ اَخِيْهِ كَذٰلِكَ كِدْنَا لِيُوْسُفَ مَا كَانَ لِيَأْخُذَ اَخَاهُ فِيْ دِيْنِ الْمَلِكِ اِلَّا اَنْ يَّشَآءَ اللّٰهُ نَرْفَعُ دَرَجٰتٍ مَّنْ نَّشَآءُ وَفَوْقَ كُلِّ ذِيْ عِلْمٍ عَلِيْمٌ ۞

قَالُوْا اِنْ يَّسْرِقْ فَقَدْ سَرَقَ اَخٌ لَّهٗ مِنْ قَبْلُ فَاَسَرَّهَا يُوْسُفُ فِيْ نَفْسِهٖ وَلَمْ يُبْدِهَا لَهُمْ قَالَ اَنْتُمْ شَرٌّ مَّكَانًا وَّاللّٰهُ اَعْلَمُ بِمَا تَصِفُوْنَ ۞

قَالُوْا يٰٓاَيُّهَا الْعَزِيْزُ اِنَّ لَهٗٓ اَبًا شَيْخًا كَبِيْرًا فَخُذْ

They pleaded: Exalted one, he has a very aged father, and, to spare him suffering, we implore thee seize one of us in his stead; we esteem thee a gracious personage. Joseph answered: Allah forbid that we should seize any save him with whom we found our property, for then we would surely be unjust. When they despaired of him, they withdrew conferring among themselves. Their leader said: Do you not recall that your father has taken from you a solemn promise in the name of Allah, and, how, aforetime, you were guilty of a default with respect to Joseph? I will, therefore, not leave this land until my father gives me special permission or Allah decrees something in my favour. He is the best of Judges. Go ye back to your father and say to him: Father, your younger son was certainly guilty of theft and we have stated to you only that which we know as a fact. We could not guard against the unseen. You may enquire of the people of the city wherein we were and of the caravan with which we travelled, we are telling you the truth. (79—83)

When they told him this, Jacob said: It cannot be thus. It seems your minds have dressed up something in a plausible guise. It behoves me to be steadfast. May be Allah will bring them to me together. He is the All-Knowing, the Wise. Then he turned away from them and made supplication: Lord I appeal to Thee again in the matter of Joseph. His eyes welled up with tears but he did not permit his sorrow to be witnessed by others. They admonished him: By Allah, it seems you will not cease worrying about Joseph, till you make yourself ill or you expire. He expostulated: I make my plaint of grief and sorrow only to Allah, and I know from Allah that which you know not. Go, my sons, and enquire after Joseph and his brother and despair not of the mercy of Allah; for none despairs of Allah's mercy save the unbelieving people. (84—88)

اَحَدَنَا مَكَانَهٗ ۚ اِنَّا نَرٰىكَ مِنَ الْمُحْسِنِيْنَ ۞

قَالَ مَعَاذَ اللّٰهِ اَنْ نَّاْخُذَ اِلَّا مَنْ وَّجَدْنَا مَتَاعَنَا عِنْدَهٗٓ ۙ اِنَّاۤ اِذًا لَّظٰلِمُوْنَ ۞

فَلَمَّا اسْتَيْـَٔسُوْا مِنْهُ خَلَصُوْا نَجِيًّا ۗ قَالَ كَبِيْرُهُمْ اَلَمْ تَعْلَمُوْۤا اَنَّ اَبَاكُمْ قَدْ اَخَذَ عَلَيْكُمْ مَّوْثِقًا مِّنَ اللّٰهِ وَمِنْ قَبْلُ مَا فَرَّطْتُّمْ فِيْ يُوْسُفَ ۚ فَلَنْ اَبْرَحَ الْاَرْضَ حَتّٰى يَاْذَنَ لِيْٓ اَبِيْٓ اَوْ يَحْكُمَ اللّٰهُ لِيْ ۚ وَهُوَ خَيْرُ الْحٰكِمِيْنَ ۞

اِرْجِعُوْۤا اِلٰٓى اَبِيْكُمْ فَقُوْلُوْا يٰٓاَبَانَاۤ اِنَّ ابْنَكَ سَرَقَ ۚ وَمَا شَهِدْنَاۤ اِلَّا بِمَا عَلِمْنَا وَمَا كُنَّا لِلْغَيْبِ حٰفِظِيْنَ ۞

وَسْـَٔلِ الْقَرْيَةَ الَّتِيْ كُنَّا فِيْهَا وَالْعِيْرَ الَّتِيْۤ اَقْبَلْنَا فِيْهَا ۚ وَاِنَّا لَصٰدِقُوْنَ ۞

قَالَ بَلْ سَوَّلَتْ لَكُمْ اَنْفُسُكُمْ اَمْرًا ۗ فَصَبْرٌ جَمِيْلٌ ۚ عَسَى اللّٰهُ اَنْ يَّاْتِيَنِيْ بِهِمْ جَمِيْعًا ۗ اِنَّهٗ هُوَ الْعَلِيْمُ الْحَكِيْمُ ۞

وَتَوَلّٰى عَنْهُمْ وَقَالَ يٰٓاَسَفٰى عَلٰى يُوْسُفَ وَابْيَضَّتْ عَيْنٰهُ مِنَ الْحُزْنِ فَهُوَ كَظِيْمٌ ۞

قَالُوْا تَاللّٰهِ تَفْتَؤُا تَذْكُرُ يُوْسُفَ حَتّٰى تَكُوْنَ حَرَضًا اَوْ تَكُوْنَ مِنَ الْهٰلِكِيْنَ ۞

قَالَ اِنَّمَاۤ اَشْكُوْا بَثِّيْ وَحُزْنِيْۤ اِلَى اللّٰهِ وَاَعْلَمُ مِنَ اللّٰهِ مَا لَا تَعْلَمُوْنَ ۞

يٰبَنِيَّ اذْهَبُوْا فَتَحَسَّسُوْا مِنْ يُّوْسُفَ وَاَخِيْهِ وَلَا

When his brothers presented themselves
before Joseph again, they pleaded: Exalted one, we and our family are sore
afflicted by want, and we have brought
only a paltry sum; so give us full measure,
and give us more out of charity; surely,
Allah rewards the charitable vastly. Joseph
asked: Do you recall what you did to
Joseph and his brother when you did not
realise the evil of what you were doing?
They exclaimed: Are you indeed Joseph?
He replied: I am Joseph and this is my
brother. Allah has indeed been gracious
to us. The truth is that whoso is righteous
and is steadfast, Allah does not suffer
the reward of such good ones to be lost.
They affirmed: We testify to Allah that
Allah has surely exalted you above us and
that no doubt we were in the wrong.
Joseph sought to comfort them: No blame
shall lie on you this day. May Allah forgive you. He is the Most Merciful of all
those who show mercy. Take this shirt of
mine and lay it before my father, he will
comprehend everything; and bring to me
the whole of your family. (89—94)

When the caravan set out from Egypt,
their father said to those around him: Were
it not that you would call me a dotard,
I would say that I certainly perceive the
fragrance of Joseph. They retorted: By
Allah, you still persist in your fixed illusion. But when the bearer of the good
news arrived, he laid Joseph's shirt before
his father, who thereupon comprehended
everything and reminded them: Did I not
say to you: I know from Allah that which
you know not! (95—97)

His sons then begged him: Father, do pray for forgiveness of our sins, we were manifestly in the wrong. He comforted them: I shall certainly pray for forgiveness for you to my Lord, most assuredly He is the Most Forgiving, Ever Merciful. (98—99)

When they approached, Joseph went forth to do honour to his parents and welcomed them: Enter ye all into Egypt in peace as is the pleasure of Allah. He installed his parents in the place of honour and they all fell down prostrate before Allah in gratitude for His favours to him. Joseph said: Father, this is the fulfilment of my dream of old. My Lord has made it come true. He was indeed gracious unto me for He took me out of prison and appointed me to a place of honour and brought you from the desert after Satan had brought about discord between me and my brethren. Surely, my Lord is benignly Gracious unto whomsoever He pleases, for He is the All-Knowing, the Wise. Then Joseph prayed: My Lord, Thou hast bestowed upon me a portion of sovereignty and taught me somewhat of the interpretation of dreams. Maker of the heavens and the earth, Thou art my Helper in this world and the Hereafter, let death when it comes find me in a state of complete submission to Thy will and join me to the company of the righteous. (100—102)

These are tidings of the unseen that We reveal to thee, O Prophet, though thou wast not present with them when they plotted and agreed upon a plan. However much dost thou desire that all men should believe, most of them will not. Thou dost not ask of them any reward in return for that which thou dost teach. On the contrary, it is but a source of honour for all mankind. (103—105)

How many a Sign is there in the heavens and the earth which they pass by, turning away from it; and most of them, even when they profess belief in Allah, at the same time attribute partners to Him.

قَالُوْا يَا أَبَانَا اسْتَغْفِرْ لَنَا ذُنُوْبَنَا إِنَّا كُنَّا خَاطِئِيْنَ ۞

قَالَ سَوْفَ أَسْتَغْفِرُ لَكُمْ رَبِّيْ إِنَّهُ هُوَ الْغَفُوْرُ الرَّحِيْمُ ۞

فَلَمَّا دَخَلُوْا عَلٰى يُوْسُفَ اٰوٰٓى إِلَيْهِ أَبَوَيْهِ وَقَالَ ادْخُلُوْا مِصْرَ إِنْ شَآءَ اللّٰهُ اٰمِنِيْنَ ۞

وَرَفَعَ أَبَوَيْهِ عَلَى الْعَرْشِ وَخَرُّوْا لَهُ سُجَّدًا ۚ وَقَالَ يَا أَبَتِ هٰذَا تَأْوِيْلُ رُؤْيَايَ مِنْ قَبْلُ قَدْ جَعَلَهَا رَبِّيْ حَقًّا ۚ وَقَدْ أَحْسَنَ بِيْٓ إِذْ أَخْرَجَنِيْ مِنَ السِّجْنِ وَجَآءَ بِكُمْ مِّنَ الْبَدْوِ مِنْ بَعْدِ أَنْ نَّزَغَ الشَّيْطٰنُ بَيْنِيْ وَبَيْنَ إِخْوَتِيْ ۚ إِنَّ رَبِّيْ لَطِيْفٌ لِّمَا يَشَآءُ إِنَّهُ هُوَ الْعَلِيْمُ الْحَكِيْمُ ۞

رَبِّ قَدْ اٰتَيْتَنِيْ مِنَ الْمُلْكِ وَعَلَّمْتَنِيْ مِنْ تَأْوِيْلِ الْأَحَادِيْثِ ۚ فَاطِرَ السَّمٰوٰتِ وَالْأَرْضِ ۗ أَنْتَ وَلِيّٖ فِي الدُّنْيَا وَالْاٰخِرَةِ ۚ تَوَفَّنِيْ مُسْلِمًا وَّأَلْحِقْنِيْ بِالصّٰلِحِيْنَ ۞

ذٰلِكَ مِنْ أَنْبَآءِ الْغَيْبِ نُوْحِيْهِ إِلَيْكَ ۚ وَمَا كُنْتَ لَدَيْهِمْ إِذْ أَجْمَعُوْا أَمْرَهُمْ وَهُمْ يَمْكُرُوْنَ ۞

وَمَآ أَكْثَرُ النَّاسِ وَلَوْ حَرَصْتَ بِمُؤْمِنِيْنَ ۞

وَمَا تَسْأَلُهُمْ عَلَيْهِ مِنْ أَجْرٍ ۚ إِنْ هُوَ إِلَّا ذِكْرٌ لِّلْعٰلَمِيْنَ ۞

وَكَأَيِّنْ مِّنْ اٰيَةٍ فِي السَّمٰوٰتِ وَالْأَرْضِ يَمُرُّوْنَ عَلَيْهَا وَهُمْ عَنْهَا مُعْرِضُوْنَ ۞

وَمَا يُؤْمِنُ أَكْثَرُهُمْ بِاللّٰهِ إِلَّا وَهُمْ مُّشْرِكُوْنَ ۞

Do they, then, feel secure against the coming on them of an overwhelming chastisement from Allah, or against the sudden coming upon them, without their perceiving it, of the Hour of which they have been forewarned? (106—108)

Announce then: This is my way; I call to Allah on the basis of sure knowledge, I and those who follow me. Holy is Allah; and I am not of those who associate partners with Allah. (109)

Before thee also, We sent as Messengers men to whom We sent revelation from among the dwellers of earthly towns. Have they not, then, travelled in the earth, so as to witness the end of those before them who rejected Our Messengers? Surely, the abode of the Hereafter is better for the righteous. Will you not, then, understand? (110)

Thus it was that when Our Messengers despaired of the disbelievers, and the latter became sure that they were being told lies, Our help came to Our Messengers and those were saved whom We desired to save. Our chastisement is not averted from the guilty. (111)

In these, their annals, there is a lesson for men of understanding. This is not a thing forged, but fulfilment of previous revelations and a detailed exposition of all things and a guidance and a mercy for people who believe. (112)

أَفَأَمِنُوٓا أَن تَأْتِيَهُمْ غَاشِيَةٌ مِّنْ عَذَابِ اللَّهِ أَوْ تَأْتِيَهُمُ السَّاعَةُ بَغْتَةً وَهُمْ لَا يَشْعُرُونَ ۝

قُلْ هَٰذِهِۦ سَبِيلِىٓ أَدْعُوٓا إِلَى اللَّهِ عَلَىٰ بَصِيرَةٍ أَنَا۠ وَمَنِ اتَّبَعَنِى وَسُبْحَانَ اللَّهِ وَمَآ أَنَا۠ مِنَ الْمُشْرِكِينَ ۝

وَمَآ أَرْسَلْنَا مِن قَبْلِكَ إِلَّا رِجَالًا نُّوحِىٓ إِلَيْهِم مِّنْ أَهْلِ الْقُرَىٰٓ أَفَلَمْ يَسِيرُوا فِى الْأَرْضِ فَيَنظُرُوا كَيْفَ كَانَ عَاقِبَةُ الَّذِينَ مِن قَبْلِهِمْ وَلَدَارُ الْآخِرَةِ خَيْرٌ لِّلَّذِينَ اتَّقَوْا أَفَلَا تَعْقِلُونَ ۝

حَتَّىٰٓ إِذَا اسْتَيْـَٔسَ الرُّسُلُ وَظَنُّوٓا أَنَّهُمْ قَدْ كُذِبُوا جَآءَهُمْ نَصْرُنَا فَنُجِّىَ مَن نَّشَآءُ وَلَا يُرَدُّ بَأْسُنَا عَنِ الْقَوْمِ الْمُجْرِمِينَ ۝

لَقَدْ كَانَ فِى قَصَصِهِمْ عِبْرَةٌ لِّأُولِى الْأَلْبَابِ مَا كَانَ حَدِيثًا يُفْتَرَىٰ وَلَٰكِن تَصْدِيقَ الَّذِى بَيْنَ يَدَيْهِ وَتَفْصِيلَ كُلِّ شَىْءٍ وَهُدًى وَرَحْمَةً لِّقَوْمٍ يُؤْمِنُونَ ۝

Chapter 13

بِسۡمِ اللهِ الرَّحۡمٰنِ الرَّحِيۡمِ۞

AL-RA'D

(Revealed before Hijra)

In the name of Allah, Most Gracious, Ever Merciful. (1)

I AM ALLAH, THE ALL-KNOWING, THE ALL-SEEING.

These are verses of the Perfect Book. That which has been revealed to thee from thy Lord is the Truth, but most men believe not. Allah is He Who raised up the heavens without any pillars that you can see. Then He settled Himself on the Throne, and constrained the sun and the moon to serve you; each planet pursues its course during an appointed term. He regulates it all and expounds the Signs, that you may have firm belief in the meeting with your Lord. He it is Who spread out the earth and made therein firmly fixed mountains and rivers, and of fruits of every kind He has made pairs. He causes the night to cover the day. In all this, verily, are Signs for a people who reflect. In the earth are diverse tracts adjoining one another, and vineyards, and corn-fields and date-palms, some growing from one root and others from separate roots, which are irrigated by the same water, and yet We make some of them excel others in the quality of their fruits. Therein also are Signs for a people who understand. (2—5)

If thou dost wonder at their saying, wondrous indeed it is: What, when we become dust, shall we enter upon a new state of creation? These are they who disbelieve in their Lord, they shall have shackles round their necks, and they shall be the inmates of the Fire, wherein they shall abide. They demand that thou

الٓمٓرٰ تِلۡكَ اٰيٰتُ الۡكِتٰبِ وَ الَّذِىۡۤ اُنۡزِلَ اِلَيۡكَ مِنۡ رَّبِّكَ الۡحَقُّ وَ لٰكِنَّ اَكۡثَرَ النَّاسِ لَا يُؤۡمِنُوۡنَ۞

اَللّٰهُ الَّذِىۡ رَفَعَ السَّمٰوٰتِ بِغَيۡرِ عَمَدٍ تَرَوۡنَهَا ثُمَّ اسۡتَوٰى عَلَى الۡعَرۡشِ وَ سَخَّرَ الشَّمۡسَ وَ الۡقَمَرَ كُلٌّ يَّجۡرِىۡ لِاَجَلٍ مُّسَمًّى يُدَبِّرُ الۡاَمۡرَ يُفَصِّلُ الۡاٰيٰتِ لَعَلَّكُمۡ بِلِقَآءِ رَبِّكُمۡ تُوۡقِنُوۡنَ۞

وَ هُوَ الَّذِىۡ مَدَّ الۡاَرۡضَ وَ جَعَلَ فِيۡهَا رَوَاسِىَ وَ اَنۡهٰرًا وَ مِنۡ كُلِّ الثَّمَرٰتِ جَعَلَ فِيۡهَا زَوۡجَيۡنِ اثۡنَيۡنِ يُغۡشِى الَّيۡلَ النَّهَارَ اِنَّ فِىۡ ذٰلِكَ لَاٰيٰتٍ لِّقَوۡمٍ يَّتَفَكَّرُوۡنَ۞

وَ فِى الۡاَرۡضِ قِطَعٌ مُّتَجٰوِرٰتٌ وَّ جَنّٰتٌ مِّنۡ اَعۡنَابٍ وَّ زَرۡعٌ وَّ نَخِيۡلٌ صِنۡوَانٌ وَّ غَيۡرُ صِنۡوَانٍ يُّسۡقٰى بِمَآءٍ وَّاحِدٍ وَّ نُفَضِّلُ بَعۡضَهَا عَلٰى بَعۡضٍ فِى الۡاُكُلِ اِنَّ فِىۡ ذٰلِكَ لَاٰيٰتٍ لِّقَوۡمٍ يَّعۡقِلُوۡنَ۞

وَ اِنۡ تَعۡجَبۡ فَعَجَبٌ قَوۡلُهُمۡ ءَاِذَا كُنَّا تُرٰبًا ءَاِنَّا لَفِىۡ خَلۡقٍ جَدِيۡدٍ اُولٰٓئِكَ الَّذِيۡنَ كَفَرُوۡا بِرَبِّهِمۡ وَ اُولٰٓئِكَ الۡاَغۡلٰلُ فِىۡۤ اَعۡنَاقِهِمۡ وَ اُولٰٓئِكَ اَصۡحٰبُ النَّارِ هُمۡ فِيۡهَا خٰلِدُوۡنَ۞

وَ يَسۡتَعۡجِلُوۡنَكَ بِالسَّيِّئَةِ قَبۡلَ الۡحَسَنَةِ وَ قَدۡ خَلَتۡ

shouldst hasten on their punishment ahead of any good that may befall them, despite the fact that exemplary punishments have been meted out to people like them before. Thy Lord is indeed Most Forgiving for mankind, despite their wrongdoing; and thy Lord is also Severe in punishment. Those who disbelieve ask: Wherefore has not a Sign been sent down to him from His Lord? Thou art but a Warner; and every people has had its guide. (6—8)

مِنْ قَبْلِهِمُ الْمَثُلَاتُ وَاِنَّ رَبَّكَ لَذُوْمَغْفِرَةٍ لِلنَّاسِ عَلَىٰ ظُلْمِهِمْ وَاِنَّ رَبَّكَ لَشَدِيْدُ الْعِقَابِ ۞ وَيَقُوْلُ الَّذِيْنَ كَفَرُوْا لَوْلَاۤ اُنْزِلَ عَلَيْهِ اٰيَةٌ مِّنْ رَّبِّهِ ؕ اِنَّمَاۤ اَنْتَ مُنْذِرٌ وَّلِكُلِّ قَوْمٍ هَادٍ ۞

اللّٰهُ يَعْلَمُ مَا تَحْمِلُ كُلُّ اُنْثٰى وَمَا تَغِيْضُ الْاَرْحَامُ وَمَا تَزْدَادُ ؕ وَكُلُّ شَيْءٍ عِنْدَهٗ بِمِقْدَارٍ ۞

عٰلِمُ الْغَيْبِ وَالشَّهَادَةِ الْكَبِيْرُ الْمُتَعَالِ ۞

Allah knows well that which every female bears and that which the wombs reject as defective and that which they foster. With Him is everything in proper measure. He is the Knower of the unseen and the seen, Great above all, Most High. He among you who talks in secret and he who talks openly are equally within His ken; and so also he who seeks to hide himself by night and he who goes forth openly by day. He has appointed a succession of angels in front of the Messenger and behind him to guard him by the command of Allah. Surely, Allah would not withdraw a favour that He has conferred upon a people, until they change their own attitude towards Him. But when Allah decrees punishment for a people, there is no repelling it, nor can they have any helper beside Him. He it is Who shows you the lightning to inspire fear and hope, and raises heavy clouds. The thunder proclaims His Praise and Holiness, and likewise do the angels for awe of Him. He directs the thunderbolts and smites therewith whom He wills, yet they dispute concerning Allah, ignoring that He is Severe in punishing. Unto Him is the true prayer. Those on whom they call beside Him, do not respond to them at all. Their case is like that of one who stretches forth his hands toward water that it may reach his mouth, but it reaches it not. The prayer of the disbelievers is but a delusion.

سَوَآءٌ مِّنْكُمْ مَّنْ اَسَرَّ الْقَوْلَ وَمَنْ جَهَرَ بِهٖ وَمَنْ هُوَ مُسْتَخْفٍ بِالَّيْلِ وَسَارِبٌ بِالنَّهَارِ ۞

لَهٗ مُعَقِّبَاتٌ مِّنْۢ بَيْنِ يَدَيْهِ وَمِنْ خَلْفِهٖ يَحْفَظُوْنَهٗ مِنْ اَمْرِ اللّٰهِ ؕ اِنَّ اللّٰهَ لَا يُغَيِّرُ مَا بِقَوْمٍ حَتّٰى يُغَيِّرُوْا مَا بِاَنْفُسِهِمْ ؕ وَاِذَاۤ اَرَادَ اللّٰهُ بِقَوْمٍ سُوْٓءًا فَلَا مَرَدَّ لَهٗ ۚ وَمَا لَهُمْ مِّنْ دُوْنِهٖ مِنْ وَّالٍ ۞

هُوَ الَّذِيْ يُرِيْكُمُ الْبَرْقَ خَوْفًا وَّطَمَعًا وَّيُنْشِئُ السَّحَابَ الثِّقَالَ ۞

وَيُسَبِّحُ الرَّعْدُ بِحَمْدِهٖ وَالْمَلٰٓئِكَةُ مِنْ خِيْفَتِهٖ ۚ وَيُرْسِلُ الصَّوَاعِقَ فَيُصِيْبُ بِهَا مَنْ يَّشَآءُ وَهُمْ يُجَادِلُوْنَ فِى اللّٰهِ ۚ وَهُوَ شَدِيْدُ الْمِحَالِ ۞

لَهٗ دَعْوَةُ الْحَقِّ ؕ وَالَّذِيْنَ يَدْعُوْنَ مِنْ دُوْنِهٖ لَا يَسْتَجِيْبُوْنَ لَهُمْ بِشَيْءٍ اِلَّا كَبَاسِطِ كَفَّيْهِ اِلَى الْمَآءِ لِيَبْلُغَ فَاهُ وَمَا هُوَ بِبَالِغِهٖ ؕ وَمَا دُعَآءُ الْكٰفِرِيْنَ اِلَّا فِيْ ضَلٰلٍ ۞

To Allah submits whosoever is in the heavens and in the earth willingly or unwillingly, and likewise do their shadows in the mornings and the evenings. (9—16)

Ask them: Who is the Lord of the heavens and the earth? Then tell them: It is Allah. Again ask them: Have you, then, taken beside Him helpers who have no power to acquire good or to repel harm even in respect of their own selves? Can the blind and the seeing be equal? Or, can darkness and light be the same? Or, do they assign to Allah partners who have created the like of His creation so that the two creations appear indistinguishable to them? Tell them: Allah alone is the Creator of all things, and He is the Single, the Most Supreme. He sends down water from the sky so that valleys begin to flow according to their capacity, and the flood carries swelling foam on its surface. In the same way foam comes up from that which they heat up in the fire, for the purpose of making ornaments or articles of domestic use. Thus does Allah illustrate truth and falsehood. The foam passes off like froth, and that which benefits people stays on in the earth. Thus does Allah expound all things. For those who respond to their Lord is the best of everything; and those who respond not to Him, if they had all that is in the earth and the like of it added thereto, they would seek to ransom themselves therewith. They shall have an evil reckoning, and their abode is hell. A wretched resting place it is! (17—19)

Is he who knows that what has been revealed to thee from thy Lord is the Truth, like one who is blind? It is only those gifted with understanding who take heed; those who fulfil Allah's pact and break not the covenant; who join together the ties of kinship that Allah has bidden

وَلِلّٰهِ يَسْجُدُ مَنْ فِى السَّمٰوٰتِ وَالْاَرْضِ طَوْعًا وَّ كَرْهًا وَّظِلٰلُهُمْ بِالْغُدُوِّ وَالْاٰصَالِ ۩

قُلْ مَنْ رَّبُّ السَّمٰوٰتِ وَالْاَرْضِ قُلِ اللّٰهُ ۚ قُلْ اَفَاتَّخَذْتُمْ مِّنْ دُوْنِهٖۤ اَوْلِيَآءَ لَا يَمْلِكُوْنَ لِاَنْفُسِهِمْ نَفْعًا وَّلَا ضَرًّا ۚ قُلْ هَلْ يَسْتَوِى الْاَعْمٰى وَالْبَصِيْرُ ۙ اَمْ هَلْ تَسْتَوِى الظُّلُمٰتُ وَالنُّوْرُ ۚ اَمْ جَعَلُوْا لِلّٰهِ شُرَكَآءَ خَلَقُوْا كَخَلْقِهٖ فَتَشَابَهَ الْخَلْقُ عَلَيْهِمْ ؕ قُلِ اللّٰهُ خَالِقُ كُلِّ شَيْءٍ وَّهُوَ الْوَاحِدُ الْقَهَّارُ ۝

اَنْزَلَ مِنَ السَّمَآءِ مَآءً فَسَالَتْ اَوْدِيَةٌ بِقَدَرِهَا فَاحْتَمَلَ السَّيْلُ زَبَدًا رَّابِيًا ؕ وَمِمَّا يُوْقِدُوْنَ عَلَيْهِ فِى النَّارِ ابْتِغَآءَ حِلْيَةٍ اَوْ مَتَاعٍ زَبَدٌ مِّثْلُهٗ ؕ كَذٰلِكَ يَضْرِبُ اللّٰهُ الْحَقَّ وَالْبَاطِلَ ۬ؕ فَاَمَّا الزَّبَدُ فَيَذْهَبُ جُفَآءً ۚ وَاَمَّا مَا يَنْفَعُ النَّاسَ فَيَمْكُثُ فِى الْاَرْضِ ؕ كَذٰلِكَ يَضْرِبُ اللّٰهُ الْاَمْثَالَ ۝

لِلَّذِيْنَ اسْتَجَابُوْا لِرَبِّهِمُ الْحُسْنٰى ۬ؕ وَالَّذِيْنَ لَمْ يَسْتَجِيْبُوْا لَهٗ لَوْ اَنَّ لَهُمْ مَّا فِى الْاَرْضِ جَمِيْعًا وَّمِثْلَهٗ مَعَهٗ لَافْتَدَوْا بِهٖ ؕ اُولٰٓئِكَ لَهُمْ سُوْءُ الْحِسَابِ ۬ۙ وَمَأْوٰىهُمْ جَهَنَّمُ ؕ وَبِئْسَ الْمِهَادُ ۝

اَفَمَنْ يَّعْلَمُ اَنَّمَاۤ اُنْزِلَ اِلَيْكَ مِنْ رَّبِّكَ الْحَقُّ كَمَنْ هُوَ اَعْمٰى ؕ اِنَّمَا يَتَذَكَّرُ اُولُوا الْاَلْبَابِ ۝

الَّذِيْنَ يُوْفُوْنَ بِعَهْدِ اللّٰهِ وَلَا يَنْقُضُوْنَ الْمِيْثَاقَ ۝

وَالَّذِيْنَ يَصِلُوْنَ مَآ اَمَرَ اللّٰهُ بِهٖۤ اَنْ يُّوْصَلَ وَ

to be joined, and fear their Lord, and dread the evil reckoning; those who are steadfast in seeking the favour of their Lord, and observe Prayer, and spend secretly and openly out of that with which We have provided them, and overcome evil with good. For them is the best reward of the Hereafter: Gardens of Eternity, which they shall enter and also those who are righteous from among their ancestors, and their consorts and their progeny. Angels will come to them from every gate, greeting them: Peace be unto you, because you were steadfast. Behold how good is the reward of this abode. Those who break the covenant of Allah after having made it firm, and cut asunder that which Allah has commanded to be joined together, and act corruptly in the land are under a curse and for them is an evil abode. Allah enlarges His provision or straitens it for whomsoever He pleases. They are content with the hither life whereas the hither life is but a temporary provision in contrast with that which is to come. (20—27)

Those who disbelieve ask: Why is not a Sign sent down to him by his Lord? Tell them: Allah lets go astray those whom He wills and guides to Himself those who turn to Him: those who believe and whose hearts find comfort in the remembrance of Allah. It is only in the remembrance of Allah that hearts can find comfort. Those who believe and act righteously, shall have happiness and an excellent retreat. (28—30)

Thus have We sent thee to a people, before whom other people have passed away waiting for a Messenger, that thou mayest recite to them that which We have revealed to thee: for they disbelieve in the bounty of the Gracious One. Tell them: He is my Lord; there is no god but He; in Him do I put my trust and towards Him is my return. If there were a Quran by which mountains could be moved or by which the earth could be cut asunder, or by which the dead could be spoken to they would still not believe in it. Indeed, the matter of their believing rests wholly with Allah. Have not the believers yet realised that, if Allah had enforced His will, He could have surely guided all mankind? Calamity shall not cease to strike the disbelievers because of that which they have wrought, or to strike near their homes, until the promise of Allah of the final triumph of the believers comes to pass. Surely, Allah fails not in His promise. (31—32)

Messengers were also mocked at before thee; but I granted respite to those who disbelieved, and at the end of it I seized them. Observe, then, how severe was My punishment. Will then He, Who watches the conduct of every one, call not to account those who mock at thee? They ascribe partners to Allah. Say to them: Name them. Or is it that you presume to inform Him of something in the earth of which He does not know? Or, is all this only your verbal assertion? The truth is that their own contrivance appears attractive to the disbelievers and they have been kept back from the right path. He whom Allah lets go astray can have no guide. For such as these there shall be a punishment in this life also; and, surely, the punishment of the Hereafter is harder to bear, and they will have no one to save them from Allah's punishment. (33—35)

The Paradise promised to the righteous is as if rivers flow through it; its fruit is everlasting and also its shade. That is the recompense of those who are righteous and the recompense of the disbelievers is the Fire.

Those to whom We have given the Book rejoice in that which has been revealed to thee; though of the different parties there are some who deny a part thereof. Say to them: I have been commanded only to worship Allah and not to associate partners with Him. Unto Him do I call and unto Him is my return. Thus have We revealed it as a detailed commandment. Then if thou follow their vain desires, after the knowledge that has come to thee, thou shalt have no friend nor anyone to save thee from the wrath of Allah. (36—38)

وَالَّذِيْنَ اٰتَيْنٰهُمُ الْكِتٰبَ يَفْرَحُوْنَ بِمَآ اُنْزِلَ اِلَيْكَ وَمِنَ الْاَحْزَابِ مَنْ يُّنْكِرُ بَعْضَهٗ ؕ قُلْ اِنَّمَآ اُمِرْتُ اَنْ اَعْبُدَ اللّٰهَ وَلَآ اُشْرِكَ بِهٖ ؕ اِلَيْهِ اَدْعُوْا وَاِلَيْهِ مَاٰبِ ۝

وَكَذٰلِكَ اَنْزَلْنٰهُ حُكْمًا عَرَبِيًّا ؕ وَلَئِنِ اتَّبَعْتَ اَهْوَآءَهُمْ بَعْدَ مَا جَآءَكَ مِنَ الْعِلْمِ ۙ مَالَكَ مِنَ اللّٰهِ مِنْ وَّلِيٍّ وَّلَا وَاقٍ ۝

We did indeed send Messengers before thee and We made for them wives and children. It is not possible for a Messenger to bring a Sign except by the command of Allah. For every design there is an appointed term. Allah effaces what He wills and establishes what He wills; with Him is the source of all commandments. Whether We bring to pass during thy lifetime some of that which We have designed for them, or whether We cause thee to die, it will all be fulfilled. Thy part is to convey the Message; it is for Us to make the reckoning. Do they not see that We are approaching from the borders of the land, reducing it as We proceed? Allah judges; no one has power to reverse His judgment. He is Swift in reckoning. Those who were before them also devised plans, but they came to naught. All planning belongs to Allah. He knows what everyone does. The disbelievers will soon know to whom belongs the true recompense of the ultimate resort. Those who disbelieve say: Thou art not a Messenger of Allah. Say to them: Sufficient is Allah as a Witness between you and me, and so also is he who possesses knowledge of the Book. (39—44)

وَلَقَدْ اَرْسَلْنَا رُسُلًا مِّنْ قَبْلِكَ وَجَعَلْنَا لَهُمْ اَزْوَاجًا وَّذُرِّيَّةً ؕ وَمَا كَانَ لِرَسُوْلٍ اَنْ يَّاْتِيَ بِاٰيَةٍ اِلَّا بِاِذْنِ اللّٰهِ ؕ لِكُلِّ اَجَلٍ كِتَابٌ ۝

يَمْحُوا اللّٰهُ مَا يَشَآءُ وَيُثْبِتُ ۖ وَعِنْدَهٗ اُمُّ الْكِتٰبِ ۝

وَاِنْ مَّا نُرِيَنَّكَ بَعْضَ الَّذِيْ نَعِدُهُمْ اَوْ نَتَوَفَّيَنَّكَ فَاِنَّمَا عَلَيْكَ الْبَلٰغُ وَعَلَيْنَا الْحِسَابُ ۝

اَوَلَمْ يَرَوْا اَنَّا نَاْتِي الْاَرْضَ نَنْقُصُهَا مِنْ اَطْرَافِهَا ؕ وَاللّٰهُ يَحْكُمُ لَا مُعَقِّبَ لِحُكْمِهٖ ؕ وَهُوَ سَرِيْعُ الْحِسَابِ ۝

وَقَدْ مَكَرَ الَّذِيْنَ مِنْ قَبْلِهِمْ فَلِلّٰهِ الْمَكْرُ جَمِيْعًا ؕ يَعْلَمُ مَا تَكْسِبُ كُلُّ نَفْسٍ ؕ وَسَيَعْلَمُ الْكُفَّارُ لِمَنْ عُقْبَى الدَّارِ ۝

وَيَقُوْلُ الَّذِيْنَ كَفَرُوْا لَسْتَ مُرْسَلًا ؕ قُلْ كَفٰى بِاللّٰهِ شَهِيْدًۢا بَيْنِيْ وَبَيْنَكُمْ ۙ وَمَنْ عِنْدَهٗ عِلْمُ الْكِتٰبِ ۝

سُوْرَةُ اِبْرَاهِيْمَ مَكِّيَّةٌ

IBRĀHĪM

(Revealed before Hijra)

In the name of Allah, Most Gracious, Ever Merciful. (1)

I AM ALLAH THE ALL-SEEING.

This is a Book that We have revealed to thee that thou mayest bring mankind out of every kind of darkness into the light, by the command of their Lord, to the path of the Mighty, the Praiseworthy Allah, to Whom belongs whatsoever is in the heavens and whatsoever is in the earth. Woe to the disbelievers for a grievous chastisement: those who have chosen the hither life in preference to the Hereafter, and hinder people from the way of Allah and seek to make it appear crooked. It is these who have gone far astray. We have sent every Messenger with revelation in the language of his people that he might make it clear to them. Then Allah lets go astray whom He wills and guides whom He wills. He is the Mighty, the Wise. (2—5)

We did send Moses with Our Signs, commanding him: Bring forth thy people from every kind of darkness into the light and remind them of the favour and chastisement of Allah; for surely therein are Signs for every steadfast and grateful person. Moses said to his people: Call to mind Allah's favour upon you when He delivered you from Pharaoh's people who afflicted you with grievous torment, slaying your male children and sparing your female ones; and therein was a great trial for you from your Lord. Call to mind also when your Lord declared: If you will use My bounties beneficently, I will surely multiply them unto you, but if you misuse

بِسْمِ اللهِ الرَّحْمٰنِ الرَّحِيْمِ ۝

الٓرٰ ۟ كِتٰبٌ اَنْزَلْنٰهُ اِلَيْكَ لِتُخْرِجَ النَّاسَ مِنَ الظُّلُمٰتِ اِلَى النُّوْرِ ۟ بِاِذْنِ رَبِّهِمْ اِلٰى صِرَاطِ الْعَزِيْزِ الْحَمِيْدِ ۝

اللهِ الَّذِيْ لَهُ مَا فِى السَّمٰوٰتِ وَ مَا فِى الْاَرْضِ ۟ وَ وَيْلٌ لِّلْكٰفِرِيْنَ مِنْ عَذَابٍ شَدِيْدِ ۝ ۟

الَّذِيْنَ يَسْتَحِبُّوْنَ الْحَيٰوةَ الدُّنْيَا عَلَى الْاٰخِرَةِ وَ يَصُدُّوْنَ عَنْ سَبِيْلِ اللهِ وَ يَبْغُوْنَهَا عِوَجًا ۟ اُولٰٓئِكَ فِيْ ضَلٰلٍۭ بَعِيْدٍ ۝

وَ مَآ اَرْسَلْنَا مِنْ رَّسُوْلٍ اِلَّا بِلِسَانِ قَوْمِهٖ لِيُبَيِّنَ لَهُمْ ۟ فَيُضِلُّ اللهُ مَنْ يَّشَآءُ وَ يَهْدِيْ مَنْ يَّشَآءُ ۟ وَ هُوَ الْعَزِيْزُ الْحَكِيْمُ ۝

وَ لَقَدْ اَرْسَلْنَا مُوْسٰى بِاٰيٰتِنَآ اَنْ اَخْرِجْ قَوْمَكَ مِنَ الظُّلُمٰتِ اِلَى النُّوْرِ ۟ وَ ذَكِّرْهُمْ بِاَيّٰمِ اللهِ ۟ اِنَّ فِيْ ذٰلِكَ لَاٰيٰتٍ لِّكُلِّ صَبَّارٍ شَكُوْرٍ ۝

وَ اِذْ قَالَ مُوْسٰى لِقَوْمِهِ اذْكُرُوْا نِعْمَةَ اللهِ عَلَيْكُمْ اِذْ اَنْجٰكُمْ مِّنْ اٰلِ فِرْعَوْنَ يَسُوْمُوْنَكُمْ سُوْٓءَ الْعَذَابِ وَ يُذَبِّحُوْنَ اَبْنَآءَكُمْ وَ يَسْتَحْيُوْنَ نِسَآءَكُمْ ۟ وَ فِيْ ذٰلِكُمْ بَلَآءٌ مِّنْ رَّبِّكُمْ عَظِيْمٌ ۝

وَ اِذْ تَاَذَّنَ رَبُّكُمْ لَئِنْ شَكَرْتُمْ لَاَزِيْدَنَّكُمْ وَ لَئِنْ

them, My punishment is severe indeed. Moses also admonished his people: If you and all others in the earth beside you were to deny Allah, it would not detract one jot from His Majesty, for Allah is Self-Sufficient, Praiseworthy. (6—9)

Have not the terrible tidings of those before you, the people of Noah, and the tribes of 'Ad and Thamud and those who came after them, reached you? They were so utterly destroyed that none knows of them now save Allah. Their Messengers came to them with clear Signs, but they repudiated them, and said: We disbelieve in that with which you have been sent, and we are in grave doubt concerning that to which you call us. Their Messengers expostulated: Are you in doubt concerning Allah, Originator of the heavens and the earth? He calls you that He may forgive you your sins, and grant you respite for an appointed term. They rejoined: You are but human like ourselves; you desire to turn us away from that which our fathers used to worship. If you are in the right, then bring us some clear proof. Their Messengers replied to them: Indeed we are human like yourselves, but Allah bestows His favour on whomsoever He wills from among His servants. It is not within our power to bring you a proof except by the command of Allah. In Allah alone should the believers put their trust. (10—12)

Wherefore should we not put our trust in Allah, when He has guided us to our appropriate ways? We will, surely, continue steadfast under your persecution. In Allah alone let those who trust put their trust. Those who disbelieved sought to intimidate their Messengers: We will, surely, expel you from our land unless you return to our religion. Whereupon their Lord reassured them with the revelation:

238

We will surely destroy these wrongdoers and will make you dwell in the land after them. This is a promise for those who are mindful of My Majesty and are mindful of My warnings. They sought Our Judgment, and every haughty enemy of truth came to naught, and found himself facing hell. He shall be given boiling water to drink; he shall sip it by mouthfuls and shall not find it easy to swallow it. Death will approach him from every quarter, yet he will not die. There shall be for him further grievous torment. (13—18)

لَنُهْلِكَنَّ الظّٰلِمِيْنَ ۞

وَلَنُسْكِنَنَّكُمُ الْاَرْضَ مِنْ بَعْدِهِمْ ذٰلِكَ لِمَنْ خَافَ مَقَامِيْ وَخَافَ وَعِيْدِ ۞

وَاسْتَفْتَحُوْا وَخَابَ كُلُّ جَبَّارٍ عَنِيْدٍ ۞

مِّنْ وَّرَآئِهٖ جَهَنَّمُ وَيُسْقٰى مِنْ مَّآءٍ صَدِيْدٍ ۞

يَّتَجَرَّعُهٗ وَلَا يَكَادُ يُسِيْغُهٗ وَيَأْتِيْهِ الْمَوْتُ مِنْ كُلِّ مَكَانٍ وَّمَا هُوَ بِمَيِّتٍ وَّمِنْ وَّرَآئِهٖ عَذَابٌ غَلِيْظٌ ۞

The works of those who deny their Lord are like ashes on which the wind blows fiercely on a stormy day. They shall not be able to avail of any portion of that which they seek to earn. That, indeed, is utter ruin. Dost thou not perceive that Allah has created the heavens and the earth in accordance with the requirements of truth and wisdom? If He pleases, He can bring you to naught and replace you with a new creation; and this is not at all difficult for Allah. They shall all stand before Allah; then shall the weak ones say to the haughty ones: We only followed you. Now can you rid us of aught of Allah's chastisement? They will reply: Had Allah guided us, we would, surely, have guided you. As it is, it is all the same whether we are patient or impatient; there is no way of deliverance for us. When the matter is concluded, Satan will say: Allah made you a true promise; and I also made you a promise, but I failed you. I had no authority over you, except that I called you and you obeyed me. So blame me not, but blame your own selves. I cannot help you, nor can you help me. I have already dis-

مَثَلُ الَّذِيْنَ كَفَرُوْا بِرَبِّهِمْ اَعْمَالُهُمْ كَرَمَادٍ اشْتَدَّتْ بِهِ الرِّيْحُ فِيْ يَوْمٍ عَاصِفٍ لَا يَقْدِرُوْنَ مِمَّا كَسَبُوْا عَلٰى شَيْءٍ ذٰلِكَ هُوَ الضَّلٰلُ الْبَعِيْدُ ۞

اَلَمْ تَرَ اَنَّ اللّٰهَ خَلَقَ السَّمٰوٰتِ وَالْاَرْضَ بِالْحَقِّ اِنْ يَّشَأْ يُذْهِبْكُمْ وَيَأْتِ بِخَلْقٍ جَدِيْدٍ ۞

وَّمَا ذٰلِكَ عَلَى اللّٰهِ بِعَزِيْزٍ ۞

وَبَرَزُوْا لِلّٰهِ جَمِيْعًا فَقَالَ الضُّعَفٰؤُا لِلَّذِيْنَ اسْتَكْبَرُوْا اِنَّا كُنَّا لَكُمْ تَبَعًا فَهَلْ اَنْتُمْ مُّغْنُوْنَ عَنَّا مِنْ عَذَابِ اللّٰهِ مِنْ شَيْءٍ قَالُوْا لَوْ هَدٰىنَا اللّٰهُ لَهَدَيْنٰكُمْ سَوَآءٌ عَلَيْنَآ اَجَزِعْنَآ اَمْ صَبَرْنَا مَا لَنَا مِنْ مَّحِيْصٍ ۞

وَقَالَ الشَّيْطٰنُ لَمَّا قُضِيَ الْاَمْرُ اِنَّ اللّٰهَ وَعَدَكُمْ وَعْدَ الْحَقِّ وَوَعَدْتُّكُمْ فَاَخْلَفْتُكُمْ وَمَا كَانَ لِيَ عَلَيْكُمْ مِّنْ سُلْطٰنٍ اِلَّا اَنْ دَعَوْتُكُمْ فَاسْتَجَبْتُمْ لِيْ فَلَا تَلُوْمُوْنِيْ وَلُوْمُوْا اَنْفُسَكُمْ مَآ اَنَا بِمُصْرِخِكُمْ

claimed your associating me with Allah. Thus for the wrongdoers there shall surely be a grievous chastisement, and those who believe and work righteousness will be admitted into Gardens beneath which rivers flow, wherein they will abide by the command of their Lord. Their greeting therein will be: Peace. (19—24)

Dost thou not see how Allah sets forth the case of a good Word, which is like a good tree whose root is firm and every one of whose branches reaches into heaven? It brings forth fresh fruit at all times by the command of its Lord. Allah sets forth for people all that they stand in need of that they may take heed. The case of an evil word is like that of an evil tree, which is uprooted from the earth and has no stability. Allah strengthens the believers with the Word that is firmly established, both in the hither life and the Hereafter; and Allah brings the wrongdoers to naught. Allah does what He wills. (25—28)

Hast thou not observed those who have ungratefully cast aside Allah's favour and landed their people in hell and an abode of ruin it is. They have set up rivals to Allah to lead people away from His path. Warn them: Enjoy yourselves awhile, you will then proceed to the Fire. Say to My servants who have believed, that they should observe Prayer and spend secretly and openly out of that which We have given them, before there comes the day wherein there will be neither bargaining nor mutual friendship. (29—32)

Allah is He Who created the heavens and the earth and caused water to come down from the clouds, and brought forth therewith fruits for your sustenance. He has constrained to your service the winds that vessels may sail through the sea by His command, and the rivers also has He constrained to your service. He has also constrained to your service the sun and the moon, both carrying out their functions incessantly; and He has subjected to you the night as well as the day. He has given you all that you asked of Him; and if you try to count the favours of Allah, you will not be able to number them. Verily, man is very unjust, very ungrateful. (33—35)

Call to mind when Abraham prayed: My Lord, make this city inviolate, and keep me and my children away from the worship of idols. My Lord, they have indeed led astray large numbers of people. So whoever follows me, he is certainly of me; and whoever disobeys me in his case also Thou art surely Most Forgiving, Ever Merciful. Our Lord, I have settled some of my progeny in a barren valley near Thy Sacred House, that they may perform Prayer with due observance, Our Lord. So make people's hearts incline towards them and provide them with fruits of all kinds that they may be grateful. Our Lord, Thou certainly knowest that which we conceal and that which we make known; nothing whatsoever is hidden from Allah, whether in the earth or in the heaven. All praise belongs to Allah Who has bestowed upon me, despite my old age, Ishmael and Isaac. Surely My Lord is the Hearer of prayer. My Lord, make me constant in observing Prayer and every one of my children also. Our Lord, of Thy grace accept my prayer.

اَللّٰهُ الَّذِىْ خَلَقَ السَّمٰوٰتِ وَ الْاَرْضَ وَ اَنْزَلَ مِنَ السَّمَآءِ مَآءً فَاَخْرَجَ بِهٖ مِنَ الثَّمَرٰتِ رِزْقًا لَّكُمْ ۚ وَ سَخَّرَ لَكُمُ الْفُلْكَ لِتَجْرِىَ فِى الْبَحْرِ بِاَمْرِهٖ ۚ وَ سَخَّرَ لَكُمُ الْاَنْهٰرَ ۞

وَ سَخَّرَ لَكُمُ الشَّمْسَ وَ الْقَمَرَ دَآئِبَيْنِ ۚ وَ سَخَّرَ لَكُمُ الَّيْلَ وَ النَّهَارَ ۞

وَ اٰتٰىكُمْ مِّنْ كُلِّ مَا سَاَلْتُمُوْهُ ۚ وَ اِنْ تَعُدُّوْا نِعْمَتَ اللّٰهِ لَا تُحْصُوْهَا ۚ اِنَّ الْاِنْسَانَ لَظَلُوْمٌ كَفَّارٌ ۞

وَ اِذْ قَالَ اِبْرٰهِيْمُ رَبِّ اجْعَلْ هٰذَا الْبَلَدَ اٰمِنًا وَّ اجْنُبْنِىْ وَ بَنِىَّ اَنْ نَّعْبُدَ الْاَصْنَامَ ۞

رَبِّ اِنَّهُنَّ اَضْلَلْنَ كَثِيْرًا مِّنَ النَّاسِ ۚ فَمَنْ تَبِعَنِىْ فَاِنَّهٗ مِنِّىْ ۚ وَ مَنْ عَصَانِىْ فَاِنَّكَ غَفُوْرٌ رَّحِيْمٌ ۞

رَبَّنَآ اِنِّىْ اَسْكَنْتُ مِنْ ذُرِّيَّتِىْ بِوَادٍ غَيْرِ ذِىْ زَرْعٍ عِنْدَ بَيْتِكَ الْمُحَرَّمِ ۙ رَبَّنَا لِيُقِيْمُوا الصَّلٰوةَ فَاجْعَلْ اَفْئِدَةً مِّنَ النَّاسِ تَهْوِىْ اِلَيْهِمْ وَ ارْزُقْهُمْ مِّنَ الثَّمَرٰتِ لَعَلَّهُمْ يَشْكُرُوْنَ ۞

رَبَّنَآ اِنَّكَ تَعْلَمُ مَا نُخْفِىْ وَ مَا نُعْلِنُ ۚ وَ مَا يَخْفٰى عَلَى اللّٰهِ مِنْ شَىْءٍ فِى الْاَرْضِ وَ لَا فِى السَّمَآءِ ۞

اَلْحَمْدُ لِلّٰهِ الَّذِىْ وَهَبَ لِىْ عَلَى الْكِبَرِ اِسْمٰعِيْلَ وَ اِسْحٰقَ ۚ اِنَّ رَبِّىْ لَسَمِيْعُ الدُّعَآءِ ۞

رَبِّ اجْعَلْنِىْ مُقِيْمَ الصَّلٰوةِ وَ مِنْ ذُرِّيَّتِىْ ۖ رَبَّنَا وَ تَقَبَّلْ دُعَآءِ ۞

Our Lord, extend Thy forgiveness to me and to my parents and to all the believers on the day when the reckoning is held. (36—42)

Think not that Allah is unaware of what these wrongdoers do. He only gives them respite till the day on which their eyes will stare fixedly in horror, and they will hurry on in fright, their heads lifted up, their gaze directed forward, their minds utterly void. (43—44)

Warn them, O Prophet, of the day when the promised chastisement will come upon them, and the wrongdoers will say: Our Lord, grant us respite for a short while; we will respond to Thy call and will follow the Messengers. They will be reminded: Are you not those who swore that you would never suffer any decline? You are a people who carried on the traditions of a wrongdoing people who passed away before you, whose dwellings you occupy, knowing how We had dealt with them. We have made everything plain to you. They devised their plans; their plans are all within Allah's knowledge. Even if their plans were such as to make the mountains move, they would be brought to naught. (45—47)

Think not that Allah is one who would fail in His promise to His Messengers. Surely, Allah is Mighty, Lord of retribution. The day will come when the heavens and the earth will be changed into other heavens and another earth, and they will all appear before Allah, the Single, the Most Supreme. Thou shalt see the guilty ones secured in chains on that day; their garments will be black as if fashioned out of pitch; and the Fire shall envelop their faces. This will be in the course of Allah's requital of each soul for what it has wrought. Surely, Allah is Swift at reckoning. This is an admonition for mankind, that they may be warned thereby and

رَبَّنَا اغۡفِرۡ لِیۡ وَ لِوَالِدَیَّ وَ لِلۡمُؤۡمِنِیۡنَ یَوۡمَ یَقُوۡمُ الۡحِسَابُ ۚ۠

وَ لَا تَحۡسَبَنَّ اللّٰهَ غَافِلًا عَمَّا یَعۡمَلُ الظّٰلِمُوۡنَ ؕ اِنَّمَا یُؤَخِّرُهُمۡ لِیَوۡمٍ تَشۡخَصُ فِیۡهِ الۡاَبۡصَارُ ۙ

مُهۡطِعِیۡنَ مُقۡنِعِیۡ رُءُوۡسِهِمۡ لَا یَرۡتَدُّ اِلَیۡهِمۡ طَرۡفُهُمۡ ۚ وَ اَفۡـِٕدَتُهُمۡ هَوَآءٌ ؕ

وَ اَنۡذِرِ النَّاسَ یَوۡمَ یَاۡتِیۡهِمُ الۡعَذَابُ فَیَقُوۡلُ الَّذِیۡنَ ظَلَمُوۡا رَبَّنَاۤ اَخِّرۡنَاۤ اِلٰۤی اَجَلٍ قَرِیۡبٍ ۙ نُّجِبۡ دَعۡوَتَكَ وَ نَتَّبِعِ الرُّسُلَ ؕ اَوَ لَمۡ تَكُوۡنُوۡۤا اَقۡسَمۡتُمۡ مِّنۡ قَبۡلُ مَا لَكُمۡ مِّنۡ زَوَالٍ ۙ

وَّ سَكَنۡتُمۡ فِیۡ مَسٰكِنِ الَّذِیۡنَ ظَلَمُوۡۤا اَنۡفُسَهُمۡ وَ تَبَیَّنَ لَكُمۡ كَیۡفَ فَعَلۡنَا بِهِمۡ وَ ضَرَبۡنَا لَكُمُ الۡاَمۡثَالَ

وَ قَدۡ مَكَرُوۡا مَكۡرَهُمۡ وَ عِنۡدَ اللّٰهِ مَكۡرُهُمۡ ؕ وَ اِنۡ كَانَ مَكۡرُهُمۡ لِتَزُوۡلَ مِنۡهُ الۡجِبَالُ

فَلَا تَحۡسَبَنَّ اللّٰهَ مُخۡلِفَ وَعۡدِهٖ رُسُلَهٗ ؕ اِنَّ اللّٰهَ عَزِیۡزٌ ذُو انۡتِقَامٍ ؕ

یَوۡمَ تُبَدَّلُ الۡاَرۡضُ غَیۡرَ الۡاَرۡضِ وَ السَّمٰوٰتُ وَ بَرَزُوۡا لِلّٰهِ الۡوَاحِدِ الۡقَهَّارِ

وَ تَرَی الۡمُجۡرِمِیۡنَ یَوۡمَئِذٍ مُّقَرَّنِیۡنَ فِی الۡاَصۡفَادِ ۚ

سَرَابِیۡلُهُمۡ مِّنۡ قَطِرَانٍ وَّ تَغۡشٰی وُجُوۡهَهُمُ النَّارُ ۙ

لِیَجۡزِیَ اللّٰهُ كُلَّ نَفۡسٍ مَّا كَسَبَتۡ ؕ اِنَّ اللّٰهَ سَرِیۡعُ الۡحِسَابِ

هٰذَا بَلٰغٌ لِّلنَّاسِ وَ لِیُنۡذَرُوۡا بِهٖ وَ لِیَعۡلَمُوۡۤا اَنَّمَا هُوَ

that they may know that Allah is the only One God, and that those possessed of understanding may take heed. (48—53)

غ إِلَٰهٌ وَّاحِدٌ وَّلِيَذَّكَّرَ أُولُوا الْأَلْبَابِ ۞

AL-ḤIJR
(Revealed before Hijra)

In the name of Allah, Most Gracious, Ever Merciful. (1)

I AM ALLAH, THE ALL-SEEING. These are verses of the Perfect Book and of the perspicuous Quran. Those who reject it would often wish that they would be its followers. Leave them occupied with eating and enjoying themselves and being beguiled by vain hopes; soon will they realise the futility of their endeavours. We have never destroyed a township except after a definite decree has gone forth concerning it. No people can outstrip its appointed term, nor can it tarry behind it. They have asserted: O thou to whom this Exhortation has been sent down, surely thou art deluded; else why dost thou not bring down the angels upon us if thou art truthful? Know they not that We do not send down angels but when they are justly due, and then the guilty ones are granted no respite; Surely, We Ourself have sent down this Exhortation, and We will, most surely, safeguard it. (2—10)

We indeed sent Messengers before thee among groups of ancient peoples; but whenever a Messenger came to any of them they mocked at him. Thus do We cause this attitude to become a characteristic of the minds of the guilty ones. Now in their turn this people do not believe in the Quran, though they have before them the example of the former peoples. Even if We were to bestow upon them some extraordinary means of perception and they were to begin to perceive the truth through it, they would be sure to say: Our senses are clouded; in fact we have been bewitched. (11—16)

We have indeed appointed stages for planets in the heaven and have adorned it for beholders; and We have safeguarded the spiritual heaven of true revelation against every rejected Satan.

But if any one having heard a portion of
it stealthily seeks to pervert it, he is pursued
by a bright flame of illuminating truth. We
have also spread out the earth and set
therein firm mountains and caused every
appropriate article to grow and multiply
therein. We have provided therein means
of livelihood for you and for such of Our
creation as you have not to provide for.
There is not a thing but We have unbounded
stores thereof, and We send it down in
regulated quantities. We put in motion winds
carrying moisture, then we send down fresh
water from the clouds, wherewith We provide you with drink. You could not have
stored it up for yourselves. Truly it is We
Who bring to life and We Who cause death
and it is We Who are the sole Inheritor of all.
We know well those of you who go ahead and
We know well those who lag behind. It is thy
Lord Who will gather them all together.
Surely, He is Wise, All-Knowing. (17—26)

We brought man into being from dry
ringing clay which was wrought from black
mud, and the Jinn We had brought into
being before from the fire of a glowing
blast. Call to mind when thy Lord said to
the angels: I am about to bring into being
a man from dry ringing clay. wrought
from black mud; so when I have perfected
him and have enlightened his mind with
My revelation, do ye all fall down in
prostration along with him. In obedience
to this command the angels all fell down
in prostration together, but Iblis did not;
he refused to join those who prostrated.

Allah asked him: What is the matter with thee, that thou wouldst not be among those who have prostrated? He answered I am not one to submit in the manner of man whom Thou hast created from dry ringing clay wrought from black mud. (27—34)

Allah decreed: Then get out hence, for thou art rejected, and be sure that on thee shall rest My curse till the Day of Judgment. He begged: My Lord, grant me respite till the day when they shall be raised up. Allah said: Thou art granted respite till that appointed day. He boasted: Lord, since Thou hast adjudged me as lost, I will make error appear attractive to them in this life and I will lead them all astray, excepting Thy chosen servants from among them. Allah said: This is the path which leads straight to Me. Surely, thou shalt have no power over My true servants, barring those erring ones who choose to follow thee; and, surely hell is the rendezvous for them all. It has seven gates, each gate has a portion of them allotted to it. The righteous will surely be amid gardens and fountains; they will be told: Enter therein, in peace and security. We shall cleanse their hearts of all traces of ill-will; they will be as brethren seated on couches facing one another. They shall never be weary, nor shall they be ejected therefrom. (35—49)

Announce to My servants, O Prophet, that I am the One Most Forgiving Ever Merciful;

قَالَ يٰٓاِبْلِيْسُ مَا لَكَ اَلَّا تَكُوْنَ مَعَ السّٰجِدِيْنَ ۝

قَالَ لَمْ اَكُنْ لِّاَسْجُدَ لِبَشَرٍ خَلَقْتَهٗ مِنْ صَلْصَالٍ مِّنْ حَمَاٍ مَّسْنُوْنٍ ۝

قَالَ فَاخْرُجْ مِنْهَا فَاِنَّكَ رَجِيْمٌ ۝

وَّاِنَّ عَلَيْكَ اللَّعْنَةَ اِلٰى يَوْمِ الدِّيْنِ ۝

قَالَ رَبِّ فَاَنْظِرْنِيْٓ اِلٰى يَوْمِ يُبْعَثُوْنَ ۝

قَالَ فَاِنَّكَ مِنَ الْمُنْظَرِيْنَ ۝

اِلٰى يَوْمِ الْوَقْتِ الْمَعْلُوْمِ ۝

قَالَ رَبِّ بِمَآ اَغْوَيْتَنِيْ لَاُزَيِّنَنَّ لَهُمْ فِى الْاَرْضِ وَلَاُغْوِيَنَّهُمْ اَجْمَعِيْنَ ۝

اِلَّا عِبَادَكَ مِنْهُمُ الْمُخْلَصِيْنَ ۝

قَالَ هٰذَا صِرَاطٌ عَلَيَّ مُسْتَقِيْمٌ ۝

اِنَّ عِبَادِيْ لَيْسَ لَكَ عَلَيْهِمْ سُلْطٰنٌ اِلَّا مَنِ اتَّبَعَكَ مِنَ الْغٰوِيْنَ ۝

وَاِنَّ جَهَنَّمَ لَمَوْعِدُهُمْ اَجْمَعِيْنَ ۝

لَهَا سَبْعَةُ اَبْوَابٍ لِكُلِّ بَابٍ مِّنْهُمْ جُزْءٌ مَّقْسُوْمٌ ۝

اِنَّ الْمُتَّقِيْنَ فِيْ جَنّٰتٍ وَّعُيُوْنٍ ۝

اُدْخُلُوْهَا بِسَلٰمٍ اٰمِنِيْنَ ۝

وَنَزَعْنَا مَا فِيْ صُدُوْرِهِمْ مِّنْ غِلٍّ اِخْوَانًا عَلٰى سُرُرٍ مُّتَقٰبِلِيْنَ ۝

لَا يَمَسُّهُمْ فِيْهَا نَصَبٌ وَّمَا هُمْ مِّنْهَا بِمُخْرَجِيْنَ ۝

نَبِّئْ عِبَادِيْٓ اَنِّيْٓ اَنَا الْغَفُوْرُ الرَّحِيْمُ ۝

and that it is My chastisement that is the truly grievous chastisement. Tell them about Abraham's guests. When they came to him they greeted him with: Peace. He said: We feel afraid of your errand. They tried to reassure him: Have no fear. We give thee glad tidings of a learned son. Abraham enquired: Do you give me the tidings despite my old age? On what do you base the tidings? They answered: We have given thee true tidings; do not, therefore, be despondent. Abraham observed: It is only the misguided ones who despair of the mercy of their Lord. Well, now, tell me what errand have you been sent on? They made answer: We have been sent to a guilty people who are condemned to ruin, excepting the family of Lot. We must save them all; only we surmise that his wife will be among those who remain behind and will be lost. (50—61)

When the messengers came to Lot and his family, he observed: You must be strangers here. They answered: The fact is we have come to thee with tidings of that about which they doubted. We have brought thee sure tidings and we are truthful. Set out with thy family some time in the latter part of the night, and do thou follow in their wake. Let none of you look back, and proceed to where you are commanded. We communicated to him Our decree that the guilty ones would be utterly destroyed by morning. (62—67)

The people of the city came to Lot rejoicing in the conviction that they would now have him securely in their power. He expostulated with them: These are my guests, so do not humiliate me;

وَاَنَّ عَذَابِیْ هُوَ الْعَذَابُ الْاَلِیْمُ ۝

وَنَبِّئْهُمْ عَنْ ضَیْفِ اِبْرٰهِیْمَ ۝

اِذْ دَخَلُوْا عَلَیْهِ فَقَالُوْا سَلٰمًا ؕ قَالَ اِنَّا مِنْكُمْ وَجِلُوْنَ ۝

قَالُوْا لَا تَوْجَلْ اِنَّا نُبَشِّرُكَ بِغُلٰمٍ عَلِیْمٍ ۝

قَالَ اَبَشَّرْتُمُوْنِیْ عَلٰۤی اَنْ مَّسَّنِیَ الْكِبَرُ فَبِمَ تُبَشِّرُوْنَ ۝

قَالُوْا بَشَّرْنٰكَ بِالْحَقِّ فَلَا تَكُنْ مِّنَ الْقٰنِطِیْنَ ۝

قَالَ وَمَنْ یَّقْنَطُ مِنْ رَّحْمَةِ رَبِّهٖۤ اِلَّا الضَّآلُّوْنَ ۝

قَالَ فَمَا خَطْبُكُمْ اَیُّهَا الْمُرْسَلُوْنَ ۝

قَالُوْۤا اِنَّاۤ اُرْسِلْنَاۤ اِلٰی قَوْمٍ مُّجْرِمِیْنَ ۝

اِلَّاۤ اٰلَ لُوْطٍ ؕ اِنَّا لَمُنَجُّوْهُمْ اَجْمَعِیْنَ ۝

اِلَّا امْرَاَتَهٗ قَدَّرْنَاۤ ۙ اِنَّهَا لَمِنَ الْغٰبِرِیْنَ ۝

فَلَمَّا جَآءَ اٰلَ لُوْطِ ۨالْمُرْسَلُوْنَ ۝

قَالَ اِنَّكُمْ قَوْمٌ مُّنْكَرُوْنَ ۝

قَالُوْا بَلْ جِئْنٰكَ بِمَا كَانُوْا فِیْهِ یَمْتَرُوْنَ ۝

وَاَتَیْنٰكَ بِالْحَقِّ وَاِنَّا لَصٰدِقُوْنَ ۝

فَاَسْرِ بِاَهْلِكَ بِقِطْعٍ مِّنَ الَّیْلِ وَاتَّبِعْ اَدْبَارَهُمْ وَلَا یَلْتَفِتْ مِنْكُمْ اَحَدٌ وَّامْضُوْا حَیْثُ تُؤْمَرُوْنَ ۝

وَقَضَیْنَاۤ اِلَیْهِ ذٰلِكَ الْاَمْرَ اَنَّ دَابِرَ هٰۤؤُلَآءِ مَقْطُوْعٌ مُّصْبِحِیْنَ ۝

وَجَآءَ اَهْلُ الْمَدِیْنَةِ یَسْتَبْشِرُوْنَ ۝

قَالَ اِنَّ هٰۤؤُلَآءِ ضَیْفِیْ فَلَا تَفْضَحُوْنِ ۝

fear Allah and disgrace me not. They said: Did we not forbid thee extending hospitality to strangers? Lot remonstrated with them: If you are bent upon taking action, there are my daughters, you can treat them as hostages for your security against any harm you may apprehend from my guests. (By thy life, O Prophet, thy opponents also are wandering distractedly in their intoxication!) Then the chastisement seized them at sunrise. We turned the city upside down, and We rained upon them stones of clay. Surely, in this there are Signs for people of intelligence. The city lies along a well known route. Surely, in this is a Sign for those who believe. The People of the Wood were also wrongdoers; and We chastised them also. Both these cities lie along an easily identifiable way. (68—80)

وَاتَّقُوا اللّٰهَ وَلَا تُخْزُونِ ۝

قَالُوٓا اَوَلَمْ نَنْهَكَ عَنِ الْعٰلَمِيْنَ ۝

قَالَ هٰٓؤُلَآءِ بَنٰتِيۤ اِنْ كُنْتُمْ فٰعِلِيْنَ ۝

لَعَمْرُكَ اِنَّهُمْ لَفِيْ سَكْرَتِهِمْ يَعْمَهُوْنَ ۝

فَاَخَذَتْهُمُ الصَّيْحَةُ مُشْرِقِيْنَ ۝

فَجَعَلْنَا عَالِيَهَا سَافِلَهَا وَ اَمْطَرْنَا عَلَيْهِمْ حِجَارَةً مِّنْ سِجِّيْلٍ ۝

اِنَّ فِيْ ذٰلِكَ لَاٰيٰتٍ لِّلْمُتَوَسِّمِيْنَ ۝

وَاِنَّهَا لَبِسَبِيْلٍ مُّقِيْمٍ ۝

اِنَّ فِيْ ذٰلِكَ لَاٰيَةً لِّلْمُؤْمِنِيْنَ ۝

وَاِنْ كَانَ اَصْحٰبُ الْاَيْكَةِ لَظٰلِمِيْنَ ۝

The People of Hijr also rejected the Messengers as liars. We gave them Our Signs too, but they turned away from them. They used to hew out houses in the mountains, dwelling therein in security. The chastisement seized them in the morning; and all that they had worked at availed them nothing. (81—85)

فَانْتَقَمْنَا مِنْهُمْ وَاِنَّهُمَا لَبِاِمَامٍ مُّبِيْنٍ ۝

وَلَقَدْ كَذَّبَ اَصْحٰبُ الْحِجْرِ الْمُرْسَلِيْنَ ۝

وَاٰتَيْنٰهُمْ اٰيٰتِنَا فَكَانُوْا عَنْهَا مُعْرِضِيْنَ ۝

وَكَانُوْا يَنْحِتُوْنَ مِنَ الْجِبَالِ بُيُوْتًا اٰمِنِيْنَ ۝

فَاَخَذَتْهُمُ الصَّيْحَةُ مُصْبِحِيْنَ ۝

فَمَآ اَغْنٰى عَنْهُمْ مَّا كَانُوْا يَكْسِبُوْنَ ۝

We have created the heavens and the earth and all that is between the two in accordance with the requirements of truth and wisdom, and the appointed Hour is sure to come; so forbear generously. Verily, thy Lord is the Great Creator, the All-Knowing. We have indeed bestowed upon thee the seven oft-recited verses of the Fatiha, and the Great Quran. So do not lift thine eyes towards that which We have bestowed upon some of them of

وَ مَا خَلَقْنَا السَّمٰوٰتِ وَ الْاَرْضَ وَمَا بَيْنَهُمَآ اِلَّا بِالْحَقِّ ۝

وَاِنَّ السَّاعَةَ لَاٰتِيَةٌ فَاصْفَحِ الصَّفْحَ الْجَمِيْلَ ۝

اِنَّ رَبَّكَ هُوَ الْخَلَّاقُ الْعَلِيْمُ ۝

وَلَقَدْ اٰتَيْنٰكَ سَبْعًا مِّنَ الْمَثَانِيْ وَالْقُرْاٰنَ الْعَظِيْمَ ۝

لَا تَمُدَّنَّ عَيْنَيْكَ اِلٰى مَا مَتَّعْنَا بِهٖٓ اَزْوَاجًا مِّنْهُمْ

temporary provision, and grieve not over them and continue to be kindly gracious towards the believers. Proclaim: I am indeed, a plain Warner; for We have determined the punishment for those who have been assigned different tasks in opposition to thee; who have pronounced the Quran a collection of falsehoods. So, by thy Lord, We shall question them all concerning that which they used to do. Declare thou openly that which thou art commanded to proclaim and turn aside from those who ascribe partners to Allah. (86—95)

لَا تَحْزَنْ عَلَيْهِمْ وَاخْفِضْ جَنَاحَكَ لِلْمُؤْمِنِيْنَ ۞

وَقُلْ اِنِّىْٓ اَنَا النَّذِيْرُ الْمُبِيْنُ ۞

كَمَآ اَنْزَلْنَا عَلَى الْمُقْتَسِمِيْنَ ۞

الَّذِيْنَ جَعَلُوا الْقُرْاٰنَ عِضِيْنَ ۞

فَوَرَبِّكَ لَنَسْئَلَنَّهُمْ اَجْمَعِيْنَ ۞

عَمَّا كَانُوْا يَعْمَلُوْنَ ۞

فَاصْدَعْ بِمَا تُؤْمَرُ وَاَعْرِضْ عَنِ الْمُشْرِكِيْنَ ۞

اِنَّا كَفَيْنٰكَ الْمُسْتَهْزِئِيْنَ ۞

We will safeguard thee against the scoffers who set up other gods with Allah; soon will they know the consequences of their enormity. Indeed, We know that thou art sore grieved by that which they say; but continue to glorify thy Lord with His praise, and be of those who render obedience to Him, and carry on the worship of thy Lord till death comes to thee. (96—100)

الَّذِيْنَ يَجْعَلُوْنَ مَعَ اللّٰهِ اِلٰهًا اٰخَرَ فَسَوْفَ يَعْلَمُوْنَ ۞

وَلَقَدْ نَعْلَمُ اَنَّكَ يَضِيْقُ صَدْرُكَ بِمَا يَقُوْلُوْنَ ۞

فَسَبِّحْ بِحَمْدِ رَبِّكَ وَكُنْ مِّنَ السّٰجِدِيْنَ ۞

وَاعْبُدْ رَبَّكَ حَتّٰى يَأْتِيَكَ الْيَقِيْنُ ۞

AL-NAHL

(Revealed before Hijra)

بِسْمِ اللهِ الرَّحْمٰنِ الرَّحِيمِ ۝

In the name of Allah, Most Gracious, Ever Merciful. (1)

اَتٰۤى اَمْرُ اللهِ فَلَا تَسْتَعْجِلُوهُ ۖ سُبْحٰنَهٗ وَتَعٰلٰى عَمَّا يُشْرِكُوْنَ ۝

The decree of Allah is at hand, so seek ye not to hasten it. Holy is He, and exalted far above that which they associate with Him. He sends down the angels with revelation by His command on whomsoever of His servants He pleases, directing: Warn people that there is no god beside Me, so make Me alone your shield against all ill. He has created the heavens and the earth in accordance with the requirements of truth and wisdom. Exalted is He far above that which they associate with Him. He has created man from a drop of fluid, and lo: he becomes a bold wrangler! He has created cattle for your benefit; they are a source of warmth for you and you have other uses for them and you also eat of their flesh; and they are a credit for you when you drive them forth to pasture in the morning and when you bring them home in the evening. They carry your loads to places which you could not reach without great hardship to yourselves. Surely, your Lord is Compassionate, Ever Merciful. He has created horses, mules and donkeys that you may ride them, and also as adornment; and He will create for that purpose other means which you do not yet know. Allah points out the right way, for some ways are devious. Had He enforced His will, He would have guided you all. (2—10)

يُنَزِّلُ الْمَلٰٓئِكَةَ بِالرُّوحِ مِنْ اَمْرِهٖ عَلٰى مَنْ يَّشَآءُ مِنْ عِبَادِهٖۤ اَنْ اَنْذِرُوۤا اَنَّهٗ لَاۤ اِلٰهَ اِلَّاۤ اَنَا فَاتَّقُوْنِ ۝

خَلَقَ السَّمٰوٰتِ وَالْاَرْضَ بِالْحَقِّ ۚ تَعٰلٰى عَمَّا يُشْرِكُوْنَ ۝

خَلَقَ الْاِنْسَانَ مِنْ نُّطْفَةٍ فَاِذَا هُوَ خَصِيْمٌ مُّبِيْنٌ ۝

وَالْاَنْعَامَ خَلَقَهَا ۚ لَكُمْ فِيْهَا دِفْءٌ وَّمَنَافِعُ وَمِنْهَا تَاْكُلُوْنَ ۝

وَلَكُمْ فِيْهَا جَمَالٌ حِيْنَ تُرِيْحُوْنَ وَحِيْنَ تَسْرَحُوْنَ ۝

وَتَحْمِلُ اَثْقَالَكُمْ اِلٰى بَلَدٍ لَّمْ تَكُوْنُوْا بٰلِغِيْهِ اِلَّا بِشِقِّ الْاَنْفُسِ ۚ اِنَّ رَبَّكُمْ لَرَءُوْفٌ رَّحِيْمٌ ۝

وَّالْخَيْلَ وَالْبِغَالَ وَالْحَمِيْرَ لِتَرْكَبُوْهَا وَزِيْنَةً ۚ وَيَخْلُقُ مَا لَا تَعْلَمُوْنَ ۝

وَعَلَى اللهِ قَصْدُ السَّبِيْلِ وَمِنْهَا جَآئِرٌ ۚ وَلَوْ شَآءَ لَهَدٰىكُمْ اَجْمَعِيْنَ ۝

He it is Who sends down water for you from the clouds, from it you drink and with it grow trees on which you pasture your cattle. (11)

هُوَ الَّذِيْۤ اَنْزَلَ مِنَ السَّمَآءِ مَآءً لَّكُمْ مِّنْهُ شَرَابٌ وَّمِنْهُ شَجَرٌ فِيْهِ تُسِيْمُوْنَ ۝

Therewith He grows for you corn, and the olive and the date-palm and the grape, and all kinds of fruits. Surely, in that is a Sign for a people who reflect. He has constrained to your service the night and the day and the sun and the moon; and the stars too have been constrained to your service by His command. Surely in all this there are Signs for a people who make use of their understanding. In that which He has created for you in the earth of diverse types of articles, there is a Sign for people who take heed. He it is Who has constrained the sea to your service that you may eat fresh sea-food therefrom and may take out therefrom articles that you wear as ornaments. Thou seest the vessels ploughing through it that you may voyage across the oceans seeking His bounty and that you may be grateful. He has set in the earth firm mountains lest it roll beneath you, and has made rivers and tracks that you may find your way; and He has set up other marks. By these and by the stars they set their course. (12—17)

Is He, then, Who creates like one who creates not? Will you not, then, take heed? If you try to count the favours of Allah, you will not be able to number them. Surely, Allah is Most Forgiving, Ever Merciful. Allah knows all that you conceal and all that you disclose. Those on whom they call beside Allah create not anything, but are themselves created; they are lifeless, not living; and they know not when they will be raised up. (18—22)

يُنْۢبِتُ لَكُمْ بِهِ الزَّرْعَ وَ الزَّيْتُوْنَ وَالنَّخِيْلَ وَالْاَعْنَابَ وَمِنْ كُلِّ الثَّمَرٰتِ ۗ اِنَّ فِيْ ذٰلِكَ لَاٰيَةً لِّقَوْمٍ يَّتَفَكَّرُوْنَ ۝

وَ سَخَّرَ لَكُمُ الَّيْلَ وَ النَّهَارَ ۙ وَ الشَّمْسَ وَالْقَمَرَ ۚ وَالنُّجُوْمُ مُسَخَّرٰتٌ بِاَمْرِهٖ ۗ اِنَّ فِيْ ذٰلِكَ لَاٰيٰتٍ لِّقَوْمٍ يَّعْقِلُوْنَ ۝

وَمَا ذَرَاَ لَكُمْ فِي الْاَرْضِ مُخْتَلِفًا اَلْوَانُهٗ ۗ اِنَّ فِيْ ذٰلِكَ لَاٰيَةً لِّقَوْمٍ يَّذَّكَّرُوْنَ ۝

وَهُوَ الَّذِيْ سَخَّرَ الْبَحْرَ لِتَأْكُلُوْا مِنْهُ لَحْمًا طَرِيًّا وَّتَسْتَخْرِجُوْا مِنْهُ حِلْيَةً تَلْبَسُوْنَهَا ۚ وَ تَرَى الْفُلْكَ مَوَاخِرَ فِيْهِ وَلِتَبْتَغُوْا مِنْ فَضْلِهٖ وَلَعَلَّكُمْ تَشْكُرُوْنَ ۝

وَاَلْقٰى فِي الْاَرْضِ رَوَاسِيَ اَنْ تَمِيْدَ بِكُمْ وَاَنْهٰرًا وَّسُبُلًا لَّعَلَّكُمْ تَهْتَدُوْنَ ۝

وَعَلٰمٰتٍ ۗ وَ بِالنَّجْمِ هُمْ يَهْتَدُوْنَ ۝

اَفَمَنْ يَّخْلُقُ كَمَنْ لَّا يَخْلُقُ ۗ اَفَلَا تَذَكَّرُوْنَ ۝

وَاِنْ تَعُدُّوْا نِعْمَةَ اللّٰهِ لَا تُحْصُوْهَا ۗ اِنَّ اللّٰهَ لَغَفُوْرٌ رَّحِيْمٌ ۝

وَاللّٰهُ يَعْلَمُ مَا تُسِرُّوْنَ وَمَا تُعْلِنُوْنَ ۝

وَالَّذِيْنَ يَدْعُوْنَ مِنْ دُوْنِ اللّٰهِ لَا يَخْلُقُوْنَ شَيْئًا وَّهُمْ يُخْلَقُوْنَ ۝

اَمْوَاتٌ غَيْرُ اَحْيَاءٍ ۚ وَمَا يَشْعُرُوْنَ ۙ اَيَّانَ يُبْعَثُوْنَ ۝

Your God is One God. The minds of those who do not believe in the Hereafter are strangers to truth, and they are arrogant. Of a surety, Allah knows that which they conceal and that which they disclose. Surely, He loves not the arrogant. When it is said to them: How glorious is that which your Lord has sent down! they retort: Only old wives' tales! The consequence will be that they shall bear their burdens in full on the Day of Judgment, and also the burdens of those ignorant ones whom they lead astray. Evil is that which they bear! (23—26)

Those who were before them also devised plans against their Messengers, but Allah approached the structure of their plans at their very foundations, so that the roof crashed upon them from above them; and the chastisement came upon them from where they knew not. Then on the Day of Judgment He will humiliate them and will enquire from them: Where are those alleged partners of Mine for whose sake you opposed My Messengers? Those endowed with knowledge will say: This day humiliation and affliction will surely befall the disbelievers. (27—28)

Those whom the angels cause to die while they are wronging their souls, will offer submission, pleading: We used not to do any evil. They will be told: Indeed? Allah knows well what you used to do. Enter now the gates of hell, to abide therein. Evil indeed is the abode of the arrogant. (29—30)

When it is said to the righteous: How glorious is that which your Lord has sent down! they answer: Indeed it is the best. For those who do good is good in this world; and the abode of the Hereafter is even better. Excellent indeed is the abode of the righteous:

اِلٰهُكُمْ اِلٰهٌ وَّاحِدٌ ۚ فَالَّذِيْنَ لَا يُؤْمِنُوْنَ بِالْاٰخِرَةِ قُلُوْبُهُمْ مُّنْكِرَةٌ وَّهُمْ مُّسْتَكْبِرُوْنَ ۞

لَا جَرَمَ اَنَّ اللّٰهَ يَعْلَمُ مَا يُسِرُّوْنَ وَمَا يُعْلِنُوْنَ ۚ اِنَّهٗ لَا يُحِبُّ الْمُسْتَكْبِرِيْنَ ۞

وَاِذَا قِيْلَ لَهُمْ مَّاذَآ اَنْزَلَ رَبُّكُمْ ۙ قَالُوْٓا اَسَاطِيْرُ الْاَوَّلِيْنَ ۞

لِيَحْمِلُوْٓا اَوْزَارَهُمْ كَامِلَةً يَّوْمَ الْقِيٰمَةِ ۙ وَمِنْ اَوْزَارِ الَّذِيْنَ يُضِلُّوْنَهُمْ بِغَيْرِ عِلْمٍ ۗ اَلَا سَآءَ مَا يَزِرُوْنَ ۞

قَدْ مَكَرَ الَّذِيْنَ مِنْ قَبْلِهِمْ فَاَتَى اللّٰهُ بُنْيَانَهُمْ مِّنَ الْقَوَاعِدِ فَخَرَّ عَلَيْهِمُ السَّقْفُ مِنْ فَوْقِهِمْ وَاَتٰىهُمُ الْعَذَابُ مِنْ حَيْثُ لَا يَشْعُرُوْنَ ۞

ثُمَّ يَوْمَ الْقِيٰمَةِ يُخْزِيْهِمْ وَيَقُوْلُ اَيْنَ شُرَكَآءِيَ الَّذِيْنَ كُنْتُمْ تُشَآقُّوْنَ فِيْهِمْ ۚ قَالَ الَّذِيْنَ اُوْتُوا الْعِلْمَ اِنَّ الْخِزْيَ الْيَوْمَ وَالسُّوْٓءَ عَلَى الْكٰفِرِيْنَ ۞

الَّذِيْنَ تَتَوَفّٰىهُمُ الْمَلٰٓئِكَةُ ظَالِمِيْٓ اَنْفُسِهِمْ ۖ فَاَلْقَوُا السَّلَمَ مَا كُنَّا نَعْمَلُ مِنْ سُوْٓءٍ ۚ بَلٰٓى اِنَّ اللّٰهَ عَلِيْمٌ بِمَا كُنْتُمْ تَعْمَلُوْنَ ۞

فَادْخُلُوْٓا اَبْوَابَ جَهَنَّمَ خٰلِدِيْنَ فِيْهَا ۖ فَلَبِئْسَ مَثْوَى الْمُتَكَبِّرِيْنَ ۞

وَقِيْلَ لِلَّذِيْنَ اتَّقَوْا مَاذَآ اَنْزَلَ رَبُّكُمْ ۗ قَالُوْا خَيْرًا ۗ لِلَّذِيْنَ اَحْسَنُوْا فِيْ هٰذِهِ الدُّنْيَا حَسَنَةٌ ۗ وَلَدَارُ الْاٰخِرَةِ خَيْرٌ ۗ وَلَنِعْمَ دَارُ الْمُتَّقِيْنَ ۞

Gardens of Eternity, which they will
enter, through which rivers flow. They will
have therein all that they wish for. Thus
does Allah reward the righteous, those
whom the angels cause to die while they
are pure, greeting them with: Upon you
is peace for all time! Enter into Paradise
because of that which you used to do.
(31—33)

جَنَّتُ عَدْنٍ يَّدْخُلُوْنَهَا تَجْرِىْ مِنْ تَحْتِهَا الْاَنْهٰرُ
لَهُمْ فِيْهَا مَا يَشَآءُوْنَ ۚ كَذٰلِكَ يَجْزِى اللّٰهُ
الْمُتَّقِيْنَ ۟
الَّذِيْنَ تَتَوَفّٰىهُمُ الْمَلٰٓئِكَةُ طَيِّبِيْنَ ۙ يَقُوْلُوْنَ سَلٰمٌ
عَلَيْكُمُ ۙ ادْخُلُوا الْجَنَّةَ بِمَا كُنْتُمْ تَعْمَلُوْنَ ۟

What do the disbelievers wait for, except that the angels should come upon
them or that the decree of thy Lord should
come to pass? Thus did those before them.
Allah did not wrong them but they used
to wrong themselves. So the evil consequences of that which they did overtook
them, and the chastisement at which they
used to mock encompassed them. (34—35)

هَلْ يَنْظُرُوْنَ اِلَّا اَنْ تَأْتِيَهُمُ الْمَلٰٓئِكَةُ اَوْ يَأْتِىَ
اَمْرُ رَبِّكَ ۚ كَذٰلِكَ فَعَلَ الَّذِيْنَ مِنْ قَبْلِهِمْ ۚ وَمَا ظَلَمَهُمُ
اللّٰهُ وَلٰكِنْ كَانُوْٓا اَنْفُسَهُمْ يَظْلِمُوْنَ ۟
فَاَصَابَهُمْ سَيِّاٰتُ مَا عَمِلُوْا وَحَاقَ بِهِمْ مَّا كَانُوْا
بِهٖ يَسْتَهْزِءُوْنَ ۟

Those who ascribe partners to Allah
assert: If Allah had so willed we would
not have worshipped anything beside
Him, neither we nor our fathers, nor would
we have forbidden anything without His
command. So did those who denied the
truth before them. Do they not consider
that the duty of the Messengers is but to
convey the Message clearly? We did raise
among every people a Messenger who
enjoined: Worship Allah alone and shun
every transgressor. Then of them there
were those who took heed and whom Allah
guided, and there were those who became
deserving of ruin. So travel through the
earth and observe what was the end of those
who rejected the Messengers. If thou art
solicitous of their being guided, then know
that Allah guides not those who lead
others astray; nor have they any helpers.
They swear their strongest oaths by Allah
that Allah will not raise up those who
die. On the contrary, this is a promise
He has charged Himself with (but most

وَقَالَ الَّذِيْنَ اَشْرَكُوْا لَوْ شَآءَ اللّٰهُ مَا عَبَدْنَا مِنْ
دُوْنِهٖ مِنْ شَيْءٍ نَّحْنُ وَلَاٰ اٰبَآؤُنَا وَلَا حَرَّمْنَا مِنْ
دُوْنِهٖ مِنْ شَيْءٍ ۚ كَذٰلِكَ فَعَلَ الَّذِيْنَ مِنْ قَبْلِهِمْ ۚ
فَهَلْ عَلَى الرُّسُلِ اِلَّا الْبَلٰغُ الْمُبِيْنُ ۟
وَلَقَدْ بَعَثْنَا فِىْ كُلِّ اُمَّةٍ رَّسُوْلًا اَنِ اعْبُدُوا اللّٰهَ
وَاجْتَنِبُوا الطَّاغُوْتَ ۚ فَمِنْهُمْ مَّنْ هَدَى اللّٰهُ
وَمِنْهُمْ مَّنْ حَقَّتْ عَلَيْهِ الضَّلٰلَةُ ۚ فَسِيْرُوْا فِى الْاَرْضِ
فَانْظُرُوْا كَيْفَ كَانَ عَاقِبَةُ الْمُكَذِّبِيْنَ ۟
اِنْ تَحْرِصْ عَلٰى هُدٰىهُمْ فَاِنَّ اللّٰهَ لَا يَهْدِىْ مَنْ
يُّضِلُّ وَمَا لَهُمْ مِّنْ نّٰصِرِيْنَ ۟
وَاَقْسَمُوْا بِاللّٰهِ جَهْدَ اَيْمَانِهِمْ ۙ لَا يَبْعَثُ اللّٰهُ مَنْ
يَّمُوْتُ ۚ بَلٰى وَعْدًا عَلَيْهِ حَقًّا وَّلٰكِنَّ اَكْثَرَ النَّاسِ

people know not) that He may make
clear to them the reality concerning which
they differ today and that those who disbelieve may realise that they had lied.
When We have willed a matter, it is for
Us only to say concerning it: Be; and
it is. (36—41)

We will surely provide those who have
migrated from their homes for the sake
of Allah after having been wronged, being
steadfast and putting their trust in their
Lord, with a goodly abode in this world; and
truly the reward of the Hereafter is even
greater if the disbelievers but knew. (42—43)

Before thee also We sent as Messengers
only men to whom We vouchsafed revelation; and if you do not know this, O disbelievers, then enquire from those who
believe in this Reminder. We sent them
with clear Signs and Scriptures. We have
sent down this Reminder to thee that thou
mayest expound to people Allah's commandments that have been sent down to
them through thee, and that they may
reflect over them. (44—45)

Do those who design evil against thee
feel secure that Allah will not humiliate
them in the land, or that the punishment
of which they have been warned will not
come upon them whence they do not
perceive; or that He will not destroy them
in the course of their journeyings to and
fro? They should know that they shall
never be able to frustrate His design. Or,
that He will not destroy them through
a process of attrition? Your Lord is indeed
Compassionate, Ever Merciful towards the
believers. Have the disbelievers, despite
their constant humiliation, never been
impelled to observe that the shadows of
everything that Allah has created move
from the right and from the left in submission to Allah? Whatever is in the
heavens and whatever creature is in the
earth, and the angels also all submit
humbly to Allah, and they behave not
proudly. They fear their Lord in Whose
power they are and do that which they
are commanded. (46—51)

Allah has ever commanded: Take not for worship two gods. There is only One God. So fear Me alone. To Him belongs whatsoever is in the heavens and in the earth, and obedience is due to Him alone. Will you then take any other than Allah as your Protector? Whatever blessing you have is from Allah, and when distress afflicts you it is to Him that you cry for help. Then as soon as He removes the distress from you, some of you ascribe partners to their Lord, thus denying that which We have bestowed upon them. Well then, enjoy yourselves awhile; you will soon realise the consequences of your conduct. They set apart a portion of that which We have bestowed upon them for the false gods of which they know nothing. Allah bears witness you will certainly be called to account for that which you fabricate. (52—57)

They ascribe daughters to Allah (Holy is He!) and for themselves they have what they desire. When one of them is told of the birth of a female child, his face is overcast with gloom and he is deeply agitated. He seeks to hide himself from the people because of the ominous news he has had. Shall he preserve it despite the disgrace involved or bury it in the ground? Evil is that which they judge. Those who do not believe in the Hereafter are in evil case. All high attributes belong to Allah alone. He is the Mighty, the Wise. (58—61)

If Allah were to punish people instantly for their wrongdoing, He would not spare a living creature on the earth, but He grants them respite till an appointed term that they may make amends. When their time

255

for punishment arrives they cannot tarry a single hour nor can they go ahead. They attribute to Allah that which they dislike for themselves, and they assert with confidence the falsehood that a happy state is assured for them. Undoubtedly, they are destined for the Fire; and therein shall they be abandoned. (62—63)

Allah bears witness: We did send Messengers to the people before thee; but Satan made their doings appear attractive to them; so he is their partner this day, and they shall have a grievous punishment. We have now sent down the Book to thee that it may expound to them that concerning which they differ and as a guidance and mercy for those who believe therein. It is Allah Who has sent down water from heaven and has quickened therewith the earth after its death. Surely, in that is a Sign for a people who would listen to the truth. (64—66)

There is a lesson for you in the cattle. We provide you with a drink out of that which is in their bellies; that is, from betwixt the faeces and the blood We provide milk pure and pleasant for those who drink it. Of the fruits of date-palms and the grapes you obtain intoxicating drinks, and also pure and wholesome food. Surely, in that is a Sign for a people who make use of their understanding. Thy Lord directed the bee: Prepare thou hives in the hills and in the trees and in the trellises that they put up, and eat of every kind of fruit and follow the ways appointed for thee by thy Lord which have been made easy for thee. There comes out of the bellies of the bees a drink of varying hues, possessing healing qualities for people. Surely, in that is a Sign for a people who reflect. Allah creates you, then He causes you to die; and there are some among you who are made to revert to a decrepit old age in which they lose all knowledge after having acquired it. Surely, Allah is All-Knowing, Determiner of the measure. (67—71)

جَآءَ اَجَلُهُمْ لَا يَسْتَأْخِرُوْنَ سَاعَةً وَّ لَا يَسْتَقْدِمُوْنَ ۞

وَ يَجْعَلُوْنَ لِلّٰهِ مَا يَكْرَهُوْنَ وَ تَصِفُ اَلْسِنَتُهُمُ الْكَذِبَ اَنَّ لَهُمُ الْحُسْنٰى لَا جَرَمَ اَنَّ لَهُمُ النَّارَ وَ اَنَّهُمْ مُّفْرَطُوْنَ ۞

تَاللّٰهِ لَقَدْ اَرْسَلْنَآ اِلٰٓى اُمَمٍ مِّنْ قَبْلِكَ فَزَيَّنَ لَهُمُ الشَّيْطٰنُ اَعْمَالَهُمْ فَهُوَ وَلِيُّهُمُ الْيَوْمَ وَ لَهُمْ عَذَابٌ اَلِيْمٌ ۞

وَمَآ اَنْزَلْنَا عَلَيْكَ الْكِتٰبَ اِلَّا لِتُبَيِّنَ لَهُمُ الَّذِى اخْتَلَفُوْا فِيْهِ وَهُدًى وَّ رَحْمَةً لِّقَوْمٍ يُّؤْمِنُوْنَ ۞

وَاللّٰهُ اَنْزَلَ مِنَ السَّمَآءِ مَآءً فَاَحْيَا بِهِ الْاَرْضَ بَعْدَ مَوْتِهَا ۚ اِنَّ فِيْ ذٰلِكَ لَاٰيَةً لِّقَوْمٍ يَّسْمَعُوْنَ ۞

وَاِنَّ لَكُمْ فِى الْاَنْعَامِ لَعِبْرَةً ۚ نُسْقِيْكُمْ مِّمَّا فِيْ بُطُوْنِهِ مِنْۢ بَيْنِ فَرْثٍ وَّ دَمٍ لَّبَنًا خَالِصًا سَآئِغًا لِّلشّٰرِبِيْنَ ۞

وَ مِنْ ثَمَرٰتِ النَّخِيْلِ وَ الْاَعْنَابِ تَتَّخِذُوْنَ مِنْهُ سَكَرًا وَّ رِزْقًا حَسَنًا ۚ اِنَّ فِيْ ذٰلِكَ لَاٰيَةً لِّقَوْمٍ يَّعْقِلُوْنَ ۞

وَ اَوْحٰى رَبُّكَ اِلَى النَّحْلِ اَنِ اتَّخِذِىْ مِنَ الْجِبَالِ بُيُوْتًا وَّ مِنَ الشَّجَرِ وَ مِمَّا يَعْرِشُوْنَ ۞

ثُمَّ كُلِىْ مِنْ كُلِّ الثَّمَرٰتِ فَاسْلُكِىْ سُبُلَ رَبِّكِ ذُلُلًا ۚ يَخْرُجُ مِنْۢ بُطُوْنِهَا شَرَابٌ مُّخْتَلِفٌ اَلْوَانُهُ فِيْهِ شِفَآءٌ لِّلنَّاسِ ۚ اِنَّ فِيْ ذٰلِكَ لَاٰيَةً لِّقَوْمٍ يَّتَفَكَّرُوْنَ ۞

وَاللّٰهُ خَلَقَكُمْ ثُمَّ يَتَوَفّٰىكُمْ وَ مِنْكُمْ مَّنْ يُّرَدُّ اِلٰٓى اَرْذَلِ الْعُمُرِ لِكَىْ لَا يَعْلَمَ بَعْدَ عِلْمٍ شَيْئًا ۚ اِنَّ اللّٰهَ عَلِيْمٌ

Allah has favoured some of you above others in the matter of worldly provision; but those more favoured will by no means restore a portion of their provision to those under their control, so that they may be equal sharers therein. Will they then deny the favour of Allah? Allah has made for you consorts of your own kind and has produced for you from your consorts, sons and grandsons, and has provided for you all manner of wholesome things. Will they then believe in that which will perish and deny the favour of Allah? They worship beside Allah such as have no power to bestow upon them anything from the heavens or the earth, nor can they have such power. Then fabricate not similitudes concerning Allah. Surely, Allah knows everything and you know nothing. (72—75)

Allah draws attention to the case of a person who is owned by another and has no power over anything, and the case of one whom We have provided with a fair provision from Ourself, and he spends thereof secretly and openly. Can they be equal? All praise belongs to Allah, but most of them know not. Allah also draws attention to the case of two men: One of them is dumb, having no capacity to achieve anything, and is a burden on his master; whithersoever he sends him, he brings back no good. Can such a one be the equal of him who enjoins justice and follows the straight path? (76—77)

To Allah belongs the knowledge of the unseen of the heavens and the earth; and the coming of the Hour is like the twinkling of an eye, or even quicker. Surely, Allah has full power over everything. (78)

257

Allah brought you forth from the wombs of your mothers, when you knew nothing, and gave you ears and eyes and hearts that you may be grateful. Do they not see the birds held under control in the vault of heaven? It is only Allah Who keeps them back from swooping down upon you. In that are Signs for a people who believe. Allah has made your homes your habitations and has made for you, of the skins of cattle, habitations which are easy for you to transport and easy to set up; and He provides for you from the wool and furs and hair of cattle, household goods and articles for use over a period. Allah has made for you, of that which He has created, trees and other means of shade, and places of shelter in the mountains; and He has made for you garments which protect you from heat and cold, and coats of mail which protect you in battle. Thus does He complete His favour unto you, that you may submit wholly to Him. Yet, if they turn away thy duty is only to convey the Message clearly. They recognise the favour of Allah and yet deny it, and most of them are confirmed disbelievers. (79—84)

وَاللّٰهُ اَخْرَجَكُمْ مِّنْ بُطُوْنِ اُمَّهٰتِكُمْ لَا تَعْلَمُوْنَ شَيْئًا وَّجَعَلَ لَكُمُ السَّمْعَ وَالْاَبْصَارَ وَالْاَفْئِدَةَ لَعَلَّكُمْ تَشْكُرُوْنَ ۝

اَلَمْ يَرَوْا اِلَى الطَّيْرِ مُسَخَّرٰتٍ فِيْ جَوِّ السَّمَآءِ مَا يُمْسِكُهُنَّ اِلَّا اللّٰهُ اِنَّ فِيْ ذٰلِكَ لَاٰيٰتٍ لِّقَوْمٍ يُّؤْمِنُوْنَ ۝

وَاللّٰهُ جَعَلَ لَكُمْ مِّنْ بُيُوْتِكُمْ سَكَنًا وَّجَعَلَ لَكُمْ مِّنْ جُلُوْدِ الْاَنْعَامِ بُيُوْتًا تَسْتَخِفُّوْنَهَا يَوْمَ ظَعْنِكُمْ وَيَوْمَ اِقَامَتِكُمْ وَمِنْ اَصْوَافِهَا وَاَوْبَارِهَا وَاَشْعَارِهَآ اَثَاثًا وَّمَتَاعًا اِلٰى حِيْنٍ ۝

وَاللّٰهُ جَعَلَ لَكُمْ مِّمَّا خَلَقَ ظِلٰلًا وَّجَعَلَ لَكُمْ مِّنَ الْجِبَالِ اَكْنَانًا وَّجَعَلَ لَكُمْ سَرَابِيْلَ تَقِيْكُمُ الْحَرَّ وَسَرَابِيْلَ تَقِيْكُمْ بَأْسَكُمْ كَذٰلِكَ يُتِمُّ نِعْمَتَهٗ عَلَيْكُمْ لَعَلَّكُمْ تُسْلِمُوْنَ ۝

فَاِنْ تَوَلَّوْا فَاِنَّمَا عَلَيْكَ الْبَلٰغُ الْمُبِيْنُ ۝

يَعْرِفُوْنَ نِعْمَتَ اللّٰهِ ثُمَّ يُنْكِرُوْنَهَا وَاَكْثَرُهُمُ الْكٰفِرُوْنَ ۝

Keep in mind the day when We shall raise up a witness from every people, then those who disbelieve shall not be permitted to put forward excuses or to beg for favours. When those who did wrong see the punishment, they will not be granted any alleviation or respite. When those who associate partners with Allah will see their associate-gods, they will exclaim: Lord these are our associate-gods, whom we used to call upon instead of Thee. Whereupon

وَيَوْمَ نَبْعَثُ مِنْ كُلِّ اُمَّةٍ شَهِيْدًا ثُمَّ لَا يُؤْذَنُ لِلَّذِيْنَ كَفَرُوْا وَلَا هُمْ يُسْتَعْتَبُوْنَ ۝

وَاِذَا رَاَ الَّذِيْنَ ظَلَمُوا الْعَذَابَ فَلَا يُخَفَّفُ عَنْهُمْ وَلَا هُمْ يُنْظَرُوْنَ ۝

وَاِذَا رَاَ الَّذِيْنَ اَشْرَكُوْا شُرَكَآءَهُمْ قَالُوْا رَبَّنَا هٰٓؤُلَآءِ شُرَكَآؤُنَا الَّذِيْنَ كُنَّا نَدْعُوْا مِنْ دُوْنِكَ

they will retort: Certainly you are liars. They will offer submission to Allah on that day, and all that they used to devise will fail them. We will add punishment to punishment in the case of those who disbelieve and turn people away from the way of Allah, because of the corruption they worked. Keep in mind the day when We will raise up in every people a witness against them from amongst themselves, and We will bring thee as a witness against all of them. We have sent down the Book to thee as an exposition of everything, and a guidance, and a mercy, and glad tidings for those who render perfect obedience. (85—90)

Allah enjoins equity and benevolence and graciousness as between kindred, and forbids evil designs, ill-behaviour and transgression. He admonishes you that you may take heed. Fulfil the covenant of Allah when you have made one; and break not your pledges after making them firm, having made Allah your surety; Allah knows that which you do. Be not like the woman who having made strong yarn, breaks it into pieces. You make your covenants a means of increasing your influence by deceit, for fear lest one people become more powerful than another. Surely, Allah tries you therewith, and on the Day of Judgment He will make clear to you that wherein you differed. Had Allah enforced His will, He would surely have made you all one people; but He lets go astray him who wishes it, and guides him who wishes it, and you will surely be called to account for that which you do. Make not your covenants a means of achieving ulterior purposes, or your foot

will slip after having been firmly established, and you will face evil consequences
because by so acting you turned people
away from Allah's way, and you will have
a severe punishment. Barter not the
covenant of Allah for a paltry price. Surely, that which is with Allah is far better for
you if you only knew. Whatever you have
shall pass away, but that which is with
Allah is lasting. We will certainly reward
those who are steadfast according to the
measure of the best of their works. Of the
believers whoso acts righteously, whether
male or female, We will surely grant such
a one a pure life; and We will certainly
reward them according to the measure
of the best of their works. (91—98)

بَعْدَ ثُبُوْتِهَا وَ تَذُوْقُوا السُّوْٓءَ بِمَا صَدَدْتُّمْ عَنْ
سَبِيْلِ اللّٰهِ ۚ وَ لَكُمْ عَذَابٌ عَظِيْمٌ ۞

وَ لَا تَشْتَرُوْا بِعَهْدِ اللّٰهِ ثَمَنًا قَلِيْلًا ۚ اِنَّمَا عِنْدَ اللّٰهِ
هُوَ خَيْرٌ لَّكُمْ اِنْ كُنْتُمْ تَعْلَمُوْنَ ۞

مَا عِنْدَكُمْ يَنْفَدُ وَ مَا عِنْدَ اللّٰهِ بَاقٍ ۗ وَ لَنَجْزِيَنَّ
الَّذِيْنَ صَبَرُوْٓا اَجْرَهُمْ بِاَحْسَنِ مَا كَانُوْا
يَعْمَلُوْنَ ۞

مَنْ عَمِلَ صَالِحًا مِّنْ ذَكَرٍ اَوْ اُنْثٰى وَهُوَ مُؤْمِنٌ
فَلَنُحْيِيَنَّهٗ حَيٰوةً طَيِّبَةً ۚ وَ لَنَجْزِيَنَّهُمْ اَجْرَهُمْ
بِاَحْسَنِ مَا كَانُوْا يَعْمَلُوْنَ ۞

When thou recitest the Quran, seek the
protection of Allah against the wiles of
Satan the rejected. Surely, he has no
power over those who believe and put their
trust in their Lord. He has power only
over those who make friends with him and
set up partners with Allah under his
incitement. (99—101)

فَاِذَا قَرَاْتَ الْقُرْاٰنَ فَاسْتَعِذْ بِاللّٰهِ مِنَ الشَّيْطٰنِ
الرَّجِيْمِ ۞

اِنَّهٗ لَيْسَ لَهٗ سُلْطٰنٌ عَلَى الَّذِيْنَ اٰمَنُوْا وَعَلٰى رَبِّهِمْ
يَتَوَكَّلُوْنَ ۞

اِنَّمَا سُلْطٰنُهٗ عَلَى الَّذِيْنَ يَتَوَلَّوْنَهٗ وَ الَّذِيْنَ هُمْ بِهٖ
مُشْرِكُوْنَ ۞

When We substitute in the Quran one
Commandment in place of another in
older scriptures (and Allah knows best the
appropriateness of that which He reveals)
they say: Thou art but a fabricator. Nay,
but most of them know not. Tell them the
Spirit of Holiness has brought it down
from thy Lord in accordance with the
requirements of truth and wisdom, that
He may strengthen those who believe, and
also as a guidance and as good tidings for
those who submit. Indeed We know that
they say: A certain person instructs him;

وَ اِذَا بَدَّلْنَآ اٰيَةً مَّكَانَ اٰيَةٍ ۙ وَّ اللّٰهُ اَعْلَمُ بِمَا
يُنَزِّلُ قَالُوْٓا اِنَّمَآ اَنْتَ مُفْتَرٍ ۚ بَلْ اَكْثَرُهُمْ
لَا يَعْلَمُوْنَ ۞

قُلْ نَزَّلَهٗ رُوْحُ الْقُدُسِ مِنْ رَّبِّكَ بِالْحَقِّ لِيُثَبِّتَ
الَّذِيْنَ اٰمَنُوْا وَ هُدًى وَّ بُشْرٰى لِلْمُسْلِمِيْنَ ۞

وَ لَقَدْ نَعْلَمُ اَنَّهُمْ يَقُوْلُوْنَ اِنَّمَا يُعَلِّمُهٗ بَشَرٌ ۗ

but the tongue of the one they have in
mind is foreign, while the language of the
Quran is plain and clear Arabic. Allah will
not guide those who do not believe in the
Signs of Allah, and they shall have a
grievous punishment. Only those fabricate
lies concerning Allah who do not believe
in the Signs of Allah, and these are confirmed liars. (102—106)

لِسَانُ الَّذِیۡ یُلْحِدُوۡنَ اِلَیۡهِ اَعۡجَمِیٌّ وَّهٰذَا لِسَانٌ
عَرَبِیٌّ مُّبِیۡنٌ ۞

اِنَّ الَّذِیۡنَ لَا یُؤۡمِنُوۡنَ بِاٰیٰتِ اللّٰهِ لَا یَهۡدِیۡهِمُ اللّٰهُ
وَلَهُمۡ عَذَابٌ اَلِیۡمٌ ۞

اِنَّمَا یَفۡتَرِی الۡکَذِبَ الَّذِیۡنَ لَا یُؤۡمِنُوۡنَ بِاٰیٰتِ
اللّٰهِ ۚ وَاُولٰٓئِکَ هُمُ الۡکٰذِبُوۡنَ ۞

Whoso disbelieves in Allah after he has
believed, excepting the case of one who is
forced to make a declaration of disbelief
while his heart rests securely in faith, but
one who opens his mind wide to disbelief,
on him is Allah's wrath and he shall have
a grievous punishment. That is because
such people love the hither life better than
the Hereafter and because Allah guides
not the disbelieving people. In consequence of their disbelief Allah has set
a seal on their hearts and ears and eyes,
and they are indeed heedless. Undoubtedly, they will be the losers in the Hereafter. Surely, thy Lord will be Most
Forgiving and Merciful towards those who
migrated after they had been persecuted
and strove hard in the cause of Allah and
continued steadfast, on the day when
every one will come pleading for himself,
and every one will be fully recompensed
for that which he did and they will not
be wronged. (107—112)

مَنۡ کَفَرَ بِاللّٰهِ مِنۡ بَعۡدِ اِیۡمَانِهٖٓ اِلَّا مَنۡ اُکۡرِهَ وَ
قَلۡبُهٗ مُطۡمَئِنٌّ بِالۡاِیۡمَانِ وَلٰکِنۡ مَّنۡ شَرَحَ بِالۡکُفۡرِ
صَدۡرًا فَعَلَیۡهِمۡ غَضَبٌ مِّنَ اللّٰهِ ۚ وَلَهُمۡ عَذَابٌ عَظِیۡمٌ ۞

ذٰلِکَ بِاَنَّهُمُ اسۡتَحَبُّوا الۡحَیٰوةَ الدُّنۡیَا عَلَی الۡاٰخِرَةِ ۙ وَ
اَنَّ اللّٰهَ لَا یَهۡدِی الۡقَوۡمَ الۡکٰفِرِیۡنَ ۞

اُولٰٓئِکَ الَّذِیۡنَ طَبَعَ اللّٰهُ عَلٰی قُلُوۡبِهِمۡ وَ سَمۡعِهِمۡ وَ
اَبۡصَارِهِمۡ ۚ وَ اُولٰٓئِکَ هُمُ الۡغٰفِلُوۡنَ ۞

لَا جَرَمَ اَنَّهُمۡ فِی الۡاٰخِرَةِ هُمُ الۡخٰسِرُوۡنَ ۞

ثُمَّ اِنَّ رَبَّکَ لِلَّذِیۡنَ هَاجَرُوۡا مِنۡۢ بَعۡدِ مَا فُتِنُوۡا
ثُمَّ جٰهَدُوۡا وَ صَبَرُوۡٓا ۙ اِنَّ رَبَّکَ مِنۡۢ بَعۡدِهَا لَغَفُوۡرٌ
رَّحِیۡمٌ ۞

یَوۡمَ تَاۡتِیۡ کُلُّ نَفۡسٍ تُجَادِلُ عَنۡ نَّفۡسِهَا وَ تُوَفّٰی
کُلُّ نَفۡسٍ مَّا عَمِلَتۡ وَ هُمۡ لَا یُظۡلَمُوۡنَ ۞

Allah sets forth for your guidance the
case of a city which enjoyed peace and
security, and its provisions came to it in
plenty from every quarter; but it proved
ungrateful for Allah's favour and in consequence, Allah enveloped it in hunger and
fear because of that which its people did.

وَ ضَرَبَ اللّٰهُ مَثَلًا قَرۡیَةً کَانَتۡ اٰمِنَةً مُّطۡمَئِنَّةً
یَّاۡتِیۡهَا رِزۡقُهَا رَغَدًا مِّنۡ کُلِّ مَکَانٍ فَکَفَرَتۡ
بِاَنۡعُمِ اللّٰهِ فَاَذَاقَهَا اللّٰهُ لِبَاسَ الۡجُوۡعِ وَ الۡخَوۡفِ

Indeed there came to them a Messenger from among themselves, but they rejected him as false, so punishment overtook them as they were wrongdoers. (113—114)

بِمَا كَانُوْا يَصْنَعُوْنَ ۝

وَلَقَدْ جَآءَهُمْ رَسُوْلٌ مِّنْهُمْ فَكَذَّبُوْهُ فَاَخَذَهُمُ الْعَذَابُ وَهُمْ ظٰلِمُوْنَ ۝

So, drawing a lesson from their case, eat of the lawful and wholesome things that Allah has provided for you; and be grateful for the bounty of Allah, if it is Him you worship. He has forbidden you only the flesh of dead animals, blood, the flesh of swine and that on which the name of any other than Allah has been invoked. But he who is impelled by necessity to partake of any of these, neither being defiant of the law, nor going beyond the limits of his immediate need, will surely find Allah Most Forgiving, Ever Merciful. Say not, because of the false utterances of your tongues: This is lawful and that is unlawful; fabricating lies against Allah. Surely, those who fabricate lies against Allah do not prosper; theirs is only a brief enjoyment to be followed by a grievous punishment. We had made unlawful for the Jews before this all that We have recited to thee. We wronged them not, but they used to wrong themselves. Surely, thy Lord is Most Forgiving, Ever Merciful towards those who do evil in ignorance and truly repent thereafter and make amends. (115—120)

فَكُلُوْا مِمَّا رَزَقَكُمُ اللّٰهُ حَلٰلًا طَيِّبًا ۪ وَّاشْكُرُوْا نِعْمَتَ اللّٰهِ اِنْ كُنْتُمْ اِيَّاهُ تَعْبُدُوْنَ ۝

اِنَّمَا حَرَّمَ عَلَيْكُمُ الْمَيْتَةَ وَالدَّمَ وَلَحْمَ الْخِنْزِيْرِ وَمَآ اُهِلَّ لِغَيْرِ اللّٰهِ بِهٖ ۚ فَمَنِ اضْطُرَّ غَيْرَ بَاغٍ وَّلَا عَادٍ فَاِنَّ اللّٰهَ غَفُوْرٌ رَّحِيْمٌ ۝

وَلَا تَقُوْلُوْا لِمَا تَصِفُ اَلْسِنَتُكُمُ الْكَذِبَ هٰذَا حَلٰلٌ وَّهٰذَا حَرَامٌ لِّتَفْتَرُوْا عَلَى اللّٰهِ الْكَذِبَ ۚ اِنَّ الَّذِيْنَ يَفْتَرُوْنَ عَلَى اللّٰهِ الْكَذِبَ لَا يُفْلِحُوْنَ ۝

مَتَاعٌ قَلِيْلٌ ۪ وَّلَهُمْ عَذَابٌ اَلِيْمٌ ۝

وَعَلَى الَّذِيْنَ هَادُوْا حَرَّمْنَا مَا قَصَصْنَا عَلَيْكَ مِنْ قَبْلُ ۚ وَمَا ظَلَمْنٰهُمْ وَلٰكِنْ كَانُوْا اَنْفُسَهُمْ يَظْلِمُوْنَ ۝

ثُمَّ اِنَّ رَبَّكَ لِلَّذِيْنَ عَمِلُوا السُّوْٓءَ بِجَهَالَةٍ ثُمَّ تَابُوْا مِنْ بَعْدِ ذٰلِكَ وَاَصْلَحُوْٓا ۙ اِنَّ رَبَّكَ مِنْ بَعْدِهَا لَغَفُوْرٌ رَّحِيْمٌ ۝

Abraham was indeed a paragon of virtue, humble for the sake of Allah, ever inclined to Him, and was not of those who ascribe partners to Allah. He was appreciative of the favours of his Lord, Who exalted him and guided him to the straight path.

اِنَّ اِبْرٰهِيْمَ كَانَ اُمَّةً قَانِتًا لِّلّٰهِ حَنِيْفًا ۪ وَلَمْ يَكُ مِنَ الْمُشْرِكِيْنَ ۝

شَاكِرًا لِّاَنْعُمِهٖ ۚ اِجْتَبٰهُ وَهَدٰهُ اِلٰى صِرَاطٍ مُّسْتَقِيْمٍ ۝

We bestowed on him great success in this world, and in the Hereafter he will surely be among the righteous. Now We have commanded thee: Follow the way of Abraham who had submitted himself wholly to Allah and was not of those who ascribe partners to Allah. The penalty for profaning the Sabbath was imposed only on those who had differed about it, and thy Lord will surely judge between them on the day of Judgment concerning that wherein they differed. (121—125)

وَاٰتَيۡنٰهُ فِى الدُّنۡيَا حَسَنَةً ۖ وَاِنَّهٗ فِى الۡاٰخِرَةِ لَمِنَ الصّٰلِحِيۡنَ ۞

ثُمَّ اَوۡحَيۡنَاۤ اِلَيۡكَ اَنِ اتَّبِعۡ مِلَّةَ اِبۡرٰهِيۡمَ حَنِيۡفًا ؕ وَمَا كَانَ مِنَ الۡمُشۡرِكِيۡنَ ۞

اِنَّمَا جُعِلَ السَّبۡتُ عَلَى الَّذِيۡنَ اخۡتَلَفُوۡا فِيۡهِ ؕ وَاِنَّ رَبَّكَ لَيَحۡكُمُ بَيۡنَهُمۡ يَوۡمَ الۡقِيٰمَةِ فِيۡمَا كَانُوۡا فِيۡهِ يَخۡتَلِفُوۡنَ ۞

Call unto the way of thy Lord with wisdom and goodly exhortation, and contend with them on the basis of that which is best. Thy Lord knows best those who have strayed away from His path, and He knows best those who are rightly guided. If you desire to exact retribution, then adjust the penalty to the wrong you have suffered, but if you endure with fortitude, that surely is best for the steadfast. Do thou endure with fortitude, and thou canst do so only with the help of Allah; and grieve not for them, nor feel distressed because of their plottings. Surely Allah is with those who restrain themselves and those who are benevolent. (126—129)

اُدۡعُ اِلٰى سَبِيۡلِ رَبِّكَ بِالۡحِكۡمَةِ وَالۡمَوۡعِظَةِ الۡحَسَنَةِ وَجَادِلۡهُمۡ بِالَّتِىۡ هِىَ اَحۡسَنُ ؕ اِنَّ رَبَّكَ هُوَ اَعۡلَمُ بِمَنۡ ضَلَّ عَنۡ سَبِيۡلِهٖ وَهُوَ اَعۡلَمُ بِالۡمُهۡتَدِيۡنَ ۞

وَاِنۡ عَاقَبۡتُمۡ فَعَاقِبُوۡا بِمِثۡلِ مَا عُوۡقِبۡتُمۡ بِهٖ ؕ وَلَئِنۡ صَبَرۡتُمۡ لَهُوَ خَيۡرٌ لِّلصّٰبِرِيۡنَ ۞

وَاصۡبِرۡ وَمَا صَبۡرُكَ اِلَّا بِاللّٰهِ وَلَا تَحۡزَنۡ عَلَيۡهِمۡ وَلَا تَكُ فِىۡ ضَيۡقٍ مِّمَّا يَمۡكُرُوۡنَ ۞

اِنَّ اللّٰهَ مَعَ الَّذِيۡنَ اتَّقَوۡا وَّالَّذِيۡنَ هُمۡ مُّحۡسِنُوۡنَ ۞

BANĪ ISRĀ'ĪL

(Revealed before Hijra)

In the name of Allah, Most Gracious, Ever Merciful. (1)

Holy is He Who took His servant by night from the Sacred Mosque to the Distant Mosque, the precincts of which We have blessed, that We might show him some of Our Signs. Surely, it is He Who is the All-Hearing, the All-Seeing. (2)

We gave Moses the Book and made it a guidance for the children of Israel, directing them: Take no partner beside Me, O descendants of those whom We carried in the Ark with Noah. He was indeed a grateful servant. We had conveyed it clearly to the children of Israel in the Book: You will twice spread corruption in the land and be elated with great insolence. When the time of the first of these warnings came, We sent against you servants of Ours, mighty in war, who penetrated into your houses. The warning was bound to be fulfilled. Then We restored to you the initiative against them, bestowed upon you an increase of wealth and children and made you more numerous than before. If you act beneficently it will be to your own good, and if you act corruptly it will be to your own loss. When the time of the second warning came, that your enemies may humiliate your leading people, and enter the Mosque as they had entered it the first time, and destroy utterly all that over which they might gain the upper hand; that too was fulfilled. It may be that your Lord may now have mercy on you; but if you revert to your old ways, We too will revert to chastising you. We have devised hell as a prison for the disbelievers. (3—9)

Surely, this Quran guides to the way which is most firm and right, and gives to the believers who work righteousness the glad tidings that they shall have a great reward and warns that for those who do not believe in the Hereafter We have prepared a grievous chastisement. (10—11)

Man calls for evil as eagerly as Allah calls him to good; man is indeed hasty. We have made the night and the day two Signs; the Sign of the night We obliterate and the Sign of the day We make sight-giving that you may seek the bounty of your Lord, and that you may know the computation of years and the method of reckoning. We have expounded everything in detail. (12—13)

Every person's doings have We fastened firmly to his neck; and on the Day of Judgment We shall place before him a book which he will find wide open, and he will be told: Read thy record, thou art sufficient as a reckoner against thyself this day. He who follows the right way follows it to his own good, and he who goes astray does it to his own loss. He who carries a responsibility cannot be relieved of it by another. We never punish a people until after We have sent a Messenger. Before We decide to destroy a township, We command the affluent section of its people to adopt the ways of righteousness, where-upon they decide on disobedience. Thus the sentence becomes due against it, and We destroy it utterly. Many generations have We destroyed after Noah. Thy Lord is well aware of the sins of His servants and sees them all. (14—18)

Whoso desires only the hither life, We bestow upon those of them We please such immediate advantage as We determine; thereafter We appoint hell for them which they enter condemned and rejected. Whoso desires the Hereafter and, being a believer, strives properly for it, the striving of such will be duly appreciated. We assist all these as well as those as a bounty from thy Lord. Thy Lord's bounty is not held back from any. Observe, how We have exalted some of them over others in respect of the provisions of this life; and surely, the life of the Hereafter will be more varied in degrees of ranks and degrees of excellence. Set not up, therefore, another god with Allah, lest thou sit down humiliated and forsaken. (19—23)

مَنۡ كَانَ يُرِيۡدُ الۡعَاجِلَةَ عَجَّلۡنَا لَهٗ فِيۡهَا مَا نَشَآءُ لِمَنۡ نُّرِيۡدُ ثُمَّ جَعَلۡنَا لَهٗ جَهَنَّمَ يَصۡلٰىهَا مَذۡمُوۡمًا مَّدۡحُوۡرًا ۞

وَ مَنۡ اَرَادَ الۡاٰخِرَةَ وَ سَعٰى لَهَا سَعۡيَهَا وَ هُوَ مُؤۡمِنٌ فَاُولٰٓئِكَ كَانَ سَعۡيُهُمۡ مَّشۡكُوۡرًا ۞

كُلًّا نُّمِدُّ هٰٓؤُلَآءِ وَ هٰٓؤُلَآءِ مِنۡ عَطَآءِ رَبِّكَ وَ مَا كَانَ عَطَآءُ رَبِّكَ مَحۡظُوۡرًا ۞

اُنۡظُرۡ كَيۡفَ فَضَّلۡنَا بَعۡضَهُمۡ عَلٰى بَعۡضٍ وَ لَلۡاٰخِرَةُ اَكۡبَرُ دَرَجٰتٍ وَّ اَكۡبَرُ تَفۡضِيۡلًا ۞

لَا تَجۡعَلۡ مَعَ اللّٰهِ اِلٰهًا اٰخَرَ فَتَقۡعُدَ مَذۡمُوۡمًا مَّخۡذُوۡلًا ۞

وَ قَضٰى رَبُّكَ اَلَّا تَعۡبُدُوۡۤا اِلَّاۤ اِيَّاهُ وَ بِالۡوَالِدَيۡنِ اِحۡسَانًا ؕ اِمَّا يَبۡلُغَنَّ عِنۡدَكَ الۡكِبَرَ اَحَدُهُمَاۤ اَوۡ كِلٰهُمَا فَلَا تَقُلۡ لَّهُمَاۤ اُفٍّ وَّ لَا تَنۡهَرۡهُمَا وَ قُلۡ لَّهُمَا قَوۡلًا كَرِيۡمًا ۞

Thy Lord has commanded that ye worship none but Him and has enjoined benevolence towards parents. Should either or both of them attain old age in thy lifetime, never say: Ugh; to them nor chide them, but always speak gently to them. Be humbly tender with them and pray: Lord, have mercy on them, even as they nurtured me when I was little. Your Lord knows best that which is in your minds; if you will be righteous, then surely He is Most Forgiving towards those who turn constantly to Him. Render to the kinsman his due and the needy and the wayfarer, and squander not thy substance extravagantly, for the extravagant fall into evil company and misuse the bounties

وَ اخۡفِضۡ لَهُمَا جَنَاحَ الذُّلِّ مِنَ الرَّحۡمَةِ وَ قُلۡ رَّبِّ ارۡحَمۡهُمَا كَمَا رَبَّيٰنِيۡ صَغِيۡرًا ۞

رَبُّكُمۡ اَعۡلَمُ بِمَا فِيۡ نُفُوۡسِكُمۡ ؕ اِنۡ تَكُوۡنُوۡا صٰلِحِيۡنَ فَاِنَّهٗ كَانَ لِلۡاَوَّابِيۡنَ غَفُوۡرًا ۞

وَ اٰتِ ذَا الۡقُرۡبٰى حَقَّهٗ وَ الۡمِسۡكِيۡنَ وَ ابۡنَ السَّبِيۡلِ وَ لَا تُبَذِّرۡ تَبۡذِيۡرًا ۞

اِنَّ الۡمُبَذِّرِيۡنَ كَانُوۡۤا اِخۡوَانَ الشَّيٰطِيۡنِ ؕ وَ كَانَ

of their Lord. On occasions when thou
must turn away from any of those who
should be the objects of thy benevolence,
while seeking thy Lord's mercy for which
thou hopest, then speak kindly to them.
Do not hold back altogether out of miserliness and render thyself blameworthy,
nor spend without restraint and exhaust
thy substance, thus becoming thyself an
object of charity. Thy Lord enlarges His
provision for whom He wills, and straitens
it for whom He wills. He is well-aware of
all that relates to His servants and sees
it all. (24—31)

الشَّيْطٰنُ لِرَبِّهٖ كَفُوْرًا ۞

وَاِمَّا تُعْرِضَنَّ عَنْهُمُ ابْتِغَآءَ رَحْمَةٍ مِّنْ رَّبِّكَ
تَرْجُوْهَا فَقُلْ لَّهُمْ قَوْلًا مَّيْسُوْرًا ۞

وَلَا تَجْعَلْ يَدَكَ مَغْلُوْلَةً اِلٰى عُنُقِكَ وَلَا تَبْسُطْهَا
كُلَّ الْبَسْطِ فَتَقْعُدَ مَلُوْمًا مَّحْسُوْرًا ۞

اِنَّ رَبَّكَ يَبْسُطُ الرِّزْقَ لِمَنْ يَّشَآءُ وَيَقْدِرُ اِنَّهٗ
كَانَ بِعِبَادِهٖ خَبِيْرًۢا بَصِيْرًا ۞

وَلَا تَقْتُلُوْٓا اَوْلَادَكُمْ خَشْيَةَ اِمْلَاقٍ نَحْنُ نَرْزُقُهُمْ
وَاِيَّاكُمْ اِنَّ قَتْلَهُمْ كَانَ خِطْأً كَبِيْرًا ۞

وَلَا تَقْرَبُوا الزِّنٰٓى اِنَّهٗ كَانَ فَاحِشَةً وَسَآءَ سَبِيْلًا ۞

وَلَا تَقْتُلُوا النَّفْسَ الَّتِيْ حَرَّمَ اللّٰهُ اِلَّا بِالْحَقِّ وَمَنْ
قُتِلَ مَظْلُوْمًا فَقَدْ جَعَلْنَا لِوَلِيِّهٖ سُلْطٰنًا فَلَا يُسْرِفْ
فِّى الْقَتْلِ اِنَّهٗ كَانَ مَنْصُوْرًا ۞

وَلَا تَقْرَبُوْا مَالَ الْيَتِيْمِ اِلَّا بِالَّتِيْ هِيَ اَحْسَنُ حَتّٰى
يَبْلُغَ اَشُدَّهٗ وَاَوْفُوْا بِالْعَهْدِ اِنَّ الْعَهْدَ كَانَ مَسْئُوْلًا ۞

وَاَوْفُوا الْكَيْلَ اِذَا كِلْتُمْ وَزِنُوْا بِالْقِسْطَاسِ الْمُسْتَقِيْمِ
ذٰلِكَ خَيْرٌ وَّاَحْسَنُ تَأْوِيْلًا ۞

Do not destroy your offspring for fear
of poverty; it is We Who provide for them
and for you. Surely, destroying them is
a great sin. Do not even approach adultery;
surely, it is a foul thing and an evil way.
Do not destroy the life that Allah has
declared sacred save for just cause. The
heir of one who is killed wrongfully has
Our authority to demand retribution, but
let him not transgress the prescribed
limits in exacting retribution, for within
the limits he is upheld by law. Do not
approach the property of the orphan
during his minority, except for the most
beneficent purpose, and fulfil every covenant, for you will be called to account for
it. Give full measure when you measure
out, and weigh out with a true balance;
that is best and most commendable in the
end. Follow not that of which thou hast
no knowledge; for the ear and the eye and
the heart shall all be called to account.
(32—37)

وَلَا تَقْفُ مَا لَيْسَ لَكَ بِهٖ عِلْمٌ اِنَّ السَّمْعَ وَالْبَصَرَ
وَالْفُؤَادَ كُلُّ اُولٰٓئِكَ كَانَ عَنْهُ مَسْئُوْلًا ۞

وَلَا تَمْشِ فِى الْاَرْضِ مَرَحًا اِنَّكَ لَنْ تَخْرِقَ الْاَرْضَ
وَلَنْ تَبْلُغَ الْجِبَالَ طُوْلًا ۞

Do not tread haughtily upon the earth,
for thou canst not thereby reach its confines nor outstrip those who are of the
highest rank. The evil of all this is hateful
in the sight of thy Lord. (38—39)

كُلُّ ذٰلِكَ كَانَ سَيِّئُهٗ عِنْدَ رَبِّكَ مَكْرُوْهًا ۞

This is part of the wisdom that thy Lord has revealed to thee. Set not up with Allah any other god, lest thou be cast into hell, condemned and rejected. Has your Lord, then, honoured you with sons and Himself adopted some of the angels as daughters? Indeed you utter an enormity. (40—41)

We have expounded the truth in this Quran in diverse ways that they may be admonished, but it only adds to their aversion. Tell them: Had there been other gods with Him, as they allege, they would surely have helped them to discover a way to find favour with the Lord of the Throne. Holy is He and exalted far above that which they allege. The seven heavens and the earth and those that are therein celebrate His praise; and there is not a thing but glorifies Him with His praise; but you do not comprehend their glorification. Verily, He is Forbearing, Most Forgiving. When thou recitest the Quran, We put between thee and those who do not believe in the Hereafter an invisible veil, and We put coverings over their hearts which disable them from comprehending it, and We afflict their ears with deafness. When thou dost mention thy Lord, the Single One, in thy recitation of the Quran, they turn their backs in aversion. We know well what they listen for, when they listen to thee, and when they confer in private, when the unjust ones say: You are only following one who is self-deceived. Observe how they invent explanations concerning thee, which lead them astray, so that they are incapacitated from discovering the right way. (42—49)

They ask: When we shall have become bones and broken particles, shall we indeed be raised up as a new creation? Tell them: Aye even if you become stones or iron or any other form of creation that you deem hardest of all, you shall be raised up. Then will they ask: Who is it that shall restore us to life? Answer them: He Who created you the first time. They will shake their heads at thee in wonder and enquire: When will all this be? Say to them: It may be that the time is nigh. When He will call you and you will respond praising Him, you will imagine that you had tarried only a short while in the world. (50—53)

Tell My servants that they should always say that which is best. Satan stirs up discord among them. Surely, Satan is man's declared enemy. Your Lord knows you best. If He please He will have mercy on you and if He please He will chastise you. We have not sent thee to be a keeper over them. Thy Lord knows best those that are in the heavens and the earth. We exalted some of the Prophets over the others and We gave David the Psalms. Point out to them, O Prophet: Call on those angels and Prophets whom you claim to be gods beside Him and you will know that they have no power to remove affliction from you or to bring about any change that you may desire. Those whom they call on themselves seek a way of approach to their Lord, trying to discover which of them is nearer to Him, and hope for His mercy and fear His punishment. Surely, the punishment of thy Lord is to be feared.

خَلْقًا جَدِيدًا ۝

قُلْ كُوْنُوْا حِجَارَةً اَوْ حَدِيْدًا ۝

اَوْ خَلْقًا مِّمَّا يَكْبُرُ فِيْ صُدُوْرِكُمْ ۚ فَسَيَقُوْلُوْنَ مَنْ يُّعِيْدُنَا ۗ قُلِ الَّذِيْ فَطَرَكُمْ اَوَّلَ مَرَّةٍ ۚ فَسَيُنْغِضُوْنَ اِلَيْكَ رُءُوْسَهُمْ وَ يَقُوْلُوْنَ مَتٰى هُوَ ۗ قُلْ عَسٰۤى اَنْ يَّكُوْنَ قَرِيْبًا ۝

يَوْمَ يَدْعُوْكُمْ فَتَسْتَجِيْبُوْنَ بِحَمْدِهٖ وَ تَظُنُّوْنَ اِنْ لَّبِثْتُمْ اِلَّا قَلِيْلًا ۝

وَ قُلْ لِّعِبَادِيْ يَقُوْلُوا الَّتِيْ هِيَ اَحْسَنُ ۗ اِنَّ الشَّيْطٰنَ يَنْزَغُ بَيْنَهُمْ ۗ اِنَّ الشَّيْطٰنَ كَانَ لِلْاِنْسَانِ عَدُوًّا مُّبِيْنًا ۝

رَبُّكُمْ اَعْلَمُ بِكُمْ ۗ اِنْ يَّشَأْ يَرْحَمْكُمْ اَوْ اِنْ يَّشَأْ يُعَذِّبْكُمْ ۗ وَ مَاۤ اَرْسَلْنٰكَ عَلَيْهِمْ وَكِيْلًا ۝

وَ رَبُّكَ اَعْلَمُ بِمَنْ فِى السَّمٰوٰتِ وَ الْاَرْضِ ۗ وَ لَقَدْ فَضَّلْنَا بَعْضَ النَّبِيّٖنَ عَلٰى بَعْضٍ وَّ اٰتَيْنَا دَاوٗدَ زَبُوْرًا ۝

قُلِ ادْعُوا الَّذِيْنَ زَعَمْتُمْ مِّنْ دُوْنِهٖ فَلَا يَمْلِكُوْنَ كَشْفَ الضُّرِّ عَنْكُمْ وَ لَا تَحْوِيْلًا ۝

اُولٰٓئِكَ الَّذِيْنَ يَدْعُوْنَ يَبْتَغُوْنَ اِلٰى رَبِّهِمُ الْوَسِيْلَةَ اَيُّهُمْ اَقْرَبُ وَ يَرْجُوْنَ رَحْمَتَهٗ وَ يَخَافُوْنَ عَذَابَهٗ ۗ اِنَّ عَذَابَ رَبِّكَ كَانَ مَحْذُوْرًا ۝

وَ اِنْ مِّنْ قَرْيَةٍ اِلَّا نَحْنُ مُهْلِكُوْهَا قَبْلَ يَوْمِ الْقِيٰمَةِ

There is not a township but We shall destroy it before the Day of Judgment or chastise its people with a severe chastisement. That is written down in the Book. People after people have rejected Our Signs, but that cannot hinder Us from sending them. We gave Thamud the she-camel as a clear Sign, but they were cruel to it. We send the Signs only to warn. When we said to thee: Thy Lord has decreed the ruin of thy enemies; and We showed thee the vision of the Distant Mosque; it was all a trial and a warning for the people concerned, as also is the pedigreed people on whom a curse has been pronounced in the Quran. We continue warning them but that only serves to impel them into greater transgression. (54—61)

Call to mind when We commanded the angels: Fall down into prostration along with Adam. They all prostrated, but Iblis did not. He protested: Shall I prostrate myself along with one whom Thou hast created of clay? Tell me, Lord, can I submit to this one whom Thou hast honoured above me? If Thou wilt grant me respite till the Day of Judgment, I will most surely reduce his posterity to subjection except a few. Allah said: Get out. Hell shall be the recompense of you all, thee and those who follow thee from among them: an adequate recompense. Go ahead and entice whomsoever of them thou canst, with thy voice, and mount assaults against them with thy horse and foot and be their partner in wealth and offspring, and make promises to them (Satan's promises are all deceit), thou shalt have no authority over My true servants. O My servant, thy Lord is sufficient as Guardian. (62—66)

Your Lord is He Who propels the vessels in the sea for your benefit, that you may seek of His bounty. Surely, He is Ever Merciful towards you.

اَوۡ مُعَذِّبُوۡهَا عَذَابًا شَدِيۡدًا ؕ كَانَ ذٰلِكَ فِى الۡكِتٰبِ مَسۡطُوۡرًا ۞

وَمَا مَنَعَنَاۤ اَنۡ نُّرۡسِلَ بِالۡاٰيٰتِ اِلَّاۤ اَنۡ كَذَّبَ بِهَا الۡاَوَّلُوۡنَ ؕ وَاٰتَيۡنَا ثَمُوۡدَ النَّاقَةَ مُبۡصِرَةً فَظَلَمُوۡا بِهَا ؕ وَمَا نُرۡسِلُ بِالۡاٰيٰتِ اِلَّا تَخۡوِيۡفًا ۞

وَاِذۡ قُلۡنَا لَكَ اِنَّ رَبَّكَ اَحَاطَ بِالنَّاسِ ؕ وَمَا جَعَلۡنَا الرُّءۡيَا الَّتِىۡۤ اَرَيۡنٰكَ اِلَّا فِتۡنَةً لِّلنَّاسِ وَالشَّجَرَةَ الۡمَلۡعُوۡنَةَ فِى الۡقُرۡاٰنِ ؕ وَنُخَوِّفُهُمۡ ۙ فَمَا يَزِيۡدُهُمۡ اِلَّا طُغۡيَانًا كَبِيۡرًا ۞

وَاِذۡ قُلۡنَا لِلۡمَلٰٓئِكَةِ اسۡجُدُوۡا لِاٰدَمَ فَسَجَدُوۡۤا اِلَّاۤ اِبۡلِيۡسَ ؕ قَالَ ءَاَسۡجُدُ لِمَنۡ خَلَقۡتَ طِيۡنًا ۞

قَالَ اَرَاَيۡتَكَ هٰذَا الَّذِىۡ كَرَّمۡتَ عَلَىَّ ۫ لَئِنۡ اَخَّرۡتَنِ اِلٰى يَوۡمِ الۡقِيٰمَةِ لَاَحۡتَنِكَنَّ ذُرِّيَّتَهٗۤ اِلَّا قَلِيۡلًا ۞

قَالَ اذۡهَبۡ فَمَنۡ تَبِعَكَ مِنۡهُمۡ فَاِنَّ جَهَنَّمَ جَزَآؤُكُمۡ جَزَآءً مَّوۡفُوۡرًا ۞

وَاسۡتَفۡزِزۡ مَنِ اسۡتَطَعۡتَ مِنۡهُمۡ بِصَوۡتِكَ وَاَجۡلِبۡ عَلَيۡهِمۡ بِخَيۡلِكَ وَرَجِلِكَ وَشَارِكۡهُمۡ فِى الۡاَمۡوَالِ وَالۡاَوۡلَادِ وَعِدۡهُمۡ ؕ وَمَا يَعِدُهُمُ الشَّيۡطٰنُ اِلَّا غُرُوۡرًا ۞

اِنَّ عِبَادِىۡ لَيۡسَ لَكَ عَلَيۡهِمۡ سُلۡطٰنٌ ؕ وَكَفٰى بِرَبِّكَ وَكِيۡلًا ۞

رَبُّكُمُ الَّذِىۡ يُزۡجِىۡ لَكُمُ الۡفُلۡكَ فِى الۡبَحۡرِ لِتَبۡتَغُوۡا مِنۡ فَضۡلِهٖ ؕ اِنَّهٗ كَانَ بِكُمۡ رَحِيۡمًا ۞

When danger threatens you in the sea you call upon Him, and forget all others upon whom you call. But when He brings you safe to land, you turn aside. Man is ever ungrateful. Do you then feel secure against His causing you to be swallowed up by the earth or His sending a sandstorm to cover you up, when you would find no one to rescue you? Or, do you feel secure against His sending you back therein once more and raising a fierce gale against you and drowning you because of your ingratitude, when you would find no one to help you against Us? We have indeed honoured the children of Adam, and provided for them means of transportation in land and sea, and given them wholesome food and exalted them high above the greater part of Our creation. (67—71)

وَ اِذَا مَسَّكُمُ الضُّرُّ فِي الْبَحْرِ ضَلَّ مَنْ تَدْعُوْنَ اِلَّا اِيَّاهُ ۚ فَلَمَّا نَجّٰىكُمْ اِلَى الْبَرِّ اَعْرَضْتُمْ ۚ وَكَانَ الْاِنْسَانُ كَفُوْرًا ۝

اَفَاَمِنْتُمْ اَنْ يَّخْسِفَ بِكُمْ جَانِبَ الْبَرِّ اَوْ يُرْسِلَ عَلَيْكُمْ حَاصِبًا ثُمَّ لَا تَجِدُوْا لَكُمْ وَكِيْلًا ۝

اَمْ اَمِنْتُمْ اَنْ يُّعِيْدَكُمْ فِيْهِ تَارَةً اُخْرٰى فَيُرْسِلَ عَلَيْكُمْ قَاصِفًا مِّنَ الرِّيْحِ فَيُغْرِقَكُمْ بِمَا كَفَرْتُمْ ثُمَّ لَا تَجِدُوْا لَكُمْ عَلَيْنَا بِهٖ تَبِيْعًا ۝

وَ لَقَدْ كَرَّمْنَا بَنِيْ اٰدَمَ وَحَمَلْنٰهُمْ فِي الْبَرِّ وَالْبَحْرِ وَرَزَقْنٰهُمْ مِّنَ الطَّيِّبٰتِ وَفَضَّلْنٰهُمْ عَلٰى كَثِيْرٍ مِّمَّنْ خَلَقْنَا تَفْضِيْلًا ۝

Keep in mind the day when We shall summon every people with its leader. Then those who are given their book in their right hands will read their record eagerly, and they will not be wronged a whit. But he who continues blind in this life will be blind in the Hereafter and even more astray from the right path. They were minded to inflict upon thee severest suffering because of that which We have revealed to thee, that thou mayest substitute in its place something of thy own, in which case they would have certainly taken thee as a fast friend. Even if We had not strengthened thee with the Quran, thou wouldst have inclined to them but little. Hadst thou done what they had wished of thee We would have afflicted thee with intensified chastisement in this life and intensified chastisement after death, and thou wouldst not have found any helper for thyself against Us. They continue to conspire against thee that they may force thee to leave the land, but in

يَوْمَ نَدْعُوْا كُلَّ اُنَاسٍ بِاِمَامِهِمْ ۚ فَمَنْ اُوْتِيَ كِتٰبَهٗ بِيَمِيْنِهٖ فَاُولٰٓئِكَ يَقْرَءُوْنَ كِتٰبَهُمْ وَلَا يُظْلَمُوْنَ فَتِيْلًا ۝

وَمَنْ كَانَ فِيْ هٰذِهٖ اَعْمٰى فَهُوَ فِي الْاٰخِرَةِ اَعْمٰى وَاَضَلُّ سَبِيْلًا ۝

وَ اِنْ كَادُوْا لَيَفْتِنُوْنَكَ عَنِ الَّذِيْٓ اَوْحَيْنَا اِلَيْكَ لِتَفْتَرِيَ عَلَيْنَا غَيْرَهٗ ۖ وَاِذًا لَّاتَّخَذُوْكَ خَلِيْلًا ۝

وَ لَوْلَآ اَنْ ثَبَّتْنٰكَ لَقَدْ كِدْتَّ تَرْكَنُ اِلَيْهِمْ شَيْئًا قَلِيْلًا ۝

اِذًا لَّاَذَقْنٰكَ ضِعْفَ الْحَيٰوةِ وَضِعْفَ الْمَمَاتِ ثُمَّ لَا تَجِدُ لَكَ عَلَيْنَا نَصِيْرًا ۝

وَ اِنْ كَادُوْا لَيَسْتَفِزُّوْنَكَ مِنَ الْاَرْضِ لِيُخْرِجُوْكَ

that case they too would not tarry long after thee. That has been Our way with Our Messengers whom We sent before thee; and thou wilt not find Our way subject to any change. (72—78)

Observe Prayer at different times between the declining of the sun and the deep darkness of the night, and recite the Quran at dawn. The recitation of the Quran at dawn is specially acceptable to Allah. At night also wake up for its recitation, an additional favour unto thee. It may be that thereby thy Lord will raise thee to a praiseworthy station. Keep praying: My Lord, make my re-entry into Mecca a beneficent event, and make my going forth from Mecca also a beneficent event, and grant me from Thyself a helper and a witness; and announce: Truth has come and falsehood has disappeared, falsehood is bound to perish. We reveal progressively of the Quran that which is a healing and a mercy for the believers; but it only impels the wrongdoers into greater ruin. When We bestow a favour upon a person, he turns arrogantly away and draws aside; and when evil afflicts him he gives himself up to despair. Say to them: Everyone acts in his own way, and your Lord knows best who is rightly guided. (79—85)

They question thee concerning the soul. Tell them: The soul has been created by the command of my Lord; and you have been granted but little knowledge concerning it. If We pleased, We could certainly take away that which We have revealed to thee and then thou wouldst find no helper for thyself against Us, except through the special mercy of thy Lord Surely, great is His grace on thee. (86—88)

272

Proclaim: If all men, high and low, were to gather together to produce the like of this Quran, they would not be able to produce the like thereof, even though they all combined in the effort. We have expounded for mankind all things necessary in this Quran, but most people adhere obstinately to disbelief. They assert: We will never believe anything thou sayest until thou cause a spring to flow for us from the earth; or thou have a garden of date-palms and vines and cause streams to flow plentifully in the midst thereof; or thou cause the heavens to fall on us in pieces, as thou hast claimed; or thou bring Allah and the angels before us face to face; or thou have a house of gold; or thou ascend up into heaven; and we will not believe in thy ascension until thou send down on us a book that we can read. Tell them: Holy is my Lord. I am but a human being sent as a Messenger. (89—94)

قُلْ لَّئِنِ اجْتَمَعَتِ الْإِنْسُ وَالْجِنُّ عَلَى اَنْ يَّأْتُوْا بِمِثْلِ هٰذَا الْقُرْاٰنِ لَا يَأْتُوْنَ بِمِثْلِهٖ وَلَوْكَانَ بَعْضُهُمْ لِبَعْضٍ ظَهِيْرًا ۝

وَلَقَدْ صَرَّفْنَا لِلنَّاسِ فِيْ هٰذَا الْقُرْاٰنِ مِنْ كُلِّ مَثَلٍ فَاَبٰى اَكْثَرُ النَّاسِ اِلَّا كُفُوْرًا ۝

وَقَالُوْا لَنْ نُّؤْمِنَ لَكَ حَتّٰى تَفْجُرَ لَنَا مِنَ الْاَرْضِ يَنْبُوْعًا ۝

اَوْ تَكُوْنَ لَكَ جَنَّةٌ مِّنْ نَّخِيْلٍ وَّعِنَبٍ فَتُفَجِّرَ الْاَنْهٰرَ خِلٰلَهَا تَفْجِيْرًا ۝

اَوْ تُسْقِطَ السَّمَآءَ كَمَا زَعَمْتَ عَلَيْنَا كِسَفًا اَوْ تَأْتِيَ بِاللّٰهِ وَالْمَلٰٓئِكَةِ قَبِيْلًا ۝

اَوْ يَكُوْنَ لَكَ بَيْتٌ مِّنْ زُخْرُفٍ اَوْ تَرْقٰى فِي السَّمَآءِ وَلَنْ نُّؤْمِنَ لِرُقِيِّكَ حَتّٰى تُنَزِّلَ عَلَيْنَا كِتٰبًا نَّقْرَؤُهٗ قُلْ سُبْحَانَ رَبِّيْ هَلْ كُنْتُ اِلَّا بَشَرًا رَّسُوْلًا ۝

وَمَا مَنَعَ النَّاسَ اَنْ يُّؤْمِنُوْا اِذْ جَآءَهُمُ الْهُدٰى اِلَّا اَنْ قَالُوْٓا اَبَعَثَ اللّٰهُ بَشَرًا رَّسُوْلًا ۝

قُلْ لَّوْ كَانَ فِي الْاَرْضِ مَلٰٓئِكَةٌ يَّمْشُوْنَ مُطْمَئِنِّيْنَ لَنَزَّلْنَا عَلَيْهِمْ مِّنَ السَّمَآءِ مَلَكًا رَّسُوْلًا ۝

قُلْ كَفٰى بِاللّٰهِ شَهِيْدًا بَيْنِيْ وَبَيْنَكُمْ اِنَّهٗ كَانَ بِعِبَادِهٖ خَبِيْرًا بَصِيْرًا ۝

The one thing that stands in the way of people believing when the guidance comes to them is, that they wonder: Has Allah sent a man as a Messenger? Tell them: Had there been angels walking about in peace and quiet in the earth, We would certainly have sent down to them an angel from heaven as a Messenger. Say to them: Sufficient is Allah for a Witness between you and me; surely He knows and sees His servants full well. Those whom Allah guides are the truly guided, and for those whom He lets go astray, thou wilt find no helper beside Him, and on the Day of Judgment We shall gather them together,

وَمَنْ يَّهْدِ اللّٰهُ فَهُوَ الْمُهْتَدِ وَمَنْ يُّضْلِلْ فَلَنْ تَجِدَ لَهُمْ اَوْلِيَآءَ مِنْ دُوْنِهٖ وَنَحْشُرُهُمْ يَوْمَ

273

blind, dumb and deaf in accordance with
their motives and designs. Their abode
shall be hell; every time its heat abates
We shall add to its fierceness. That is
their recompense, because they rejected
Our Signs and said: When we are reduced to bones and broken particles
shall we indeed be raised up as a new
creation? Do they not realise that Allah
Who created the heavens and the earth
has the power to create the like of them?
He has appointed a definite term for
them; there is no doubt about it, but
the wrongdoers persist in disbelief. Say to
them: Even if you possessed the limitless
treasures of my Lord's mercy, you would
surely hold them back for fear of exhaust-
ing them. Man is indeed niggardly. (95—
101)

We did indeed give Moses nine manifest
Signs; thou canst enquire from the children
of Israel. When he came to them, Pharaoh's
response to him was: Moses, I am sure thou
art self-deceived. He said: Thou knowest
well that these Signs have been sent down
by the Lord of the heavens and the earth
as manifest demonstrations and, Pharaoh,
I am sure thou art destined to perish. So
Pharaoh resolved to remove Moses and his
people from the earth; but We drowned
him and those who were with him, all
together. Thereafter We said to the
children of Israel: Dwell in the Promised
land; and when the time of the second
promise in respect of the Muslims approaches, We shall bring you back, a
mingled crowd. (102—105)

We have sent down this Discourse in
accordance with the requirements of truth
and wisdom, and with truth and wisdom
has it descended; and We have sent thee
only as a bearer of good tidings and a
Warner. The Quran We have divided into
parts that thou mayest recite it to the
people slowly and deliberately, and We
have sent it down a little at a time.

Say to them: Whether you believe in it or not, those to whom knowledge has been given before it fall down prostrate in token of complete submission when it is recited to them, and say: Holy is our Lord, surely, the promise of our Lord is bound to be fulfilled. They weep while they prostrate, and this adds to their humility. Say to them: Call upon Him as Allah or call upon Him as Rahman; by whichever name you call upon Him, His are the best attributes. Do not utter the words of Prayer aloud, nor too low, but seek a way in between. Proclaim widely: All praise belongs to Allah Who has taken unto Himself no son, and Who has no partner in His kingdom, nor does anyone befriend Him because of any weakness of His. Proclaim His Greatness on every occasion. (106—112)

قُلْ اٰمِنُوْا بِهٖٓ اَوْ لَا تُؤْمِنُوْاۚ اِنَّ الَّذِيْنَ اُوْتُوا الْعِلْمَ مِنْ قَبْلِهٖٓ اِذَا يُتْلٰى عَلَيْهِمْ يَخِرُّوْنَ لِلْاَذْقَانِ سُجَّدًا ۝

وَّ يَقُوْلُوْنَ سُبْحٰنَ رَبِّنَاۤ اِنْ كَانَ وَعْدُ رَبِّنَا لَمَفْعُوْلًا ۝ وَ يَخِرُّوْنَ لِلْاَذْقَانِ يَبْكُوْنَ وَ يَزِيْدُهُمْ خُشُوْعًا ۩ ۝

قُلِ ادْعُوا اللّٰهَ اَوِ ادْعُوا الرَّحْمٰنَۚ اَيًّا مَّا تَدْعُوْا فَلَهُ الْاَسْمَآءُ الْحُسْنٰىۚ وَ لَا تَجْهَرْ بِصَلَاتِكَ وَ لَا تُخَافِتْ بِهَا وَ ابْتَغِ بَيْنَ ذٰلِكَ سَبِيْلًا ۝

وَ قُلِ الْحَمْدُ لِلّٰهِ الَّذِيْ لَمْ يَتَّخِذْ وَلَدًا وَّ لَمْ يَكُنْ لَّهٗ شَرِيْكٌ فِي الْمُلْكِ وَ لَمْ يَكُنْ لَّهٗ وَلِيٌّ مِّنَ الذُّلِّ وَ كَبِّرْهُ تَكْبِيْرًا ۝

AL-KAHF

(Revealed before Hijra)

In the name of Allah, Most Gracious, Ever Merciful. (1)

All praise belongs to Allah Who has sent down the Book to His servant, free from all distortion, full of truth and guidance, that it may give warning of a grievous chastisement proceeding from Him, and that it may give the believers who work righteousness the glad tidings that they shall have a good reward which they shall enjoy for ever; and that it may warn those who say: Allah has taken unto Himself a son. They have no knowledge whatever concerning it, nor had their fathers. Grievous is the assertion that they make; they only utter a falsehood. Wilt thou grieve thyself to death for sorrow over them, if they believe not in this Discourse? We have made all that is on the earth an ornament for it, that We may try the dwellers thereof which of them is best in conduct. The time will come when We shall turn all that is on it into a barren waste. (2—9)

Dost thou think that the People of the Cave and Inscription were one of Our wondrous Signs? When the young men betook themselves to the wide cave for refuge, they prayed: Our Lord, bestow on us special mercy from Thyself and provide for us right guidance in our affair. So, for a number of years We

276

deprived them of news of the outside world. Then We raised them up that We might know which of the parties of their co-religionists had a better recollection of the period that they had sojourned in the Cave. Now We will recite to thee their true narrative. They were a party of young men who believed truly in their Lord, and We had bestowed further guidance on them. When they made up their minds to leave their homes, We strengthened their hearts, and they said one to another: Our Lord is the Lord of the heavens and the earth; we shall never call upon any god beside Him; for if we did so, we would utter a preposterous thing. These, our people, have adopted other gods beside Him. Why do they not produce some clear authority in their support, and, failing that, why do they not realise that there can be no one more unjust than one who fabricates a lie concerning Allah? Now that you have withdrawn from them and from that which they worship beside Allah, continue secure in the Cave; your Lord will extend His mercy to you and will provide facilities for you in your present situation. The sun could be observed to move away from their Cave on the right, as it rose, and to turn away from them on the left, when it set; and they were in a spacious hollow in the Cave. This is one of the Signs of Allah. He whom Allah guides is rightly guided; but for him whom He lets go astray, thou wilt find no helper or guide. (10—18)

Thou wouldst deem them awake but they are asleep. We shall cause them to turn to the right and to the left; their dog stretching out its forelegs on the

مِنْ لَّدُنْكَ رَحْمَةً وَّهَيِّئْ لَنَا مِنْ اَمْرِنَا رَشَدًا ۞

فَضَرَبْنَا عَلٰۤ اٰذَانِهِمْ فِى الْكَهْفِ سِنِيْنَ عَدَدًا ۞

ثُمَّ بَعَثْنٰهُمْ لِنَعْلَمَ اَىُّ الْحِزْبَيْنِ اَحْصٰى لِمَا لَبِثُوْۤا اَمَدًا ۞

نَحْنُ نَقُصُّ عَلَيْكَ نَبَاَهُمْ بِالْحَقِّ اِنَّهُمْ فِتْيَةٌ اٰمَنُوْا بِرَبِّهِمْ وَزِدْنٰهُمْ هُدًى ۞

وَّرَبَطْنَا عَلٰى قُلُوْبِهِمْ اِذْ قَامُوْا فَقَالُوْا رَبُّنَا رَبُّ السَّمٰوٰتِ وَالْاَرْضِ لَنْ نَّدْعُوَا مِنْ دُوْنِهٖ اِلٰهًا لَّقَدْ قُلْنَاۤ اِذًا شَطَطًا ۞

هٰۤؤُلَاۤءِ قَوْمُنَا اتَّخَذُوْا مِنْ دُوْنِهٖۤ اٰلِهَةً لَوْ لَا يَاْتُوْنَ عَلَيْهِمْ بِسُلْطٰنٍۭ بَيِّنٍ فَمَنْ اَظْلَمُ مِمَّنِ افْتَرٰى عَلَى اللّٰهِ كَذِبًا ۞

وَاِذِ اعْتَزَلْتُمُوْهُمْ وَمَا يَعْبُدُوْنَ اِلَّا اللّٰهَ فَاْوٗۤا اِلَى الْكَهْفِ يَنْشُرْ لَكُمْ رَبُّكُمْ مِّنْ رَّحْمَتِهٖ وَيُهَيِّئْ لَكُمْ مِّنْ اَمْرِكُمْ مِّرْفَقًا ۞

وَتَرَى الشَّمْسَ اِذَا طَلَعَتْ تَّزٰوَرُ عَنْ كَهْفِهِمْ ذَاتَ الْيَمِيْنِ وَاِذَا غَرَبَتْ تَّقْرِضُهُمْ ذَاتَ الشِّمَالِ وَهُمْ فِىْ فَجْوَةٍ مِّنْهُ ذٰلِكَ مِنْ اٰيٰتِ اللّٰهِ مَنْ يَّهْدِ اللّٰهُ فَهُوَ الْمُهْتَدِ وَمَنْ يُّضْلِلْ فَلَنْ تَجِدَ لَهٗ وَلِيًّا مُّرْشِدًا ۞

وَتَحْسَبُهُمْ اَيْقَاظًا وَّهُمْ رُقُوْدٌ ۖ وَّنُقَلِّبُهُمْ ذَاتَ الْيَمِيْنِ وَذَاتَ الشِّمَالِ ۖ وَكَلْبُهُمْ بَاسِطٌ

threshold. If thou were to come to
know of their pomp and power, thou
wouldst surely turn away from them in
fright, and be filled with awe of them.
So We raised them up from their lowly
condition, and they began to question
one another. One of them asked; How
long have you tarried here? Some of them
said: We have tarried a day or part of a
day. Others said: Your Lord knows best
how long you have tarried. Now send one
of you with these coins to the city, and
let him see which of them has the best
food, and let him bring you some provisions therefrom. He should be courteously
alert, and should not inform any one
about you. For, should they come to
know of you, they would stone you or
force you to return to their faith and then
you will have no chance whatever to
prosper. Thus did We acquaint the people
with their condition that they might know
that Allah's promise is true and that
there is no doubt about the Hour. Call to
mind the time when people disputed
among themselves concerning them and
some said: Raise a building above them.
Their Lord knew them best. Those who
won their point said: We will, surely, build
a place of worship above them. (19—22)

Those who have no definite knowledge
concerning them will make guesses: They
were three, the fourth was their dog; or
they will say: They were five, the sixth
was their dog; or they will say: They were
seven, the eighth was their dog. Say to
them: My Lord knows their number best;
none knows them save a few. So argue
about them only on the strength of knowledge, nor seek information about them
from any of them. Never say about anything I shall certainly do this tomorrow;

but say only: I shall do as Allah wills.
Shouldst thou forget, call to mind the
assurance of thy Lord and say: I trust
my Lord will guide me to that which is
even nearer to the right path than this.
Some will say they remained in their cave
three hundred years plus nine. Say to
them: Allah knows best how long they
remained there. He alone has knowledge
of the secrets of the heavens and the
earth. He sees all and hears all. They
have no helper beside Him and He does
not let any one share His authority.
(23—27)

إِلَّا أَن يَشَاءَ اللَّهُ وَاذْكُر رَّبَّكَ إِذَا نَسِيتَ وَقُل
عَسَى أَن يَهْدِيَنِ رَبِّي لِأَقْرَبَ مِنْ هَٰذَا رَشَدًا ۞

وَلَبِثُوا فِي كَهْفِهِمْ ثَلَٰثَ مِائَةٍ سِنِينَ وَ
ازْدَادُوا تِسْعًا ۞

قُلِ اللَّهُ أَعْلَمُ بِمَا لَبِثُوا لَهُ غَيْبُ السَّمَٰوَٰتِ وَالْأَرْضِ
أَبْصِرْ بِهِ وَأَسْمِعْ مَا لَهُم مِّن دُونِهِ مِن وَلِيٍّ
وَلَا يُشْرِكُ فِي حُكْمِهِ أَحَدًا ۞

وَاتْلُ مَا أُوحِيَ إِلَيْكَ مِن كِتَابِ رَبِّكَ لَا مُبَدِّلَ
لِكَلِمَٰتِهِ وَلَن تَجِدَ مِن دُونِهِ مُلْتَحَدًا ۞

وَاصْبِرْ نَفْسَكَ مَعَ الَّذِينَ يَدْعُونَ رَبَّهُم بِالْغَدَٰوةِ
وَالْعَشِيِّ يُرِيدُونَ وَجْهَهُ وَلَا تَعْدُ عَيْنَاكَ عَنْهُمْ
تُرِيدُ زِينَةَ الْحَيَوٰةِ الدُّنْيَا وَلَا تُطِعْ مَنْ
أَغْفَلْنَا قَلْبَهُ عَن ذِكْرِنَا وَاتَّبَعَ هَوَٰهُ
وَكَانَ أَمْرُهُ فُرُطًا ۞

Recite that which has been revealed to
thee of the Book of thy Lord. There is
none who can change His words; nor wilt
thou find a place of refuge beside Him.
Continue thy companionship with those
who call on their Lord, morning and
evening, seeking His pleasure, and look
not beyond them, for if thou dost that
thou wouldst be seeking the values of this
life; and follow not him whom We have
caused to be heedless of Our remembrance
who pursues his low desires, and whose
case exceeds all bounds. Proclaim: This is
the truth from your Lord; then let him
who will, believe, and let him who will,
disbelieve. We have prepared for the
wrongdoers a fire which already covers
them like a canopy. If they cry for help
their only help will be boiling water like
molten brass which will scorch their faces.
A terrible drink and an evil resting place!
Those who believe and work righteousness
shall have their reward; We suffer not
the reward of those who act virtuously to
be lost. They will have Gardens of Eternity
beneath which rivers flow, wherein they

وَقُلِ الْحَقُّ مِن رَّبِّكُمْ فَمَن شَاءَ فَلْيُؤْمِن
وَمَن شَاءَ فَلْيَكْفُرْ إِنَّا أَعْتَدْنَا لِلظَّٰلِمِينَ نَارًا
أَحَاطَ بِهِمْ سُرَادِقُهَا وَإِن يَسْتَغِيثُوا يُغَاثُوا بِمَاءٍ
كَالْمُهْلِ يَشْوِي الْوُجُوهَ بِئْسَ الشَّرَابُ وَسَاءَتْ
مُرْتَفَقًا ۞

إِنَّ الَّذِينَ آمَنُوا وَعَمِلُوا الصَّٰلِحَٰتِ إِنَّا لَا نُضِيعُ
أَجْرَ مَنْ أَحْسَنَ عَمَلًا ۞

أُولَٰئِكَ لَهُمْ جَنَّٰتُ عَدْنٍ تَجْرِي مِن تَحْتِهِمُ

will be adorned with bracelets of gold,
and will wear green robes of fine and
heavy silk, reclining upon raised couches.
An excellent reward and a delightful resting place. (28—32)

الْأَنْهَارُ يُحَلَّوْنَ فِيهَا مِنْ اَسَاوِرَ مِنْ ذَهَبٍ
وَّيَلْبَسُوْنَ ثِيَابًا خُضْرًا مِّنْ سُنْدُسٍ وَّ
اِسْتَبْرَقٍ مُّتَّكِئِيْنَ فِيهَا عَلَى الْاَرَآئِكِ نِعْمَ
الثَّوَابُ وَحَسُنَتْ مُرْتَفَقًا ۞

وَاضْرِبْ لَهُمْ مَّثَلًا رَّجُلَيْنِ جَعَلْنَا لِاَحَدِهِمَا
جَنَّتَيْنِ مِنْ اَعْنَابٍ وَّحَفَفْنٰهُمَا بِنَخْلٍ وَّجَعَلْنَا
بَيْنَهُمَا زَرْعًا ۞

كِلْتَا الْجَنَّتَيْنِ اٰتَتْ اُكُلَهَا وَلَمْ تَظْلِمْ مِّنْهُ شَيْئًا
وَّفَجَّرْنَا خِلٰلَهُمَا نَهَرًا ۞

Recite to them the case of two men:
One of them We had provided with two
vineyards which We had surrounded with
date-palms, and between the two We had
placed corn-fields. Each garden yielded its
fruit in abundance without failure: and
between the two We caused a stream to
flow. The owner gathered large quantities
of fruit, and boasted to his companion:
I am richer in wealth than thou and have
a stronger company of retainers. On one
occasion he entered his garden in a mood
of self-righteousness and vainglory and
said: I am sure this will never perish; and
I do not think the Hour will ever come.
But even if I am brought back to my
Lord, I shall, surely, find a better resort
than this. His companion admonished
him: Dost thou deny Him Who created
thee from dust, then from a sperm-drop,
then fashioned thee into a whole man?
As for me Allah alone is my Lord, and I
do not associate anyone with my Lord.
When thou didst enter thy garden why
didst thou not say: All will go as Allah
wills, for it is only by the grace of Allah
that any power is bestowed. If thou dost
consider me as less than thyself in the
matter of riches and offspring,

وَكَانَ لَهُ ثَمَرٌ فَقَالَ لِصَاحِبِهِ وَهُوَ يُحَاوِرُهُ
اَنَا اَكْثَرُ مِنْكَ مَالًا وَّاَعَزُّ نَفَرًا ۞

وَدَخَلَ جَنَّتَهُ وَهُوَ ظَالِمٌ لِّنَفْسِهِ قَالَ مَآ
اَظُنُّ اَنْ تَبِيْدَ هٰذِهِ اَبَدًا ۞

وَّمَآ اَظُنُّ السَّاعَةَ قَائِمَةً وَّلَئِنْ رُّدِدْتُّ اِلٰى
رَبِّيْ لَاَجِدَنَّ خَيْرًا مِّنْهَا مُنْقَلَبًا ۞

قَالَ لَهُ صَاحِبُهُ وَهُوَ يُحَاوِرُهُ اَكَفَرْتَ بِالَّذِيْ
خَلَقَكَ مِنْ تُرَابٍ ثُمَّ مِنْ نُّطْفَةٍ ثُمَّ سَوّٰىكَ
رَجُلًا ۞

لٰكِنَّا هُوَ اللّٰهُ رَبِّيْ وَلَا اُشْرِكُ بِرَبِّيْ اَحَدًا ۞

وَلَوْلَآ اِذْ دَخَلْتَ جَنَّتَكَ قُلْتَ مَا شَآءَ اللّٰهُ
لَا قُوَّةَ اِلَّا بِاللّٰهِ اِنْ تَرَنِ اَنَا اَقَلَّ مِنْكَ مَالًا
وَّوَلَدًا ۞

it is quite likely that my Lord will bestow upon me a garden better than thine, and may direct against thy garden a thunderbolt from heaven, converting it into barren slippery ground. Or, its water may sink into the earth, so that thou wilt not be able to find it. So it was and all his fruit was destroyed. The garden had all fallen down on its trellises, and its owner wrung his hands bewailing all that he had spent on it, and said: Would that I had not associated anyone with my Lord. He had no party to help him against Allah, nor could he avenge himself. At such time it is only the support of Allah, the True, that can be of avail. He is the Best in rewarding and the Best in respect of the final outcome. (33—45)

Expound to them the case of the life of this world. It is like the water that We send down from the sky, and the vegetation of the earth grows and mingles with it and all becomes stubble which is scattered about by the winds. Allah has full power over everything. Wealth and children are an ornament of the life of this world; then of these that which is converted into a source of permanent beneficence is best in the sight of thy Lord, both in respect of immediate reward and in respect of expected benefits. Keep in mind the day when We shall remove the mountains, and thou wilt see the nations of the earth march forth against one another and We shall gather them together and shall not leave any one of them out. They will be presented to thy Lord, all lined up, and will be greeted with: You have, indeed, come to Us as We created you at first, though you did think that We would not fix the Hour for the fulfilment of Our promise to you. The Book will be placed before them and thou wilt

فَعَسٰى رَبِّيٓ اَنْ يُّؤْتِيَنِ خَيْرًا مِّنْ جَنَّتِكَ وَيُرْسِلَ عَلَيْهَا حُسْبَانًا مِّنَ السَّمَآءِ فَتُصْبِحَ صَعِيْدًا زَلَقًا ۙ

اَوْ يُصْبِحَ مَآؤُهَا غَوْرًا فَلَنْ تَسْتَطِيْعَ لَهٗ طَلَبًا ۟

وَاُحِيْطَ بِثَمَرِهٖ فَاَصْبَحَ يُقَلِّبُ كَفَّيْهِ عَلٰى مَآ اَنْفَقَ فِيْهَا وَهِيَ خَاوِيَةٌ عَلٰى عُرُوْشِهَا وَيَقُوْلُ يٰلَيْتَنِيْ لَمْ اُشْرِكْ بِرَبِّيْٓ اَحَدًا ۟

وَلَمْ تَكُنْ لَّهٗ فِئَةٌ يَّنْصُرُوْنَهٗ مِنْ دُوْنِ اللّٰهِ وَمَا كَانَ مُنْتَصِرًا ۟

هُنَالِكَ الْوَلَايَةُ لِلّٰهِ الْحَقِّ هُوَ خَيْرٌ ثَوَابًا وَّ خَيْرٌ عُقْبًا ۟

وَاضْرِبْ لَهُمْ مَّثَلَ الْحَيٰوةِ الدُّنْيَا كَمَآءٍ اَنْزَلْنٰهُ مِنَ السَّمَآءِ فَاخْتَلَطَ بِهٖ نَبَاتُ الْاَرْضِ فَاَصْبَحَ هَشِيْمًا تَذْرُوْهُ الرِّيٰحُ وَكَانَ اللّٰهُ عَلٰى كُلِّ شَيْءٍ مُّقْتَدِرًا ۟

اَلْمَالُ وَالْبَنُوْنَ زِيْنَةُ الْحَيٰوةِ الدُّنْيَا وَالْبٰقِيٰتُ الصّٰلِحٰتُ خَيْرٌ عِنْدَ رَبِّكَ ثَوَابًا وَّخَيْرٌ اَمَلًا ۟

وَيَوْمَ نُسَيِّرُ الْجِبَالَ وَتَرَى الْاَرْضَ بَارِزَةً وَّحَشَرْنٰهُمْ فَلَمْ نُغَادِرْ مِنْهُمْ اَحَدًا ۟

وَعُرِضُوْا عَلٰى رَبِّكَ صَفًّا لَقَدْ جِئْتُمُوْنَا كَمَا خَلَقْنٰكُمْ اَوَّلَ مَرَّةٍ بَلْ زَعَمْتُمْ اَلَّنْ نَّجْعَلَ لَكُمْ مَوْعِدًا ۟

وَوُضِعَ الْكِتٰبُ فَتَرَى الْمُجْرِمِيْنَ مُشْفِقِيْنَ مِمَّا

see the guilty ones terrified at its contents. They will cry out: Woe to us, What is the matter with this Book that it leaves out nothing, small or great, but has recorded it. They will find all that they did confronting them. Thy Lord does not wrong any one. (46—50)

Call to mind when We commanded the angels: Fall down prostrate along with Adam. They did so, but Iblis did not. He was one of the fiery-tempered arrogant ones, so he disobeyed the command of his Lord. Will you then take him and his progeny, all of whom are your enemies, for friends instead of Me? Evil is this exchange for the wrongdoers. I did not have them witness the creation of the heavens and the earth, nor their own creation; nor could I take as helpers those who lead people astray. On the day when He will say to them: Now call those whom you deemed to be My partners; they will call on them but they will receive no answer, and We shall place a barrier between them. The guilty ones shall see the Fire and realise that they are going to fall therein, but they shall find no way of deliverance from it. (51—54)

We have, indeed, expounded all necessary things, in diverse ways, in this Quran for the benefit of mankind, but man is most contentious. That which prevents people from believing when the guidance comes to them, or from asking forgiveness of their Lord is their desire that they should be afflicted in the same manner as the ancients or that punishment should come upon them face to face. We send the Messengers only as bearers of glad tidings and as Warners. Those who disbelieve contend by means of falsehood that they may nullify the truth thereby. They treat My Signs and that which they are warned against as a jest. Who can be more unjust than one who is reminded of the Signs of his Lord, but

فِيهِ وَيَقُوْلُوْنَ يٰوَيْلَتَنَا مَالِ هٰذَا الْكِتٰبِ لَا يُغَادِرُ صَغِيْرَةً وَّلَا كَبِيْرَةً اِلَّا اَحْصٰهَا وَوَجَدُوْا مَا عَمِلُوْا حَاضِرًا وَلَا يَظْلِمُ رَبُّكَ اَحَدًا ۞

وَاِذْ قُلْنَا لِلْمَلٰٓئِكَةِ اسْجُدُوْا لِاٰدَمَ فَسَجَدُوْۤا اِلَّاۤ اِبْلِيْسَ كَانَ مِنَ الْجِنِّ فَفَسَقَ عَنْ اَمْرِ رَبِّهٖ اَفَتَتَّخِذُوْنَهٗ وَذُرِّيَّتَهٗۤ اَوْلِيَآءَ مِنْ دُوْنِيْ وَهُمْ لَكُمْ عَدُوٌّ بِئْسَ لِلظّٰلِمِيْنَ بَدَلًا ۞

مَاۤ اَشْهَدْتُّهُمْ خَلْقَ السَّمٰوٰتِ وَالْاَرْضِ وَلَا خَلْقَ اَنْفُسِهِمْ وَمَا كُنْتُ مُتَّخِذَ الْمُضِلِّيْنَ عَضُدًا ۞

وَيَوْمَ يَقُوْلُ نَادُوْا شُرَكَآءِيَ الَّذِيْنَ زَعَمْتُمْ فَدَعَوْهُمْ فَلَمْ يَسْتَجِيْبُوْا لَهُمْ وَجَعَلْنَا بَيْنَهُمْ مَّوْبِقًا ۞

وَرَاَ الْمُجْرِمُوْنَ النَّارَ فَظَنُّوْۤا اَنَّهُمْ مُّوَاقِعُوْهَا وَلَمْ يَجِدُوْا عَنْهَا مَصْرِفًا ۞

وَلَقَدْ صَرَّفْنَا فِيْ هٰذَا الْقُرْاٰنِ لِلنَّاسِ مِنْ كُلِّ مَثَلٍ وَكَانَ الْاِنْسَانُ اَكْثَرَ شَيْءٍ جَدَلًا ۞

وَمَا مَنَعَ النَّاسَ اَنْ يُّؤْمِنُوْۤا اِذْ جَآءَهُمُ الْهُدٰى وَيَسْتَغْفِرُوْا رَبَّهُمْ اِلَّاۤ اَنْ تَأْتِيَهُمْ سُنَّةُ الْاَوَّلِيْنَ اَوْ يَأْتِيَهُمُ الْعَذَابُ قُبُلًا ۞

وَمَا نُرْسِلُ الْمُرْسَلِيْنَ اِلَّا مُبَشِّرِيْنَ وَمُنْذِرِيْنَ وَيُجَادِلُ الَّذِيْنَ كَفَرُوْا بِالْبَاطِلِ لِيُدْحِضُوْا بِهِ الْحَقَّ وَاتَّخَذُوْۤا اٰيٰتِيْ وَمَاۤ اُنْذِرُوْا هُزُوًا ۞

وَمَنْ اَظْلَمُ مِمَّنْ ذُكِّرَ بِاٰيٰتِ رَبِّهٖ فَاَعْرَضَ عَنْهَا

turns away from them, and forgets his own misconduct which is the provision he has laid up for the Hereafter. We have placed several coverings over their hearts and have afflicted their ears with deafness that they may not understand. If thou call them to guidance, they will not follow it out of sheer perversity. Thy Lord is Most Forgiving, Lord of Mercy. Had He wished to destroy them on account of their evil conduct, He would have afflicted them with punishment quickly; but they have an appointed time, whereafter they will find no deliverance except through suffering the punishment. We destroyed these towns because of the iniquities of their people, and We had appointed a term for their destruction. (55—60)

In his vision Moses said to his young man: I will not quit until I arrive at the junction of the two seas, or else I will journey on for ages. When they arrived at the junction between them, they forgot to take care of their fish and it made its way into the sea swiftly. After they had passed the place, Moses said to his young man: Bring us our morning meal; we have surely been fatigued by this journey of ours. He answered: Look, what shall we do now? When we betook ourselves to the rock for rest I forgot to look after the fish (it is only Satan who made me forget it) and the fish made its way into the sea in a strange manner. Moses said: That is the place we have been seeking; so they returned retracing their footsteps. (61—65)

There they found a Servant of Ours upon whom We had bestowed Our mercy and whom We had taught knowledge from Ourself. Moses said to him: May I follow thee that thou mayest teach me part of the guidance that thou hast been taught? He answered: Keeping company with me will not be easy for you, as you will not be able to restrain your curiosity, and, in truth, how can you keep quiet concerning matters which you do not comprehend? Moses said: If Allah please, you will find me patient, and I will not disobey you in anything. He said: Well, then, if thou wouldst follow me ask me no question about anything till I speak to thee of it. (66—71)

So they set out till, when they embarked in a boat, he made a hole in it. Moses exclaimed: Have you made a hole in the boat to drown the people in it? You have, indeed, done a strange thing! He answered: Did I not tell you that you would not be able to restrain yourself in my company? Moses pleaded: Do not take me to task, because I forgot your instruction; and do not be hard on me for this lapse on my part. So they proceeded till, when they met a boy, he slew him. On this Moses protested: Is it not that you have slain an innocent person without his having slain any one? Surely you have committed an heinous act! He repeated: Did I not tell you that you would not be able to restrain yourself in my company? Moses was full of remorse: If I question you about anything after this, do not keep me with you. You will then be fully justified. So they went on till, when they came to a town, they asked its people for food, but they refused to extend hospitality to them. They found a wall in the town which was about to fall down, and he buttressed it. Moses said: If you had so desired, you could have asked payment for it. (72—78)

مِمَّا عُلِّمْتَ رُشْدًا ۝

قَالَ إِنَّكَ لَنْ تَسْتَطِيعَ مَعِيَ صَبْرًا ۝

وَكَيْفَ تَصْبِرُ عَلَى مَا لَمْ تُحِطْ بِهِ خُبْرًا ۝

قَالَ سَتَجِدُنِي إِنْ شَاءَ اللَّهُ صَابِرًا وَّلَا أَعْصِي لَكَ أَمْرًا ۝

قَالَ فَإِنِ اتَّبَعْتَنِي فَلَا تَسْأَلْنِي عَنْ شَيْءٍ حَتَّى أُحْدِثَ لَكَ مِنْهُ ذِكْرًا ۝

فَانْطَلَقَا ۟ حَتَّى إِذَا رَكِبَا فِي السَّفِينَةِ خَرَقَهَا ۚ قَالَ أَخَرَقْتَهَا لِتُغْرِقَ أَهْلَهَا ۚ لَقَدْ جِئْتَ شَيْئًا إِمْرًا ۝

قَالَ أَلَمْ أَقُلْ إِنَّكَ لَنْ تَسْتَطِيعَ مَعِيَ صَبْرًا ۝

قَالَ لَا تُؤَاخِذْنِي بِمَا نَسِيتُ وَلَا تُرْهِقْنِي مِنْ أَمْرِي عُسْرًا ۝

فَانْطَلَقَا ۟ حَتَّى إِذَا لَقِيَا غُلَامًا فَقَتَلَهُ ۚ قَالَ أَقَتَلْتَ نَفْسًا زَكِيَّةً بِغَيْرِ نَفْسٍ ۚ لَقَدْ جِئْتَ شَيْئًا نُّكْرًا ۝

قَالَ أَلَمْ أَقُلْ لَّكَ إِنَّكَ لَنْ تَسْتَطِيعَ مَعِيَ صَبْرًا ۝

قَالَ إِنْ سَأَلْتُكَ عَنْ شَيْءٍ بَعْدَهَا فَلَا تُصَاحِبْنِي ۖ قَدْ بَلَغْتَ مِنْ لَّدُنِّي عُذْرًا ۝

فَانْطَلَقَا ۟ حَتَّى إِذَا أَتَيَا أَهْلَ قَرْيَةٍ اسْتَطْعَمَا أَهْلَهَا فَأَبَوْا أَنْ يُّضَيِّفُوهُمَا فَوَجَدَا فِيهَا جِدَارًا يُّرِيدُ أَنْ يَّنْقَضَّ فَأَقَامَهُ ۚ قَالَ لَوْ شِئْتَ لَتَّخَذْتَ عَلَيْهِ أَجْرًا ۝

He said: This must be the parting between us. I shall now explain to you the meaning of that concerning which you were not able to restrain your curiosity. The boat belonged to some poor people who worked on the river, across which was a tyrant who seized every boat by force, so I decided to make a hole in it. The boy's parents were believers, and we apprehended lest on growing up he should afflict them with distress through rebellion and disbelief; so we desired that their Lord may bestow upon them in his place a child better than him in purity and closer in affection. The wall belonged to two orphan boys in the town, and beneath it was a treasure belonging to them; their father had been a righteous man, so thy Lord desired that they should arrive at their full maturity and bring out their treasure, as a mercy from thy Lord. I did not do it of my own accord. This is the explanation of that which you were not able to contemplate with equanimity. (79—83)

They ask thee concerning Dhul Qarnain also. Tell them: I shall certainly recite something about him to you. We established him in the earth and provided him with the means of achieving everything. He followed a certain way and when he arrived at the place of the setting of the sun, he discovered as if it was setting in an expanse of murky water, and found in its vicinity a people. We said to him: Dhul Qarnain, you may punish them or treat

قَالَ هٰذَا فِرَاقُ بَيۡنِیۡ وَ بَيۡنِكَ ۚ سَاُنَبِّئُكَ بِتَاۡوِيۡلِ مَا لَمۡ تَسۡتَطِعۡ عَّلَيۡهِ صَبۡرًا ۞

اَمَّا السَّفِيۡنَةُ فَكَانَتۡ لِسَكِيۡنَ يَعۡمَلُوۡنَ فِی الۡبَحۡرِ فَاَرَدۡتُّ اَنۡ اَعِيۡبَهَا وَ كَانَ وَرَآءَهُمۡ مَّلِكٌ يَّاۡخُذُ كُلَّ سَفِيۡنَةٍ غَصۡبًا ۞

وَ اَمَّا الۡغُلٰمُ فَكَانَ اَبَوٰهُ مُؤۡمِنَيۡنِ فَخَشِيۡنَاۤ اَنۡ يُّرۡهِقَهُمَا طُغۡيَانًا وَّ كُفۡرًا ۞

فَاَرَدۡنَاۤ اَنۡ يُّبۡدِلَهُمَا رَبُّهُمَا خَيۡرًا مِّنۡهُ زَكٰوةً وَّ اَقۡرَبَ رُحۡمًا ۞

وَ اَمَّا الۡجِدَارُ فَكَانَ لِغُلٰمَيۡنِ يَتِيۡمَيۡنِ فِی الۡمَدِيۡنَةِ وَ كَانَ تَحۡتَهٗ كَنۡزٌ لَّهُمَا وَ كَانَ اَبُوۡهُمَا صَالِحًا ۚ فَاَرَادَ رَبُّكَ اَنۡ يَّبۡلُغَاۤ اَشُدَّهُمَا وَ يَسۡتَخۡرِجَا كَنۡزَهُمَا ۖ رَحۡمَةً مِّنۡ رَّبِّكَ ۚ وَ مَا فَعَلۡتُهٗ عَنۡ اَمۡرِیۡ ؕ ذٰلِكَ تَاۡوِيۡلُ مَا لَمۡ تَسۡطِعۡ عَّلَيۡهِ صَبۡرًا ۞

وَ يَسۡئَلُوۡنَكَ عَنۡ ذِی الۡقَرۡنَيۡنِ ؕ قُلۡ سَاَتۡلُوۡا عَلَيۡكُمۡ مِّنۡهُ ذِكۡرًا ۞

اِنَّا مَكَّنَّا لَهٗ فِی الۡاَرۡضِ وَ اٰتَيۡنٰهُ مِنۡ كُلِّ شَیۡءٍ سَبَبًا ۞

فَاَتۡبَعَ سَبَبًا ۞

حَتّٰۤی اِذَا بَلَغَ مَغۡرِبَ الشَّمۡسِ وَجَدَهَا تَغۡرُبُ فِیۡ عَيۡنٍ حَمِئَةٍ وَّ وَجَدَ عِنۡدَهَا قَوۡمًا ۬ؕ قُلۡنَا يٰذَا الۡقَرۡنَيۡنِ اِمَّاۤ اَنۡ تُعَذِّبَ وَ اِمَّاۤ اَنۡ تَتَّخِذَ فِيۡهِمۡ

them with kindness. He said: We shall certainly punish him who does wrong; then shall he be brought back to his Lord, Who will chastise him with a grievous chastisement. He who believes and works righteousness will have a good reward in the Hereafter, and We shall also facilitate everything for him by Our command. Then he followed another way, and when he arrived at the place of the rising of the sun, he found it rising on a people for whom We had made no shelter against it. Thus indeed it was, and We have securely preserved all knowledge concerning him. (84—92)

Then he followed still another way. When he reached between the two barriers, he found on either side a people who could scarcely understand what he said. They said to him: Dhul Qarnain, verily, Gog and Magog are creating disorder in the land. Shall we appoint a tribute to be paid to thee on condition that thou set up a barrier between them and us? He said to them: The resources which my Lord has made available to me for such purposes are far better than those of my enemies, but you may help me according to your means and I will set up a rampart between them and you. So bring me lumps of iron. When he had filled up the space between the two natural barriers, the mountain and the sea, he said to them: Now blow on the fire with your bellows. When he had made it as fire, he said: Now bring me molten copper that I may pour it thereon. When all was finished Gog and Magog were not able to scale it, nor were they able to bore through it. (93—98)

حُسْنًا ۸۵

قَالَ اَمَّا مَنْ ظَلَمَ فَسَوْفَ نُعَذِّبُهٗ ثُمَّ يُرَدُّ اِلٰى رَبِّهٖ فَيُعَذِّبُهٗ عَذَابًا نُّكْرًا ۸۶

وَاَمَّا مَنْ اٰمَنَ وَعَمِلَ صَالِحًا فَلَهٗ جَزَآءَ ﹰ الْحُسْنٰى ۚ وَسَنَقُوْلُ لَهٗ مِنْ اَمْرِنَا يُسْرًا ۸۷

ثُمَّ اَتْبَعَ سَبَبًا ۸۸

حَتّٰى اِذَا بَلَغَ مَطْلِعَ الشَّمْسِ وَجَدَهَا تَطْلُعُ عَلٰى قَوْمٍ لَّمْ نَجْعَلْ لَّهُمْ مِّنْ دُوْنِهَا سِتْرًا ۸۹

كَذٰلِكَ ۚ وَقَدْ اَحَطْنَا بِمَا لَدَيْهِ خُبْرًا ۹۰

ثُمَّ اَتْبَعَ سَبَبًا ۹۱

حَتّٰى اِذَا بَلَغَ بَيْنَ السَّدَّيْنِ وَجَدَ مِنْ دُوْنِهِمَا قَوْمًا لَّا يَكَادُوْنَ يَفْقَهُوْنَ قَوْلًا ۹۲

قَالُوْا يٰذَا الْقَرْنَيْنِ اِنَّ يَأْجُوْجَ وَمَأْجُوْجَ مُفْسِدُوْنَ فِى الْاَرْضِ فَهَلْ نَجْعَلُ لَكَ خَرْجًا عَلٰٓى اَنْ تَجْعَلَ بَيْنَنَا وَبَيْنَهُمْ سَدًّا ۹۳

قَالَ مَا مَكَّنِّيْ فِيْهِ رَبِّيْ خَيْرٌ فَاَعِيْنُوْنِيْ بِقُوَّةٍ اَجْعَلْ بَيْنَكُمْ وَبَيْنَهُمْ رَدْمًا ۹۴

اٰتُوْنِيْ زُبَرَ الْحَدِيْدِ ۚ حَتّٰٓى اِذَا سَاوٰى بَيْنَ الصَّدَفَيْنِ قَالَ انْفُخُوْا ۚ حَتّٰٓى اِذَا جَعَلَهٗ نَارًا ۙ قَالَ اٰتُوْنِيْ اُفْرِغْ عَلَيْهِ قِطْرًا ۹۵

فَمَا اسْطَاعُوْا اَنْ يَّظْهَرُوْهُ وَمَا اسْتَطَاعُوْا لَهٗ نَقْبًا ۹۶

Dhul Qarnain said: All this has been accomplished through the mercy of my Lord. When my Lord's warning of universal catastrophe is to be fulfilled, He will knock it down into a flat mound. My Lord's warning is bound to be fulfilled. (99)

قَالَ هٰذَا رَحْمَةٌ مِّنْ رَّبِّيْ فَاِذَا جَآءَ وَعْدُ رَبِّيْ جَعَلَهُ دَكَّآءَ وَكَانَ وَعْدُ رَبِّيْ حَقًّا ۞

وَّتَرَكْنَا بَعْضَهُمْ يَوْمَئِذٍ يَّمُوْجُ فِيْ بَعْضٍ وَّنُفِخَ فِي الصُّوْرِ فَجَمَعْنٰهُمْ جَمْعًا ۞

وَّعَرَضْنَا جَهَنَّمَ يَوْمَئِذٍ لِّلْكٰفِرِيْنَ عَرْضَا ۞

When that day comes We shall let some of them surge against others like the waves of the ocean, and the trumpet will be blown, and We shall gather them all together. On that day We shall present hell, face to face, to the disbelievers whose eyes were veiled against My Reminder (the Quran) so that they heeded it not, and who could not even afford to listen. Do the disbelievers imagine that they can take My servants as helpers instead of Me? We have prepared hell as entertainment for the disbelievers. Ask them: Shall We tell you of those who are the greatest losers in respect of their works? It is those whose effort is devoted wholly to the life of this world, and they imagine that they are engaged in producing excellent works. They are those who reject the Signs of their Lord and disbelieve in the meeting with Him. So their works are vain, and on the Day of Judgment We shall attach no weight to them. Hell will be their reward, because they disbelieved, and made a jest of My Signs and My Messengers. Those who believe and work righteousness will have Gardens of Paradise for an abode, wherein they will abide. They will desire no change therefrom. (100—109)

اَلَّذِيْنَ كَانَتْ اَعْيُنُهُمْ فِيْ غِطَآءٍ عَنْ ذِكْرِيْ وَكَانُوْا لَا يَسْتَطِيْعُوْنَ سَمْعًا ۞

اَفَحَسِبَ الَّذِيْنَ كَفَرُوْا اَنْ يَّتَّخِذُوْا عِبَادِيْ مِنْ دُوْنِيْ اَوْلِيَآءَ ۚ اِنَّآ اَعْتَدْنَا جَهَنَّمَ لِلْكٰفِرِيْنَ نُزُلَا ۞

قُلْ هَلْ نُنَبِّئُكُمْ بِالْاَخْسَرِيْنَ اَعْمَالًا ۞

اَلَّذِيْنَ ضَلَّ سَعْيُهُمْ فِي الْحَيٰوةِ الدُّنْيَا وَهُمْ يَحْسَبُوْنَ اَنَّهُمْ يُحْسِنُوْنَ صُنْعًا ۞

اُولٰٓئِكَ الَّذِيْنَ كَفَرُوْا بِاٰيٰتِ رَبِّهِمْ وَلِقَآئِهٖ فَحَبِطَتْ اَعْمَالُهُمْ فَلَا نُقِيْمُ لَهُمْ يَوْمَ الْقِيٰمَةِ وَزْنًا ۞

ذٰلِكَ جَزَآؤُهُمْ جَهَنَّمُ بِمَا كَفَرُوْا وَاتَّخَذُوْا اٰيٰتِيْ وَرُسُلِيْ هُزُوًا ۞

اِنَّ الَّذِيْنَ اٰمَنُوْا وَعَمِلُوا الصّٰلِحٰتِ كَانَتْ لَهُمْ جَنّٰتُ الْفِرْدَوْسِ نُزُلَا ۞

خٰلِدِيْنَ فِيْهَا لَا يَبْغُوْنَ عَنْهَا حِوَلَا ۞

Tell them: If the ocean became ink for transcribing the words of my Lord, surely

قُلْ لَّوْ كَانَ الْبَحْرُ مِدَادًا لِّكَلِمٰتِ رَبِّيْ لَنَفِدَ

the ocean would be exhausted before the words of my Lord came to an end, even though We augmented it with the like thereof. Tell them: I am but a man like yourselves; only it is revealed to me that your God is One God. So let him who hopes to meet his Lord work righteousness and let him associate no one in the worship of his Lord. (110—111)

الْبَحْرُ قَبْلَ اَنْ تَنْفَدَ كَلِمٰتُ رَبِّیْ وَلَوْ جِئْنَا بِمِثْلِهٖ مَدَدًا ۞

قُلْ اِنَّمَاۤ اَنَا بَشَرٌ مِّثْلُكُمْ یُوْحٰۤی اِلَیَّ اَنَّمَاۤ اِلٰهُكُمْ اِلٰهٌ وَّاحِدٌ ۚ فَمَنْ كَانَ یَرْجُوْا لِقَآءَ رَبِّهٖ فَلْیَعْمَلْ عَمَلًا صَالِحًا وَّلَا یُشْرِكْ بِعِبَادَةِ رَبِّهٖۤ اَحَدًا ۞

MARYAM

(Revealed before Hijra)

In the name of Allah, Most Gracious,
Ever Merciful. (1)

THOU ART SUFFICIENT AND THOU
ART THE GUIDE, ALL-KNOWING
TRUTHFUL ONE. (2)

This is an account of the mercy of thy
Lord bestowed upon His servant Zachariah, when he called upon his Lord in low
tones, praying: My Lord, my very bones
have become feeble, and my head has
turned hoary with age, but never have my
supplications to Thee, O Lord, remained
unfruitful. I am apprehensive of the
behaviour of my relations after my death,
and my wife is barren. I beg Thee, therefore, do Thou bestow upon me from
Thyself a successor to be my heir and to
be the heir of the blessings of the House
of Jacob; and make him one who should
be pleasing in Thy sight, O Lord. His
Lord responded: Zachariah, We give thee
glad tidings of a son who shall grow up
to maturity and whose name shall be
Yahya. We have designated no one before
him by this name. Zachariah exclaimed:
My Lord, how shall it be that I shall have
a son grown up, seeing that my wife is
barren and that I have arrived at extreme
old age. His Lord answered: So it is, but
thy Lord sayeth: It is easy for Me; seest
thou not that I created thee before, when
thou wast nothing. Zachariah begged:
My Lord, lay a command upon me. His
Lord said: Thou art commanded not to
speak to anyone for three successive days
and nights. Thereupon Zachariah came
forth from the chamber unto his people
and conveyed to them by signs to glorify
the Lord morn and eve. (3—12)

289

We commanded Yahya: Hold fast the Book; and We bestowed upon him wisdom while he was still young, as a token of tenderness from Ourself and to purify him. He grew up righteous, and was dutiful towards his parents and was not haughty or rebellious. Peace was on him on the day of his birth, and on the day of his death, and peace will be on him on the day he will be raised up to life again. (13—16)

اَنْ سَبِّحُوْا بُكْرَةً وَّعَشِيًّا ۞

يٰيَحْيٰى خُذِ الْكِتٰبَ بِقُوَّةٍ ۚ وَاٰتَيْنٰهُ الْحُكْمَ صَبِيًّا ۞

وَّحَنَانًا مِّنْ لَّدُنَّا وَزَكٰوةً ۚ وَكَانَ تَقِيًّا ۞

وَّبَرًّا بِوَالِدَيْهِ وَلَمْ يَكُنْ جَبَّارًا عَصِيًّا ۞

وَسَلٰمٌ عَلَيْهِ يَوْمَ وُلِدَ وَيَوْمَ يَمُوْتُ وَيَوْمَ يُبْعَثُ حَيًّا ۞

Recite the account of Mary according to this Book, when she withdrew from her people to a place towards the east, and screened herself off from them. Then We sent Our angel to her and he appeared to her in the form of a well proportioned man. On perceiving him she exclaimed: I seek refuge with the Gracious One from thee if thou art at all righteous. The angel reassured her: I am but a messenger from thy Lord, that I may give thee a righteous son who will grow up to maturity. She marvelled: How shall it be that I shall have a grown son, seeing that no man has touched me and I have not been unchaste? The angel said: So it is, but thy Lord sayeth: It is easy for Me. It is so ordained that We may make him a Sign unto people and a source of Our mercy. This has been decreed. (17—22)

وَاذْكُرْ فِى الْكِتٰبِ مَرْيَمَ ۘ اِذِ انْتَبَذَتْ مِنْ اَهْلِهَا مَكَانًا شَرْقِيًّا ۞

فَاتَّخَذَتْ مِنْ دُوْنِهِمْ حِجَابًا ۗ فَاَرْسَلْنَا اِلَيْهَا رُوْحَنَا فَتَمَثَّلَ لَهَا بَشَرًا سَوِيًّا ۞

قَالَتْ اِنِّىْ اَعُوْذُ بِالرَّحْمٰنِ مِنْكَ اِنْ كُنْتَ تَقِيًّا ۞

قَالَ اِنَّمَآ اَنَا رَسُوْلُ رَبِّكِ ۖ لِاَهَبَ لَكِ غُلٰمًا زَكِيًّا ۞

قَالَتْ اَنّٰى يَكُوْنُ لِىْ غُلٰمٌ وَّلَمْ يَمْسَسْنِىْ بَشَرٌ وَّلَمْ اَكُ بَغِيًّا ۞

قَالَ كَذٰلِكِ ۚ قَالَ رَبُّكِ هُوَ عَلَىَّ هَيِّنٌ ۚ وَلِنَجْعَلَهٗٓ اٰيَةً لِّلنَّاسِ وَرَحْمَةً مِّنَّا ۚ وَكَانَ اَمْرًا مَّقْضِيًّا ۞

Thus she conceived him, and withdrew with him to a remote place. When her time came the pains of childbirth drove her to the trunk of a palm-tree. Realising her condition, she cried out: Would that I had died before this and had been quite forgotten. The voice of the angel reached her from below: Grieve not; for thy Lord has provided a rivulet below

فَحَمَلَتْهُ فَانْتَبَذَتْ بِهٖ مَكَانًا قَصِيًّا ۞

فَاَجَآءَهَا الْمَخَاضُ اِلٰى جِذْعِ النَّخْلَةِ ۚ قَالَتْ يٰلَيْتَنِىْ مِتُّ قَبْلَ هٰذَا وَكُنْتُ نَسْيًا مَّنْسِيًّا ۞

فَنَادٰىهَا مِنْ تَحْتِهَآ اَلَّا تَحْزَنِىْ قَدْ جَعَلَ رَبُّكِ

thee, wherein thou mayest wash thyself and the child. Then take hold of the branch of the palm-tree and shake it; it will shed fresh ripe dates upon thee. Thus eat and drink and be at rest. Shouldst thou see anyone approaching, call out: I have this day vowed a fast to the Gracious One. I will, therefore, hold no converse with any person. (23—27)

تَحْتَكِ سَرِيًّا ۝

وَهُزِّىٓ إِلَيْكِ بِجِذْعِ النَّخْلَةِ تُسَٰقِطْ عَلَيْكِ رُطَبًا جَنِيًّا ۝

فَكُلِى وَاشْرَبِى وَقَرِّى عَيْنًا ۚ فَإِمَّا تَرَيِنَّ مِنَ الْبَشَرِ أَحَدًا ۙ فَقُولِىٓ إِنِّى نَذَرْتُ لِلرَّحْمٰنِ صَوْمًا فَلَنْ أُكَلِّمَ الْيَوْمَ إِنْسِيًّا ۝

She accompanied him to her people, while he was riding. They upbraided her: Mary, thou hast perpetrated an abominable thing. O sister of Aaron, thy father was not a wicked man, nor was thy mother an unchaste woman. She pointed to him. They said: How can we hold converse with one who was but yesterday a child being rocked in a cradle? (28—30)

فَأَتَتْ بِهِ قَوْمَهَا تَحْمِلُهُ ۖ قَالُوا يٰمَرْيَمُ لَقَدْ جِئْتِ شَيْئًا فَرِيًّا ۝

يٰٓأُخْتَ هٰرُونَ مَا كَانَ أَبُوكِ امْرَأَ سَوْءٍ وَّمَا كَانَتْ أُمُّكِ بَغِيًّا ۝

فَأَشَارَتْ إِلَيْهِ ۖ قَالُوا كَيْفَ نُكَلِّمُ مَنْ كَانَ فِى الْمَهْدِ صَبِيًّا ۝

Jesus taught: I am a servant of Allah, He has given me the Book, and has appointed me a Prophet; He has made me blessed wheresoever I may be, and has enjoined upon me Prayer and almsgiving throughout my life. He has made me dutiful towards my mother, and has not made me haughty and graceless. Peace was ordained for me the day I was born, the day I shall die and the day I shall be raised up to life again. (31—34)

قَالَ إِنِّى عَبْدُ اللَّهِ ۖ ءَاتٰنِىَ الْكِتٰبَ وَجَعَلَنِى نَبِيًّا ۝

وَّجَعَلَنِى مُبَارَكًا أَيْنَ مَا كُنْتُ وَأَوْصٰنِى بِالصَّلٰوةِ وَالزَّكٰوةِ مَا دُمْتُ حَيًّا ۝

وَّبَرًّا بِوَالِدَتِى وَلَمْ يَجْعَلْنِى جَبَّارًا شَقِيًّا ۝

وَالسَّلٰمُ عَلَىَّ يَوْمَ وُلِدْتُّ وَيَوْمَ أَمُوتُ وَيَوْمَ أُبْعَثُ حَيًّا ۝

Such was Jesus son of Mary. This is a statement of the truth about that concerning which they entertain doubt. It is not in accord with the Majesty of Allah that He should take unto Himself a son. Holy is He. When He decrees a thing, He says concerning it: Be, and it is.

ذٰلِكَ عِيسَى ابْنُ مَرْيَمَ ۚ قَوْلَ الْحَقِّ الَّذِى فِيهِ يَمْتَرُونَ ۝

مَا كَانَ لِلَّهِ أَنْ يَّتَّخِذَ مِنْ وَّلَدٍ ۙ سُبْحٰنَهُ ۚ إِذَا قَضَىٰ أَمْرًا فَإِنَّمَا يَقُولُ لَهُ كُنْ فَيَكُونُ ۝

Jesus taught: Allah is my Lord and your Lord; so worship Him alone. This is the right path. (35—37)

وَاِنَّ اللّٰهَ رَبِّیۡ وَرَبُّکُمۡ فَاعۡبُدُوۡہُ ؕ ہٰذَا صِرَاطٌ مُّسۡتَقِیۡمٌ ۩

فَاخۡتَلَفَ الۡاَحۡزَابُ مِنۡۢ بَیۡنِہِمۡ ۚ فَوَیۡلٌ لِّلَّذِیۡنَ کَفَرُوۡا مِنۡ مَّشۡہَدِ یَوۡمٍ عَظِیۡمٍ ۩

Thereafter, different groups differed among themselves. Woe to those who disbelieve in the meeting of the great day. The day they present themselves before Us, how keen will be their hearing and sight, but the wrongdoers are in manifest error today. Warn them of the day of remorse when the affair will be conclusively determined, while today they are heedless and believe not. Of a surety, it is We Ourself Who will inherit the earth and all who are thereon; and to Us will they all be returned. (38—41)

اَسۡمِعۡ بِہِمۡ وَاَبۡصِرۡ ۙ یَوۡمَ یَاۡتُوۡنَنَا لٰکِنِ الظّٰلِمُوۡنَ الۡیَوۡمَ فِیۡ ضَلٰلٍ مُّبِیۡنٍ ۩

وَاَنۡذِرۡہُمۡ یَوۡمَ الۡحَسۡرَۃِ اِذۡ قُضِیَ الۡاَمۡرُ ۚ وَہُمۡ فِیۡ غَفۡلَۃٍ وَّہُمۡ لَا یُؤۡمِنُوۡنَ ۩

اِنَّا نَحۡنُ نَرِثُ الۡاَرۡضَ وَمَنۡ عَلَیۡہَا وَاِلَیۡنَا یُرۡجَعُوۡنَ ۩

وَاذۡکُرۡ فِی الۡکِتٰبِ اِبۡرٰہِیۡمَ ۬ اِنَّہٗ کَانَ صِدِّیۡقًا نَّبِیًّا ۩

Recite the account of Abraham according to this Book; he was indeed a righteous person and a Prophet. Call to mind when he said to his father: Father, wherefore dost thou worship that which hears not, nor sees, nor can avail thee aught? Father, there has indeed been given to me knowledge such as has not been given to thee. Follow me, therefore, I shall guide thee along a straight path. Father, serve not Satan; surely, Satan is persistently disobedient to the Gracious One. Father, indeed I fear lest a chastisement from the Gracious One afflict thee, and thou become a companion of Satan. His father rebuked him: Is it that thou art turning away from my gods, Abraham? If thou desist not, I shall surely cause thee to be stoned to death. Now leave me alone for a while, lest I do thee some injury.

اِذۡ قَالَ لِاَبِیۡہِ یٰۤاَبَتِ لِمَ تَعۡبُدُ مَا لَا یَسۡمَعُ وَلَا یُبۡصِرُ وَلَا یُغۡنِیۡ عَنۡکَ شَیۡئًا ۩

یٰۤاَبَتِ اِنِّیۡ قَدۡ جَآءَنِیۡ مِنَ الۡعِلۡمِ مَا لَمۡ یَاۡتِکَ فَاتَّبِعۡنِیۡۤ اَہۡدِکَ صِرَاطًا سَوِیًّا ۩

یٰۤاَبَتِ لَا تَعۡبُدِ الشَّیۡطٰنَ ؕ اِنَّ الشَّیۡطٰنَ کَانَ لِلرَّحۡمٰنِ عَصِیًّا ۩

یٰۤاَبَتِ اِنِّیۡۤ اَخَافُ اَنۡ یَّمَسَّکَ عَذَابٌ مِّنَ الرَّحۡمٰنِ فَتَکُوۡنَ لِلشَّیۡطٰنِ وَلِیًّا ۩

قَالَ اَرَاغِبٌ اَنۡتَ عَنۡ اٰلِہَتِیۡ یٰۤاِبۡرٰہِیۡمُ ۚ لَئِنۡ لَّمۡ تَنۡتَہِ لَاَرۡجُمَنَّکَ وَاہۡجُرۡنِیۡ مَلِیًّا ۩

Abraham made answer: Peace be on thee;
I will ask forgiveness of my Lord for thee;
He is indeed gracious unto me. I shall
keep away from you and from that which
you call upon beside Allah; and I will
supplicate my Lord, and surely I will
encounter no ill fortune by virtue of my
supplications. So when he left them and
that which they worshipped beside Allah,
We bestowed on him Isaac and after him
Jacob, and each of them We made a
Prophet; and We granted them of Our
mercy and bestowed on them true and
high renown. (42—51)

Recite the account of Moses according
to this Book. He was indeed a chosen
one, and was a Messenger and a Prophet.
We called him from the right side of the
Mount and made him draw near to Us
through close communion; and We bestowed upon him, as his helper, out of Our
mercy, his brother Aaron, having made
him a Prophet. (52—54)

Recite the account of Ishmael according to this Book. He was indeed always
true to his promise and was a Messenger
and a Prophet. He exhorted his people
to Prayer and almsgiving, and was well
liked by his Lord. (55—56)

Recite the account of Idris according
to this Book; he was indeed a righteous
person and a Prophet, and We exalted
him to a lofty station. (57—58)

These were the people on whom Allah
bestowed His blessings from among the
Prophets, of the posterity of Adam and
of those whom We carried in the Ark
with Noah, and of the posterity of

قَالَ سَلٰمٌ عَلَيْكَ ۚ سَاَسْتَغْفِرُ لَكَ رَبِّيْ ۚ اِنَّهٗ كَانَ بِيْ حَفِيًّا ۝

وَاَعْتَزِلُكُمْ وَمَا تَدْعُوْنَ مِنْ دُوْنِ اللّٰهِ وَاَدْعُوْا رَبِّيْ ۖ عَسَىٰٓ اَلَّاۤ اَكُوْنَ بِدُعَآءِ رَبِّيْ شَقِيًّا ۝

فَلَمَّا اعْتَزَلَهُمْ وَمَا يَعْبُدُوْنَ مِنْ دُوْنِ اللّٰهِ ۙ وَهَبْنَا لَهٗۤ اِسْحٰقَ وَيَعْقُوْبَ ۚ وَكُلًّا جَعَلْنَا نَبِيًّا ۝

وَوَهَبْنَا لَهُمْ مِّنْ رَّحْمَتِنَا وَجَعَلْنَا لَهُمْ لِسَانَ صِدْقٍ عَلِيًّا ۝

وَاذْكُرْ فِى الْكِتٰبِ مُوْسٰىۤ ۖ اِنَّهٗ كَانَ مُخْلَصًا وَّكَانَ رَسُوْلًا نَّبِيًّا ۝

وَنَادَيْنٰهُ مِنْ جَانِبِ الطُّوْرِ الْاَيْمَنِ وَقَرَّبْنٰهُ نَجِيًّا ۝

وَوَهَبْنَا لَهٗ مِنْ رَّحْمَتِنَاۤ اَخَاهُ هٰرُوْنَ نَبِيًّا ۝

وَاذْكُرْ فِى الْكِتٰبِ اِسْمٰعِيْلَ ۖ اِنَّهٗ كَانَ صَادِقَ الْوَعْدِ وَكَانَ رَسُوْلًا نَّبِيًّا ۝

وَكَانَ يَأْمُرُ اَهْلَهٗ بِالصَّلٰوةِ وَالزَّكٰوةِ ۖ وَكَانَ عِنْدَ رَبِّهٖ مَرْضِيًّا ۝

وَاذْكُرْ فِى الْكِتٰبِ اِدْرِيْسَ ۚ اِنَّهٗ كَانَ صِدِّيْقًا نَّبِيًّا ۝

وَّرَفَعْنٰهُ مَكَانًا عَلِيًّا ۝

اُولٰٓئِكَ الَّذِيْنَ اَنْعَمَ اللّٰهُ عَلَيْهِمْ مِّنَ النَّبِيّٖنَ مِنْ ذُرِّيَّةِ اٰدَمَ ۖ وَمِمَّنْ حَمَلْنَا مَعَ نُوْحٍ ۖ وَمِنْ ذُرِّيَّةِ

Abraham and Israel; and they were of those whom We guided and chose for Our service. When the Word of the Gracious One was recited to them their hearts were moved and they fell down into prostration. Then they were followed by a people who laid aside Prayer and followed evil desires; they will be seized with ruin, except those of them who repent and believe and act righteously. Such will enter Paradise — not being wronged in the least — Gardens of Eternity, which the Gracious One has promised to His servants without their having seen them. His promise is always fulfilled. They will not hear therein anything vain, only greetings of Peace; and they will have their sustenance therein, morning and evening. This is the Paradise that We bestow as an inheritance on those of Our servants who are righteous. (59—64)

اِبْرٰهِيْمَ وَاِسْرَآءِيْلَ وَمِمَّنْ هَدَيْنَا وَاجْتَبَيْنَا ۖ

اِذَا تُتْلٰى عَلَيْهِمْ اٰيٰتُ الرَّحْمٰنِ خَرُّوْا سُجَّدًا وَّبُكِيًّا ۩

فَخَلَفَ مِنْ بَعْدِهِمْ خَلْفٌ اَضَاعُوا الصَّلٰوةَ وَاتَّبَعُوا الشَّهَوٰتِ فَسَوْفَ يَلْقَوْنَ غَيًّا ۙ

اِلَّا مَنْ تَابَ وَاٰمَنَ وَعَمِلَ صَالِحًا فَاُولٰٓئِكَ يَدْخُلُوْنَ الْجَنَّةَ وَلَا يُظْلَمُوْنَ شَيْئًا ۙ

جَنّٰتِ عَدْنِ ِۨالَّتِىْ وَعَدَ الرَّحْمٰنُ عِبَادَهٗ بِالْغَيْبِ ۖ اِنَّهٗ كَانَ وَعْدُهٗ مَاْتِيًّا ۞

لَا يَسْمَعُوْنَ فِيْهَا لَغْوًا اِلَّا سَلٰمًا ۖ وَلَهُمْ رِزْقُهُمْ فِيْهَا بُكْرَةً وَّعَشِيًّا ۞

تِلْكَ الْجَنَّةُ الَّتِىْ نُوْرِثُ مِنْ عِبَادِنَا مَنْ كَانَ تَقِيًّا ۞

The angels declare: We descend not save by the command of thy Lord; to Him belongs all that is before us and all that is behind us and all that is between. Thy Lord is not forgetful in the least. He is the Lord of the heavens and of the earth and of all that is between the two. So worship Him alone and be steadfast in His service. Knowest thou anyone who possesses attributes like unto His? (65—66)

وَمَا نَتَنَزَّلُ اِلَّا بِاَمْرِ رَبِّكَ ۖ لَهٗ مَا بَيْنَ اَيْدِيْنَا وَمَا خَلْفَنَا وَمَا بَيْنَ ذٰلِكَ ۖ وَمَا كَانَ رَبُّكَ نَسِيًّا ۚ

رَبُّ السَّمٰوٰتِ وَالْاَرْضِ وَمَا بَيْنَهُمَا فَاعْبُدْهُ وَاصْطَبِرْ لِعِبَادَتِهٖ ۚ هَلْ تَعْلَمُ لَهٗ سَمِيًّا ۞

Man will ever ask: When I am dead, shall I be brought forth alive? Does not man remember that We created him before when he was naught? By thy Lord, We shall most surely gather them together, men and satans alike, and bring them close to hell on their knees. Then We shall select from every group those who

وَيَقُوْلُ الْاِنْسَانُ ءَاِذَا مَا مِتُّ لَسَوْفَ اُخْرَجُ حَيًّا ۞

اَوَلَا يَذْكُرُ الْاِنْسَانُ اَنَّا خَلَقْنٰهُ مِنْ قَبْلُ وَلَمْ يَكُ شَيْئًا ۞

فَوَرَبِّكَ لَنَحْشُرَنَّهُمْ وَالشَّيٰطِيْنَ ثُمَّ لَنُحْضِرَنَّهُمْ حَوْلَ جَهَنَّمَ جِثِيًّا ۞

ثُمَّ لَنَنْزِعَنَّ مِنْ كُلِّ شِيْعَةٍ اَيُّهُمْ اَشَدُّ عَلَى الرَّحْمٰنِ

were most stubborn in their opposition to the Gracious One. We know best those most deserving of arriving therein. There is not one of you but will come to it in this life or the next; this is an unalterable decree of thy Lord. Then shall We save the righteous and shall leave the wrongdoers therein, on their knees. (67—73)

عِتِيًّا ۝

ثُمَّ لَنَحْنُ اَعْلَمُ بِالَّذِيْنَ هُمْ اَوْلٰى بِهَا صِلِيًّا ۝

وَاِنْ مِّنْكُمْ اِلَّا وَارِدُهَا ۚ كَانَ عَلٰى رَبِّكَ حَتْمًا مَّقْضِيًّا ۝

ثُمَّ نُنَجِّى الَّذِيْنَ اتَّقَوْا وَّنَذَرُ الظّٰلِمِيْنَ فِيْهَا جِثِيًّا ۝

When Our manifest Signs are recited unto them, the disbelievers ask the believers: Which of us two groups is better in status and more desirable as company? How many a generation have We destroyed before them, who were better off than these in belongings and outward display! Tell them: The Gracious One grants respite for a time to those who are in error until, when they are confronted with that which they are promised, torment or ruin, they realise who is worse situated and is weaker in numbers. Allah increases in guidance those who follow guidance; and lasting good works are better in the sight of thy Lord in respect of reward and in respect of the end. (74—77)

وَاِذَا تُتْلٰى عَلَيْهِمْ اٰيٰتُنَا بَيِّنٰتٍ قَالَ الَّذِيْنَ كَفَرُوْا لِلَّذِيْنَ اٰمَنُوْا اَىُّ الْفَرِيْقَيْنِ خَيْرٌ مَّقَامًا وَّاَحْسَنُ نَدِيًّا ۝

وَكَمْ اَهْلَكْنَا قَبْلَهُمْ مِّنْ قَرْنٍ هُمْ اَحْسَنُ اَثَاثًا وَّرِءْيًا ۝

قُلْ مَنْ كَانَ فِى الضَّلٰلَةِ فَلْيَمْدُدْ لَهُ الرَّحْمٰنُ مَدًّا ۚ حَتّٰى اِذَا رَاَوْا مَا يُوْعَدُوْنَ اِمَّا الْعَذَابَ وَاِمَّا السَّاعَةَ ۚ فَسَيَعْلَمُوْنَ مَنْ هُوَ شَرٌّ مَّكَانًا وَّاَضْعَفُ جُنْدًا ۝

وَيَزِيْدُ اللّٰهُ الَّذِيْنَ اهْتَدَوْا هُدًى ۚ وَالْبٰقِيٰتُ الصّٰلِحٰتُ خَيْرٌ عِنْدَ رَبِّكَ ثَوَابًا وَّخَيْرٌ مَّرَدًّا ۝

Knowest thou of him who disbelieved in Our Signs and boasted: I shall certainly be given wealth and children? Has he been apprised of the unseen or taken a promise from the Gracious One? Indeed not. We shall note down what he says and shall prolong his agony, and We shall inherit that of which he boasts, and he shall come to us empty-handed. They have taken other gods than Allah, that they may be a source of honour for them.

اَفَرَءَيْتَ الَّذِيْ كَفَرَ بِاٰيٰتِنَا وَقَالَ لَاُوْتَيَنَّ مَالًا وَّوَلَدًا ۝

اَطَّلَعَ الْغَيْبَ اَمِ اتَّخَذَ عِنْدَ الرَّحْمٰنِ عَهْدًا ۝

كَلَّا ۚ سَنَكْتُبُ مَا يَقُوْلُ وَنَمُدُّ لَهُ مِنَ الْعَذَابِ مَدًّا ۝

وَّنَرِثُهُ مَا يَقُوْلُ وَيَأْتِيْنَا فَرْدًا ۝

وَاتَّخَذُوْا مِنْ دُوْنِ اللّٰهِ اٰلِهَةً لِّيَكُوْنُوْا لَهُمْ عِزًّا ۝

That will not be. Their false gods will reject their worship and will stand in opposition to them. (78—83)

وَكَلَّا سَيَكْفُرُوْنَ بِعِبَادَتِهِمْ وَيَكُوْنُوْنَ عَلَيْهِمْ ضِدًّا ۝

اَلَمْ تَرَ اَنَّا اَرْسَلْنَا الشَّيٰطِيْنَ عَلَى الْكٰفِرِيْنَ تَؤُزُّهُمْ اَزًّا ۝

فَلَا تَعْجَلْ عَلَيْهِمْ اِنَّمَا نَعُدُّ لَهُمْ عَدًّا ۝

يَوْمَ نَحْشُرُ الْمُتَّقِيْنَ اِلَى الرَّحْمٰنِ وَفْدًا ۝

وَّنَسُوْقُ الْمُجْرِمِيْنَ اِلٰى جَهَنَّمَ وِرْدًا ۝

Knowest thou not that We have appointed satans to incite the disbelievers to disobedience? So move not against them in haste; We have fixed a reckoning for them. Keep in mind the day when We shall gather the righteous ones in honour before the Gracious One, and shall drive the guilty ones to hell in disgrace. On that day no one will have the capacity to intercede, save he who has received a promise from the Gracious One. (84—88)

لَا يَمْلِكُوْنَ الشَّفَاعَةَ اِلَّا مَنِ اتَّخَذَ عِنْدَ الرَّحْمٰنِ عَهْدًا ۝

وَ قَالُوا اتَّخَذَ الرَّحْمٰنُ وَلَدًا ۝

لَقَدْ جِئْتُمْ شَيْئًا اِدًّا ۝

تَكَادُ السَّمٰوٰتُ يَتَفَطَّرْنَ مِنْهُ وَ تَنْشَقُّ الْاَرْضُ وَ تَخِرُّ الْجِبَالُ هَدًّا ۝

They allege: The Gracious One has taken unto Himself a son. Assuredly, you have uttered a monstrous thing! The heavens might well-nigh burst thereat, and the earth cleave asunder, and the mountains fall down in pieces, because they ascribe a son to the Gracious One; whereas it becomes not the Gracious One to take unto Himself a son. There is no one in the heavens and the earth but he shall come to the Gracious One as a bondman. Verily He encompasses them and has numbered them all. Each one of them shall come to Him singly on the Day of Judgment. The Gracious One will create enduring love for those who believe and work righteousness. So We have made the Quran easy in thy tongue that thou mayest convey thereby glad tidings to the righteous, and warn thereby a contentious people.

اَنْ دَعَوْا لِلرَّحْمٰنِ وَلَدًا ۝

وَ مَا يَنْبَغِيْ لِلرَّحْمٰنِ اَنْ يَّتَّخِذَ وَلَدًا ۝

اِنْ كُلُّ مَنْ فِى السَّمٰوٰتِ وَ الْاَرْضِ اِلَّا اٰتِى الرَّحْمٰنِ عَبْدًا ۝

لَقَدْ اَحْصٰهُمْ وَعَدَّهُمْ عَدًّا ۝

وَ كُلُّهُمْ اٰتِيْهِ يَوْمَ الْقِيٰمَةِ فَرْدًا ۝

اِنَّ الَّذِيْنَ اٰمَنُوْا وَ عَمِلُوا الصّٰلِحٰتِ سَيَجْعَلُ لَهُمُ الرَّحْمٰنُ وُدًّا ۝

فَاِنَّمَا يَسَّرْنٰهُ بِلِسَانِكَ لِتُبَشِّرَ بِهِ الْمُتَّقِيْنَ وَ تُنْذِرَ بِهِ قَوْمًا لُّدًّا ۝

How many a generation have We destroyed before them! Canst thou perceive a single one of them, or hear even a whisper of them? (89—99)

وَكَمْ اَهْلَكْنَا قَبْلَهُمْ مِّنْ قَرْنٍ هَلْ تُحِسُّ مِنْهُمْ مِّنْ اَحَدٍ اَوْ تَسْمَعُ لَهُمْ رِكْزًا ۝

ṬĀ HĀ

(Revealed before Hijra)

In the name of Allah, Most Gracious,
Ever Merciful. (1)

بِسْمِ اللهِ الرَّحْمٰنِ الرَّحِيْمِ ۝

طٰهٰ ۝

مَآ اَنْزَلْنَا عَلَيْكَ الْقُرْاٰنَ لِتَشْقٰٓى ۝

اِلَّا تَذْكِرَةً لِّمَنْ يَّخْشٰى ۝

O man of perfect capacities, We have
not sent down the Quran to thee that
thou may be distressed, but as an exhortation for him who fears Allah. It is a
revelation from Him Who created the
earth and the high heavens, the Gracious
One Who has settled Himself on the
Throne. To Him belongs whatsoever is in
the heavens and whatsoever is in the earth,
and whatsoever is between them, and
whatsoever is beneath the moist subsoil.
If thou speakest aloud or speakest in a
low voice, He hears all, for He knows all
that is secret and most hidden. Allah is
He beside Whom there is no god. His are
the most excellent attributes. (2—9)

تَنْزِيْلًا مِّمَّنْ خَلَقَ الْاَرْضَ وَ السَّمٰوٰتِ الْعُلٰى ۝

اَلرَّحْمٰنُ عَلَى الْعَرْشِ اسْتَوٰى ۝

لَهٗ مَا فِى السَّمٰوٰتِ وَ مَا فِى الْاَرْضِ وَ مَا بَيْنَهُمَا وَ مَا
تَحْتَ الثَّرٰى ۝

وَ اِنْ تَجْهَرْ بِالْقَوْلِ فَاِنَّهٗ يَعْلَمُ السِّرَّ وَ اَخْفٰى ۝

اَللّٰهُ لَآ اِلٰهَ اِلَّا هُوَ لَهُ الْاَسْمَآءُ الْحُسْنٰى ۝

وَ هَلْ اَتٰىكَ حَدِيْثُ مُوْسٰى ۝

اِذْ رَاٰ نَارًا فَقَالَ لِاَهْلِهِ امْكُثُوْٓا اِنِّيْ اٰنَسْتُ نَارًا
لَّعَلِّيْٓ اٰتِيْكُمْ مِّنْهَا بِقَبَسٍ اَوْ اَجِدُ عَلَى النَّارِ
هُدًى ۝

Has an account of Moses reached thee,
when he perceived a fire and said to his
family: Tarry ye awhile. I have perceived
a fire, perchance I may bring you a brand
therefrom or find guidance at the fire.
When he came to it he heard a call:
Moses, verily I am thy Lord. Cast off thy
shoes; for thou art in the sacred vale of
Tuwa. I have chosen thee; so hearken to
what is revealed. Verily, I am Allah; there
is no god beside Me; so worship Me alone,
and observe Prayer for My remembrance.

فَلَمَّآ اَتٰىهَا نُوْدِيَ يٰمُوْسٰى ۝

اِنِّيْٓ اَنَا رَبُّكَ فَاخْلَعْ نَعْلَيْكَ اِنَّكَ بِالْوَادِ الْمُقَدَّسِ
طُوًى ۝

وَ اَنَا اخْتَرْتُكَ فَاسْتَمِعْ لِمَا يُوْحٰى ۝

اِنَّنِيْٓ اَنَا اللّٰهُ لَآ اِلٰهَ اِلَّآ اَنَا فَاعْبُدْنِيْ وَ اَقِمِ
الصَّلٰوةَ لِذِكْرِيْ ۝

Of a surety, the Hour is coming; I will manifest it, so that every one may be recompensed according to his endeavour. So let not him who believes not therein and follows his own evil inclinations turn thee away from believing firmly in it, lest thou perish. (10—17)

اِنَّ السَّاعَةَ اٰتِيَةٌ اَكَادُ اُخْفِيهَا لِتُجْزٰى كُلُّ نَفْسٍ بِمَا تَسْعٰى ۝

فَلَا يَصُدَّنَّكَ عَنْهَا مَنْ لَّا يُؤْمِنُ بِهَا وَ اتَّبَعَ هَوٰىهُ فَتَرْدٰى ۝

وَ مَا تِلْكَ بِيَمِينِكَ يٰمُوْسٰى ۝

قَالَ هِيَ عَصَايَ اَتَوَكَّؤُا عَلَيْهَا وَاَهُشُّ بِهَا عَلٰى غَنَمِيْ وَلِيَ فِيْهَا مَاٰرِبُ اُخْرٰى ۝

قَالَ اَلْقِهَا يٰمُوْسٰى ۝

فَاَلْقٰهَا فَاِذَا هِيَ حَيَّةٌ تَسْعٰى ۝

قَالَ خُذْهَا وَ لَا تَخَفْ سَنُعِيْدُهَا سِيْرَتَهَا الْاُوْلٰى ۝

وَاضْمُمْ يَدَكَ اِلٰى جَنَاحِكَ تَخْرُجْ بَيْضَاءَ مِنْ غَيْرِ سُوْءٍ اٰيَةً اُخْرٰى ۝

لِنُرِيَكَ مِنْ اٰيٰتِنَا الْكُبْرٰى ۝

Allah asked: What is that in thy right hand, Moses? He replied: It is my rod. I lean on it, and beat down therewith leaves from the trees for my sheep, and I have also other uses for it. Allah directed: Cast it down, Moses. So he cast it down, and lo! It was a running serpent. Allah reassured him: Catch hold of it and be not afraid. We shall restore it to its former condition. Now draw thy hand close under thy other arm; it shall come forth white, without any blemish — another Sign. All this is a preparation that We may show thee some of Our greater Signs. Go thou to Pharaoh, he has transgressed grievously. (18—25)

اِذْهَبْ اِلٰى فِرْعَوْنَ اِنَّهُ طَغٰى ۝

قَالَ رَبِّ اشْرَحْ لِيْ صَدْرِيْ ۝

وَ يَسِّرْ لِيْ اَمْرِيْ ۝

وَاحْلُلْ عُقْدَةً مِّنْ لِّسَانِيْ ۝

يَفْقَهُوْا قَوْلِيْ ۝

وَاجْعَلْ لِّيْ وَزِيْرًا مِّنْ اَهْلِيْ ۝

هٰرُوْنَ اَخِيْ ۝

اشْدُدْ بِهٖ اَزْرِيْ ۝

Moses supplicated: Lord, expand my mind, and make it easy for me to carry out Thy behest, and remove every impediment from my speech that people may understand easily what I say, and appoint for me a helper from among my family, even Aaron, my brother. Make him my collaborator in my task and thus add to my strength, that we may glorify Thee constantly and remember Thee much. Thou hast full knowledge of us. (26—36)

وَاَشْرِكْهُ فِيۤ اَمْرِیۡ ۝

كَیۡ نُّسَبِّحَكَ كَثِيۡرًا ۝

وَّنَذۡكُرَكَ كَثِيۡرًا ۝

اِنَّكَ كُنۡتَ بِنَا بَصِيۡرًا ۝

قَالَ قَدۡ اُوۡتِيۡتَ سُؤۡلَكَ يٰمُوۡسٰی ۝

وَلَقَدۡ مَنَنَّا عَلَيۡكَ مَرَّةً اُخۡرٰیۤ ۝

اِذۡ اَوۡحَيۡنَاۤ اِلٰۤی اُمِّكَ مَا يُوۡحٰیۤ ۝

Allah responded to him: Granted is thy prayer, Moses. I have been gracious towards thee before also when I revealed to thy mother all that was needed to be revealed, to wit: Put him in the ark, and place it in the river. The river will cast it on to the bank and one who is an enemy of Mine and his will take him up. I surrounded thee with My love, so that thou mightest be reared under My care. Thy sister walked along, repeating: Shall I inform you of one who will take care of him? Thus We restored thee to thy mother so that she might be comforted and might not grieve. Then thou didst kill a man, and We delivered thee from sorrow. Then We proved thee in diverse ways and thou didst tarry several years among the people of Midian. Then thou camest up to the standard, Moses, and I chose thee for Myself. Now go, thou and thy brother, with My Signs, and be diligent in remembering Me. Go, both of you, to Pharaoh, for he has transgressed grievously; but speak gently to him, perchance he may take heed or be humble.

اَنِ اقۡذِفِيۡهِ فِی التَّابُوۡتِ فَاقۡذِفِيۡهِ فِی الۡيَمِّ فَلۡيُلۡقِهِ الۡيَمُّ بِالسَّاحِلِ يَاۡخُذۡهُ عَدُوٌّ لِّیۡ وَعَدُوٌّ لَّهٗ ؕ وَ اَلۡقَيۡتُ عَلَيۡكَ مَحَبَّةً مِّنِّیۡ ۖ وَلِتُصۡنَعَ عَلٰی عَيۡنِیۡ ۝

اِذۡ تَمۡشِیۡۤ اُخۡتُكَ فَتَقُوۡلُ هَلۡ اَدُلُّكُمۡ عَلٰی مَنۡ يَّكۡفُلُهٗ ؕ فَرَجَعۡنٰكَ اِلٰۤی اُمِّكَ كَیۡ تَقَرَّ عَيۡنُهَا وَلَا تَحۡزَنَ ؕ وَقَتَلۡتَ نَفۡسًا فَنَجَّيۡنٰكَ مِنَ الۡغَمِّ وَفَتَنّٰكَ فُتُوۡنًا ۖ فَلَبِثۡتَ سِنِيۡنَ فِیۡۤ اَهۡلِ مَدۡيَنَ ۙ ثُمَّ جِئۡتَ عَلٰی قَدَرٍ يّٰمُوۡسٰی ۝

وَاصۡطَنَعۡتُكَ لِنَفۡسِیۡ ۝

اِذۡهَبۡ اَنۡتَ وَاَخُوۡكَ بِاٰيٰتِیۡ وَلَا تَنِيَا فِیۡ ذِكۡرِیۡ ۝

اِذۡهَبَاۤ اِلٰی فِرۡعَوۡنَ اِنَّهٗ طَغٰی ۝

فَقُوۡلَا لَهٗ قَوۡلًا لَّيِّنًا لَّعَلَّهٗ يَتَذَكَّرُ اَوۡ يَخۡشٰی ۝

They urged: Lord, we fear lest he commit some excess against us or press us hard. Allah reassured them: Fear not at all; for I am with you both, hearing and seeing. Go ye both to him and say: We are the Messengers of thy Lord; so let the children of Israel go with us, and oppress

قَالَا رَبَّنَاۤ اِنَّنَا نَخَافُ اَنۡ يَّفۡرُطَ عَلَيۡنَاۤ اَوۡ اَنۡ يَّطۡغٰی ۝

قَالَ لَا تَخَافَاۤ اِنَّنِیۡ مَعَكُمَاۤ اَسۡمَعُ وَاَرٰی ۝

فَاۡتِيٰهُ فَقُوۡلَاۤ اِنَّا رَسُوۡلَا رَبِّكَ فَاَرۡسِلۡ مَعَنَا بَنِیۤۡ

them not. We have indeed brought thee
a Sign from thy Lord. Allah's peace shall
be on him who follows the guidance
brought by us, and, it has been revealed
to us, that punishment shall overtake
him who rejects it and turns away from it.
(37—49)

اِسۡرَآءِیۡلَ ۬ وَلَا تُعَذِّبۡهُمۡ قَدۡ جِئۡنٰكَ بِاٰیَةٍ مِّنۡ رَّبِّكَ ؕ وَالسَّلٰمُ عَلٰی مَنِ اتَّبَعَ الۡهُدٰی ۞

اِنَّا قَدۡ اُوۡحِیَ اِلَیۡنَاۤ اَنَّ الۡعَذَابَ عَلٰی مَنۡ كَذَّبَ وَتَوَلّٰی ۞

قَالَ فَمَنۡ رَّبُّكُمَا یٰمُوۡسٰی ۞

قَالَ رَبُّنَا الَّذِیۡۤ اَعۡطٰی كُلَّ شَیۡءٍ خَلۡقَهٗ ثُمَّ هَدٰی ۞

قَالَ فَمَا بَالُ الۡقُرُوۡنِ الۡاُوۡلٰی ۞

قَالَ عِلۡمُهَا عِنۡدَ رَبِّیۡ فِیۡ كِتٰبٍ ۚ لَا یَضِلُّ رَبِّیۡ وَلَا یَنۡسَی ۬

Pharaoh enquired: Who then is the
Lord of you both, Moses? He said: Our
Lord is He Who has bestowed upon
everything its appropriate faculties and
then guided it to their proper use. Pharaoh
asked: What then will be the fate of
former peoples who knew nought of it?
Moses said: The knowledge thereof is
with my Lord all recorded in a Book.
My Lord errs not, nor forgets. Moses
added: My Lord is He Who has made the
earth a cradle for you, and has caused
pathways to run through it for your
benefit and Who sends down rain from
the sky. My Lord says: Thereby We bring
forth diverse kinds of vegetation, so eat
ye of them and also pasture your cattle.
Verily, in this are Signs for those endowed
with reason. From the earth have We
created you, and into it We shall cause
you to return and from it shall We bring
you forth once more. (50—56)

الَّذِیۡ جَعَلَ لَكُمُ الۡاَرۡضَ مَهۡدًا وَّسَلَكَ لَكُمۡ فِیۡهَا سُبُلًا وَّاَنۡزَلَ مِنَ السَّمَآءِ مَآءً ؕ فَاَخۡرَجۡنَا بِهٖۤ اَزۡوَاجًا مِّنۡ نَّبَاتٍ شَتّٰی ۞

كُلُوۡا وَارۡعَوۡا اَنۡعَامَكُمۡ ؕ اِنَّ فِیۡ ذٰلِكَ لَاٰیٰتٍ لِّاُولِی النُّهٰی ۞

مِنۡهَا خَلَقۡنٰكُمۡ وَفِیۡهَا نُعِیۡدُكُمۡ وَمِنۡهَا نُخۡرِجُكُمۡ تَارَةً اُخۡرٰی ۞

وَلَقَدۡ اَرَیۡنٰهُ اٰیٰتِنَا كُلَّهَا فَكَذَّبَ وَاَبٰی ۞

We did show Pharaoh Our Signs of all
kinds, but he rejected them and persisted in disbelief. He said: Hast thou
come to us, Moses, to drive us out of our
land by thy magic? If so, we shall assuredly oppose thee with the like magic; so
make an appointment between thyself
and us which we should not fail to keep,
neither thou nor we, at a place alike for
us both. (57—59)

قَالَ اَجِئۡتَنَا لِتُخۡرِجَنَا مِنۡ اَرۡضِنَا بِسِحۡرِكَ یٰمُوۡسٰی ۞

فَلَنَأۡتِیَنَّكَ بِسِحۡرٍ مِّثۡلِهٖ فَاجۡعَلۡ بَیۡنَنَا وَبَیۡنَكَ مَوۡعِدًا لَّا نُخۡلِفُهٗ نَحۡنُ وَلَاۤ اَنۡتَ مَكَانًا سُوًی ۞

301

Moses said: Let your appointment be for the day of the Festival, and let the people be assembled when the sun is risen high. Thereupon Pharaoh withdrew and concerted his plan and returned for the appointment. Moses admonished Pharaoh and his party: Woe unto you; concert not a lie against Allah, lest He destroy you by some calamity. Surely, he who fabricates a lie shall perish. Thereupon they began to argue amongst themselves and conferred in secret. They argued: These two are big magicians, who desire to drive you out from your land by their magic and to destroy your excellent way of life; therefore, concert your plan and go forward in a body. Surely, he who gains the ascendancy this day will flourish. (60—65)

Those who came forward against Moses enquired: Moses, will you make the first cast, or shall we be the first to make the cast? He said: Do you make the cast. And lo! their cords and their staves appeared to him, by their magic, as though they scurried about. Moses conceived a fear in his mind, but We reassured him: Fear not, for surely thou wilt have the upper hand. Put down that which is in thy right hand, it will swallow up that which they have wrought, for that which they have wrought is but a magician's trick, and a magician shall not thrive, come whence he may. When Moses put down his rod and the magicians were exposed, they were impelled to fall down prostrate and cried: We believe in the Lord of Aaron and Moses. Pharaoh was incensed thereat and stormed: What? Do you believe in him before I give you leave? He must be your chief who has taught you magic. Therefore, I will certainly cut off your hands and your

feet on alternate sides, and I will surely crucify you on the trunks of palm-
trees. Then shall you know which of us
can inflict severer and more lasting
punishment. They retorted: We cannot
prefer thee to the manifest Signs that
have come to us, nor to Him Who created us. So decree what thou wilt decree,
thou canst but terminate this present
life. We have believed in our Lord that
He may forgive us our sins and forgive
us the deceit that thou hast forced us to
practise. Allah is the Best and Most
Abiding. (66—74)

اَرْجُلَكُمْ مِّنْ خِلَافٍ وَّلَاُوصَلِّبَنَّكُمْ فِىْ جُذُوْعِ
التَّخْلِ وَلَتَعْلَمُنَّ اَيُّنَاۤ اَشَدُّ عَذَابًا وَّاَبْقٰى ۝
قَالُوْا لَنْ نُّؤْثِرَكَ عَلٰى مَا جَآءَنَا مِنَ الْبَيِّنٰتِ وَ
الَّذِىْ فَطَرَنَا فَاقْضِ مَاۤ اَنْتَ قَاضٍ اِنَّمَا تَقْضِىْ
هٰذِهِ الْحَيٰوةَ الدُّنْيَا ۝
اِنَّاۤ اٰمَنَّا بِرَبِّنَا لِيَغْفِرَ لَنَا خَطٰيٰنَا وَمَاۤ اَكْرَهْتَنَا
عَلَيْهِ مِنَ السِّحْرِ وَاللّٰهُ خَيْرٌ وَّاَبْقٰى ۝
اِنَّهٗ مَنْ يَّأْتِ رَبَّهٗ مُجْرِمًا فَاِنَّ لَهٗ جَهَنَّمَ لَا
يَمُوْتُ فِيْهَا وَلَا يَحْيٰى ۝
وَمَنْ يَّأْتِهٖ مُؤْمِنًا قَدْ عَمِلَ الصّٰلِحٰتِ فَاُولٰٓئِكَ
لَهُمُ الدَّرَجٰتُ الْعُلٰى ۝

The truth is, that the portion of him
who comes to his Lord a sinner is hell;
he shall neither die therein nor live. But
he who comes to Him a believer, having
acted righteously, for such are the highest
ranks in Gardens of Eternity, beneath
which rivers flow; they will abide therein
for ever. That is the recompense of those
who keep themselves pure. (75—77)

جَنّٰتُ عَدْنٍ تَجْرِىْ مِنْ تَحْتِهَا الْاَنْهٰرُ خٰلِدِيْنَ
فِيْهَا وَذٰلِكَ جَزٰٓؤُا مَنْ تَزَكّٰى ۝
وَلَقَدْ اَوْحَيْنَاۤ اِلٰى مُوْسٰٓى اَنْ اَسْرِ بِعِبَادِىْ فَاضْرِبْ
لَهُمْ طَرِيْقًا فِى الْبَحْرِ يَبَسًا لَّا تَخٰفُ دَرَكًا وَّلَا
تَخْشٰى ۝

We directed Moses: Set forth with My
servants in the darkness of the night and
show them a dry path in the sea. Thou
wilt not have any apprehension of being
overtaken nor wilt thou be oppressed by
any other fear. Pharaoh pursued them
with his hosts and a great volume of the
waters of the sea overwhelmed them.
Pharaoh led his people astray and did not
guide them aright. (78—80)

فَاَتْبَعَهُمْ فِرْعَوْنُ بِجُنُوْدِهٖ فَغَشِيَهُمْ مِّنَ الْيَمِّ
مَا غَشِيَهُمْ ۝
وَاَضَلَّ فِرْعَوْنُ قَوْمَهٗ وَمَا هَدٰى ۝

Children of Israel, We delivered you
from your enemy, and We made a covenant with you on the right side of the
Mount, and We sent down on you Manna
and Salwa, and admonished you: Eat of the

يٰبَنِىْۤ اِسْرَآءِيْلَ قَدْ اَنْجَيْنٰكُمْ مِّنْ عَدُوِّكُمْ وَ
وٰعَدْنٰكُمْ جَانِبَ الطُّوْرِ الْاَيْمَنَ وَنَزَّلْنَا عَلَيْكُمُ
الْمَنَّ وَالسَّلْوٰى ۝

good things that We have provided for you, and transgress not therein, lest My wrath descend upon you; and he on whom My wrath descends is surely ruined. But I am Most Forgiving towards him who repents and believes and acts righteously and follows the guidance. (81—83)

كُلُوْا مِنْ طَيِّبٰتِ مَا رَزَقْنٰكُمْ وَلَا تَطْغَوْا فِيْهِ فَيَحِلَّ عَلَيْكُمْ غَضَبِيْ وَمَنْ يَّحْلِلْ عَلَيْهِ غَضَبِيْ فَقَدْ هَوٰى ۝

وَاِنِّيْ لَغَفَّارٌ لِّمَنْ تَابَ وَاٰمَنَ وَعَمِلَ صَالِحًا ثُمَّ اهْتَدٰى ۝

وَمَآ اَعْجَلَكَ عَنْ قَوْمِكَ يٰمُوْسٰى ۝

When Moses arrived for his tryst with his Lord he was asked: What has brought thee away in haste from thy people, Moses? He answered: They are close behind me, and I have hastened to Thee, my Lord, that Thou mightest be pleased. His Lord told him: We have tried thy people in thy absence, and the Samiri has led them astray. So Moses returned to his people chagrined and in a rage and up-braided them: O my people, did not your Lord make you a gracious promise? Did, then, the appointed time appear too long to you, and did you desire that your Lord's wrath should descend upon you, that you went against your promise to me? They made answer: We did not go against our promise to thee of our own accord; but we were heavily laden with orna- ments of Pharaoh's people and cast them away and so did Samiri. Then he pro- duced a calf for them, a lifeless body which made a meaningless sound. He and those with him said: This is your god and the god of Moses. He has forgotten it and left it behind. Did they not see that it made no answer to them and had no power to do them harm or good? (84—90)

قَالَ هُمْ اُولَآءِ عَلٰى اَثَرِيْ وَعَجِلْتُ اِلَيْكَ رَبِّ لِتَرْضٰى ۝

قَالَ فَاِنَّا قَدْ فَتَنَّا قَوْمَكَ مِنْ بَعْدِكَ وَاَضَلَّهُمُ السَّامِرِيُّ ۝

فَرَجَعَ مُوْسٰى اِلٰى قَوْمِهٖ غَضْبَانَ اَسِفًا قَالَ يٰقَوْمِ اَلَمْ يَعِدْكُمْ رَبُّكُمْ وَعْدًا حَسَنًا اَفَطَالَ عَلَيْكُمُ الْعَهْدُ اَمْ اَرَدْتُّمْ اَنْ يَّحِلَّ عَلَيْكُمْ غَضَبٌ مِّنْ رَّبِّكُمْ فَاَخْلَفْتُمْ مَّوْعِدِيْ ۝

قَالُوْا مَآ اَخْلَفْنَا مَوْعِدَكَ بِمَلْكِنَا وَلٰكِنَّا حُمِّلْنَا اَوْزَارًا مِّنْ زِيْنَةِ الْقَوْمِ فَقَذَفْنٰهَا فَكَذٰلِكَ اَلْقَى السَّامِرِيُّ ۝

فَاَخْرَجَ لَهُمْ عِجْلًا جَسَدًا لَّهٗ خُوَارٌ فَقَالُوْا هٰذَآ اِلٰهُكُمْ وَاِلٰهُ مُوْسٰى ە فَنَسِيَ ۝

اَفَلَا يَرَوْنَ اَلَّا يَرْجِعُ اِلَيْهِمْ قَوْلًا وَّلَا يَمْلِكُ لَهُمْ ضَرًّا وَّلَا نَفْعًا ۝

Even before the return of Moses, Aaron had warned them: O my people you have been tried by reason of the calf. Surely,

وَلَقَدْ قَالَ لَهُمْ هٰرُوْنُ مِنْ قَبْلُ يٰقَوْمِ اِنَّمَا

the Gracious One is your Lord; so follow me and obey my command. They replied: We shall not cease to worship it till Moses return to us. Moses upbraided his brother: Aaron, what hindered thee from following me, when thou didst see them go astray? Didst thou, then, disobey my command? Aaron answered: Son of my mother, seize me not by my beard, nor by the hair of my head. I feared lest thou shouldst say: Thou hast caused a division among the children of Israel and didst not mind my word. Then Moses turned to Samiri and asked him: What hast thou to say, Samiri? He said: I perceived what they had not perceived. I had adopted only part of the teaching of the Messenger and then even that I cast away, and my mind commended to me that which I did.

Moses said to him: Go thy way. Thou art unclean and shalt throughout thy life warn people: Touch me not. There is a term appointed for thee which thou shalt not outstrip. Now look at thy god before whom thou didst devotedly sit in adoration. We will certainly burn it and scatter its remains in the sea. (91—98)

Your God is only Allah, beside Whom there is no god. He embraces all things within His knowledge. Thus do We relate to thee the tidings of what has gone before and We have given thee from Ourself the Quran as a Reminder. Whoso turns away from it will surely bear a heavy burden on the Day of Judgment, abiding thereunder. It will be a sore burden for them on the Day of Judgment,

فُتِنْتُمْ بِهٖ ۚ وَاِنَّ رَبَّكُمُ الرَّحْمٰنُ فَاتَّبِعُوْنِیْ وَاَطِیْعُوْۤا اَمْرِیْ ۝

قَالُوْا لَنْ نَّبْرَحَ عَلَیْهِ عٰكِفِیْنَ حَتّٰی یَرْجِعَ اِلَیْنَا مُوْسٰی ۝

قَالَ یٰهٰرُوْنُ مَا مَنَعَكَ اِذْ رَاَیْتَهُمْ ضَلُّوْۤا ۝ اَلَّا تَتَّبِعَنِ ۚ اَفَعَصَیْتَ اَمْرِیْ ۝

قَالَ یَبْنَؤُمَّ لَا تَاْخُذْ بِلِحْیَتِیْ وَلَا بِرَاْسِیْ ۚ اِنِّیْ خَشِیْتُ اَنْ تَقُوْلَ فَرَّقْتَ بَیْنَ بَنِیْۤ اِسْرَآءِیْلَ وَلَمْ تَرْقُبْ قَوْلِیْ ۝

قَالَ فَمَا خَطْبُكَ یٰسَامِرِیُّ ۝

قَالَ بَصُرْتُ بِمَا لَمْ یَبْصُرُوْا بِهٖ فَقَبَضْتُ قَبْضَةً مِّنْ اَثَرِ الرَّسُوْلِ فَنَبَذْتُهَا وَكَذٰلِكَ سَوَّلَتْ لِیْ نَفْسِیْ ۝

قَالَ فَاذْهَبْ فَاِنَّ لَكَ فِی الْحَیٰوةِ اَنْ تَقُوْلَ لَا مِسَاسَ ۚ وَاِنَّ لَكَ مَوْعِدًا لَّنْ تُخْلَفَهٗ ۚ وَانْظُرْ اِلٰۤی اِلٰهِكَ الَّذِیْ ظَلْتَ عَلَیْهِ عَاكِفًا ۚ لَّنُحَرِّقَنَّهٗ ثُمَّ لَنَنْسِفَنَّهٗ فِی الْیَمِّ نَسْفًا ۝

اِنَّمَاۤ اِلٰهُكُمُ اللّٰهُ الَّذِیْ لَاۤ اِلٰهَ اِلَّا هُوَ ۚ وَسِعَ كُلَّ شَیْءٍ عِلْمًا ۝

كَذٰلِكَ نَقُصُّ عَلَیْكَ مِنْ اَنْۢبَآءِ مَا قَدْ سَبَقَ ۚ وَقَدْ اٰتَیْنٰكَ مِنْ لَّدُنَّا ذِكْرًا ۝

مَنْ اَعْرَضَ عَنْهُ فَاِنَّهٗ یَحْمِلُ یَوْمَ الْقِیٰمَةِ وِزْرًا ۝ خٰلِدِیْنَ فِیْهِ ۚ وَسَآءَ لَهُمْ یَوْمَ الْقِیٰمَةِ حِمْلًا ۝

the day when the trumpet will be blown. On that day We shall gather the sinful ones together, blue-eyed. They will commiserate with each other in low tones: Your period of supremacy lasted but ten centuries. We know best their meaning, when their leading dignitary will say: You flourished only during a brief period of time. (99—105)

يَوْمَ يُنْفَخُ فِى الصُّوْرِ وَنَحْشُرُ الْمُجْرِمِيْنَ يَوْمَئِذٍ زُرْقًا ۞

يَّتَخَافَتُوْنَ بَيْنَهُمْ اِنْ لَّبِثْتُمْ اِلَّا عَشْرًا ۞

نَحْنُ اَعْلَمُ بِمَا يَقُوْلُوْنَ اِذْ يَقُوْلُ اَمْثَلُهُمْ طَرِيْقَةً اِنْ لَّبِثْتُمْ اِلَّا يَوْمًا ۞

They ask thee concerning the mountains. Tell them: My Lord will uproot them and scatter them as dust, leaving them as a barren level plain, in which there is no depression or elevation. On that day people will all follow the Caller in whose teaching there will be no deviation; and all voices will be hushed before the Gracious One and nothing will be heard except a subdued murmur. On that day no intercession shall avail, except on the part of one to whom permission is granted by the Gracious One and with whose word He is pleased. He knows all that is ahead of them and all that is behind them, but they cannot compass Him with their knowledge. On that day all leading personalities shall humble themselves before the Living, Self-Subsisting and All-Sustaining One, and he who bears the burden of iniquity will be ruined. But he who works righteousness being a believer, shall apprehend no injustice or loss. (106—113)

وَيَسْئَلُوْنَكَ عَنِ الْجِبَالِ فَقُلْ يَنْسِفُهَا رَبِّىْ نَسْفًا ۞

فَيَذَرُهَا قَاعًا صَفْصَفًا ۞

لَّا تَرٰى فِيْهَا عِوَجًا وَّلَا اَمْتًا ۞

يَوْمَئِذٍ يَّتَّبِعُوْنَ الدَّاعِىَ لَا عِوَجَ لَهُ وَخَشَعَتِ الْاَصْوَاتُ لِلرَّحْمٰنِ فَلَا تَسْمَعُ اِلَّا هَمْسًا ۞

يَوْمَئِذٍ لَّا تَنْفَعُ الشَّفَاعَةُ اِلَّا مَنْ اَذِنَ لَهُ الرَّحْمٰنُ وَرَضِىَ لَهُ قَوْلًا ۞

يَعْلَمُ مَا بَيْنَ اَيْدِيْهِمْ وَمَا خَلْفَهُمْ وَلَا يُحِيْطُوْنَ بِهٖ عِلْمًا ۞

وَعَنَتِ الْوُجُوْهُ لِلْحَىِّ الْقَيُّوْمِ وَقَدْ خَابَ مَنْ حَمَلَ ظُلْمًا ۞

وَمَنْ يَّعْمَلْ مِنَ الصّٰلِحٰتِ وَهُوَ مُؤْمِنٌ فَلَا يَخٰفُ ظُلْمًا وَّلَا هَضْمًا ۞

Thus have We sent it down, the Quran, in Arabic and have expounded therein every kind of warning, that they may be mindful of their duty or that it may serve them as a reminder afresh. Exalted then is Allah, the True King. Be not too eager to anticipate the Quran ere its revelation is completed unto thee; but

وَكَذٰلِكَ اَنْزَلْنٰهُ قُرْاٰنًا عَرَبِيًّا وَّصَرَّفْنَا فِيْهِ مِنَ الْوَعِيْدِ لَعَلَّهُمْ يَتَّقُوْنَ اَوْ يُحْدِثُ لَهُمْ ذِكْرًا ۞

فَتَعٰلَى اللّٰهُ الْمَلِكُ الْحَقُّ وَلَا تَعْجَلْ بِالْقُرْاٰنِ مِنْ قَبْلِ اَنْ يُّقْضٰى اِلَيْكَ وَحْيُهٗ وَقُلْ رَّبِّ زِدْنِىْ

keep up the supplication: Lord, bestow on me an increase of knowledge. (114—115)

We indeed laid a commandment on Adam aforetime, but he forgot, yet We did not discover in him any determination to disobey. When We commanded the angels to prostrate themselves before Us in gratitude for the creation of Adam, they all fell down in prostration, but Iblis did not, he refused to obey. So We warned Adam: Satan is thy enemy and the enemy of thy companion, so let him not drive you out of the garden, lest each of you come to grief. It is ordained for you that you shall not be hungry in the garden nor shall you be naked, and that you shall not thirst therein nor shall you be exposed to the sun. But Satan tried to entice him away and said: Adam, shall I lead you to the tree of eternity and to a kingdom that never declines?

So they ate of the tree and their nakedness became manifest to them and they began to cover it up with the adornments of the garden. Adam thus disobeyed his Lord and fell into error. Then his Lord chose him for His grace and turned to him with mercy and guided him. Allah commanded: Go forth, both parties, all together from the garden; some of you will be enemies of others. If there comes to you guidance from Me, then whoso follows My guidance will not go astray, nor will he come to grief. But whoso will turn away from My Reminder, his will be a strait life and on the Day of Judgment We shall raise him up blind. He will ask: Lord, why hast Thou raised me up blind, while I had good sight before? Allah will answer: Thus it is. Our Signs came to thee and thou didst disregard them; in like manner wilt thou be disregarded on this day of the manifestation of My mercy.

عِلْمًا ۝

وَلَقَدْ عَهِدْنَا إِلٰٓى اٰدَمَ مِنْ قَبْلُ فَنَسِىَ وَلَمْ نَجِدْ لَهٗ عَزْمًا ۝

وَاِذْ قُلْنَا لِلْمَلٰٓئِكَةِ اسْجُدُوْا لِاٰدَمَ فَسَجَدُوْۤا اِلَّاۤ اِبْلِيْسَ ؕ اَبٰى ۝

فَقُلْنَا يٰٓاٰدَمُ اِنَّ هٰذَا عَدُوٌّ لَّكَ وَلِزَوْجِكَ فَلَا يُخْرِجَنَّكُمَا مِنَ الْجَنَّةِ فَتَشْقٰى ۝

اِنَّ لَكَ اَلَّا تَجُوْعَ فِيْهَا وَلَا تَعْرٰى ۝

وَاَنَّكَ لَا تَظْمَؤُا فِيْهَا وَلَا تَضْحٰى ۝

فَوَسْوَسَ اِلَيْهِ الشَّيْطٰنُ قَالَ يٰٓاٰدَمُ هَلْ اَدُلُّكَ عَلٰى شَجَرَةِ الْخُلْدِ وَمُلْكٍ لَّا يَبْلٰى ۝

فَاَكَلَا مِنْهَا فَبَدَتْ لَهُمَا سَوْاٰتُهُمَا وَطَفِقَا يَخْصِفٰنِ عَلَيْهِمَا مِنْ وَّرَقِ الْجَنَّةِ ۫ وَعَصٰٓى اٰدَمُ رَبَّهٗ فَغَوٰى ۝

ثُمَّ اجْتَبٰهُ رَبُّهٗ فَتَابَ عَلَيْهِ وَهَدٰى ۝

قَالَ اهْبِطَا مِنْهَا جَمِيْعًۢا بَعْضُكُمْ لِبَعْضٍ عَدُوٌّ ۚ فَاِمَّا يَاْتِيَنَّكُمْ مِّنِّيْ هُدًى ۙ فَمَنِ اتَّبَعَ هُدَايَ فَلَا يَضِلُّ وَلَا يَشْقٰى ۝

وَمَنْ اَعْرَضَ عَنْ ذِكْرِيْ فَاِنَّ لَهٗ مَعِيْشَةً ضَنْكًا وَّنَحْشُرُهٗ يَوْمَ الْقِيٰمَةِ اَعْمٰى ۝

قَالَ رَبِّ لِمَ حَشَرْتَنِيْۤ اَعْمٰى وَقَدْ كُنْتُ بَصِيْرًا ۝

قَالَ كَذٰلِكَ اَتَتْكَ اٰيٰتُنَا فَنَسِيْتَهَا ۚ وَكَذٰلِكَ الْيَوْمَ تُنْسٰى ۝

Thus do We recompense him who casts aside Divine guidance and believes not in the Signs of his Lord; and the chastisement of the Hereafter is severer and more lasting. Does it not furnish guidance to them how many a generation We destroyed before them, in whose dwellings they now move about? Therein indeed are Signs for those who are possessed of wisdom. Were it not for a word already gone forth from thy Lord, and a term already fixed, their punishment would have been everlasting. (116—130)

Therefore, be steadfast under their calumnies and glorify thy Lord with His praise before the rising of the sun and before its setting; and glorify Him in the hours of the night and in different parts of the day, so that through His grace thou mayest win true happiness. Do not look covetously upon that which We have bestowed upon some classes of them for a brief enjoyment, of the embellishments of worldly life, that We may try them thereby. The provision bestowed upon thee by thy Lord is better and more lasting. Enjoin Prayer on thy people, and be constant therein. We ask thee not for provision; it is We Who provide for thee. The best end is that of righteousness. (131—133)

They ask: Why does he not bring us a Sign from his Lord? Has there not come to them a Sign like that mentioned in the former Books? Had We destroyed them through some calamity before the coming of this Messenger, they would surely have said: Lord, wherefore didst Thou not send to us a Messenger that we might have followed Thy commandments before we were humbled and disgraced? Tell them: Everyone is waiting for his end; wait ye on, therefore, and soon will you know who are the people of the right path and who follow true guidance and who do not. (134—136)

308

سُوْرَةُ الْاَنْبِيَاءِ مَكِّيَّةٌ

AL-ANBIYĀ'

(Revealed before Hijra)

بِسْمِ اللهِ الرَّحْمٰنِ الرَّحِيْمِ ۟

In the name of Allah, Most Gracious, Ever Merciful. (1)

اِقْتَرَبَ لِلنَّاسِ حِسَابُهُمْ وَ هُمْ فِیْ غَفْلَةٍ مُّعْرِضُوْنَ ۟

The time of reckoning is drawing nigh for the people, yet they are heedless and turn away. Whenever any fresh admonition comes to them from their Lord, they listen to it and make sport of it. Their minds are indifferent towards it. The wrongdoers confer together in secret and then counsel others: See you not, is this one other than a man like yourselves? Will you then, being intelligent, be beguiled by his deceptive talk? The Prophet's response is: My Lord knows well what is spoken in the heaven and in the earth; He is the All-Hearing, the All-Knowing.

مَا یَاْتِیْهِمْ مِنْ ذِكْرٍ مِنْ رَّبِّهِمْ مُّحْدَثٍ اِلَّا اسْتَمَعُوْهُ وَ هُمْ یَلْعَبُوْنَ ۟

لَاهِیَةً قُلُوْبُهُمْ وَ اَسَرُّوا النَّجْوَی الَّذِیْنَ ظَلَمُوْا ۚ هَلْ هٰذَا اِلَّا بَشَرٌ مِّثْلُكُمْ ۚ اَفَتَاْتُوْنَ السِّحْرَ وَاَنْتُمْ تُبْصِرُوْنَ ۟

قُلْ رَبِّیْ یَعْلَمُ الْقَوْلَ فِی السَّمَاءِ وَالْاَرْضِ وَهُوَ السَّمِیْعُ الْعَلِیْمُ ۟

بَلْ قَالُوْا اَضْغَاثُ اَحْلَامٍ بَلِ افْتَرٰىهُ بَلْ هُوَ شَاعِرٌ ۚ فَلْیَاْتِنَا بِاٰیَةٍ كَمَا اُرْسِلَ الْاَوَّلُوْنَ ۟

They go on to say: These are his confused dreams; nay, he has invented it all; he is but a poet with a fertile imagination. Let him bring us a Sign, as he alleges the former Prophets did. Of the townships that We destroyed before them no one believed; would these then believe? Before thee also We sent as Messengers men to whom We vouchsafed revelation. If you who disbelieve know it not, then ask the People of the Book. We did not give them bodies that needed no food, nor were they to live for ever. But We fulfilled the promise We made them; and We saved them and those with them whom We pleased, and We destroyed the transgressors.

مَا اٰمَنَتْ قَبْلَهُمْ مِنْ قَرْیَةٍ اَهْلَكْنٰهَا ۚ اَفَهُمْ یُؤْمِنُوْنَ ۟

وَ مَا اَرْسَلْنَا قَبْلَكَ اِلَّا رِجَالًا نُّوْحِیْ اِلَیْهِمْ فَسْـَٔلُوْا اَهْلَ الذِّكْرِ اِنْ كُنْتُمْ لَا تَعْلَمُوْنَ ۟

وَ مَا جَعَلْنٰهُمْ جَسَدًا لَّا یَاْكُلُوْنَ الطَّعَامَ وَ مَا كَانُوْا خٰلِدِیْنَ ۟

ثُمَّ صَدَقْنٰهُمُ الْوَعْدَ فَاَنْجَیْنٰهُمْ وَ مَنْ نَّشَاءُ وَاَهْلَكْنَا الْمُسْرِفِیْنَ ۟

We have now sent down to you a Book which makes provision for your uplift; will you not then understand? How many a township that acted wrongfully have We utterly destroyed, and raised up after it another people? When they perceived Our chastisement, they prepared to flee from it. Flee not, but return to the comforts and luxuries in which you exulted so that you may be interrogated. At this they exclaimed: Alas, we were indeed wrongdoers. They continued thus to bewail till We mowed them down into stubble. (2—16)

We created not the heaven and the earth and all that is between the two in sport. Had We wished to find a pastime, We would surely have found it in that which is with Us, if at all We would have been inclined in that way. Nay, We hurl the truth at falsehood and it crushes it and it disappears. Woe unto you for that which you spin out. To Him belongs whosoever is in the heavens and in the earth. Those who are in His presence do not disdain to worship Him, nor do they weary of it; they glorify Him night and day, and cease not. (17—21)

Have they taken gods from the earth who create? If there had been in the heavens and the earth other gods beside Allah, then surely both would have gone to ruin. Then glorified be Allah, the Lord of the Throne, above that which they ascribe to Him. He cannot be questioned concerning what He does, but they will be questioned. Have they taken gods beside Him? Say to them: Bring your proof.

لَقَدْ اَنْزَلْنَاۤ اِلَيْكُمْ كِتٰبًا فِيْهِ ذِكْرُكُمْ ؕ اَفَلَا تَعْقِلُوْنَ ۟۞

وَكَمْ قَصَمْنَا مِنْ قَرْيَةٍ كَانَتْ ظَالِمَةً وَّاَنْشَاْنَا بَعْدَهَا قَوْمًا اٰخَرِيْنَ ۟

فَلَمَّاۤ اَحَسُّوْا بَاْسَنَاۤ اِذَا هُمْ مِّنْهَا يَرْكُضُوْنَ ۟

لَا تَرْكُضُوْا وَارْجِعُوْۤا اِلٰى مَاۤ اُتْرِفْتُمْ فِيْهِ وَمَسٰكِنِكُمْ لَعَلَّكُمْ تُسْـَٔلُوْنَ ۟

قَالُوْا يٰوَيْلَنَاۤ اِنَّا كُنَّا ظٰلِمِيْنَ ۟

فَمَا زَالَتْ تِّلْكَ دَعْوٰىهُمْ حَتّٰى جَعَلْنٰهُمْ حَصِيْدًا خٰمِدِيْنَ ۟

وَمَا خَلَقْنَا السَّمَآءَ وَالْاَرْضَ وَمَا بَيْنَهُمَا لٰعِبِيْنَ ۟

لَوْ اَرَدْنَاۤ اَنْ نَّتَّخِذَ لَهْوًا لَّاتَّخَذْنٰهُ مِنْ لَّدُنَّاۤ ۖ اِنْ كُنَّا فٰعِلِيْنَ ۟

بَلْ نَقْذِفُ بِالْحَقِّ عَلَى الْبَاطِلِ فَيَدْمَغُهُ فَاِذَا هُوَ زَاهِقٌ ؕ وَلَكُمُ الْوَيْلُ مِمَّا تَصِفُوْنَ ۟

وَلَهٗ مَنْ فِى السَّمٰوٰتِ وَالْاَرْضِ ؕ وَمَنْ عِنْدَهٗ لَا يَسْتَكْبِرُوْنَ عَنْ عِبَادَتِهٖ وَلَا يَسْتَحْسِرُوْنَ ۟

يُسَبِّحُوْنَ الَّيْلَ وَالنَّهَارَ لَا يَفْتُرُوْنَ ۟

اَمِ اتَّخَذُوْۤا اٰلِهَةً مِّنَ الْاَرْضِ هُمْ يُنْشِرُوْنَ ۟

لَوْ كَانَ فِيْهِمَاۤ اٰلِهَةٌ اِلَّا اللّٰهُ لَفَسَدَتَا ۚ فَسُبْحٰنَ اللّٰهِ رَبِّ الْعَرْشِ عَمَّا يَصِفُوْنَ ۟

لَا يُسْـَٔلُ عَمَّا يَفْعَلُ وَهُمْ يُسْـَٔلُوْنَ ۟

اَمِ اتَّخَذُوْا مِنْ دُوْنِهٖۤ اٰلِهَةً ؕ قُلْ هَاتُوْا بُرْهَانَكُمْ ۚ

This Quran is a source of honour for those who are with me and is also a source of honour for those who were before me. But most of them know not the truth, and so they turn away from it. We sent no Messenger before thee but We directed him: There is no god but I; so worship Me alone. But they say: The Gracious One has taken to Himself a son. Holy is He. Those whom they so designate are only His honoured servants. They utter not a word more than He directs, and they only carry out His commands. He knows what lies ahead of them and what is left behind them, and they intercede not except only he whose intercession He permits and they tremble with fear of Him. Whosoever of them should say: I am a god beside Him We shall requite him with hell. Thus do We requite the wrongdoers. (22—30)

Do not the disbelievers realise that the heavens and the earth were a solid mass, then We split them asunder, and We made from water every living thing? Will they not then believe? We have placed in the earth firm mountains lest it roll beneath them; and We have made wide pathways therein that they may thereby journey from place to place. We have made the heaven a guarded and protecting roof; yet they turn away from its Signs. He it is Who created the night and the day, and the sun and the moon each gliding freely in its orbit. (31—34)

We granted not everlasting life to any human being before thee; then if thou shouldst die will they live on for ever?

هٰذَا ذِكْرُ مَنْ مَّعِيَ وَ ذِكْرُ مَنْ قَبْلِيْ بَلْ اَكْثَرُهُمْ لَا يَعْلَمُوْنَ الْحَقَّ فَهُمْ مُّعْرِضُوْنَ ۟

وَ مَآ اَرْسَلْنَا مِنْ قَبْلِكَ مِنْ رَّسُوْلٍ اِلَّا نُوْحِيْ اِلَيْهِ اَنَّهٗ لَاۤ اِلٰهَ اِلَّاۤ اَنَا فَاعْبُدُوْنِ ۟

وَ قَالُوا اتَّخَذَ الرَّحْمٰنُ وَلَدًا سُبْحٰنَهٗ بَلْ عِبَادٌ مُّكْرَمُوْنَ ۟

لَا يَسْبِقُوْنَهٗ بِالْقَوْلِ وَ هُمْ بِاَمْرِهٖ يَعْمَلُوْنَ ۟

يَعْلَمُ مَا بَيْنَ اَيْدِيْهِمْ وَ مَا خَلْفَهُمْ وَ لَا يَشْفَعُوْنَ اِلَّا لِمَنِ ارْتَضٰى وَ هُمْ مِّنْ خَشْيَتِهٖ مُشْفِقُوْنَ ۟

وَ مَنْ يَّقُلْ مِنْهُمْ اِنِّيْۤ اِلٰهٌ مِّنْ دُوْنِهٖ فَذٰلِكَ نَجْزِيْهِ جَهَنَّمَ كَذٰلِكَ نَجْزِى الظّٰلِمِيْنَ ۟

اَوَلَمْ يَرَ الَّذِيْنَ كَفَرُوْۤا اَنَّ السَّمٰوٰتِ وَ الْاَرْضَ كَانَتَا رَتْقًا فَفَتَقْنٰهُمَا وَ جَعَلْنَا مِنَ الْمَآءِ كُلَّ شَيْءٍ حَيٍّ اَفَلَا يُؤْمِنُوْنَ ۟

وَ جَعَلْنَا فِى الْاَرْضِ رَوَاسِيَ اَنْ تَمِيْدَ بِهِمْ وَ جَعَلْنَا فِيْهَا فِجَاجًا سُبُلًا لَّعَلَّهُمْ يَهْتَدُوْنَ ۟

وَ جَعَلْنَا السَّمَآءَ سَقْفًا مَّحْفُوْظًا وَ هُمْ عَنْ اٰيٰتِهَا مُعْرِضُوْنَ ۟

وَ هُوَ الَّذِيْ خَلَقَ الَّيْلَ وَ النَّهَارَ وَ الشَّمْسَ وَ الْقَمَرَ كُلٌّ فِيْ فَلَكٍ يَّسْبَحُوْنَ ۟

وَ مَا جَعَلْنَا لِبَشَرٍ مِّنْ قَبْلِكَ الْخُلْدَ اَفَاۡئِنْ مِّتَّ فَهُمُ الْخٰلِدُوْنَ ۟

Every one shall suffer death; and We shall prove you through good and ill by way of trial, and to Us shall you be returned. When the disbelievers see thee they make light of thee: Is this the one who decries your gods? Yet it is they who reject with disdain the mention of the Gracious One. (35—37)

كُلُّ نَفْسٍ ذَآئِقَةُ الْمَوْتِ ۗ وَنَبْلُوْكُمْ بِالشَّرِّ وَ الْخَيْرِ فِتْنَةً ۗ وَ اِلَيْنَا تُرْجَعُوْنَ ۞

وَ اِذَا رَاٰكَ الَّذِيْنَ كَفَرُوْۤا اِنْ يَّتَّخِذُوْنَكَ اِلَّا هُزُوًا ؕ اَهٰذَا الَّذِيْ يَذْكُرُ اٰلِهَتَكُمْ ۚ وَ هُمْ بِذِكْرِ الرَّحْمٰنِ هُمْ كٰفِرُوْنَ ۞

Man is hasty by nature. I will certainly show you My Signs, but do not be impatient. They ask: When will this promise be fulfilled, if you are truthful? If only the disbelievers knew the hour when they would not be able to keep off the fire from their faces nor from their backs, nor will they be helped. Indeed it will come upon them unawares so that it will utterly confound them; and they will not be able to repel it, nor will they be granted respite. Messengers have been mocked at before thee, but that whereat they mocked encompassed those of them who scoffed. (38—42)

خُلِقَ الْاِنْسَانُ مِنْ عَجَلٍ ؕ سَاُورِيْكُمْ اٰيٰتِيْ فَلَا تَسْتَعْجِلُوْنِ ۞

وَ يَقُوْلُوْنَ مَتٰى هٰذَا الْوَعْدُ اِنْ كُنْتُمْ صٰدِقِيْنَ ۞ لَوْ يَعْلَمُ الَّذِيْنَ كَفَرُوْا حِيْنَ لَا يَكُفُّوْنَ عَنْ وُّجُوْهِهِمُ النَّارَ وَ لَا عَنْ ظُهُوْرِهِمْ وَ لَا هُمْ يُنْصَرُوْنَ ۞ بَلْ تَأْتِيْهِمْ بَغْتَةً فَتَبْهَتُهُمْ فَلَا يَسْتَطِيْعُوْنَ رَدَّهَا وَ لَا هُمْ يُنْظَرُوْنَ ۞

Ask them: Who can save you from the chastisement of the Gracious One by night and by day? In truth they turn away from being reminded of their Lord. Have they any gods who can save them from Our chastisement? They cannot even help themselves, nor can their devotees be befriended by any one against Us. The truth is that We provided generously for them and their fathers and they remained in enjoyment of Our provision for a long time. Do they not perceive that We are advancing into their territory and are reducing it from its borders? Do they still hope to win? (43—45)

وَ لَقَدِ اسْتُهْزِئَ بِرُسُلٍ مِّنْ قَبْلِكَ فَحَاقَ بِالَّذِيْنَ سَخِرُوْا مِنْهُمْ مَّا كَانُوْا بِهٖ يَسْتَهْزِءُوْنَ ۞

قُلْ مَنْ يَّكْلَؤُكُمْ بِالَّيْلِ وَ النَّهَارِ مِنَ الرَّحْمٰنِ ؕ بَلْ هُمْ عَنْ ذِكْرِ رَبِّهِمْ مُّعْرِضُوْنَ ۞

اَمْ لَهُمْ اٰلِهَةٌ تَمْنَعُهُمْ مِّنْ دُوْنِنَا ؕ لَا يَسْتَطِيْعُوْنَ نَصْرَ اَنْفُسِهِمْ وَ لَا هُمْ مِّنَّا يُصْحَبُوْنَ ۞

بَلْ مَتَّعْنَا هٰؤُلَآءِ وَ اٰبَآءَهُمْ حَتّٰى طَالَ عَلَيْهِمُ الْعُمُرُ ؕ اَفَلَا يَرَوْنَ اَنَّا نَأْتِى الْاَرْضَ نَنْقُصُهَا مِنْ اَطْرَافِهَا ؕ اَفَهُمُ الْغٰلِبُوْنَ ۞

Tell them: I warn you only according to divine revelation, and I know that when the deaf are warned they cannot

قُلْ اِنَّمَاۤ اُنْذِرُكُمْ بِالْوَحْىِ ۖ وَ لَا يَسْمَعُ الصُّمُّ

312

hear the call. But if even a breath of
the chastisement of thy Lord were to
touch them, they will surely cry out:
Woe to us! We were indeed wrongdoers. We shall set up just scales for the
Day of Judgment so that no one will be
wronged at all. If there is good or evil
equal to the weight of a mustard seed,
We would bring it forth. Sufficient are
We as a reckoner. We gave Moses and
Aaron the Discrimination and a Light and
a Reminder for the righteous, who fear
their Lord in secret, and who dread the
Hour of Judgment. Now this is a blessed
Reminder that We have sent down. Will
you then reject it? (46—51)

اَلدُّعَآءُ اِذَا مَا يُنْذَرُوْنَ ۞

وَ لَئِنْ مَّسَّتْهُمْ نَفْحَةٌ مِّنْ عَذَابِ رَبِّكَ لَيَقُوْلُنَّ
يٰوَيْلَنَاۤ اِنَّا كُنَّا ظٰلِمِيْنَ ۞

وَ نَضَعُ الْمَوَازِيْنَ الْقِسْطَ لِيَوْمِ الْقِيٰمَةِ فَلَا تُظْلَمُ
نَفْسٌ شَيْئًا ؕ وَ اِنْ كَانَ مِثْقَالَ حَبَّةٍ مِّنْ خَرْدَلٍ
اَتَيْنَا بِهَا ؕ وَ كَفٰى بِنَا حٰسِبِيْنَ ۞

وَ لَقَدْ اٰتَيْنَا مُوْسٰى وَ هٰرُوْنَ الْفُرْقَانَ وَ ضِيَآءً
وَّ ذِكْرًا لِّلْمُتَّقِيْنَ ۞

الَّذِيْنَ يَخْشَوْنَ رَبَّهُمْ بِالْغَيْبِ وَ هُمْ مِّنَ السَّاعَةِ
مُشْفِقُوْنَ ۞

وَ هٰذَا ذِكْرٌ مُّبٰرَكٌ اَنْزَلْنٰهُ ؕ اَفَاَنْتُمْ لَهٗ مُنْكِرُوْنَ ۞

وَ لَقَدْ اٰتَيْنَاۤ اِبْرٰهِيْمَ رُشْدَهٗ مِنْ قَبْلُ وَ كُنَّا
بِهٖ عٰلِمِيْنَ ۞

اِذْ قَالَ لِاَبِيْهِ وَ قَوْمِهٖ مَا هٰذِهِ التَّمَاثِيْلُ الَّتِىۤ
اَنْتُمْ لَهَا عٰكِفُوْنَ ۞

قَالُوْا وَجَدْنَاۤ اٰبَآءَنَا لَهَا عٰبِدِيْنَ ۞

قَالَ لَقَدْ كُنْتُمْ اَنْتُمْ وَ اٰبَآؤُكُمْ فِيْ ضَلٰلٍ مُّبِيْنٍ ۞

قَالُوْۤا اَجِئْتَنَا بِالْحَقِّ اَمْ اَنْتَ مِنَ اللّٰعِبِيْنَ ۞

قَالَ بَلْ رَّبُّكُمْ رَبُّ السَّمٰوٰتِ وَ الْاَرْضِ الَّذِىْ
فَطَرَهُنَّ ۫ وَ اَنَا عَلٰى ذٰلِكُمْ مِّنَ الشّٰهِدِيْنَ ۞

وَ تَاللّٰهِ لَاَكِيْدَنَّ اَصْنَامَكُمْ بَعْدَ اَنْ تُوَلُّوْا
مُدْبِرِيْنَ ۞

We had bestowed upon Abraham his
wisdom before this and We knew him
well. He said to his father and his people:
What are these images to which you are
so devoted? They said: We saw our fathers
worshipping them. He observed: Then you
and your fathers have been in manifest
error. They enquired: Are you telling us
the truth or are you jesting? He replied:
The truth is that your Lord is the Lord
of the heavens and the earth, Who
created them, and I bear witness to that
before you. By Allah, after you have gone
away and turned your backs I will certainly devise a plan against your idols.

He broke them all to pieces, except the principal one, so that they might return to it. When they saw this they protested: Whoever has done this to our gods is surely a malefactor. Some of them said: We heard a young man, called Abraham, malign them. They said: Then bring him before the people that they may judge him. When he came, they asked him: Abraham, have you done this to our gods?

فَجَعَلَهُمْ جُذٰذًا اِلَّا كَبِيْرًا لَّهُمْ لَعَلَّهُمْ اِلَيْهِ يَرْجِعُوْنَ ۝ قَالُوْا مَنْ فَعَلَ هٰذَا بِاٰلِهَتِنَا اِنَّهٗ لَمِنَ الظّٰلِمِيْنَ ۝ قَالُوْا سَمِعْنَا فَتًى يَّذْكُرُهُمْ يُقَالُ لَهٗۤ اِبْرٰهِيْمُ ۝ قَالُوْا فَأْتُوْا بِهٖ عَلٰۤى اَعْيُنِ النَّاسِ لَعَلَّهُمْ يَشْهَدُوْنَ ۝ قَالُوْۤا ءَاَنْتَ فَعَلْتَ هٰذَا بِاٰلِهَتِنَا يٰۤاِبْرٰهِيْمُ ۝

He answered: Somebody must have done it. This is the principal one. Ask him and the others, if they can speak. Then they conferred among themselves, and confessed: Indeed you yourselves are in the wrong; and being confounded, they said to Abraham: Thou knowest well that these do not speak. He rebuked them: Then do you worship instead of Allah that which cannot profit you at all nor harm you?

قَالَ بَلْ فَعَلَهٗ كَبِيْرُهُمْ هٰذَا فَسْـَٔلُوْهُمْ اِنْ كَانُوْا يَنْطِقُوْنَ ۝ فَرَجَعُوْۤا اِلٰۤى اَنْفُسِهِمْ فَقَالُوْۤا اِنَّكُمْ اَنْتُمُ الظّٰلِمُوْنَ ۝ ثُمَّ نُكِسُوْا عَلٰى رُءُوْسِهِمْ لَقَدْ عَلِمْتَ مَا هٰۤؤُلَآءِ يَنْطِقُوْنَ ۝ قَالَ اَفَتَعْبُدُوْنَ مِنْ دُوْنِ اللّٰهِ مَا لَا يَنْفَعُكُمْ شَيْئًا وَّلَا يَضُرُّكُمْ ۝

Fie on you and on that which you worship in place of Allah. Can you not understand? They were chagrined and said: Burn him and thus help your gods, if you mean to do something. When they cast him into the fire We commanded it: Be cool and a means of safety for Abraham.

اُفٍّ لَّكُمْ وَلِمَا تَعْبُدُوْنَ مِنْ دُوْنِ اللّٰهِ اَفَلَا تَعْقِلُوْنَ ۝ قَالُوْا حَرِّقُوْهُ وَانْصُرُوْۤا اٰلِهَتَكُمْ اِنْ كُنْتُمْ فٰعِلِيْنَ ۝ قُلْنَا يٰنَارُ كُوْنِيْ بَرْدًا وَّسَلٰمًا عَلٰۤى اِبْرٰهِيْمَ ۝

They had sought to do him harm, but We frustrated them, and brought him and Lot in safety to the land which We had blessed for the peoples. We bestowed upon him Isaac, and a grandson Jacob, and We made all of them righteous. We made them leaders who guided people by Our command, and We enjoined on them the

وَاَرَادُوْا بِهٖ كَيْدًا فَجَعَلْنٰهُمُ الْاَخْسَرِيْنَ ۝ وَنَجَّيْنٰهُ وَلُوْطًا اِلَى الْاَرْضِ الَّتِيْ بٰرَكْنَا فِيْهَا لِلْعٰلَمِيْنَ ۝ وَوَهَبْنَا لَهٗۤ اِسْحٰقَ وَيَعْقُوْبَ نَافِلَةً وَكُلًّا جَعَلْنَا صٰلِحِيْنَ ۝ وَجَعَلْنٰهُمْ اَئِمَّةً يَّهْدُوْنَ بِاَمْرِنَا وَاَوْحَيْنَاۤ

doing of good, observance of Prayer and the giving of alms. They were all Our devoted servants. To Lot also we gave wisdom and knowledge and We delivered him from the city which practised abominations. They were indeed a wicked and rebellious people. We admitted him to Our mercy; surely he was of the righteous. (52—76)

اِلَيْهِمْ فِعْلَ الْخَيْرٰتِ وَاِقَامَ الصَّلٰوةِ وَاِيْتَاءَ الزَّكٰوةِ ۚ وَكَانُوْا لَنَا عٰبِدِيْنَ ۝

وَلُوْطًا اٰتَيْنٰهُ حُكْمًا وَّعِلْمًا وَّنَجَّيْنٰهُ مِنَ الْقَرْيَةِ الَّتِيْ كَانَتْ تَّعْمَلُ الْخَبٰٓئِثَ ۗ اِنَّهُمْ كَانُوْا قَوْمَ سَوْءٍ فٰسِقِيْنَ ۝

وَاَدْخَلْنٰهُ فِيْ رَحْمَتِنَا ۗ اِنَّهُ مِنَ الصّٰلِحِيْنَ ۝

Call to mind Noah, when he called on Us aforetime, and We heard his prayer and delivered him and his family from great distress, and helped him against his people who rejected Our Signs. They were surely a wicked people, so We drowned them all. (77—78)

وَنُوْحًا اِذْ نَادٰى مِنْ قَبْلُ فَاسْتَجَبْنَا لَهُ فَنَجَّيْنٰهُ وَاَهْلَهُ مِنَ الْكَرْبِ الْعَظِيْمِ ۝

وَنَصَرْنٰهُ مِنَ الْقَوْمِ الَّذِيْنَ كَذَّبُوْا بِاٰيٰتِنَا ۗ اِنَّهُمْ كَانُوْا قَوْمَ سَوْءٍ فَاَغْرَقْنٰهُمْ اَجْمَعِيْنَ ۝

وَدَاوٗدَ وَسُلَيْمٰنَ اِذْ يَحْكُمٰنِ فِي الْحَرْثِ اِذْ نَفَشَتْ فِيْهِ غَنَمُ الْقَوْمِ ۚ وَكُنَّا لِحُكْمِهِمْ شٰهِدِيْنَ ۝

Call to mind David and Solomon, when they exercised their judgment concerning the crop which had been destroyed by a mob and We were witness to their judgment. We gave Solomon the right understanding of the matter, and upon each We bestowed wisdom and knowledge. We constrained to David's service the people of the mountains who celebrated the praises of Allah, and also the birds. We had power to do all this. We taught him the fashioning of coats of mail for you, to protect you in battle. Will you then be grateful? We constrained to Solomon's service the fierce wind, which blew at his bidding towards the land which We had blessed. We are fully conversant with all things. We also subjected to him expert divers who dived for him and performed other tasks; and it was We who watched over them. (79—83)

فَفَهَّمْنٰهَا سُلَيْمٰنَ ۚ وَكُلًّا اٰتَيْنَا حُكْمًا وَّعِلْمًا ۙ وَّسَخَّرْنَا مَعَ دَاوٗدَ الْجِبَالَ يُسَبِّحْنَ وَالطَّيْرَ ۚ وَكُنَّا فٰعِلِيْنَ ۝

وَعَلَّمْنٰهُ صَنْعَةَ لَبُوْسٍ لَّكُمْ لِتُحْصِنَكُمْ مِّنْ بَاْسِكُمْ ۚ فَهَلْ اَنْتُمْ شٰكِرُوْنَ ۝

وَلِسُلَيْمٰنَ الرِّيْحَ عَاصِفَةً تَجْرِيْ بِاَمْرِهٖ اِلَى الْاَرْضِ الَّتِيْ بٰرَكْنَا فِيْهَا ۚ وَكُنَّا بِكُلِّ شَيْءٍ عٰلِمِيْنَ ۝

وَمِنَ الشَّيٰطِيْنِ مَنْ يَّغُوْصُوْنَ لَهُ وَيَعْمَلُوْنَ عَمَلًا دُوْنَ ذٰلِكَ ۚ وَكُنَّا لَهُمْ حٰفِظِيْنَ ۝

Call to mind Job when he called on his Lord: I have been afflicted with distress and Thou art the Most Merciful of all who show mercy. So We heard his prayer and removed the distress from which he suffered and bestowed upon him his family, and the like thereof with them as a mercy from Us, and as a reminder for those devoted to Our worship. (84—85)

Call to mind also Ishmael and Idris and Dhul-Kifl. All of them were steadfast, and We admitted them to Our mercy. Surely, they were of the righteous. (86—87)

Call to mind also Dhul Nun, when he went away in dudgeon, but was sure in his mind that We would not cause him distress, and he cried out in the midst of his afflictions: There is no god except Thee, Holy art Thou. I have indeed been a wrongdoer. So We heard his prayer and delivered him from sorrow. Thus do We deliver those who believe. (88—89)

Call to mind Zachariah also when he called on his Lord: Leave me not alone, Lord, Thou art the Best of heirs. So We heard his prayer and bestowed upon him Yahya, and made his wife whole for his sake. They used to hasten to do good and they called on Us in hope and in fear, and they humbled themselves before Us. (90—91)

Call to mind her also who safeguarded her chastity; so We blessed her with Our revelation and We made her and her son a Sign for peoples. (92)

These your people are one people and I am your Lord, so worship Me alone.

وَاَيُّوْبَ اِذْ نَادٰى رَبَّهٗٓ اَنِّىۡ مَسَّنِىَ الضُّرُّ وَاَنْتَ اَرْحَمُ الرّٰحِمِيْنَ ۞

فَاسْتَجَبْنَا لَهٗ فَكَشَفْنَا مَا بِهٖ مِنْ ضُرٍّ وَّاٰتَيْنٰهُ اَهْلَهٗ وَمِثْلَهُمْ مَّعَهُمْ رَحْمَةً مِّنْ عِنْدِنَا وَذِكْرٰى لِلْعٰبِدِيْنَ ۞

وَاِسْمٰعِيْلَ وَاِدْرِيْسَ وَذَا الْكِفْلِ كُلٌّ مِّنَ الصّٰبِرِيْنَ ۞

وَاَدْخَلْنٰهُمْ فِىْ رَحْمَتِنَا اِنَّهُمْ مِّنَ الصّٰلِحِيْنَ ۞

وَذَا النُّوْنِ اِذْ ذَّهَبَ مُغَاضِبًا فَظَنَّ اَنْ لَّنْ نَّقْدِرَ عَلَيْهِ فَنَادٰى فِى الظُّلُمٰتِ اَنْ لَّآ اِلٰهَ اِلَّآ اَنْتَ سُبْحٰنَكَ اِنِّىْ كُنْتُ مِنَ الظّٰلِمِيْنَ ۞

فَاسْتَجَبْنَا لَهٗ وَنَجَّيْنٰهُ مِنَ الْغَمِّ وَكَذٰلِكَ نُجِى الْمُؤْمِنِيْنَ ۞

وَزَكَرِيَّآ اِذْ نَادٰى رَبَّهٗ رَبِّ لَا تَذَرْنِىْ فَرْدًا وَّاَنْتَ خَيْرُ الْوٰرِثِيْنَ ۞

فَاسْتَجَبْنَا لَهٗ وَوَهَبْنَا لَهٗ يَحْيٰى وَاَصْلَحْنَا لَهٗ زَوْجَهٗ اِنَّهُمْ كَانُوْا يُسٰرِعُوْنَ فِى الْخَيْرٰتِ وَيَدْعُوْنَنَا رَغَبًا وَّرَهَبًا وَكَانُوْا لَنَا خٰشِعِيْنَ ۞

وَالَّتِىْٓ اَحْصَنَتْ فَرْجَهَا فَنَفَخْنَا فِيْهَا مِنْ رُّوْحِنَا وَجَعَلْنٰهَا وَابْنَهَآ اٰيَةً لِّلْعٰلَمِيْنَ ۞

اِنَّ هٰذِهٖٓ اُمَّتُكُمْ اُمَّةً وَّاحِدَةً وَّاَنَا رَبُّكُمْ فَاعْبُدُوْنِ ۞

They have cut up the teachings of the Prophets into bits; but they will all return to Us. Whoever works righteousness, being a believer, his effort will not be disregarded and We shall surely record it. (93—95)

It is ordained for every township We have destroyed that its dwellers shall not return to this life. When Gog and Magog are let loose, and they spread out leaping across every barrier of land and sea and the true promise of Allah draws nigh, the eyes of those who disbelieved will stare fixedly, and they will exclaim: Woe unto us, we were indeed heedless of this; nay, we were wrongdoers. They will be told: Surely, you and that which you worship beside Allah, are destined to be the fuel of hell. You will also enter therein.

If these had been gods, as you allege, they would not have come to it; but long will they abide therein. Screaming will be their lot therein, and they will not be able to lend ear to admonition. Those who have been promised a good reward by Us, will be removed far from it. They will not hear the slightest sound thereof; and they will abide in a state of bliss that their souls desire. The Great Terror will not grieve them, and the angels will greet them with: This is your day that you were promised. Be mindful of the day when We shall roll up the heavens like the rolling up of the scrolls by a scribe. As We began the first creation, so shall We repeat it. We have charged Ourself with it, and so shall We do. (96—105)

وَتَقَطَّعُوٓا أَمْرَهُم بَيْنَهُمْ ۖ كُلٌّ إِلَيْنَا رَاجِعُونَ ۩

فَمَن يَعْمَلْ مِنَ الصَّالِحَاتِ وَهُوَ مُؤْمِنٌ فَلَا كُفْرَانَ لِسَعْيِهِ وَإِنَّا لَهُ كَاتِبُونَ ۩

وَحَرَامٌ عَلَىٰ قَرْيَةٍ أَهْلَكْنَاهَآ أَنَّهُمْ لَا يَرْجِعُونَ ۩

حَتَّىٰٓ إِذَا فُتِحَتْ يَأْجُوجُ وَمَأْجُوجُ وَهُم مِّن كُلِّ حَدَبٍ يَنسِلُونَ ۩

وَاقْتَرَبَ الْوَعْدُ الْحَقُّ فَإِذَا هِيَ شَاخِصَةٌ أَبْصَارُ الَّذِينَ كَفَرُوا يَٰوَيْلَنَا قَدْ كُنَّا فِي غَفْلَةٍ مِّنْ هَٰذَا بَلْ كُنَّا ظَالِمِينَ ۩

إِنَّكُمْ وَمَا تَعْبُدُونَ مِن دُونِ اللَّهِ حَصَبُ جَهَنَّمَ أَنتُمْ لَهَا وَارِدُونَ ۩

لَوْ كَانَ هَٰٓؤُلَآءِ آلِهَةً مَّا وَرَدُوهَا ۖ وَكُلٌّ فِيهَا خَالِدُونَ ۩

لَهُمْ فِيهَا زَفِيرٌ وَهُمْ فِيهَا لَا يَسْمَعُونَ ۩

إِنَّ الَّذِينَ سَبَقَتْ لَهُم مِّنَّا الْحُسْنَىٰٓ أُولَٰٓئِكَ عَنْهَا مُبْعَدُونَ ۩

لَا يَسْمَعُونَ حَسِيسَهَا ۖ وَهُمْ فِي مَا اشْتَهَتْ أَنفُسُهُمْ خَالِدُونَ ۩

لَا يَحْزُنُهُمُ الْفَزَعُ الْأَكْبَرُ وَتَتَلَقَّاهُمُ الْمَلَائِكَةُ هَٰذَا يَوْمُكُمُ الَّذِي كُنتُمْ تُوعَدُونَ ۩

يَوْمَ نَطْوِي السَّمَآءَ كَطَيِّ السِّجِلِّ لِلْكُتُبِ ۚ كَمَا بَدَأْنَآ أَوَّلَ خَلْقٍ نُّعِيدُهُ ۚ وَعْدًا عَلَيْنَا ۚ إِنَّا كُنَّا

We have recorded in the Book of David, after the exhortation, that My righteous servants shall inherit the Land. Herein, surely, is a message for those who are devoted to worship. We have sent thee only as a mercy for the universe. (106—108)

فَعِلِيْنَ ۞

وَلَقَدْ كَتَبْنَا فِى الزَّبُوْرِ مِنْ بَعْدِ الذِّكْرِ اَنَّ الْاَرْضَ يَرِثُهَا عِبَادِىَ الصّٰلِحُوْنَ ۞

اِنَّ فِىْ هٰذَا لَبَلٰغًا لِّقَوْمٍ عٰبِدِيْنَ ۞

وَمَاۤ اَرْسَلْنٰكَ اِلَّا رَحْمَةً لِّلْعٰلَمِيْنَ ۞

قُلْ اِنَّمَا يُوْحٰىۤ اِلَىَّ اَنَّمَاۤ اِلٰهُكُمْ اِلٰهٌ وَّاحِدٌ ۚ فَهَلْ اَنْتُمْ مُّسْلِمُوْنَ ۞

Proclaim: It has been revealed to me that your God is but One God. Will you then submit? If they turn away, tell them: I have warned you all alike and I know not whether that which you are promised is near or distant. Allah surely knows that which you say openly and also knows that which you conceal. Nor do I know whether that which you are promised is a trial for you, or is an enjoyment for a while. On this the Prophet prayed: Lord, judge Thou with truth. Our Lord is the Gracious One Whose help is to be sought against that which you assert. (109—113)

فَاِنْ تَوَلَّوْا فَقُلْ اٰذَنْتُكُمْ عَلٰى سَوَآءٍ ۚ وَاِنْ اَدْرِىْ اَقَرِيْبٌ اَمْ بَعِيْدٌ مَّا تُوْعَدُوْنَ ۞

اِنَّهٗ يَعْلَمُ الْجَهْرَ مِنَ الْقَوْلِ وَيَعْلَمُ مَا تَكْتُمُوْنَ ۞

وَاِنْ اَدْرِىْ لَعَلَّهٗ فِتْنَةٌ لَّكُمْ وَمَتَاعٌ اِلٰى حِيْنٍ ۞

قٰلَ رَبِّ احْكُمْ بِالْحَقِّ ۗ وَرَبُّنَا الرَّحْمٰنُ الْمُسْتَعَانُ عَلٰى مَا تَصِفُوْنَ ۞

318

سُوْرَةُ الْحَجِّ مَدَنِيَّةٌ ﴿٢٢﴾

AL-ḤAJJ

(Revealed after Hijra)

In the name of Allah, Most Gracious, Ever Merciful. (1)

بِسْمِ اللهِ الرَّحْمٰنِ الرَّحِيْمِ۝

يَآيُّهَا النَّاسُ اتَّقُوْا رَبَّكُمْ اِنَّ زَلْزَلَةَ السَّاعَةِ شَيْءٌ عَظِيْمٌ۝

O people, be mindful of your duty to your Lord; verily the earthquake of the Judgment is a tremendous thing. On that day, every woman giving suck shall forget her suckling and every pregnant woman shall cast her burden; and everyone will appear intoxicated, while they will not be intoxicated, but the chastisement of Allah will be severe indeed. There are some among men who dispute concerning Allah without knowledge and follow every rebellious misguided one, concerning whom it is decreed that whosoever makes friends with him, he will lead him astray and will guide him to the torment of the Fire. (2—5)

يَوْمَ تَرَوْنَهَا تَذْهَلُ كُلُّ مُرْضِعَةٍ عَمَّا اَرْضَعَتْ وَتَضَعُ كُلُّ ذَاتِ حَمْلٍ حَمْلَهَا وَتَرَى النَّاسَ سُكَارٰى وَمَا هُمْ بِسُكَارٰى وَلٰكِنَّ عَذَابَ اللهِ شَدِيْدٌ۝

وَمِنَ النَّاسِ مَنْ يُّجَادِلُ فِى اللهِ بِغَيْرِ عِلْمٍ وَّيَتَّبِعُ كُلَّ شَيْطٰنٍ مَّرِيْدٍۙ۝

كُتِبَ عَلَيْهِ اَنَّهٗ مَنْ تَوَلَّاهُ فَاَنَّهٗ يُضِلُّهٗ وَيَهْدِيْهِ اِلٰى عَذَابِ السَّعِيْرِ۝

O people, if you are in doubt concerning being raised up again, then consider that We created you from dust, then from a spermdrop, then from clotted blood, then from a lump of flesh, formed and unformed. We cause that which We will to stay in the wombs for an appointed term, then We bring you forth as babes; then We cause you to grow that you may attain to your full strength. Then some of you die and some of you reach extreme old age, when after having acquired much knowledge you become empty of it. You observe the earth lose all its capacity, but when We send water thereon, it stirs

يَآيُّهَا النَّاسُ اِنْ كُنْتُمْ فِىْ رَيْبٍ مِّنَ الْبَعْثِ فَاِنَّا خَلَقْنٰكُمْ مِّنْ تُرَابٍ ثُمَّ مِنْ نُّطْفَةٍ ثُمَّ مِنْ عَلَقَةٍ ثُمَّ مِنْ مُّضْغَةٍ مُّخَلَّقَةٍ وَّغَيْرِ مُخَلَّقَةٍ لِّنُبَيِّنَ لَكُمْ وَنُقِرُّ فِى الْاَرْحَامِ مَا نَشَآءُ اِلٰى اَجَلٍ مُّسَمًّى ثُمَّ نُخْرِجُكُمْ طِفْلًا ثُمَّ لِتَبْلُغُوْا اَشُدَّكُمْ وَمِنْكُمْ مَّنْ يُّتَوَفّٰى وَمِنْكُمْ مَّنْ يُّرَدُّ اِلٰى اَرْذَلِ الْعُمُرِ لِكَيْلَا يَعْلَمَ مِنْ بَعْدِ عِلْمٍ شَيْئًا وَتَرَى الْاَرْضَ هَامِدَةً فَاِذَآ اَنْزَلْنَا عَلَيْهَا الْمَآءَ اهْتَزَّتْ وَرَبَتْ وَاَنْبَتَتْ

319

and swells, and grows every kind of beauteous vegetation. This shows that Allah is Self-Subsisting and All-Sustaining, and that it is He Who brings the dead to life and that He has power over all things; and that the time appointed for everything is bound to come there is no doubt in it, and that Allah will raise up those who are in the graves. (6—8)

مِنْ كُلِّ زَوْجٍ بَهِيْجٍ ۞

ذٰلِكَ بِاَنَّ اللّٰهَ هُوَ الْحَقُّ وَ اَنَّهٗ يُحْيِ الْمَوْتٰى وَ اَنَّهٗ عَلٰى كُلِّ شَىْءٍ قَدِيْرٌ ۞

وَّاَنَّ السَّاعَةَ اٰتِيَةٌ لَّا رَيْبَ فِيْهَا ۙ وَ اَنَّ اللّٰهَ يَبْعَثُ مَنْ فِى الْقُبُوْرِ ۞

وَ مِنَ النَّاسِ مَنْ يُّجَادِلُ فِى اللّٰهِ بِغَيْرِ عِلْمٍ وَّ لَا هُدًى وَّ لَا كِتٰبٍ مُّنِيْرٍ ۞

There are some among men who dispute concerning Allah without knowledge, without guidance, and without the authority of an enlightening Book, disdainfully, that they may lead people astray from Allah's way. For such is disgrace in this world, and on the Day of Judgment We shall inflict upon them the torment of burning. That is the consequence of your conduct. Allah is not unjust to His servants. There are some among men who worship Allah half-heartedly. Then if good befall them they are content therewith; and if they encounter a trial they return to their former way. They lose in this world as well as in the Hereafter. That is a clear loss. They call beside Allah on that which can neither harm them nor benefit them. That is indeed straying far away.

ثَانِىَ عِطْفِهٖ لِيُضِلَّ عَنْ سَبِيْلِ اللّٰهِ ۖ لَهٗ فِى الدُّنْيَا خِزْيٌ وَّ نُذِيْقُهٗ يَوْمَ الْقِيٰمَةِ عَذَابَ الْحَرِيْقِ ۞

ذٰلِكَ بِمَا قَدَّمَتْ يَدٰكَ وَ اَنَّ اللّٰهَ لَيْسَ بِظَلَّامٍ لِّلْعَبِيْدِ ۞

وَ مِنَ النَّاسِ مَنْ يَّعْبُدُ اللّٰهَ عَلٰى حَرْفٍ ۚ فَاِنْ اَصَابَهٗ خَيْرُ اطْمَاَنَّ بِهٖ ۚ وَ اِنْ اَصَابَتْهُ فِتْنَةُ اِنْقَلَبَ عَلٰى وَجْهِهٖ ۚ خَسِرَ الدُّنْيَا وَ الْاٰخِرَةَ ۚ ذٰلِكَ هُوَ الْخُسْرَانُ الْمُبِيْنُ ۞

يَدْعُوْا مِنْ دُوْنِ اللّٰهِ مَا لَا يَضُرُّهٗ وَ مَا لَا يَنْفَعُهٗ ۚ ذٰلِكَ هُوَ الضَّلٰلُ الْبَعِيْدُ ۞

يَدْعُوْا لَمَنْ ضَرُّهٗ اَقْرَبُ مِنْ نَّفْعِهٖ ۚ لَبِئْسَ الْمَوْلٰى وَ لَبِئْسَ الْعَشِيْرُ ۞

They call on him whose harm is much more likely than his benefit. Evil indeed is such a patron and evil indeed is such an associate. Allah will admit those who believe and act righteously into Gardens beneath which rivers flow. Allah does

اِنَّ اللّٰهَ يُدْخِلُ الَّذِيْنَ اٰمَنُوْا وَ عَمِلُوا الصّٰلِحٰتِ جَنّٰتٍ تَجْرِيْ مِنْ تَحْتِهَا الْاَنْهٰرُ ۚ اِنَّ اللّٰهَ يَفْعَلُ

that which He wills. Whoso believes that Allah will not help the Prophet in this world and the Hereafter, let him make his way to heaven by means of a rope and then cut it off and see whether his device can help to remove that which enrages him. Thus have We sent down the Quran comprising Manifest Signs. Surely Allah guides whom He wills. (9—17)

مَا يُرِيُدُ ۝

مَنْ كَانَ يَظُنُّ اَنْ لَّنْ يَّنْصُرَهُ اللّٰهُ فِى الدُّنْيَا وَ الْاٰخِرَةِ فَلْيَمْدُدْ بِسَبَبٍ اِلَى السَّمَآءِ ثُمَّ لِيَقْطَعْ فَلْيَنْظُرْ هَلْ يُذْهِبَنَّ كَيْدُهُ مَا يَغِيْظُ ۝

وَ كَذٰلِكَ اَنْزَلْنٰهُ اٰيٰتٍۭ بَيِّنٰتٍ ۙ وَّ اَنَّ اللّٰهَ يَهْدِىْ مَنْ يُّرِيْدُ ۝

Verily Allah will judge between those who believe, and the Jews, and the Sabians, and the Christians, and the Magians and the idolaters, on the Day of Judgment. Surely, Allah watches over everything. Hast thou not seen, that to Allah submits whosoever is in the heavens and whosoever is in the earth, and the sun, and the moon, and the stars, and the mountains, and the trees and the beasts and many of mankind? But there are many who have been condemned to punishment. Whomsoever Allah disgraces, none can raise him to honour. Verily, Allah does what He pleases. These two groups, the believers and the disbelievers, dispute concerning their Lord. Those who disbelieve will have garments of fire cut out for them; and boiling water will be poured down over their heads, whereby that which is in their bellies will be melted and also their skins; and maces of iron will be prepared for their chastisement.

اِنَّ الَّذِيْنَ اٰمَنُوْا وَ الَّذِيْنَ هَادُوْا وَ الصّٰبِئِيْنَ وَ النَّصٰرٰى وَ الْمَجُوْسَ وَ الَّذِيْنَ اَشْرَكُوْۤا ۖ اِنَّ اللّٰهَ يَفْصِلُ بَيْنَهُمْ يَوْمَ الْقِيٰمَةِ ؕ اِنَّ اللّٰهَ عَلٰى كُلِّ شَىْءٍ شَهِيْدٌ ۝

اَلَمْ تَرَ اَنَّ اللّٰهَ يَسْجُدُ لَهٗ مَنْ فِى السَّمٰوٰتِ وَ مَنْ فِى الْاَرْضِ وَ الشَّمْسُ وَ الْقَمَرُ وَ النُّجُوْمُ وَ الْجِبَالُ وَ الشَّجَرُ وَ الدَّوَآبُّ وَ كَثِيْرٌ مِّنَ النَّاسِ ؕ وَ كَثِيْرٌ حَقَّ عَلَيْهِ الْعَذَابُ ؕ وَ مَنْ يُّهِنِ اللّٰهُ فَمَا لَهٗ مِنْ مُّكْرِمٍ ؕ اِنَّ اللّٰهَ يَفْعَلُ مَا يَشَآءُ ۩ ۝

هٰذٰنِ خَصْمٰنِ اخْتَصَمُوْا فِىْ رَبِّهِمْ ۫ فَالَّذِيْنَ كَفَرُوْا قُطِّعَتْ لَهُمْ ثِيَابٌ مِّنْ نَّارٍ ؕ يُصَبُّ مِنْ فَوْقِ رُءُوْسِهِمُ الْحَمِيْمُ ۝

يُصْهَرُ بِهٖ مَا فِىْ بُطُوْنِهِمْ وَ الْجُلُوْدُ ۝

وَ لَهُمْ مَّقَامِعُ مِنْ حَدِيْدٍ ۝

Whenever, out of anguish, they will seek to get out of it, they will be turned back into it and they will be told: Continue in the torment of burning. (18—23)

كُلَّمَاۤ اَرَادُوْۤا اَنْ يَّخْرُجُوْا مِنْهَا مِنْ غَمٍّ اُعِيْدُوْا فِيْهَا ۗ وَ ذُوْقُوْا عَذَابَ الْحَرِيْقِ ۝

Allah will admit those who believe and act righteously into Gardens beneath which rivers flow. They will be given bracelets of gold and pearls to wear, and their raiment therein will be of silk. They will be guided to purity of speech and to praiseworthy courses. Those who disbelieve and hinder people from the way of Allah, and from the Sacred Mosque, which We have appointed equally for all people, for those who stay therein for continuous worship of Allah as well as those who are visitors from the desert, whoso seeks wrongfully to deviate therein from the right path shall be subjected by Us to grievous torment. (24—26)

إِنَّ اللّٰهَ يُدْخِلُ الَّذِيْنَ اٰمَنُوْا وَعَمِلُوا الصّٰلِحٰتِ جَنّٰتٍ تَجْرِىْ مِنْ تَحْتِهَا الْاَنْهٰرُ يُحَلَّوْنَ فِيْهَا مِنْ اَسَاوِرَ مِنْ ذَهَبٍ وَّلُؤْلُؤًا ۚ وَلِبَاسُهُمْ فِيْهَا حَرِيْرٌ ۝

وَهُدُوْٓا اِلَى الطَّيِّبِ مِنَ الْقَوْلِ ۚ وَهُدُوْٓا اِلٰى صِرَاطِ الْحَمِيْدِ ۝

اِنَّ الَّذِيْنَ كَفَرُوْا وَيَصُدُّوْنَ عَنْ سَبِيْلِ اللّٰهِ وَالْمَسْجِدِ الْحَرَامِ الَّذِىْ جَعَلْنٰهُ لِلنَّاسِ سَوَآءَ اِلْعَاكِفُ فِيْهِ وَالْبَادِ ۚ وَمَنْ يُّرِدْ فِيْهِ بِاِلْحَادٍ بِظُلْمٍ نُّذِقْهُ مِنْ عَذَابٍ اَلِيْمٍ ۝

Call to mind when We assigned to Abraham the site of the House and commanded him: Associate not anything with Me, and purify My House for those who perform the circuits, and those who stand and bow down and fall down prostrate in Prayer; and call mankind to the Pilgrimage. They will come to thee on foot, and on every lean camel, proceeding by every distant track that they may witness its benefits for them and may pronounce the name of Allah, during the appointed days, in gratitude for His bounties, over that which He has bestowed upon them in the shape of cattle. So eat thereof and feed the distressed and the needy. Then let them carry out their needful acts of cleansing and fulfil their vows and perform the circuits of the Ancient House. That is the commandment. Whoso honours that which is declared sacred by Allah, may be sure that it counts for good with his Lord. Cattle are made lawful for you, except that

وَاِذْ بَوَّاْنَا لِاِبْرٰهِيْمَ مَكَانَ الْبَيْتِ اَنْ لَّا تُشْرِكْ بِىْ شَيْئًا وَّطَهِّرْ بَيْتِىَ لِلطَّآئِفِيْنَ وَالْقَآئِمِيْنَ وَالرُّكَّعِ السُّجُوْدِ ۝

وَاَذِّنْ فِى النَّاسِ بِالْحَجِّ يَأْتُوْكَ رِجَالًا وَّعَلٰى كُلِّ ضَامِرٍ يَّأْتِيْنَ مِنْ كُلِّ فَجٍّ عَمِيْقٍ ۝

لِّيَشْهَدُوْا مَنَافِعَ لَهُمْ وَيَذْكُرُوا اسْمَ اللّٰهِ فِىْٓ اَيَّامٍ مَّعْلُوْمٰتٍ عَلٰى مَا رَزَقَهُمْ مِّنْ بَهِيْمَةِ الْاَنْعَامِ ۚ فَكُلُوْا مِنْهَا وَاَطْعِمُوا الْبَآئِسَ الْفَقِيْرَ ۝

ثُمَّ لْيَقْضُوْا تَفَثَهُمْ وَلْيُوْفُوْا نُذُوْرَهُمْ وَلْيَطَّوَّفُوْا بِالْبَيْتِ الْعَتِيْقِ ۝

ذٰلِكَ ۚ وَمَنْ يُّعَظِّمْ حُرُمٰتِ اللّٰهِ فَهُوَ خَيْرٌ لَّهُ عِنْدَ رَبِّهٖ ۚ وَاُحِلَّتْ لَكُمُ الْاَنْعَامُ اِلَّا مَا يُتْلٰى عَلَيْكُمْ

which has already been announced to you in the Quran. Then shun the abomination of idols, and shun all words of falsehood, devoting yourselves wholly to Allah, not associating anything with Him. Whoso associates anything with Allah, his case is, as if he fell from a height, and the birds snatched him up, or the wind blew him away to a distant place. That is the admonition. Whoso venerates the sacred Signs of Allah may be sure that it counts as righteousness of the heart for him. You may draw benefits from the animals designed for sacrifice, for an appointed term, then they must be conveyed to the Ancient House. (27—34)

For every people We appointed rites of sacrifice, that they might pronounce the name of Allah over the quadrupeds of the class of cattle that He has provided for them. Remember then that your God is One God, and submit yourselves, therefore, wholly to Him; and give glad tidings to the humble, whose hearts are filled with awe when Allah's name is mentioned, and to those who endure patiently whatever befalls them, and who observe Prayer and spend for the pleasure of Allah out of that which We have provided for them. We have appointed the sacrificial camels also as the Signs of Allah, for you. In them there is much good for you. So pronounce the name of Allah over them when they are tied up in lines; and when they fall down on their sides slaughtered, eat thereof yourselves and feed the needy, those who are content and those who are distressed. Thus have We subjected them to you that you may be grateful. Their flesh reaches not Allah, nor their blood, but it is your righteousness that reaches Him. Thus has He subjected them to you that you may glorify Allah for guiding you; and give glad tidings to those who carry out all commandments to the full. (35—38)

Allah will surely defend those who believe, Allah loves not the perfidious and the ungrateful. Permission to fight is granted to those against whom war is made, because they have been wronged, and Allah indeed has the power to help them. They are those who have been driven out of their homes unjustly only because they affirmed: Our Lord is Allah. If Allah did not repel the aggression of some people by means of others, cloisters and churches and synagogues and mosques, wherein the name of Allah is oft commemorated, would surely be destroyed. Allah will surely help him who helps His cause; Allah is indeed Powerful, Mighty. If We establish these persecuted ones in the earth, they will observe Prayer and pay the Zakat and enjoin good and forbid evil. With Allah rests the final issue of all affairs. (39—42)

اِنَّ اللّٰهَ يُدٰفِعُ عَنِ الَّذِيۡنَ اٰمَنُوۡا ؕ اِنَّ اللّٰهَ لَا يُحِبُّ كُلَّ خَوَّانٍ كَفُوۡرٍ ۝

اُذِنَ لِلَّذِيۡنَ يُقَاتَلُوۡنَ بِاَنَّهُمۡ ظُلِمُوۡا ؕ وَاِنَّ اللّٰهَ عَلٰى نَصۡرِهِمۡ لَقَدِيۡرُ ۝

الَّذِيۡنَ اُخۡرِجُوۡا مِنۡ دِيَارِهِمۡ بِغَيۡرِ حَقٍّ اِلَّاۤ اَنۡ يَّقُوۡلُوۡا رَبُّنَا اللّٰهُ ؕ وَلَوۡ لَا دَفۡعُ اللّٰهِ النَّاسَ بَعۡضَهُمۡ بِبَعۡضٍ لَّهُدِّمَتۡ صَوَامِعُ وَبِيَعٌ وَّصَلَوٰتٌ وَّمَسٰجِدُ يُذۡكَرُ فِيۡهَا اسۡمُ اللّٰهِ كَثِيۡرًا ؕ وَلَيَنۡصُرَنَّ اللّٰهُ مَنۡ يَّنۡصُرُهٗ ؕ اِنَّ اللّٰهَ لَقَوِيٌّ عَزِيۡزٌ ۝

اَلَّذِيۡنَ اِنۡ مَّكَّنّٰهُمۡ فِى الۡاَرۡضِ اَقَامُوا الصَّلٰوةَ وَاٰتَوُا الزَّكٰوةَ وَاَمَرُوۡا بِالۡمَعۡرُوۡفِ وَنَهَوۡا عَنِ الۡمُنۡكَرِ ؕ وَلِلّٰهِ عَاقِبَةُ الۡاُمُوۡرِ ۝

If thy opponents charge thee with falsehood, even so did, before them, the people of Noah and the tribes of 'Ad and Thamud and the people of Abraham and the people of Lot; and the inhabitants of Midian also charged their Prophets with falsehood. Moses was also charged with falsehood. But I gave respite to the disbelievers and then I seized them. Consider then, how terrible were the consequences of rejecting My message. How many a city have We destroyed which was given to wrongdoing, so that it is fallen down on its roofs, and how many a well is deserted and how many a lofty castle is in ruins! Have they not travelled in the earth that they may have hearts wherewith to understand or ears wherewith to hear? The truth is that it is not the eyes

وَاِنۡ يُّكَذِّبُوۡكَ فَقَدۡ كَذَّبَتۡ قَبۡلَهُمۡ قَوۡمُ نُوۡحٍ وَّعَادٌ وَّثَمُوۡدُ ۝

وَقَوۡمُ اِبۡرٰهِيۡمَ وَقَوۡمُ لُوۡطٍ ۝

وَّاَصۡحٰبُ مَدۡيَنَ ۚ وَكُذِّبَ مُوۡسٰى فَاَمۡلَيۡتُ لِلۡكٰفِرِيۡنَ ثُمَّ اَخَذۡتُهُمۡ ۚ فَكَيۡفَ كَانَ نَكِيۡرِ ۝

فَكَاَيِّنۡ مِّنۡ قَرۡيَةٍ اَهۡلَكۡنٰهَا وَهِىَ ظَالِمَةٌ فَهِىَ خَاوِيَةٌ عَلٰى عُرُوۡشِهَا وَبِئۡرٍ مُّعَطَّلَةٍ وَّقَصۡرٍ مَّشِيۡدٍ ۝

اَفَلَمۡ يَسِيۡرُوۡا فِى الۡاَرۡضِ فَتَكُوۡنَ لَهُمۡ قُلُوۡبٌ يَّعۡقِلُوۡنَ بِهَاۤ اَوۡ اٰذَانٌ يَّسۡمَعُوۡنَ بِهَا ۚ فَاِنَّهَا لَا

that are blind, but blinded are the hearts that are in the breasts. They ask thee to hasten on the punishment. Allah never fails in His promise; only, a day in thy Lord's reckoning is as a thousand years in your counting. To how many a city I gave respite while it was given to wrongdoing and then I seized it. Unto Me is the return. (43—49)

تَعْمَى الْاَبْصَارُ وَلٰكِنْ تَعْمَى الْقُلُوْبُ الَّتِيْ فِى الصُّدُوْرِ ۞

وَيَسْتَعْجِلُوْنَكَ بِالْعَذَابِ وَلَنْ يُخْلِفَ اللّٰهُ وَعْدَهٗ ۖ وَاِنَّ يَوْمًا عِنْدَ رَبِّكَ كَاَلْفِ سَنَةٍ مِّمَّا تَعُدُّوْنَ ۞

وَكَاَيِّنْ مِّنْ قَرْيَةٍ اَمْلَيْتُ لَهَا وَهِيَ ظَالِمَةٌ ثُمَّ اَخَذْتُهَا ۚ وَاِلَيَّ الْمَصِيْرُ ۞

قُلْ يٰۤاَيُّهَا النَّاسُ اِنَّمَاۤ اَنَا لَكُمْ نَذِيْرٌ مُّبِيْنٌ ۞

فَالَّذِيْنَ اٰمَنُوْا وَعَمِلُوا الصّٰلِحٰتِ لَهُمْ مَّغْفِرَةٌ وَّرِزْقٌ كَرِيْمٌ ۞

وَالَّذِيْنَ سَعَوْا فِيْۤ اٰيٰتِنَا مُعٰجِزِيْنَ اُولٰٓئِكَ اَصْحٰبُ الْجَحِيْمِ ۞

Proclaim: O ye people, I am but a plain Warner sent to you. Then those who believe and act righteously, will have forgiveness and an honourable provision; but those who strive against Our Signs seeking to frustrate Our purpose shall be the inmates of the Fire. Whenever We send a Messenger or a Prophet and he forms a design to fulfil Our purpose Satan puts obstacles in the way of his design. Then Allah removes the obstacles placed by Satan, and Allah firmly establishes His Signs. Allah is All-Knowing, Wise. The result is that the obstacles raised by Satan prove a trial for the sick and hard of heart, and surely the wrongdoers are always bent on opposition. But those to whom knowledge has been given realise that the Quran is the truth from thy Lord, so that they may believe therein and their hearts may submit to it. Surely Allah guides those who believe to the right path. Those who disbelieve will continue in doubt concerning it until the Hour comes

وَمَاۤ اَرْسَلْنَا مِنْ قَبْلِكَ مِنْ رَّسُوْلٍ وَّلَا نَبِيٍّ اِلَّاۤ اِذَا تَمَنّٰٓى اَلْقَى الشَّيْطٰنُ فِيْۤ اُمْنِيَّتِهٖ ۚ فَيَنْسَخُ اللّٰهُ مَا يُلْقِى الشَّيْطٰنُ ثُمَّ يُحْكِمُ اللّٰهُ اٰيٰتِهٖ ۖ وَاللّٰهُ عَلِيْمٌ حَكِيْمٌ ۞

لِّيَجْعَلَ مَا يُلْقِى الشَّيْطٰنُ فِتْنَةً لِّلَّذِيْنَ فِيْ قُلُوْبِهِمْ مَّرَضٌ وَّالْقَاسِيَةِ قُلُوْبُهُمْ ۚ وَاِنَّ الظّٰلِمِيْنَ لَفِيْ شِقَاقٍ بَعِيْدٍ ۞

وَّلِيَعْلَمَ الَّذِيْنَ اُوْتُوا الْعِلْمَ اَنَّهُ الْحَقُّ مِنْ رَّبِّكَ فَيُؤْمِنُوْا بِهٖ فَتُخْبِتَ لَهٗ قُلُوْبُهُمْ ۚ وَاِنَّ اللّٰهَ لَهَادِ الَّذِيْنَ اٰمَنُوْۤا اِلٰى صِرَاطٍ مُّسْتَقِيْمٍ ۞

وَلَا يَزَالُ الَّذِيْنَ كَفَرُوْا فِيْ مِرْيَةٍ مِّنْهُ حَتّٰى

suddenly upon them or a devastating punishment overtakes them. On that day the kingdom shall be Allah's and He will judge between them. Those who believe and act righteously will be in Gardens of Delight; but for those who disbelieve and reject Our Signs there will be an humiliating chastisement. (50—58)

Allah will surely provide a goodly provision for those who migrate from their homes in the cause of Allah and are then slain or die. Surely Allah is the Best of providers. He will surely admit them to a resort with which they will be well pleased. Allah is indeed All-Knowing, Forbearing. That indeed is so. (59—60)

Whoso exacts a penalty in proportion to the injury done to him and is nevertheless transgressed against will surely be helped by Allah. Verily, Allah is Most Forgiving, Forbearing. This system of retribution proves that it is Allah Who causes the night to enter into the day, and causes the day to enter into the night, and that Allah is All-Hearing, All-Seeing. That is because Allah is Self-Subsisting and All-Sustaining, and that which they call on beside Him is bound to perish, and because Allah is the High, the Great. Seest thou not that Allah sends down water from the sky and the earth thereby becomes green? Allah is indeed Beneficent, All-Aware. To Him belongs all that is in the heavens and all that is in the earth. Surely Allah is Self-Sufficient, Praiseworthy. (61—65)

Seest thou not that Allah has subjected to you whatever is in the earth, and that the vessels sail in the sea by His command? He holds back the punishment from overtaking you without His command. Surely, Allah is Compassionate and Ever Merciful towards people. He it is Who gave you life, then He will cause you to die, then will He give you life again. Surely, man is most ungrateful. (66—67)

تَجْرِىْ فِى الْبَحْرِ بِاَمْرِهٖ وَيُمْسِكُ السَّمَآءَ اَنْ تَقَعَ عَلَى الْاَرْضِ اِلَّا بِاِذْنِهٖ اِنَّ اللّٰهَ بِالنَّاسِ لَرَءُوْفٌ رَّحِيْمٌ ۞

وَهُوَ الَّذِىْٓ اَحْيَاكُمْ ثُمَّ يُمِيْتُكُمْ ثُمَّ يُحْيِيْكُمْ اِنَّ الْاِنْسَانَ لَكَفُوْرٌ ۞

For every people have We appointed ways of worship which they observe, so let them not dispute with thee over Islamic ways of worship; and invite them to thy Lord, for surely thou followest the right guidance. If they contend with thee, say to them: Allah knows best that which you do. Allah will judge between you and me on the Day of Judgment concerning that about which you differ. Knowest thou not that Allah knows whatsoever is in the heavens and the earth? Surely, it is all preserved in a Book, and that is easy for Allah. They worship beside Allah that for which He has sent down no authority and concerning which they have no knowledge. The wrongdoers will have no helper. When Our clear Signs are recited unto them, thou seest on the countenances of the disbelievers manifest signs of displeasure. They would well-nigh assault those who recite Our Signs to them. Say to them: Shall I tell you of something worse than this? It is the Fire that Allah has promised to those who disbelieve; and an evil destination it is. (68—73)

لِكُلِّ اُمَّةٍ جَعَلْنَا مَنْسَكًا هُمْ نَاسِكُوْهُ فَلَا يُنَازِعُنَّكَ فِى الْاَمْرِ وَادْعُ اِلٰى رَبِّكَ اِنَّكَ لَعَلٰى هُدًى مُّسْتَقِيْمٍ ۞

وَاِنْ جَادَلُوْكَ فَقُلِ اللّٰهُ اَعْلَمُ بِمَا تَعْمَلُوْنَ ۞

اَللّٰهُ يَحْكُمُ بَيْنَكُمْ يَوْمَ الْقِيٰمَةِ فِيْمَا كُنْتُمْ فِيْهِ تَخْتَلِفُوْنَ ۞

اَلَمْ تَعْلَمْ اَنَّ اللّٰهَ يَعْلَمُ مَا فِى السَّمَآءِ وَالْاَرْضِ اِنَّ ذٰلِكَ فِىْ كِتٰبٍ اِنَّ ذٰلِكَ عَلَى اللّٰهِ يَسِيْرٌ ۞

وَيَعْبُدُوْنَ مِنْ دُوْنِ اللّٰهِ مَا لَمْ يُنَزِّلْ بِهٖ سُلْطٰنًا وَّمَا لَيْسَ لَهُمْ بِهٖ عِلْمٌ وَمَا لِلظّٰلِمِيْنَ مِنْ نَّصِيْرٍ ۞

وَاِذَا تُتْلٰى عَلَيْهِمْ اٰيٰتُنَا بَيِّنٰتٍ تَعْرِفُ فِىْ وُجُوْهِ الَّذِيْنَ كَفَرُوا الْمُنْكَرَ يَكَادُوْنَ يَسْطُوْنَ بِالَّذِيْنَ يَتْلُوْنَ عَلَيْهِمْ اٰيٰتِنَا قُلْ اَفَاُنَبِّئُكُمْ بِشَرٍّ مِّنْ ذٰلِكُمُ النَّارُ وَعَدَهَا اللّٰهُ الَّذِيْنَ كَفَرُوْا وَبِئْسَ الْمَصِيْرُ ۞

Listen, O people, carefully to this illustration. Surely, those on whom you call instead of Allah cannot create even a fly, though they should all combine together

يٰٓاَيُّهَا النَّاسُ ضُرِبَ مَثَلٌ فَاسْتَمِعُوْا لَهٗ اِنَّ الَّذِيْنَ تَدْعُوْنَ مِنْ دُوْنِ اللّٰهِ لَنْ يَّخْلُقُوْا ذُبَابًا

for the purpose; and if a fly should snatch away anything from them, they cannot recover it therefrom. How helpless is he who calls on them and how helpless are those on whom he calls! They have not a true concept of Allah's attributes. Surely, Allah is Powerful, Mighty. Allah chooses His Messengers from among angels and from among men. Surely, Allah is All-Hearing, All-Seeing. He knows what lies ahead of them and what is left behind them; and to Allah are all affairs returned. (74—77)

وَّلَوِ اجْتَمَعُوْا لَهٗ ۚ وَاِنْ يَّسْلُبْهُمُ الذُّبَابُ شَيْئًا

لَّا يَسْتَنْقِذُوْهُ مِنْهُ ۚ ضَعُفَ الطَّالِبُ وَالْمَطْلُوْبُ ۞

مَا قَدَرُوا اللّٰهَ حَقَّ قَدْرِهٖ ۚ اِنَّ اللّٰهَ لَقَوِيٌّ عَزِيْزٌ ۞

اَللّٰهُ يَصْطَفِيْ مِنَ الْمَلٰٓئِكَةِ رُسُلًا وَّمِنَ النَّاسِ ۚ

اِنَّ اللّٰهَ سَمِيْعٌۢ بَصِيْرٌ ۞

يَعْلَمُ مَا بَيْنَ اَيْدِيْهِمْ وَمَا خَلْفَهُمْ ۚ وَاِلَى اللّٰهِ تُرْجَعُ

الْاُمُوْرُ ۞

يٰٓاَيُّهَا الَّذِيْنَ اٰمَنُوا ارْكَعُوْا وَاسْجُدُوْا وَاعْبُدُوْا

رَبَّكُمْ وَافْعَلُوا الْخَيْرَ لَعَلَّكُمْ تُفْلِحُوْنَ ۩ ۞

O ye who believe, bow down and prostrate yourselves in Prayer, and worship your Lord, and work righteousness that you may prosper. Strive in the cause of Allah a perfect striving, for He has exalted you and has laid no hardship upon you in the matter of religion. Follow the faith of your father Abraham. Allah has named you Muslims in this Book and also in previous Books, so that the Messenger may be a witness over you, and that you may be witnesses over mankind. Then observe Prayer, and pay the Zakat, and hold fast to Allah. He is your Master; an excellent Master and an excellent Helper. (78—79)

وَجَاهِدُوْا فِي اللّٰهِ حَقَّ جِهَادِهٖ ۚ هُوَ اجْتَبٰىكُمْ

وَمَا جَعَلَ عَلَيْكُمْ فِي الدِّيْنِ مِنْ حَرَجٍ ۚ مِلَّةَ

اَبِيْكُمْ اِبْرٰهِيْمَ ۚ هُوَ سَمّٰىكُمُ الْمُسْلِمِيْنَ ۙ مِنْ

قَبْلُ وَفِيْ هٰذَا لِيَكُوْنَ الرَّسُوْلُ شَهِيْدًا عَلَيْكُمْ

وَتَكُوْنُوْا شُهَدَآءَ عَلَى النَّاسِ ۚ فَاَقِيْمُوا الصَّلٰوةَ

وَاٰتُوا الزَّكٰوةَ وَاعْتَصِمُوْا بِاللّٰهِ ۚ هُوَ مَوْلٰىكُمْ ۚ فَنِعْمَ

الْمَوْلٰى وَنِعْمَ النَّصِيْرُ ۞

Chapter 23

سُوْرَةُ الْمُؤْمِنُوْنَ مَكِّيَّةٌ

AL-MU'MINŪN

(Revealed before Hijra)

In the name of Allah, Most Gracious, Ever Merciful. (1)

بِسْمِ اللّٰهِ الرَّحْمٰنِ الرَّحِيْمِ ۚ ۝

قَدْ اَفْلَحَ الْمُؤْمِنُوْنَ ۝

الَّذِيْنَ هُمْ فِيْ صَلَاتِهِمْ خَاشِعُوْنَ ۙ ۝

وَ الَّذِيْنَ هُمْ عَنِ اللَّغْوِ مُعْرِضُوْنَ ۝

وَ الَّذِيْنَ هُمْ لِلزَّكٰوةِ فٰعِلُوْنَ ۝

The believers shall attain their goal; those who are humble in their Prayers, who shun all that is vain, who are prompt in paying the Zakat, who safeguard their chastity — there shall be no blame on them in respect of their wives and those under their control; but whoever seeks anything beyond that is a transgressor — who are watchful of their trusts and their covenants, and who are strict in the observance of their Prayers. These are the true heirs who will inherit Paradise; they will abide therein. (2—12)

وَ الَّذِيْنَ هُمْ لِفُرُوْجِهِمْ حٰفِظُوْنَ ۙ ۝

اِلَّا عَلٰۤى اَزْوَاجِهِمْ اَوْ مَا مَلَكَتْ اَيْمَانُهُمْ فَاِنَّهُمْ غَيْرُ مَلُوْمِيْنَ ۝

فَمَنِ ابْتَغٰى وَرَآءَ ذٰلِكَ فَاُولٰٓئِكَ هُمُ الْعٰدُوْنَ ۝

وَ الَّذِيْنَ هُمْ لِاَمٰنٰتِهِمْ وَ عَهْدِهِمْ رٰعُوْنَ ۙ ۝

وَ الَّذِيْنَ هُمْ عَلٰى صَلَوٰتِهِمْ يُحَافِظُوْنَ ۝

اُولٰٓئِكَ هُمُ الْوٰرِثُوْنَ ۙ ۝

الَّذِيْنَ يَرِثُوْنَ الْفِرْدَوْسَ ۗ هُمْ فِيْهَا خٰلِدُوْنَ ۝

وَ لَقَدْ خَلَقْنَا الْاِنْسَانَ مِنْ سُلٰلَةٍ مِّنْ طِيْنٍ ۚ ۝

ثُمَّ جَعَلْنٰهُ نُطْفَةً فِيْ قَرَارٍ مَّكِيْنٍ ۪ ۝

Verily, We created man from an extract of clay; then We placed him as a drop of sperm in a safe depository; then We fashioned the sperm into a clot; then We fashioned the clot into a shapeless lump; then out of this shapeless lump We fashioned bones; then We clothed the bones with flesh; then We developed it into a new creation. So blessed is Allah, the Best of creators.

ثُمَّ خَلَقْنَا النُّطْفَةَ عَلَقَةً فَخَلَقْنَا الْعَلَقَةَ مُضْغَةً فَخَلَقْنَا الْمُضْغَةَ عِظٰمًا فَكَسَوْنَا الْعِظٰمَ لَحْمًا ثُمَّ اَنْشَأْنٰهُ خَلْقًا اٰخَرَ ۚ فَتَبٰرَكَ اللّٰهُ اَحْسَنُ الْخٰلِقِيْنَ ۝

ثُمَّ اِنَّكُمْ بَعْدَ ذٰلِكَ لَمَيِّتُوْنَ ۝

After this you will surely die, and on the Day of Judgment you will be raised up. For your advancement in that life We have fashioned seven spiritual paths. We were not neglectful of Our creation. (13—18)

We sent down water from the sky according to measure, and We caused it to stay in the earth — surely We have power to take it away — and We produced for you thereby gardens of date-palms and vineyards, in which there are for you abundant fruits; and of them you eat. We have also created for you the tree which springs forth from Mount Sinai containing within it oil and a sauce for those who eat. In the cattle also there is a lesson for you. We provide for you drink out of that which is in their bellies, and you derive many other benefits from them, and the flesh of some of them you eat; and on them and on ships you are borne. (19—23)

We sent Noah to his people and he admonished them: O my people, worship Allah alone; you have no god other than Him. Will you not be mindful of your duty to Him? The leaders of his people, who disbelieved, said to them: He is only a human being like yourselves who desires to exalt himself above you. If Allah had wished to send a Messenger, He could have sent down angels. We have not heard of any such event happening in the time of our forefathers. He is but a man stricken with madness; wait, therefore, for his end for a while. Thereupon Noah prayed: Lord, come to my help, for they treat me as a liar. So We directed him: Construct the Ark under Our eyes and according to Our directions. When Our command comes and the fountains of the earth gush forth, take into it two of every kind, as directed by Us, male and female, and thy family, except those of them concerning whom Our decree has already

ثُمَّ اِنَّكُمْ يَوْمَ الْقِيٰمَةِ تُبْعَثُوْنَ ۝

وَلَقَدْ خَلَقْنَا فَوْقَكُمْ سَبْعَ طَرَآئِقَ ۖ وَمَا كُنَّا عَنِ الْخَلْقِ غٰفِلِيْنَ ۝

وَاَنْزَلْنَا مِنَ السَّمَآءِ مَآءً بِقَدَرٍ فَاَسْكَنّٰهُ فِى الْاَرْضِ ۖ وَاِنَّا عَلٰى ذَهَابٍ بِهٖ لَقٰدِرُوْنَ ۝

فَاَنْشَاْنَا لَكُمْ بِهٖ جَنّٰتٍ مِّنْ نَّخِيْلٍ وَّاَعْنَابٍ ۘ لَكُمْ فِيْهَا فَوَاكِهُ كَثِيْرَةٌ وَّمِنْهَا تَاْكُلُوْنَ ۝

وَشَجَرَةً تَخْرُجُ مِنْ طُوْرِ سَيْنَآءَ تَنْبُتُ بِالدُّهْنِ وَصِبْغٍ لِّلْاٰكِلِيْنَ ۝

وَاِنَّ لَكُمْ فِى الْاَنْعَامِ لَعِبْرَةً ۖ نُسْقِيْكُمْ مِّمَّا فِىْ بُطُوْنِهَا وَلَكُمْ فِيْهَا مَنَافِعُ كَثِيْرَةٌ وَّمِنْهَا تَاْكُلُوْنَ ۝

وَعَلَيْهَا وَعَلَى الْفُلْكِ تُحْمَلُوْنَ ۝

وَلَقَدْ اَرْسَلْنَا نُوْحًا اِلٰى قَوْمِهٖ فَقَالَ يٰقَوْمِ اعْبُدُوا اللّٰهَ مَا لَكُمْ مِّنْ اِلٰهٍ غَيْرُهٗ ۗ اَفَلَا تَتَّقُوْنَ ۝

فَقَالَ الْمَلَؤُا الَّذِيْنَ كَفَرُوْا مِنْ قَوْمِهٖ مَا هٰذَآ اِلَّا بَشَرٌ مِّثْلُكُمْ ۙ يُرِيْدُ اَنْ يَّتَفَضَّلَ عَلَيْكُمْ ۗ وَلَوْ شَآءَ اللّٰهُ لَاَنْزَلَ مَلٰٓئِكَةً ۖ مَّا سَمِعْنَا بِهٰذَا فِىْۤ اٰبَآئِنَا الْاَوَّلِيْنَ ۝

اِنْ هُوَ اِلَّا رَجُلٌۢ بِهٖ جِنَّةٌ فَتَرَبَّصُوْا بِهٖ حَتّٰى حِيْنٍ ۝

قَالَ رَبِّ انْصُرْنِىْ بِمَا كَذَّبُوْنِ ۝

فَاَوْحَيْنَآ اِلَيْهِ اَنِ اصْنَعِ الْفُلْكَ بِاَعْيُنِنَا وَوَحْيِنَا فَاِذَا جَآءَ اَمْرُنَا وَفَارَ التَّنُّوْرُ ۙ فَاسْلُكْ فِيْهَا مِنْ كُلٍّ زَوْجَيْنِ اثْنَيْنِ وَاَهْلَكَ اِلَّا مَنْ سَبَقَ عَلَيْهِ

issued; and do not entreat Me concerning the wrongdoers; they shall be drowned. When thou and those who are with thee have settled in the Ark, let each of you say: All praise belongs to Allah Who has delivered us from the unjust people; and when thou art about to land pray: Lord, make my landing full of every kind of blessing, for Thou art the Best of those who cause people to land. In this there are Signs; and of a surety We make a trial of people. (24—31)

القَوْلُ مِنْهُمْ وَلَا تُخَاطِبْنِيْ فِي الَّذِيْنَ ظَلَمُوْا اِنَّهُمْ مُّغْرَقُوْنَ ۞

فَاِذَا اسْتَوَيْتَ اَنْتَ وَمَنْ مَّعَكَ عَلَى الْفُلْكِ فَقُلِ الْحَمْدُ لِلّٰهِ الَّذِيْ نَجّٰنَا مِنَ الْقَوْمِ الظّٰلِمِيْنَ ۞

وَقُلْ رَّبِّ اَنْزِلْنِيْ مُنْزَلًا مُّبٰرَكًا وَّاَنْتَ خَيْرُ الْمُنْزِلِيْنَ ۞

اِنَّ فِيْ ذٰلِكَ لَاٰيٰتٍ وَّاِنْ كُنَّا لَمُبْتَلِيْنَ ۞

ثُمَّ اَنْشَاْنَا مِنْ بَعْدِهِمْ قَرْنًا اٰخَرِيْنَ ۞

فَاَرْسَلْنَا فِيْهِمْ رَسُوْلًا مِّنْهُمْ اَنِ اعْبُدُوا اللّٰهَ مَا لَكُمْ مِّنْ اِلٰهٍ غَيْرُهٗ ۖ اَفَلَا تَتَّقُوْنَ ۞

Then We raised after them another generation; and We sent among them a Messenger from among themselves who exhorted them: Worship Allah alone. You have no god other than Him. Will you not then make Him your shield against all calamities? The leaders of his people, who disbelieved and denied the meeting of the Hereafter and upon whom We had bestowed ease and comfort in this life, said to the people: He is but a human being like yourselves. He eats of that which you eat and drinks of that which you drink. If you obey a human being like yourselves, you will then surely be losers. Does he promise you that when you are dead and have become dust and bones, you will be brought forth again?

وَقَالَ الْمَلَاُ مِنْ قَوْمِهِ الَّذِيْنَ كَفَرُوْا وَكَذَّبُوْا بِلِقَآءِ الْاٰخِرَةِ وَاَتْرَفْنٰهُمْ فِي الْحَيٰوةِ الدُّنْيَا مَا هٰذَآ اِلَّا بَشَرٌ مِّثْلُكُمْ يَاْكُلُ مِمَّا تَاْكُلُوْنَ مِنْهُ وَيَشْرَبُ مِمَّا تَشْرَبُوْنَ ۞

وَلَئِنْ اَطَعْتُمْ بَشَرًا مِّثْلَكُمْ اِنَّكُمْ اِذًا لَّخٰسِرُوْنَ ۞

اَيَعِدُكُمْ اَنَّكُمْ اِذَا مِتُّمْ وَكُنْتُمْ تُرَابًا وَّعِظَامًا اَنَّكُمْ مُّخْرَجُوْنَ ۞

هَيْهَاتَ هَيْهَاتَ لِمَا تُوْعَدُوْنَ ۞

That which you are promised is utterly opposed to reason. There is no life other than our present life; we were without life and now we live, but we shall not be raised up again. He is only a man who has fabricated a lie against Allah; and we are not going to believe in him.

اِنْ هِيَ اِلَّا حَيَاتُنَا الدُّنْيَا نَمُوْتُ وَنَحْيَا وَمَا نَحْنُ بِمَبْعُوْثِيْنَ ۞

اِنْ هُوَ اِلَّا رَجُلُ افْتَرٰى عَلَى اللّٰهِ كَذِبًا وَّمَا نَحْنُ لَهٗ بِمُؤْمِنِيْنَ ۞

He beseeched Allah: Lord, come to my help, for they treat me as a liar. Allah decreed: A little while and they will be full of remorse. They were overtaken by punishment which had been firmly predicted and We reduced them to rubble. Ruined are the unjust people. (32—42)

Then We raised after them other generations. No people can go ahead of their appointed time, nor can they linger behind. Then We sent Our Messengers, one after another. Every time their Messenger came to a people, they treated him as a liar. So We despatched them to ruin one after another and We made them mere tales. Ruined are the people who do not believe. (43—45)

Then We sent Moses and his brother Aaron, with Our Signs and a clear authority, to Pharaoh and his chiefs; but they behaved arrogantly and took up a haughty attitude. They said: Shall we believe in two human beings like ourselves, whose people are our servants? So they called them liars and became a ruined people. We gave Moses the Book that his people might be guided; and We made the son of Mary and his mother a Sign, and gave them shelter on a pleasant plateau with springs of running water. (46—51)

O ye Messengers, eat of the things that are pure and act righteously. I am well aware of that which you do. This community of yours is one community and I am your Lord, so make Me your shield against

قَالَ رَبِّ انْصُرْنِي بِمَا كَذَّبُونِ ۞

قَالَ عَمَّا قَلِيلٍ لَّيُصْبِحُنَّ نٰدِمِينَ ۞

فَأَخَذَتْهُمُ الصَّيْحَةُ بِالْحَقِّ فَجَعَلْنٰهُمْ غُثَآءً فَبُعْدًا لِّلْقَوْمِ الظّٰلِمِينَ ۞

ثُمَّ أَنْشَأْنَا مِنْ بَعْدِهِمْ قُرُونًا اٰخَرِينَ ۞

مَا تَسْبِقُ مِنْ أُمَّةٍ أَجَلَهَا وَمَا يَسْتَأْخِرُونَ ۞

ثُمَّ أَرْسَلْنَا رُسُلَنَا تَتْرَا ۗ كُلَّمَا جَآءَ أُمَّةً رَّسُولُهَا كَذَّبُوهُ فَأَتْبَعْنَا بَعْضَهُمْ بَعْضًا وَّجَعَلْنٰهُمْ أَحَادِيثَ فَبُعْدًا لِّقَوْمٍ لَّا يُؤْمِنُونَ ۞

ثُمَّ أَرْسَلْنَا مُوسٰى وَأَخَاهُ هٰرُونَ ۙ بِاٰيٰتِنَا وَسُلْطٰنٍ مُّبِينٍ ۞

إِلٰى فِرْعَوْنَ وَمَلَائِهِ فَاسْتَكْبَرُوا وَكَانُوا قَوْمًا عَالِينَ ۞

فَقَالُوا أَنُؤْمِنُ لِبَشَرَيْنِ مِثْلِنَا وَقَوْمُهُمَا لَنَا عٰبِدُونَ ۞

فَكَذَّبُوهُمَا فَكَانُوا مِنَ الْمُهْلَكِينَ ۞

وَلَقَدْ اٰتَيْنَا مُوسَى الْكِتٰبَ لَعَلَّهُمْ يَهْتَدُونَ ۞

وَجَعَلْنَا ابْنَ مَرْيَمَ وَأُمَّهُ اٰيَةً وَّاٰوَيْنٰهُمَا إِلٰى رَبْوَةٍ ذَاتِ قَرَارٍ وَّمَعِينٍ ۞

يٰأَيُّهَا الرُّسُلُ كُلُوا مِنَ الطَّيِّبٰتِ وَاعْمَلُوا صَالِحًا ۗ إِنِّي بِمَا تَعْمَلُونَ عَلِيمٌ ۞

وَإِنَّ هٰذِهِ أُمَّتُكُمْ أُمَّةً وَّاحِدَةً وَّأَنَا رَبُّكُمْ

all harm. But their people have cut up the guidance into bits among themselves, each party rejoicing in what they have. So leave them in their confusion for a while.

Do they imagine that Our helping them with wealth and children is to make them advance rapidly in good? Nay, they do not realise the true values. Those who tremble with fear of their Lord, and believe in His Signs, and ascribe not partners to Him, and give to others what has been bestowed upon them, and their hearts are full of fear because one day they must return to their Lord; it is these who advance rapidly in doing good, outstripping each other in that respect.

We do not charge any one beyond his capacity, and with Us is a Book which speaks the truth and they will not be wronged. But their hearts are heedless of this Book, and in addition they indulge in questionable practices. So that when We afflict with punishment those of them who are well off, they immediately cry for help.

Call not for help this day, surely you shall not be helped by Us. My Signs were recited unto you, but you used to turn away from them arrogantly. making fun, talking nonsense. (52—68)

فَٱتَّقُونِ ۞

فَتَقَطَّعُوٓا أَمْرَهُم بَيْنَهُمْ زُبُرًا ۖ كُلُّ حِزْبٍ بِمَا لَدَيْهِمْ فَرِحُونَ ۞

فَذَرْهُمْ فِى غَمْرَتِهِمْ حَتَّىٰ حِينٍ ۞

أَيَحْسَبُونَ أَنَّمَا نُمِدُّهُم بِهِۦ مِن مَّالٍ وَبَنِينَ ۞

نُسَارِعُ لَهُمْ فِى ٱلْخَيْرَٰتِ ۚ بَل لَّا يَشْعُرُونَ ۞

إِنَّ ٱلَّذِينَ هُم مِّنْ خَشْيَةِ رَبِّهِم مُّشْفِقُونَ ۞

وَٱلَّذِينَ هُم بِـَٔايَٰتِ رَبِّهِمْ يُؤْمِنُونَ ۞

وَٱلَّذِينَ هُم بِرَبِّهِمْ لَا يُشْرِكُونَ ۞

وَٱلَّذِينَ يُؤْتُونَ مَآ ءَاتَوا وَّقُلُوبُهُمْ وَجِلَةٌ أَنَّهُمْ إِلَىٰ رَبِّهِمْ رَٰجِعُونَ ۞

أُو۟لَٰٓئِكَ يُسَٰرِعُونَ فِى ٱلْخَيْرَٰتِ وَهُمْ لَهَا سَٰبِقُونَ ۞

وَلَا نُكَلِّفُ نَفْسًا إِلَّا وُسْعَهَا ۖ وَلَدَيْنَا كِتَٰبٌ يَنطِقُ بِٱلْحَقِّ ۚ وَهُمْ لَا يُظْلَمُونَ ۞

بَلْ قُلُوبُهُمْ فِى غَمْرَةٍ مِّنْ هَٰذَا وَلَهُمْ أَعْمَٰلٌ مِّن دُونِ ذَٰلِكَ هُمْ لَهَا عَٰمِلُونَ ۞

حَتَّىٰٓ إِذَآ أَخَذْنَا مُتْرَفِيهِم بِٱلْعَذَابِ إِذَا هُمْ يَجْـَٔرُونَ ۞

لَا تَجْـَٔرُوا ٱلْيَوْمَ ۖ إِنَّكُم مِّنَّا لَا تُنصَرُونَ ۞

قَدْ كَانَتْ ءَايَٰتِى تُتْلَىٰ عَلَيْكُمْ فَكُنتُمْ عَلَىٰٓ أَعْقَٰبِكُمْ تَنكِصُونَ ۞

مُسْتَكْبِرِينَ بِهِۦ سَٰمِرًا تَهْجُرُونَ ۞

Have they, then, not pondered over the Divine Word, or have they received a promise of immunity which was not given to their fathers of old? Or, do they not recognise their Messenger that they deny him? Or, do they say he is possessed? Nay, he has brought them the truth and most of them dislike the truth. If the truth had followed their desires, the heavens and the earth and whosoever dwells therein would have been corrupted. Nay, We have provided them with a source of honour, and it is from their source of honour that they turn away. Or, is it that thou dost demand an imposition from them? That is not so, because that which thy Lord has bestowed on thee is best; and He is the Best of providers.

أَفَلَمْ يَدَّبَّرُوا الْقَوْلَ أَمْ جَاءَهُمْ مَّا لَمْ يَأْتِ
آبَاءَهُمُ الْأَوَّلِينَ ۞

أَمْ لَمْ يَعْرِفُوا رَسُولَهُمْ فَهُمْ لَهُ مُنْكِرُونَ ۞

أَمْ يَقُولُونَ بِهِ جِنَّةٌ ۚ بَلْ جَاءَهُمْ بِالْحَقِّ وَأَكْثَرُهُمْ
لِلْحَقِّ كَارِهُونَ ۞

وَلَوِ اتَّبَعَ الْحَقُّ أَهْوَاءَهُمْ لَفَسَدَتِ السَّمٰوٰتُ
وَالْأَرْضُ وَمَنْ فِيهِنَّ ۚ بَلْ أَتَيْنٰهُمْ بِذِكْرِهِمْ فَهُمْ
عَنْ ذِكْرِهِمْ مُعْرِضُونَ ۞

أَمْ تَسْأَلُهُمْ خَرْجًا فَخَرَاجُ رَبِّكَ خَيْرٌ ۖ وَهُوَ خَيْرُ
الرَّازِقِينَ ۞

Thou dost but call them to the straight path, and those who do not believe in the Hereafter are indeed deviating from that path. If We were to have mercy on them and relieve them of their affliction, they would advance in their transgression blindly. We have inflicted punishment on them, but even so have they not humbled themselves before their Lord, nor entreated Him. But when We afflict them with severe chastisement they will be in despair. (69—78)

وَإِنَّكَ لَتَدْعُوهُمْ إِلٰى صِرَاطٍ مُّسْتَقِيمٍ ۞

وَإِنَّ الَّذِينَ لَا يُؤْمِنُونَ بِالْآخِرَةِ عَنِ الصِّرَاطِ
لَنَاكِبُونَ ۞

وَلَوْ رَحِمْنٰهُمْ وَكَشَفْنَا مَا بِهِمْ مِّنْ ضُرٍّ لَّجُّوا
فِي طُغْيَانِهِمْ يَعْمَهُونَ ۞

وَلَقَدْ أَخَذْنٰهُمْ بِالْعَذَابِ فَمَا اسْتَكَانُوا لِرَبِّهِمْ
وَمَا يَتَضَرَّعُونَ ۞

حَتّٰى إِذَا فَتَحْنَا عَلَيْهِمْ بَابًا ذَا عَذَابٍ شَدِيدٍ
إِذَا هُمْ فِيهِ مُبْلِسُونَ ۞

He it is Who has made for you ears, and eyes, and hearts; but little thanks do you give. He it is Who has multiplied you in the earth, and unto Him shall you be gathered.

وَهُوَ الَّذِي أَنْشَأَ لَكُمُ السَّمْعَ وَالْأَبْصَارَ وَالْأَفْئِدَةَ
قَلِيلًا مَا تَشْكُرُونَ ۞

وَهُوَ الَّذِي ذَرَأَكُمْ فِي الْأَرْضِ وَإِلَيْهِ تُحْشَرُونَ ۞

He it is Who gives life and causes death, and He controls the alternation of night and day. Will you not then understand? In truth they say the same that the former people said. They said: Is it that when we are dead and have become dust and bones, we shall be raised up again? This is what we and our fathers have been promised before. This is nothing but old wives' tales. Ask them: To whom do the earth and all therein belong, if you happen to know? They will say: To Allah. Say to them: Will you not then be admonished? Ask them: Who is the Lord of the seven heavens, and the Lord of the Great Throne? They will say: They belong to Allah. Say to them: Will you not then take Him as your Protector? Ask them: In Whose hand is the dominion over all things and Who grants asylum, but against Whom no asylum is available, if indeed you know? They will say: All this pertains to Allah alone. Say to them: How are you then deluded? Yea, We have brought them the truth, and they reject it. Allah has not taken unto Himself any son, nor is there any other god along with Him; in that case each god would have walked away with that which he had created, and some of them would surely have dominated over others. Holy is Allah and above all that they ascribe to Him. He knows the unseen and the seen, and is, therefore, exalted above all that which they associate with Him. (79—93)

Pray: Lord, if Thou wilt show me that of which they have been warned, then place me not, Lord, with the wrongdoing people.

وَهُوَ الَّذِى يُحْىِ وَيُمِيتُ وَلَهُ اخْتِلَافُ الَّيْلِ وَ النَّهَارِ اَفَلَا تَعْقِلُوْنَ ۝

بَلْ قَالُوْا مِثْلَ مَا قَالَ الْاَوَّلُوْنَ ۝

قَالُوْٓا ءَاِذَا مِتْنَا وَكُنَّا تُرَابًا وَّعِظَامًا ءَاِنَّا لَمَبْعُوْثُوْنَ ۝

لَقَدْ وُعِدْنَا نَحْنُ وَاٰبَآؤُنَا هٰذَا مِنْ قَبْلُ اِنْ هٰذَا اِلَّاۤ اَسَاطِيْرُ الْاَوَّلِيْنَ ۝

قُلْ لِّمَنِ الْاَرْضُ وَمَنْ فِيْهَاۤ اِنْ كُنْتُمْ تَعْلَمُوْنَ ۝

سَيَقُوْلُوْنَ لِلّٰهِ قُلْ اَفَلَا تَذَكَّرُوْنَ ۝

قُلْ مَنْ رَّبُّ السَّمٰوٰتِ السَّبْعِ وَرَبُّ الْعَرْشِ الْعَظِيْمِ ۝

سَيَقُوْلُوْنَ لِلّٰهِ قُلْ اَفَلَا تَتَّقُوْنَ ۝

قُلْ مَنْ بِيَدِهٖ مَلَكُوْتُ كُلِّ شَىْءٍ وَّهُوَ يُجِيْرُ وَلَا يُجَارُ عَلَيْهِ اِنْ كُنْتُمْ تَعْلَمُوْنَ ۝

سَيَقُوْلُوْنَ لِلّٰهِ قُلْ فَاَنّٰى تُسْحَرُوْنَ ۝

بَلْ اَتَيْنٰهُمْ بِالْحَقِّ وَاِنَّهُمْ لَكٰذِبُوْنَ ۝

مَا اتَّخَذَ اللّٰهُ مِنْ وَّلَدٍ وَّمَا كَانَ مَعَهٗ مِنْ اِلٰهٍ اِذًا لَّذَهَبَ كُلُّ اِلٰهٍ بِمَا خَلَقَ وَلَعَلَا بَعْضُهُمْ عَلٰى بَعْضٍ سُبْحٰنَ اللّٰهِ عَمَّا يَصِفُوْنَ ۝

عٰلِمِ الْغَيْبِ وَالشَّهَادَةِ فَتَعٰلٰى عَمَّا يُشْرِكُوْنَ ۝

قُلْ رَّبِّ اِمَّا تُرِيَنِّىْ مَا يُوْعَدُوْنَ ۝

رَبِّ فَلَا تَجْعَلْنِىْ فِى الْقَوْمِ الظّٰلِمِيْنَ ۝

We certainly have power to show thee that of which they have been warned. Repel evil with that which is best. We know well that which they allege. Pray: Lord, I seek refuge with Thee from the incitements of the rebellious ones, and I seek refuge with Thee, Lord, lest they should approach me. (94—99)

وَاِنَّا عَلٰۤى اَنْ نُّرِيَكَ مَا نَعِدُهُمْ لَقٰدِرُوۡنَ ۞

اِدۡفَعۡ بِالَّتِىۡ هِىَ اَحۡسَنُ السَّيِّئَةَ ۚ نَحۡنُ اَعۡلَمُ بِمَا يَصِفُوۡنَ ۞

وَقُلْ رَّبِّ اَعُوۡذُ بِكَ مِنۡ هَمَزٰتِ الشَّيٰطِيۡنِ ۞

وَاَعُوۡذُ بِكَ رَبِّ اَنۡ يَّحۡضُرُوۡنِ ۞

حَتّٰۤى اِذَا جَآءَ اَحَدَهُمُ الْمَوۡتُ قَالَ رَبِّ ارۡجِعُوۡنِ ۞

لَعَلِّىۡۤ اَعۡمَلُ صَالِحًا فِيۡمَا تَرَكۡتُ كَلَّا ؕ اِنَّهَا كَلِمَةٌ هُوَ قَآئِلُهَا ؕ وَمِنۡ وَّرَآئِهِمۡ بَرۡزَخٌ اِلٰى يَوۡمِ يُبۡعَثُوۡنَ ۞

When death approaches one of them, he will supplicate: Lord, send me back, that I may act righteously in the life that I have departed from. That cannot be; it is only an utterance of his. Behind them is a barrier right up to the day when they shall be raised up again. When the trumpet is blown there will be no ties of relationship between them on that day, nor will they ask after one another. Then those whose scales are heavy with good works will prosper; and those whose scales are light will have ruined their souls; in hell will they abide. The Fire will stain their faces and they will be twisted with torment. They will be asked: Were not My Signs recited unto you, and did you not reject them? They will answer: Lord, our misfortune overpowered us, and we were an erring people. Lord, take us out of this, then if we revert to misconduct, we shall indeed be wrong-doers. He will say: Away with you, continue therein and speak not unto Me.

فَاِذَا نُفِخَ فِى الصُّوۡرِ فَلَاۤ اَنۡسَابَ بَيۡنَهُمۡ يَوۡمَئِذٍ وَّلَا يَتَسَآءَلُوۡنَ ۞

فَمَنۡ ثَقُلَتۡ مَوَازِيۡنُهٗ فَاُولٰٓئِكَ هُمُ الْمُفۡلِحُوۡنَ ۞

وَمَنۡ خَفَّتۡ مَوَازِيۡنُهٗ فَاُولٰٓئِكَ الَّذِيۡنَ خَسِرُوۡۤا اَنۡفُسَهُمۡ فِىۡ جَهَنَّمَ خٰلِدُوۡنَ ۞

تَلۡفَحُ وُجُوۡهَهُمُ النَّارُ وَهُمۡ فِيۡهَا كٰلِحُوۡنَ ۞

اَلَمۡ تَكُنۡ اٰيٰتِىۡ تُتۡلٰى عَلَيۡكُمۡ فَكُنۡتُمۡ بِهَا تُكَذِّبُوۡنَ ۞

قَالُوۡا رَبَّنَا غَلَبَتۡ عَلَيۡنَا شِقۡوَتُنَا وَكُنَّا قَوۡمًا ضَآلِّيۡنَ ۞

رَبَّنَاۤ اَخۡرِجۡنَا مِنۡهَا فَاِنۡ عُدۡنَا فَاِنَّا ظٰلِمُوۡنَ ۞

قَالَ اخۡسَـُٔوۡا فِيۡهَا وَلَا تُكَلِّمُوۡنِ ۞

There was a party of My servants who affirmed: Lord, we believe; so forgive us

اِنَّهٗ كَانَ فَرِيۡقٌ مِّنۡ عِبَادِىۡ يَقُوۡلُوۡنَ رَبَّنَاۤ اٰمَنَّا

and have mercy on us; for Thou art the
Best of those who show mercy. But you
made of them a laughing stock, and continued making fun of them, whereby you
forgot My remembrance. I have rewarded them this day for their steadfastness, and it is they who have triumphed. Allah will then ask: Now tell me:
How many years did you tarry in the
earth? They will say: We tarried only
for a day or a part of a day, but enquire
from those who keep count. He will say:
You tarried only a short while, if you did
but understand. Did you imagine that We
had created you without purpose, and
that you would not be brought back
to Us? Then exalted be Allah, the True King.
There is no god but He, the Lord of the
Glorious Throne. He who calls on another
god than Allah, for which he has no authority,
shall render an account of it to his Lord.

Certainly the disbelievers never prosper.
Pray: Lord, forgive and have mercy, for
Thou art the Best of those who show
mercy. (100—119)

فَاغْفِرْ لَنَا وَارْحَمْنَا وَأَنْتَ خَيْرُ الرَّاحِمِينَ ۞

فَاتَّخَذْتُمُوهُمْ سِخْرِيًّا حَتَّى أَنْسَوْكُمْ ذِكْرِي وَكُنْتُمْ
مِنْهُمْ تَضْحَكُونَ ۞

إِنِّي جَزَيْتُهُمُ الْيَوْمَ بِمَا صَبَرُوا أَنَّهُمْ هُمُ الْفَائِزُونَ ۞

قَالَ كَمْ لَبِثْتُمْ فِي الْأَرْضِ عَدَدَ سِنِينَ ۞

قَالُوا لَبِثْنَا يَوْمًا أَوْ بَعْضَ يَوْمٍ فَسْئَلِ الْعَادِّينَ ۞

قَالَ إِنْ لَبِثْتُمْ إِلَّا قَلِيلًا لَوْ أَنَّكُمْ كُنْتُمْ تَعْلَمُونَ ۞

أَفَحَسِبْتُمْ أَنَّمَا خَلَقْنَاكُمْ عَبَثًا وَأَنَّكُمْ إِلَيْنَا لَا
تُرْجَعُونَ ۞

فَتَعَالَى اللَّهُ الْمَلِكُ الْحَقُّ لَا إِلَهَ إِلَّا هُوَ رَبُّ الْعَرْشِ
الْكَرِيمِ ۞

وَمَنْ يَدْعُ مَعَ اللَّهِ إِلَهًا آخَرَ لَا بُرْهَانَ لَهُ بِهِ
فَإِنَّمَا حِسَابُهُ عِنْدَ رَبِّهِ إِنَّهُ لَا يُفْلِحُ الْكَافِرُونَ ۞

وَقُلْ رَبِّ اغْفِرْ وَارْحَمْ وَأَنْتَ خَيْرُ الرَّاحِمِينَ ۞

Chapter 24

بِسْمِ اللهِ الرَّحْمٰنِ الرَّحِيْمِ ۞

سُوْرَةُ التَّوْرِ مَدَنِيَّةٌ

AL-NŪR

(Revealed after Hijra)

In the name of Allah, Most Gracious, Ever Merciful. (1)

بِسْمِ اللهِ الرَّحْمٰنِ الرَّحِيْمِ ۞

سُوْرَةٌ اَنْزَلْنٰهَا وَفَرَضْنٰهَا وَاَنْزَلْنَا فِيْهَآ اٰيٰتٍ بَيِّنٰتٍ لَّعَلَّكُمْ تَذَكَّرُوْنَ ۞

This is a Sura which We have revealed and which We have made obligatory; and We have revealed therein clear commandments that you may take heed. Flog the adulteress and the adulterer, each one of them, with a hundred stripes, and let not pity for them restrain you from executing the judgment of Allah, if you believe in Allah and the Last Day. Let a party of the believers witness their punishment. An adulterer does not consort except with an adulteress or an idolatrous woman, and an adulteress does not consort except with an adulterer or with an idolatrous man. Such conduct is forbidden to the believers. (2—4)

اَلزَّانِيَةُ وَالزَّانِيْ فَاجْلِدُوْا كُلَّ وَاحِدٍ مِّنْهُمَا مِائَةَ جَلْدَةٍ ۠ وَّلَا تَأْخُذْكُمْ بِهِمَا رَأْفَةٌ فِيْ دِيْنِ اللهِ اِنْ كُنْتُمْ تُؤْمِنُوْنَ بِاللهِ وَالْيَوْمِ الْاٰخِرِ ۚ وَلْيَشْهَدْ عَذَابَهُمَا طَآئِفَةٌ مِّنَ الْمُؤْمِنِيْنَ ۞

اَلزَّانِيْ لَا يَنْكِحُ اِلَّا زَانِيَةً اَوْ مُشْرِكَةً ۫ وَّالزَّانِيَةُ لَا يَنْكِحُهَآ اِلَّا زَانٍ اَوْ مُشْرِكٌ ۚ وَحُرِّمَ ذٰلِكَ عَلَى الْمُؤْمِنِيْنَ ۞

The penalty of those who calumniate chaste women and then bring not four witnesses, is flogging with eighty stripes. Do not admit their evidence ever after, for it is they that are the transgressors; except in the case of those who repent thereafter and make amends, for surely Allah is Most Forgiving, Ever Merciful. (5—6)

وَالَّذِيْنَ يَرْمُوْنَ الْمُحْصَنٰتِ ثُمَّ لَمْ يَأْتُوْا بِاَرْبَعَةِ شُهَدَآءَ فَاجْلِدُوْهُمْ ثَمٰنِيْنَ جَلْدَةً وَّلَا تَقْبَلُوْا لَهُمْ شَهَادَةً اَبَدًا ۚ وَاُولٰٓئِكَ هُمُ الْفٰسِقُوْنَ ۞

اِلَّا الَّذِيْنَ تَابُوْا مِنْ بَعْدِ ذٰلِكَ وَاَصْلَحُوْا ۚ فَاِنَّ اللهَ غَفُوْرٌ رَّحِيْمٌ ۞

In the case of those who charge their wives with misconduct, and have not witnesses except their own selves, the evidence of such a one will suffice, if he bears witness four times in the name of Allah that he is telling the truth, and a fifth time that Allah's curse be upon him if he lies.

وَالَّذِيْنَ يَرْمُوْنَ اَزْوَاجَهُمْ وَلَمْ يَكُنْ لَّهُمْ شُهَدَآءُ اِلَّآ اَنْفُسُهُمْ فَشَهَادَةُ اَحَدِهِمْ اَرْبَعُ شَهٰدٰتٍ ۢ بِاللهِ ۙ اِنَّهُ لَمِنَ الصّٰدِقِيْنَ ۞

وَالْخَامِسَةُ اَنَّ لَعْنَتَ اللهِ عَلَيْهِ اِنْ كَانَ مِنَ

The punishment shall be averted from her, if she bears witness four times in the name of Allah that he has lied, and a fifth time that the wrath of Allah be upon her if he has spoken the truth. Were it not for Allah's grace and His mercy upon you, and that Allah is Compassionate and Wise, you would have come to grief. (7—11)

الْكٰذِبِيْنَ ۞

وَ يَدْرَؤُا عَنْهَا الْعَذَابَ اَنْ تَشْهَدَ اَرْبَعَ شَهٰدٰتٍۭ بِاللّٰهِ ۙ اِنَّهٗ لَمِنَ الْكٰذِبِيْنَ ۞

وَالْخَامِسَةَ اَنَّ غَضَبَ اللّٰهِ عَلَيْهَاۤ اِنْ كَانَ مِنَ الصّٰدِقِيْنَ ۞

وَ لَوْ لَا فَضْلُ اللّٰهِ عَلَيْكُمْ وَ رَحْمَتُهٗ وَ اَنَّ اللّٰهَ تَوَّابٌ حَكِيْمٌ ۞

Those who invented the great calumny are a party from among you. Do not consider their conduct as productive of evil for you; nay, it has been productive of good for you. Every one of them shall account for what he has earned of the sin; and he who took the principal part therein shall have a grievous punishment.

اِنَّ الَّذِيْنَ جَآءُوْ بِالْاِفْكِ عُصْبَةٌ مِّنْكُمْ لَا تَحْسَبُوْهُ شَرًّا لَّكُمْ بَلْ هُوَ خَيْرٌ لَّكُمْ لِكُلِّ امْرِئٍ مِّنْهُمْ مَّا اكْتَسَبَ مِنَ الْاِثْمِ وَ الَّذِيْ تَوَلّٰى كِبْرَهٗ مِنْهُمْ لَهٗ عَذَابٌ عَظِيْمٌ ۞

When you heard of it, why did not the believing men and believing women think well of their own people, and say: This is a manifest lie. Why did not they who made the charge bring four witnesses in support of it? Not having brought the witnesses, they are indeed liars in the sight of Allah. Were it not for the grace of Allah and His mercy upon you, in this world and the Hereafter, a great chastisement would have befallen you for that into which you plunged; for you began to learn it from one another and to speak about it, and you uttered with your mouths that of which you had no knowledge. You thought it to be a light matter, while in the sight of Allah it was a grievous thing. When you heard of it, wherefore did you not say: It is not proper for us to talk about it. Holy art Thou, O Lord, this is a grievous calumny?

لَوْ لَاۤ اِذْ سَمِعْتُمُوْهُ ظَنَّ الْمُؤْمِنُوْنَ وَ الْمُؤْمِنٰتُ بِاَنْفُسِهِمْ خَيْرًا ۙ وَّ قَالُوْا هٰذَاۤ اِفْكٌ مُّبِيْنٌ ۞

لَوْ لَا جَآءُوْ عَلَيْهِ بِاَرْبَعَةِ شُهَدَآءَ ۚ فَاِذْ لَمْ يَاْتُوْا بِالشُّهَدَآءِ فَاُولٰٓئِكَ عِنْدَ اللّٰهِ هُمُ الْكٰذِبُوْنَ ۞

وَ لَوْ لَا فَضْلُ اللّٰهِ عَلَيْكُمْ وَ رَحْمَتُهٗ فِي الدُّنْيَا وَ الْاٰخِرَةِ لَمَسَّكُمْ فِيْ مَاۤ اَفَضْتُمْ فِيْهِ عَذَابٌ عَظِيْمٌ ۞

اِذْ تَلَقَّوْنَهٗ بِاَلْسِنَتِكُمْ وَ تَقُوْلُوْنَ بِاَفْوَاهِكُمْ مَّا لَيْسَ لَكُمْ بِهٖ عِلْمٌ وَّ تَحْسَبُوْنَهٗ هَيِّنًا ۖ وَّ هُوَ عِنْدَ اللّٰهِ عَظِيْمٌ ۞

وَ لَوْ لَاۤ اِذْ سَمِعْتُمُوْهُ قُلْتُمْ مَّا يَكُوْنُ لَنَاۤ اَنْ نَّتَكَلَّمَ بِهٰذَا ۖ سُبْحٰنَكَ هٰذَا بُهْتَانٌ عَظِيْمٌ ۞

339

Allah admonishes you never to return to the like thereof, if you are believers. Allah explains the commandments to you. Allah is All-Knowing, Wise. Those who desire that indecencies should spread among the believers, will have a painful chastisement in this world and the Hereafter. Allah knows, and you know not. But for the grace of Allah and His Mercy upon you, and that Allah is Compassionate and Merciful, you would have come to grief. (12—21)

O ye who believe, follow not in the footsteps of Satan, and whoso follows in the footsteps of Satan should know that he but enjoins indecency and manifest evil. But for the grace of Allah and His Mercy upon you, not one of you would ever be purified; but Allah purifies whom He pleases. Allah is All-Hearing, All-Knowing. Let not those who are possessed of means and plenty among you resolve to withhold their bounty from the kindred and the needy and those who have migrated from their homes in the cause of Allah, because of some default on the part of the recipient. Let them forgive and forbear. Do you not desire that Allah should forgive you? Allah is Most Forgiving, Ever Merciful. Those who calumniate chaste, unwary, believing women are cursed in this world and the Hereafter; and for them is a grievous chastisement, on the day when their tongues and their hands and their feet will bear witness against them as to that which they used to do.

يَعِظُكُمُ اللّٰهُ اَنْ تَعُوْدُوْا لِمِثْلِهٖ اَبَدًا اِنْ كُنْتُمْ مُّؤْمِنِيْنَ ۝

وَ يُبَيِّنُ اللّٰهُ لَكُمُ الْاٰيٰتِ ۚ وَاللّٰهُ عَلِيْمٌ حَكِيْمٌ ۝

اِنَّ الَّذِيْنَ يُحِبُّوْنَ اَنْ تَشِيْعَ الْفَاحِشَةُ فِى الَّذِيْنَ اٰمَنُوْا لَهُمْ عَذَابٌ اَلِيْمٌ ۙ فِى الدُّنْيَا وَالْاٰخِرَةِ ۚ وَاللّٰهُ يَعْلَمُ وَاَنْتُمْ لَا تَعْلَمُوْنَ ۝

وَلَوْلَا فَضْلُ اللّٰهِ عَلَيْكُمْ وَرَحْمَتُهٗ وَاَنَّ اللّٰهَ رَءُوْفٌ رَّحِيْمٌ ۝

يٰٓاَيُّهَا الَّذِيْنَ اٰمَنُوْا لَا تَتَّبِعُوْا خُطُوٰتِ الشَّيْطٰنِ ۚ وَمَنْ يَّتَّبِعْ خُطُوٰتِ الشَّيْطٰنِ فَاِنَّهٗ يَأْمُرُ بِالْفَحْشَاءِ وَالْمُنْكَرِ ۚ وَلَوْلَا فَضْلُ اللّٰهِ عَلَيْكُمْ وَرَحْمَتُهٗ مَا زَكٰى مِنْكُمْ مِّنْ اَحَدٍ اَبَدًا ۙ وَّلٰكِنَّ اللّٰهَ يُزَكِّيْ مَنْ يَّشَاءُ ۚ وَاللّٰهُ سَمِيْعٌ عَلِيْمٌ ۝

وَلَا يَأْتَلِ اُولُوا الْفَضْلِ مِنْكُمْ وَالسَّعَةِ اَنْ يُّؤْتُوْٓا اُولِى الْقُرْبٰى وَالْمَسٰكِيْنَ وَالْمُهٰجِرِيْنَ فِى سَبِيْلِ اللّٰهِ ۖ وَلْيَعْفُوْا وَلْيَصْفَحُوْا ۗ اَلَا تُحِبُّوْنَ اَنْ يَّغْفِرَ اللّٰهُ لَكُمْ ۗ وَاللّٰهُ غَفُوْرٌ رَّحِيْمٌ ۝

اِنَّ الَّذِيْنَ يَرْمُوْنَ الْمُحْصَنٰتِ الْغٰفِلٰتِ الْمُؤْمِنٰتِ لُعِنُوْا فِى الدُّنْيَا وَالْاٰخِرَةِ ۖ وَلَهُمْ عَذَابٌ عَظِيْمٌ ۝

يَّوْمَ تَشْهَدُ عَلَيْهِمْ اَلْسِنَتُهُمْ وَاَيْدِيْهِمْ وَاَرْجُلُهُمْ بِمَا كَانُوْا يَعْمَلُوْنَ ۝

On that day Allah will pay them their just due and they will know that Allah is the Perfect and Manifest Truth. Evil things are a characteristic of evil people, and evil people are inclined towards evil things; and good things are a character-istic of good people and good people are inclined towards good things; these are innocent of what their calumniators allege. For them is forgiveness and an honour-able provision. (22—27)

O ye who believe, enter not houses other than your own until you have obtained leave and have saluted the in-mates thereof. That will be the better for you, that you may be heedful. If you find no one therein, then enter them not until leave is given you. If it is said to you: Go back just now: then go back; that is purer for you. Allah knows well that which you do. It is no sin on your part to enter uninhabited houses wherein are your goods. Allah knows that which you dis-close and that which you conceal. (28—30)

Direct the believing men to restrain their looks and to guard their senses. That is purer for them. Surely, Allah is well aware of that which they do. Direct the believing women to restrain their looks and to guard their senses and not to disclose any part of their beauty or their adornments, save that which is apparent thereof. They should draw their head-coverings across their bosoms; and should not disclose any part of their beauty or their adornments save to their husbands or to their fathers, or the fathers of their husbands or their sons or the sons of their husbands, or their brothers, or the sons of their brothers, or the sons of their sisters, or gentlewomen,

يَوۡمَئِذٍ يُّوَفِّيۡهِمُ اللّٰهُ دِيۡنَهُمُ الۡحَقَّ وَيَعۡلَمُوۡنَ اَنَّ اللّٰهَ هُوَ الۡحَقُّ الۡمُبِيۡنُ ۞

اَلۡخَبِيۡثٰتُ لِلۡخَبِيۡثِيۡنَ وَ الۡخَبِيۡثُوۡنَ لِلۡخَبِيۡثٰتِ ۚ وَ الطَّيِّبٰتُ لِلطَّيِّبِيۡنَ وَ الطَّيِّبُوۡنَ لِلطَّيِّبٰتِ ۚ اُولٰٓئِكَ مُبَرَّءُوۡنَ مِمَّا يَقُوۡلُوۡنَ ۚ لَهُمۡ مَّغۡفِرَةٌ وَّرِزۡقٌ كَرِيۡمٌ ۞

يٰۤاَيُّهَا الَّذِيۡنَ اٰمَنُوۡا لَا تَدۡخُلُوۡا بُيُوۡتًا غَيۡرَ بُيُوۡتِكُمۡ حَتّٰى تَسۡتَاۡنِسُوۡا وَ تُسَلِّمُوۡا عَلٰۤى اَهۡلِهَا ؕ ذٰلِكُمۡ خَيۡرٌ لَّكُمۡ لَعَلَّكُمۡ تَذَكَّرُوۡنَ ۞

فَاِنۡ لَّمۡ تَجِدُوۡا فِيۡهَاۤ اَحَدًا فَلَا تَدۡخُلُوۡهَا حَتّٰى يُؤۡذَنَ لَكُمۡ ۚ وَ اِنۡ قِيۡلَ لَكُمُ ارۡجِعُوۡا فَارۡجِعُوۡا هُوَ اَزۡكٰى لَكُمۡ ؕ وَ اللّٰهُ بِمَا تَعۡمَلُوۡنَ عَلِيۡمٌ ۞

لَيۡسَ عَلَيۡكُمۡ جُنَاحٌ اَنۡ تَدۡخُلُوۡا بُيُوۡتًا غَيۡرَ مَسۡكُوۡنَةٍ فِيۡهَا مَتَاعٌ لَّكُمۡ ؕ وَ اللّٰهُ يَعۡلَمُ مَا تُبۡدُوۡنَ وَ مَا تَكۡتُمُوۡنَ ۞

قُلۡ لِّلۡمُؤۡمِنِيۡنَ يَغُضُّوۡا مِنۡ اَبۡصَارِهِمۡ وَ يَحۡفَظُوۡا فُرُوۡجَهُمۡ ؕ ذٰلِكَ اَزۡكٰى لَهُمۡ ؕ اِنَّ اللّٰهَ خَبِيۡرٌ بِمَا يَصۡنَعُوۡنَ ۞

وَ قُلۡ لِّلۡمُؤۡمِنٰتِ يَغۡضُضۡنَ مِنۡ اَبۡصَارِهِنَّ وَ يَحۡفَظۡنَ فُرُوۡجَهُنَّ وَ لَا يُبۡدِيۡنَ زِيۡنَتَهُنَّ اِلَّا مَا ظَهَرَ مِنۡهَا وَ لۡيَضۡرِبۡنَ بِخُمُرِهِنَّ عَلٰى جُيُوۡبِهِنَّ ۪ وَ لَا يُبۡدِيۡنَ زِيۡنَتَهُنَّ اِلَّا لِبُعُوۡلَتِهِنَّ اَوۡ اٰبَآئِهِنَّ اَوۡ اٰبَآءِ بُعُوۡلَتِهِنَّ اَوۡ اَبۡنَآئِهِنَّ اَوۡ اَبۡنَآءِ بُعُوۡلَتِهِنَّ اَوۡ اِخۡوَانِهِنَّ اَوۡ بَنِىۡۤ اِخۡوَانِهِنَّ اَوۡ بَنِىۡۤ اَخَوٰتِهِنَّ اَوۡ نِسَآئِهِنَّ اَوۡ مَا

or their maidservants, or such attendants who have no desire for women, or such children who have no knowledge of the relationship between the sexes; nor should they strike their feet on the ground in such manner as to disclose their ornaments which they ought not to disclose. Turn ye to Allah all together, O believers, that you may prosper. (31—32)

Arrange the marriages of widows from among you, and of the righteous from among those under your control, male and female. If they be poor, Allah will grant them means out of His bounty. Allah is Vastly Bountiful, All-Knowing. Those who find no means of marriage should keep themselves chaste, until Allah grants them means out of His bounty. Write out a deed of manumission for such out of those under your control as desire it, if you see some good in them, and help them to secure their freedom with a portion of the wealth of Allah which He has bestowed upon you. Force not females under your control into unchastity by restraining them from marriage should they desire to safeguard their chastity through marriage, in order that you may add to your worldly gains through their labour. If anyone forces them into unchastity by restraining them from marriage, surely Allah will, thereafter, be towards them Most Forgiving, Merciful. We have sent down to you manifest Signs, and the example of those who have passed away before you, and an exhortation for the God-fearing. (33—35)

Allah is the Light of the heavens and of the earth. His light is as if there were a lustrous niche, wherein is a lamp contained in a crystal globe, the globe as bright as a glittering star. The lamp is lit with the oil of a blessed tree, an olive, neither of the east nor of the west. The oil would well-nigh glow forth even though no fire were to touch it. Light upon light! Allah guides to His light whomsoever He wills.

مَلَكَتْ اَيْمَانُهُنَّ اَوِ التَّابِعِيْنَ غَيْرِ اُولِي الْاِرْبَةِ مِنَ الرِّجَالِ اَوِ الطِّفْلِ الَّذِيْنَ لَمْ يَظْهَرُوْا عَلٰى عَوْرٰتِ النِّسَاءِ وَلَا يَضْرِبْنَ بِاَرْجُلِهِنَّ لِيُعْلَمَ مَا يُخْفِيْنَ مِنْ زِيْنَتِهِنَّ وَتُوْبُوْا اِلَى اللّٰهِ جَمِيْعًا اَيُّهَ الْمُؤْمِنُوْنَ لَعَلَّكُمْ تُفْلِحُوْنَ ۝

وَاَنْكِحُوا الْاَيَامٰى مِنْكُمْ وَالصّٰلِحِيْنَ مِنْ عِبَادِكُمْ وَاِمَآئِكُمْ اِنْ يَّكُوْنُوْا فُقَرَاءَ يُغْنِهِمُ اللّٰهُ مِنْ فَضْلِهِ وَاللّٰهُ وَاسِعٌ عَلِيْمٌ ۝

وَلْيَسْتَعْفِفِ الَّذِيْنَ لَا يَجِدُوْنَ نِكَاحًا حَتّٰى يُغْنِيَهُمُ اللّٰهُ مِنْ فَضْلِهِ وَالَّذِيْنَ يَبْتَغُوْنَ الْكِتٰبَ مِمَّا مَلَكَتْ اَيْمَانُكُمْ فَكَاتِبُوْهُمْ اِنْ عَلِمْتُمْ فِيْهِمْ خَيْرًا وَاٰتُوْهُمْ مِّنْ مَّالِ اللّٰهِ الَّذِيْٓ اٰتٰكُمْ وَلَا تُكْرِهُوْا فَتَيٰتِكُمْ عَلَى الْبِغَاءِ اِنْ اَرَدْنَ تَحَصُّنًا لِّتَبْتَغُوْا عَرَضَ الْحَيٰوةِ الدُّنْيَا وَمَنْ يُّكْرِهْهُّنَّ فَاِنَّ اللّٰهَ مِنْ بَعْدِ اِكْرَاهِهِنَّ غَفُوْرٌ رَّحِيْمٌ ۝

وَلَقَدْ اَنْزَلْنَآ اِلَيْكُمْ اٰيٰتٍ مُّبَيِّنٰتٍ وَّمَثَلًا مِّنَ الَّذِيْنَ خَلَوْا مِنْ قَبْلِكُمْ وَمَوْعِظَةً لِّلْمُتَّقِيْنَ ۝

اَللّٰهُ نُوْرُ السَّمٰوٰتِ وَالْاَرْضِ مَثَلُ نُوْرِهِ كَمِشْكٰوةٍ فِيْهَا مِصْبَاحٌ اَلْمِصْبَاحُ فِيْ زُجَاجَةٍ اَلزُّجَاجَةُ كَاَنَّهَا كَوْكَبٌ دُرِّيٌّ يُّوْقَدُ مِنْ شَجَرَةٍ مُّبٰرَكَةٍ زَيْتُوْنَةٍ لَّا شَرْقِيَّةٍ وَّلَا غَرْبِيَّةٍ يَّكَادُ زَيْتُهَا يُضِيْءُ وَلَوْ لَمْ تَمْسَسْهُ نَارٌ نُوْرٌ عَلٰى نُوْرٍ يَهْدِى اللّٰهُ لِنُوْرِهِ مَنْ يَّشَاءُ

Allah sets forth all that is needful for mankind. Allah knows all things well. This light now illumines houses which Allah has ordained that they be exalted and in which His name is commemorated. Therein is He glorified morn and eve by men whom neither trade nor traffic beguiles from the remembrance of Allah and the observance of Prayer and the payment of Zakat. They fear a day on which hearts and eyes will be agitated, so that Allah may bestow upon them the best reward for their deeds, and give them more out of His bounty. Allah provides for whomsoever He wills without measure. (36—39)

The works of those who disbelieve are like a mirage in a wide plain. A thirsty one imagines it to be water until, when he comes up to it, he finds it to be nothing, and he finds Allah near him, Who then pays him his account in full. Allah is Swift at reckoning. Or, their works are like thick darknesses spread over a vast and deep sea, the surface of which is agitated by waves rolling upon waves, above which are clouds; layers of darkness one upon another so thick that when a person holds out his hand he can hardly see it. For him whom Allah grants not light, there is no light at all. (40—41)

Seest thou not that all who are in the heavens and the earth celebrate the praises of Allah, and also the birds in rows upon rows. Each one knows his own mode of prayer and praise, and Allah knows well that which they do. To Allah belongs the kingdom of the heavens and the earth, and to Allah shall be the return. Seest thou not that Allah wafts the clouds gently, then joins them together, then piles them up so that thou seest the rain issue forth from the midst thereof?

وَيَضْرِبُ اللهُ الْأَمْثَالَ لِلنَّاسِ ۖ وَاللهُ بِكُلِّ شَىْءٍ عَلِيْمٌ ۞

فِىْ بُيُوْتٍ أَذِنَ اللهُ أَنْ تُرْفَعَ وَيُذْكَرَ فِيْهَا اسْمُهٗ ۙ يُسَبِّحُ لَهٗ فِيْهَا بِالْغُدُوِّ وَالْأَصَالِ ۞

رِجَالٌ ۙ لَّا تُلْهِيْهِمْ تِجَارَةٌ وَّلَا بَيْعٌ عَنْ ذِكْرِ اللهِ وَإِقَامِ الصَّلٰوةِ وَإِيْتَآءِ الزَّكٰوةِ ۙ يَخَافُوْنَ يَوْمًا تَتَقَلَّبُ فِيْهِ الْقُلُوْبُ وَالْأَبْصَارُ ۞

لِيَجْزِيَهُمُ اللهُ أَحْسَنَ مَا عَمِلُوْا وَيَزِيْدَهُمْ مِّنْ فَضْلِهٖ ۖ وَاللهُ يَرْزُقُ مَنْ يَّشَآءُ بِغَيْرِ حِسَابٍ ۞

وَالَّذِيْنَ كَفَرُوْا أَعْمَالُهُمْ كَسَرَابٍ بِقِيْعَةٍ يَّحْسَبُهُ الظَّمْآنُ مَآءً ۖ حَتّٰى إِذَا جَآءَهٗ لَمْ يَجِدْهُ شَيْئًا وَّوَجَدَ اللهَ عِنْدَهٗ فَوَفّٰهُ حِسَابَهٗ ۖ وَاللهُ سَرِيْعُ الْحِسَابِ ۞

أَوْ كَظُلُمٰتٍ فِىْ بَحْرٍ لُّجِّيٍّ يَّغْشٰهُ مَوْجٌ مِّنْ فَوْقِهٖ مَوْجٌ مِّنْ فَوْقِهٖ سَحَابٌ ۚ ظُلُمٰتٌ بَعْضُهَا فَوْقَ بَعْضٍ ۚ إِذَا أَخْرَجَ يَدَهٗ لَمْ يَكَدْ يَرٰىهَا ۗ وَمَنْ لَّمْ يَجْعَلِ اللهُ لَهٗ نُوْرًا فَمَا لَهٗ مِنْ نُّوْرٍ ۞

أَلَمْ تَرَ أَنَّ اللهَ يُسَبِّحُ لَهٗ مَنْ فِى السَّمٰوٰتِ وَالْأَرْضِ وَالطَّيْرُ صٰٓفّٰتٍ ۗ كُلٌّ قَدْ عَلِمَ صَلَاتَهٗ وَتَسْبِيْحَهٗ ۗ وَاللهُ عَلِيْمٌ بِمَا يَفْعَلُوْنَ ۞

وَلِلّٰهِ مُلْكُ السَّمٰوٰتِ وَالْأَرْضِ ۖ وَإِلَى اللهِ الْمَصِيْرُ ۞ أَلَمْ تَرَ أَنَّ اللهَ يُزْجِىْ سَحَابًا ثُمَّ يُؤَلِّفُ بَيْنَهٗ ثُمَّ يَجْعَلُهٗ رُكَامًا فَتَرَى الْوَدْقَ يَخْرُجُ مِنْ خِلٰلِهٖ ۖ وَ

He sends down from the clouds mountains of frozen matter and He causes it to fall on whom He pleases and turns it away from whom He pleases. The flash of His lightning may well-nigh take away the sight of some eyes. Allah alternates the night and the day. Therein surely is a lesson for those gifted with understanding. Allah has created every animal from water. Some of them move on their bellies, some of them on two feet and some on four. Allah creates what He pleases. Surely, Allah has power to do all that He wills. We have sent down manifest Signs. Allah guides whom He wills to the right path. (42—47)

They affirm: We believe in Allah and in the Messenger and we shall obey. Thereafter some of them turn away from their affirmation. These are not believers. When they are called to Allah and His Messenger that he may judge between them, a party of them turn away; but if they consider the right to be on their side they hasten to him in all submission. Are their minds diseased, or do they doubt, or do they fear that Allah and His Messenger will be unjust to them? The truth is that they themselves are wrongdoers. The response of the believers, when they are called to Allah and His Messenger that he may judge between them is; We hear and we obey. It is they who will prosper. Those who obey Allah and His Messenger, and fear Allah, and are mindful of their duty to Him, are the ones

يُنَزِّلُ مِنَ السَّمَآءِ مِنْ جِبَالٍ فِيْهَا مِنْۢ بَرَدٍ فَيُصِيْبُ بِهٖ مَنْ يَّشَآءُ وَ يَصْرِفُهٗ عَنْ مَّنْ يَّشَآءُ ۭ يَكَادُ سَنَا بَرْقِهٖ يَذْهَبُ بِالْاَبْصَارِ ۞

يُقَلِّبُ اللّٰهُ الَّيْلَ وَ النَّهَارَ ۭ اِنَّ فِيْ ذٰلِكَ لَعِبْرَةً لِّاُولِى الْاَبْصَارِ ۞

وَاللّٰهُ خَلَقَ كُلَّ دَآبَّةٍ مِّنْ مَّآءٍ ۚ فَمِنْهُمْ مَّنْ يَّمْشِيْ عَلٰى بَطْنِهٖ ۚ وَ مِنْهُمْ مَّنْ يَّمْشِيْ عَلٰى رِجْلَيْنِ ۚ وَمِنْهُمْ مَّنْ يَّمْشِيْ عَلٰۤى اَرْبَعٍ ۭ يَخْلُقُ اللّٰهُ مَا يَشَآءُ ۭ اِنَّ اللّٰهَ عَلٰى كُلِّ شَيْءٍ قَدِيْرٌ ۞

لَقَدْ اَنْزَلْنَآ اٰيٰتٍ مُّبَيِّنٰتٍ ۭ وَاللّٰهُ يَهْدِيْ مَنْ يَّشَآءُ اِلٰى صِرَاطٍ مُّسْتَقِيْمٍ ۞

وَ يَقُوْلُوْنَ اٰمَنَّا بِاللّٰهِ وَ بِالرَّسُوْلِ وَاَطَعْنَا ثُمَّ يَتَوَلّٰى فَرِيْقٌ مِّنْهُمْ مِّنْۢ بَعْدِ ذٰلِكَ ۭ وَمَآ اُولٰٓئِكَ بِالْمُؤْمِنِيْنَ ۞ وَاِذَا دُعُوْٓا اِلَى اللّٰهِ وَرَسُوْلِهٖ لِيَحْكُمَ بَيْنَهُمْ اِذَا فَرِيْقٌ مِّنْهُمْ مُّعْرِضُوْنَ ۞

وَاِنْ يَّكُنْ لَّهُمُ الْحَقُّ يَأْتُوْٓا اِلَيْهِ مُذْعِنِيْنَ ۭ اَفِيْ قُلُوْبِهِمْ مَّرَضٌ اَمِ ارْتَابُوْٓا اَمْ يَخَافُوْنَ اَنْ يَّحِيْفَ اللّٰهُ عَلَيْهِمْ وَرَسُوْلُهٗ ۭ بَلْ اُولٰٓئِكَ هُمُ الظّٰلِمُوْنَ ۞

اِنَّمَا كَانَ قَوْلَ الْمُؤْمِنِيْنَ اِذَا دُعُوْٓا اِلَى اللّٰهِ وَرَسُوْلِهٖ لِيَحْكُمَ بَيْنَهُمْ اَنْ يَّقُوْلُوْا سَمِعْنَا وَ اَطَعْنَا ۭ وَ اُولٰٓئِكَ هُمُ الْمُفْلِحُوْنَ ۞

وَمَنْ يُّطِعِ اللّٰهَ وَرَسُوْلَهٗ وَيَخْشَ اللّٰهَ وَيَتَّقْهِ فَاُولٰٓئِكَ

who will triumph. They swear firm oaths
by Allah that if thou command them
they will surely go forth. Say to them:
You are not required to affirm on oath;
all that is required of you is normal
obedience. Surely, Allah is well aware of
that which you do. Tell them: Obey
Allah and obey the Messenger. If you
turn away, then he is responsible for that
which he is charged with and you are
responsible for that which you are charged
with. If you obey him you will be rightly
guided. The Messenger is responsible only
for conveying the Message clearly. (48—
55)

Allah has promised those among you
who believe and act righteously that He
will surely make them Successors in the
earth, as He made Successors those who
were before them; and that He will surely
establish for them their religion which He
has chosen for them; and that after their
state of fear He will grant them peace
and security. They will worship Me and
will not associate anything with Me.
Those who disbelieve thereafter, they will
be the rebellious ones. Observe Prayer and
pay the Zakat and obey the Messenger
that you may be shown mercy. Imagine
not that the disbelievers can frustrate
Our design in the earth; their abode is
hell; and an evil resort it is. (56—58)

O ye who believe, let those who are
under your control and those of you who
have not yet attained puberty, ask leave
of you at three times before coming in;
before the morning Prayer, and when
you put aside your clothes at noon, and
after the night Prayer. These are three
periods of privacy for you. Outside of
these there is no restriction on you or on
them, for some of you have occasion to
attend upon others.

Thus does Allah expound His commandments to you. Allah is All-Knowing, Wise. When your children attain puberty they should ask leave in the same manner as their seniors. Thus does Allah expound His commandments to you. Allah is All-Knowing, Wise. There is no blame on elderly women who are past the age of marriage, if they lay aside their outer coverings, without displaying their adornment. But it would be better for them to guard themselves. Allah is All-Hearing, All-Knowing. (59—61)

طَوّٰفُوْنَ عَلَيْكُمْ بَعْضُكُمْ عَلٰى بَعْضٍ كَذٰلِكَ يُبَيِّنُ اللّٰهُ لَكُمُ الْاٰيٰتِ وَاللّٰهُ عَلِيْمٌ حَكِيْمٌ ۝ وَاِذَا بَلَغَ الْاَطْفَالُ مِنْكُمُ الْحُلُمَ فَلْيَسْتَأْذِنُوْا كَمَا اسْتَأْذَنَ الَّذِيْنَ مِنْ قَبْلِهِمْ كَذٰلِكَ يُبَيِّنُ اللّٰهُ لَكُمْ اٰيٰتِهٖ وَاللّٰهُ عَلِيْمٌ حَكِيْمٌ ۝ وَالْقَوَاعِدُ مِنَ النِّسَآءِ الّٰتِيْ لَا يَرْجُوْنَ نِكَاحًا فَلَيْسَ عَلَيْهِنَّ جُنَاحٌ اَنْ يَّضَعْنَ ثِيَابَهُنَّ غَيْرَ مُتَبَرِّجٰتٍ بِزِيْنَةٍ وَاَنْ يَّسْتَعْفِفْنَ خَيْرٌ لَّهُنَّ وَاللّٰهُ سَمِيْعٌ عَلِيْمٌ ۝

There is no harm for the blind, the lame, the sick or yourselves that you eat from your own houses, or from the houses of your fathers, or mothers, or brothers, or sisters, or paternal uncles, or paternal aunts, or maternal uncles, or maternal aunts, or from those that you are in charge of, or from the house of a friend. Nor is there any harm whether you eat together or separately. But when you enter houses, salute your people with the greeting of peace, a greeting from your Lord full of blessings and purity. Thus does Allah expound to you His commandments that you may understand. (62)

لَيْسَ عَلَى الْاَعْمٰى حَرَجٌ وَّلَا عَلَى الْاَعْرَجِ حَرَجٌ وَّلَا عَلَى الْمَرِيْضِ حَرَجٌ وَّلَا عَلٰٓى اَنْفُسِكُمْ اَنْ تَأْكُلُوْا مِنْ بُيُوْتِكُمْ اَوْ بُيُوْتِ اٰبَآئِكُمْ اَوْ بُيُوْتِ اُمَّهٰتِكُمْ اَوْ بُيُوْتِ اِخْوَانِكُمْ اَوْ بُيُوْتِ اَخَوٰتِكُمْ اَوْ بُيُوْتِ اَعْمَامِكُمْ اَوْ بُيُوْتِ عَمّٰتِكُمْ اَوْ بُيُوْتِ اَخْوَالِكُمْ اَوْ بُيُوْتِ خٰلٰتِكُمْ اَوْ مَا مَلَكْتُمْ مَّفَاتِحَهٗٓ اَوْ صَدِيْقِكُمْ لَيْسَ عَلَيْكُمْ جُنَاحٌ اَنْ تَأْكُلُوْا جَمِيْعًا اَوْ اَشْتَاتًا فَاِذَا دَخَلْتُمْ بُيُوْتًا فَسَلِّمُوْا عَلٰٓى اَنْفُسِكُمْ تَحِيَّةً مِّنْ عِنْدِ اللّٰهِ مُبٰرَكَةً طَيِّبَةً كَذٰلِكَ يُبَيِّنُ اللّٰهُ لَكُمُ الْاٰيٰتِ لَعَلَّكُمْ تَعْقِلُوْنَ ۝

Those alone are true believers who believe in Allah and His Messenger, and who when they are together with him considering some public affair, go not away without obtaining his leave. It is only those who ask leave of thee that believe truly in Allah and His Messenger.

اِنَّمَا الْمُؤْمِنُوْنَ الَّذِيْنَ اٰمَنُوْا بِاللّٰهِ وَرَسُوْلِهٖ وَاِذَا كَانُوْا مَعَهٗ عَلٰٓى اَمْرٍ جَامِعٍ لَّمْ يَذْهَبُوْا حَتّٰى يَسْتَأْذِنُوْهُ اِنَّ الَّذِيْنَ يَسْتَأْذِنُوْنَكَ اُولٰٓئِكَ الَّذِيْنَ يُؤْمِنُوْنَ

So when they ask leave of thee for some affair of theirs, give leave to those of them whom thou pleasest, and ask forgiveness for them of Allah. Surely, Allah is Most-Forgiving, Ever Merciful. Do not consider that your being called by the Messenger is the same as your being called by one another. Surely, Allah knows those of you who steal away covertly. Let those who oppose the command of the Messenger beware lest a trial afflict them or a grievous punishment overtake them.

Hearken: To Allah belongs whatever is in the heavens and in the earth. Allah knows well what condition you are in. On the day when they will be returned unto Him, He will inform them of that which they did. Allah knows everything full well. (63—65)

بِاللّٰهِ وَرَسُوْلِهٖ ۚ فَاِذَا اسْتَأْذَنُوْكَ لِبَعْضِ شَأْنِهِمْ فَأْذَنْ لِّمَنْ شِئْتَ مِنْهُمْ وَاسْتَغْفِرْ لَهُمُ اللّٰهَ ۚ اِنَّ اللّٰهَ غَفُوْرٌ رَّحِيْمٌ ۞

لَا تَجْعَلُوْا دُعَآءَ الرَّسُوْلِ بَيْنَكُمْ كَدُعَآءِ بَعْضِكُمْ بَعْضًا ۚ قَدْ يَعْلَمُ اللّٰهُ الَّذِيْنَ يَتَسَلَّلُوْنَ مِنْكُمْ لِوَاذًا ۚ فَلْيَحْذَرِ الَّذِيْنَ يُخَالِفُوْنَ عَنْ اَمْرِهٖۤ اَنْ تُصِيْبَهُمْ فِتْنَةٌ اَوْ يُصِيْبَهُمْ عَذَابٌ اَلِيْمٌ ۞

اَلَاۤ اِنَّ لِلّٰهِ مَا فِى السَّمٰوٰتِ وَالْاَرْضِ ۚ قَدْ يَعْلَمُ مَاۤ اَنْتُمْ عَلَيْهِ ۚ وَيَوْمَ يُرْجَعُوْنَ اِلَيْهِ فَيُنَبِّئُهُمْ بِمَا عَمِلُوْا ۚ وَاللّٰهُ بِكُلِّ شَيْءٍ عَلِيْمٌ ۞

AL-FURQĀN

(Revealed before Hijra)

In the name of Allah, Most Gracious,
Ever Merciful. (1)

إِسْمِ اللّٰهِ الرَّحْمٰنِ الرَّحِيْمِ ۝

تَبٰرَكَ الَّذِىْ نَزَّلَ الْفُرْقَانَ عَلٰى عَبْدِهٖ لِيَكُوْنَ لِلْعٰلَمِيْنَ نَذِيْرَا ۝

Blessed is He Who has sent down the Discriminating Book to His servant, that he may be a Warner to all the peoples. He it is to Whom belongs the Kingdom of the heavens and the earth. He has taken unto Himself no son, and has no partner in the Kingdom. He has created everything and has determined its measure. Yet they have taken beside Him gods, who create nothing and are themselves created, and who have no power to harm, or benefit themselves and control neither death, nor life, nor resurrection. The dis-believers say: This Quran is naught but a lie that he has fabricated, and other people have helped him with it. They have, thereby, perpetrated an injustice and an untruth. They also say: These are fables of the ancients which he has got someone to write down for him and they are recited to him morn and eve. Say to them: The Quran has been revealed by Him Who knows every secret that is in the heavens and the earth. Verily, He is Most Forgiving, Ever Merciful. (2—7)

الَّذِىْ لَهٗ مُلْكُ السَّمٰوٰتِ وَالْاَرْضِ وَلَمْ يَتَّخِذْ وَلَدًا وَّلَمْ يَكُنْ لَّهٗ شَرِيْكٌ فِى الْمُلْكِ وَخَلَقَ كُلَّ شَىْءٍ فَقَدَّرَهٗ تَقْدِيْرًا ۝

وَاتَّخَذُوْا مِنْ دُوْنِهٖۤ اٰلِهَةً لَّا يَخْلُقُوْنَ شَيْئًا وَّهُمْ يُخْلَقُوْنَ وَلَا يَمْلِكُوْنَ لِاَنْفُسِهِمْ ضَرًّا وَّلَا نَفْعًا وَّلَا يَمْلِكُوْنَ مَوْتًا وَّلَا حَيٰوةً وَّلَا نُشُوْرًا ۝

وَقَالَ الَّذِيْنَ كَفَرُوْۤا اِنْ هٰذَاۤ اِلَّاۤ اِفْكُ افْتَرٰىهُ وَاَعَانَهٗ عَلَيْهِ قَوْمٌ اٰخَرُوْنَ ۚ فَقَدْ جَآءُوْ ظُلْمًا وَّزُوْرًا ۝

وَقَالُوْۤا اَسَاطِيْرُ الْاَوَّلِيْنَ اكْتَتَبَهَا فَهِىَ تُمْلٰى عَلَيْهِ بُكْرَةً وَّاَصِيْلًا ۝

قُلْ اَنْزَلَهُ الَّذِىْ يَعْلَمُ السِّرَّ فِى السَّمٰوٰتِ وَالْاَرْضِ ۚ اِنَّهٗ كَانَ غَفُوْرًا رَّحِيْمًا ۝

وَقَالُوْا مَالِ هٰذَا الرَّسُوْلِ يَأْكُلُ الطَّعَامَ وَيَمْشِىْ فِى الْاَسْوَاقِ ۚ لَوْلَاۤ اُنْزِلَ اِلَيْهِ مَلَكٌ فَيَكُوْنَ مَعَهٗ نَذِيْرَا ۝

They say: What kind of a Messenger is this who eats food and walks in the streets! Why has not an angel been sent down to him that he might be a warner along with him?

Or, a treasure should have been poured down to him, or he should have had a garden to eat therefrom. The wrongdoers aver: You but follow a man who is in the pay of others. Observe, what kind of things do they attribute to thee. They have gone astray and cannot find a way to saying anything sensible. (8—10)

أَوْ يُلْقَىٰ إِلَيْهِ كَنْزٌ أَوْ تَكُونُ لَهُ جَنَّةٌ يَأْكُلُ مِنْهَا ۚ وَقَالَ الظَّٰلِمُونَ إِن تَتَّبِعُونَ إِلَّا رَجُلًا مَّسْحُورًا ۝

انْظُرْ كَيْفَ ضَرَبُوا لَكَ الْأَمْثَالَ فَضَلُّوا فَلَا يَسْتَطِيعُونَ سَبِيلًا ۝

Blessed is He Who, if He please, will assign thee better than that which they have in mind, Gardens beneath which rivers flow, and will assign thee palaces. The truth is they deny the Hour, and for those who deny the Hour We have prepared a blazing fire. When it sees them from a place far off, they will hear its raging and roaring. When they are thrown into a narrow corner thereof, chained together, they will at once pray for annihilation; and they will be told: Call not today for only one annihilation, but call for manifold annihilations. Ask them: Will that be better or the Garden of Eternity promised to the righteous, which will be their reward and resort? They will have therein whatsoever they desire, abiding therein for ever. This is a promise which thy Lord has made incumbent upon Himself. (11—17)

تَبَارَكَ الَّذِي إِن شَاءَ جَعَلَ لَكَ خَيْرًا مِّن ذَٰلِكَ جَنَّٰتٍ تَجْرِي مِن تَحْتِهَا الْأَنْهَٰرُ وَيَجْعَل لَّكَ قُصُورًا ۝

بَلْ كَذَّبُوا بِالسَّاعَةِ ۖ وَأَعْتَدْنَا لِمَن كَذَّبَ بِالسَّاعَةِ سَعِيرًا ۝

إِذَا رَأَتْهُم مِّن مَّكَانٍ بَعِيدٍ سَمِعُوا لَهَا تَغَيُّظًا وَزَفِيرًا ۝

وَإِذَا أُلْقُوا مِنْهَا مَكَانًا ضَيِّقًا مُّقَرَّنِينَ دَعَوْا هُنَالِكَ ثُبُورًا ۝

لَّا تَدْعُوا الْيَوْمَ ثُبُورًا وَاحِدًا وَادْعُوا ثُبُورًا كَثِيرًا ۝ قُلْ أَذَٰلِكَ خَيْرٌ أَمْ جَنَّةُ الْخُلْدِ الَّتِي وُعِدَ الْمُتَّقُونَ ۚ كَانَتْ لَهُمْ جَزَاءً وَمَصِيرًا ۝

لَّهُمْ فِيهَا مَا يَشَاءُونَ خَالِدِينَ ۚ كَانَ عَلَىٰ رَبِّكَ وَعْدًا مَّسْئُولًا ۝

On the day when He will assemble the disbelievers along with those whom they worship beside Allah, He will ask the latter: Was it you who led astray these My servants, or did they stray away from the right path on their own? They will answer: Holy art Thou! It was not right for us to take protectors beside Thee;

وَيَوْمَ يَحْشُرُهُمْ وَمَا يَعْبُدُونَ مِن دُونِ اللَّهِ فَيَقُولُ أَأَنتُمْ أَضْلَلْتُمْ عِبَادِي هَٰؤُلَاءِ أَمْ هُمْ ضَلُّوا السَّبِيلَ ۝

قَالُوا سُبْحَانَكَ مَا كَانَ يَنبَغِي لَنَا أَن نَّتَّخِذَ مِن

but Thou didst bestow on these and on their fathers provision for this life until they forgot Thy remembrance, and became a ruined people. Then Allah will say to their worshippers: You see how they have given the lie to that which you asserted; so you cannot avert the punishment, nor can you obtain help. Whosoever from among you did wrong, We shall afflict him with grievous chastisement. We sent no Messengers before thee but that they all ate food and walked in the streets. We make some of you a means of trial for others, to see whether you are steadfast. Thy Lord is All-Seeing. (18—21)

Those who do not expect a meeting with Us ask: Why are not angels sent down to us? Or, why do we not see our Lord? Surely, they esteem themselves too highly and have greatly exceeded the bounds in rebellion. There will be no good tidings for the guilty on the day they see the angels; and they will cry out: Keep away, keep away! We shall turn to all that they did and We shall scatter it like particles of dust. On that day the inmates of heaven shall be better off as regards their abode and better off in respect of their place of repose. (22—25)

On the day when the heaven shall be rent asunder with lowering clouds, and the angels shall be sent down in large numbers, the kingdom shall belong on that day truly to the Gracious One. That day will be hard on the disbelievers.

دُوْنِكَ مِنْ اَوْلِيَآءَ وَلٰكِنْ مَّتَّعْتَهُمْ وَاٰبَآءَهُمْ حَتّٰى نَسُوا الذِّكْرَ وَكَانُوْا قَوْمًا بُوْرًا ۝

فَقَدْ كَذَّبُوْكُمْ بِمَا تَقُوْلُوْنَ فَمَا تَسْتَطِيْعُوْنَ صَرْفًا وَّلَا نَصْرًا وَمَنْ يَّظْلِمْ مِّنْكُمْ نُذِقْهُ عَذَابًا كَبِيْرًا ۝

وَمَآ اَرْسَلْنَا قَبْلَكَ مِنَ الْمُرْسَلِيْنَ اِلَّا اِنَّهُمْ لَيَأْكُلُوْنَ الطَّعَامَ وَيَمْشُوْنَ فِى الْاَسْوَاقِ وَجَعَلْنَا بَعْضَكُمْ لِبَعْضٍ فِتْنَةً اَتَصْبِرُوْنَ وَكَانَ رَبُّكَ بَصِيْرًا ۝

وَقَالَ الَّذِيْنَ لَا يَرْجُوْنَ لِقَآءَنَا لَوْلَآ اُنْزِلَ عَلَيْنَا الْمَلٰٓئِكَةُ اَوْ نَرٰى رَبَّنَا لَقَدِ اسْتَكْبَرُوْا فِيْ اَنْفُسِهِمْ وَعَتَوْ عُتُوًّا كَبِيْرًا ۝

يَوْمَ يَرَوْنَ الْمَلٰٓئِكَةَ لَا بُشْرٰى يَوْمَئِذٍ لِّلْمُجْرِمِيْنَ وَيَقُوْلُوْنَ حِجْرًا مَّحْجُوْرًا ۝

وَقَدِمْنَآ اِلٰى مَا عَمِلُوْا مِنْ عَمَلٍ فَجَعَلْنٰهُ هَبَآءً مَّنْثُوْرًا ۝

اَصْحٰبُ الْجَنَّةِ يَوْمَئِذٍ خَيْرٌ مُّسْتَقَرًّا وَّاَحْسَنُ مَقِيْلًا ۝

وَيَوْمَ تَشَقَّقُ السَّمَآءُ بِالْغَمَامِ وَنُزِّلَ الْمَلٰٓئِكَةُ تَنْزِيْلًا ۝

اَلْمُلْكُ يَوْمَئِذِ الْحَقُّ لِلرَّحْمٰنِ وَكَانَ يَوْمًا عَلَى الْكٰفِرِيْنَ عَسِيْرًا ۝

On that day the wrongdoer will bite on his hands, and will exclaim: Would that I had taken up with the Messenger. Woe is me! Would that I had never taken such a one as a friend. He made me forgetful of the Reminder when it came to me. Satan always deserts man in the end. The Messenger will say: Lord, my people did indeed discard the Quran utterly. Thus did We make for every Prophet enemies from among the sinners; and thy Lord is Sufficient as a Guide and a Helper. (26—32)

وَيَوْمَ يَعَضُّ الظَّالِمُ عَلَى يَدَيْهِ يَقُوْلُ يٰلَيْتَنِى اتَّخَذْتُ مَعَ الرَّسُوْلِ سَبِيْلًا ۝

يٰوَيْلَتٰى لَيْتَنِى لَمْ اَتَّخِذْ فُلَانًا خَلِيْلًا ۝

لَقَدْ اَضَلَّنِى عَنِ الذِّكْرِ بَعْدَ اِذْ جَآءَنِىْ ۚ وَكَانَ الشَّيْطٰنُ لِلْاِنْسَانِ خَذُوْلًا ۝

وَقَالَ الرَّسُوْلُ يٰرَبِّ اِنَّ قَوْمِى اتَّخَذُوْا هٰذَا الْقُرْاٰنَ مَهْجُوْرًا ۝

وَكَذٰلِكَ جَعَلْنَا لِكُلِّ نَبِيٍّ عَدُوًّا مِّنَ الْمُجْرِمِيْنَ ۚ وَكَفٰى بِرَبِّكَ هَادِيًا وَّنَصِيْرًا ۝

The disbelievers object: Why was not the Quran revealed to him all at once? It is revealed progressively that We may strengthen thy heart therewith. We have arranged it in the best form. Whenever they raise an objection, We refute it with a firm argument, and We provide thee with an excellent explanation. Those who will be gathered unto hell along with their leaders will be the worst in plight and most astray from the right path. (33—35)

وَقَالَ الَّذِيْنَ كَفَرُوْا لَوْلَا نُزِّلَ عَلَيْهِ الْقُرْاٰنُ جُمْلَةً وَّاحِدَةً ۛ كَذٰلِكَ ۛ لِنُثَبِّتَ بِهٖ فُؤَادَكَ وَرَتَّلْنٰهُ تَرْتِيْلًا ۝

وَلَا يَأْتُوْنَكَ بِمَثَلٍ اِلَّا جِئْنٰكَ بِالْحَقِّ وَاَحْسَنَ تَفْسِيْرًا ۝

اَلَّذِيْنَ يُحْشَرُوْنَ عَلٰى وُجُوْهِهِمْ اِلٰى جَهَنَّمَ ۙ اُولٰٓئِكَ شَرٌّ مَّكَانًا وَّاَضَلُّ سَبِيْلًا ۝

We gave Moses the Book, and appointed his brother Aaron with him as his assistant. We directed them: Go both of you to the people who have rejected Our Signs. After they had carried out Our direction, We destroyed the disbelieving people utterly. We drowned the people of Noah when they rejected the Messengers, and We made them a Sign for mankind. We have prepared a painful chastisement for the wrongdoers. To 'Ad and Thamud and the People of the Well and to many a generation between them,

وَلَقَدْ اٰتَيْنَا مُوْسَى الْكِتٰبَ وَجَعَلْنَا مَعَهٗٓ اَخَاهُ هٰرُوْنَ وَزِيْرًا ۝

فَقُلْنَا اذْهَبَآ اِلَى الْقَوْمِ الَّذِيْنَ كَذَّبُوْا بِاٰيٰتِنَا ۚ فَدَمَّرْنٰهُمْ تَدْمِيْرًا ۝

وَقَوْمَ نُوْحٍ لَّمَّا كَذَّبُوا الرُّسُلَ اَغْرَقْنٰهُمْ وَجَعَلْنٰهُمْ لِلنَّاسِ اٰيَةً ۖ وَاَعْتَدْنَا لِلظّٰلِمِيْنَ عَذَابًا اَلِيْمًا ۝

وَّعَادًا وَّثَمُوْدَا۟ وَاَصْحٰبَ الرَّسِّ وَقُرُوْنًا بَيْنَ ذٰلِكَ

We expounded the truth separately, and when they rejected it We destroyed each one utterly. The disbelievers of Mecca have come upon the ruins of the city on which a distressing rain fell. Have they not contemplated them? But the truth is they do not expect to be raised up after death. When they see thee they make fun of thee and say: Is this the one whom Allah has sent as a Messenger? He had well-nigh beguiled us away from our gods had we not adhered to them steadily. When they behold the punishment they shall realise who was most astray from the right path. Hast thou considered the case of one who has made his own evil inclinations his god? Canst thou be a guardian over him to force him into ways of righteousness? Dost thou imagine that most of them hear or understand? They are but like cattle, and in their conduct even more astray. (36—45)

كَثِيْرًا ۝

وَكُلًّا ضَرَبْنَا لَهُ الْاَمْثَالَ وَكُلًّا تَبَّرْنَا تَتْبِيْرًا ۝

وَلَقَدْ اَتَوْا عَلَى الْقَرْيَةِ الَّتِىْ اُمْطِرَتْ مَطَرَ السَّوْءِ ۚ

اَفَلَمْ يَكُوْنُوْا يَرَوْنَهَا ۚ بَلْ كَانُوْا لَا يَرْجُوْنَ نُشُوْرًا ۝

وَاِذَا رَاَوْكَ اِنْ يَّتَّخِذُوْنَكَ اِلَّا هُزُوًا ۚ اَهٰذَا الَّذِىْ

بَعَثَ اللّٰهُ رَسُوْلًا ۝

اِنْ كَادَ لَيُضِلُّنَا عَنْ اٰلِهَتِنَا لَوْلَاۤ اَنْ صَبَرْنَا عَلَيْهَا ۚ

وَسَوْفَ يَعْلَمُوْنَ حِيْنَ يَرَوْنَ الْعَذَابَ مَنْ اَضَلُّ

سَبِيْلًا ۝

اَرَءَيْتَ مَنِ اتَّخَذَ اِلٰهَهٗ هَوٰىهُ ۚ اَفَاَنْتَ تَكُوْنُ

عَلَيْهِ وَكِيْلًا ۝

اَمْ تَحْسَبُ اَنَّ اَكْثَرَهُمْ يَسْمَعُوْنَ اَوْ يَعْقِلُوْنَ ۚ اِنْ

هُمْ اِلَّا كَالْاَنْعَامِ بَلْ هُمْ اَضَلُّ سَبِيْلًا ۝

اَلَمْ تَرَ اِلٰى رَبِّكَ كَيْفَ مَدَّ الظِّلَّ ۚ وَلَوْ شَآءَ لَجَعَلَهٗ

سَاكِنًا ۚ ثُمَّ جَعَلْنَا الشَّمْسَ عَلَيْهِ دَلِيْلًا ۝

ثُمَّ قَبَضْنٰهُ اِلَيْنَا قَبْضًا يَّسِيْرًا ۝

وَهُوَ الَّذِىْ جَعَلَ لَكُمُ الَّيْلَ لِبَاسًا وَّالنَّوْمَ سُبَاتًا

وَّجَعَلَ النَّهَارَ نُشُوْرًا ۝

وَهُوَ الَّذِىْۤ اَرْسَلَ الرِّيٰحَ بُشْرًۢا بَيْنَ يَدَىْ رَحْمَتِهٖ ۚ

وَاَنْزَلْنَا مِنَ السَّمَآءِ مَآءً طَهُوْرًا ۝

لِّنُحْۦِىَ بِهٖ بَلْدَةً مَّيْتًا وَّنُسْقِيَهٗ مِمَّا خَلَقْنَاۤ اَنْعَامًا

وَّاَنَاسِىَّ كَثِيْرًا ۝

Seest thou not how thy Lord spreads out the shade? Had He pleased He could have made it stationary. Then We made the position of the sun an indicator of it. Then We draw it in towards Ourself slowly. He it is Who has made the night a covering for you, and sleep a source of rest, and the day for going about. He it is Who sends the breezes as heralds of His mercy, and We send down pure water from the sky, that We may thereby revive a dead land, and give it for drink to Our creation, cattle and men in great numbers.

We have expounded the Quran to them in diverse ways that they may take heed, but most people reject everything but disbelief. If We had pleased, We could surely have raised a Warner in every city. So do not give way to the disbelievers and put forth against them by means of the Quran, a great effort. (46—53)

He it is Who has caused the two waters to flow, one of the rivers and springs, sweet and palatable, and the other of the oceans, salt and bitter; and between them He has placed as a barrier a system that keeps them apart. He it is Who has created man from water and has made for him kindred by descent and kindred by marriage. Thy Lord is Powerful. They worship beside Allah that which can neither benefit them nor harm them. The disbeliever is ever opposed to the designs of his Lord. (54—56)

We have sent thee only as a bearer of glad tidings and as a Warner. Say to them: I ask of you no recompense for conveying Allah's message to you, save that whoso wishes may follow the way that leads to his Lord. Put thy trust in the One Who is Ever Living and is the Source of life, Who dies not, and glorify Him with His praise. He is fully Aware of the sins of His servants; Who created the heavens and the earth and all that is between them in six periods, then settled Himself on the Throne — the Gracious One. Ask thou concerning Him one who knows. When it is said to them: Prostrate yourselves before the Gracious One, they ask: And what is this Gracious One? Shall we prostrate ourselves before whatever thou biddest us? and it increases their aversion. (57—61)

وَلَقَدْ صَرَّفْنَهُ بَيْنَهُمْ لِيَذَّكَّرُوا فَأَبَى اَكْثَرُ النَّاسِ اِلَّا كُفُوْرًا ۝

وَلَوْ شِئْنَا لَبَعَثْنَا فِىْ كُلِّ قَرْيَةٍ نَّذِيْرًا ۝

فَلَا تُطِعِ الْكٰفِرِيْنَ وَجَاهِدْهُمْ بِهٖ جِهَادًا كَبِيْرًا ۝

وَهُوَ الَّذِىْ مَرَجَ الْبَحْرَيْنِ هٰذَا عَذْبٌ فُرَاتٌ وَّ هٰذَا مِلْحٌ اُجَاجٌ ۚ وَجَعَلَ بَيْنَهُمَا بَرْزَخًا وَّحِجْرًا مَّحْجُوْرًا ۝

وَهُوَ الَّذِىْ خَلَقَ مِنَ الْمَآءِ بَشَرًا فَجَعَلَهُ نَسَبًا وَّصِهْرًا ۚ وَكَانَ رَبُّكَ قَدِيْرًا ۝

وَيَعْبُدُوْنَ مِنْ دُوْنِ اللّٰهِ مَا لَا يَنْفَعُهُمْ وَلَا يَضُرُّهُمْ ۚ وَكَانَ الْكَافِرُ عَلٰى رَبِّهٖ ظَهِيْرًا ۝

وَمَآ اَرْسَلْنٰكَ اِلَّا مُبَشِّرًا وَّ نَذِيْرًا ۝

قُلْ مَآ اَسْـَٔلُكُمْ عَلَيْهِ مِنْ اَجْرٍ اِلَّا مَنْ شَآءَ اَنْ يَّتَّخِذَ اِلٰى رَبِّهٖ سَبِيْلًا ۝

وَتَوَكَّلْ عَلَى الْحَىِّ الَّذِىْ لَا يَمُوْتُ وَسَبِّحْ بِحَمْدِهٖ ۚ وَكَفٰى بِهٖ بِذُنُوْبِ عِبَادِهٖ خَبِيْرًا ۝

اَلَّذِىْ خَلَقَ السَّمٰوٰتِ وَالْاَرْضَ وَمَا بَيْنَهُمَا فِىْ سِتَّةِ اَيَّامٍ ثُمَّ اسْتَوٰى عَلَى الْعَرْشِ ۚ اَلرَّحْمٰنُ فَسْـَٔلْ بِهٖ خَبِيْرًا ۝

وَاِذَا قِيْلَ لَهُمُ اسْجُدُوْا لِلرَّحْمٰنِ قَالُوْا وَمَا الرَّحْمٰنُ ۗ اَنَسْجُدُ لِمَا تَأْمُرُنَا وَزَادَهُمْ نُفُوْرًا ۩

تَبٰرَكَ الَّذِىْ جَعَلَ فِى السَّمَآءِ بُرُوْجًا وَّجَعَلَ فِيْهَا

Blessed is He Who has made mansions in the heavens and has placed therein an illuminating lamp and a bright moon. He it is Who has made the night and the day to follow each other, for him who would take heed and would be grateful.

سِرَاجًا وَّقَمَرًا مُّنِيْرًا ۝

وَهُوَ الَّذِيْ جَعَلَ الَّيْلَ وَالنَّهَارَ خِلْفَةً لِّمَنْ اَرَادَ اَنْ يَّذَّكَّرَ اَوْ اَرَادَ شُكُوْرًا ۝

وَعِبَادُ الرَّحْمٰنِ الَّذِيْنَ يَمْشُوْنَ عَلَى الْاَرْضِ هَوْنًا وَّاِذَا خَاطَبَهُمُ الْجٰهِلُوْنَ قَالُوْا سَلٰمًا ۝

وَالَّذِيْنَ يَبِيْتُوْنَ لِرَبِّهِمْ سُجَّدًا وَّقِيَامًا ۝

وَالَّذِيْنَ يَقُوْلُوْنَ رَبَّنَا اصْرِفْ عَنَّا عَذَابَ جَهَنَّمَ اِنَّ عَذَابَهَا كَانَ غَرَامًا ۝

اِنَّهَا سَآءَتْ مُسْتَقَرًّا وَّمُقَامًا ۝

The true servants of the Gracious One are those who walk upon the earth with humility and when they are accosted by the ignorant ones, their response is: Peace; who pass the hours of the night in prostration and standing before their Lord; who entreat: Lord, avert from us the punishment of hell, it is a heavy torment, it is indeed an evil resort and dwelling-place; who are neither extravagant nor niggardly in spending, but keep a balance between the two; who call not on any god beside Allah, nor destroy a life that Allah has declared sacred except for just cause, and commit not adultery, for whoso does that shall meet with the punishment of his sin and his punishment will be intensified on the Day of Judgment and he will abide therein disgraced, except for those who repent and believe and work righteousness, whose evil deeds Allah will convert into good ones, Allah being Most Forgiving, Ever Merciful (and he who repents and works righteousness indeed turns to Allah with true repentance); who bear not false witness and when they come upon anything vain, they pass on with dignity; who, when

وَالَّذِيْنَ اِذَآ اَنْفَقُوْا لَمْ يُسْرِفُوْا وَلَمْ يَقْتُرُوْا وَكَانَ بَيْنَ ذٰلِكَ قَوَامًا ۝

وَالَّذِيْنَ لَا يَدْعُوْنَ مَعَ اللّٰهِ اِلٰهًا اٰخَرَ وَلَا يَقْتُلُوْنَ النَّفْسَ الَّتِيْ حَرَّمَ اللّٰهُ اِلَّا بِالْحَقِّ وَلَا يَزْنُوْنَ وَمَنْ يَّفْعَلْ ذٰلِكَ يَلْقَ اَثَامًا ۝

يُّضٰعَفْ لَهُ الْعَذَابُ يَوْمَ الْقِيٰمَةِ وَيَخْلُدْ فِيْهِ مُهَانًا ۝

اِلَّا مَنْ تَابَ وَاٰمَنَ وَعَمِلَ عَمَلًا صَالِحًا فَاُولٰٓئِكَ يُبَدِّلُ اللّٰهُ سَيِّاٰتِهِمْ حَسَنٰتٍ وَكَانَ اللّٰهُ غَفُوْرًا رَّحِيْمًا ۝

وَمَنْ تَابَ وَعَمِلَ صَالِحًا فَاِنَّهٗ يَتُوْبُ اِلَى اللّٰهِ مَتَابًا ۝

وَالَّذِيْنَ لَا يَشْهَدُوْنَ الزُّوْرَ وَاِذَا مَرُّوْا بِاللَّغْوِ

they are reminded of the Signs of their
Lord do not contemplate them like one
without hearing and sight; and who
implore: Lord, grant us of our spouses
and our offspring the delight of our eyes,
and make us a model for the righteous.
These are the ones who will be rewarded
with lofty mansions in Paradise, because
they were steadfast, and they will be
welcomed thereunto with greetings and
salutations of peace, abiding therein.
Excellent it is as a resort and dwelling-
place. (62—77)

مَرُّوْا كِرَامًا ۝

وَالَّذِيْنَ اِذَا ذُكِّرُوْا بِاٰيٰتِ رَبِّهِمْ لَمْ يَخِرُّوْا عَلَيْهَا

صُمًّا وَّعُمْيَانًا ۝

وَالَّذِيْنَ يَقُوْلُوْنَ رَبَّنَا هَبْ لَنَا مِنْ اَزْوَاجِنَا وَ

ذُرِّيّٰتِنَا قُرَّةَ اَعْيُنٍ وَّاجْعَلْنَا لِلْمُتَّقِيْنَ اِمَامًا ۝

اُولٰٓئِكَ يُجْزَوْنَ الْغُرْفَةَ بِمَا صَبَرُوْا وَيُلَقَّوْنَ فِيْهَا

تَحِيَّةً وَّسَلٰمًا ۝

خٰلِدِيْنَ فِيْهَا حَسُنَتْ مُسْتَقَرًّا وَّمُقَامًا ۝

Say to the disbelievers: What would
my Lord care for you, were it not for your
prayers. You have indeed rejected the
Truth and the chastisement will now
cleave to you. (78)

قُلْ مَا يَعْبَؤُا بِكُمْ رَبِّيْ لَوْلَا دُعَاؤُكُمْ فَقَدْ

كَذَّبْتُمْ فَسَوْفَ يَكُوْنُ لِزَامًا ۝

Chapter 26

AL-SHU‘ARĀ’

(Revealed before Hijra)

In the name of Allah, Most Gracious, Ever Merciful. (1)

بِسۡمِ اللهِ الرَّحۡمٰنِ الرَّحِیۡمِ ۟

THE PURE, ALL-HEARING, EX-ALTED. (2)

طٰسٓمّٓ ۟

These are verses of the clear Book. Haply thou wilt risk death grieving that they do not believe. If We pleased We could send down a Sign to them from heaven which would compel their submission. There never comes a new Reminder to the people from the Gracious One, but they turn away from it. Accordingly, these people have also rejected it, but soon the consequences of their mockery will begin to be manifested to them. Do they not observe how many a pair of excellent species have We caused to grow in the earth? In that there is a Sign indeed; but most of these would not believe. Verily, it is thy Lord Who is the Mighty, the Ever Merciful. (3—10)

تِلۡكَ اٰیٰتُ الۡكِتٰبِ الۡمُبِیۡنِ ۟

لَعَلَّكَ بَاخِعٌ نَّفۡسَكَ اَلَّا یَكُوۡنُوۡا مُؤۡمِنِیۡنَ ۟

اِنۡ نَّشَاۡ نُنَزِّلۡ عَلَیۡهِمۡ مِّنَ السَّمَاۤءِ اٰیَةً فَظَلَّتۡ اَعۡنَاقُهُمۡ لَهَا خٰضِعِیۡنَ ۟

وَ مَا یَاۡتِیۡهِمۡ مِّنۡ ذِكۡرٍ مِّنَ الرَّحۡمٰنِ مُحۡدَثٍ اِلَّا كَانُوۡا عَنۡهُ مُعۡرِضِیۡنَ ۟

فَقَدۡ كَذَّبُوۡا فَسَیَاۡتِیۡهِمۡ اَنۡۢبٰٓؤُا مَا كَانُوۡا بِهٖ یَسۡتَهۡزِءُوۡنَ ۟

اَوَلَمۡ یَرَوۡا اِلَی الۡاَرۡضِ كَمۡ اَنۡۢبَتۡنَا فِیۡهَا مِنۡ كُلِّ زَوۡجٍ كَرِیۡمٍ ۟

اِنَّ فِیۡ ذٰلِكَ لَاٰیَةً ؕ وَ مَا كَانَ اَكۡثَرُهُمۡ مُّؤۡمِنِیۡنَ ۟

وَ اِنَّ رَبَّكَ لَهُوَ الۡعَزِیۡزُ الرَّحِیۡمُ ۟

Call to mind when thy Lord called Moses and directed him: Go to the wrong-doing people, the people of Pharaoh, and remind them: Will you not be righteous? He pleaded: Lord, I fear lest they should reject me; and I may feel oppressed and tongue-tied, so appoint Aaron also along with me. Besides, they have a charge against me, and I am afraid they might put me to death ere I am able to deliver Thy message. His Lord reassured him: That shall not be. Go, then, both of you with Our Signs. We are with you, hearing your prayers.

وَ اِذۡ نَادٰی رَبُّكَ مُوۡسٰۤی اَنِ ائۡتِ الۡقَوۡمَ الظّٰلِمِیۡنَ ۟

قَوۡمَ فِرۡعَوۡنَ ؕ اَلَا یَتَّقُوۡنَ ۟

قَالَ رَبِّ اِنِّیۡۤ اَخَافُ اَنۡ یُّكَذِّبُوۡنِ ۟

وَ یَضِیۡقُ صَدۡرِیۡ وَ لَا یَنۡطَلِقُ لِسَانِیۡ فَاَرۡسِلۡ اِلٰی هٰرُوۡنَ ۟

وَ لَهُمۡ عَلَیَّ ذَنۡۢبٌ فَاَخَافُ اَنۡ یَّقۡتُلُوۡنِ ۟

قَالَ كَلَّا ۚ فَاذۡهَبَا بِاٰیٰتِنَاۤ اِنَّا مَعَكُمۡ مُّسۡتَمِعُوۡنَ ۟

So, go to Pharaoh, and say to him: We are the Messengers of the Lord of the worlds, and our message is: Send the children of Israel with us. (11—18)

Pharaoh said to Moses: Did we not bring thee up among us as a child, and thou didst spend many years of thy life among us? Then thou didst commit thy deed and proved thyself ungrateful. Moses said: Indeed I did it, but I was then ignorant, and being afraid of you I fled from you. Then my Lord granted me proper judgment and made me a Messenger. Now thou tauntest me with the favour done me, as against thy having enslaved the children of Israel. Pharaoh asked: What is this Lord of the worlds? Moses said: The Lord of the heavens and the earth and of all that is between the two, if you would believe. Pharaoh said to those around him: Have you heard what he has said? Moses went on to say: The same Who is your Lord, and the Lord of your forefathers. Pharaoh observed: Most surely this Messenger of yours who has been sent to you is a madman.

Moses added: He is the Lord of the East and of the West, and of all that is between the two, if you did but understand. Pharaoh said in a rage: If thou dost adopt a God other than me, I will certainly put thee in prison. Moses exclaimed: What, even though I bring thee a manifest Sign? Pharaoh said: Bring it then, if thou speakest truth. Thereupon Moses put down his rod, and suddenly it appeared as a serpent clearly visible; and he drew

فَأْتِيَا فِرْعَوْنَ فَقُوْلَا إِنَّا رَسُوْلُ رَبِّ الْعٰلَمِيْنَ ۙ

اَنْ اَرْسِلْ مَعَنَا بَنِيْ اِسْرَآءِيْلَ ؕ

قَالَ اَلَمْ نُرَبِّكَ فِيْنَا وَلِيْدًا وَّ لَبِثْتَ فِيْنَا مِنْ عُمُرِكَ سِنِيْنَ ۙ

وَ فَعَلْتَ فَعْلَتَكَ الَّتِيْ فَعَلْتَ وَاَنْتَ مِنَ الْكٰفِرِيْنَ

قَالَ فَعَلْتُهَآ اِذًا وَّ اَنَا مِنَ الضَّآلِّيْنَ ؕ

فَفَرَرْتُ مِنْكُمْ لَمَّا خِفْتُكُمْ فَوَهَبَ لِيْ رَبِّيْ حُكْمًا وَّ جَعَلَنِيْ مِنَ الْمُرْسَلِيْنَ

وَ تِلْكَ نِعْمَةٌ تَمُنُّهَا عَلَيَّ اَنْ عَبَّدْتَّ بَنِيْ اِسْرَآءِيْلَ ؕ

قَالَ فِرْعَوْنُ وَ مَا رَبُّ الْعٰلَمِيْنَ

قَالَ رَبُّ السَّمٰوٰتِ وَ الْاَرْضِ وَ مَا بَيْنَهُمَا ؕ اِنْ كُنْتُمْ مُّوْقِنِيْنَ

قَالَ لِمَنْ حَوْلَهٗٓ اَلَا تَسْتَمِعُوْنَ

قَالَ رَبُّكُمْ وَ رَبُّ اٰبَآئِكُمُ الْاَوَّلِيْنَ

قَالَ اِنَّ رَسُوْلَكُمُ الَّذِيْٓ اُرْسِلَ اِلَيْكُمْ لَمَجْنُوْنٌ

قَالَ رَبُّ الْمَشْرِقِ وَ الْمَغْرِبِ وَ مَا بَيْنَهُمَا ؕ اِنْ كُنْتُمْ تَعْقِلُوْنَ

قَالَ لَئِنِ اتَّخَذْتَ اِلٰهًا غَيْرِيْ لَاَجْعَلَنَّكَ مِنَ الْمَسْجُوْنِيْنَ

قَالَ اَوَ لَوْ جِئْتُكَ بِشَيْءٍ مُّبِيْنٍ

قَالَ فَأْتِ بِهٖٓ اِنْ كُنْتَ مِنَ الصّٰدِقِيْنَ

فَاَلْقٰى عَصَاهُ فَاِذَا هِيَ ثُعْبَانٌ مُّبِيْنٌ ۚ

forth his hand and it appeared white to
the beholders. (19—34)

وَنَزَعَ يَدَهُ فَإِذَا هِيَ بَيْضَآءُ لِلنَّظِرِيْنَ ۞

قَالَ لِلْمَلَإِ حَوْلَهُ إِنَّ هٰذَا لَسٰحِرٌ عَلِيْمٌ ۞

يُّرِيْدُ أَنْ يُّخْرِجَكُمْ مِّنْ أَرْضِكُمْ بِسِحْرِهٖ ۖ فَمَا ذَا
تَأْمُرُوْنَ ۞

Pharaoh said to the chiefs around him:
This is surely a skilful magician who seeks
to drive you out of your land by his
magic. Now what do you advise? They
said: Put him and his brother off awhile,
and send summoners into the cities who
should bring to thee every skilful sorcerer.
Accordingly, the sorcerers were assembled
together at the appointed time on the
day fixed. The people were told: Will you
also gather together, so that we may
follow the magicians, if they be the winners. When the magicians came they
asked Pharaoh: Shall we have a reward,
if we are the winners? He replied: Certainly, and you will also become part of
my entourage. Moses said to the magicians:
Go ahead, and do whatever you have in
mind. So they cast down their cords and
their rods and proclaimed: By the honour
of Pharaoh, it is we who will have the
upper hand! Then Moses put down his rod
and it proceeded to demolish all that they
had fabricated. Whereupon the magicians
were impelled to fall down prostrate and
announced: We believe in the Lord of the
worlds, the Lord of Moses, and of Aaron.

قَالُوْٓا أَرْجِهْ وَأَخَاهُ وَابْعَثْ فِي الْمَدَآئِنِ حٰشِرِيْنَ ۞

يَأْتُوْكَ بِكُلِّ سَحَّارٍ عَلِيْمٍ ۞

فَجُمِعَ السَّحَرَةُ لِمِيْقَاتِ يَوْمٍ مَّعْلُوْمٍ ۞

وَقِيْلَ لِلنَّاسِ هَلْ أَنْتُمْ مُّجْتَمِعُوْنَ ۞

لَعَلَّنَا نَتَّبِعُ السَّحَرَةَ إِنْ كَانُوْا هُمُ الْغٰلِبِيْنَ ۞

فَلَمَّا جَآءَ السَّحَرَةُ قَالُوْا لِفِرْعَوْنَ أَئِنَّ لَنَا لَأَجْرًا
إِنْ كُنَّا نَحْنُ الْغٰلِبِيْنَ ۞

قَالَ نَعَمْ وَإِنَّكُمْ إِذًا لَّمِنَ الْمُقَرَّبِيْنَ ۞

قَالَ لَهُمْ مُّوْسَى أَلْقُوْا مَآ أَنْتُمْ مُّلْقُوْنَ ۞

فَأَلْقَوْا حِبَالَهُمْ وَعِصِيَّهُمْ وَقَالُوْا بِعِزَّةِ فِرْعَوْنَ
إِنَّا لَنَحْنُ الْغٰلِبُوْنَ ۞

فَأَلْقَى مُوْسَى عَصَاهُ فَإِذَا هِيَ تَلْقَفُ مَا يَأْفِكُوْنَ ۞

فَأُلْقِيَ السَّحَرَةُ سٰجِدِيْنَ ۞

قَالُوْٓا أٰمَنَّا بِرَبِّ الْعٰلَمِيْنَ ۞

رَبِّ مُوْسَى وَهٰرُوْنَ ۞

Pharaoh was incensed and shouted: Have
you believed in him before I gave you
leave? He is surely your chief who has
taught you magic. Soon will you learn
your doom. I shall cut off your hands
and your feet on alternate sides, and shall
crucify you all.

قَالَ أٰمَنْتُمْ لَهُ قَبْلَ أَنْ أٰذَنَ لَكُمْ إِنَّهُ لَكَبِيْرُكُمُ
الَّذِيْ عَلَّمَكُمُ السِّحْرَ فَلَسَوْفَ تَعْلَمُوْنَ ۚ لَأُقَطِّعَنَّ
أَيْدِيَكُمْ وَأَرْجُلَكُمْ مِّنْ خِلَافٍ وَّلَأُصَلِّبَنَّكُمْ

They made answer: It matters not. To our
Lord shall we return. We hope our Lord
will forgive us our sins, since we are the
first to believe. (35—52)

أَجْمَعِيْنَ ۞

قَالُوْا لَا ضَيْرَ ۖ اِنَّآ اِلٰى رَبِّنَا مُنْقَلِبُوْنَ ۞

اِنَّا نَطْمَعُ اَنْ يَّغْفِرَ لَنَا رَبُّنَا خَطٰيٰنَآ اَنْ كُنَّآ اَوَّلَ

الْمُؤْمِنِيْنَ ۞

وَاَوْحَيْنَآ اِلٰى مُوْسٰٓى اَنْ اَسْرِ بِعِبَادِيْٓ اِنَّكُمْ مُّتَّبَعُوْنَ ۞

فَاَرْسَلَ فِرْعَوْنُ فِى الْمَدَآئِنِ حٰشِرِيْنَ ۞

اِنَّ هٰٓؤُلَآءِ لَشِرْذِمَةٌ قَلِيْلُوْنَ ۞

We directed Moses: Set forth with My
servants by night. You will surely be
pursued. When Pharaoh discovered this,
he sent summoners into the cities announcing: These are a small party and
they have provoked us. We are a large
and watchful force, we must frustrate
their design. Thus We drove them forth
out of gardens and springs, and treasures
and pleasant abodes and made the
children of Israel inheritors of these
bounties. Thus it was. They pursued them in
the morning, and when the two hosts came
in sight of one another, the companions
of Moses said: We are caught. Said Moses:
Never! My Lord is with me. He will
direct me aright; whereupon We directed
Moses: Strike the sea with thy rod.
On this the sea was divided into sections
and every section looked like a big dune.

وَاِنَّهُمْ لَنَا لَغَآئِظُوْنَ ۞

وَاِنَّا لَجَمِيْعٌ حٰذِرُوْنَ ۞

فَاَخْرَجْنٰهُمْ مِّنْ جَنّٰتٍ وَّعُيُوْنٍ ۞

وَّكُنُوْزٍ وَّمَقَامٍ كَرِيْمٍ ۞

كَذٰلِكَ ۚ وَاَوْرَثْنٰهَا بَنِيْٓ اِسْرَآءِيْلَ ۞

فَاَتْبَعُوْهُمْ مُّشْرِقِيْنَ ۞

فَلَمَّا تَرَآءَ الْجَمْعٰنِ قَالَ اَصْحٰبُ مُوْسٰٓى اِنَّا لَمُدْرَكُوْنَ ۞

قَالَ كَلَّا ۚ اِنَّ مَعِيَ رَبِّيْ سَيَهْدِيْنِ ۞

فَاَوْحَيْنَآ اِلٰى مُوْسٰٓى اَنِ اضْرِبْ بِّعَصَاكَ الْبَحْرَ ۖ

فَانْفَلَقَ فَكَانَ كُلُّ فِرْقٍ كَالطَّوْدِ الْعَظِيْمِ ۞

وَاَزْلَفْنَا ثَمَّ الْاٰخَرِيْنَ ۞

In the meantime We made the others
approach nearer. We delivered Moses and
those who were with him, all of them.
Then We drowned the others. In this,
verily, there is a Sign; but most of these
would not believe. Surely, it is thy Lord
Who is the Mighty, the Ever Merciful.
(53—69)

وَاَنْجَيْنَا مُوْسٰى وَمَنْ مَّعَهٗٓ اَجْمَعِيْنَ ۞

ثُمَّ اَغْرَقْنَا الْاٰخَرِيْنَ ۞

اِنَّ فِيْ ذٰلِكَ لَاٰيَةً ۖ وَمَا كَانَ اَكْثَرُهُمْ مُّؤْمِنِيْنَ ۞

وَاِنَّ رَبَّكَ لَهُوَ الْعَزِيْزُ الرَّحِيْمُ ۞

Recite unto them the account of Abraham, when he asked his father and his people; What do you worship? They replied: We worship idols and we sit in devotion before them. He asked them: Do they listen to you when you call on them, or do they benefit you in any way or do you any harm? They answered: Not so; but we found our fathers doing the same. (70—75)

Abraham said: Do you realise that those objects that you and your fathers have been worshipping all seek my ruin? It is only the Lord of the worlds, Who has created me, Who guides me, and Who gives me to eat and to drink; and when I fall ill, it is He Who restores me to health; and Who will cause me to die, and then bring me to life again, and Who, I hope, will forgive me my faults on the Day of Judgment. (76—83)

Abraham supplicated: Lord, bestow right judgment upon me and join me with the righteous; and give me a true and lasting reputation among posterity; and include me among the inheritors of the Garden of Bliss; and forgive my father, he is one of the erring ones; and humiliate me not on the day when people will be raised up, the day when wealth and sons will not avail, and he alone will be saved who comes to Allah with a submissive heart. (84—90)

Heaven shall be brought near to the righteous and hell shall be uncovered for those who have gone astray. They will be asked: Where are those whom you worshipped beside Allah? Can they help you or procure help for themselves? Then will they all be thrown headlong therein, the worshippers, and the worshipped, and the hosts of Iblis, all together. They will dispute between themselves therein and the worshippers will say: By Allah, we were in manifest error when we held you as equal with the Lord of the worlds, and we were led astray by the guilty ones. Now we have no one to intercede for us, nor any sincere friend. If we could but return to the world and be among the believers. In this, verily, there is a Sign, but most of these would not believe. Surely, it is thy Lord Who is the Mighty, the Ever Merciful. (91—105)

وَبُرِّزَتِ الْجَحِيْمُ لِلْغَاوِيْنَ ۞

وَقِيْلَ لَهُمْ اَيْنَمَا كُنْتُمْ تَعْبُدُوْنَ ۞

مِنْ دُوْنِ اللّٰهِ هَلْ يَنْصُرُوْنَكُمْ اَوْ يَنْتَصِرُوْنَ ۞

فَكُبْكِبُوْا فِيْهَا هُمْ وَالْغَاوٗنَ ۞

وَجُنُوْدُ اِبْلِيْسَ اَجْمَعُوْنَ ۞

قَالُوْا وَهُمْ فِيْهَا يَخْتَصِمُوْنَ ۞

تَاللّٰهِ اِنْ كُنَّا لَفِيْ ضَلٰلٍ مُّبِيْنٍ ۞

اِذْ نُسَوِّيْكُمْ بِرَبِّ الْعٰلَمِيْنَ ۞

وَمَا اَضَلَّنَا اِلَّا الْمُجْرِمُوْنَ ۞

فَمَا لَنَا مِنْ شَافِعِيْنَ ۞

وَلَا صَدِيْقٍ حَمِيْمٍ ۞

فَلَوْ اَنَّ لَنَا كَرَّةً فَنَكُوْنَ مِنَ الْمُؤْمِنِيْنَ ۞

اِنَّ فِيْ ذٰلِكَ لَاٰيَةً ۚ وَمَا كَانَ اَكْثَرُهُمْ مُّؤْمِنِيْنَ ۞

وَاِنَّ رَبَّكَ لَهُوَ الْعَزِيْزُ الرَّحِيْمُ ۞

كَذَّبَتْ قَوْمُ نُوْحِ الْمُرْسَلِيْنَ ۞

اِذْ قَالَ لَهُمْ اَخُوْهُمْ نُوْحٌ اَلَا تَتَّقُوْنَ ۞

اِنِّيْ لَكُمْ رَسُوْلٌ اَمِيْنٌ ۞

فَاتَّقُوا اللّٰهَ وَاَطِيْعُوْنِ ۞

وَمَا اَسْئَلُكُمْ عَلَيْهِ مِنْ اَجْرٍ ۚ اِنْ اَجْرِيَ اِلَّا عَلٰى رَبِّ الْعٰلَمِيْنَ ۞

فَاتَّقُوا اللّٰهَ وَاَطِيْعُوْنِ ۞

قَالُوْا اَنُؤْمِنُ لَكَ وَاتَّبَعَكَ الْاَرْذَلُوْنَ ۞

The People of Noah rejected the Messengers, when their brother Noah said to them: Will you not be righteous? I am sent to you as a trusty Messenger. So be mindful of your duty to Allah, and obey me. I ask of you no recompense for it; my recompense is with the Lord of the worlds. So fear Allah, and obey me. His people retorted: Shall we believe in thee, when it is the meanest who follow thee?

Noah remonstrated with them: What knowledge have I of their doings? It is only my Lord who can call them to account, could you but understand. I am not going to drive away those who believe. I am only a plain Warner. The disbelievers warned: If you do not desist, Noah, you shall certainly be stoned to death. Noah implored his Lord: My people have rejected me Lord, therefore, do Thou judge finally between them and me, and deliver me and the believers that are with me from our enemies. So We delivered him and those who were with him in the fully laden Ark; and We drowned all the rest. In this, verily, there is a Sign, but most of these would not believe. Surely, it is thy Lord Who is the Mighty, the Ever Merciful. (106—123)

قَالَ وَمَا عِلْمِیْ بِمَا كَانُوْا یَعْمَلُوْنَ ۞

اِنْ حِسَابُهُمْ اِلَّا عَلٰى رَبِّیْ لَوْ تَشْعُرُوْنَ ۞

وَمَاۤ اَنَا بِطَارِدِ الْمُؤْمِنِیْنَ ۞

اِنْ اَنَا اِلَّا نَذِیْرٌ مُّبِیْنٌ ۞

قَالُوْا لَئِنْ لَّمْ تَنْتَهِ یٰنُوْحُ لَتَكُوْنَنَّ مِنَ الْمَرْجُوْمِیْنَ ۞

قَالَ رَبِّ اِنَّ قَوْمِیْ كَذَّبُوْنِ ۞

فَافْتَحْ بَیْنِیْ وَبَیْنَهُمْ فَتْحًا وَّنَجِّنِیْ وَمَنْ مَّعِیَ مِنَ الْمُؤْمِنِیْنَ ۞

فَاَنْجَیْنٰهُ وَمَنْ مَّعَهٗ فِی الْفُلْكِ الْمَشْحُوْنِ ۞

ثُمَّ اَغْرَقْنَا بَعْدُ الْبٰقِیْنَ ۞

اِنَّ فِیْ ذٰلِكَ لَاٰیَةً وَمَا كَانَ اَكْثَرُهُمْ مُّؤْمِنِیْنَ ۞

وَاِنَّ رَبَّكَ لَهُوَ الْعَزِیْزُ الرَّحِیْمُ ۞

كَذَّبَتْ عَادُ الْمُرْسَلِیْنَ ۞

اِذْ قَالَ لَهُمْ اَخُوْهُمْ هُوْدٌ اَلَا تَتَّقُوْنَ ۞

اِنِّیْ لَكُمْ رَسُوْلٌ اَمِیْنٌ ۞

فَاتَّقُوا اللهَ وَاَطِیْعُوْنِ ۞

وَمَاۤ اَسْـَٔلُكُمْ عَلَیْهِ مِنْ اَجْرٍ اِنْ اَجْرِیَ اِلَّا عَلٰى رَبِّ الْعٰلَمِیْنَ ۞

اَتَبْنُوْنَ بِكُلِّ رِیْعٍ اٰیَةً تَعْبَثُوْنَ ۞

وَتَتَّخِذُوْنَ مَصَانِعَ لَعَلَّكُمْ تَخْلُدُوْنَ ۞

وَاِذَا بَطَشْتُمْ بَطَشْتُمْ جَبَّارِیْنَ ۞

فَاتَّقُوا اللهَ وَاَطِیْعُوْنِ ۞

The 'Ad rejected the Messengers, when their brother Hud said to them: Will you not be righteous? I am sent to you as a trusty Messenger. So be mindful of your duty to Allah, and obey me. I ask of you no recompense for it; my recompense is with the Lord of the worlds. Do you build monuments on every eminence out of vanity, and erect palaces as though you will live for ever? When you lay hands upon any one you do so as tyrants. So fear Allah, and obey me.

Fear Him Who has helped you with that which you know. He has helped you with cattle, and sons, and gardens, and springs. I fear for you the torment of an awful day. They retorted: It is the same to us whether thou admonish us or not, this is a habit which has been current among the ancients, and we shall never be punished. So they rejected him; and We destroyed them. In that indeed there is a Sign; but most of these would not believe. Surely, it is thy Lord Who is the Mighty, the Ever Merciful. (124—141)

وَ اتَّقُوا الَّذِىٓ اَمَدَّكُمۡ بِمَا تَعۡلَمُوۡنَ ۟

اَمَدَّكُمۡ بِاَنۡعَامٍ وَّ بَنِيۡنَ ۟

وَ جَنّٰتٍ وَّ عُيُوۡنٍ ۟

اِنِّيۡٓ اَخَافُ عَلَيۡكُمۡ عَذَابَ يَوۡمٍ عَظِيۡمٍ ۟

قَالُوۡا سَوَآءٌ عَلَيۡنَآ اَوَعَظۡتَ اَمۡ لَمۡ تَكُنۡ مِّنَ الۡوٰعِظِيۡنَ ۟

اِنۡ هٰذَآ اِلَّا خُلُقُ الۡاَوَّلِيۡنَ ۟

وَ مَا نَحۡنُ بِمُعَذَّبِيۡنَ ۟

فَكَذَّبُوۡهُ فَاَهۡلَكۡنٰهُمۡ ؕ اِنَّ فِىۡ ذٰلِكَ لَاٰيَةً ؕ وَ مَا كَانَ اَكۡثَرُهُمۡ مُّؤۡمِنِيۡنَ ۟

وَ اِنَّ رَبَّكَ لَهُوَ الۡعَزِيۡزُ الرَّحِيۡمُ ۟

The Thamud rejected the Messengers, when their brother Saleh said to them: Will you not be righteous? I am sent to you as a trusty Messenger. So be mindful of your duty to Allah, and obey me. I ask of you no recompense for it; my recompense is with the Lord of the worlds.

كَذَّبَتۡ ثَمُوۡدُ الۡمُرۡسَلِيۡنَ ۟

اِذۡ قَالَ لَهُمۡ اَخُوۡهُمۡ صٰلِحٌ اَلَا تَتَّقُوۡنَ ۟

اِنِّيۡ لَكُمۡ رَسُوۡلٌ اَمِيۡنٌ ۟

فَاتَّقُوا اللّٰهَ وَ اَطِيۡعُوۡنِ ۟

وَ مَآ اَسۡـَٔلُكُمۡ عَلَيۡهِ مِنۡ اَجۡرٍ ۚ اِنۡ اَجۡرِىَ اِلَّا عَلٰى رَبِّ الۡعٰلَمِيۡنَ ۟

Do you imagine that you will be left secure amidst all this here, gardens and springs, and waving cornfields, and date-palms with heavy spathes near breaking? You hew out mansions in the mountains taking pride in your skill. So fear Allah and obey me; and obey not the bidding of those who exceed the bounds, who create disorder in the land and do not promote order and security.

اَتُتۡرَكُوۡنَ فِىۡ مَا هٰهُنَآ اٰمِنِيۡنَ ۟

فِىۡ جَنّٰتٍ وَّ عُيُوۡنٍ ۟

وَّ زُرُوۡعٍ وَّ نَخۡلٍ طَلۡعُهَا هَضِيۡمٌ ۟

وَ تَنۡحِتُوۡنَ مِنَ الۡجِبَالِ بُيُوۡتًا فٰرِهِيۡنَ ۟

فَاتَّقُوا اللّٰهَ وَ اَطِيۡعُوۡنِ ۟

وَ لَا تُطِيۡعُوۡٓا اَمۡرَ الۡمُسۡرِفِيۡنَ ۟

They retorted: Thou art being put up to this by others who support thee. Thou art but a human being like ourselves. Bring us then a Sign, if thou art truthful. He replied: Here is a she-camel, it has its appointed day of drinking at the place of watering, and you have your appointed day. Do her no harm, else you will be afflicted with the chastisement of an awful day. But they hamstrung her and then became remorseful. So the punishment overtook them. In that surely there is a Sign, but most of these would not believe. Surely, it is thy Lord Who is the Mighty, the Ever Merciful. (142—160)

الَّذِيْنَ يُفْسِدُوْنَ فِى الْاَرْضِ وَلَا يُصْلِحُوْنَ ۞

قَالُوْۤا اِنَّمَاۤ اَنْتَ مِنَ الْمُسَحَّرِيْنَ ۞

مَاۤ اَنْتَ اِلَّا بَشَرٌ مِّثْلُنَا ۚ فَاْتِ بِاٰيَةٍ اِنْ كُنْتَ مِنَ الصّٰدِقِيْنَ ۞

قَالَ هٰذِهٖ نَاقَةٌ لَّهَا شِرْبٌ وَّلَكُمْ شِرْبُ يَوْمٍ مَّعْلُوْمٍ ۞

وَلَا تَمَسُّوْهَا بِسُوْٓءٍ فَيَاْخُذَكُمْ عَذَابُ يَوْمٍ عَظِيْمٍ ۞

فَعَقَرُوْهَا فَاَصْبَحُوْا نٰدِمِيْنَ ۞

فَاَخَذَهُمُ الْعَذَابُ ؕ اِنَّ فِىْ ذٰلِكَ لَاٰيَةً ؕ وَمَا كَانَ اَكْثَرُهُمْ مُّؤْمِنِيْنَ ۞

وَاِنَّ رَبَّكَ لَهُوَ الْعَزِيْزُ الرَّحِيْمُ ۞

The people of Lot rejected the Messengers, when their brother Lot said to them: Will you not be righteous? I am sent to you as a trusty Messenger. So be mindful of your duty to Allah, and obey me. I ask of you no recompense for it; my recompense is with the Lord of the worlds.

كَذَّبَتْ قَوْمُ لُوْطِ ِۨالْمُرْسَلِيْنَ ۞

اِذْ قَالَ لَهُمْ اَخُوْهُمْ لُوْطٌ اَلَا تَتَّقُوْنَ ۞

اِنِّىْ لَكُمْ رَسُوْلٌ اَمِيْنٌ ۞

فَاتَّقُوا اللّٰهَ وَاَطِيْعُوْنِ ۞

وَمَاۤ اَسْـَٔلُكُمْ عَلَيْهِ مِنْ اَجْرٍ ۚ اِنْ اَجْرِىَ اِلَّا عَلٰى رَبِّ الْعٰلَمِيْنَ ۞

اَتَاْتُوْنَ الذُّكْرَانَ مِنَ الْعٰلَمِيْنَ ۞

Out of all creation have you selected only males for yourselves, and do you leave aside your wives whom your Lord created for you? You are a people who transgress the limits set by nature. They retorted: If thou desist not, Lot, thou wilt surely be banished. He observed: Certainly I detest your practice; and

وَتَذَرُوْنَ مَا خَلَقَ لَكُمْ رَبُّكُمْ مِّنْ اَزْوَاجِكُمْ ؕ بَلْ اَنْتُمْ قَوْمٌ عٰدُوْنَ ۞

قَالُوْا لَئِنْ لَّمْ تَنْتَهِ يٰلُوْطُ لَتَكُوْنَنَّ مِنَ الْمُخْرَجِيْنَ ۞

قَالَ اِنِّىْ لِعَمَلِكُمْ مِّنَ الْقَالِيْنَ ۞

he prayed: Lord, deliver me and my family from their vile conduct. So We delivered him and his family, all of them, except an old woman who stayed behind. Then We destroyed the rest. We sent upon them a rain of stones, and evil is the rain that descends upon those who are warned and disregard the warning. In that surely is a Sign; but most of these would not believe. Surely, it is thy Lord Who is the Mighty, the Ever Merciful. (161—176)

رَبِّ نَجِّنِیْ وَ اَهْلِیْ مِمَّا یَعْمَلُوْنَ ۞

فَنَجَّیْنٰهُ وَ اَهْلَهٗۤ اَجْمَعِیْنَ ۞

اِلَّا عَجُوْزًا فِی الْغٰبِرِیْنَ ۞

ثُمَّ دَمَّرْنَا الْاٰخَرِیْنَ ۞

وَ اَمْطَرْنَا عَلَیْهِمْ مَّطَرًا ۚ فَسَآءَ مَطَرُ الْمُنْذَرِیْنَ ۞

اِنَّ فِیْ ذٰلِكَ لَاٰیَةً ؕ وَ مَا كَانَ اَكْثَرُهُمْ مُّؤْمِنِیْنَ ۞

وَ اِنَّ رَبَّكَ لَهُوَ الْعَزِیْزُ الرَّحِیْمُ ۞

كَذَّبَ اَصْحٰبُ لْـَٔیْكَةِ الْمُرْسَلِیْنَ ۞

اِذْ قَالَ لَهُمْ شُعَیْبٌ اَلَا تَتَّقُوْنَ ۞

اِنِّیْ لَكُمْ رَسُوْلٌ اَمِیْنٌ ۞

فَاتَّقُوا اللّٰهَ وَ اَطِیْعُوْنِ ۞

The People of the Wood rejected the Messengers when Shuaib said to them: Will you not be righteous? I am sent to you as a trusty Messenger. So be mindful of your duty to Allah, and obey me. I ask of you no recompense for it; my recompense is with the Lord of the worlds.

وَ مَاۤ اَسْـَٔلُكُمْ عَلَیْهِ مِنْ اَجْرٍ ۚ اِنْ اَجْرِیَ اِلَّا عَلٰی رَبِّ الْعٰلَمِیْنَ ۞

اَوْفُوا الْكَیْلَ وَ لَا تَكُوْنُوْا مِنَ الْمُخْسِرِیْنَ ۞

وَ زِنُوْا بِالْقِسْطَاسِ الْمُسْتَقِیْمِ ۞

وَ لَا تَبْخَسُوا النَّاسَ اَشْیَآءَهُمْ وَ لَا تَعْثَوْا فِی الْاَرْضِ مُفْسِدِیْنَ ۞

Give full measure, and do not occasion loss to other parties; and weigh out with a true balance. Do not deliver short; and do not go about creating disorder in the land. Fear Him Who created you and the earlier peoples. They retorted: Thou art being put up to this by others who support thee. Thou art but a human being like ourselves, and we are convinced thou art a liar. So cause a fragment of a cloud to fall on us, if thou art truthful.

وَ اتَّقُوا الَّذِیْ خَلَقَكُمْ وَ الْجِبِلَّةَ الْاَوَّلِیْنَ ۞

قَالُوْۤا اِنَّمَاۤ اَنْتَ مِنَ الْمُسَحَّرِیْنَ ۞

وَ مَاۤ اَنْتَ اِلَّا بَشَرٌ مِّثْلُنَا وَ اِنْ نَّظُنُّكَ لَمِنَ الْكٰذِبِیْنَ ۞

فَاَسْقِطْ عَلَیْنَا كِسَفًا مِّنَ السَّمَآءِ اِنْ كُنْتَ مِنَ الصّٰدِقِیْنَ ۞

He observed: My Lord knows your conduct well. Thus they rejected him, and
they were afflicted with the chastisement
of the day of overshadowing gloom. That
was indeed the chastisement of a dreadful
day. In that surely is a Sign, but most of
these would not believe. Surely, it is thy
Lord Who is the Mighty, the Ever Merciful. (177—192)

قَالَ رَبِّيْ اَعْلَمُ بِمَا تَعْمَلُوْنَ ۞

فَكَذَّبُوْهُ فَاَخَذَهُمْ عَذَابُ يَوْمِ الظُّلَّةِ ۗ اِنَّهٗ كَانَ عَذَابَ يَوْمٍ عَظِيْمٍ ۞

اِنَّ فِيْ ذٰلِكَ لَاٰيَةً ۗ وَمَا كَانَ اَكْثَرُهُمْ مُّؤْمِنِيْنَ ۞

وَاِنَّ رَبَّكَ لَهُوَ الْعَزِيْزُ الرَّحِيْمُ ۞

وَاِنَّهٗ لَتَنْزِيْلُ رَبِّ الْعٰلَمِيْنَ ۞

نَزَلَ بِهِ الرُّوْحُ الْاَمِيْنُ ۞

عَلٰى قَلْبِكَ لِتَكُوْنَ مِنَ الْمُنْذِرِيْنَ ۞

بِلِسَانٍ عَرَبِيٍّ مُّبِيْنٍ ۞

وَاِنَّهٗ لَفِيْ زُبُرِ الْاَوَّلِيْنَ ۞

اَوَلَمْ يَكُنْ لَّهُمْ اٰيَةً اَنْ يَّعْلَمَهٗ عُلَمٰٓؤُا بَنِيْٓ اِسْرَآءِيْلَ ۞

Verily, this Quran is a revelation from
the Lord of the worlds. The Faithful
Spirit has descended with it on thy heart,
that thou mayest be a Warner, in plain
and clear Arabic tongue. Surely, it is
mentioned in the former Scriptures. Is it
not a Sign for them that the learned
among the children of Israel recognise it?

وَلَوْ نَزَّلْنٰهُ عَلٰى بَعْضِ الْاَعْجَمِيْنَ ۞

فَقَرَاَهٗ عَلَيْهِمْ مَّا كَانُوْا بِهٖ مُؤْمِنِيْنَ ۞

كَذٰلِكَ سَلَكْنٰهُ فِيْ قُلُوْبِ الْمُجْرِمِيْنَ ۞

لَا يُؤْمِنُوْنَ بِهٖ حَتّٰى يَرَوُا الْعَذَابَ الْاَلِيْمَ ۞

فَيَاْتِيَهُمْ بَغْتَةً وَّهُمْ لَا يَشْعُرُوْنَ ۞

فَيَقُوْلُوْا هَلْ نَحْنُ مُنْظَرُوْنَ ۞

اَفَبِعَذَابِنَا يَسْتَعْجِلُوْنَ ۞

اَفَرَءَيْتَ اِنْ مَّتَّعْنٰهُمْ سِنِيْنَ ۞

ثُمَّ جَآءَهُمْ مَّا كَانُوْا يُوْعَدُوْنَ ۞

مَاۤ اَغْنٰى عَنْهُمْ مَّا كَانُوْا يُمَتَّعُوْنَ ۞

Had We sent it down to one of the non-
Arabs, and he had recited it to them,
they would never have believed in it.
Thus have We caused disbelief to enter
into the hearts of the sinful. They will not
believe in it till they see the grievous
chastisement. It will come upon them
suddenly unperceived, and they will say:
Shall we be given a respite? Do these
people now seek to hasten Our punishment? Seest thou not that if We were to
provide for them over the years and then
they were afflicted with the promised
punishment, that with which We would
have provided them would be of no avail
to them.

We have never destroyed a township but it has had its Warners, so that its people may be admonished. We are not unjust. (193—210)

وَ مَاۤ اَهْلَكْنَا مِنْ قَرْيَةٍ اِلَّا لَهَا مُنْذِرُوْنَ ۟ۚ ۲۰۹

ذِكْرٰی ۫ۛ وَ مَا کُنَّا ظٰلِمِیْنَ ۲۱۰

وَ مَا تَنَزَّلَتْ بِهِ الشَّیٰطِیْنُ ۲۱۱

وَ مَا یَنْۢبَغِیْ لَهُمْ وَ مَا یَسْتَطِیْعُوْنَ ؕ ۲۱۲

اِنَّهُمْ عَنِ السَّمْعِ لَمَعْزُوْلُوْنَ ؕ ۲۱۳

The Quran has not been brought down by evil agencies. They would not be worthy of it, nor do they possess the capacity. Surely they are debarred from listening to the Divine Word. Call not, therefore, on any god beside Allah, lest thou become one of those chastised. At the outset warn thy nearest kinsmen, and extend kindness and affection to the believers who follow thee. Should they disobey thee in anything warn them: I dissociate myself from that which you do; and put thy trust in the Mighty, the Ever Merciful, Who sees thee when thou standest alone for Prayer, and also sees thy movements in the company of those who prostrate themselves in Prayer along with thee. He is indeed the All-Hearing, the All-Knowing. (211—221)

فَلَا تَدْعُ مَعَ اللّٰهِ اِلٰهًا اٰخَرَ فَتَکُوْنَ مِنَ الْمُعَذَّبِیْنَ ۚ ۲۱۴

وَ اَنْذِرْ عَشِیْرَتَکَ الْاَقْرَبِیْنَ ۙ ۲۱۵

وَ اخْفِضْ جَنَاحَکَ لِمَنِ اتَّبَعَکَ مِنَ الْمُؤْمِنِیْنَ ۚ ۲۱۶

فَاِنْ عَصَوْکَ فَقُلْ اِنِّیْ بَرِیْٓءٌ مِّمَّا تَعْمَلُوْنَ ۚ ۲۱۷

وَ تَوَکَّلْ عَلَی الْعَزِیْزِ الرَّحِیْمِ ۙ ۲۱۸

الَّذِیْ یَرٰىکَ حِیْنَ تَقُوْمُ ۙ ۲۱۹

وَ تَقَلُّبَکَ فِی السّٰجِدِیْنَ ۲۲۰

اِنَّهٗ هُوَ السَّمِیْعُ الْعَلِیْمُ ۲۲۱

هَلْ اُنَبِّئُکُمْ عَلٰی مَنْ تَنَزَّلُ الشَّیٰطِیْنُ ؕ ۲۲۲

تَنَزَّلُ عَلٰی کُلِّ اَفَّاکٍ اَثِیْمٍ ۙ ۲۲۳

یُّلْقُوْنَ السَّمْعَ وَ اَکْثَرُهُمْ کٰذِبُوْنَ ؕ ۲۲۴

Shall I inform you on whom do the evil ones descend? They descend on every lying sinner, repeating what they hear and most of them are liars. It is the erring ones who follow the poets. Seest thou not how the poets wander distracted in every valley and say that which they do not; except those who believe and act righteously, and remember Allah much, and exact retribution only when they are wronged. The wrongdoers will soon know to what place they will return. (222—228)

وَ الشُّعَرَآءُ یَتَّبِعُهُمُ الْغَاوٗنَ ؕ ۲۲۵

اَلَمْ تَرَ اَنَّهُمْ فِیْ کُلِّ وَادٍ یَّهِیْمُوْنَ ۙ ۲۲۶

وَ اَنَّهُمْ یَقُوْلُوْنَ مَا لَا یَفْعَلُوْنَ ۙ ۲۲۷

اِلَّا الَّذِیْنَ اٰمَنُوْا وَ عَمِلُوا الصّٰلِحٰتِ وَ ذَکَرُوا اللّٰهَ کَثِیْرًا وَّ انْتَصَرُوْا مِنْۢ بَعْدِ مَا ظُلِمُوْا ؕ وَ سَیَعْلَمُ الَّذِیْنَ ظَلَمُوْۤا اَیَّ مُنْقَلَبٍ یَّنْقَلِبُوْنَ ۠ ۲۲۸

AL-NAML

(Revealed before Hijra)

In the name of Allah, Most Gracious, Ever Merciful. (1)

THE PURE, THE ALL-HEARING.

These are verses of the Quran and of a perspicuous Book, a guidance and glad tidings for the believers who observe Prayer, and pay the Zakat and have firm faith in the Hereafter. We have made their deeds appear attractive to those who do not believe in the Hereafter, so they wander blindly. It is they who shall suffer a grievous torment and they shall be the greatest losers in the Hereafter. (2—6)

Verily. thou receivest the Quran from the presence of One Wise, All-Knowing. Call to mind when Moses said to the members of his family: I perceive a fire. I will bring back to you thence some news of great import or I will bring you a flaming brand that you may warm yourselves thereat. So when he approached it he was addressed: Blessed is he who is in the fire and he who is near it, and glorified be Allah, the Lord of the worlds. Moses, verily, I am Allah, the Mighty, the Wise.

Put down thy rod. When Moses saw his rod move agitatedly, as though it were a small serpent, he turned back running and did not look back. He was called: Moses, fear not. I am the One in Whose presence the Messengers need have no fear.

368

I am Most Forgiving, Ever Merciful towards him who does wrong and then substitutes good in place of evil. Now put thy hand inside thy cloak next to thy bosom, it will come forth white, without any blemish. This is among nine Signs for Pharaoh and his people: for they are a rebellious people. But when Our sight-giving Signs came to them, they said: This is plain magic; and they persisted in rejecting them wrongfully and arrogantly, while their hearts were convinced of their truth. Observe, then, how evil was the end of those who acted corruptly. (7—15)

اِلَّا مَنْ ظَلَمَ ثُمَّ بَدَّلَ حُسْنًا بَعْدَ سُوٓءٍ فَاِنِّیْ غَفُوْرٌ رَّحِیْمٌ ۝

وَاَدْخِلْ یَدَکَ فِیْ جَیْبِکَ تَخْرُجْ بَیْضَآءَ مِنْ غَیْرِ سُوٓءٍ فِیْ تِسْعِ اٰیٰتٍ اِلٰی فِرْعَوْنَ وَقَوْمِهٖ اِنَّهُمْ کَانُوْا قَوْمًا فٰسِقِیْنَ ۝

فَلَمَّا جَآءَتْهُمْ اٰیٰتُنَا مُبْصِرَةً قَالُوْا هٰذَا سِحْرٌ مُّبِیْنٌ ۝

وَجَحَدُوْا بِهَا وَاسْتَیْقَنَتْهَاۤ اَنْفُسُهُمْ ظُلْمًا وَّعُلُوًّا ۚ فَانْظُرْ کَیْفَ کَانَ عَاقِبَةُ الْمُفْسِدِیْنَ ۝

We bestowed knowledge on David and Solomon, and both affirmed: All praise belongs to Allah, Who has exalted us above many of His believing servants. Solomon succeeded David and said: O ye people, we have been taught the speech of birds; and we have been given all necessary knowledge. This indeed is Allah's manifest grace. On one occasion Solomon's hosts of Jinn and men and birds were assembled before him in separate divisions and they were ordered to march. When they came to the Valley of Al-Naml a woman of the tribe of the Naml said: O ye Naml, go into your habitations, lest Solomon and his hosts crush you unknowingly.

وَلَقَدْ اٰتَیْنَا دَاوٗدَ وَسُلَیْمٰنَ عِلْمًا وَّقَالَا الْحَمْدُ لِلّٰهِ الَّذِیْ فَضَّلَنَا عَلٰی کَثِیْرٍ مِّنْ عِبَادِهِ الْمُؤْمِنِیْنَ ۝

وَوَرِثَ سُلَیْمٰنُ دَاوٗدَ وَقَالَ یٰۤاَیُّهَا النَّاسُ عُلِّمْنَا مَنْطِقَ الطَّیْرِ وَاُوْتِیْنَا مِنْ کُلِّ شَیْءٍ ؕ اِنَّ هٰذَا لَهُوَ الْفَضْلُ الْمُبِیْنُ ۝

وَحُشِرَ لِسُلَیْمٰنَ جُنُوْدُهٗ مِنَ الْجِنِّ وَالْاِنْسِ وَالطَّیْرِ فَهُمْ یُوْزَعُوْنَ ۝

حَتّٰۤی اِذَاۤ اَتَوْا عَلٰی وَادِ النَّمْلِ ۙ قَالَتْ نَمْلَةٌ یٰۤاَیُّهَا النَّمْلُ ادْخُلُوْا مَسٰکِنَکُمْ ۚ لَا یَحْطِمَنَّکُمْ سُلَیْمٰنُ وَجُنُوْدُهٗ ۙ وَهُمْ لَا یَشْعُرُوْنَ ۝

Solomon laughed at her words and prayed: Lord, grant me the capacity to be grateful for Thy favour which Thou hast bestowed upon me and upon my parents and to act righteously so as to win Thy pleasure; and admit me, by Thy mercy, among Thy righteous servants.

فَتَبَسَّمَ ضَاحِکًا مِّنْ قَوْلِهَا وَقَالَ رَبِّ اَوْزِعْنِیْۤ اَنْ اَشْکُرَ نِعْمَتَکَ الَّتِیْۤ اَنْعَمْتَ عَلَیَّ وَعَلٰی وَالِدَیَّ وَاَنْ اَعْمَلَ صَالِحًا تَرْضٰهُ وَاَدْخِلْنِیْ بِرَحْمَتِکَ

Then Solomon reviewed the birds, and said: How is it that I do not see Hudhud? Is he, then, absent? I will surely punish him severely or shall order him to be executed, unless he furnishes me with a good reason for his absence. Shortly after, Hudhud appeared and said: I have obtained information which thou dost not possess. I have come to thee from Saba with sure tidings. I found a woman ruling over all of them; she has been granted everything and she has a wondrous throne. I found her and her people worshipping the sun, instead of Allah. Satan has made their conduct look handsome to them, and has thus hindered them from the right way, so that they follow not guidance. He has bidden them not to worship Allah; while Allah is He Who brings to light the hidden measure of all that is in the heavens and the earth, and Who knows that which you conceal and that which you make known. Allah, there is no god but He, the Lord of the Mighty Throne. Solomon said: We shall see whether thou hast spoken the truth, or whether thou art a liar. Go with this letter of mine and lay it before them; then withdraw from them and see what answer they return. (16—29)

The Queen took counsel. Ye chiefs, a noble letter has been delivered to me. It is from Solomon. It reads: In the name of Allah, Most Gracious, Ever Merciful. Behave not arrogantly towards me in this matter, but come to me in submission. Now counsel me in this, ye Chiefs.

فِىْ عِبَادِكَ الصّٰلِحِيْنَ ۞

وَ تَفَقَّدَ الطَّيْرَ فَقَالَ مَالِىَ لَاۤ اَرَى الْهُدْهُدَ ۖ اَمْ كَانَ مِنَ الْغَآئِبِيْنَ ۞

لَاُعَذِّبَنَّهٗ عَذَابًا شَدِيْدًا اَوْ لَاَاذْبَحَنَّهٗۤ اَوْ لَيَاْتِيَنِّىْ بِسُلْطٰنٍ مُّبِيْنٍ ۞

فَمَكَثَ غَيْرَ بَعِيْدٍ فَقَالَ اَحَطْتُّ بِمَا لَمْ تُحِطْ بِهٖ وَجِئْتُكَ مِنْ سَبَاٍ بِنَبَاٍ يَّقِيْنٍ ۞

اِنِّىْ وَجَدْتُّ امْرَاَةً تَمْلِكُهُمْ وَاُوْتِيَتْ مِنْ كُلِّ شَىْءٍ وَّلَهَا عَرْشٌ عَظِيْمٌ ۞

وَجَدْتُّهَا وَقَوْمَهَا يَسْجُدُوْنَ لِلشَّمْسِ مِنْ دُوْنِ اللهِ وَزَيَّنَ لَهُمُ الشَّيْطٰنُ اَعْمَالَهُمْ فَصَدَّهُمْ عَنِ السَّبِيْلِ فَهُمْ لَا يَهْتَدُوْنَ ۞

اَلَّا يَسْجُدُوْا لِلّٰهِ الَّذِىْ يُخْرِجُ الْخَبْءَ فِى السَّمٰوٰتِ وَالْاَرْضِ وَيَعْلَمُ مَا تُخْفُوْنَ وَمَا تُعْلِنُوْنَ ۞

اَللهُ لَاۤ اِلٰهَ اِلَّا هُوَ رَبُّ الْعَرْشِ الْعَظِيْمِ ۩ ۞

قَالَ سَنَنْظُرُ اَصَدَقْتَ اَمْ كُنْتَ مِنَ الْكٰذِبِيْنَ ۞

اِذْهَبْ بِّكِتٰبِىْ هٰذَا فَاَلْقِهْ اِلَيْهِمْ ثُمَّ تَوَلَّ عَنْهُمْ فَانْظُرْ مَاذَا يَرْجِعُوْنَ ۞

قَالَتْ يٰۤاَيُّهَا الْمَلَؤُا اِنِّىْۤ اُلْقِىَ اِلَىَّ كِتٰبٌ كَرِيْمٌ ۞

اِنَّهٗ مِنْ سُلَيْمٰنَ وَاِنَّهٗ بِسْمِ اللهِ الرَّحْمٰنِ الرَّحِيْمِ ۞

اَلَّا تَعْلُوْا عَلَىَّ وَاْتُوْنِىْ مُسْلِمِيْنَ ۞

قَالَتْ يٰۤاَيُّهَا الْمَلَؤُا اَفْتُوْنِىْ فِىْۤ اَمْرِىْ مَا كُنْتُ

I never decide any affair till I have conferred with you. They said: We are strong
and we possess great prowess in battle,
but the decision is in thy hands. Consider
then what thou wilt command. She said:
Surely, when mighty kings invade a
country they despoil it and humiliate its
leading people. That has been their way.
I have decided to send them gifts and will
see what answer the envoys bring back.
When the embassy came to Solomon, he
said: Do you seek to win my favour by
adding to my wealth? Surely that which
Allah has bestowed on me is better than
that which He has bestowed on you.
It seems to me you take pride in your
gifts. Hudhud, do thou go back to them
and tell them I shall invade them with a
force which they shall not be able to
withstand, and we shall drive them out in
disgrace after they have lost their authority. (30—38)

Solomon asked his nobles: Which of you
will bring me a throne the like of her
throne, before they come to me in submission? A powerful chieftain from among
the people of the hills said: I shall bring
it to thee before thou move camp; and
indeed I possess the means therefor and
I am trustworthy. Thereupon one who had
knowledge of the Book said: I will bring
it to thee in the twinkling of an eye.
When Solomon saw it set before him, he
exclaimed: This is by the grace of my
Lord, that He may try me whether I am
grateful or ungrateful. Whosoever is grateful it is for the good of his own self;
and whosoever is ungrateful, then surely
my Lord is Self-Sufficient, Generous.
Solomon directed: Make this throne even
better than her own so that her own
should appear common to her, and let us
see whether she follows the right way or
remains misguided.

قَاطِعَةً اَمْرًا حَتّٰى تَشْهَدُوْنِ ۞

قَالُوْا نَحْنُ اُولُوْا قُوَّةٍ وَّ اُولُوْا بَأْسٍ شَدِيْدٍ ۙ وَّ
الْاَمْرُ اِلَيْكِ فَانْظُرِىْ مَاذَا تَأْمُرِيْنَ ۞

قَالَتْ اِنَّ الْمُلُوْكَ اِذَا دَخَلُوْا قَرْيَةً اَفْسَدُوْهَا وَ
جَعَلُوْا اَعِزَّةَ اَهْلِهَآ اَذِلَّةً ۚ وَكَذٰلِكَ يَفْعَلُوْنَ ۞

وَاِنِّىْ مُرْسِلَةٌ اِلَيْهِمْ بِهَدِيَّةٍ فَنٰظِرَةٌ ۢ بِمَ يَرْجِعُ
الْمُرْسَلُوْنَ ۞

فَلَمَّا جَآءَ سُلَيْمٰنَ قَالَ اَتُمِدُّوْنَنِ بِمَالٍ ۫ فَمَآ اٰتٰىنِۦَ
اللّٰهُ خَيْرٌ مِّمَّآ اٰتٰىكُمْ ۚ بَلْ اَنْتُمْ بِهَدِيَّتِكُمْ تَفْرَحُوْنَ ۞

اِرْجِعْ اِلَيْهِمْ فَلَنَأْتِيَنَّهُمْ بِجُنُوْدٍ لَّا قِبَلَ لَهُمْ بِهَا
وَلَنُخْرِجَنَّهُمْ مِّنْهَآ اَذِلَّةً وَّهُمْ صٰغِرُوْنَ ۞

قَالَ يٰٓاَيُّهَا الْمَلَؤُا اَيُّكُمْ يَأْتِيْنِىْ بِعَرْشِهَا قَبْلَ اَنْ
يَّأْتُوْنِىْ مُسْلِمِيْنَ ۞

قَالَ عِفْرِيْتٌ مِّنَ الْجِنِّ اَنَا اٰتِيْكَ بِهٖ قَبْلَ اَنْ
تَقُوْمَ مِنْ مَّقَامِكَ ۚ وَاِنِّىْ عَلَيْهِ لَقَوِىٌّ اَمِيْنٌ ۞

قَالَ الَّذِىْ عِنْدَهٗ عِلْمٌ مِّنَ الْكِتٰبِ اَنَا اٰتِيْكَ بِهٖ
قَبْلَ اَنْ يَّرْتَدَّ اِلَيْكَ طَرْفُكَ ۚ فَلَمَّا رَاٰهُ مُسْتَقِرًّا عِنْدَهٗ
قَالَ هٰذَا مِنْ فَضْلِ رَبِّىْ ۖ لِيَبْلُوَنِىْٓ ءَاَشْكُرُ اَمْ
اَكْفُرُ ۚ وَمَنْ شَكَرَ فَاِنَّمَا يَشْكُرُ لِنَفْسِهٖ ۚ وَمَنْ كَفَرَ
فَاِنَّ رَبِّىْ غَنِىٌّ كَرِيْمٌ ۞

قَالَ نَكِّرُوْا لَهَا عَرْشَهَا نَنْظُرْ اَتَهْتَدِىْٓ اَمْ تَكُوْنُ
مِنَ الَّذِيْنَ لَا يَهْتَدُوْنَ ۞

371

So when she came, she was asked: Is thy throne like this? She replied: It looks exactly like it; and we had been informed already of the vastness of your resources and we had submitted. Solomon asked her to desist from worshipping that which she used to worship beside Allah; for she came of a disbelieving people. She was asked to enter the palace. When she saw it she imagined it to be a great expanse of water and was taken aback. Solomon explained: It is a great hall paved smooth with slabs of glass. Thereupon she confessed: Lord, indeed I wronged my soul; and like Solomon I submit myself to Allah, the Lord of the worlds. (39—45)

فَلَمَّا جَآءَتْ قِيلَ اَهٰكَذَا عَرْشُكِ قَالَتْ كَاَنَّهُ هُوَ وَاُوْتِيْنَا الْعِلْمَ مِنْ قَبْلِهَا وَكُنَّا مُسْلِمِيْنَ ۝

وَصَدَّهَا مَا كَانَتْ تَّعْبُدُ مِنْ دُوْنِ اللّٰهِ اِنَّهَا كَانَتْ مِنْ قَوْمٍ كٰفِرِيْنَ ۝

قِيْلَ لَهَا ادْخُلِى الصَّرْحَ فَلَمَّا رَاَتْهُ حَسِبَتْهُ لُجَّةً وَّكَشَفَتْ عَنْ سَاقَيْهَا قَالَ اِنَّهٗ صَرْحٌ مُّمَرَّدٌ مِّنْ قَوَارِيْرَ قَالَتْ رَبِّ اِنِّى ظَلَمْتُ نَفْسِى وَاَسْلَمْتُ مَعَ سُلَيْمٰنَ لِلّٰهِ رَبِّ الْعٰلَمِيْنَ ۝

وَلَقَدْ اَرْسَلْنَآ اِلٰى ثَمُوْدَ اَخَاهُمْ صٰلِحًا اَنِ اعْبُدُوا اللّٰهَ فَاِذَا هُمْ فَرِيْقٰنِ يَخْتَصِمُوْنَ ۝

We sent to Thamud their brother Saleh who admonished them: Worship Allah alone; and at once they were divided into two contending groups. He urged them: O my people, why do you wish to hasten on the evil rather than the good? Wherefore do you not ask forgiveness of Allah that you may be shown mercy? They retorted: We have found thee and those with thee to be ill-omened. He said: The true cause of your ill-fortune is with Allah. The truth is that you are a people that is being tried. There were in the town nine persons who were bent on mischief and were averse to any reform. They conferred together and said: Let us bind ourselves by an oath sworn in the name of Allah that we shall despatch Saleh and his family by night, and to his heir who demands retribution we shall say: We have not witnessed the destruction of his family, and most surely we are telling the truth. Thus they devised a plan, and We also devised a plan, but they were not aware of it. Observe, then, what was the end of their plan. We destroyed them and their people utterly, all together.

قَالَ يٰقَوْمِ لِمَ تَسْتَعْجِلُوْنَ بِالسَّيِّئَةِ قَبْلَ الْحَسَنَةِ لَوْ لَا تَسْتَغْفِرُوْنَ اللّٰهَ لَعَلَّكُمْ تُرْحَمُوْنَ ۝

قَالُوا اطَّيَّرْنَا بِكَ وَبِمَنْ مَّعَكَ قَالَ طٰٓئِرُكُمْ عِنْدَ اللّٰهِ بَلْ اَنْتُمْ قَوْمٌ تُفْتَنُوْنَ ۝

وَكَانَ فِى الْمَدِيْنَةِ تِسْعَةُ رَهْطٍ يُّفْسِدُوْنَ فِى الْاَرْضِ وَلَا يُصْلِحُوْنَ ۝

قَالُوْا تَقَاسَمُوْا بِاللّٰهِ لَنُبَيِّتَنَّهٗ وَاَهْلَهٗ ثُمَّ لَنَقُوْلَنَّ لِوَلِيِّهٖ مَا شَهِدْنَا مَهْلِكَ اَهْلِهٖ وَاِنَّا لَصٰدِقُوْنَ ۝

وَمَكَرُوْا مَكْرًا وَّمَكَرْنَا مَكْرًا وَّهُمْ لَا يَشْعُرُوْنَ ۝

فَانْظُرْ كَيْفَ كَانَ عَاقِبَةُ مَكْرِهِمْ اَنَّا دَمَّرْنٰهُمْ وَقَوْمَهُمْ اَجْمَعِيْنَ ۝

فَتِلْكَ بُيُوْتُهُمْ خَاوِيَةً بِمَا ظَلَمُوْا اِنَّ فِى ذٰلِكَ

Behold their houses in ruin, because of their wrongdoing. In that surely is a Sign for a people who have knowledge. We saved those who had believed and were mindful of their duty to Allah. (46—54)

لَاٰيَةً لِّقَوْمٍ يَّعْلَمُوْنَ ۵۳

وَاَنْجَيْنَا الَّذِيْنَ اٰمَنُوْا وَكَانُوْا يَتَّقُوْنَ ۵۴

وَلُوْطًا اِذْ قَالَ لِقَوْمِهٖۤ اَتَأْتُوْنَ الْفَاحِشَةَ وَاَنْتُمْ تُبْصِرُوْنَ ۵۵

We also sent Lot who admonished his people: Do you commit evil deliberately? Do you approach men lustfully rather than women? You are indeed a perverse people. The only answer of his people was: Drive out Lot and his family from the city. They are people who take pride in their purity. So We delivered him and his family except his wife, whom We held to be of those who stayed behind; and We caused a rain to descend upon them. Evil is the rain that falls upon those who are warned. (55—59)

اَئِنَّكُمْ لَتَأْتُوْنَ الرِّجَالَ شَهْوَةً مِّنْ دُوْنِ النِّسَآءِ ۚ بَلْ اَنْتُمْ قَوْمٌ تَجْهَلُوْنَ ۵۶

فَمَا كَانَ جَوَابَ قَوْمِهٖۤ اِلَّاۤ اَنْ قَالُوْۤا اَخْرِجُوْۤا اٰلَ لُوْطٍ مِّنْ قَرْيَتِكُمْ ۚ اِنَّهُمْ اُنَاسٌ يَّتَطَهَّرُوْنَ ۵۷

فَاَنْجَيْنٰهُ وَاَهْلَهٗۤ اِلَّا امْرَاَتَهٗ ۫ قَدَّرْنٰهَا مِنَ الْغٰبِرِيْنَ ۵۸

وَاَمْطَرْنَا عَلَيْهِمْ مَّطَرًا ۚ فَسَآءَ مَطَرُ الْمُنْذَرِيْنَ ۵۹

قُلِ الْحَمْدُ لِلّٰهِ وَسَلٰمٌ عَلٰى عِبَادِهِ الَّذِيْنَ اصْطَفٰى ۚ آٰللّٰهُ خَيْرٌ اَمَّا يُشْرِكُوْنَ ۶۰

Proclaim: All praise belongs to Allah, and peace be upon those servants of His whom He has chosen. Ask them: Is Allah better or that which they associate with Him? Who created the heavens and the earth, and sent down water from the clouds with which We raise beautiful orchards? You could not raise the trees thereof. Then, is there a god beside Allah? Yet, they are a people who set up equals with Allah. Or, Who made the earth a place of resort, and placed rivers in its midst, and placed upon it firm mountains, and put a barrier between the two waters? Then, is there a god beside Allah? But most of them lack knowledge. Or, Who responds to the afflicted person when he calls upon Him, and removes the affliction, and will make you inheritors of the earth? Then, is there a god beside Allah? Little is it that you heed.

اَمَّنْ خَلَقَ السَّمٰوٰتِ وَالْاَرْضَ وَاَنْزَلَ لَكُمْ مِّنَ السَّمَآءِ مَآءً ۚ فَاَنْبَتْنَا بِهٖ حَدَآئِقَ ذَاتَ بَهْجَةٍ ۚ مَا كَانَ لَكُمْ اَنْ تُنْۢبِتُوْا شَجَرَهَا ۚ ءَاِلٰهٌ مَّعَ اللّٰهِ ۚ بَلْ هُمْ قَوْمٌ يَّعْدِلُوْنَ ۶۱

اَمَّنْ جَعَلَ الْاَرْضَ قَرَارًا وَّجَعَلَ خِلٰلَهَاۤ اَنْهٰرًا وَّجَعَلَ لَهَا رَوَاسِيَ وَجَعَلَ بَيْنَ الْبَحْرَيْنِ حَاجِزًا ۚ ءَاِلٰهٌ مَّعَ اللّٰهِ ۚ بَلْ اَكْثَرُهُمْ لَا يَعْلَمُوْنَ ۶۲

اَمَّنْ يُّجِيْبُ الْمُضْطَرَّ اِذَا دَعَاهُ وَيَكْشِفُ السُّوْٓءَ وَيَجْعَلُكُمْ خُلَفَآءَ الْاَرْضِ ۚ ءَاِلٰهٌ مَّعَ اللّٰهِ ۚ قَلِيْلًا مَّا تَذَكَّرُوْنَ ۶۳

Or, Who guides you in every kind of darkness of the land and of the sea, and Who sends the breezes as heralds of His mercy? Then, is there a god beside Allah? Exalted is Allah above that which they associate with Him. Or, Who originates creation and then repeats it, and Who provides for you from the heaven and the earth? Then, is there a god beside Allah? Urge them: Bring forward your proofs, if you are telling the truth. Declare: None save Allah knows the unseen in the heavens and the earth; nor do they know when will they be raised up. The truth is, their knowledge respecting the Hereafter has reached its limit; they are in doubt concerning it; indeed they are totally blind to it. (60—67)

اَمَّنْ يَّهْدِيْكُمْ فِىْ ظُلُمٰتِ الْبَرِّ وَالْبَحْرِ وَمَنْ يُّرْسِلُ الرِّيٰحَ بُشْرًۢا بَيْنَ يَدَيْ رَحْمَتِهٖؕ ءَاِلٰهٌ مَّعَ اللّٰهِؕ تَعٰلَى اللّٰهُ عَمَّا يُشْرِكُوْنَ ۝

اَمَّنْ يَّبْدَؤُا الْخَلْقَ ثُمَّ يُعِيْدُهٗ وَمَنْ يَّرْزُقُكُمْ مِّنَ السَّمَآءِ وَالْاَرْضِؕ ءَاِلٰهٌ مَّعَ اللّٰهِؕ قُلْ هَاتُوْا بُرْهَانَكُمْ اِنْ كُنْتُمْ صٰدِقِيْنَ ۝

قُلْ لَّا يَعْلَمُ مَنْ فِى السَّمٰوٰتِ وَالْاَرْضِ الْغَيْبَ اِلَّا اللّٰهُؕ وَمَا يَشْعُرُوْنَ اَيَّانَ يُبْعَثُوْنَ ۝

بَلِ ادّٰرَكَ عِلْمُهُمْ فِى الْاٰخِرَةِۗ بَلْ هُمْ فِىْ شَكٍّ مِّنْهَاۗ بَلْ هُمْ مِّنْهَا عَمُوْنَ ۝

وَقَالَ الَّذِيْنَ كَفَرُوْٓا ءَاِذَا كُنَّا تُرٰبًا وَّاٰبَآؤُنَآ اَئِنَّا لَمُخْرَجُوْنَ ۝

لَقَدْ وُعِدْنَا هٰذَا نَحْنُ وَاٰبَآؤُنَا مِنْ قَبْلُۙ اِنْ هٰذَآ اِلَّآ اَسَاطِيْرُ الْاَوَّلِيْنَ ۝

قُلْ سِيْرُوْا فِى الْاَرْضِ فَانْظُرُوْا كَيْفَ كَانَ عَاقِبَةُ الْمُجْرِمِيْنَ ۝

The disbelievers ask: When we and our fathers have become dust, shall we indeed be brought forth again? We and our fathers were promised this before; these are but old stories. Tell them: Travel in the earth and observe what was the end of the sinful ones. Grieve not over them, nor feel distressed at their designs. They ask: When will this promise be fulfilled if you are truthful? Tell them: May be that a part of that which you would hasten on is close behind you. Truly, thy Lord is gracious towards mankind, but most of them are not grateful.

وَلَا تَحْزَنْ عَلَيْهِمْ وَلَا تَكُنْ فِىْ ضَيْقٍ مِّمَّا يَمْكُرُوْنَ ۝

وَيَقُوْلُوْنَ مَتٰى هٰذَا الْوَعْدُ اِنْ كُنْتُمْ صٰدِقِيْنَ ۝

قُلْ عَسٰٓى اَنْ يَّكُوْنَ رَدِفَ لَكُمْ بَعْضُ الَّذِىْ تَسْتَعْجِلُوْنَ ۝

وَاِنَّ رَبَّكَ لَذُوْ فَضْلٍ عَلَى النَّاسِ وَلٰكِنَّ اَكْثَرَهُمْ لَا يَشْكُرُوْنَ ۝

Thy Lord knows well that which they conceal in their minds and that which they disclose. There is nothing hidden in the heaven and the earth, but is recorded in a clear Book. (68—76)

وَاِنَّ رَبَّكَ لَيَعْلَمُ مَا تُكِنُّ صُدُوْرُهُمْ وَمَا يُعْلِنُوْنَ ۞

وَمَا مِنْ غَآئِبَةٍ فِى السَّمَآءِ وَالْاَرْضِ اِلَّا فِىْ كِتٰبٍ مُّبِيْنٍ ۞

اِنَّ هٰذَا الْقُرْاٰنَ يَقُصُّ عَلٰى بَنِىْ اِسْرَآءِيْلَ اَكْثَرَ الَّذِىْ هُمْ فِيْهِ يَخْتَلِفُوْنَ ۞

This Quran expounds to the children of Israel most of that concerning which they differ; and it is a guidance and a mercy for the believers. Thy Lord decides between them by His judgment set forth in the Quran. He is the Mighty, the All-Knowing. So put thy trust in Allah; surely, thou dost take thy stand on manifest truth. Thou canst not make the dead to hear, nor canst thou make the deaf to hear the call, when they turn their backs on it; nor canst thou guide the blind out of their error. Thou canst make only those to hear who believe in Our Signs, for they submit. When the sentence is pronounced against them, We shall bring forth for them an insect out of the earth, which shall bite them because people did not believe in Our Signs. (77—83)

وَاِنَّهٗ لَهُدًى وَّرَحْمَةٌ لِّلْمُؤْمِنِيْنَ ۞

اِنَّ رَبَّكَ يَقْضِىْ بَيْنَهُمْ بِحُكْمِهٖ ۚ وَهُوَ الْعَزِيْزُ الْعَلِيْمُ ۞

فَتَوَكَّلْ عَلَى اللّٰهِ ۚ اِنَّكَ عَلَى الْحَقِّ الْمُبِيْنِ ۞

اِنَّكَ لَا تُسْمِعُ الْمَوْتٰى وَلَا تُسْمِعُ الصُّمَّ الدُّعَآءَ اِذَا وَلَّوْا مُدْبِرِيْنَ ۞

وَمَا اَنْتَ بِهٰدِى الْعُمْىِ عَنْ ضَلٰلَتِهِمْ ۚ اِنْ تُسْمِعُ اِلَّا مَنْ يُّؤْمِنُ بِاٰيٰتِنَا فَهُمْ مُّسْلِمُوْنَ ۞

وَاِذَا وَقَعَ الْقَوْلُ عَلَيْهِمْ اَخْرَجْنَا لَهُمْ دَآبَّةً مِّنَ الْاَرْضِ تُكَلِّمُهُمْ ۙ اَنَّ النَّاسَ كَانُوْا بِاٰيٰتِنَا لَا يُوْقِنُوْنَ ۞

On the day when We shall assemble together from every people a large group from among those who rejected Our Signs, they shall be divided into companies; and when they have all arrived they will be interrogated: Did you reject My Signs because you had not considered them on the basis of knowledge or reason or, else, what were you engaged in? The sentence will be pronounced against them because they did wrong, and they will be speechless. Know they not that We have made the night that they may rest therein and the day sight-giving?

وَيَوْمَ نَحْشُرُ مِنْ كُلِّ اُمَّةٍ فَوْجًا مِّمَّنْ يُّكَذِّبُ بِاٰيٰتِنَا فَهُمْ يُوْزَعُوْنَ ۞

حَتّٰى اِذَا جَآءُوْ قَالَ اَكَذَّبْتُمْ بِاٰيٰتِىْ وَلَمْ تُحِيْطُوْا بِهَا عِلْمًا اَمَّا ذَا كُنْتُمْ تَعْمَلُوْنَ ۞

وَوَقَعَ الْقَوْلُ عَلَيْهِمْ بِمَا ظَلَمُوْا فَهُمْ لَا يَنْطِقُوْنَ ۞

اَلَمْ يَرَوْا اَنَّا جَعَلْنَا الَّيْلَ لِيَسْكُنُوْا فِيْهِ وَالنَّهَارَ

In this there are Signs for a people who believe. On the day when the trumpet is blown, whoever is in the heavens and whoever is in the earth will be terror-stricken, save him whom Allah pleases. All shall come to Him humbled. You see the mountains as if they were firmly fixed, but they shall pass away like the passing of the clouds. This is the work of Allah Who has co-ordinated everything. He knows well what you do. Whoever does good shall have better than that, and they will be secure against terror that day. Whoever does evil shall fall into the Fire face downwards, and will be asked: Are you not rewarded according to your actions? (84—91)

Proclaim: I am commanded to worship the Lord of this city which He has made sacred, and to Him belong all things; and I am commanded to submit wholly to Him, and to recite the Quran. So whoever guides himself thereby, does so to the good of his own self; and whoever goes astray is responsible for himself. Say: I am but a Warner. Proclaim also: All praise belongs to Allah. Soon will He show you His Signs, and you will know them. Thy Lord is not unaware of that which you do. (92—94)

مُبْصِرًا ۙ اِنَّ فِیْ ذٰلِكَ لَاٰیٰتٍ لِّقَوْمٍ یُّؤْمِنُوْنَ ۝

وَیَوْمَ یُنْفَخُ فِی الصُّوْرِ فَفَزِعَ مَنْ فِی السَّمٰوٰتِ وَ مَنْ فِی الْاَرْضِ اِلَّا مَنْ شَآءَ اللّٰهُ ؕ وَكُلٌّ اَتَوْهُ دٰخِرِیْنَ ۝

وَتَرَی الْجِبَالَ تَحْسَبُهَا جَامِدَةً وَّهِیَ تَمُرُّ مَرَّ السَّحَابِ ؕ صُنْعَ اللّٰهِ الَّذِیْۤ اَتْقَنَ كُلَّ شَیْءٍ ؕ اِنَّهٗ خَبِیْرٌۢ بِمَا تَفْعَلُوْنَ ۝

مَنْ جَآءَ بِالْحَسَنَةِ فَلَهٗ خَیْرٌ مِّنْهَا ۚ وَهُمْ مِّنْ فَزَعٍ یَّوْمَئِذٍ اٰمِنُوْنَ ۝

وَمَنْ جَآءَ بِالسَّیِّئَةِ فَكُبَّتْ وُجُوْهُهُمْ فِی النَّارِ ؕ هَلْ تُجْزَوْنَ اِلَّا مَا كُنْتُمْ تَعْمَلُوْنَ ۝

اِنَّمَاۤ اُمِرْتُ اَنْ اَعْبُدَ رَبَّ هٰذِهِ الْبَلْدَةِ الَّذِیْ حَرَّمَهَا وَلَهٗ كُلُّ شَیْءٍ ؗ وَّاُمِرْتُ اَنْ اَكُوْنَ مِنَ الْمُسْلِمِیْنَ ۝

وَاَنْ اَتْلُوَا الْقُرْاٰنَ ۚ فَمَنِ اهْتَدٰی فَاِنَّمَا یَهْتَدِیْ لِنَفْسِهٖ ۚ وَمَنْ ضَلَّ فَقُلْ اِنَّمَاۤ اَنَا مِنَ الْمُنْذِرِیْنَ ۝

وَقُلِ الْحَمْدُ لِلّٰهِ سَیُرِیْكُمْ اٰیٰتِهٖ فَتَعْرِفُوْنَهَا ؕ وَمَا رَبُّكَ بِغَافِلٍ عَمَّا تَعْمَلُوْنَ ۝

AL-QAṢAṢ

(Revealed before Hijra)

In the name of Allah, Most Gracious, Ever Merciful. (1)

بِسْمِ اللهِ الرَّحْمٰنِ الرَّحِيْمِ ۞

THE PURE THE ALL-HEARING EXALTED. (2)

طٰسٓمّٓ ۞

These are verses of the perspicuous Book. (3)

تِلْكَ اٰيٰتُ الْكِتٰبِ الْمُبِيْنِ ۞

نَتْلُوْا عَلَيْكَ مِنْ نَّبَاِ مُوْسٰى وَفِرْعَوْنَ بِالْحَقِّ لِقَوْمٍ يُّؤْمِنُوْنَ ۞

We rehearse unto thee a true account of Moses and Pharaoh, for the benefit of a people who believe. Pharaoh behaved arrogantly in the land, and divided the people thereof into sections, seeking to weaken one section, slaying their male children and sparing the female ones. He was a worker of corruption. We desired to show favour to those who were considered weak in the land, and to make them leaders and make them inheritors of Our bounties, and to establish them in the earth and to show Pharaoh and Haman and their hosts that which they feared. We directed the mother of Moses: Suckle him; and when thou fearest for his life cast him afloat into the river and fear not nor grieve; for We shall restore him to thee and shall make him a Messenger. Then a member of Pharaoh's family picked him up from the river that he might become an enemy and a source of sorrow for them. Verily, Pharaoh and Haman and their hosts were in error. (4—9)

اِنَّ فِرْعَوْنَ عَلَا فِى الْاَرْضِ وَجَعَلَ اَهْلَهَا شِيَعًا يَّسْتَضْعِفُ طَآئِفَةً مِّنْهُمْ يُذَبِّحُ اَبْنَآءَهُمْ وَيَسْتَحْيٖ نِسَآءَهُمْ اِنَّهٗ كَانَ مِنَ الْمُفْسِدِيْنَ ۞

وَنُرِيْدُ اَنْ نَّمُنَّ عَلَى الَّذِيْنَ اسْتُضْعِفُوْا فِى الْاَرْضِ وَنَجْعَلَهُمْ اَئِمَّةً وَّنَجْعَلَهُمُ الْوٰرِثِيْنَ ۞

وَنُمَكِّنَ لَهُمْ فِى الْاَرْضِ وَنُرِىَ فِرْعَوْنَ وَهَامٰنَ وَجُنُوْدَهُمَا مِنْهُمْ مَّا كَانُوْا يَحْذَرُوْنَ ۞

وَاَوْحَيْنَا اِلٰى اُمِّ مُوْسٰى اَنْ اَرْضِعِيْهِ فَاِذَا خِفْتِ عَلَيْهِ فَاَلْقِيْهِ فِى الْيَمِّ وَلَا تَخَافِيْ وَلَا تَحْزَنِيْ اِنَّا رَآدُّوْهُ اِلَيْكِ وَجَاعِلُوْهُ مِنَ الْمُرْسَلِيْنَ ۞

فَالْتَقَطَهٗ اٰلُ فِرْعَوْنَ لِيَكُوْنَ لَهُمْ عَدُوًّا وَّحَزَنًا ۚ اِنَّ فِرْعَوْنَ وَهَامٰنَ وَجُنُوْدَهُمَا كَانُوْا خٰطِئِيْنَ ۞

Pharaoh's wife said: He will prove a source of joy for thee and me. Slay him not; haply he may prove useful for us, or we may even adopt him as a son. They perceived not Allah's purpose.

وَقَالَتِ امْرَاَتُ فِرْعَوْنَ قُرَّتُ عَيْنٍ لِّيْ وَلَكَ ۖ لَا تَقْتُلُوْهُ عَسٰى اَنْ يَّنْفَعَنَا اَوْ نَتَّخِذَهٗ وَلَدًا وَّهُمْ

The heart of the mother of Moses became free from anxiety. Had We not strengthened her heart so that she might be a firm believer in Our grace and mercy, she would have disclosed his identity. She said to his sister: Follow in his wake. So she observed him from afar, but they were not aware of this. We had decreed in advance that he shall refuse the wet-nurses; so his sister said to them: Shall I tell you of a household who will take care of him for you and will be his sincere wellwishers? Thus did We restore him to his mother so that her heart might be at rest and that she might not grieve and should know that Allah's promise always comes to pass. But most of them know not. (10—14)

When Moses reached his age of full strength and attained maturity, We bestowed wisdom and knowledge upon him. Thus do We reward the virtuous. This is how it came about. One day he entered the city at the time of repose and he found therein two men fighting; one of them of his own people and the other from his enemies. He who was of his own people called for his help against the one who was of his enemies. Thereupon Moses smote the latter with his fist and finished him. When Moses perceived this, he exclaimed: This is of Satan's doing; he is indeed an enemy, a manifest misleader; and he prayed: Lord, I have indeed wronged my soul, do Thou forgive me. So He forgave him; He is Most Forgiving, Ever Merciful. Moses affirmed: Lord, because of the favour that Thou hast bestowed upon me, I will never be a helper of the guilty. In the morning he came to the city, apprehensive, watchful; and again the one who had sought his help the day before cried out to him for help. Moses said to him: Thou art mani-

festly a misguided fellow. When he decided to lay hold of the man who was
an enemy of both of them, he called out:
Moses, dost thou desire to kill me as thou
didst kill a man yesterday? It seems thou
wouldst be a tyrant in the land and desirest
not to be a peacemaker. At that moment
there came a man from the far side of the
city, running; and said: Moses, the nobles are
taking counsel together to put thee to
death. Then listen to me and depart from
the city. I am one of thy well-wishers.
So Moses departed, fearful and alert,
praying: Lord, deliver me from the unjust
people. (15—22)

When he started towards Midian, he
said: I am sure, my Lord will guide me
to the right way. When he arrived at the
spring of Midian, he found around it a
crowd of people who were watering their
flocks, and beyond them he saw two
damsels who were holding their flocks
back. Moses asked them: What is your
problem? They replied: We cannot water
our flocks, till the shepherds take away
their flocks; and our father is a very old
man. So Moses watered their flocks for
them; and retired into the shade and
prayed: Lord, I am in need of whatever
of good Thou mayest send down to me.

Presently, one of the two damsels came
up to him walking modestly and said:
My father calls thee that he may reward
thee for thy having watered our flocks
for us. When Moses came to their father
and gave him an account of himself, he
said: Be not afraid; thou hast escaped
from the unjust people.

إِنَّكَ لَغَوِيٌّ مُّبِينٌ ۝

فَلَمَّآ أَنْ أَرَادَ أَن يَبْطِشَ بِالَّذِى هُوَ عَدُوٌّ لَّهُمَا

قَالَ يَا مُوسَى أَتُرِيدُ أَن تَقْتُلَنِى كَمَا قَتَلْتَ نَفْسًا

بِالْأَمْسِ إِن تُرِيدُ إِلَّا أَن تَكُونَ جَبَّارًا فِى الْأَرْضِ

وَمَا تُرِيدُ أَن تَكُونَ مِنَ الْمُصْلِحِينَ ۝

وَجَآءَ رَجُلٌ مِّنْ أَقْصَا الْمَدِينَةِ يَسْعَى قَالَ يَا مُوسَى

إِنَّ الْمَلَأَ يَأْتَمِرُونَ بِكَ لِيَقْتُلُوكَ فَاخْرُجْ إِنِّى لَكَ

مِنَ النَّاصِحِينَ ۝

فَخَرَجَ مِنْهَا خَآئِفًا يَتَرَقَّبُ قَالَ رَبِّ نَجِّنِى مِنَ

الْقَوْمِ الظَّالِمِينَ ۝

وَلَمَّا تَوَجَّهَ تِلْقَآءَ مَدْيَنَ قَالَ عَسَى رَبِّى أَن

يَهْدِيَنِى سَوَآءَ السَّبِيلِ ۝

وَلَمَّا وَرَدَ مَآءَ مَدْيَنَ وَجَدَ عَلَيْهِ أُمَّةً مِّنَ

النَّاسِ يَسْقُونَ وَوَجَدَ مِن دُونِهِمُ امْرَأَتَيْنِ

تَذُودَانِ قَالَ مَا خَطْبُكُمَا قَالَتَا لَا نَسْقِى حَتَّى

يُصْدِرَ الرِّعَآءُ وَأَبُونَا شَيْخٌ كَبِيرٌ ۝

فَسَقَى لَهُمَا ثُمَّ تَوَلَّى إِلَى الظِّلِّ فَقَالَ رَبِّ إِنِّى لِمَآ

أَنزَلْتَ إِلَىَّ مِنْ خَيْرٍ فَقِيرٌ ۝

فَجَآءَتْهُ إِحْدَاهُمَا تَمْشِى عَلَى اسْتِحْيَآءٍ قَالَتْ إِنَّ

أَبِى يَدْعُوكَ لِيَجْزِيَكَ أَجْرَ مَا سَقَيْتَ لَنَا فَلَمَّا

جَآءَهُ وَقَصَّ عَلَيْهِ الْقَصَصَ قَالَ لَا تَخَفْ نَجَوْتَ

مِنَ الْقَوْمِ الظَّالِمِينَ ۝

One of the two damsels suggested: Father, hire him, for the best man thou canst hire is one who is strong and trustworthy. Their father said to Moses: I am willing to give in marriage to thee one of these two daughters of mine on condition that thou serve me on hire for eight years. But if thou dost complete the term of ten years, it will be of thine own accord, I do not desire to be hard on thee; thou wilt find me, if Allah wills, a fair person. Moses said: Then that is settled between thee and me. Whichever of the two terms I complete, there will be no blame on me. Allah is a witness to what we say. (23—29)

When Moses completed the term and set out with his family, he perceived a fire in the direction of the Mount, and said to his family: Wait here awhile, I perceive a fire. May be I can bring you some piece of important news therefrom, or a burning brand from the fire that you may warm yourselves at it. When he came to it, he was called by a voice from a blessed spot in the blessed Valley, from near a tree: Moses, I am Allah, Lord of the worlds; put down thy rod. When he saw it move as if it were a serpent, he turned his back and ran and did not turn to look. Then he was called again: Moses, come forward and be not afraid; surely, thou art safe.

Insert thy hand inside thy cloak; it will come forth white, without blemish; and draw thy arm close to thy body to still thy fear. These two are of the Signs of thy Lord to Pharaoh and his nobles. Surely, they are a disobedient people.

قَالَتْ اِحْدٰىهُمَا يٰٓاَبَتِ اسْتَأْجِرْهُ اِنَّ خَيْرَ مَنِ اسْتَأْجَرْتَ الْقَوِىُّ الْاَمِيْنُ ۞

قَالَ اِنِّىْٓ اُرِيْدُ اَنْ اُنْكِحَكَ اِحْدَى ابْنَتَىَّ هٰتَيْنِ عَلٰٓى اَنْ تَأْجُرَنِىْ ثَمٰنِىَ حِجَجٍ فَاِنْ اَتْمَمْتَ عَشْرًا فَمِنْ عِنْدِكَ وَمَآ اُرِيْدُ اَنْ اَشُقَّ عَلَيْكَ سَتَجِدُنِىْٓ اِنْ شَآءَ اللّٰهُ مِنَ الصّٰلِحِيْنَ ۞

قَالَ ذٰلِكَ بَيْنِىْ وَبَيْنَكَ اَيَّمَا الْاَجَلَيْنِ قَضَيْتُ فَلَا عُدْوَانَ عَلَىَّ وَاللّٰهُ عَلٰى مَا نَقُوْلُ وَكِيْلٌ ۞

فَلَمَّا قَضٰى مُوْسَى الْاَجَلَ وَسَارَ بِاَهْلِهٖٓ اٰنَسَ مِنْ جَانِبِ الطُّوْرِ نَارًا قَالَ لِاَهْلِهِ امْكُثُوْٓا اِنِّىْٓ اٰنَسْتُ نَارًا لَّعَلِّىْٓ اٰتِيْكُمْ مِّنْهَا بِخَبَرٍ اَوْ جَذْوَةٍ مِّنَ النَّارِ لَعَلَّكُمْ تَصْطَلُوْنَ ۞

فَلَمَّآ اَتٰىهَا نُوْدِىَ مِنْ شَاطِئِ الْوَادِ الْاَيْمَنِ فِى الْبُقْعَةِ الْمُبٰرَكَةِ مِنَ الشَّجَرَةِ اَنْ يّٰمُوْسٰىٓ اِنِّىْٓ اَنَا اللّٰهُ رَبُّ الْعٰلَمِيْنَ ۞

وَاَنْ اَلْقِ عَصَاكَ فَلَمَّا رَاٰهَا تَهْتَزُّ كَاَنَّهَا جَآنٌّ وَّلّٰى مُدْبِرًا وَّلَمْ يُعَقِّبْ يٰمُوْسٰىٓ اَقْبِلْ وَلَا تَخَفْ اِنَّكَ مِنَ الْاٰمِنِيْنَ ۞

اُسْلُكْ يَدَكَ فِىْ جَيْبِكَ تَخْرُجْ بَيْضَآءَ مِنْ غَيْرِ سُوْٓءٍ وَّاضْمُمْ اِلَيْكَ جَنَاحَكَ مِنَ الرَّهْبِ فَذٰنِكَ بُرْهَانٰنِ مِنْ رَّبِّكَ اِلٰى فِرْعَوْنَ وَمَلَا۟ىِٕهٖ اِنَّهُمْ كَانُوْا قَوْمًا فٰسِقِيْنَ ۞

Moses pleaded: Lord, I killed one of their people, and I fear that they may kill me and thus prevent me from carrying out Thy behest. My brother Aaron possesses greater facility of speech than I do; send him, therefore, with me as a helper, that he may bear witness to my truth. I fear that they will charge me with falsehood. Allah reassured him: We will strengthen thy arm with thy brother, and We will furnish you both with the means of overcoming them, so that they will not be able to reach you. You two and those who follow you will prevail, through Our Signs. (30—36)

قَالَ رَبِّ اِنِّیْ قَتَلْتُ مِنْهُمْ نَفْسًا فَاَخَافُ اَنْ یَّقْتُلُوْنِ ۝

وَاَخِیْ هٰرُوْنُ هُوَ اَفْصَحُ مِنِّیْ لِسَانًا فَاَرْسِلْهُ مَعِیَ رِدْاً یُّصَدِّقُنِیْ اِنِّیْ اَخَافُ اَنْ یُّکَذِّبُوْنِ ۝

قَالَ سَنَشُدُّ عَضُدَکَ بِاَخِیْکَ وَنَجْعَلُ لَکُمَا سُلْطٰنًا فَلَا یَصِلُوْنَ اِلَیْکُمَا ۚ بِاٰیٰتِنَا ۚ اَنْتُمَا وَمَنِ اتَّبَعَکُمَا الْغٰلِبُوْنَ ۝

فَلَمَّا جَآءَهُمْ مُّوْسٰی بِاٰیٰتِنَا بَیِّنٰتٍ قَالُوْا مَا هٰذَآ اِلَّا سِحْرٌ مُّفْتَرًی وَّمَا سَمِعْنَا بِهٰذَا فِیْۤ اٰبَآئِنَا الْاَوَّلِیْنَ ۝

وَقَالَ مُوْسٰی رَبِّیْۤ اَعْلَمُ بِمَنْ جَآءَ بِالْهُدٰی مِنْ عِنْدِهٖ وَمَنْ تَکُوْنُ لَهٗ عَاقِبَةُ الدَّارِ ۚ اِنَّهٗ لَا یُفْلِحُ الظّٰلِمُوْنَ ۝

وَقَالَ فِرْعَوْنُ یٰۤاَیُّهَا الْمَلَاُ مَا عَلِمْتُ لَکُمْ مِّنْ اِلٰهٍ غَیْرِیْ ۚ فَاَوْقِدْ لِیْ یٰهَامٰنُ عَلَی الطِّیْنِ فَاجْعَلْ لِّیْ صَرْحًا لَّعَلِّیْۤ اَطَّلِعُ اِلٰۤی اِلٰهِ مُوْسٰی ۙ وَاِنِّیْ لَاَظُنُّهٗ مِنَ الْکٰذِبِیْنَ ۝

When Moses came to Pharaoh and his people with Our clear Signs, they exclaimed: This is but sorcery cleverly devised; we never heard of the like of this happening in the time of our forefathers. Moses replied: My Lord knows best who it is that has brought guidance from Him, and who it is who ends up well. The truth is the wrongdoers do not prosper. Pharaoh declared: Ye nobles, I know of no god for you except myself. Burn me bricks of clay, Haman, and build me a high tower, perhaps I may come upon the God of Moses, though I am convinced he is a liar.

وَاسْتَکْبَرَ هُوَ وَجُنُوْدُهٗ فِی الْاَرْضِ بِغَیْرِ الْحَقِّ وَ ظَنُّوْۤا اَنَّهُمْ اِلَیْنَا لَا یُرْجَعُوْنَ ۝

فَاَخَذْنٰهُ وَجُنُوْدَهٗ فَنَبَذْنٰهُمْ فِی الْیَمِّ ۚ فَانْظُرْ کَیْفَ کَانَ عَاقِبَةُ الظّٰلِمِیْنَ ۝

وَجَعَلْنٰهُمْ اَئِمَّةً یَّدْعُوْنَ اِلَی النَّارِ ۚ وَیَوْمَ الْقِیٰمَةِ

He and his hosts behaved arrogantly in the land without justification, and they thought they would never be brought back to Us. So We seized him and his hosts, and cast them into the sea. Observe, then, what was the end of the wrongdoers. We had made them leaders, but they called people to the Fire; and on the Day of Judgment they will not be helped.

We caused them to be followed by a curse in this world and on the Day of Judgment they will be among the wretched. (37—43)

لَا يُنْصَرُوْنَ ۞

وَاَتْبَعْنٰهُمْ فِىْ هٰذِهِ الدُّنْيَا لَعْنَةً ۖ وَيَوْمَ الْقِيٰمَةِ هُمْ مِّنَ الْمَقْبُوْحِيْنَ ۞

وَلَقَدْ اٰتَيْنَا مُوْسَى الْكِتٰبَ مِنْ بَعْدِ مَآ اَهْلَكْنَا الْقُرُوْنَ الْاُوْلٰى بَصَآئِرَ لِلنَّاسِ وَهُدًى وَّرَحْمَةً لَّعَلَّهُمْ يَتَذَكَّرُوْنَ ۞

After We had destroyed the earlier generations, We gave Moses the Book which bestowed spiritual vision on people, and was a guidance and a mercy that they may reflect. Thou wast not present on the western side of the Mount when We committed the matter to Moses, nor wast thou among the witnesses. But We created many generations and a long time passed away for them, and they forgot the prophecies contained in the Torah concerning thy advent. Nor wast thou a dweller among the people of Midian rehearsing Our Signs unto them; but it is We Who send Messengers; so We sent Moses in his time, and generations after him We sent thee in accordance with the prophecies made by Us through Moses in the Torah. Thou wast not on the side of the Mount when We called Moses, and prophesied through him thy advent. We have sent thee as a mercy from thy Lord, that thou mayest warn a people to whom no Warner had come before thee, that they may take heed. It was lest, if an affliction should befall them because of their misconduct, they should say: Lord, wherefore didst thou not send a Messenger to us that we might have followed Thy Signs and been of the believers? But when the truth came to them from Us, they said: Why has he not been given the like of that which Moses was given? But did they not reject that which Moses was given before? They had said: Moses and Aaron are but two sorcerers who back up each other; and We disbelieve in both. Say to them: Then bring a book revealed by Allah which is a better guide than the Torah and the Quran that I may follow it, if you are truthful.

وَمَا كُنْتَ بِجَانِبِ الْغَرْبِيِّ اِذْ قَضَيْنَآ اِلٰى مُوْسَى الْاَمْرَ وَمَا كُنْتَ مِنَ الشّٰهِدِيْنَ ۞

وَلٰكِنَّآ اَنْشَاْنَا قُرُوْنًا فَتَطَاوَلَ عَلَيْهِمُ الْعُمُرُ ۚ وَمَا كُنْتَ ثَاوِيًا فِىْٓ اَهْلِ مَدْيَنَ تَتْلُوْا عَلَيْهِمْ اٰيٰتِنَا ۙ وَلٰكِنَّا كُنَّا مُرْسِلِيْنَ ۞

وَمَا كُنْتَ بِجَانِبِ الطُّوْرِ اِذْ نَادَيْنَا وَلٰكِنْ رَّحْمَةً مِّنْ رَّبِّكَ لِتُنْذِرَ قَوْمًا مَّآ اَتٰىهُمْ مِّنْ نَّذِيْرٍ مِّنْ قَبْلِكَ لَعَلَّهُمْ يَتَذَكَّرُوْنَ ۞

وَلَوْلَآ اَنْ تُصِيْبَهُمْ مُّصِيْبَةٌ بِمَا قَدَّمَتْ اَيْدِيْهِمْ فَيَقُوْلُوْا رَبَّنَا لَوْلَآ اَرْسَلْتَ اِلَيْنَا رَسُوْلًا فَنَتَّبِعَ اٰيٰتِكَ وَنَكُوْنَ مِنَ الْمُؤْمِنِيْنَ ۞

فَلَمَّا جَآءَهُمُ الْحَقُّ مِنْ عِنْدِنَا قَالُوْا لَوْلَآ اُوْتِىَ مِثْلَ مَآ اُوْتِىَ مُوْسٰى ۚ اَوَلَمْ يَكْفُرُوْا بِمَآ اُوْتِىَ مُوْسٰى مِنْ قَبْلُ ۚ قَالُوْا سِحْرٰنِ تَظَاهَرَا ۗ وَقَالُوْٓا اِنَّا بِكُلٍّ كٰفِرُوْنَ ۞

قُلْ فَاْتُوْا بِكِتٰبٍ مِّنْ عِنْدِ اللّٰهِ هُوَ اَهْدٰى مِنْهُمَآ

Then, if they respond not to thee, know that they but follow their own evil inclinations; and who is more erring than one who follows his evil inclinations without any guidance from Allah? Allah guides not the unjust people. (44—51)

اَتَّبِعْهُ اِنْ كُنْتُمْ صَادِقِيْنَ ۞

فَاِنْ لَّمْ يَسْتَجِيْبُوْا لَكَ فَاعْلَمْ اَنَّمَا يَتَّبِعُوْنَ اَهْوَآءَهُمْ

وَمَنْ اَضَلُّ مِمَّنِ اتَّبَعَ هَوَاهُ بِغَيْرِ هُدًى مِّنَ اللّٰهِ

اِنَّ اللّٰهَ لَا يَهْدِى الْقَوْمَ الظّٰلِمِيْنَ ۞

وَلَقَدْ وَصَّلْنَا لَهُمُ الْقَوْلَ لَعَلَّهُمْ يَتَذَكَّرُوْنَ ۞

Those to whom We gave the Book before the Quran, and to whom We sent revelation, time after time, that they may take heed, recognise the Quran as the truth. When it is recited unto them, they say: We believe in it. Surely, it is the truth from our Lord. We had already submitted to Allah before it. These will receive a double reward, because they have been steadfast. They repel evil with good, and spend out of that which We have given them; and when they hear idle talk, they turn away from it and say: We are responsible for our deeds and you are responsible for yours. Peace unto you, we seek not the ignorant. Surely, thou canst not guide whomsoever thou pleasest; but Allah guides whomsoever He pleases; and He knows well those who would be guided. They say: If we were to follow the guidance with thee we would be destroyed by the people. Have We not established for them a safe Sanctuary, to which are brought fruits of all kinds, as a provision from Us? But most of them know not. How many a township have We destroyed the people of which had become arrogant on account of their affluence! These are their dwellings, inhabited but little after them. It is We Who became the Inheritor.

الَّذِيْنَ اٰتَيْنٰهُمُ الْكِتٰبَ مِنْ قَبْلِهٖ هُمْ بِهٖ يُؤْمِنُوْنَ ۞

وَاِذَا يُتْلٰى عَلَيْهِمْ قَالُوْٓا اٰمَنَّا بِهٖٓ اِنَّهُ الْحَقُّ مِنْ رَّبِّنَآ

اِنَّا كُنَّا مِنْ قَبْلِهٖ مُسْلِمِيْنَ ۞

اُولٰٓئِكَ يُؤْتَوْنَ اَجْرَهُمْ مَّرَّتَيْنِ بِمَا صَبَرُوْا وَ

يَدْرَءُوْنَ بِالْحَسَنَةِ السَّيِّئَةَ وَمِمَّا رَزَقْنٰهُمْ يُنْفِقُوْنَ ۞

وَاِذَا سَمِعُوا اللَّغْوَ اَعْرَضُوْا عَنْهُ وَقَالُوْا لَنَآ اَعْمَالُنَا

وَلَكُمْ اَعْمَالُكُمْ سَلٰمٌ عَلَيْكُمْ لَا نَبْتَغِى الْجٰهِلِيْنَ ۞

اِنَّكَ لَا تَهْدِيْ مَنْ اَحْبَبْتَ وَلٰكِنَّ اللّٰهَ يَهْدِيْ مَنْ

يَّشَآءُ وَهُوَ اَعْلَمُ بِالْمُهْتَدِيْنَ ۞

وَقَالُوْٓا اِنْ نَّتَّبِعِ الْهُدٰى مَعَكَ نُتَخَطَّفْ مِنْ اَرْضِنَا

اَوَلَمْ نُمَكِّنْ لَّهُمْ حَرَمًا اٰمِنًا يُّجْبٰٓى اِلَيْهِ ثَمَرٰتُ

كُلِّ شَيْءٍ رِّزْقًا مِّنْ لَّدُنَّا وَلٰكِنَّ اَكْثَرَهُمْ لَا يَعْلَمُوْنَ ۞

وَكَمْ اَهْلَكْنَا مِنْ قَرْيَةٍۭ بَطِرَتْ مَعِيْشَتَهَا فَتِلْكَ

مَسٰكِنُهُمْ لَمْ تُسْكَنْ مِّنْ بَعْدِهِمْ اِلَّا قَلِيْلًا وَ

Thy Lord would never destroy a people until He had raised among them a Messenger, reciting unto them Our Signs; nor would We destroy a town unless the people thereof were wrongdoers.

كُنَّا نَحْنُ الْوٰرِثِيْنَ ۞

وَمَا كَانَ رَبُّكَ مُهْلِكَ الْقُرٰى حَتّٰى يَبْعَثَ فِيْٓ اُمِّهَا

رَسُوْلًا يَّتْلُوْا عَلَيْهِمْ اٰيٰتِنَا وَمَا كُنَّا مُهْلِكِى الْقُرٰى

Whatever you are given in this life is but a temporary provision and an ornament therefor; and that which is with Allah is better and more lasting. Will you not then understand? Can he to whom We have promised good in the life to come, and he is sure to see Our promise fulfilled, be like the one whom We have provided with the good things of this life, and then on the Day of Judgment he will be brought up for his accounting? (52—62)

Be mindful of the day when He will call to them: Where are those who, you alleged, were My partners? Those against whom sentence will have been passed, will say: These are those whom we led astray. We led them astray, even as we ourselves had gone astray. We dissociate ourselves from our past. It was not us that these people worshipped. It will be said: Then call your alleged partners; and they will call them, but they will not answer them. They shall witness the punishment. Would that they had followed the guidance. Be mindful of the day when He will call to them and ask: What answer did you make to the Messengers? They will forget all reasoning on that day, and they will not be able to ask each other. But he who repents and believes and works righteousness will surely be among the prosperous. (63—68) Thy Lord creates what He pleases and chooses whomsoever He pleases. They have no choice. Holy is Allah and far above that which they associate with Him. Thy Lord knows that which they conceal in their minds and that which they disclose. He is Allah; there is no god but He. To Him belongs all praise in the beginning and in the end; and His is the judgment and to Him shall you be brought back. (69—71)

Ask them: Tell me, if Allah were to extend the night over you perpetually till the Day of Judgment, what god is there beside Allah who could bring you light? Will you

إِلَّا وَاَهْلُهَا ظٰلِمُوْنَ ۞

وَمَاۤ اُوْتِيْتُمْ مِّنْ شَىْءٍ فَمَتَاعُ الْحَيٰوةِ الدُّنْيَا وَزِيْنَتُهَا ۚ وَمَا عِنْدَ اللّٰهِ خَيْرٌ وَّاَبْقٰى ۖ اَفَلَا تَعْقِلُوْنَ ۞

اَفَمَنْ وَّعَدْنٰهُ وَعْدًا حَسَنًا فَهُوَ لَاقِيْهِ كَمَنْ مَّتَّعْنٰهُ مَتَاعَ الْحَيٰوةِ الدُّنْيَا ثُمَّ هُوَ يَوْمَ الْقِيٰمَةِ مِنَ الْمُحْضَرِيْنَ ۞

وَيَوْمَ يُنَادِيْهِمْ فَيَقُوْلُ اَيْنَ شُرَكَآءِيَ الَّذِيْنَ كُنْتُمْ تَزْعُمُوْنَ ۞

قَالَ الَّذِيْنَ حَقَّ عَلَيْهِمُ الْقَوْلُ رَبَّنَا هٰۤؤُلَاءِ الَّذِيْنَ اَغْوَيْنَا ۚ اَغْوَيْنٰهُمْ كَمَا غَوَيْنَا ۖ تَبَرَّاْنَاۤ اِلَيْكَ ۖ مَا كَانُوْۤا اِيَّانَا يَعْبُدُوْنَ ۞

وَقِيْلَ ادْعُوْا شُرَكَآءَكُمْ فَدَعَوْهُمْ فَلَمْ يَسْتَجِيْبُوْا لَهُمْ وَرَاَوُا الْعَذَابَ ۚ لَوْ اَنَّهُمْ كَانُوْا يَهْتَدُوْنَ ۞

وَيَوْمَ يُنَادِيْهِمْ فَيَقُوْلُ مَاذَاۤ اَجَبْتُمُ الْمُرْسَلِيْنَ ۞

فَعَمِيَتْ عَلَيْهِمُ الْاَنْۢبَآءُ يَوْمَئِذٍ فَهُمْ لَا يَتَسَآءَلُوْنَ ۞

فَاَمَّا مَنْ تَابَ وَاٰمَنَ وَعَمِلَ صَالِحًا فَعَسٰۤى اَنْ يَّكُوْنَ مِنَ الْمُفْلِحِيْنَ ۞

وَرَبُّكَ يَخْلُقُ مَا يَشَآءُ وَيَخْتَارُ ۗ مَا كَانَ لَهُمُ الْخِيَرَةُ ۚ سُبْحٰنَ اللّٰهِ وَتَعٰلٰى عَمَّا يُشْرِكُوْنَ ۞

وَرَبُّكَ يَعْلَمُ مَا تُكِنُّ صُدُوْرُهُمْ وَمَا يُعْلِنُوْنَ ۞

وَهُوَ اللّٰهُ لَاۤ اِلٰهَ اِلَّا هُوَ ۖ لَهُ الْحَمْدُ فِى الْاُوْلٰى وَالْاٰخِرَةِ ۖ وَلَهُ الْحُكْمُ وَاِلَيْهِ تُرْجَعُوْنَ ۞

قُلْ اَرَءَيْتُمْ اِنْ جَعَلَ اللّٰهُ عَلَيْكُمُ الَّيْلَ سَرْمَدًا

384

not then hearken? Ask them also: Tell me, if Allah were to extend the day over you perpetually till the Day of Judgment, what god is there beside Allah who could bring you night wherein you could rest? Will you not then see? Of His mercy has He made for you the night and the day, that you may rest therein and that you may seek of His bounty, and that you may be grateful. (72—74)

إِلَى يَوْمِ الْقِيَامَةِ مَنْ إِلٰهٌ غَيْرُ اللّٰهِ يَأْتِيكُمْ بِضِيَآءٍ ۗ أَفَلَا تَسْمَعُوْنَ ۝

قُلْ أَرَءَيْتُمْ إِنْ جَعَلَ اللّٰهُ عَلَيْكُمُ النَّهَارَ سَرْمَدًا إِلَى يَوْمِ الْقِيَامَةِ مَنْ إِلٰهٌ غَيْرُ اللّٰهِ يَأْتِيكُمْ بِلَيْلٍ تَسْكُنُوْنَ فِيْهِ ۚ أَفَلَا تُبْصِرُوْنَ ۝

وَمِنْ رَّحْمَتِهِ جَعَلَ لَكُمُ الَّيْلَ وَالنَّهَارَ لِتَسْكُنُوْا فِيْهِ وَلِتَبْتَغُوْا مِنْ فَضْلِهِ وَلَعَلَّكُمْ تَشْكُرُوْنَ ۝

On the day when He will call to them and ask: Where are those whom you alleged were My partners? We shall draw from every people a witness and We shall say to them: Bring your proof. Then will they know that the truth belongs to Allah, and that which they used to invent will fall away from them. (75—76)

وَيَوْمَ يُنَادِيْهِمْ فَيَقُوْلُ أَيْنَ شُرَكَآءِيَ الَّذِيْنَ كُنْتُمْ تَزْعُمُوْنَ ۝

وَنَزَعْنَا مِنْ كُلِّ أُمَّةٍ شَهِيْدًا فَقُلْنَا هَاتُوْا بُرْهَانَكُمْ فَعَلِمُوْا أَنَّ الْحَقَّ لِلّٰهِ وَضَلَّ عَنْهُمْ مَّا كَانُوْا يَفْتَرُوْنَ ۝

إِنَّ قَارُوْنَ كَانَ مِنْ قَوْمِ مُوْسَى فَبَغَى عَلَيْهِمْ ۖ وَآتَيْنٰهُ مِنَ الْكُنُوْزِ مَآ إِنَّ مَفَاتِحَهُ لَتَنُوْأُ بِالْعُصْبَةِ أُولِي الْقُوَّةِ ۖ إِذْ قَالَ لَهُ قَوْمُهُ لَا تَفْرَحْ إِنَّ اللّٰهَ لَا يُحِبُّ الْفَرِحِيْنَ ۝

Korah was of the people of Moses, but he oppressed them. We had given him so much treasure that his keys would have weighed down a party of strong men. When his people said to him: Exult not, surely Allah loves not those who exult; and seek the Home of the Hereafter through that which Allah has bestowed on thee; and neglect not thy lot in this world; and do good to people as Allah has done good to thee; and seek not to create mischief in the land, surely Allah loves not the mischief makers; he retorted: All this has been given to me because of my expert knowledge. Did he not know that Allah had destroyed before him people who were mightier and richer than he? The guilty ones are not required to offer explanations of their sins.

وَابْتَغِ فِيْمَآ آتٰىكَ اللّٰهُ الدَّارَ الْآخِرَةَ وَلَا تَنْسَ نَصِيْبَكَ مِنَ الدُّنْيَا وَأَحْسِنْ كَمَآ أَحْسَنَ اللّٰهُ إِلَيْكَ وَلَا تَبْغِ الْفَسَادَ فِي الْأَرْضِ إِنَّ اللّٰهَ لَا يُحِبُّ الْمُفْسِدِيْنَ ۝

قَالَ إِنَّمَآ أُوْتِيْتُهُ عَلٰى عِلْمٍ عِنْدِيْ ۚ أَوَلَمْ يَعْلَمْ أَنَّ اللّٰهَ قَدْ أَهْلَكَ مِنْ قَبْلِهِ مِنَ الْقُرُوْنِ مَنْ هُوَ أَشَدُّ مِنْهُ قُوَّةً وَّأَكْثَرُ جَمْعًا ۚ وَلَا يُسْئَلُ عَنْ ذُنُوْبِهِمُ

One day he went forth before his people in his panoply, and those who were eager for the life of this world exclaimed: Would that we had the like of that which Korah has been given. Indeed, he is the master of a great fortune. But those who had been given true knowledge rebuked them: Ruin seize you, Allah's reward is best for those who believe and act righteously; and it is awarded only to those who are steadfast. Then We caused the earth to swallow him up and his dwelling. There was no party that could help him against Allah, nor could he contrive deliverance for himself. Those who had coveted his position only the day before began to say: Ruin on you! It is only Allah Who enlarges the provision for such of His servants as He pleases, and also straitens it. Had not Allah been gracious to us, He would have caused us to be swallowed up also. Ruin seize you! The ungrateful never prosper. (77—83)

We bestow the Home of the Hereafter on those who desire not self aggrandisement in the earth, nor corruption; and the happy end is for the righteous. He who does good will be given better than that; and he who does evil, such shall not be punished but in proportion to that which they used to do. (84—85)

He Who has made the teaching of the Quran obligatory on thee, will most surely bring thee back to the place of resort. Tell them: My Lord knows best who follows the guidance firmly, and who is in manifest error. Thou didst have no expectation that this perfect Book would be revealed to thee; but it came as a mercy from thy Lord; so never lend thy support to the disbelievers; and let not anyone turn thee away from the Signs of Allah after they have been sent down to thee; and call people to thy Lord, and have no concern with those who ascribe partners to Him. Call not on any other god beside Allah. There is no god but He. Everything will perish except that which is under His care. His is the judgment and to Him will you be brought back. (86—89)

وَادْعُ اِلٰى رَبِّكَ وَلَا تَكُوْنَنَّ مِنَ الْمُشْرِكِيْنَ ۚ وَلَا تَدْعُ مَعَ اللّٰهِ اِلٰهًا اٰخَرَ ۘ لَاۤ اِلٰهَ اِلَّا هُوَ ۟ كُلُّ شَيْءٍ هَالِكٌ اِلَّا وَجْهَهٗ ۚ لَهُ الْحُكْمُ وَاِلَيْهِ تُرْجَعُوْنَ ۞

AL-'ANKABŪT

(Revealed before Hijra)

In the name of Allah, Most Gracious, Ever Merciful. (1)

I AM ALLAH, THE ALL-KNOWING. (2)

Do people imagine that it is enough for them to say: We believe; and that they will not be tried? We certainly tried those who were before them, and now also Allah will bring into the open those who are truthful and those who lie. Do those who do evil imagine that they will escape Us? Ill it is that they judge. He who hopes to meet Allah should know that Allah's appointed time is certainly coming. He is the All-Hearing, All-Knowing. Whoso strives in the cause of Allah, strives but for the good of his own self; verily, Allah is Independent of all creatures. From those who believe and work righteousness, We shall surely remove their ills, and We shall give them the best reward in return for that which they do. (3—8)

We have enjoined on man benevolence towards his parents; but should they contend with thee that thou associate with Me that of which thou hast no knowledge, then in this obey them not. Unto Me is your return, and I shall enlighten you concerning that which you did. Those who believe and work righteousness, them We shall surely admit to the company of the righteous. (9—10)

There are some who say: We believe in Allah; but when they are put to trouble in the cause of Allah, they take the persecution inflicted on them by the people as punishment from Allah. When help comes to you from Allah, they are sure to say: We were with you through all this. Is not Allah well aware of all that passes through the minds of all His creatures? Allah will surely bring into the open those who believe, and will also bring into the open the hypocrites. Those who disbelieve say to those who believe: Follow our way, and we will bear your sins. But they cannot bear aught of their sins. They are certainly liars. It is true, however, that their own burdens will be augmented with other burdens, and they will be questioned on the Day of Judgment concerning that which they fabricated. (11—14)

We sent Noah to his people and he remained with them fifty years short of one thousand. Then the deluge overtook them as they were wrongdoers. But We saved him and those who were with him in the Ark, and made it a Sign for the peoples. (15—16)

We sent Abraham to his people and he said to them: Worship Allah and be mindful of your duty to Him. That is better for you if you but knew. You worship idols beside Allah, and fabricate lies in the matter of religion. Those whom you worship beside Allah have no power to provide sustenance for you. Then seek your sustenance from Allah, and worship Him and be grateful to Him. Unto Him will you be brought back. But if you reject that which I urge upon you, that is nothing new, for people before you also rejected the truth. The Messenger's responsibility is only to convey the message clearly. (17—19)

وَمِنَ النَّاسِ مَنْ يَّقُوْلُ اٰمَنَّا بِاللّٰهِ فَاِذَآ اُوْذِيَ فِى اللّٰهِ جَعَلَ فِتْنَةَ النَّاسِ كَعَذَابِ اللّٰهِ وَلَئِنْ جَآءَ نَصْرٌ مِّنْ رَّبِّكَ لَيَقُوْلُنَّ اِنَّا كُنَّا مَعَكُمْ اَوَلَيْسَ اللّٰهُ بِاَعْلَمَ بِمَا فِىْ صُدُوْرِ الْعٰلَمِيْنَ ۝

وَلَيَعْلَمَنَّ اللّٰهُ الَّذِيْنَ اٰمَنُوْا وَلَيَعْلَمَنَّ الْمُنٰفِقِيْنَ ۝

وَقَالَ الَّذِيْنَ كَفَرُوْا لِلَّذِيْنَ اٰمَنُوا اتَّبِعُوْا سَبِيْلَنَا وَلْنَحْمِلْ خَطٰيٰكُمْ وَمَا هُمْ بِحٰمِلِيْنَ مِنْ خَطٰيٰهُمْ مِّنْ شَىْءٍ اِنَّهُمْ لَكٰذِبُوْنَ ۝

وَلَيَحْمِلُنَّ اَثْقَالَهُمْ وَاَثْقَالًا مَّعَ اَثْقَالِهِمْ وَلَيُسْـَٔلُنَّ يَوْمَ الْقِيٰمَةِ عَمَّا كَانُوْا يَفْتَرُوْنَ ۝

وَلَقَدْ اَرْسَلْنَا نُوْحًا اِلٰى قَوْمِهٖ فَلَبِثَ فِيْهِمْ اَلْفَ سَنَةٍ اِلَّا خَمْسِيْنَ عَامًا فَاَخَذَهُمُ الطُّوْفَانُ وَ هُمْ ظٰلِمُوْنَ ۝

فَاَنْجَيْنٰهُ وَاَصْحٰبَ السَّفِيْنَةِ وَجَعَلْنٰهَآ اٰيَةً لِّلْعٰلَمِيْنَ ۝

وَاِبْرٰهِيْمَ اِذْ قَالَ لِقَوْمِهِ اعْبُدُوا اللّٰهَ وَاتَّقُوْهُ ذٰلِكُمْ خَيْرٌ لَّكُمْ اِنْ كُنْتُمْ تَعْلَمُوْنَ ۝

اِنَّمَا تَعْبُدُوْنَ مِنْ دُوْنِ اللّٰهِ اَوْثَانًا وَّتَخْلُقُوْنَ اِفْكًا اِنَّ الَّذِيْنَ تَعْبُدُوْنَ مِنْ دُوْنِ اللّٰهِ لَا يَمْلِكُوْنَ لَكُمْ رِزْقًا فَابْتَغُوْا عِنْدَ اللّٰهِ الرِّزْقَ وَاعْبُدُوْهُ وَاشْكُرُوْا لَهٗ اِلَيْهِ تُرْجَعُوْنَ ۝

وَاِنْ تُكَذِّبُوْا فَقَدْ كَذَّبَ اُمَمٌ مِّنْ قَبْلِكُمْ وَمَا عَلَى الرَّسُوْلِ اِلَّا الْبَلٰغُ الْمُبِيْنُ ۝

Know they not how Allah originates creation, then repeats it? That indeed is easy for Allah. Tell them: Travel in the earth, and observe how Allah originated the creation, then will He provide the second creation. Surely, Allah has power to do all that He wills. He punishes whom He pleases, and has mercy on whom He pleases; and to Him will you be returned. You cannot defeat His purpose in the earth or in the heaven; nor have you any friend or helper beside Allah. It is those who disbelieve in the Signs of Allah and the meeting with Him, who have despaired of My mercy. They will have a grievous punishment. (20—24)

اَوَلَمْ يَرَوْا كَيْفَ يُبْدِئُ اللّٰهُ الْخَلْقَ ثُمَّ يُعِيْدُهٗ ؕ اِنَّ ذٰلِكَ عَلَى اللّٰهِ يَسِيْرٌ ۝

قُلْ سِيْرُوْا فِى الْاَرْضِ فَانْظُرُوْا كَيْفَ بَدَاَ الْخَلْقَ ثُمَّ اللّٰهُ يُنْشِئُ النَّشْاَةَ الْاٰخِرَةَ ؕ اِنَّ اللّٰهَ عَلٰى كُلِّ شَىْءٍ قَدِيْرٌ ۝

يُعَذِّبُ مَنْ يَّشَآءُ وَيَرْحَمُ مَنْ يَّشَآءُ ۚ وَاِلَيْهِ تُقْلَبُوْنَ ۝ وَمَاۤ اَنْتُمْ بِمُعْجِزِيْنَ فِى الْاَرْضِ وَلَا فِى السَّمَآءِ ۖ وَمَا لَكُمْ مِّنْ دُوْنِ اللّٰهِ مِنْ وَّلِيٍّ وَّلَا نَصِيْرٍ ۝

وَالَّذِيْنَ كَفَرُوْا بِاٰيٰتِ اللّٰهِ وَلِقَآئِهٖۤ اُولٰٓئِكَ يَئِسُوْا مِنْ رَّحْمَتِىْ وَاُولٰٓئِكَ لَهُمْ عَذَابٌ اَلِيْمٌ ۝

The only response of Abraham's people to his exhortations was: Slay him or burn him alive. But Allah delivered him from the fire. In that surely are Signs for a people who would believe. Abraham warned his people: You have taken up the worship of idols, leaving Allah, to promote friendship between yourselves in the present life. But on the Day of Judgment you will deny each other and curse each other. Your abode will be the Fire; and you will have no helpers. Lot was the one who believed in him. Abraham declared: I shall migrate to another land for the sake of my Lord. He is the Mighty, the Wise. We bestowed on him Isaac and Jacob, and We bestowed on his descendants the gifts of Prophethood and the Book, and We gave him his reward in this life, and in the Hereafter he will surely be among the righteous. (25—28)

فَمَا كَانَ جَوَابَ قَوْمِهٖۤ اِلَّاۤ اَنْ قَالُوا اقْتُلُوْهُ اَوْ حَرِّقُوْهُ فَاَنْجٰهُ اللّٰهُ مِنَ النَّارِ ؕ اِنَّ فِىْ ذٰلِكَ لَاٰيٰتٍ لِّقَوْمٍ يُّؤْمِنُوْنَ ۝

وَقَالَ اِنَّمَا اتَّخَذْتُمْ مِّنْ دُوْنِ اللّٰهِ اَوْثَانًا ۙ مَّوَدَّةَ بَيْنِكُمْ فِى الْحَيٰوةِ الدُّنْيَا ۚ ثُمَّ يَوْمَ الْقِيٰمَةِ يَكْفُرُ بَعْضُكُمْ بِبَعْضٍ وَّيَلْعَنُ بَعْضُكُمْ بَعْضًا ۫ وَّمَأْوٰىكُمُ النَّارُ وَمَا لَكُمْ مِّنْ نّٰصِرِيْنَ ۝

فَاٰمَنَ لَهٗ لُوْطٌ ۘ وَقَالَ اِنِّىْ مُهَاجِرٌ اِلٰى رَبِّىْ ؕ اِنَّهٗ هُوَ الْعَزِيْزُ الْحَكِيْمُ ۝

وَوَهَبْنَا لَهٗۤ اِسْحٰقَ وَيَعْقُوْبَ وَجَعَلْنَا فِىْ ذُرِّيَّتِهِ النُّبُوَّةَ وَالْكِتٰبَ وَاٰتَيْنٰهُ اَجْرَهٗ فِى الدُّنْيَا ۚ وَاِنَّهٗ فِى

We sent Lot to his people and he admonished them: You commit an abomination which none among mankind has ever committed before you. Do you indeed approach men lustfully, and commit highway robberies and behave indecently in your meetings? The only response of his people was: Then bring upon us the chastisement of Allah, if thou speakest the truth. Lot prayed: Lord, help me against this wicked people. When Our messengers came to Abraham with glad tidings of the birth of a son, they told him: We are about to destroy the people of this city; surely they are wrongdoers. Abraham said: But Lot lives there. They said: We know well who lives therein. We will surely help save him and his family, except his wife, who will be among those who stay behind.

الْاٰخِرَةِ لَمِنَ الصّٰلِحِیْنَ ۟

وَلُوْطًا اِذْ قَالَ لِقَوْمِهٖۤ اِنَّکُمْ لَتَاْتُوْنَ الْفَاحِشَةَ ۫ مَا سَبَقَکُمْ بِهَا مِنْ اَحَدٍ مِّنَ الْعٰلَمِیْنَ ۟

اَئِنَّکُمْ لَتَاْتُوْنَ الرِّجَالَ وَتَقْطَعُوْنَ السَّبِیْلَ ۬ ۬ ۙ وَ تَاْتُوْنَ فِیْ نَادِیْکُمُ الْمُنْکَرَ ؕ فَمَا کَانَ جَوَابَ قَوْمِهٖۤ اِلَّاۤ اَنْ قَالُوا ائْتِنَا بِعَذَابِ اللّٰهِ اِنْ کُنْتَ مِنَ الصّٰدِقِیْنَ ۟

قَالَ رَبِّ انْصُرْنِیْ عَلَی الْقَوْمِ الْمُفْسِدِیْنَ ۟

وَلَمَّا جَآءَتْ رُسُلُنَاۤ اِبْرٰهِیْمَ بِالْبُشْرٰی ۙ قَالُوْۤا اِنَّا مُهْلِکُوْۤا اَهْلِ هٰذِهِ الْقَرْیَةِ ۚ اِنَّ اَهْلَهَا کَانُوْا ظٰلِمِیْنَ ۟

When Our messengers came to Lot, he was distressed on their account and was greatly embarrassed. They said to him: Fear not, nor grieve. We will deliver thee and thy family, except thy wife, who will be among those who stay behind. We are about to inflict upon the people of this city a punishment from heaven, because of their disobedience. We have left a clear Sign thereof for a people who would understand. (29—36)

قَالَ اِنَّ فِیْهَا لُوْطًا ؕ قَالُوْا نَحْنُ اَعْلَمُ بِمَنْ فِیْهَا ۫ لَنُنَجِّیَنَّهٗ وَاَهْلَهٗۤ اِلَّا امْرَاَتَهٗ ۫ کَانَتْ مِنَ الْغٰبِرِیْنَ ۟

وَلَمَّاۤ اَنْ جَآءَتْ رُسُلُنَا لُوْطًا سِیْٓءَ بِهِمْ وَضَاقَ بِهِمْ ذَرْعًا وَّقَالُوْا لَا تَخَفْ وَلَا تَحْزَنْ ۫ اِنَّا مُنَجُّوْکَ وَاَهْلَکَ اِلَّا امْرَاَتَکَ کَانَتْ مِنَ الْغٰبِرِیْنَ ۟

اِنَّا مُنْزِلُوْنَ عَلٰۤی اَهْلِ هٰذِهِ الْقَرْیَةِ رِجْزًا مِّنَ السَّمَآءِ بِمَا کَانُوْا یَفْسُقُوْنَ ۟

وَلَقَدْ تَّرَکْنَا مِنْهَاۤ اٰیَةً بَیِّنَةً لِّقَوْمٍ یَّعْقِلُوْنَ ۟

We sent to the people of Midian their brother Shuaib, who admonished them: Worship Allah, be mindful of the Last Day, and commit not iniquity in the land, creating disorder.

وَاِلٰی مَدْیَنَ اَخَاهُمْ شُعَیْبًا ۙ فَقَالَ یٰقَوْمِ اعْبُدُوا اللّٰهَ وَارْجُوا الْیَوْمَ الْاٰخِرَ وَلَا تَعْثَوْا فِی الْاَرْضِ مُفْسِدِیْنَ ۟

But they rejected him, and a violent earthquake seized them and they were left prostrate on the ground in their homes. The same happened to 'Ad and Thamud, and their fate is discernible by you by looking at their dwelling places. Satan made their ways appear good to them, and thereby turned them away from the straight path, for all that they were intelligent people. Korah, and Pharoah and Haman were also destroyed. Moses came to them with manifest Signs, but they were arrogant in the land, and they could not outstrip Our chastisement. We seized every one of them on account of their sins; against some of them We sent a violent sandstorm; some were overtaken by a roaring blast; some were swallowed up by the earth; and some We drowned. Allah would not wrong them, but they wronged their own selves. (37—41)

The case of those who take helpers beside Allah is like the case of the spider, who builds itself a house, but the frailest of all structures is the house of the spider, if they but knew. Surely, Allah knows whatever they call upon beside Him. He is the Mighty, the Wise. These are illustrations that We set forth for people, but only those who possess knowledge comprehend them. Allah has created the heavens and the earth for a purpose. In that surely is a Sign for the believers. (42—45)

Recite that which has been revealed to thee of the Book, and observe Prayer. Surely, Prayer shields a votary against indecency and misbehaviour. Verily, the remembrance of Allah possesses the highest beneficence.

Allah knows well that with which you occupy yourselves. Contend not with the people of the Book except on the basis of that which is best, but contend not at all with such of them as are unjust. Tell them: We believe in that which has been revealed to us, and in that which has been revealed to you; our God and your God is One; and to Him we submit. In like manner We sent down this Perfect Book to thee, so those to whom We have given true knowledge of the Torah believe also in the Quran and of these Meccans also there are some who believe in it. It is only the disbelievers who persist in rejecting Our Signs. Thou didst not recite any Book before the revelation of the Quran, nor didst thou write one with thy right hand; in that case those who reject it as a fabrication would have had further cause for doubt. As it is, the Quran is a whole series of clear Signs preserved in the hearts of those who have been given the knowledge; and it is only the unjust who persist in denying Our Signs. They ask: Why are not Signs sent down to him from his Lord? Tell them: Allah has all the Signs; I am but a clear Warner. Does it not suffice them that We have sent down to thee the Perfect Book which is recited to them? In this, surely, there is mercy and admonition for a people who believe. Say to them: Allah is sufficient as a Witness between you and me. He knows all that is in the heavens and the earth. Those who act upon falsehood and disbelieve in Allah are the losers. (46—53)

They challenge thee to hasten on for them the punishment of this life. Had there not been an appointed term, that punishment would have overtaken them already. But it shall surely overtake them unexpectedly, without their being aware of its approach. Then they ask thee to hasten on the punishment of the Hereafter; but surely hell is already encompassing the disbelievers. Then the day is approaching when the torment will overwhelm them from above and from underneath their feet, and Allah will say: Now taste ye the fruit of your actions. (54—56)

393

O My servants who believe, verily My
earth is vast, so worship Me alone. Every
one shall suffer death; then to Us shall you
be brought back. We shall house those who
believe and act righteously, in lofty mansions of Paradise, beneath which rivers
flow. They will abide therein. Excellent is
the reward of those who labour for good,
those who are steadfast and put their trust
in their Lord. (57—60)

اَرْجُلِهِمْ وَيَقُوْلُ ذُوْقُوْا مَا كُنْتُمْ تَعْمَلُوْنَ ۞

يٰعِبَادِيَ الَّذِيْنَ اٰمَنُوْۤا اِنَّ اَرْضِيْ وَاسِعَةٌ فَاِيَّايَ
فَاعْبُدُوْنِ ۞

كُلُّ نَفْسٍ ذَآئِقَةُ الْمَوْتِ ثُمَّ اِلَيْنَا تُرْجَعُوْنَ ۞

وَالَّذِيْنَ اٰمَنُوْا وَعَمِلُوا الصّٰلِحٰتِ لَنُبَوِّئَنَّهُمْ مِّنَ
الْجَنَّةِ غُرَفًا تَجْرِيْ مِنْ تَحْتِهَا الْاَنْهٰرُ خٰلِدِيْنَ فِيْهَا ۚ
نِعْمَ اَجْرُ الْعٰمِلِيْنَ ۙ

Many an animal there is that carries not
its own sustenance about. Allah provides
for them and for you. He is the All-Hearing, the All-Knowing. If thou wert to ask
them: Who has created the heavens and
the earth and pressed into service the sun
and the moon? they will surely answer:
Allah. How then are they being led away!
Allah enlarges the provision for such of
His servants as He pleases, and straitens it
for whom He pleases. Surely, Allah has
full knowledge of all things. If thou wert
to ask them: Who sends down water from
the clouds, and therewith revives the earth
after its death? they will surely answer:
Allah. Say: All praise belongs to Allah.
But most of them understand not. (61—
64)

الَّذِيْنَ صَبَرُوْا وَعَلٰى رَبِّهِمْ يَتَوَكَّلُوْنَ ۞

وَكَاَيِّنْ مِّنْ دَآبَّةٍ لَّا تَحْمِلُ رِزْقَهَا ۖ اللّٰهُ يَرْزُقُهَا
وَاِيَّاكُمْ ۖ وَهُوَ السَّمِيْعُ الْعَلِيْمُ ۞

وَلَئِنْ سَاَلْتَهُمْ مَّنْ خَلَقَ السَّمٰوٰتِ وَالْاَرْضَ وَسَخَّرَ
الشَّمْسَ وَالْقَمَرَ لَيَقُوْلُنَّ اللّٰهُ ۖ فَاَنّٰى يُؤْفَكُوْنَ ۞

اَللّٰهُ يَبْسُطُ الرِّزْقَ لِمَنْ يَّشَآءُ مِنْ عِبَادِهٖ وَيَقْدِرُ
لَهٗ ۚ اِنَّ اللّٰهَ بِكُلِّ شَيْءٍ عَلِيْمٌ ۞

وَلَئِنْ سَاَلْتَهُمْ مَّنْ نَّزَّلَ مِنَ السَّمَآءِ مَآءً فَاَحْيَا بِهِ
الْاَرْضَ مِنْ بَعْدِ مَوْتِهَا لَيَقُوْلُنَّ اللّٰهُ ۚ قُلِ الْحَمْدُ
لِلّٰهِ ۚ بَلْ اَكْثَرُهُمْ لَا يَعْقِلُوْنَ ۞

The hither life is nothing but sport and
pastime, and the Home of the Hereafter
is the only true life, if they but knew.
When they board a vessel, they call on
Allah, with sincere and perfect faith in
Him, to keep them safe; but when He
brings them safe to land, they begin to
ascribe partners to Him; that they may
deny that which We have bestowed on
them and they may enjoy themselves for
a time. But soon will they know the consequences of their conduct.

وَمَا هٰذِهِ الْحَيٰوةُ الدُّنْيَاۤ اِلَّا لَهْوٌ وَّلَعِبٌ ۚ وَاِنَّ
الدَّارَ الْاٰخِرَةَ لَهِيَ الْحَيَوَانُ ۘ لَوْ كَانُوْا يَعْلَمُوْنَ ۞

فَاِذَا رَكِبُوْا فِى الْفُلْكِ دَعَوُا اللّٰهَ مُخْلِصِيْنَ لَهُ الدِّيْنَ ۚ
فَلَمَّا نَجّٰهُمْ اِلَى الْبَرِّ اِذَا هُمْ يُشْرِكُوْنَ ۞

لِيَكْفُرُوْا بِمَاۤ اٰتَيْنٰهُمْ ۙ وَلِيَتَمَتَّعُوْا ۖ فَسَوْفَ يَعْلَمُوْنَ ۞

Do they not know that We have made the
Sanctuary at Mecca a place of security,
while people are snatched away from all
around them? Would they then believe in
falsehood and deny the favour of Allah?
Who is more unjust than one who fabricates a lie concerning Allah, or rejects the
truth when it comes to him? Is there not
a resort in hell for the disbelievers? We
will surely guide in Our ways those who
strive after Us. Verily Allah is with those
who do good. (65—70)

أَوَلَمْ يَرَوْا أَنَّا جَعَلْنَا حَرَمًا اٰمِنًا وَّيُتَخَطَّفُ النَّاسُ مِنْ

حَوْلِهِمْ أَفَبِالْبَاطِلِ يُؤْمِنُوْنَ وَبِنِعْمَةِ اللّٰهِ يَكْفُرُوْنَ ۝

وَمَنْ أَظْلَمُ مِمَّنِ افْتَرٰى عَلَى اللّٰهِ كَذِبًا أَوْ كَذَّبَ

بِالْحَقِّ لَمَّا جَاءَهٗ أَلَيْسَ فِيْ جَهَنَّمَ مَثْوًى لِّلْكٰفِرِيْنَ ۝

وَالَّذِيْنَ جَاهَدُوْا فِيْنَا لَنَهْدِيَنَّهُمْ سُبُلَنَا وَإِنَّ اللّٰهَ

لَمَعَ الْمُحْسِنِيْنَ ۝

Chapter 30

AL-RŪM

(Revealed before Hijra)

In the name of Allah, Most Gracious Ever Merciful. (1)

بِسْمِ اللهِ الرَّحْمٰنِ الرَّحِيْمِ ۝

الٓمّٓ ۝

غُلِبَتِ الرُّوْمُ ۝

I AM ALLAH, THE ALL-KNOWING. (2)

فِىْٓ اَدْنَى الْاَرْضِ وَهُمْ مِّنْ بَعْدِ غَلَبِهِمْ سَيَغْلِبُوْنَ ۝

فِىْ بِضْعِ سِنِيْنَ ۟ لِلّٰهِ الْاَمْرُ مِنْ قَبْلُ وَمِنْ بَعْدُ ۟

وَيَوْمَئِذٍ يَّفْرَحُ الْمُؤْمِنُوْنَ ۝

بِنَصْرِ اللهِ ۘ يَنْصُرُ مَنْ يَّشَآءُ ۘ وَهُوَ الْعَزِيْزُ الرَّحِيْمُ ۝

وَعْدَ اللهِ ۘ لَا يُخْلِفُ اللهُ وَعْدَهٗ وَلٰكِنَّ اَكْثَرَ النَّاسِ لَا يَعْلَمُوْنَ ۝

The Byzantines have been defeated in the land nearby, but after their defeat they will be victorious within a few years; Allah's is the supreme authority before and after, and the believers will rejoice on that day, with the help of Allah. He helps whom He pleases; He is the Mighty, the Ever Merciful. This is the promise of Allah. Allah goes not back on His promise, but most people know it not. They know only the outer aspect of the life of this world, and of the Hereafter they are utterly unmindful. Have they not reflected in their own minds that Allah has created the heavens and the earth and all that is between the two with a purpose and for a fixed term? But most men believe not in the meeting with their Lord. Have they not travelled in the earth and observed what was the end of those before them? They were stronger than these in power, and they tilled the soil and populated the earth more than these have populated it. Their Messengers came to them with manifest Signs. Allah would not wrong them, but they wronged their own selves. The

يَعْلَمُوْنَ ظَاهِرًا مِّنَ الْحَيٰوةِ الدُّنْيَا ۚ وَهُمْ عَنِ الْاٰخِرَةِ هُمْ غٰفِلُوْنَ ۝

اَوَلَمْ يَتَفَكَّرُوْا فِىْٓ اَنْفُسِهِمْ ۗ مَا خَلَقَ اللهُ السَّمٰوٰتِ وَالْاَرْضَ وَمَا بَيْنَهُمَآ اِلَّا بِالْحَقِّ وَاَجَلٍ مُّسَمًّى ۗ وَاِنَّ كَثِيْرًا مِّنَ النَّاسِ بِلِقَآئِ رَبِّهِمْ لَكٰفِرُوْنَ ۝

اَوَلَمْ يَسِيْرُوْا فِى الْاَرْضِ فَيَنْظُرُوْا كَيْفَ كَانَ عَاقِبَةُ الَّذِيْنَ مِنْ قَبْلِهِمْ ۗ كَانُوْٓا اَشَدَّ مِنْهُمْ قُوَّةً وَّاَثَارُوا الْاَرْضَ وَعَمَرُوْهَآ اَكْثَرَ مِمَّا عَمَرُوْهَا وَجَآءَتْهُمْ رُسُلُهُمْ بِالْبَيِّنٰتِ ۗ فَمَا كَانَ اللهُ لِيَظْلِمَهُمْ وَلٰكِنْ كَانُوْٓا اَنْفُسَهُمْ يَظْلِمُوْنَ ۝

end of those who did evil was evil, because they rejected the Signs of Allah and mocked at them. (3—11)

ثُمَّ كَانَ عَاقِبَةَ الَّذِيْنَ اَسَآءُوا السُّوْٓاٰى اَنْ كَذَّبُوْا بِاٰيٰتِ اللّٰهِ وَكَانُوْا بِهَا يَسْتَهْزِءُوْنَ ⑪

اَللّٰهُ يَبْدَؤُا الْخَلْقَ ثُمَّ يُعِيْدُهٗ ثُمَّ اِلَيْهِ تُرْجَعُوْنَ ⑫

وَيَوْمَ تَقُوْمُ السَّاعَةُ يُبْلِسُ الْمُجْرِمُوْنَ ⑬

وَلَمْ يَكُنْ لَّهُمْ مِّنْ شُرَكَآئِهِمْ شُفَعٰٓؤُا وَكَانُوْا بِشُرَكَآئِهِمْ كٰفِرِيْنَ ⑭

Allah originates creation; then He repeats it; then to Him shall you be brought back. On the Day of Judgment the guilty ones will be in despair. They will have no intercessors from among those whom they associate with Allah; in fact they will repudiate such associates. On the Day of Judgment they will become separated from one another. Those who believed and acted righteously will be made happy in a splendid Garden. Those who disbelieved and rejected Our Signs and the meeting of the Hereafter will be brought face to face with punishment. So glorify Allah when you begin the evening and when you begin the morning — to Him belongs all praise in the heavens and the earth — and in the afternoon and when the sun begins to decline. He brings forth the living from the dead, and He brings forth the dead from the living; and revives the earth after its death. In like manner shall you be brought forth. (12—20)

وَيَوْمَ تَقُوْمُ السَّاعَةُ يَوْمَئِذٍ يَّتَفَرَّقُوْنَ ⑮

فَاَمَّا الَّذِيْنَ اٰمَنُوْا وَعَمِلُوا الصّٰلِحٰتِ فَهُمْ فِيْ رَوْضَةٍ يُّحْبَرُوْنَ ⑯

وَاَمَّا الَّذِيْنَ كَفَرُوْا وَكَذَّبُوْا بِاٰيٰتِنَا وَلِقَآئِ الْاٰخِرَةِ فَاُولٰٓئِكَ فِى الْعَذَابِ مُحْضَرُوْنَ ⑰

فَسُبْحٰنَ اللّٰهِ حِيْنَ تُمْسُوْنَ وَحِيْنَ تُصْبِحُوْنَ ⑱

وَلَهُ الْحَمْدُ فِى السَّمٰوٰتِ وَالْاَرْضِ وَعَشِيًّا وَّحِيْنَ تُظْهِرُوْنَ ⑲

يُخْرِجُ الْحَيَّ مِنَ الْمَيِّتِ وَيُخْرِجُ الْمَيِّتَ مِنَ الْحَيِّ وَيُحْيِ الْاَرْضَ بَعْدَ مَوْتِهَاٰ وَكَذٰلِكَ تُخْرَجُوْنَ ⑳

Of His Signs it is that He created you from dust, and lo! you are human beings spread over the earth. Of His Signs it is that He has created mates for you of your own kind that you may find peace of mind through them, and He has put love and tenderness between you. In that surely are Signs for a people who reflect. Of His

وَمِنْ اٰيٰتِهٖ اَنْ خَلَقَكُمْ مِّنْ تُرَابٍ ثُمَّ اِذَآ اَنْتُمْ بَشَرٌ تَنْتَشِرُوْنَ ㉑

وَمِنْ اٰيٰتِهٖ اَنْ خَلَقَ لَكُمْ مِّنْ اَنْفُسِكُمْ اَزْوَاجًا لِّتَسْكُنُوْٓا اِلَيْهَا وَجَعَلَ بَيْنَكُمْ مَّوَدَّةً وَّرَحْمَةً اِنَّ فِيْ ذٰلِكَ لَاٰيٰتٍ لِّقَوْمٍ يَّتَفَكَّرُوْنَ ㉒

Signs is the creation of the heavens and the earth, and the diversity of your tongues and colours. In that surely are Signs for those who possess knowledge. Of His Signs is your sleep by night and by day, and your seeking of His bounty. In that surely are Signs for a people who listen. Of His Signs it is that He shows you the lightning to inspire fear and hope, and He sends down water from the clouds, and quickens therewith the earth after its death. In that surely are Signs for a people who understand. Of His Signs it is that the heaven and the earth stand firm by His command. Then when He calls you to come forth from the earth, at once you will come forth. To Him belongs whosoever is in the heavens and in the earth. All are obedient to Him. He it is Who originates the creation and then repeats it, and it is most easy for Him. His is the most exalted state in the heavens and the earth. He is the Mighty, the Wise. (21—28)

He sets forth an illustration for you from your own selves. Have you, among those whom you possess, partners in that which We have provided for you so that you become equal sharers therein and fear them as you fear each other? Thus do We expound the Signs to a people who understand. But those who are unjust follow their own low desires without any knowledge. Then who can guide him whom Allah adjudges as lost? They will have no helpers. Devote thyself single-mindedly to the Faith, and thus follow the nature designed by Allah, the nature according to which He has fashioned mankind. There is no altering the creation of Allah. That is the everlasting faith. But most people know not.

وَ مِنْ اٰيٰتِهٖ خَلْقُ السَّمٰوٰتِ وَالْاَرْضِ وَاخْتِلَافُ اَلْسِنَتِكُمْ وَ اَلْوَانِكُمْ اِنَّ فِيْ ذٰلِكَ لَاٰيٰتٍ لِّلْعٰلِمِيْنَ ۝

وَ مِنْ اٰيٰتِهٖ مَنَامُكُمْ بِالَّيْلِ وَ النَّهَارِ وَابْتِغَآؤُكُمْ مِّنْ فَضْلِهٖ اِنَّ فِيْ ذٰلِكَ لَاٰيٰتٍ لِّقَوْمٍ يَّسْمَعُوْنَ ۝

وَ مِنْ اٰيٰتِهٖ يُرِيْكُمُ الْبَرْقَ خَوْفًا وَّطَمَعًا وَّيُنَزِّلُ مِنَ السَّمَآءِ مَآءً فَيُحْيٖ بِهِ الْاَرْضَ بَعْدَ مَوْتِهَا اِنَّ فِيْ ذٰلِكَ لَاٰيٰتٍ لِّقَوْمٍ يَّعْقِلُوْنَ ۝

وَ مِنْ اٰيٰتِهٖٓ اَنْ تَقُوْمَ السَّمَآءُ وَالْاَرْضُ بِاَمْرِهٖ ثُمَّ اِذَا دَعَاكُمْ دَعْوَةً مِّنَ الْاَرْضِ اِذَآ اَنْتُمْ تَخْرُجُوْنَ ۝

وَ لَهٗ مَنْ فِي السَّمٰوٰتِ وَالْاَرْضِ كُلٌّ لَّهٗ قٰنِتُوْنَ ۝

وَ هُوَ الَّذِيْ يَبْدَؤُا الْخَلْقَ ثُمَّ يُعِيْدُهٗ وَهُوَ اَهْوَنُ عَلَيْهِ وَ لَهُ الْمَثَلُ الْاَعْلٰى فِي السَّمٰوٰتِ وَالْاَرْضِ وَهُوَ الْعَزِيْزُ الْحَكِيْمُ ۝

ضَرَبَ لَكُمْ مَّثَلًا مِّنْ اَنْفُسِكُمْ هَلْ لَّكُمْ مِّنْ مَّا مَلَكَتْ اَيْمَانُكُمْ مِّنْ شُرَكَآءَ فِيْ مَا رَزَقْنٰكُمْ فَاَنْتُمْ فِيْهِ سَوَآءٌ تَخَافُوْنَهُمْ كَخِيْفَتِكُمْ اَنْفُسَكُمْ كَذٰلِكَ نُفَصِّلُ الْاٰيٰتِ لِقَوْمٍ يَّعْقِلُوْنَ ۝

بَلِ اتَّبَعَ الَّذِيْنَ ظَلَمُوْٓا اَهْوَآءَهُمْ بِغَيْرِ عِلْمٍ فَمَنْ يَّهْدِيْ مَنْ اَضَلَّ اللّٰهُ وَمَا لَهُمْ مِّنْ نّٰصِرِيْنَ ۝

فَاَقِمْ وَجْهَكَ لِلدِّيْنِ حَنِيْفًا فِطْرَتَ اللّٰهِ الَّتِيْ فَطَرَ النَّاسَ عَلَيْهَا لَا تَبْدِيْلَ لِخَلْقِ اللّٰهِ ذٰلِكَ الدِّيْنُ

Adopt the faith, setting your faces towards Him, and be mindful of your duty
to Him, and observe Prayer, and be not
of those who ascribe partners to Allah,
those who split up their religion and became divided into sects; every party
rejoicing in that which they have. (29—
33)

الْقَيِّمُ وَلٰكِنَّ اَكْثَرَ النَّاسِ لَا يَعْلَمُوْنَ ۞

مُنِيْبِيْنَ اِلَيْهِ وَاتَّقُوْهُ وَاَقِيْمُوا الصَّلٰوةَ وَلَا تَكُوْنُوْا
مِنَ الْمُشْرِكِيْنَ ۞

مِنَ الَّذِيْنَ فَرَّقُوْا دِيْنَهُمْ وَكَانُوْا شِيَعًا ۖ كُلُّ حِزْبٍ
بِمَا لَدَيْهِمْ فَرِحُوْنَ ۞

وَاِذَا مَسَّ النَّاسَ ضُرٌّ دَعَوْا رَبَّهُمْ مُّنِيْبِيْنَ اِلَيْهِ
ثُمَّ اِذَآ اَذَاقَهُمْ مِّنْهُ رَحْمَةً اِذَا فَرِيْقٌ مِّنْهُمْ بِرَبِّهِمْ
يُشْرِكُوْنَ ۞

لِيَكْفُرُوْا بِمَآ اٰتَيْنٰهُمْ ۚ فَتَمَتَّعُوْا ۚ فَسَوْفَ تَعْلَمُوْنَ ۞

اَمْ اَنْزَلْنَا عَلَيْهِمْ سُلْطٰنًا فَهُوَ يَتَكَلَّمُ بِمَا كَانُوْا بِهٖ
يُشْرِكُوْنَ ۞

When an affliction befalls people, they
cry unto their Lord, turning wholly to Him.
Then, when they receive mercy from Him,
a section of them associate partners with
their Lord, with the consequence that they
begin to deny that which We have bestowed upon them. So enjoy yourselves
awhile, soon will you know that to which
you are condemned. Have we sent down to
them any authority that speaks in support of
that which they associate with Him? When
people experience Our mercy, they rejoice
therein; but if they encounter tribulation in
consequence of their own actions, they are
in despair. Know they not that Allah
enlarges the provision for whomsoever He
pleases, and straitens it for whomsoever
He pleases? In that surely are Signs for
a people who believe. So render to the
kinsman his due, and to the needy and to
the wayfarer. That is best for those who
seek the pleasure of Allah, and it is they
who will prosper. Whatever you lay out
at interest that it may foster the wealth
of the people, it does not increase in the
sight of Allah; but whatever you remit as
Zakat, seeking the pleasure of Allah, that
is multiplied manifold. Allah is He who
created you, then He provided for you;

وَاِذَآ اَذَقْنَا النَّاسَ رَحْمَةً فَرِحُوْا بِهَا ۚ وَاِنْ تُصِبْهُمْ
سَيِّئَةٌۢ بِمَا قَدَّمَتْ اَيْدِيْهِمْ اِذَا هُمْ يَقْنَطُوْنَ ۞

اَوَلَمْ يَرَوْا اَنَّ اللّٰهَ يَبْسُطُ الرِّزْقَ لِمَنْ يَّشَآءُ وَ
يَقْدِرُ ۚ اِنَّ فِيْ ذٰلِكَ لَاٰيٰتٍ لِّقَوْمٍ يُّؤْمِنُوْنَ ۞

فَاٰتِ ذَا الْقُرْبٰى حَقَّهٗ وَالْمِسْكِيْنَ وَابْنَ السَّبِيْلِ ۚ
ذٰلِكَ خَيْرٌ لِّلَّذِيْنَ يُرِيْدُوْنَ وَجْهَ اللّٰهِ ۚ وَاُولٰٓئِكَ
هُمُ الْمُفْلِحُوْنَ ۞

وَمَآ اٰتَيْتُمْ مِّنْ رِّبًا لِّيَرْبُوَا۟ فِيْٓ اَمْوَالِ النَّاسِ فَلَا
يَرْبُوْا عِنْدَ اللّٰهِ ۚ وَمَآ اٰتَيْتُمْ مِّنْ زَكٰوةٍ تُرِيْدُوْنَ
وَجْهَ اللّٰهِ فَاُولٰٓئِكَ هُمُ الْمُضْعِفُوْنَ ۞

اَللّٰهُ الَّذِيْ خَلَقَكُمْ ثُمَّ رَزَقَكُمْ ثُمَّ يُمِيْتُكُمْ ثُمَّ

then He will cause you to die and thereafter will bring you to life. Is there any
of your alleged partners who can do any
of these things? Holy is He and exalted
above that which they associate with
Him. (34—41)

يُحْيِيْكُمْ ۚ هَلْ مِنْ شُرَكَآئِكُمْ مَّنْ يَّفْعَلُ مِنْ ذٰلِكُمْ مِّنْ شَىْءٍ ۚ سُبْحٰنَهٗ وَ تَعٰلٰى عَمَّا يُشْرِكُوْنَ ۟

ظَهَرَ الْفَسَادُ فِى الْبَرِّ وَالْبَحْرِ بِمَا كَسَبَتْ اَيْدِى النَّاسِ لِيُذِيْقَهُمْ بَعْضَ الَّذِىْ عَمِلُوْا لَعَلَّهُمْ يَرْجِعُوْنَ ۟

Corruption has appeared on land and
sea in consequence of people's misdeeds,
that Allah may afflict them with the consequences of their misconduct, so that
they may turn back from evil. Urge them:
Travel in the earth and observe what was
the end of those who were before you.
Most of them were idolaters. So devote
thyself wholly to the everlasting faith,
before the coming of the day which in
Allah's design cannot be averted, and on
which people will sort themselves out.
Those who disbelieve will bear the consequences thereof, and those who act
righteously will only have prepared for
their own good, that He may reward, out
of His bounty, those who believe and act
righteously. Surely, He loves not the disbelievers. (42—46)

قُلْ سِيْرُوْا فِى الْاَرْضِ فَانْظُرُوْا كَيْفَ كَانَ عَاقِبَةُ الَّذِيْنَ مِنْ قَبْلُ ۚ كَانَ اَكْثَرُهُمْ مُّشْرِكِيْنَ ۟

فَاَقِمْ وَجْهَكَ لِلدِّيْنِ الْقَيِّمِ مِنْ قَبْلِ اَنْ يَّأْتِىَ يَوْمٌ لَّا مَرَدَّ لَهٗ مِنَ اللّٰهِ يَوْمَئِذٍ يَّصَّدَّعُوْنَ ۟

مَنْ كَفَرَ فَعَلَيْهِ كُفْرُهٗ ۚ وَمَنْ عَمِلَ صَالِحًا فَلِاَنْفُسِهِمْ يَمْهَدُوْنَ ۟

لِيَجْزِىَ الَّذِيْنَ اٰمَنُوْا وَعَمِلُوا الصّٰلِحٰتِ مِنْ فَضْلِهٖ ۚ اِنَّهٗ لَا يُحِبُّ الْكٰفِرِيْنَ ۟

Of His Signs it is that He sends the breezes as heralds of good fortune, that He
may grant you of His mercy, and that
vessels may sail at His command, and
that you may seek of His bounty, and
that you may be grateful. Surely We sent
Messengers before thee to their respective
peoples, and they brought them clear
Signs. Then We punished those who were
guilty; it is incumbent upon Us to help
the believers. Allah is He Who sends the
winds, so that they raise the vapours in
the form of clouds which He spreads in
the sky as He pleases, layer upon layer,
and thou seest the rain issuing forth from
their midst. When He causes it to fall on
whom He pleases of His servants, they

وَمِنْ اٰيٰتِهٖ اَنْ يُّرْسِلَ الرِّيَاحَ مُبَشِّرٰتٍ وَّلِيُذِيْقَكُمْ مِّنْ رَّحْمَتِهٖ وَلِتَجْرِىَ الْفُلْكُ بِاَمْرِهٖ وَلِتَبْتَغُوْا مِنْ فَضْلِهٖ وَلَعَلَّكُمْ تَشْكُرُوْنَ ۟

وَلَقَدْ اَرْسَلْنَا مِنْ قَبْلِكَ رُسُلًا اِلٰى قَوْمِهِمْ فَجَآءُوْهُمْ بِالْبَيِّنٰتِ فَانْتَقَمْنَا مِنَ الَّذِيْنَ اَجْرَمُوْا ۚ وَكَانَ حَقًّا عَلَيْنَا نَصْرُ الْمُؤْمِنِيْنَ ۟

اَللّٰهُ الَّذِىْ يُرْسِلُ الرِّيٰحَ فَتُثِيْرُ سَحَابًا فَيَبْسُطُهٗ فِى السَّمَآءِ كَيْفَ يَشَآءُ وَيَجْعَلُهٗ كِسَفًا فَتَرَى الْوَدْقَ يَخْرُجُ مِنْ خِلٰلِهٖ ۚ فَاِذَآ اَصَابَ بِهٖ مَنْ يَّشَآءُ مِنْ

rejoice thereat; though before its coming down they were in despair. Observe, then, the token of Allah's mercy; how He revives the earth after its death. He is the One Who will quicken the dead; for He has power over all things. But if We sent a hot wind and they saw their crops turn yellow, they would certainly begin to show ingratitude.

عِبَادِهٖۤ اِذَا هُمْ يَسْتَبْشِرُوْنَ ۞

وَاِنْ كَانُوْا مِنْ قَبْلِ اَنْ يُّنَزَّلَ عَلَيْهِمْ مِّنْ قَبْلِهٖ لَمُبْلِسِيْنَ ۞

فَانْظُرْ اِلٰۤى اٰثَارِ رَحْمَتِ اللّٰهِ كَيْفَ يُحْيِ الْاَرْضَ بَعْدَ مَوْتِهَا ؕ اِنَّ ذٰلِكَ لَمُحْيِ الْمَوْتٰى ۚ وَهُوَ عَلٰى كُلِّ شَىْءٍ قَدِيْرٌ ۞

Thou canst not make the dead hear, nor the deaf when they turn their backs; nor canst thou guide the blind out of their error. Thou canst make only those hear who would believe in Our Signs and submit. (47—54)

وَلَئِنْ اَرْسَلْنَا رِيْحًا فَرَاَوْهُ مُصْفَرًّا لَّظَلُّوْا مِنْ بَعْدِهٖ يَكْفُرُوْنَ ۞

فَاِنَّكَ لَا تُسْمِعُ الْمَوْتٰى وَلَا تُسْمِعُ الصُّمَّ الدُّعَآءَ اِذَا وَلَّوْا مُدْبِرِيْنَ ۞

وَمَاۤ اَنْتَ بِهٰدِ الْعُمْيِ عَنْ ضَلٰلَتِهِمْ ؕ اِنْ تُسْمِعُ اِلَّا مَنْ يُّؤْمِنُ بِاٰيٰتِنَا فَهُمْ مُّسْلِمُوْنَ ۞

Allah is He Who created you in a state of weakness, and after weakness gave you strength; then, after strength, caused weakness and old age. He creates what He pleases. He is the All-Knowing, the Determiner of the measure. On the day when the Hour arrives the guilty will swear that they stayed in the world only a brief period. Thus did they use to prevaricate.

اَللّٰهُ الَّذِيْ خَلَقَكُمْ مِّنْ ضُعْفٍ ثُمَّ جَعَلَ مِنْ بَعْدِ ضُعْفٍ قُوَّةً ثُمَّ جَعَلَ مِنْ بَعْدِ قُوَّةٍ ضُعْفًا وَّشَيْبَةً ؕ يَخْلُقُ مَا يَشَآءُ ۚ وَهُوَ الْعَلِيْمُ الْقَدِيْرُ ۞

وَيَوْمَ تَقُوْمُ السَّاعَةُ يُقْسِمُ الْمُجْرِمُوْنَ ۚ۬ مَا لَبِثُوْا غَيْرَ سَاعَةٍ ؕ كَذٰلِكَ كَانُوْا يُؤْفَكُوْنَ ۞

But those who are given knowledge and faith will say: You have indeed tarried according to the Book of Allah, till the Day of Revival and this is the Day of Revival, but you do not realise. On that day their excuses will not avail the wrong-doers, nor will they be granted respite. (55—58)

وَقَالَ الَّذِيْنَ اُوْتُوا الْعِلْمَ وَالْاِيْمَانَ لَقَدْ لَبِثْتُمْ فِيْ كِتٰبِ اللّٰهِ اِلٰى يَوْمِ الْبَعْثِ ۫ فَهٰذَا يَوْمُ الْبَعْثِ وَلٰكِنَّكُمْ كُنْتُمْ لَا تَعْلَمُوْنَ ۞

فَيَوْمَئِذٍ لَّا يَنْفَعُ الَّذِيْنَ ظَلَمُوْا مَعْذِرَتُهُمْ وَلَا هُمْ يُسْتَعْتَبُوْنَ ۞

We have expounded in this Quran every type of illustration for the people; yet if thou were to bring a Sign, those who disbelieve will surely say: You are but liars. Thus does Allah seal up the hearts of those who have no knowledge. So be steadfast; the promise of Allah is sure to be fulfilled. Let not those who lack certainty cause thee to shift thy stand. (59—61)

وَلَقَدْ ضَرَبْنَا لِلنَّاسِ فِيْ هٰذَا الْقُرْاٰنِ مِنْ كُلِّ مَثَلٍ وَلَئِنْ جِئْتَهُمْ بِاٰيَةٍ لَّيَقُوْلَنَّ الَّذِيْنَ كَفَرُوْۤا اِنْ اَنْتُمْ اِلَّا مُبْطِلُوْنَ ۝

كَذٰلِكَ يَطْبَعُ اللّٰهُ عَلٰى قُلُوْبِ الَّذِيْنَ لَا يَعْلَمُوْنَ ۝

فَاصْبِرْ اِنَّ وَعْدَ اللّٰهِ حَقٌّ وَّلَا يَسْتَخِفَّنَّكَ الَّذِيْنَ لَا يُوْقِنُوْنَ ۝

سُوْرَةُ لُقْمٰنَ مَكِّيَّةٌ (٣١)

LUQMĀN

(Revealed before Hijra)

In the name of Allah, Most Gracious, Ever Merciful. (1)

بِسْمِ اللهِ الرَّحْمٰنِ الرَّحِيْمِ ۞

الٓمّٓ ۞

تِلْكَ اٰيٰتُ الْكِتٰبِ الْحَكِيْمِ ۞

I AM ALLAH, THE ALL-KNOWING. (2)

هُدًى وَّ رَحْمَةً لِّلْمُحْسِنِيْنَ ۞

الَّذِيْنَ يُقِيْمُوْنَ الصَّلٰوةَ وَيُؤْتُوْنَ الزَّكٰوةَ وَهُمْ بِالْاٰخِرَةِ هُمْ يُوْقِنُوْنَ ۞

اُولٰٓئِكَ عَلٰى هُدًى مِّنْ رَّبِّهِمْ وَ اُولٰٓئِكَ هُمُ الْمُفْلِحُوْنَ ۞

These are verses of the Perfect Book which is full of wisdom, and is a guidance and a mercy for those who discharge their obligations to the full; those who observe Prayer, pay the Zakat and have firm faith in the Hereafter. It is they who follow guidance from their Lord and it is they who shall prosper. Some people spend their time and substance in acquiring idle diversions to lead people astray from the path of Allah, without knowledge, and to make fun of it. For them there will be a humiliating punishment. When Our Signs are recited to such a one, he turns away arrogantly, as though he heard them not, as if there were a heaviness in his ears. So announce to him a painful punishment. For those who believe and work righteousness, there will be Gardens of Delight, wherein they will abide. Allah's promise is true. He is the Mighty, the Wise. He has created the heavens without any visible pillars, and He has placed in the earth firm mountains lest it roll beneath you, and has spread therein all kinds of creatures. We have sent down water from the clouds, and have caused to grow therein every fine species. This is

وَ مِنَ النَّاسِ مَنْ يَّشْتَرِىْ لَهْوَ الْحَدِيْثِ لِيُضِلَّ عَنْ سَبِيْلِ اللهِ بِغَيْرِ عِلْمٍ ۙ وَّيَتَّخِذَهَا هُزُوًا ؕ اُولٰٓئِكَ لَهُمْ عَذَابٌ مُّهِيْنٌ ۞

وَ اِذَا تُتْلٰى عَلَيْهِ اٰيٰتُنَا وَلّٰى مُسْتَكْبِرًا كَاَنْ لَّمْ يَسْمَعْهَا كَاَنَّ فِىْ اُذُنَيْهِ وَقْرًا ۚ فَبَشِّرْهُ بِعَذَابٍ اَلِيْمٍ ۞

اِنَّ الَّذِيْنَ اٰمَنُوْا وَ عَمِلُوا الصّٰلِحٰتِ لَهُمْ جَنّٰتُ النَّعِيْمِ ۙ

خٰلِدِيْنَ فِيْهَا ؕ وَعْدَ اللهِ حَقًّا ؕ وَ هُوَ الْعَزِيْزُ الْحَكِيْمُ ۞

خَلَقَ السَّمٰوٰتِ بِغَيْرِ عَمَدٍ تَرَوْنَهَا وَ اَلْقٰى فِى الْاَرْضِ رَوَاسِىَ اَنْ تَمِيْدَ بِكُمْ وَبَثَّ فِيْهَا مِنْ كُلِّ دَآبَّةٍ ؕ وَ اَنْزَلْنَا مِنَ السَّمَآءِ مَآءً فَاَنْبَتْنَا فِيْهَا مِنْ كُلِّ زَوْجٍ كَرِيْمٍ ۞

Allah's creation. Now show me what those others beside Him have created. The wrongdoers are in manifest error. (3—12)

We bestowed wisdom upon Luqman, and enjoined on him: Be grateful to Allah. Whoso is grateful, is grateful for the good of his own self, and whoso is ungrateful should know that Allah is Self-Sufficient, Praiseworthy. Call to mind when Luqman exhorted his son: Dear son, associate not partners with Allah. Surely, associating partners with Allah is a grievous wrong. (13—14)

We have enjoined upon man concerning his parents: Be grateful to Me and to thy parents. Unto Me is the final return. His mother bears him in travail after travail, and his weaning takes two years. Should they contend with thee to associate with Me that of which thou hast no knowledge, obey them not in that, but keep up thy kindly co-operation with them in worldly matters, and follow the way of him who turns to Me in humility. Then unto Me will be your return and I shall inform you of that which you used to do. (15—16)

Luqman said to his son: Dear son, Allah will surely bring forth the slightest action even if it be of no greater weight than a grain of mustard seed, and be hidden inside a rock or anywhere in the heavens or in the earth. Verily, Allah is the Knower of the most secret matters, All-Aware. Dear son, observe Prayer and enjoin good and forbid evil, and endure steadfastly whatever may befall thee. That is indeed a matter of high resolve. Do not puff up thy cheeks with pride before people, nor tread haughtily upon the earth. Surely, Allah loves not any arrogant boaster. Walk at a moderate pace and restrain thy voice; verily, the most disagreeable sound is the bray of a donkey. (17—20)

هٰذَا خَلْقُ اللّٰهِ فَاَرُوۡنِیۡ مَاذَا خَلَقَ الَّذِیۡنَ مِنۡ دُوۡنِهٖ ۚ بَلِ الظّٰلِمُوۡنَ فِیۡ ضَلٰلٍ مُّبِیۡنٍ ۞

وَلَقَدۡ اٰتَیۡنَا لُقۡمٰنَ الۡحِکۡمَةَ اَنِ اشۡکُرۡ لِلّٰهِ ؕ وَمَنۡ یَّشۡکُرۡ فَاِنَّمَا یَشۡکُرُ لِنَفۡسِهٖ ۚ وَمَنۡ کَفَرَ فَاِنَّ اللّٰهَ غَنِیٌّ حَمِیۡدٌ ۞

وَاِذۡ قَالَ لُقۡمٰنُ لِابۡنِهٖ وَهُوَ یَعِظُهٗ یٰبُنَیَّ لَا تُشۡرِکۡ بِاللّٰهِ ؕ اِنَّ الشِّرۡکَ لَظُلۡمٌ عَظِیۡمٌ ۞

وَوَصَّیۡنَا الۡاِنۡسَانَ بِوَالِدَیۡهِ ۚ حَمَلَتۡهُ اُمُّهٗ وَهۡنًا عَلٰی وَهۡنٍ وَّفِصَالُهٗ فِیۡ عَامَیۡنِ اَنِ اشۡکُرۡ لِیۡ وَلِوَالِدَیۡکَ ؕ اِلَیَّ الۡمَصِیۡرُ ۞

وَاِنۡ جَاهَدٰکَ عَلٰۤی اَنۡ تُشۡرِکَ بِیۡ مَا لَیۡسَ لَکَ بِهٖ عِلۡمٌ ۙ فَلَا تُطِعۡهُمَا وَصَاحِبۡهُمَا فِی الدُّنۡیَا مَعۡرُوۡفًا ۫ وَّاتَّبِعۡ سَبِیۡلَ مَنۡ اَنَابَ اِلَیَّ ۚ ثُمَّ اِلَیَّ مَرۡجِعُکُمۡ فَاُنَبِّئُکُمۡ بِمَا کُنۡتُمۡ تَعۡمَلُوۡنَ ۞

یٰبُنَیَّ اِنَّهَاۤ اِنۡ تَکُ مِثۡقَالَ حَبَّةٍ مِّنۡ خَرۡدَلٍ فَتَکُنۡ فِیۡ صَخۡرَةٍ اَوۡ فِی السَّمٰوٰتِ اَوۡ فِی الۡاَرۡضِ یَاۡتِ بِهَا اللّٰهُ ؕ اِنَّ اللّٰهَ لَطِیۡفٌ خَبِیۡرٌ ۞

یٰبُنَیَّ اَقِمِ الصَّلٰوةَ وَاۡمُرۡ بِالۡمَعۡرُوۡفِ وَانۡهَ عَنِ الۡمُنۡکَرِ وَاصۡبِرۡ عَلٰی مَاۤ اَصَابَکَ ؕ اِنَّ ذٰلِکَ مِنۡ عَزۡمِ الۡاُمُوۡرِ ۞ وَلَا تُصَعِّرۡ خَدَّکَ لِلنَّاسِ وَلَا تَمۡشِ فِی الۡاَرۡضِ مَرَحًا ؕ اِنَّ اللّٰهَ لَا یُحِبُّ کُلَّ مُخۡتَالٍ فَخُوۡرٍ ۞

وَاقۡصِدۡ فِیۡ مَشۡیِکَ وَاغۡضُضۡ مِنۡ صَوۡتِکَ ؕ اِنَّ

Have you not seen that Allah has constrained to your service whatever is in the heavens and whatever is in the earth, and poured out His favours to you, visible and invisible? Yet there are some among men who dispute concerning Allah, without knowledge or guidance, or the authority of an illuminating Book. When it is said to them: Follow that which Allah has revealed; they retort: Indeed not; We shall follow only that which our fathers did. What! Even though Satan should be inviting them to the torment of the Fire, by holding up before them the example of their fathers? He who submits himself completely to Allah and is mindful of all his obligations, is as if he has firmly grasped a strong handle. With Allah rests the end of all affairs. (21—23)

The disbelief of him who does not believe, should not grieve thee. Unto Us will they return and We shall inform them of that which they did. Surely, Allah knows well even their secret thoughts. We shall let them enjoy themselves awhile; then shall We drive them to a severe torment. If thou were to ask them: Who created the heavens and the earth?; they will surely answer: Allah. Say: All praise belongs to Allah. But most of them know not. To Allah belongs whatever is in the heavens and the earth. Verily, Allah is Self-Sufficient, Praiseworthy. If all the trees that are in the earth became pens, and the ocean, reinforced by seven oceans, became ink for transcribing the words of Allah, these would not be exhausted. Surely, Allah is Mighty, Wise. Your creation and your being raised up are like that of a single person. Verily, Allah is All-Hearing, All-Seeing.

Seest thou not that Allah makes the night pass into the day, and makes the day pass into the night, and He has constrained the sun and the moon into service, each pursuing its course during an appointed term, and that Allah is well aware of that which you do? That is because Allah is the Truth and Everlasting, and that which they call upon beside Him is false and perishing, and because it is Allah Who is the Most High and the Incomparably Great. (24—31)

Seest thou not that the vessels sail on the sea carrying the bounty of Allah, that He may show you of His Signs? Therein are surely Signs for every truly steadfast, grateful person. When waves engulf them like so many coverings, they call upon Allah, in full sincerity of faith; but when He brings them safe to land, then some of them adhere to the right course, and the rest revert to their former ways. None denies Our Signs, except a perfidious, ungrateful person. Ye people, be mindful of your duty to your Lord, and fear the day when a father will not be of any avail to his son, and a son will not be of any avail to his father. Allah's promise will surely be fulfilled. So let not the life of this world beguile you, nor let the Arch-Deceiver deceive you concerning Allah. With Allah alone is the knowledge of the Hour. He sends down the rain and knows that which is in the wombs. No person knows what he will earn tomorrow and no person knows in what land he will die. Surely, it is Allah Who is All-Knowing, All-Aware. (32—35)

Chapter 32

سُوْرَةُ السَّجْدَةِ مَكِّيَّة

AL-SAJDAH

(Revealed before Hijra)

In the name of Allah, Most Gracious, Ever Merciful. (1)

بِسْمِ اللهِ الرَّحْمٰنِ الرَّحِيْمِ ۝

الٓمّٓ ۝

I AM ALLAH, THE ALL-KNOWING. (2)

تَنْزِيْلُ الْكِتٰبِ لَا رَيْبَ فِيْهِ مِنْ رَّبِّ الْعٰلَمِيْنَ ۝

أَمْ يَقُوْلُوْنَ افْتَرٰىهُ بَلْ هُوَ الْحَقُّ مِنْ رَّبِّكَ لِتُنْذِرَ قَوْمًا مَّا أَتٰىهُمْ مِّنْ نَّذِيْرٍ مِّنْ قَبْلِكَ لَعَلَّهُمْ يَهْتَدُوْنَ ۝

The revelation of this Book is from the Lord of the worlds; this is a truth beyond doubt. Do they say: He has fabricated it? Nay, it is the everlasting truth from thy Lord, that thou mayest warn a people to whom no Warner has come before thee, that they may be guided. Allah is He Who has created the heavens and the earth, and that which is between the two, in six periods; then He settled Himself on the Throne. You have no helper or intercessor beside Him. Will you not, then, take heed? He will establish His command from the heaven to the earth according to His plan, then it will ascend to Him during a period, which, according to your reckoning, will extend to a thousand years. Such is the Knower of the unseen and the seen, the Mighty, the Ever Merciful Who has created everything in the best condition, and Who began the creation of man from clay. Then He made his progeny from an extract of an insignificant fluid. Then He perfected his faculties and breathed into him of His spirit. He has bestowed upon you hearing and sight and understanding; but little thanks do you give. They ask: Is it, that when we are lost in the earth, we shall then become a new creation? In fact they disbelieve in the meeting with their Lord. Say to them: The angel of death that has been appointed over you will cause you to die; then to your Lord will you be brought back. (3—12)

اللهُ الَّذِيْ خَلَقَ السَّمٰوٰتِ وَالْأَرْضَ وَمَا بَيْنَهُمَا فِيْ سِتَّةِ أَيَّامٍ ثُمَّ اسْتَوٰى عَلَى الْعَرْشِ مَا لَكُمْ مِّنْ دُوْنِهِ مِنْ وَّلِيٍّ وَّلَا شَفِيْعٍ أَفَلَا تَتَذَكَّرُوْنَ ۝

يُدَبِّرُ الْأَمْرَ مِنَ السَّمَآءِ إِلَى الْأَرْضِ ثُمَّ يَعْرُجُ إِلَيْهِ فِيْ يَوْمٍ كَانَ مِقْدَارُهُ أَلْفَ سَنَةٍ مِّمَّا تَعُدُّوْنَ ۝

ذٰلِكَ عٰلِمُ الْغَيْبِ وَالشَّهَادَةِ الْعَزِيْزُ الرَّحِيْمُ ۝

الَّذِيْ أَحْسَنَ كُلَّ شَيْءٍ خَلَقَهُ وَبَدَأَ خَلْقَ الْإِنْسَانِ مِنْ طِيْنٍ ۝

ثُمَّ جَعَلَ نَسْلَهُ مِنْ سُلٰلَةٍ مِّنْ مَّآءٍ مَّهِيْنٍ ۝

ثُمَّ سَوّٰىهُ وَنَفَخَ فِيْهِ مِنْ رُّوْحِهِ وَجَعَلَ لَكُمُ السَّمْعَ وَالْأَبْصَارَ وَالْأَفْئِدَةَ قَلِيْلًا مَّا تَشْكُرُوْنَ ۝

وَقَالُوْٓا أَإِذَا ضَلَلْنَا فِي الْأَرْضِ أَإِنَّا لَفِيْ خَلْقٍ جَدِيْدٍ بَلْ هُمْ بِلِقَآءِ رَبِّهِمْ كٰفِرُوْنَ ۝

قُلْ يَتَوَفّٰىكُمْ مَّلَكُ الْمَوْتِ الَّذِيْ وُكِّلَ بِكُمْ ثُمَّ

If only thou couldst see the guilty ones hanging down their heads before their Lord. They will plead: Lord we have seen and we have heard, so now send us back that we may act righteously. We are now convinced of the truth of what we were told. If We had enforced Our will, We would have given every person his appropriate guidance, but My word has been fulfilled: I will certainly fill hell with men, high and low, all together. Then suffer today — because you forgot today's meeting and in consequence We also forgot you — the lasting torment, which is the reward of what you used to do. (13—15)

إِلَىٰ رَبِّكُمْ تُرْجَعُونَ ۞

وَلَوْ تَرَىٰٓ إِذِ الْمُجْرِمُونَ نَاكِسُوا رُءُوسِهِمْ عِندَ رَبِّهِمْ رَبَّنَآ أَبْصَرْنَا وَسَمِعْنَا فَارْجِعْنَا نَعْمَلْ صَالِحًا إِنَّا مُوقِنُونَ ۞

وَلَوْ شِئْنَا لَاٰتَيْنَا كُلَّ نَفْسٍ هُدَىٰهَا وَلَٰكِنْ حَقَّ الْقَوْلُ مِنِّى لَاَمْلَأَنَّ جَهَنَّمَ مِنَ الْجِنَّةِ وَالنَّاسِ أَجْمَعِينَ ۞

فَذُوقُوا بِمَا نَسِيتُمْ لِقَآءَ يَوْمِكُمْ هَٰذَآ إِنَّا نَسِينَٰكُمْ وَذُوقُوا عَذَابَ الْخُلْدِ بِمَا كُنتُمْ تَعْمَلُونَ ۞

إِنَّمَا يُؤْمِنُ بِـَٔايَٰتِنَا الَّذِينَ إِذَا ذُكِّرُوا بِهَا خَرُّوا سُجَّدًا وَسَبَّحُوا بِحَمْدِ رَبِّهِمْ وَهُمْ لَا يَسْتَكْبِرُونَ ۩ ۞

تَتَجَافَىٰ جُنُوبُهُمْ عَنِ الْمَضَاجِعِ يَدْعُونَ رَبَّهُمْ خَوْفًا وَطَمَعًا وَمِمَّا رَزَقْنَٰهُمْ يُنفِقُونَ ۞

فَلَا تَعْلَمُ نَفْسٌ مَّآ أُخْفِىَ لَهُم مِّن قُرَّةِ أَعْيُنٍ جَزَآءً بِمَا كَانُوا يَعْمَلُونَ ۞

Only those believe in Our Signs who, when they are reminded of them, fall down prostrate and celebrate the praises of their Lord, and are not arrogant. They withdraw themselves from their beds in the latter part of the night for prayers, and they call on their Lord in fear and hope, and spend out of that which We have bestowed on them. No one knows what bliss is kept hidden from them, as a reward for what they used to do. Is he, then, who is a believer, like one who is disobedient? They cannot be held equal. Those who believe and work righteousness, will have Gardens of Eternal Abode, as an entertainment because of that which they used to do. Of those who are disobedient the abode will be the Fire. Every time they desire to come out of it, they will be turned back into it, and they will be told: Suffer the torment of the Fire which you used to deny. We shall afflict them with punishment in this world before the severer chastisement of the Hereafter that they may turn to repentance. Who is

أَفَمَن كَانَ مُؤْمِنًا كَمَن كَانَ فَاسِقًا لَّا يَسْتَوُۥنَ ۞

أَمَّا الَّذِينَ ءَامَنُوا وَعَمِلُوا الصَّٰلِحَٰتِ فَلَهُمْ جَنَّٰتُ الْمَأْوَىٰ نُزُلًا بِمَا كَانُوا يَعْمَلُونَ ۞

وَأَمَّا الَّذِينَ فَسَقُوا فَمَأْوَىٰهُمُ النَّارُ كُلَّمَآ أَرَادُوٓا أَن يَخْرُجُوا مِنْهَآ أُعِيدُوا فِيهَا وَقِيلَ لَهُمْ ذُوقُوا عَذَابَ النَّارِ الَّذِى كُنتُم بِهِ تُكَذِّبُونَ ۞

وَلَنُذِيقَنَّهُم مِّنَ الْعَذَابِ الْأَدْنَىٰ دُونَ الْعَذَابِ الْأَكْبَرِ لَعَلَّهُمْ يَرْجِعُونَ ۞

more unjust than one who is reminded of
the Signs of his Lord and then turns away
from them? We shall certainly exact retribution from the guilty. (16--23)

وَمَنْ أَظْلَمُ مِمَّنْ ذُكِّرَ بِاٰيٰتِ رَبِّهٖ ثُمَّ أَعْرَضَ عَنْهَا ۚ إِنَّا مِنَ الْمُجْرِمِيْنَ مُنْتَقِمُوْنَ ۝

We gave Moses the Book and made it
a guidance for the children of Israel. So be
thou in no doubt concerning Our giving
thee the Book. We made from among the
children of Israel leaders, those who had
been steadfast and had firm faith in Our
Signs, who guided the people by Our
command. Thy Lord will surely judge
between them on the Day of Judgment
concerning that in which they disagreed.

وَلَقَدْ اٰتَيْنَا مُوْسَى الْكِتٰبَ فَلَا تَكُنْ فِيْ مِرْيَةٍ مِّنْ لِّقَآئِهٖ وَجَعَلْنٰهُ هُدًى لِّبَنِيْۤ إِسْرَآءِيْلَ ۝

وَجَعَلْنَا مِنْهُمْ أَئِمَّةً يَّهْدُوْنَ بِأَمْرِنَا لَمَّا صَبَرُوْا ۚ وَكَانُوْا بِاٰيٰتِنَا يُوْقِنُوْنَ ۝

إِنَّ رَبَّكَ هُوَ يَفْصِلُ بَيْنَهُمْ يَوْمَ الْقِيٰمَةِ فِيْمَا كَانُوْا فِيْهِ يَخْتَلِفُوْنَ ۝

Does it not afford them guidance how many
a people have We destroyed amidst whose
dwellings they now move about? In that
surely are Signs. Will they not then
listen? Have they not seen that We drive
the water to the dry land and produce
thereby crops of which their cattle and
they themselves eat? Do they not observe?

أَوَلَمْ يَهْدِ لَهُمْ كَمْ أَهْلَكْنَا مِنْ قَبْلِهِمْ مِّنَ الْقُرُوْنِ يَمْشُوْنَ فِيْ مَسٰكِنِهِمْ ۚ إِنَّ فِيْ ذٰلِكَ لَاٰيٰتٍ ۚ أَفَلَا يَسْمَعُوْنَ ۝

أَوَلَمْ يَرَوْا أَنَّا نَسُوْقُ الْمَآءَ إِلَى الْأَرْضِ الْجُرُزِ فَنُخْرِجُ بِهٖ زَرْعًا تَأْكُلُ مِنْهُ أَنْعَامُهُمْ وَأَنْفُسُهُمْ ۚ أَفَلَا يُبْصِرُوْنَ ۝

They ask: When will this victory be, if you
are truthful? Tell them: On the day of
victory their profession of belief will not
avail the disbelievers, nor will they be
granted respite. So turn away from them
and wait; they too are waiting. (24--31)

وَيَقُوْلُوْنَ مَتٰى هٰذَا الْفَتْحُ إِنْ كُنْتُمْ صٰدِقِيْنَ ۝

قُلْ يَوْمَ الْفَتْحِ لَا يَنْفَعُ الَّذِيْنَ كَفَرُوْۤا إِيْمَانُهُمْ وَلَا هُمْ يُنْظَرُوْنَ ۝

فَأَعْرِضْ عَنْهُمْ وَانْتَظِرْ إِنَّهُمْ مُّنْتَظِرُوْنَ ۝

Chapter 33

AL-AḤZĀB

(Revealed after Hijra)

In the name of Allah, Most Gracious, Ever Merciful. (1)

بِسْمِ اللّٰهِ الرَّحْمٰنِ الرَّحِيْمِ ۝

يٰۤاَيُّهَا النَّبِيُّ اتَّقِ اللّٰهَ وَلَا تُطِعِ الْكٰفِرِيْنَ وَالْمُنٰفِقِيْنَ ۗ اِنَّ اللّٰهَ كَانَ عَلِيْمًا حَكِيْمًا ۝

O Prophet, make Allah your shield and follow not the wishes of the disbelievers, and the hypocrites. Verily, Allah is All-Knowing, Wise. Follow that which is revealed to thee from thy Lord. Verily, Allah is Well Aware of that which you do. Put thy trust in Allah; sufficient is Allah as a Guardian. (2—4)

وَّاتَّبِعْ مَا يُوْحٰۤى اِلَيْكَ مِنْ رَّبِّكَ ۗ اِنَّ اللّٰهَ كَانَ بِمَا تَعْمَلُوْنَ خَبِيْرًا ۝

وَّتَوَكَّلْ عَلَى اللّٰهِ ۗ وَكَفٰى بِاللّٰهِ وَكِيْلًا ۝

Allah has not made for any man two hearts in his bosom; nor has He made those of your wives from whom you separate by calling them your mothers, your mothers in fact; nor has He made those whom you adopt as sons, your sons in fact. These are merely the utterances of your mouths. Allah sets forth the truth, and He guides to the right path. Call them after their fathers; that is most just in the sight of Allah. But if you know not their fathers, still they are your brothers in faith and your friends. There is no blame on you concerning anything done by you in this matter by mistake; but you are accountable for anything you do of set purpose. Allah is Most Forgiving, Ever Merciful. The Prophet has priority with the believers even over their own selves, and his wives stand to them as their mothers; and blood relations are nearer to one another in the Book of Allah, than the rest of the believers, including the Emigrants, except that you show kindness to your friends. That is written down in the Book. (5—7)

مَا جَعَلَ اللّٰهُ لِرَجُلٍ مِّنْ قَلْبَيْنِ فِيْ جَوْفِهٖ ۚ وَمَا جَعَلَ اَزْوَاجَكُمُ الّٰٓئِيْ تُظٰهِرُوْنَ مِنْهُنَّ اُمَّهٰتِكُمْ ۚ وَمَا جَعَلَ اَدْعِيَآءَكُمْ اَبْنَآءَكُمْ ۚ ذٰلِكُمْ قَوْلُكُمْ بِاَفْوَاهِكُمْ ۗ وَاللّٰهُ يَقُوْلُ الْحَقَّ وَهُوَ يَهْدِى السَّبِيْلَ ۝

اُدْعُوْهُمْ لِاٰبَآئِهِمْ هُوَ اَقْسَطُ عِنْدَ اللّٰهِ ۚ فَاِنْ لَّمْ تَعْلَمُوْۤا اٰبَآءَهُمْ فَاِخْوَانُكُمْ فِى الدِّيْنِ وَمَوَالِيْكُمْ ۗ وَلَيْسَ عَلَيْكُمْ جُنَاحٌ فِيْمَاۤ اَخْطَأْتُمْ بِهٖ ۙ وَلٰكِنْ مَّا تَعَمَّدَتْ قُلُوْبُكُمْ ۗ وَكَانَ اللّٰهُ غَفُوْرًا رَّحِيْمًا ۝

اَلنَّبِيُّ اَوْلٰى بِالْمُؤْمِنِيْنَ مِنْ اَنْفُسِهِمْ وَاَزْوَاجُهٗۤ اُمَّهٰتُهُمْ ۗ وَاُولُوا الْاَرْحَامِ بَعْضُهُمْ اَوْلٰى بِبَعْضٍ فِيْ كِتٰبِ اللّٰهِ مِنَ الْمُؤْمِنِيْنَ وَالْمُهٰجِرِيْنَ اِلَّاۤ اَنْ تَفْعَلُوْۤا اِلٰۤى اَوْلِيَآئِكُمْ مَّعْرُوْفًا ۗ كَانَ ذٰلِكَ فِى الْكِتٰبِ مَسْطُوْرًا ۝

Call to mind when We took from the Prophets a special covenant, and from thee, and from Noah, and Abraham, and Moses, and Jesus son of Mary; and We indeed took from them a solemn covenant, that Allah may question the truthful about their truthfulness. For the disbelievers He has prepared a painful punishment. (8—9)

وَاِذْ اَخَذْنَا مِنَ النَّبِيّٖنَ مِيْثَاقَهُمْ وَمِنْكَ وَمِنْ
نُّوْحٍ وَّاِبْرٰهِيْمَ وَمُوْسٰى وَعِيْسَى ابْنِ مَرْيَمَ ۚ
وَاَخَذْنَا مِنْهُمْ مِّيْثَاقًا غَلِيْظًا ۙ

لِّيَسْئَلَ الصّٰدِقِيْنَ عَنْ صِدْقِهِمْ ۚ وَاَعَدَّ لِلْكٰفِرِيْنَ
عَذَابًا اَلِيْمًا ۚ

O ye who believe, call to mind the favour of Allah which He did you when you were invaded by hosts, and We sent against them a wind and hosts that you saw not. Allah sees well that which you do. When they came upon you from above you and from below you, your eyes became distracted, and your hearts rose up to your throats, and you began to entertain diverse thoughts about Allah. Then were the believers sorely tried, and were violently shaken. The hypocrites and those whose minds were diseased exclaimed: Allah and His Messenger have merely deluded us. A party of them went so far as to urge: O people of Yathrib, you have no way of deliverance left, so turn back from your faith. A section of them asked leave of the Prophet, pleading: Our houses are exposed. Their houses were not exposed, they only sought a way of escape.

يٰۤاَيُّهَا الَّذِيْنَ اٰمَنُوا اذْكُرُوْا نِعْمَةَ اللهِ عَلَيْكُمْ اِذْ
جَآءَتْكُمْ جُنُوْدٌ فَاَرْسَلْنَا عَلَيْهِمْ رِيْحًا وَّجُنُوْدًا لَّمْ
تَرَوْهَا ۚ وَكَانَ اللهُ بِمَا تَعْمَلُوْنَ بَصِيْرًا ۚ

اِذْ جَآءُوْكُمْ مِّنْ فَوْقِكُمْ وَمِنْ اَسْفَلَ مِنْكُمْ وَاِذْ
زَاغَتِ الْاَبْصَارُ وَبَلَغَتِ الْقُلُوْبُ الْحَنَاجِرَ وَتَظُنُّوْنَ
بِاللهِ الظُّنُوْنَا ۚ

هُنَالِكَ ابْتُلِيَ الْمُؤْمِنُوْنَ وَزُلْزِلُوْا زِلْزَالًا شَدِيْدًا ۚ
وَاِذْ يَقُوْلُ الْمُنٰفِقُوْنَ وَالَّذِيْنَ فِيْ قُلُوْبِهِمْ مَّرَضٌ
مَّا وَعَدَنَا اللهُ وَرَسُوْلُهٗۤ اِلَّا غُرُوْرًا ۚ

وَاِذْ قَالَتْ طَّآئِفَةٌ مِّنْهُمْ يٰۤاَهْلَ يَثْرِبَ لَا مُقَامَ
لَكُمْ فَارْجِعُوْا ۚ وَيَسْتَأْذِنُ فَرِيْقٌ مِّنْهُمُ النَّبِيَّ يَقُوْلُوْنَ
اِنَّ بُيُوْتَنَا عَوْرَةٌ ۚ وَمَا هِيَ بِعَوْرَةٍ ۚ اِنْ يُّرِيْدُوْنَ
اِلَّا فِرَارًا ۚ

If the enemy were to enter the town from various directions, and these people were asked to turn back from their faith, they would do it. But then they would not tarry long in Medina. They had covenanted with Allah, before the advent of the hosts, that they would not turn their backs. The covenant with Allah will have to be accounted for.

وَلَوْ دُخِلَتْ عَلَيْهِمْ مِّنْ اَقْطَارِهَا ثُمَّ سُئِلُوا الْفِتْنَةَ
لَاٰتَوْهَا وَمَا تَلَبَّثُوْا بِهَاۤ اِلَّا يَسِيْرًا ۚ

وَلَقَدْ كَانُوْا عَاهَدُوا اللهَ مِنْ قَبْلُ لَا يُوَلُّوْنَ
الْاَدْبَارَ ۚ وَكَانَ عَهْدُ اللهِ مَسْئُوْلًا ۚ

Say to them: Flight shall not avail you if you flee from death or slaughter, and little would you gain. Say to them: Who is it that can save you from Allah, if He wished to do you harm, or can stop Him, if He wished to show you mercy? They will not find for themselves any friend or helper other than Allah. Verily, Allah knows well those among you who hindered others from fighting, and said to their brethren: Come to us; and themselves they fight but little. They are very miserly concerning you. When danger threatens, thou seest them looking towards thee, their eyes rolling like those of one who is fainting at the approach of death. But when the fear passes away they assail you with sharp tongues, being niggardly of any good coming your way. These have never truly believed; so Allah has rendered all their efforts vain. That is easy for Allah. They still hope the Confederates may not have withdrawn; but if the Confederates should come again, they would wish to be with the nomad Arabs in the desert, asking for news of you. If they were among you, little would they fight. (10—21)

قُلْ لَّنْ يَّنْفَعَكُمُ الْفِرَارُ اِنْ فَرَرْتُمْ مِّنَ الْمَوْتِ اَوِ الْقَتْلِ وَاِذًا لَّا تُمَتَّعُوْنَ اِلَّا قَلِيْلًا ۝

قُلْ مَنْ ذَا الَّذِيْ يَعْصِمُكُمْ مِّنَ اللّٰهِ اِنْ اَرَادَ بِكُمْ سُوْٓءًا اَوْ اَرَادَ بِكُمْ رَحْمَةً ۗ وَلَا يَجِدُوْنَ لَهُمْ مِّنْ دُوْنِ اللّٰهِ وَلِيًّا وَّلَا نَصِيْرًا ۝

قَدْ يَعْلَمُ اللّٰهُ الْمُعَوِّقِيْنَ مِنْكُمْ وَالْقَآئِلِيْنَ لِاِخْوَانِهِمْ هَلُمَّ اِلَيْنَا ۚ وَلَا يَأْتُوْنَ الْبَأْسَ اِلَّا قَلِيْلًا ۝

اَشِحَّةً عَلَيْكُمْ ۖ فَاِذَا جَآءَ الْخَوْفُ رَاَيْتَهُمْ يَنْظُرُوْنَ اِلَيْكَ تَدُوْرُ اَعْيُنُهُمْ كَالَّذِيْ يُغْشٰى عَلَيْهِ مِنَ الْمَوْتِ ۚ فَاِذَا ذَهَبَ الْخَوْفُ سَلَقُوْكُمْ بِاَلْسِنَةٍ حِدَادٍ اَشِحَّةً عَلَى الْخَيْرِ ۚ اُولٰٓئِكَ لَمْ يُؤْمِنُوْا فَاَحْبَطَ اللّٰهُ اَعْمَالَهُمْ ۚ وَكَانَ ذٰلِكَ عَلَى اللّٰهِ يَسِيْرًا ۝

يَحْسَبُوْنَ الْاَحْزَابَ لَمْ يَذْهَبُوْا ۚ وَاِنْ يَّأْتِ الْاَحْزَابُ يَوَدُّوْا لَوْ اَنَّهُمْ بَادُوْنَ فِي الْاَعْرَابِ يَسْاَلُوْنَ عَنْ اَنْبَآئِكُمْ ۚ وَلَوْ كَانُوْا فِيْكُمْ مَّا قَاتَلُوْٓا اِلَّا قَلِيْلًا ۝

You have in the Messenger of Allah an excellent exemplar, for him who hopes to meet with Allah and the Last Day, and who remembers Allah much. (22)

لَقَدْ كَانَ لَكُمْ فِيْ رَسُوْلِ اللّٰهِ اُسْوَةٌ حَسَنَةٌ لِّمَنْ كَانَ يَرْجُوا اللّٰهَ وَالْيَوْمَ الْاٰخِرَ وَذَكَرَ اللّٰهَ كَثِيْرًا ۝

When the true believers saw the Confederates, they said: Here is what Allah and His Messenger had promised us; Allah and His Messenger have been proved right. It only added to their faith and spirit of submission. Among the believers are men who have been true to the covenant they made with Allah. Some have fulfilled

وَلَمَّا رَاَ الْمُؤْمِنُوْنَ الْاَحْزَابَ ۙ قَالُوْا هٰذَا مَا وَعَدَنَا اللّٰهُ وَرَسُوْلُهٗ وَصَدَقَ اللّٰهُ وَرَسُوْلُهٗ ۖ وَمَا زَادَهُمْ اِلَّآ اِيْمَانًا وَّتَسْلِيْمًا ۝

مِنَ الْمُؤْمِنِيْنَ رِجَالٌ صَدَقُوْا مَا عَاهَدُوا اللّٰهَ عَلَيْهِ

their vow, and laid down their lives in
battle, and there are others who wait.
They have not weakened in their resolve
in the least; that Allah may reward
the faithful for keeping their troth, and
punish the hypocrites if He so please, or
turn to them in mercy. Verily, Allah is
Most Forgiving, Ever Merciful. Allah
turned back the disbelievers in their rage;
they gained nothing. Allah fought on
behalf of the believers. Allah is Powerful,
Mighty. He brought those of the people
of the Book who had backed up the confederates, down from their fortresses and
cast terror into their hearts; so that some
of them you slew and some you took
captive. He made you inheritors of their
land and their houses and their wealth,
and of a land on which you have not yet
set foot. Allah has power over all things.
(23—28)

Say, O Prophet, to thy wives: If you
desire the life of this world and its adornment, come then, I shall make provision
for you and send you away in a handsome
manner. But if you desire Allah and His
Messenger and the Home of the Hereafter,
then Allah has prepared for those of you
who carry out their obligations fully a
great reward. Wives of the Prophet, if any
of you should act in a manner incom-
patible with the highest standard of piety,
her punishment will be doubled. That is
easy for Allah. But whoever of you is
completely obedient to Allah and His
Messenger and acts righteously, We shall
double her reward; and We have prepared

فَمِنْهُمْ مَّنْ قَضٰى نَحْبَهٗ وَمِنْهُمْ مَّنْ يَّنْتَظِرُ ۖ وَمَا
بَدَّلُوْا تَبْدِيْلًا ۙ ۝

لِّيَجْزِيَ اللهُ الصّٰدِقِيْنَ بِصِدْقِهِمْ وَيُعَذِّبَ الْمُنٰفِقِيْنَ
اِنْ شَآءَ اَوْ يَتُوْبَ عَلَيْهِمْ ۚ اِنَّ اللهَ كَانَ غَفُوْرًا
رَّحِيْمًا ۝

وَرَدَّ اللهُ الَّذِيْنَ كَفَرُوْا بِغَيْظِهِمْ لَمْ يَنَالُوْا خَيْرًا ۚ
وَكَفَى اللهُ الْمُؤْمِنِيْنَ الْقِتَالَ ۚ وَكَانَ اللهُ قَوِيًّا
عَزِيْزًا ۝

وَاَنْزَلَ الَّذِيْنَ ظَاهَرُوْهُمْ مِّنْ اَهْلِ الْكِتٰبِ مِنْ
صَيَاصِيْهِمْ وَقَذَفَ فِيْ قُلُوْبِهِمُ الرُّعْبَ فَرِيْقًا
تَقْتُلُوْنَ وَتَأْسِرُوْنَ فَرِيْقًا ۝

وَاَوْرَثَكُمْ اَرْضَهُمْ وَدِيَارَهُمْ وَاَمْوَالَهُمْ وَاَرْضًا
لَّمْ تَطَـُٔوْهَا ۚ وَكَانَ اللهُ عَلٰى كُلِّ شَيْءٍ قَدِيْرًا ۝

يٰٓاَيُّهَا النَّبِيُّ قُلْ لِّاَزْوَاجِكَ اِنْ كُنْتُنَّ تُرِدْنَ الْحَيٰوةَ
الدُّنْيَا وَزِيْنَتَهَا فَتَعَالَيْنَ اُمَتِّعْكُنَّ وَاُسَرِّحْكُنَّ
سَرَاحًا جَمِيْلًا ۝

وَاِنْ كُنْتُنَّ تُرِدْنَ اللهَ وَرَسُوْلَهٗ وَالدَّارَ الْاٰخِرَةَ
فَاِنَّ اللهَ اَعَدَّ لِلْمُحْسِنٰتِ مِنْكُنَّ اَجْرًا عَظِيْمًا ۝

يٰنِسَآءَ النَّبِيِّ مَنْ يَّأْتِ مِنْكُنَّ بِفَاحِشَةٍ مُّبَيِّنَةٍ
يُّضٰعَفْ لَهَا الْعَذَابُ ضِعْفَيْنِ ۚ وَكَانَ ذٰلِكَ عَلَى
اللهِ يَسِيْرًا ۝

وَمَنْ يَّقْنُتْ مِنْكُنَّ لِلهِ وَرَسُوْلِهٖ وَتَعْمَلْ صَالِحًا

an honourable provision for her. Wives of the Prophet, if you safeguard your dignity, you are not like any other women. So speak in a simple straightforward manner, lest he whose mind is diseased should form an ill design; and always say the good word. Stay at home and do not show off in the manner of the women of the days of ignorance, and observe Prayer, and pay the Zakat, and obey Allah and His Messenger. Allah desires to remove from you all uncleanness, members of the Household, and to purify you completely. Remember that which is rehearsed in your homes of the Signs of Allah and of wisdom. Verily, Allah is the Knower of minutest things, All-Aware. (29—35)

For men who submit themselves wholly to Allah, and women who submit themselves wholly to Him, and men who believe and women who believe, and men who are obedient and women who are obedient, and men who are truthful and women who are truthful, and men who are steadfast and women who are steadfast, and men who are humble and women who are humble, and men who give alms and women who give alms, and men who fast and women who fast, and men who guard their chastity and women who guard their chastity, and men who remember Allah much and women who remember Him, Allah has prepared forgiveness and a great reward. (36)

It is not open to a believing man or a believing woman, when Allah and His Messenger have decided a matter, to exercise their own choice in deciding it. Whoso disobeys Allah and His Messenger, falls into open error. Call to mind when thou didst say to him on whom Allah had bestowed favours and thou also hadst bestowed favours: Cleave to thy wife and be mindful of thy obligation to Allah; and

تُؤْتِيهَآ اَجْرَهَا مَرَّتَيْنِ وَاَعْتَدْنَا لَهَا رِزْقًا كَرِيْمًا ۞

يٰنِسَآءَ النَّبِيِّ لَسْتُنَّ كَاَحَدٍ مِّنَ النِّسَآءِ اِنِ اتَّقَيْتُنَّ فَلَا تَخْضَعْنَ بِالْقَوْلِ فَيَطْمَعَ الَّذِيْ فِيْ قَلْبِهِ مَرَضٌ وَّقُلْنَ قَوْلًا مَّعْرُوْفًا ۞

وَقَرْنَ فِيْ بُيُوْتِكُنَّ وَلَا تَبَرَّجْنَ تَبَرُّجَ الْجَاهِلِيَّةِ الْاُوْلٰى وَاَقِمْنَ الصَّلٰوةَ وَاٰتِيْنَ الزَّكٰوةَ وَاَطِعْنَ اللّٰهَ وَرَسُوْلَهٗ ؕ اِنَّمَا يُرِيْدُ اللّٰهُ لِيُذْهِبَ عَنْكُمُ الرِّجْسَ اَهْلَ الْبَيْتِ وَيُطَهِّرَكُمْ تَطْهِيْرًا ۞

وَاذْكُرْنَ مَا يُتْلٰى فِيْ بُيُوْتِكُنَّ مِنْ اٰيٰتِ اللّٰهِ وَالْحِكْمَةِ ؕ اِنَّ اللّٰهَ كَانَ لَطِيْفًا خَبِيْرًا ۞

اِنَّ الْمُسْلِمِيْنَ وَالْمُسْلِمٰتِ وَالْمُؤْمِنِيْنَ وَالْمُؤْمِنٰتِ وَالْقٰنِتِيْنَ وَالْقٰنِتٰتِ وَالصّٰدِقِيْنَ وَالصّٰدِقٰتِ وَالصّٰبِرِيْنَ وَالصّٰبِرٰتِ وَالْخٰشِعِيْنَ وَالْخٰشِعٰتِ وَالْمُتَصَدِّقِيْنَ وَالْمُتَصَدِّقٰتِ وَالصَّآئِمِيْنَ وَالصّٰٓئِمٰتِ وَالْحٰفِظِيْنَ فُرُوْجَهُمْ وَالْحٰفِظٰتِ وَالذّٰكِرِيْنَ اللّٰهَ كَثِيْرًا وَّالذّٰكِرٰتِ ۙ اَعَدَّ اللّٰهُ لَهُمْ مَّغْفِرَةً وَّ اَجْرًا عَظِيْمًا ۞

وَمَا كَانَ لِمُؤْمِنٍ وَّلَا مُؤْمِنَةٍ اِذَا قَضَى اللّٰهُ وَرَسُوْلُهٗٓ اَمْرًا اَنْ يَّكُوْنَ لَهُمُ الْخِيَرَةُ مِنْ اَمْرِهِمْ ؕ وَمَنْ يَّعْصِ اللّٰهَ وَرَسُوْلَهٗ فَقَدْ ضَلَّ ضَلٰلًا مُّبِيْنًا ۞

وَاِذْ تَقُوْلُ لِلَّذِيْٓ اَنْعَمَ اللّٰهُ عَلَيْهِ وَاَنْعَمْتَ عَلَيْهِ اَمْسِكْ عَلَيْكَ زَوْجَكَ وَاتَّقِ اللّٰهَ وَتُخْفِيْ فِيْ نَفْسِكَ

thou didst conceal in thy mind that which Allah was about to bring to light (that Zaid had decided to divorce his wife) and thou wast afraid of the people, whereas Allah has better right that thou shouldst fear Him. Then, when Zaid had carried into effect his decision concerning her, We joined her in marriage with thee, so that there should be no constraint in the minds of the believers in the matter of marrying the wives of their adopted sons after they had divorced them. Allah's decree is bound to be fulfilled. There could be no hindrance for the Prophet with regard to that which Allah has made incumbent upon him. The command of Allah is a decree which has been determined. Such has been the way of Allah with the Prophets who have passed away before, those who delivered the messages of Allah and feared Him, and feared none but Allah. Sufficient is Allah as a Reckoner. (37—40)

Muhammad is not the father of any of your men, but he is the Messenger of Allah and the Seal of the Prophets. Allah has full knowledge of all things. (41)

O ye who believe, remember Allah much; and glorify Him morn and eve. He it is Who sends His blessings on you, and His angels call down blessings on you, that He may bring you forth from all kinds of darkness into light. He is Ever Merciful to the believers. On the day when they meet Him they will be greeted with: Peace; and He has prepared for them a noble recompense. (42—45)

O Prophet, We have sent thee as a witness, and a bearer of glad tidings and a warner, and as a summoner unto Allah by His command and a light-giving sun. Announce to the believers the glad tidings that they will receive great bounty from Allah. Follow not the wishes of the disbelievers and the hypocrites and ignore their persecution and put thy trust in Allah. Sufficient is Allah as a Guardian. (46—49)

مَا اللّٰهُ مُبْدِيْهِ وَتَخْشَى النَّاسَ وَاللّٰهُ اَحَقُّ اَنْ تَخْشٰهُ ۗ فَلَمَّا قَضٰى زَيْدٌ مِّنْهَا وَطَرًا زَوَّجْنٰكَهَا لِكَىْ لَا يَكُوْنَ عَلَى الْمُؤْمِنِيْنَ حَرَجٌ فِيْٓ اَزْوَاجِ اَدْعِيَآئِهِمْ اِذَا قَضَوْا مِنْهُنَّ وَطَرًا ۚ وَكَانَ اَمْرُ اللّٰهِ مَفْعُوْلًا ۞

مَا كَانَ عَلَى النَّبِيِّ مِنْ حَرَجٍ فِيْمَا فَرَضَ اللّٰهُ لَهٗ ۗ سُنَّةَ اللّٰهِ فِى الَّذِيْنَ خَلَوْا مِنْ قَبْلُ ۚ وَكَانَ اَمْرُ اللّٰهِ قَدَرًا مَّقْدُوْرَا ۞

اِلَّذِيْنَ يُبَلِّغُوْنَ رِسٰلٰتِ اللّٰهِ وَيَخْشَوْنَهٗ وَلَا يَخْشَوْنَ اَحَدًا اِلَّا اللّٰهَ ۗ وَكَفٰى بِاللّٰهِ حَسِيْبًا ۞

مَا كَانَ مُحَمَّدٌ اَبَآ اَحَدٍ مِّنْ رِّجَالِكُمْ وَلٰكِنْ رَّسُوْلَ اللّٰهِ وَخَاتَمَ النَّبِيّٖنَ ۗ وَكَانَ اللّٰهُ بِكُلِّ شَيْءٍ عَلِيْمًا ۞ يٰٓاَيُّهَا الَّذِيْنَ اٰمَنُوا اذْكُرُوا اللّٰهَ ذِكْرًا كَثِيْرًا ۞

وَّسَبِّحُوْهُ بُكْرَةً وَّاَصِيْلًا ۞

هُوَ الَّذِيْ يُصَلِّيْ عَلَيْكُمْ وَمَلٰٓئِكَتُهٗ لِيُخْرِجَكُمْ مِّنَ الظُّلُمٰتِ اِلَى النُّوْرِ ۚ وَكَانَ بِالْمُؤْمِنِيْنَ رَحِيْمًا ۞ تَحِيَّتُهُمْ يَوْمَ يَلْقَوْنَهٗ سَلٰمٌ ۚ وَاَعَدَّ لَهُمْ اَجْرًا كَرِيْمًا ۞

يٰٓاَيُّهَا النَّبِيُّ اِنَّآ اَرْسَلْنٰكَ شَاهِدًا وَّمُبَشِّرًا وَّنَذِيْرًا ۞

وَّدَاعِيًا اِلَى اللّٰهِ بِاِذْنِهٖ وَسِرَاجًا مُّنِيْرًا ۞ وَبَشِّرِ الْمُؤْمِنِيْنَ بِاَنَّ لَهُمْ مِّنَ اللّٰهِ فَضْلًا كَبِيْرًا ۞ وَلَا تُطِعِ الْكٰفِرِيْنَ وَالْمُنٰفِقِيْنَ وَدَعْ اَذٰىهُمْ وَتَوَكَّلْ

O ye who believe, when you marry believing women and then divorce them before you have consorted with them, you are not entitled to demand in their case the period of waiting before they can re-marry. So make some provision for them and send them away in a handsome manner. (50)

O Prophet, We have made lawful for thee thy wives whose dower thou hast paid, and those under thy control from among prisoners of war, and daughters of thy paternal and maternal uncles and aunts who have emigrated with thee, and any other believing woman who dedicates herself to the Prophet provided the Prophet desires to marry her, so that there may be no hindrance for thee in the discharge of thy responsibilities. This ordinance is only for thee and not for the other believers. We have already made known that which We have prescribed for them in the matter of their wives and those under their control. Allah is Most Forgiving, Ever Merciful. It is permitted to thee to put away any of thy wives that thou pleasest or to retain any of them thou pleasest; and if thou shouldst desire to take back any of those thou hast put away, it shall be no blame on thee. In this way it is more likely that they may be comforted, and that they may not be grieved, and that they may all be pleased with that which thou hast given them. Allah knows all that is in your minds. Allah is All-Knowing, Forbearing. It is not lawful for thee to marry any women beyond these categories, nor to change them for other wives even though their goodness please thee, except those under thy control. Allah is Watchful over all things. (51—53)

O ye who believe, enter not the houses of the Prophet, unless you are invited to a meal, and then not in anticipation of its getting ready. But enter when you are

called, and when you have eaten, disperse;
linger not in eagerness for talk. This was
a cause of embarrassment for the Prophet,
but he felt shy in asking you to leave.
Allah is not shy in pointing out the right
course. When you ask any of the wives of
the Prophet for something, ask from
behind a curtain. That is purer for your
hearts and for their hearts. It behoves you
not to cause annoyance to the Messenger
of Allah, nor that you should ever marry
any of his wives after his death. That
would be an enormity in the sight of Allah.
Whether you disclose a thing or conceal
it, Allah knows all things well. There is no
restriction on them in the matter of their
facing their fathers or their sons or their
brothers or the sons of their brothers or
the sons of their sisters or gentlewomen
or those under their control. Be mindful
of your duty to Allah, wives of the Prophet, verily, Allah watches over everything. (54—56)

Allah sends down blessings on the
Prophet, and His angels invoke blessings
on him. O ye who believe, do you also
invoke blessings on him and salute him
with the salutation of peace. Verily, those
who malign Allah and His Messenger,
are cast aside by Allah in this world and in
the Hereafter and Allah has prepared an
humiliating punishment for them. Those
who malign believing men and believing
women for that which they have not done
shall bear the guilt of a calumny and
a manifest sin. (57—59)

O Prophet, direct thy wives and daughters and the women of the believers that
they should pull down their outer cloaks
from their heads over their faces. This will
make it possible for them to be distinguished so that they will not be molested.
Allah is Most Forgiving, Ever Merciful.
(60)

إِذَا دُعِيتُمْ فَادْخُلُوا فَإِذَا طَعِمْتُمْ فَانْتَشِرُوا وَ
لَا مُسْتَأْنِسِينَ لِحَدِيثٍ إِنَّ ذٰلِكُمْ كَانَ يُؤْذِى
النَّبِيَّ فَيَسْتَحْيِ مِنْكُمْ وَاللّٰهُ لَا يَسْتَحْيِ مِنَ الْحَقِّ
وَإِذَا سَأَلْتُمُوهُنَّ مَتَاعًا فَسْئَلُوهُنَّ مِنْ وَرَاءِ حِجَابٍ
ذٰلِكُمْ أَطْهَرُ لِقُلُوبِكُمْ وَقُلُوبِهِنَّ وَمَا كَانَ لَكُمْ
أَنْ تُؤْذُوا رَسُولَ اللّٰهِ وَلَا أَنْ تَنْكِحُوا أَزْوَاجَهُ مِنْ
بَعْدِهِ أَبَدًا إِنَّ ذٰلِكُمْ كَانَ عِنْدَ اللّٰهِ عَظِيمًا ۝
إِنْ تُبْدُوا شَيْئًا أَوْ تُخْفُوهُ فَإِنَّ اللّٰهَ كَانَ بِكُلِّ شَيْءٍ
عَلِيمًا ۝
لَا جُنَاحَ عَلَيْهِنَّ فِي آبَائِهِنَّ وَلَا أَبْنَائِهِنَّ وَلَا
إِخْوَانِهِنَّ وَلَا أَبْنَاءِ إِخْوَانِهِنَّ وَلَا أَبْنَاءِ أَخَوَاتِهِنَّ
وَلَا نِسَائِهِنَّ وَلَا مَا مَلَكَتْ أَيْمَانُهُنَّ وَاتَّقِينَ
اللّٰهَ إِنَّ اللّٰهَ كَانَ عَلَى كُلِّ شَيْءٍ شَهِيدًا ۝
إِنَّ اللّٰهَ وَمَلَائِكَتَهُ يُصَلُّونَ عَلَى النَّبِيِّ يَا أَيُّهَا الَّذِينَ
آمَنُوا صَلُّوا عَلَيْهِ وَسَلِّمُوا تَسْلِيمًا ۝
إِنَّ الَّذِينَ يُؤْذُونَ اللّٰهَ وَرَسُولَهُ لَعَنَهُمُ اللّٰهُ فِي
الدُّنْيَا وَالْآخِرَةِ وَأَعَدَّ لَهُمْ عَذَابًا مُهِينًا ۝
وَالَّذِينَ يُؤْذُونَ الْمُؤْمِنِينَ وَالْمُؤْمِنَاتِ بِغَيْرِ مَا
اكْتَسَبُوا فَقَدِ احْتَمَلُوا بُهْتَانًا وَإِثْمًا مُبِينًا ۝
يَا أَيُّهَا النَّبِيُّ قُلْ لِأَزْوَاجِكَ وَبَنَاتِكَ وَنِسَاءِ الْمُؤْمِنِينَ
يُدْنِينَ عَلَيْهِنَّ مِنْ جَلَابِيبِهِنَّ ذٰلِكَ أَدْنَى أَنْ
يُعْرَفْنَ فَلَا يُؤْذَيْنَ وَكَانَ اللّٰهُ غَفُورًا رَحِيمًا ۝

417

If the hypocrites, and those whose minds are diseased, and those who cause agitation in the city by circulating false rumours, desist not, We shall set thee up against them; then they will not long continue thy neighbours in the city. Such people are accursed and liable to be seized and cut down wherever found. This has been the way of Allah with those who passed away before you; never wilt thou find a change in the way of Allah. (61—63)

لَّئِنْ لَّمْ يَنْتَهِ الْمُنٰفِقُوْنَ وَالَّذِيْنَ فِيْ قُلُوْبِهِمْ مَرَضٌ وَّالْمُرْجِفُوْنَ فِى الْمَدِيْنَةِ لَنُغْرِيَنَّكَ بِهِمْ ثُمَّ لَا يُجَاوِرُوْنَكَ فِيْهَآ اِلَّا قَلِيْلًا ۟

مَّلْعُوْنِيْنَ ۛ اَيْنَمَا ثُقِفُوْٓا اُخِذُوْا وَقُتِّلُوْا تَقْتِيْلًا ۟

سُنَّةَ اللّٰهِ فِى الَّذِيْنَ خَلَوْا مِنْ قَبْلُ ۚ وَلَنْ تَجِدَ لِسُنَّةِ اللّٰهِ تَبْدِيْلًا ۟

People ask thee concerning the Hour. Tell them: Allah alone has knowledge of it. How wouldst thou know that the Hour may be nigh? Allah has banished the disbelievers from His mercy and has prepared for them a burning torment, wherein they will abide. They will find therein no friend or helper. On the day when their faces are turned over the Fire, they will exclaim: Would that we had obeyed Allah and obeyed the Messenger. They will plead: Lord, we obeyed our leaders and great ones and they led us astray from the right path. Lord, intensify their punishment and deprive them utterly of Thy mercy. (64—69)

يَسْـَٔلُكَ النَّاسُ عَنِ السَّاعَةِ ۭ قُلْ اِنَّمَا عِلْمُهَا عِنْدَ اللّٰهِ ۭ وَمَا يُدْرِيْكَ لَعَلَّ السَّاعَةَ تَكُوْنُ قَرِيْبًا ۟

اِنَّ اللّٰهَ لَعَنَ الْكٰفِرِيْنَ وَاَعَدَّ لَهُمْ سَعِيْرًا ۟

خٰلِدِيْنَ فِيْهَآ اَبَدًا ۚ لَا يَجِدُوْنَ وَلِيًّا وَّلَا نَصِيْرًا ۟

يَوْمَ تُقَلَّبُ وُجُوْهُهُمْ فِى النَّارِ يَقُوْلُوْنَ يٰلَيْتَنَآ اَطَعْنَا اللّٰهَ وَاَطَعْنَا الرَّسُوْلَا ۟

وَقَالُوْا رَبَّنَآ اِنَّآ اَطَعْنَا سَادَتَنَا وَكُبَرَآءَنَا فَاَضَلُّوْنَا السَّبِيْلَا ۟

رَبَّنَآ اٰتِهِمْ ضِعْفَيْنِ مِنَ الْعَذَابِ وَالْعَنْهُمْ لَعْنًا كَبِيْرًا ۟

O ye who believe, do not behave like those who distressed Moses with their calumnies, and then Allah cleared him of that which they alleged. He had a high standing with Allah. O ye who believe, be mindful of your duty to Allah, and say the straightforward thing. He will enable you to act righteously and will forgive you your defaults. Whoso obeys Allah and His Messenger achieves a great triumph. (70—72)

يٰٓاَيُّهَا الَّذِيْنَ اٰمَنُوْا لَا تَكُوْنُوْا كَالَّذِيْنَ اٰذَوْا مُوْسٰى فَبَرَّاَهُ اللّٰهُ مِمَّا قَالُوْا ۭ وَكَانَ عِنْدَ اللّٰهِ وَجِيْهًا ۟

يٰٓاَيُّهَا الَّذِيْنَ اٰمَنُوا اتَّقُوا اللّٰهَ وَقُوْلُوْا قَوْلًا سَدِيْدًا ۟

يُّصْلِحْ لَكُمْ اَعْمَالَكُمْ وَيَغْفِرْ لَكُمْ ذُنُوْبَكُمْ ۭ وَمَنْ يُّطِعِ اللّٰهَ وَرَسُوْلَهُ فَقَدْ فَازَ فَوْزًا عَظِيْمًا ۟

اِنَّا عَرَضْنَا الْاَمَانَةَ عَلَى السَّمٰوٰتِ وَالْاَرْضِ وَ

We offered the Trust to the heavens and the earth and the mountains, but they refused to undertake it and were afraid of it. But man undertook it. Indeed he is capable of inflicting great hardship upon himself, disregardful of consequences. The consequence of assumption of responsibility under the Law is that Allah will punish the hypocrites, men and women, and the idolaters, men and women; and Allah will turn in mercy to the believers, men and women. Allah is Most Forgiving, Ever Merciful. (73—74)

الْجِبَالِ فَاَبَيْنَ اَنْ يَّحْمِلْنَهَا وَاَشْفَقْنَ مِنْهَا وَحَمَلَهَا الْاِنْسَانُ ۚ اِنَّهٗ كَانَ ظَلُوْمًا جَهُوْلًا ۟

لِّيُعَذِّبَ اللّٰهُ الْمُنٰفِقِيْنَ وَالْمُنٰفِقٰتِ وَالْمُشْرِكِيْنَ وَالْمُشْرِكٰتِ وَيَتُوْبَ اللّٰهُ عَلَى الْمُؤْمِنِيْنَ وَالْمُؤْمِنٰتِ ؕ وَكَانَ اللّٰهُ غَفُوْرًا رَّحِيْمًا ۟

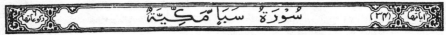

Chapter 34

AL-SABA'

(*Revealed before Hijra*)

بِسْمِ اللهِ الرَّحْمٰنِ الرَّحِيْمِ ۝

In the name of Allah, Most Gracious, Ever Merciful. (1)

اَلْحَمْدُ لِلهِ الَّذِىْ لَهٗ مَا فِى السَّمٰوٰتِ وَمَا فِى الْاَرْضِ وَلَهُ الْحَمْدُ فِى الْاٰخِرَةِ ؕ وَهُوَ الْحَكِيْمُ الْخَبِيْرُ ۝

يَعْلَمُ مَا يَلِجُ فِى الْاَرْضِ وَمَا يَخْرُجُ مِنْهَا وَمَا يَنْزِلُ مِنَ السَّمَاءِ وَمَا يَعْرُجُ فِيْهَا ؕ وَهُوَ الرَّحِيْمُ الْغَفُوْرُ ۝

All praise is due to Allah, to Whom belongs whatever is in the heavens and whatever is in the earth. His is all praise, as in the beginning, so in the end. He is the Wise, the All-Aware. He knows whatever goes into the earth and whatever comes forth from it, and whatever descends from the heaven and whatever ascends into it. He is Ever Merciful, Most Forgiving. (2—3)

وَقَالَ الَّذِيْنَ كَفَرُوْا لَا تَأْتِيْنَا السَّاعَةُ ؕ قُلْ بَلٰى وَرَبِّىْ لَتَأْتِيَنَّكُمْ ۙ عٰلِمِ الْغَيْبِ ۚ لَا يَعْزُبُ عَنْهُ مِثْقَالُ ذَرَّةٍ فِى السَّمٰوٰتِ وَلَا فِى الْاَرْضِ وَلَا اَصْغَرُ مِنْ ذٰلِكَ وَلَا اَكْبَرُ اِلَّا فِىْ كِتٰبٍ مُّبِيْنٍ ۝

لِيَجْزِىَ الَّذِيْنَ اٰمَنُوْا وَعَمِلُوا الصّٰلِحٰتِ ؕ اُولٰٓئِكَ لَهُمْ مَغْفِرَةٌ وَّرِزْقٌ كَرِيْمٌ ۝

Those who disbelieve assert: The Hour will never come upon us. Tell them: On the contrary, by my Lord, the Knower of the unseen, it will surely come upon you. Not the smallest particle in the heavens or the earth, or anything less than that or greater escapes Him, but all is recorded in an open Book, that He may reward those who believe and work righteousness. These will have forgiveness and honourable provision. Those who strive to frustrate Us, in the matter of Our Signs, will suffer a painful torment. Those who have been given knowledge know that what has been revealed to thee from thy Lord is the truth, and that it guides unto the path of the Mighty, the Praiseworthy. Those who disbelieve say: Shall we point out to you a man who will tell you that when you are broken up into particles, you will be put together again in a new creation?

وَالَّذِيْنَ سَعَوْا فِىْ اٰيٰتِنَا مُعٰجِزِيْنَ اُولٰٓئِكَ لَهُمْ عَذَابٌ مِّنْ رِّجْزٍ اَلِيْمٌ ۝

وَيَرَى الَّذِيْنَ اُوْتُوا الْعِلْمَ الَّذِىْۤ اُنْزِلَ اِلَيْكَ مِنْ رَّبِّكَ هُوَ الْحَقَّ ۙ وَيَهْدِىْۤ اِلٰى صِرَاطِ الْعَزِيْزِ الْحَمِيْدِ ۝

وَقَالَ الَّذِيْنَ كَفَرُوْا هَلْ نَدُلُّكُمْ عَلٰى رَجُلٍ يُّنَبِّئُكُمْ اِذَا مُزِّقْتُمْ كُلَّ مُمَزَّقٍ ۙ اِنَّكُمْ لَفِىْ خَلْقٍ جَدِيْدٍ ۝

Has he fabricated a lie against Allah, or is he afflicted with madness? Indeed no. It is those who believe not in the Hereafter that are already afflicted with the chastisement and are far gone in error. Do they not observe how they are encompassed by that which is before them and that which is behind them of the heaven and the earth? We could, if We please, cause the earth to swallow them up, or cause the clouds to fall upon them in a deluge. In that verily is a Sign for every servant of Ours who turns to Us. (4—10)

We bestowed Our grace upon David, and commanded: O ye dwellers of the mountains and ye birds join with him in celebrating Our praise; and We taught him the art of smelting iron ore. We commanded him: Fashion full-length coats of mail, and keep their rings small; and act righteously, all of you. I am watching all that you do. We subjected the wind to Solomon; its morning course was a month and its evening course a month; and We caused a fount of molten copper to flow for him. We subjected experts to him who worked under him, by the command of his Lord. We had decreed that if any of them turned away from Our command, We would afflict him with the torment of burning. They made for him whatever he desired of temples, and statues, and basins large as reservoirs, and huge cooking vessels fixed in their places. We directed: Carry on gratefully, ye of the House of David; but few of My servants are truly grateful. When We decreed Solomon's death, those in subjection to him learnt of the decline of his power only through a worm of the earth that ate away his staff. So when he tottered and fell, the experts realised that had they known that which was hidden from their sight, they would not have continued in the torment of humiliating subjection. (11—15)

For the people of Saba there was a Sign in their home-land; two gardens, one on the right hand and the other on the left. Allah commanded them: Eat of that which your Lord has provided for you, and be grateful. You have a pleasant land and a Lord Most Forgiving. Yet they turned away from the truth. So We afflicted them with a devastating flood, and converted their two excellent gardens into gardens bearing bitter fruits, tamarisk, and a few lote trees. We requited them in that way because of their ingratitude; and none do We requite in that way but the ungrateful. We had placed between them and the towns that We had blessed, other towns situated close to each other, and We fixed easy stages between them, and reassured them: Move back and forth between them, night and day, in security. But they were unappreciative of Our bounties and beseeched Us: Lord, make the stages of our journeys longer. Thus they wronged their own selves and We made them bygone tales, grinding them into particles. In that verily are Signs for every steadfast grateful person. Iblis proved his estimate of them to be true, for they all followed him except a party of the believers, though he had no authority over them; only We desired to distinguish those who believed in the Hereafter from those who were in doubt concerning it. Thy Lord is Watchful over all things. (16—22)

Say to them: Call those on whose behalf you make a claim beside Allah. They are not masters of the smallest particle in the heavens or in the earth, nor have they any share in either, nor is any of them His helper. No intercession avails with Him, except on the part of him whom He grants permission. When their hearts are relieved of fear, they will enquire from those to whom permission is granted: What has your Lord said? They will answer: The truth. He is the High, the Great.

الْحَقُّ وَهُوَ الْعَلِيُّ الْكَبِيرُ ۝

قُلْ مَنْ يَرْزُقُكُمْ مِنَ السَّمٰوٰتِ وَ الْأَرْضِ قُلِ اللّٰهُ

وَ اِنَّا أَوْ اِيَّاكُمْ لَعَلٰى هُدًى أَوْ فِيْ ضَلٰلٍ مُّبِيْنٍ ۝

قُلْ لَّا تُسْئَلُوْنَ عَمَّا أَجْرَمْنَا وَ لَا نُسْئَلُ عَمَّا تَعْمَلُوْنَ ۝

قُلْ يَجْمَعُ بَيْنَنَا رَبُّنَا ثُمَّ يَفْتَحُ بَيْنَنَا بِالْحَقِّ وَهُوَ

الْفَتَّاحُ الْعَلِيْمُ ۝

قُلْ أَرُوْنِيَ الَّذِيْنَ أَلْحَقْتُمْ بِهِ شُرَكَآءَ كَلَّا بَلْ هُوَ

اللّٰهُ الْعَزِيْزُ الْحَكِيْمُ ۝

وَ مَا أَرْسَلْنٰكَ اِلَّا كَآفَّةً لِلنَّاسِ بَشِيْرًا وَّ نَذِيْرًا وَّ

لٰكِنَّ أَكْثَرَ النَّاسِ لَا يَعْلَمُوْنَ ۝

وَ يَقُوْلُوْنَ مَتٰى هٰذَا الْوَعْدُ اِنْ كُنْتُمْ صٰدِقِيْنَ ۝

قُلْ لَّكُمْ مِّيْعَادُ يَوْمٍ لَّا تَسْتَأْخِرُوْنَ عَنْهُ سَاعَةً

وَّ لَا تَسْتَقْدِمُوْنَ ۝

وَ قَالَ الَّذِيْنَ كَفَرُوْا لَنْ نُّؤْمِنَ بِهٰذَا الْقُرْاٰنِ وَلَا

بِالَّذِيْ بَيْنَ يَدَيْهِ وَ لَوْ تَرٰى اِذِ الظّٰلِمُوْنَ مَوْقُوْفُوْنَ

عِنْدَ رَبِّهِمْ يَرْجِعُ بَعْضُهُمْ اِلٰى بَعْضٍ الْقَوْلَ

يَقُوْلُ الَّذِيْنَ اسْتُضْعِفُوْا لِلَّذِيْنَ اسْتَكْبَرُوْا لَوْلَا أَنْتُمْ

لَكُنَّا مُؤْمِنِيْنَ ۝

قَالَ الَّذِيْنَ اسْتَكْبَرُوْا لِلَّذِيْنَ اسْتُضْعِفُوْا أَنَحْنُ

صَدَدْنٰكُمْ عَنِ الْهُدٰى بَعْدَ اِذْ جَآءَكُمْ بَلْ كُنْتُمْ

مُّجْرِمِيْنَ ۝

وَ قَالَ الَّذِيْنَ اسْتُضْعِفُوْا لِلَّذِيْنَ اسْتَكْبَرُوْا بَلْ مَكْرُ

Ask them: Who provides sustenance for you from the heavens and the earth? Then tell them: Allah; and add: Either you or we are rightly guided, and the other of us is in manifest error. Say to them: You will not be called to account for our sins and we shall not be called to account for that which you do. Tell them: Our Lord will bring us face to face; then will He judge between us with truth. He is the Judge, the All-Knowing. Say to them: Show me those whom you have joined with Him as partners. You can never do that; for He is Allah; the Mighty, the Wise. We have sent thee only as a bearer of glad tidings and a Warner for the whole of mankind, but most people know not. They ask: When will this promise be fulfilled, if you are truthful? Tell them: Your term is a period, which you can neither outstrip nor anticipate by an hour. (23—31)

The disbelievers say: We will never believe in this Quran nor in that which was revealed before it. Couldst thou but see the wrongdoers standing before their Lord, contending back and forth. Those who had been considered weak will say to the haughty ones: Had it not been for you, we would certainly have believed. The haughty ones will reply to the weak ones: Did we keep you away from the guidance when it came to you? Indeed not. You yourselves were the guilty ones. The weak ones will retort: Surely, it was your scheming day and night, when you bade us disbelieve in Allah and set up equals with Him, that has brought us to this pass. They will try to cover up their discomfiture when they are confronted with the punishment. We shall put chains round the necks of those who had disbelieved. They will be requited only in proportion to their misdeeds. (32—34)

الَّيْلِ وَ النَّهَارِ اِذْ تَاْمُرُوْنَنَاۤ اَنْ نَّكْفُرَ بِاللّٰهِ وَ نَجْعَلَ لَهۤ اَنْدَادًا ؕ وَاَسَرُّوا النَّدَامَةَ لَمَّا رَاَوُا الْعَذَابَ ؕ وَ جَعَلْنَا الْاَغْلٰلَ فِیۤ اَعْنَاقِ الَّذِیْنَ كَفَرُوْا ؕ هَلْ یُجْزَوْنَ اِلَّا مَا كَانُوْا یَعْمَلُوْنَ ۝

وَمَاۤ اَرْسَلْنَا فِیْ قَرْیَةٍ مِّنْ نَّذِیْرٍ اِلَّا قَالَ مُتْرَفُوْهَاۤ ۙ اِنَّا بِمَاۤ اُرْسِلْتُمْ بِهٖ كٰفِرُوْنَ ۝

We never sent a Warner to any city but its wealthy ones asserted: We disbelieve in that which you have been sent with. We have more wealth and children than you have; and we are not going to be punished. Say to them: My Lord enlarges the provision for whomsoever He pleases and straitens it for whomsoever He pleases; but most people know it not. It is not your wealth or your children that will confer on you nearness to Us. It is those who believe and act righteously that will have manifold reward for their good deeds and will enjoy security in lofty mansions. Those who strive to frustrate Our purpose in the matter of Our Signs will be confronted with chastisement. Say to them: It is my Lord who enlarges the provision for such of His servants as He pleases, and straitens it for such of them as He pleases. Whatever you spend He will foster it. He is the Best of providers. (35—40)

وَ قَالُوْا نَحْنُ اَكْثَرُ اَمْوَالًا وَّ اَوْلَادًا ۙ وَّ مَا نَحْنُ بِمُعَذَّبِیْنَ ۝ قُلْ اِنَّ رَبِّیْ یَبْسُطُ الرِّزْقَ لِمَنْ یَّشَاۤءُ وَ یَقْدِرُ وَلٰكِنَّ اَكْثَرَ النَّاسِ لَا یَعْلَمُوْنَ ع ۝

وَمَاۤ اَمْوَالُكُمْ وَ لَاۤ اَوْلَادُكُمْ بِالَّتِیْ تُقَرِّبُكُمْ عِنْدَنَا زُلْفٰۤی اِلَّا مَنْ اٰمَنَ وَ عَمِلَ صَالِحًا ۫ فَاُولٰٓئِكَ لَهُمْ جَزَاۤءُ الضِّعْفِ بِمَا عَمِلُوْا وَ هُمْ فِی الْغُرُفٰتِ اٰمِنُوْنَ ۝ وَالَّذِیْنَ یَسْعَوْنَ فِیْۤ اٰیٰتِنَا مُعٰجِزِیْنَ اُولٰٓئِكَ فِی الْعَذَابِ مُحْضَرُوْنَ ۝

قُلْ اِنَّ رَبِّیْ یَبْسُطُ الرِّزْقَ لِمَنْ یَّشَاۤءُ مِنْ عِبَادِهٖ وَ یَقْدِرُ لَهٗ ؕ وَ مَاۤ اَنْفَقْتُمْ مِّنْ شَیْءٍ فَهُوَ یُخْلِفُهٗ ۚ وَ هُوَ خَیْرُ الرّٰزِقِیْنَ ۝

وَ یَوْمَ یَحْشُرُهُمْ جَمِیْعًا ثُمَّ یَقُوْلُ لِلْمَلٰٓئِكَةِ اَهٰٓؤُلَاۤءِ اِیَّاكُمْ كَانُوْا یَعْبُدُوْنَ ۝

On the day when He gathers them all together, He will ask the angels: Was it you that these people worshipped? They will reply: Holy art Thou! Thou art our Protector against them. They worshipped imaginary beings; it was in them that most of them believed.

قَالُوْا سُبْحٰنَكَ اَنْتَ وَلِیُّنَا مِنْ دُوْنِهِمْ ۚ بَلْ كَانُوْا یَعْبُدُوْنَ الْجِنَّ ۚ اَكْثَرُهُمْ بِهِمْ مُّؤْمِنُوْنَ ۝

فَالْیَوْمَ لَا یَمْلِكُ بَعْضُكُمْ لِبَعْضٍ نَّفْعًا وَّ لَا ضَرًّا ۚ

On that day you will have no capacity to benefit or harm one another; and We shall say to the wrongdoers: Suffer the punishment of the Fire that you denied. When Our manifest Signs are recited to them they say: This is only a man who seeks to turn you away from that which your fathers worshipped. They say of the Quran: It is falsehood fabricated by him. Those who disbelieve, say of the truth when it comes to them: This is clear magic. We have given them no books in which they have read this, nor have We sent them a Warner before thee, who may have told them this. Those who were before them also rejected the truth. These have not attained to one tenth of the power that We had bestowed upon those who were before them, yet when they rejected My Messengers, how terrible was My chastisement! (41—46)

Say to them: I exhort you to do one thing: and that is that you stand before Allah two and two or singly and reflect. You will thus realise that your companion is not afflicted with madness. He is only a Warner, warning you of an impending severe chastisement. Tell them: Whatever recompense I might ask of you, you can keep it. My recompense is with Allah; and He is Witness over all things. Say to them: My Lord hurls the Truth at falsehood and smashes it. He is the Great Knower of the unseen. Say to them: The Truth has come and will endure. Falsehood has no power to originate anything, nor to revive it. Affirm: If I am in error, I shall carry the burden thereof; and if I am rightly guided, it is because of that which my Lord has revealed to me. Verily, He is All-Hearing, Nigh. (47—51)

Couldst thou but see when they will be smitten with fear and there will be no way of escape; and they will be seized from a place nearby.

وَّ نَقُوْلُ لِلَّذِيْنَ ظَلَمُوْا ذُوْقُوْا عَذَابَ النَّارِ الَّتِيْ كُنْتُمْ بِهَا تُكَذِّبُوْنَ ۝

وَ إِذَا تُتْلٰى عَلَيْهِمْ اٰيٰتُنَا بَيِّنٰتٍ قَالُوْا مَا هٰذَا إِلَّا رَجُلٌ يُّرِيْدُ أَنْ يَّصُدَّكُمْ عَمَّا كَانَ يَعْبُدُ اٰبَآؤُكُمْ ۚ وَ قَالُوْا مَا هٰذَا إِلَّا إِفْكٌ مُّفْتَرًى ۚ وَ قَالَ الَّذِيْنَ كَفَرُوْا لِلْحَقِّ لَمَّا جَآءَهُمْ ۙ إِنْ هٰذَا إِلَّا سِحْرٌ مُّبِيْنٌ ۝

وَ مَآ اٰتَيْنٰهُمْ مِّنْ كُتُبٍ يَّدْرُسُوْنَهَا وَ مَآ أَرْسَلْنَآ إِلَيْهِمْ قَبْلَكَ مِنْ نَّذِيْرٍ ۝

وَ كَذَّبَ الَّذِيْنَ مِنْ قَبْلِهِمْ ۙ وَ مَا بَلَغُوْا مِعْشَارَ مَآ اٰتَيْنٰهُمْ فَكَذَّبُوْا رُسُلِيْ ۟ فَكَيْفَ كَانَ نَكِيْرِ ۝

قُلْ إِنَّمَآ أَعِظُكُمْ بِوَاحِدَةٍ ۚ أَنْ تَقُوْمُوْا لِلّٰهِ مَثْنٰى وَ فُرَادٰى ثُمَّ تَتَفَكَّرُوْا ۟ مَا بِصَاحِبِكُمْ مِّنْ جِنَّةٍ ۚ إِنْ هُوَ إِلَّا نَذِيْرٌ لَّكُمْ بَيْنَ يَدَيْ عَذَابٍ شَدِيْدٍ ۝

قُلْ مَا سَأَلْتُكُمْ مِّنْ أَجْرٍ فَهُوَ لَكُمْ ۚ إِنْ أَجْرِيَ إِلَّا عَلَى اللّٰهِ ۚ وَ هُوَ عَلٰى كُلِّ شَيْءٍ شَهِيْدٌ ۝

قُلْ إِنَّ رَبِّيْ يَقْذِفُ بِالْحَقِّ ۚ عَلَّامُ الْغُيُوْبِ ۝

قُلْ جَآءَ الْحَقُّ وَ مَا يُبْدِئُ الْبَاطِلُ وَ مَا يُعِيْدُ ۝

قُلْ إِنْ ضَلَلْتُ فَإِنَّمَآ أَضِلُّ عَلٰى نَفْسِيْ ۚ وَ إِنِ اهْتَدَيْتُ فَبِمَا يُوْحِيْ إِلَيَّ رَبِّيْ ۚ إِنَّهُ سَمِيْعٌ قَرِيْبٌ ۝

وَ لَوْ تَرٰى إِذْ فَزِعُوْا فَلَا فَوْتَ وَ أُخِذُوْا مِنْ مَّكَانٍ قَرِيْبٍ ۝

وَّ قَالُوْا اٰمَنَّا بِهٖ ۚ وَ أَنّٰى لَهُمُ التَّنَاوُشُ مِنْ مَّكَانٍ

Then they will say: We now believe
therein; but how will they achieve this,
having gone so far? They had rejected it
before, while they indulged in conjectures
from a place far off. A barrier will be
placed between them and that which they
yearn after, as was done with the likes
of them before. They too were afflicted
with distracting doubt. (52—55)

بَعِيدٌ ۟

وَقَدْ كَفَرُوا بِهِ مِنْ قَبْلُ ۚ وَيَقْذِفُونَ بِالْغَيْبِ مِنْ

مَّكَانٍ بَعِيدٍ ۟

وَحِيلَ بَيْنَهُمْ وَبَيْنَ مَا يَشْتَهُونَ كَمَا فُعِلَ

بِأَشْيَاعِهِمْ مِّنْ قَبْلُ ۚ إِنَّهُمْ كَانُوا فِي شَكٍّ مُرِيبٍ ۟

بِسۡمِ اللهِ الرَّحۡمٰنِ الرَّحِیۡمِ ۝

سُوۡرَةُ فَاطِرمَکِّیَّة ۩

AL-FĀṬIR
(Revealed before Hijra)

In the name of Allah, Most Gracious, Ever Merciful. (1)

All praise belongs to Allah, Who is about to fashion the heavens and the earth in a new pattern; and Who will make the angels His messengers having two, three or four wings. He adds to His creation whatever He pleases. Allah has power over all things. Whatever of mercy Allah grants to people may be withheld by none; and whatever He withholds, may not be released by any thereafter. He is the Mighty, the Wise. Ye people, keep in mind the favour that Allah has bestowed upon you. Is there any creator other than Allah Who provides for you from the heaven and the earth? There is no god but He. Whither then are you turned away? If they reject thee, Messengers before thee were also rejected. All matters are brought back to Allah for final determination. (2—5)

Ye people, assuredly the promise of Allah is true, so let not the hither life beguile you, nor let any deceiver deceive you concerning Allah. Satan is your enemy; so treat him as an enemy. He calls his followers that they may become inmates of the Fire. For those who disbelieve there is a severe chastisement; and for those who believe and work righteousness, there is forgiveness and a great reward.

بِسۡمِ اللهِ الرَّحۡمٰنِ الرَّحِیۡمِ ۝

اَلۡحَمۡدُ لِلّٰهِ فَاطِرِ السَّمٰوٰتِ وَالۡاَرۡضِ جَاعِلِ الۡمَلٰٓئِکَةِ رُسُلًا اُولِیۡۤ اَجۡنِحَةٍ مَّثۡنٰی وَ ثُلٰثَ وَرُبٰعَ ؕ یَزِیۡدُ فِی الۡخَلۡقِ مَا یَشَآءُ ؕ اِنَّ اللهَ عَلٰی کُلِّ شَیۡءٍ قَدِیۡرٌ ۝

مَا یَفۡتَحِ اللهُ لِلنَّاسِ مِنۡ رَّحۡمَةٍ فَلَا مُمۡسِکَ لَهَا ۚ وَمَا یُمۡسِکۡ ۙ فَلَا مُرۡسِلَ لَهٗ مِنۡ بَعۡدِهٖ ؕ وَهُوَ الۡعَزِیۡزُ الۡحَکِیۡمُ ۝

یٰۤاَیُّهَا النَّاسُ اذۡکُرُوۡا نِعۡمَتَ اللهِ عَلَیۡکُمۡ ؕ هَلۡ مِنۡ خَالِقٍ غَیۡرُ اللهِ یَرۡزُقُکُمۡ مِّنَ السَّمَآءِ وَالۡاَرۡضِ ؕ لَاۤ اِلٰهَ اِلَّا هُوَ ۫ فَاَنّٰی تُؤۡفَکُوۡنَ ۝

وَاِنۡ یُّکَذِّبُوۡکَ فَقَدۡ کُذِّبَتۡ رُسُلٌ مِّنۡ قَبۡلِکَ ؕ وَ اِلَی اللهِ تُرۡجَعُ الۡاُمُوۡرُ ۝

یٰۤاَیُّهَا النَّاسُ اِنَّ وَعۡدَ اللهِ حَقٌّ فَلَا تَغُرَّنَّکُمُ الۡحَیٰوةُ الدُّنۡیَا ٭ وَلَا یَغُرَّنَّکُمۡ بِاللهِ الۡغَرُوۡرُ ۝

اِنَّ الشَّیۡطٰنَ لَکُمۡ عَدُوٌّ فَاتَّخِذُوۡهُ عَدُوًّا ؕ اِنَّمَا یَدۡعُوۡا حِزۡبَهٗ لِیَکُوۡنُوۡا مِنۡ اَصۡحٰبِ السَّعِیۡرِ ۝

اَلَّذِیۡنَ کَفَرُوۡا لَهُمۡ عَذَابٌ شَدِیۡدٌ ۬ؕ وَالَّذِیۡنَ اٰمَنُوۡا وَعَمِلُوا الصّٰلِحٰتِ لَهُمۡ مَّغۡفِرَةٌ وَّاَجۡرٌ کَبِیۡرٌ ۝

Can he be guided, the evil of whose conduct appears pleasing to him and he looks upon it as good? Surely, Allah adjudges astray whom He will and guides whom He will. So let not thy soul waste away in sighing after them. Surely, Allah knows that which they do. (6—9)

Allah it is Who sends the winds that raise the clouds; then We drive them to a region that has become lifeless, and quicken thereby the earth after its death. Likewise is the process of raising the dead. Whoso seeks honour should realise that all honour belongs to Allah. Unto Him ascend good words and righteous conduct exalts them. Those who plan evil will suffer severe chastisement and their planning will come to naught. Allah created you from dust, then from a sperm-drop, then he made you pairs. No female conceives, nor does she give birth but it is within His knowledge nor is anyone's life prolonged nor is it cut short, but it is in accordance with a law laid down. That surely is easy for Allah. (10—12)

The two waters are not alike; this one of the rivers and springs sweet, palatable and pleasant to drink, and the other of the sea, salt and bitter. From each you eat fresh meat, and fish out articles that you wear as ornaments. Thou seest the vessels ploughing through each that you may seek of His bounty, and that you may be grateful. He merges the night into the day, and merges the day into the night; and He has bound the sun and the moon into service, each running its course for an appointed term. Such is Allah, your Lord; His is the kingdom.

اَفَمَنْ زُيِّنَ لَهٗ سُوْٓءُ عَمَلِهٖ فَرَاٰهُ حَسَنًا ۚ فَاِنَّ اللّٰهَ يُضِلُّ مَنْ يَّشَآءُ وَيَهْدِىْ مَنْ يَّشَآءُ ۖ فَلَا تَذْهَبْ نَفْسُكَ عَلَيْهِمْ حَسَرٰتٍ ۭ اِنَّ اللّٰهَ عَلِيْمٌۢ بِمَا يَصْنَعُوْنَ ۞

وَاللّٰهُ الَّذِىْٓ اَرْسَلَ الرِّيٰحَ فَتُثِيْرُ سَحَابًا فَسُقْنٰهُ اِلٰى بَلَدٍ مَّيِّتٍ فَاَحْيَيْنَا بِهِ الْاَرْضَ بَعْدَ مَوْتِهَا ۭ كَذٰلِكَ النُّشُوْرُ ۞

مَنْ كَانَ يُرِيْدُ الْعِزَّةَ فَلِلّٰهِ الْعِزَّةُ جَمِيْعًا ۭ اِلَيْهِ يَصْعَدُ الْكَلِمُ الطَّيِّبُ وَالْعَمَلُ الصَّالِحُ يَرْفَعُهٗ ۭ وَالَّذِيْنَ يَمْكُرُوْنَ السَّيِّاٰتِ لَهُمْ عَذَابٌ شَدِيْدٌ ۭ وَمَكْرُ اُولٰٓئِكَ هُوَ يَبُوْرُ ۞

وَاللّٰهُ خَلَقَكُمْ مِّنْ تُرَابٍ ثُمَّ مِنْ نُّطْفَةٍ ثُمَّ جَعَلَكُمْ اَزْوَاجًا ۭ وَمَا تَحْمِلُ مِنْ اُنْثٰى وَلَا تَضَعُ اِلَّا بِعِلْمِهٖ ۭ وَمَا يُعَمَّرُ مِنْ مُّعَمَّرٍ وَّلَا يُنْقَصُ مِنْ عُمُرِهٖٓ اِلَّا فِىْ كِتٰبٍ ۭ اِنَّ ذٰلِكَ عَلَى اللّٰهِ يَسِيْرٌ ۞

وَمَا يَسْتَوِى الْبَحْرٰنِ ۖ هٰذَا عَذْبٌ فُرَاتٌ سَآئِغٌ شَرَابُهٗ وَهٰذَا مِلْحٌ اُجَاجٌ ۭ وَمِنْ كُلٍّ تَاْكُلُوْنَ لَحْمًا طَرِيًّا وَّتَسْتَخْرِجُوْنَ حِلْيَةً تَلْبَسُوْنَهَا ۚ وَتَرَى الْفُلْكَ فِيْهِ مَوَاخِرَ لِتَبْتَغُوْا مِنْ فَضْلِهٖ وَلَعَلَّكُمْ تَشْكُرُوْنَ ۞

يُوْلِجُ الَّيْلَ فِى النَّهَارِ وَيُوْلِجُ النَّهَارَ فِى الَّيْلِ ۙ وَسَخَّرَ الشَّمْسَ وَالْقَمَرَ ۖ كُلٌّ يَّجْرِىْ لِاَجَلٍ مُّسَمًّى ۭ ذٰلِكُمُ اللّٰهُ رَبُّكُمْ لَهُ الْمُلْكُ ۭ وَالَّذِيْنَ تَدْعُوْنَ

Those whom you call upon beside Him possess not even the membraneous covering of a date stone. If you call on them, they will not hear your call; and could they have heard it, they could not answer you. On the Day of Judgment they will repudiate your having associated them with Allah. None can inform thee so well as One, All-Aware. (13—15)

مِنْ دُوْنِهٖ مَا يَمْلِكُوْنَ مِنْ قِطْمِيْرٍ ۞

اِنْ تَدْعُوْهُمْ لَا يَسْمَعُوْا دُعَآءَكُمْ ۚ وَلَوْ سَمِعُوْا مَا اسْتَجَابُوْا لَكُمْ ۚ وَيَوْمَ الْقِيٰمَةِ يَكْفُرُوْنَ بِشِرْكِكُمْ ۚ وَلَا يُنَبِّئُكَ مِثْلُ خَبِيْرٍ ۞

يٰٓاَيُّهَا النَّاسُ اَنْتُمُ الْفُقَرَآءُ اِلَى اللّٰهِ ۚ وَاللّٰهُ هُوَ الْغَنِيُّ الْحَمِيْدُ ۞

Ye people, it is you who are dependent upon Allah, while Allah is Self-Sufficient, Praiseworthy. If He please, He could destroy you and put in your place a new creation. That is not difficult for Allah. (16—18)

اِنْ يَّشَاْ يُذْهِبْكُمْ وَيَاْتِ بِخَلْقٍ جَدِيْدٍ ۞

وَمَا ذٰلِكَ عَلَى اللّٰهِ بِعَزِيْزٍ ۞

No one can bear the burden of another. If a heavily laden one should call another to carry his load, naught of it shall be carried by the other, even though he be a kinsman. Thou canst warn only those who fear their Lord in secret and observe Prayer. Whoso purifies himself does so to his own benefit. To Allah is the final return. (19)

وَلَا تَزِرُ وَازِرَةٌ وِّزْرَ اُخْرٰى ۚ وَاِنْ تَدْعُ مُثْقَلَةٌ اِلٰى حِمْلِهَا لَا يُحْمَلْ مِنْهُ شَيْءٌ وَّلَوْ كَانَ ذَا قُرْبٰى ۚ اِنَّمَا تُنْذِرُ الَّذِيْنَ يَخْشَوْنَ رَبَّهُمْ بِالْغَيْبِ وَ اَقَامُوا الصَّلٰوةَ ۚ وَمَنْ تَزَكّٰى فَاِنَّمَا يَتَزَكّٰى لِنَفْسِهٖ ۚ وَاِلَى اللّٰهِ الْمَصِيْرُ ۞

وَمَا يَسْتَوِى الْاَعْمٰى وَالْبَصِيْرُ ۞

وَلَا الظُّلُمٰتُ وَلَا النُّوْرُ ۞

وَلَا الظِّلُّ وَلَا الْحَرُوْرُ ۞

The blind and the seeing are not alike, nor the darkness and light, nor the shade and sun, nor the living and the dead. Surely, Allah causes to hear whomsoever He wills, and thou canst not make those to hear who are buried in the graves. Thou art but a Warner. Verily, We have sent thee with enduring truth, as a bearer of glad tidings and as a Warner. There is no people to whom a Warner has not been sent.

وَمَا يَسْتَوِى الْاَحْيَآءُ وَلَا الْاَمْوَاتُ ۚ اِنَّ اللّٰهَ يُسْمِعُ مَنْ يَّشَآءُ ۚ وَمَا اَنْتَ بِمُسْمِعٍ مَّنْ فِى الْقُبُوْرِ ۞

اِنْ اَنْتَ اِلَّا نَذِيْرٌ ۞

اِنَّا اَرْسَلْنٰكَ بِالْحَقِّ بَشِيْرًا وَّنَذِيْرًا ۚ وَاِنْ مِّنْ اُمَّةٍ اِلَّا خَلَا فِيْهَا نَذِيْرٌ ۞

وَاِنْ يُّكَذِّبُوْكَ فَقَدْ كَذَّبَ الَّذِيْنَ مِنْ قَبْلِهِمْ

If they reject thee, those who were before them also rejected those who came to warn them. Their Messengers came to them with clear Signs, and with commandments, and with the enlightening Book. Then I seized those who disbelieved. Let them recall then how terrible was My chastisement. (20—27)

Seest thou not that Allah sends down water from the clouds, and We bring forth therewith fruits of diverse colours; and of the mountains some are white and red, and of diverse hues and others raven black; and in like manner there are people, and beasts and cattle of various colours? Of the servants of Allah, it is those who possess knowledge that fear Him. Allah is Mighty, Most Forgiving. Those who follow the Book of Allah and observe Prayer and spend out of that which We have provided for them, secretly and openly, are pursuing a commerce that suffers no loss; for Allah will give them their full rewards and will add to them out of His bounty. He is surely Most Forgiving, Most Appreciating. (28—31)

That which We have revealed to thee of the Book is the truth, fulfilling that which was revealed before it. Surely, Allah is All-Aware, All-Seeing concerning His servants. Then We make inheritors of the Book those of Our servants whom We choose. Some of them are hard upon themselves, some follow the middle course, some excel others in goodness, by Allah's command. This is a great bounty of Allah. Their reward will be Gardens of Eternity which they will enter. They will be adorned therein with bracelets of gold, and pearls; and their garments therein will be of silk.

They will say: All praise belongs to Allah,
Who has rid us of all grief. Surely, our
Lord is Most Forgiving, Most Appreciating, Who has, out of His bounty, settled
us in an abode wherein neither toil nor
weariness affects us. The disbelievers will
be in the fire of hell; death will not be
decreed for them that they could escape
by way of death, nor will its torment be
lightened for them in any other way. Thus
do We requite every ungrateful person.
Therein will they beseech for help: Lord
take us out of this, we will act righteously
contrary to that which we used to do.
They will be told: Did We not grant you
a long enough span of life to enable those
to reflect who might desire to reflect; and
did not a Warner come to you? Now suffer
the torment; for the wrongdoers there is
no helper. (32—38)

وَقَالُوا الْحَمْدُ لِلّٰهِ الَّذِىٓ اَذْهَبَ عَنَّا الْحَزَنَ ؕ اِنَّ
رَبَّنَا لَغَفُوْرٌ شَكُوْرُۨ ۝

الَّذِىٓ اَحَلَّنَا دَارَ الْمُقَامَةِ مِنْ فَضْلِهٖ ۚ لَا يَمَسُّنَا
فِيْهَا نَصَبٌ وَّلَا يَمَسُّنَا فِيْهَا لُغُوْبٌ ۝

وَالَّذِيْنَ كَفَرُوْا لَهُمْ نَارُ جَهَنَّمَ ۚ لَا يُقْضٰى عَلَيْهِمْ
فَيَمُوْتُوْا وَلَا يُخَفَّفُ عَنْهُمْ مِّنْ عَذَابِهَا ؕ كَذٰلِكَ
نَجْزِىْ كُلَّ كَفُوْرٍ ۝

وَهُمْ يَصْطَرِخُوْنَ فِيْهَا ۚ رَبَّنَآ اَخْرِجْنَا نَعْمَلْ صَالِحًا
غَيْرَ الَّذِىْ كُنَّا نَعْمَلُ ؕ اَوَلَمْ نُعَمِّرْكُمْ مَّا يَتَذَكَّرُ
فِيْهِ مَنْ تَذَكَّرَ وَجَآءَكُمُ النَّذِيْرُ ؕ فَذُوْقُوْا فَمَا
لِلظّٰلِمِيْنَ مِنْ نَّصِيْرٍ ۝

اِنَّ اللّٰهَ عٰلِمُ غَيْبِ السَّمٰوٰتِ وَالْاَرْضِ ؕ اِنَّهٗ عَلِيْمٌ
بِذَاتِ الصُّدُوْرِ ۝

هُوَ الَّذِىْ جَعَلَكُمْ خَلٰٓئِفَ فِى الْاَرْضِ ؕ فَمَنْ كَفَرَ
فَعَلَيْهِ كُفْرُهٗ ؕ وَلَا يَزِيْدُ الْكٰفِرِيْنَ كُفْرُهُمْ عِنْدَ
رَبِّهِمْ اِلَّا مَقْتًا ۚ وَلَا يَزِيْدُ الْكٰفِرِيْنَ كُفْرُهُمْ اِلَّا
خَسَارًا ۝

Allah knows the secrets of the heavens
and the earth; He knows well all that is in
the minds. He it is Who made you vicegerents in the earth; so he who disbelieves
will bear the burden of his disbelief. Their
disbelief will only increase the displeasure
of their Lord with the disbelievers: it will
only augment their loss. Ask them: Show
me what have these associate gods of
yours whom you call on beside Allah
created of the earth? Or have they a share
in the creation of the heavens? Or have
We given them a Book that furnishes
them with a proof? None of this. Indeed
the wrongdoers promise one another nothing but deception. (39—41)

قُلْ اَرَءَيْتُمْ شُرَكَآءَكُمُ الَّذِيْنَ تَدْعُوْنَ مِنْ دُوْنِ
اللّٰهِ ؕ اَرُوْنِىْ مَاذَا خَلَقُوْا مِنَ الْاَرْضِ اَمْ لَهُمْ شِرْكٌ
فِى السَّمٰوٰتِ ۚ اَمْ اٰتَيْنٰهُمْ كِتٰبًا فَهُمْ عَلٰى بَيِّنَتٍ مِّنْهُ ۚ
بَلْ اِنْ يَّعِدُ الظّٰلِمُوْنَ بَعْضُهُمْ بَعْضًا اِلَّا غُرُوْرًا ۝

اِنَّ اللّٰهَ يُمْسِكُ السَّمٰوٰتِ وَالْاَرْضَ اَنْ تَزُوْلَا ۚ وَ

Allah holds the heavens and the earth, lest they should deviate from their places. Were they to deviate none could keep them from destruction thereafter save Him. Surely, He is Forbearing, Most Forgiving. (42)

They swore their strongest oaths by Allah, that if a Warner came to them, they would be better guided than any other people. But when a Warner did come to them, it only increased them in aversion, because of their desire to dominate in the earth, and of their evil designs. Evil designs encompass none but the authors thereof. Do they then look for anything, except that which happened to those before them? But thou wilt never find any change in the way of Allah, nor wilt thou find Allah's decree ever averted. Have they not travelled in the earth and seen what was the end of those before them? Yet, those were stronger than these in power. Nothing in the heavens or the earth could frustrate Allah's designs. Verily, He is All-Knowing, All-Powerful. If Allah were to call people to account for all that they do, He would not leave a living creature on the surface of the earth; but He grants them respite during an appointed term; and when their appointed time comes, it is seen that Allah was watching His servants. (43—46)

لَئِنْ زَالَتَآ إِنْ أَمْسَكَهُمَا مِنْ أَحَدٍ مِّنْ بَعْدِهٖ ۗ إِنَّهٗ كَانَ حَلِيمًا غَفُورًا ۝

وَأَقْسَمُوا بِاللّٰهِ جَهْدَ أَيْمَانِهِمْ لَئِنْ جَآءَهُمْ نَذِيرٌ لَّيَكُونُنَّ أَهْدٰى مِنْ إِحْدَى الْأُمَمِ ۖ فَلَمَّا جَآءَهُمْ نَذِيرٌ مَّا زَادَهُمْ إِلَّا نُفُورًا ۝

اسْتِكْبَارًا فِي الْأَرْضِ وَمَكْرَ السَّيِّئِ ۚ وَلَا يَحِيقُ الْمَكْرُ السَّيِّئُ إِلَّا بِأَهْلِهٖ ۚ فَهَلْ يَنْظُرُونَ إِلَّا سُنَّتَ الْأَوَّلِينَ ۚ فَلَنْ تَجِدَ لِسُنَّتِ اللّٰهِ تَبْدِيلًا ۚ وَلَنْ تَجِدَ لِسُنَّتِ اللّٰهِ تَحْوِيلًا ۝

أَوَلَمْ يَسِيرُوا فِي الْأَرْضِ فَيَنْظُرُوا كَيْفَ كَانَ عَاقِبَةُ الَّذِينَ مِنْ قَبْلِهِمْ وَكَانُوا أَشَدَّ مِنْهُمْ قُوَّةً ۚ وَمَا كَانَ اللّٰهُ لِيُعْجِزَهٗ مِنْ شَيْءٍ فِي السَّمٰوٰتِ وَلَا فِي الْأَرْضِ ۚ إِنَّهٗ كَانَ عَلِيمًا قَدِيرًا ۝

وَلَوْ يُؤَاخِذُ اللّٰهُ النَّاسَ بِمَا كَسَبُوا مَا تَرَكَ عَلٰى ظَهْرِهَا مِنْ دَآبَّةٍ وَلٰكِنْ يُؤَخِّرُهُمْ إِلٰى أَجَلٍ مُّسَمًّى ۚ فَإِذَا جَآءَ أَجَلُهُمْ فَإِنَّ اللّٰهَ كَانَ بِعِبَادِهٖ بَصِيرًا ۝

YĀ SĪN

(Revealed before Hijra)

In the name of Allah, Most Gracious, Ever Merciful. (1)

بِسْمِ اللهِ الرَّحْمٰنِ الرَّحِيْمِ ۟

يٰسٓ ۟

وَالْقُرْاٰنِ الْحَكِيْمِ ۟

اِنَّكَ لَمِنَ الْمُرْسَلِيْنَ ۟

عَلٰى صِرَاطٍ مُّسْتَقِيْمٍ ۟

تَنْزِيْلَ الْعَزِيْزِ الرَّحِيْمِ ۟

لِتُنْذِرَ قَوْمًا مَّا اُنْذِرَ اٰبَآؤُهُمْ فَهُمْ غٰفِلُوْنَ ۟

لَقَدْ حَقَّ الْقَوْلُ عَلٰۤى اَكْثَرِهِمْ فَهُمْ لَا يُؤْمِنُوْنَ ۟

اِنَّا جَعَلْنَا فِيْۤ اَعْنَاقِهِمْ اَغْلٰلًا فَهِيَ اِلَى الْاَذْقَانِ فَهُمْ مُّقْمَحُوْنَ ۟

وَجَعَلْنَا مِنْۢ بَيْنِ اَيْدِيْهِمْ سَدًّا وَّ مِنْ خَلْفِهِمْ سَدًّا فَاَغْشَيْنٰهُمْ فَهُمْ لَا يُبْصِرُوْنَ ۟

وَسَوَآءٌ عَلَيْهِمْ ءَاَنْذَرْتَهُمْ اَمْ لَمْ تُنْذِرْهُمْ لَا يُؤْمِنُوْنَ ۟

اِنَّمَا تُنْذِرُ مَنِ اتَّبَعَ الذِّكْرَ وَخَشِيَ الرَّحْمٰنَ بِالْغَيْبِ ۚ فَبَشِّرْهُ بِمَغْفِرَةٍ وَّ اَجْرٍ كَرِيْمٍ ۟

اِنَّا نَحْنُ نُحْيِ الْمَوْتٰى وَنَكْتُبُ مَا قَدَّمُوْا وَاٰثَارَهُمْ ۚ وَكُلَّ شَيْءٍ اَحْصَيْنٰهُ فِيْۤ اِمَامٍ مُّبِيْنٍ ۟

وَاضْرِبْ لَهُمْ مَّثَلًا اَصْحٰبَ الْقَرْيَةِ ۘ اِذْ جَآءَهَا

O Perfect Leader! We cite the Quran full of wisdom as proof thereof. Thou art indeed one of the Messengers, pursuing the right path. The Quran is a revelation from the Mighty, the Ever Merciful, that thou mayest warn a people whose fathers were not warned, and so they are heedless. Surely Our word has proved true concerning most of them, for they do not believe. We have put round their necks chains of habits and custom, which reach up to their chins, thus forcing up their heads. We have set a barrier before them and a barrier behind them, and have covered them up so that they cannot see. Thus in their present state it is the same to them whether thou warn them or warn them not; they will not believe. Thou canst warn only him who would follow the Reminder and fear the Gracious One in secret. To such a one give glad tidings of forgiveness and a noble reward. Surely, it is We who give life to the dead, and We record that which they send forward and that which they leave behind. We have recorded everything in a clear Book. (2—13)

Recite to them the case of the people of a town when the Messengers came to it. We sent to them two Messengers, and they rejected them both; so We strengthened them with a third, and they said to the people: Indeed, We have been sent to you as Messengers. They retorted: You are but human beings like us, and the Gracious One has not sent down anything. You are only lying. The Messengers said: Our Lord knows that we are Messengers sent to you; and our duty is to convey the message to you clearly. The people rejoined: We believe you to be persons of evil augury; if you desist not, we will surely stone you and you will experience a painful torment at our hands. The Messengers replied: Your evil fortune is with your own selves. Do you attribute it to us because we admonish you? The truth is you are a people exceeding all bounds in disobedience. (14—20)

الْمُرْسَلُوْنَ ۞

اِذْ اَرْسَلْنَآ اِلَيْهِمُ اثْنَيْنِ فَكَذَّبُوْهُمَا فَعَزَّزْنَا بِثَالِثٍ فَقَالُوْٓا اِنَّآ اِلَيْكُمْ مُّرْسَلُوْنَ ۞

قَالُوْا مَآ اَنْتُمْ اِلَّا بَشَرٌ مِّثْلُنَا ۙ وَمَآ اَنْزَلَ الرَّحْمٰنُ مِنْ شَيْءٍ ۙ اِنْ اَنْتُمْ اِلَّا تَكْذِبُوْنَ ۞

قَالُوْا رَبُّنَا يَعْلَمُ اِنَّآ اِلَيْكُمْ لَمُرْسَلُوْنَ ۞

وَمَا عَلَيْنَآ اِلَّا الْبَلٰغُ الْمُبِيْنُ ۞

قَالُوْٓا اِنَّا تَطَيَّرْنَا بِكُمْ ۚ لَئِنْ لَّمْ تَنْتَهُوْا لَنَرْجُمَنَّكُمْ وَلَيَمَسَّنَّكُمْ مِّنَّا عَذَابٌ اَلِيْمٌ ۞

قَالُوْا طَآئِرُكُمْ مَّعَكُمْ ؕ اَئِنْ ذُكِّرْتُمْ ؕ بَلْ اَنْتُمْ قَوْمٌ مُّسْرِفُوْنَ ۞

وَجَآءَ مِنْ اَقْصَا الْمَدِيْنَةِ رَجُلٌ يَّسْعٰى ۫ قَالَ يٰقَوْمِ اتَّبِعُوا الْمُرْسَلِيْنَ ۞

اتَّبِعُوْا مَنْ لَّا يَسْئَلُكُمْ اَجْرًا وَّهُمْ مُّهْتَدُوْنَ ۞

A man came running from the other side of the town and addressed them thus: O my people, follow the Messengers, follow those who ask of you no recompense, and who are rightly guided. Why should I not worship Him Who has created me, and unto Whom you will be brought back? Shall I adopt others beside Him as gods? If the Gracious One should intend me any harm, their intercession would avail me naught, nor could they safeguard me against it. In such case I would indeed be in manifest error. I have believed in your Lord; so listen to me. His Lord said to him: Enter thou into Paradise. Thereupon he exclaimed: Would that my people knew how my Lord has granted me forgiveness and has joined me to the honoured ones.

وَمَا لِيَ لَآ اَعْبُدُ الَّذِيْ فَطَرَنِيْ وَاِلَيْهِ تُرْجَعُوْنَ ۞

ءَاَتَّخِذُ مِنْ دُوْنِهٖٓ اٰلِهَةً اِنْ يُّرِدْنِ الرَّحْمٰنُ بِضُرٍّ لَّا تُغْنِ عَنِّيْ شَفَاعَتُهُمْ شَيْئًا وَّلَا يُنْقِذُوْنِ ۞

اِنِّيْٓ اِذًا لَّفِيْ ضَلٰلٍ مُّبِيْنٍ ۞

اِنِّيْٓ اٰمَنْتُ بِرَبِّكُمْ فَاسْمَعُوْنِ ۞

قِيْلَ ادْخُلِ الْجَنَّةَ ؕ قَالَ يٰلَيْتَ قَوْمِيْ يَعْلَمُوْنَ ۞

بِمَا غَفَرَ لِيْ رَبِّيْ وَجَعَلَنِيْ مِنَ الْمُكْرَمِيْنَ ۞

وَمَآ اَنْزَلْنَا عَلٰى قَوْمِهٖ مِنْ بَعْدِهٖ مِنْ جُنْدٍ مِّنَ

We did not send down on his people after him any host from heaven, nor do We send down such hosts. It was but a single blast and they were stripped of everything. (21—30)

السَّمَاءِ وَمَا كُنَّا مُنْزِلِيْنَ ۞

اِنْ كَانَتْ اِلَّا صَيْحَةً وَّاحِدَةً فَاِذَا هُمْ خٰمِدُوْنَ ۞

يٰحَسْرَةً عَلَى الْعِبَادِ مَا يَأْتِيْهِمْ مِّنْ رَّسُوْلٍ اِلَّا كَانُوْا بِهِ يَسْتَهْزِءُوْنَ ۞

Alas for My creatures! Whenever a Messenger comes to them they deride him and make fun of him. Have they not seen how many generations have We destroyed before them, and that they never return to them? All of them, gathered together, will certainly be brought before Us. (31—33)

اَلَمْ يَرَوْا كَمْ اَهْلَكْنَا قَبْلَهُمْ مِّنَ الْقُرُوْنِ اَنَّهُمْ اِلَيْهِمْ لَا يَرْجِعُوْنَ ۞

وَاِنْ كُلٌّ لَّمَّا جَمِيْعٌ لَّدَيْنَا مُحْضَرُوْنَ ۞

وَاٰيَةٌ لَّهُمُ الْاَرْضُ الْمَيْتَةُ ۚ اَحْيَيْنٰهَا وَاَخْرَجْنَا مِنْهَا حَبًّا فَمِنْهُ يَأْكُلُوْنَ ۞

The dead earth is a Sign for the disbelievers. We revive it and We bring forth therefrom grain, of which they eat. We have made in it gardens of date-palms and vines, and We have caused springs to gush forth therein, that they may eat of the fruits thereof. It was not their hands that made them. Will they not then be grateful? Holy is He Who created all things in pairs, of that which the earth grows, and of themselves, and of that which they know not. (34—37)

وَجَعَلْنَا فِيْهَا جَنّٰتٍ مِّنْ نَّخِيْلٍ وَّاَعْنَابٍ وَّفَجَّرْنَا فِيْهَا مِنَ الْعُيُوْنِ ۞

لِيَأْكُلُوْا مِنْ ثَمَرِهٖ وَمَا عَمِلَتْهُ اَيْدِيْهِمْ ۚ اَفَلَا يَشْكُرُوْنَ ۞

سُبْحٰنَ الَّذِيْ خَلَقَ الْاَزْوَاجَ كُلَّهَا مِمَّا تُنْبِتُ الْاَرْضُ وَمِنْ اَنْفُسِهِمْ وَمِمَّا لَا يَعْلَمُوْنَ ۞

وَاٰيَةٌ لَّهُمُ الَّيْلُ ۚ نَسْلَخُ مِنْهُ النَّهَارَ فَاِذَا هُمْ مُّظْلِمُوْنَ ۞

The night is also a Sign for them. We strip off the day from it, and they are left in darkness. The sun is moving towards an appointed goal. That is the decree of the Almighty, the All-Knowing. We have appointed stages for the moon, till it wanes into the shape of an old dry branch of a palm-tree. It is not permissible for the sun to approach the moon, nor may the night outstrip the day. All glide along in an orbit. (38—41)

وَالشَّمْسُ تَجْرِيْ لِمُسْتَقَرٍّ لَّهَا ۚ ذٰلِكَ تَقْدِيْرُ الْعَزِيْزِ الْعَلِيْمِ ۞

وَالْقَمَرَ قَدَّرْنٰهُ مَنَازِلَ حَتّٰى عَادَ كَالْعُرْجُوْنِ الْقَدِيْمِ ۞

لَا الشَّمْسُ يَنْبَغِيْ لَهَآ اَنْ تُدْرِكَ الْقَمَرَ وَلَا

It is also a Sign for them that We carry their offspring in crowded vessels, and We have created for them other like means of transportation whereon they ride. If We so willed, We could drown them; then they would have no one to respond to their cries of distress nor would they be rescued except by Our mercy, and as a provision for a time. When it is said to them: Guard yourselves against that which is ahead of you, through prayer and righteous action, and against that which is behind you, through sincere repentance, that you may be shown mercy, they turn away. No Sign comes to them out of the Signs of their Lord, but they turn away from it. When it is said to them: Spend out of that with which Allah has provided you; those who disbelieve say to those who believe: Shall we feed him whom Allah would have fed had He so willed? You are but in manifest error. Then they ask: When will this warning of chastisement be carried out, if indeed you are truthful? They wait only for a single blast that will afflict them while they are still disputing. They will have no time to advise one another, or to return to their families to take care of them. (42—51)

الَّيْلُ سَابِقُ النَّهَارِ وَكُلٌّ فِى فَلَكٍ يَّسْبَحُوْنَ ۞

وَ اٰيَةٌ لَّهُمْ اَنَّا حَمَلْنَا ذُرِّيَّتَهُمْ فِى الْفُلْكِ الْمَشْحُوْنِ ۞

وَخَلَقْنَا لَهُمْ مِّنْ مِّثْلِهٖ مَا يَرْكَبُوْنَ ۞

وَ اِنْ نَّشَأْ نُغْرِقْهُمْ فَلَا صَرِيْخَ لَهُمْ وَ لَا هُمْ يُنْقَذُوْنَ ۞

اِلَّا رَحْمَةً مِّنَّا وَ مَتَاعًا اِلٰى حِيْنٍ ۞

وَ اِذَا قِيْلَ لَهُمُ اتَّقُوْا مَا بَيْنَ اَيْدِيْكُمْ وَ مَا خَلْفَكُمْ لَعَلَّكُمْ تُرْحَمُوْنَ ۞

وَ مَا تَأْتِيْهِمْ مِّنْ اٰيَةٍ مِّنْ اٰيٰتِ رَبِّهِمْ اِلَّا كَانُوْا عَنْهَا مُعْرِضِيْنَ ۞

وَ اِذَا قِيْلَ لَهُمْ اَنْفِقُوْا مِمَّا رَزَقَكُمُ اللّٰهُ قَالَ الَّذِيْنَ كَفَرُوْا لِلَّذِيْنَ اٰمَنُوْا اَنُطْعِمُ مَنْ لَّوْ يَشَاءُ اللّٰهُ اَطْعَمَهٗ اِنْ اَنْتُمْ اِلَّا فِى ضَلٰلٍ مُّبِيْنٍ ۞

وَ يَقُوْلُوْنَ مَتٰى هٰذَا الْوَعْدُ اِنْ كُنْتُمْ صٰدِقِيْنَ ۞

مَا يَنْظُرُوْنَ اِلَّا صَيْحَةً وَّاحِدَةً تَأْخُذُهُمْ وَهُمْ يَخِصِّمُوْنَ ۞

فَلَا يَسْتَطِيْعُوْنَ تَوْصِيَةً وَّلَا اِلٰى اَهْلِهِمْ يَرْجِعُوْنَ ۞

وَ نُفِخَ فِى الصُّوْرِ فَاِذَا هُمْ مِّنَ الْاَجْدَاثِ اِلٰى رَبِّهِمْ يَنْسِلُوْنَ ۞

قَالُوْا يٰوَيْلَنَا مَنْ بَعَثَنَا مِنْ مَّرْقَدِنَا هٰذَا مَا وَعَدَ الرَّحْمٰنُ وَ صَدَقَ الْمُرْسَلُوْنَ ۞

اِنْ كَانَتْ اِلَّا صَيْحَةً وَّاحِدَةً فَاِذَا هُمْ جَمِيْعٌ لَّدَيْنَا

The trumpet shall be blown and they will hasten on to their Lord from their graves, exclaiming: Woe to us, who has raised us up from our graves? This is what the Gracious One had warned us of, and the Messengers spoke the truth. It will be but one blast, and they will all be brought before Us together.

On that day, no one will be wronged in the least; and you will be recompensed according to what you did. The inmates of heaven will be happily occupied that day. They and their companions will be under the shades of Allah's mercy, reclining on raised couches. They will be provided therein with fruits and whatever else they call for. Peace! will be the greeting conveyed to them from the Ever Merciful Lord. (52—59)

مُّحْضَرُوْنَ ۝

فَالْيَوْمَ لَا تُظْلَمُ نَفْسٌ شَيْئًا وَّلَا تُجْزَوْنَ اِلَّا مَا كُنْتُمْ تَعْمَلُوْنَ ۝

اِنَّ اَصْحٰبَ الْجَنَّةِ الْيَوْمَ فِيْ شُغُلٍ فٰكِهُوْنَ ۝

هُمْ وَاَزْوَاجُهُمْ فِيْ ظِلٰلٍ عَلَى الْاَرَآئِكِ مُتَّكِئُوْنَ ۝

لَهُمْ فِيْهَا فَاكِهَةٌ وَّلَهُمْ مَّا يَدَّعُوْنَ ۝

سَلٰمٌ قَوْلًا مِّنْ رَّبٍّ رَّحِيْمٍ ۝

وَامْتَازُوا الْيَوْمَ اَيُّهَا الْمُجْرِمُوْنَ ۝

A command will go forth: Separate yourselves from the righteous this day, ye guilty ones. Did I not enjoin on you, sons of Adam, that you worship not Satan, for he is your declared enemy, and that you worship Me alone; this is the right path?

اَلَمْ اَعْهَدْ اِلَيْكُمْ يٰبَنِيْ اٰدَمَ اَنْ لَّا تَعْبُدُوا الشَّيْطٰنَ اِنَّهُ لَكُمْ عَدُوٌّ مُّبِيْنٌ ۝

وَّاَنِ اعْبُدُوْنِيْ هٰذَا صِرَاطٌ مُّسْتَقِيْمٌ ۝

وَلَقَدْ اَضَلَّ مِنْكُمْ جِبِلًّا كَثِيْرًا اَفَلَمْ تَكُوْنُوْا تَعْقِلُوْنَ ۝

هٰذِهٖ جَهَنَّمُ الَّتِيْ كُنْتُمْ تُوْعَدُوْنَ ۝

اِصْلَوْهَا الْيَوْمَ بِمَا كُنْتُمْ تَكْفُرُوْنَ ۝

He has led astray a great multitude of you. Did you not then understand? This is the hell of which you were warned. Enter it this day, because of your having disbelieved. On that day We shall put a seal on their mouths, and their hands will speak to Us, and their feet will bear witness to their doings. If We so willed, We could put out their eyes, then they would rush to find the way; but how would they see? If We so willed, We could root them to the spot, then they would not be able to go forward or turn back. He to whom We grant long life is afflicted by Us with a decline in his faculties. Do they not understand? (60—69)

الْيَوْمَ نَخْتِمُ عَلٰى اَفْوَاهِهِمْ وَتُكَلِّمُنَا اَيْدِيْهِمْ وَتَشْهَدُ اَرْجُلُهُمْ بِمَا كَانُوْا يَكْسِبُوْنَ ۝

وَلَوْ نَشَآءُ لَطَمَسْنَا عَلٰى اَعْيُنِهِمْ فَاسْتَبَقُوا الصِّرَاطَ فَاَنّٰى يُبْصِرُوْنَ ۝

وَلَوْ نَشَآءُ لَمَسَخْنٰهُمْ عَلٰى مَكَانَتِهِمْ فَمَا اسْتَطَاعُوْا مُضِيًّا وَّلَا يَرْجِعُوْنَ ۝

وَمَنْ نُّعَمِّرْهُ نُنَكِّسْهُ فِي الْخَلْقِ اَفَلَا يَعْقِلُوْنَ ۝

We have not taught the Prophet poetry, nor would it be compatible with his dignity. The revelation sent to him is but an admonition and a Book to be read repeatedly which makes things plain, so that it may warn him who is alive, and that Allah's word may be fulfilled concerning the disbelievers. (70—71)

وَمَا عَلَّمْنٰهُ الشِّعْرَ وَمَا يَنۢبَغِيۡ لَهٗ ؕ اِنۡ هُوَ اِلَّا ذِكْرٌ وَّقُرْاٰنٌ مُّبِيۡنٌ ۟ۙ

لِيُنۡذِرَ مَنۡ كَانَ حَيًّا وَّيَحِقَّ الْقَوۡلُ عَلَى الْكٰفِرِيۡنَ ۟

اَوَلَمۡ يَرَوۡا اَنَّا خَلَقْنَا لَهُمۡ مِّمَّا عَمِلَتۡ اَيۡدِيۡنَاۤ اَنۡعَامًا فَهُمۡ لَهَا مٰلِكُوۡنَ ۟

Do they not see that, among Our handiwork, We have created for them cattle which they own? We have subjected the same to them, so that some of them they ride, and of the flesh of others they eat. They derive other benefits from them and also obtain from them drink. Will they not then be grateful? They have adopted other gods beside Allah, that they might be helped. They are not able to help them, but they will testify against them in a large body. So let not that which they say cause thee concern. We know all that they conceal and that they disclose. (72—77)

وَذَلَّلْنٰهَا لَهُمۡ فَمِنۡهَا رَكُوۡبُهُمۡ وَمِنۡهَا يَاۡكُلُوۡنَ ۟

وَلَهُمۡ فِيۡهَا مَنَافِعُ وَمَشَارِبُ ؕ اَفَلَا يَشْكُرُوۡنَ ۟

وَاتَّخَذُوۡا مِنۡ دُوۡنِ اللهِ اٰلِهَةً لَّعَلَّهُمۡ يُنۡصَرُوۡنَ ۟ؕ

لَا يَسْتَطِيۡعُوۡنَ نَصْرَهُمۡ ۙ وَهُمۡ لَهُمۡ جُنۡدٌ مُّحْضَرُوۡنَ ۟

فَلَا يَحْزُنۡكَ قَوۡلُهُمۡ ۘ اِنَّا نَعْلَمُ مَا يُسِرُّوۡنَ وَمَا يُعْلِنُوۡنَ ۟

اَوَلَمۡ يَرَ الْاِنۡسَانُ اَنَّا خَلَقْنٰهُ مِنۡ نُّطۡفَةٍ فَاِذَا هُوَ خَصِيۡمٌ مُّبِيۡنٌ ۟

Does not man know that We have created him from a mere sperm-drop? Then he becomes a persistent disputer; he forgets the process of his own creation but has a lot to say concerning Us. He asks: Who will quicken the bones when they are decayed? Tell them: He Who created them the first time will quicken them. He knows well every type of creation; the One Who produces fire for you out of the green tree, which you kindle. Has not He Who created the heavens and the earth the power to create the like of them? Yea, and He is indeed the Supreme Creator, the All-Knowing. His power is such that when He intends a thing He says concerning it Be; and it is.

وَضَرَبَ لَنَا مَثَلًا وَّنَسِيَ خَلْقَهٗ ؕ قَالَ مَنۡ يُّحۡيِ الْعِظَامَ وَهِيَ رَمِيۡمٌ ۟

قُلۡ يُحۡيِيۡهَا الَّذِيۡۤ اَنۡشَاَهَاۤ اَوَّلَ مَرَّةٍ ؕ وَهُوَ بِكُلِّ خَلْقٍ عَلِيۡمٌ ۟ۙ

الَّذِيۡ جَعَلَ لَكُمۡ مِّنَ الشَّجَرِ الْاَخْضَرِ نَارًا فَاِذَاۤ اَنۡتُمۡ مِّنۡهُ تُوۡقِدُوۡنَ ۟

اَوَلَيۡسَ الَّذِيۡ خَلَقَ السَّمٰوٰتِ وَالْاَرۡضَ بِقٰدِرٍ عَلٰۤى اَنۡ يَّخْلُقَ مِثْلَهُمۡ ؕ بَلٰى ۗ وَهُوَ الْخَلّٰقُ الْعَلِيۡمُ ۟

اِنَّمَاۤ اَمْرُهٗۤ اِذَاۤ اَرَادَ شَيْئًا اَنۡ يَّقُوۡلَ لَهٗ كُنۡ فَيَكُوۡنُ ۟

Thus Holy is He, in Whose hand is the kingdom over all things. To Him will you all be brought back. (78—84)

فَسُبْحٰنَ الَّذِى بِيَدِهٖ مَلَكُوْتُ كُلِّ شَىْءٍ وَّاِلَيْهِ

تُرْجَعُوْنَ ۝

AL-ṢĀFFĀT

(Revealed before Hijra)

In the name of Allah, Most Gracious, Ever Merciful. (1)

We call to witness those who range themselves in close ranks, in support of the Truth; who are stern admonishers against evil; who are constant in reciting the Reminder; that most surely your God is One, the Lord of the heavens and the earth and all that is between them and the Lord of the sources of light. We have adorned the lowest heaven with the adornment of the planets, and have guarded it against all rebellious satans. They cannot penetrate to the meaning of that which is spoken in the Assembly on High and are pelted from every direction and repulsed; and for them is a lasting punishment. But if any of them snatches away something by stealth and perverts it, he is pursued by a piercing flame. (2—11)

Then ask them whether it is they who were harder to create or the rest of the universe that We have created? Them We created of cohesive clay. Thou dost wonder at their talk, and they ridicule what thou sayest. When they are admonished, they pay no heed; and when they see a Sign, they laugh at it, and say: This is plain magic.

440

What! when we are dead and have become dust and bones, shall we be raised up again, and our forefathers of old also? Tell them: Yea; and you will then be in disgrace. It will be a single stern call, and they will be roused into consciousness and will exclaim: Woe for us! This is the Day of Judgment. They will be told: This is the Day of Final Decision that you used to deny. (12—22)

ءَاِذَا مِتْنَا وَكُنَّا تُرَابًا وَّعِظَامًا ءَاِنَّا لَمَبْعُوْثُوْنَ ۞

اَوَ اٰبَآؤُنَا الْاَوَّلُوْنَ ۞

قُلْ نَعَمْ وَاَنْتُمْ دَاخِرُوْنَ ۞

فَاِنَّمَا هِيَ زَجْرَةٌ وَّاحِدَةٌ فَاِذَا هُمْ يَنْظُرُوْنَ ۞

وَقَالُوْا يٰوَيْلَنَا هٰذَا يَوْمُ الدِّيْنِ ۞

هٰذَا يَوْمُ الْفَصْلِ الَّذِيْ كُنْتُمْ بِهٖ تُكَذِّبُوْنَ ۞

اُحْشُرُوا الَّذِيْنَ ظَلَمُوْا وَاَزْوَاجَهُمْ وَمَا كَانُوْا يَعْبُدُوْنَ ۞

Allah will command: Assemble the wrongdoers along with their companions and that which they used to worship beside Allah; and lead them along the path of hell and make them stand there, for they will be questioned. Then they will be asked: How is it that you do not help one another? On that day they will surrender completely; and one party of them will dispute with the other.

مِنْ دُوْنِ اللّٰهِ فَاهْدُوْهُمْ اِلٰى صِرَاطِ الْجَحِيْمِ ۞

وَقِفُوْهُمْ اِنَّهُمْ مَّسْئُوْلُوْنَ ۞

مَا لَكُمْ لَا تَنَاصَرُوْنَ ۞

بَلْ هُمُ الْيَوْمَ مُسْتَسْلِمُوْنَ ۞

وَاَقْبَلَ بَعْضُهُمْ عَلٰى بَعْضٍ يَّتَسَآءَلُوْنَ ۞

قَالُوْا اِنَّكُمْ كُنْتُمْ تَأْتُوْنَنَا عَنِ الْيَمِيْنِ ۞

قَالُوْا بَلْ لَّمْ تَكُوْنُوْا مُؤْمِنِيْنَ ۞

وَمَا كَانَ لَنَا عَلَيْكُمْ مِّنْ سُلْطٰنٍ بَلْ كُنْتُمْ قَوْمًا طٰغِيْنَ ۞

They will say: You used to come at us from our right, seeking to mislead us. The others will retort: You yourselves had no faith. We possessed no authority over you; but you yourselves were a rebellious people. Now the word of our Lord has been justified in our case, and we must suffer the torment. We led you astray, for we ourselves had gone astray. On that day they will all share in the chastisement. Thus do We deal with the guilty ones.

فَحَقَّ عَلَيْنَا قَوْلُ رَبِّنَا اِنَّا لَذَآئِقُوْنَ ۞

فَاَغْوَيْنٰكُمْ اِنَّا كُنَّا غٰوِيْنَ ۞

فَاِنَّهُمْ يَوْمَئِذٍ فِي الْعَذَابِ مُشْتَرِكُوْنَ ۞

اِنَّا كَذٰلِكَ نَفْعَلُ بِالْمُجْرِمِيْنَ ۞

اِنَّهُمْ كَانُوْا اِذَا قِيْلَ لَهُمْ لَا اِلٰهَ اِلَّا اللّٰهُ

When it was said to them: There is no god but Allah; they were arrogant, and said: Shall we give up our gods at the bidding of a distracted versifier? But he has brought the truth and has testified to the truth of all the Messengers. You shall surely suffer the painful torment, being requited in proportion to that which you wrought. (23—40)

But the chosen servants of Allah will have a provision already announced, fruits of various kinds; and they will be honoured in Gardens of Bliss, seated on thrones, facing one another. They will be served with goblets from a flowing fountain, containing sparkling white drink, delicious to the taste, wherein there will be neither intoxication nor heaviness. With them will be pure women, with restrained looks and large beautiful eyes, as though they were eggs with their glossy shine well taken care of.

Then some of them will start a conversation. One of them will say: I had a companion who asked me: Art thou indeed of those who believe that when we are dead and have become dust and bones, we shall be requited? He will say: Will you have a look, if you can find him? Then he will have a look and will find him in the midst of hell; and will say to him: By Allah, thou didst almost cause my ruin. Had it not been for the favour of my

يَسْتَكْبِرُوْنَ ۞

وَ يَقُوْلُوْنَ اَئِنَّا لَتَارِكُوْۤا اٰلِهَتِنَا لِشَاعِرٍ مَّجْنُوْنٍ ۞

بَلْ جَآءَ بِالْحَقِّ وَصَدَّقَ الْمُرْسَلِيْنَ ۞

اِنَّكُمْ لَذَآئِقُوا الْعَذَابِ الْاَلِيْمِ ۞

وَمَا تُجْزَوْنَ اِلَّا مَا كُنْتُمْ تَعْمَلُوْنَ ۞

اِلَّا عِبَادَ اللّٰهِ الْمُخْلَصِيْنَ ۞

اُولٰٓئِكَ لَهُمْ رِزْقٌ مَّعْلُوْمٌ ۞

فَوَاكِهُ ۚ وَ هُمْ مُّكْرَمُوْنَ ۞

فِيْ جَنّٰتِ النَّعِيْمِ ۞

عَلٰى سُرُرٍ مُّتَقٰبِلِيْنَ ۞

يُطَافُ عَلَيْهِمْ بِكَأْسٍ مِّنْ مَّعِيْنٍ ۞

بَيْضَآءَ لَذَّةٍ لِّلشّٰرِبِيْنَ ۞

لَا فِيْهَا غَوْلٌ وَّلَا هُمْ عَنْهَا يُنْزَفُوْنَ ۞

وَعِنْدَهُمْ قٰصِرٰتُ الطَّرْفِ عِيْنٌ ۞

كَاَنَّهُنَّ بَيْضٌ مَّكْنُوْنٌ ۞

فَاَقْبَلَ بَعْضُهُمْ عَلٰى بَعْضٍ يَّتَسَآءَلُوْنَ ۞

قَالَ قَآئِلٌ مِّنْهُمْ اِنِّيْ كَانَ لِيْ قَرِيْنٌ ۞

يَّقُوْلُ اَئِنَّكَ لَمِنَ الْمُصَدِّقِيْنَ ۞

ءَاِذَا مِتْنَا وَكُنَّا تُرَابًا وَّعِظَامًا ءَاِنَّا لَمَدِيْنُوْنَ ۞

قَالَ هَلْ اَنْتُمْ مُّطَّلِعُوْنَ ۞

فَاطَّلَعَ فَرَاٰهُ فِيْ سَوَآءِ الْجَحِيْمِ ۞

قَالَ تَاللّٰهِ اِنْ كِدْتَّ لَتُرْدِيْنِ ۞

Lord, I too would have been of those called up in front of hell. Now tell me: Is there no death other than our first death, and are we not liable to chastisement? (41—60)

وَلَوْلَا نِعْمَةُ رَبِّي لَكُنْتُ مِنَ الْمُحْضَرِينَ ۝

أَفَمَا نَحْنُ بِمَيِّتِينَ ۝

إِلَّا مَوْتَتَنَا الْأُولَى وَمَا نَحْنُ بِمُعَذَّبِينَ ۝

إِنَّ هٰذَا لَهُوَ الْفَوْزُ الْعَظِيمُ ۝

لِمِثْلِ هٰذَا فَلْيَعْمَلِ الْعَامِلُونَ ۝

أَذٰلِكَ خَيْرٌ نُزُلًا أَمْ شَجَرَةُ الزَّقُّومِ ۝

إِنَّا جَعَلْنَاهَا فِتْنَةً لِلظَّالِمِينَ ۝

Surely, the state of Our chosen servants in the Hereafter is the supreme triumph. For the like of this should every worker work. Is that better entertainment or the tree Zaqqum? We have made it a means of trial for the wrongdoers. It is a tree that springs forth in the bottom of hell; its fruit is as though it were the heads of serpents. They shall eat of it and fill their bellies with it; and boiling water shall be added to their drink. Then their return will be to hell. They found their fathers erring and themselves rushed on in their footsteps. Many of the ancient peoples had erred before them, and We had sent Warners among them. Observe, then, how was the end of those who had been warned, excepting the chosen servants of Allah. (61—75)

إِنَّهَا شَجَرَةٌ تَخْرُجُ فِي أَصْلِ الْجَحِيمِ ۝

طَلْعُهَا كَأَنَّهُ رُءُوسُ الشَّيَاطِينِ ۝

فَإِنَّهُمْ لَآكِلُونَ مِنْهَا فَمَالِئُونَ مِنْهَا الْبُطُونَ ۝

ثُمَّ إِنَّ لَهُمْ عَلَيْهَا لَشَوْبًا مِنْ حَمِيمٍ ۝

ثُمَّ إِنَّ مَرْجِعَهُمْ لَإِلَى الْجَحِيمِ ۝

إِنَّهُمْ أَلْفَوْا آبَاءَهُمْ ضَالِّينَ ۝

فَهُمْ عَلَى آثَارِهِمْ يُهْرَعُونَ ۝

وَلَقَدْ ضَلَّ قَبْلَهُمْ أَكْثَرُ الْأَوَّلِينَ ۝

وَلَقَدْ أَرْسَلْنَا فِيهِمْ مُنْذِرِينَ ۝

فَانْظُرْ كَيْفَ كَانَ عَاقِبَةُ الْمُنْذَرِينَ ۝

إِلَّا عِبَادَ اللهِ الْمُخْلَصِينَ ۝

Noah cried unto Us in his distress; and what excellent answer did We return! We delivered him and his family from the great distress; and We made his offspring the only survivors; and established for him a good name among succeeding gener-

وَلَقَدْ نَادَانَا نُوحٌ فَلَنِعْمَ الْمُجِيبُونَ ۝

وَنَجَّيْنَاهُ وَأَهْلَهُ مِنَ الْكَرْبِ الْعَظِيمِ ۝

وَجَعَلْنَا ذُرِّيَّتَهُ هُمُ الْبَاقِينَ ۝

وَتَرَكْنَا عَلَيْهِ فِي الْآخِرِينَ ۝

ations. Peace be upon Noah, is the greeting among the peoples. Thus do We requite those who do good. He was indeed of Our believing servants. Then We drowned the others. (76—83)

سَلَامٌ عَلَى نُوحٍ فِى الْعَلَمِيْنَ ۞

اِنَّا كَذَلِكَ نَجْزِى الْمُحْسِنِيْنَ ۞

اِنَّهُ مِنْ عِبَادِنَا الْمُؤْمِنِيْنَ ۞

ثُمَّ اَغْرَقْنَا الْاٰخَرِيْنَ ۞

وَاِنَّ مِنْ شِيْعَتِهِ لَاِبْرٰهِيْمَ ۞

اِذْ جَاءَ رَبَّهُ بِقَلْبٍ سَلِيْمٍ ۞

اِذْ قَالَ لِاَبِيْهِ وَقَوْمِهِ مَاذَا تَعْبُدُوْنَ ۞

اَئِفْكًا اٰلِهَةً دُوْنَ اللّٰهِ تُرِيْدُوْنَ ۞

فَمَا ظَنُّكُمْ بِرَبِّ الْعَلَمِيْنَ ۞

فَنَظَرَ نَظْرَةً فِى النُّجُوْمِ ۞

فَقَالَ اِنِّى سَقِيْمٌ ۞

فَتَوَلَّوْا عَنْهُ مُدْبِرِيْنَ ۞

فَرَاغَ اِلٰى اٰلِهَتِهِمْ فَقَالَ اَلَا تَأْكُلُوْنَ ۞

مَا لَكُمْ لَا تَنْطِقُوْنَ ۞

فَرَاغَ عَلَيْهِمْ ضَرْبًا بِالْيَمِيْنِ ۞

فَاَقْبَلُوْا اِلَيْهِ يَزِفُّوْنَ ۞

قَالَ اَتَعْبُدُوْنَ مَا تَنْحِتُوْنَ ۞

وَاللّٰهُ خَلَقَكُمْ وَمَا تَعْمَلُوْنَ ۞

قَالُوا ابْنُوْا لَهُ بُنْيَانًا فَاَلْقُوْهُ فِى الْجَحِيْمِ ۞

فَاَرَادُوْا بِهِ كَيْدًا فَجَعَلْنَاهُمُ الْاَسْفَلِيْنَ ۞

وَقَالَ اِنِّى ذَاهِبٌ اِلٰى رَبِّى سَيَهْدِيْنِ ۞

رَبِّ هَبْ لِى مِنَ الصّٰلِحِيْنَ ۞

Of his party was Abraham, when he came to his Lord with a submissive heart. He asked his father and his people: What is it that you worship? Do you falsely seek gods beside Allah? Then what do you think of the Lord of the worlds? Then he cast a glance at the stars and said: I am about to fall ill. So they left him alone and turned away. Then he went quietly to their gods and questioned them: Do you not eat? Why do you not speak? Then he struck them forcibly with his right hand. When the people learnt of it they came to him running. He said to them: Do you worship that which you yourselves have carved out, whereas Allah has created you and your handiwork? They decided: Build around him a structure, and kindle a fire therein, and then cast him into the blaze. Thus they devised a plan against him, but We humiliated them. (84—99)

Abraham said: I am going to my Lord. He will surely guide me. He prayed: Lord, grant me righteous progeny. So We gave him glad tidings of a gentle son. When the boy began to run about with him, Abraham said to him: Son, I have seen in my dream that I am slaughtering thee. So consider what thou thinkest of it. The boy replied: Father, do what thou art commanded; thou wilt find me, if Allah please, steadfast. When both were ready to submit to Allah's will, and he had thrown him down on his forehead, We called to him: Abraham, thou hast indeed fulfilled the dream. Thus do We reward those who do their duty to the utmost. That was surely a manifest trial. We ransomed the boy with a great sacrifice, and We preserved for Abraham a good name in succeeding generations. Peace be upon Abraham.

Thus do We reward those who do their duty to the utmost. Surely, he was of Our believing servants. We gave him the glad tidings of Isaac, a Prophet, and one of the righteous. We bestowed blessings on him and on Isaac. Among their progeny were those who did good and those who manifestly wronged themselves. (100—114)

We bestowed Our favours on Moses and Aaron; and We delivered them and their people from the great distress. We helped them and theirs was the upper hand. We gave them the enlightening Book, and We guided them to the right path. We

فَبَشَّرْنَاهُ بِغُلَامٍ حَلِيمٍ ۝

فَلَمَّا بَلَغَ مَعَهُ السَّعْيَ قَالَ يَا بُنَيَّ إِنِّيٓ أَرَى فِي الْمَنَامِ أَنِّيٓ أَذْبَحُكَ فَانْظُرْ مَاذَا تَرَىٰ ۚ قَالَ يَا أَبَتِ افْعَلْ مَا تُؤْمَرُ ۖ سَتَجِدُنِيٓ إِنْ شَاءَ اللَّهُ مِنَ الصَّابِرِينَ ۝

فَلَمَّآ أَسْلَمَا وَتَلَّهُ لِلْجَبِينِ ۝

وَنَادَيْنَاهُ أَنْ يَّا إِبْرَاهِيمُ ۝

قَدْ صَدَّقْتَ الرُّؤْيَا ۚ إِنَّا كَذَٰلِكَ نَجْزِي الْمُحْسِنِينَ ۝

إِنَّ هٰذَا لَهُوَ الْبَلَاءُ الْمُبِينُ ۝

وَفَدَيْنَاهُ بِذِبْحٍ عَظِيمٍ ۝

وَتَرَكْنَا عَلَيْهِ فِي الْآخِرِينَ ۝

سَلَامٌ عَلَىٰ إِبْرَاهِيمَ ۝

كَذَٰلِكَ نَجْزِي الْمُحْسِنِينَ ۝

إِنَّهُ مِنْ عِبَادِنَا الْمُؤْمِنِينَ ۝

وَبَشَّرْنَاهُ بِإِسْحَاقَ نَبِيًّا مِنَ الصَّالِحِينَ ۝

وَبَارَكْنَا عَلَيْهِ وَعَلَىٰ إِسْحَاقَ ۚ وَمِنْ ذُرِّيَّتِهِمَا مُحْسِنٌ وَظَالِمٌ لِنَفْسِهِ مُبِينٌ ۝

وَلَقَدْ مَنَنَّا عَلَىٰ مُوسَىٰ وَهَارُونَ ۝

وَنَجَّيْنَاهُمَا وَقَوْمَهُمَا مِنَ الْكَرْبِ الْعَظِيمِ ۝

وَنَصَرْنَاهُمْ فَكَانُوا هُمُ الْغَالِبِينَ ۝

وَآتَيْنَاهُمَا الْكِتَابَ الْمُسْتَبِينَ ۝

وَهَدَيْنَاهُمَا الصِّرَاطَ الْمُسْتَقِيمَ ۝

established a good name for them among succeeding generations. Peace on Moses and Aaaron. Thus do We reward those who do their duty to the utmost. They were of Our believing servants. (115—123)

وَتَرَكْنَا عَلَيْهِمَا فِي الْآخِرِينَ ۟

سَلٰمٌ عَلٰى مُوسٰى وَهٰرُوْنَ ۟

إِنَّا كَذٰلِكَ نَجْزِى الْمُحْسِنِيْنَ ۟

إِنَّهُمَا مِنْ عِبَادِنَا الْمُؤْمِنِيْنَ ۟

وَإِنَّ إِلْيَاسَ لَمِنَ الْمُرْسَلِيْنَ ۟

إِذْ قَالَ لِقَوْمِهٖ أَلَا تَتَّقُوْنَ ۟

Elias was certainly one of the Messengers. He admonished his people: Will you not be mindful of your duty to Allah? Do you call on Baal, and forsake the Best of creators, Allah, your Lord and the Lord of your forefathers of old? But they rejected him, and surely they will be summoned to an accounting and punishment, except the chosen servants of Allah. We established a good name for him among succeeding generations. Peace be on Eliaseen. Thus do We reward those who do their duty to the utmost. He was of Our believing servants. (124—133)

أَتَدْعُوْنَ بَعْلًا وَّتَذَرُوْنَ أَحْسَنَ الْخَالِقِيْنَ ۟

اللّٰهَ رَبَّكُمْ وَرَبَّ اٰبَآئِكُمُ الْأَوَّلِيْنَ ۟

فَكَذَّبُوْهُ فَإِنَّهُمْ لَمُحْضَرُوْنَ ۟

إِلَّا عِبَادَ اللّٰهِ الْمُخْلَصِيْنَ ۟

وَتَرَكْنَا عَلَيْهِ فِي الْآخِرِينَ ۟

سَلٰمٌ عَلٰى إِلْ يَاسِيْنَ ۟

إِنَّا كَذٰلِكَ نَجْزِى الْمُحْسِنِيْنَ ۟

إِنَّهٗ مِنْ عِبَادِنَا الْمُؤْمِنِيْنَ ۟

وَإِنَّ لُوْطًا لَّمِنَ الْمُرْسَلِيْنَ ۟

إِذْ نَجَّيْنٰهُ وَأَهْلَهٗ أَجْمَعِيْنَ ۟

Lot was also one of the Messengers. We delivered him and the whole of his family, except an old woman who stayed behind; and then We utterly destroyed the others. You pass by their ruins in the morning and by night, then why do you not understand? (134—139)

إِلَّا عَجُوْزًا فِي الْغٰبِرِيْنَ ۟

ثُمَّ دَمَّرْنَا الْآخَرِيْنَ ۟

وَإِنَّكُمْ لَتَمُرُّوْنَ عَلَيْهِمْ مُّصْبِحِيْنَ ۟

وَبِالَّيْلِ أَفَلَا تَعْقِلُوْنَ ۟

Jonah was also one of the Messengers. He fled to the crowded vessel, and cast

وَإِنَّ يُوْنُسَ لَمِنَ الْمُرْسَلِيْنَ ۟

إِذْ أَبَقَ إِلَى الْفُلْكِ الْمَشْحُوْنِ ۟

lots with the others and was chosen as one to be thrown overboard. A large fish swallowed him, while he was rebuking himself. Had he not been one of the glorifiers of Allah, he would surely have tarried in its belly till Judgment Day. Then We caused him to be cast upon a wide bare tract of land; and he was sick; and We caused a gourd-plant to grow beside him. Then We sent him as a Messenger to a hundred thousand people or more, and they believed. So We provided for them for a long while. (140—149)

Then ask these disbelievers of Mecca whether thy Lord has daughters while they have sons? Did We create the angels females in their presence? Hearken! It is one of their fabrications that they say: Allah has begotten children. They are certainly liars. Has He chosen daughters in preference to sons? What ails you? How ill do you judge! Do you not reflect? Or have you a clear authority? Then produce your Book, if you are truthful.

They allege a blood relationship between Allah and the Jinn, while the Jinn are aware that they will be produced before Allah for judgment. Holy is Allah and above that which they attribute to Him. But the chosen servants of Allah are not among these calumniators. Surely, you and that which you worship have no power to mis-

فَسَاهَمَ فَكَانَ مِنَ الْمُدْحَضِيْنَ ۞

فَالْتَقَمَهُ الْحُوْتُ وَهُوَ مُلِيْمٌ ۞

فَلَوْلَا اَنَّهُ كَانَ مِنَ الْمُسَبِّحِيْنَ ۞

لَلَبِثَ فِيْ بَطْنِهٖ اِلٰى يَوْمِ يُبْعَثُوْنَ ۞

فَنَبَذْنٰهُ بِالْعَرَآءِ وَهُوَ سَقِيْمٌ ۞

وَاَنْبَتْنَا عَلَيْهِ شَجَرَةً مِّنْ يَّقْطِيْنٍ ۞

وَاَرْسَلْنٰهُ اِلٰى مِائَةِ اَلْفٍ اَوْ يَزِيْدُوْنَ ۞

فَاٰمَنُوْا فَمَتَّعْنٰهُمْ اِلٰى حِيْنٍ ۞

فَاسْتَفْتِهِمْ اَلِرَبِّكَ الْبَنَاتُ وَلَهُمُ الْبَنُوْنَ ۞

اَمْ خَلَقْنَا الْمَلٰٓئِكَةَ اِنَاثًا وَّهُمْ شٰهِدُوْنَ ۞

اَلَآ اِنَّهُمْ مِّنْ اِفْكِهِمْ لَيَقُوْلُوْنَ ۞

وَلَدَ اللّٰهُ وَاِنَّهُمْ لَكٰذِبُوْنَ ۞

اَصْطَفَى الْبَنَاتِ عَلَى الْبَنِيْنَ ۞

مَا لَكُمْ كَيْفَ تَحْكُمُوْنَ ۞

اَفَلَا تَذَكَّرُوْنَ ۞

اَمْ لَكُمْ سُلْطٰنٌ مُّبِيْنٌ ۞

فَأْتُوْا بِكِتٰبِكُمْ اِنْ كُنْتُمْ صٰدِقِيْنَ ۞

وَجَعَلُوْا بَيْنَهُ وَبَيْنَ الْجِنَّةِ نَسَبًا وَلَقَدْ عَلِمَتِ

الْجِنَّةُ اِنَّهُمْ لَمُحْضَرُوْنَ ۞

سُبْحٰنَ اللّٰهِ عَمَّا يَصِفُوْنَ ۞

اِلَّا عِبَادَ اللّٰهِ الْمُخْلَصِيْنَ ۞

فَاِنَّكُمْ وَمَا تَعْبُدُوْنَ ۞

lead anyone away from Him, except one who is destined for hell. (150—164)

مَآ أَنتُمْ عَلَيْهِ بِفَٰتِنِينَ ۝

إِلَّا مَنْ هُوَ صَالِ الْجَحِيمِ ۝

وَمَا مِنَّآ إِلَّا لَهُ مَقَامٌ مَّعْلُومٌ ۝

Tell them: Every one of us, the believers, has an appointed station. We are all standing in rows in Prayer, and verily, we are those who glorify Allah. (165—167)

وَإِنَّا لَنَحْنُ الصَّآفُّونَ ۝

وَإِنَّا لَنَحْنُ الْمُسَبِّحُونَ ۝

وَإِن كَانُوا لَيَقُولُونَ ۝

لَوْ أَنَّ عِندَنَا ذِكْرًا مِّنَ الْأَوَّلِينَ ۝

The Meccans used to say: If a Messenger had come to us, as they came to the people of old, we would surely have been Allah's chosen servants. But when he came to them, they disbelieved. They will soon come to know.

لَكُنَّا عِبَادَ اللَّهِ الْمُخْلَصِينَ ۝

فَكَفَرُوا بِهِ فَسَوْفَ يَعْلَمُونَ ۝

وَلَقَدْ سَبَقَتْ كَلِمَتُنَا لِعِبَادِنَا الْمُرْسَلِينَ ۝

إِنَّهُمْ لَهُمُ الْمَنصُورُونَ ۝

وَإِنَّ جُندَنَا لَهُمُ الْغَٰلِبُونَ ۝

Our word has gone forth respecting Our servants, the Messengers, that it is they who will be helped, and that it is Our host that would triumph. So turn away from them for a while and watch them; they will soon see. Do they ask for Our punishment to be hastened? When it descends into their courtyard, evil will that morning be for those who were warned. So turn away from them for a while and watch them; they will soon see.

فَتَوَلَّ عَنْهُمْ حَتَّىٰ حِينٍ ۝

وَأَبْصِرْهُمْ فَسَوْفَ يُبْصِرُونَ ۝

أَفَبِعَذَابِنَا يَسْتَعْجِلُونَ ۝

فَإِذَا نَزَلَ بِسَاحَتِهِمْ فَسَآءَ صَبَاحُ الْمُنذَرِينَ ۝

وَتَوَلَّ عَنْهُمْ حَتَّىٰ حِينٍ ۝

وَأَبْصِرْ فَسَوْفَ يُبْصِرُونَ ۝

سُبْحَٰنَ رَبِّكَ رَبِّ الْعِزَّةِ عَمَّا يَصِفُونَ ۝

Holy is thy Lord, the Lord of Honour, far above that which they assert. Peace be upon the Messengers. All praise belongs to Allah, the Lord of the worlds. (168—183)

وَسَلَٰمٌ عَلَى الْمُرْسَلِينَ ۝

وَالْحَمْدُ لِلَّهِ رَبِّ الْعَٰلَمِينَ ۝

سُوۡرَةُ صّ مَكِّيَّة

ṢĀD

(Revealed before Hijra)

In the name of Allah, Most Gracious, Ever Merciful. (1)

This revelation is from the Truthful One, and the Quran, which is full of exhortation, is a witness to it. Those who disbelieve are moved by arrogance and a spirit of opposition. How many a generation before them have We destroyed. They cried out for help, but the time for deliverance had sped.

They wonder that a Warner has come to them from among themselves; and the disbelievers say: This is a lying sorcerer. Has he rolled the gods into One God? That is indeed an astounding thing! Their leading men called out: Disperse, and stick to your gods. There is some design behind this. We have not heard of anything like this even among the latest community. This is mere fabrication.

Has the exhortation been sent down to him, of all our people? But they are in doubt concerning My exhortation itself. They are so daring, as they have not experienced My chastisement. Do they possess the treasures of the mercy of thy Lord, the Mighty, the Great Bestower?

Do they possess the kingdom of the heavens and the earth and all that is between them? If so, let them ascend into heaven and bring down a book in support of their claim. On the contrary, a host from among the confederates shall be routed here.

Before them the people of Noah, the tribe of 'Ad, and Pharaoh, wielding great power, and the tribe of Thamud, and the people of Lot and the dwellers of the Wood had rejected the Messengers. They were an organised host. Each one of them rejected the Messengers, and in each case My punishment came down upon them. (2—15)

كَذَّبَتْ قَبْلَهُمْ قَوْمُ نُوحٍ وَّعَادٌ وَّفِرْعَوْنُ ذُو الْاَوْتَادِ ﴿١٣﴾

وَثَمُوْدُ وَقَوْمُ لُوْطٍ وَّاَصْحٰبُ الْاَيْكَةِ ؕ اُولٰٓئِكَ الْاَحْزَابُ ﴿١٣﴾

اِنْ كُلٌّ اِلَّا كَذَّبَ الرُّسُلَ فَحَقَّ عِقَابِ ﴿١٤﴾

وَمَا يَنْظُرُ هٰٓؤُلَاءِ اِلَّا صَيْحَةً وَّاحِدَةً مَّا لَهَا مِنْ فَوَاقٍ ﴿١٥﴾

The disbelievers of Mecca wait for a calamity that would overtake them suddenly, and there is nothing to delay it. They say: Lord, give us our portion quickly, before the Day of Reckoning. Bear patiently that which they say, and call to mind Our servant David, a man of great power, who turned constantly to Us. We subjected the people of the mountains to him. They celebrated Allah's praises with him morn and eve. We had also gathered round him the high-soaring ones; they were all inclined towards Allah. We made his kingdom strong, and bestowed upon him wisdom and decisive judgment.

وَقَالُوْا رَبَّنَا عَجِّلْ لَّنَا قِطَّنَا قَبْلَ يَوْمِ الْحِسَابِ ﴿١٦﴾

اِصْبِرْ عَلٰى مَا يَقُوْلُوْنَ وَاذْكُرْ عَبْدَنَا دَاوٗدَ ذَا الْاَيْدِ ۚ اِنَّهٗۤ اَوَّابٌ ﴿١٧﴾

اِنَّا سَخَّرْنَا الْجِبَالَ مَعَهٗ يُسَبِّحْنَ بِالْعَشِيِّ وَالْاِشْرَاقِ ﴿١٨﴾

وَالطَّيْرَ مَحْشُوْرَةً ؕ كُلٌّ لَّهٗۤ اَوَّابٌ ﴿١٩﴾

وَشَدَدْنَا مُلْكَهٗ وَاٰتَيْنٰهُ الْحِكْمَةَ وَفَصْلَ الْخِطَابِ ﴿٢٠﴾

Has the story of the disputants reached thee who climbed over the wall of his chamber? When they entered in upon David, he felt afraid of them. They reassured him: Be not afraid. We are but two disputants; one of us transgresses against the other; so judge between us with justice and do not deviate from the right course, and guide us to the right path. This is my brother; he has ninety-nine ewes, and I have only a single ewe. Yet he says: Hand it over to me; and persists in pressing his demand upon me. David said: He has done thee wrong in demanding thy ewe to add it to his own ewes.

وَهَلْ اَتٰىكَ نَبَؤُا الْخَصْمِ ۘ اِذْ تَسَوَّرُوا الْمِحْرَابَ ﴿٢١﴾

اِذْ دَخَلُوْا عَلٰى دَاوٗدَ فَفَزِعَ مِنْهُمْ قَالُوْا لَا تَخَفْ ۚ خَصْمٰنِ بَغٰى بَعْضُنَا عَلٰى بَعْضٍ فَاحْكُمْ بَيْنَنَا بِالْحَقِّ وَلَا تُشْطِطْ وَاهْدِنَاۤ اِلٰى سَوَآءِ الصِّرَاطِ ﴿٢٢﴾

اِنَّ هٰذَاۤ اَخِيْ ۗ لَهٗ تِسْعٌ وَّتِسْعُوْنَ نَعْجَةً وَّلِيَ نَعْجَةٌ وَّاحِدَةٌ ۚ فَقَالَ اَكْفِلْنِيْهَا وَعَزَّنِيْ فِى الْخِطَابِ ﴿٢٣﴾

قَالَ لَقَدْ ظَلَمَكَ بِسُؤَالِ نَعْجَتِكَ اِلٰى نِعَاجِهٖ ؕ

Certainly many partners transgress against one another, except those who believe and act righteously; and they are but few. David perceived that We had warned him of a difficult situation; so he asked forgiveness of his Lord, and fell down bowing in worship and turned to Him. So We covered up his weaknesses, and indeed he was in a position of nearness to Us and will have an excellent retreat. We commanded him: David, We have made thee a vicegerent in the earth; so judge between people with justice, and follow not vain desire, lest it should lead thee astray from the way of Allah. Surely those who go astray from the way of Allah will have a severe punishment, because they forgot the Day of Reckoning. (16—27)

We have not created the heaven and the earth and all that is between them in vain. That is the view of those who disbelieve. Woe, then, to the disbelievers because of the punishment of the Fire. Shall We treat those who believe and act righteously like those who act corruptly in the earth? Shall We treat the righteous like the wicked? We have revealed this Book to thee, replete with excellences of every description, that they may reflect over its verses, and that those gifted with understanding may take heed. (28—30)

We bestowed on David, Solomon an excellent servant of Ours. He turned to Us constantly. Call to mind when swift horses of noble breed were brought before him at eventide, and he said: I love good things because they are reminders of my Lord. When the horses disappeared from sight, he said:

Bring them back to me; and he started stroking their legs and necks. We warned Solomon that We had decided to place on his throne a soulless body. So he turned to Us and prayed: Lord grant me forgiveness and bestow on me the kingdom of the spirit, that will not pass by inheritance after me. Surely, Thou art the Great Bestower. We subjected to him the wind, blowing gently by his command whithersoever he desired to go, and the giants, all types of builders and divers, and others bound in fetters. This is Our unlimited bounty; treat thy subject peoples generously or with due restraint. Surely, he had a position of nearness to Us, and will have an excellent retreat. (31—41)

Call to mind Our servant Job. When he cried unto his Lord: My wicked enemy has afflicted me with toil and torment; We directed him: Strike thy riding beast with thy heels. Here is cool water to wash with and to drink. We bestowed on him his family and as many more with him by Our mercy and as a reminder to those possessing understanding. We had commanded him: Take hold of a twig of the date-palm tree and urge on thy mount with it, and incline not towards falsehood. Indeed We found him steadfast; he was an excellent servant. Surely, he turned constantly to Us. (42—45)

Call to mind Our servants Abraham and Isaac and Jacob, men of might and vision. We chose them for a special purpose; the remembrance of the Home of the Hereafter. In Our sight they were among the elect and the best.

رُدُّوهَا عَلَيَّ ۖ فَطَفِقَ مَسْحًۢا بِالسُّوقِ وَالْأَعْنَاقِ ۝

وَلَقَدْ فَتَنَّا سُلَيْمَانَ وَأَلْقَيْنَا عَلَىٰ كُرْسِيِّهِ جَسَدًا ثُمَّ أَنَابَ ۝

قَالَ رَبِّ اغْفِرْ لِي وَهَبْ لِي مُلْكًا لَّا يَنْۢبَغِي لِأَحَدٍ مِّنْۢ بَعْدِي ۖ إِنَّكَ أَنتَ الْوَهَّابُ ۝

فَسَخَّرْنَا لَهُ الرِّيحَ تَجْرِي بِأَمْرِهِ رُخَآءً حَيْثُ أَصَابَ ۝

وَالشَّيَاطِينَ كُلَّ بَنَّآءٍ وَغَوَّاصٍ ۝

وَآخَرِينَ مُقَرَّنِينَ فِي الْأَصْفَادِ ۝

هَٰذَا عَطَآؤُنَا فَامْنُنْ أَوْ أَمْسِكْ بِغَيْرِ حِسَابٍ ۝

وَإِنَّ لَهُ عِندَنَا لَزُلْفَىٰ وَحُسْنَ مَآبٍ ۝

وَاذْكُرْ عَبْدَنَآ أَيُّوبَ إِذْ نَادَىٰ رَبَّهُ أَنِّي مَسَّنِيَ الشَّيْطَانُ بِنُصْبٍ وَعَذَابٍ ۝

ارْكُضْ بِرِجْلِكَ ۖ هَٰذَا مُغْتَسَلٌۢ بَارِدٌ وَشَرَابٌ ۝

وَوَهَبْنَا لَهُ أَهْلَهُ وَمِثْلَهُم مَّعَهُمْ رَحْمَةً مِّنَّا وَذِكْرَىٰ لِأُولِي الْأَلْبَابِ ۝

وَخُذْ بِيَدِكَ ضِغْثًا فَاضْرِب بِّهِ وَلَا تَحْنَثْ ۗ إِنَّا وَجَدْنَاهُ صَابِرًا ۚ نِّعْمَ الْعَبْدُ ۖ إِنَّهُ أَوَّابٌ ۝

وَاذْكُرْ عِبَادَنَآ إِبْرَاهِيمَ وَإِسْحَاقَ وَيَعْقُوبَ أُولِي الْأَيْدِي وَالْأَبْصَارِ ۝

إِنَّآ أَخْلَصْنَاهُم بِخَالِصَةٍ ذِكْرَى الدَّارِ ۝

وَإِنَّهُمْ عِندَنَا لَمِنَ الْمُصْطَفَيْنَ الْأَخْيَارِ ۝

452

Call to mind also Ishmael and Isaaiah and Ezekiel: All were of the best. This is a reminder; and the righteous will surely have an excellent retreat — Gardens of Eternity, with their gates thrown open to them, reclining therein on cushions. They will call therein at pleasure for plenteous fruit and drink. With them will be pure women with eyes downcast, companions of equal age. This is that which you are promised for the Day of Reckoning. This is Our provision which will never be exhausted. This much for the believers. (46—56)

وَاذْكُرْ اِسْمٰعِيْلَ وَالْيَسَعَ وَذَا الْكِفْلِ ؕ وَكُلٌّ مِّنَ الْاَخْيَارِ ۟۳۹

هٰذَا ذِكْرٌ ؕ وَاِنَّ لِلْمُتَّقِيْنَ لَحُسْنَ مَاٰبٍ ۟۴۹

جَنّٰتِ عَدْنٍ مُّفَتَّحَةً لَّهُمُ الْاَبْوَابُ ۟۵۰

مُّتَّكِئِيْنَ فِيْهَا يَدْعُوْنَ فِيْهَا بِفَاكِهَةٍ كَثِيْرَةٍ وَّشَرَابٍ ۟۵۱

وَعِنْدَهُمْ قٰصِرٰتُ الطَّرْفِ اَتْرَابٌ ۟۵۲

هٰذَا مَا تُوْعَدُوْنَ لِيَوْمِ الْحِسَابِ ۟۵۳

اِنَّ هٰذَا لَرِزْقُنَا مَا لَهٗ مِنْ نَّفَادٍ ۚ۵۴

هٰذَا ؕ وَاِنَّ لِلطّٰغِيْنَ لَشَرَّ مَاٰبٍ ۟۵۵

جَهَنَّمَ ۚ يَصْلَوْنَهَا ۚ فَبِئْسَ الْمِهَادُ ۟۵۶

هٰذَا ۚ فَلْيَذُوْقُوْهُ حَمِيْمٌ وَّغَسَّاقٌ ۟۵۷

وَّاٰخَرُ مِنْ شَكْلِهٖۤ اَزْوَاجٌ ؕ۵۸

هٰذَا فَوْجٌ مُّقْتَحِمٌ مَّعَكُمْ ۚ لَا مَرْحَبًۢا بِهِمْ ؕ اِنَّهُمْ صَالُوا النَّارِ ۟۵۹

قَالُوْا بَلْ اَنْتُمْ ۟ لَا مَرْحَبًۢا بِكُمْ ؕ اَنْتُمْ قَدَّمْتُمُوْهُ لَنَا ۚ فَبِئْسَ الْقَرَارُ ۟۶۰

قَالُوْا رَبَّنَا مَنْ قَدَّمَ لَنَا هٰذَا فَزِدْهُ عَذَابًا ضِعْفًا فِى النَّارِ ۟۶۱

وَقَالُوْا مَا لَنَا لَا نَرٰى رِجَالًا كُنَّا نَعُدُّهُمْ مِّنَ الْاَشْرَارِ ۟۶۲

اَتَّخَذْنٰهُمْ سِخْرِيًّا اَمْ زَاغَتْ عَنْهُمُ الْاَبْصَارُ ۟۶۳

But for the rebellious there is an evil resort: hell which they will enter — an evil resting place! This is their reward. So let them sample it: a boiling fluid, and an intensely cold and stinking drink; and various kinds of similar torments. Those condemned to hell will carry on an acrimonious exchange. One group will point to another and say: This is a group that will accompany you. No welcome for them. They are headed for the Fire. They will retort: It is you. No welcome for you either. It is you who prepared this for us, and an evil resting place it is! They will add: Lord, whosoever has prepared this for us, do Thou intensify his torment in the Fire. The inmates of hell will be puzzled and will say: How is it that we do not see among us men whom we used to reckon among the wicked? Is it that we ridiculed them unjustly, or has our vision become defective that we miss them?

Surely, this is a fact: this bickering between the inmates of hell. (56—65)

اِنَّ ذٰلِكَ لَحَقٌّ تَخَاصُمُ اَهْلِ النَّارِ ۞

قُلْ اِنَّمَاۤ اَنَا مُنْذِرٌ ۖ وَّمَا مِنْ اِلٰهٍ اِلَّا اللّٰهُ
الْوَاحِدُ الْقَهَّارُ ۞

Say to them: I am but a Warner. There is no god but Allah, the One, the Most Supreme, the Lord of the heavens and the earth and of all that which is between the two, the Mighty, the Most Forgiving. Tell them: This is an announcement of tremendous import, from which you are turning away. I had no knowledge of the Exalted Assembly when they discussed the matter among themselves, except that it has been revealed to me, that I am a plain Warner. (66—71)

رَبُّ السَّمٰوٰتِ وَالْاَرْضِ وَمَا بَيْنَهُمَا الْعَزِيْزُ
الْغَفَّارُ ۞

قُلْ هُوَ نَبَؤٌا عَظِيْمٌ ۞

اَنْتُمْ عَنْهُ مُعْرِضُوْنَ ۞

مَا كَانَ لِيَ مِنْ عِلْمٍ بِالْمَلَاِ الْاَعْلٰۤ اِذْ يَخْتَصِمُوْنَ ۞

اِنْ يُّوْحٰۤ اِلَيَّ اِلَّاۤ اَنَّمَاۤ اَنَا نَذِيْرٌ مُّبِيْنٌ ۞

اِذْ قَالَ رَبُّكَ لِلْمَلٰٓئِكَةِ اِنِّيْ خَالِقٌۢ بَشَرًا مِّنْ طِيْنٍ ۞

فَاِذَا سَوَّيْتُهٗ وَنَفَخْتُ فِيْهِ مِنْ رُّوْحِيْ فَقَعُوْا لَهٗ
سٰجِدِيْنَ ۞

Call to mind when thy Lord apprised the angels: I am about to create man from clay, so when I have brought his faculties to perfection and have breathed into him of My Spirit, fall ye down in submission to him. The angels submitted, all of them together, but Iblis did not. He behaved arrogantly, and he was of the disbelievers. Allah demanded of him: Iblis, what hindered thee from submitting to one whom I had created of My own power? Art thou too proud, or dost thou fancy thyself as being too exalted? Iblis replied: I am better then he. Me Thou hast created of fire and him hast Thou created of clay. Thereupon Allah commanded: Get out hence, for thou art rejected, and thou shalt be under My curse till the Day of Judgment. He pleaded: Lord, then grant me respite till the day when they shall be raised up. Allah said: Thou art granted respite till the appointed time.

فَسَجَدَ الْمَلٰٓئِكَةُ كُلُّهُمْ اَجْمَعُوْنَ ۞

اِلَّاۤ اِبْلِيْسَ ۖ اِسْتَكْبَرَ وَكَانَ مِنَ الْكٰفِرِيْنَ ۞

قَالَ يٰۤاِبْلِيْسُ مَا مَنَعَكَ اَنْ تَسْجُدَ لِمَا خَلَقْتُ
بِيَدَيَّ ۖ اَسْتَكْبَرْتَ اَمْ كُنْتَ مِنَ الْعَالِيْنَ ۞

قَالَ اَنَا خَيْرٌ مِّنْهُ ۖ خَلَقْتَنِيْ مِنْ نَّارٍ وَّخَلَقْتَهٗ
مِنْ طِيْنٍ ۞

قَالَ فَاخْرُجْ مِنْهَا فَاِنَّكَ رَجِيْمٌ ۞

وَّاِنَّ عَلَيْكَ لَعْنَتِيْۤ اِلٰى يَوْمِ الدِّيْنِ ۞

قَالَ رَبِّ فَاَنْظِرْنِيْۤ اِلٰى يَوْمِ يُبْعَثُوْنَ ۞

قَالَ فَاِنَّكَ مِنَ الْمُنْظَرِيْنَ ۞

Iblis said: Then by Thy Honour, I will lead them all astray, except Thy chosen servants from among them. Allah announced: The truth is, and the truth I ever proclaim, that I will surely fill hell with thee and with those who follow thee from among them, all together. (72—86)

إِلٰى يَوْمِ الْوَقْتِ الْمَعْلُوْمِ ۞

قَالَ فَبِعِزَّتِكَ لَاُغْوِيَنَّهُمْ اَجْمَعِيْنَ ۟ۙ

اِلَّا عِبَادَكَ مِنْهُمُ الْمُخْلَصِيْنَ ۞

قَالَ فَالْحَقُّ ۫ وَالْحَقَّ اَقُوْلُ ۞

لَاَمْلَئَنَّ جَهَنَّمَ مِنْكَ وَمِمَّنْ تَبِعَكَ مِنْهُمْ اَجْمَعِيْنَ ۞

Say to the people, O Prophet: I ask not of you any recompense for conveying Allah's message to you, nor am I one given to affectation. The Quran is a Reminder for all peoples, and you will witness the fulfilment of its warnings after a while. (87—89)

قُلْ مَاۤ اَسْئَلُكُمْ عَلَيْهِ مِنْ اَجْرٍ وَّمَاۤ اَنَا مِنَ الْمُتَكَلِّفِيْنَ ۞

اِنْ هُوَ اِلَّا ذِكْرٌ لِّلْعٰلَمِيْنَ ۞

وَلَتَعْلَمُنَّ نَبَاَهٗ بَعْدَ حِيْنٍ ۞

AL-ZUMAR

(Revealed before Hijra)

In the name of Allah, Most Gracious, Ever Merciful. (1)

بِسْمِ اللّٰهِ الرَّحْمٰنِ الرَّحِيْمِ ۞

تَنْزِيْلُ الْكِتٰبِ مِنَ اللّٰهِ الْعَزِيْزِ الْحَكِيْمِ ۞

اِنَّاۤ اَنْزَلْنَاۤ اِلَيْكَ الْكِتٰبَ بِالْحَقِّ فَاعْبُدِ اللّٰهَ مُخْلِصًا لَّهُ الدِّيْنَ ۞

The revelation of this Book is from Allah, the Mighty, the Wise. We have revealed this Book to thee comprising the truth; so worship Allah in sincere obedience. Hearken, it is to Allah that sincere obedience is due. Those who adopt patrons other than Him allege: We worship them only that they may bring us near to Allah. Surely, Allah will judge between them concerning that wherein they differ. Surely, Allah guides no one who is an ungrateful liar. (2—4)

اَلَا لِلّٰهِ الدِّيْنُ الْخَالِصُ ۚ وَالَّذِيْنَ اتَّخَذُوْا مِنْ دُوْنِهٖۤ اَوْلِيَآءَ ۘ مَا نَعْبُدُهُمْ اِلَّا لِيُقَرِّبُوْنَاۤ اِلَى اللّٰهِ زُلْفٰى ؕ اِنَّ اللّٰهَ يَحْكُمُ بَيْنَهُمْ فِيْ مَا هُمْ فِيْهِ يَخْتَلِفُوْنَ ۙ اِنَّ اللّٰهَ لَا يَهْدِيْ مَنْ هُوَ كٰذِبٌ كَفَّارٌ ۞

If Allah had desired to make any one His son, He could have chosen whom He pleased out of His creation. Holy is He ! He is Allah, the One, the Most Supreme. He has created the heavens and the earth with a true purpose. He makes the night overspread the day, and makes the day overspread the night. He has constrained the sun and the moon into service; each pursues its course until an appointed time. Take note, He is the Mighty, the Most Forgiving. He created you from a single being; then of the same kind He made its mate. He has provided for you eight heads of cattle in pairs. He creates you in the wombs of your mothers, creation after creation, passing through three stages of darkness. This is Allah, your Lord. His is the kingdom. There is no god but He. Whither then are you being turned away ? (5—7)

لَوْ اَرَادَ اللّٰهُ اَنْ يَّتَّخِذَ وَلَدًا لَّاصْطَفٰى مِمَّا يَخْلُقُ مَا يَشَآءُ ۙ سُبْحٰنَهٗ ؕ هُوَ اللّٰهُ الْوَاحِدُ الْقَهَّارُ ۞

خَلَقَ السَّمٰوٰتِ وَالْاَرْضَ بِالْحَقِّ ۚ يُكَوِّرُ الَّيْلَ عَلَى النَّهَارِ وَيُكَوِّرُ النَّهَارَ عَلَى الَّيْلِ وَسَخَّرَ الشَّمْسَ وَالْقَمَرَ ؕ كُلٌّ يَّجْرِيْ لِاَجَلٍ مُّسَمًّى ؕ اَلَا هُوَ الْعَزِيْزُ الْغَفَّارُ ۞

خَلَقَكُمْ مِّنْ نَّفْسٍ وَّاحِدَةٍ ثُمَّ جَعَلَ مِنْهَا زَوْجَهَا وَاَنْزَلَ لَكُمْ مِّنَ الْاَنْعَامِ ثَمٰنِيَةَ اَزْوَاجٍ ؕ يَخْلُقُكُمْ فِيْ بُطُوْنِ اُمَّهٰتِكُمْ خَلْقًا مِّنْ بَعْدِ خَلْقٍ فِيْ ظُلُمٰتٍ ثَلٰثٍ ؕ ذٰلِكُمُ اللّٰهُ رَبُّكُمْ لَهُ الْمُلْكُ ؕ لَاۤ اِلٰهَ

If you are ungrateful, surely Allah is Self-Sufficient, and He is not pleased with ingratitude in His servants; but if you are grateful, He likes it for you. No one can bear the burden of another. To your Lord is your return; and He will inform you of that which you used to do. Surely, He is Well-Aware of your secret thoughts. When a person is afflicted, he calls upon his Lord, turning penitently to Him. Then, when He confers a favour upon him from Himself, he forgets that which he used to pray for before, and starts assigning rivals to Allah, that he may lead people astray from His way. Say to such a one: Profit from thy disbelief a short while; thou art surely of the inmates of the Fire. Then observe one who is devout in prayer, standing and in prostration, during the hours of the night, and who fears the Hereafter, and hopes for the mercy of his Lord. Ask them: Can those who know be like those who know not? It is only those endowed with understanding that take heed. (8—10)

Say: O ye creatures of Allah who believe' be mindful of your duty to your Lord. For those who perform their duty to the utmost in this life, there is a good recompense. Allah's earth is spacious. Verily, the steadfast will have their reward without measure. Tell them: I am commanded to worship Allah, in sincerest obedience to Him; and am commanded to be the foremost in submission to Him. Say: Indeed I fear, were I to disobey my Lord, the punishment of a great day. Tell them: It is Allah I worship, in sincerest obedience.

إِلَّا هُوَ فَأَنّٰى تُصۡرَفُوۡنَ ۞

اِنۡ تَكۡفُرُوۡا فَاِنَّ اللّٰهَ غَنِیٌّ عَنۡكُمۡ وَلَا یَرۡضٰی لِعِبَادِهِ الۡكُفۡرَ وَاِنۡ تَشۡكُرُوۡا یَرۡضَهُ لَكُمۡ وَلَا تَزِرُ وَازِرَةٌ وِّزۡرَ اُخۡرٰی ثُمَّ اِلٰی رَبِّكُمۡ مَّرۡجِعُكُمۡ فَیُنَبِّئُكُمۡ بِمَا كُنۡتُمۡ تَعۡمَلُوۡنَ ؕ اِنَّهُ عَلِیۡمٌۢ بِذَاتِ الصُّدُوۡرِ ۞

وَاِذَا مَسَّ الۡاِنۡسَانَ ضُرٌّ دَعَا رَبَّهُ مُنِیۡبًا اِلَیۡهِ ثُمَّ اِذَا خَوَّلَهُ نِعۡمَةً مِّنۡهُ نَسِیَ مَا كَانَ یَدۡعُوۡا اِلَیۡهِ مِنۡ قَبۡلُ وَجَعَلَ لِلّٰهِ اَنۡدَادًا لِّیُضِلَّ عَنۡ سَبِیۡلِهِ ؕ قُلۡ تَمَتَّعۡ بِكُفۡرِكَ قَلِیۡلًا ۖ اِنَّكَ مِنۡ اَصۡحٰبِ النَّارِ ۞

اَمَّنۡ هُوَ قَانِتٌ اٰنَآءَ الَّیۡلِ سَاجِدًا وَّقَآئِمًا یَّحۡذَرُ الۡاٰخِرَةَ وَیَرۡجُوۡا رَحۡمَةَ رَبِّهٖ ؕ قُلۡ هَلۡ یَسۡتَوِی الَّذِیۡنَ یَعۡلَمُوۡنَ وَالَّذِیۡنَ لَا یَعۡلَمُوۡنَ ؕ اِنَّمَا یَتَذَكَّرُ اُولُوا الۡاَلۡبَابِ ۞

قُلۡ یٰعِبَادِ الَّذِیۡنَ اٰمَنُوا اتَّقُوۡا رَبَّكُمۡ ؕ لِلَّذِیۡنَ اَحۡسَنُوۡا فِیۡ هٰذِهِ الدُّنۡیَا حَسَنَةٌ ؕ وَاَرۡضُ اللّٰهِ وَاسِعَةٌ ؕ اِنَّمَا یُوَفَّی الصّٰبِرُوۡنَ اَجۡرَهُمۡ بِغَیۡرِ حِسَابٍ ۞

قُلۡ اِنِّیۡۤ اُمِرۡتُ اَنۡ اَعۡبُدَ اللّٰهَ مُخۡلِصًا لَّهُ الدِّیۡنَ ۞ وَاُمِرۡتُ لِاَنۡ اَكُوۡنَ اَوَّلَ الۡمُسۡلِمِیۡنَ ۞

قُلۡ اِنِّیۡۤ اَخَافُ اِنۡ عَصَیۡتُ رَبِّیۡ عَذَابَ یَوۡمٍ عَظِیۡمٍ ۞

قُلِ اللّٰهَ اَعۡبُدُ مُخۡلِصًا لَّهُ دِیۡنِیۡ ۙ ۞

Then worship what you like beside Him, but be warned that the real losers will be those who ruin themselves and their families on the Day of Judgment. That truly is the manifest loss. They will have coverings of fire over them and beneath them. It is against this that Allah warns His servants: O My servants make Me your shield. (11—17)

فَاعْبُدُوْا مَا شِئْتُمْ مِّنْ دُوْنِهٖ ۗ قُلْ اِنَّ الْخٰسِرِيْنَ الَّذِيْنَ خَسِرُوْۤا اَنْفُسَهُمْ وَاَهْلِيْهِمْ يَوْمَ الْقِيٰمَةِ ۗ اَلَا ذٰلِكَ هُوَ الْخُسْرَانُ الْمُبِيْنُ ۞

لَهُمْ مِّنْ فَوْقِهِمْ ظُلَلٌ مِّنَ النَّارِ وَمِنْ تَحْتِهِمْ ظُلَلٌ ۗ ذٰلِكَ يُخَوِّفُ اللّٰهُ بِهٖ عِبَادَهٗ ۗ يٰعِبَادِ فَاتَّقُوْنِ ۞

وَالَّذِيْنَ اجْتَنَبُوا الطَّاغُوْتَ اَنْ يَّعْبُدُوْهَا وَاَنَابُوْۤا اِلَى اللّٰهِ لَهُمُ الْبُشْرٰى ۚ فَبَشِّرْ عِبَادِۙ ۞

Those who shun the worship of false gods and turn to Allah, shall have good news. So give glad tidings to My servants; who listen to the Word and follow the best thereof, that it is they whom Allah has guided and it is they who are possessed of understanding. But what of him against whom the sentence of punishment has become due? Canst thou deliver him who is in the Fire? For them who are mindful of their duty to Allah are lofty mansions built over lofty mansions, beneath which rivers flow. This is Allah's promise; Allah goes not back on His promise. Hast not thou seen that Allah sends down water from the sky, then causes it to flow in the earth in streams, and then brings forth thereby herbage, varying in colours? Then it dries up and turns yellow; then He reduces it to broken straw. In that surely is a reminder for those possessed of understanding. (18—22)

الَّذِيْنَ يَسْتَمِعُوْنَ الْقَوْلَ فَيَتَّبِعُوْنَ اَحْسَنَهٗ ۗ اُولٰٓئِكَ الَّذِيْنَ هَدٰىهُمُ اللّٰهُ وَاُولٰٓئِكَ هُمْ اُولُوا الْاَلْبَابِ ۞

اَفَمَنْ حَقَّ عَلَيْهِ كَلِمَةُ الْعَذَابِ ۗ اَفَاَنْتَ تُنْقِذُ مَنْ فِى النَّارِ ۞

لٰكِنِ الَّذِيْنَ اتَّقَوْا رَبَّهُمْ لَهُمْ غُرَفٌ مِّنْ فَوْقِهَا غُرَفٌ مَّبْنِيَّةٌ ۙ تَجْرِيْ مِنْ تَحْتِهَا الْاَنْهٰرُ ۗ وَعْدَ اللّٰهِ ۗ لَا يُخْلِفُ اللّٰهُ الْمِيْعَادَ ۞

اَلَمْ تَرَ اَنَّ اللّٰهَ اَنْزَلَ مِنَ السَّمَاءِ مَاءً فَسَلَكَهٗ يَنَابِيْعَ فِى الْاَرْضِ ثُمَّ يُخْرِجُ بِهٖ زَرْعًا مُّخْتَلِفًا اَلْوَانُهٗ ثُمَّ يَهِيْجُ فَتَرٰىهُ مُصْفَرًّا ثُمَّ يَجْعَلُهٗ حُطَامًا ۗ اِنَّ فِيْ ذٰلِكَ لَذِكْرٰى لِاُولِى الْاَلْبَابِ ۞

How enviable is the case of one whose mind Allah has prepared for the acceptance of Islam, so that he possesses a light from his Lord. Woe, then, to those whose hearts are hardened against the remembrance of Allah. They are in manifest error. (23)

اَفَمَنْ شَرَحَ اللّٰهُ صَدْرَهٗ لِلْاِسْلَامِ فَهُوَ عَلٰى نُوْرٍ مِّنْ رَّبِّهٖ ۗ فَوَيْلٌ لِّلْقٰسِيَةِ قُلُوْبُهُمْ مِّنْ ذِكْرِ اللّٰهِ ۗ اُولٰٓئِكَ فِيْ ضَلٰلٍ مُّبِيْنٍ ۞

اَللّٰهُ نَزَّلَ اَحْسَنَ الْحَدِيْثِ كِتٰبًا مُّتَشَابِهًا مَّثَانِيَ ۙ

Allah has sent down the best Message in the form of a Book, part of which resembles that which was revealed before, and part is new comprising the highest wisdom, whereby the skins of those who fear their Lord are set tingling, and then their skins and their hearts soften into the remembrance of Allah. This Quran is the guidance of Allah; He guides therewith whom He pleases. He whom Allah adjudges astray, has no one to guide him. How desperate is the case of one who seeks to shield himself from severe torment on the Day of Judgment by presenting his face to it. The wrongdoers will be told: Suffer now the consequences of that which you did. Those who were before them also rejected the Messengers; so the punishment came upon them whence they knew not. Allah afflicted them with humiliation in the present life, and the punishment of the Hereafter will certainly be greater, if they but knew. (24—27)

We have expounded for mankind everything in this Quran that they may take heed; a Quran expressed in clear language, wherein there is no deviation from the truth, that they may become righteous. Allah sets forth the case of a man belonging to several partners who are at odds with one another, and of another who belongs wholly to one man. Are the two in equal case? All praise belongs to Allah, but most of them know not. Thou wilt die and they will die, then on the Day of Judgment you will contend with one another before your Lord. Then who is more unjust than one who fabricates lies against Allah, or than one who rejects the truth when it comes to him? Is not hell an abode for disbelievers? But he who has brought the Truth and he who testifies to it, these are the righteous.

تَقْشَعِرُّ مِنْهُ جُلُوْدُ الَّذِيْنَ يَخْشَوْنَ رَبَّهُمْ ثُمَّ تَلِيْنُ جُلُوْدُهُمْ وَ قُلُوْبُهُمْ اِلٰى ذِكْرِ اللّٰهِ ذٰلِكَ هُدَى اللّٰهِ يَهْدِيْ بِهٖ مَنْ يَّشَآءُ وَ مَنْ يُّضْلِلِ اللّٰهُ فَمَا لَهٗ مِنْ هَادٍ ۝

اَفَمَنْ يَّتَّقِيْ بِوَجْهِهٖ سُوْٓءَ الْعَذَابِ يَوْمَ الْقِيٰمَةِ وَقِيْلَ لِلظّٰلِمِيْنَ ذُوْقُوْا مَا كُنْتُمْ تَكْسِبُوْنَ ۝

كَذَّبَ الَّذِيْنَ مِنْ قَبْلِهِمْ فَاَتٰىهُمُ الْعَذَابُ مِنْ حَيْثُ لَا يَشْعُرُوْنَ ۝

فَاَذَاقَهُمُ اللّٰهُ الْخِزْيَ فِى الْحَيٰوةِ الدُّنْيَا وَ لَعَذَابُ الْاٰخِرَةِ اَكْبَرُ لَوْ كَانُوْا يَعْلَمُوْنَ ۝

وَ لَقَدْ ضَرَبْنَا لِلنَّاسِ فِىْ هٰذَا الْقُرْاٰنِ مِنْ كُلِّ مَثَلٍ لَّعَلَّهُمْ يَتَذَكَّرُوْنَ ۝

قُرْاٰنًا عَرَبِيًّا غَيْرَ ذِىْ عِوَجٍ لَّعَلَّهُمْ يَتَّقُوْنَ ۝

ضَرَبَ اللّٰهُ مَثَلًا رَّجُلًا فِيْهِ شُرَكَآءُ مُتَشٰكِسُوْنَ وَ رَجُلًا سَلَمًا لِّرَجُلٍ هَلْ يَسْتَوِيٰنِ مَثَلًا اَلْحَمْدُ لِلّٰهِ بَلْ اَكْثَرُهُمْ لَا يَعْلَمُوْنَ ۝

اِنَّكَ مَيِّتٌ وَّ اِنَّهُمْ مَّيِّتُوْنَ ۝

ثُمَّ اِنَّكُمْ يَوْمَ الْقِيٰمَةِ عِنْدَ رَبِّكُمْ تَخْتَصِمُوْنَ ۝

فَمَنْ اَظْلَمُ مِمَّنْ كَذَبَ عَلَى اللّٰهِ وَ كَذَّبَ بِالصِّدْقِ اِذْ جَآءَهٗ اَلَيْسَ فِىْ جَهَنَّمَ مَثْوًى لِّلْكٰفِرِيْنَ ۝

وَ الَّذِىْ جَآءَ بِالصِّدْقِ وَ صَدَّقَ بِهٖٓ اُولٰٓئِكَ هُمُ

They will have with their Lord whatever they desire; that is the reward of those who do their duty to the utmost. So that Allah may cover up the undesirable portion of their acts and reward them according to the best of their actions. (28—36)

Is not Allah Sufficient for His servant? Yet they would frighten thee with those beside Him. There is no one to guide him whom Allah adjudges astray; and no one can lead astray him whom Allah guides. Is not Allah the Mighty, the Lord of Retribution? If thou were to ask them: Who created the heavens and the earth?; they will surely answer: Allah. Then ask them: Tell me, if Allah decided to inflict an injury upon me, could those whom you call upon beside Allah remove the injury inflicted by Him? Or, if He decided to show me mercy, could they withhold His mercy from me? Tell them: Allah is sufficient for me. In Him trust those who would trust. Say O my people, carry on, on your side; I shall carry on, on my side; soon shall you know which side is afflicted with a degrading and abiding punishment.

We have revealed to thee the Book, comprising truth and wisdom for the benefit of mankind. Then whoever follows the guidance, does so to his own good; and whoever goes astray does so to his own loss. Thou art not a guardian over them. (37—42)

الْمُتَّقُوْنَ ۞

لَهُمْ مَّا يَشَآءُوْنَ عِنْدَ رَبِّهِمْ ذٰلِكَ جَزَآءُ الْمُحْسِنِيْنَ ۞

لِيُكَفِّرَ اللّٰهُ عَنْهُمْ اَسْوَاَ الَّذِيْ عَمِلُوْا وَيَجْزِيَهُمْ اَجْرَهُمْ بِاَحْسَنِ الَّذِيْ كَانُوْا يَعْمَلُوْنَ ۞

اَلَيْسَ اللّٰهُ بِكَافٍ عَبْدَهٗ وَيُخَوِّفُوْنَكَ بِالَّذِيْنَ مِنْ دُوْنِهٖ وَمَنْ يُّضْلِلِ اللّٰهُ فَمَا لَهٗ مِنْ هَادٍ ۞

وَمَنْ يَّهْدِ اللّٰهُ فَمَا لَهٗ مِنْ مُّضِلٍّ اَلَيْسَ اللّٰهُ بِعَزِيْزٍ ذِى انْتِقَامٍ ۞

وَلَئِنْ سَاَلْتَهُمْ مَّنْ خَلَقَ السَّمٰوٰتِ وَالْاَرْضَ لَيَقُوْلُنَّ اللّٰهُ قُلْ اَفَرَءَيْتُمْ مَّا تَدْعُوْنَ مِنْ دُوْنِ اللّٰهِ اِنْ اَرَادَنِيَ اللّٰهُ بِضُرٍّ هَلْ هُنَّ كٰشِفٰتُ ضُرِّهٖ اَوْ اَرَادَنِيْ بِرَحْمَةٍ هَلْ هُنَّ مُمْسِكٰتُ رَحْمَتِهٖ قُلْ حَسْبِيَ اللّٰهُ عَلَيْهِ يَتَوَكَّلُ الْمُتَوَكِّلُوْنَ ۞

قُلْ يٰقَوْمِ اعْمَلُوْا عَلٰى مَكَانَتِكُمْ اِنِّيْ عَامِلٌ فَسَوْفَ تَعْلَمُوْنَ ۞

مَنْ يَّأْتِيْهِ عَذَابٌ يُّخْزِيْهِ وَيَحِلُّ عَلَيْهِ عَذَابٌ مُّقِيْمٌ ۞

اِنَّا اَنْزَلْنَا عَلَيْكَ الْكِتٰبَ لِلنَّاسِ بِالْحَقِّ فَمَنِ اهْتَدٰى فَلِنَفْسِهٖ وَمَنْ ضَلَّ فَاِنَّمَا يَضِلُّ عَلَيْهَا وَمَآ اَنْتَ عَلَيْهِمْ بِوَكِيْلٍ ۞

اَللّٰهُ يَتَوَفَّى الْاَنْفُسَ حِيْنَ مَوْتِهَا وَالَّتِيْ لَمْ تَمُتْ

Allah takes charge of souls at the time of death, and of those not yet dead during their sleep. Then He retains those in respect of which He has decreed death, and sends back the others for an appointed term. In that surely are Signs for a people who reflect. Have they chosen intercessors beside Allah? Ask them: Would they intercede for you even if they have no power over anything and possess no intelligence? Say to them: All intercession rests with Allah. To Him belongs the kingdom of the heavens and the earth; and to Him shall you be brought back. (43—45)

When Allah the One is mentioned, the hearts of those who do not believe in the Hereafter shrink with aversion; but when those beside Him are mentioned, they at once cheer up. Say: O Allah! Originator of the heavens and the earth, Knower of the unseen and the seen, Thou alone will judge between Thy servants concerning that in which they differ. If the wrongdoers possessed all that is in the earth, and the like thereof in addition, they would seek to ransom themselves with it from the severe punishment on the Day of Judgment; but there shall appear unto them from Allah, that which they never thought of. The evil consequences of their actions will become manifest to them, and that which they used to mock at will encompass them. (46—49)

When a person is afflicted, he cries unto Us; but when We confer upon him a favour from Ourself, he says: This has been given to me on account of my own knowledge. He does not realise that it is a trial: but most of them know not.

Those who were before them said the same thing, yet all that they had earned availed them not; and the evil consequences of their actions caught up with them. Those who do wrong out of these disbelievers will also be overtaken by the evil consequences of their actions; and they will not be able to frustrate Allah's design. Know they not that Allah enlarges the provision for whom He pleases, and straitens it for whom He pleases. Verily, in that are Signs for a people who believe. (50—53)

Convey to them: O My servants who have committed excesses against your own selves despair not of the mercy of Allah, surely Allah forgives all sins; He is Most Forgiving. Ever Merciful. Turn ye to your Lord and submit yourselves to Him, before the punishment overtakes you and no one is able to help you. Follow the highest of the commandments that have been sent down to you from your Lord, before the punishment comes upon you unawares while you perceive not its approach; lest a person should say: O my grief over my remissness in respect of my duty to Allah, and certainly I was one of the scoffers; or should say: If Allah had guided me I would certainly have been among the righteous; or should say, when he sees the punishment: Would that I could return to the world, I would then be among those who do their duty to the utmost. He will be told: Aye, My Signs did come to thee, but thou didst reject them, wast arrogant and wast of the disbelievers. On the Day of Judgment thou wilt see those who fabricated lies against Allah with their faces overcast with gloom. Is there not in hell an abode for the arrogant? Allah will deliver the righteous and bestow success on them; no evil shall afflict them, nor shall they grieve.

Allah is the Creator of all things and He is Guardian over all. To Him belong the keys of the heavens and the earth; and it is those who deny the Signs of Allah that are the losers. (54—64)

Say: O ignorant ones, do you bid me that I worship other gods than Allah? Verily, it has been revealed to thee and to every one of the Prophets before thee: If thou attribute partners to Allah, thy work shall be vain, and thou shalt certainly be of the losers. Aye, worship Allah and be among the grateful. They have not appreciated Allah's attributes as they should be appreciated. The earth will be completely under His control on the Day of Judgment, and the heavens will be rolled up in His right hand. Holy is He, and exalted above that which they associate with Him. The trumpet will be blown and all that are in the heavens and all that are in the earth will be struck senseless, save only those that Allah pleases. Then will it be blown a second time, and they will be standing, waiting. The earth will be lit up with the light of her Lord, and the Book will be laid open, and the Prophets and witnesses will be brought, and judgment will be given between them with justice, and they will not be wronged. Every soul will be fully rewarded for what it did. He is well aware of what they do. (65—71)

The disbelievers will be driven to hell in groups, until when they approach it, its gates will be thrown open, and its keepers will say to them: Did not Messengers from among yourselves come to you reciting unto you the Signs of your Lord, and warning you of your meeting of this day? They will say: That is so; but the sentence of punishment was bound to be carried out against the disbelievers.

They will be told: Enter the gates of hell, abiding therein. Evil is the abode of the arrogant. Those who were mindful of their duty to their Lord will be conducted to the Garden in groups. When they approach it and its gates are thrown open, its keepers will greet them with: Peace be upon you, you have attained to the state of bliss, so enter it, abiding therein.

They will respond: All praise belongs to Allah, Who has fulfilled His promise to us and has bestowed upon us this vast region as an inheritance to make our abode in the Garden wherever we please. How excellent, then, is the reward of the righteous workers. Thou wilt see the angels circling the Throne, glorifying their Lord with His praise. It will be judged between the people with justice; and it will be announced: All praise belongs to Allah, the Lord of the worlds. (72—76)

حَقَّتْ كَلِمَةُ الْعَذَابِ عَلَى الْكٰفِرِيْنَ ۝

قِيْلَ ادْخُلُوْٓا اَبْوَابَ جَهَنَّمَ خٰلِدِيْنَ فِيْهَا فَبِئْسَ مَثْوَى الْمُتَكَبِّرِيْنَ ۝

وَسِيْقَ الَّذِيْنَ اتَّقَوْا رَبَّهُمْ اِلَى الْجَنَّةِ زُمَرًا ۤ حَتّٰٓى اِذَا جَآءُوْهَا وَفُتِحَتْ اَبْوَابُهَا وَقَالَ لَهُمْ خَزَنَتُهَا سَلٰمٌ عَلَيْكُمْ طِبْتُمْ فَادْخُلُوْهَا خٰلِدِيْنَ ۝

وَقَالُوا الْحَمْدُ لِلّٰهِ الَّذِيْ صَدَقَنَا وَعْدَهٗ وَاَوْرَثَنَا الْاَرْضَ نَتَبَوَّاُ مِنَ الْجَنَّةِ حَيْثُ نَشَآءُ ۚ فَنِعْمَ اَجْرُ الْعٰمِلِيْنَ ۝

وَتَرَى الْمَلٰٓئِكَةَ حَآفِّيْنَ مِنْ حَوْلِ الْعَرْشِ يُسَبِّحُوْنَ بِحَمْدِ رَبِّهِمْ ۚ وَقُضِيَ بَيْنَهُمْ بِالْحَقِّ وَقِيْلَ الْحَمْدُ لِلّٰهِ رَبِّ الْعٰلَمِيْنَ ۝

بِسْمِ اللهِ الرَّحْمٰنِ الرَّحِيْمِ ۝

AL-MU'MIN
(Revealed before Hijra)

In the name of Allah, Most Gracious, Ever Merciful. (1)

بِسْمِ اللهِ الرَّحْمٰنِ الرَّحِيْمِ ۝

حٰمٓ ۝

THE PRAISEWORTHY, THE LORD OF HONOUR. (2)

تَنْزِيْلُ الْكِتٰبِ مِنَ اللهِ الْعَزِيْزِ الْعَلِيْمِ ۝

غَافِرِ الذَّنْبِ وَقَابِلِ التَّوْبِ شَدِيْدِ الْعِقَابِ

ذِى الطَّوْلِ ۚ لَآ اِلٰهَ اِلَّا هُوَ ۚ اِلَيْهِ الْمَصِيْرُ ۝

The revelation of this Book is from Allah, the Mighty, the All-Knowing, Who forgives sins and accepts repentance, Whose punishment is severe, the Lord of Bounty. There is no god but He. Towards Him is the final return. None contends against the Signs of Allah except those who disbelieve. Let not their going about freely in the land mislead thee. Before them also many people rejected their Messengers, the people of Noah and after them those who ranged themselves in opposition to their Messengers. Every people strove to seize their Messenger, and put forth false arguments striving thereby to shake the Truth. Then I seized them and how terrible was My retribution! Thus was the judgment of thy Lord fulfilled against the disbelievers that they are the inmates of the Fire. (3—7)

مَا يُجَادِلُ فِيْۤ اٰيٰتِ اللهِ اِلَّا الَّذِيْنَ كَفَرُوْا فَلَا يَغْرُرْكَ تَقَلُّبُهُمْ فِى الْبِلَادِ ۝

كَذَّبَتْ قَبْلَهُمْ قَوْمُ نُوْحٍ وَّالْاَحْزَابُ مِنْۢ بَعْدِهِمْ وَهَمَّتْ كُلُّ اُمَّةٍۭ بِرَسُوْلِهِمْ لِيَاْخُذُوْهُ وَجَادَلُوْا بِالْبَاطِلِ لِيُدْحِضُوْا بِهِ الْحَقَّ فَاَخَذْتُهُمْ ۖ فَكَيْفَ كَانَ عِقَابِ ۝

وَكَذٰلِكَ حَقَّتْ كَلِمَتُ رَبِّكَ عَلَى الَّذِيْنَ كَفَرُوْۤا اَنَّهُمْ اَصْحٰبُ النَّارِ ۝

Those who uphold the Throne and those who are around it, glorify their Lord with His praise, believing fully in Him, and pray for forgiveness for those who believe: Lord, Thou dost comprehend all things in Thy mercy and knowledge, so grant Thy forgiveness to those who repent and follow Thy way and safeguard them against the punishment of hell; and, Lord, admit

اَلَّذِيْنَ يَحْمِلُوْنَ الْعَرْشَ وَمَنْ حَوْلَهٗ يُسَبِّحُوْنَ بِحَمْدِ رَبِّهِمْ وَيُؤْمِنُوْنَ بِهٖ وَيَسْتَغْفِرُوْنَ لِلَّذِيْنَ اٰمَنُوْا ۚ رَبَّنَا وَسِعْتَ كُلَّ شَىْءٍ رَّحْمَةً وَّعِلْمًا فَاغْفِرْ لِلَّذِيْنَ تَابُوْا وَاتَّبَعُوْا سَبِيْلَكَ وَقِهِمْ عَذَابَ الْجَحِيْمِ ۝

رَبَّنَا وَاَدْخِلْهُمْ جَنّٰتِ عَدْنِ ِۨالَّتِىْ وَعَدْتَّهُمْ

them and the virtuous from among their fathers and their wives and their children to the Gardens of Eternity which Thou hast promised them. Surely, Thou art the Mighty, the Wise. Safeguard them against all ill, for to him whom Thou dost safeguard against all ill that day hast Thou surely shown mercy. That indeed is the supreme triumph.(8—10)

وَمَنْ صَلَحَ مِنْ اٰبَآئِهِمْ وَاَزْوَاجِهِمْ وَذُرِّيّٰتِهِمْ ؕ اِنَّكَ اَنْتَ الْعَزِيْزُ الْحَكِيْمُ ۟

وَقِهِمُ السَّيِّاٰتِ ؕ وَمَنْ تَقِ السَّيِّاٰتِ يَوْمَئِذٍ فَقَدْ رَحِمْتَهٗ ؕ وَذٰلِكَ هُوَ الْفَوْزُ الْعَظِيْمُ ۟

اِنَّ الَّذِيْنَ كَفَرُوْا يُنَادَوْنَ لَمَقْتُ اللّٰهِ اَكْبَرُ مِنْ مَقْتِكُمْ اَنْفُسَكُمْ اِذْ تُدْعَوْنَ اِلَى الْاِيْمَانِ فَتَكْفُرُوْنَ ۟

Those who disbelieve will be told: Far greater than your abhorrence of yourselves this day was the displeasure of Allah with you when you were being called to the faith and you disbelieved. They will say: Lord, Thou hast made us pass through death twice and hast given us life twice, we now confess our faults. Is there, then, a way of escape? They will be told: You find yourselves in this plight, because when it was Allah, the One, Who was called on you disbelieved, but when partners were assigned to Him you believed. Now the judgment rests with Allah, the High, the Great. (11—13)

قَالُوْا رَبَّنَآ اَمَتَّنَا اثْنَتَيْنِ وَاَحْيَيْتَنَا اثْنَتَيْنِ فَاعْتَرَفْنَا بِذُنُوْبِنَا فَهَلْ اِلٰى خُرُوْجٍ مِّنْ سَبِيْلٍ ۟

ذٰلِكُمْ بِاَنَّهٗۤ اِذَا دُعِيَ اللّٰهُ وَحْدَهٗ كَفَرْتُمْ ؕ وَاِنْ يُّشْرَكْ بِهٖ تُؤْمِنُوْا ؕ فَالْحُكْمُ لِلّٰهِ الْعَلِيِّ الْكَبِيْرِ ۟

هُوَ الَّذِيْ يُرِيْكُمْ اٰيٰتِهٖ وَيُنَزِّلُ لَكُمْ مِّنَ السَّمَآءِ رِزْقًا ؕ وَمَا يَتَذَكَّرُ اِلَّا مَنْ يُّنِيْبُ ۟

It is He Who shows you His Signs, and sends down provision for you from heaven but none pays heed save he who turns to Allah. So call on Him with perfect sincerity of faith, though the disbelievers may be averse. His are the most exalted attributes, He is the Lord of the Throne. He causes His Word to descend by His command on whomsoever of His servants He pleases, that he may warn people of the Day of Meeting, the Day when they will all come forth; nothing concerning them will be hidden from Allah. Whose is the Kingdom this day? Of Allah, the One, the Most Supreme.

فَادْعُوا اللّٰهَ مُخْلِصِيْنَ لَهُ الدِّيْنَ وَلَوْ كَرِهَ الْكٰفِرُوْنَ ۟

رَفِيْعُ الدَّرَجٰتِ ذُو الْعَرْشِ ۚ يُلْقِى الرُّوْحَ مِنْ اَمْرِهٖ عَلٰى مَنْ يَّشَآءُ مِنْ عِبَادِهٖ لِيُنْذِرَ يَوْمَ التَّلَاقِ ۟

يَوْمَ هُمْ بَارِزُوْنَ ۚ لَا يَخْفٰى عَلَى اللّٰهِ مِنْهُمْ شَيْءٌ ؕ لِمَنِ الْمُلْكُ الْيَوْمَ ؕ لِلّٰهِ الْوَاحِدِ الْقَهَّارِ ۟

This day will every one be requited for
that which he has earned, there will be no
injustice this day. Surely Allah is Swift
at reckoning. Then warn them of the
Approaching Day, when people's hearts,
full of suppressed grief, will reach up to
their throats, and the wrongdoers will
have neither friend nor any effective intercessor. He knows the treachery of the eyes
and that which the minds conceal. Allah
judges with truth, and those whom they
call on beside Him have no power to judge
at all. Surely Allah is All-Hearing, All-
Seeing. (14—21)

Have they not travelled in the earth
that they could see what was the end of
those before them? They were mightier
than these in the power that they wielded
and more skilled as witnessed by the
remains that they have left in the earth;
but Allah seized them with ruin because
of their sins, and there was none who could
shield them against Allah's wrath. That
was because their Messengers came to
them with manifest Signs, but they disbelieved; so Allah seized them with ruin.
Surely He is Powerful, Severe in punishment. (22—23)

We sent Moses, with Our Signs and
manifest authority unto Pharaoh and
Haman and Korah; but they said: He is
only a magician and impostor. When he
came to them with truth from Us, they
said: Slay the male children of those who
have believed with him and spare their
female children. But the design of the disbelievers is ever frustrated. Pharaoh announced: Hinder me not in putting Moses
to death; and let him call on his Lord
to save him. I fear lest he should change

اَلْيَوْمَ تُجْزٰى كُلُّ نَفْسٍ بِمَا كَسَبَتْ ۚ لَا ظُلْمَ

الْيَوْمَ ۚ اِنَّ اللّٰهَ سَرِيْعُ الْحِسَابِ ۝

وَاَنْذِرْهُمْ يَوْمَ الْاٰزِفَةِ اِذِ الْقُلُوْبُ لَدَى

الْحَنَاجِرِ كٰظِمِيْنَ ۚ مَا لِلظّٰلِمِيْنَ مِنْ حَمِيْمٍ

وَّلَا شَفِيْعٍ يُّطَاعُ ۝

يَعْلَمُ خَآئِنَةَ الْاَعْيُنِ وَمَا تُخْفِى الصُّدُوْرُ ۝

وَاللّٰهُ يَقْضِيْ بِالْحَقِّ ۚ وَالَّذِيْنَ يَدْعُوْنَ مِنْ

دُوْنِهٖ لَا يَقْضُوْنَ بِشَيْءٍ ۚ اِنَّ اللّٰهَ هُوَ السَّمِيْعُ

الْبَصِيْرُ ۝

اَوَلَمْ يَسِيْرُوْا فِى الْاَرْضِ فَيَنْظُرُوْا كَيْفَ

كَانَ عَاقِبَةُ الَّذِيْنَ كَانُوْا مِنْ قَبْلِهِمْ ۚ كَانُوْا اَشَدَّ

مِنْهُمْ قُوَّةً وَّاٰثَارًا فِى الْاَرْضِ فَاَخَذَهُمُ اللّٰهُ بِذُنُوْبِهِمْ

وَمَا كَانَ لَهُمْ مِّنَ اللّٰهِ مِنْ وَّاقٍ ۝

ذٰلِكَ بِاَنَّهُمْ كَانَتْ تَّاْتِيْهِمْ رُسُلُهُمْ بِالْبَيِّنٰتِ فَكَفَرُوْا

فَاَخَذَهُمُ اللّٰهُ ۚ اِنَّهٗ قَوِيٌّ شَدِيْدُ الْعِقَابِ ۝

وَلَقَدْ اَرْسَلْنَا مُوْسٰى بِاٰيٰتِنَا وَسُلْطٰنٍ مُّبِيْنٍ ۝

اِلٰى فِرْعَوْنَ وَهَامٰنَ وَقَارُوْنَ فَقَالُوْا سٰحِرٌ كَذَّابٌ ۝

فَلَمَّا جَآءَهُمْ بِالْحَقِّ مِنْ عِنْدِنَا قَالُوا اقْتُلُوْا اَبْنَآءَ

الَّذِيْنَ اٰمَنُوْا مَعَهٗ وَاسْتَحْيُوْا نِسَآءَهُمْ ۚ وَمَا كَيْدُ

الْكٰفِرِيْنَ اِلَّا فِيْ ضَلٰلٍ ۝

وَقَالَ فِرْعَوْنُ ذَرُوْنِيْۤ اَقْتُلْ مُوْسٰى وَلْيَدْعُ

رَبَّهٗ ۚ اِنِّيْۤ اَخَافُ اَنْ يُّبَدِّلَ دِيْنَكُمْ اَوْ اَنْ يُّظْهِرَ

your religion or cause disturbance in the land. Moses replied: I seek refuge with my Lord and your Lord against the mischief of every arrogant one who believes not in the Day of Reckoning. (24—28)

فِى الْاَرْضِ الْفَسَادَ ۝

وَقَالَ مُوْسٰۤى اِنِّىْ عُذْتُ بِرَبِّىْ وَرَبِّكُمْ مِّنْ كُلِّ مُتَكَبِّرٍ لَّا يُؤْمِنُ بِيَوْمِ الْحِسَابِ ۝

وَقَالَ رَجُلٌ مُّؤْمِنٌ مِّنْ اٰلِ فِرْعَوْنَ يَكْتُمُ اِيْمَانَهٗٓ اَتَقْتُلُوْنَ رَجُلًا اَنْ يَّقُوْلَ رَبِّىَ اللّٰهُ وَقَدْ جَآءَكُمْ

A believing man from among the people of Pharaoh, who concealed his faith, said: Will you slay a man simply because he says: Allah is my Lord; and he has brought you clear proofs from your Lord? If he is an impostor, he will be called to account for his imposture; but if he tells the truth, then some of that with which he threatens you will surely befall you. Certainly Allah guides not any extravagant impostor.

بِالْبَيِّنٰتِ مِنْ رَّبِّكُمْ وَاِنْ يَّكُ كَاذِبًا فَعَلَيْهِ كَذِبُهٗ وَاِنْ يَّكُ صَادِقًا يُّصِبْكُمْ بَعْضُ الَّذِىْ يَعِدُكُمْ اِنَّ اللّٰهَ لَا يَهْدِىْ مَنْ هُوَ مُسْرِفٌ كَذَّابٌ ۝

يٰقَوْمِ لَكُمُ الْمُلْكُ الْيَوْمَ ظٰهِرِيْنَ فِى الْاَرْضِ فَمَنْ يَّنْصُرُنَا مِنْ بَأْسِ اللّٰهِ اِنْ جَآءَنَا قَالَ فِرْعَوْنُ مَآ اُرِيْكُمْ اِلَّا مَآ اَرٰى وَمَآ اَهْدِيْكُمْ اِلَّا سَبِيْلَ الرَّشَادِ ۝

O my people, today you have dominant authority in the land; but who will safeguard us against the chastisement of Allah if it comes upon us? Pharaoh said: I point out to you only that which I consider right and seek only to guide you along the right path. He who believed said: O my people, I fear for you a day like the day which overtook erring people before you, like the people of Noah, and the tribes of 'Ad and Thamud and those who came after them. Allah wills no injustice for His creatures. O my people, I fear for you the day of wailing and calling for help, the day when you will turn your backs and flee from the wrath of Allah, and there will be no one to shield you from Allah. For him whom Allah adjudges astray there is no guide. Joseph came to you before this with clear proofs, but you continued in doubt concerning that which he brought you till, when he died, you said: Allah will

وَقَالَ الَّذِىْ اٰمَنَ يٰقَوْمِ اِنِّىْ اَخَافُ عَلَيْكُمْ مِّثْلَ يَوْمِ الْاَحْزَابِ ۝

مِثْلَ دَأْبِ قَوْمِ نُوْحٍ وَّعَادٍ وَّثَمُوْدَ وَالَّذِيْنَ مِنْ بَعْدِهِمْ وَمَا اللّٰهُ يُرِيْدُ ظُلْمًا لِّلْعِبَادِ ۝

وَيٰقَوْمِ اِنِّىْ اَخَافُ عَلَيْكُمْ يَوْمَ التَّنَادِ ۝

يَوْمَ تُوَلُّوْنَ مُدْبِرِيْنَ مَا لَكُمْ مِّنَ اللّٰهِ مِنْ عَاصِمٍ وَمَنْ يُّضْلِلِ اللّٰهُ فَمَا لَهٗ مِنْ هَادٍ ۝

وَلَقَدْ جَآءَكُمْ يُوْسُفُ مِنْ قَبْلُ بِالْبَيِّنٰتِ فَمَا زِلْتُمْ فِىْ شَكٍّ مِّمَّا جَآءَكُمْ بِهٖ حَتّٰى اِذَا هَلَكَ قُلْتُمْ

never raise up a Messenger after him.
Thus does Allah adjudge astray every
extravagant doubter; those who contend against the Signs of Allah, without any authority furnished to them by
Allah. Grievously displeasing is this in the
sight of Allah and of those who believe.
Thus does Allah set a seal on the heart of
every arrogant, haughty one. (29—36)

لَنْ يَّبْعَثَ اللّٰهُ مِنْۢ بَعْدِهٖ رَسُوْلًا ۫ كَذٰلِكَ يُضِلُّ
اللّٰهُ مَنْ هُوَ مُسْرِفٌ مُّرْتَابُۨ ۙ

الَّذِيْنَ يُجَادِلُوْنَ فِيْٓ اٰيٰتِ اللّٰهِ بِغَيْرِ سُلْطٰنٍ اَتٰىهُمْ ؕ
كَبُرَ مَقْتًا عِنْدَ اللّٰهِ وَعِنْدَ الَّذِيْنَ اٰمَنُوْا ؕ كَذٰلِكَ
يَطْبَعُ اللّٰهُ عَلٰى كُلِّ قَلْبِ مُتَكَبِّرٍ جَبَّارٍ ۟

وَقَالَ فِرْعَوْنُ يٰهَامٰنُ ابْنِ لِيْ صَرْحًا لَّعَلِّيْٓ
اَبْلُغُ الْاَسْبَابَ ۙ

Pharaoh commanded Haman: Build me
a lofty structure that I may scale the
approaches that lead to heaven and discover the God of Moses, for I consider him
a liar. Thus was his evil conduct made to
seem fair to Pharaoh, and he was hindered
from the right path. The design of Pharaoh
all tended to his ruin. (37—38)

اَسْبَابَ السَّمٰوٰتِ فَاَطَّلِعَ اِلٰٓى اِلٰهِ مُوْسٰى وَاِنِّيْ
لَاَظُنُّهٗ كَاذِبًا ؕ وَكَذٰلِكَ زُيِّنَ لِفِرْعَوْنَ سُوْٓءُ عَمَلِهٖ
وَصُدَّ عَنِ السَّبِيْلِ ؕ وَمَا كَيْدُ فِرْعَوْنَ اِلَّا فِيْ
تَبَابٍ ۟

وَقَالَ الَّذِيْٓ اٰمَنَ يٰقَوْمِ اتَّبِعُوْنِ اَهْدِكُمْ سَبِيْلَ
الرَّشَادِ ۚ

يٰقَوْمِ اِنَّمَا هٰذِهِ الْحَيٰوةُ الدُّنْيَا مَتَاعٌ ۫ وَّاِنَّ الْاٰخِرَةَ
هِيَ دَارُ الْقَرَارِ ۟

He who believed said: O my people,
follow me, I shall guide you to the straight
path. The life of this world is but a temporary provision; and the Hereafter is the
permanent abode. Whoso does evil will be
requited only with the like thereof; but
whoso does good, whether male or female,
and is a believer, these will enter the
Garden; they will be provided therein
without measure. O my people, how strange
it is that I call you to salvation and
you call me to the Fire. You invite me
to deny Allah and to associate with Him
that of which I have no knowledge, while
I invite you to the Mighty, the Most
Forgiving.

مَنْ عَمِلَ سَيِّئَةً فَلَا يُجْزٰٓى اِلَّا مِثْلَهَا ۚ وَمَنْ
عَمِلَ صَالِحًا مِّنْ ذَكَرٍ اَوْ اُنْثٰى وَهُوَ مُؤْمِنٌ فَاُولٰٓئِكَ
يَدْخُلُوْنَ الْجَنَّةَ يُرْزَقُوْنَ فِيْهَا بِغَيْرِ حِسَابٍ ۟

وَيٰقَوْمِ مَا لِيْٓ اَدْعُوْكُمْ اِلَى النَّجَاةِ وَتَدْعُوْنَنِيْٓ
اِلَى النَّارِ ۟

تَدْعُوْنَنِيْ لِاَكْفُرَ بِاللّٰهِ وَاُشْرِكَ بِهٖ مَا لَيْسَ
لِيْ بِهٖ عِلْمٌ ۫ وَّاَنَا اَدْعُوْكُمْ اِلَى الْعَزِيْزِ الْغَفَّارِ ۟

Surely that to which you call me has no title to be called upon in this world or in the Hereafter; and certainly our return is to Allah and the transgressors will be the inmates of the Fire. You will soon recall my admonition. I commit my cause to Allah; surely Allah is watchful of His servants.

So Allah safeguarded him against the mischief of that which they contrived, and a grievous chastisement encompassed the people of Pharaoh: the Fire, to which they are exposed morning and evening. When the Hour arrives, the decree will go forth: Cast the people of Pharaoh into severe torment. They will wrangle with one another in the Fire. The weak will say to the mighty ones: We were under your authority. Can you, then, relieve us of a portion of the fiery torment? Those who had considered themselves mighty will say: We are all in it. Allah has already judged between His servants. Those in the Fire will beg the keepers of hell: Pray to your Lord that He may reduce our torment for a period. They will make answer: Did not your Messengers come to you with manifest Signs? The reply will be: Surely. The keepers will retort: Then, pray on. But the prayer of the disbelievers is in vain. (39—51)

Most surely do We help Our Messengers and those who believe in this life as well as on the day when the witnesses shall step forth; the day when their excuses will not

لَا جَرَمَ اَنَّمَا تَدْعُوْنَنِى اِلَيْهِ لَيْسَ لَهُ دَعْوَةٌ فِى الدُّنْيَا وَلَا فِى الْاٰخِرَةِ وَاَنَّ مَرَدَّنَآ اِلَى اللّٰهِ وَاَنَّ الْمُسْرِفِيْنَ هُمْ اَصْحٰبُ النَّارِ ۞

فَسَتَذْكُرُوْنَ مَآ اَقُوْلُ لَكُمْ وَاُفَوِّضُ اَمْرِىْ اِلَى اللّٰهِ اِنَّ اللّٰهَ بَصِيْرٌ بِالْعِبَادِ ۞

فَوَقٰهُ اللّٰهُ سَيِّاٰتِ مَا مَكَرُوْا وَحَاقَ بِاٰلِ فِرْعَوْنَ سُوْٓءُ الْعَذَابِ ۞

اَلنَّارُ يُعْرَضُوْنَ عَلَيْهَا غُدُوًّا وَّعَشِيًّا ۚ وَيَوْمَ تَقُوْمُ السَّاعَةُ ۗ اَدْخِلُوْٓا اٰلَ فِرْعَوْنَ اَشَدَّ الْعَذَابِ ۞

وَاِذْ يَتَحَآجُّوْنَ فِى النَّارِ فَيَقُوْلُ الضُّعَفٰٓؤُا لِلَّذِيْنَ اسْتَكْبَرُوْٓا اِنَّا كُنَّا لَكُمْ تَبَعًا فَهَلْ اَنْتُمْ مُّغْنُوْنَ عَنَّا نَصِيْبًا مِّنَ النَّارِ ۞

قَالَ الَّذِيْنَ اسْتَكْبَرُوْٓا اِنَّا كُلٌّ فِيْهَآ اِنَّ اللّٰهَ قَدْ حَكَمَ بَيْنَ الْعِبَادِ ۞

وَقَالَ الَّذِيْنَ فِى النَّارِ لِخَزَنَةِ جَهَنَّمَ ادْعُوْا رَبَّكُمْ يُخَفِّفْ عَنَّا يَوْمًا مِّنَ الْعَذَابِ ۞

قَالُوْٓا اَوَلَمْ تَكُ تَأْتِيْكُمْ رُسُلُكُمْ بِالْبَيِّنٰتِ ۗ قَالُوْا بَلٰى ۗ قَالُوْا فَادْعُوْا ۚ وَمَا دُعٰٓؤُا الْكٰفِرِيْنَ اِلَّا فِىْ ضَلٰلٍ ۞

اِنَّا لَنَنْصُرُ رُسُلَنَا وَالَّذِيْنَ اٰمَنُوْا فِى الْحَيٰوةِ الدُّنْيَا وَيَوْمَ يَقُوْمُ الْاَشْهَادُ ۞

profit the wrongdoers, and they will be cast aside and evil will be their abode. Certainly We gave Moses the guidance, and made the children of Israel the inheritors of the Book: a guidance and a reminder for men of understanding. So be patient. Surely, the promise of Allah is true. Ask forgiveness for those who wrong thee, and glorify thy Lord with His praise, morning and evening. Those who contend against the Signs of Allah without any authority having come to them from Allah are merely puffed up with vain pride and desires which they shall never attain. So seek refuge with Allah. Surely He is All-Hearing, All-Seeing. (52—57)

Surely, the creation of the heavens and the earth is greater than the creation of mankind; but most people know not. The blind and the seeing are not equal; nor are those who believe and act righteously and those who do evil. Little do you reflect. The Hour will surely come; in that there is no doubt; yet most men believe not. Your Lord has said: Call on Me; I will respond to you. Those who consider themselves above worshipping Me will surely enter hell, despised. (58—61)

Allah is He Who has made the night that you may seek repose in it, and the day illuminating. Verily, Allah is Most Bountiful towards mankind, but most people are not grateful. Such is Allah, your Lord,

يَوْمَ لَا يَنْفَعُ الظّٰلِمِيْنَ مَعْذِرَتُهُمْ وَلَهُمُ اللَّعْنَةُ وَلَهُمْ سُوْٓءُ الدَّارِ ۞

وَلَقَدْ اٰتَيْنَا مُوْسَى الْهُدٰى وَاَوْرَثْنَا بَنِيْٓ اِسْرَآءِيْلَ الْكِتٰبَ ۙ۞

هُدًى وَّذِكْرٰى لِاُولِى الْاَلْبَابِ ۞

فَاصْبِرْ اِنَّ وَعْدَ اللّٰهِ حَقٌّ وَّاسْتَغْفِرْ لِذَنْۢبِكَ وَسَبِّحْ بِحَمْدِ رَبِّكَ بِالْعَشِيِّ وَالْاِبْكَارِ ۞

اِنَّ الَّذِيْنَ يُجَادِلُوْنَ فِيْٓ اٰيٰتِ اللّٰهِ بِغَيْرِ سُلْطٰنٍ اَتٰىهُمْ ۙ اِنْ فِيْ صُدُوْرِهِمْ اِلَّا كِبْرٌ مَّا هُمْ بِبَالِغِيْهِ ۚ فَاسْتَعِذْ بِاللّٰهِ ۚ اِنَّهُ هُوَ السَّمِيْعُ الْبَصِيْرُ ۞

لَخَلْقُ السَّمٰوٰتِ وَالْاَرْضِ اَكْبَرُ مِنْ خَلْقِ النَّاسِ وَلٰكِنَّ اَكْثَرَ النَّاسِ لَا يَعْلَمُوْنَ ۞

وَمَا يَسْتَوِى الْاَعْمٰى وَالْبَصِيْرُ ۙ وَالَّذِيْنَ اٰمَنُوْا وَعَمِلُوا الصّٰلِحٰتِ وَلَا الْمُسِيْٓءُ ۭ قَلِيْلًا مَّا تَتَذَكَّرُوْنَ ۞

اِنَّ السَّاعَةَ لَاٰتِيَةٌ لَّا رَيْبَ فِيْهَا وَلٰكِنَّ اَكْثَرَ النَّاسِ لَا يُؤْمِنُوْنَ ۞

وَقَالَ رَبُّكُمُ ادْعُوْنِيْٓ اَسْتَجِبْ لَكُمْ ۭ اِنَّ الَّذِيْنَ يَسْتَكْبِرُوْنَ عَنْ عِبَادَتِيْ سَيَدْخُلُوْنَ جَهَنَّمَ دٰخِرِيْنَ ۞

اَللّٰهُ الَّذِيْ جَعَلَ لَكُمُ الَّيْلَ لِتَسْكُنُوْا فِيْهِ وَالنَّهَارَ مُبْصِرًا ۭ اِنَّ اللّٰهَ لَذُوْ فَضْلٍ عَلَى النَّاسِ وَلٰكِنَّ اَكْثَرَ النَّاسِ لَا يَشْكُرُوْنَ ۞

Creator of all things. There is no god but He. How then are you being turned away? Thus indeed are turned away those who deny His Signs stubbornly without reflection. Allah is He Who has made the earth a resting place for you, and the heaven a canopy, and has endowed you with faculties and capacities and has made them strong and perfect, and has provided you with good things. Such is Allah, your Lord. Blessed is Allah, the Lord of the worlds. He is Ever Living, the Bestower of Life; there is no god but He. So call on Him in utter sincerity of faith. All praise belongs to Allah, the Lord of the worlds.

ذٰلِكُمُ اللهُ رَبُّكُمْ خَالِقُ كُلِّ شَىْءٍ لَّا اِلٰهَ اِلَّا هُوَ ۖ فَاَنّٰى تُؤْفَكُوْنَ ۝

كَذٰلِكَ يُؤْفَكُ الَّذِيْنَ كَانُوْا بِاٰيٰتِ اللهِ يَجْحَدُوْنَ ۝

اَللهُ الَّذِيْ جَعَلَ لَكُمُ الْاَرْضَ قَرَارًا وَّ السَّمَاءَ بِنَآءً وَّصَوَّرَكُمْ فَاَحْسَنَ صُوَرَكُمْ وَرَزَقَكُمْ مِّنَ الطَّيِّبٰتِ ذٰلِكُمُ اللهُ رَبُّكُمْ ۚ فَتَبٰرَكَ اللهُ رَبُّ الْعٰلَمِيْنَ ۝

هُوَ الْحَيُّ لَا اِلٰهَ اِلَّا هُوَ فَادْعُوْهُ مُخْلِصِيْنَ لَهُ الدِّيْنَ ۭ اَلْحَمْدُ لِلهِ رَبِّ الْعٰلَمِيْنَ ۝

Proclaim: I have been forbidden to worship those whom you call upon beside Allah, since there have come unto me clear proofs from my Lord; and I have been commanded to submit myself wholly to the Lord of the worlds. He it is Who created you from dust, then from a sperm-drop, then from a clot; then He brings you forth a child; then He lets you attain your full strength; then He lets you become old — some of you are caused to die before — that you may reach an appointed term and that through all this you may exercise your understanding. He it is Who gives life and causes death. When He decrees a thing He says concerning it: Be; and it is. (62—69)

قُلْ اِنِّيْ نُهِيْتُ اَنْ اَعْبُدَ الَّذِيْنَ تَدْعُوْنَ مِنْ دُوْنِ اللهِ لَمَّا جَاءَنِيَ الْبَيِّنٰتُ مِنْ رَّبِّيْ وَاُمِرْتُ اَنْ اُسْلِمَ لِرَبِّ الْعٰلَمِيْنَ ۝

هُوَ الَّذِيْ خَلَقَكُمْ مِّنْ تُرَابٍ ثُمَّ مِنْ نُّطْفَةٍ ثُمَّ مِنْ عَلَقَةٍ ثُمَّ يُخْرِجُكُمْ طِفْلًا ثُمَّ لِتَبْلُغُوْٓا اَشُدَّكُمْ ثُمَّ لِتَكُوْنُوْا شُيُوْخًا ۚ وَمِنْكُمْ مَّنْ يُّتَوَفّٰى مِنْ قَبْلُ وَلِتَبْلُغُوْٓا اَجَلًا مُّسَمًّى وَّ لَعَلَّكُمْ تَعْقِلُوْنَ ۝

هُوَ الَّذِيْ يُحْىٖ وَيُمِيْتُ ۚ فَاِذَا قَضٰٓى اَمْرًا فَاِنَّمَا يَقُوْلُ لَهُ كُنْ فَيَكُوْنُ ۝

Seest thou not those who contend against the Signs of Allah, whither are they being turned away; those who reject the Book and that with which We sent Our Messengers?

اَلَمْ تَرَ اِلَى الَّذِيْنَ يُجَادِلُوْنَ فِيْٓ اٰيٰتِ اللهِ ۭ اَنّٰى يُصْرَفُوْنَ ۝

الَّذِيْنَ كَذَّبُوْا بِالْكِتٰبِ وَ بِمَآ اَرْسَلْنَا بِهٖ رُسُلَنَا ۖ

But soon will they come to know, when with iron collars round their necks and with chains they will be dragged into boiling water and will then be fed into the Fire. Then they will be asked: Where are those who were your associate gods beside Allah? They will answer: We have lost them. Nay, we never prayed to anything before. Thus does Allah confound the disbelievers. That is what you exulted in, without justification, during your earthly life, and on account of which you behaved insolently. Enter now the gates of hell, to abide therein. Evil is the abode of the arrogant.

So be patient. Surely the promise of Allah is true. Whether We show thee part of that which We have promised them, or We cause thee to die, to Us will they be brought back and they shall then learn the truth. We did send Messengers before thee; of them are those that We have mentioned to thee, and of them are those that We have not mentioned to thee. It behoves not a Messenger to bring a Sign except by the leave of Allah. When Allah's decree goes forth, the matter is settled with justice, and those who pursue falsehood are the losers. (70—79)

Allah is He Who has created cattle for you, that you may ride some of them, and eat of the flesh of some — and you have other uses for them— and that through them you may attain your desires; and on them and on vessels are you borne. He shows you His Signs; then which of the Signs of Allah will you deny?

فَسَوْفَ يَعْلَمُوْنَ ۞

اِذِ الْاَغْلٰلُ فِىْۤ اَعْنَاقِهِمْ وَالسَّلٰسِلُ ۖ يُسْحَبُوْنَ ۞

فِى الْحَمِيْمِ ۖ ثُمَّ فِى النَّارِ يُسْجَرُوْنَ ۞

ثُمَّ قِيْلَ لَهُمْ اَيْنَ مَا كُنْتُمْ تُشْرِكُوْنَ ۞

مِنْ دُوْنِ اللّٰهِ ۖ قَالُوْا ضَلُّوْا عَنَّا بَلْ لَّمْ نَكُنْ نَّدْعُوْا مِنْ قَبْلُ شَيْئًا ۚ كَذٰلِكَ يُضِلُّ اللّٰهُ الْكٰفِرِيْنَ ۞

ذٰلِكُمْ بِمَا كُنْتُمْ تَفْرَحُوْنَ فِى الْاَرْضِ بِغَيْرِ الْحَقِّ وَبِمَا كُنْتُمْ تَمْرَحُوْنَ ۞

اُدْخُلُوْۤا اَبْوَابَ جَهَنَّمَ خٰلِدِيْنَ فِيْهَا ۖ فَبِئْسَ مَثْوَى الْمُتَكَبِّرِيْنَ ۞

فَاصْبِرْ اِنَّ وَعْدَ اللّٰهِ حَقٌّ ۚ فَاِمَّا نُرِيَنَّكَ بَعْضَ الَّذِىْ نَعِدُهُمْ اَوْ نَتَوَفَّيَنَّكَ فَاِلَيْنَا يُرْجَعُوْنَ ۞

وَلَقَدْ اَرْسَلْنَا رُسُلًا مِّنْ قَبْلِكَ مِنْهُمْ مَّنْ قَصَصْنَا عَلَيْكَ وَمِنْهُمْ مَّنْ لَّمْ نَقْصُصْ عَلَيْكَ ۗ وَمَا كَانَ لِرَسُوْلٍ اَنْ يَّأْتِىَ بِاٰيَةٍ اِلَّا بِاِذْنِ اللّٰهِ ۚ فَاِذَا جَآءَ اَمْرُ اللّٰهِ قُضِىَ بِالْحَقِّ وَخَسِرَ هُنَالِكَ الْمُبْطِلُوْنَ ۞

اَللّٰهُ الَّذِىْ جَعَلَ لَكُمُ الْاَنْعَامَ لِتَرْكَبُوْا مِنْهَا وَمِنْهَا تَأْكُلُوْنَ ۞

وَلَكُمْ فِيْهَا مَنَافِعُ وَلِتَبْلُغُوْا عَلَيْهَا حَاجَةً فِىْ صُدُوْرِكُمْ وَعَلَيْهَا وَعَلَى الْفُلْكِ تُحْمَلُوْنَ ۞

وَيُرِيْكُمْ اٰيٰتِهٖ ۖ فَاَىَّ اٰيٰتِ اللّٰهِ تُنْكِرُوْنَ ۞

Have they not travelled in the earth that they could see the end of those before them? They were more numerous than these, and mightier in power, and more skilled as witnessed by the remains they have left behind in the earth, but all that they practised was of no avail to them.

اَفَلَمْ يَسِيْرُوْا فِي الْاَرْضِ فَيَنْظُرُوْا كَيْفَ كَانَ عَاقِبَةُ الَّذِيْنَ مِنْ قَبْلِهِمْ ۭ كَانُوْٓا اَكْثَرَ مِنْهُمْ وَاَشَدَّ قُوَّةً وَّاٰثَارًا فِي الْاَرْضِ فَمَآ اَغْنٰى عَنْهُمْ مَّا كَانُوْا يَكْسِبُوْنَ ۝

فَلَمَّا جَآءَتْهُمْ رُسُلُهُمْ بِالْبَيِّنٰتِ فَرِحُوْا بِمَا عِنْدَهُمْ مِّنَ الْعِلْمِ وَحَاقَ بِهِمْ مَّا كَانُوْا بِهٖ يَسْتَهْزِءُوْنَ ۝

When their Messengers came to them with manifest Signs, they exulted in the knowledge which they possessed; and the chastisement at which they mocked encompassed them. When they perceived Our punishment they cried out: We believe now in Allah, the One, and reject all that we used to associate with Him. But when they had perceived Our chastisement, their believing could not profit them. That is Allah's law which has ever been in operation in respect of His servants. Thus the disbelievers were the losers. (80— 86)

فَلَمَّا رَاَوْا بَاْسَنَا قَالُوْٓا اٰمَنَّا بِاللّٰهِ وَحْدَهٗ وَكَفَرْنَا بِمَا كُنَّا بِهٖ مُشْرِكِيْنَ ۝

فَلَمْ يَكُ يَنْفَعُهُمْ اِيْمَانُهُمْ لَمَّا رَاَوْا بَاْسَنَا ۭ سُنَّتَ اللّٰهِ الَّتِيْ قَدْ خَلَتْ فِيْ عِبَادِهٖ ۚ وَخَسِرَ هُنَالِكَ الْكٰفِرُوْنَ ۝

ḤĀ MĪM SAJDAH

(Revealed before Hijra)

In the name of Allah, Most Gracious, Ever Merciful. (1)

THE PRAISEWORTHY, THE LORD OF HONOUR (2)

This Quran is a revelation from the Most Gracious, Ever Merciful; a Book whose commandments have been expounded in detail, which will be repeatedly read, couched in clear, eloquent language, for the benefit of people who possess knowledge; bearer of glad tidings and a warner. But most of them turn away and do not choose even to listen. They say: Our hearts are securely wrapped up against that to which thou callest us, and there is deafness in our ears and between thee and us there is a barrier. Do thou carry on in thy way and we shall carry on in ours. Tell them: I am but a human being like you. It is revealed to me that your God is One God; so be steadfast in your relationship with Him, and ask forgiveness of Him. Woe to the idolaters, who do not pay the Zakat, and who deny the Hereafter. Those who believe and act righteously, will surely have a never-ending reward. (3—9)

Ask them: Do you disbelieve in Him Who created the earth in two periods, and set up equals to Him? He is the Lord of the worlds. He placed in the earth firm mountains, rising above its surface, and blessed it with abundance, and provided therein nurture for its dwellers in proper measure, equally for all seekers, in four periods. Then He turned to the heaven, which was all mist, and said to it and to the earth: Submit ye to My command, willingly or unwillingly. They said: We have submitted willingly. He arranged them in seven heavens, in two periods, and He invested each heaven with capacity to discharge its function. We adorned the lowest heaven with lights and for protection. This is the decree of the Mighty, the All-Knowing. But if they turn away, tell them: I have warned you of a sudden destructive punishment like the one that overtook the tribes of 'Ad and Thamud.

وَقَدَّرَ فِيهَآ أَقْوَاتَهَا فِىٓ أَرْبَعَةِ أَيَّامٍ سَوَآءً لِّلسَّآئِلِيْنَ ۞

ثُمَّ اسْتَوٰىٓ إِلَى السَّمَآءِ وَهِىَ دُخَانٌ فَقَالَ لَهَا وَلِلْأَرْضِ ائْتِيَا طَوْعًا أَوْ كَرْهًا ۖ قَالَتَآ أَتَيْنَا طَآئِعِيْنَ ۞

فَقَضٰهُنَّ سَبْعَ سَمٰوٰتٍ فِىْ يَوْمَيْنِ وَأَوْحٰى فِىْ كُلِّ سَمَآءٍ أَمْرَهَا ۚ وَزَيَّنَّا السَّمَآءَ الدُّنْيَا بِمَصَابِيْحَ ۖ وَحِفْظًا ۚ ذٰلِكَ تَقْدِيْرُ الْعَزِيْزِ الْعَلِيْمِ ۞

فَإِنْ أَعْرَضُوْا فَقُلْ أَنْذَرْتُكُمْ صٰعِقَةً مِّثْلَ صٰعِقَةِ عَادٍ وَّثَمُوْدَ ۞

إِذْ جَآءَتْهُمُ الرُّسُلُ مِنْۢ بَيْنِ أَيْدِيْهِمْ وَمِنْ خَلْفِهِمْ أَلَّا تَعْبُدُوْٓا إِلَّا اللّٰهَ ۚ قَالُوْا لَوْ شَآءَ رَبُّنَا لَأَنْزَلَ مَلٰٓئِكَةً فَإِنَّا بِمَآ أُرْسِلْتُمْ بِهٖ كٰفِرُوْنَ ۞

فَأَمَّا عَادٌ فَاسْتَكْبَرُوْا فِى الْأَرْضِ بِغَيْرِ الْحَقِّ وَقَالُوْا مَنْ أَشَدُّ مِنَّا قُوَّةً ۖ أَوَلَمْ يَرَوْا أَنَّ اللّٰهَ الَّذِىْ خَلَقَهُمْ هُوَ أَشَدُّ مِنْهُمْ قُوَّةً ۖ وَكَانُوْا بِآيٰتِنَا يَجْحَدُوْنَ ۞

فَأَرْسَلْنَا عَلَيْهِمْ رِيْحًا صَرْصَرًا فِىٓ أَيَّامٍ نَّحِسَاتٍ لِّنُذِيْقَهُمْ عَذَابَ الْخِزْيِ فِى الْحَيٰوةِ الدُّنْيَا ۖ وَلَعَذَابُ الْآخِرَةِ أَخْزٰى وَهُمْ لَا يُنْصَرُوْنَ ۞

وَأَمَّا ثَمُوْدُ فَهَدَيْنٰهُمْ فَاسْتَحَبُّوا الْعَمٰى عَلَى

When their Messengers came to them in a continuous succession, admonishing them: Worship none but Allah; they retorted: Had our Lord so willed, He would have sent down angels. We reject that with which you have been sent. The tribe of 'Ad behaved arrogantly in the earth without any justification and said: Who is mightier than we are in power? Did they not see that Allah, Who created them, is mightier than they in power? Yet they persisted in rejecting Our Signs. So We sent against them a fierce wind for several ominous days, that We might afflict them with humiliating chastisement in this life and the chastisement of the Hereafter is even more humiliating, and they will not be helped. To Thamud We gave guidance, but they preferred blindness to guidance, so they were afflicted with the calamity of an humiliating chastisement, on account of that which they practised. But We saved those who believed and acted righteously. (10—19)

On the day when the enemies of Allah are gathered together and driven to the Fire, they will be sorted out, till when they approach it, their ears and their eyes and their skins will bear witness against them concerning that which they used to do. They will inquire from their skins: Why bear ye witness against us? These will make answer: Allah, Who has made everything else to speak, has made us to speak also. He it is Who created you the first time, and unto Him have you been brought back. You did not attempt to conceal your vices out of an apprehension that your ears and your eyes and your skins would bear witness against you; nay, you imagined that even Allah did not know much of that which you did. That notion of yours that you entertained concerning your Lord, has been your ruin, and you became losers. Now if they will endure, the Fire is their abode; but if they desire to be heard they will not be granted a hearing.

We assigned to them associates who made their doings appear fair to them, and the same decree went forth against them as had gone forth against communities of Jinn and mankind before them, that they will be among the losers. (20—26)

الۡهُدٰى فَاَخَذَتۡهُمۡ صٰعِقَةُ الۡعَذَابِ الۡهُوۡنِ بِمَا كَانُوۡا يَكۡسِبُوۡنَ ۞

وَ نَجَّيۡنَا الَّذِيۡنَ اٰمَنُوۡا وَ كَانُوۡا يَتَّقُوۡنَ ۞

وَ يَوۡمَ يُحۡشَرُ اَعۡدَآءُ اللّٰهِ اِلَى النَّارِ فَهُمۡ يُوۡزَعُوۡنَ ۞

حَتّٰى اِذَا مَا جَآءُوۡهَا شَهِدَ عَلَيۡهِمۡ سَمۡعُهُمۡ وَ اَبۡصَارُهُمۡ وَ جُلُوۡدُهُمۡ بِمَا كَانُوۡا يَعۡمَلُوۡنَ ۞

وَ قَالُوۡا لِجُلُوۡدِهِمۡ لِمَ شَهِدۡتُّمۡ عَلَيۡنَا ؕ قَالُوۡۤا اَنۡطَقَنَا اللّٰهُ الَّذِىۡۤ اَنۡطَقَ كُلَّ شَىۡءٍ وَّ هُوَ خَلَقَكُمۡ اَوَّلَ مَرَّةٍ وَّ اِلَيۡهِ تُرۡجَعُوۡنَ ۞

وَ مَا كُنۡتُمۡ تَسۡتَتِرُوۡنَ اَنۡ يَّشۡهَدَ عَلَيۡكُمۡ سَمۡعُكُمۡ وَ لَاۤ اَبۡصَارُكُمۡ وَ لَا جُلُوۡدُكُمۡ وَ لٰكِنۡ ظَنَنۡتُمۡ اَنَّ اللّٰهَ لَا يَعۡلَمُ كَثِيۡرًا مِّمَّا تَعۡمَلُوۡنَ ۞

وَ ذٰلِكُمۡ ظَنُّكُمُ الَّذِىۡ ظَنَنۡتُمۡ بِرَبِّكُمۡ اَرۡدٰىكُمۡ فَاَصۡبَحۡتُمۡ مِّنَ الۡخٰسِرِيۡنَ ۞

فَاِنۡ يَّصۡبِرُوۡا فَالنَّارُ مَثۡوًى لَّهُمۡ ۚ وَ اِنۡ يَّسۡتَعۡتِبُوۡا فَمَا هُمۡ مِّنَ الۡمُعۡتَبِيۡنَ ۞

وَ قَيَّضۡنَا لَهُمۡ قُرَنَآءَ فَزَيَّنُوۡا لَهُمۡ مَّا بَيۡنَ اَيۡدِيۡهِمۡ وَ مَا خَلۡفَهُمۡ وَ حَقَّ عَلَيۡهِمُ الۡقَوۡلُ فِىۡۤ اُمَمٍ قَدۡ خَلَتۡ مِنۡ قَبۡلِهِمۡ مِّنَ الۡجِنِّ وَ الۡاِنۡسِ ۚ اِنَّهُمۡ كَانُوۡا خٰسِرِيۡنَ ۞

وَ قَالَ الَّذِيۡنَ كَفَرُوۡا لَا تَسۡمَعُوۡا لِهٰذَا الۡقُرۡاٰنِ

The disbelievers say: Listen not to this Quran, and interrupt its recital with noise that you may have the upper hand. Most certainly will We afflict the disbelievers with severe torment, and, most certainly, will We requite them for the worst of their deeds. That is the requital of the enemies of Allah, the Fire, which will be their abiding home, as a requital for their obstinate rejection of Our Signs. The disbelievers will say: Lord, show us those from among the Jinn and men who led us astray, that we may trample them under foot and reduce them to an abject condition.

وَالْغَوْا فِيْهِ لَعَلَّكُمْ تَغْلِبُوْنَ ۞

فَلَنُذِيْقَنَّ الَّذِيْنَ كَفَرُوْا عَذَابًا شَدِيْدًا ۙ وَّ لَنَجْزِيَنَّهُمْ اَسْوَاَ الَّذِيْ كَانُوْا يَعْمَلُوْنَ ۞

ذٰلِكَ جَزَآءُ اَعْدَآءِ اللهِ النَّارُ ۚ لَهُمْ فِيْهَا دَارُ الْخُلْدِ ۚ جَزَآءً ۢ بِمَا كَانُوْا بِاٰيٰتِنَا يَجْحَدُوْنَ ۞

وَقَالَ الَّذِيْنَ كَفَرُوْا رَبَّنَاۤ اَرِنَا الَّذَيْنِ اَضَلّٰنَا مِنَ الْجِنِّ وَالْاِنْسِ نَجْعَلْهُمَا تَحْتَ اَقْدَامِنَا لِيَكُوْنَا مِنَ الْاَسْفَلِيْنَ ۞

While on them who affirm: Our Lord is Allah, and then remain steadfast, angels descend, reassuring them: Fear not nor grieve, and rejoice in the Garden that you were promised. We are your friends in this life and in the Hereafter. Therein you will have all that you desire, and therein you will have all that you ask for: an entertainment from the Most Forgiving, the Ever Merciful. (27—33)

اِنَّ الَّذِيْنَ قَالُوْا رَبُّنَا اللهُ ثُمَّ اسْتَقَامُوْا تَتَنَزَّلُ عَلَيْهِمُ الْمَلٰٓئِكَةُ اَلَّا تَخَافُوْا وَلَا تَحْزَنُوْا وَاَبْشِرُوْا بِالْجَنَّةِ الَّتِيْ كُنْتُمْ تُوْعَدُوْنَ ۞

نَحْنُ اَوْلِيٰۤؤُكُمْ فِي الْحَيٰوةِ الدُّنْيَا وَفِي الْاٰخِرَةِ ۚ وَلَكُمْ فِيْهَا مَا تَشْتَهِيْۤ اَنْفُسُكُمْ وَلَكُمْ فِيْهَا مَا تَدَّعُوْنَ ۞

نُزُلًا مِّنْ غَفُوْرٍ رَّحِيْمٍ ۞

Who speaks better than one who invites people to Allah and works righteousness and affirms: Truly, I am of those who submit wholly to Allah? Good and evil are not alike. Repel evil with that which is best, and lo, he between whom and thyself was enmity is as though he were a warm friend. But none attains to this save those who are steadfast, and none attains to this save those who are granted a large share of good. Should a tribulation on the

وَمَنْ اَحْسَنُ قَوْلًا مِّمَّنْ دَعَاۤ اِلَى اللهِ وَعَمِلَ صَالِحًا وَّقَالَ اِنَّنِيْ مِنَ الْمُسْلِمِيْنَ ۞

وَلَا تَسْتَوِى الْحَسَنَةُ وَلَا السَّيِّئَةُ ۚ اِدْفَعْ بِالَّتِيْ هِيَ اَحْسَنُ فَاِذَا الَّذِيْ بَيْنَكَ وَبَيْنَهُ عَدَاوَةٌ كَاَنَّهُ وَلِيٌّ حَمِيْمٌ ۞

وَمَا يُلَقّٰهَاۤ اِلَّا الَّذِيْنَ صَبَرُوْا ۚ وَمَا يُلَقّٰهَاۤ اِلَّا ذُوْ حَظٍّ عَظِيْمٍ ۞

part of Satan assail thee, do thou seek refuge with Allah. Surely, He is the All-Hearing, the All-Knowing. (34—37)

وَ اِمَّا يَنْزَغَنَّكَ مِنَ الشَّيْطٰنِ نَزْغٌ فَاسْتَعِذْ بِاللّٰهِ ط اِنَّهُ هُوَ السَّمِيْعُ الْعَلِيْمُ ۝

وَ مِنْ اٰيٰتِهِ الَّيْلُ وَ النَّهَارُ وَ الشَّمْسُ وَ الْقَمَرُ ؕ لَا تَسْجُدُوْا لِلشَّمْسِ وَ لَا لِلْقَمَرِ وَ اسْجُدُوْا لِلّٰهِ الَّذِيْ خَلَقَهُنَّ اِنْ كُنْتُمْ اِيَّاهُ تَعْبُدُوْنَ ۝

Of His Signs are the night and the day and the sun and the moon. Prostrate not yourselves before the sun, nor before the moon, but prostrate yourselves before Allah, Who created them, if it is He Whom you truly worship. Then, if they turn away in disdain, surely those who are with thy Lord glorify Him night and day, and are never wearied. Of His Signs is it that thou seest the earth withered, but when We send down water on it, it stirs and swells with verdure. Surely, He Who quickens it will quicken the dead. Verily He has power over all things. Those who seek to pervert Our Signs are not hidden from Us. Then is he better who is cast into the Fire, or he who comes to Us secure on the Day of Judgment? Do as you wish. Surely He sees all that you do. (38—41)

فَاِنِ اسْتَكْبَرُوْا فَالَّذِيْنَ عِنْدَ رَبِّكَ يُسَبِّحُوْنَ لَهٗ بِالَّيْلِ وَ النَّهَارِ وَ هُمْ لَا يَسْـَٔمُوْنَ ۩ۚ

وَ مِنْ اٰيٰتِهٖٓ اَنَّكَ تَرَى الْاَرْضَ خَاشِعَةً فَاِذَآ اَنْزَلْنَا عَلَيْهَا الْمَآءَ اهْتَزَّتْ وَ رَبَتْ ؕ اِنَّ الَّذِيْٓ اَحْيَاهَا لَمُحْيِ الْمَوْتٰى ؕ اِنَّهٗ عَلٰى كُلِّ شَيْءٍ قَدِيْرٌ ۝

اِنَّ الَّذِيْنَ يُلْحِدُوْنَ فِيْٓ اٰيٰتِنَا لَا يَخْفَوْنَ عَلَيْنَا ؕ اَفَمَنْ يُّلْقٰى فِي النَّارِ خَيْرٌ اَمْ مَّنْ يَّأْتِيْٓ اٰمِنًا يَّوْمَ الْقِيٰمَةِ ؕ اِعْمَلُوْا مَا شِئْتُمْ ۙ اِنَّهٗ بِمَا تَعْمَلُوْنَ بَصِيْرٌ ۝

اِنَّ الَّذِيْنَ كَفَرُوْا بِالذِّكْرِ لَمَّا جَآءَهُمْ ۚ وَ اِنَّهٗ لَكِتٰبٌ عَزِيْزٌ ۝ۙ

Those who reject the Reminder when it has come to them are in evil case, for it is a Mighty Book: falsehood cannot approach it from fore or aft; it is a revelation from the Wise, the Praiseworthy. Nothing is said to thee but that which was said to the Messengers before thee. Thy Lord is Most Forgiving, also Master of painful chastisement. Had We revealed the Quran in a foreign tongue, they would have said: Why have not its verses been expounded clearly? What! An Arab Prophet, and a scripture in a foreign tongue? Tell them: It is a guidance and a healing for those who believe, and those who do not believe are deaf of ears and it is hidden from them. They are like a person who is called from a far-off place.

لَا يَأْتِيْهِ الْبَاطِلُ مِنْ بَيْنِ يَدَيْهِ وَ لَا مِنْ خَلْفِهٖ ؕ تَنْزِيْلٌ مِّنْ حَكِيْمٍ حَمِيْدٍ ۝

مَا يُقَالُ لَكَ اِلَّا مَا قَدْ قِيْلَ لِلرُّسُلِ مِنْ قَبْلِكَ ؕ اِنَّ رَبَّكَ لَذُوْ مَغْفِرَةٍ وَّ ذُوْ عِقَابٍ اَلِيْمٍ ۝

وَ لَوْ جَعَلْنٰهُ قُرْاٰنًا اَعْجَمِيًّا لَّقَالُوْا لَوْ لَا فُصِّلَتْ اٰيٰتُهٗ ؕ ءَاَعْجَمِيٌّ وَّ عَرَبِيٌّ ؕ قُلْ هُوَ لِلَّذِيْنَ اٰمَنُوْا هُدًى وَّ شِفَآءٌ ؕ وَ الَّذِيْنَ لَا يُؤْمِنُوْنَ فِيْٓ اٰذَانِهِمْ وَقْرٌ

We also gave Moses a Book, and concerning it also there were differences. Had it not been for a word that had gone forth before from thy Lord, the matter would have been decided between them. They are certainly in a disquieting doubt concerning the Quran. (42—46)

وَهُوَ عَلَيْهِمْ عَمًى ۖ أُولَٰئِكَ يُنَادَوْنَ مِن مَّكَانٍ بَعِيدٍ ﴿٤٤﴾

وَلَقَدْ اٰتَيْنَا مُوسَى الْكِتٰبَ فَاخْتُلِفَ فِيْهِ ۚ وَلَوْلَا كَلِمَةٌ سَبَقَتْ مِنْ رَّبِّكَ لَقُضِيَ بَيْنَهُمْ ۚ وَإِنَّهُمْ لَفِىْ شَكٍّ مِّنْهُ مُرِيْبٍ ﴿٤٥﴾

مَنْ عَمِلَ صَالِحًا فَلِنَفْسِهِ ۚ وَمَنْ أَسَآءَ فَعَلَيْهَا ۗ وَمَا رَبُّكَ بِظَلَّامٍ لِّلْعَبِيْدِ ﴿٤٦﴾

Whoso acts righteously, it is for the good of his own self; and whoso does evil bears the burden thereof. Thy Lord is not in the least unjust to His creatures. Knowledge of the Hour rests entirely with Him. No fruit comes forth from its spathes, nor does any female conceive, nor give birth to a child, but it is within His knowledge. On the day when He will call unto them: Where are My partners?; they will make answer: We declare it unto Thee, not one of us is a witness of it. All that they used to call upon before will be lost to them, and they will know for certain that they have no place of escape. (47—49)

إِلَيْهِ يُرَدُّ عِلْمُ السَّاعَةِ ۚ وَمَا تَخْرُجُ مِن ثَمَرَاتٍ مِّنْ أَكْمَامِهَا وَمَا تَحْمِلُ مِنْ أُنثَىٰ وَلَا تَضَعُ إِلَّا بِعِلْمِهِ ۚ وَيَوْمَ يُنَادِيْهِمْ أَيْنَ شُرَكَآئِيْ قَالُوٓا اٰذَنّٰكَ مَا مِنَّا مِن شَهِيْدٍ ﴿٤٨﴾

وَضَلَّ عَنْهُم مَّا كَانُوا يَدْعُوْنَ مِن قَبْلُ وَظَنُّوْا مَا لَهُم مِّن مَّحِيْصٍ ﴿٤٩﴾

لَا يَسْأَمُ الْإِنسَانُ مِن دُعَآءِ الْخَيْرِ ۖ وَإِن مَّسَّهُ الشَّرُّ فَيَـُٔوْسٌ قَنُوْطٌ ﴿٥٠﴾

Man does not tire of praying for good, but if he is afflicted with evil, he despairs and gives up all hope. If after an affliction that has befallen him, We bestow Our mercy upon him, he is sure to say: This is my due; and I do not think the Hour will ever come, but even if I am returned to my Lord, I shall surely have with Him the very best. We will surely inform the disbelievers of all that they did, and We will certainly afflict them with severe torment. When We bestow a favour on man, he turns away and veers aside; but when evil afflicts him, he makes lengthy supplications.

وَلَئِنْ أَذَقْنٰهُ رَحْمَةً مِّنَّا مِنْ بَعْدِ ضَرَّآءَ مَسَّتْهُ لَيَقُوْلَنَّ هٰذَا لِيْ وَمَآ أَظُنُّ السَّاعَةَ قَآئِمَةً ۙ وَلَئِن رُّجِعْتُ إِلَىٰ رَبِّيْ إِنَّ لِيْ عِنْدَهُ لَلْحُسْنَىٰ ۚ فَلَنُنَبِّئَنَّ الَّذِيْنَ كَفَرُوْا بِمَا عَمِلُوْا ۖ وَلَنُذِيْقَنَّهُم مِّنْ عَذَابٍ غَلِيْظٍ ﴿٥١﴾

وَإِذَآ أَنْعَمْنَا عَلَى الْإِنسَانِ أَعْرَضَ وَنَأَىٰ بِجَانِبِهِ ۖ وَإِذَا مَسَّهُ الشَّرُّ فَذُوْ دُعَآءٍ عَرِيْضٍ ﴿٥٢﴾

Ask them: Have you considered, if this Quran is from Allah and you reject it, then who is more astray than one who has drifted far away from the Truth? We will show them Our Signs in the universe and also among their own selves, until it becomes manifest to them that the Quran is the Truth. Is it not enough that thy Lord is Witness over all things? Hearken! they are in doubt concerning the meeting with their Lord. Hearken! He certainly encompasses all things. (50—55)

قُلْ اَرَءَيْتُمْ اِنْ كَانَ مِنْ عِنْدِ اللّٰهِ ثُمَّ كَفَرْتُمْ بِهٖ مَنْ اَضَلُّ مِمَّنْ هُوَ فِىْ شِقَاقٍۭ بَعِيْدٍ ۞

سَنُرِيْهِمْ اٰيٰتِنَا فِى الْاٰفَاقِ وَفِىْٓ اَنْفُسِهِمْ حَتّٰى يَتَبَيَّنَ لَهُمْ اَنَّهُ الْحَقُّ ۗ اَوَلَمْ يَكْفِ بِرَبِّكَ اَنَّهٗ عَلٰى كُلِّ شَىْءٍ شَهِيْدٌ ۞

اَلَاۤ اِنَّهُمْ فِىْ مِرْيَةٍ مِّنْ لِّقَآءِ رَبِّهِمْ ۗ اَلَاۤ اِنَّهٗ بِكُلِّ شَىْءٍ مُّحِيْطٌ ۞

Chapter 42

AL-SHŪRĀ
(Revealed before Hijra)

In the name of Allah, Most Gracious, Ever Merciful. (1)

بِسْمِ اللهِ الرَّحْمٰنِ الرَّحِيْمِ ۟

حٰمۤ ۟

عۤسۤقۤ ۟

THE PRAISEWORTHY, THE LORD OF HONOUR, THE ALL-KNOWING, THE ALL-HEARING, THE ALL-POWERFUL (2—3)

كَذٰلِكَ يُوْحِىٓ اِلَيْكَ وَاِلَى الَّذِيْنَ مِنْ قَبْلِكَ ۙ اللهُ الْعَزِيْزُ الْحَكِيْمُ ۟

لَهٗ مَا فِى السَّمٰوٰتِ وَمَا فِى الْاَرْضِ ۭ وَهُوَ الْعَلِىُّ الْعَظِيْمُ ۟

Thus has Allah, the Mighty, the Wise, sent revelation to thee and to those who were before thee. To Him belongs whatever is in the heavens and whatever is in the earth. He is the High, the Great. The heavens may well-nigh rend asunder from above them on account of their misdeeds while the angels glorify their Lord with His praise and ask forgiveness for those on the earth. Behold it is surely Allah Who is the Most Forgiving, the Ever Merciful. Allah encompasses those who have taken protectors beside Him; thou art not a guardian over them. Thus have We revealed the Quran to thee in Arabic, that thou mayest warn the people of the central township of the land and those around it; and that thou mayest warn them of the Day of the Gathering, of which there is no doubt, when a party will be in the Garden and a party will be in the blazing Fire. Had Allah so pleased, He could have made them one people; but He admits into His mercy whomsoever He pleases. For the wrongdoers there is neither protector nor helper. Have they taken for themselves protectors other than Him? It is Allah alone Who is the Protector; it is He Who quickens the dead, and it is He Who has power over all things. (4—10)

تَكَادُ السَّمٰوٰتُ يَتَفَطَّرْنَ مِنْ فَوْقِهِنَّ وَالْمَلٰٓئِكَةُ يُسَبِّحُوْنَ بِحَمْدِ رَبِّهِمْ وَ يَسْتَغْفِرُوْنَ لِمَنْ فِى الْاَرْضِ ۭ اَلَآ اِنَّ اللهَ هُوَ الْغَفُوْرُ الرَّحِيْمُ ۟

وَالَّذِيْنَ اتَّخَذُوْا مِنْ دُوْنِهٖٓ اَوْلِيَآءَ اللهُ حَفِيْظٌ عَلَيْهِمْ ۡ وَمَآ اَنْتَ عَلَيْهِمْ بِوَكِيْلٍ ۟

وَكَذٰلِكَ اَوْحَيْنَآ اِلَيْكَ قُرْاٰنًا عَرَبِيًّا لِّتُنْذِرَ اُمَّ الْقُرٰى وَمَنْ حَوْلَهَا وَتُنْذِرَ يَوْمَ الْجَمْعِ لَا رَيْبَ فِيْهِ ۭ فَرِيْقٌ فِى الْجَنَّةِ وَفَرِيْقٌ فِى السَّعِيْرِ ۟

وَلَوْ شَآءَ اللهُ لَجَعَلَهُمْ اُمَّةً وَّاحِدَةً وَّلٰكِنْ يُّدْخِلُ مَنْ يَّشَآءُ فِيْ رَحْمَتِهٖ ۭ وَالظّٰلِمُوْنَ مَا لَهُمْ مِّنْ وَّلِيٍّ وَّلَا نَصِيْرٍ ۟

اَمِ اتَّخَذُوْا مِنْ دُوْنِهٖٓ اَوْلِيَآءَ ۚ فَاللهُ هُوَ الْوَلِىُّ

482

In whatsoever you differ, the final decision thereof rests with Allah. Such is Allah, my Lord; in Him I put my trust and to Him I turn. He is the Maker of the heavens and the earth. He has made for you spouses of your own kind, and of the cattle also He has made pairs. He multiplies you in the earth. There is nothing whatever like unto Him. He is All-Hearing, All-Seeing. To Him belong the keys of the heavens and the earth. He enlarges the provision for whomsoever He pleases and straitens it for whomsoever He pleases. Surely, He knows all things well. (11—13)

He has prescribed for you the religion which He enjoined on Noah, and which We have revealed to thee, and which We enjoined on Abraham and Moses and Jesus, that is: Be steadfast in obedience, and be not divided therein. Hard upon the idolaters is that to which thou callest them. Allah chooses for Himself whom He pleases, and guides to Himself him who turns to Him. The disbelievers did not differ in the matter of religion till after knowledge had come to them by means of the Quran, and then only on account of jealousy among themselves. Had it not been for a word that had gone forth from thy Lord for an appointed term, the matter would have been long before decided between them. Surely those who have been made inheritors of the Book after the earlier people are in a disquieting doubt about it. To this, then, do thou invite mankind, and be steadfast as thou art commanded, and follow not their low desires, and affirm: I believe in whatever of the Book Allah has sent down, and I am commanded to judge justly between you. Allah is our Lord and your Lord. We are responsible for that which we do, and you are responsible for that which you do. There is no contention between us. Allah will gather us together, and to Him is the return.

Those who dispute concerning Allah, after He has been accepted, futile is their contention in the sight of their Lord. On them is Allah's wrath and for them will be a seve e chastisement. Allah it is Who has sent down the Book with truth, and also the Balance. How wouldst thou know that the Hour may be nigh? Those who believe not in it seek to hasten it; but those who believe are fearful of it and know that it is bound to come. Hearken! those who entertain doubt concerning the Hour are far gone in error. Allah is aware of the most secret thoughts and doings of His creatures. He provides for whom He pleases. He is the Powerful, the Mighty. (14—20)

وَالَّذِيْنَ يُحَآجُّوْنَ فِى اللهِ مِنْۢ بَعْدِ مَا اسْتُجِيْبَ لَهٗ حُجَّتُهُمْ دَاحِضَةٌ عِنْدَ رَبِّهِمْ وَ عَلَيْهِمْ غَضَبٌ وَّلَهُمْ عَذَابٌ شَدِيْدٌ ۝

اَللهُ الَّذِىْٓ اَنْزَلَ الْكِتٰبَ بِالْحَقِّ وَ الْمِيْزَانَ وَمَا يُدْرِيْكَ لَعَلَّ السَّاعَةَ قَرِيْبٌ ۝

يَسْتَعْجِلُ بِهَا الَّذِيْنَ لَا يُؤْمِنُوْنَ بِهَا ۚ وَالَّذِيْنَ اٰمَنُوْا مُشْفِقُوْنَ مِنْهَا ۙ وَيَعْلَمُوْنَ اَنَّهَا الْحَقُّ ؕ اَلَآ اِنَّ الَّذِيْنَ يُمَارُوْنَ فِى السَّاعَةِ لَفِىْ ضَلٰلٍۭ بَعِيْدٍ ۝

اَللهُ لَطِيْفٌۢ بِعِبَادِهٖ يَرْزُقُ مَنْ يَّشَآءُ ۚ وَ هُوَ الْقَوِىُّ الْعَزِيْزُ ۞

مَنْ كَانَ يُرِيْدُ حَرْثَ الْاٰخِرَةِ نَزِدْ لَهٗ فِىْ حَرْثِهٖ ۚ وَمَنْ كَانَ يُرِيْدُ حَرْثَ الدُّنْيَا نُؤْتِهٖ مِنْهَا وَ مَا لَهٗ فِى الْاٰخِرَةِ مِنْ نَّصِيْبٍ ۝

اَمْ لَهُمْ شُرَكٰٓؤُا شَرَعُوْا لَهُمْ مِّنَ الدِّيْنِ مَالَمْ يَأْذَنْۢ بِهِ اللهُ ؕ وَلَوْلَا كَلِمَةُ الْفَصْلِ لَقُضِىَ بَيْنَهُمْ ؕ وَ اِنَّ الظّٰلِمِيْنَ لَهُمْ عَذَابٌ اَلِيْمٌ ۝

تَرَى الظّٰلِمِيْنَ مُشْفِقِيْنَ مِمَّا كَسَبُوْا وَهُوَ وَاقِعٌۢ بِهِمْ ؕ وَالَّذِيْنَ اٰمَنُوْا وَعَمِلُوا الصّٰلِحٰتِ فِىْ رَوْضٰتِ الْجَنّٰتِ ۚ لَهُمْ مَّا يَشَآءُوْنَ عِنْدَ رَبِّهِمْ ؕ ذٰلِكَ هُوَ الْفَضْلُ الْكَبِيْرُ ۝

ذٰلِكَ الَّذِىْ يُبَشِّرُ اللهُ عِبَادَهُ الَّذِيْنَ اٰمَنُوْا وَعَمِلُوا

Whoso desires the harvest of the Hereafter, We give him increase in his harvest; and whoso desires the harvest of this world, We give him thereof, but in the Hereafter he has no share. Have they any associate gods who have enjoined on them in matters of faith that which Allah has not commanded? Had it not been for Our decisive word, the matter would have been decided between them. Surely the wrongdoers have a grievous punishment. Thou seest the wrongdoers fearful on account of that which they have practised, but the requital thereof is sure to befall them; while those who believe and work righteousness will be in the Gardens of Paradise. They shall have with their Lord whatever they desire. This is the great bounty. This it is whereof Allah gives the glad tidings to His servants who believe and act righteously. Tell them: I ask of you no recompense in return for it, except love as between kindred. Whoso practises good We increase its charm for him. Surely, Allah is Most Forgiving, Most Appreciating. (21—24)

Do they allege: He has fabricated a lie against Allah? Had Allah so willed He could seal up thy heart. Allah blots out falsehood and establishes the truth by His words. Surely, He knows well even secret thoughts. He it is who accepts repentance from His servants and forgives sins and knows all that you do. He accepts the prayers of those who believe and work righteousness, and bestows upon them in excess of their supplications out of His grace. For the disbelievers there is a severe punishment. Were Allah to enlarge greatly the provision for His servants, they would behave arrogantly in the earth; but He sends down what He pleases according to measure. Indeed, He is Well-Aware concerning His servants and All-Seeing. He it is Who sends down rain after they despair of it, and spreads out His mercy. He is the Protector, the Praiseworthy. Of His Signs is the creation of the heavens and the earth, and of whatever living creatures He has spread out in both. He has the power to gather them together when He pleases. (25—30)

Whatever misfortune befalls you, is in consequence of that which you practise. He overlooks many of your defaults. You cannot frustrate God's design in the earth; nor have you any friend or helper beside Allah.

Of His Signs are vessels sailing across the sea, like mountain tops. If He were so to will, He could cause the winds to drop so that they would become motionless upon its surface. In that, surely, are Signs for every steadfast grateful one. Or, He could destroy those in them on account of their doings. But He overlooks many of their defaults. He well knows those who contend against Our Signs. They have no place of refuge. (31—36)

وَمِنْ اٰيٰتِهِ الْجَوَارِ فِى الْبَحْرِ كَالْاَعْلَامِ ۞

اِنْ يَّشَاْ يُسْكِنِ الرِّيْحَ فَيَظْلَلْنَ رَوَاكِدَ عَلٰى ظَهْرِهٖ

اِنَّ فِىْ ذٰلِكَ لَاٰيٰتٍ لِّكُلِّ صَبَّارٍ شَكُوْرٍ ۞

اَوْ يُوْبِقْهُنَّ بِمَا كَسَبُوْا وَيَعْفُ عَنْ كَثِيْرٍ ۞

وَيَعْلَمَ الَّذِيْنَ يُجَادِلُوْنَ فِىْۤ اٰيٰتِنَا مَا لَهُمْ مِّنْ

مَّحِيْصٍ ۞

فَمَاۤ اُوْتِيْتُمْ مِّنْ شَىْءٍ فَمَتَاعُ الْحَيٰوةِ الدُّنْيَا ۚ

وَمَا عِنْدَ اللّٰهِ خَيْرٌ وَّاَبْقٰى لِلَّذِيْنَ اٰمَنُوْا وَعَلٰى

رَبِّهِمْ يَتَوَكَّلُوْنَ ۞

Whatever you have been given is only a temporary provision of this life, but that which is with Allah is better and more lasting for those who believe and put their trust in their Lord; those who eschew the graver sins and indecencies, and when they are wroth they forgive; those who hearken to their Lord, and observe Prayer and whose affairs are administered by mutual consultation, and who spend out of whatever We have provided for them; and those who, when a wrong is done them, defend themselves.

وَالَّذِيْنَ يَجْتَنِبُوْنَ كَبٰٓئِرَ الْاِثْمِ وَالْفَوَاحِشَ وَاِذَا

مَا غَضِبُوْا هُمْ يَغْفِرُوْنَ ۞

وَالَّذِيْنَ اسْتَجَابُوْا لِرَبِّهِمْ وَاَقَامُوا الصَّلٰوةَ ۪ وَاَمْرُهُمْ

شُوْرٰى بَيْنَهُمْ ۪ وَمِمَّا رَزَقْنٰهُمْ يُنْفِقُوْنَ ۞

وَالَّذِيْنَ اِذَاۤ اَصَابَهُمُ الْبَغْيُ هُمْ يَنْتَصِرُوْنَ ۞

وَجَزٰٓؤُا سَيِّئَةٍ سَيِّئَةٌ مِّثْلُهَا ۚ فَمَنْ عَفَا وَاَصْلَحَ

فَاَجْرُهٗ عَلَى اللّٰهِ ۪ اِنَّهٗ لَا يُحِبُّ الظّٰلِمِيْنَ ۞

وَلَمَنِ انْتَصَرَ بَعْدَ ظُلْمِهٖ فَاُولٰٓئِكَ مَا عَلَيْهِمْ مِّنْ

سَبِيْلٍ ۞

The recompense of an injury is a penalty in proportion thereto; but whoso forgives and effects a reform thereby has his reward with Allah. Surely He loves not the wrong-doers. No blame attaches to those who exact due retribution when they are wronged; blame attaches only to those who wrong others and transgress in the earth without justification. They will have a painful chas-tisement. But the wronged one who endures with fortitude and forgives, achieves a matter of high resolve. (37—44)

اِنَّمَا السَّبِيْلُ عَلَى الَّذِيْنَ يَظْلِمُوْنَ النَّاسَ وَيَبْغُوْنَ

فِى الْاَرْضِ بِغَيْرِ الْحَقِّ ۪ اُولٰٓئِكَ لَهُمْ عَذَابٌ اَلِيْمٌ ۞

وَلَمَنْ صَبَرَ وَغَفَرَ اِنَّ ذٰلِكَ لَمِنْ عَزْمِ الْاُمُوْرِ ۞

وَمَنْ يُّضْلِلِ اللّٰهُ فَمَا لَهٗ مِنْ وَّلِيٍّ مِّنْ بَعْدِهٖ ۪

He whom Allah adjudges astray shall have no helper thereafter. Thou wilt find the wrongdoers saying, when they perceive the punishment: Is there any way of repelling it? Thou wilt see them brought face to face with it, casting down their eyes in humiliation, looking at it with a stealthy glance. The believers will say: Losers indeed are those who ruin themselves and their families on the Day of Judgment. Hearken! the wrongdoers will be afflicted with a lasting torment. They will have no helpers to help them against Allah. For him whom Allah judges astray there is no way at all. Hearken ye to your Lord, before there comes the day for which there is no averting against the decree of Allah. There will be no refuge for you that day, nor any possibility of denial. Then, if they turn away, We have not sent thee as a guardian over them. Thy duty is only to convey the Message. When We bestow mercy upon man, he rejoices therein; but if, in consequence of his default, he is afflicted with evil, he is ungrateful. (45—49)

To Allah belongs the kingdom of the heavens and the earth. He creates what He pleases. He bestows females upon whom He pleases and He bestows males upon whom He pleases; or He mixes them, males and females; and He makes whom He pleases barren. He is All-Knowing, Determiner of the measure. (50—51)

It is not given to a man that Allah should speak to him except by revelation or from behind a veil or by sending a messenger to reveal by His command that which He pleases. Surely, He is High, Wise.

Thus have We revealed to thee the Word by Our command. Thou didst not know what the Book was, nor what was the Faith. But We have made thy revelation a light, whereby We guide such of Our servants as We please. Truly, thou dost guide mankind to the right path; the path of Allah, to Whom belongs whatever is in the heavens and whatever is in the earth. Behold ! to Allah do all things return. (52—54)

مَا يَشَآءُ ۚ اِنَّهٗ عَلِيٌّ حَكِيمٌ ۞

وَكَذٰلِكَ اَوْحَيْنَآ اِلَيْكَ رُوْحًا مِّنْ اَمْرِنَا ۚ مَا كُنْتَ تَدْرِيْ مَا الْكِتٰبُ وَلَا الْاِيْمَانُ وَلٰكِنْ جَعَلْنٰهُ نُوْرًا نَّهْدِيْ بِهٖ مَنْ نَّشَآءُ مِنْ عِبَادِنَا ۚ وَاِنَّكَ لَتَهْدِيْۤ اِلٰى صِرَاطٍ مُّسْتَقِيْمٍ ۞

صِرَاطِ اللّٰهِ الَّذِيْ لَهٗ مَا فِى السَّمٰوٰتِ وَمَا فِى الْاَرْضِ ۗ اَلَاۤ اِلَى اللّٰهِ تَصِيْرُ الْاُمُوْرُ ۞

Chapter 43

سُوْرَةُ الزُّخْرُفِ مَكِّيَّةٌ

AL-ZUKHRUF
(Revealed before Hijra)

In the name of Allah, Most Gracious, Ever Merciful. (1)

بِسْمِ اللهِ الرَّحْمٰنِ الرَّحِيْمِ ۞

حٰمٓ ۞

THE PRAISEWORTHY, THE LORD OF HONOUR. (2)

وَالْكِتٰبِ الْمُبِيْنِ ۞

اِنَّا جَعَلْنٰهُ قُرْءٰنًا عَرَبِيًّا لَّعَلَّكُمْ تَعْقِلُوْنَ ۞

This perspicuous Book is proof that We have made it a Book to be repeatedly read, easily comprehensible, that you may understand. It forms part of Our Eternal Guidance, exalted and full of wisdom.

وَاِنَّهٗ فِيْٓ اُمِّ الْكِتٰبِ لَدَيْنَا لَعَلِيٌّ حَكِيْمٌ ۞

اَفَنَضْرِبُ عَنْكُمُ الذِّكْرَ صَفْحًا اَنْ كُنْتُمْ قَوْمًا مُّسْرِفِيْنَ ۞

وَكَمْ اَرْسَلْنَا مِنْ نَّبِيٍّ فِى الْاَوَّلِيْنَ ۞

Shall We deprive you of the Remembrance because you are a people far gone in transgression? How many a Prophet did We send among the earlier peoples! But whenever a Prophet came to them, they mocked at him. Then We destroyed those who were much more powerful than these, and they have before them the example of earlier peoples. Were thou to ask them: Who created the heavens and the earth? they would say: The Mighty, the All-Knowing created them. He it is Who has made the earth a cradle for you, and has made pathways therein for you, that you may be rightly guided, and Who sends down water from the sky in proper measure, and We thereby quicken a dead land — even so will you be raised — and Who has created everything in pairs, and has made vessels and beasts whereon you ride, that you may settle yourselves firmly on their backs and when you are securely seated thereon you may remember the favour of your Lord and say:

وَ مَا يَاْتِيْهِمْ مِّنْ نَّبِيٍّ اِلَّا كَانُوْا بِهٖ يَسْتَهْزِءُوْنَ ۞

فَاَهْلَكْنَآ اَشَدَّ مِنْهُمْ بَطْشًا وَّمَضٰى مَثَلُ الْاَوَّلِيْنَ ۞

وَ لَئِنْ سَاَلْتَهُمْ مَّنْ خَلَقَ السَّمٰوٰتِ وَ الْاَرْضَ لَيَقُوْلُنَّ خَلَقَهُنَّ الْعَزِيْزُ الْعَلِيْمُ ۞

الَّذِىْ جَعَلَ لَكُمُ الْاَرْضَ مَهْدًا وَّ جَعَلَ لَكُمْ فِيْهَا سُبُلًا لَّعَلَّكُمْ تَهْتَدُوْنَ ۞

وَالَّذِىْ نَزَّلَ مِنَ السَّمَآءِ مَآءً بِقَدَرٍ فَاَنْشَرْنَا بِهٖ بَلْدَةً مَّيْتًا كَذٰلِكَ تُخْرَجُوْنَ ۞

وَ الَّذِىْ خَلَقَ الْاَزْوَاجَ كُلَّهَا وَجَعَلَ لَكُمْ مِّنَ الْفُلْكِ وَالْاَنْعَامِ مَا تَرْكَبُوْنَ ۞

لِتَسْتَوٗا عَلٰى ظُهُوْرِهٖ ثُمَّ تَذْكُرُوْا نِعْمَةَ رَبِّكُمْ اِذَا اسْتَوَيْتُمْ عَلَيْهِ وَ تَقُوْلُوْا سُبْحٰنَ الَّذِىْ سَخَّرَ

Holy is He Who has subjected this to us, while we had not the strength to subdue it by ourselves. To our Lord surely shall we return. Yet they make some of His servants partners in His Divinity. Surely, man is plainly ungrateful. (3 —16)

لَنَا هٰذَا وَ مَا كُنَّا لَهُ مُقْرِنِيْنَ ۞
وَ اِنَّآ اِلٰى رَبِّنَا لَمُنْقَلِبُوْنَ ۞
وَ جَعَلُوْا لَهُ مِنْ عِبَادِهِ جُزْءًا ۭ اِنَّ الْاِنْسَانَ لَكَفُوْرٌ
مُّبِيْنٌ ۞

Has He chosen for Himself daughters out of that which He has created, and honoured you with sons? Yet when tidings are given to one of them of that which he ascribes to the Gracious One, his face is flushed and he is choked with grief. What! One who is nurtured in ornaments and can scarcely express its meaning in a contention! They make out the angels, who are the servants of the Gracious One, to be females. Did they witness their creation? If so, their testimony shall be recorded, and they shall be questioned.

اَمِ اتَّخَذَ مِمَّا يَخْلُقُ بَنٰتٍ وَّ اَصْفٰكُمْ بِالْبَنِيْنَ ۞
وَ اِذَا بُشِّرَ اَحَدُهُمْ بِمَا ضَرَبَ لِلرَّحْمٰنِ مَثَلًا
ظَلَّ وَجْهُهُ مُسْوَدًّا وَّ هُوَ كَظِيْمٌ ۞
اَوَ مَنْ يُّنَشَّؤُا فِى الْحِلْيَةِ وَ هُوَ فِى الْخِصَامِ غَيْرُ
مُبِيْنٍ ۞
وَ جَعَلُوا الْمَلٰٓئِكَةَ الَّذِيْنَ هُمْ عِبٰدُ الرَّحْمٰنِ اِنَاثًا ۭ
اَشَهِدُوْا خَلْقَهُمْ ۭ سَتُكْتَبُ شَهَادَتُهُمْ وَ يُسْئَلُوْنَ ۞

They say: If the Gracious One had so willed we would not have worshipped any beside Him. They have no knowledge whatsoever of it; they do nothing but conjecture. Have We given them a Book before this, so that they base themselves on it? Instead they say: We found our fathers holding to a certain course, and we are guided by their footsteps. Thus whenever We sent a Warner before thee to a township, its affluent people said: We found our fathers holding to a course, and we are following in their footsteps. The Warner queried: Even though I bring you better guidance than that which you found your fathers following? to which they retorted: But we reject that with which you are sent. Then We exacted retribution from them. Observe, then, what was the end of those who rejected Our Messengers. (17—26)

وَ قَالُوْا لَوْ شَآءَ الرَّحْمٰنُ مَا عَبَدْنٰهُمْ ۭ مَا لَهُمْ
بِذٰلِكَ مِنْ عِلْمٍ ۭ اِنْ هُمْ اِلَّا يَخْرُصُوْنَ ۞
اَمْ اٰتَيْنٰهُمْ كِتٰبًا مِّنْ قَبْلِهٖ فَهُمْ بِهٖ مُسْتَمْسِكُوْنَ ۞
بَلْ قَالُوْٓا اِنَّا وَجَدْنَآ اٰبَآءَنَا عَلٰٓى اُمَّةٍ وَّ اِنَّا عَلٰٓى اٰثٰرِهِمْ
مُّهْتَدُوْنَ ۞
وَ كَذٰلِكَ مَآ اَرْسَلْنَا مِنْ قَبْلِكَ فِىْ قَرْيَةٍ مِّنْ نَّذِيْرٍ
اِلَّا قَالَ مُتْرَفُوْهَآ ۙ اِنَّا وَجَدْنَآ اٰبَآءَنَا عَلٰٓى اُمَّةٍ وَّ
اِنَّا عَلٰٓى اٰثٰرِهِمْ مُّقْتَدُوْنَ ۞
قُلْ اَوَ لَوْ جِئْتُكُمْ بِاَهْدٰى مِمَّا وَجَدْتُّمْ عَلَيْهِ
اٰبَآءَكُمْ ۭ قَالُوْٓا اِنَّا بِمَآ اُرْسِلْتُمْ بِهٖ كٰفِرُوْنَ ۞
فَانْتَقَمْنَا مِنْهُمْ فَانْظُرْ كَيْفَ كَانَ عَاقِبَةُ

Call to mind when Abraham said to his father and his people: I disown utterly that which you worship, except Him Who created me and He will surely guide me. This he established as a firm doctrine among his posterity, that they might shun idol worship. Now I bestowed upon these people and their fathers worldly provision until there came to them the Truth and a Messenger expounding it clearly. But when the Truth came to them they said: This is magic, and we reject it.

They ask: Why has not this Quran been sent down to some great man of the two towns, Mecca or Taif? Is it they who presume to distribute the mercy of thy Lord? It is We who distribute among them their livelihood in this life, and We exalt some of them above others in rank, so that they may serve each other mutually. The mercy of thy Lord is better than that which they amass.

Were it not that mankind would in consequence thereof all tread the same path, We would have provided those who disbelieve in the Gracious One, with roofs of silver for their houses, and stairways by which they could climb, and the doors of their houses and couches on which they could recline, of the same, or of gold. But all that is only a temporary provision of the present life; and the Hereafter according to thy Lord is for the righteous. (27—36)

For him who turns away from the remembrance of the Gracious One, We appoint a satan, who becomes his boon companion. These hinder them from the right path, but they imagine that they are rightly guided; until when such a one comes to Us, he says to his boon companion: Would that there had been between thee and me the whole expanse of the earth. He then realises what an evil companion the other was. Having been wrongdoers, it will in no wise profit you this day that you and your companions are joined together in punishment. Canst thou, then, make the deaf hear, or guide the blind or him who is in manifest error?

If We cause thee to die, We shall still exact retribution from them; or We shall show thee in this life that which We have promised them; for surely We have complete power over them. So hold fast to that which has been revealed to thee; surely thou art on the right path. Thy revelation is a source of honour for thee and for thy people; and you will surely be called to account. Seek among the teachings of those of Our Messengers whom We sent before thee. Did We appoint any deities beside the Gracious One to be worshipped? (37—46)

We sent Moses with Our Signs to Pharaoh and his nobles, and he said to them: Truly I am a Messenger of the Lord of the worlds. When he came to them with Our Signs, they greeted them with laughter. Every Sign We showed them was greater than the one preceding it. We afflicted them with chastisement, that they might turn away from their evil courses. But they kept on saying to Moses: O magician, pray for us to thy Lord, according to the promise He has made thee, that if He will but remove this affliction, we will surely be guided.

But each time We removed the affliction from them, they broke their word. Pharaoh made a proclamation among his people: O my people, does not the kingdom of Egypt belong to me, and these streams that run under my control? Then do you not see? Is it not that I am better than this base fellow, who can scarcely make his meaning clear? If he is truthful, why have not bracelets of gold been bestowed upon him, or angels accompanied him in closed ranks to guard him? Thus did he beguile his people and they followed him. They were indeed a wicked people. So, when they incurred Our wrath, We exacted retribution from them, and drowned them all; and they became a tale told and a lesson for those coming after. (47—57)

When the son of Mary is mentioned in the Quran as an example, thy people raise a clamour at it, and ask: Are our gods better or he? They mention this only as a contention; they are a disputatious people. He was only a servant of Ours on whom We bestowed Our favour, and We made him an example for the children of Israel. If We so willed, We could make some of you angels to be successors in the earth. This Quran sets out indications of the Hour; so have no doubt about it, but follow Me. This is the right path. Let not

اِنَّنَا لَمُهْتَدُوْنَ ۝

فَلَمَّا كَشَفْنَا عَنْهُمُ الْعَذَابَ اِذَا هُمْ يَنْكُثُوْنَ ۝

وَنَادٰى فِرْعَوْنُ فِىْ قَوْمِهٖ قَالَ يٰقَوْمِ اَلَيْسَ لِىْ مُلْكُ مِصْرَ وَهٰذِهِ الْاَنْهٰرُ تَجْرِىْ مِنْ تَحْتِىْ ۚ اَفَلَا تُبْصِرُوْنَ ۝

اَمْ اَنَا خَيْرٌ مِّنْ هٰذَا الَّذِىْ هُوَ مَهِيْنٌ ۙ وَّلَا يَكَادُ يُبِيْنُ ۝

فَلَوْلَآ اُلْقِىَ عَلَيْهِ اَسْوِرَةٌ مِّنْ ذَهَبٍ اَوْ جَآءَ مَعَهُ الْمَلٰٓئِكَةُ مُقْتَرِنِيْنَ ۝

فَاسْتَخَفَّ قَوْمَهٗ فَاَطَاعُوْهُ ۚ اِنَّهُمْ كَانُوْا قَوْمًا فٰسِقِيْنَ ۝

فَلَمَّآ اٰسَفُوْنَا انْتَقَمْنَا مِنْهُمْ فَاَغْرَقْنٰهُمْ اَجْمَعِيْنَ ۝

فَجَعَلْنٰهُمْ سَلَفًا وَّمَثَلًا لِّلْاٰخِرِيْنَ ۝

وَلَمَّا ضُرِبَ ابْنُ مَرْيَمَ مَثَلًا اِذَا قَوْمُكَ مِنْهُ يَصِدُّوْنَ ۝

وَقَالُوْٓا ءَاٰلِهَتُنَا خَيْرٌ اَمْ هُوَ ۗ مَا ضَرَبُوْهُ لَكَ اِلَّا جَدَلًا ۗ بَلْ هُمْ قَوْمٌ خَصِمُوْنَ ۝

اِنْ هُوَ اِلَّا عَبْدٌ اَنْعَمْنَا عَلَيْهِ وَجَعَلْنٰهُ مَثَلًا لِّبَنِىْ اِسْرَآءِيْلَ ۝

وَلَوْ نَشَآءُ لَجَعَلْنَا مِنْكُمْ مَّلٰٓئِكَةً فِى الْاَرْضِ يَخْلُفُوْنَ ۝

وَاِنَّهٗ لَعِلْمٌ لِّلسَّاعَةِ فَلَا تَمْتَرُنَّ بِهَا وَاتَّبِعُوْنِ ۚ هٰذَا صِرَاطٌ مُّسْتَقِيْمٌ ۝

Satan hinder you. Surely he is your declared enemy. (58—63)

وَلَا يَصُدَّنَّكُمُ الشَّيْطٰنُ إِنَّهُ لَكُمْ عَدُوٌّ مُّبِيْنٌ ۝

وَلَمَّا جَآءَ عِيْسٰى بِالْبَيِّنٰتِ قَالَ قَدْ جِئْتُكُمْ بِالْحِكْمَةِ

وَلِاُبَيِّنَ لَكُمْ بَعْضَ الَّذِىْ تَخْتَلِفُوْنَ فِيْهِ ۚ

فَاتَّقُوا اللّٰهَ وَ اَطِيْعُوْنِ ۝

اِنَّ اللّٰهَ هُوَ رَبِّىْ وَ رَبُّكُمْ فَاعْبُدُوْهُ ۗ هٰذَا صِرَاطٌ مُّسْتَقِيْمٌ ۝

When Jesus came with clear proofs, he said: I have come to you with wisdom, and to make clear to you some of that about which you differ. So fear Allah and obey me. Verily Allah it is Who is my Lord and your Lord; so worship Him. This is the right path. But the parties differed among themselves. So woe to the wrongdoers because of the chastisement of a painful day. They but wait for the Hour to come suddenly upon them, while they perceive it not. Friends on that day will be enemies of each other, except the righteous, who believed in Our Signs and submitted. (64—68)

فَاخْتَلَفَ الْاَحْزَابُ مِنْ بَيْنِهِمْ ۚ فَوَيْلٌ لِّلَّذِيْنَ ظَلَمُوْا مِنْ عَذَابِ يَوْمٍ اَلِيْمٍ ۝

هَلْ يَنْظُرُوْنَ اِلَّا السَّاعَةَ اَنْ تَأْتِيَهُمْ بَغْتَةً وَّ هُمْ لَا يَشْعُرُوْنَ ۝

اَلْاَخِلَّآءُ يَوْمَئِذٍ بَعْضُهُمْ لِبَعْضٍ عَدُوٌّ اِلَّا الْمُتَّقِيْنَ ۚ۠ ۝

O My servants, there is no fear for you this day, nor shall you grieve. Enter the Garden, you and your companions, delighted and joyful. Dishes and cups of gold will be passed round to them, and in them will be all that the hearts desire and in which the eyes delight. Therein will you abide. This is the Garden to which you have been made heirs, because of that which you practised. Therein for you is fruit in abundance, of which you will eat. The guilty will abide in the torment of hell; it will not be reduced, and they will be a prey to despair.

يٰعِبَادِ لَا خَوْفٌ عَلَيْكُمُ الْيَوْمَ وَلَا اَنْتُمْ تَحْزَنُوْنَ ۝

اَلَّذِيْنَ اٰمَنُوْا بِاٰيٰتِنَا وَ كَانُوْا مُسْلِمِيْنَ ۚ ۝

اُدْخُلُوا الْجَنَّةَ اَنْتُمْ وَ اَزْوَاجُكُمْ تُحْبَرُوْنَ ۝

يُطَافُ عَلَيْهِمْ بِصِحَافٍ مِّنْ ذَهَبٍ وَّ اَكْوَابٍ ۚ وَ فِيْهَا مَا تَشْتَهِيْهِ الْاَنْفُسُ وَ تَلَذُّ الْاَعْيُنُ ۚ وَ اَنْتُمْ فِيْهَا خٰلِدُوْنَ ۝

وَ تِلْكَ الْجَنَّةُ الَّتِىْ اُوْرِثْتُمُوْهَا بِمَا كُنْتُمْ تَعْمَلُوْنَ ۝

لَكُمْ فِيْهَا فَاكِهَةٌ كَثِيْرَةٌ مِّنْهَا تَأْكُلُوْنَ ۝

اِنَّ الْمُجْرِمِيْنَ فِىْ عَذَابِ جَهَنَّمَ خٰلِدُوْنَ ۝

لَا يُفَتَّرُ عَنْهُمْ وَ هُمْ فِيْهِ مُبْلِسُوْنَ ۝

We wronged them not; they themselves were the wrongdoers. They will cry: O master, let thy Lord make an end of us. He will answer: You will tarry therein. We brought you the truth; but most of you were averse to the truth. (69—79)

Have these disbelievers of Mecca determined upon a course? Then We too are determined upon their ruin. Do they imagine that We hear not their secrets and their private counsels? Yea, Our envoys are with them recording everything. (80—81)

Say to them: Had there been a son of the Gracious One, I would have been the first of worshippers. Holy is Allah, Lord of the heavens and the earth, Lord of the Throne above all that which they ascribe to Him. Leave them alone to indulge in vain discourse and to amuse themselves until they come face to face with that Day of theirs which they have been promised. He it is Who is God in heaven and God on earth; and He is the Wise, the All-Knowing. Blessed is He to Whom belongs the kingdom of the heavens and the earth and of all that is between them; and with Him is the knowledge of the Hour and to Him will you be brought back. Those on whom they call beside Allah have no power of intercession; but only he who bears witness to the truth and well they know it. Were thou to ask them Who created them, they will surely say: Allah. How then are they being turned away? We call to witness the cry of the Messenger: These are a people who will not believe; and Our reply: Then turn away from them, and say: Peace. Soon will they know. (82—90)

Chapter 44

سُوْرَةُ الدُّخَانِ مَكِّيَّة

AL-DUKHĀN

(Revealed before Hijra)

In the name of Allah, Most Gracious, Ever Merciful. (1)

بِسْمِ اللهِ الرَّحْمٰنِ الرَّحِيْمِ ۝

حٰمٓ ۝

THE PRAISEWORTHY, THE LORD OF HONOUR (2)

وَالْكِتٰبِ الْمُبِيْنِ ۝

اِنَّآ اَنْزَلْنٰهُ فِيْ لَيْلَةٍ مُّبٰرَكَةٍ اِنَّا كُنَّا مُنْذِرِيْنَ ۝

فِيْهَا يُفْرَقُ كُلُّ اَمْرٍ حَكِيْمٍ ۝

We call to witness this clear Book. We revealed it in a blessed Night, We have ever been warning. In it are all matters of wisdom expounded with discrimination by Our command. We have ever sent Messengers, as a mercy from thy Lord. He indeed is the All-Hearing, the All-Knowing, the Lord of the heavens and the earth and all that is between them, if you would only have faith. There is no god but He. He bestows life and He causes death. He is your Lord and the Lord of your forefathers. Yet they play about in doubt. Then watch for the day when a pall of smoke will appear in the sky and envelop the people. That will be a painful torment. The cry will go up: Lord, remove from us the torment; we do believe. How will they be admonished, seeing that there came to them a Messenger, expounding matters clearly, and they turned away from him declaring: He is tutored, a man possessed! Yet, We shall remove the torment for a while, but you will certainly revert to your misdeeds.

اَمْرًا مِّنْ عِنْدِنَا اِنَّا كُنَّا مُرْسِلِيْنَ ۝

رَحْمَةً مِّنْ رَّبِّكَ اِنَّهُ هُوَ السَّمِيْعُ الْعَلِيْمُ ۝

رَبِّ السَّمٰوٰتِ وَالْاَرْضِ وَمَا بَيْنَهُمَا اِنْ كُنْتُمْ مُّوْقِنِيْنَ ۝

لَاۤ اِلٰهَ اِلَّا هُوَ يُحْيٖ وَيُمِيْتُ رَبُّكُمْ وَرَبُّ اٰبَآئِكُمُ الْاَوَّلِيْنَ ۝

بَلْ هُمْ فِيْ شَكٍّ يَّلْعَبُوْنَ ۝

فَارْتَقِبْ يَوْمَ تَأْتِي السَّمَآءُ بِدُخَانٍ مُّبِيْنٍ ۝

يَّغْشَى النَّاسَ هٰذَا عَذَابٌ اَلِيْمٌ ۝

رَبَّنَا اكْشِفْ عَنَّا الْعَذَابَ اِنَّا مُؤْمِنُوْنَ ۝

اَنّٰى لَهُمُ الذِّكْرٰى وَقَدْ جَآءَهُمْ رَسُوْلٌ مُّبِيْنٌ ۝

ثُمَّ تَوَلَّوْا عَنْهُ وَقَالُوْا مُعَلَّمٌ مَّجْنُوْنٌ ۝

Keep in mind, however, that on the day when We afflict you with the Great Affliction, We will certainly exact retribution. (3—17)

اِنَّا كَاشِفُوا الْعَذَابِ قَلِيْلًا اِنَّكُمْ عَآئِدُوْنَ ۝

يَوْمَ نَبْطِشُ الْبَطْشَةَ الْكُبْرٰى اِنَّا مُنْتَقِمُوْنَ ۝

We tried the people of Pharaoh before them. There came to them a noble Messenger, who said to them: Restore to me the servants of Allah; I am a trusty Messenger sent to you, to warn you not to exalt yourselves in defiance of Allah. I come to you with a clear authority. I seek the protection of my Lord and your Lord lest you seek to stone me. If you believe not in me, then leave me alone. Then he called on his Lord: This is indeed a sinful people; and his Lord directed him: Set forth with My servants by night; you will surely be pursued. Then leave the sea behind, treading along the furrows of the dunes. Surely, Pharaoh's host are doomed to be drowned. They left behind many a garden and spring, and cornfield, and comfortable dwelling, and luxury in which they delighted. Thus it was; and We made another people inherit all that. The heaven and the earth mourned them not, nor were they granted respite. (18—30)

وَلَقَدْ فَتَنَّا قَبْلَهُمْ قَوْمَ فِرْعَوْنَ وَجَاءَهُمْ رَسُوْلٌ كَرِيْمٌ ۝

أَنْ أَدُّوْٓا إِلَيَّ عِبَادَ اللّٰهِ إِنِّيْ لَكُمْ رَسُوْلٌ أَمِيْنٌ ۝

وَأَنْ لَّا تَعْلُوْا عَلَى اللّٰهِ إِنِّيْ اٰتِيْكُمْ بِسُلْطٰنٍ مُّبِيْنٍ ۝

وَإِنِّيْ عُذْتُ بِرَبِّيْ وَرَبِّكُمْ أَنْ تَرْجُمُوْنِ ۝

وَإِنْ لَّمْ تُؤْمِنُوْا لِيْ فَاعْتَزِلُوْنِ ۝

فَدَعَا رَبَّهٗٓ أَنَّ هٰٓؤُلَاءِ قَوْمٌ مُّجْرِمُوْنَ ۝

فَأَسْرِ بِعِبَادِيْ لَيْلًا إِنَّكُمْ مُّتَّبَعُوْنَ ۝

وَاتْرُكِ الْبَحْرَ رَهْوًا إِنَّهُمْ جُنْدٌ مُّغْرَقُوْنَ ۝

كَمْ تَرَكُوْا مِنْ جَنّٰتٍ وَّعُيُوْنٍ ۝

وَّزُرُوْعٍ وَّمَقَامٍ كَرِيْمٍ ۝

وَّنَعْمَةٍ كَانُوْا فِيْهَا فٰكِهِيْنَ ۝

كَذٰلِكَ وَأَوْرَثْنٰهَا قَوْمًا اٰخَرِيْنَ ۝

فَمَا بَكَتْ عَلَيْهِمُ السَّمَاءُ وَالْأَرْضُ وَمَا كَانُوْا مُنْظَرِيْنَ ۝

We delivered the children of Israel from the humiliating torment inflicted on them by Pharaoh. He was surely haughty and of the extravagant. We chose them deliberately above the peoples of their time. We gave them Signs, wherein was a clear trial for them. (31—34)

وَلَقَدْ نَجَّيْنَا بَنِيْٓ إِسْرَاءِيْلَ مِنَ الْعَذَابِ الْمُهِيْنِ ۝

مِنْ فِرْعَوْنَ إِنَّهٗ كَانَ عَالِيًا مِّنَ الْمُسْرِفِيْنَ ۝

وَلَقَدِ اخْتَرْنٰهُمْ عَلٰى عِلْمٍ عَلَى الْعٰلَمِيْنَ ۝

وَاٰتَيْنٰهُمْ مِّنَ الْاٰيٰتِ مَا فِيْهِ بَلٰٓؤٌا مُّبِيْنٌ ۝

إِنَّ هٰٓؤُلَاءِ لَيَقُوْلُوْنَ ۝

The disbelievers of Mecca say: There is only one death for us and we shall not be raised up again. Bring back our fathers if you speak the truth.

إِنْ هِيَ إِلَّا مَوْتَتُنَا الْأُوْلٰى وَمَا نَحْنُ بِمُنْشَرِيْنَ ۝

فَأْتُوْا بِاٰبَائِنَا إِنْ كُنْتُمْ صٰدِقِيْنَ ۝

Are they better than the people of Tubba and those before them? We destroyed them because they were sinful. We did not create the heavens and the earth, and all that is between them, in sport. We created them for an enduring purpose, but most of them know not. The Day of Judgment is the appointed time for all of them; the Day when a friend shall not avail a friend at all, nor shall they be helped, save those to whom Allah shows mercy. Surely, He is the Mighty, the Ever Merciful. (35—43)

أَهُمْ خَيْرٌ أَمْ قَوْمُ تُبَّعٍ وَّالَّذِيْنَ مِنْ قَبْلِهِمْ أَهْلَكْنٰهُمْ ۖ إِنَّهُمْ كَانُوْا مُجْرِمِيْنَ ۝

وَمَا خَلَقْنَا السَّمٰوٰتِ وَالْأَرْضَ وَمَا بَيْنَهُمَا لٰعِبِيْنَ ۝

مَا خَلَقْنٰهُمَا إِلَّا بِالْحَقِّ وَلٰكِنَّ أَكْثَرَهُمْ لَا يَعْلَمُوْنَ ۝

إِنَّ يَوْمَ الْفَصْلِ مِيْقَاتُهُمْ أَجْمَعِيْنَ ۝

يَوْمَ لَا يُغْنِيْ مَوْلًى عَنْ مَوْلًى شَيْئًا وَّلَا هُمْ يُنْصَرُوْنَ ۝

إِلَّا مَنْ رَّحِمَ اللّٰهُ ۚ إِنَّهُ هُوَ الْعَزِيْزُ الرَّحِيْمُ ۝

إِنَّ شَجَرَتَ الزَّقُّوْمِ ۝

طَعَامُ الْأَثِيْمِ ۝

كَالْمُهْلِ ۚ يَغْلِيْ فِي الْبُطُوْنِ ۝

كَغَلْيِ الْحَمِيْمِ ۝

خُذُوْهُ فَاعْتِلُوْهُ إِلٰى سَوَاءِ الْجَحِيْمِ ۝

ثُمَّ صُبُّوْا فَوْقَ رَأْسِهٖ مِنْ عَذَابِ الْحَمِيْمِ ۝

ذُقْ ۚ إِنَّكَ أَنْتَ الْعَزِيْزُ الْكَرِيْمُ ۝

إِنَّ هٰذَا مَا كُنْتُمْ بِهٖ تَمْتَرُوْنَ ۝

إِنَّ الْمُتَّقِيْنَ فِيْ مَقَامٍ أَمِيْنٍ ۝

فِيْ جَنّٰتٍ وَّعُيُوْنٍ ۝

The tree of Zaqqum is the food of the sinful; like dregs of oil, it will boil in their bellies, like the boiling of scalding water. The angels will be commanded: Seize this sinful one, and drag him into the midst of the blazing Fire; then pour upon his head the torment of boiling water. He will be told: Now suffer this, thou who didst hold thyself mighty and noble. This is that which you doubted. (44—51)

يَلْبَسُوْنَ مِنْ سُنْدُسٍ وَّإِسْتَبْرَقٍ مُّتَقَابِلِيْنَ ۝

كَذٰلِكَ ۚ وَزَوَّجْنٰهُمْ بِحُوْرٍ عِيْنٍ ۝

يَدْعُوْنَ فِيْهَا بِكُلِّ فَاكِهَةٍ آمِنِيْنَ ۝

لَا يَذُوْقُوْنَ فِيْهَا الْمَوْتَ إِلَّا الْمَوْتَةَ الْأُوْلٰى ۖ وَوَقٰهُمْ عَذَابَ الْجَحِيْمِ ۝

Verily, the righteous will be in a place of security, amid gardens and springs, attired in fine silk and heavy brocade, facing one another. Thus will it be. We shall give them as companions fair maidens, having wide lustrous eyes. They will call therein for every kind of fruit, dwelling in security. They will not suffer any death therein after the first death, and Allah will safeguard them against the torment of the Fire,

as an act of grace from thy Lord. That
is the supreme triumph. We have made
the Quran easy in thy tongue, that they
may take heed. So wait on; they too are
waiting. (52—60)

فَضْلًا مِّنْ رَّبِّكَ ذٰلِكَ هُوَ الْفَوْزُ الْعَظِيْمُۚ ۞

فَاِنَّمَا يَسَّرْنٰهُ بِلِسَانِكَ لَعَلَّهُمْ يَتَذَكَّرُوْنَ ۞

فَارْتَقِبْ اِنَّهُمْ مُّرْتَقِبُوْنَ ۞

In the name of Allah, Most Gracious,
Ever Merciful. (1)

بِسْمِ اللهِ الرَّحْمٰنِ الرَّحِيْمِ ۞

حٰمٓ ۞

تَنْزِيْلُ الْكِتٰبِ مِنَ اللهِ الْعَزِيْزِ الْحَكِيْمِ ۞

THE PRAISEWORTHY, THE LORD
OF HONOUR. (2)

اِنَّ فِى السَّمٰوٰتِ وَالْاَرْضِ لَاٰيٰتٍ لِّلْمُؤْمِنِيْنَ ۞

وَفِىْ خَلْقِكُمْ وَمَا يَبُثُّ مِنْ دَآبَّةٍ اٰيٰتٌ لِّقَوْمٍ
يُّوْقِنُوْنَ ۞

The revelation of this Book is from
Allah, the Mighty, the Wise. Verily, in
the heavens and the earth are Signs for
those who believe. Likewise in your own
creation, and in that of all the creatures
that He spreads out in the earth are
Signs for a people who possess firm faith.
Also in the alternation of the night and
the day, and in the provision that Allah
sends down from the sky, whereby He
quickens the earth after its death, and in
the courses of the winds, are Signs for a
people who use their understanding. These
are the Signs of Allah that We rehearse
unto thee with truth. Then leaving aside
Allah and His Signs, what is it that they
will believe? Woe to every sinful liar who
hears the Signs of Allah recited unto him,
and then haughtily persists in his denial,
as though he heard them not. So give him
the tidings of a painful torment. When he
learns something of Our Signs, he makes

وَاخْتِلَافِ الَّيْلِ وَالنَّهَارِ وَمَا اَنْزَلَ اللهُ مِنَ السَّمَآءِ
مِنْ رِّزْقٍ فَاَحْيَا بِهِ الْاَرْضَ بَعْدَ مَوْتِهَا وَتَصْرِيْفِ
الرِّيٰحِ اٰيٰتٌ لِّقَوْمٍ يَّعْقِلُوْنَ ۞

تِلْكَ اٰيٰتُ اللهِ نَتْلُوْهَا عَلَيْكَ بِالْحَقِّ فَبِاَيِّ حَدِيْثٍ
بَعْدَ اللهِ وَاٰيٰتِهِ يُؤْمِنُوْنَ ۞

وَيْلٌ لِّكُلِّ اَفَّاكٍ اَثِيْمٍ ۞

يَّسْمَعُ اٰيٰتِ اللهِ تُتْلٰى عَلَيْهِ ثُمَّ يُصِرُّ مُسْتَكْبِرًا كَاَنْ
لَّمْ يَسْمَعْهَا فَبَشِّرْهُ بِعَذَابٍ اَلِيْمٍ ۞

وَاِذَا عَلِمَ مِنْ اٰيٰتِنَا شَيْئًا اتَّخَذَهَا هُزُوًا اُولٰٓئِكَ

a jest of them. For these there is a humiliating punishment. Hell is in front of them, and that which they practised shall not avail them aught, nor shall those whom they have taken up as protectors beside Allah. They will suffer a great chastisement. This is guidance; and for those who disbelieve in the Signs of their Lord is the torment of a painful chastisement. (3—12)

لَهُمْ عَذَابٌ مُّهِيْنٌ ۞

مِنْ وَّرَآئِهِمْ جَهَنَّمُ ۚ وَلَا يُغْنِيْ عَنْهُمْ مَّا كَسَبُوْا شَيْئًا وَّلَا مَا اتَّخَذُوْا مِنْ دُوْنِ اللّٰهِ اَوْلِيَآءَ ۚ وَلَهُمْ عَذَابٌ عَظِيْمٌ ۞

هٰذَا هُدًى ۚ وَالَّذِيْنَ كَفَرُوْا بِاٰيٰتِ رَبِّهِمْ لَهُمْ عَذَابٌ مِّنْ رِّجْزٍ اَلِيْمٌ ۞

Allah is He Who has subjected the sea to you that vessels may sail thereon by His command, and that you may seek of His bounty and that you may be grateful. He has subjected to you whatsoever is in the heavens and whatsoever is in the earth, all of it. In that surely are Signs for a people who reflect. Tell those who believe to forgive those who do not fear the Days appointed by Allah for their chastisement, that He may requite a people for that which they practised. Whoso does good, does it for his own benefit; and whoso does evil, does it to his own loss. Then to your Lord will you be brought back. (13—16)

اَللّٰهُ الَّذِيْ سَخَّرَ لَكُمُ الْبَحْرَ لِتَجْرِيَ الْفُلْكُ فِيْهِ بِاَمْرِهٖ وَلِتَبْتَغُوْا مِنْ فَضْلِهٖ وَلَعَلَّكُمْ تَشْكُرُوْنَ ۞

وَسَخَّرَ لَكُمْ مَّا فِي السَّمٰوٰتِ وَمَا فِي الْاَرْضِ جَمِيْعًا مِّنْهُ ۚ اِنَّ فِيْ ذٰلِكَ لَاٰيٰتٍ لِّقَوْمٍ يَّتَفَكَّرُوْنَ ۞

قُلْ لِّلَّذِيْنَ اٰمَنُوْا يَغْفِرُوْا لِلَّذِيْنَ لَا يَرْجُوْنَ اَيَّامَ اللّٰهِ لِيَجْزِيَ قَوْمًا بِمَا كَانُوْا يَكْسِبُوْنَ ۞

مَنْ عَمِلَ صَالِحًا فَلِنَفْسِهٖ ۚ وَمَنْ اَسَآءَ فَعَلَيْهَا ۖ ثُمَّ اِلٰى رَبِّكُمْ تُرْجَعُوْنَ ۞

We gave the children of Israel the Book, and sovereignty, and Prophethood; and We provided them with pure things, and We exalted them above the peoples of their time. We also bestowed on them clear Signs and commandments. They did not differ among themselves except through mutual envy till after clear knowledge had come to them. Verily, thy Lord will judge between them on the Day of Judgment concerning that wherein they differed. Now We have set thee on a clear path in the matter of the Law; so follow it, and follow not the wishes of those who have no knowledge.

وَلَقَدْ اٰتَيْنَا بَنِيْ اِسْرَآءِيْلَ الْكِتٰبَ وَالْحُكْمَ وَالنُّبُوَّةَ وَرَزَقْنٰهُمْ مِّنَ الطَّيِّبٰتِ وَفَضَّلْنٰهُمْ عَلَى الْعٰلَمِيْنَ ۞

وَاٰتَيْنٰهُمْ بَيِّنٰتٍ مِّنَ الْاَمْرِ ۚ فَمَا اخْتَلَفُوْا اِلَّا مِنْ بَعْدِ مَا جَآءَهُمُ الْعِلْمُ ۙ بَغْيًا بَيْنَهُمْ ۚ اِنَّ رَبَّكَ يَقْضِيْ بَيْنَهُمْ يَوْمَ الْقِيٰمَةِ فِيْمَا كَانُوْا فِيْهِ يَخْتَلِفُوْنَ ۞

ثُمَّ جَعَلْنٰكَ عَلٰى شَرِيْعَةٍ مِّنَ الْاَمْرِ فَاتَّبِعْهَا وَلَا تَتَّبِعْ اَهْوَآءَ الَّذِيْنَ لَا يَعْلَمُوْنَ ۞

They will not avail thee aught against Allah. The wrongdoers are friends, one of another; and Allah is the Friend of the righteous. The teachings revealed to thee are manifest proofs for people, and a guidance and a mercy for a people who have faith. Do those who seek to do evil imagine that We shall make them the equal of those who believe and act righteously, in life and in death? Evil indeed is that which they judge. (17—22)

اِنَّهُمْ لَنْ يُّغْنُوْا عَنْكَ مِنَ اللّٰهِ شَيْئًا وَاِنَّ الظّٰلِمِيْنَ بَعْضُهُمْ اَوْلِيَآءُ بَعْضٍ وَاللّٰهُ وَلِيُّ الْمُتَّقِيْنَ ۞

هٰذَا بَصَآئِرُ لِلنَّاسِ وَهُدًى وَّرَحْمَةٌ لِّقَوْمٍ يُّوْقِنُوْنَ ۞

اَمْ حَسِبَ الَّذِيْنَ اجْتَرَحُوا السَّيِّاٰتِ اَنْ نَّجْعَلَهُمْ كَالَّذِيْنَ اٰمَنُوْا وَعَمِلُوا الصّٰلِحٰتِ سَوَآءً مَّحْيَاهُمْ وَمَمَاتُهُمْ سَآءَ مَا يَحْكُمُوْنَ ۞

Allah has created the heavens and the earth in accordance with an eternal law, so that everyone may be requited according to that which he practises; and they shall not be wronged. Hast thou reflected over the case of him who has made his desires his god, and whom Allah has adjudged astray on the basis of His knowledge, and whose ears and whose heart He has sealed up, and on whose eyes He has put a covering? Who will, then, guide him, after Allah has thus condemned him? Will you not then take heed? They assert: There is nothing but our present life; we live and we die and it is the passage of time that kills us. But they have no real knowledge of the matter; they do nothing but conjecture. When Our manifest Signs are recited to them, their only contention is: Bring back our fathers if you are truthful. Tell them: It is Allah Who gives you life, then causes you to die; then will He gather you together unto the Day of Judgment about which there is no doubt. But most people know it not. (23—27)

وَخَلَقَ اللّٰهُ السَّمٰوٰتِ وَالْاَرْضَ بِالْحَقِّ وَلِتُجْزٰى كُلُّ نَفْسٍ بِمَا كَسَبَتْ وَهُمْ لَا يُظْلَمُوْنَ ۞

اَفَرَءَيْتَ مَنِ اتَّخَذَ اِلٰهَهُ هَوٰهُ وَاَضَلَّهُ اللّٰهُ عَلٰى عِلْمٍ وَّخَتَمَ عَلٰى سَمْعِهِ وَقَلْبِهِ وَجَعَلَ عَلٰى بَصَرِهِ غِشَاوَةً فَمَنْ يَّهْدِيْهِ مِنْ بَعْدِ اللّٰهِ اَفَلَا تَذَكَّرُوْنَ ۞

وَقَالُوْا مَا هِيَ اِلَّا حَيَاتُنَا الدُّنْيَا نَمُوْتُ وَنَحْيَا وَمَا يُهْلِكُنَا اِلَّا الدَّهْرُ وَمَا لَهُمْ بِذٰلِكَ مِنْ عِلْمٍ اِنْ هُمْ اِلَّا يَظُنُّوْنَ ۞

وَاِذَا تُتْلٰى عَلَيْهِمْ اٰيٰتُنَا بَيِّنٰتٍ مَّا كَانَ حُجَّتَهُمْ اِلَّا اَنْ قَالُوا ائْتُوْا بِاٰبَآئِنَا اِنْ كُنْتُمْ صٰدِقِيْنَ ۞

قُلِ اللّٰهُ يُحْيِيْكُمْ ثُمَّ يُمِيْتُكُمْ ثُمَّ يَجْمَعُكُمْ اِلٰى يَوْمِ الْقِيٰمَةِ لَا رَيْبَ فِيْهِ وَلٰكِنَّ اَكْثَرَ النَّاسِ لَا يَعْلَمُوْنَ ۞

To Allah belongs the kingdom of the heavens and the earth. On the day when the Hour shall come, those who follow

وَلِلّٰهِ مُلْكُ السَّمٰوٰتِ وَالْاَرْضِ وَيَوْمَ تَقُوْمُ السَّاعَةُ

falsehood will be the losers. Thou wilt see every people on their knees. Every people will be summoned to its record, and they will be told: This day shall you be requited for that which you did. This is Our Book; it speaks against you with truth. We caused to be recorded all that you did.

يَوْمَئِذٍ يَّخْسَرُ الْمُبْطِلُوْنَ ۞

وَتَرٰى كُلَّ اُمَّةٍ جَاثِيَةً ۖ كُلُّ اُمَّةٍ تُدْعٰى اِلٰى كِتٰبِهَا ۭ اَلْيَوْمَ تُجْزَوْنَ مَا كُنْتُمْ تَعْمَلُوْنَ ۞

هٰذَا كِتٰبُنَا يَنْطِقُ عَلَيْكُمْ بِالْحَقِّ ۭ اِنَّا كُنَّا نَسْتَنْسِخُ مَا كُنْتُمْ تَعْمَلُوْنَ ۞

فَاَمَّا الَّذِيْنَ اٰمَنُوْا وَعَمِلُوا الصّٰلِحٰتِ فَيُدْخِلُهُمْ رَبُّهُمْ فِىْ رَحْمَتِهٖ ۭ ذٰلِكَ هُوَ الْفَوْزُ الْمُبِيْنُ ۞

Their Lord will admit into His mercy those who believed and acted righteously. That is the manifest triumph. Those who disbelieved will be told: Were not My Signs recited unto you? But you were arrogant and became a guilty people. When you were told: Allah's promise is true and there is no doubt about the coming of the Hour; you said: We know not what the Hour is, we can only conjecture, and we are not convinced. The evil nature of their deeds will become manifest to them, and that which they used to mock at will encompass them. They will be told: This day We shall leave you helpless, as you forgot the meeting of this day of yours. Your resort is the Fire, and you will have no helpers. This is so, because you made a jest of the Signs of Allah, and the life of the world beguiled you. Thus that day they will not be taken out of the torment, nor will they be taken back into favour.

وَاَمَّا الَّذِيْنَ كَفَرُوْا ۣ اَفَلَمْ تَكُنْ اٰيٰتِىْ تُتْلٰى عَلَيْكُمْ فَاسْتَكْبَرْتُمْ وَكُنْتُمْ قَوْمًا مُّجْرِمِيْنَ ۞

وَاِذَا قِيْلَ اِنَّ وَعْدَ اللّٰهِ حَقٌّ وَّالسَّاعَةُ لَا رَيْبَ فِيْهَا قُلْتُمْ مَّا نَدْرِىْ مَا السَّاعَةُ ۙ اِنْ نَّظُنُّ اِلَّا ظَنًّا وَّمَا نَحْنُ بِمُسْتَيْقِنِيْنَ ۞

وَبَدَا لَهُمْ سَيِّاٰتُ مَا عَمِلُوْا وَحَاقَ بِهِمْ مَّا كَانُوْا بِهٖ يَسْتَهْزِءُوْنَ ۞

وَقِيْلَ الْيَوْمَ نَنْسٰكُمْ كَمَا نَسِيْتُمْ لِقَآءَ يَوْمِكُمْ هٰذَا وَمَاْوٰىكُمُ النَّارُ وَمَا لَكُمْ مِّنْ نّٰصِرِيْنَ ۞

ذٰلِكُمْ بِاَنَّكُمُ اتَّخَذْتُمْ اٰيٰتِ اللّٰهِ هُزُوًا وَّغَرَّتْكُمُ الْحَيٰوةُ الدُّنْيَا ۚ فَالْيَوْمَ لَا يُخْرَجُوْنَ مِنْهَا وَلَا هُمْ يُسْتَعْتَبُوْنَ ۞

All praise, then, belongs to Allah, Lord of the heavens, and Lord of the earth, Lord of all the worlds. His is the Greatness in the heavens and the earth;

فَلِلّٰهِ الْحَمْدُ رَبِّ السَّمٰوٰتِ وَرَبِّ الْاَرْضِ رَبِّ الْعٰلَمِيْنَ ۞

وَلَهُ الْكِبْرِيَآءُ فِى السَّمٰوٰتِ وَالْاَرْضِ ۗ وَهُوَ الْعَزِيْزُ

and He is the Mighty, the Wise. (28—38)

الْحَكِيمُ ۞

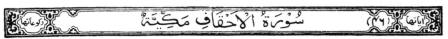

Part 26   AL-AḤQĀF   Chapter 46
(Revealed before Hijra)

In the name of Allah, Most Gracious, Ever Merciful. (1)

بِسْمِ اللهِ الرَّحْمٰنِ الرَّحِيمِ ۞

حٰمٓ ۞

THE PRAISEWORTHY, THE LORD OF HONOUR. (2)

تَنْزِيلُ الْكِتٰبِ مِنَ اللهِ الْعَزِيزِ الْحَكِيمِ ۞

مَا خَلَقْنَا السَّمٰوٰتِ وَالْأَرْضَ وَمَا بَيْنَهُمَا إِلَّا

بِالْحَقِّ وَأَجَلٍ مُّسَمًّى ۚ وَالَّذِينَ كَفَرُوا عَمَّا أُنْذِرُوا

مُعْرِضُونَ ۞

The revelation of this Book is from Allah, the Mighty, the Wise. We have created the heavens and the earth, and all that is between them with an enduring purpose, and for an appointed term; but those who disbelieve turn away from that of which they have been warned. Ask them: Have you considered that which you worship beside Allah? Show me what have they created of the earth; or, have they a share in the creation of the heavens? Produce a Book revealed before this, in support of your claim, or some vestige of knowledge, if you are telling the truth.

قُلْ أَرَأَيْتُمْ مَّا تَدْعُونَ مِنْ دُونِ اللهِ أَرُونِي

مَاذَا خَلَقُوا مِنَ الْأَرْضِ أَمْ لَهُمْ شِرْكٌ فِي السَّمٰوٰتِ

اِيْتُونِي بِكِتٰبٍ مِّنْ قَبْلِ هٰذَا أَوْ أَثٰرَةٍ مِّنْ عِلْمٍ

اِنْ كُنْتُمْ صٰدِقِينَ ۞

وَمَنْ أَضَلُّ مِمَّنْ يَّدْعُوا مِنْ دُونِ اللهِ مَنْ

لَّا يَسْتَجِيبُ لَهُ إِلٰى يَوْمِ الْقِيٰمَةِ وَهُمْ عَنْ دُعَآئِهِمْ

غٰفِلُونَ ۞

Who is more astray than one who calls on that beside Allah which will not answer him till Judgment Day? Indeed they are not even conscious of their prayer. When mankind are gathered together, those to whom prayer was addressed will be the enemies of their votaries and will repudiate their worship. When Our clear Signs are recited to them, the disbelievers on hearing the truth exclaim: Why, this is manifest sorcery.

وَإِذَا حُشِرَ النَّاسُ كَانُوا لَهُمْ أَعْدَآءً وَّكَانُوا

بِعِبَادَتِهِمْ كٰفِرِينَ ۞

وَإِذَا تُتْلٰى عَلَيْهِمْ اٰيٰتُنَا بَيِّنٰتٍ قَالَ الَّذِينَ كَفَرُوا

لِلْحَقِّ لَمَّا جَآءَهُمْ هٰذَا سِحْرٌ مُّبِينٌ ۞

Do they say: He has fabricated the Quran? Tell them: If I have fabricated it, you cannot avail me aught against Allah's chastisement. He knows well the idle talk that you indulge in. Sufficient is He as a witness between you and me. He is the Most Forgiving, the Ever Merciful. Tell them: I am no innovation among Messengers, nor do I know what will be done with me or with you. I only follow that which is revealed to me; and I am but a plain Warner. Ask them: If my revelation is from Allah, and you reject it, would it not be strange that a witness from among the children of Israel should have foretold the advent of one like himself and should have believed in him, while you deny him in your arrogance? Surely, Allah guides not the wrongdoing people. (3—11)

Those who disbelieve say of those who believe: If the Quran had been any good they would not have accepted it ahead of us. Since they have not appreciated its truth, they are sure to say: This is only a repetition of old fabrications. Before it was the Book of Moses, a guide and a mercy; and this is a Book in Arabic fulfilling previous Books, that it may warn the wrongdoers and give glad tidings to those who do good. Those who say: Allah is our Lord, and then remain steadfast, will be subject to no fear, nor will they grieve. These are the dwellers of the Garden; they shall abide therein; a recompense for that which they did. (12—15)

We have enjoined on man to act bene-volently towards his parents. His mother bears him in pain and brings him forth in pain; and the bearing of him and his weaning extends over thirty months.

504

When he attains his full maturity at forty years, he prays: Lord, grant me the favour that I may be grateful to Thee for the bounty that Thou hast bestowed upon me and upon my parents, and that I may act righteously so as to please Thee, and make my progeny righteous also. I do turn to Thee and truly I am of Thy obedient servants. Of these We shall accept the best of their works, and We shall overlook their defaults. They shall be among the inmates of the Garden. That is a true promise that is held out to them. Then there is he who upbraids his parents: Fie on you. Do you threaten me that I shall be brought forth again, when generations have already passed on before me and not one of them has come back? They beseech Allah for help and adjure him: Woe unto thee, believe; for Allah's promise is true. But he shrugs it off with: These are but old wives' tales!

These are those concerning whom the sentence of punishment was executed, from among communities of Jinn and men who had passed on before. They were indeed the losers. They shall all be requited fully according to the quality of their conduct; and they shall not be wronged. On the day when the disbelievers will be brought to the Fire, they will be told: You have exhausted your bounties in your life in the earth, and have benefited from them. Now this day you will be requited with ignominious punishment because you were arrogant in the earth without justification and because you were rebellious. (16—21)

Call to mind Hud, brother of the tribe of 'Ad, when he warned his people among the sand dunes, and there have been Warners before him and after him: Worship none but Allah, I am fearful of your being afflicted with the torment of a great day. They retorted: Hast thou come to us to turn us away from our gods? Then if that which thou sayest is true bring upon us that with which thou dost threaten us. He replied: The knowledge of it is with Allah. I convey to you that with which I have been sent. I perceive, however, that you are an ignorant people. Then when they saw the portent advancing towards their valleys in the shape of a cloud, they said: Here is a cloud bringing us rain. Indeed not! This is that which you asked to be hastened: a wind carrying a grievous punishment. It will destroy everything by the command of its Lord. When morning arrived there was nothing left to be seen except their dwellings. Thus do We requite a guilty people.

قَدْ خَلَتِ النُّذُرُ مِنْ بَيْنِ يَدَيْهِ وَمِنْ خَلْفِهٖۤ اَلَّا تَعْبُدُوْۤا اِلَّا اللّٰهَ اِنِّیْۤ اَخَافُ عَلَيْكُمْ عَذَابَ يَوْمٍ عَظِيْمٍ ۝

قَالُوْۤا اَجِئْتَنَا لِتَأْفِكَنَا عَنْ اٰلِهَتِنَا فَأْتِنَا بِمَا تَعِدُنَاۤ اِنْ كُنْتَ مِنَ الصّٰدِقِيْنَ ۝

قَالَ اِنَّمَا الْعِلْمُ عِنْدَ اللّٰهِ ۙ وَ اُبَلِّغُكُمْ مَّاۤ اُرْسِلْتُ بِهٖ وَ لٰكِنِّیْۤ اَرٰىكُمْ قَوْمًا تَجْهَلُوْنَ ۝

فَلَمَّا رَاَوْهُ عَارِضًا مُّسْتَقْبِلَ اَوْدِيَتِهِمْ ۙ قَالُوْا هٰذَا عَارِضٌ مُّمْطِرُنَا ؕ بَلْ هُوَ مَا اسْتَعْجَلْتُمْ بِهٖ ؕ رِيْحٌ فِيْهَا عَذَابٌ اَلِيْمٌ ۝

تُدَمِّرُ كُلَّ شَیْءٍۢ بِاَمْرِ رَبِّهَا فَاَصْبَحُوْا لَا يُرٰۤی اِلَّا مَسٰكِنُهُمْ ؕ كَذٰلِكَ نَجْزِی الْقَوْمَ الْمُجْرِمِيْنَ ۝

We had provided them with resources with which We have not provided you; and We had given them ears and eyes and hearts, the same as We have given you. But their ears and their eyes and their hearts availed them naught since they persisted in denying the Signs of Allah; and that which they used to mock at encompassed them. (22—27)

وَ لَقَدْ مَكَّنّٰهُمْ فِيْمَاۤ اِنْ مَّكَّنّٰكُمْ فِيْهِ وَجَعَلْنَا لَهُمْ سَمْعًا وَّ اَبْصَارًا وَّ اَفْئِدَةً ۖ فَمَاۤ اَغْنٰی عَنْهُمْ سَمْعُهُمْ وَلَاۤ اَبْصَارُهُمْ وَ لَاۤ اَفْئِدَتُهُمْ مِّنْ شَیْءٍ اِذْ كَانُوْا يَجْحَدُوْنَ ۙ بِاٰيٰتِ اللّٰهِ وَحَاقَ بِهِمْ مَّا كَانُوْا بِهٖ يَسْتَهْزِءُوْنَ ۝

We have also destroyed the townships around you; and We had expounded Our Signs in diverse ways that they might turn to them. Why did not those help them whom they had set up as gods beside Allah, that they might bring them near to Him? Instead they left them in the lurch. This was the end of their lies and of that which they fabricated. (28—29)

وَ لَقَدْ اَهْلَكْنَا مَا حَوْلَكُمْ مِّنَ الْقُرٰی وَ صَرَّفْنَا الْاٰيٰتِ لَعَلَّهُمْ يَرْجِعُوْنَ ۝

فَلَوْلَا نَصَرَهُمُ الَّذِيْنَ اتَّخَذُوْا مِنْ دُوْنِ اللّٰهِ قُرْبَانًا اٰلِهَةً ؕ بَلْ ضَلُّوْا عَنْهُمْ ۚ وَ ذٰلِكَ اِفْكُهُمْ وَ مَا كَانُوْا يَفْتَرُوْنَ ۝

Call to mind when We diverted towards thee a party who came to thee secretly, desiring to hear the Quran, and when they came to the recitation, they said to one another: Listen in silence; and when it was finished, they went back to their people, warning them. They told them: Our people, we have listened to a Book, which has been sent down after Moses, fulfilling that which has been revealed before it; it guides to the truth and to the straight path. Our people, respond to one who calls to Allah, and believe in him. Allah will forgive you your sins, and will safeguard you against a painful chastisement. Whoso does not respond to him who calls to Allah, cannot frustrate His design in the earth, nor can he have any protector beside Him. Such are in manifest error. Do they not realise that Allah Who has created the heavens and the earth and was not wearied in the process, has the power to bring the dead to life? Indeed, He has power over all things.

وَإِذْ صَرَفْنَآ إِلَيْكَ نَفَرًا مِّنَ الْجِنِّ يَسْتَمِعُوْنَ الْقُرْاٰنَ ۚ فَلَمَّا حَضَرُوْهُ قَالُوْۤا أَنْصِتُوْا ۚ فَلَمَّا قُضِيَ وَلَّوْا إِلٰى قَوْمِهِمْ مُّنْذِرِيْنَ ۝

قَالُوْا يٰقَوْمَنَآ إِنَّا سَمِعْنَا كِتٰبًا أُنْزِلَ مِنْ بَعْدِ مُوْسٰى مُصَدِّقًا لِّمَا بَيْنَ يَدَيْهِ يَهْدِيْۤ إِلَى الْحَقِّ وَإِلٰى طَرِيْقٍ مُّسْتَقِيْمٍ ۝

يٰقَوْمَنَآ أَجِيْبُوْا دَاعِيَ اللّٰهِ وَاٰمِنُوْا بِهٖ يَغْفِرْ لَكُمْ مِّنْ ذُنُوْبِكُمْ وَيُجِرْكُمْ مِّنْ عَذَابٍ أَلِيْمٍ ۝

وَمَنْ لَّا يُجِبْ دَاعِيَ اللّٰهِ فَلَيْسَ بِمُعْجِزٍ فِي الْأَرْضِ وَلَيْسَ لَهٗ مِنْ دُوْنِهٖۤ أَوْلِيَآءُ ۚ أُولٰٓئِكَ فِيْ ضَلٰلٍ مُّبِيْنٍ ۝

أَوَلَمْ يَرَوْا أَنَّ اللّٰهَ الَّذِيْ خَلَقَ السَّمٰوٰتِ وَالْأَرْضَ وَلَمْ يَعْيَ بِخَلْقِهِنَّ بِقٰدِرٍ عَلٰۤى أَنْ يُّحْيِۦَ الْمَوْتٰى ۚ بَلٰۤى إِنَّهٗ عَلٰى كُلِّ شَيْءٍ قَدِيْرٌ ۝

وَيَوْمَ يُعْرَضُ الَّذِيْنَ كَفَرُوْا عَلَى النَّارِ ۚ أَلَيْسَ هٰذَا بِالْحَقِّ ۚ قَالُوْا بَلٰى وَرَبِّنَا ۚ قَالَ فَذُوْقُوا الْعَذَابَ بِمَا كُنْتُمْ تَكْفُرُوْنَ ۝

On the day when those who disbelieve will be brought to the Fire, they will be asked: Is not this the truth? They will answer: Indeed, by our Lord. He will say: Then suffer the punishment because you disbelieved. Continue steadfast then, as were steadfast the Messengers of high resolve, and desire not their quick chastisement. On the day when they perceive that which they are promised, they will imagine as if they had not tarried in this life but for a short while. This is but a warning; and none but the disobedient people will be destroyed. (30—36)

فَاصْبِرْ كَمَا صَبَرَ أُولُوا الْعَزْمِ مِنَ الرُّسُلِ وَلَا تَسْتَعْجِلْ لَّهُمْ ۚ كَأَنَّهُمْ يَوْمَ يَرَوْنَ مَا يُوْعَدُوْنَ ۙ لَمْ يَلْبَثُوْۤا إِلَّا سَاعَةً مِّنْ نَّهَارٍ ۚ بَلٰغٌ ۚ فَهَلْ يُهْلَكُ إِلَّا الْقَوْمُ الْفٰسِقُوْنَ ۝

MUḤAMMAD

(Revealed after Hijra)

In the name of Allah, Most Gracious, Ever Merciful. (1)

بِسْمِ اللهِ الرَّحْمٰنِ الرَّحِيْمِ ۝

الَّذِيْنَ كَفَرُوْا وَصَدُّوْا عَنْ سَبِيْلِ اللهِ اَضَلَّ اَعْمَالَهُمْ ۝

Allah renders vain the works of those who disbelieve and hinder people from the way of Allah; and from those who believe and work righteousness and believe in that which has been revealed to Muhammad, and it is the truth from their Lord, He removes their ills and improves their condition. That is because those who disbelieve follow falsehood, while those who believe follow the truth from their Lord. Thus does Allah set forth to people their true condition. (2—4)

وَالَّذِيْنَ اٰمَنُوْا وَعَمِلُوا الصّٰلِحٰتِ وَاٰمَنُوْا بِمَا نُزِّلَ عَلٰى مُحَمَّدٍ وَّهُوَ الْحَقُّ مِنْ رَّبِّهِمْ لِكَفَّرَ عَنْهُمْ سَيِّاٰتِهِمْ وَاَصْلَحَ بَالَهُمْ ۝

ذٰلِكَ بِاَنَّ الَّذِيْنَ كَفَرُوا اتَّبَعُوا الْبَاطِلَ وَاَنَّ الَّذِيْنَ اٰمَنُوا اتَّبَعُوا الْحَقَّ مِنْ رَّبِّهِمْ كَذٰلِكَ يَضْرِبُ اللهُ لِلنَّاسِ اَمْثَالَهُمْ ۝

When you meet in battle those who have disbelieved, smite their necks; and after the slaughter fasten tight the bonds, until the war lays aside its burdens. Then either release them as a favour, or in return for ransom. That is the ordinance. Had Allah so pleased He could have punished them Himself; but He has willed that He may try some of you by means of others. Allah will never render vain the works of those who are slain in His cause. He will guide them and improve their condition, and admit them into the Garden which He has made known to them. O ye who believe, if you help the cause of Allah, He will help you and make your steps firm; while ruin will seize those who disbelieve, and He will render their works vain.

فَاِذَا لَقِيْتُمُ الَّذِيْنَ كَفَرُوْا فَضَرْبَ الرِّقَابِ حَتّٰى اِذَآ اَثْخَنْتُمُوْهُمْ فَشُدُّوا الْوَثَاقَ فَاِمَّا مَنًّا بَعْدُ وَاِمَّا فِدَآءً حَتّٰى تَضَعَ الْحَرْبُ اَوْزَارَهَاقَ ذٰلِكَ وَلَوْ يَشَآءُ اللهُ لَانْتَصَرَ مِنْهُمْ وَلٰكِنْ لِيَبْلُوَا بَعْضَكُمْ بِبَعْضٍ وَ الَّذِيْنَ قُتِلُوْا فِيْ سَبِيْلِ اللهِ فَلَنْ يُّضِلَّ اَعْمَالَهُمْ ۝

سَيَهْدِيْهِمْ وَيُصْلِحُ بَالَهُمْ ۝

وَيُدْخِلُهُمُ الْجَنَّةَ عَرَّفَهَا لَهُمْ ۝

يٰٓاَيُّهَا الَّذِيْنَ اٰمَنُوْا اِنْ تَنْصُرُوا اللهَ يَنْصُرْكُمْ وَ يُثَبِّتْ اَقْدَامَكُمْ ۝

وَالَّذِيْنَ كَفَرُوْا فَتَعْسًا لَّهُمْ وَاَضَلَّ اَعْمَالَهُمْ ۝

508

That is because they are averse to that which Allah has revealed; so He has rendered their works futile. Have they not travelled in the earth and observed what was the end of those who were before them? Allah destroyed them utterly, and the same will be the case of these disbelievers. That is because Allah is the Helper of those who believe, and the disbelievers have no helper. (5—12)

ذٰلِكَ بِاَنَّهُمْ كَرِهُوْا مَاۤ اَنْزَلَ اللّٰهُ فَاَحْبَطَ اَعْمَالَهُمْ ۟

اَفَلَمْ يَسِيْرُوْا فِي الْاَرْضِ فَيَنْظُرُوْا كَيْفَ كَانَ عَاقِبَةُ الَّذِيْنَ مِنْ قَبْلِهِمْ دَمَّرَ اللّٰهُ عَلَيْهِمْ ۫ وَ لِلْكٰفِرِيْنَ اَمْثَالُهَا ۟

ذٰلِكَ بِاَنَّ اللّٰهَ مَوْلَى الَّذِيْنَ اٰمَنُوْا وَاَنَّ الْكٰفِرِيْنَ لَا مَوْلٰى لَهُمْ ۟

اِنَّ اللّٰهَ يُدْخِلُ الَّذِيْنَ اٰمَنُوْا وَ عَمِلُوا الصّٰلِحٰتِ جَنّٰتٍ تَجْرِيْ مِنْ تَحْتِهَا الْاَنْهٰرُ ۚ وَالَّذِيْنَ كَفَرُوْا يَتَمَتَّعُوْنَ وَ يَأْكُلُوْنَ كَمَا تَأْكُلُ الْاَنْعَامُ وَالنَّارُ مَثْوًى لَّهُمْ ۟

Allah will surely cause those who believe and work righteousness to enter the Gardens beneath which rivers flow; while those who disbelieve enjoy themselves in this life and eat and drink as do the animals, and the Fire will be their ultimate resort. How many a township, mightier than thy town which has driven thee out, have We destroyed, and no one came to their help! Is he then who bases himself upon a clear proof from his Lord like one to whom the evil of his conduct appears fair, and he is of those who pursue their low desires?

وَ كَاَيِّنْ مِّنْ قَرْيَةٍ هِيَ اَشَدُّ قُوَّةً مِّنْ قَرْيَتِكَ الَّتِيْۤ اَخْرَجَتْكَ ۚ اَهْلَكْنٰهُمْ فَلَا نَاصِرَ لَهُمْ ۟

اَفَمَنْ كَانَ عَلٰى بَيِّنَةٍ مِّنْ رَّبِّهٖ كَمَنْ زُيِّنَ لَهٗ سُوْٓءُ عَمَلِهٖ وَ اتَّبَعُوْۤا اَهْوَآءَهُمْ ۟

The Garden promised to the righteous has rivers of water that is not corrupted; and rivers of milk of which the taste changes not; and rivers of wine, a delight for those who drink; and rivers of pure honey. They will have all kinds of fruits therein, and forgiveness from their Lord. Can these be like those who abide in the Fire and are given boiling water to drink which tears out their bowels? Some of them appear to listen to thee, but when they go forth from thy presence they ask those who have been given knowledge: What has he been talking about just now?

مَثَلُ الْجَنَّةِ الَّتِيْ وُعِدَ الْمُتَّقُوْنَ ۚ فِيْهَاۤ اَنْهٰرٌ مِّنْ مَّآءٍ غَيْرِ اٰسِنٍ ۚ وَاَنْهٰرٌ مِّنْ لَّبَنٍ لَّمْ يَتَغَيَّرْ طَعْمُهٗ ۚ وَاَنْهٰرٌ مِّنْ خَمْرٍ لَّذَّةٍ لِّلشّٰرِبِيْنَ ۚ وَاَنْهٰرٌ مِّنْ عَسَلٍ مُّصَفًّى ۚ وَلَهُمْ فِيْهَا مِنْ كُلِّ الثَّمَرٰتِ وَمَغْفِرَةٌ مِّنْ رَّبِّهِمْ ۚ كَمَنْ هُوَ خَالِدٌ فِي النَّارِ وَسُقُوْا مَآءً حَمِيْمًا فَقَطَّعَ اَمْعَآءَهُمْ ۟

وَ مِنْهُمْ مَّنْ يَّسْتَمِعُ اِلَيْكَ ۚ حَتّٰۤى اِذَا خَرَجُوْا مِنْ عِنْدِكَ قَالُوْا لِلَّذِيْنَ اُوْتُوا الْعِلْمَ مَاذَا قَالَ اٰنِفًا

These are they whose hearts Allah has sealed up and who pursue their low desires. Allah adds to the guidance of those who follow the guidance, and bestows righteousness upon them. The others but wait for the Hour to come upon them suddenly. The signs thereof have already appeared. But when it actually comes upon them, what admonition will profit them? Know, then, that there is no god other than Allah, and beseech for the suppression of thy frailties and ask forgiveness, and for the believing men and the believing women. Allah knows well your moving about and your abiding place. (13—20)

أُولٰٓئِكَ الَّذِيْنَ طَبَعَ اللّٰهُ عَلٰى قُلُوْبِهِمْ وَاتَّبَعُوْٓا اَهْوَآءَهُمْ ۞

وَالَّذِيْنَ اهْتَدَوْا زَادَهُمْ هُدًى وَّ اٰتٰهُمْ تَقْوٰىهُمْ ۞

فَهَلْ يَنْظُرُوْنَ اِلَّا السَّاعَةَ اَنْ تَأْتِيَهُمْ بَغْتَةً ۚ فَقَدْ جَآءَ اَشْرَاطُهَا ۚ فَاَنّٰى لَهُمْ اِذَا جَآءَتْهُمْ ذِكْرٰىهُمْ ۞

فَاعْلَمْ اَنَّهٗ لَاۤ اِلٰهَ اِلَّا اللّٰهُ وَاسْتَغْفِرْ لِذَنْبِكَ وَ لِلْمُؤْمِنِيْنَ وَالْمُؤْمِنٰتِ ۚ وَاللّٰهُ يَعْلَمُ مُتَقَلَّبَكُمْ وَ مَثْوٰىكُمْ ۞

Those who believe enquire eagerly: Why is not a Sura revealed, permitting the taking up of arms? But when a decisive Sura is revealed in which fighting is mentioned, thou seest the sick of heart looking towards thee like one in the grip of death. For them is ruin. Their part was to obey and to call people to that which is becoming. Then when the matter was determined upon, had they been true to their duty to Allah, it would have been the better for them. Is it not likely that if you turn away, you will by your conduct create disorder in the land and sever the ties of kinship? It is these whom Allah has cast away and has made them deaf and blinded their eyes. Do they not ponder over the Quran, or is it that their hearts are locked up from within?

وَيَقُوْلُ الَّذِيْنَ اٰمَنُوْا لَوْلَا نُزِّلَتْ سُوْرَةٌ ۚ فَاِذَاۤ اُنْزِلَتْ سُوْرَةٌ مُّحْكَمَةٌ وَّ ذُكِرَ فِيْهَا الْقِتَالُ ۙ رَاَيْتَ الَّذِيْنَ فِيْ قُلُوْبِهِمْ مَّرَضٌ يَّنْظُرُوْنَ اِلَيْكَ نَظَرَ الْمَغْشِيِّ عَلَيْهِ مِنَ الْمَوْتِ ۚ فَاَوْلٰى لَهُمْ ۞

طَاعَةٌ وَّ قَوْلٌ مَّعْرُوْفٌ ۫ فَاِذَا عَزَمَ الْاَمْرُ ۫ فَلَوْ صَدَقُوا اللّٰهَ لَكَانَ خَيْرًا لَّهُمْ ۞

فَهَلْ عَسَيْتُمْ اِنْ تَوَلَّيْتُمْ اَنْ تُفْسِدُوْا فِي الْاَرْضِ وَتُقَطِّعُوْٓا اَرْحَامَكُمْ ۞

أُولٰٓئِكَ الَّذِيْنَ لَعَنَهُمُ اللّٰهُ فَاَصَمَّهُمْ وَ اَعْمٰىۤ اَبْصَارَهُمْ ۞

اَفَلَا يَتَدَبَّرُوْنَ الْقُرْاٰنَ اَمْ عَلٰى قُلُوْبٍ اَقْفَالُهَا ۞

اِنَّ الَّذِيْنَ ارْتَدُّوْا عَلٰٓى اَدْبَارِهِمْ مِّنْ بَعْدِ مَا

Surely, those who have turned away after guidance has been made manifest to them have been deceived by Satan who has beguiled them with false hopes. That is because they said to those who are averse to that which Allah has revealed: We will obey you in certain matters. Allah knows well their secrets. Then how will it be when the angels will cause them to die, smiting their faces and their backs? That will be because they followed that which displeased Allah, and were averse to that which would please Him. So He rendered their works vain. (21—29)

تَبَيَّنَ لَهُمُ الْهُدَى الشَّيْطُنُ سَوَّلَ لَهُمْ وَاَمْلٰى لَهُمْ ۝

ذٰلِكَ بِاَنَّهُمْ قَالُوْا لِلَّذِيْنَ كَرِهُوْا مَا نَزَّلَ اللّٰهُ سَنُطِيْعُكُمْ فِيْ بَعْضِ الْاَمْرِ ۚ وَاللّٰهُ يَعْلَمُ اِسْرَارَهُمْ ۝

فَكَيْفَ اِذَا تَوَفَّتْهُمُ الْمَلٰٓئِكَةُ يَضْرِبُوْنَ وُجُوْهَهُمْ وَاَدْبَارَهُمْ ۝

ذٰلِكَ بِاَنَّهُمُ اتَّبَعُوْا مَا اَسْخَطَ اللّٰهَ وَكَرِهُوْا رِضْوَانَهٗ فَاَحْبَطَ اَعْمَالَهُمْ ۝

Do those who are sick of heart imagine that Allah will not bring to light their malice? If We pleased We could show them to thee so that thou couldst know them by their features. Even so thou knowest them by the tone of their utterances. Allah knows well your practices.

اَمْ حَسِبَ الَّذِيْنَ فِيْ قُلُوْبِهِمْ مَّرَضٌ اَنْ لَّنْ يُّخْرِجَ اللّٰهُ اَضْغَانَهُمْ ۝

وَلَوْ نَشَآءُ لَاَرَيْنٰكَهُمْ فَلَعَرَفْتَهُمْ بِسِيْمٰهُمْ وَلَتَعْرِفَنَّهُمْ فِيْ لَحْنِ الْقَوْلِ ۚ وَاللّٰهُ يَعْلَمُ اَعْمَالَكُمْ ۝

وَلَنَبْلُوَنَّكُمْ حَتّٰى نَعْلَمَ الْمُجٰهِدِيْنَ مِنْكُمْ وَالصّٰبِرِيْنَ ۙ وَنَبْلُوَا اَخْبَارَكُمْ ۝

We will surely try you until We make known those from among you who strive in the cause of Allah, and those who are steadfast; and We will bring to light your true condition. Those who disbelieve, and hinder people from the way of Allah and oppose the Messenger after guidance has become manifest to them, shall not harm Allah in the least; and He will render their works vain. O ye who believe, obey Allah and obey the Messenger and let not your works go vain. Verily, those who disbelieve and hinder people from the way of Allah and die in their disbelief will not be forgiven by Allah.

اِنَّ الَّذِيْنَ كَفَرُوْا وَصَدُّوْا عَنْ سَبِيْلِ اللّٰهِ وَشَآقُّوا الرَّسُوْلَ مِنْ بَعْدِ مَا تَبَيَّنَ لَهُمُ الْهُدٰى ۙ لَنْ يَّضُرُّوا اللّٰهَ شَيْئًا ۚ وَسَيُحْبِطُ اَعْمَالَهُمْ ۝

يٰٓاَيُّهَا الَّذِيْنَ اٰمَنُوْٓا اَطِيْعُوا اللّٰهَ وَاَطِيْعُوا الرَّسُوْلَ وَلَا تُبْطِلُوْٓا اَعْمَالَكُمْ ۝

اِنَّ الَّذِيْنَ كَفَرُوْا وَصَدُّوْا عَنْ سَبِيْلِ اللّٰهِ ثُمَّ مَاتُوْا وَهُمْ كُفَّارٌ فَلَنْ يَّغْفِرَ اللّٰهُ لَهُمْ ۝

Then sue not for peace because of your slackness; for you will certainly have the upper hand. Allah is with you, and He will not diminish aught from your works.

فَلَا تَهِنُوْا وَتَدْعُوْۤا اِلَى السَّلْمِ وَاَنْتُمُ الْاَعْلَوْنَ ۖ وَاللّٰهُ مَعَكُمْ وَلَنْ يَّتِرَكُمْ اَعْمَالَكُمْ ۝

The life of this world is but sport and pastime, and if you believe and are righteous, He will give you your due and will not require of you your belongings. Were He to require them of you and to press you for them, you would be niggardly, and He would bring to light your ill-will. Hearken, you are those who are called upon to spend in the cause of Allah; but of you there are some who hold back, and whoso holds back, does so only against himself. Allah is Self-Sufficient; it is you who are needy. If you turn away, He will bring in your stead another people who will not be such laggards as you. (30—39)

اِنَّمَا الْحَيٰوةُ الدُّنْيَا لَعِبٌ وَّلَهْوٌ ۖ وَاِنْ تُؤْمِنُوْا وَتَتَّقُوْا يُؤْتِكُمْ اُجُوْرَكُمْ وَلَا يَسْـَٔلْكُمْ اَمْوَالَكُمْ ۝

اِنْ يَّسْـَٔلْكُمُوْهَا فَيُحْفِكُمْ تَبْخَلُوْا وَيُخْرِجْ اَضْغَانَكُمْ ۝

هٰۤاَنْتُمْ هٰۤؤُلَاۤءِ تُدْعَوْنَ لِتُنْفِقُوْا فِيْ سَبِيْلِ اللّٰهِ ۚ فَمِنْكُمْ مَّنْ يَّبْخَلُ ۚ وَمَنْ يَّبْخَلْ فَاِنَّمَا يَبْخَلُ عَنْ نَّفْسِهٖ ۚ وَاللّٰهُ الْغَنِيُّ وَاَنْتُمُ الْفُقَرَاۤءُ ۚ وَاِنْ تَتَوَلَّوْا يَسْتَبْدِلْ قَوْمًا غَيْرَكُمْ ثُمَّ لَا يَكُوْنُوْۤا اَمْثَالَكُمْ ۝

سُوْرَةُ الْفَتْحِ مَدَنِيَّةٌ ۝

(*Revealed after Hijra*)

In the name of Allah, Most Gracious, Ever Merciful. (1)

بِسْمِ اللّٰهِ الرَّحْمٰنِ الرَّحِيْمِ ۝

اِنَّا فَتَحْنَا لَكَ فَتْحًا مُّبِيْنًا ۝

Surely, We have granted thee a clear victory, that Allah may cover up thy shortcomings, past and future, and that He may complete His favour unto thee, and may guide thee along the right path; and that Allah may help thee with a mighty help. He it is Who sent down tranquillity upon the hearts of the believers that they might add faith to their faith — to Allah belong the hosts of the heavens and the earth, and Allah is All-Knowing, Wise —

لِّيَغْفِرَ لَكَ اللّٰهُ مَا تَقَدَّمَ مِنْ ذَنْبِكَ وَمَا تَاَخَّرَ وَيُتِمَّ نِعْمَتَهٗ عَلَيْكَ وَيَهْدِيَكَ صِرَاطًا مُّسْتَقِيْمًا ۝

وَّيَنْصُرَكَ اللّٰهُ نَصْرًا عَزِيْزًا ۝

هُوَ الَّذِيْۤ اَنْزَلَ السَّكِيْنَةَ فِيْ قُلُوْبِ الْمُؤْمِنِيْنَ لِيَزْدَادُوْۤا اِيْمَانًا مَّعَ اِيْمَانِهِمْ ۗ وَلِلّٰهِ جُنُوْدُ السَّمٰوٰتِ وَالْاَرْضِ ۚ وَكَانَ اللّٰهُ عَلِيْمًا حَكِيْمًا ۝

that He may admit the believers, men and women, into Gardens beneath which rivers flow, wherein they will abide, and that He may remove their ills from them — that, in the sight of Allah, is the supreme triumph — and that He may punish the hypocrites, men and women, and the idolaters, men and women, who entertain unworthy thoughts concerning Allah. They will be afflicted with calamity. Allah is wroth with them and has cast them aside, and has prepared hell for them. It is an evil destination. To Allah belong the hosts of the heaven and the earth. Allah is Mighty, Wise. We have sent thee as a witness and a bearer of glad tidings and a Warner, that you may believe in Allah and His Messenger, and may help the Messenger, and honour Allah and the Messenger, and glorify Allah, morning and evening. Those who swear allegiance to thee swear allegiance to Allah; Allah's hand is above their hands. So whoever breaks the covenant, does so to his own loss; and whoever fulfils the covenant he has made with Allah, upon him will He bestow a great reward. (2—11)

Those of the desert Arabs who contrived to be left behind, will say to thee: Our belongings and our families kept us occupied, so ask forgiveness for us. They say with their tongues that which is not in their hearts. Say to them: Who can avail you aught against Allah, if He should intend you some harm or should intend you some good? Allah is indeed well aware of that which you do. You had imagined that the Messenger and the believers would never come back to their families, and this prospect appeared pleasing to your hearts. You indulged in evil thinking, and became a ruined people.

إِلَىٰ أَهْلِيهِمْ أَبَدًا وَّزُيِّنَ ذٰلِكَ فِيْ قُلُوْبِكُمْ وَظَنَنْتُمْ ظَنَّ السَّوْءِ ۚ وَكُنْتُمْ قَوْمًا بُوْرًا ۝

وَمَنْ لَّمْ يُؤْمِنْ بِاللّٰهِ وَرَسُوْلِهٖ فَإِنَّآ أَعْتَدْنَا لِلْكٰفِرِيْنَ سَعِيْرًا ۝

He who believes not in Allah and His Messenger should know that We have prepared a blazing torment for the disbelievers. To Allah belongs the kingdom of the heavens and the earth. He forgives whom He so wills, and punishes whom He so wills. Allah is Most Forgiving, Ever Merciful. When you go forth to gather the spoils, those who were left behind will say: Permit us to follow you. They will seek to alter Allah's decree. Tell them: You shall not follow us. Thus has Allah determined already. Then will they say: Indeed, you are jealous of us. The truth is they have little understanding. Say to the desert Arabs who were left behind: You will be called to fight against a people possessing great valour; you shall fight them until they submit. Then, if you respond to Allah's call, Allah will bestow on you a good reward, but if you turn away, as you turned away before, He will chastise you with a painful chastisement. The blind, the lame and the sick are under no obligation to go forth to fight. Allah will admit those who obey Him and His Messenger into Gardens beneath which rivers flow; and will chastise with a grievous chastisement those who turn away from His command. (12—18)

وَلِلّٰهِ مُلْكُ السَّمٰوٰتِ وَالْأَرْضِ ۚ يَغْفِرُ لِمَنْ يَّشَآءُ وَيُعَذِّبُ مَنْ يَّشَآءُ ۚ وَكَانَ اللّٰهُ غَفُوْرًا رَّحِيْمًا ۝

سَيَقُوْلُ الْمُخَلَّفُوْنَ إِذَا انْطَلَقْتُمْ إِلَىٰ مَغَانِمَ لِتَأْخُذُوْهَا ذَرُوْنَا نَتَّبِعْكُمْ ۚ يُرِيْدُوْنَ أَنْ يُّبَدِّلُوْا كَلٰمَ اللّٰهِ ۚ قُلْ لَّنْ تَتَّبِعُوْنَا كَذٰلِكُمْ قَالَ اللّٰهُ مِنْ قَبْلُ ۚ فَسَيَقُوْلُوْنَ بَلْ تَحْسُدُوْنَنَا ۚ بَلْ كَانُوْا لَا يَفْقَهُوْنَ إِلَّا قَلِيْلًا ۝

قُلْ لِّلْمُخَلَّفِيْنَ مِنَ الْأَعْرَابِ سَتُدْعَوْنَ إِلَىٰ قَوْمٍ أُولِيْ بَأْسٍ شَدِيْدٍ تُقَاتِلُوْنَهُمْ أَوْ يُسْلِمُوْنَ ۚ فَإِنْ تُطِيْعُوْا يُؤْتِكُمُ اللّٰهُ أَجْرًا حَسَنًا ۚ وَإِنْ تَتَوَلَّوْا كَمَا تَوَلَّيْتُمْ مِّنْ قَبْلُ يُعَذِّبْكُمْ عَذَابًا أَلِيْمًا ۝

لَيْسَ عَلَى الْأَعْمٰى حَرَجٌ وَّلَا عَلَى الْأَعْرَجِ حَرَجٌ وَّلَا عَلَى الْمَرِيْضِ حَرَجٌ ۚ وَمَنْ يُّطِعِ اللّٰهَ وَرَسُوْلَهٗ يُدْخِلْهُ جَنّٰتٍ تَجْرِيْ مِنْ تَحْتِهَا الْأَنْهٰرُ ۚ وَمَنْ يَّتَوَلَّ يُعَذِّبْهُ عَذَابًا أَلِيْمًا ۝

Allah was indeed well pleased with the believers when they swore allegiance to thee under the Tree, and He appreciated the surge of faith in their hearts, and

لَقَدْ رَضِيَ اللّٰهُ عَنِ الْمُؤْمِنِيْنَ إِذْ يُبَايِعُوْنَكَ تَحْتَ الشَّجَرَةِ فَعَلِمَ مَا فِيْ قُلُوْبِهِمْ فَأَنْزَلَ السَّكِيْنَةَ

He sent down tranquillity on them, and He rewarded them with a victory near at hand, and great spoils that they gathered. Allah is Mighty, Wise. Allah has promised you great spoils that you will gather, and He has bestowed on you these in advance; and He held back people's hands from you that all this may be a Sign for the believers, and that He may guide you along the right path. There is another victory that you have not yet achieved, but Allah has compassed it. Allah has full power to compass all that He wills. Had those who disbelieve fought you at Hudaibiyyah, they would certainly have turned their backs; and they would have found neither protector nor helper.

Such has ever been the way of Allah; and thou shalt never find any change in the way of Allah. He it is Who held back their hands from you and held back your hands from them in the Valley of Mecca, after He had granted you victory over them. Allah knew all that you did. It is these who disbelieved and hindered you from the Sacred Mosque, and prevented the animals which had been designated for sacrifice from reaching their place of sacrifice. Had it not been for believing men and women of whom you had no knowledge, who were then in Mecca, and whom you might have trampled down unknowingly and thus incurred blame on their account, Allah would have let you fight your way into Mecca; but He held you back that He might admit into His mercy whom He will. Had these believing men and women drawn apart from the rest, We would surely have chastised the disbelievers with a grievous chastisement.

Call to mind when the disbelievers whipped up in their minds a feeling of indignation resembling the indignation of pre-Islamic times, whereupon Allah sent down His tranquillity on His Messenger and on the believers, and established them firmly on the principle of righteousness; and they were indeed better entitled to it and more worthy of it. Allah knows all things well. (19—27)

Allah has in truth completely fulfilled for His Messenger the vision that He vouchsafed him, namely, that you will surely enter the Sacred Mosque, if Allah so wills, in security, with your heads shaven or close cropped and having no fear. He knew that which you knew not; and He has ordained for you besides that a victory near at hand. He it is Who has sent His Messenger with guidance and the Religion of Truth, that He may cause it to prevail over all other religions. Sufficient is Allah as a Witness. Muhammad is the Messenger of Allah. Those who are with him are unyielding towards the disbelievers, compassionate towards one another. Thou seest them single-minded in their devotion and obedience to Allah, seeking His grace and pleasure. Their identification mark is visible on their foreheads in the impression of prostrations. This is their description in the Torah. Their description in the Gospel is that of a seed that sends forth its sprout, then makes it strong; it then becomes thick and stands firm on its stem, delighting the sowers; that the disbelievers may be incensed thereat. Allah has promised forgiveness and a great reward to those of them who believe and work righteousness. (28—30)

الْجَاهِلِيَّةِ فَأَنْزَلَ اللّٰهُ سَكِينَتَهُ عَلٰى رَسُوْلِهٖ وَ عَلَى الْمُؤْمِنِيْنَ وَ اَلْزَمَهُمْ كَلِمَةَ التَّقْوٰى وَكَانُوْٓا اَحَقَّ بِهَا وَاَهْلَهَا ۚ وَكَانَ اللّٰهُ بِكُلِّ شَيْءٍ عَلِيْمًا ۝

لَقَدْ صَدَقَ اللّٰهُ رَسُوْلَهُ الرُّءْيَا بِالْحَقِّ ۚ لَتَدْخُلُنَّ الْمَسْجِدَ الْحَرَامَ اِنْ شَآءَ اللّٰهُ اٰمِنِيْنَ ۙ مُحَلِّقِيْنَ رُءُوْسَكُمْ وَمُقَصِّرِيْنَ ۙ لَا تَخَافُوْنَ ۚ فَعَلِمَ مَا لَمْ تَعْلَمُوْا فَجَعَلَ مِنْ دُوْنِ ذٰلِكَ فَتْحًا قَرِيْبًا ۝

هُوَ الَّذِيْٓ اَرْسَلَ رَسُوْلَهٗ بِالْهُدٰى وَدِيْنِ الْحَقِّ لِيُظْهِرَهٗ عَلَى الدِّيْنِ كُلِّهٖ ۚ وَكَفٰى بِاللّٰهِ شَهِيْدًا ۝

مُحَمَّدٌ رَّسُوْلُ اللّٰهِ ۚ وَالَّذِيْنَ مَعَهٗٓ اَشِدَّآءُ عَلَى الْكُفَّارِ رُحَمَآءُ بَيْنَهُمْ تَرٰىهُمْ رُكَّعًا سُجَّدًا يَّبْتَغُوْنَ فَضْلًا مِّنَ اللّٰهِ وَرِضْوَانًا ۙ سِيْمَاهُمْ فِيْ وُجُوْهِهِمْ مِّنْ اَثَرِ السُّجُوْدِ ۚ ذٰلِكَ مَثَلُهُمْ فِي التَّوْرٰىةِ ۛ وَمَثَلُهُمْ فِي الْاِنْجِيْلِ ۛ كَزَرْعٍ اَخْرَجَ شَطْـَٔهٗ فَاٰزَرَهٗ فَاسْتَغْلَظَ فَاسْتَوٰى عَلٰى سُوْقِهٖ يُعْجِبُ الزُّرَّاعَ لِيَغِيْظَ بِهِمُ الْكُفَّارَ ۗ وَعَدَ اللّٰهُ الَّذِيْنَ اٰمَنُوْا وَعَمِلُوا الصّٰلِحٰتِ مِنْهُمْ مَّغْفِرَةً وَّاَجْرًا عَظِيْمًا ۝

سُوْرَةُ الْحُجُرَاتِ مَدَنِيَّةٌ ‏(٤٩)

AL-HUJURAT
(Revealed after Hijra)

In the name of Allah, Most Gracious, Ever Merciful. (1)

بِسْمِ اللّٰهِ الرَّحْمٰنِ الرَّحِيْمِ ۝

يٰۤاَيُّهَا الَّذِيْنَ اٰمَنُوْا لَا تُقَدِّمُوْا بَيْنَ يَدَيِ اللّٰهِ وَرَسُوْلِهٖ وَاتَّقُوا اللّٰهَ ؕ اِنَّ اللّٰهَ سَمِيْعٌ عَلِيْمٌ ۝

يٰۤاَيُّهَا الَّذِيْنَ اٰمَنُوْا لَا تَرْفَعُوْۤا اَصْوَاتَكُمْ فَوْقَ صَوْتِ النَّبِيِّ وَلَا تَجْهَرُوْا لَهٗ بِالْقَوْلِ كَجَهْرِ بَعْضِكُمْ لِبَعْضٍ اَنْ تَحْبَطَ اَعْمَالُكُمْ وَاَنْتُمْ لَا تَشْعُرُوْنَ ۝

O ye who believe, be not forward in the presence of Allah and His Messenger, and be mindful of your duty to Allah. Allah is **All-Hearing, All-Knowing. O ye who** believe, do not raise your voices above the voice of the Prophet, and speak not aloud to him, as you speak aloud to one another, lest your works become vain without your knowing it. Those who lower their voices in the presence of the Messenger of Allah are the ones whose hearts Allah has disposed towards righteousness. For them is forgiveness and a great reward. Most of those who call out to thee from without thy apartments are lacking in understanding. Were they to wait until thou camest out to them, it would be the better for them. But Allah is Most Forgiving, Ever Merciful. (2—6)

اِنَّ الَّذِيْنَ يَغُضُّوْنَ اَصْوَاتَهُمْ عِنْدَ رَسُوْلِ اللّٰهِ اُولٰٓئِكَ الَّذِيْنَ امْتَحَنَ اللّٰهُ قُلُوْبَهُمْ لِلتَّقْوٰى ؕ لَهُمْ مَغْفِرَةٌ وَّاَجْرٌ عَظِيْمٌ ۝

اِنَّ الَّذِيْنَ يُنَادُوْنَكَ مِنْ وَّرَآءِ الْحُجُرَاتِ اَكْثَرُهُمْ لَا يَعْقِلُوْنَ ۝

وَلَوْ اَنَّهُمْ صَبَرُوْا حَتّٰى تَخْرُجَ اِلَيْهِمْ لَكَانَ خَيْرًا لَّهُمْ ؕ وَاللّٰهُ غَفُوْرٌ رَّحِيْمٌ ۝

O ye who believe, when an untrustworthy person comes to you with serious intelligence, do check up on it, lest you harm a people in ignorance, and then be remorseful over that which you have done. Remember, you have the Messenger of Allah among you. Were he to follow your wishes in most matters, you would be involved in trouble. But Allah has endeared faith to you and has made

يٰۤاَيُّهَا الَّذِيْنَ اٰمَنُوْۤا اِنْ جَآءَكُمْ فَاسِقٌۢ بِنَبَاٍ فَتَبَيَّنُوْۤا اَنْ تُصِيْبُوْا قَوْمًاۢ بِجَهَالَةٍ فَتُصْبِحُوْا عَلٰى مَا فَعَلْتُمْ نٰدِمِيْنَ ۝

وَاعْلَمُوْۤا اَنَّ فِيْكُمْ رَسُوْلَ اللّٰهِ ؕ لَوْ يُطِيْعُكُمْ فِيْ كَثِيْرٍ مِّنَ الْاَمْرِ لَعَنِتُّمْ وَلٰكِنَّ اللّٰهَ حَبَّبَ اِلَيْكُمُ

it look fair to your hearts and He has made you averse to disbelief, wickedness and disobedience. Such are those who follow the right course, through the grace and favour of Allah. Allah is All-Knowing, Wise. (7—9)

الْاِيْمَانَ وَ زَيَّنَهٗ فِيْ قُلُوْبِكُمْ وَكَرَّهَ اِلَيْكُمُ الْكُفْرَ وَالْفُسُوْقَ وَالْعِصْيَانَ اُولٰٓئِكَ هُمُ الرّٰشِدُوْنَۙ فَضْلًا مِّنَ اللّٰهِ وَنِعْمَةً وَاللّٰهُ عَلِيْمٌ حَكِيْمٌ۠ وَاِنْ طَآئِفَتٰنِ مِنَ الْمُؤْمِنِيْنَ اقْتَتَلُوْا فَاَصْلِحُوْا

If two parties of believers should fall out with each other and start fighting, make peace between them. If one of them should transgress against the other, fight the one that transgresses until it submits to the command of Allah. Then if it should so submit, make peace between them with equity, and act justly. Verily, Allah loves the just. All believers are brothers; so make peace between your brothers, and be mindful of your duty to Allah that you may be shown mercy. (10—11)

بَيْنَهُمَا ۚ فَاِنْ بَغَتْ اِحْدٰىهُمَا عَلَى الْاُخْرٰى فَقَاتِلُوا الَّتِيْ تَبْغِيْ حَتّٰى تَفِيْٓءَ اِلٰٓى اَمْرِ اللّٰهِ ۚ فَاِنْ فَآءَتْ فَاَصْلِحُوْا بَيْنَهُمَا بِالْعَدْلِ وَاَقْسِطُوْا ۚ اِنَّ اللّٰهَ يُحِبُّ الْمُقْسِطِيْنَ اِنَّمَا الْمُؤْمِنُوْنَ اِخْوَةٌ فَاَصْلِحُوْا بَيْنَ اَخَوَيْكُمْ وَاتَّقُوا اللّٰهَ لَعَلَّكُمْ تُرْحَمُوْنَ

O ye who believe, let no people deride another people, haply they may be better than themselves; nor let one group of women deride another, haply the last may be better than the first. Defame not your people, nor call them names. Ill indeed it is to earn an evil reputation after having believed. Those who do not repent are the wrongdoers. O ye who believe, eschew too much suspicion; for some suspicion may do much harm. Also spy not, nor backbite one another. Would any of you like to eat the flesh of his dead brother? Surely you would loathe such an imputation. Be mindful of your duty to Allah. Surely, Allah is Oft-Returning with Compassion, and is Ever Merciful. (12—13)

يٰٓاَيُّهَا الَّذِيْنَ اٰمَنُوْا لَا يَسْخَرْ قَوْمٌ مِّنْ قَوْمٍ عَسٰٓى اَنْ يَّكُوْنُوْا خَيْرًا مِّنْهُمْ وَلَا نِسَآءٌ مِّنْ نِّسَآءٍ عَسٰٓى اَنْ يَّكُنَّ خَيْرًا مِّنْهُنَّ ۚ وَلَا تَلْمِزُوْٓا اَنْفُسَكُمْ وَلَا تَنَابَزُوْا بِالْاَلْقَابِ ۚ بِئْسَ الْاِسْمُ الْفُسُوْقُ بَعْدَ الْاِيْمَانِ ۚ وَمَنْ لَّمْ يَتُبْ فَاُولٰٓئِكَ هُمُ الظّٰلِمُوْنَ يٰٓاَيُّهَا الَّذِيْنَ اٰمَنُوا اجْتَنِبُوْا كَثِيْرًا مِّنَ الظَّنِّ ۖ اِنَّ بَعْضَ الظَّنِّ اِثْمٌ وَّلَا تَجَسَّسُوْا وَلَا يَغْتَبْ بَّعْضُكُمْ بَعْضًا ۚ اَيُحِبُّ اَحَدُكُمْ اَنْ يَّأْكُلَ لَحْمَ اَخِيْهِ مَيْتًا فَكَرِهْتُمُوْهُ ۚ وَاتَّقُوا اللّٰهَ ۚ اِنَّ اللّٰهَ تَوَّابٌ رَّحِيْمٌ

O mankind, We have created you from male and female; and We have divided you into tribes and sub-tribes for greater facility of intercourse.

يٰٓاَيُّهَا النَّاسُ اِنَّا خَلَقْنٰكُمْ مِّنْ ذَكَرٍ وَّاُنْثٰى وَجَعَلْنٰكُمْ شُعُوْبًا وَّقَبَآئِلَ لِتَعَارَفُوْا ۚ اِنَّ

Verily, the most honoured among you in the sight of Allah is he who is the most righteous among you. Surely, Allah is All-Knowing, All-Aware. (14)

اَكْرَمَكُمْ عِنْدَ اللهِ اَتْقَكُمْ اِنَّ اللهَ عَلِيْمٌ خَبِيْرٌ ۝

The Arabs of the desert say: We have believed. Say to them: You have not believed yet, but say rather: We have submitted; for faith has not yet entered into your hearts. But if you will obey Allah and His Messenger, He will not detract anything from your good deeds. Allah is Most Forgiving, Ever Merciful.

قَالَتِ الْاَعْرَابُ اٰمَنَّا ۚ قُلْ لَّمْ تُؤْمِنُوْا وَلٰكِنْ قُوْلُوْۤا اَسْلَمْنَا وَلَمَّا يَدْخُلِ الْاِيْمَانُ فِيْ قُلُوْبِكُمْ ۚ وَاِنْ تُطِيْعُوا اللهَ وَرَسُوْلَهٗ لَا يَلِتْكُمْ مِّنْ اَعْمَالِكُمْ شَيْئًا ۚ اِنَّ اللهَ غَفُوْرٌ رَّحِيْمٌ ۝

The believers are only those who have faith in Allah and His Messenger and then doubt not, but strive with their belongings and their persons in the cause of Allah. It is they who are truthful. Say to them: Will you acquaint Allah with your faith, while Allah knows whatever is in the heavens and whatever is in the earth, and Allah knows all things well. They behave as if they have done thee a favour by embracing Islam. Say to them: Deem not your embracing Islam a favour done to me. On the contrary, Allah has done you a favour in that He has guided you to the faith, if you are truthful. Allah knows the secrets of the heavens and the earth. Allah sees all that you do. (15—19)

اِنَّمَا الْمُؤْمِنُوْنَ الَّذِيْنَ اٰمَنُوْا بِاللهِ وَرَسُوْلِهٖ ثُمَّ لَمْ يَرْتَابُوْا وَجَاهَدُوْا بِاَمْوَالِهِمْ وَاَنْفُسِهِمْ فِيْ سَبِيْلِ اللهِ ۚ اُولٰۤئِكَ هُمُ الصّٰدِقُوْنَ ۝

قُلْ اَتُعَلِّمُوْنَ اللهَ بِدِيْنِكُمْ ۚ وَاللهُ يَعْلَمُ مَا فِي السَّمٰوٰتِ وَمَا فِي الْاَرْضِ ۚ وَاللهُ بِكُلِّ شَيْءٍ عَلِيْمٌ ۝

يَمُنُّوْنَ عَلَيْكَ اَنْ اَسْلَمُوْا ۖ قُلْ لَّا تَمُنُّوْا عَلَيَّ اِسْلَامَكُمْ ۚ بَلِ اللهُ يَمُنُّ عَلَيْكُمْ اَنْ هَدٰىكُمْ لِلْاِيْمَانِ اِنْ كُنْتُمْ صٰدِقِيْنَ ۝

اِنَّ اللهَ يَعْلَمُ غَيْبَ السَّمٰوٰتِ وَالْاَرْضِ ۚ وَاللهُ بَصِيْرٌ بِمَا تَعْمَلُوْنَ ۞

QĀF

(Revealed before Hijra)

In the name of Allah, Most Gracious, Ever Merciful. (1)

THE LORD OF POWER

We cite the Glorious Quran in support of the truth of this Sura. They wonder that there should come to them a Warner from among themselves. The disbelievers exclaim: This is a thing strange. Is it that when we are dead and have become dust, we shall be raised up again? That is a return which passes understanding. We know well what part of them the earth consumes, and with Us is a Book that preserves everything. They rejected the truth when it came to them, so they are in a state of confusion. Have they not looked at the sky above them, and considered how We have made it and adorned it, and that there are no flaws in it?

We have spread out the earth, and placed therein firm mountains; and We have caused to grow therein all kinds of beautiful species in pairs; a matter for contemplation and a source of admonition for every servant that turns to Us. We send down from the sky water which is full of blessings, and We produce therewith gardens and grain harvests, and tall palmtrees with spathes piled one above the other, as a provision for Our servants; and We quicken thereby a dead land. Even so shall be the Resurrection.

بِسْمِ اللهِ الرَّحْمٰنِ الرَّحِيْمِ ۞

قۤ ۚ وَالْقُرْاٰنِ الْمَجِيْدِ ۞

بَلْ عَجِبُوْۤا اَنْ جَآءَهُمْ مُّنْذِرٌ مِّنْهُمْ فَقَالَ الْكٰفِرُوْنَ هٰذَا شَیْءٌ عَجِیْبٌ ۞

ءَاِذَا مِتْنَا وَكُنَّا تُرَابًا ۚ ذٰلِكَ رَجْعٌۢ بَعِیْدٌ ۞

قَدْ عَلِمْنَا مَا تَنْقُصُ الْاَرْضُ مِنْهُمْ ۚ وَعِنْدَنَا كِتٰبٌ حَفِیْظٌ ۞

بَلْ كَذَّبُوْا بِالْحَقِّ لَمَّا جَآءَهُمْ فَهُمْ فِیْۤ اَمْرٍ مَّرِیْجٍ ۞

اَفَلَمْ یَنْظُرُوْۤا اِلَی السَّمَآءِ فَوْقَهُمْ كَیْفَ بَنَیْنٰهَا وَزَیَّنّٰهَا وَمَا لَهَا مِنْ فُرُوْجٍ ۞

وَالْاَرْضَ مَدَدْنٰهَا وَاَلْقَیْنَا فِیْهَا رَوَاسِیَ وَاَنْۢبَتْنَا فِیْهَا مِنْ كُلِّ زَوْجٍۭ بَهِیْجٍ ۞

تَبْصِرَةً وَّ ذِكْرٰی لِكُلِّ عَبْدٍ مُّنِیْبٍ ۞

وَنَزَّلْنَا مِنَ السَّمَآءِ مَآءً مُّبٰرَكًا فَاَنْۢبَتْنَا بِهٖ جَنّٰتٍ وَّحَبَّ الْحَصِیْدِ ۞

وَالنَّخْلَ بٰسِقٰتٍ لَّهَا طَلْعٌ نَّضِیْدٌ ۞

رِّزْقًا لِّلْعِبَادِ ۙ وَاَحْیَیْنَا بِهٖ بَلْدَةً مَّیْتًا ۚ كَذٰلِكَ الْخُرُوْجُ ۞

The people of Noah rejected the Messengers before them and the People of the Well and the tribes of 'Ad and Thamud, and Pharaoh, and the people of Lot and the Dwellers of the Wood, and the people of Tubba. All of them rejected the Messengers, so that My promise of chastisement was fulfilled. Did We then become weary in consequence of the first creation? Nay, but they are in confusion in the matter of the new creation. (2—16)

كَذَّبَتْ قَبْلَهُمْ قَوْمُ نُوحٍ وَّأَصْحَبُ الرَّسِّ وَثَمُوْدُ ۝

وَّعَادٌ وَّفِرْعَوْنُ وَإِخْوَانُ لُوْطٍ ۝

وَّأَصْحَبُ الْأَيْكَةِ وَقَوْمُ تُبَّعٍ كُلٌّ كَذَّبَ الرُّسُلَ فَحَقَّ وَعِيْدِ ۝

أَفَعَيِيْنَا بِالْخَلْقِ الْأَوَّلِ بَلْ هُمْ فِىْ لَبْسٍ مِّنْ خَلْقٍ جَدِيْدٍ ۝

Assuredly, We have created man and We know well what kind of doubt his mind throws up. We are closer to him than his jugular vein. There are two, one sitting on his right and the other on his left, who learn everything concerning him and preserve it. He utters not a word, but there is by him an alert watcher who takes care to preserve it. The stupor of death shall surely approach and he will be told: This is what thou wast seeking to avert. The trumpet shall be blown. This is the Day of the Promised chastisement.

وَلَقَدْ خَلَقْنَا الْإِنْسَانَ وَنَعْلَمُ مَا تُوَسْوِسُ بِهٖ نَفْسُهٗ وَنَحْنُ أَقْرَبُ إِلَيْهِ مِنْ حَبْلِ الْوَرِيْدِ ۝

إِذْ يَتَلَقَّى الْمُتَلَقِّيَانِ عَنِ الْيَمِيْنِ وَعَنِ الشِّمَالِ قَعِيْدٌ ۝

مَا يَلْفِظُ مِنْ قَوْلٍ إِلَّا لَدَيْهِ رَقِيْبٌ عَتِيْدٌ ۝

وَجَآءَتْ سَكْرَةُ الْمَوْتِ بِالْحَقِّ ذٰلِكَ مَا كُنْتَ مِنْهُ تَحِيْدُ ۝

وَنُفِخَ فِى الصُّوْرِ ذٰلِكَ يَوْمُ الْوَعِيْدِ ۝

وَجَآءَتْ كُلُّ نَفْسٍ مَّعَهَا سَآئِقٌ وَّشَهِيْدٌ ۝

Every one shall come forth, accompanied by a driver and a witness. He will be told: Thou wast heedless of this Day; now have We removed thy veil from thee, and today thy vision is sharpened. His companion will say: I have here his record ready; and the verdict will be: Cast ye twain into hell every ungrateful enemy of truth, hinderer of good, transgressor, doubter, who set up other gods beside Allah. So cast him into grievous torment.

لَقَدْ كُنْتَ فِىْ غَفْلَةٍ مِّنْ هٰذَا فَكَشَفْنَا عَنْكَ غِطَآءَكَ فَبَصَرُكَ الْيَوْمَ حَدِيْدٌ ۝

وَقَالَ قَرِيْنُهٗ هٰذَا مَا لَدَىَّ عَتِيْدٌ ۝

أَلْقِيَا فِىْ جَهَنَّمَ كُلَّ كَفَّارٍ عَنِيْدٍ ۝

مَّنَّاعٍ لِّلْخَيْرِ مُعْتَدٍ مُّرِيْبٍ ۝

إِلَّذِىْ جَعَلَ مَعَ اللهِ إِلٰهًا اٰخَرَ فَأَلْقِيَاهُ فِى الْعَذَابِ الشَّدِيْدِ ۝

His companion will say: Lord, I did not incite him to rebel; he was far gone in error on his own. Allah will rebuke them: Do not indulge in recrimination in My presence. I had forewarned you of the chastisement. No one can pervert anything presented before Me; and I am not in the least unjust to My servants. (17—30)

On that day We will ask hell: Art thou filled up? and it will answer: Is there more? And heaven will be brought close to the righteous. They will be told: This is that which you were promised, for everyone who turned to Allah and was watchful of his actions; who feared the Gracious One in solitude and approached Him with a penitent heart. They will be told: Enter therein in peace. This is the Day of Eternity. They will have therein whatever they desire, and with Us is more. (31—36)

How many a generation have We destroyed before them, who were mightier than these in power! They burrowed under their cities to save themselves, but was there a place of refuge? Therein, verily, is a reminder for him who has a comprehending heart, or who gives ear and observes. (37—38)

We created the heavens and the earth and all that is between them in six periods, and We suffered no weariness. So endure with patience that which they say, and glorify thy Lord with His praise, before the rising of the sun and before its setting, and glorify Him during the night, and after each Prayer. (39—41)

Hearken! The day when the caller will call from a place nearby, the day when they will hear the inevitable blast; that will be the day of coming forth. It is We who give life and cause death, and to Us is the return. On the day when the earth will cleave from above them while they rush forth; that will be a raising up quite easy for Us. We know well what they say, and thou hast not been appointed a despot over them. So admonish, by means of the Quran, him who fears My warning. (42—46)

يَوْمَ يَسْمَعُوْنَ الصَّيْحَةَ بِالْحَقِّ ذٰلِكَ يَوْمُ الْخُرُوْجِ ۞

اِنَّا نَحْنُ نُحْيِ وَنُمِيْتُ وَاِلَيْنَا الْمَصِيْرُ ۞

يَوْمَ تَشَقَّقُ الْاَرْضُ عَنْهُمْ سِرَاعًا ذٰلِكَ حَشْرٌ عَلَيْنَا يَسِيْرٌ ۞

نَحْنُ اَعْلَمُ بِمَا يَقُوْلُوْنَ وَمَآ اَنْتَ عَلَيْهِمْ بِجَبَّارٍ

فَذَكِّرْ بِالْقُرْاٰنِ مَنْ يَّخَافُ وَعِيْدِ ۞

In the name of Allah, Most Gracious, Ever Merciful. (1)

بِسْمِ اللهِ الرَّحْمٰنِ الرَّحِيْمِ ۞

وَالذّٰرِيٰتِ ذَرْوًا ۞

فَالْحٰمِلٰتِ وِقْرًا ۞

فَالْجٰرِيٰتِ يُسْرًا ۞

فَالْمُقَسِّمٰتِ اَمْرًا ۞

We call to witness the winds that waft the vapours, and carry the load of moisture, and blow gently and distribute the command of Allah in the shape of rain, that that which you are promised is true, and the judgment will surely come to pass.

اِنَّمَا تُوْعَدُوْنَ لَصَادِقٌ ۞

وَاِنَّ الدِّيْنَ لَوَاقِعٌ ۞

وَالسَّمَآءِ ذَاتِ الْحُبُكِ ۞

اِنَّكُمْ لَفِيْ قَوْلٍ مُّخْتَلِفٍ ۞

يُّؤْفَكُ عَنْهُ مَنْ اُفِكَ ۞

قُتِلَ الْخَرّٰصُوْنَ ۞

We call to witness heaven which is traversed by diverse tracks, you are caught in contradictory assertions, through which he is turned away from the truth who is destined to be so turned away. Ruined are the liars who flounder about in ignorance.

الَّذِيْنَ هُمْ فِيْ غَمْرَةٍ سَاهُوْنَ ۞

They ask: When will the Day of Judgment be? It will be on the day when they are afflicted with the Fire, and are told: Suffer your torment. This is what you sought to hasten. The righteous will be in the midst of gardens and springs, receiving that which their Lord will bestow on them. Before this they carried out their obligations to the full. They slept but little at night and sought forgiveness at dawn; and in their wealth was a share for those who asked for help and for those who could not. In the earth are Signs for those who believe firmly, and also in your own selves. Will you not then see? In heaven is your sustenance, and also that which you are promised. By the Lord of the heaven and the earth, the Quran is certainly the truth even as it is true that you speak. (2 – 24)

يَسْـَٔلُوْنَ اَيَّانَ يَوْمُ الدِّيْنِ ۟ۚ

يَوْمَ هُمْ عَلَى النَّارِ يُفْتَنُوْنَ ۟

ذُوْقُوْا فِتْنَتَكُمْ ۖ هٰذَا الَّذِيْ كُنْتُمْ بِهٖ تَسْتَعْجِلُوْنَ ۟

اِنَّ الْمُتَّقِيْنَ فِيْ جَنّٰتٍ وَّعُيُوْنٍ ۟ۙ

اٰخِذِيْنَ مَاۤ اٰتٰىهُمْ رَبُّهُمْ ۖ اِنَّهُمْ كَانُوْا قَبْلَ ذٰلِكَ مُحْسِنِيْنَ ۟ؕ

كَانُوْا قَلِيْلًا مِّنَ الَّيْلِ مَا يَهْجَعُوْنَ ۟

وَبِالْاَسْحَارِ هُمْ يَسْتَغْفِرُوْنَ ۟

وَفِيْۤ اَمْوَالِهِمْ حَقٌّ لِّلسَّآئِلِ وَالْمَحْرُوْمِ ۟

وَفِي الْاَرْضِ اٰيٰتٌ لِّلْمُوْقِنِيْنَ ۟ۙ

وَفِيْۤ اَنْفُسِكُمْ ۚ اَفَلَا تُبْصِرُوْنَ ۟

وَفِي السَّمَآءِ رِزْقُكُمْ وَمَا تُوْعَدُوْنَ ۟

فَوَرَبِّ السَّمَآءِ وَالْاَرْضِ اِنَّهٗ لَحَقٌّ مِّثْلَ مَاۤ اَنَّكُمْ تَنْطِقُوْنَ ۟

هَلْ اَتٰىكَ حَدِيْثُ ضَيْفِ اِبْرٰهِيْمَ الْمُكْرَمِيْنَ ۟ۘ

اِذْ دَخَلُوْا عَلَيْهِ فَقَالُوْا سَلٰمًا ۖ قَالَ سَلٰمٌ ۚ قَوْمٌ مُّنْكَرُوْنَ ۟

فَرَاغَ اِلٰۤى اَهْلِهٖ فَجَآءَ بِعِجْلٍ سَمِيْنٍ ۟ۙ

فَقَرَّبَهٗۤ اِلَيْهِمْ قَالَ اَلَا تَاْكُلُوْنَ ۟

فَاَوْجَسَ مِنْهُمْ خِيْفَةً ۖ قَالُوْا لَا تَخَفْ ۖ وَبَشَّرُوْهُ بِغُلٰمٍ عَلِيْمٍ ۟

فَاَقْبَلَتِ امْرَاَتُهٗ فِيْ صَرَّةٍ فَصَكَّتْ وَجْهَهَا وَ

Has an account of the honoured guests of Abraham reached thee? When they came to him they said: Peace on you. He returned their salutation: On you be peace; and murmured to himself: They seem to be strangers. Then he went quietly to his household and brought a fat roasted calf, and placed it before them and said: Will you not eat? He conceived a fear of them. They reassured him: Fear not; and gave him glad tidings of the birth of a wise son. Then his wife came forward in agitation and smote her face and said: A barren old woman!

They said: Even so has thy Lord said. Surely, He is the Wise, the All-Knowing. Abraham asked them: Now what is your errand, ye messengers? They answered: We have been sent to a sinful people, that we may send down upon them stones of clay, which are marked by thy Lord for the punishment of those guilty of excesses. We brought forth therefrom all those who were believers, and We found therein only one household of those obedient to Us. We left therein a Sign for those who fear the painful chastisement; and also in Moses, when We sent him to Pharaoh with clear authority; but he turned away to his idols, and said: Moses is a sorcerer or a madman. So We seized him and his hosts and threw them into the sea; and he was the one to blame.

We also left a Sign in the tribe of 'Ad, when We sent against them a blasting wind, which destroyed everything over which it passed and left it like a rotten bone. Also in the tribe of Thamud, when it was said to them: Enjoy yourselves for a while. But they rebelled against the command of their Lord; so a torment seized them while they gazed. They were not able to rise up to save themselves, nor could they obtain help. We had destroyed the people of Noah before them; they were a disobedient people. (25—47)

525

We have built the heavens as a manifestation of several of Our attributes, and surely We go on expanding the universe. We have spread out the earth like a bed, and how excellently do We spread out. Of everything We have created pairs that you may reflect. Flee ye, therefore, unto Allah; surely, I am a plain Warner unto you from Him. Do not set up any other god along with Allah. Surely, I am a plain Warner unto you from Him. Thus there came no Messenger to those before them, but they said: He is a sorcerer or a madman. Have they left this as a legacy to one another? In truth they were all a rebellious people. So turn away from them; there will be no blame upon thee. But keep on exhorting; for exhortation benefits the believers. (48—56)

وَالسَّمَآءَ بَنَيْنٰهَا بِاَيْدٍ وَّاِنَّا لَمُوْسِعُوْنَ ۝

وَالْاَرْضَ فَرَشْنٰهَا فَنِعْمَ الْمٰهِدُوْنَ ۝

وَمِنْ كُلِّ شَيْءٍ خَلَقْنَا زَوْجَيْنِ لَعَلَّكُمْ تَذَكَّرُوْنَ ۝

فَفِرُّوْۤا اِلَى اللّٰهِ اِنِّيْ لَكُمْ مِّنْهُ نَذِيْرٌ مُّبِيْنٌ ۝

وَلَا تَجْعَلُوْا مَعَ اللّٰهِ اِلٰهًا اٰخَرَ اِنِّيْ لَكُمْ مِّنْهُ نَذِيْرٌ مُّبِيْنٌ ۝

كَذٰلِكَ مَاۤ اَتَى الَّذِيْنَ مِنْ قَبْلِهِمْ مِّنْ رَّسُوْلٍ اِلَّا قَالُوْا سَاحِرٌ اَوْ مَجْنُوْنٌ ۝

اَتَوَاصَوْا بِهٖ بَلْ هُمْ قَوْمٌ طَاغُوْنَ ۝

فَتَوَلَّ عَنْهُمْ فَمَاۤ اَنْتَ بِمَلُوْمٍ ۝

وَّذَكِّرْ فَاِنَّ الذِّكْرٰى تَنْفَعُ الْمُؤْمِنِيْنَ ۝

I have created men, high and low, that they may worship Me. I desire no support from them, nor do I desire that they should feed Me. Surely, it is Allah Who is the Great Sustainer, the Lord of Power, the Strong. The lot of the wrongdoers is like that of their fellows who preceded them; so let them not ask Me to hasten on the punishment. Woe, then, to those who disbelieve, because of that day of theirs which they have been promised. (57—61)

وَمَا خَلَقْتُ الْجِنَّ وَالْاِنْسَ اِلَّا لِيَعْبُدُوْنِ ۝

مَاۤ اُرِيْدُ مِنْهُمْ مِّنْ رِّزْقٍ وَّمَاۤ اُرِيْدُ اَنْ يُّطْعِمُوْنِ ۝

اِنَّ اللّٰهَ هُوَ الرَّزَّاقُ ذُو الْقُوَّةِ الْمَتِيْنُ ۝

فَاِنَّ لِلَّذِيْنَ ظَلَمُوْا ذَنُوْبًا مِّثْلَ ذَنُوْبِ اَصْحٰبِهِمْ فَلَا يَسْتَعْجِلُوْنِ ۝

فَوَيْلٌ لِّلَّذِيْنَ كَفَرُوْا مِنْ يَّوْمِهِمُ الَّذِيْ يُوْعَدُوْنَ ۝

AL-ṬŪR
(Revealed before Hijra)

بِسْمِ اللهِ الرَّحْمٰنِ الرَّحِيْمِ ۝

In the name of Allah, Most Gracious, Ever Merciful. (1)

وَالطُّوْرِ ۝

وَكِتٰبٍ مَّسْطُوْرٍ ۝

فِيْ رَقٍّ مَّنْشُوْرٍ ۝

وَّالْبَيْتِ الْمَعْمُوْرِ ۝

وَّالسَّقْفِ الْمَرْفُوْعِ ۝

وَّالْبَحْرِ الْمَسْجُوْرِ ۝

We cite as evidence the Mount, that is, the revelation sent down to Moses; and this Book inscribed on unfolded parchment; and the frequently visited House; and the exalted roof; and the swollen sea; that the punishment of thy Lord will certainly come to pass; there is none that can avert it. (2—9)

اِنَّ عَذَابَ رَبِّكَ لَوَاقِعٌ ۝

مَّا لَهٗ مِنْ دَافِعٍ ۝

يَّوْمَ تَمُوْرُ السَّمَآءُ مَوْرًا ۝

وَّتَسِيْرُ الْجِبَالُ سَيْرًا ۝

فَوَيْلٌ يَّوْمَئِذٍ لِّلْمُكَذِّبِيْنَ ۝

الَّذِيْنَ هُمْ فِيْ خَوْضٍ يَّلْعَبُوْنَ ۝

يَوْمَ يُدَعُّوْنَ اِلٰى نَارِ جَهَنَّمَ دَعًّا ۝

هٰذِهِ النَّارُ الَّتِيْ كُنْتُمْ بِهَا تُكَذِّبُوْنَ ۝

On the day when the heaven will be greatly agitated and the mountains will move fast, woe on that day unto those who reject the truth, who take pleasure in vain discourse. The day on which they shall be thrust into the fire of hell with a violent thrust, and they will be told: This is the Fire which you denied. Is this magic, or do you still not see? Now enter it, and whether you endure it with fortitude or not, it will be the same for you. You are requited with that which you practised. The righteous will be in Gardens and bliss,

اَفَسِحْرٌ هٰذَاۤ اَمْ اَنْتُمْ لَا تُبْصِرُوْنَ ۝

اِصْلَوْهَا فَاصْبِرُوْاۤ اَوْ لَا تَصْبِرُوْا سَوَآءٌ عَلَيْكُمْ اِنَّمَا تُجْزَوْنَ مَا كُنْتُمْ تَعْمَلُوْنَ ۝

اِنَّ الْمُتَّقِيْنَ فِيْ جَنّٰتٍ وَّنَعِيْمٍ ۝

happy with that which their Lord has bestowed on them; and their Lord will save them from the torment of the Fire. They will be told: Eat and drink joyfully, because of that which you did, reclining on couches arranged in rows. We shall bestow upon them as companions maidens with large beautiful eyes. In the case of those believers whose children follow in their footsteps in the matter of faith, We shall join their children with them, and We shall not in any way reduce the reward of their works. Every person will be held to that which he did. We shall bestow upon them an abundance of fruits and meat, such as they will desire. Therein will they present one to another cups containing a drink that induces neither levity nor sin; and they will be waited upon by their children, pure as carefully guarded pearls. They will turn one to another asking questions. They will say: Before this among our people, we were apprehensive; but Allah has been gracious unto us, and has saved us from the torment of the burning blast. We used to pray to Him aforetime. Surely, He is the Beneficent, the Ever Merciful. (10—29)

Then continue to admonish them. By the grace of thy Lord, thou art neither a soothsayer, nor a madman. Do they assert: He is but a poet; we are waiting for his adverse fortune to manifest itself? Tell them: Wait on. I too am with you, waiting! Are they so directed by their understanding, or, are they a rebellious people? Or, do they say: He has fabricated it? Indeed, they do not believe in revelation.

فَكِهِيْنَ بِمَاۤ اٰتٰىهُمْ رَبُّهُمْ ۚ وَوَقٰىهُمْ رَبُّهُمْ عَذَابَ الْجَحِيْمِ ۟ۙ ۱۹

كُلُوْا وَ اشْرَبُوْا هَنِيْٓئًۢا بِمَا كُنْتُمْ تَعْمَلُوْنَ ۟ۙ ۲۰

مُتَّكِـِٕيْنَ عَلٰى سُرُرٍ مَّصْفُوْفَةٍ ۚ وَزَوَّجْنٰهُمْ بِحُوْرٍ عِيْنٍ ۟ ۲۱

وَالَّذِيْنَ اٰمَنُوْا وَاتَّبَعَتْهُمْ ذُرِّيَّتُهُمْ بِاِيْمَانٍ اَلْحَقْنَا بِهِمْ ذُرِّيَّتَهُمْ وَمَاۤ اَلَتْنٰهُمْ مِّنْ عَمَلِهِمْ مِّنْ شَيْءٍ ۚ كُلُّ امْرِئٍۢ بِمَا كَسَبَ رَهِيْنٌ ۟ ۲۲

وَاَمْدَدْنٰهُمْ بِفَاكِهَةٍ وَّلَحْمٍ مِّمَّا يَشْتَهُوْنَ ۟ ۲۳

يَتَنَازَعُوْنَ فِيْهَا كَاْسًا لَّا لَغْوٌ فِيْهَا وَلَا تَاْثِيْمٌ ۟ ۲۴

وَيَطُوْفُ عَلَيْهِمْ غِلْمَانٌ لَّهُمْ كَاَنَّهُمْ لُؤْلُؤٌ مَّكْنُوْنٌ ۟ ۲۵

وَاَقْبَلَ بَعْضُهُمْ عَلٰى بَعْضٍ يَّتَسَآءَلُوْنَ ۟ ۲۶

قَالُوْۤا اِنَّا كُنَّا قَبْلُ فِيْۤ اَهْلِنَا مُشْفِقِيْنَ ۟ ۲۷

فَمَنَّ اللّٰهُ عَلَيْنَا وَوَقٰىنَا عَذَابَ السَّمُوْمِ ۟ ۲۸

اِنَّا كُنَّا مِنْ قَبْلُ نَدْعُوْهُ ۚ اِنَّهٗ هُوَ الْبَرُّ الرَّحِيْمُ ۟ؔ ۲۹

فَذَكِّرْ فَمَاۤ اَنْتَ بِنِعْمَتِ رَبِّكَ بِكَاهِنٍ وَّلَا مَجْنُوْنٍ ۟ؕ ۳۰

اَمْ يَقُوْلُوْنَ شَاعِرٌ نَّتَرَبَّصُ بِهٖ رَيْبَ الْمَنُوْنِ ۟ ۳۱

قُلْ تَرَبَّصُوْا فَاِنِّيْ مَعَكُمْ مِّنَ الْمُتَرَبِّصِيْنَ ۟ؕ ۳۲

اَمْ تَاْمُرُهُمْ اَحْلَامُهُمْ بِهٰذَاۤ اَمْ هُمْ قَوْمٌ طَاغُوْنَ ۟ۚ ۳۳

اَمْ يَقُوْلُوْنَ تَقَوَّلَهٗ ۚ بَلْ لَّا يُؤْمِنُوْنَ ۟ؕ ۳۴

If they are truthful, let them produce a discourse like unto this. Have they been created from nothing, or are they their own creators? Have they created the heavens and the earth? In truth they put no faith in anything. Do they own the treasures of thy Lord, or are they the guardians thereof? Have they a ladder by means of which they can surprise the secrets of heaven? If so, let their listener produce a manifest authority. Has He only daughters, while you have sons? Dost thou demand a recompense from them, so that they are weighed down by the impost? Do they possess knowledge of the unseen, which they write down? Do they contemplate contriving a stratagem against thee? But it is the disbelievers that will be the victims of the stratagem. Have they a god other than Allah? Exalted is Allah above all that which they associate with Him. If they should see a fragment of the sky descending, they would say: Piled up clouds! Then leave them alone until they encounter the day on which they will be stunned with terror; the day on which no stratagem shall avail them aught, nor shall they be helped. Verily, for the wrongdoers there is a punishment besides that; but most of them know not.

So adhere steadfastly to the command of thy Lord, for thou art under Our protection; and glorify thy Lord with His praise when thou art standing in Prayer, and during part of the night and at the time of the setting of the stars. (30—50)

فَلْيَأْتُوْا بِحَدِيثٍ مِّثْلِهٖٓ اِنْ كَانُوْا صٰدِقِيْنَ ۝

اَمْ خُلِقُوْا مِنْ غَيْرِ شَيْءٍ اَمْ هُمُ الْخٰلِقُوْنَ ۝

اَمْ خَلَقُوا السَّمٰوٰتِ وَالْاَرْضَ بَلْ لَّا يُوْقِنُوْنَ ۝

اَمْ عِنْدَهُمْ خَزَآئِنُ رَبِّكَ اَمْ هُمُ الْمُصَۜيْطِرُوْنَ ۝

اَمْ لَهُمْ سُلَّمٌ يَّسْتَمِعُوْنَ فِيْهِ فَلْيَأْتِ مُسْتَمِعُهُمْ بِسُلْطٰنٍ مُّبِيْنٍ ۝

اَمْ لَهُ الْبَنٰتُ وَلَكُمُ الْبَنُوْنَ ۝

اَمْ تَسْئَلُهُمْ اَجْرًا فَهُمْ مِّنْ مَّغْرَمٍ مُّثْقَلُوْنَ ۝

اَمْ عِنْدَهُمُ الْغَيْبُ فَهُمْ يَكْتُبُوْنَ ۝

اَمْ يُرِيْدُوْنَ كَيْدًا فَالَّذِيْنَ كَفَرُوْا هُمُ الْمَكِيْدُوْنَ ۝

اَمْ لَهُمْ اِلٰهٌ غَيْرُ اللّٰهِ سُبْحٰنَ اللّٰهِ عَمَّا يُشْرِكُوْنَ ۝

وَاِنْ يَّرَوْا كِسْفًا مِّنَ السَّمَآءِ سَاقِطًا يَّقُوْلُوْا سَحَابٌ مَّرْكُوْمٌ ۝

فَذَرْهُمْ حَتّٰى يُلٰقُوْا يَوْمَهُمُ الَّذِيْ فِيْهِ يُصْعَقُوْنَ ۝

يَوْمَ لَا يُغْنِيْ عَنْهُمْ كَيْدُهُمْ شَيْئًا وَّلَا هُمْ يُنْصَرُوْنَ ۝

وَاِنَّ لِلَّذِيْنَ ظَلَمُوْا عَذَابًا دُوْنَ ذٰلِكَ وَلٰكِنَّ اَكْثَرَهُمْ لَا يَعْلَمُوْنَ ۝

وَاصْبِرْ لِحُكْمِ رَبِّكَ فَاِنَّكَ بِاَعْيُنِنَا وَسَبِّحْ بِحَمْدِ رَبِّكَ حِيْنَ تَقُوْمُ ۝

وَمِنَ الَّيْلِ فَسَبِّحْهُ وَاِدْبَارَ النُّجُوْمِ ۝

AL-NAJM
(Revealed before Hijra)

In the name of Allah, Most Gracious, Ever Merciful. (1)

بِسْمِ اللهِ الرَّحْمٰنِ الرَّحِيْمِ ۝

وَالنَّجْمِ اِذَا هَوٰى ۝

مَا ضَلَّ صَاحِبُكُمْ وَمَا غَوٰى ۝

وَمَا يَنْطِقُ عَنِ الْهَوٰى ۝

اِنْ هُوَ اِلَّا وَحْيٌ يُّوْحٰى ۝

عَلَّمَهٗ شَدِيْدُ الْقُوٰى ۝

ذُوْ مِرَّةٍ فَاسْتَوٰى ۝

وَهُوَ بِالْاُفُقِ الْاَعْلٰى ۝

ثُمَّ دَنَا فَتَدَلّٰى ۝

We cite the Pleidas as evidence, when it will draw close, that your companion, Muhammad, has neither erred, nor has he gone astray. He does not speak out of his own desire; the Quran is pure revelation sent to him; taught him by the Lord of mighty powers, Whose powers are manifested repeatedly and Who has established Himself firmly on the Throne.

فَكَانَ قَابَ قَوْسَيْنِ اَوْ اَدْنٰى ۝

فَاَوْحٰى اِلٰى عَبْدِهٖ مَا اَوْحٰى ۝

مَا كَذَبَ الْفُؤَادُ مَا رَاٰى ۝

اَفَتُمٰرُوْنَهٗ عَلٰى مَا يَرٰى ۝

وَلَقَدْ رَاٰهُ نَزْلَةً اُخْرٰى ۝

This manifestation is now visible on the spiritual horizons. Muhammad approached closer to Allah, and Allah leaned down towards him, so that it became as it were a case of one chord serving two bows or closer still. Then He revealed to His servant that which He had willed to reveal.

عِنْدَ سِدْرَةِ الْمُنْتَهٰى ۝

عِنْدَهَا جَنَّةُ الْمَأْوٰى ۝

اِذْ يَغْشَى السِّدْرَةَ مَا يَغْشٰى ۝

مَا زَاغَ الْبَصَرُ وَمَا طَغٰى ۝

لَقَدْ رَاٰى مِنْ اٰيٰتِ رَبِّهِ الْكُبْرٰى ۝

The Prophet stated truly that which his heart had experienced. Then will you dispute with him concerning that which he experienced? He experienced it a second time, near the farthest lote-tree, close to which is the Garden of Eternal Abode, at the time when the lote-tree was enveloped in Divine glory. The Prophet's eye did not deviate or wander. Thus did he witness one of the greatest Signs of his Lord. (2—19)

Now tell me about your goddesses Lot and Uzza, and the third one Manat, another of them. Is it that for you are sons, and for Him only daughters? That is indeed an unfair apportionment. These are but names which you and your fathers have devised; Allah has sent down no authority concerning them. They follow naught but conjecture and their own desires, despite guidance having come to them from their Lord. Is it that man can have whatever he desires? Nay, to Allah belong the bounties of this life and of the Hereafter. (20—26)

أَفَرَءَيْتُمُ اللّٰتَ وَالْعُزّٰى ۞

وَمَنٰوةَ الثَّالِثَةَ الْاُخْرٰى ۞

اَلَكُمُ الذَّكَرُ وَلَهُ الْاُنْثٰى ۞

تِلْكَ اِذًا قِسْمَةٌ ضِيْزٰى ۞

اِنْ هِيَ اِلَّا اَسْمَآءٌ سَمَّيْتُمُوْهَآ اَنْتُمْ وَاٰبَآؤُكُمْ مَّآ اَنْزَلَ اللّٰهُ بِهَا مِنْ سُلْطٰنٍ اِنْ يَّتَّبِعُوْنَ اِلَّا الظَّنَّ وَمَا تَهْوَى الْاَنْفُسُ وَلَقَدْ جَآءَهُمْ مِّنْ رَّبِّهِمُ الْهُدٰى ۞

اَمْ لِلْاِنْسَانِ مَا تَمَنّٰى ۞

فَلِلّٰهِ الْاٰخِرَةُ وَالْاُوْلٰى ۞

وَكَمْ مِّنْ مَّلَكٍ فِى السَّمٰوٰتِ لَا تُغْنِىْ شَفَاعَتُهُمْ شَيْئًا اِلَّا مِنْ بَعْدِ اَنْ يَّاْذَنَ اللّٰهُ لِمَنْ يَّشَآءُ وَيَرْضٰى ۞

اِنَّ الَّذِيْنَ لَا يُؤْمِنُوْنَ بِالْاٰخِرَةِ لَيُسَمُّوْنَ الْمَلٰٓئِكَةَ تَسْمِيَةَ الْاُنْثٰى ۞

Many an angel is there in the heavens whose intercession will be of no avail to anyone, except after Allah has given permission to whomsoever He wills and pleases. Those who do not believe in the Hereafter give the angels female names; but they have no knowledge thereof. They but follow conjecture; and conjecture avails naught against truth. So turn aside from him who turns away from Our remembrance, and seeks nothing except the life of this world. That is the extreme limit of their knowledge. Verily, thy Lord knows best him who strays from His way, and He knows best him who follows guidance. To Allah belongs whatever is in

وَمَا لَهُمْ بِهٖ مِنْ عِلْمٍ اِنْ يَّتَّبِعُوْنَ اِلَّا الظَّنَّ وَاِنَّ الظَّنَّ لَا يُغْنِىْ مِنَ الْحَقِّ شَيْئًا ۞

فَاَعْرِضْ عَنْ مَّنْ تَوَلّٰى ۬ عَنْ ذِكْرِنَا وَلَمْ يُرِدْ اِلَّا الْحَيٰوةَ الدُّنْيَا ۞

ذٰلِكَ مَبْلَغُهُمْ مِّنَ الْعِلْمِ اِنَّ رَبَّكَ هُوَ اَعْلَمُ بِمَنْ ضَلَّ عَنْ سَبِيْلِهٖ وَهُوَ اَعْلَمُ بِمَنِ اهْتَدٰى ۞

وَلِلّٰهِ مَا فِى السَّمٰوٰتِ وَمَا فِى الْاَرْضِ لِيَجْزِىَ

the heavens and whatever is in the earth, that He may requite those who do evil according to that which they have wrought and that He may reward those who do good with that which is best. Thy Lord is Master of vast forgiveness for those who shun the graver sins and all indecencies, excepting only minor defaults. He knows you well from the time when He created you from the earth, and when you were covered up in the wombs of your mothers. So ascribe not purity to yourselves. He knows best him who is truly righteous. (27—33)

الَّذِيْنَ اَسَآءُوْا بِمَا عَمِلُوْا وَيَجْزِيَ الَّذِيْنَ اَحْسَنُوْا بِالْحُسْنَى ۚ ۝

الَّذِيْنَ يَجْتَنِبُوْنَ كَبٰٓئِرَ الْاِثْمِ وَالْفَوَاحِشَ اِلَّا اللَّمَمَ ۗ اِنَّ رَبَّكَ وَاسِعُ الْمَغْفِرَةِ ۗ هُوَ اَعْلَمُ بِكُمْ اِذْ اَنْشَاَكُمْ مِّنَ الْاَرْضِ وَاِذْ اَنْتُمْ اَجِنَّةٌ فِيْ بُطُوْنِ اُمَّهٰتِكُمْ ۚ فَلَا تُزَكُّوْا اَنْفُسَكُمْ ۗ هُوَ اَعْلَمُ بِمَنِ اتَّقٰى ۝

اَفَرَءَيْتَ الَّذِيْ تَوَلّٰى ۝

وَاَعْطٰى قَلِيْلًا وَّاَكْدٰى ۝

اَعِنْدَهٗ عِلْمُ الْغَيْبِ فَهُوَ يَرٰى ۝

اَمْ لَمْ يُنَبَّاْ بِمَا فِيْ صُحُفِ مُوْسٰى ۝

وَاِبْرٰهِيْمَ الَّذِيْ وَفّٰى ۝

اَلَّا تَزِرُ وَازِرَةٌ وِّزْرَ اُخْرٰى ۝

وَاَنْ لَّيْسَ لِلْاِنْسَانِ اِلَّا مَا سَعٰى ۝

وَاَنَّ سَعْيَهٗ سَوْفَ يُرٰى ۝

ثُمَّ يُجْزٰىهُ الْجَزَآءَ الْاَوْفٰى ۝

وَاَنَّ اِلٰى رَبِّكَ الْمُنْتَهٰى ۝

وَاَنَّهٗ هُوَ اَضْحَكَ وَاَبْكٰى ۝

وَاَنَّهٗ هُوَ اَمَاتَ وَاَحْيَا ۝

وَاَنَّهٗ خَلَقَ الزَّوْجَيْنِ الذَّكَرَ وَالْاُنْثٰى ۝

مِنْ نُّطْفَةٍ اِذَا تُمْنٰى ۝

وَاَنَّ عَلَيْهِ النَّشْاَةَ الْاُخْرٰى ۝

Seest thou him who turns away from the truth, and gives only a little in the cause of Allah, and is niggardly? Has he the knowledge of the unseen, so that he can see his own end? Has he not been told of that which is in the Scriptures of Moses and of Abraham the Faithful, that no bearer of burden shall bear the burden of another; that man will have nothing but that which he strives for; that the result of his striving shall soon be known and he will then be fully recompensed; that the final decision rests with thy Lord; that He makes people laugh and He makes them weep; that He causes death and He gives life; that He creates the pairs, male and female, from a sperm-drop when it is emitted; that it is for Him to initiate the second creation;

that it is He who bestows wealth and makes content; that He is the Lord of Sirius; that He destroyed the first tribe of 'Ad and the tribe of Thamud, and spared no one, and the people of Noah before them; verily, they were most unjust and most rebellious; and He overthrew the subverted cities, and they were covered up by Allah's chastisement? Which, then, of the bounties of thy Lord wilt thou dispute? (34—56)

وَأَنَّهُ هُوَ أَغْنَى وَأَقْنَى ۞

وَأَنَّهُ هُوَ رَبُّ الشِّعْرَىٰ ۞

وَأَنَّهُ أَهْلَكَ عَادَا الْأُولَىٰ ۞

وَثَمُودَا فَمَا أَبْقَى ۞

وَقَوْمَ نُوحٍ مِّنْ قَبْلُ إِنَّهُمْ كَانُوا هُمْ أَظْلَمَ وَأَطْغَى ۞

وَالْمُؤْتَفِكَةَ أَهْوَىٰ ۞

فَغَشَّهَا مَا غَشَّىٰ ۞

فَبِأَيِّ آلَاءِ رَبِّكَ تَتَمَارَىٰ ۞

هَٰذَا نَذِيرٌ مِّنَ النُّذُرِ الْأُولَىٰ ۞

أَزِفَتِ الْآزِفَةُ ۞

لَيْسَ لَهَا مِن دُونِ اللَّهِ كَاشِفَةٌ ۞

أَفَمِنْ هَٰذَا الْحَدِيثِ تَعْجَبُونَ ۞

وَتَضْحَكُونَ وَلَا تَبْكُونَ ۞

وَأَنتُمْ سَامِدُونَ ۞

فَاسْجُدُوا لِلَّهِ وَاعْبُدُوا ۞

This Prophet is a Warner, like the Warners of old. The Hour of judgment is approaching, none but Allah can avert it. Do you then wonder at this announcement, and laugh at it, and do not weep, and continue preoccupied with vanities? Arise, and prostrate yourselves before Allah, and worship Him. (57—63)

Part 27   **AL-QAMAR**   Chapter 54
(Revealed before Hijra)

In the name of Allah, Most Gracious, Ever Merciful. (1)

بِسْمِ اللَّهِ الرَّحْمَٰنِ الرَّحِيمِ ۞

The Hour of the Great Event has drawn nigh and the moon is rent asunder. If they see a Sign they turn away and say: A power-

اقْتَرَبَتِ السَّاعَةُ وَانشَقَّ الْقَمَرُ ۞

وَإِن يَرَوْا آيَةً يُعْرِضُوا وَيَقُولُوا سِحْرٌ

ful feat of magic! They have rejected the truth and followed their own fancies; but every divine decree will inevitably be fulfilled. They have already been told of prophecies wherein there are warnings, and consummate wisdom, but warnings profit them not. Therefore, turn away from them and await the day when the Summoner will summon them to a thing distasteful. Their eyes will be cast down, and they will come forth from their graves as though they were locusts scattered about, hastening towards the Summoner. The disbelievers will say: This is a distressing day. (2—9)

مُسْتَمِرٌّ ۞

وَكَذَّبُوۡا وَاتَّبَعُوۡۤا اَهۡوَآءَهُمۡ وَكُلُّ اَمۡرٍ مُّسۡتَقِرٌّ ۞

وَلَقَدۡ جَآءَهُمۡ مِّنَ الۡاَنۡبَآءِ مَا فِيۡهِ مُزۡدَجَرٌ ۞

حِكۡمَةٌ ۢ بَالِغَةٌ فَمَا تُغۡنِ النُّذُرُ ۞

فَتَوَلَّ عَنۡهُمۡ یَوۡمَ یَدۡعُ الدَّاعِ اِلٰی شَیۡءٍ نُّکُرٍ ۞

خُشَّعًا اَبۡصَارُهُمۡ یَخۡرُجُوۡنَ مِنَ الۡاَجۡدَاثِ کَاَنَّهُمۡ جَرَادٌ مُّنۡتَشِرٌ ۞

مُّهۡطِعِیۡنَ اِلَی الدَّاعِ ؕ یَقُوۡلُ الۡکٰفِرُوۡنَ هٰذَا یَوۡمٌ عَسِرٌ ۞

The people of Noah rejected the truth before them; they rejected Our servant and said: A madman, spurned by our gods. He called on his Lord: I am overcome; do Thou avenge me. Thereupon We opened the gates of heaven with water pouring down; and We caused the earth to burst forth with springs, so the two waters met for a purpose which had been determined. We carried Noah in the Ark constructed with planks and nails. It sailed along under Our eyes: a reward for him who had been rejected. We made this event a Sign for coming generations. Then is there anyone who would take heed? How terrible, then, was My chastisement and My warning! Indeed, We have made the Quran easy to follow; but is there anyone who would take heed? The tribe of 'Ad also rejected the truth. How terrible then was My chastisement and My warning! We sent against them a furious wind, on a day of unending ill-luck, which tore

کَذَّبَتۡ قَبۡلَهُمۡ قَوۡمُ نُوۡحٍ فَکَذَّبُوۡا عَبۡدَنَا وَقَالُوۡا مَجۡنُوۡنٌ وَّازۡدُجِرَ ۞

فَدَعَا رَبَّهٗۤ اَنِّیۡ مَغۡلُوۡبٌ فَانۡتَصِرۡ ۞

فَفَتَحۡنَاۤ اَبۡوَابَ السَّمَآءِ بِمَآءٍ مُّنۡهَمِرٍ ۞

وَّفَجَّرۡنَا الۡاَرۡضَ عُیُوۡنًا فَالۡتَقَی الۡمَآءُ عَلٰۤی اَمۡرٍ قَدۡ قُدِرَ ۞

وَحَمَلۡنٰهُ عَلٰی ذَاتِ اَلۡوَاحٍ وَّدُسُرٍ ۞

تَجۡرِیۡ بِاَعۡیُنِنَا ۚ جَزَآءً لِّمَنۡ کَانَ کُفِرَ ۞

وَلَقَدۡ تَّرَکۡنٰهَاۤ اٰیَةً فَهَلۡ مِنۡ مُّدَّکِرٍ ۞

فَکَیۡفَ کَانَ عَذَابِیۡ وَنُذُرِ ۞

وَلَقَدۡ یَسَّرۡنَا الۡقُرۡاٰنَ لِلذِّکۡرِ فَهَلۡ مِنۡ مُّدَّکِرٍ ۞

کَذَّبَتۡ عَادٌ فَکَیۡفَ کَانَ عَذَابِیۡ وَنُذُرِ ۞

اِنَّاۤ اَرۡسَلۡنَا عَلَیۡهِمۡ رِیۡحًا صَرۡصَرًا فِیۡ یَوۡمِ نَحۡسٍ

people away as though they were the trunks of uprooted palm-trees. How terrible then was My chastisement and My warning! Indeed, We have made the Quran easy to follow; but is there anyone who would take heed? (10—23)

The tribe of Thamud also rejected Our warnings, and said: What! Shall we follow a single human being from among us? If we did that, we would certainly be in manifest error and bereft of sense. Has the revelation been sent down to him alone from among us? He is but a boastful liar. We said to their Messenger Saleh: Tomorrow will they know who the boastful liar is. We will send the she-camel as a trial for them. So watch them and be patient. Tell them that the water has been apportioned between them; let each party attend at its appointed time. On this they called their chief, who came and hamstrung the she-camel. How terrible then was My chastisement and My warning! We sent against them a single blast, and they became like dry stubble, trampled upon.

Indeed, We have made the Quran easy to follow; but is there anyone who would take heed? Lot's people also rejected Our warnings. We sent a storm of stones upon them, except the family of Lot, whom We delivered by early dawn,

مُسْتَمِرٌّ ۞

تَنْزِعُ النَّاسَ كَاَنَّهُمْ اَعْجَازُ نَخْلٍ مُّنْقَعِرٍ ۞

فَكَيْفَ كَانَ عَذَابِىْ وَ نُذُرِ ۞

وَ لَقَدْ يَسَّرْنَا الْقُرْاٰنَ لِلذِّكْرِ فَهَلْ مِنْ مُّدَّكِرٍ ۞

كَذَّبَتْ ثَمُوْدُ بِالنُّذُرِ ۞

فَقَالُوْٓا اَبَشَرًا مِّنَّا وَاحِدًا نَّتَّبِعُهٗٓ اِنَّآ اِذًا لَّفِىْ ضَلٰلٍ وَّ سُعُرٍ ۞

ءَاُلْقِىَ الذِّكْرُ عَلَيْهِ مِنْ بَيْنِنَا بَلْ هُوَ كَذَّابٌ اَشِرٌ ۞

سَيَعْلَمُوْنَ غَدًا مَّنِ الْكَذَّابُ الْاَشِرُ ۞

اِنَّا مُرْسِلُوا النَّاقَةِ فِتْنَةً لَّهُمْ فَارْتَقِبْهُمْ وَاصْطَبِرْ ۞

وَ نَبِّئْهُمْ اَنَّ الْمَاءَ قِسْمَةٌ بَيْنَهُمْ كُلُّ شِرْبٍ مُّحْتَضَرٌ ۞

فَنَادَوْا صَاحِبَهُمْ فَتَعَاطٰى فَعَقَرَ ۞

فَكَيْفَ كَانَ عَذَابِىْ وَ نُذُرِ ۞

اِنَّآ اَرْسَلْنَا عَلَيْهِمْ صَيْحَةً وَّاحِدَةً فَكَانُوْا كَهَشِيْمِ الْمُحْتَظِرِ ۞

وَ لَقَدْ يَسَّرْنَا الْقُرْاٰنَ لِلذِّكْرِ فَهَلْ مِنْ مُّدَّكِرٍ ۞

كَذَّبَتْ قَوْمُ لُوْطٍ بِالنُّذُرِ ۞

اِنَّآ اَرْسَلْنَا عَلَيْهِمْ حَاصِبًا اِلَّآ اٰلَ لُوْطٍ نَجَّيْنٰهُمْ بِسَحَرٍ ۞

535

as a favour from Ourself. Thus do We requite him who is grateful. He had indeed warned them of Our chastisement, but they disputed about the warning. They tried to turn him against his guests; so We blinded their eyes, and said: Suffer My chastisement and My warning. There came upon them early in the morning the inevitable chastisement. Suffer, then, My chastisement and My warning. Indeed, We have made the Quran easy to follow. But is there anyone who would take heed? Surely to the people of Pharaoh also came Warners. They rejected all Our Signs; so We seized them, with the seizure of One Mighty, Omnipotent. (24—43)

نِعْمَةً مِّنْ عِنْدِنَا ۚ كَذٰلِكَ نَجْزِیْ مَنْ شَکَرَ ۟۳۵

وَلَقَدْ اَنْذَرَهُمْ بَطْشَتَنَا فَتَمَارَوْا بِالنُّذُرِ ۟۳۶

وَلَقَدْ رَاوَدُوْهُ عَنْ ضَیْفِهٖ فَطَمَسْنَاۤ اَعْیُنَهُمْ فَذُوْقُوْا عَذَابِیْ وَ نُذُرِ ۟۳۷

وَلَقَدْ صَبَّحَهُمْ بُکْرَةً عَذَابٌ مُّسْتَقِرٌّ ۟۳۸

فَذُوْقُوْا عَذَابِیْ وَ نُذُرِ ۟۳۹

وَلَقَدْ یَسَّرْنَا الْقُرْاٰنَ لِلذِّکْرِ فَهَلْ مِنْ مُّدَّکِرٍ ۟۴۰

وَلَقَدْ جَآءَ اٰلَ فِرْعَوْنَ النُّذُرُ ۟۴۱

کَذَّبُوْا بِاٰیٰتِنَا کُلِّهَا فَاَخَذْنٰهُمْ اَخْذَ عَزِیْزٍ مُّقْتَدِرٍ ۟۴۲

اَکُفَّارُکُمْ خَیْرٌ مِّنْ اُولٰٓئِکُمْ اَمْ لَکُمْ بَرَآءَةٌ فِی الزُّبُرِ ۟۴۳

اَمْ یَقُوْلُوْنَ نَحْنُ جَمِیْعٌ مُّنْتَصِرٌ ۟۴۴

سَیُهْزَمُ الْجَمْعُ وَیُوَلُّوْنَ الدُّبُرَ ۟۴۵

بَلِ السَّاعَةُ مَوْعِدُهُمْ وَالسَّاعَةُ اَدْهٰی وَاَمَرُّ ۟۴۶

اِنَّ الْمُجْرِمِیْنَ فِیْ ضَلٰلٍ وَّسُعُرٍ ۟۴۷

یَوْمَ یُسْحَبُوْنَ فِی النَّارِ عَلٰی وُجُوْهِهِمْ ؕ ذُوْقُوْا مَسَّ سَقَرَ ۟۴۸

اِنَّا کُلَّ شَیْءٍ خَلَقْنٰهُ بِقَدَرٍ ۟۴۹

وَمَاۤ اَمْرُنَاۤ اِلَّا وَاحِدَةٌ کَلَمْحٍ بِالْبَصَرِ ۟۵۰

وَلَقَدْ اَهْلَکْنَاۤ اَشْیَاعَکُمْ فَهَلْ مِنْ مُّدَّکِرٍ ۟۵۱

وَکُلُّ شَیْءٍ فَعَلُوْهُ فِی الزُّبُرِ ۟۵۲

وَکُلُّ صَغِیْرٍ وَّکَبِیْرٍ مُّسْتَطَرٌ ۟۵۳

Are your disbelievers, then, better than those? Or, have you been granted an exemption in the Scriptures? Or, do they boast: We are a strong host, well succoured? The hosts shall soon be routed, and they will turn their backs in flight. Aye, the Hour is their appointed time, and the Hour will be most grievous and most bitter. The guilty ones are in manifest error and are afflicted with madness. On the day when they will be dragged into the Fire on their faces, they will be told: Suffer the torment of hell. We have created everything in due measure; and Our command is carried out instantaneously, like the twinkling of an eye. Indeed We have destroyed people like you before; but is there anyone who would take heed? Everything they have done is recorded in the Books. Every matter, small and great, is written down.

The righteous will be in the midst of Gardens and streams, in the seat of truth with the Omnipotent King. (44—56)

اِنَّ الْمُتَّقِيْنَ فِيْ جَنّٰتٍ وَّنَهَرٍ ۞

فِيْ مَقْعَدِ صِدْقٍ عِنْدَ مَلِيْكٍ مُّقْتَدِرٍ ۞

(Revealed before Hijra)

In the name of Allah, Most Gracious, Ever Merciful. (1)

بِسْمِ اللهِ الرَّحْمٰنِ الرَّحِيْمِ ۞

اَلرَّحْمٰنُ ۞

عَلَّمَ الْقُرْاٰنَ ۞

خَلَقَ الْاِنْسَانَ ۞

عَلَّمَهُ الْبَيَانَ ۞

اَلشَّمْسُ وَ الْقَمَرُ بِحُسْبَانٍ ۞

وَّ النَّجْمُ وَ الشَّجَرُ يَسْجُدٰنِ ۞

The Gracious One has taught the Quran. He has created man and taught him the art of speech and exposition. The sun and the moon move according to a fixed reckoning; and the stars and trees submit to Him. He has raised the heaven high and set up the measure, that you may not transgress the measure. So weigh all things in justice and fall not short of the measure.

وَ السَّمَآءَ رَفَعَهَا وَ وَضَعَ الْمِيْزَانَ ۞

اَلَّا تَطْغَوْا فِى الْمِيْزَانِ ۞

وَ اَقِيْمُوا الْوَزْنَ بِالْقِسْطِ وَ لَا تُخْسِرُوا الْمِيْزَانَ ۞

وَ الْاَرْضَ وَضَعَهَا لِلْاَنَامِ ۞

فِيْهَا فَاكِهَةٌ ۙ وَّ النَّخْلُ ذَاتُ الْاَكْمَامِ ۞

He has set the earth for His creatures; therein are all kinds of fruits and palm-trees with sheaths, and grain inside its husk and fragrant flowers. Which, then, of the favours of your Lord will you twain, jinn and men, deny? He created man from dry ringing clay, like earthenware; and the jinn He created from a flame of fire.

وَ الْحَبُّ ذُو الْعَصْفِ وَ الرَّيْحَانُ ۞

فَبِاَيِّ اٰلَآءِ رَبِّكُمَا تُكَذِّبٰنِ ۞

خَلَقَ الْاِنْسَانَ مِنْ صَلْصَالٍ كَالْفَخَّارِ ۞

وَ خَلَقَ الْجَآنَّ مِنْ مَّارِجٍ مِّنْ نَّارٍ ۞

Which, then, of the favours of your Lord will you twain deny? He is the Lord of the two Easts and the Lord of the two Wests. Which, then, of the favours of your Lord will you twain deny? He has put the two oceans in motion; they will meet. Just now there is a barrier between them; they cannot encroach one upon the other. Which, then, of the favours of your Lord will you twain deny? Pearls and coral are taken out of both. Which, then, of the favours of your Lord will you twain deny? His are the vessels with lofty sails raised high on the ocean like mountains. Which, then, of the favours of your Lord will you twain deny? (2—26)

فَبِاَیِّ اٰلَآءِ رَبِّكُمَا تُكَذِّبٰنِ ۝

رَبُّ الْمَشْرِقَیْنِ وَرَبُّ الْمَغْرِبَیْنِ ۝

فَبِاَیِّ اٰلَآءِ رَبِّكُمَا تُكَذِّبٰنِ ۝

مَرَجَ الْبَحْرَیْنِ یَلْتَقِیٰنِ ۝

بَیْنَهُمَا بَرْزَخٌ لَّا یَبْغِیٰنِ ۝

فَبِاَیِّ اٰلَآءِ رَبِّكُمَا تُكَذِّبٰنِ ۝

یَخْرُجُ مِنْهُمَا اللُّؤْلُؤُ وَالْمَرْجَانُ ۝

فَبِاَیِّ اٰلَآءِ رَبِّكُمَا تُكَذِّبٰنِ ۝

وَلَهُ الْجَوَارِ الْمُنْشَاٰتُ فِی الْبَحْرِ كَالْاَعْلَامِ ۝

فَبِاَیِّ اٰلَآءِ رَبِّكُمَا تُكَذِّبٰنِ ۝

كُلُّ مَنْ عَلَیْهَا فَانٍ ۝

وَّیَبْقٰی وَجْهُ رَبِّكَ ذُو الْجَلٰلِ وَالْاِكْرَامِ ۝

فَبِاَیِّ اٰلَآءِ رَبِّكُمَا تُكَذِّبٰنِ ۝

یَسْـَٔلُهُ مَنْ فِی السَّمٰوٰتِ وَالْاَرْضِ كُلَّ یَوْمٍ هُوَ فِی شَاْنٍ ۝

فَبِاَیِّ اٰلَآءِ رَبِّكُمَا تُكَذِّبٰنِ ۝

سَنَفْرُغُ لَكُمْ اَیُّهَ الثَّقَلٰنِ ۝

فَبِاَیِّ اٰلَآءِ رَبِّكُمَا تُكَذِّبٰنِ ۝

یٰمَعْشَرَ الْجِنِّ وَالْاِنْسِ اِنِ اسْتَطَعْتُمْ اَنْ تَنْفُذُوْا مِنْ اَقْطَارِ السَّمٰوٰتِ وَالْاَرْضِ فَانْفُذُوْا لَا تَنْفُذُوْنَ اِلَّا بِسُلْطٰنٍ ۝

فَبِاَیِّ اٰلَآءِ رَبِّكُمَا تُكَذِّبٰنِ ۝

All that is on the earth will perish, and only that will survive which is under the care of thy Lord, Master of Glory and Honour. Which, then, of the favours of your Lord will you twain deny? All that are in the heavens and the earth beseech Him. Everyday He manifests Himself in a new state. Which, then, of the favours of your Lord will you twain deny? Soon shall We attend to you two mighty ones. Which, then, of the favours of your Lord will you twain deny? O company of jinn and men, if you have the capacity to penetrate beyond the confines of the heavens and the earth, by all means do so; but you cannot do so except with authority. Which, then, of the favours of your Lord will you twain deny?

You will be afflicted with smokeless fire, and with smoke without flame, and you will not be able to help yourselves. Which, then, of the favours of your Lord will you twain deny? When the heaven is rent asunder, and assumes a rosy hue like red leather (which, then, of the favours of your Lord will you twain deny?) neither jinn nor man will be asked about his sin on that day (which, then, of the favours of your Lord will you twain deny?) and the guilty will be known by their marks and will be seized by the forelocks and the feet (which, then, of the favours of your Lord will you twain deny) and will be told: This is the hell which the guilty deny. Now between it and fierce boiling water will they go round; which, then, of the favours of your Lord will you twain deny? (27—46)

But for him who fears to stand before his Lord there are two Gardens (which, then, of the favours of your Lord will you twain deny?) having many varieties of trees (which, then, of the favours of your Lord will you twain deny?) and two springs flowing full (which, then, of the favours of your Lord will you twain deny?) and of every type of fruit two kinds. Which, then, of the favours of your Lord will you twain deny? They will recline on couches above carpets the linings of which will be of thick bro-

يُرْسَلُ عَلَيْكُمَا شُوَاظٌ مِّنْ نَّارٍ ۙ وَّ نُحَاسٌ فَلَا تَنْتَصِرٰنِ ۚ

فَبِاَيِّ اٰلَآءِ رَبِّكُمَا تُكَذِّبٰنِ ۚ

فَاِذَا انْشَقَّتِ السَّمَآءُ فَكَانَتْ وَرْدَةً كَالدِّهَانِ ۚ

فَبِاَيِّ اٰلَآءِ رَبِّكُمَا تُكَذِّبٰنِ ۚ

فَيَوْمَئِذٍ لَّا يُسْـَٔلُ عَنْ ذَنْۢبِهٖۤ اِنْسٌ وَّ لَا جَآنٌّ ۚ

فَبِاَيِّ اٰلَآءِ رَبِّكُمَا تُكَذِّبٰنِ ۚ

يُعْرَفُ الْمُجْرِمُوْنَ بِسِيْمٰهُمْ فَيُؤْخَذُ بِالنَّوَاصِيْ وَ الْاَقْدَامِ ۚ

فَبِاَيِّ اٰلَآءِ رَبِّكُمَا تُكَذِّبٰنِ ۚ

هٰذِهٖ جَهَنَّمُ الَّتِيْ يُكَذِّبُ بِهَا الْمُجْرِمُوْنَ ۘ

يَطُوْفُوْنَ بَيْنَهَا وَ بَيْنَ حَمِيْمٍ اٰنٍ ۚ

فَبِاَيِّ اٰلَآءِ رَبِّكُمَا تُكَذِّبٰنِ ۚ

وَلِمَنْ خَافَ مَقَامَ رَبِّهٖ جَنَّتٰنِ ۚ

فَبِاَيِّ اٰلَآءِ رَبِّكُمَا تُكَذِّبٰنِ ۚ

ذَوَاتَاۤ اَفْنَانٍ ۚ

فَبِاَيِّ اٰلَآءِ رَبِّكُمَا تُكَذِّبٰنِ ۚ

فِيْهِمَا عَيْنٰنِ تَجْرِيٰنِ ۚ

فَبِاَيِّ اٰلَآءِ رَبِّكُمَا تُكَذِّبٰنِ ۚ

فِيْهِمَا مِنْ كُلِّ فَاكِهَةٍ زَوْجٰنِ ۚ

فَبِاَيِّ اٰلَآءِ رَبِّكُمَا تُكَذِّبٰنِ ۚ

مُتَّكِئِيْنَ عَلٰى فُرُشٍۭ بَطَآئِنُهَا مِنْ اِسْتَبْرَقٍ ؕ وَ

cade; and the fruits of the two Gardens will be hanging low within easy reach. Which, then, of the favours of your Lord will you twain deny? Therein will be chaste maidens of modest gaze, untouched by man or jinn (which, then, of the favours of your Lord will you twain deny?) as if they were rubies and small pearls. Which, then, of the favours of your Lord will you twain deny? Can the reward of goodness be anything but goodness? Which, then, of the favours of your Lord will you twain deny? (47—62)

Besides these two there will be two other Gardens (which, then, of the favours of your Lord will you twain deny?) dark green with foliage. Which, then, of the favours of your Lord will you twain deny? Therein will also be two springs gushing with water. Which, then, of the favours of your Lord will you twain deny? In both of them there will be all kinds of fruit, and dates and pomegranates. Which, then, of the favours of your Lord will you twain deny? (63—70)

Therein will be good and beautiful women (which, then, of the favours of your Lord will you twain deny?) black-eyed, guarded in pavilions (which, then, of the favours of your Lord will you twain deny?) untouched by man or jinn

540

(which, then, of the favours of your Lord will you twain deny?) reclining on green cushions and beautiful carpets. Which, then, of the favours of your Lord will you twain deny? Blessed is the name of thy Lord, Master of Glory and Honour. (71—79)

فَبِاَيِّ اٰلَاۤءِ رَبِّكُمَا تُكَذِّبٰنِ ۞

مُتَّكِـِٕيْنَ عَلٰى رَفْرَفٍ خُضْرٍ وَّعَبْقَرِيٍّ حِسَانٍ ۞

فَبِاَيِّ اٰلَاۤءِ رَبِّكُمَا تُكَذِّبٰنِ ۞

تَبٰرَكَ اسْمُ رَبِّكَ ذِى الْجَلٰلِ وَالْاِكْرَامِ ۞

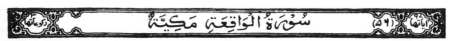

سُوْرَةُ الْوَاقِعَةِ مَكِّيَّةٌ

Part 27   **AL-WĀQI'AH**   Chapter 56
(Revealed before Hijra)

In the name of Allah, Most Gracious, Ever Merciful. (1)

بِسْمِ اللّٰهِ الرَّحْمٰنِ الرَّحِيْمِ ۞

اِذَا وَقَعَتِ الْوَاقِعَةُ ۞

لَيْسَ لِوَقْعَتِهَا كَاذِبَةٌ ۞

خَافِضَةٌ رَّافِعَةٌ ۞

When the Event comes to pass, the coming of which no one can avert, some it will bring low and others it will exalt.

اِذَا رُجَّتِ الْاَرْضُ رَجًّا ۞

وَّبُسَّتِ الْجِبَالُ بَسًّا ۞

فَكَانَتْ هَبَاۤءً مُّنْبَثًّا ۞

وَّكُنْتُمْ اَزْوَاجًا ثَلٰثَةً ۞

فَاَصْحٰبُ الْمَيْمَنَةِ مَاۤ اَصْحٰبُ الْمَيْمَنَةِ ۞

When the earth is shaken violently, and the mountains are crumbled into dust and become like motes floating in the air, you will be divided into three groups: those on the right (and what will those on the right be?) and those on the left (and what will those on the left be?) and those who are foremost — they verily are the foremost. They will be the honoured ones, dwelling in the Gardens of Bliss; a large party from the early believers,

وَاَصْحٰبُ الْمَشْـَٔمَةِ مَاۤ اَصْحٰبُ الْمَشْـَٔمَةِ ۞

وَالسّٰبِقُوْنَ السّٰبِقُوْنَ ۞

اُولٰٓئِكَ الْمُقَرَّبُوْنَ ۞

فِيْ جَنّٰتِ النَّعِيْمِ ۞

ثُلَّةٌ مِّنَ الْاَوَّلِيْنَ ۞

and a few from the late-comers, reclining on couches inwrought with gold and jewels, facing one another. They will be waited on by ageless youths, carrying goblets and ewers and cups filled out of a flowing spring, neither causing headache nor inebriating, and such fruits as they choose, and the flesh of birds as they may desire.

وَ قَلِيلٌ مِّنَ الْاٰخِرِيْنَ ۝

عَلٰى سُرُرٍ مَّوْضُوْنَةٍ ۝

مُّتَّكِـئِيْنَ عَلَيْهَا مُتَقٰبِلِيْنَ ۝

يَطُوْفُ عَلَيْهِمْ وِلْدَانٌ مُّخَلَّدُوْنَ ۝

بِاَكْوَابٍ وَّ اَبَارِيْقَ ۙ وَ كَأْسٍ مِّنْ مَّعِيْنٍ ۝

لَّا يُصَدَّعُوْنَ عَنْهَا وَ لَا يُنْزِفُوْنَ ۝

وَ فَاكِهَةٍ مِّمَّا يَتَخَيَّرُوْنَ ۝

وَ لَحْمِ طَيْرٍ مِّمَّا يَشْتَهُوْنَ ۝

وَ حُوْرٌ عِيْنٌ ۝

They will have as companions maidens with lovely black eyes, pure as pearls well guarded; a recompense for what they did. They will not hear therein any vain or sinful talk, but only the salutation: Peace, peace.

كَاَمْثَالِ اللُّؤْلُؤِ الْمَكْنُوْنِ ۝

جَزَآءً بِمَا كَانُوْا يَعْمَلُوْنَ ۝

لَا يَسْمَعُوْنَ فِيْهَا لَغْوًا وَّ لَا تَأْثِيْمًا ۝

اِلَّا قِيْلًا سَلٰمًا سَلٰمًا ۝

وَ اَصْحٰبُ الْيَمِيْنِ ۙ مَا اَصْحٰبُ الْيَمِيْنِ ۝

فِيْ سِدْرٍ مَّخْضُوْدٍ ۝

وَّ طَلْحٍ مَّنْضُوْدٍ ۝

وَّ ظِلٍّ مَّمْدُوْدٍ ۝

وَّ مَآءٍ مَّسْكُوْبٍ ۝

وَّ فَاكِهَةٍ كَثِيْرَةٍ ۝

لَّا مَقْطُوْعَةٍ وَّ لَا مَمْنُوْعَةٍ ۝

وَّ فُرُشٍ مَّرْفُوْعَةٍ ۝

اِنَّا اَنْشَأْنٰهُنَّ اِنْشَآءً ۝

Those on the right; how fortunate will those on the right be! They will be amidst thornless lote-trees, and clustered bananas, and extensive shades, and falling water, and varieties of fruit, endless and unforbidden. They will have noble spouses, whom We specially created, and made virgins, loving and matching in age, for those in the right. They will be a large party from the early believers and a large party from the late comers. (2—41)

Those on the left; how unfortunate will those on the left be! They will be in the midst of scorching wind and scalding water, and in the shadow of black smoke, neither cool nor agreeable. Before this they had lived in ease and comfort and had persisted in extreme wickedness, and were wont to say: When we are dead and have become dust and bones, shall we be raised up again, and also our fathers of yore?

Tell them: Indeed, the earlier ones and the later ones will all be gathered together for the appointment of a day which has been determined upon. Then you erring deniers of truth will eat of the tree of Zaqqum, and will fill your bellies with it and drink boiling water on top of it, drinking like camels afflicted with raging thirst. This will be their entertainment on the Day of Judgment.

543

It is We Who created you, then why do you not accept the truth? Reflect on the sperm-drop that you emit. Do you create it, or are We its Creator? It is We Who have decreed death for all of you, and We cannot be frustrated in replacing you with others like you, and in developing you into a form you know not. You have certainly known the first creation, then why do you not take heed? Reflect on that which you sow. Is it you who cause it to grow, or do We? If We so pleased, We could reduce it all to broken particles, then you would start lamenting: We have been heavily burdened; indeed we have been bereft of all the fruits of our labour.

Reflect on the water that you drink. Is it you who cause it to descend from the clouds, or do We? If We so pleased, We could make it bitter. Then, why are you not grateful? Reflect on the fire that you kindle. Is it you who produce the tree from which you take the wood, or do We? We have made it a reminder, and a provision for voyagers. So glorify the name of thy Lord, the Great. (42—75)

I cite as proof the falling of the stars, and that, if you only knew, is very strong proof, that this is indeed a noble Quran,

544

in a well-preserved Book, into the meaning of which only the purified can penetrate. It is revelation from the Lord of the worlds.

فِىۡ كِتٰبٍ مَّكۡنُوۡنٍ ۝

لَّا يَمَسُّهٗۤ اِلَّا الۡمُطَهَّرُوۡنَ ۝

تَنۡزِيۡلٌ مِّنۡ رَّبِّ الۡعٰلَمِيۡنَ ۝

اَفَبِهٰذَا الۡحَدِيۡثِ اَنۡتُمۡ مُّدۡهِنُوۡنَ ۝

وَ تَجۡعَلُوۡنَ رِزۡقَكُمۡ اَنَّكُمۡ تُكَذِّبُوۡنَ ۝

Is it this Divine discourse that you would pass by? Do you make it your business that you reject it? Why is it that when a person is in the throes of death, and you are at that moment looking on, and We are nearer to him than you are, that you do not realise the truth? How is it that if you are not to be called to account, you are unable to reverse his condition, if you are truthful in your claim?

فَلَوۡلَاۤ اِذَا بَلَغَتِ الۡحُلۡقُوۡمَ ۝

وَ اَنۡتُمۡ حِيۡنَئِذٍ تَنۡظُرُوۡنَ ۝

وَ نَحۡنُ اَقۡرَبُ اِلَيۡهِ مِنۡكُمۡ وَ لٰكِنۡ لَّا تُبۡصِرُوۡنَ ۝

فَلَوۡلَاۤ اِنۡ كُنۡتُمۡ غَيۡرَ مَدِيۡنِيۡنَ ۝

تَرۡجِعُوۡنَهَاۤ اِنۡ كُنۡتُمۡ صٰدِقِيۡنَ ۝

فَاَمَّاۤ اِنۡ كَانَ مِنَ الۡمُقَرَّبِيۡنَ ۝

Now, if he be one of the honoured ones, then for him is ease and comfort and the Garden of Bliss; and if he be of those of the right, he will be greeted with: Peace be on thee, O thou of those of the right. But if he be one of those who reject the truth and are in error, then his entertainment will be boiling water and an abode in hell. This is the certain truth.

فَرَوۡحٌ وَّ رَيۡحَانٌ ۙ وَّ جَنَّتُ نَعِيۡمٍ ۝

وَ اَمَّاۤ اِنۡ كَانَ مِنۡ اَصۡحٰبِ الۡيَمِيۡنِ ۝

فَسَلٰمٌ لَّكَ مِنۡ اَصۡحٰبِ الۡيَمِيۡنِ ۝

وَ اَمَّاۤ اِنۡ كَانَ مِنَ الۡمُكَذِّبِيۡنَ الضَّآلِّيۡنَ ۝

فَنُزُلٌ مِّنۡ حَمِيۡمٍ ۝

وَّ تَصۡلِيَةُ جَحِيۡمٍ ۝

اِنَّ هٰذَا لَهُوَ حَقُّ الۡيَقِيۡنِ ۝

So glorify the name of thy Lord, the Great. (76—97)

فَسَبِّحۡ بِاسۡمِ رَبِّكَ الۡعَظِيۡمِ ۝

Chapter 57

AL-ḤADĪD

(Revealed after Hijra)

In the name of Allah, Most Gracious, Ever Merciful. (1)

بِسْمِ اللهِ الرَّحْمٰنِ الرَّحِيْمِ ۞

سَبَّحَ لِلّٰهِ مَا فِى السَّمٰوٰتِ وَالْاَرْضِ ۚ وَ هُوَ الْعَزِيْزُ الْحَكِيْمُ ۞

لَهٗ مُلْكُ السَّمٰوٰتِ وَالْاَرْضِ ۚ يُحْىٖ وَ يُمِيْتُ ۚ وَهُوَ عَلٰى كُلِّ شَىْءٍ قَدِيْرٌ ۞

هُوَ الْاَوَّلُ وَ الْاٰخِرُ وَ الظَّاهِرُ وَ الْبَاطِنُ ۚ وَهُوَ بِكُلِّ شَىْءٍ عَلِيْمٌ ۞

هُوَ الَّذِىْ خَلَقَ السَّمٰوٰتِ وَالْاَرْضَ فِىْ سِتَّةِ اَيَّامٍ ثُمَّ اسْتَوٰى عَلَى الْعَرْشِ ۚ يَعْلَمُ مَا يَلِجُ فِى الْاَرْضِ وَ مَا يَخْرُجُ مِنْهَا وَمَا يَنْزِلُ مِنَ السَّمَآءِ وَ مَا يَعْرُجُ فِيْهَا ۚ وَهُوَ مَعَكُمْ اَيْنَ مَا كُنْتُمْ ۚ وَاللهُ بِمَا تَعْمَلُوْنَ بَصِيْرٌ ۞

لَهٗ مُلْكُ السَّمٰوٰتِ وَ الْاَرْضِ ۚ وَاِلَى اللهِ تُرْجَعُ الْاُمُوْرُ ۞

يُوْلِجُ الَّيْلَ فِى النَّهَارِ وَ يُوْلِجُ النَّهَارَ فِى الَّيْلِ ۚ وَهُوَ عَلِيْمٌۢ بِذَاتِ الصُّدُوْرِ ۞

اٰمِنُوْا بِاللهِ وَرَسُوْلِهٖ وَ اَنْفِقُوْا مِمَّا جَعَلَكُمْ مُّسْتَخْلَفِيْنَ فِيْهِ ۚ فَالَّذِيْنَ اٰمَنُوْا مِنْكُمْ وَاَنْفَقُوْا لَهُمْ اَجْرٌ كَبِيْرٌ ۞

Whatever is in the heavens and the earth glorifies Allah. He is the Mighty, the Wise. His is the kingdom of the heavens and the earth; He bestows life and He causes death; and He has power to do all that He wills. He is the First and the Last and the Manifest and the Hidden, and He has full knowledge of all things. He it is Who created the heavens and the earth in six periods, then He settled Himself on the Throne. He knows that which enters the earth and that which comes out of it, and that which comes down from heaven and that which goes up into it. He is with you wheresoever you may be. Allah sees all that you do. His is the Kingdom of the heavens and the earth; and to Allah are all affairs returned for final determination.

He causes the night to pass into the day and causes the day to pass into the night. He has full knowledge of all that passes through people's minds. Believe in Allah and His Messenger, and spend in the cause of Allah out of that to which He has made you heirs. Those of you who believe and keep spending in the cause of Allah will have a great reward.

What ails you that you believe not in Allah, while the Messenger calls you to believe in your Lord, and He has already taken a covenant from you, if indeed you are believers? He it is Who sends down clear Signs to His servant that He may bring you out of every kind of darkness into the light. Surely, Allah is Compassionate and Merciful towards you. What ails you that you spend not in the cause of Allah, while to Allah belongs the heritage of the heavens and the earth? Those of you who spent in the cause of Allah and fought before the victory are higher in rank than those who spent and fought after the victory; the two are not equal. To both has Allah promised a good reward. Allah is Well-Aware of that which you do. (2—11)

وَ مَا لَكُمْ لَا تُؤْمِنُوْنَ بِاللّٰهِ وَ الرَّسُوْلُ يَدْعُوْكُمْ لِتُؤْمِنُوْا بِرَبِّكُمْ وَ قَدْ اَخَذَ مِيْثَاقَكُمْ اِنْ كُنْتُمْ مُّؤْمِنِيْنَ ۝

هُوَ الَّذِيْ يُنَزِّلُ عَلٰى عَبْدِهٖ اٰيٰتٍۭ بَيِّنٰتٍ لِّيُخْرِجَكُمْ مِّنَ الظُّلُمٰتِ اِلَى النُّوْرِ وَ اِنَّ اللّٰهَ بِكُمْ لَرَءُوْفٌ رَّحِيْمٌ ۝

وَ مَا لَكُمْ اَلَّا تُنْفِقُوْا فِيْ سَبِيْلِ اللّٰهِ وَ لِلّٰهِ مِيْرَاثُ السَّمٰوٰتِ وَ الْاَرْضِ لَا يَسْتَوِيْ مِنْكُمْ مَّنْ اَنْفَقَ مِنْ قَبْلِ الْفَتْحِ وَ قٰتَلَ اُولٰٓئِكَ اَعْظَمُ دَرَجَةً مِّنَ الَّذِيْنَ اَنْفَقُوْا مِنْۢ بَعْدُ وَ قٰتَلُوْا وَ كُلًّا وَّعَدَ اللّٰهُ الْحُسْنٰى وَ اللّٰهُ بِمَا تَعْمَلُوْنَ خَبِيْرٌ ۝

مَنْ ذَا الَّذِيْ يُقْرِضُ اللّٰهَ قَرْضًا حَسَنًا فَيُضٰعِفَهٗ لَهٗ وَ لَهٗٓ اَجْرٌ كَرِيْمٌ ۝

Who is he who will lend to Allah a goodly loan that He may increase it for him manifold, and he will have a generous reward? Keep in mind the day when thou wilt see the believing men and believing women, their light running before them and on their right hands, and they will be greeted with: Glad tidings for you this day of Gardens beneath which rivers flow, wherein you will abide. That is the supreme triumph. That is the day when the hypocrites, men and women, will say to those who believe: Wait a while for us that we may take light from your light. They will be told: Go back and seek for light. Then a wall will be set up between them with a door in it, on the inside of which there will be all mercy, and outside of it, in front, will appear torment.

يَوْمَ تَرَى الْمُؤْمِنِيْنَ وَ الْمُؤْمِنٰتِ يَسْعٰى نُوْرُهُمْ بَيْنَ اَيْدِيْهِمْ وَ بِاَيْمَانِهِمْ بُشْرٰىكُمُ الْيَوْمَ جَنّٰتٌ تَجْرِيْ مِنْ تَحْتِهَا الْاَنْهٰرُ خٰلِدِيْنَ فِيْهَا ذٰلِكَ هُوَ الْفَوْزُ الْعَظِيْمُ ۝

يَوْمَ يَقُوْلُ الْمُنٰفِقُوْنَ وَ الْمُنٰفِقٰتُ لِلَّذِيْنَ اٰمَنُوا انْظُرُوْنَا نَقْتَبِسْ مِنْ نُّوْرِكُمْ قِيْلَ ارْجِعُوْا وَرَآءَكُمْ فَالْتَمِسُوْا نُوْرًا فَضُرِبَ بَيْنَهُمْ بِسُوْرٍ لَّهٗ بَابٌ بَاطِنُهٗ فِيْهِ الرَّحْمَةُ وَ ظَاهِرُهٗ مِنْ قِبَلِهِ الْعَذَابُ ۝

The hypocrites will call out to the believers: Were we not with you? They will answer: Indeed, but you involved yourselves in risk and you hesitated and doubted and your vain desires misled you till the decree of Allah came to pass. Thus Satan deceived you concerning Allah. So this day no ransom will be accepted from you, nor from those who disbelieved. Your abode is the Fire; that is your guardian, and an evil destination it is. (12—16)

Is it not time that the hearts of those who believe should feel humbled at the remembrance of Allah and of that which has come down to them of the truth? Let them not be like those who were given the Book before them and the term of Allah's favour was prolonged for them, so that their hearts were hardened, and most of them became disobedient. Keep in mind that Allah quickens the earth after its death. We have made the Signs manifest to you that you may understand. For the men who give alms and the women who give alms and for those who lend to Allah a goodly loan, that which they spend will be increased manifold, and theirs will be a generous reward. Those who believe in Allah and His Messengers are the Faithful and the Witnesses in the sight of their Lord. They will have their reward and their light. Those who disbelieve and reject Our Signs, these are the inmates of hell. (17—20)

Keep in mind that the life of this world is only sport and pastime, and a display, and a subject of boasting among yourselves, and rivalry in multiplying riches and children. It is like vegetation produced by the rain which rejoices the tiller. Then it dries up and takes on a yellow colour; then it becomes broken particles of stubble.

يُنَادُوْنَهُمْ اَلَمْ نَكُنْ مَّعَكُمْ قَالُوْا بَلٰى وَلٰكِنَّكُمْ فَتَنْتُمْ اَنْفُسَكُمْ وَتَرَبَّصْتُمْ وَارْتَبْتُمْ وَغَرَّتْكُمُ الْاَمَانِيُّ حَتّٰى جَآءَ اَمْرُ اللّٰهِ وَغَرَّكُمْ بِاللّٰهِ الْغَرُوْرُ ۞ فَالْيَوْمَ لَا يُؤْخَذُ مِنْكُمْ فِدْيَةٌ وَّلَا مِنَ الَّذِيْنَ كَفَرُوْا مَاْوٰىكُمُ النَّارُ هِيَ مَوْلٰىكُمْ وَبِئْسَ الْمَصِيْرُ ۞

اَلَمْ يَاْنِ لِلَّذِيْنَ اٰمَنُوْا اَنْ تَخْشَعَ قُلُوْبُهُمْ لِذِكْرِ اللّٰهِ وَمَا نَزَلَ مِنَ الْحَقِّ وَلَا يَكُوْنُوْا كَالَّذِيْنَ اُوْتُوا الْكِتٰبَ مِنْ قَبْلُ فَطَالَ عَلَيْهِمُ الْاَمَدُ فَقَسَتْ قُلُوْبُهُمْ وَكَثِيْرٌ مِّنْهُمْ فٰسِقُوْنَ ۞ اِعْلَمُوْا اَنَّ اللّٰهَ يُحْيِ الْاَرْضَ بَعْدَ مَوْتِهَا قَدْ بَيَّنَّا لَكُمُ الْاٰيٰتِ لَعَلَّكُمْ تَعْقِلُوْنَ ۞ اِنَّ الْمُصَّدِّقِيْنَ وَالْمُصَّدِّقٰتِ وَاَقْرَضُوا اللّٰهَ قَرْضًا حَسَنًا يُّضٰعَفُ لَهُمْ وَلَهُمْ اَجْرٌ كَرِيْمٌ ۞ وَالَّذِيْنَ اٰمَنُوْا بِاللّٰهِ وَرُسُلِهٖ اُولٰٓئِكَ هُمُ الصِّدِّيْقُوْنَ وَالشُّهَدَآءُ عِنْدَ رَبِّهِمْ لَهُمْ اَجْرُهُمْ وَنُوْرُهُمْ وَالَّذِيْنَ كَفَرُوْا وَكَذَّبُوْا بِاٰيٰتِنَا اُولٰٓئِكَ اَصْحٰبُ الْجَحِيْمِ ۞

اِعْلَمُوْا اَنَّمَا الْحَيٰوةُ الدُّنْيَا لَعِبٌ وَّلَهْوٌ وَّزِيْنَةٌ وَّتَفَاخُرٌ بَيْنَكُمْ وَتَكَاثُرٌ فِي الْاَمْوَالِ وَالْاَوْلَادِ كَمَثَلِ غَيْثٍ اَعْجَبَ الْكُفَّارَ نَبَاتُهُ ثُمَّ يَهِيْجُ فَتَرٰىهُ مُصْفَرًّا ثُمَّ يَكُوْنُ حُطَامًا وَفِي الْاٰخِرَةِ

In the Hereafter there is severe chastisement and also forgiveness from Allah and His pleasure. The life of this world is nothing but illusory enjoyment. Vie with one another in seeking forgiveness from your Lord and for a Garden the value of which is equal to the value of the heaven and the earth, which has been prepared for those who believe in Allah and His Messengers. That is Allah's grace; He bestows it upon whomsoever He pleases. Allah is Lord of immense grace.

عَذَابٌ شَدِيْدٌ وَّمَغْفِرَةٌ مِّنَ اللّٰهِ وَرِضْوَانٌ ۭ وَمَا الْحَيٰوةُ الدُّنْيَآ اِلَّا مَتَاعُ الْغُرُوْرِ ۞

سَابِقُوْا اِلٰى مَغْفِرَةٍ مِّنْ رَّبِّكُمْ وَجَنَّةٍ عَرْضُهَا كَعَرْضِ السَّمَآءِ وَالْاَرْضِ ۙ اُعِدَّتْ لِلَّذِيْنَ اٰمَنُوْا بِاللّٰهِ وَرُسُلِهٖ ۭ ذٰلِكَ فَضْلُ اللّٰهِ يُؤْتِيْهِ مَنْ يَّشَآءُ ۭ وَاللّٰهُ ذُو الْفَضْلِ الْعَظِيْمِ ۞

No calamity afflicts those on the earth or your own persons but is recorded in a Book before We make it manifest. Surely, that is easy for Allah. Thus it is, so that you may not grieve over that which you miss, nor exult over that which He bestows on you. Allah loves not any vainglorious boaster, who is niggardly himself and urges others to be niggardly. Whoso turns away should know that Allah is Self-Sufficient, Praiseworthy. We have sent Our Messengers with manifest Signs and have sent down with them the Book and the Balance, that people may act with justice. We sent down iron which furnishes weapons for violent warfare, and also provides many benefits, that Allah may make known those who help Him and His Messengers out of faith. Surely, Allah is Powerful, Mighty. (21—26)

مَا اَصَابَ مِنْ مُّصِيْبَةٍ فِى الْاَرْضِ وَلَا فِىْ اَنْفُسِكُمْ اِلَّا فِىْ كِتٰبٍ مِّنْ قَبْلِ اَنْ نَّبْرَاَهَا ۭ اِنَّ ذٰلِكَ عَلَى اللّٰهِ يَسِيْرٌ ۞

لِّكَيْلَا تَاْسَوْا عَلٰى مَا فَاتَكُمْ وَلَا تَفْرَحُوْا بِمَآ اٰتٰكُمْ ۭ وَاللّٰهُ لَا يُحِبُّ كُلَّ مُخْتَالٍ فَخُوْرِ ۞

اِلَّذِيْنَ يَبْخَلُوْنَ وَيَاْمُرُوْنَ النَّاسَ بِالْبُخْلِ ۭ وَمَنْ يَّتَوَلَّ فَاِنَّ اللّٰهَ هُوَ الْغَنِيُّ الْحَمِيْدُ ۞

لَقَدْ اَرْسَلْنَا رُسُلَنَا بِالْبَيِّنٰتِ وَاَنْزَلْنَا مَعَهُمُ الْكِتٰبَ وَالْمِيْزَانَ لِيَقُوْمَ النَّاسُ بِالْقِسْطِ ۚ وَاَنْزَلْنَا الْحَدِيْدَ فِيْهِ بَاْسٌ شَدِيْدٌ وَّمَنَافِعُ لِلنَّاسِ وَلِيَعْلَمَ اللّٰهُ مَنْ يَّنْصُرُهٗ وَرُسُلَهٗ بِالْغَيْبِ ۭ اِنَّ اللّٰهَ قَوِيٌّ عَزِيْزٌ ۞

We sent Noah and Abraham, and We bestowed Prophethood and the Book upon their descendants. Some of them followed the guidance but many of them were rebellious. Then We caused Our Messengers to follow in their footsteps; and We

وَلَقَدْ اَرْسَلْنَا نُوْحًا وَّاِبْرٰهِيْمَ وَجَعَلْنَا فِىْ ذُرِّيَّتِهِمَا النُّبُوَّةَ وَالْكِتٰبَ فَمِنْهُمْ مُّهْتَدٍ ۚ وَكَثِيْرٌ مِّنْهُمْ فٰسِقُوْنَ ۞

ثُمَّ قَفَّيْنَا عَلٰٓى اٰثَارِهِمْ بِرُسُلِنَا وَقَفَّيْنَا بِعِيْسَى

caused Jesus son of Mary to follow them, and We gave him the Gospel. We put compassion and mercy in the hearts of those who followed him. They took up monasticism for the seeking of Allah's pleasure. We did not prescribe it for them; but then they did not observe it duly. We bestowed upon those of them who believed their due reward, but many of them are rebellious. (27—28)

ابْنِ مَرْيَمَ وَاٰتَيْنٰهُ الْاِنْجِيْلَ ەۙ وَجَعَلْنَا فِيْ قُلُوْبِ الَّذِيْنَ اتَّبَعُوْهُ رَاْفَةً وَّرَحْمَةً ۭ وَرَهْبَانِيَّةَ ِ۟ ابْتَدَعُوْهَا مَا كَتَبْنٰهَا عَلَيْهِمْ اِلَّا ابْتِغَآءَ رِضْوَانِ اللّٰهِ فَمَا رَعَوْهَا حَقَّ رِعَايَتِهَا ۚ فَاٰتَيْنَا الَّذِيْنَ اٰمَنُوْا مِنْهُمْ اَجْرَهُمْ ۚ وَكَثِيْرٌ مِّنْهُمْ فٰسِقُوْنَ ۝

O ye who believe, be mindful of your duty to Allah and have firm faith in His Messenger; He will bestow a double portion of His mercy on you, and will provide for you a light wherein you will walk and will grant you forgiveness. Verily Allah is Most Forgiving, Ever Merciful. Thus it is, so that the people of the Book may not think that the Muslims are not capable of attaining aught of Allah's grace; and may know that grace is entirely in the hands of Allah; He bestows it on whomsoever He pleases. Allah is the Lord of immense grace. (29—30)

يٰٓاَيُّهَا الَّذِيْنَ اٰمَنُوا اتَّقُوا اللّٰهَ وَاٰمِنُوْا بِرَسُوْلِهٖ يُؤْتِكُمْ كِفْلَيْنِ مِنْ رَّحْمَتِهٖ وَيَجْعَلْ لَّكُمْ نُوْرًا تَمْشُوْنَ بِهٖ وَيَغْفِرْ لَكُمْ ۭ وَاللّٰهُ غَفُوْرٌ رَّحِيْمٌ ۝

لِّئَلَّا يَعْلَمَ اَهْلُ الْكِتٰبِ اَلَّا يَقْدِرُوْنَ عَلٰى شَيْءٍ مِّنْ فَضْلِ اللّٰهِ وَاَنَّ الْفَضْلَ بِيَدِ اللّٰهِ يُؤْتِيْهِ مَنْ يَّشَآءُ ۭ وَاللّٰهُ ذُو الْفَضْلِ الْعَظِيْمِ ۝

سُوْرَةُ الْمُجَادِلَةِ مَدَنِيَّةٌ

Chapter 58   **AL-MUJĀDILAH**   **Part 28**
(Revealed after Hijra)

In the name of Allah, Most Gracious, Ever Merciful. (1)

بِسْمِ اللّٰهِ الرَّحْمٰنِ الرَّحِيْمِ ۝

قَدْ سَمِعَ اللّٰهُ قَوْلَ الَّتِيْ تُجَادِلُكَ فِيْ زَوْجِهَا وَتَشْتَكِيْٓ اِلَى اللّٰهِ ۖ وَاللّٰهُ يَسْمَعُ تَحَاوُرَكُمَا ۭ اِنَّ اللّٰهَ سَمِيْعٌۢ بَصِيْرٌ ۝

Allah has heard the prayer of her who pleaded with thee concerning her husband and beseeched Allah. Allah heard the dialogue between you. Allah is All-Hearing, All-Seeing. Those among you who put away their wives by calling them mothers

اَلَّذِيْنَ يُظٰهِرُوْنَ مِنْكُمْ مِّنْ نِّسَآئِهِمْ مَّا هُنَّ

are surely guilty of uttering words that are manifestly evil and untrue. Their wives do not thereby become their mothers. Their mothers are only those who gave them birth. But Allah is surely Forbearing, Most Forgiving. Those who call their wives mothers and would then repair that which they have said must procure the freedom of one held in bondage before they touch each other. This is what you are admonished with, and Allah is Well-Aware of that which you do. But whoso is not able to procure a slave to set free, must fast consecutively for two months before the two touch each other; and whoso is not able to do that, must feed sixty poor people. This penalty is prescribed to enforce obedience on your part to Allah and His Messenger. These are the limits set by Allah, and for those who repudiate them is a painful chastisement. Those who oppose Allah and His Messenger will surely be humiliated even as those before them were humiliated. We have sent down Our clear commands. Those who repudiate them shall suffer an humiliating chastisement, on the day when Allah will raise them all together, and will inform them of that which they did. Allah has kept count of it, while they forgot it. Allah is witness over all things. (2—7)

Knowest thou not that Allah has knowledge of all that is in the heavens and all that is in the earth? There is no secret counsel of three, but He is the fourth thereat, nor of five, but He is the sixth, nor of less than that, nor of more, but He is with them wheresoever they may be. Then on the Day of Judgment He will inform them of that which they did. Surely, Allah knows all things well. Seest thou not those who were forbidden to conspire secretly and who keep returning to that which they were forbidden, and conspire in support of sin and transgression and disobedience to the Messenger? When they come to thee they greet thee with a greeting with which Allah has not greeted thee, and they think in their hearts: Why does not Allah punish us for our hypocritical greeting? Sufficient for them is hell, wherein they will enter; and an evil destination it is. O ye who believe, when you confer together in secret, confer not in support of sin and transgression and disobedience to the Messenger, but confer for the promotion of virtue and righteousness, and be mindful of your duty to Allah unto Whom you shall all be gathered. Secret conspiracy is a device of Satan, that he may make the believers anxious; but it cannot harm them in the least, except by Allah's leave. In Allah should the believers put their trust. (8—11)

O ye who believe, when you are asked to make room in your assemblies then do make room, Allah will bestow amplitude upon you. When you are asked to rise up, then rise up, Allah will exalt in rank those from among you who believe and those to whom knowledge is given. Allah is Well-Aware of that which you do. O ye who believe, when you consult the Messenger in private, make an offering for charity before your consultation. That is better for you and purer. But if you find not anything to offer, then Allah is Most Forgiving, Ever Merciful. Are you afraid of making an inadequate offering before your consultation? Then, if you are not able to make an adequate offering and Allah has already turned to you with grace, observe Prayer and pay the Zakat and obey Allah and His Messenger. Allah is Well-Aware of that which you do. (12—14)

Seest thou not those who make friends with a people with whom Allah is wroth ? They are neither of you nor of them, and they swear to falsehood knowingly. Allah has prepared for them a severe chastisement. Evil indeed is that which they used to practise. They have made their oaths a cloak, by means of which they turn people away from the path of Allah. They shall suffer an humiliating chastisement.

Their wealth and their progeny shall not avail them aught against Allah. They are the inmates of the Fire wherein they will abide. On the day when Allah will raise them all together, they will swear to Him even as they swear to you, thinking they are making a strong stand. Despite all their protestations they are liars. Satan has got the better of them, and has made them neglect the remembrance of Allah. They are the party of Satan; and it is Satan's party that are the losers.

Surely, those who oppose Allah and His Messenger are among the vilest. Allah has decreed: Most surely, it is I who will prevail, I and My Messengers. Verily, Allah is Powerful, Mighty. Thou wilt not find any people who believe in Allah and the Last Day, and yet love those who oppose Allah and His Messenger, even though they be

ع رَسُوْلَهٗ ۚ وَاللّٰهُ خَبِيْرٌۢ بِمَا تَعْمَلُوْنَ ۞

اَلَمْ تَرَ اِلَى الَّذِيْنَ تَوَلَّوْا قَوْمًا غَضِبَ اللّٰهُ عَلَيْهِمْ ؕ

مَا هُمْ مِّنْكُمْ وَلَا مِنْهُمْ ۙ وَيَحْلِفُوْنَ عَلَى الْكَذِبِ

وَهُمْ يَعْلَمُوْنَ ۞

اَعَدَّ اللّٰهُ لَهُمْ عَذَابًا شَدِيْدًا ؕ اِنَّهُمْ سَاۤءَ مَا

كَانُوْا يَعْمَلُوْنَ ۞

اِتَّخَذُوْۤا اَيْمَانَهُمْ جُنَّةً فَصَدُّوْا عَنْ سَبِيْلِ

اللّٰهِ فَلَهُمْ عَذَابٌ مُّهِيْنٌ ۞

لَنْ تُغْنِيَ عَنْهُمْ اَمْوَالُهُمْ وَلَاۤ اَوْلَادُهُمْ مِّنَ

اللّٰهِ شَيْئًا ؕ اُولٰٓئِكَ اَصْحٰبُ النَّارِ ۚ هُمْ فِيْهَا خٰلِدُوْنَ ۞

يَوْمَ يَبْعَثُهُمُ اللّٰهُ جَمِيْعًا فَيَحْلِفُوْنَ لَهٗ كَمَا

يَحْلِفُوْنَ لَكُمْ وَيَحْسَبُوْنَ اَنَّهُمْ عَلٰى شَيْءٍ ؕ اَلَاۤ

اِنَّهُمْ هُمُ الْكٰذِبُوْنَ ۞

اِسْتَحْوَذَ عَلَيْهِمُ الشَّيْطٰنُ فَاَنْسٰهُمْ ذِكْرَ اللّٰهِ ؕ

اُولٰٓئِكَ حِزْبُ الشَّيْطٰنِ ؕ اَلَاۤ اِنَّ حِزْبَ الشَّيْطٰنِ

هُمُ الْخٰسِرُوْنَ ۞

اِنَّ الَّذِيْنَ يُحَاۤدُّوْنَ اللّٰهَ وَرَسُوْلَهٗۤ اُولٰٓئِكَ فِى

الْاَذَلِّيْنَ ۞

كَتَبَ اللّٰهُ لَاَغْلِبَنَّ اَنَا وَرُسُلِيْ ؕ اِنَّ اللّٰهَ قَوِيٌّ

عَزِيْزٌ ۞

لَا تَجِدُ قَوْمًا يُّؤْمِنُوْنَ بِاللّٰهِ وَالْيَوْمِ الْاٰخِرِ

يُوَاۤدُّوْنَ مَنْ حَاۤدَّ اللّٰهَ وَرَسُوْلَهٗ وَلَوْ كَانُوْۤا اٰبَاۤءَهُمْ

their fathers, or their sons, or their brethren, or their kindred. These are they in whose hearts Allah has inscribed true faith and whom He has strengthened with revelation from Himself. He will admit them to Gardens through which streams flow; therein will they abide. Allah is well pleased with them and they are well pleased with Him. They are Allah's party. Take note, it is Allah's party who will prosper. (15—23)

اَوۡ اَبۡنَآءَهُمۡ اَوۡ اِخۡوَانَهُمۡ اَوۡ عَشِيۡرَتَهُمۡ ۚ اُولٰٓئِكَ كَتَبَ فِىۡ قُلُوۡبِهِمُ الۡاِيۡمَانَ وَ اَيَّدَهُمۡ بِرُوۡحٍ مِّنۡهُ ؕ وَ يُدۡخِلُهُمۡ جَنّٰتٍ تَجۡرِىۡ مِنۡ تَحۡتِهَا الۡاَنۡهٰرُ خٰلِدِيۡنَ فِيۡهَا ؕ رَضِىَ اللّٰهُ عَنۡهُمۡ وَ رَضُوۡا عَنۡهُ ؕ اُولٰٓئِكَ حِزۡبُ اللّٰهِ ؕ اَلَاۤ اِنَّ حِزۡبَ اللّٰهِ هُمُ الۡمُفۡلِحُوۡنَ ۞

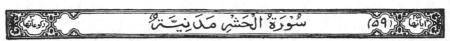

سُوۡرَةُ الۡحَشۡرِ مَدَنِيَّةٌ

(*Revealed after Hijra*)

In the name of Allah, Most Gracious, Ever Merciful. (1)

بِسۡمِ اللّٰهِ الرَّحۡمٰنِ الرَّحِيۡمِ ۞

سَبَّحَ لِلّٰهِ مَا فِى السَّمٰوٰتِ وَ مَا فِى الۡاَرۡضِ ۚ وَ هُوَ الۡعَزِيۡزُ الۡحَكِيۡمُ ۞

All that is in the heavens and all that is in the earth glorifies Allah. He is the Mighty, the Wise. He it is Who turned out the disbelievers from among the People of the Book from their homes at the time of the first banishment. You did not think that they would go forth and they thought that their fortresses would protect them against Allah. But Allah came upon them whence they did not expect and cast terror into their hearts, so that they destroyed their homes with their own hands and the hands of the believers. So take warning, O ye who possess understanding. Had it not been that Allah had decreed exile for them, He would surely have chastised them in this life also. In the Hereafter they will certainly undergo the chastisement of the Fire. That is because they opposed Allah and His Messenger; and whoso oppo-

هُوَ الَّذِىۡۤ اَخۡرَجَ الَّذِيۡنَ كَفَرُوۡا مِنۡ اَهۡلِ الۡكِتٰبِ مِنۡ دِيَارِهِمۡ لِاَوَّلِ الۡحَشۡرِ ؔؕ مَا ظَنَنۡتُمۡ اَنۡ يَّخۡرُجُوۡا وَ ظَنُّوۡۤا اَنَّهُمۡ مَّانِعَتُهُمۡ حُصُوۡنُهُمۡ مِّنَ اللّٰهِ فَاَتٰىهُمُ اللّٰهُ مِنۡ حَيۡثُ لَمۡ يَحۡتَسِبُوۡا ۫ وَ قَذَفَ فِىۡ قُلُوۡبِهِمُ الرُّعۡبَ يُخۡرِبُوۡنَ بُيُوۡتَهُمۡ بِاَيۡدِيۡهِمۡ وَ اَيۡدِى الۡمُؤۡمِنِيۡنَ ۫ فَاعۡتَبِرُوۡا يٰۤاُولِى الۡاَبۡصَارِ ۞

وَ لَوۡ لَاۤ اَنۡ كَتَبَ اللّٰهُ عَلَيۡهِمُ الۡجَلَآءَ لَعَذَّبَهُمۡ فِى الدُّنۡيَا ؕ وَ لَهُمۡ فِى الۡاٰخِرَةِ عَذَابُ النَّارِ ۞

ذٰلِكَ بِاَنَّهُمۡ شَآقُّوا اللّٰهَ وَ رَسُوۡلَهٗ ۚ وَ مَنۡ يُّشَآقِّ

ses Allah will find that Allah is Severe in retribution. Whatever palm-trees you cut down or left them standing on their roots was by Allah's command, that He might disgrace the transgressors. Whatever Allah has given to His Messenger as spoils from them, is of His grace. You urged neither horse nor camel for it; but Allah grants power to His Messengers over whomsoever He pleases. Allah has power over all things.

Whatever Allah has bestowed on His Messenger as spoils, from the people of Khaibar and its suburbs, is for Allah and for the Messenger and for the near of kin and the orphans and the needy and the wayfarer, that it may not circulate only among those of you who are rich. Whatever the Messenger gives you, that take; and whatsoever he forbids you, from that abstain. Be mindful of your duty to Allah; surely, Allah is severe in retribution. It is also for the poor Refugees who have been driven out from their homes and their possessions, who seek Allah's grace and His pleasure and constantly help the cause of Allah and His Messenger. These are the sincere in faith. It is also for those who had established their home in Medina and had accepted the faith before the coming of the Refugees. They love those who come to them for refuge and do not hanker after that which is given to the Refugees, but give them preference over their own selves, even when they themselves are poor. Whoso is rid of the covetousness of his own mind, it is these who will be successful.

It is also for those who came after them. They pray: Lord, forgive us and our brethren who preceded us in the faith, and permit not any feeling of rancour to arise in our hearts against those who believe, Lord; Thou art indeed Compassionate, Merciful. (2—11)

اللهَ فَاِنَّ اللهَ شَدِيْدُ الْعِقَابِ ۞

مَا قَطَعْتُمْ مِّنْ لِّيْنَةٍ اَوْ تَرَكْتُمُوْهَا قَآئِمَةً عَلٰى اُصُوْلِهَا فَبِاِذْنِ اللهِ وَلِيُخْزِيَ الْفٰسِقِيْنَ ۞

وَمَآ اَفَآءَ اللهُ عَلٰى رَسُوْلِهٖ مِنْهُمْ فَمَآ اَوْجَفْتُمْ عَلَيْهِ مِنْ خَيْلٍ وَّلَا رِكَابٍ وَّلٰكِنَّ اللهَ يُسَلِّطُ رُسُلَهٗ عَلٰى مَنْ يَّشَآءُ وَاللهُ عَلٰى كُلِّ شَيْءٍ قَدِيْرٌ ۞

مَآ اَفَآءَ اللهُ عَلٰى رَسُوْلِهٖ مِنْ اَهْلِ الْقُرٰى فَلِلّٰهِ وَلِلرَّسُوْلِ وَلِذِى الْقُرْبٰى وَالْيَتٰمٰى وَالْمَسٰكِيْنِ وَابْنِ السَّبِيْلِ كَيْ لَا يَكُوْنَ دُوْلَةً بَيْنَ الْاَغْنِيَآءِ مِنْكُمْ وَمَآ اٰتٰكُمُ الرَّسُوْلُ فَخُذُوْهُ وَمَا نَهٰكُمْ عَنْهُ فَانْتَهُوْا وَاتَّقُوا اللهَ اِنَّ اللهَ شَدِيْدُ الْعِقَابِ ۞

لِلْفُقَرَآءِ الْمُهٰجِرِيْنَ الَّذِيْنَ اُخْرِجُوْا مِنْ دِيَارِهِمْ وَاَمْوَالِهِمْ يَبْتَغُوْنَ فَضْلًا مِّنَ اللهِ وَرِضْوَانًا وَّيَنْصُرُوْنَ اللهَ وَرَسُوْلَهٗ اُولٰئِكَ هُمُ الصّٰدِقُوْنَ ۞

وَالَّذِيْنَ تَبَوَّءُوا الدَّارَ وَالْاِيْمَانَ مِنْ قَبْلِهِمْ يُحِبُّوْنَ مَنْ هَاجَرَ اِلَيْهِمْ وَلَا يَجِدُوْنَ فِيْ صُدُوْرِهِمْ حَاجَةً مِّمَّا اُوْتُوْا وَيُؤْثِرُوْنَ عَلٰى اَنْفُسِهِمْ وَلَوْ كَانَ بِهِمْ خَصَاصَةٌ وَمَنْ يُّوْقَ شُحَّ نَفْسِهٖ فَاُولٰئِكَ هُمُ الْمُفْلِحُوْنَ ۞

وَالَّذِيْنَ جَآءُوْ مِنْ بَعْدِهِمْ يَقُوْلُوْنَ رَبَّنَا اغْفِرْ لَنَا وَلِاِخْوَانِنَا الَّذِيْنَ سَبَقُوْنَا بِالْاِيْمَانِ وَلَا تَجْعَلْ فِيْ قُلُوْبِنَا غِلًّا لِّلَّذِيْنَ اٰمَنُوْا رَبَّنَآ اِنَّكَ

Knowest thou not the hypocrites who say to their disbelieving companions among the people of the Book: If you are turned out of Medina, we will surely go out with you, and we will never obey any one at all against you, and if you are fought against we will certainly help you. Allah bears witness that they are certainly liars. If their companions are turned out, they will never go out with them; and if they are fought against they will never help them; and were they to help them they would assuredly turn their backs, and they themselves will not be helped. In truth they have greater fear of you in their hearts than of Allah. That is because they are a people without understanding. They will not fight you in a body except in fortified towns or from behind walls. Their boast of their fighting prowess to each other is fierce. Thou thinkest them to be united but their hearts are divided. That is because they are a people without sense.

They are like people who have shortly before been afflicted with the consequences of their evil conduct, and suffered a painful chastisement. They are like Satan, when he says to man: Disbelieve; and when he disbelieves, Satan says to him: I am quit of you; I fear Allah, the Lord of the worlds. They will both end up in the Fire, abiding therein. Such is the reward of the wrongdoers. (12—18)

O ye who believe, be mindful of your duty to Allah, and let every one look to that which he lays up for the morrow. Fear Allah; verily Allah is Well-Aware of that which you do. Be not like those who forgot Allah, and in consequence He caused them to forget their own true interests. It is they that are the rebellious. The inmates of the Fire and the inmates of the Garden are not alike. It is the inmates of the Garden who will triumph. (19—21)

أُولٰٓئِكَ هُمُ الْفٰسِقُوْنَ ۝

لَا يَسْتَوِىْٓ اَصْحٰبُ النَّارِ وَاَصْحٰبُ الْجَنَّةِ اَصْحٰبُ الْجَنَّةِ هُمُ الْفَآئِزُوْنَ ۝

Had We sent down this Quran on a mountain, thou wouldst certainly have seen it bend down in humility and rent asunder in awe of Allah's Majesty. These are illustrations that We set forth for mankind that they may reflect. (22)

لَوْ اَنْزَلْنَا هٰذَا الْقُرْاٰنَ عَلٰى جَبَلٍ لَّرَاَيْتَهٗ خَاشِعًا مُّتَصَدِّعًا مِّنْ خَشْيَةِ اللّٰهِ ۚ وَتِلْكَ الْاَمْثَالُ نَضْرِبُهَا لِلنَّاسِ لَعَلَّهُمْ يَتَفَكَّرُوْنَ ۝

هُوَ اللّٰهُ الَّذِىْ لَآ اِلٰهَ اِلَّا هُوَ ۚ عٰلِمُ الْغَيْبِ وَالشَّهَادَةِ ۚ هُوَ الرَّحْمٰنُ الرَّحِيْمُ ۝

Allah is He beside Whom there is no god, Knower of the unseen and the seen. He is the Most Gracious, the Ever Merciful. Allah is He beside Whom there is no god, the Sovereign, the Most Holy, the Source of Peace, the Bestower of Security, the Protector, the Mighty, the Subduer, the Exalted. Holy is Allah, far above that which they associate with Him. He is Allah, the Creator, the Maker, the Fashioner; His are the most beautiful names. All that is in the heavens and the earth glorifies Him. He is the Mighty, the Wise. (23—25)

هُوَ اللّٰهُ الَّذِىْ لَآ اِلٰهَ اِلَّا هُوَ ۚ اَلْمَلِكُ الْقُدُّوْسُ السَّلٰمُ الْمُؤْمِنُ الْمُهَيْمِنُ الْعَزِيْزُ الْجَبَّارُ الْمُتَكَبِّرُ ۚ سُبْحٰنَ اللّٰهِ عَمَّا يُشْرِكُوْنَ ۝

هُوَ اللّٰهُ الْخَالِقُ الْبَارِئُ الْمُصَوِّرُ لَهُ الْاَسْمَآءُ الْحُسْنٰى ۚ يُسَبِّحُ لَهٗ مَا فِى السَّمٰوٰتِ وَالْاَرْضِ ۚ وَهُوَ الْعَزِيْزُ الْحَكِيْمُ ۝

(Revealed after Hijra)

In the name of Allah, Most Gracious, Ever Merciful. (1)

بِسْمِ اللّٰهِ الرَّحْمٰنِ الرَّحِيْمِ ۝

O ye who believe, make not friends with My enemy and your enemy. You send them messages of affection, while they disbelieve in the truth that has come to you, and call out the Messenger and your-

يٰٓاَيُّهَا الَّذِيْنَ اٰمَنُوْا لَا تَتَّخِذُوْا عَدُوِّىْ وَعَدُوَّكُمْ اَوْلِيَآءَ تُلْقُوْنَ اِلَيْهِمْ بِالْمَوَدَّةِ وَقَدْ كَفَرُوْا بِمَا جَآءَكُمْ مِّنَ الْحَقِّ ۚ يُخْرِجُوْنَ الرَّسُوْلَ وَاِيَّاكُمْ اَنْ

selves to battle solely because you believe in Allah, your Lord. When you go forth to strive in My cause and to seek My pleasure, some of you send them friendly messages in secret; while I know well that which you conceal and that which you disclose. Whoever of you does so, has surely slipped from the right path. Should they gain mastery over you, you will realise that they are your enemies and are employing their hands and tongues to your injury; ardently desiring that you should become disbelievers.

تُؤْمِنُوْا بِاللّٰهِ رَبِّكُمْ ۚ اِنْ كُنْتُمْ خَرَجْتُمْ جِهَادًا فِیْ سَبِیْلِیْ وَ ابْتِغَآءَ مَرْضَاتِیْ ۙ تُسِرُّوْنَ اِلَیْهِمْ بِالْمَوَدَّةِ ۖ وَ اَنَا اَعْلَمُ بِمَاۤ اَخْفَیْتُمْ وَمَاۤ اَعْلَنْتُمْ ؕ وَمَنْ یَّفْعَلْهُ مِنْكُمْ فَقَدْ ضَلَّ سَوَآءَ السَّبِیْلِ ۟

اِنْ یَّثْقَفُوْكُمْ یَكُوْنُوْا لَكُمْ اَعْدَآءً وَّ یَبْسُطُوْۤا اِلَیْكُمْ اَیْدِیَهُمْ وَاَلْسِنَتَهُمْ بِالسُّوْٓءِ وَ وَدُّوْا لَوْ تَكْفُرُوْنَ ۟

Neither your ties of kinship nor your children will avail you aught on the Day of Judgment; He will decide between you. Allah sees all that you do. For you there is a good example in Abraham and his companions, when they said to their people: We dissociate ourselves utterly from you and from that which you worship beside Allah. We totally reject you. Enmity and hatred have become manifest between you and us for ever, until you believe in Allah, the One. Abraham's saying to his father: I shall ask forgiveness for thee, though I have no power to help thee in the least against Allah; was a thing apart. Their prayer was: Lord, in Thee do we put our trust, and to Thee do we turn in repentance, and to Thee is the final return. Lord, make us not a trial for those who disbelieve, and forgive us, Lord, for Thou alone art the Mighty, the Wise. In them there is a good example for you, for all those who desire the favour of Allah and look forward to the Last Day. Whoso turns away shall find that Allah is Self-Sufficient, Praiseworthy. (2—7)

لَنْ تَنْفَعَكُمْ اَرْحَامُكُمْ وَلَاۤ اَوْلَادُكُمْ ۛ یَوْمَ الْقِیٰمَةِ ۛ یَفْصِلُ بَیْنَكُمْ ؕ وَاللّٰهُ بِمَا تَعْمَلُوْنَ بَصِیْرٌ ۟

قَدْ كَانَتْ لَكُمْ اُسْوَةٌ حَسَنَةٌ فِیْۤ اِبْرٰهِیْمَ وَالَّذِیْنَ مَعَهٗ ۚ اِذْ قَالُوْا لِقَوْمِهِمْ اِنَّا بُرَءٰٓؤُا مِنْكُمْ وَمِمَّا تَعْبُدُوْنَ مِنْ دُوْنِ اللّٰهِ ۫ كَفَرْنَا بِكُمْ وَبَدَا بَیْنَنَا وَبَیْنَكُمُ الْعَدَاوَةُ وَالْبَغْضَآءُ اَبَدًا حَتّٰی تُؤْمِنُوْا بِاللّٰهِ وَحْدَهٗۤ اِلَّا قَوْلَ اِبْرٰهِیْمَ لِاَبِیْهِ لَاَسْتَغْفِرَنَّ لَكَ وَمَاۤ اَمْلِكُ لَكَ مِنَ اللّٰهِ مِنْ شَیْءٍ ؕ رَبَّنَا عَلَیْكَ تَوَكَّلْنَا وَاِلَیْكَ اَنَبْنَا وَاِلَیْكَ الْمَصِیْرُ ۟

رَبَّنَا لَا تَجْعَلْنَا فِتْنَةً لِّلَّذِیْنَ كَفَرُوْا وَاغْفِرْ لَنَا رَبَّنَا ۚ اِنَّكَ اَنْتَ الْعَزِیْزُ الْحَكِیْمُ ۟

لَقَدْ كَانَ لَكُمْ فِیْهِمْ اُسْوَةٌ حَسَنَةٌ لِّمَنْ كَانَ یَرْجُوا اللّٰهَ وَالْیَوْمَ الْاٰخِرَ ؕ وَمَنْ یَّتَوَلَّ فَاِنَّ اللّٰهَ هُوَ الْغَنِیُّ الْحَمِیْدُ ۟

It may be that Allah will bring about amity between you and those with whom you are at enmity. Allah has the Power;

عَسَی اللّٰهُ اَنْ یَّجْعَلَ بَیْنَكُمْ وَبَیْنَ الَّذِیْنَ عَادَیْتُمْ

Allah is Most Forgiving, Ever Merciful.
Allah does not forbid you to be kind and
to act equitably towards those who have
not fought you because of your religion,
and who have not driven you forth from
your homes. Surely, Allah loves those who
are equitable. Allah only forbids you that
you make friends with those who have
fought against you because of your religion, and have driven you out of your
homes and have aided others in driving
you out. Whoso makes friends with them,
those are the transgressors. (8—10)

O ye who believe, when believing women
come to you as Refugees, satisfy yourselves as to their faith. Allah knows well
their faith. Then if you find them true
believers send them not back to the disbelievers. These women are not lawful for
them, nor are they lawful for these women;
but remit to their disbelieving husbands
what they have spent on them. Thereafter, it is no sin for you to marry them
on payment of their dowers. Do not hold
disbelieving women to their marriage ties,
but demand the return of that which you
have spent on them; and let the disbelievers demand that which they have
spent. This is the judgment of Allah. He
judges between you. Allah is All-Knowing, Wise. If any of your wives goes over
to the disbelievers, and thereafter any
disbelieving women become your prisoners, then pay to those whose wives have
gone away the equivalent of that which
they had spent. Be mindful of your duty
to Allah in whom you believe. (11—12)

O Prophet, when believing women come
to thee, offering their allegiance that they
will not associate anything with Allah, and
that they will not steal, and will not commit adultery, nor kill their children, nor
make a false accusation of unchastity, nor
disobey thee in that which is right, then

مِّنْهُمْ مَّوَدَّةً ۚ وَاللّٰهُ قَدِيرٌ ۚ وَاللّٰهُ غَفُوْرٌ رَّحِيْمٌ ۝

لَا يَنْهٰىكُمُ اللّٰهُ عَنِ الَّذِيْنَ لَمْ يُقَاتِلُوْكُمْ فِى
الدِّيْنِ وَلَمْ يُخْرِجُوْكُمْ مِّنْ دِيَارِكُمْ اَنْ تَبَرُّوْهُمْ
وَتُقْسِطُوْۤا اِلَيْهِمْ ۚ اِنَّ اللّٰهَ يُحِبُّ الْمُقْسِطِيْنَ ۝

اِنَّمَا يَنْهٰىكُمُ اللّٰهُ عَنِ الَّذِيْنَ قَاتَلُوْكُمْ فِى الدِّيْنِ
وَاَخْرَجُوْكُمْ مِّنْ دِيَارِكُمْ وَظَاهَرُوْا عَلٰۤى اِخْرَاجِكُمْ
اَنْ تَوَلَّوْهُمْ ۚ وَمَنْ يَّتَوَلَّهُمْ فَاُولٰۤئِكَ هُمُ الظّٰلِمُوْنَ ۝

يٰۤاَيُّهَا الَّذِيْنَ اٰمَنُوْۤا اِذَا جَآءَكُمُ الْمُؤْمِنٰتُ مُهٰجِرٰتٍ
فَامْتَحِنُوْهُنَّ ۚ اَللّٰهُ اَعْلَمُ بِاِيْمَانِهِنَّ ۚ فَاِنْ عَلِمْتُمُوْهُنَّ
مُؤْمِنٰتٍ فَلَا تَرْجِعُوْهُنَّ اِلَى الْكُفَّارِ ۚ لَا هُنَّ حِلٌّ
لَّهُمْ وَلَا هُمْ يَحِلُّوْنَ لَهُنَّ ۚ وَاٰتُوْهُمْ مَّاۤ اَنْفَقُوْا ۚ
وَلَا جُنَاحَ عَلَيْكُمْ اَنْ تَنْكِحُوْهُنَّ اِذَاۤ اٰتَيْتُمُوْهُنَّ
اُجُوْرَهُنَّ ۚ وَلَا تُمْسِكُوْا بِعِصَمِ الْكَوَافِرِ وَاسْـَٔلُوْا
مَاۤ اَنْفَقْتُمْ وَلْيَسْـَٔلُوْا مَاۤ اَنْفَقُوْا ۚ ذٰلِكُمْ حُكْمُ اللّٰهِ ۚ
يَحْكُمُ بَيْنَكُمْ ۚ وَاللّٰهُ عَلِيْمٌ حَكِيْمٌ ۝

وَاِنْ فَاتَكُمْ شَيْءٌ مِّنْ اَزْوَاجِكُمْ اِلَى الْكُفَّارِ
فَعَاقَبْتُمْ فَاٰتُوا الَّذِيْنَ ذَهَبَتْ اَزْوَاجُهُمْ مِّثْلَ
مَاۤ اَنْفَقُوْا ۚ وَاتَّقُوا اللّٰهَ الَّذِيْۤ اَنْتُمْ بِهٖ مُؤْمِنُوْنَ ۝

يٰۤاَيُّهَا النَّبِيُّ اِذَا جَآءَكَ الْمُؤْمِنٰتُ يُبَايِعْنَكَ عَلٰۤى
اَنْ لَّا يُشْرِكْنَ بِاللّٰهِ شَيْـًٔا وَّلَا يَسْرِقْنَ وَلَا يَزْنِيْنَ
وَلَا يَقْتُلْنَ اَوْلَادَهُنَّ وَلَا يَأْتِيْنَ بِبُهْتَانٍ يَّفْتَرِيْنَهٗ
بَيْنَ اَيْدِيْهِنَّ وَاَرْجُلِهِنَّ وَلَا يَعْصِيْنَكَ فِيْ مَعْرُوْفٍ

accept their allegiance and ask Allah to forgive them. Verily, Allah is Most Forgiving, Ever Merciful. O ye who believe, make not friends with people with whom Allah is wroth; they have despaired of the Hereafter, as the disbelievers have despaired of those who are in the graves. (13—14)

فَبَايِعْهُنَّ وَاسْتَغْفِرْ لَهُنَّ اللَّهَ اِنَّ اللَّهَ غَفُوْرٌ رَّحِيْمٌ ۞

يٰاَيُّهَا الَّذِيْنَ اٰمَنُوْا لَا تَتَوَلَّوْا قَوْمًا غَضِبَ اللَّهُ عَلَيْهِمْ قَدْ يَئِسُوْا مِنَ الْاٰخِرَةِ كَمَا يَئِسَ الْكُفَّارُ مِنْ اَصْحٰبِ الْقُبُوْرِ ۞

(Revealed after Hijra)

In the name of Allah, Most Gracious, Ever Merciful. (1)

بِسْمِ اللَّهِ الرَّحْمٰنِ الرَّحِيْمِ ۞

سَبَّحَ لِلَّهِ مَا فِي السَّمٰوٰتِ وَمَا فِي الْاَرْضِ وَهُوَ الْعَزِيْزُ الْحَكِيْمُ ۞

Whatever is in the heavens and whatever is in the earth glorifies Allah. He is the Mighty, the Wise. O ye who believe, why do you say that which you do not? Most odious is it in the sight of Allah that you should say that which you do not. Allah loves those who fight in His cause arrayed in serried ranks, as though they were a strong wall cemented with molten lead. (2—5)

يٰاَيُّهَا الَّذِيْنَ اٰمَنُوْا لِمَ تَقُوْلُوْنَ مَا لَا تَفْعَلُوْنَ ۞

كَبُرَ مَقْتًا عِنْدَ اللَّهِ اَنْ تَقُوْلُوْا مَا لَا تَفْعَلُوْنَ ۞

اِنَّ اللَّهَ يُحِبُّ الَّذِيْنَ يُقَاتِلُوْنَ فِيْ سَبِيْلِهِ صَفًّا كَاَنَّهُمْ بُنْيَانٌ مَرْصُوْصٌ ۞

Call to mind when Moses said to his people; O my people, why do you vex me when you know that I am Allah's Messenger unto you? So when they deviated from the right course, Allah made their hearts perverse. Allah guides not a rebellious people. Call to mind also when Jesus son of Mary said: O children of Israel, surely I am Allah's Messenger unto you, fulfilling the prophecies contained in the Torah, which was revealed before me, and giving glad tidings of a Messenger who will come after me whose name will be Ahmad. But when he came to them with clear proofs, they said: This is clear

وَاِذْ قَالَ مُوْسٰى لِقَوْمِهِ يٰقَوْمِ لِمَ تُؤْذُوْنَنِيْ وَقَدْ تَعْلَمُوْنَ اَنِّيْ رَسُوْلُ اللَّهِ اِلَيْكُمْ فَلَمَّا زَاغُوْا اَزَاغَ اللَّهُ قُلُوْبَهُمْ وَاللَّهُ لَا يَهْدِي الْقَوْمَ الْفٰسِقِيْنَ ۞

وَاِذْ قَالَ عِيْسَى ابْنُ مَرْيَمَ يٰبَنِيْ اِسْرَآءِيْلَ اِنِّيْ رَسُوْلُ اللَّهِ اِلَيْكُمْ مُصَدِّقًا لِّمَا بَيْنَ يَدَيَّ مِنَ التَّوْرٰىةِ وَمُبَشِّرًا بِرَسُوْلٍ يَّأْتِيْ مِنْ بَعْدِي اسْمُهُ اَحْمَدُ فَلَمَّا جَآءَهُمْ بِالْبَيِّنٰتِ قَالُوْا هٰذَا

deception. Who could be more unjust than one who fabricates a lie against Allah, while he is called to Islam? Allah guides not a wrongdoing people. They desire to extinguish the light of Allah with the breath of their mouths, but Allah will perfect His light, however much the disbelievers may dislike it. He it is Who has sent His Messenger with the guidance and the Religion of Truth, that He may cause it to prevail over all religions, however much those who associate partners with Allah may dislike it. (6—10)

O ye who believe, shall I guide you to a commerce that will save you from a painful chastisement? It is that you believe in Allah and His Messenger, and strive in the cause of Allah with your belongings and your persons. That is the better for you, did you but know. He will forgive you your sins, and will admit you to Gardens beneath which rivers flow, and to pure and pleasant dwellings in Gardens of Eternity. That is the supreme triumph.

There is another favour that you greatly desire that He will bestow upon you, namely, help from Allah and a speedy victory. So give glad tidings of it to the believers. O ye who believe, become helpers in the cause of Allah, as said Jesus son of Mary to his disciples: Who will be my helpers in the cause of Allah? The disciples answered: We are helpers in the cause of Allah. So a party of the children of Israel believed and a party disbelieved.

سِحْرٌ مُّبِيْنٌ ۞

وَمَنْ اَظْلَمُ مِمَّنِ افْتَرٰى عَلَى اللّٰهِ الْكَذِبَ وَهُوَ يُدْعٰى اِلَى الْاِسْلَامِ ۚ وَاللّٰهُ لَا يَهْدِے الْقَوْمَ الظّٰلِمِيْنَ ۞

يُرِيْدُوْنَ لِيُطْفِئُوْا نُوْرَاللّٰهِ بِاَفْوَاهِهِمْ وَاللّٰهُ مُتِمُّ نُوْرِهٖ وَلَوْ كَرِهَ الْكٰفِرُوْنَ ۞

هُوَالَّذِيْٓ اَرْسَلَ رَسُوْلَهٗ بِالْهُدٰى وَدِيْنِ الْحَقِّ لِيُظْهِرَهٗ عَلَى الدِّيْنِ كُلِّهٖ وَلَوْ كَرِهَ الْمُشْرِكُوْنَ ۞

يٰٓاَيُّهَا الَّذِيْنَ اٰمَنُوْا هَلْ اَدُلُّكُمْ عَلٰى تِجَارَةٍ تُنْجِيْكُمْ مِّنْ عَذَابٍ اَلِيْمٍ ۞

تُؤْمِنُوْنَ بِاللّٰهِ وَرَسُوْلِهٖ وَتُجَاهِدُوْنَ فِيْ سَبِيْلِ اللّٰهِ بِاَمْوَالِكُمْ وَاَنْفُسِكُمْ ۚ ذٰلِكُمْ خَيْرٌ لَّكُمْ اِنْ كُنْتُمْ تَعْلَمُوْنَ ۞

يَغْفِرْ لَكُمْ ذُنُوْبَكُمْ وَيُدْخِلْكُمْ جَنّٰتٍ تَجْرِيْ مِنْ تَحْتِهَا الْاَنْهٰرُ وَمَسٰكِنَ طَيِّبَةً فِيْ جَنّٰتِ عَدْنٍ ۚ ذٰلِكَ الْفَوْزُ الْعَظِيْمُ ۞

وَاُخْرٰى تُحِبُّوْنَهَا ۚ نَصْرٌ مِّنَ اللّٰهِ وَفَتْحٌ قَرِيْبٌ ۚ وَبَشِّرِ الْمُؤْمِنِيْنَ ۞

يٰٓاَيُّهَا الَّذِيْنَ اٰمَنُوْا كُوْنُوْٓا اَنْصَارَ اللّٰهِ كَمَا قَالَ عِيْسَى ابْنُ مَرْيَمَ لِلْحَوَارِيّـٖنَ مَنْ اَنْصَارِيْٓ اِلَى اللّٰهِ ۚ قَالَ الْحَوَارِيُّوْنَ نَحْنُ اَنْصَارُ اللّٰهِ ۚ فَاٰمَنَتْ طَّائِفَةٌ مِّنْ بَنِيْٓ اِسْرَآءِيْلَ وَكَفَرَتْ طَّائِفَةٌ ۚ

Then We supported those who believed against their enemies, and they gained the mastery over them. (11—15)

فَاَيَّدْنَا الَّذِيْنَ اٰمَنُوْا عَلٰى عَدُوِّهِمْ فَاَصْبَحُوْا

ظٰهِرِيْنَ ۝

     سُوْرَةُ الْجُمْعَةِ مَدَنِيَّةٌ

Chapter 62   AL-JUMU‘AH   Part 28
(Revealed after Hijra)

In the name of Allah, Most Gracious, Ever Merciful. (1)

بِسْمِ اللّٰهِ الرَّحْمٰنِ الرَّحِيْمِ ۝

يُسَبِّحُ لِلّٰهِ مَا فِى السَّمٰوٰتِ وَمَا فِى الْاَرْضِ الْمَلِكِ

الْقُدُّوْسِ الْعَزِيْزِ الْحَكِيْمِ ۝

هُوَ الَّذِيْ بَعَثَ فِى الْاُمِّيّٖنَ رَسُوْلًا مِّنْهُمْ يَتْلُوْا

عَلَيْهِمْ اٰيٰتِهٖ وَيُزَكِّيْهِمْ وَيُعَلِّمُهُمُ الْكِتٰبَ وَ

الْحِكْمَةَ ۖ وَاِنْ كَانُوْا مِنْ قَبْلُ لَفِيْ ضَلٰلٍ

مُّبِيْنٍ ۝

Whatever is in the heavens and whatever is in the earth glorifies Allah, the Sovereign, the Most Holy, the Mighty, the Wise. He it is Who has raised among the unlettered people, and will raise among others from among them who have not yet joined them, a Messenger from among themselves who recites unto them His Signs, and purifies them, and fosters their welfare, and teaches them the Book and wisdom, though before this they had been in manifest error. He is the Mighty, the Wise. That is Allah's grace; He bestows it on whom He pleases. Allah is the Master of immense grace. The case of those who were made subject to the Law of the Torah, but did not carry out their obligations under it, is like that of a donkey carrying a load of books. Evil is the case of the people who reject the Signs of Allah. Allah guides not the wrongdoing people.

وَّاٰخَرِيْنَ مِنْهُمْ لَمَّا يَلْحَقُوْا بِهِمْ ۚ وَهُوَ الْعَزِيْزُ

الْحَكِيْمُ ۝

ذٰلِكَ فَضْلُ اللّٰهِ يُؤْتِيْهِ مَنْ يَّشَآءُ ۚ وَاللّٰهُ ذُوالْفَضْلِ

الْعَظِيْمِ ۝

مَثَلُ الَّذِيْنَ حُمِّلُوا التَّوْرٰةَ ثُمَّ لَمْ يَحْمِلُوْهَا

كَمَثَلِ الْحِمَارِ يَحْمِلُ اَسْفَارًا ۚ بِئْسَ مَثَلُ

الْقَوْمِ الَّذِيْنَ كَذَّبُوْا بِاٰيٰتِ اللّٰهِ ۚ وَاللّٰهُ لَايَهْدِى

الْقَوْمَ الظّٰلِمِيْنَ ۝

Say to them; O ye who are Jews, if you fancy that you are the friends of Allah to

قُلْ يٰاَيُّهَا الَّذِيْنَ هَادُوْا اِنْ زَعَمْتُمْ اَنَّكُمْ اَوْلِيَآءُ

the exclusion of all other people, then agree to pray that death may overtake you if your claim is false. But they will never agree to do so because of that which they have wrought. Allah knows the wrongdoers well. Tell them: The death from which you shrink will surely overtake you. Then will you be ushered before Him Who knows the unseen and the seen, and He will inform you of that which you had been doing. (2—9)

O ye who believe, when the call is made for Prayer on Friday, hasten to the remembrance of Allah and leave off all business. That is the better for you, did you but know. When the Prayer is finished then disperse in the land and seek of Allah's grace, and remember Allah much that you may prosper. When they perceive a matter of commerce or amusement they drift away from thee towards it and leave thee standing by thyself. Tell them: That which Allah has to bestow is better than any matter of amusement or commerce. Allah is the Best Provider. (10—12)

(Revealed after Hijra)

In the name of Allah, Most Gracious, Ever Merciful. (1)

When the hypocrites come to thee they say: We bear witness on oath that thou art indeed the Messenger of Allah. Allah knows that thou art indeed His Messenger, but Allah bears witness that the hypocrites are liars. They have made their oaths a cloak that they may thereby turn people away from the way of Allah. Evil is that which they practise. That is because they believed and thereafter disbelieved; so a seal was set upon their hearts and they have no understanding.

اللّٰهُ وَ اللّٰهُ يَعْلَمُ اِنَّكَ لَرَسُوْلُهٗ ؕ وَ اللّٰهُ يَشْهَدُ اِنَّ الْمُنٰفِقِيْنَ لَكٰذِبُوْنَ ۞

اِتَّخَذُوْۤا اَيْمَانَهُمْ جُنَّةً فَصَدُّوْا عَنْ سَبِيْلِ اللّٰهِ ؕ اِنَّهُمْ سَآءَ مَا كَانُوْا يَعْمَلُوْنَ ۞

ذٰلِكَ بِاَنَّهُمْ اٰمَنُوْا ثُمَّ كَفَرُوْا فَطُبِعَ عَلٰى قُلُوْبِهِمْ فَهُمْ لَا يَفْقَهُوْنَ ۞

وَاِذَا رَاَيْتَهُمْ تُعْجِبُكَ اَجْسَامُهُمْ ؕ وَاِنْ يَّقُوْلُوْا تَسْمَعْ لِقَوْلِهِمْ ؕ كَاَنَّهُمْ خُشُبٌ مُّسَنَّدَةٌ ؕ يَحْسَبُوْنَ كُلَّ صَيْحَةٍ عَلَيْهِمْ ؕ هُمُ الْعَدُوُّ فَاحْذَرْهُمْ ؕ قٰتَلَهُمُ اللّٰهُ ؗ اَنّٰى يُؤْفَكُوْنَ ۞

When thou seest them their persons please thee; and when they speak thou dost lend ear to what they say. They appear as if they were blocks of wood propped up. They imagine that every warning of chastisement relates to them. They are the enemy, so beware! Ruin seize them! How are they being turned away! When it is said to them: Come, that the Messenger of Allah may ask forgiveness for you, they turn aside their heads and thou seest them holding back in pride. It is the same for them whether thou ask for forgiveness for them or not, Allah will never forgive them. Surely, Allah guides not a rebellious people.

وَاِذَا قِيْلَ لَهُمْ تَعَالَوْا يَسْتَغْفِرْ لَكُمْ رَسُوْلُ اللّٰهِ لَوَّوْا رُءُوْسَهُمْ وَرَاَيْتَهُمْ يَصُدُّوْنَ وَهُمْ مُّسْتَكْبِرُوْنَ ۞

سَوَآءٌ عَلَيْهِمْ اَسْتَغْفَرْتَ لَهُمْ اَمْ لَمْ تَسْتَغْفِرْ لَهُمْ ؕ لَنْ يَّغْفِرَ اللّٰهُ لَهُمْ ؕ اِنَّ اللّٰهَ لَا يَهْدِى الْقَوْمَ الْفٰسِقِيْنَ ۞

They are the ones who say: Do not spend on those who are with the Messenger of Allah that they may disperse; whereas to Allah belong the treasures of the heavens and the earth; but the hypocrites comprehend it not. They say: When we return to Medina, the one most honourable will surely drive out therefrom the one most mean; whereas true honour belongs to Allah and to His Messenger and the believers; but the hypocrites know it not.

هُمُ الَّذِيْنَ يَقُوْلُوْنَ لَا تُنْفِقُوْا عَلٰى مَنْ عِنْدَ رَسُوْلِ اللّٰهِ حَتّٰى يَنْفَضُّوْا ؕ وَلِلّٰهِ خَزَآئِنُ السَّمٰوٰتِ وَالْاَرْضِ وَلٰكِنَّ الْمُنٰفِقِيْنَ لَا يَفْقَهُوْنَ ۞

يَقُوْلُوْنَ لَئِنْ رَّجَعْنَاۤ اِلَى الْمَدِيْنَةِ لَيُخْرِجَنَّ الْاَعَزُّ مِنْهَا الْاَذَلَّ ؕ وَلِلّٰهِ الْعِزَّةُ وَلِرَسُوْلِهٖ وَلِلْمُؤْمِنِيْنَ وَلٰكِنَّ الْمُنٰفِقِيْنَ لَا يَعْلَمُوْنَ ۞

O ye who believe, let not your properties and your children divert you from the remembrance of Allah. Whoever behaves in that way, it is they who are the losers.

يَّاَيُّهَا الَّذِيْنَ اٰمَنُوْا لَا تُلْهِكُمْ اَمْوَالُكُمْ وَلَا اَوْلَادُكُمْ عَنْ ذِكْرِ اللّٰهِ ۚ وَمَنْ يَّفْعَلْ ذٰلِكَ فَاُولٰٓئِكَ هُمُ الْخٰسِرُوْنَ ۞

Spend out of that with which We have provided you before death comes upon one of you and he should say: Lord, why didst Thou not grant me respite for a while, that I could give alms and be among the righteous! Allah will not grant respite to one when his appointed time has come. Allah is Well-Aware of that which you do. (2—12)

وَاَنْفِقُوْا مِنْ مَّا رَزَقْنٰكُمْ مِّنْ قَبْلِ اَنْ يَّاْتِيَ اَحَدَكُمُ الْمَوْتُ فَيَقُوْلَ رَبِّ لَوْلَا اَخَّرْتَنِيْ اِلٰٓى اَجَلٍ قَرِيْبٍ ۙ فَاَصَّدَّقَ وَاَكُنْ مِّنَ الصّٰلِحِيْنَ ۞ وَلَنْ يُّؤَخِّرَ اللّٰهُ نَفْسًا اِذَا جَآءَ اَجَلُهَا ۚ وَاللّٰهُ خَبِيْرٌ بِمَا تَعْمَلُوْنَ ۞

(Revealed after Hijra)

In the name of Allah, Most Gracious, Ever Merciful. (1)

بِسْمِ اللّٰهِ الرَّحْمٰنِ الرَّحِيْمِ ۞

يُسَبِّحُ لِلّٰهِ مَا فِى السَّمٰوٰتِ وَمَا فِى الْاَرْضِ ۚ لَهُ الْمُلْكُ وَلَهُ الْحَمْدُ ۫ وَهُوَ عَلٰى كُلِّ شَيْءٍ قَدِيْرٌ ۞

Whatever is in the heavens and whatever is in the earth glorifies Allah. His is the Kingdom and His the praise; and He has power over all things. It is He Who has created you; then some of you are disbelievers and some are believers. Allah sees all that you do. He has created the heavens and the earth with a determined purpose, and He gave you form and made your forms good. To Him is the final return. He knows whatever is in the heavens and the earth, and He knows that which you conceal and that which you disclose. Allah knows well all that passes through your minds. Have you not learnt what befell those who disbelieved before you?

هُوَ الَّذِيْ خَلَقَكُمْ فَمِنْكُمْ كَافِرٌ وَّمِنْكُمْ مُّؤْمِنٌ ۚ وَاللّٰهُ بِمَا تَعْمَلُوْنَ بَصِيْرٌ ۞ خَلَقَ السَّمٰوٰتِ وَالْاَرْضَ بِالْحَقِّ وَصَوَّرَكُمْ فَاَحْسَنَ صُوَرَكُمْ ۚ وَاِلَيْهِ الْمَصِيْرُ ۞ يَعْلَمُ مَا فِى السَّمٰوٰتِ وَالْاَرْضِ وَيَعْلَمُ مَا تُسِرُّوْنَ وَمَا تُعْلِنُوْنَ ۚ وَاللّٰهُ عَلِيْمٌۢ بِذَاتِ الصُّدُوْرِ ۞ اَلَمْ يَاْتِكُمْ نَبَؤُا الَّذِيْنَ كَفَرُوْا مِنْ قَبْلُ ۫ فَذَاقُوْا

They suffered the consequences of their conduct, and they had a painful chastisement. That was because their Messengers came to them with manifest Signs, but they said: Shall mortals guide us? So they disbelieved and turned away. Allah had no need of them. Allah is Self-Sufficient, Praiseworthy. Those who disbelieve assert that they will not be raised up. Tell them: Yea, by my Lord, you shall surely be raised up; then shall you surely be informed of that which you did. That is easy for Allah. Believe, therefore, in Allah and His Messenger, and in the Light that We have sent down; Allah is Well-Aware of all that you do. The day when He shall gather you for the Day of Gathering, that will be the day of the determination of gains and losses. Allah will remove the ills of those who believe in Allah and work righteousness, and will admit them to Gardens beneath which rivers flow, to abide therein for ever. That is the supreme triumph. Those who disbelieve and reject Our Signs shall be the inmates of the Fire, wherein they shall abide; and an evil destination it is. (2—11)

وَبَالَ اَمْرِهِمْ وَلَهُمْ عَذَابٌ اَلِيْمٌ ۝

ذٰلِكَ بِاَنَّهٗ كَانَتْ تَّاْتِيْهِمْ رُسُلُهُمْ بِالْبَيِّنٰتِ فَقَالُوْۤا اَبَشَرٌ يَّهْدُوْنَنَا ۖ فَكَفَرُوْا وَتَوَلَّوْا ۚ وَّاسْتَغْنَى اللّٰهُ ؕ وَاللّٰهُ غَنِيٌّ حَمِيْدٌ ۝

زَعَمَ الَّذِيْنَ كَفَرُوْۤا اَنْ لَّنْ يُّبْعَثُوْا ؕ قُلْ بَلٰى وَرَبِّيْ لَتُبْعَثُنَّ ثُمَّ لَتُنَبَّؤُنَّ بِمَا عَمِلْتُمْ ؕ وَذٰلِكَ عَلَى اللّٰهِ يَسِيْرٌ ۝

فَاٰمِنُوْا بِاللّٰهِ وَرَسُوْلِهٖ وَالنُّوْرِ الَّذِيْۤ اَنْزَلْنَا ؕ وَاللّٰهُ بِمَا تَعْمَلُوْنَ خَبِيْرٌ ۝

يَوْمَ يَجْمَعُكُمْ لِيَوْمِ الْجَمْعِ ذٰلِكَ يَوْمُ التَّغَابُنِ ؕ وَمَنْ يُّؤْمِنْ بِاللّٰهِ وَيَعْمَلْ صَالِحًا يُّكَفِّرْ عَنْهُ سَيِّاٰتِهٖ وَيُدْخِلْهُ جَنّٰتٍ تَجْرِيْ مِنْ تَحْتِهَا الْاَنْهٰرُ خٰلِدِيْنَ فِيْهَاۤ اَبَدًا ؕ ذٰلِكَ الْفَوْزُ الْعَظِيْمُ ۝

وَالَّذِيْنَ كَفَرُوْا وَكَذَّبُوْا بِاٰيٰتِنَاۤ اُولٰٓئِكَ اَصْحٰبُ النَّارِ خٰلِدِيْنَ فِيْهَا ؕ وَبِئْسَ الْمَصِيْرُ ۝

مَاۤ اَصَابَ مِنْ مُّصِيْبَةٍ اِلَّا بِاِذْنِ اللّٰهِ ؕ وَمَنْ يُّؤْمِنْ بِاللّٰهِ يَهْدِ قَلْبَهٗ ؕ وَاللّٰهُ بِكُلِّ شَيْءٍ عَلِيْمٌ ۝

وَاَطِيْعُوا اللّٰهَ وَاَطِيْعُوا الرَّسُوْلَ ۚ فَاِنْ تَوَلَّيْتُمْ فَاِنَّمَا عَلٰى رَسُوْلِنَا الْبَلٰغُ الْمُبِيْنُ ۝

اَللّٰهُ لَاۤ اِلٰهَ اِلَّا هُوَ ؕ وَعَلَى اللّٰهِ فَلْيَتَوَكَّلِ الْمُؤْمِنُوْنَ ۝

يٰۤاَيُّهَا الَّذِيْنَ اٰمَنُوْۤا اِنَّ مِنْ اَزْوَاجِكُمْ وَاَوْلَادِكُمْ

Whatever affliction befalls you is by Allah's leave. Allah guides aright the heart of whoever truly believes in Him. Allah knows all things well. Obey Allah and obey the Messenger; but if you turn away Our Messenger is only charged with conveying the Message clearly. Allah is He beside Whom there is no god; so in Allah should the believers put their trust. O ye who believe, surely of your wives and your children some are your enemies, so beware of them. But if you forbear and forgive and pardon, then surely, Allah is Most Forgiving, Ever Merciful. Your belongings and your children are a trial for you; but with Allah is an immense reward.

عَدُوًّا لَّكُمْ فَاحْذَرُوهُمْ ۚ وَإِنْ تَعْفُوا وَتَصْفَحُوا وَتَغْفِرُوا فَإِنَّ اللّٰهَ غَفُوْرٌ رَّحِيْمٌ ۞

إِنَّمَا أَمْوَالُكُمْ وَأَوْلَادُكُمْ فِتْنَةٌ ۚ وَاللّٰهُ عِنْدَهُ أَجْرٌ عَظِيْمٌ ۞

So be mindful of your duty to Allah as best you can, and listen and obey, and spend in His cause. That will be the best for yourselves. Whoso is rid of the covetousness of his mind, it is those who shall be successful. If you lend to Allah a goodly loan, He will multiply it for you, and will forgive you. Allah is Most Appreciating, Compassionate, Knower of the unseen and the seen, the Mighty, the Wise. (12—19)

فَاتَّقُوا اللّٰهَ مَا اسْتَطَعْتُمْ وَاسْمَعُوا وَأَطِيْعُوا وَأَنْفِقُوا خَيْرًا لِّأَنْفُسِكُمْ ۚ وَمَنْ يُّوْقَ شُحَّ نَفْسِهِ فَأُولٰٓئِكَ هُمُ الْمُفْلِحُوْنَ ۞

إِنْ تُقْرِضُوا اللّٰهَ قَرْضًا حَسَنًا يُّضَاعِفْهُ لَكُمْ وَيَغْفِرْ لَكُمْ ۚ وَاللّٰهُ شَكُوْرٌ حَلِيْمٌ ۞

عٰلِمُ الْغَيْبِ وَالشَّهَادَةِ الْعَزِيْزُ الْحَكِيْمُ ۞

سُوْرَةُ الطَّلَاقِ مَدَنِيَّةٌ

(Revealed after Hijra)

In the name of Allah, Most Gracious, Ever Merciful. (1)

بِسْمِ اللّٰهِ الرَّحْمٰنِ الرَّحِيْمِ ۞

O Prophet, when you divorce your wives, observe the period prescribed for making the divorce effective, and reckon the period, and be mindful of your duty to Allah your Lord. Turn them not out of their houses, nor should they leave their houses, during that period, unless they are guilty of manifest indecency. These are the limits set by Allah. Whoso transgresses the limits set by Allah wrongs himself. The period is prescribed as you do not know that Allah may bring about something new. When they arrive at the end of the prescribed period, then retain them in a suitable manner or send them away

يٰٓأَيُّهَا النَّبِيُّ إِذَا طَلَّقْتُمُ النِّسَآءَ فَطَلِّقُوْهُنَّ لِعِدَّتِهِنَّ وَأَحْصُوا الْعِدَّةَ ۚ وَاتَّقُوا اللّٰهَ رَبَّكُمْ ۚ لَا تُخْرِجُوْهُنَّ مِنْ بُيُوْتِهِنَّ وَلَا يَخْرُجْنَ إِلَّا أَنْ يَّأْتِيْنَ بِفَاحِشَةٍ مُّبَيِّنَةٍ ۚ وَتِلْكَ حُدُوْدُ اللّٰهِ ۚ وَمَنْ يَّتَعَدَّ حُدُوْدَ اللّٰهِ فَقَدْ ظَلَمَ نَفْسَهُ ۚ لَا تَدْرِيْ لَعَلَّ اللّٰهَ يُحْدِثُ بَعْدَ ذٰلِكَ أَمْرًا ۞

فَإِذَا بَلَغْنَ أَجَلَهُنَّ فَأَمْسِكُوْهُنَّ بِمَعْرُوْفٍ أَوْ

in a suitable manner and appoint two just persons from among you as witnesses; and bear true witness for the sake of Allah. This is an admonition for him who believes in Allah and the Last Day. Allah will prepare a way out of his difficulties for him who is mindful of his duty to Allah, and will provide for him whence he expects not. Allah is sufficient for him who puts his trust in Allah. Allah is sure to attain His purpose. Allah has appointed a measure for everything.

The prescribed period for those of your wives who have lost all expectation of monthly courses, in case of doubt, is three months and also in case of those who have not had their monthly courses. In case of those who are with child, the prescribed period shall be until they are delivered. Allah will provide facilities in the matter of him who is mindful of his duty to Allah. This is the command of Allah which He has revealed to you. Allah will remove the ills of him who is mindful of his duty to Allah, and will enlarge his reward. Lodge them during the prescribed period in the houses wherein you dwell, according to your means; and harass them not that you may create hardships for them. If they be with child provide for them until they are delivered. If they give suck to the child for you, give them their due recompense, and settle the matter between yourselves equitably; but if you encounter difficulty from each other, then let another woman suckle the child for the father.

Let one who is in easy circumstances spend according to his means, and let him whose means of subsistence are straitened spend out of that which Allah has given him. Allah does not require of anyone beyond that which He has bestowed on him. For those suffering from hardship, Allah will soon bring about ease. (2—8)

فَارِقُوهُنَّ بِمَعْرُوفٍ وَّاَشْهِدُوْا ذَوَىْ عَدْلٍ مِّنْكُمْ وَاَقِيْمُوا الشَّهَادَةَ لِلّٰهِ ذٰلِكُمْ يُوْعَظُ بِهٖ مَنْ كَانَ يُؤْمِنُ بِاللّٰهِ وَالْيَوْمِ الْاٰخِرِ وَمَنْ يَّتَّقِ اللّٰهَ يَجْعَلْ لَّهٗ مَخْرَجًا ۞

وَّيَرْزُقْهُ مِنْ حَيْثُ لَا يَحْتَسِبُ وَمَنْ يَّتَوَكَّلْ عَلَى اللّٰهِ فَهُوَ حَسْبُهٗ اِنَّ اللّٰهَ بَالِغُ اَمْرِهٖ قَدْ جَعَلَ اللّٰهُ لِكُلِّ شَىْءٍ قَدْرًا ۞

وَالّٰٓئِیْ يَئِسْنَ مِنَ الْمَحِيْضِ مِنْ نِّسَآئِكُمْ اِنِ ارْتَبْتُمْ فَعِدَّتُهُنَّ ثَلٰثَةُ اَشْهُرٍ وَّالّٰٓئِیْ لَمْ يَحِضْنَ وَاُولَاتُ الْاَحْمَالِ اَجَلُهُنَّ اَنْ يَّضَعْنَ حَمْلَهُنَّ وَمَنْ يَّتَّقِ اللّٰهَ يَجْعَلْ لَّهٗ مِنْ اَمْرِهٖ يُسْرًا ۞

ذٰلِكَ اَمْرُ اللّٰهِ اَنْزَلَهٗ اِلَيْكُمْ وَمَنْ يَّتَّقِ اللّٰهَ يُكَفِّرْ عَنْهُ سَيِّاٰتِهٖ وَيُعْظِمْ لَهٗ اَجْرًا ۞

اَسْكِنُوْهُنَّ مِنْ حَيْثُ سَكَنْتُمْ مِّنْ وُّجْدِكُمْ وَ لَا تُضَآرُّوْهُنَّ لِتُضَيِّقُوْا عَلَيْهِنَّ وَاِنْ كُنَّ اُولَاتِ حَمْلٍ فَاَنْفِقُوْا عَلَيْهِنَّ حَتّٰى يَضَعْنَ حَمْلَهُنَّ فَاِنْ اَرْضَعْنَ لَكُمْ فَاٰتُوْهُنَّ اُجُوْرَهُنَّ وَاْتَمِرُوْا بَيْنَكُمْ بِمَعْرُوْفٍ وَاِنْ تَعَاسَرْتُمْ فَسَتُرْضِعُ لَهٗٓ اُخْرٰى ۞

لِيُنْفِقْ ذُوْ سَعَةٍ مِّنْ سَعَتِهٖ وَمَنْ قُدِرَ عَلَيْهِ رِزْقُهٗ فَلْيُنْفِقْ مِمَّآ اٰتٰهُ اللّٰهُ لَا يُكَلِّفُ اللّٰهُ نَفْسًا اِلَّا مَآ اٰتٰهَا سَيَجْعَلُ اللّٰهُ بَعْدَ عُسْرٍ يُّسْرًا ۞

وَكَاَيِّنْ مِّنْ قَرْيَةٍ عَتَتْ عَنْ اَمْرِ رَبِّهَا وَرُسُلِهٖ

568

Many a town insolently rejected the command of its Lord and His Messengers. Then We called it to a severe accounting, and chastised it with a dire chastisement. Thus it suffered the evil consequences of its conduct and the end of its affairs was ruin. For such Allah has prepared a severe torment. So fear Allah, O ye men of understanding, who have believed. Allah has sent down to you a source of honour, a Messenger, who recites unto you the clear Signs of Allah, that he may bring those who believe and act righteously out of every kind of darkness into the light. Whoso believes in Allah and acts righteously, will be admitted by Him to Gardens beneath which rivers flow, to abide therein for ever. Allah has indeed made excellent provision for him. (9—12)

فَحَاسَبْنَٰهَا حِسَابًا شَدِيدًا وَّعَذَّبْنَٰهَا عَذَابًا نُّكْرًا ۙ

فَذَاقَتْ وَبَالَ أَمْرِهَا وَكَانَ عَاقِبَةُ أَمْرِهَا خُسْرًا ۞

أَعَدَّ اللّٰهُ لَهُمْ عَذَابًا شَدِيدًا ۖ فَاتَّقُوا اللّٰهَ يٰٓأُولِي الْأَلْبَابِ ۛ الَّذِينَ آمَنُوا ۛ قَدْ أَنْزَلَ اللّٰهُ إِلَيْكُمْ ذِكْرًا ۙ

رَّسُولًا يَّتْلُوا عَلَيْكُمْ اٰيٰتِ اللّٰهِ مُبَيِّنٰتٍ لِّيُخْرِجَ الَّذِينَ آمَنُوا وَعَمِلُوا الصّٰلِحٰتِ مِنَ الظُّلُمٰتِ إِلَى النُّورِ ۚ وَمَنْ يُّؤْمِنْ بِاللّٰهِ وَيَعْمَلْ صَالِحًا يُّدْخِلْهُ جَنّٰتٍ تَجْرِى مِنْ تَحْتِهَا الْأَنْهٰرُ خٰلِدِينَ فِيهَا أَبَدًا ۖ قَدْ أَحْسَنَ اللّٰهُ لَهُ رِزْقًا ۞

Allah is He Who created seven heavens, and of the earth the like thereof. The divine command comes down in their midst that you may know that Allah has power over all things in His knowledge. (13)

اللّٰهُ الَّذِى خَلَقَ سَبْعَ سَمٰوٰتٍ وَّمِنَ الْأَرْضِ مِثْلَهُنَّ ۖ يَتَنَزَّلُ الْأَمْرُ بَيْنَهُنَّ لِتَعْلَمُوا أَنَّ اللّٰهَ عَلٰى كُلِّ شَىْءٍ قَدِيرٌ ۙ وَّأَنَّ اللّٰهَ قَدْ أَحَاطَ بِكُلِّ شَىْءٍ عِلْمًا ۞

 سُورَةُ التَّحْرِيمِ مَدَنِيَّةٌ

In the name of Allah, Most Gracious, Ever Merciful. (1)

بِسْمِ اللّٰهِ الرَّحْمٰنِ الرَّحِيمِ ۞

O Prophet, why dost thou forbid thyself that which Allah has made lawful for thee, seeking the pleasure of thy wives? Allah is Most Forgiving, Ever Merciful. Allah has sanctioned the dissolution of your vows; and He is your Patron.

يٰٓأَيُّهَا النَّبِيُّ لِمَ تُحَرِّمُ مَآ أَحَلَّ اللّٰهُ لَكَ ۖ تَبْتَغِى مَرْضَاتَ أَزْوَاجِكَ ۚ وَاللّٰهُ غَفُورٌ رَّحِيمٌ ۞

قَدْ فَرَضَ اللّٰهُ لَكُمْ تَحِلَّةَ أَيْمَانِكُمْ ۚ وَاللّٰهُ مَوْلٰىكُمْ

He is All-Knowing, Wise. When the Prophet confided a matter to one of his wives and she divulged it, and Allah informed him of it, he made known to her part thereof and refrained from disclosing the rest. When he told her of it, she said: Who has told thee this? He replied: The All-Knowing, the All-Aware has told me. If you two turn unto Allah in repentance, your hearts being already so inclined, that would be well. But if you back each other up against him, surely Allah is His Helper and Gabriel and the righteous among the believers; and beyond that all the angels do support him. It may be that, if he divorce you, his Lord will give him instead wives better than you, submissive, believing, obedient, repentant, devout in worship, observers of the fast, both widows and virgins. (2—6)

وَهُوَ الْعَلِيْمُ الْحَكِيْمُ ۞

وَاِذْ اَسَرَّ النَّبِيُّ اِلٰى بَعْضِ اَزْوَاجِهٖ حَدِيْثًا ۚ فَلَمَّا نَبَّاَتْ بِهٖ وَاَظْهَرَهُ اللّٰهُ عَلَيْهِ عَرَّفَ بَعْضَهٗ وَاَعْرَضَ عَنْ بَعْضٍ ۚ فَلَمَّا نَبَّاَهَا بِهٖ قَالَتْ مَنْ اَنْبَاَكَ هٰذَا ۗ قَالَ نَبَّاَنِيَ الْعَلِيْمُ الْخَبِيْرُ ۞

اِنْ تَتُوْبَآ اِلَى اللّٰهِ فَقَدْ صَغَتْ قُلُوْبُكُمَا ۚ وَاِنْ تَظٰهَرَا عَلَيْهِ فَاِنَّ اللّٰهَ هُوَ مَوْلٰىهُ وَجِبْرِيْلُ وَصَالِحُ الْمُؤْمِنِيْنَ ۚ وَالْمَلٰٓئِكَةُ بَعْدَ ذٰلِكَ ظَهِيْرٌ ۞

عَسٰى رَبُّهٗٓ اِنْ طَلَّقَكُنَّ اَنْ يُّبْدِلَهٗٓ اَزْوَاجًا خَيْرًا مِّنْكُنَّ مُسْلِمٰتٍ مُّؤْمِنٰتٍ قٰنِتٰتٍ تٰٓئِبٰتٍ عٰبِدٰتٍ سٰٓئِحٰتٍ ثَيِّبٰتٍ وَّاَبْكَارًا ۞

O ye who believe, safeguard yourselves and your families against a fire whose fuel is men and stones, over which are appointed angels, stern and severe, who disobey not Allah in that which He commands them and do as they are directed. O ye who disbelieve, put forth no excuses this day. You will surely be requited for that which you did. (7—8)

يٰٓاَيُّهَا الَّذِيْنَ اٰمَنُوْا قُوْٓا اَنْفُسَكُمْ وَاَهْلِيْكُمْ نَارًا وَّقُوْدُهَا النَّاسُ وَالْحِجَارَةُ عَلَيْهَا مَلٰٓئِكَةٌ غِلَاظٌ شِدَادٌ لَّا يَعْصُوْنَ اللّٰهَ مَآ اَمَرَهُمْ وَيَفْعَلُوْنَ مَا يُؤْمَرُوْنَ ۞

يٰٓاَيُّهَا الَّذِيْنَ كَفَرُوْا لَا تَعْتَذِرُوا الْيَوْمَ ۗ اِنَّمَا تُجْزَوْنَ مَا كُنْتُمْ تَعْمَلُوْنَ ۞

O ye who believe turn to Allah in sincere repentance. It may be that your Lord will remove your ills and admit you to Gardens beneath which rivers flow, on the day when Allah will not humiliate the Prophet and those who have believed with him. Their light will run before them and on their right hands. They will pray: Lord,

يٰٓاَيُّهَا الَّذِيْنَ اٰمَنُوْا تُوْبُوْٓا اِلَى اللّٰهِ تَوْبَةً نَّصُوْحًا ۗ عَسٰى رَبُّكُمْ اَنْ يُّكَفِّرَ عَنْكُمْ سَيِّاٰتِكُمْ وَيُدْخِلَكُمْ جَنّٰتٍ تَجْرِيْ مِنْ تَحْتِهَا الْاَنْهٰرُ ۙ يَوْمَ لَا يُخْزِى اللّٰهُ النَّبِيَّ وَالَّذِيْنَ اٰمَنُوْا مَعَهٗ ۚ نُوْرُهُمْ يَسْعٰى بَيْنَ اَيْدِيْهِمْ وَبِاَيْمَانِهِمْ يَقُوْلُوْنَ رَبَّنَآ اَتْمِمْ

perfect our light for us and forgive us, surely Thou hast power over all things. O Prophet, strive hard against the disbelievers and the hypocrites; and be firm against them. Their abode is hell, and an evil destination it is. (9—10)

لَنَا نُوْرَنَا وَاغْفِرْ لَنَا ۚ إِنَّكَ عَلَى كُلِّ شَيْءٍ قَدِيْرٌ ۝

يٰٓاَيُّهَا النَّبِيُّ جَاهِدِ الْكُفَّارَ وَالْمُنٰفِقِيْنَ وَاغْلُظْ عَلَيْهِمْ ۚ وَمَأْوٰىهُمْ جَهَنَّمُ ۚ وَبِئْسَ الْمَصِيْرُ ۝

ضَرَبَ اللهُ مَثَلًا لِّلَّذِيْنَ كَفَرُوا امْرَاَتَ نُوْحٍ وَّ امْرَاَتَ لُوْطٍ ۚ كَانَتَا تَحْتَ عَبْدَيْنِ مِنْ عِبَادِنَا صَالِحَيْنِ فَخَانَتٰهُمَا فَلَمْ يُغْنِيَا عَنْهُمَا مِنَ اللهِ شَيْئًا وَّقِيْلَ ادْخُلَا النَّارَ مَعَ الدّٰخِلِيْنَ ۝

Allah cites as examples of disbelievers the wife of Noah and the wife of Lot. They were married to two righteous servants of Ours, but they acted disloyally towards them. So their husbands availed them naught against Allah, and they were told: Enter the Fire along with those who enter therein. Allah also cites as examples of believers the wife of Pharaoh who prayed: Lord, build for me a house near Thee in the Garden; and deliver me from Pharaoh and his work, and deliver me from the wrongdoing people; and Mary, the daughter of Imran, who guarded her chastity and We sent Our Word to her, and she fulfilled the words of her Lord and His Books and was one of the obedient. (11—13)

وَضَرَبَ اللهُ مَثَلًا لِّلَّذِيْنَ اٰمَنُوا امْرَاَتَ فِرْعَوْنَ ۘ إِذْ قَالَتْ رَبِّ ابْنِ لِيْ عِنْدَكَ بَيْتًا فِي الْجَنَّةِ وَ نَجِّنِيْ مِنْ فِرْعَوْنَ وَعَمَلِهٖ وَنَجِّنِيْ مِنَ الْقَوْمِ الظّٰلِمِيْنَ ۝

وَمَرْيَمَ ابْنَتَ عِمْرٰنَ الَّتِيْ اَحْصَنَتْ فَرْجَهَا فَنَفَخْنَا فِيْهِ مِنْ رُّوْحِنَا وَصَدَّقَتْ بِكَلِمٰتِ رَبِّهَا وَكُتُبِهٖ وَكَانَتْ مِنَ الْقٰنِتِيْنَ ۝

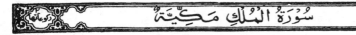

سُوْرَةُ الْمُلْكِ مَكِّيَّةٌ

(Revealed before Hijra)

In the name of Allah, Most Gracious, Ever Merciful. (1)

بِسْمِ اللهِ الرَّحْمٰنِ الرَّحِيْمِ ۝

Blessed is He in Whose hand is the kingdom and He has the power to do all that He wills, Who has created death and life that He might try you which of you is best in conduct.

تَبٰرَكَ الَّذِيْ بِيَدِهِ الْمُلْكُ ۖ وَهُوَ عَلٰى كُلِّ شَيْءٍ قَدِيْرٌ ۝

الَّذِيْ خَلَقَ الْمَوْتَ وَالْحَيٰوةَ لِيَبْلُوَكُمْ اَيُّكُمْ

He is the Mighty, the Most Forgiving,
Who has created the seven heavens in
order, one above the other. Thou canst
not discover a flaw in the creation of the
Gracious One. Then look again: Seest thou
any disparity? Look again, and yet again,
thy sight will return to thee frustrated
and fatigued. (2—5)

أَحْسَنُ عَمَلاً ۖ وَهُوَ الْعَزِيزُ الْغَفُورُ ۝

الَّذِي خَلَقَ سَبْعَ سَمٰوٰتٍ طِبَاقًا ۖ مَا تَرٰى فِي

خَلْقِ الرَّحْمٰنِ مِنْ تَفٰوُتٍ ۖ فَارْجِعِ الْبَصَرَ ۙ هَلْ

تَرٰى مِنْ فُطُوْرٍ ۝

ثُمَّ ارْجِعِ الْبَصَرَ كَرَّتَيْنِ يَنْقَلِبْ إِلَيْكَ الْبَصَرُ

خَاسِئًا وَّهُوَ حَسِيْرٌ ۝

وَلَقَدْ زَيَّنَّا السَّمَآءَ الدُّنْيَا بِمَصَابِيْحَ وَجَعَلْنٰهَا

We have adorned the lowest heaven
with lamps and We have made them
the means of driving away Satans. We
have prepared for them a blazing torment. For those who disbelieve in their
Lord is the chastisement of hell, and an
evil resort it is. When they are cast into
it they will hear it roar, as it boils up. It
would almost burst with fury. Whenever
a host of disbelievers is cast into it
the wardens thereof will ask them: Did no
Warner come to you? They will answer:
A Warner did indeed come to us, but we
rejected him and said: Allah has not
revealed anything; you are surely in great
error. They will add: Had we but listened
or exercised our judgment, we would not
have been among the inmates of the
Blaze. Thus will they confess their sins.
Then cast far away are the inmates of the
Blaze.

رُجُوْمًا لِّلشَّيٰطِيْنِ ۖ وَأَعْتَدْنَا لَهُمْ عَذَابَ السَّعِيْرِ ۝

وَلِلَّذِيْنَ كَفَرُوْا بِرَبِّهِمْ عَذَابُ جَهَنَّمَ ۖ وَبِئْسَ

الْمَصِيْرُ ۝

إِذَآ أُلْقُوْا فِيْهَا سَمِعُوْا لَهَا شَهِيْقًا وَّهِيَ تَفُوْرُ ۝

تَكَادُ تَمَيَّزُ مِنَ الْغَيْظِ ۖ كُلَّمَآ أُلْقِيَ فِيْهَا فَوْجٌ

سَأَلَهُمْ خَزَنَتُهَآ أَلَمْ يَأْتِكُمْ نَذِيْرٌ ۝

قَالُوْا بَلٰى قَدْ جَآءَنَا نَذِيْرٌ ۖ فَكَذَّبْنَا وَقُلْنَا مَا

نَزَّلَ اللهُ مِنْ شَيْءٍ ۙ إِنْ أَنْتُمْ إِلَّا فِيْ ضَلٰلٍ

كَبِيْرٍ ۝

وَقَالُوْا لَوْ كُنَّا نَسْمَعُ أَوْ نَعْقِلُ مَا كُنَّا فِيْ أَصْحٰبِ

السَّعِيْرِ ۝

فَاعْتَرَفُوْا بِذَنْبِهِمْ ۖ فَسُحْقًا لِّأَصْحٰبِ السَّعِيْرِ ۝

For those who fear their Lord in secret
there is forgiveness and a great reward.
Whether you conceal that which you
say or publish it abroad, He knows
well that which passess in your minds.

إِنَّ الَّذِيْنَ يَخْشَوْنَ رَبَّهُمْ بِالْغَيْبِ لَهُمْ مَّغْفِرَةٌ

وَأَجْرٌ كَبِيْرٌ ۝

وَأَسِرُّوْا قَوْلَكُمْ أَوِ اجْهَرُوْا بِهِ ۖ إِنَّهُ عَلِيْمٌ بِذَاتِ

Would He not know Who created you?
He knows the most secret thoughts. He is
the Imperceptible, the All-Aware. (6—15)

He it is Who has made the earth submissive to you, so traverse along its sides,
and eat of His provision. Towards Him is
the return. Do you feel secure that He Who
is in the heaven may not cause the earth
to sink with you when it passes round?
Do you feel secure that He Who is in the
heaven may not send against you a storm
of stones? Then will you know how terrible
was My warning. Those before them also
rejected the Messengers; then how grievous was My chastisement! Have they not
observed the birds above them spreading
their wings in flight and then drawing
them in? None withholds them but the
Gracious One. He sees all things well. Can
those who constitute your host help you
against the Gracious One? The disbelievers are caught in deception. Who is he
that will provide for you, if He should
withhold His provision? But they persist
obstinately in rebellion and aversion.

Is he who walks grovelling upon his face
better guided, or he who walks upright on
the straight path? Say to them: He it is
Who brought you into being and provided
you with ears and eyes and hearts: but
little thanks do you give. Say to them: He it
is Who multiplied you in the earth and unto
Him will you be gathered. They ask: When
will this promise come to pass, if you are
truthful? Tell them: The knowledge of it is
with Allah.

الصُّدُورِ ۝

ع أَلَا يَعْلَمُ مَنْ خَلَقَ وَهُوَ اللَّطِيفُ الْخَبِيرُ ۝

هُوَ الَّذِي جَعَلَ لَكُمُ الْأَرْضَ ذَلُولًا فَامْشُوا فِي
مَنَاكِبِهَا وَكُلُوا مِنْ رِزْقِهِ وَإِلَيْهِ النُّشُورُ ۝

ءَأَمِنْتُمْ مَنْ فِي السَّمَاءِ أَنْ يَخْسِفَ بِكُمُ الْأَرْضَ
فَإِذَا هِيَ تَمُورُ ۝

أَمْ أَمِنْتُمْ مَنْ فِي السَّمَاءِ أَنْ يُرْسِلَ عَلَيْكُمْ حَاصِبًا
فَسَتَعْلَمُونَ كَيْفَ نَذِيرِ ۝

وَلَقَدْ كَذَّبَ الَّذِينَ مِنْ قَبْلِهِمْ فَكَيْفَ كَانَ نَكِيرِ ۝

أَوَلَمْ يَرَوْا إِلَى الطَّيْرِ فَوْقَهُمْ صَافَّاتٍ وَيَقْبِضْنَ
مَا يُمْسِكُهُنَّ إِلَّا الرَّحْمَنُ إِنَّهُ بِكُلِّ شَيْءٍ بَصِيرٌ ۝

أَمَّنْ هَذَا الَّذِي هُوَ جُنْدٌ لَكُمْ يَنْصُرُكُمْ مِنْ
دُونِ الرَّحْمَنِ إِنِ الْكَافِرُونَ إِلَّا فِي غُرُورٍ ۝

أَمَّنْ هَذَا الَّذِي يَرْزُقُكُمْ إِنْ أَمْسَكَ رِزْقَهُ
بَلْ لَجُّوا فِي عُتُوٍّ وَنُفُورٍ ۝

أَفَمَنْ يَمْشِي مُكِبًّا عَلَى وَجْهِهِ أَهْدَى أَمَّنْ يَمْشِي
سَوِيًّا عَلَى صِرَاطٍ مُسْتَقِيمٍ ۝

قُلْ هُوَ الَّذِي أَنْشَأَكُمْ وَجَعَلَ لَكُمُ السَّمْعَ
وَالْأَبْصَارَ وَالْأَفْئِدَةَ قَلِيلًا مَا تَشْكُرُونَ ۝

قُلْ هُوَ الَّذِي ذَرَأَكُمْ فِي الْأَرْضِ وَإِلَيْهِ تُحْشَرُونَ ۝

وَيَقُولُونَ مَتَى هَذَا الْوَعْدُ إِنْ كُنْتُمْ صَادِقِينَ ۝

قُلْ إِنَّمَا الْعِلْمُ عِنْدَ اللَّهِ وَإِنَّمَا أَنَا نَذِيرٌ

I am but a plain Warner. When they see it approaching, the faces of those who disbelieve will become gloomy, and they will be told: This is that which you used to call for. (16—28)

قُمِبِينٌ ۞

فَلَمَّا رَاَوْهُ زُلْفَةً سِيْئَتْ وُجُوْهُ الَّذِيْنَ كَفَرُوْا وَقِيْلَ هٰذَا الَّذِيْ كُنْتُمْ بِهٖ تَدَّعُوْنَ ۞

قُلْ اَرَءَيْتُمْ اِنْ اَهْلَكَنِيَ اللّٰهُ وَمَنْ مَّعِىَ اَوْ رَحِمْنَا فَمَنْ يُّجِيْرُ الْكٰفِرِيْنَ مِنْ عَذَابٍ اَلِيْمٍ ۞

Ask them: Tell me, whether Allah should destroy me and those who are with me, or have mercy on us, who will shield the disbelievers from a painful chastisement? Tell them: He is the Gracious One; in Him have we believed and in Him have we put our trust. Soon will you know who is in manifest error. Ask them: Tell me, if all your water were to disappear in the earth, then who will bring you clear flowing water? (29—31)

قُلْ هُوَ الرَّحْمٰنُ اٰمَنَّا بِهٖ وَعَلَيْهِ تَوَكَّلْنَا فَسَتَعْلَمُوْنَ مَنْ هُوَ فِيْ ضَلٰلٍ مُّبِيْنٍ ۞

قُلْ اَرَءَيْتُمْ اِنْ اَصْبَحَ مَآؤُكُمْ غَوْرًا فَمَنْ يَّأْتِيْكُمْ بِمَآءٍ مَّعِيْنٍ ۞

In the name of Allah, Most Gracious, Ever Merciful. (1)

بِسْمِ اللّٰهِ الرَّحْمٰنِ الرَّحِيْمِ ۞

نٓ وَالْقَلَمِ وَمَا يَسْطُرُوْنَ ۞

مَآ اَنْتَ بِنِعْمَةِ رَبِّكَ بِمَجْنُوْنٍ ۞

وَاِنَّ لَكَ لَاَجْرًا غَيْرَ مَمْنُوْنٍ ۞

وَاِنَّكَ لَعَلٰى خُلُقٍ عَظِيْمٍ ۞

فَسَتُبْصِرُ وَيُبْصِرُوْنَ ۞

We cite the inkstand, and the pen, and that which is thereby written, that thou art not, by the grace of thy Lord, afflicted with madness. For thee, most surely, there is an unending reward. Thou dost most surely possess high moral excellences. Thou wilt soon see and they too will see which of you is demented.

بِاَيِّكُمُ الْمَفْتُوْنُ ۞

Surely, thy Lord knows best those who go astray from His way, and He knows best those who follow guidance;

اِنَّ رَبَّكَ هُوَ اَعْلَمُ بِمَنْ ضَلَّ عَنْ سَبِيْلِهٖ وَهُوَ اَعْلَمُ بِالْمُهْتَدِيْنَ ۞

so comply not with the wishes of those who reject the truth. They wish that thou shouldst be a little accommodating so that they may also be accommodating. But yield thou not to any low swearer, back-biter, slanderer, forbidder of good, trans-gressor, sinner, unmannerly lout and mis-begotten knave, because he is wealthy and has a number of children and retainers.

فَلَا تُطِعِ الْمُكَذِّبِيْنَ ۟

وَدُّوْا لَوْ تُدْهِنُ فَيُدْهِنُوْنَ ۟

وَلَا تُطِعْ كُلَّ حَلَّافٍ مَّهِيْنٍ ۙ

هَمَّازٍ مَّشَّآءٍ بِنَمِيْمٍ ۙ

مَّنَّاعٍ لِّلْخَيْرِ مُعْتَدٍ اَثِيْمٍ ۙ

عُتُلٍّ بَعْدَ ذٰلِكَ زَنِيْمٍ ۙ

اَنْ كَانَ ذَا مَالٍ وَّبَنِيْنَ ۟

اِذَا تُتْلٰى عَلَيْهِ اٰيٰتُنَا قَالَ اَسَاطِيْرُ الْاَوَّلِيْنَ ۟

سَنَسِمُهٗ عَلَى الْخُرْطُوْمِ ۟

When Our Signs are recited unto him, he says: Old wives' tales! We will brand him on the snout. We will try them as We tried the owners of the garden who vowed that they would for certain gather its fruit in the morning, and they made no exception by way of: If Allah wills. Then a visitation from thy Lord passed over it while they were asleep, and by morning it became as if all its fruit had been cut down. They called to one another at the break of dawn: Go forth early to your orchard, if you would gather its fruit. So they set out, talking to one another in low tones: Let no poor man intrude on you in the orchard today.

اِنَّا بَلَوْنٰهُمْ كَمَا بَلَوْنَآ اَصْحٰبَ الْجَنَّةِ ۚ اِذْ اَقْسَمُوْا لَيَصْرِمُنَّهَا مُصْبِحِيْنَ ۙ

وَلَا يَسْتَثْنُوْنَ ۟

فَطَافَ عَلَيْهَا طَآئِفٌ مِّنْ رَّبِّكَ وَهُمْ نَآئِمُوْنَ ۟

فَاَصْبَحَتْ كَالصَّرِيْمِ ۙ

فَتَنَادَوْا مُصْبِحِيْنَ ۙ

اَنِ اغْدُوْا عَلٰى حَرْثِكُمْ اِنْ كُنْتُمْ صٰرِمِيْنَ ۟

فَانْطَلَقُوْا وَهُمْ يَتَخَافَتُوْنَ ۙ

اَنْ لَّا يَدْخُلَنَّهَا الْيَوْمَ عَلَيْكُمْ مِّسْكِيْنٌ ۙ

Thus they set forth in the morning deter-mined to be niggardly. When they saw it, they exclaimed: Surely, we have lost our way! Oh no, we have been stripped of everything! The worthiest of them said: Did I not say to you: Why do you not glorify Allah?

وَّغَدَوْا عَلٰى حَرْدٍ قٰدِرِيْنَ ۟

فَلَمَّا رَاَوْهَا قَالُوْٓا اِنَّا لَضَآلُّوْنَ ۟

بَلْ نَحْنُ مَحْرُوْمُوْنَ ۟

قَالَ اَوْسَطُهُمْ اَلَمْ اَقُلْ لَّكُمْ لَوْلَا تُسَبِّحُوْنَ ۟

Thereupon they said: Glory be to our Lord. Surely, we have been wrongdoers. Then some of them turned to the others with reproaches and said: Woe to us. We were indeed rebellious. May be our Lord will give us instead a better orchard than this. We shall humbly beseech our Lord. Such is the punishment. Surely, the punishment of the Hereafter is greater by far; did they but know. (2—34)

قَالُوْا سُبْحٰنَ رَبِّنَاۤ اِنَّا كُنَّا ظٰلِمِيْنَ ۝

فَاَقْبَلَ بَعْضُهُمْ عَلٰى بَعْضٍ يَّتَلَاوَمُوْنَ ۝

قَالُوْا يٰوَيْلَنَاۤ اِنَّا كُنَّا طٰغِيْنَ ۝

عَسٰى رَبُّنَاۤ اَنْ يُّبْدِلَنَا خَيْرًا مِّنْهَاۤ اِنَّاۤ اِلٰى رَبِّنَا رٰغِبُوْنَ ۝

كَذٰلِكَ الْعَذَابُ ۭ وَلَعَذَابُ الْاٰخِرَةِ اَكْبَرُ ۘ لَوْ كَانُوْا يَعْلَمُوْنَ ۝

For the righteous, indeed, there are Gardens of Bliss with their Lord. Could We treat those who submit to Us, like the guilty? What ails you? How ill do you judge! Have you a Book wherein you read that you shall have whatever you choose? Or have you any covenant binding on Us till the Day of Judgment that you shall have all that you command? Ask them which of them will vouch for that? Or have they any alleged partners of Allah? Let them, then, produce those partners of theirs, if they speak the truth.

اِنَّ لِلْمُتَّقِيْنَ عِنْدَ رَبِّهِمْ جَنّٰتِ النَّعِيْمِ ۝

اَفَنَجْعَلُ الْمُسْلِمِيْنَ كَالْمُجْرِمِيْنَ ۝

مَا لَكُمْ ۟ كَيْفَ تَحْكُمُوْنَ ۝

اَمْ لَكُمْ كِتٰبٌ فِيْهِ تَدْرُسُوْنَ ۝

اِنَّ لَكُمْ فِيْهِ لَمَا تَخَيَّرُوْنَ ۝

اَمْ لَكُمْ اَيْمَانٌ عَلَيْنَا بَالِغَةٌ اِلٰى يَوْمِ الْقِيٰمَةِ ۙ اِنَّ لَكُمْ لَمَا تَحْكُمُوْنَ ۝

سَلْهُمْ اَيُّهُمْ بِذٰلِكَ زَعِيْمٌ ۝

اَمْ لَهُمْ شُرَكَآءُ ۚۛ فَلْيَأْتُوْا بِشُرَكَآئِهِمْ اِنْ كَانُوْا صٰدِقِيْنَ ۝

On the day when the calamity overtakes them and they are called upon to prostrate themselves, they will not be able to do so; their eyes will be cast down and they will be covered with ignominy. They were indeed called upon to prostrate themselves when they were whole, but they did not obey. So leave Me to deal with those who reject this discourse. We shall draw them step by step towards destruction whence they know not.

يَوْمَ يُكْشَفُ عَنْ سَاقٍ وَّيُدْعَوْنَ اِلَى السُّجُوْدِ فَلَا يَسْتَطِيْعُوْنَ ۝

خَاشِعَةً اَبْصَارُهُمْ تَرْهَقُهُمْ ذِلَّةٌ ۭ وَقَدْ كَانُوْا يُدْعَوْنَ اِلَى السُّجُوْدِ وَهُمْ سٰلِمُوْنَ ۝

فَذَرْنِيْ وَمَنْ يُّكَذِّبُ بِهٰذَا الْحَدِيْثِ ۭ سَنَسْتَدْرِجُهُمْ

I grant them respite, for My design is powerful. Dost thou demand a reward from them that they feel weighed down by the impost? Do they possess knowledge of the unseen, so that they write it down? So, be thou steadfast in carrying out the command of thy Lord, and be not like Jonah, the Man of the Fish, who called on his Lord when he was full of suppressed grief. Had not his Lord's favour reached him, he would have been cast disgraced upon a barren tract of land. But his Lord chose him and made him one of the righteous.

مِنْ حَيْثُ لَا يَعْلَمُوْنَ ۞

وَأُمْلِيْ لَهُمْ ۖ إِنَّ كَيْدِيْ مَتِيْنٌ ۞

أَمْ تَسْئَلُهُمْ أَجْرًا فَهُمْ مِّنْ مَّغْرَمٍ مُّثْقَلُوْنَ ۞

أَمْ عِنْدَهُمُ الْغَيْبُ فَهُمْ يَكْتُبُوْنَ ۞

فَاصْبِرْ لِحُكْمِ رَبِّكَ وَلَا تَكُنْ كَصَاحِبِ الْحُوْتِ ۚ

إِذْ نَادٰى وَهُوَ مَكْظُوْمٌ ۞

لَوْلَا أَنْ تَدَارَكَهُ نِعْمَةٌ مِّنْ رَّبِّهِ لَنُبِذَ بِالْعَرَاءِ وَهُوَ مَذْمُوْمٌ ۞

فَاجْتَبٰهُ رَبُّهُ فَجَعَلَهُ مِنَ الصّٰلِحِيْنَ ۞

وَإِنْ يَّكَادُ الَّذِيْنَ كَفَرُوْا لَيُزْلِقُوْنَكَ بِأَبْصَارِهِمْ لَمَّا سَمِعُوا الذِّكْرَ وَيَقُوْلُوْنَ إِنَّهُ لَمَجْنُوْنٌ ۞

وَمَا هُوَ إِلَّا ذِكْرٌ لِّلْعٰلَمِيْنَ ۞

Those who disbelieve would fain have caused thee to stumble with their angry looks when they heard the Quran; and they keep saying: He is certainly mad. But the truth is that it is a source of honour for all the worlds. (35—53)

سُوْرَةُ الْحَاقَّةِ مَكِّيَّةٌ

Part 29   AL-ḤĀQQAH   Chapter 69
(Revealed before Hijra)

In the name of Allah, Most Gracious, Ever Merciful. (1)

بِسْمِ اللهِ الرَّحْمٰنِ الرَّحِيْمِ ۞

The Inevitable. What is the Inevitable? What has made thee know what the Inevitable is? (2—4)

الْحَاقَّةُ ۞

مَا الْحَاقَّةُ ۞

وَمَا أَدْرٰىكَ مَا الْحَاقَّةُ ۞

The tribes of 'Ad and Thamud rejected the warning of the calamity. Then the tribe of Thamud were destroyed with a violent blast,

كَذَّبَتْ ثَمُوْدُ وَعَادٌ بِالْقَارِعَةِ ۞

فَأَمَّا ثَمُوْدُ فَأُهْلِكُوْا بِالطَّاغِيَةِ ۞

577

and the tribe of 'Ad were destroyed by a fierce roaring wind, which He caused to blow against them for seven nights and eight days in succession, so that thou mightest have seen the people lying prostrate therein, as though they were roots of palm-trees fallen down. Do you perceive any sign of them? Pharaoh and those before him and the people of the overthrown cities were guilty of sins, and they disobeyed the Messenger of their Lord, He therefore inflicted a severe punishment upon them. When the waters rose high in the time of Noah, We carried you in the Ark, that We might make it a reminder for you, and that retaining ears might retain it.

When a single blast is sounded on the trumpet, and the earth and the mountains are heaved up and then crushed in a single crash, on that day will the great Event come to pass; and the heaven will cleave asunder and appear very frail that day. The angels will be standing on its sides, and above them eight of them will that day bear the Throne of thy Lord.

On that day you will be presented before Allah and no secret action of yours will remain hidden from you. He who is given his record in his right hand will say: Come read my record; I knew I would meet my reckoning. So he will have a delightful life, in a lofty Garden, the clusters of whose fruits will be within easy reach.

They will be told: Eat and drink without care, because of that which you did in days gone by. But he who is given his record in his left hand will say: Would that I had not been given my record, nor known what my reckoning was. Would that my death had made an end of me. My wealth has been of no avail to me; and my power has perished.

The angels will be commanded: Seize him and fetter him; and cast him into hell, and bind him with a chain of seventy links. He did not believe in Allah of vast power, and did not urge the feeding of the poor. He has, therefore, no friend here to-day; nor any food except the corruption that flows from the bodies of the damned, which none but the sinners eat. (5—38)

We cite in evidence all that which you see and all that which you see not, that the Quran is surely the Word brought by a noble Messenger; and it is not the word of a poet; little it is that you believe. Nor is it the word of a soothsayer, but little it is that you heed. It is a revelation from the Lord of the worlds.

كُلُوا وَاشْرَبُوا هَنِيئًا بِمَا أَسْلَفْتُمْ فِي الْأَيَّامِ الْخَالِيَةِ ۝

وَأَمَّا مَنْ أُوتِيَ كِتَابَهُ بِشِمَالِهِ فَيَقُولُ يَا لَيْتَنِي لَمْ أُوتَ كِتَابِيَهْ ۝

وَلَمْ أَدْرِ مَا حِسَابِيَهْ ۝

يَا لَيْتَهَا كَانَتِ الْقَاضِيَةَ ۝

مَا أَغْنَى عَنِّي مَالِيَهْ ۝

هَلَكَ عَنِّي سُلْطَانِيَهْ ۝

خُذُوهُ فَغُلُّوهُ ۝

ثُمَّ الْجَحِيمَ صَلُّوهُ ۝

ثُمَّ فِي سِلْسِلَةٍ ذَرْعُهَا سَبْعُونَ ذِرَاعًا فَاسْلُكُوهُ ۝

إِنَّهُ كَانَ لَا يُؤْمِنُ بِاللَّهِ الْعَظِيمِ ۝

وَلَا يَحُضُّ عَلَى طَعَامِ الْمِسْكِينِ ۝

فَلَيْسَ لَهُ الْيَوْمَ هَاهُنَا حَمِيمٌ ۝

وَلَا طَعَامٌ إِلَّا مِنْ غِسْلِينٍ ۝

لَا يَأْكُلُهُ إِلَّا الْخَاطِئُونَ ۝

فَلَا أُقْسِمُ بِمَا تُبْصِرُونَ ۝

وَمَا لَا تُبْصِرُونَ ۝

إِنَّهُ لَقَوْلُ رَسُولٍ كَرِيمٍ ۝

وَمَا هُوَ بِقَوْلِ شَاعِرٍ قَلِيلًا مَا تُؤْمِنُونَ ۝

وَلَا بِقَوْلِ كَاهِنٍ قَلِيلًا مَا تَذَكَّرُونَ ۝

تَنْزِيلٌ مِنْ رَبِّ الْعَالَمِينَ ۝

If he had fabricated any saying and attributed it to Us, We would surely have seized him by the right hand, and then surely We would have severed his large artery, and not one of you could have kept Us from it.

وَلَوْ تَقَوَّلَ عَلَيْنَا بَعْضَ الْاَقَاوِيلِ ۙ

لَاَخَذْنَا مِنْهُ بِالْيَمِينِ ۙ

ثُمَّ لَقَطَعْنَا مِنْهُ الْوَتِينَ ۖ

فَمَا مِنْكُمْ مِّنْ اَحَدٍ عَنْهُ حٰجِزِينَ ۚ

وَاِنَّهٗ لَتَذْكِرَةٌ لِّلْمُتَّقِينَ

Verily, this Quran is a source of guidance and honour for those who are mindful of their duty to Allah. We know that there are some among you who reject it, and that it is a source of regret for the disbelievers. Surely, it is the true certainty. So glorify the name of thy Lord the Great. (39—53)

وَاِنَّا لَنَعْلَمُ اَنَّ مِنْكُمْ مُّكَذِّبِينَ

وَاِنَّهٗ لَحَسْرَةٌ عَلَى الْكٰفِرِينَ ۚ

وَاِنَّهٗ لَحَقُّ الْيَقِينِ ۚ

فَسَبِّحْ بِاسْمِ رَبِّكَ الْعَظِيمِ ۖ

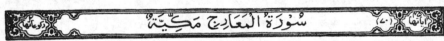

(Revealed before Hijra)

In the name of Allah, Most Gracious, Ever Merciful. (1)

بِسْمِ اللّٰهِ الرَّحْمٰنِ الرَّحِيمِ ۚ

سَاَلَ سَآئِلٌ بِعَذَابٍ وَّاقِعٍ ۙ

لِّلْكٰفِرِينَ لَيْسَ لَهٗ دَافِعٌ ۙ

An enquirer inquires concerning the punishment that will afflict the disbelievers, which none can repel, from Allah, Lord of great heights.

مِّنَ اللّٰهِ ذِي الْمَعَارِجِ ۙ

تَعْرُجُ الْمَلٰئِكَةُ وَالرُّوحُ اِلَيْهِ فِيْ يَوْمٍ كَانَ

مِقْدَارُهٗ خَمْسِينَ اَلْفَ سَنَةٍ ۚ

The angels and the Spirit ascend to Him in a day, the measure of which is fifty thousand years. So continue patient in a becoming manner. They imagine it to be far off, but We see it nigh.

فَاصْبِرْ صَبْرًا جَمِيلًا

اِنَّهُمْ يَرَوْنَهٗ بَعِيدًا ۙ

وَّنَرٰىهُ قَرِيبًا ۙ

On that day the heaven will be like molten copper, and the mountains will be like flakes of wool, and a friend will not inquire after a friend, for they will be within sight of one another. A guilty one would fain ransom himself from the torment of that day by offering his children and his wife and his brother, and his kinsfolk who gave him shelter, and all those who are on the earth, if only thus he might save himself. All in vain ! It will be a fierce blaze, stripping off the skin to the scalp. It will encompass him who turns his back on it and retreats, and who hoarded wealth and withheld it. (2—19)

يَوْمَ تَكُوْنُ السَّمَآءُ كَالْمُهْلِ ۞

وَتَكُوْنُ الْجِبَالُ كَالْعِهْنِ ۞

وَلَا يَسْـَٔلُ حَمِيْمٌ حَمِيْمًا ۚ

يُبَصَّرُوْنَهُمْ يَوَدُّ الْمُجْرِمُ لَوْ يَفْتَدِيْ مِنْ عَذَابِ يَوْمِئِذٍ بِبَنِيْهِ ۞

وَصَاحِبَتِهِ وَاَخِيْهِ ۞

وَفَصِيْلَتِهِ الَّتِيْ تُـْٔوِيْهِ ۞

وَمَنْ فِى الْاَرْضِ جَمِيْعًا ثُمَّ يُنْجِيْهِ ۞

كَلَّا ۚ اِنَّهَا لَظٰى ۞

نَزَّاعَةً لِّلشَّوٰى ۞

تَدْعُوْا مَنْ اَدْبَرَ وَتَوَلّٰى ۞

وَجَمَعَ فَاَوْعٰى ۞

اِنَّ الْاِنْسَانَ خُلِقَ هَلُوْعًا ۞

اِذَا مَسَّهُ الشَّرُّ جَزُوْعًا ۞

وَّاِذَا مَسَّهُ الْخَيْرُ مَنُوْعًا ۞

اِلَّا الْمُصَلِّيْنَ ۞

الَّذِيْنَ هُمْ عَلٰى صَلَاتِهِمْ دَآئِمُوْنَ ۞

وَالَّذِيْنَ فِيْٓ اَمْوَالِهِمْ حَقٌّ مَّعْلُوْمٌ ۞

لِّلسَّآئِلِ وَالْمَحْرُوْمِ ۞

وَالَّذِيْنَ يُصَدِّقُوْنَ بِيَوْمِ الدِّيْنِ ۞

وَالَّذِيْنَ هُمْ مِّنْ عَذَابِ رَبِّهِمْ مُّشْفِقُوْنَ ۞

اِنَّ عَذَابَ رَبِّهِمْ غَيْرُ مَأْمُوْنٍ ۞

Verily, it is in man's nature to be impatient. When evil afflicts him, he is full of lamentation; but when good befalls him, he is niggardly; except those who pray and are constant in their Prayer; and those in whose wealth there is a well-ascertained share for those who ask and those who do not; and those who affirm faith in the Day of Judgment; and those who are fearful of the chastisement of their Lord, the chastisement of their Lord is surely not a thing to feel secure from;

and those who guard their senses, except
in respect of their wives and those under
their control; such are not to blame, but
those who seek to go beyond that are the
transgressors; and those who are watchful
of their trusts and their covenants; and
those who are steadfast in their testi-
monies; and those who are strict in the
observance of Prayer. These will be honoured in the Garden. (20—36)

وَالَّذِيْنَ هُمْ لِفُرُوْجِهِمْ حٰفِظُوْنَ ۞

اِلَّا عَلٰٓى اَزْوَاجِهِمْ اَوْ مَا مَلَكَتْ اَيْمَانُهُمْ فَاِنَّهُمْ
غَيْرُ مَلُوْمِيْنَ ۞

فَمَنِ ابْتَغٰى وَرَآءَ ذٰلِكَ فَاُولٰٓئِكَ هُمُ الْعٰدُوْنَ ۞

وَالَّذِيْنَ هُمْ لِاَمٰنٰتِهِمْ وَعَهْدِهِمْ رٰعُوْنَ ۞

وَالَّذِيْنَ هُمْ بِشَهٰدٰتِهِمْ قَآئِمُوْنَ ۞

وَالَّذِيْنَ هُمْ عَلٰى صَلَاتِهِمْ يُحَافِظُوْنَ ۞

اُولٰٓئِكَ فِيْ جَنّٰتٍ مُّكْرَمُوْنَ ۞

What ails the disbelievers that they
come hastening towards thee with extended necks from the right hand and the left,
in parties? Does every man among them
hope to be admitted to the Garden of Bliss?
That cannot be. We have created them of
that which they know. I affirm by the Lord of
the Easts and the Wests, that We have
the power to bring in their place better
than they, and We cannot be frustrated.

فَمَالِ الَّذِيْنَ كَفَرُوْا قِبَلَكَ مُهْطِعِيْنَ ۞

عَنِ الْيَمِيْنِ وَعَنِ الشِّمَالِ عِزِيْنَ ۞

اَيَطْمَعُ كُلُّ امْرِئٍ مِّنْهُمْ اَنْ يُّدْخَلَ جَنَّةَ نَعِيْمٍ ۞

كَلَّا ۭ اِنَّا خَلَقْنٰهُمْ مِّمَّا يَعْلَمُوْنَ ۞

فَلَآ اُقْسِمُ بِرَبِّ الْمَشٰرِقِ وَالْمَغٰرِبِ اِنَّا لَقٰدِرُوْنَ ۞

عَلٰٓى اَنْ نُّبَدِّلَ خَيْرًا مِّنْهُمْ ۙ وَمَا نَحْنُ بِمَسْبُوْقِيْنَ ۞

فَذَرْهُمْ يَخُوْضُوْا وَيَلْعَبُوْا حَتّٰى يُلٰقُوْا يَوْمَهُمُ
الَّذِيْ يُوْعَدُوْنَ ۞

So leave them occupied with vain discourse and sport until they are confronted
with the day that they are promised, the
day that they will come forth from their
graves hastening, as though they were
running to join their standards, their eyes
cast down, covered with ignominy. That
is the day which they are promised. (37—
45)

يَوْمَ يَخْرُجُوْنَ مِنَ الْاَجْدَاثِ سِرَاعًا كَاَنَّهُمْ اِلٰى
نُصُبٍ يُّوْفِضُوْنَ ۞

خَاشِعَةً اَبْصَارُهُمْ تَرْهَقُهُمْ ذِلَّةٌ ۭ ذٰلِكَ الْيَوْمُ
الَّذِيْ كَانُوْا يُوْعَدُوْنَ ۞

سُوْرَةُ نُوْحٍ مَكِّيَّةٌ

NŪḤ

(Revealed before Hijra)

In the name of Allah, Most Gracious, Ever Merciful. (1)

بِسْمِ اللهِ الرَّحْمٰنِ الرَّحِيْمِ ۞

اِنَّاۤ اَرْسَلْنَا نُوْحًا اِلٰى قَوْمِهٖۤ اَنْ اَنْذِرْ قَوْمَكَ مِنْ قَبْلِ اَنْ يَّأْتِيَهُمْ عَذَابٌ اَلِيْمٌ ۞

قَالَ يٰقَوْمِ اِنِّيْ لَكُمْ نَذِيْرٌ مُّبِيْنٌ ۞

اَنِ اعْبُدُوا اللهَ وَاتَّقُوْهُ وَاَطِيْعُوْنِ ۞

يَغْفِرْ لَكُمْ مِّنْ ذُنُوْبِكُمْ وَيُؤَخِّرْكُمْ اِلٰۤى اَجَلٍ مُّسَمًّى ؕ اِنَّ اَجَلَ اللهِ اِذَا جَآءَ لَا يُؤَخَّرُ ۘ لَوْ كُنْتُمْ تَعْلَمُوْنَ ۞

We sent Noah to his people directing him: Warn thy people before there comes upon them a grievous punishment. He exhorted them: O my people, I am sent as a plain Warner unto you, that you worship only Allah and be mindful of your duty to Him and obey me. He will forgive you your sins and will grant you respite till an appointed time. When the time appointed by Allah arrives, it cannot be put back, if only you knew.

قَالَ رَبِّ اِنِّيْ دَعَوْتُ قَوْمِيْ لَيْلًا وَّنَهَارًا ۞

فَلَمْ يَزِدْهُمْ دُعَآئِيْۤ اِلَّا فِرَارًا ۞

وَاِنِّيْ كُلَّمَا دَعَوْتُهُمْ لِتَغْفِرَ لَهُمْ جَعَلُوْۤا اَصَابِعَهُمْ فِيْۤ اٰذَانِهِمْ وَاسْتَغْشَوْا ثِيَابَهُمْ وَاَصَرُّوْا وَاسْتَكْبَرُوا اسْتِكْبَارًا ۞

Then Noah supplicated: Lord, I have called my people night and day, but my calling only made them flee me more. Every time I called them that Thou mightest forgive them they put their fingers into their ears, and drew close their garments and were obstinate and behaved with pride and arrogance.

ثُمَّ اِنِّيْ دَعَوْتُهُمْ جِهَارًا ۞

ثُمَّ اِنِّيْۤ اَعْلَنْتُ لَهُمْ وَاَسْرَرْتُ لَهُمْ اِسْرَارًا ۞

فَقُلْتُ اسْتَغْفِرُوْا رَبَّكُمْ اِنَّهٗ كَانَ غَفَّارًا ۞

يُّرْسِلِ السَّمَآءَ عَلَيْكُمْ مِّدْرَارًا ۞

وَّيُمْدِدْكُمْ بِاَمْوَالٍ وَّبَنِيْنَ وَيَجْعَلْ لَّكُمْ جَنّٰتٍ وَّيَجْعَلْ لَّكُمْ اَنْهَارًا ۞

Then I called them openly, and spoke to them in public and in private. I said to them: Seek forgiveness of your Lord; He is the Great Forgiver. He will send down rain on you in abundance, and will help you with wealth and children, and will bestow gardens on you, and will cause rivers to flow for you.

What ails you that you do not expect wisdom from Allah? He has created you through different stages of existence. Have you not seen how Allah has created seven heavens in perfect harmony, and has placed the moon therein as a light, and made the sun as a lamp? Allah has produced you from the earth and caused you to grow; then will He cause you to return thereto, and will bring you forth as a new creation. Allah has made the earth a carpet for you that you may traverse its wide paths. (2—21)

مَا لَكُمْ لَا تَرْجُوْنَ لِلّٰهِ وَقَارًا ۟

وَقَدْ خَلَقَكُمْ اَطْوَارًا ۟

اَلَمْ تَرَوْا كَيْفَ خَلَقَ اللّٰهُ سَبْعَ سَمٰوٰتٍ طِبَاقًا ۟

وَّجَعَلَ الْقَمَرَ فِيْهِنَّ نُوْرًا وَّجَعَلَ الشَّمْسَ سِرَاجًا ۟

وَاللّٰهُ اَنْبَتَكُمْ مِّنَ الْاَرْضِ نَبَاتًا ۟

ثُمَّ يُعِيْدُكُمْ فِيْهَا وَيُخْرِجُكُمْ اِخْرَاجًا ۟

وَاللّٰهُ جَعَلَ لَكُمُ الْاَرْضَ بِسَاطًا ۟

لِّتَسْلُكُوْا مِنْهَا سُبُلًا فِجَاجًا ۟

Noah supplicated: Lord, they have disobeyed me, and followed one whose wealth and children have only added to his ruin. They have planned mightily against me, and have exhorted one another: Forsake not your gods, neither Wadd, nor Suwa, nor Yaghuth and Yauq and Nasr. They have led many astray; so increase Thou not the wrongdoers but in error. Because of their sins they were drowned and cast into fire; and they found no helpers for themselves beside Allah.

قَالَ نُوْحٌ رَّبِّ اِنَّهُمْ عَصَوْنِيْ وَاتَّبَعُوْا مَنْ لَّمْ يَزِدْهُ مَالُهٗ وَوَلَدُهٗٓ اِلَّا خَسَارًا ۟

وَمَكَرُوْا مَكْرًا كُبَّارًا ۟

وَقَالُوْا لَا تَذَرُنَّ اٰلِهَتَكُمْ وَلَا تَذَرُنَّ وَدًّا وَّلَا سُوَاعًا ۙ وَّلَا يَغُوْثَ وَيَعُوْقَ وَنَسْرًا ۟

وَقَدْ اَضَلُّوْا كَثِيْرًا ۚ وَلَا تَزِدِ الظّٰلِمِيْنَ اِلَّا ضَلٰلًا ۟

مِمَّا خَطِيْٓئٰتِهِمْ اُغْرِقُوْا فَاُدْخِلُوْا نَارًا ۙ فَلَمْ يَجِدُوْا لَهُمْ مِّنْ دُوْنِ اللّٰهِ اَنْصَارًا ۟

وَقَالَ نُوْحٌ رَّبِّ لَا تَذَرْ عَلَى الْاَرْضِ مِنَ الْكٰفِرِيْنَ دَيَّارًا ۟

Noah implored: Lord, leave not in the land a single dweller from among the disbelievers; for if Thou leave them, they will only lead Thy servants astray, and will beget only sinners and disbelievers.

اِنَّكَ اِنْ تَذَرْهُمْ يُضِلُّوْا عِبَادَكَ وَلَا يَلِدُوْٓا اِلَّا فَاجِرًا كَفَّارًا ۟

Lord, forgive me and my parents, and
whoever enters my house a believer, and
the believing men and the believing
women; and bestow no increase upon the
wrongdoers except in ruin (22—29)

رَبِّ اغْفِرْلِيْ وَلِوَالِدَيَّ وَلِمَنْ دَخَلَ بَيْتِيَ مُؤْمِنًا وَّ
لِلْمُؤْمِنِيْنَ وَالْمُؤْمِنَاتِ وَلَا تَزِدِ الظَّالِمِيْنَ اِلَّا تَبَارًا ۝

(Revealed before Hijra)

In the name of Allah, Most Gracious,
Ever Merciful. (1)

بِسْمِ اللهِ الرَّحْمٰنِ الرَّحِيْمِ ۝

قُلْ اُوْحِيَ اِلَيَّ اَنَّهُ اسْتَمَعَ نَفَرٌ مِّنَ الْجِنِّ فَقَالُوْٓا
اِنَّا سَمِعْنَا قُرْاٰنًا عَجَبًا ۝

Announce: It has been revealed to me
that a company of the Jinn listened to
the Quran being recited, and when they
returned to their people they said: We
have heard a wonderful Quran, which
guides to the right way; so we have believed in it and we will never associate
anyone with our Lord. The truth is that
the Majesty of our Lord is exalted, and
that He has taken neither wife nor son
unto Himself. The foolish amongst us
used to utter extravagant lies concerning
Allah. We had imagined that men and
jinn would never utter a lie concerning
Allah. Some individuals from among men
used to seek the protection of some individuals from among the jinn and thus
augmented their insolence. They fancied,
even as you fancy, that Allah would never
raise anyone as a Prophet.

يَّهْدِيْٓ اِلَى الرُّشْدِ فَاٰمَنَّا بِهٖ وَلَنْ نُّشْرِكَ بِرَبِّنَآ
اَحَدًا ۝

وَّاَنَّهٗ تَعٰلٰى جَدُّ رَبِّنَا مَا اتَّخَذَ صَاحِبَةً وَّلَا وَلَدًا ۝
وَّاَنَّهٗ كَانَ يَقُوْلُ سَفِيْهُنَا عَلَى اللهِ شَطَطًا ۝
وَّاَنَّا ظَنَنَّآ اَنْ لَّنْ تَقُوْلَ الْاِنْسُ وَالْجِنُّ عَلَى اللهِ
كَذِبًا ۝
وَّاَنَّهٗ كَانَ رِجَالٌ مِّنَ الْاِنْسِ يَعُوْذُوْنَ بِرِجَالٍ
مِّنَ الْجِنِّ فَزَادُوْهُمْ رَهَقًا ۝
وَّاَنَّهُمْ ظَنُّوْا كَمَا ظَنَنْتُمْ اَنْ لَّنْ يَّبْعَثَ اللهُ اَحَدًا ۝
وَّاَنَّا لَمَسْنَا السَّمَآءَ فَوَجَدْنٰهَا مُلِئَتْ حَرَسًا
شَدِيْدًا وَّشُهُبًا ۝

We sought to obtain some knowledge
of divine revelation, but we found it guarded by strong guards and flaming fire.
We used to take up stations to listen;
but whoso listens now finds a flaming
fire lying in wait for him.

وَّاَنَّا كُنَّا نَقْعُدُ مِنْهَا مَقَاعِدَ لِلسَّمْعِ فَمَنْ يَّسْتَمِعِ
الْاٰنَ يَجِدْ لَهٗ شِهَابًا رَّصَدًا ۝

We know not whether, through the Quran, misfortune is designed for those who are in the earth, or their Lord designs to lead them aright. Some of us are righteous and some of us are otherwise; we follow different ways. We know that we cannot frustrate Allah's design in the earth, nor can we frustrate it by flight. When we heard the call to guidance, we believed in it. He who believes in his Lord has no fear of loss or of injustice. Some of us are obedient and some are unjust; it is the obedient who seek guidance. The unjust are the fuel of hell.

If the people of Mecca had adhered to the straight path, We would have provided them with abundant water to drink, that We may try them thereby. Whoso turns away from the remembrance of his Lord is subjected by Him to severe torment. All places of worship belong to Allah alone; so call not therein on anyone beside Allah. When the Servant of Allah stands up praying to Him, they cluster round him in a dense crowd. (2—20)

Tell them: I pray only to my Lord, and I associate no one with Him. I have no power to do you either harm or good. Surely, none can protect me against Allah, nor can I find any place of refuge beside Him.

وَّاَنَّا لَا نَدْرِىٓ اَشَرٌّ اُرِيْدَ بِمَنْ فِى الْاَرْضِ اَمْ اَرَادَ بِهِمْ رَبُّهُمْ رَشَدًا ۞

وَّاَنَّا مِنَّا الصّٰلِحُوْنَ وَمِنَّا دُوْنَ ذٰلِكَ ۚ كُنَّا طَرَآئِقَ قِدَدًا ۞

وَّاَنَّا ظَنَنَّاۤ اَنْ لَّنْ نُّعْجِزَ اللّٰهَ فِى الْاَرْضِ وَلَنْ نُّعْجِزَهٗ هَرَبًا ۞

وَّاَنَّا لَمَّا سَمِعْنَا الْهُدٰىٓ اٰمَنَّا بِهٖ ۚ فَمَنْ يُّؤْمِنْۢ بِرَبِّهٖ فَلَا يَخَافُ بَخْسًا وَّلَا رَهَقًا ۞

وَّاَنَّا مِنَّا الْمُسْلِمُوْنَ وَمِنَّا الْقَاسِطُوْنَ ۚ فَمَنْ اَسْلَمَ فَاُولٰٓئِكَ تَحَرَّوْا رَشَدًا ۞

وَاَمَّا الْقَاسِطُوْنَ فَكَانُوْا لِجَهَنَّمَ حَطَبًا ۞

وَّاَنْ لَّوِ اسْتَقَامُوْا عَلَى الطَّرِيْقَةِ لَاَسْقَيْنٰهُمْ مَّآءً غَدَقًا ۞

لِّنَفْتِنَهُمْ فِيْهِ ۚ وَمَنْ يُّعْرِضْ عَنْ ذِكْرِ رَبِّهٖ يَسْلُكْهُ عَذَابًا صَعَدًا ۞

وَّاَنَّ الْمَسٰجِدَ لِلّٰهِ فَلَا تَدْعُوْا مَعَ اللّٰهِ اَحَدًا ۞

وَّاَنَّهٗ لَمَّا قَامَ عَبْدُ اللّٰهِ يَدْعُوْهُ كَادُوْا يَكُوْنُوْنَ عَلَيْهِ لِبَدًا ۞

قُلْ اِنَّمَاۤ اَدْعُوْا رَبِّيْ وَلَاۤ اُشْرِكُ بِهٖۤ اَحَدًا ۞

قُلْ اِنِّيْ لَاۤ اَمْلِكُ لَكُمْ ضَرًّا وَّلَا رَشَدًا ۞

قُلْ اِنِّيْ لَنْ يُّجِيْرَنِيْ مِنَ اللّٰهِ اَحَدٌ ۙ وَّلَنْ اَجِدَ مِنْ دُوْنِهٖ مُلْتَحَدًا ۞

My duty is to convey that which I receive from Him and His Messages. For those who disobey Allah and His Messenger there is the fire of hell, wherein they will abide for long. When they perceive that which they are promised, they will know who has fewer helpers and is fewer in numbers. Tell them: I know not whether that which you are promised is nigh or whether my Lord has fixed a term for it.

إِلَّا بَلَاغًا مِّنَ اللّٰهِ وَرِسٰلٰتِهٖ ۗ وَمَنْ يَّعْصِ اللّٰهَ وَ

رَسُوْلَهٗ فَاِنَّ لَهٗ نَارَ جَهَنَّمَ خٰلِدِيْنَ فِيْهَاۤ اَبَدًا ۟

حَتّٰۤى اِذَا رَاَوْا مَا يُوْعَدُوْنَ فَسَيَعْلَمُوْنَ مَنْ

اَضْعَفُ نَاصِرًا وَّ اَقَلُّ عَدَدًا ۟

قُلْ اِنْ اَدْرِىۤ اَقَرِيْبٌ مَّا تُوْعَدُوْنَ اَمْ يَجْعَلُ لَهٗ

رَبِّىْۤ اَمَدًا ۟

عٰلِمُ الْغَيْبِ فَلَا يُظْهِرُ عَلٰى غَيْبِهٖۤ اَحَدًا ۟

He is the Knower of the unseen; and He reveals not His secrets to anyone, except to him whom He chooses from among His Messengers. Then He appoints an escort of angels to go before him and behind him, that He may know that the Messenger has delivered the Messages of his Lord. He encompasses all that is with them and He keeps count of all things. (21—29)

اِلَّا مَنِ ارْتَضٰى مِنْ رَّسُوْلٍ فَاِنَّهٗ يَسْلُكُ مِنْۢ بَيْنِ

يَدَيْهِ وَمِنْ خَلْفِهٖ رَصَدًا ۟

لِّيَعْلَمَ اَنْ قَدْ اَبْلَغُوْا رِسٰلٰتِ رَبِّهِمْ وَاَحَاطَ بِمَا

لَدَيْهِمْ وَاَحْصٰى كُلَّ شَىْءٍ عَدَدًا ۟

In the name of Allah, Most Gracious, Ever Merciful. (1)

بِسْمِ اللّٰهِ الرَّحْمٰنِ الرَّحِيْمِ ۟

يٰۤاَيُّهَا الْمُزَّمِّلُ ۟

قُمِ الَّيْلَ اِلَّا قَلِيْلًا ۟

نِّصْفَهٗۤ اَوِ انْقُصْ مِنْهُ قَلِيْلًا ۟

اَوْ زِدْ عَلَيْهِ وَرَتِّلِ الْقُرْاٰنَ تَرْتِيْلًا ۟

اِنَّا سَنُلْقِىْ عَلَيْكَ قَوْلًا ثَقِيْلًا ۟

اِنَّ نَاشِئَةَ الَّيْلِ هِىَ اَشَدُّ وَطْاً وَّاَقْوَمُ قِيْلًا ۟

O thou wrapped up in thy mantle, stand up in Prayer at night except a small portion thereof, half of it, or a little less or a little more, and recite the Quran in a slow and distinct manner. We are about to charge thee with a weighty Word. Getting up at night for worship is the most potent means of subduing the self and of achieving effectiveness in discourse.

Thou hast much occupation during the day. So remind thyself of the attributes of thy Lord and devote thyself wholly to His service. He is the Lord of the East and of the West, there is no god but He, so take Him as thy Guardian. Endure patiently whatever they say; and withdraw from them in a becoming manner. Leave Me alone with those wealthy and self-indulgent ones who reject the truth and give them a little respite. Surely, We have with us ready all types of fetters and a raging fire for them, and food that chokes and a painful chastisement against the day when the earth and the mountains shall be in violent motion, and the mountains will become like crumbling sandhills. (2—15)

Verily, We have sent unto you a Messenger, who is a witness over you, even as We sent a Messenger unto Pharaoh. But Pharaoh disobeyed the Messenger, so We afflicted him with a grievous chastisement. How will you then, if you disbelieve, guard yourselves against a day which will turn children grey-headed, and when the heaven will be rent asunder? This is His promise which must be fulfilled. This is a reminder. So let him who will, take a way to his Lord. (16—20)

Thy Lord knows that thou standest up praying a little less than two-thirds of the night, and sometimes a half or a third thereof, and also a party of those who are with thee. Allah determines the measure of the night and the day. He knows that you cannot keep its measure, so He has turned to you in mercy. Recite, then, as much of the Quran as is easy for you. He knows that there will be some among you who may be sick and others who may travel in the land seeking Allah's bounty, and yet others who may be called on to fight in the cause of Allah. So recite of it that which is easy for you, and observe Prayer, and pay the Zakat, and lend to Allah a goodly loan. Whatever of good you send on for yourselves, you will find it with Allah. He is the Best and Greatest in bestowing reward. Seek forgiveness of Allah. Surely, Allah is Most Forgiving, Ever Merciful. (21)

فِى الْاَرْضِ يَبْتَغُوْنَ مِنْ فَضْلِ اللّٰهِ ۙ وَاٰخَرُوْنَ

يُقَاتِلُوْنَ فِىْ سَبِيْلِ اللّٰهِ ۖ فَاقْرَءُوْا مَا تَيَسَّرَ مِنْهُ ۙ وَ

اَقِيْمُوا الصَّلٰوةَ وَاٰتُوا الزَّكٰوةَ وَاَقْرِضُوا اللّٰهَ قَرْضًا

حَسَنًا ؕ وَمَا تُقَدِّمُوْا لِاَنْفُسِكُمْ مِّنْ خَيْرٍ تَجِدُوْهُ

عِنْدَ اللّٰهِ هُوَ خَيْرًا وَّاَعْظَمَ اَجْرًا ؕ وَاسْتَغْفِرُوا

اللّٰهَ ؕ اِنَّ اللّٰهَ غَفُوْرٌ رَّحِيْمٌ ۠ ۧ

سُوْرَةُ الْمُدَّثِّرِ مَكِّيَّةٌ

(Revealed before Hijra)

In the name of Allah, Most Gracious, Ever Merciful. (1)

بِسْمِ اللّٰهِ الرَّحْمٰنِ الرَّحِيْمِ ۠

يٰٓاَيُّهَا الْمُدَّثِّرُ ۠

قُمْ فَاَنْذِرْ ۠

وَرَبَّكَ فَكَبِّرْ ۠

وَثِيَابَكَ فَطَهِّرْ ۠

وَالرُّجْزَ فَاهْجُرْ ۠

O thou standing ready, wearing thy cloak, up and warn; and magnify thy Lord; and purify those around thee; and stamp out idolatry; and do not bestow a favour in the expectation of receiving more in return; and endure hardship steadfastly for the sake of thy Lord.

وَلَا تَمْنُنْ تَسْتَكْثِرُ ۠

وَلِرَبِّكَ فَاصْبِرْ ۠

فَاِذَا نُقِرَ فِى النَّاقُوْرِ ۠

فَذٰلِكَ يَوْمَئِذٍ يَّوْمٌ عَسِيْرٌ ۠

عَلَى الْكٰفِرِيْنَ غَيْرُ يَسِيْرٍ ۠

When the trumpet is sounded, it will be a distressing day for the disbelievers, not at all easy. Leave Me alone with him whom I created when he was bereft of every-

ذَرْنِىْ وَمَنْ خَلَقْتُ وَحِيْدًا ۠

thing, and then I gave him abundant
wealth, and sons who remain present with
him, and provided for him every resource.
Yet he desires that I should give him more.

وَجَعَلْتُ لَهُ مَالًا مَّمْدُوْدًا ۟

وَّبَنِيْنَ شُهُوْدًا ۟

وَّمَهَّدْتُّ لَهُ تَمْهِيْدًا ۟

ثُمَّ يَطْمَعُ اَنْ اَزِيْدَ ۟

كَلَّا ۖ اِنَّهُ كَانَ لِاٰيٰتِنَا عَنِيْدًا ۟

سَاُرْهِقُهُ صَعُوْدًا ۟

اِنَّهُ فَكَّرَ وَقَدَّرَ ۟

فَقُتِلَ كَيْفَ قَدَّرَ ۟

ثُمَّ قُتِلَ كَيْفَ قَدَّرَ ۟

ثُمَّ نَظَرَ ۟

Not at all. He was contumacious towards
Our Signs. I shall afflict him with a painful
chastisement. He reflected over Our Signs
and calculated; ruin seize him, how he
calculated; again, ruin seize him how he
calculated! Then he reflected once more,
then he frowned and scowled, then he
turned away and was disdainful and said:
This is a lie copied from the ancients; it is
nothing but the word of a man. I shall
soon cast him into the fire of hell. How
wouldst thou know what the fire of hell
is? It spares not and omits no torment; it
scorches the skin. It has nineteen wardens.

ثُمَّ عَبَسَ وَ بَسَرَ ۟

ثُمَّ اَدْبَرَ وَاسْتَكْبَرَ ۟

فَقَالَ اِنْ هٰذَآ اِلَّا سِحْرٌ يُّؤْثَرُ ۟

اِنْ هٰذَآ اِلَّا قَوْلُ الْبَشَرِ ۟

سَاُصْلِيْهِ سَقَرَ ۟

وَ مَآ اَدْرٰىكَ مَا سَقَرُ ۟

لَا تُبْقِيْ وَلَا تَذَرُ ۟

لَوَّاحَةٌ لِّلْبَشَرِ ۖ

عَلَيْهَا تِسْعَةَ عَشَرَ ۟

We have only appointed angels as wardens
of the Fire. We have fixed their number
only as a trial for those who disbelieve, so
that those who have been given the Book
may be certain and those who believe

وَ مَا جَعَلْنَآ اَصْحٰبَ النَّارِ اِلَّا مَلٰٓئِكَةً ۖ وَّ مَا جَعَلْنَا
عِدَّتَهُمْ اِلَّا فِتْنَةً لِّلَّذِيْنَ كَفَرُوْا ۙ لِيَسْتَيْقِنَ الَّذِيْنَ
اُوْتُوا الْكِتٰبَ وَ يَزْدَادَ الَّذِيْنَ اٰمَنُوْٓا اِيْمَانًا وَّ لَا يَرْتَابَ

may increase in faith, and both may not have any doubt, and that those sick at heart and the disbelievers may say: What does Allah mean by such an illustration? Thus does Allah adjudge as having gone astray whom He wills and guides whom He wills. None knows the hosts of thy Lord but He. This is but a Reminder for man. (2—32)

الَّذِيْنَ اُوْتُوا الْكِتٰبَ وَالْمُؤْمِنُوْنَ وَلِيَقُوْلَ الَّذِيْنَ فِيْ

قُلُوْبِهِمْ مَّرَضٌ وَّالْكٰفِرُوْنَ مَاذَآ اَرَادَ اللّٰهُ بِهٰذَا

مَثَلًا ۟ كَذٰلِكَ يُضِلُّ اللّٰهُ مَنْ يَّشَآءُ وَيَهْدِيْ مَنْ

يَّشَآءُ ۟ وَمَا يَعْلَمُ جُنُوْدَ رَبِّكَ اِلَّا هُوَ ۟ وَمَا هِيَ اِلَّا

ذِكْرٰى لِلْبَشَرِ ۟

كَلَّا وَالْقَمَرِ ۟

وَالَّيْلِ اِذْ اَدْبَرَ ۟

وَالصُّبْحِ اِذَآ اَسْفَرَ ۟

اِنَّهَا لَاِحْدَى الْكُبَرِ ۟

نَذِيْرًا لِّلْبَشَرِ ۟

لِمَنْ شَآءَ مِنْكُمْ اَنْ يَّتَقَدَّمَ اَوْ يَتَاَخَّرَ ۟

كُلُّ نَفْسٍ بِمَا كَسَبَتْ رَهِيْنَةٌ ۟

اِلَّا اَصْحٰبَ الْيَمِيْنِ ۟

فِيْ جَنّٰتٍ ۟ يَتَسَآءَلُوْنَ ۟

عَنِ الْمُجْرِمِيْنَ ۟

مَا سَلَكَكُمْ فِيْ سَقَرَ ۟

قَالُوْا لَمْ نَكُ مِنَ الْمُصَلِّيْنَ ۟

وَلَمْ نَكُ نُطْعِمُ الْمِسْكِيْنَ ۟

وَكُنَّا نَخُوْضُ مَعَ الْخَآئِضِيْنَ ۟

وَكُنَّا نُكَذِّبُ بِيَوْمِ الدِّيْنِ ۟

حَتّٰى اَتٰىنَا الْيَقِيْنُ ۟

فَمَا تَنْفَعُهُمْ شَفَاعَةُ الشّٰفِعِيْنَ ۟

We cite the moon in evidence, and the night when it retreats, and the morn when it brightens, that the promised chastisement is one of the greatest events. It is a warning to man, to him among you who desires to advance in virtue or to draw back from vice.

Every one is pledged in respect of that which he practised; except those of the right hand. They will be in Gardens and will ask the guilty ones: What has brought you to the fire of hell? They will answer: We were not of those who offered Prayers, nor did we feed the poor. We indulged in vain discourse along with those who indulged in it, and we denied the Day of Judgment until death overtook us. So no intercession will avail them.

What ails them that they turn away from the exhortation, as if they are frightened asses fleeing from a lion? Every one of them desires to be given unfolded sheets of revelation. In truth they do not fear the Hereafter.

فَمَا لَهُمْ عَنِ التَّذْكِرَةِ مُعْرِضِيْنَ ۝

كَاَنَّهُمْ حُمُرٌ مُّسْتَنْفِرَةٌ ۝

فَرَّتْ مِنْ قَسْوَرَةٍ ۝

بَلْ يُرِيْدُ كُلُّ امْرِئٍ مِّنْهُمْ اَنْ يُّؤْتٰى صُحُفًا

مُّنَشَّرَةً ۝

كَلَّا بَلْ لَّا يَخَافُوْنَ الْاٰخِرَةَ ۝

كَلَّا اِنَّهٗ تَذْكِرَةٌ ۝

فَمَنْ شَآءَ ذَكَرَهٗ ۝

Hearken, verily this is an exhortation. Let him, then, who will, remember it. But they will not remember unless Allah so please. He bestows righteousness and He bestows forgiveness. (33—57)

وَمَا يَذْكُرُوْنَ اِلَّا اَنْ يَّشَآءَ اللّٰهُ هُوَ اَهْلُ التَّقْوٰى

وَاَهْلُ الْمَغْفِرَةِ ۝

 سُوْرَةُ الْقِيٰمَةِ مَكِّيَّةٌ

Chapter 75   AL-QIYĀMAH   Part 29
(Revealed before Hijra)

In the name of Allah, Most Gracious, Ever Merciful. (1)

بِسْمِ اللّٰهِ الرَّحْمٰنِ الرَّحِيْمِ ۝

لَاۤ اُقْسِمُ بِيَوْمِ الْقِيٰمَةِ ۝

I call to witness the Judgment Day; and in support thereof I call to witness the self-accusing faculty.

وَلَاۤ اُقْسِمُ بِالنَّفْسِ اللَّوَّامَةِ ۝

اَيَحْسَبُ الْاِنْسَانُ اَلَّنْ نَّجْمَعَ عِظَامَهٗ ۝

بَلٰى قٰدِرِيْنَ عَلٰۤى اَنْ نُّسَوِّيَ بَنَانَهٗ ۝

Does man imagine that We shall not assemble his bones? Indeed, We have the power to restore his very finger tips. But man desires to continue in his evil courses. He keeps asking: When will the Day of Judgment be? When the eye is dazzled,

بَلْ يُرِيْدُ الْاِنْسَانُ لِيَفْجُرَ اَمَامَهٗ ۝

يَسْـَٔلُ اَيَّانَ يَوْمُ الْقِيٰمَةِ ۝

فَاِذَا بَرِقَ الْبَصَرُ ۝

and the moon is eclipsed, and the sun and
the moon exhibit the same phenomenon,
on that day man will say: Is there a place
of refuge? Not at all: there is nowhere to
take refuge. On that day, with thy Lord
alone will be the place of rest. Man will
be informed that day of that which he had
committed and of that which he had
neglected. In truth man is aware of the
working of his mind; even though he put
forward his excuses. (2—16)

Do not move thy tongue with the words
of the revelation that thou mayest hurry
over it. Upon Us rests its collection and
its recital. So when We recite it, do thou
follow its recital. Then upon Us rests the
expounding thereof. (17—20)

You love that which is transitory; and
you neglect that which is lasting. On that
day some faces will be bright, looking
eagerly towards their Lord; and some
faces will be dismal, fearing that a back-
breaking calamity would befall them.
Hearken, when life is fluttering, and it is
said: Can anyone save him by incantations
and the like? and everyone is sure it is
the hour of parting, and the extreme
moment is reached,

593

towards thy Lord alone at that hour is the advance.

He neither gave alms, nor offered Prayers; but he rejected the truth and turned his back on it; then went to his family strutting haughtily. Ruin upon thee and ruin again!

Does man think that he is to be left purposeless? Was he not a drop of fluid emitted forth? Then he became a clot, and then Allah shaped and proportioned him, and He made of him a pair, male and female. Has not such a One the power to bring the dead to life? (21—41)

سُوْرَةُ الدَّهْرِ مَكِّيَّةٌ

Chapter 76   AL-DAHR   Part 29
(Revealed before Hijra)

In the name of Allah, Most Gracious, Ever Merciful. (1)

Has not man passed through a space of time when he was not anything made mention of? We created man from a sperm-drop comprising many qualities, that We might try him; so We made him hearing and seeing; and We showed him the Way. He is either appreciative, and follows it, or is ungrateful, and rejects it. We have prepared chains and collars and a blazing Fire for the disbelievers.

594

The virtuous shall drink of a cup tempered with camphor, from a spring wherefrom the servants of Allah drink. They cause it to gush forth through their efforts. They fulfil their vows, and fear a day the mischief of which is widespread.

إِنَّ الْأَبْرَارَ يَشْرَبُوْنَ مِنْ كَأْسٍ كَانَ مِزَاجُهَا كَافُوْرًا ۞

عَيْنًا يَّشْرَبُ بِهَا عِبَادُ اللّٰهِ يُفَجِّرُوْنَهَا تَفْجِيْرًا ۞

يُوْفُوْنَ بِالنَّذْرِ وَيَخَافُوْنَ يَوْمًا كَانَ شَرُّهُ مُسْتَطِيْرًا ۞

وَيُطْعِمُوْنَ الطَّعَامَ عَلٰى حُبِّهٖ مِسْكِيْنًا وَّيَتِيْمًا وَّاَسِيْرًا ۞

They feed the poor, the orphan and the captive for the love of Allah, assuring them: We feed you only for Allah's pleasure. We desire no return nor thanks from you. We fear our Lord against a dismal and calamitous day. So Allah will shield them against the mischief of that day, and will grant them brightness and joy. He will reward them for their steadfastness, with a Garden and raiment of silk. They will recline upon couches, suffering no extreme either of heat or of cold.

إِنَّمَا نُطْعِمُكُمْ لِوَجْهِ اللّٰهِ لَا نُرِيْدُ مِنْكُمْ جَزَآءً وَّلَا شُكُوْرًا ۞

إِنَّا نَخَافُ مِنْ رَّبِّنَا يَوْمًا عَبُوْسًا قَمْطَرِيْرًا ۞

فَوَقٰىهُمُ اللّٰهُ شَرَّ ذٰلِكَ الْيَوْمِ وَلَقّٰىهُمْ نَضْرَةً وَّسُرُوْرًا ۞

وَجَزٰىهُمْ بِمَا صَبَرُوْا جَنَّةً وَّحَرِيْرًا ۞

مُّتَّكِئِيْنَ فِيْهَا عَلَى الْاَرَآئِكِ لَا يَرَوْنَ فِيْهَا شَمْسًا وَّلَا زَمْهَرِيْرًا ۞

وَدَانِيَةً عَلَيْهِمْ ظِلٰلُهَا وَذُلِّلَتْ قُطُوْفُهَا تَذْلِيْلًا ۞

وَيُطَافُ عَلَيْهِمْ بِاٰنِيَةٍ مِّنْ فِضَّةٍ وَّاَكْوَابٍ كَانَتْ قَوَارِيْرَا ۞

Its shades will be close over them and its clustered fruits will be brought within their easy reach. They will be served in vessels of silver and goblets, sparkling like crystal, exquisitely fashioned. They will be given to drink therein a cup tempered with ginger, from a spring named Salsabil. They will be waited on by ageless youths, looking like scattered pearls.

قَوَارِيْرَا مِنْ فِضَّةٍ قَدَّرُوْهَا تَقْدِيْرًا ۞

وَيُسْقَوْنَ فِيْهَا كَأْسًا كَانَ مِزَاجُهَا زَنْجَبِيْلًا ۞

عَيْنًا فِيْهَا تُسَمّٰى سَلْسَبِيْلًا ۞

وَيَطُوْفُ عَلَيْهِمْ وِلْدَانٌ مُّخَلَّدُوْنَ ۚ اِذَا رَاَيْتَهُمْ

It will be a spectacle of bliss and a vast kingdom. They will wear garments of fine green silk and thick brocade, and bracelets of silver. Their Lord will give them to drink a pure beverage. They will be told: This is your reward, Your effort is appreciated. (2—23)

حَسِبْتَهُمْ لُؤْلُؤًا مَّنْثُوْرًا ۞

وَاِذَا رَاَيْتَ ثَمَّ رَاَيْتَ نَعِيْمًا وَّمُلْكًا كَبِيْرًا ۞

عٰلِيَهُمْ ثِيَابُ سُنْدُسٍ خُضْرٌ وَّاِسْتَبْرَقٌ وَّحُلُّوْٓا اَسَاوِرَ مِنْ فِضَّةٍ وَسَقٰهُمْ رَبُّهُمْ شَرَابًا طَهُوْرًا ۞

اِنَّ هٰذَا كَانَ لَكُمْ جَزَآءً وَّكَانَ سَعْيُكُمْ مَّشْكُوْرًا ۞

We have revealed the Quran unto thee piecemeal. So adhere steadfastly to the command of thy Lord, and do not yield to any sinful, ungrateful one from among them. Remember thy Lord morning and evening, and prostrate thyself before Him at night, and extol His glory for a long part of the night.

اِنَّا نَحْنُ نَزَّلْنَا عَلَيْكَ الْقُرْاٰنَ تَنْزِيْلًا ۞

فَاصْبِرْ لِحُكْمِ رَبِّكَ وَلَا تُطِعْ مِنْهُمْ اٰثِمًا اَوْ كَفُوْرًا ۞

وَاذْكُرِ اسْمَ رَبِّكَ بُكْرَةً وَّاَصِيْلًا ۞

وَمِنَ الَّيْلِ فَاسْجُدْ لَهُ وَسَبِّحْهُ لَيْلًا طَوِيْلًا ۞

These people love that which is transitory, and neglect the hard day ahead. We have created them and made their joints strong; and We can replace them with others like them when We will.

اِنَّ هٰٓؤُلَآءِ يُحِبُّوْنَ الْعَاجِلَةَ وَيَذَرُوْنَ وَرَآءَهُمْ يَوْمًا ثَقِيْلًا ۞

نَحْنُ خَلَقْنٰهُمْ وَشَدَدْنَآ اَسْرَهُمْ وَاِذَا شِئْنَا بَدَّلْنَآ اَمْثَالَهُمْ تَبْدِيْلًا ۞

Verily, this is a Reminder; so whoever wishes may take to the way that leads to his Lord. But you can wish only if Allah pleases. Verily, Allah is All-Knowing, Wise. He admits to His mercy whom He pleases and for the wrongdoers He has prepared a painful chastisement. (24—32)

اِنَّ هٰذِهٖ تَذْكِرَةٌ فَمَنْ شَآءَ اتَّخَذَ اِلٰى رَبِّهٖ سَبِيْلًا ۞

وَمَا تَشَآءُوْنَ اِلَّآ اَنْ يَّشَآءَ اللّٰهُ اِنَّ اللّٰهَ كَانَ عَلِيْمًا حَكِيْمًا ۞

يُدْخِلُ مَنْ يَّشَآءُ فِيْ رَحْمَتِهٖ وَالظّٰلِمِيْنَ اَعَدَّ لَهُمْ عَذَابًا اَلِيْمًا ۞

سُوْرَةُ الْمُرْسَلْتِ مَكِّيَةٌ

AL-MURSALĀT
(Revealed before Hijra)

In the name of Allah, Most Gracious, Ever Merciful. (1)

بِسْمِ اللهِ الرَّحْمٰنِ الرَّحِيْمِ ۝

وَالْمُرْسَلٰتِ عُرْفًا ۝

فَالْعٰصِفٰتِ عَصْفًا ۝

وَّالنّٰشِرٰتِ نَشْرًا ۝

فَالْفٰرِقٰتِ فَرْقًا ۝

فَالْمُلْقِيٰتِ ذِكْرًا ۝

عُذْرًا اَوْ نُذْرًا ۝

We cite in evidence those who proceed slowly, and then they push on fast, spreading the Message abroad, discriminating between truth and falsehood, announcing the Exhortation, excusing and warning, that what you are promised must come to pass.

اِنَّمَا تُوْعَدُوْنَ لَوَاقِعٌ ۝

فَاِذَا النُّجُوْمُ طُمِسَتْ ۝

وَاِذَا السَّمَآءُ فُرِجَتْ ۝

وَاِذَا الْجِبَالُ نُسِفَتْ ۝

وَاِذَا الرُّسُلُ اُقِّتَتْ ۝

When the stars are dimmed, and the heaven is rent asunder, and the mountains are blown away, and the Messengers appear at the appointed time, and it is asked: What do these portents portend? They portend the Day of Judgment.

لِاَيِّ يَوْمٍ اُجِّلَتْ ۝

لِيَوْمِ الْفَصْلِ ۝

وَمَآ اَدْرٰىكَ مَا يَوْمُ الْفَصْلِ ۝

وَيْلٌ يَّوْمَئِذٍ لِّلْمُكَذِّبِيْنَ ۝

اَلَمْ نُهْلِكِ الْاَوَّلِيْنَ ۝

How do you know what the Day of Judgment is? Woe on that day unto those who reject the truth. Did We not destroy the earlier peoples? We will now cause the later ones to follow them. Thus do We deal with the guilty.

ثُمَّ نُتْبِعُهُمُ الْاٰخِرِيْنَ ۝

كَذٰلِكَ نَفْعَلُ بِالْمُجْرِمِيْنَ ۝

Woe on that day unto those who reject the truth. Did We not create you from an insignificant fluid? We placed it in a secure repository, for a fixed period, then We determined its stages of development, and how excellently do We determine! Woe on that day unto those who reject the truth.

وَيْلٌ يَوْمَئِذٍ لِّلْمُكَذِّبِينَ ۞

أَلَمْ نَخْلُقْكُّم مِّن مَّآءٍ مَّهِينٍ ۞

فَجَعَلْنَاهُ فِى قَرَارٍ مَّكِينٍ ۞

إِلَىٰ قَدَرٍ مَّعْلُومٍ ۞

فَقَدَرْنَا فَنِعْمَ الْقَادِرُونَ ۞

وَيْلٌ يَوْمَئِذٍ لِّلْمُكَذِّبِينَ ۞

Have We not made the earth vast enough to gather the living and the dead? We placed thereon high mountains and provided for you sweet water to drink. Woe on that day unto those who reject the truth.

أَلَمْ نَجْعَلِ الْأَرْضَ كِفَاتًا ۞

أَحْيَآءً وَأَمْوَاتًا ۞

وَجَعَلْنَا فِيهَا رَوَاسِىَ شَامِخَاتٍ وَأَسْقَيْنَاكُم مَّآءً فُرَاتًا ۞

They will be told: Proceed towards that which you denied; proceed towards a shelter which has three sections, neither affording shade, nor protecting from the blaze. It throws up sparks like huge castles, as if they were camels of yellow colour. Woe on that day unto those who reject the truth.

وَيْلٌ يَوْمَئِذٍ لِّلْمُكَذِّبِينَ ۞

انطَلِقُوا إِلَىٰ مَا كُنتُم بِهِ تُكَذِّبُونَ ۞

انطَلِقُوا إِلَىٰ ظِلٍّ ذِى ثَلَٰثِ شُعَبٍ ۞

لَّا ظَلِيلٍ وَلَا يُغْنِى مِنَ اللَّهَبِ ۞

إِنَّهَا تَرْمِى بِشَرَرٍ كَالْقَصْرِ ۞

كَأَنَّهُ جِمَالَتٌ صُفْرٌ ۞

وَيْلٌ يَوْمَئِذٍ لِّلْمُكَذِّبِينَ ۞

That is a day on which they will not be able to speak; nor shall they be permitted to offer excuses. Woe on that day unto those who reject the truth.

هَٰذَا يَوْمُ لَا يَنطِقُونَ ۞

وَلَا يُؤْذَنُ لَهُمْ فَيَعْتَذِرُونَ ۞

وَيْلٌ يَوْمَئِذٍ لِّلْمُكَذِّبِينَ ۞

This is the Day of Judgment on which We shall gather you and all the earlier peoples together. If you have any stratagem, employ it against me.

هَٰذَا يَوْمُ الْفَصْلِ جَمَعْنَاكُمْ وَالْأَوَّلِينَ ۞

فَإِن كَانَ لَكُمْ كَيْدٌ فَكِيدُونِ ۞

Woe on that day unto those who **reject** the truth. (2—41)

وَيْلٌ يَّوْمَئِذٍ لِّلْمُكَذِّبِيْنَ ۞

اِنَّ الْمُتَّقِيْنَ فِيْ ظِلَالٍ وَّعُيُوْنٍ ۞

وَّفَوَاكِهَ مِمَّا يَشْتَهُوْنَ ۞

كُلُوْا وَاشْرَبُوْا هَنِيْئًا بِمَا كُنْتُمْ تَعْمَلُوْنَ ۞

اِنَّا كَذٰلِكَ نَجْزِى الْمُحْسِنِيْنَ ۞

وَيْلٌ يَّوْمَئِذٍ لِّلْمُكَذِّبِيْنَ ۞

The righteous will be in the midst of shades and springs, and fruits such as they desire. They will be told: Eat and drink agreeably as a reward for that which you did. Thus do We reward those who do good. Woe on that day unto those who reject the truth. They will be told: While you are in this world, eat and enjoy yourselves a little. Surely, you are the guilty ones. Woe on that day unto those who reject the truth. When they were told to hold fast to the Unity of Allah, they rejected it. Woe on that day unto those who reject the truth. Then in which discourse, after the Quran, will they believe? (42—51)

كُلُوْا وَتَمَتَّعُوْا قَلِيْلًا اِنَّكُمْ مُّجْرِمُوْنَ ۞

وَيْلٌ يَّوْمَئِذٍ لِّلْمُكَذِّبِيْنَ ۞

وَاِذَا قِيْلَ لَهُمُ ارْكَعُوْا لَا يَرْكَعُوْنَ ۞

وَيْلٌ يَّوْمَئِذٍ لِّلْمُكَذِّبِيْنَ ۞

فَبِأَيِّ حَدِيْثٍ بَعْدَهٗ يُؤْمِنُوْنَ ۞

(Revealed before Hijra)

In the name of Allah, Most Gracious, Ever Merciful. (1)

بِسْمِ اللهِ الرَّحْمٰنِ الرَّحِيْمِ ۞

عَمَّ يَتَسَآءَلُوْنَ ۞

عَنِ النَّبَأِ الْعَظِيْمِ ۞

الَّذِيْ هُمْ فِيْهِ مُخْتَلِفُوْنَ ۞

كَلَّا سَيَعْلَمُوْنَ ۞

ثُمَّ كَلَّا سَيَعْلَمُوْنَ ۞

What do they question one another about? Is it about the great Event, the Day of Judgment, concerning which they differ? Soon indeed will they come to know. We repeat, soon surely will they come to know.

Have We not made the earth a bed,

اَلَمْ نَجْعَلِ الْاَرْضَ مِهَادًا ۞

and driven in the mountains as stakes?
We have created you in pairs, and made
your sleep a source of rest, and made the
night a covering, and made the day for
the activities of life.

وَّالْجِبَالَ اَوْتَادًا ۞

وَّخَلَقْنٰكُمْ اَزْوَاجًا ۞

وَّجَعَلْنَا نَوْمَكُمْ سُبَاتًا ۞

وَّجَعَلْنَا الَّيْلَ لِبَاسًا ۞

وَّجَعَلْنَا النَّهَارَ مَعَاشًا ۞

وَبَنَيْنَا فَوْقَكُمْ سَبْعًا شِدَادًا ۞

We have built above you seven strong
heavens, and made the sun a brightly
burning lamp. We send down from the
dripping clouds water pouring forth abundantly, that We may bring forth thereby
grain and vegetation, and luxuriant gardens.

وَّجَعَلْنَا سِرَاجًا وَّهَّاجًا ۞

وَّاَنْزَلْنَا مِنَ الْمُعْصِرٰتِ مَآءً ثَجَّاجًا ۞

لِنُخْرِجَ بِهٖ حَبًّا وَّنَبَاتًا ۞

وَّجَنّٰتٍ اَلْفَافًا ۞

اِنَّ يَوْمَ الْفَصْلِ كَانَ مِيْقَاتًا ۞

يَّوْمَ يُنْفَخُ فِى الصُّوْرِ فَتَأْتُوْنَ اَفْوَاجًا ۞

Surely, the Day of Judgment has an
appointed time: the day when the trumpet
will be blown; and you will come in large
groups; and the heaven shall be opened
and will be all doors; and the mountains
shall pass away and shall become a mirage.

وَّفُتِحَتِ السَّمَآءُ فَكَانَتْ اَبْوَابًا ۞

وَّسُيِّرَتِ الْجِبَالُ فَكَانَتْ سَرَابًا ۞

اِنَّ جَهَنَّمَ كَانَتْ مِرْصَادًا ۙ ۞

لِّلطَّاغِيْنَ مَاٰبًا ۞

لّٰبِثِيْنَ فِيْهَا اَحْقَابًا ۞

لَا يَذُوْقُوْنَ فِيْهَا بَرْدًا وَّلَا شَرَابًا ۙ ۞

اِلَّا حَمِيْمًا وَّغَسَّاقًا ۞

Surely, hell lies in wait, a resort for the
rebellious, who will tarry therein for ages.
They will taste therein neither coolness
nor any pleasant drink save boiling water
and a nauseating fluid: a meet requital.
They feared not the reckoning and utterly
rejected Our Signs.

جَزَآءً وِّفَاقًا ۞

اِنَّهُمْ كَانُوْا لَا يَرْجُوْنَ حِسَابًا ۙ ۞

وَّكَذَّبُوْا بِاٰيٰتِنَا كِذَّابًا ۞

We have recorded everything in a Book. Then suffer the chastisement; We shall only add torment to your torment. (2—31)

وَكُلَّ شَىْءٍ اَحْصَيْنٰهُ كِتَابًا ۞

فَذُوْقُوْا فَلَنْ نَّزِيْدَكُمْ اِلَّا عَذَابًا ۞

اِنَّ لِلْمُتَّقِيْنَ مَفَازًا ۞

حَدَائِقَ وَاَعْنَابًا ۞

وَّكَوَاعِبَ اَتْرَابًا ۞

وَّكَاْسًا دِهَاقًا ۞

Verily, for the righteous there is felicity: walled gardens and grape-vines, and young maidens of equal age, and overflowing cups. Therein will they hear no idle talk, nor any untruth: a recompense in proportion to their works from thy Lord, the Lord of the heavens and the earth and of all that is between them, the Gracious One. They will not have the capacity to address Him; on the day when the Spirit and the angels will stand in rows, and they shall not speak, except he whom the Gracious One will permit, and he will only speak that which is right. That day is bound to come. So let him who will seek a resort with his Lord.

لَا يَسْمَعُوْنَ فِيْهَا لَغْوًا وَّلَا كِذَّابًا ۞

جَزَاءً مِّنْ رَّبِّكَ عَطَاءً حِسَابًا ۞

رَّبِّ السَّمٰوٰتِ وَالْاَرْضِ وَمَا بَيْنَهُمَا الرَّحْمٰنِ لَا يَمْلِكُوْنَ مِنْهُ خِطَابًا ۞

يَوْمَ يَقُوْمُ الرُّوْحُ وَالْمَلٰئِكَةُ صَفًّا لَّا يَتَكَلَّمُوْنَ اِلَّا مَنْ اَذِنَ لَهُ الرَّحْمٰنُ وَقَالَ صَوَابًا ۞

ذٰلِكَ الْيَوْمُ الْحَقُّ فَمَنْ شَاءَ اتَّخَذَ اِلٰى رَبِّهِ مَاٰبًا ۞

We have warned you of a chastisement which is near at hand: a day on which a man will see all that he has wrought, and the disbeliever will say: Would that I were mere dust. (32—41)

اِنَّا اَنْذَرْنٰكُمْ عَذَابًا قَرِيْبًا يَّوْمَ يَنْظُرُ الْمَرْءُ مَا قَدَّمَتْ يَدٰهُ وَيَقُوْلُ الْكٰفِرُ يٰلَيْتَنِيْ كُنْتُ تُرٰبًا ۞

سُوْرَةُ النَّازِعٰتِ مَكِّيَّةٌ

In the name of Allah, Most Gracious, Ever Merciful. (1)
We cite in evidence those who pursue their efforts vigorously,

بِسْمِ اللّٰهِ الرَّحْمٰنِ الرَّحِيْمِ ۞

وَالنّٰزِعٰتِ غَرْقًا ۞

and strengthen their relationship with Allah, and proceed far afield with ease, and outstrip their rivals, and manage well the affair entrusted to them.

وَّ النّٰشِطٰتِ نَشْطًا ۙ

وَّ السّٰبِحٰتِ سَبْحًا ۙ

فَالسّٰبِقٰتِ سَبْقًا ۙ

فَالْمُدَبِّرٰتِ اَمْرًا ۘ

يَوْمَ تَرْجُفُ الرَّاجِفَةُ ۙ

تَتْبَعُهَا الرَّادِفَةُ ؕ

On the day on which people shall prepare for battle, to be followed by another one like it, the hearts of some will tremble and their eyes will be cast down. They will exclaim: Shall we be restored to our former state, even when we have become rotten bones? That indeed would be a losing return. It will be only a single cry, and they will all come out in the open. (2—15)

قُلُوْبٌ يَّوْمَئِذٍ وَّاجِفَةٌ ۙ

اَبْصَارُهَا خَاشِعَةٌ ۘ

يَقُوْلُوْنَ ءَ اِنَّا لَمَرْدُوْدُوْنَ فِى الْحَافِرَةِ ؕ

ءَ اِذَا كُنَّا عِظَامًا نَّخِرَةً ؕ

قَالُوْا تِلْكَ اِذًا كَرَّةٌ خَاسِرَةٌ ۘ

فَاِنَّمَا هِىَ زَجْرَةٌ وَّاحِدَةٌ ۙ

فَاِذَا هُمْ بِالسَّاهِرَةِ ؕ

Has the account of Moses reached thee, when his Lord called him in the sacred valley of Tuwa, and directed him: Go thou to Pharaoh, he is in rebellion, and say to him: Wouldst thou be purified, and shall I guide thee to thy Lord so that thou mayest fear Him?

هَلْ اَتٰىكَ حَدِيْثُ مُوْسٰى ۘ

اِذْ نَادٰىهُ رَبُّهٗ بِالْوَادِ الْمُقَدَّسِ طُوًى ۚ

اِذْهَبْ اِلٰى فِرْعَوْنَ اِنَّهٗ طَغٰى ۖ

فَقُلْ هَلْ لَّكَ اِلٰى اَنْ تَزَكّٰى ۙ

وَاَهْدِيَكَ اِلٰى رَبِّكَ فَتَخْشٰى ۚ

فَاَرٰىهُ الْاٰيَةَ الْكُبْرٰى ۖ

Then Moses showed him the great Sign. But he rejected him and was disobedient. Then he turned away and busied himself with devising his scheme. He gathered his people and proclaimed:

فَكَذَّبَ وَعَصٰى ۖ

ثُمَّ اَدْبَرَ يَسْعٰى ۖ

فَحَشَرَ فَنَادٰى ۖ

I am your most high lord. So Allah seized him for the chastisement of this world and the Hereafter. In this surely is a lesson for him who fears Allah. (16—27)

فَقَالَ اَنَا رَبُّكُمُ الْاَعْلٰى ۟

فَاَخَذَهُ اللّٰهُ نَكَالَ الْاٰخِرَةِ وَالْاُوْلٰى ۟

اِنَّ فِىْ ذٰلِكَ لَعِبْرَةً لِّمَنْ يَّخْشٰى ۟

ءَاَنْتُمْ اَشَدُّ خَلْقًا اَمِ السَّمَآءُ ۭ بَنٰىهَا ۟

رَفَعَ سَمْكَهَا فَسَوّٰىهَا ۟

وَاَغْطَشَ لَيْلَهَا وَاَخْرَجَ ضُحٰىهَا ۟

وَالْاَرْضَ بَعْدَ ذٰلِكَ دَحٰىهَا ۟

اَخْرَجَ مِنْهَا مَآءَهَا وَمَرْعٰىهَا ۟

وَالْجِبَالَ اَرْسٰىهَا ۟

Are you harder to create or the sky? He made it and he has raised its height and fashioned it flawless. He has made its night dark and its morn bright. He spread forth the earth along with it. He produced therefrom its water and its pasture. He made the mountains firm. All this is a provision for you and your cattle.

مَتَاعًا لَّكُمْ وَلِاَنْعَامِكُمْ ۟

فَاِذَا جَآءَتِ الطَّآمَّةُ الْكُبْرٰى ۟

يَوْمَ يَتَذَكَّرُ الْاِنْسَانُ مَا سَعٰى ۟

وَبُرِّزَتِ الْجَحِيْمُ لِمَنْ يَّرٰى ۟

فَاَمَّا مَنْ طَغٰى ۟

وَاٰثَرَ الْحَيٰوةَ الدُّنْيَا ۟

فَاِنَّ الْجَحِيْمَ هِىَ الْمَاْوٰى ۟

When the great calamity comes, when man will recall all that he strove for, and hell will be made manifest to him who can see, then for him who rebelled and chose the life of this world, hell will be a resort. But for him who feared to stand before his Lord and restrained his evil desires, the Garden will be a resort.

وَاَمَّا مَنْ خَافَ مَقَامَ رَبِّهٖ وَنَهَى النَّفْسَ عَنِ الْهَوٰى ۟

فَاِنَّ الْجَنَّةَ هِىَ الْمَاْوٰى ۟

يَسْـَٔلُوْنَكَ عَنِ السَّاعَةِ اَيَّانَ مُرْسٰىهَا ۟

They ask thee concerning the Hour: When will it arrive? What concern hast thou with talk of it? Thy Lord alone knows the ultimate limit of its happening.

فِيْمَ اَنْتَ مِنْ ذِكْرٰىهَا ۟

اِلٰى رَبِّكَ مُنْتَهٰىهَا ۟

Thou art only a Warner unto him who fears it. On the day they see it, they will feel as if they had not tarried in the world but an evening or a morn thereof. (28—47)

اِنَّمَاۤ اَنۡتَ مُنۡذِرُ مَنۡ یَّخۡشٰهَا ۙ

کَاَنَّهُمۡ یَوۡمَ یَرَوۡنَهَا لَمۡ یَلۡبَثُوۡۤا اِلَّا عَشِیَّةً اَوۡ

ضُحٰهَا ۙ

In the name of Allah, Most Gracious, Ever Merciful. (1)

بِسۡمِ اللّٰهِ الرَّحۡمٰنِ الرَّحِیۡمِ ۝

عَبَسَ وَتَوَلّٰۤی ۙ۝

اَنۡ جَآءَهُ الۡاَعۡمٰی ؕ۝

وَمَا یُدۡرِیۡکَ لَعَلَّهٗ یَزَّکّٰۤی ۙ۝

اَوۡ یَذَّکَّرُ فَتَنۡفَعَهُ الذِّکۡرٰی ؕ۝

اَمَّا مَنِ اسۡتَغۡنٰی ۙ۝

فَاَنۡتَ لَهٗ تَصَدّٰی ؕ۝

وَمَا عَلَیۡکَ اَلَّا یَزَّکّٰی ؕ۝

وَاَمَّا مَنۡ جَآءَکَ یَسۡعٰی ۙ۝

وَهُوَ یَخۡشٰی ۙ۝

فَاَنۡتَ عَنۡهُ تَلَهّٰی ۚ۝

کَلَّاۤ اِنَّهَا تَذۡکِرَةٌ ۚ۝

فَمَنۡ شَآءَ ذَکَرَهٗ ۘ۝

فِیۡ صُحُفٍ مُّکَرَّمَةٍ ۙ۝

مَّرۡفُوۡعَةٍ مُّطَهَّرَةٍ ۙ۝

(The Prophet's visitor) frowned and withdrew because the blind man came to him (the Prophet). (Grieve not over his having turned away) for how couldst thou have known that the one with whom thou wast engaged would purify himself, or would take heed and derive benefit from the Reminder? How could it be that thou shouldst do honour to one who is indifferent, whereas thou art not charged with his purifying himself, and that thou shouldst neglect one who fears Allah and comes running to thee? By no means could that be so.

Surely, the Quran is an admonition, so let him who will, pay heed to it. It is contained in honoured sheets, exalted and purified, in the hands of noble and virtuous scribes. (2—17)

Ruin seize man, how ungrateful he is!
Let him reflect out of what did He create
him ? Out of a sperm-drop ! He created him
and set a measure for him; then He made
the Way easy for him, then He causes him
to die and assigns a grave to him. Then,
when He pleases, He will raise him up
again. Nay, man has not yet completed
that which He had prescribed for him.
(18—24)

بِأَيْدِىْ سَفَرَةٍ ۝

كِرَامٍ بَرَرَةٍ ۝

قُتِلَ الْاِنْسَانُ مَآ اَكْفَرَهُ ۝

مِنْ اَىِّ شَىْءٍ خَلَقَهُ ۝

مِنْ نُّطْفَةٍ خَلَقَهُ فَقَدَّرَهُ ۝

ثُمَّ السَّبِيْلَ يَسَّرَهُ ۝

ثُمَّ اَمَاتَهُ فَاَقْبَرَهُ ۝

ثُمَّ اِذَا شَآءَ اَنْشَرَهُ ۝

كَلَّا لَمَّا يَقْضِ مَآ اَمَرَهُ ۝

فَلْيَنْظُرِ الْاِنْسَانُ اِلٰى طَعَامِهٖ ۝

اَنَّا صَبَبْنَا الْمَآءَ صَبًّا ۝

Now let man look at his food. We poured
down water from the sky in abundance,
then We split the earth thoroughly, and
caused to grow therein grain, and grapes,
and vegetables, and the olive and the date-
palm, and walled gardens thickly planted,
and fruits and herbage, as provision for
you and your cattle. (25—33)

ثُمَّ شَقَقْنَا الْاَرْضَ شَقًّا ۝

فَاَنْبَتْنَا فِيْهَا حَبًّا ۝

وَّعِنَبًا وَّقَضْبًا ۝

وَّزَيْتُوْنًا وَّنَخْلًا ۝

وَّحَدَآئِقَ غُلْبًا ۝

وَّفَاكِهَةً وَّاَبًّا ۝

مَتَاعًا لَّكُمْ وَلِاَنْعَامِكُمْ ۝

فَاِذَا جَآءَتِ الصَّآخَّةُ ۝

When the ear-splitting calamity comes
on the day when a man shall flee from his
brother, his mother, his father, his wife
and his sons,

يَوْمَ يَفِرُّ الْمَرْءُ مِنْ اَخِيْهِ ۝

وَاُمِّهٖ وَاَبِيْهِ ۝

وَصَاحِبَتِهٖ وَبَنِيْهِ ۝

on that day every man among them will be preoccupied with himself alone.

لِكُلِّ امْرِئٍ مِّنْهُمْ يَوْمَئِذٍ شَأْنٌ يُغْنِيهِ ۟

وُجُوهٌ يَوْمَئِذٍ مُّسْفِرَةٌ ۟

ضَاحِكَةٌ مُّسْتَبْشِرَةٌ ۟

وَوُجُوهٌ يَوْمَئِذٍ عَلَيْهَا غَبَرَةٌ ۟

تَرْهَقُهَا قَتَرَةٌ ۟

On that day some faces will be bright, laughing, joyous; and some faces will be covered with dust and gloom. These will be the disbelieving evil-doers. (34—43)

أُولٰٓئِكَ هُمُ الْكَفَرَةُ الْفَجَرَةُ ۟

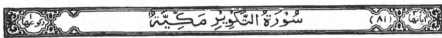

سُوْرَةُ التَّكْوِيْرِ مَكِّيَّةٌ (٨١)

(Revealed before Hijra)

In the name of Allah, Most Gracious, Ever Merciful. (1)

بِسْمِ اللهِ الرَّحْمٰنِ الرَّحِيْمِ ۟

إِذَا الشَّمْسُ كُوِّرَتْ ۟

وَإِذَا النُّجُوْمُ انْكَدَرَتْ ۟

وَإِذَا الْجِبَالُ سُيِّرَتْ ۟

وَإِذَا الْعِشَارُ عُطِّلَتْ ۟

When the sun is veiled, and the stars are dimmed, and the mountains are made to move, and ten-months pregnant she-camels are discarded as a means of transportation and the wild ones are gathered together, and the rivers are diverted, and people are brought together, and when the female infant buried alive is questioned about: For what crime was she killed?

وَإِذَا الْوُحُوْشُ حُشِرَتْ ۟

وَإِذَا الْبِحَارُ سُجِّرَتْ ۟

وَإِذَا النُّفُوْسُ زُوِّجَتْ ۟

وَإِذَا الْمَوْءُدَةُ سُئِلَتْ ۟

بِأَيِّ ذَنْبٍ قُتِلَتْ ۟

And when books are spread abroad, and when the heaven is laid bare,

وَإِذَا الصُّحُفُ نُشِرَتْ ۟

وَإِذَا السَّمَاءُ كُشِطَتْ ۟

and when hell is stoked up, and when the Garden is brought nigh, then everyone will know that which he has wrought.

وَإِذَا الْجَحِيمُ سُعِّرَتْ ۝

وَإِذَا الْجَنَّةُ أُزْلِفَتْ ۝

عَلِمَتْ نَفْسٌ مَّا أَحْضَرَتْ ۝

فَلَا أُقْسِمُ بِالْخُنَّسِ ۝

الْجَوَارِ الْكُنَّسِ ۝

وَالَّيْلِ إِذَا عَسْعَسَ ۝

I call to witness the planets that recede and advance, and seem to disappear, and the night as it sneaks away, and the dawn when its breath blows away the darkness, that the Quran is the Word revealed to a noble Messenger, mighty and established in the presence of the Lord of the Throne, entitled to obedience and faithful to his trust. Your companion is not mad. Indeed he saw Him on the clear horizon, and he is not niggardly in disclosing that which he has been vouchsafed of the unseen. This is not the word of Satan the rejected.

وَالصُّبْحِ إِذَا تَنَفَّسَ ۝

إِنَّهُ لَقَوْلُ رَسُولٍ كَرِيمٍ ۝

ذِي قُوَّةٍ عِنْدَ ذِي الْعَرْشِ مَكِينٍ ۝

مُّطَاعٍ ثَمَّ أَمِينٍ ۝

وَمَا صَاحِبُكُمْ بِمَجْنُونٍ ۝

وَلَقَدْ رَآهُ بِالْأُفُقِ الْمُبِينِ ۝

وَمَا هُوَ عَلَى الْغَيْبِ بِضَنِينٍ ۝

وَمَا هُوَ بِقَوْلِ شَيْطَانٍ رَجِيمٍ ۝

فَأَيْنَ تَذْهَبُونَ ۝

إِنْ هُوَ إِلَّا ذِكْرٌ لِّلْعَالَمِينَ ۝

Then whither are you bent? This is but a Reminder unto all the worlds, unto such of you as desire to go straight. But you can desire nothing except that Allah, the Lord of the worlds, should desire it. (2—30)

لِمَنْ شَاءَ مِنْكُمْ أَنْ يَسْتَقِيمَ ۝

وَمَا تَشَاؤُونَ إِلَّا أَنْ يَشَاءَ اللَّهُ رَبُّ الْعَالَمِينَ ۝

607

AL-INFITĀR
(Revealed before Hijra)

بِسْمِ اللهِ الرَّحْمٰنِ الرَّحِيْمِ ۝

اِذَا السَّمَآءُ انْفَطَرَتْ ۝

وَ اِذَا الْكَوَاكِبُ انْتَثَرَتْ ۝

وَ اِذَا الْبِحَارُ فُجِّرَتْ ۝

وَ اِذَا الْقُبُوْرُ بُعْثِرَتْ ۝

عَلِمَتْ نَفْسٌ مَّا قَدَّمَتْ وَ اَخَّرَتْ ۝

يٰٓاَيُّهَا الْاِنْسَانُ مَا غَرَّكَ بِرَبِّكَ الْكَرِيْمِ ۝

الَّذِىْ خَلَقَكَ فَسَوّٰىكَ فَعَدَلَكَ ۝

فِىْ اَىِّ صُوْرَةٍ مَّا شَآءَ رَكَّبَكَ ۝

كَلَّا بَلْ تُكَذِّبُوْنَ بِالدِّيْنِ ۝

وَ اِنَّ عَلَيْكُمْ لَحٰفِظِيْنَ ۝

كِرَامًا كَاتِبِيْنَ ۝

يَعْلَمُوْنَ مَا تَفْعَلُوْنَ ۝

اِنَّ الْاَبْرَارَ لَفِىْ نَعِيْمٍ ۝

وَ اِنَّ الْفُجَّارَ لَفِىْ جَحِيْمٍ ۝

يَّصْلَوْنَهَا يَوْمَ الدِّيْنِ ۝

وَ مَا هُمْ عَنْهَا بِغَآئِبِيْنَ ۝

وَ مَآ اَدْرٰىكَ مَا يَوْمُ الدِّيْنِ ۝

ثُمَّ مَآ اَدْرٰىكَ مَا يَوْمُ الدِّيْنِ ۝

In the name of Allah, Most Gracious, Ever Merciful. (1)

When the heaven is cleft asunder and the stars are scattered, and the rivers are diverted, and the graves are laid open, then everyone will know that which he has brought forward, and that which he has left behind.

Man, what has emboldened thee against thy Gracious Lord, Who created thee, then perfected thee, then proportioned thee aright? He fashioned thee in whatever form He pleased.

In effect you deny the Judgment. But there are guardians over you, honoured recorders, who know all that you do.

Verily the virtuous will be in bliss, and the wicked will be in hell; they will enter therein on the Day of Judgment, and they will not be able to escape therefrom.

How should you know what the Day of Judgment is?

608

Again, how should you know what the Day of Judgment is? It is the day on which no one shall have power to do aught for another, and the command on that day will be Allah's. (2—20)

يَوْمَ لَا تَمْلِكُ نَفْسٌ لِّنَفْسٍ شَيْئًا ۖ وَالْأَمْرُ يَوْمَئِذٍ لِّلَّهِ ۞

(Revealed before Hijra)

In the name of Allah, Most Gracious, Ever Merciful. (1)

بِسْمِ اللهِ الرَّحْمٰنِ الرَّحِيْمِ ۞

وَيْلٌ لِّلْمُطَفِّفِيْنَ ۞

الَّذِيْنَ إِذَا اكْتَالُوْا عَلَى النَّاسِ يَسْتَوْفُوْنَ ۞

وَإِذَا كَالُوْهُمْ أَوْ وَّزَنُوْهُمْ يُخْسِرُوْنَ ۞

Woe unto those who give short measure; those who, when they take by measure from other people, take it full; but when they give by measure to others or weigh out to them, give them less. Do not such people know that they will be raised up again unto a terrible day, the day when mankind will stand before the Lord of the worlds? (2—7)

أَلَا يَظُنُّ أُولٰئِكَ أَنَّهُمْ مَّبْعُوْثُوْنَ ۞

لِيَوْمٍ عَظِيْمٍ ۞

يَوْمَ يَقُوْمُ النَّاسُ لِرَبِّ الْعٰلَمِيْنَ ۞

كَلَّا إِنَّ كِتٰبَ الْفُجَّارِ لَفِيْ سِجِّيْنٍ ۞

وَمَا أَدْرٰىكَ مَا سِجِّيْنٌ ۞

كِتٰبٌ مَّرْقُوْمٌ ۞

وَيْلٌ يَّوْمَئِذٍ لِّلْمُكَذِّبِيْنَ ۞

Indeed the record of the wicked is in Sijjîn. How should you know what Sijjîn is? It is a Book inscribed. Woe on that day unto those who reject the Signs of Allah, who deny the Day of Judgment. None denies it save every sinful transgressor, who, when Our Signs are recited to him says: Old wives' tales! The truth is that their hearts have been rusted by that which they practised. They will surely be debarred on that day from the presence of their Lord.

الَّذِيْنَ يُكَذِّبُوْنَ بِيَوْمِ الدِّيْنِ ۞

وَمَا يُكَذِّبُ بِهِ إِلَّا كُلُّ مُعْتَدٍ أَثِيْمٍ ۞

إِذَا تُتْلٰى عَلَيْهِ اٰيٰتُنَا قَالَ أَسَاطِيْرُ الْأَوَّلِيْنَ ۞

كَلَّا بَلْ رَانَ عَلٰى قُلُوْبِهِمْ مَّا كَانُوْا يَكْسِبُوْنَ ۞

كَلَّا إِنَّهُمْ عَنْ رَّبِّهِمْ يَوْمَئِذٍ لَّمَحْجُوْبُوْنَ ۞

Then they will enter hell, and it will be
said to them: This is what you used to deny.
(8—18)

ثُمَّ اِنَّهُمْ لَصَالُوا الْجَحِيْمِ ۞

ثُمَّ يُقَالُ هٰذَا الَّذِىْ كُنْتُمْ بِهٖ تُكَذِّبُوْنَ ۞

كَلَّآ اِنَّ كِتٰبَ الْاَبْرَارِ لَفِىْ عِلِّيِّيْنَ ۞

وَمَآ اَدْرٰىكَ مَا عِلِّيُّوْنَ ۞

كِتٰبٌ مَّرْقُوْمٌ ۞

يَّشْهَدُهُ الْمُقَرَّبُوْنَ ۞

اِنَّ الْاَبْرَارَ لَفِىْ نَعِيْمٍ ۞

عَلَى الْاَرَآئِكِ يَنْظُرُوْنَ ۞

تَعْرِفُ فِىْ وُجُوْهِهِمْ نَضْرَةَ النَّعِيْمِ ۞

يُسْقَوْنَ مِنْ رَّحِيْقٍ مَّخْتُوْمٍ ۞

Indeed the record of the virtuous is in
Illiyyin. How should you know what Illiyyin
is? It is a Book inscribed. The chosen ones
of Allah will witness it. Surely, the virtuous will be in bliss, seated on couches,
viewing everything. Thou wilt discern in
their faces the freshness of bliss. They will
be given to drink of a pure sealed beverage, sealed with musk, and tempered with
the water of Tasnim, a spring of which the
chosen ones will drink. After this should
the aspirants aspire. (19—29)

خِتٰمُهٗ مِسْكٌ ۖ وَفِىْ ذٰلِكَ فَلْيَتَنَافَسِ الْمُتَنَافِسُوْنَ ۞

وَمِزَاجُهٗ مِنْ تَسْنِيْمٍ ۞

عَيْنًا يَّشْرَبُ بِهَا الْمُقَرَّبُوْنَ ۞

اِنَّ الَّذِيْنَ اَجْرَمُوْا كَانُوْا مِنَ الَّذِيْنَ اٰمَنُوْا

يَضْحَكُوْنَ ۞

وَاِذَا مَرُّوْا بِهِمْ يَتَغَامَزُوْنَ ۞

وَاِذَا انْقَلَبُوْٓا اِلٰٓى اَهْلِهِمُ انْقَلَبُوْا فَكِهِيْنَ ۞

وَاِذَا رَاَوْهُمْ قَالُوْٓا اِنَّ هٰٓؤُلَآءِ لَضَآلُّوْنَ ۞

وَمَآ اُرْسِلُوْا عَلَيْهِمْ حٰفِظِيْنَ ۞

Those who were guilty used to laugh at
those who believed; and when they passed
by them they winked at one another.
When they came back to their families,
they exulted over them; and when they
saw them they exclaimed: These indeed
are the lost ones. But they were not
appointed keepers over them. On this day,
it is the believers who will laugh at the
disbelievers, seated on couches, viewing
everything. Have the disbelievers been
repaid for what they did? (30—37)

فَالْيَوْمَ الَّذِيْنَ اٰمَنُوْا مِنَ الْكُفَّارِ يَضْحَكُوْنَ ۞

عَلَى الْاَرَآئِكِ يَنْظُرُوْنَ ۞

هَلْ ثُوِّبَ الْكُفَّارُ مَا كَانُوْا يَفْعَلُوْنَ ۞

سُوْرَةُ الْاِنْشِقَاقِ مَكِّيَّةٌ

AL-INSHIQĀQ
(Revealed before Hijra)

بِسْمِ اللهِ الرَّحْمٰنِ الرَّحِيْمِ ۝

In the name of Allah, Most Gracious, Ever Merciful. (1)

اِذَا السَّمَآءُ انْشَقَّتْ ۝

وَاَذِنَتْ لِرَبِّهَا وَحُقَّتْ ۝

وَاِذَا الْاَرْضُ مُدَّتْ ۝

وَاَلْقَتْ مَا فِيْهَا وَتَخَلَّتْ ۝

وَاَذِنَتْ لِرَبِّهَا وَحُقَّتْ ۝

يٰۤاَيُّهَا الْاِنْسَانُ اِنَّكَ كَادِحٌ اِلٰى رَبِّكَ كَدْحًا فَمُلٰقِيْهِ ۝

Watch for the time when the heaven is cleft asunder, and those conversant with it give ear to their Lord, and this was incumbent upon them anyhow; and when the earth is stretched forth and pours out its contents and becomes empty, and those conversant with it give ear to their Lord, and this was incumbent upon them anyhow; thou, O man, having striven hard towards thy Lord, shalt face Him.

فَاَمَّا مَنْ اُوْتِيَ كِتٰبَهٗ بِيَمِيْنِهٖ ۝

فَسَوْفَ يُحَاسَبُ حِسَابًا يَّسِيْرًا ۝

وَّيَنْقَلِبُ اِلٰۤى اَهْلِهٖ مَسْرُوْرًا ۝

وَاَمَّا مَنْ اُوْتِيَ كِتٰبَهٗ وَرَآءَ ظَهْرِهٖ ۝

فَسَوْفَ يَدْعُوْا ثُبُوْرًا ۝

وَّيَصْلٰى سَعِيْرًا ۝

Then he who is handed his statement of account in his right hand, will soon have an easy reckoning, and will return to his people rejoicing; but he to whom his statement of account is passed on behind his back, will soon cry ruin, and will enter a blazing Fire. He was joyful among his people, and fancied that his condition would never change. But, surely, his Lord observed everything concerning him.

اِنَّهٗ كَانَ فِيْۤ اَهْلِهٖ مَسْرُوْرًا ۝

اِنَّهٗ ظَنَّ اَنْ لَّنْ يَّحُوْرَ ۝

بَلٰۤى اِنَّ رَبَّهٗ كَانَ بِهٖ بَصِيْرًا ۝

فَلَاۤ اُقْسِمُ بِالشَّفَقِ ۝

I call to witness the post-sunset glow, and the night and all that it envelops,

وَالَّيْلِ وَمَا وَسَقَ ۝

and the moon when it becomes full, that you shall assuredly ascend from stage to stage.

وَالْقَمَرِ اِذَا اتَّسَقَ ۙ

لَتَرْكَبُنَّ طَبَقًا عَنْ طَبَقٍ ۚ

فَمَا لَهُمْ لَا يُؤْمِنُوْنَ ۙ

وَاِذَا قُرِئَ عَلَيْهِمُ الْقُرْاٰنُ لَا يَسْجُدُوْنَ ۩

بَلِ الَّذِيْنَ كَفَرُوْا يُكَذِّبُوْنَ ۖ

وَاللّٰهُ اَعْلَمُ بِمَا يُوْعُوْنَ ۖ

So what ails them that they believe not, and when the Quran is recited to them, they do not submit? On the contrary, those who disbelieve reject it. Allah knows best that which they keep hidden in their minds. So give them tidings of a painful chastisement. But those who believe and work righteousness, theirs is an unending reward. (2—26)

فَبَشِّرْهُمْ بِعَذَابٍ اَلِيْمٍ ۙ

اِلَّا الَّذِيْنَ اٰمَنُوْا وَعَمِلُوا الصّٰلِحٰتِ لَهُمْ

اَجْرٌ غَيْرُ مَمْنُوْنٍ ۟

سُوْرَةُ الْبُرُوْجِ مَكِّيَّةٌ

(Revealed before Hijra)

In the name of Allah, Most Gracious, Ever Merciful. (1)

بِسْمِ اللّٰهِ الرَّحْمٰنِ الرَّحِيْمِ ۟

وَالسَّمَآءِ ذَاتِ الْبُرُوْجِ ۙ

وَالْيَوْمِ الْمَوْعُوْدِ ۙ

We call to witness the heaven having mansions of stars, and the Promised Day, and the Witness and the one witnessed to, that ruined are the makers of the pit of fire constantly fed with fuel, as they sat by it and witnessed what they did to the believers.

وَشَاهِدٍ وَّمَشْهُوْدٍ ۙ

قُتِلَ اَصْحٰبُ الْاُخْدُوْدِ ۙ

النَّارِ ذَاتِ الْوَقُوْدِ ۙ

اِذْ هُمْ عَلَيْهَا قُعُوْدٌ ۙ

وَّهُمْ عَلٰى مَا يَفْعَلُوْنَ بِالْمُؤْمِنِيْنَ شُهُوْدٌ ۙ

They wreaked vengeance upon them solely because they believed in Allah, the Mighty,

وَمَا نَقَمُوْا مِنْهُمْ اِلَّا اَنْ يُّؤْمِنُوْا بِاللّٰهِ الْعَزِيْزِ

the Praiseworthy, to Whom belongs the kingdom of the heavens and the earth. Allah is Witness over all things.

الْحَمِيْدِ ۟

الَّذِىْ لَهٗ مُلْكُ السَّمٰوٰتِ وَالْاَرْضِ وَاللّٰهُ عَلٰى كُلِّ شَىْءٍ شَهِيْدٌ ۟

Those who persecute the believing men and the believing women, and then do not repent, will surely suffer the chastisement of hell, and the torment of burning. Those who believe and work righteousness will have Gardens beneath which rivers flow. That is the great triumph. (2—12)

اِنَّ الَّذِيْنَ فَتَنُوا الْمُؤْمِنِيْنَ وَالْمُؤْمِنٰتِ ثُمَّ لَمْ يَتُوْبُوْا فَلَهُمْ عَذَابُ جَهَنَّمَ وَلَهُمْ عَذَابُ الْحَرِيْقِ ۟

اِنَّ الَّذِيْنَ اٰمَنُوْا وَعَمِلُوا الصّٰلِحٰتِ لَهُمْ جَنّٰتٌ تَجْرِىْ مِنْ تَحْتِهَا الْاَنْهٰرُ ۟ ذٰلِكَ الْفَوْزُ الْكَبِيْرُ ۟

اِنَّ بَطْشَ رَبِّكَ لَشَدِيْدٌ ۟

اِنَّهٗ هُوَ يُبْدِئُ وَيُعِيْدُ ۟

Surely, the vengeance of thy Lord is severe. He originates and repeats; and He is the Most Forgiving, the Most Loving; the Lord of the Throne, the Lord of Honour; Who achieves without fail whatever He wills.

وَهُوَ الْغَفُوْرُ الْوَدُوْدُ ۟

ذُو الْعَرْشِ الْمَجِيْدُ ۟

فَعَّالٌ لِّمَا يُرِيْدُ ۟

هَلْ اَتٰىكَ حَدِيْثُ الْجُنُوْدِ ۟

فِرْعَوْنَ وَ ثَمُوْدَ ۟

بَلِ الَّذِيْنَ كَفَرُوْا فِيْ تَكْذِيْبٍ ۟

وَّاللّٰهُ مِنْ وَّرَآئِهِمْ مُّحِيْطٌ ۟

Has not an account reached thee of the hosts of Pharaoh and of Thamud? Indeed those who disbelieve persist in rejecting the truth; and Allah encompasses them from all sides. Surely, this is a glorious Quran, in a well-guarded tablet. (13—23)

بَلْ هُوَ قُرْاٰنٌ مَّجِيْدٌ ۟

فِيْ لَوْحٍ مَّحْفُوْظٍ ۟

AL-ṬĀRIQ
(Revealed before Hijra)

In the name of Allah, Most Forgiving, Ever Merciful. (1)

We cite as witnesses the heaven and the morning star. How should you know what the morning star is? It is the star of piercing brightness.

There is no being but has a guardian over it. Let man consider what he is created from. He is created from a fluid poured forth, which issues forth from between the loins and the breastbones. Surely, He has the power to bring him back to life, on the day when the secrets are disclosed. He will then have neither strength nor helper.

We cite as witness the cloud that pours forth rain repeatedly, and the earth that opens out with herbage, that the Quran is a decisive discourse and is not vain talk.

They will devise plans against it, and I will devise plans in its support. So bear with the disbelievers; aye, bear with them a little while. (2—18)

614

سُوْرَةُ الْاَعْلٰى مَكِّيَّةٌ

AL-A'LĀ
(Revealed before Hijra)

In the name of Allah, Most Gracious, Ever Merciful. (1)

بِسْمِ اللّٰهِ الرَّحْمٰنِ الرَّحِيْمِ ۝

سَبِّحِ اسْمَ رَبِّكَ الْاَعْلَى ۝

الَّذِيْ خَلَقَ فَسَوّٰى ۝

وَالَّذِيْ قَدَّرَ فَهَدٰى ۝

وَالَّذِيْٓ اَخْرَجَ الْمَرْعٰى ۝

فَجَعَلَهٗ غُثَآءً اَحْوٰى ۝

Glorify the name of thy Lord the Most High, Who created and made man flawless, Who determined the measure of his faculties and guided him accordingly, Who brings forth the pasturage and turns it into black stubble. We shall teach thee in a manner that thou shalt not forget, except as Allah wills. He knows that which is manifest and that which is hidden. We shall facilitate for thee the way to success and ease.

سَنُقْرِئُكَ فَلَا تَنْسٰى ۝

اِلَّا مَا شَآءَ اللّٰهُ ۗ اِنَّهٗ يَعْلَمُ الْجَهْرَ وَمَا يَخْفٰى ۝

وَنُيَسِّرُكَ لِلْيُسْرٰى ۝

فَذَكِّرْ اِنْ نَّفَعَتِ الذِّكْرٰى ۝

سَيَذَّكَّرُ مَنْ يَّخْشٰى ۝

وَيَتَجَنَّبُهَا الْاَشْقَى ۝

So continue to admonish for admonition always helps. He who fears Allah will certainly take heed; but the reprobate who is headed towards the great Fire will turn away from it. Then he will neither die therein nor live.

الَّذِيْ يَصْلَى النَّارَ الْكُبْرٰى ۝

ثُمَّ لَا يَمُوْتُ فِيْهَا وَلَا يَحْيٰى ۝

قَدْ اَفْلَحَ مَنْ تَزَكّٰى ۝

وَذَكَرَ اسْمَ رَبِّهٖ فَصَلّٰى ۝

بَلْ تُؤْثِرُوْنَ الْحَيٰوةَ الدُّنْيَا ۝

وَالْاٰخِرَةُ خَيْرٌ وَّاَبْقٰى ۝

اِنَّ هٰذَا لَفِى الصُّحُفِ الْاُوْلٰى ۝

He who purifies himself and remembers the name of his Lord and offers Prayer will surely prosper. But you prefer the hither life, whereas the Hereafter is better and more lasting. The same is set forth in the earlier Scriptures,

the Scriptures of Abraham and Moses.
(2—20)

Chapter 88   AL-GHĀSHIYAH   art 30

(Revealed before Hijra)

**In the name of Allah, Most Gracious,
Ever Merciful. (1)**

بِسْمِ اللهِ الرَّحْمٰنِ الرَّحِيْمِ ۝

هَلْ اَتٰىكَ حَدِيْثُ الْغَاشِيَةِ ۝

وُجُوْهٌ يَّوْمَئِذٍ خَاشِعَةٌ ۝

عَامِلَةٌ نَّاصِبَةٌ ۝

تَصْلٰى نَارًا حَامِيَةً ۝

تُسْقٰى مِنْ عَيْنٍ اٰنِيَةٍ ۝

لَيْسَ لَهُمْ طَعَامٌ اِلَّا مِنْ ضَرِيْعٍ ۝

لَا يُسْمِنُ وَلَا يُغْنِيْ مِنْ جُوْعٍ ۝

وُجُوْهٌ يَّوْمَئِذٍ نَّاعِمَةٌ ۝

لِسَعْيِهَا رَاضِيَةٌ ۝

فِيْ جَنَّةٍ عَالِيَةٍ ۝

لَا تَسْمَعُ فِيْهَا لَاغِيَةً ۝

فِيْهَا عَيْنٌ جَارِيَةٌ ۝

فِيْهَا سُرُرٌ مَّرْفُوْعَةٌ ۝

وَّاَكْوَابٌ مَّوْضُوْعَةٌ ۝

وَّنَمَارِقُ مَصْفُوْفَةٌ ۝

وَّزَرَابِيُّ مَبْثُوْثَةٌ ۝

Has an account reached thee of the
overspreading calamity? Some faces on
that day will be downcast; toiling, weary.
They shall enter a blazing fire, will be
given to drink from a boiling spring, and
will have no food save dry, bitter and
thorny herbage, which will neither nourish,
nor satisfy hunger.

Other faces, on that day, will be joyful,
well pleased with the result of their striving. They will be in a lofty Garden,
wherein no idle talk will be heard. In it
there is a running spring, and raised
couches, and goblets laid out, and cushions
arranged in order, and rich carpets laid
down.

Do they not observe the clouds, how they are created? and the heaven, how it is raised high? and the mountains, how they are set up? and the earth, how it is spread out?

اَفَلَا يَنْظُرُوْنَ اِلَى الْاِبِلِ كَيْفَ خُلِقَتْ ۞

وَاِلَى السَّمَآءِ كَيْفَ رُفِعَتْ ۞

وَاِلَى الْجِبَالِ كَيْفَ نُصِبَتْ ۞

وَاِلَى الْاَرْضِ كَيْفَ سُطِحَتْ ۞

فَذَكِّرْ اِنَّمَآ اَنْتَ مُذَكِّرٌ ۞

لَسْتَ عَلَيْهِمْ بِمُصَيْطِرٍ ۞

اِلَّا مَنْ تَوَلّٰى وَكَفَرَ ۞

فَيُعَذِّبُهُ اللّٰهُ الْعَذَابَ الْاَكْبَرَ ۞

اِنَّ اِلَيْنَآ اِيَابَهُمْ ۞

ثُمَّ اِنَّ عَلَيْنَا حِسَابَهُمْ ۞

Then, continue to admonish for thou art but an admonisher; thou hast no authority to compel them. But whoever turns away and rejects the admonition will be chastised by Allah with the great chastisement. Unto Us is their return, and it is for Us to call them to account. (2—27)

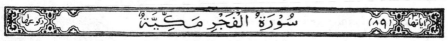

سُوْرَةُ الْفَجْرِ مَكِّيَّةٌ

(Revealed before Hijra)

In the name of Allah, Most Gracious, Ever Merciful. (1)

بِسْمِ اللّٰهِ الرَّحْمٰنِ الرَّحِيْمِ ۞

وَالْفَجْرِ ۞

وَلَيَالٍ عَشْرٍ ۞

وَّالشَّفْعِ وَالْوَتْرِ ۞

وَالَّيْلِ اِذَا يَسْرِ ۞

هَلْ فِيْ ذٰلِكَ قَسَمٌ لِّذِيْ حِجْرٍ ۞

اَلَمْ تَرَ كَيْفَ فَعَلَ رَبُّكَ بِعَادٍ ۞

اِرَمَ ذَاتِ الْعِمَادِ ۞

We call to witness the approaching Dawn, and the Ten Nights, and the Even and the Odd, and the Night when it is on the move. Is there not in all this strong evidence for one gifted with understanding?

Knowest thou not how thy Lord dealt with the tribe of 'Ad, of the city of Iram of lofty structures,

the like of which has not been created in
these parts; and with the tribe of Thamud
who hewed out rocks in the valley, and
with Pharaoh, lord of vast camps, who
transgressed in the land and wrought much
corruption therein? Thy Lord then laid
upon them the scourge of chastisement.
Surely, thy Lord is on the watch. (2—15)

It is characteristic of man that when his
Lord tries him and bestows honours and
favours upon him, he boasts: Even my
Lord honours me! But when He tries him
and limits his means, he laments: My Lord
has humiliated me without cause. Not so,
but you honour not the orphan, and you
urge not one another to feed the poor, and
you squander inherited wealth extravagantly, and you love affluence inordinately.

Hearken, when the earth is pound-
ed into level sand, and thy Lord comes
with the angels ranged in order; and hell
is brought near; on that day, man would
desire to take advantage of the admonition, but how can he then do so? He will
lament: Would that I had laid up something for this life! On that day none can
punish like unto His punishment, and
none can bind so securely as His binding.

الَّتِىْ لَمْ يُخْلَقْ مِثْلُهَا فِى الْبِلَادِۙ ٩

وَّثَمُوْدَ الَّذِيْنَ جَابُوا الصَّخْرَ بِالْوَادِۙ ٱ٠

وَّفِرْعَوْنَ ذِى الْاَوْتَادِۙ ۱۱

الَّذِيْنَ طَغَوْا فِى الْبِلَادِۙ ۱۲

فَاَكْثَرُوْا فِيْهَا الْفَسَادَۙ ۱۳

فَصَبَّ عَلَيْهِمْ رَبُّكَ سَوْطَ عَذَابٍۚ ۱۴

اِنَّ رَبَّكَ لَبِالْمِرْصَادِؕ ۱۵

فَاَمَّا الْاِنْسَانُ اِذَا مَا ابْتَلٰىهُ رَبُّهٗ فَاَكْرَمَهٗ وَ
نَعَّمَهٗ ۙ فَيَقُوْلُ رَبِّىْٓ اَكْرَمَنِؕ ۱۶

وَاَمَّآ اِذَا مَا ابْتَلٰىهُ فَقَدَرَ عَلَيْهِ رِزْقَهٗ ۙ فَيَقُوْلُ
رَبِّىْٓ اَهَانَنِۚ ۱۷

كَلَّا بَلْ لَّا تُكْرِمُوْنَ الْيَتِيْمَۙ ۱۸

وَلَا تَحٰٓضُّوْنَ عَلٰى طَعَامِ الْمِسْكِيْنِۙ ۱۹

وَتَاْكُلُوْنَ التُّرَاثَ اَكْلًا لَّمًّاۙ ۲۰

وَّتُحِبُّوْنَ الْمَالَ حُبًّا جَمًّاؕ ۲۱

كَلَّآ اِذَا دُكَّتِ الْاَرْضُ دَكًّا دَكًّاۙ ۲۲

وَّجَآءَ رَبُّكَ وَالْمَلَكُ صَفًّا صَفًّاۚ ۲۳

وَجِاْىٓءَ يَوْمَىِٕذٍۢ بِجَهَنَّمَ ۙ يَوْمَىِٕذٍ يَّتَذَكَّرُ
الْاِنْسَانُ وَاَنّٰى لَهُ الذِّكْرٰىؕ ۲۴

يَقُوْلُ يٰلَيْتَنِىْ قَدَّمْتُ لِحَيَاتِىْۚ ۲۵

فَيَوْمَىِٕذٍ لَّا يُعَذِّبُ عَذَابَهٗٓ اَحَدٌۙ ۲۶

وَّلَا يُوْثِقُ وَثَاقَهٗٓ اَحَدٌؕ ۲۷

The righteous will be greeted with: O soul at rest, return to thy Lord, thou well pleased with Him and He well pleased with thee. So enter among My chosen servants and enter My Garden. (16—31)

يَاۤيَّتُهَا النَّفْسُ الْمُطْمَئِنَّةُ ۞

ارْجِعِىۤ اِلٰى رَبِّكِ رَاضِيَةً مَّرْضِيَّةً ۞

فَادْخُلِىۡ فِىۡ عِبَادِىۡ ۞

وَادْخُلِىۡ جَنَّتِىۡ ۞

سُوۡرَةُ الْبَلَدِ مَكِّيَّةٌ ۹۰

(Revealed before Hijra)

In the name of Allah, Most Gracious, Ever Merciful. (1)

بِسۡمِ اللهِ الرَّحۡمٰنِ الرَّحِيۡمِ ۞

لَاۤ اُقْسِمُ بِهٰذَا الْبَلَدِ ۞

وَاَنْتَ حِلٌّ بِهٰذَا الْبَلَدِ ۞

We cite this city, Mecca, as a witness, and affirm that thou wilt surely alight in this city; and We cite the father, Abraham, and the son, Ishmael.

وَوَالِدٍ وَّمَا وَلَدَ ۞

لَقَدْ خَلَقْنَا الْاِنْسَانَ فِىۡ كَبَدٍ ۞

اَيَحْسَبُ اَنْ لَّنْ يَّقْدِرَ عَلَيْهِ اَحَدٌ ۞

يَقُوْلُ اَهْلَكْتُ مَالًا لُّبَدًا ۞

We have created man committed to toil. Does he think no one has power over him? He says: I have spent enormous wealth. Does he think no one watches him? Have We not given him two eyes, and a tongue and two lips, and pointed out to him the two highways of good and evil?

اَيَحْسَبُ اَنْ لَّمْ يَرَهُ اَحَدٌ ۞

اَلَمْ نَجْعَلْ لَّهُ عَيْنَيْنِ ۞

وَلِسَانًا وَّشَفَتَيْنِ ۞

وَهَدَيْنٰهُ النَّجْدَيْنِ ۞

فَلَا اقْتَحَمَ الْعَقَبَةَ ۞

وَمَاۤ اَدْرٰىكَ مَا الْعَقَبَةُ ۞

فَكُّ رَقَبَةٍ ۞

But he attempted not the scaling of the height. How shouldst thou know what the scaling of the height is? It is the freeing of a slave, or feeding, on a day of scarcity, an orphan near of kin, or a poor person reduced to penury; and to be of those who believe and exhort one another to steadfastness and exhort one another to mercy. These are the people of the right. Those who deny Our Signs, they are the people of the left. They will be chastised with furnace fire. (2—21)

أَوْ إِطْعُمُ فِيْ يَوْمٍ ذِيْ مَسْغَبَةٍ ۙ

يَتِيْمًا ذَا مَقْرَبَةٍ ۙ

أَوْ مِسْكِيْنًا ذَا مَتْرَبَةٍ ۙ

ثُمَّ كَانَ مِنَ الَّذِيْنَ اٰمَنُوْا وَتَوَاصَوْا بِالصَّبْرِ وَتَوَاصَوْا بِالْمَرْحَمَةِ ۙ

أُولٰٓئِكَ أَصْحٰبُ الْمَيْمَنَةِ ۙ

وَالَّذِيْنَ كَفَرُوْا بِاٰيٰتِنَا هُمْ أَصْحٰبُ الْمَشْـَٔمَةِ ۙ

عَلَيْهِمْ نَارٌ مُّؤْصَدَةٌ ۰

سُوْرَةُ الشَّمْسِ مَكِّيَّةٌ

Chapter 91   **AL-SHAMS**   Part 30
(Revealed before Hijra)

In the name of Allah, Most Gracious, Ever Merciful. (1)

بِسْمِ اللهِ الرَّحْمٰنِ الرَّحِيْمِ ۰

وَالشَّمْسِ وَضُحٰىهَا ۙ

وَالْقَمَرِ إِذَا تَلٰىهَا ۙ

وَالنَّهَارِ إِذَا جَلّٰىهَا ۙ

وَالَّيْلِ إِذَا يَغْشٰىهَا ۙ

وَالسَّمَآءِ وَمَا بَنٰىهَا ۙ

وَالْأَرْضِ وَمَا طَحٰىهَا ۙ

وَنَفْسٍ وَّمَا سَوّٰىهَا ۙ

فَأَلْهَمَهَا فُجُوْرَهَا وَتَقْوٰىهَا ۙ

قَدْ أَفْلَحَ مَنْ زَكّٰىهَا ۙ

وَقَدْ خَابَ مَنْ دَسّٰىهَا ۰

We call to witness the sun and its growing brightness, and the moon when it follows it, and the day when it reveals its glory, and the night when it draws a veil over it, and the heaven and the purpose of its making, and the earth and the purpose of its spreading out, and the soul and its perfect proportioning (He revealed to it the right and wrong of everything), he indeed prospers who purifies it, and he is ruined who corrupts it. (2—11)

The tribe of Thamud rejected the truth because of their rebelliousness, when the most wretched of them stood up in opposition to it. The Messenger of Allah warned them; Beware of doing any harm to the she-camel of Allah and interfering with her drink. But they rejected him and hamstrung her. So their Lord destroyed them utterly, all alike, because of their sin, and He cared not for the consequences thereof. (12—16)

كَذَّبَتْ ثَمُوْدُ بِطَغْوٰىهَآ ۞

اِذِ انْبَعَثَ اَشْقٰىهَا ۞

فَقَالَ لَهُمْ رَسُوْلُ اللّٰهِ نَاقَةَ اللّٰهِ وَسُقْيٰهَا ۞

فَكَذَّبُوْهُ فَعَقَرُوْهَا فَدَمْدَمَ عَلَيْهِمْ رَبُّهُمْ بِذَنْۢبِهِمْ فَسَوّٰىهَا ۞

وَلَا يَخَافُ عُقْبٰهَا ۞

(Revealed before Hijra)

In the name of Allah, Most Gracious, Ever Merciful. (1)

بِسْمِ اللّٰهِ الرَّحْمٰنِ الرَّحِيْمِ ۞

وَالَّيْلِ اِذَا يَغْشٰى ۞

وَالنَّهَارِ اِذَا تَجَلّٰى ۞

We call to witness the night when it covers up, and the day when it brightens up, and the creation of male and female, that your strivings are divergent.

وَمَا خَلَقَ الذَّكَرَ وَالْاُنْثٰى ۞

اِنَّ سَعْيَكُمْ لَشَتّٰى ۞

He who spends to promote the cause of Allah, and works righteousness, and testifies to the truth of that which is right, will have his way to prosperity made easy by Us.

فَاَمَّا مَنْ اَعْطٰى وَاتَّقٰى ۞

وَصَدَّقَ بِالْحُسْنٰى ۞

فَسَنُيَسِّرُهُ لِلْيُسْرٰى ۞

But he who is niggardly and is indifferent, and rejects that which is right, will have his way to misery made easy by Us. His wealth shall not avail him when he perishes.

وَاَمَّا مَنْۢ بَخِلَ وَاسْتَغْنٰى ۞

وَكَذَّبَ بِالْحُسْنٰى ۞

فَسَنُيَسِّرُهُ لِلْعُسْرٰى ۞

وَمَا يُغْنِيْ عَنْهُ مَالُهٗ اِذَا تَرَدّٰى ۞

Surely, it is for Us to provide guidance,

اِنَّ عَلَيْنَا لَلْهُدٰى ۞

and to Us belong the end and beginning of all things. So, I have warned you of a flaming fire; it is only the most wicked who reject the truth and turn their backs on it, that will enter it. But the righteous one who spends his wealth to be purified, and who owes no favour to anyone, which is to be repaid, his purpose being only to win the pleasure of his Lord, the Most High, shall be kept away from it. Surely will he be well pleased with Him. (2—22)

وَاِنَّ لَنَا لَلْاٰخِرَةَ وَالْاُوْلٰی ۞

فَاَنْذَرْتُكُمْ نَارًا تَلَظّٰی ۞

لَا يَصْلٰىهَاۤ اِلَّا الْاَشْقَی ۞

الَّذِیْ كَذَّبَ وَتَوَلّٰی ۞

وَسَيُجَنَّبُهَا الْاَتْقَی ۞

الَّذِیْ يُؤْتِیْ مَالَهٗ يَتَزَكّٰی ۞

وَمَا لِاَحَدٍ عِنْدَهٗ مِنْ نِّعْمَةٍ تُجْزٰی ۞

اِلَّا ابْتِغَآءَ وَجْهِ رَبِّهِ الْاَعْلٰی ۞

وَلَسَوْفَ يَرْضٰی ۞

Chapter 93   **AL-DUHĀ**   Part 30
(Revealed before Hijra)

In the name of Allah, Most Gracious, Ever Merciful. (1)

بِسْمِ اللهِ الرَّحْمٰنِ الرَّحِيْمِ ۞

وَالضُّحٰی ۞

وَالَّيْلِ اِذَا سَجٰی ۞

مَا وَدَّعَكَ رَبُّكَ وَمَا قَلٰی ۞

We call to witness the growing brightness of the day, and We call to witness the stillness of the night, that thy Lord has not forsaken thee, nor is He displeased with thee. Surely, every succeeding hour is better for thee than the preceding one. Thy Lord will keep on bestowing His favours upon thee so that thou wilt be well pleased. Did He not find thee an orphan and give thee shelter? and find thee enamoured of thy people and in search of guidance for them, and showed thee the right way for them? and find thee having numerous dependants and bestowed plenty on thee?

وَلَلْاٰخِرَةُ خَيْرٌ لَّكَ مِنَ الْاُوْلٰی ۞

وَلَسَوْفَ يُعْطِيْكَ رَبُّكَ فَتَرْضٰی ۞

اَلَمْ يَجِدْكَ يَتِيْمًا فَاٰوٰی ۞

وَوَجَدَكَ ضَآلًّا فَهَدٰی ۞

وَوَجَدَكَ عَآئِلًا فَاَغْنٰی ۞

Then oppress not the orphan and chide not him who asks, and keep proclaiming the bounty of thy Lord. (2--12)

فَاَمَّا الْيَتِيْمَ فَلَا تَقْهَرْ ۝

وَاَمَّا السَّآئِلَ فَلَا تَنْهَرْ ۝

وَاَمَّا بِنِعْمَةِ رَبِّكَ فَحَدِّثْ ۝

Part 30   **AL-INSHIRĀH**   Chapter 94
(Revealed before Hijra)

In the name of Allah, Most Gracious, Ever Merciful. (1)

بِسْمِ اللهِ الرَّحْمٰنِ الرَّحِيْمِ ۝

اَلَمْ نَشْرَحْ لَكَ صَدْرَكَ ۝

وَوَضَعْنَا عَنْكَ وِزْرَكَ ۝

الَّذِيْٓ اَنْقَضَ ظَهْرَكَ ۝

وَرَفَعْنَا لَكَ ذِكْرَكَ ۝

Have We not broadened thy mind, and relieved thee of thy burden which had well-nigh broken thy back, and exalted thy name? Surely, there is ease after hardship, most surely there is continuation of ease after hardship. So when thou art free, strive hard to meet thy Lord, and turn towards Him. (2—9)

فَاِنَّ مَعَ الْعُسْرِ يُسْرًا ۝

اِنَّ مَعَ الْعُسْرِ يُسْرًا ۝

فَاِذَا فَرَغْتَ فَانْصَبْ ۝

وَاِلٰى رَبِّكَ فَارْغَبْ ۝

Part 30   **AL-TĪN**   Chapter 95
(Revealed before Hijra)

In the name of Allah, Most Gracious, Ever Merciful. (1)

بِسْمِ اللهِ الرَّحْمٰنِ الرَّحِيْمِ ۝

وَالتِّيْنِ وَالزَّيْتُوْنِ ۝

We call to witness the Fig and the Olive, and Mount Sinai, and this Inviolate City, that We have created man in the best mould; then, if he works iniquity We cast him down as the lowest of the low, except those who believe and work righteousness, for them is an unending reward. After this, what is there to refute thee concerning the Judgment? Is not Allah the Best of Judges? (2—9)

وَطُوْرِ سِيْنِيْنَ ۙ

وَهٰذَا الْبَلَدِ الْاَمِيْنِ ۙ

لَقَدْ خَلَقْنَا الْاِنْسَانَ فِيْٓ اَحْسَنِ تَقْوِيْمٍ ۙ

ثُمَّ رَدَدْنٰهُ اَسْفَلَ سَافِلِيْنَ ۙ

اِلَّا الَّذِيْنَ اٰمَنُوْا وَعَمِلُوا الصّٰلِحٰتِ فَلَهُمْ اَجْرٌ
غَيْرُ مَمْنُوْنٍ ۙ

فَمَا يُكَذِّبُكَ بَعْدُ بِالدِّيْنِ ۙ

اَلَيْسَ اللّٰهُ بِاَحْكَمِ الْحٰكِمِيْنَ ۠

سُوْرَةُ الْعَلَقِ مَكِّيَّةٌ (٩٦)

In the name of Allah, Most Gracious, Ever Merciful. (1)

بِسْمِ اللّٰهِ الرَّحْمٰنِ الرَّحِيْمِ ۟

اِقْرَاْ بِاسْمِ رَبِّكَ الَّذِيْ خَلَقَ ۚ

خَلَقَ الْاِنْسَانَ مِنْ عَلَقٍ ۚ

اِقْرَاْ وَرَبُّكَ الْاَكْرَمُ ۙ

الَّذِيْ عَلَّمَ بِالْقَلَمِ ۙ

عَلَّمَ الْاِنْسَانَ مَا لَمْ يَعْلَمْ ۚ

كَلَّا اِنَّ الْاِنْسَانَ لَيَطْغٰٓى ۙ

اَنْ رَّاٰهُ اسْتَغْنٰى ۚ

Recite in the name of thy Lord Who created everything. He created man from a clot of blood. Recite, for thy Lord is Most Beneficent, Who has taught by the pen, taught man that which he knew not.

اِنَّ اِلٰى رَبِّكَ الرُّجْعٰى ۚ

اَرَءَيْتَ الَّذِيْ يَنْهٰى ۙ

Man does indeed transgress, because he considers himself self-sufficient. Surely, unto thy Lord is the return. Knowest thou him who obstructs a servant of Ours when he stands in Prayer?

عَبْدًا اِذَا صَلّٰى ۙ۞

اَرَءَيْتَ اِنْ كَانَ عَلَى الْهُدٰى ۙ۞

اَوْ اَمَرَ بِالتَّقْوٰى ۙ۞

Tell me, if he who prays follows the guidance and enjoins righteousness, and he who obstructs rejects the truth and turns his back on it, what will be the end of this last one? Does he not know that Allah watches his conduct? Then, if he desist not, We will surely drag him by the forelock, the forelock of a lying, sinful one. Then let him call his associates, We too will call Our guardians of hell.

اَرَءَيْتَ اِنْ كَذَّبَ وَتَوَلّٰى ۞

اَلَمْ يَعْلَمْ بِاَنَّ اللّٰهَ يَرٰى ۞

كَلَّا لَئِنْ لَّمْ يَنْتَهِ ۙ۬ لَنَسْفَعًا بِالنَّاصِيَةِ ۙ۞

نَاصِيَةٍ كَاذِبَةٍ خَاطِئَةٍ ۚ۞

فَلْيَدْعُ نَادِيَهٗ ۙ۞

سَنَدْعُ الزَّبَانِيَةَ ۙ۞

Then follow not him, but prostrate thyself and draw nearer to Us. (2—20)

كَلَّا ۚ لَا تُطِعْهُ وَاسْجُدْ وَاقْتَرِبْ ۩۞

(Revealed before Hijra)

In the name of Allah, Most Gracious, Ever Merciful. (1)

بِسْمِ اللّٰهِ الرَّحْمٰنِ الرَّحِيْمِ ۞

اِنَّا اَنْزَلْنٰهُ فِيْ لَيْلَةِ الْقَدْرِ ۞

وَمَا اَدْرٰىكَ مَا لَيْلَةُ الْقَدْرِ ۞

Surely, We sent down the Quran during the Night of Decrees. How shouldst thou know what is the Night of Decrees. The Night of Decrees is better than a thousand months. Therein descend angels and the Spirit by the command of their Lord with their Lord's decrees concerning every matter. It is all peace, till the break of dawn. (2—6)

لَيْلَةُ الْقَدْرِ ۙ۬ خَيْرٌ مِّنْ اَلْفِ شَهْرٍ ۞

تَنَزَّلُ الْمَلٰئِكَةُ وَالرُّوْحُ فِيْهَا بِاِذْنِ رَبِّهِمْ ۚ مِنْ كُلِّ اَمْرٍ ۙ۞

سَلٰمٌ ۙ۬ هِيَ حَتّٰى مَطْلَعِ الْفَجْرِ ۞

Chapter 98

سُوۡرَةُ الۡبَيِّنَةِ مَدَنِيَّةٌ

AL-BAYYINAH
(Revealed before Hijra)

In the name of Allah, Most Gracious, Ever Merciful. (1)

بِسۡمِ اللهِ الرَّحۡمٰنِ الرَّحِيۡمِ ۝

لَمۡ يَكُنِ الَّذِيۡنَ كَفَرُوۡا مِنۡ اَهۡلِ الۡكِتٰبِ وَالۡمُشۡرِكِيۡنَ مُنۡفَكِّيۡنَ حَتّٰى تَأۡتِيَهُمُ الۡبَيِّنَةُ ۝

رَسُوۡلٌ مِّنَ اللهِ يَتۡلُوۡا صُحُفًا مُّطَهَّرَةً ۝

فِيۡهَا كُتُبٌ قَيِّمَةٌ ۝

Those who disbelieve from among the People of the Book and the idolaters would not desist from disbelief until clear proof came to them: a Messenger from Allah, reciting pure Scriptures, wherein are lasting commandments. Those to whom the Book was given did not become divided until after clear proof had come to them; whereas, they had only been commanded to worship Allah, devoting themselves wholly to Him in full sincerity, and to observe Prayer, and pay the Zakat. This is the enduring faith.

وَمَا تَفَرَّقَ الَّذِيۡنَ اُوۡتُوا الۡكِتٰبَ اِلَّا مِنۡ بَعۡدِ مَا جَآءَتۡهُمُ الۡبَيِّنَةُ ۝

وَمَآ اُمِرُوۡۤا اِلَّا لِيَعۡبُدُوا اللهَ مُخۡلِصِيۡنَ لَهُ الدِّيۡنَ ۙ حُنَفَآءَ وَيُقِيۡمُوا الصَّلٰوةَ وَيُؤۡتُوا الزَّكٰوةَ وَذٰلِكَ دِيۡنُ الۡقَيِّمَةِ ۝

اِنَّ الَّذِيۡنَ كَفَرُوۡا مِنۡ اَهۡلِ الۡكِتٰبِ وَالۡمُشۡرِكِيۡنَ فِيۡ نَارِ جَهَنَّمَ خٰلِدِيۡنَ فِيۡهَا ؕ اُولٰٓئِكَ هُمۡ شَرُّ الۡبَرِيَّةِ ۝

Verily, those who disbelieve from among the People of the Book and the idolaters will be in the fire of hell, abiding therein. They are the worst of creatures. Those who believe and work righteousness, they are the best of creatures. Their reward with their Lord is Gardens of Eternity, beneath which rivers flow; they will abide therein for ever. Allah is well pleased with them and they are well pleased with Him. That is the reward of those who fear their Lord. (2—9)

اِنَّ الَّذِيۡنَ اٰمَنُوۡا وَعَمِلُوا الصّٰلِحٰتِ ۙ اُولٰٓئِكَ هُمۡ خَيۡرُ الۡبَرِيَّةِ ۝

جَزَآؤُهُمۡ عِنۡدَ رَبِّهِمۡ جَنّٰتُ عَدۡنٍ تَجۡرِيۡ مِنۡ تَحۡتِهَا الۡاَنۡهٰرُ خٰلِدِيۡنَ فِيۡهَآ اَبَدًا ؕ رَضِيَ اللهُ عَنۡهُمۡ وَرَضُوۡا عَنۡهُ ؕ ذٰلِكَ لِمَنۡ خَشِيَ رَبَّهٗ ۝

سُوْرَةُ الزِّلْزَالِ مَكِّيَّةٌ ﴿٩٩﴾

AL-ZILZĀL
(Revealed before Hijra)

In the name of Allah, Most Gracious, Ever Merciful. (1)

بِسْمِ اللهِ الرَّحْمٰنِ الرَّحِيْمِ ۝

اِذَا زُلْزِلَتِ الْاَرْضُ زِلْزَالَهَا ۝

وَاَخْرَجَتِ الْاَرْضُ اَثْقَالَهَا ۝

وَقَالَ الْاِنْسَانُ مَا لَهَا ۝

يَوْمَئِذٍ تُحَدِّثُ اَخْبَارَهَا ۝

بِاَنَّ رَبَّكَ اَوْحٰى لَهَا ۝

When the earth is shaken violently and brings forth its burdens, and man cries out: What is the matter with it? On that day it will narrate its account, for thy Lord has so directed it. On that day people will come forth in diverse groups that they may be shown the consequences of their actions. Then whoso will have done the smallest particle of good will see it, and whoso will have done the smallest particle of ill will also see it. (2—9)

يَوْمَئِذٍ يَّصْدُرُ النَّاسُ اَشْتَاتًا لِّيُرَوْا اَعْمَالَهُمْ ۝

فَمَنْ يَّعْمَلْ مِثْقَالَ ذَرَّةٍ خَيْرًا يَّرَهٗ ۝

وَمَنْ يَّعْمَلْ مِثْقَالَ ذَرَّةٍ شَرًّا يَّرَهٗ ۝

سُوْرَةُ الْعٰدِيٰتِ مَكِّيَّةٌ ﴿١٠٠﴾

(Revealed before Hijra)

In the name of Allah, Most Gracious, Ever Merciful. (1)

بِسْمِ اللهِ الرَّحْمٰنِ الرَّحِيْمِ ۝

وَالْعٰدِيٰتِ ضَبْحًا ۝

فَالْمُوْرِيٰتِ قَدْحًا ۝

فَالْمُغِيْرٰتِ صُبْحًا ۝

فَاَثَرْنَ بِهٖ نَقْعًا ۝

We call to witness the snorting chargers, striking sparks of fire, charging at dawn, raising clouds of dust, and penetrating into the enemy ranks,

فَوَسَطْنَ بِهٖ جَمْعًا ۝

that man, surely, is ungrateful to his Lord, and he bears witness to it by word and deed, and he is inordinately fond of wealth. Does he not know that when those in the graves are raised, and their very secret thoughts are exposed, on that day their Lord will watch over them? (2—12)

اِنَّ الْاِنْسَانَ لِرَبِّهٖ لَكَنُوْدٌ ۞

وَاِنَّهٗ عَلٰى ذٰلِكَ لَشَهِيْدٌ ۞

وَاِنَّهٗ لِحُبِّ الْخَيْرِ لَشَدِيْدٌ ۞

اَفَلَا يَعْلَمُ اِذَا بُعْثِرَ مَا فِى الْقُبُوْرِ ۞

وَحُصِّلَ مَا فِى الصُّدُوْرِ ۞

اِنَّ رَبَّهُمْ بِهِمْ يَوْمَئِذٍ لَّخَبِيْرٌ ۞

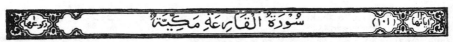

(Revealed before Hijra)

In the name of Allah, Most Gracious, Ever Merciful. (1)

بِسْمِ اللّٰهِ الرَّحْمٰنِ الرَّحِيْمِ ۞

الْقَارِعَةُ ۞

مَا الْقَارِعَةُ ۞

وَمَآ اَدْرٰىكَ مَا الْقَارِعَةُ ۞

The world will be overtaken by a great calamity. What is the great calamity? How shouldst thou know what the great calamity is?

يَوْمَ يَكُوْنُ النَّاسُ كَالْفَرَاشِ الْمَبْثُوْثِ ۞

وَتَكُوْنُ الْجِبَالُ كَالْعِهْنِ الْمَنْفُوْشِ ۞

فَاَمَّا مَنْ ثَقُلَتْ مَوَازِيْنُهٗ ۞

فَهُوَ فِىْ عِيْشَةٍ رَّاضِيَةٍ ۞

This will be the day when mankind will be like scattered moths, and the mountains will be like carded wool; when he whose scales will be heavy, with good deeds, will have a pleasant life; but he whose scales are light, for want of good deeds, will have hell as a resort. How shouldst thou know what that is? It is a burning fire. (2—12)

وَاَمَّا مَنْ خَفَّتْ مَوَازِيْنُهٗ ۞

فَاُمُّهٗ هَاوِيَةٌ ۞

وَمَآ اَدْرٰىكَ مَاهِيَهْ ۞

نَارٌ حَامِيَةٌ ۞

Chapter 102

سُوْرَةُ التَّكَاثُرِ مَكِّيَّةٌ (١٠٢)

AL-TAKĀTHUR
(Revealed before Hijra)

In the name of Allah, Most Gracious, Ever Merciful. (1)

بِسْمِ اللهِ الرَّحْمٰنِ الرَّحِيْمِ ۞

اَلْهٰكُمُ التَّكَاثُرُ ۞

حَتّٰى زُرْتُمُ الْمَقَابِرَ ۞

كَلَّا سَوْفَ تَعْلَمُوْنَ ۞

ثُمَّ كَلَّا سَوْفَ تَعْلَمُوْنَ ۞

كَلَّا لَوْ تَعْلَمُوْنَ عِلْمَ الْيَقِيْنِ ۞

لَتَرَوُنَّ الْجَحِيْمَ ۞

ثُمَّ لَتَرَوُنَّهَا عَيْنَ الْيَقِيْنِ ۞

ثُمَّ لَتُسْئَلُنَّ يَوْمَئِذٍ عَنِ النَّعِيْمِ ۞

The desire of increase in worldly possessions beguiles you till you reach the graves. Surely you will soon come to know the vanity of your pursuits; again, you surely will soon come to know how mistaken you are. Indeed if you only knew with the certainty of knowledge, you would surely see hell in this very life. But you will see it with the certainty of sight in the life to come, and then you shall be called to account, on that day, in respect of the worldly favours conferred on you. (2—9)

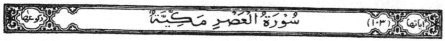

سُوْرَةُ الْعَصْرِ مَكِّيَّةٌ (١٠٣)

Chapter 103

AL-'AṢR
(Revealed before Hijra)

In the name of Allah, Most Gracious Ever Merciful. (1)

بِسْمِ اللهِ الرَّحْمٰنِ الرَّحِيْمِ ۞

وَالْعَصْرِ ۞

إِنَّ الْإِنْسَانَ لَفِيْ خُسْرٍ ۞

إِلَّا الَّذِيْنَ اٰمَنُوْا وَعَمِلُوا الصّٰلِحٰتِ وَتَوَاصَوْا بِالْحَقِّ ەۙ وَتَوَاصَوْا بِالصَّبْرِ ۞

We call to witness the passing time, that surely man suffers continuous loss, except those who believe and work righteousness, and exhort one another to hold fast to the Truth, and exhort one another to be steadfast. (2—4)

629

Chapter 104

سُوْرَةُ الْهُمَزَةِ مَكِّيَّةٌ

AL-HUMAZAH
(Revealed before Hijra)

In the name of Allah, Most Gracious,
Ever Merciful. (1)

بِسْمِ اللهِ الرَّحْمٰنِ الرَّحِيْمِ ۝

وَيْلٌ لِّكُلِّ هُمَزَةٍ لُّمَزَةٍ ۝

الَّذِيْ جَمَعَ مَالًا وَّعَدَّدَهٗ ۝

يَحْسَبُ اَنَّ مَالَهٗٓ اَخْلَدَهٗ ۝

كَلَّا لَيُنْبَذَنَّ فِى الْحُطَمَةِ ۝

وَمَآ اَدْرٰىكَ مَا الْحُطَمَةُ ۝

Woe to every backbiter, slanderer, who
amasses wealth and keeps counting it.
He thinks that his wealth will make him
immortal. Nay, he shall surely be cast
into the crushing torment. How shouldst
thou know what the crushing torment is?
It is Allah's kindled fire which rises over
the hearts. It will be closed in on them,
in widely extended columns. (2—10)

نَارُ اللهِ الْمُوْقَدَةُ ۝

الَّتِيْ تَطَّلِعُ عَلَى الْاَفْـِٕدَةِ ۝

اِنَّهَا عَلَيْهِمْ مُّؤْصَدَةٌ ۝

فِيْ عَمَدٍ مُّمَدَّدَةٍ ۝

سُوْرَةُ الْفِيْلِ مَكِّيَّةٌ

Chapter 105

AL-FĪL
(Revealed before Hijra)

In the name of Allah, Most Gracious,
Ever Merciful. (1)

بِسْمِ اللهِ الرَّحْمٰنِ الرَّحِيْمِ ۝

اَلَمْ تَرَ كَيْفَ فَعَلَ رَبُّكَ بِاَصْحٰبِ الْفِيْلِ ۝

اَلَمْ يَجْعَلْ كَيْدَهُمْ فِيْ تَضْلِيْلٍ ۝

وَاَرْسَلَ عَلَيْهِمْ طَيْرًا اَبَابِيْلَ ۝

Dost thou not recall how thy Lord dealt
with the People of the Elephant? Did He
not destroy them and thus cause their
design to miscarry? Then He sent upon
their corpses swarms of birds, which
beat them against hard lumps of clay,
and thus made them like broken straw,
left over. (2—6)

تَرْمِيْهِمْ بِحِجَارَةٍ مِّنْ سِجِّيْلٍ ۝

فَجَعَلَهُمْ كَعَصْفٍ مَّأْكُوْلٍ ۝

سُوْرَةُ الْقُرَيْشِ مَكِّيَّةٌ

AL-QURAISH
(Revealed before Hijra)

In the name of Allah, Most Gracious.
Ever Merciful. (1)

بِسْمِ اللهِ الرَّحْمٰنِ الرَّحِيْمِ ۞

لِاِيْلٰفِ قُرَيْشٍ ۞

اٖلٰفِهِمْ رِحْلَةَ الشِّتَآءِ وَالصَّيْفِ ۞

فَلْيَعْبُدُوْا رَبَّ هٰذَا الْبَيْتِ ۞

الَّذِيْٓ اَطْعَمَهُمْ مِّنْ جُوْعٍ ۙ وَّاٰمَنَهُمْ مِّنْ خَوْفٍ ۞

We destroyed the People of the Elephant to attach the hearts of the Quraish to their summer and winter journeys and to facilitate them. They should, therefore, worship the Lord of this House, Who has fed them in hunger and given them security against fear. (2—5)

سُوْرَةُ الْمَاعُوْنِ مَكِّيَّةٌ

AL-MĀ'ŪN
(Revealed before Hijra)

In the name of Allah, Most Gracious,
Ever Merciful. (1)

بِسْمِ اللهِ الرَّحْمٰنِ الرَّحِيْمِ ۞

اَرَءَيْتَ الَّذِيْ يُكَذِّبُ بِالدِّيْنِ ۞

فَذٰلِكَ الَّذِيْ يَدُعُّ الْيَتِيْمَ ۞

وَلَا يَحُضُّ عَلٰى طَعَامِ الْمِسْكِيْنِ ۞

فَوَيْلٌ لِّلْمُصَلِّيْنَ ۞

الَّذِيْنَ هُمْ عَنْ صَلَاتِهِمْ سَاهُوْنَ ۞

الَّذِيْنَ هُمْ يُرَآءُوْنَ ۞

وَيَمْنَعُوْنَ الْمَاعُوْنَ ۞

Knowest thou him who rejects the faith? That is the one who drives away the orphan and urges not the feeding of the poor. Woe unto those also who pray but are unmindful of their Prayer and pray only to be seen of people, and they hold back the least beneficence. (2—8)

631

Chapter 108

AL-KAUTHAR
(Revealed before Hijra)

In the name of Allah, Most Gracious, Ever Merciful. (1)

بِسْمِ اللهِ الرَّحْمٰنِ الرَّحِيْمِ ۝

اِنَّاۤ اَعْطَيْنٰكَ الْكَوْثَرَ ۝

فَصَلِّ لِرَبِّكَ وَانْحَرْ ۝

اِنَّ شَانِئَكَ هُوَ الْاَبْتَرُ ۝

Surely We have bestowed upon thee abundance of every kind of good. So pray to thy Lord in gratitude and offer Him sacrifice. Surely, it is thine enemy whose line will be cut off. (2—4)

Chapter 109

AL-KĀFIRŪN
(Revealed before Hijra)

In the name of Allah, Most Gracious, Ever Merciful. (1)

بِسْمِ اللهِ الرَّحْمٰنِ الرَّحِيْمِ ۝

قُلْ يٰۤاَيُّهَا الْكٰفِرُوْنَ ۝

لَاۤ اَعْبُدُ مَا تَعْبُدُوْنَ ۝

وَلَاۤ اَنْتُمْ عٰبِدُوْنَ مَاۤ اَعْبُدُ ۝

وَلَاۤ اَنَا عَابِدٌ مَّا عَبَدْتُّمْ ۝

وَلَاۤ اَنْتُمْ عٰبِدُوْنَ مَاۤ اَعْبُدُ ۝

لَكُمْ دِيْنُكُمْ وَلِيَ دِيْنِ ۝

Proclaim: Hearken ye who disbelieve! I do not worship as you worship, nor do you worship as I worship. I do not worship those that you worship, nor do you worship Him Whom I worship; that is because you follow one faith and I follow another faith. (2—7)

سُوْرَةُ النَّصْرِ مَدَنِيَّةٌ　

AL-NAṢR
(Revealed after Hijra)

In the name of Allah, Most Gracious, Ever Merciful. (1)

Now that Allah's succour has become manifest and victory has been achieved and thou hast seen people join the religion of Allah in large numbers, then glorify thy Lord, with His praise, and seek forgiveness of Him for their frailties. Surely He is oft-Returning with compassion. (2—4)

بِسْمِ اللهِ الرَّحْمٰنِ الرَّحِيْمِ ۝

اِذَا جَآءَ نَصْرُ اللهِ وَالْفَتْحُ ۝

وَرَاَيْتَ النَّاسَ يَدْخُلُوْنَ فِيْ دِيْنِ اللهِ اَفْوَاجًا ۝

فَسَبِّحْ بِحَمْدِ رَبِّكَ وَاسْتَغْفِرْهُ اِنَّهُ كَانَ تَوَّابًا ۝

　سُوْرَةُ اللَّهَبِ مَكِّيَّةٌ　

AL-LAHAB
(Revealed before Hijra)

In the name of Allah, Most Gracious, Ever Merciful. (1)

بِسْمِ اللهِ الرَّحْمٰنِ الرَّحِيْمِ ۝

تَبَّتْ يَدَا اَبِيْ لَهَبٍ وَّتَبَّ ۝

مَآ اَغْنٰى عَنْهُ مَالُهُ وَمَا كَسَبَ ۝

سَيَصْلٰى نَارًا ذَاتَ لَهَبٍ ۝

وَّامْرَاَتُهُ حَمَّالَةَ الْحَطَبِ ۝

فِيْ جِيْدِهَا حَبْلٌ مِّنْ مَّسَدٍ ۝

The two supporters of the master of flames shall perish and so shall he perish. His wealth and all his acquisitions shall avail him not. He shall enter a blazing fire, and also his wife, who carries the fuel. Round her neck will be a halter of coir. (2—6)

Chapter 112

سُوْرَةُ الْاِخْلَاصِ مَكِّيَّةٌ

AL-IKHLĀṢ
(Revealed before Hijra)

In the name of Allah, Most Gracious, Ever Merciful. (1)

بِسْمِ اللهِ الرَّحْمٰنِ الرَّحِيْمِ ۝

قُلْ هُوَ اللهُ اَحَدٌ ۝

اَللهُ الصَّمَدُ ۝

Proclaim: He is Allah, the Single; Allah, the Self-Existing and Besought of all. He begets not, nor is He begotten; and there is none equal to Him in His attributes. (2—5)

لَمْ يَلِدْ ۙ وَلَمْ يُوْلَدْ ۝

وَلَمْ يَكُنْ لَّهٗ كُفُوًا اَحَدٌ ۝

 سُوْرَةُ الْفَلَقِ مَدَنِيَّةٌ

Chapter 113

AL-FALAQ
(Revealed before Hijra)

In the name of Allah, Most Gracious, Ever Merciful. (1)

بِسْمِ اللهِ الرَّحْمٰنِ الرَّحِيْمِ ۝

قُلْ اَعُوْذُ بِرَبِّ الْفَلَقِ ۝

مِنْ شَرِّ مَا خَلَقَ ۝

Proclaim: I seek the protection of the Lord of the break of dawn, from the mischief of every created thing, from the mischief of the darkness when the moon is eclipsed, from the mischief of those who seek to promote discord, and from the mischief of every persistently envious person. (2—6)

وَمِنْ شَرِّ غَاسِقٍ اِذَا وَقَبَ ۝

وَمِنْ شَرِّ النَّفّٰثٰتِ فِی الْعُقَدِ ۝

وَمِنْ شَرِّ حَاسِدٍ اِذَا حَسَدَ ۝

 سُوْرَةُ النَّاسِ مَدَنِيَّةٌ

AL-NĀS
(Revealed before Hijra)

In the name of Allah, Most Gracious, Ever Merciful. (1)

بِسْمِ اللهِ الرَّحْمٰنِ الرَّحِيْمِ ۟

قُلْ اَعُوْذُ بِرَبِّ النَّاسِ ۟

مَلِكِ النَّاسِ ۟

اِلٰهِ النَّاسِ ۟

مِنْ شَرِّ الْوَسْوَاسِ ۙ الْخَنَّاسِ ۟

الَّذِىْ يُوَسْوِسُ فِىْ صُدُوْرِ النَّاسِ ۟

مِنَ الْجِنَّةِ وَ النَّاسِ ۟

Proclaim: I seek the protection of the Lord of mankind, the King of mankind, the God of mankind, against the mischief of every sneaking whisperer, who whispers into the minds of people, whether he be hidden from sight or be one of the common people. (2—7)

-- was instructed in elementary cultural values. 20: 119, 120.
— dwelt in garden. 2: 36.
— was commanded to emigrate. 2: 37, 39.
— was created out of clay. 3: 60.
— had two sons. 5: 28.

ADMINISTRATION OF PUBLIC AFFAIRS
Entrusting authority in the hands of those best fitted to discharge it. 4: 59.
Chosen representatives of people to consult them in —. 3: 160.
— by mutual consultation. 42: 39.
Obligatory to obey Allah and His messenger and those in authority. 4: 60.
Exercising authority over people equitably and with justice. 4: 59.
Safeguarding defence and security of state. 3: 201.

ADOPTION
Adopted sons not recognised. 33: 5.

ADORNMENT
— of oneself is allowed. 2: 13; 3: 1;5 7: 32.

ADULTERY
— is forbidden. 17: 33; 25: 69.
—, punishment of 24: 4.
Evidence required to prove charge of —. 24: 5.
Approaches to — barred. 24: 28—31, 32.
Punishment for loose behaviour short of —. 4: 16, 17.
Accusing wife of — and punishment for false accusation. 24: 7—11.
Accusing chaste women of —. 24: 5.
Adulterer marrying an adultress or idolatress. 24: 3.

AFFLICTIONS
Purpose behind —. 2: 156—158.

AGREEMENTS (See Covenants)

AL-A'RAF
People of — means the true believers. 7: 47.

ALLAH
Existence of —. 2: 22; 2: 29; 3: 3; 3: 19; 6: 74; 13: 3, 4; 22: 19; 87: 2—6.
Unity of —. 2: 164; 112: 2.

None is to be worshipped except —. 2: 117; 2: 164; 2: 256; 3: 3; 3: 19.
— is the Light of the heavens and the earth. 24: 36.
None is like unto —. 42: 12; 112: 5.
Human eyes cannot see —. 6: 104.
— manifests Himself through attributes. 6: 104.
— shows His servants way to reach Him. 29: 70.
Effort to meet — necessary. 84: 7.
All creation needs —. 112: 3.
— has detailed knowledge of everything. 2: 256; 10: 62.
-- closer to man than his jugular vein. 50: 17.
— alone knows the unknown. 27: 66.
— knows the overt and the hidden. 3: 30.
— has all power to fulfil His decrees. 2: 21.
— chooses Messengers to guide mankind. 22: 76.
— makes His Messengers prevail over opponents. 58: 22.
— sends angels to help the steadfast. 41: 31, 32.
— has no partners. 2: 117; 6: 164; 25: 3.
— is free from all defects. 2: 33.
— has no progeny. 2: 117; 4: 172; 6: 101; 18: 5, 6.
— didnot take any wife or son unto Himself. 6: 102; 72: 4.
— did not beget nor is begotten. 112: 4.
— has no associates. 9: 31.
— is Holy and Exalted and is far above attributes which idolators claim for their gods. 17: 44.
— not subject to slumber. 2: 256.
— not burdened by care of heavens or earth. 2: 256.
— not tired by creating heavens or earth. 50: 39.
— never forgets. 19: 65; 20: 53.
— does not wrong anyone. 3: 183; 10: 45.
— is the First, the Last, the Manifest and the Hidden. 57: 4.
— never enjoins foul deeds. 7: 29.
— is not fed. 6: 15; 51: 58.
— never destroys any township without warning. 17: 16; 26: 209; 28: 60.
All things submit to His will and are obedient to the laws made by — alone. 13: 16.
Laws of — never change. 13: 78; 35: 44.

— alone has knowledge of future and past. 20: 111.

One should not despair of the mercy of —. 6: 13, 55; 7: 157; 10: 59; 11: 120; 12: 88; 39: 54; 40: 8.

— alone has power to bestow life. 15: 24.

—'s Will prevails. 22: 15; 22: 19; 85: 17.

— has full power over His decree. 12: 22.

— takes into account every action howsoever small it may be. 31: 17.

Manifold reward for people spending in cause of —. 2: 262.

— helps believers. 30: 48.

Allah's throne rests on water. 11: 8.

Forgerer of lie against — never prospers. 10: 18.

— shall punish the mockery of unbelievers. 2: 16.

Man's nature bears witness to Existence of —. 7: 173, 174.

— is the Creator of heavens and earth. 2: 165; 14: 33, 34; 29: 62; 45: 5; 50: 7—12; 67: 4, 5.

— answers the prayers of supplicant. 2: 187.

The Will of — and His Messenger always prevails. 58: 22.

Consequences of rejecting —'s commandments. 3: 138.

— provides sustenance for all. 11: 7; 29: 61.

Meeting with — alone gives real peace of mind. 89: 28—30.

— has many attributes. 7: 181; 59: 23—25.

Perfect attributes belong to — alone. 7: 181; 59: 25.

(i) *ALLAH. ASSOCIATING PARTNERS WITH* (Shirk)
— is forbidden. 4: 49; 22: 32.
— is a grievous wrong. 31: 14.
No forgiveness for —. 4: 49; 4: 117.
One should not obey parents in —. 29: 9.
Discordance in universe if there were more gods than one. 21: 23; 23: 92.
People — are misguided. 39: 4.
— in Allah's person is Wrong. 12: 41; 112: 2, 3.
— in the attributes of Allah is disallowed, 112: 5.
Asking forgiveness for idolaters is forbidden. 9: 113.
People seeking help from others than Allah can never prosper. 23: 118.
Reasons against —. 27: 60—66.

People take other gods than Allah so that they may be a source of power for them. 19: 82.

Weakness of those who take other gods beside Allah. 21: 24, 25.

Arguments against —. 10: 69; 13: 34; 16: 53; 17: 43, 44.

False gods do not create anything but are themselves created. 16: 21.

False gods are dead. 16: 22.

Human nature rejects —. 16: 54.

(ii) *ALLAH, ATTRIBUTES OF*
Abaser of the haughty, (Al-Mudhill) 3: 27.
All-Aware, (Al-Khabir) 4: 36; 22: 64; 64: 9; 66: 4; 67: 15.
All-Hearing, (Al-Sami) 4: 59; 22: 62; 24: 61; 40: 21.
All-Knowing, (Al-Alim) 4: 36,71; 22: 60; 34: 27; 59: 23; 64: 12.
All-Seeing, (Al-Basir) 4: 59; 22: 76; 40: 21,57; 60: 4.
Answerer of prayers, (Al-Mujib) 11: 62.
Appreciating, the Most (Al-Shakur) 35: 35.
Attributes, One of Exalted (Rafee-ud-daraja't) 40: 16.
Awarder of appropriate punishment; Avenger. (Al-Muntaqim) 3: 4; 39: 38.

Beneficent, (Al-Barr) 52: 29.
Besought of all; the Independent; (Al-Samad) 112: 3.
Bestower, The Great (Al-Wahhab) 3: 9; 38: 36.
Bestower of Favours, (Al-Mun'im) 1: 7.
Bestower of Honour, (Al-Muizz) 3: 27.
Bestower of Security, (Al-Mu'min) 59: 24.
Bounty, The Possessor of 40: 4.
Bountiful; All-Embracing; (Al-Wasi) 4: 131; 24: 33.

Compassionate, (Al-Ra'uf) 3: 31; 24: 21.
Creator, (Al-Khaliq) 36: 82; 59: 25.
Creators, The Best of (Ahsan-ul-Khaleqeen) 23: 15.

Destroyer; The (Al-Mumit) 40: 69; 50: 44; 57: 3.
Director to the right way, (Al-Rashid) 72: 3.
Disposer of Affairs; The Keeper. (Al-Wakil) 3: 174; 4: 82; 11: 13; 17: 3; 33: 4.

639

Effacer of Sins, (Al-'Afuww) 4: 150; 22: 61; 58: 3.
Enlarger of the means of subsistence; (Al-Basit) 17: 31; 30: 38; 42: 13.
Equitable, (Al-Muqsit) 60: 9.
Exalted, (Al-Mutakabbir) 59: 24.
Exalter, (Al-Rafi) 40: 16.

Fashioner, (Al-Musawwir) 59: 25.
First, (Al-Awwal) 57: 4.
Forbearing, (Al-Halim) 2: 226; 22: 60; 33: 52; 64: 18.
Forgiver; The Great (Al-Ghaffar) 22: 61; 38: 67; 64: 15.
Forgiver of Sin, (Ghafer-izambe) 40: 4.
Forgiving; Liberal in (Wasse-ul-Magh-ferate) 53: 33.
Forgiving; The Most (Al-Ghafur) 4: 25, 44, 57; 22: 61; 58: 3, 60: 13; 64: 15.
Friend; (Al-Waliyy) 4: 46; 12: 102; 42: 10, 29.

Gatherer; Assembler of mankind on the Day of Judgement; (Al-Jami') 3: 10; 34: 27.
Generous; The Most (Al-Akra'm) 96: 4.
Glorious; (Al-Majid) 85: 16.
Gracious; (Al-Rahman) 1: 3.
Great; (Al-Azim) 42: 5; 56: 97.
Great; Incomparably (Al-Kabir) 4: 35; 22: 63; 31: 31; 34: 24.
Guardian; (Al-Hafiz) 34: 22.
Guardian; (Al-Vakil) 4: 172.
Guide; (Al-Hadi) 22: 55.

Healer; (Al-Shafi) 17: 83; 41: 45.
Helper; (Al-Naseer) 4: 46.
Hidden; One through whom hidden reality of everything is revealed; (al-Batin) 57: 4.
High; (Al-Aliyy) 4: 35; 22: 63; 31: 31; 42: 5; 43: 52.
High; The Most (Al-Muta'ali) 13: 10; 42: 5; 87: 2; 92: 21.
Holy One; (Al:Quddus) 59: 24.

Incomprehensible; The knower of all subtleties; The Benignant; (Al-Latif) 6: 104; 12: 101; 22: 64; 31: 17; 42: 20.
Indulgent; The Most (Al-Afuww) 4: 44.
Inheritor; (Al-Warith) 15: 24; 21: 90; 28: 59.

Judge; (Al-Fattah) 34: 27.
Judges; The Best of (Khair-ul-Ha'-kemeen) 10: 110; 95: 9.

Judge; The Wise. 35: 3.

King of Mankind; (Malik-inna's) 114: 3.
Knower of the unseen and the seen; 59: 23.

Last; (Al-Akhir) 57: 4.
Life-giver; (Al-Muhyi) 21: 51; 40: 69.
Light; (Al-Nur) 24: 36.
Living; (Al-Hayy) 2: 256; 3: 3.
Lord; (Al-Rabb) 1: 2; 5: 28.
Lord of Great Ascents; (Dhil Mua'rij) 70: 4.
Lord of Honour; (Al-Majid) 85: 16.
Lord of Majesty; (Al-Jalil) 55: 28.
Lord of Retribution; (dhu-Intiquam) 39: 38.
Lord of Sovereignty; (Malik-al-Mulk) 62: 2.
Lord of the Throne; (dhul Arsh) 21: 21; 40: 16; 85: 16.
Loving; (Al-Wadud) 11: 91; 85: 15.

Maker; (Al-Bari) 59: 25.
Manifest Truth; (Haqq-ul-Mobeen) 24: 26.
Manifest; He to whose existence every created thing clearly points. (Al-Zahir) 57: 4.
Master of the Day of Judgement; (M'alike Yaum-ud-Din) 1: 4.
Master; The Excellent (Namul-Mau-la') 22: 79.
Merciful; (Al-Rahim) 1: 3; 4: 24, 57; 97.
Mighty; (Al-Aziz) 4: 57; 22: 75; 59: 24; 64: 19.

Nigh; The Nearest One; (Al-Qureeb) 34: 51.
Noble; (Al-Karim) 27: 41.

Oft-returning with Compassion; The Acceptor of Repentance; (Al Tuwwab) 2: 55; 4: 65; 24: 11; 49: 13; 110: 4.
Omnipotent; (Al-Muqtadir) 54: 43, 56.
One; The (Al-Wahid) 13: 17; 38: 66; 39: 5.
Opener of doors of success for mankind; (Al-Fattah) 34: 27.
Originator; The Author of Life; (Al-Badi) 2: 118; 30: 28; 85: 14.

Peace; The Source of (Al-Salam) 59: 24.
Possessor of Power and Authority; (Al-Qadir) 16: 71; 30: 55; 64: 2.

Powerful; (Al-Qawiyy) 22: 75; 33: 26; 40: 23; 51: 59.

Praiseworthy; (Al-Hamid) 22: 65; 31: 27; 41: 43; 42: 29; 60: 7.

Preserver; He who preserves the faculties of all living things; The powerful; (Al-Muqit) 4: 86.

Protector; (Al-Muhaimin) 59: 24.

Provider; Best (Khairul-Ra'zequin) 22: 59; 34: 40; 62: 12.

Punishment; Severe in (Shadeed-il-Iquab) 40: 4.

Reckoner; (Al-Hasib) 4: 7, 87.

Reckoning; Swift at (Saree-ul-Hisab) 13: 42.

Repeater; Reproducer of life; (Al-Mu'id) 30: 28; 85: 14.

Repentance; Acceptor of (Qabil-e-Taub) 40: 4.

Requite; Possessor of the Power to (Dhun-teqa'm) 3: 5.

Ruler; (Al-Wali) 42: 5.

Self-subsisting and All-sustaining; (Al-Quyyum) 40: 4.

Self-sufficient; (Al-Ghaniyy) 2: 268; 22: 65; 27: 41; 31: 27; 60: 7; 64: 7.

Sovereign; (Al-Malik) 59: 29.

Strong; (Al-Matin) 51: 59.

Subduer or Reformer; (Al-Jabbar) 59: 24.

Sufficient (Al-Kafi) 39: 37.

Supreme; The Most (Al-Qahhar) 12: 40; 38: 66; 39: 5.

Sustainer; The Great (Al-Razzaq) 22: 59; 51: 59; 62: 12.

Swift to take Account; (Sari-ul-Hisab) 3: 200.

True; The (Al-Haqq) 10: 33.

Unique; The Lord of Unity; (Al-Ahad) 112: 2.

Watchful; (Al-Raqib) 33: 53.

Wise; The (Al-Hakim) 4: 57; 59: 25; 64: 19.

Witness; The Observer; (Al-Shahid) 4: 80; 33: 56; 34: 48.

(iii) *ALLAH, FAVOURS OF*
— are countless. 14: 35; 16: 19.
Allah is gracious to mankind. 27: 74.

(iv) *ALLAH, FRIENDSHIP WITH*
— is for those who are mindful of their duty. 45: 20.
— is for those who believe. 2: 258.
— is sufficient. 4: 46.
Allah is the guardian friend. 42: 10.

(v) *ALLAH, GLORIFICATION OF WITH HIS PRAISE*
Everything glorifies Allah. 17: 45; 24: 42; 59: 2; 62: 2.
Allah enjoins all to glorify Him with His praise. 33: 43; 40: 56; 87: 2.
Glorify Allah before sunrise and at sunset and at night. 50: 40, 41.
Glorify Allah at the setting of the stars. 52: 50.
Glorify Allah during the greater part of the night. 76: 27.
Angels glorify Allah. 2: 31; 40: 8.
Thunder glorifies Allah with His praise. 13: 14.
Birds (i.e. spiritually exalted people) and the mountains (i.e. the chiefs) glorify Allah. 38: 19, 20.
Mountains and birds (i.e. righteous people) celebrated Allah's praise with David. 21: 80; 34: 11.

(vi) *ALLAH, KNOWLEDGE OF*
— extends over heavens and earth. 2: 256.
— of what troubles the mind of man. 50: 17.
— about the Hour and all that is in the wombs. 41: 48.
— concerning the secret and hidden. 20: 8.
— of secret thoughts and open words. 6: 4.
— of every falling leaf. 6: 60.
— of secret counsels. 58: 8.

(vii) *ALLAH, LOVE OF*
— for those who trust in Him. 3: 160.
— gains one His blessings. 27: 9.
— secured by turning to Him. 2: 223
— for the steadfast. 3: 147.
— those who fulfil their duty. 3: 77; 9: 4, 7.
— for those who judge equitably. 5: 43.
— for those who do good to others. 2: 196; 3: 135, 149.
— can be won by all who strive for it. 29: 70.

(viii) *ALLAH, MEETING WITH*
Those who do not believe in — are arrogant. 16: 23; 25: 22.
In — wordly desires fall off. 26: 46—52.

(ix) *ALLAH, MERCY OF*
Sinners can obtain —. 39: 54.
— embraces every thing. 6: 148; 7: 157; 40: 8.

— is boundless. 10: 59; 39: 54; 40: 8.
Allah has charged Himself with
mercy. 6: 13, 55.
ne should despair of —. 12: 88;
39: 54.
Man has been created to be recipient
of —. 11: 120.
— is for him who sues for forgiveness.
4: 111.

(x) ALLAH, REMEMBRANCE OF
Peace of mind is attained through —.
13: 29.
Increase of courage and faith through
—. 8: 46.
Prosperity is attained through —.
62: 11.

(xi) ALLAH'S REVEALING HIMSELF TO MAN
Allah reveals Himself through His
chosen servants. 4: 164—166.
Allah has revealed Himself through
Messengers to every nation. 10: 48.
Allah has sent Warners to all people.
35: 25.
Allah reveals Himself in various
forms. 42: 52, 53.
Disbelievers are also shown significant
true dreams. 12: 37, 44.

(xii) ALLAH, SEEKING FORGIVENESS OF
— is a means of attaining prosperity
and strength. 11: 53; 71: 11—13.
By — one absorbs His mercy. 4: 65.
By — one protects oneself from His
punishment. 8: 34.

(xiii) ALLAH, SIGNS OF
— means His commandments. 2: 243.
Believers are commanded to keep
away from those who mock at —.
4: 141.

(xiv) ALLAH, SPENDING IN THE CAUSE OF
— is obligatory. 2: 196; 57: 8, 11;
64: 17.
Warning against holding back from
—. 2: 196; 47: 39.
— should be of the best. 2: 268;
3: 93.
Benefit of —. 64: 17, 18.
— after victory does not equal —
before it. 57: 11.
— should not be followed by reproaches. 2: 263, 265.
Allah multiplies His favours unto
those who are —. 2: 246, 262.

How much should one be —. 2: 220.
On whom should one spend for
Allah's cause. 2: 216.
— openly as well as secretly. 2: 275.
Those who are — shall prosper.
2: 4—6.
Glad tidings for those who are —.
22: 35, 36.
Recompense of those who are —.
2: 273.

ANGELS
— bear witness to the unity of Allah.
3: 19.
The righteous believe in —. 2: 178.
Disbelieving in — is straying away
from right path. 4: 137.
— do as they are commanded by
Allah. 66: 7.
— have no sex. 37: 151.
Coming of —. 6: 112, 159; 16: 34;
25: 22, 23.
— and spirits descend by command
of Allah. 97: 5.
— have only that much knowledge
as they are given. 2: 33.
— differ in their capacities and
strength. 35: 2.
— bear the throne (i.e. the attributes
of the Lord). 69: 18.
Guardian —. 13: 12.
Recording —. 82: 11—13.

ANGELS, DUTIES OF
i. Convey the word of Allah. 22: 76.
ii. Take charge of souls. 32: 12.
iii. Bring punishment on enemies of
prophets. 6: 159; 96: 19.
iv. Help believers and give them glad
tidings. 41: 31—33.
v. Create awe and fear in the minds
of enemies of Prophets. 3: 125.
vi. Bear witness to unity of Allah.
3: 19.
vii. Vouchsafe the truth of Prophets.
4: 167.
viii. Glorify Allah with His praise.
39: 76.
ix. Ask forgiveness for those who
believe. 40: 8; 42: 6.
x. Pray for blessings to be sent on
believers and on the Holy Prophet. 33: 44, 57.
xi. Keep peoples' records. 82: 11—13.
xii. Make believers firm. 8: 13.

ANSARS (THE HELPERS)
Allah is pleased with —. 9: 100.
Allah has turned with mercy to —.
9: 117.

APOSTATE

No damage is caused to Allah's religion by anyone becoming an —. 3: 145.

Promise of guiding large numbers of people in place of person who becomes an —. 5: 55.

No secular penalty for an —. 2: 218; 3: 87—91; 3: 145; 4: 138; 5: 55; 16: 107.

ARABS, THE

— before the Holy Prophet's advent made human sacrifices to idols. 6: 138.

— regarded the birth of a daughter as a misfortune. 16: 59, 60; 43: 18.

— buried their daughters alive. 16: 60.

— denied beneficence of Allah. 21: 37.

ARK, THE

Noah was commanded to make —. 11: 38; 23: 28.

Moses was placed in — by his mother and was put in the river. 20: 40.

— restored to Beni Israel. 2: 249.

ATONEMENT

— rejected. 6: 165.

BADR, THE BATTLE OF

Prophecies concerning — in the Holy Quran. 30: 5; 54: 45—49.

Enemy's demand of judgment at —. 8: 20.

Sign in —. 3: 14.

Divine help in —. 3: 124; 8: 10; 8: 18.

Muslims strengthened in —. 8: 12.

Position of the parties in —. 8: 43.

Unbelievers marched in exultation to —. 8: 48, 49.

Unbelievers smitten in —. 8: 51, 52.

Prisoners of war taken in —. 8: 71.

BAIAT (INITIATION)

— of the Prophet is the — of Allah. 48: 11.

Prophet took the — of his companions at Hudaibiyya. 48: 19.

Prophet was commanded to accept the — of women. 60: 13.

The words of the —. 60: 13.

BAIT-UL-HARAM (KA'BA)

— First House established for mankind. 3: 97.

— is made a resort for mankind. 2: 126.

— is the place of Abraham and Pilgrimage to the House is a duty. 3: 98.

— is made a place of security. 2: 126; 3: 98.

— is called Ka'ba. 5: 98.

— is also called Masjid-ul-Haram. 17: 2.

Prophecy of — remaining secure from attack. 52: 5, 6.

BANQUET (MA'IDA)

Jesus' prayer for — for his people. 5: 115.

BAPTISM, THE DIVINE

Invitation to adopt the religion of Allah. 2: 139.

BARZAKH

After death there is a barrier against returning to this world. 23: 101.

BATTLE

— of Ahzab. 33: 11—26.

— of Badr. (See under BADR.)

— of Hunain. 9: 25.

— of Khaiber. 33: 28.

— of Tabuk. 48: 12.

— of Uhd. 3: 122, 123, 128, 153—156.

BEGGING

— is discountenanced. 2: 274; 4: 33.

BELIEF (IMA'N)

— explained. 49: 15, 16.

— alone is not enough. 3: 180; 29: 3, 4.

Difference between — and satisfaction of mind. 2: 261.

Commandment of believing in Allah and the Messenger. 3: 180; 4: 171; 7: 159; 57: 8; 64: 9.

— in all Prophets and their Books. 2: 137; 29: 47.

Reward of — and sacrifice of wealth and person for the cause of Allah. 61: 11—13; 64: 10.

— in life Hereafter. 2: 5.

— goes with good deeds. 2: 26; 18: 89; 41: 9; 95: 7.

Seeing Signs of Allah strengthens faith. 9: 124; 33: 22, 23; 47: 18.

— at the approach of punishment is not acceptable. 10: 52, 53, 91—93; 40: 86.

BELIEVERS, THE TRUE

Qualities of —. 2: 4—6, 166, 286; 8: 3—5, 75, 76; 9: 124; 24: 52, 53

63; 31: 5, 6; 32: 16, 17; 42: 24; 58: 23.
— firmly stand on sure knowledge. 12: 109.
Allah is the friend of —. 2: 258; 3: 69; 8: 20; 47: 12.
Allah takes it upon Himself to help —. 22: 39; 30: 48.
High ranks for —. 9: 20; 20: 76; 58: 12.
— will receive great bounties from Allah. 33: 48.
Allah guides — out of darkness into the light. 2: 258.
— are free from fear or grief. 5: 70; 6: 49.
Allah adds to the guidance of —. 47: 18.
Seeking pleasure of Allah is the main objective of —. 9: 72.
Successful believers. 23: 2—12.
Good actions of — will not be disregarded. 21: 95.
— are promised delightful abodes and Gardens of Eternity. 9: 72.
— are honoured. 30: 16.
— will have forgiveness and honourable provision. 8: 5, 75.
Honourable reward prepared for —. 33: 45.
Great reward promised for —. 4: 147; 17: 10.
Unending reward for —. 41: 9; 84: 26; 95: 7.
— hasten to do good works and are foremost in them. 23: 62.

BIBLE, *The*
Perversion of —. 2: 80; 5: 14, 16.

BOOKS
Prophecy of the spread of —. 81: 11.

BOOKS, THE MOTHER OF THE (UMM-UL-KITAB)
Holy Quran is —. 3: 8; 13: 40; 43: 5.
— is the exalted Book full of wisdom. 43: 5.

BOOK, THE PEOPLE OF THE (AHL-E-KITAB)
— could not be reformed without the advent of the Holy Prophet. 97: 2—4.
— refers to Jews and Christians. 4: 154, 172.
— called to Unity of Allah. 3: 65.
— will continue to believe in Jesus' death on the cross. 4: 160.

BROTHERHOOD
— of man is ordained by Islam. 3: 104; 49: 11, 14.

BURDEN
Bearing one's own —. 29: 13, 14; 35: 19.

CAIN
— son of Adam. 5: 28—32.

CALF, THE GOLDEN
Worship of —. 2: 52; 7: 149; 20: 91.

CAMELS
Prophecy relating to — given up as means of transportation. 81: 5.

CATTLE
— created for the benefit of man. 6: 143—145; 16: 6, 67, 81; 23: 22; 39: 7; 40: 80, 81.

CHARITY
Reward of —. 2: 262, 266.
— rendered worthless by reproach or injury. 2: 263—265.
Kind word and forgiveness is better than — followed by reproach or injury. 2: 264.
Good things alone to be given in —. 2: 268.
Secret — better than open —. 2: 272.
Allah rewards those who give in —. 2: 275.

CHILDREN
— should not cause diversion from remembrance of Allah. 63: 10.
Destroying — or not giving them education or not bringing them up properly, for fear of poverty forbidden. 6: 152; 17: 32.
Prayer for pure offspring. 3: 39.
Prayer for righteousness among offspring. 25: 75; 46: 16.
Birth of daughter no cause for grief. 16: 59, 60.
Supervision of — in religious matters. 19: 56; 20: 133.
Good treatment of parents by —. 46: 16, 18.
— to treat their parents kindly. 17: 24, 25.

CHRISTIANITY
— has exceeded limits in deifying a mortal. 4: 172.
Wrong doctrine of the Sonship of God. 9: 30, 31.
Doctrine of Trinity is unacceptable. 5: 74, 75.

Doctrine of Vicarious Atonement is wrong. 6: 165; 53: 39.
Prophecy of the rise of —. 18: 19.
Prophecy of fall of — after its second success. 18: 33—45; 20: 103—105.
Period of the rise of — is ten centuries. 20: 104.
Wealth of Christians is a trial for them. 20: 132.
Western philosophy and its refutation. 82: 7—13.

CLOUDS, THE
Allah raises —. 13: 13.
Provision of water on earth by —. 15: 23.
Allah sends — wherever He pleases. 24: 44.
Rain, hailstones and irrigation of vast areas. 24: 44; 30: 49—51.
Rain from — proof of Allah's existence and unity. 2: 165.

COMMUNITY, THE SPIRITUAL
Persons included in the blessed group. 4: 70, 71.

CONJUGAL RELATIONSHIP
Object of —. 30: 22.

CONTRACTS
— should be reduced to writing. 2: 283.
Two witnesses for —. 2: 283.

CONTROVERSY
The proper method of —. 16: 126; 29: 47.

CORAH (QUAROON)
— was from amongst Beni Israel. 28: 77.
—'s arrogance towards Beni Israel. 28: 77.
— was the keeper of the treasury. 28: 77.
—'s arrogance and his punishment. 28: 79, 82.

COUNSEL
— is necessary in all important administrative matters. 3:160; 42: 39.

COVENANTS
Fulfilment of —. 5: 2; 6: 92, 93.
Repudiation of —. 8: 59.

CREATION, SPIRITUAL
— like that of the body is gradual. 22: 6, 7.

For each stage of physical creation there is a stage of —. 23: 13—18.

CREATION OF MAN
Man was not created without purpose. 23: 116; 75: 37.
Stages in the —. 22:6; 23: 13—15; 35: 12; 39: 7; 40: 68; 86: 6—8.
Man created in the best of moulds. 95: 5.
Purpose of the —. 51: 57.
Man created of one species. 4: 2; 16: 73; 30: 22.

CREATION OF UNIVERSE
— was not without purpose. 21: 17, 18.
— was in accordance with requirements of wisdom. 15: 86; 39: 6; 46: 4.
Everything in universe is coordinated and adjusted, and there is no disorder, discord, or incongruity. 67: 2—5.
Universe subjected to man. 14:33—35; 16:11—15; 45:13,14.

DACOITS AND ROBBERS
Punishment of —. 5: 34.

DAVID (PROPHET DA'UD)
— fights people of Palestine. 2: 252.
— defeats his enemies and establishes his kingdom. 2: 252.
Allah strengthens —'s kingdom. 38: 21.
— was made vicegerent on earth. 38: 27.
Allah honoured — with great knowledge. 27: 16.
Allah bestowed His grace upon —. 34: 11.
— was taught skill of making coats of mail. 21: 81.
—'s manufacture of coats of mail. 34: 11, 12.
Subjection of (the dwellers of) Mountains and the Birds (righteous people) to celebrate Allah's praises with —. 21: 80; 34: 11; 38: 19, 20.
Unsuccessful attempts of —'s enemies to attack him. 38: 22.
— and the simile of the ewes. 38: 24.
— seeking forgiveness of his Lord. 38: 25.
Supplications of — for forgiveness were not due to the commision of any sin. 38: 26.
— and Solomon decide case of the crop. 21: 79, 80.

Book of — was not a law-giving
Book. 17: 56.

DAY
One — equal to 1,000 years. 22: 48;
32: 6.
One — equal to fifty thousand years.
70: 5.

DEAD PEOPLE
— never return to this world. 2: 29;
21: 96; 23: 100, 101; 39: 59, 60.
Spiritually — could be raised in this
world. 8: 25, 43.

DEATH
— meaning departing this life. 19: 24.
— meaning pain and torment. 14: 18.
— meaning sleep. 39: 43.
No one dies except by Allah's command. 3: 146.
Each person must taste —. 3: 186;
21: 36; 29: 58.
No everlasting life in this world. 21:
35, 36.
No return to this world possible
after —. 21: 96; 23: 100, 101;
39: 43.
Two lives (i.e. worldly life and life
after death) and two —s (i.e. state
before birth and death after life).
40: 12.
— also means low spiritual state.
2: 57.
— and life refer to the rise and fall
of peoples and nations. 29: 21.
Raising dead to life. 6: 123; 75: 38—
41.
The spiritually dead. 6: 37.

DEATH, LIFE AFTER
Promise of a second life after death.
2: 29; 53: 48.
Need for the life Hereafter. 10: 5.
— is permanent life. 29: 65; 40: 40.
— is better than life in this world.
4: 78; 12: 110; 17:-22.
Mercy for believers in — and punishment for non-believers. 58: 21.
Only the believers will gain from —.
17: 72, 73.
Every action will be taken into
account in the world Hereafter.
18: 50; 20: 16.
Believers will be rewarded in the —.
2: 26.
Those who strive for gains in the —
will be favoured by Allah. 17: 20.
Believers will see Allah in —. 75: 24.
Punishment in — will be greater.
39: 27.

Grievous punishment for disbelievers in —. 17: 11.
Disbelievers have no firm ground to
stand on concerning the second
life. 6: 30, 31; 16: 39; 17: 50—52;
36: 79—82.

DEEDS
Holy Prophet had the excellent
morals. 68: 5.
Holy Prophet was the excellent
exemplar. 33: 22.
Evil — are the result of disbelief in
the life Hereafter. 27: 5, 6.
Weighing of good and evil —. 7: 9, 10.

DEEDS, GOOD
— will be rewarded tenfold. 6: 161.
— endure. 18: 47.
Basic principles of —. 2: 208; 4: 75;
5: 17; 6: 163; 60: 2; 92: 19—22.
Covenants; fulfilment of 2: 178; 5: 2;
16: 92; 17: 35; 23: 9; 70: 33.
Chastity; 17: 33; 23: 6—8; 24: 31, 34,
61; 25: 69; 33: 36; 70: 30—32.
Cleanliness; 2: 223; 4: 44; 5: 7; 22:
30; 74: 5, 6.
Controlling anger; 3: 135.
Cooperation; 5: 3.
Courage; 2: 178; 3: 173—175; 9: 40;
20: 73, 74; 33: 40; 46: 14.
Employees; good treatment of 4: 37.
Enjoining good and forbidding evil;
3: 111.
Evidence; giving of true 4: 136; 5: 9;
25: 73.
Excelling in doing good; 2: 149.
Feeding the hungry; 76: 9; 90: 15—17.
Forgiveness; 2: 110; 3: 135, 160; 4:
150; 5: 14; 7: 200; 12: 93; 24: 23;
41: 35; 42: 38—41.
Good; doing of 2: 196; 3: 135; 5: 94;
7: 57.
Gratefulness; 2: 153, 173, 186, 244;
3: 145; 5: 7, 90; 14: 8; 39: 8, 67;
46: 16.
Humility; 6: 64; 7: 14, 56, 147; 16:
24, 30; 17: 38; 28: 84; 31: 19, 20;
40: 36.
Justice; 5: 9; 6: 153; 16: 91; 49: 10.
Looks; casting down of 24: 31, 32.
Neighbours; good treatment of 4: 37.
Parents; good treatment of 4: 37; 17:
24, 25.
Patience; 2: 46, 154, 156, 178; 11: 12;
13: 23; 16: 127, 128; 28: 81; 29:
61; 39: 11; 42: 44; 103: 4.
Peace-making between people; 4: 115;
49: 10.
Perseverance; 13: 23; 41: 31—33.

People of — afflicted with plagues. 7: 134—136.

ELEPHANTS, THE PEOPLE OF THE
— were the hordes of Abraha, the Abyssinian Governor of Yamen, who had come to invade Mecca. 105: 2.

ELIAS
— was one of the Messengers. 37: 124.
— warned his people against the worship of idols. 37: 126.
People treated — as liar. 37: 127.
Generations which followed him revered him. 37: 130.

ELISHA
— was of the best. 38: 49.

ENOCH (PROPHET IDRIS)
— was steadfast. 21: 86.
— was truthful man and a Prophet. 19: 57.
— was exalted to a lofty station. 19: 58.

EQUALITY
All believers are brothers. 3: 104; 49: 11.
Mankind are equal. 49: 14.

EVIDENCE
Calling of witnesses and putting everything in writing in their presence while borrowing or contracting and entering into agreements. 2: 283.
Two female witnesses in lieu of one male witness so that one may refresh the memory of the other. 2: 283.
Witnesses to a will. 5: 107—109.
Witnesses of eyes, ears and skins. 41: 21—24.
-- when doubtful can be rebutted. 5: 107.

EVIL
Human beings are created pure and have option of following good or —. 76: 3, 40; 90: 9—11; 91: 8, 9.
Prohibition of overt and secret —. 6: 121, 152; 7: 34.
Punishment of — should be proportionate thereto. 6: 161; 10: 28; 28: 85; 40: 41.
Persistence of non-believers in — courses. 7: 29.

Man's conscience reprimands him on — actions. 7: 23; 75: 3.
Excessive — leads to hell. 2: 82.
Good overcomes —. 11: 115.
— forgiven through repentance. 3: 136, 137; 4: 111; 16: 120; 42: 26.
Hatred of — is innate in man. 40: 11; 49: 9; 91: 8, 9.
Following in the footsteps of the Holy Prophet guards from —. 3: 32.
Prayer guards from —. 29: 46.
— is to be accounted for when it is deliberate. 2: 226; 5: 90; 20: 116.

EVOLUTION
Allah has created man in different forms and in different conditios. 71: 15, 18.

EZECHIEL (DHUL-KIFL)
Nebuchadnazar's destruction of Jerusalem and —'s seeing in a vision the town and its inhabitants over a hundred years' time. 2: 260.

EZRA
Jews taking — as the Son of God. 9: 30.

FAITH, THE LIGHT OF
Allah brings the believers out of every kind of darkness into light. 2: 258; 57: 13.

FASTING (See under WORSHIP)

FIG
— refers to Adam and to the fact that human mind has been created in the image of Allah. 95: 2.

FIRE
— meaning war. 5: 65.
Moses sees — in a vision on his return from Midian. 20: 11; 27: 8; 28: 30.
Simile of — in wet wood. 36: 81; 56: 72—74.
Smokeless — in the latter days. 55: 36.

FLAMES, LUMINOUS
— pursue those who listen stealthily. 15: 19; 37: 11; 72: 10.

FOOD
Guidance for —. 5: 5.
Eating — that is good in addition to being lawful —. 2: 169; 16: 115.
— affects conduct. 23: 52.

648

All good — is lawful for believers. 5: 94.

Earth and the problem of — supply. 2: 262; 41: 11.

FOOD, FORBIDDEN
That which dies of itself is —. 2: 174; 5: 4.

Blood is —. 2: 174; 5: 4; 16: 116.

Flesh of swine is —. 2: 174; 5: 4; 6: 146; 16: 116.

That on which the name of any other than Allah has been invoked. 2: 174; 5: 4; 6: 146; 16: 116.

Flesh of animal which has been strangled or beaten to death, or killed by a fall or gored to death is —. 5: 4.

Flesh of animal which a wild animal has killed except which has been properly slaughtered is —. 5: 4.

Flesh of an animal which has been slaughtered at an altar is —. 5: 4.

Eating that on which the name of Allah has not been pronounced is —. 6: 122.

FORGIVENESS
Reward of — of an injury is with Allah. 42: 41.

FORNICATION
— is forbidden. 17: 33; 25: 69.

Punishment for —. 24: 3.

GABRIEL
Disbelieving in —. 2: 98, 99.

GAMBLING (See under DEEDS, EVIL)

GOG AND MAGOG
Gog Easterns and Magog Westerns. 18: 95, 100.

War between —. 18: 100.

— will spread over the whole world. 21: 97.

Believers will not taste the punishment of —. 21: 101—103.

Islam will rise again after the eruption of —. 21: 98.

GOLIATH (JALUT)
Defeat of —. 2: 250, 251.

GOSPEL
Revelation of —. 3: 4; 5: 47, 48.

Description of the followers of the Holy Prophet in the —. 48: 30.

GRAVE
Spiritual — in addition to the ordinary —. 80: 22.

Prophecy of old —s being opened up in latter days. 82: 5.

Being raised from the — meaning being spiritually lifted. 100: 10.

GROVE, DWELLERS OF THE
Allah's punishment fell on — because they rejected His Messengers. 50: 15.

GUARDIANSHIP
Guardian acting for ward. 2: 283.

Guardian in cases of minor or of persons of weak understanding. 4: 6, 7.

GUIDANCE
— for proper function after Allah had given everything its form. 20: 51.

Allah guides whomsoever He pleases towards right path. 24: 47; 28: 57.

Allah adds to — of those who follow —. 47: 18.

Without Allah's help no one can have —. 7: 44.

For — faith and righteous conduct are needed. 10: 10.

— does not help those who turn away. 27: 81, 82.

Prayer for perfect —. 1: 6.

— is promised to those who submit completely. 3: 21.

Following — is the way to prosperity. 2: 6.

HA'RUT AND MA'RUT
Wise men of Babylon were —. 2: 103.

HAJJ (See under WORSHIP)

HAMAN
— was the commander of Pharaoh's army. 28: 9.

— was Pharaoh's Minister of Public works. 28: 39; 40: 37.

HEART
Veil on —. 18: 58.

Blindness of —. 22: 47.

Sealing up of —. 30: 60; 40: 36; 42: 25; 63: 4.

HEAVEN (SKY)
— created with purpose. 16: 4.

— built with Allah's hands. 51: 48.

Early state of — a gaseous form. 41: 12.

—s and earth were a solid mass which was split asunder. 21: 31.

Seven —s created in two different periods or stages. 41: 13.

— and earth created in six different periods. 10: 4.
— is a roof. 2: 23.
— is a roof wellguarded and affording protection. 21: 33.
Planets move round their orbits in —. 36: 41.
Paths of stars in —. 51: 8.
— is without a support. 31: 11.
Relation of food with —. 10: 32.
—s rolled up in Allah's right hand i.e. exercising full control over them. 39: 68.
— opening up and becoming all doors (i.e. several signs appearing and believers being favoured with His blessings and punishment descending on non-believers. 78: 20.
-- being laid bare (i.e. sciences of astronomy and space making progress). 81: 12.
— being rent asunder. 77: 10; 82: 2.
— becoming like molten copper (i.e. because of intense heat). 70: 9.
— adorned with planets. 37: 7; 41: 13; 67: 6.
Pieces of — falling down as punishment by way of rain and storm. 17: 93; 26: 188; 34: 10.
All things are sent down from —. 15: 22; 40: 14.

HELL
— worst abode and a wretched place of rest. 13: 19.
— Hereafter in addition to the — in this world. 18: 101; 19: 72; 29: 55.
— helps towards spiritual rebirth. 101: 9—12.
— not everlasting. 11: 108.
Foods of —. 88: 7, 8.
Freezing cold water and boiling hot water drinks for inmates of —. 78: 26, 27.
Dwellers of — in this world moving between it and boiling water (i.e. facing trouble on all sides). 55: 45.
Zaqqum food of inmates of —. 56: 53.
— results from spiritual blindness. 17: 73.
— is a state of being amidst death but not dying. 14: 18.
Being debarred from Allah is —. 83: 16, 17.
Fire of — rises within the heart. 104: 7, 8.
— is hidden from eyes. 26: 92.
— lies in ambush for the rebellious. 78: 22—31.

Manifestation of — in this life. 79: 37.
Nineteen angels guard the fire of —. 74: 31, 32.
Roar of — fire, (i.e. excessive heat). 25: 13; 67: 8.
Seven gates of — and passage of allotted number of non-believers through each of them. 15: 45.
Stones fuel of — fire. 2: 25; 66: 7.
Every stubborn rebellious one will enter into — fire. 19: 70—72.
Righteous people shall not hear a whisper of —. 21: 102, 103.
— fire being caused to blaze up; (i.e. in latter days sin will spread so much that — fire will be near the sinners). 81: 13.

HOLY LAND, THE
— i.e. Palestine. 5: 22.
Bani Israel disobeyed Moses and so were turned away from —. 5: 27.
Jews to be gathered together in — in the latter days. 17: 105.
— will ultimately belong to the Muslims. 21: 106—113.

HOLY SPIRIT, THE
Jesus was strengthened with —. 2: 88.
— descends from Allah with the truth and strengthens believers. 16: 103.

HOME LIFE
Privacy of —. 24: 28—30.
Intermingling of sexes prohibited. 24: 31, 32; 33: 60.

HOMICIDE
— is forbidden. 4: 93, 94.
Punishment for —. 4: 93.
Kinds of murder. 4: 93, 94.

HOUSE, THE ANCIENT
Circuits of —. 22: 30.

HOUSEHOLD, THE PEOPLE OF THE (AHL-E-BAIT)
— meaning the spouses of Abraham. 11: 74.
— meaning spouses of Holy Prophet Muhammad. 33: 34; 66: 5.
Purity of —. 33: 34.

HUDAIBIYYAH, TRUCE OF
— secured the Safety of the Muslims in Mecca. 48: 25, 26.
Victory gained at —. 48: 2.

HUDHUD
— was Commander of Solomon's forces. 27: 21.

HUMILITY
Turning away from others in pride or walking haughtily on earth is forbidden. 31: 19.

Believers enjoined to observe — 31: 20.

HUNAIN
Allah helped the believers on the day of —. 9: 25—27.

HUNTING
Lawful to eat what birds of prey and beasts trained and taught by you have hunted or caught for you. 5: 5.

HUSBAND & WIFE RELATION-SHIP (See under WOMEN)

HYPOCRITES
— tried to turn Immigrants against the Helpers and both against the Holy Prophet. 63: 8, 9.

— find fault with the Holy Prophet. 9: 50, 58, 61.

— incited the disbelievers. 59: 12.

— attempted to frighten the Muslims. 4: 84.

— have a diseased heart. 2: 11.

— create disorder. 2: 13.

Leaders of — are satans. 2: 15.

Excuses of —. 2: 15.

— actually disbelieve but they pretend that they believe. 2: 18.

Two faces of —. 4: 73, 74.

Double policy of —. 4: 144.

Grievous punishment in store for — 4: 139.

— take disbelievers as their friends. 4: 140.

IBLIS
— refused to make obeisance to Adam. 2: 35; 7: 12, 13; 15: 31, 32; 17: 62; 18: 51; 20: 117.

Reason of refusal of — to make obeisance was arrogance. 2: 35; 38: 75.

— was not an angel but was one of the jinn. 18: 51.

IDOL WORSHIP
Reason for —. 39: 4.

Noah's people had different idols as their gods. 71: 24.

Noah preached unity of Allah to his people but they insisted on —. 71: 8, 9.

Hud's people were idol worshippers. 11: 54.

Abraham's people worshipped idols. 26: 72.

Reason for not worshipping Lat, Uzza, and Manat. 53: 20—24.

Helplessness of idols. 22: 74.

Reason for not worshipping false gods. 21: 23.

Every prophet has a mission to wipe away —. 16: 37.

Abraham's prayer for security from —. 14: 36.

INFANTICIDE
— is forbidden. 17: 32.

INFIDELS
Taking error in exchange for guidance is a losing business for —. 2: 17.

— are called deaf because they insist on doing evil. 2: 19.

— are called dumb because they cannot express themselves to remove their doubts. 2: 19.

— are called blind because they do not see the beneficial change that Islam had brought in Muslims. 2: 19.

Hearts of — are like stones. 2: 25.

All actions of — will be in vain. 2: 218.

Reason why — will not get reward. 78: 28.

— will get external as well as internal burning punishment. 85: 11.

— will be surrounded by punishment from all sides. 85: 20, 21.

Angels will descend on — merely to punish them. 25: 23, 24.

INHERITANCE
Law of —. 4: 8, 9, 12, 13, 177.

Making a will of one's property and its distribution. 2: 181.

Changing a will is a sin. 2: 182.

Partiality or a wrong by a testator may be corrected. 2: 183.

Division of the property left is fixed by Allah. 4: 12.

At the time of distribution other relatives, orphans, the poor and the needy should not be forgotten. 4: 9.

Share of heirs. 4: 12.

Husbands are heirs of their wives. 4: 13.

Wives are heirs of their husbands.
4: 13.
Distribution of the property of one
dying without any issue. 4: 13,
177.

INTERCESSION
No one can intercede with Allah
- without His permission. 2: 256.
Those whom they call beside Allah
possess no power of —. 43: 87.
Holy Prophet could intercede as he
bore witness to the truth. 20: 110;
34: 24; 43: 87.
— with Allah for non-believers. 6: 52.
Angels can intercede with Allah with
His permission. 53: 27.
Righteous and evil —. 4: 86.

INTOXICANTS
— forbidden. 2: 220; 5: 91, 92.

INVOKING ALLAH IN SUPPORT
OF THE TRUTH (MUBAHALA)
Invitation to Jews for —. 62: 7.
Invitation to Christians for —. 3: 62.

ISAAC
Abraham was given glad tidings of
—'s birth. 11: 72; 37: 113; 51: 29.
—'s mother was frightened on hearing the news. 11: 72.
—'s mother beat her face on the glad
news and cried. 51: 30.
Allah bestowed His blessing on —.
37: 114.
Abraham, —, and Jacob men of
strong hands and powerful vision
i.e. active and far-sighted. 38: 46.
— and Jacob were leaders who guided
their people and were the recipients of revelation. 21: 73, 74.

ISHMAEL
Truth in the Quran about — 19: 55.
— was the eldest son of Abraham.
37: 102.
Abraham's dream about slaughtering
his son —. 37: 103.
— rather than Isaac was the one to
be sacrificed. 37: 103—105, 106.
Sacrificing — meant to leave him in
the waterless and foodless valley
of Mecca. 37: 108; 14: 38.
— was the Messenger and Prophet.
19: 55.
— strictly kept his promise. 19: 55.
— enjoined prayer and alms-giving
on his people. 19: 56.

ISLAM
Name — was given so that its followers be completely submerged
in Allah. 2: 113; 6: 154, 163.
Allah gave the name of — to this
religion. 22: 79.
Fundamental principles of —. 2: 4, 5.
— is a complete religion. 5: 4.
— is the only acceptable religion. 3:
86.
— is the true religion with Allah.
3: 20.
There is no compulsion in —. 2: 257;
18: 30; 25: 58; 28: 57.
By embracing — one does not confer
a favour on anyone. 49: 18.
Guidance is found in — alone. 3: 21;
72: 15.
No other religion is better than —.
4: 126.
No hardship in —. 2: 186; 5: 7; 22: 79.
— is a strong handle to grasp. 31: 23.
One can enter the favoured group by
following —. 1: 6, 7; 4: 70.
— is likened unto a good tree. 14: 25.
— does not recognise any privilege.
49: 14.
— enjoins justice even towards an
enemy. 5: 9.
— enjoins kindness and justice towards non-believers. 60: 9.
— enjoins good treatment of all.
4: 37.
— is the same as the religion of
Noah, Abraham, Moses and Jesus.
42: 14.
Prophecy of triumph of —. 13: 42.
Prophecy of rise of — in the first
three centuries and of its decline
in the following ten centuries.
32: 6.
— requires faith in all prophets. 2:
137.
Preaching of — made obligatory for
believers. 9: 123.

ISRAEL, THE CHILDREN OF
(BANI ISRAEL)
Israel was the name of Jacob. 3: 94;
19: 59.
— had a superiority over other
nations during their time. 2: 48;
2: 123.
Allah's continuous favour on —. 2:
48; 2: 123.
Cruelties of Pharaoh on —. 2: 50;
7: 142; 14: 7; 28: 5.
Moses was sent to rescue — from
Pharaoh's tyranny. 28: 6.
Moses calls on Pharaoh not to afflict

— and seeks their freedom. 7: 106; 20: 48.

Pharaoh and his chiefs promised to set — free if their affliction was removed but they broke their promise. 43: 50, 51.

Allah's direction to Moses to lead — out of Egypt. 20: 78; 26: 53; 44: 24.

Crossing the sea by — and drowning of Pharaoh and his people. 2: 51; 7: 137; 17: 104.

Number of — at the time of exodus. 2: 244.

Shade of clouds over — as they marched through Sinai desert. 2: 58; 7: 161.

Desire of — to revert to idol worship after safely crossing the sea. 7: 139.

— demand water from Moses who under Divine direction strikes a particular rock and water flows out. 2: 61; 7: 161.

Sending down of manna and salwa. 2: 58.

Moses left for the Mount and in his absence — took a calf for worship. 2: 52, 94.

Moses punished the idol worshippers. 2: 55.

Burning of the calf. 20: 98.

Allah commands — to slaughter a cow. 2: 68—70.

Desire of — to eat vegetables an other produce instead of manna and salwa. 2: 62.

— were taken to the foot of the Mount for a covenant. 2: 64, 94; 7: 172.

Chiefs of — were overtaken by an earthquake. 7: 156.

— ask Moses to see Allah face to face. 2: 56.

Moses orders — to enter Palestine but they refuse. 5: 22.

— rejected the signs of Allah and killed the Prophets. 2: 62.

— transgressed in the matter of Sabbath and became despised like apes. 2: 66; 7: 167.

Prophecy of Jews being afflicted till the Day of Resurrection. 7: 168.

Demand of — for a king, the appointment of Jaddoon, and their test through rivulet i.e. excessive wealth. 2: 247, 250.

Establishment of kingship in — through David. 2: 252.

Twelve spiritual leaders in —. 5: 13.

Prophethood and kingship in — 5: 21.

— cursed by Jesus and David. 5: 79.

Perversion of the Book by —. 2: 80.

ITAKA'AF
Observance of —. 2: 188.

JACOB
Abraham's wife was given the glad news of the birth of —. 11: 72.

Israel was —'s name. 3: 94.

— abstained from certain articles of food. 3: 94.

—'s admonition to his sons to stand firm on the Unity of Allah and to worship Him at all times. 2: 133, 134.

JEHA'D (STRIVING FOR THE CAUSE OF ALLAH)
— is enjoined on the believers. 22: 79.

The great —, (i.e. preaching the Word of Allah). 25: 53.

— with one's wealth. 8: 73.

In — one should not transgress limits. 2: 191.

Reward for the believer whether he becomes a martyr or is victorious in —. 4: 75.

Commandment of — was not only for the Holy Prophet but was also for the the believers. 4: 85.

JERUSALEM
Destruction and rebuilding of —. 2: 260.

Destruction of — by the Babylonians. 17: 6.

— destroyed by the Romans. 17: 8.

JESUS
Mary was given the glad news of the birth of —. 3: 46; 19: 21.

Mary's surprise at the good news. 3: 48; 19: 21.

After —' birth Mary was commanded to keep a fast of silence. 19:27.

— was born at a time when the dates had become ripe. 19: 26.

— talked wisely in his childhood. 3: 47.

Mary takes — to her people. 19: 28.

— was prophet in Israel. 3: 50.

Creation of birds by —; (i.e. he gave spiritual training to ordinary human beings who thereafter soared high in the spiritual atmosphere. 3: 50; 5: 3.

653

— declared clean the blind and lepers.
3: 50; 5: 111.
— gave life to the (spiritually) dead.
5: 111.
— was given the knowledge of Torah.
5: 111; 3: 49.
Jews disbelieved in — while the
disciples believed in him. 3: 53.
Revelation was vouchsafed to the
disciples of —. 5: 112.
— was sent with clear signs and was
strengthened by the holy spirit.
2: 254; 5: 111.
Jews planned to crucify — but Allah
had promised to save from death
on the cross. 3: 55, 56.
— was put upon the cross. 4: 158.
— did not die on the cross, but faint-
ed and was taken down while
still in that condition. 2: 73; 4:
158.
Jews did not succeed in killing —. 5:
111.
— went to an elevated region with
running streams (Kashmir) after
having escaped death on the cross.
23: 51.
— died a natural death. 5: 115.
—' prayer for a banquet (worldly
provision) for his people. 5: 115.
— was born as the word (prophecy)
of God. 3: 46; 4: 172.
Kalematohu used for — meaning
the sign of Allah. 4: 172; 31: 28.
— was granted high spiritual status.
3: 46.
— came in fulfilment of the Old
Testament prophecies. 3: 51; 5:
47; 61: 7.
— was Allah's servant and His
Prophet. 19: 31.
— was merely a Messenger of Allah.
5: 76.
— was enjoined to say his prayers,
give alms and treat his mother
well. 19: 22, 23.
— preached the Unity of Allah to his
people. 3: 52; 5: 118; 19: 37; 43:
65.
They are disbelievers who take — as
God. 5: 18, 73, 74.
Proof that — and his mother were not
gods. 5: 76.
— was created out of clay. 3: 60.
Jews and Christians will continue to
believe in the death of — on the
cross. 4: 160.
— not son of Allah. 9: 20.
— was born without the agency of a
father. 3: 48; 19: 21, 22.

Verses of the Holy Quran testifying
to the death of —. 3: 56, 145; 5:
76, 118; 7: 26; 17: 94; 21: 35.

JEWS
— are those who have incurred
Allah's displeasure. 1: 7.
— are enjoined not to exceed the
limits in the matter of religion.
5: 78.
Betrayal of Muslims by — at the
battle of Ahza'b and their disgrace.
33: 27, 28.
Expedition against Banu Nuzair and
their expulsion. 59: 3—7.

JINN
Allah has created — and the *Ins* for
His worship. 51: 57.
— are people who dominate. 6: 129.
Iblis was amongst the —. 18: 51.
— are the dominant ones and Ins are
common people. 55: 34.
— (i.e. the dwellers of mountains)
under David's suzerainty. 27: 40.
— who came to meet the Holy
Prophet were the Jews of Nasbain.
46: 30.
— who listened to the recitation of
the Holy Quran were Jews from
places outside Mecca. 72: 2.
Meaning of — having been created
from fire is that they are easily
roused. 15: 28.

JOB (PROPHET AYUB)
Mention of —. 4: 164; 6: 85; 21: 84,
85; 38: 42.
— lived in a hilly territory. 38: 45.
— was tormented by his enemies.
38: 42.
— was directed to emigrate. 38: 43.
— meets his family after emigrating.
21: 85; 38: 44.

JOHN (PROPHET YAHYA)
—'s birth was announced by the
angels to Zachariah while praying. 3: 40; 19: 8.
— was given the name by Allah
Himself. 19: 8.
— was given the knowledge of Torah
and judgment from early childhood. 19: 13.
—'s piety and righteousness. 19: 14.
— fulfils some of the old prophecies.
3: 40.
—'s kind treatment of his parents.
19: 15.

Peace on — on the day of his birth and death and the day when he would be raised up to life again. 19: 16.

JONAH (PROPHET YUNUS)
—'s name was Dunnoon. 21: 88.
— was amongst the Messengers. 4: 164; 6: 87; 37: 140.
— was exalted above his people. 6: 87.
—'s attempt to travel by boat. 37: 141.
Boat faced a storm and — was thrown overboard. 37: 142.
A whale swallowed — and then it vomitted him out. 37: 143—146.
Gourd plant was caused to grow over him. 37: 147.
— was sent as a messenger to a hundred thousand people. 37: 148.
—'s people believed in him and their punishment was removed. 10: 99.
—'s people, because of their believing in him, were provided for in this world. 37: 149.

JOSEPH (PROPHET YUSAF)
Prophecy about the Holy Prophet in the events of the life of —. 12: 8.
—'s devotion to Allah in his childhood and his seeing true dreams. 12: 5.
Jacob advises — not to relate his dream to his brothers. 12: 6.
—'s brothers were jealous of him. 12: 9.
—'s brothers plan to kill him. 12: 10.
—'s brothers take him to the wood and cast him in a deep well. 12: 16.
—'s brothers report falsely to Jacob that a wolf had devoured him. 12: 18.
— taken out of the well by an Ismaeli caravan who sold him as a slave. 12: 20, 21.
— bought by Aziz of Egypt. 12: 22.
Aziz's wife tried to seduce — against his will. 12: 25.
Aziz's wife invites women of the town who acclaim — as an angel. 12: 32, 33.
— was imprisoned. 12: 36.
— was given knowledge of the interpretation of the dreams. 12: 38.
—'s interpretation of the King's vision. 12: 48, 49.
— was released from prison and appointed Chief Treasurer of Egypt. 12: 55, 56.

Famine in Egypt and —'s brothers came to him for corn. 12: 59.
—'s brothers came twice to Egypt and brought their brother Ben Yamin (Benjamin) with them. 12: 64—70.
Jacob instructs them to enter through different gates. 12: 68, 69.
Allah's plan to keep Ben Yamin in Egypt. 12: 77.
— puts his drinking cup in his brother's sack. 12: 71.
— forgives his brothers. 12: 93.
Holy Prophet's forgiveness in contrast to —'s forgiveness. 12: 93.
— sends his shirt to his father. 12: 94.
Jacob goes with his family to Egypt and — receives him. 12: 100.
—'s followers believed after his death that no Prophet would appear after him. 40: 35. .

JUDGMENT, THE DAY OF
The answer to what — is. 51: 13—15; 82: 18—20.

JUSTICE
Believers are enjoined to act with —. 5: 9.

JUSTICE, ADMINISTRATION OF PUBLIC
Obligation of judicial determination of disputes. 4: 66.
Decision of the judge must be accepted. 4: 66.
Injunction on —. 4: 136; 5: 9.

KA'BA (See BAIT-UL-HARAM)

KAUTHAR (i.e. ABUNDANCE OF GOOD)
Holy Prophet given —. 108: 2.

KHATUM-E-NABUWAT
Door of Prophethood not closed. 2: 39; 40: 35; 72: 8.
Prophet Muhammad as Khatum-en-Nabiyyeen, (i.e. the most exalted Messenger). 33: 41.

KHILAFAT
Promise to establish — in Islam. 24: 56.

KNOWLEDGE
A person with — is better than one without it. 39: 10.
— bestows understanding. 39: 10.
Acquisition of — is urged. 96: 4—6
Travelling in search of —. 18: 66, 67

People with true — alone fear Allah. 35: 29.

Allah will raise the status of those who possess —. 58: 12.

Believers are enjoined to get religious —. 9: 122.

Prophet enjoined to pray for increase of —. 20: 115.

Prophets are favoured with — from Allah. 21: 80.

Prophets are raised to be teachers of mankind. 2: 152.

Quran enjoins the study of Nature. 3: 191, 192; 10: 6, 7; 13: 4, 5; 16: 11—17; 17: 13; 35: 28, 29.

Quran enjoins the study of the conditions of different countries. 17: 22; 22: 46, 47; 29: 21.

Quran enjoins the study of the history of different nations. 12: 112; 30: 10; 33: 63; 35: 44, 45; 40: 22.

Man can rule the forces of nature with —. 17: 71; 21: 80—83; 45: 13, 14.

LAILA-TUL-QUADR (NIGHT OF DESTINY)
Meaning of —. 97: 2—6.

LAW (SHARIYAT)
Object of the — is to lighten the burden of mankind. 4: 29.

LIFE
— is a struggle with hardships. 90: 5.
— here is but a pastime and Hereafter is the true —. 29: 65.
Contrast between this — and the Hereafter. 57: 21.
Man created with purpose. 23: 116.
Water is the source of —. 21: 31.
Everything is created in pairs. 36: 37; 51: 50.
Evolution of man. 18: 38; 23: 13—15; 40: 68; 53: 33; 71: 15—19.

LIFE, THE GOAL OF
— is the meeting with Allah. 6: 32; 10: 46; 13: 3; 30: 9; 84: 7.

LIFE HEREAFTER
— is determined by man's deeds in this life. 17: 14, 15; 21: 95; 43: 81; 45: 30; 50: 19; 82: 11—13; 83: 8—19.
— begins to manifest itself in this life. 41: 31—33; 55: 47; 89: 28—31.
— is fuller manifestation of values. 39: 70; 50: 22—24; 57: 13; 69: 19; 86: 9, 10; 99: 7—9.

Progress in the — will be unceasing. 35: 35, 36; 39: 21; 66: 9.

LIFE, WORLDLY
Non-believers desire the —. 2: 201, 213.
— is inferior to the life Hereafter. 3: 16; 4: 78; 9: 38.
— is a brief sojourn in contrast to the world Hereafter. 23: 115.

LIQUOR (See under INTOXICANTS)

LOAN
Transaction of — should be in writing. 2: 283.
Period of — must be fixed. 2: 283.
Presence of witnesses. 2: 287.

LOT (PROPHET LUT)
— was one of the Messengers. 37: 134.
— mentioned along with Abraham and Ishmael. 6: 86.
— believed in Abraham and migrated with him. 21: 72; 29: 27.
Evil ways of the people of —. 26: 166, 167; 29: 30.
— warns his people to stop their evil ways. 26: 166; 27: 55, 56.
—'s people forbid his entertaining strangers. 15: 71.
—'s people reject him and threaten to exile him. 26: 168; 27: 57.
—'s people ask for punishment. 29: 30.
—'s prayer. 29: 31.
Warning of the destruction of —'s people. 15: 61; 27: 58; 29: 34; 37: 135, 136.
— is perturbed on arrival of messengers. 29: 34.
People of — visited him on the arrival of messengers. 11: 79; 15: 68.
— commanded to leave town during night. 11: 82; 15: 66.
— told not to look back. 15: 66.
—'s people were smothered under rain of stones. 7: 85; 11: 83, 84; 15: 75; 26: 174; 27: 59; 54: 35.
Rejecting — was to reject all the prophets. 54: 34.
Disbelievers are like the wife of Noah and of —. 66: 11.
— given wisdom and knowledge and was righteous. 21: 75, 76.

LOTE — TREE OF THE BOUNDARY (SIDRA-TUL-MUNTAHA'A)
Mention of —. 53: 15.

MAN (INS)
— is hasty by nature. 21: 38.
Object of creating —. 51: 57.

— is created to worship. Allah. 1: 5;
51: 57.

Nature of — is to believe in Allah.
57: 9.

— is born with nature made by
Allah. 30: 31; 91: 8, 9.

— has unlimited capacity for progress. 87: 3.

— was created in the best make. 95: 5.

— has capacity of receiving revelation. 15: 29, 30.

Allah has shown the way of good and
evil to —. 76: 14; 90: 11; 91: 9.

— is free to act as he chooses. 41:
41.

Allah provides facilities for — according to his action. 92: 6—11.

All things have been subordinated
to —. 2: 30; 22: 66; 31: 21; 45: 14.

— should seek the protection of Allah
alone. 2: 42.

Allah does not require of any — that
which is beyond his capacity. 2:
234, 287; 23: 63; 65: 8.

— desiring only this world shall have
no share in the Hereafter. 2: 201;
4: 135; 42: 21.

— is created weak. 4: 29.

Those who desire good in this life
and in the Hereafter will have a
good reward. 2: 202; 42: 21.

— is enjoined to treat his parents
kindly. 17: 24; 29: 9; 31: 15;
46: 16.

— has been created from nothing-
ness. 76: 2.

Mankind were one community in the
beginning. 2: 214.

— is created out of clay. 3: 60; 7: 13;
18: 38.

Allah fashioned — in the womb. 3: 7.

-- should repel evil with that which
is best. 23: 97.

Divine spirit is breathed into —.
32: 10.

Ungratefulness of —. 10: 13; 11:
10—12; 41: 52.

Threefold duty of —. 5: 93—94.

— will live and die on earth. 7: 26.

Best garment for — is righteousness.
7: 27.

Stages in the physical growth of —.
22: 6; 23: 13—15.

Punishment of — for disbelieving
after believing. 3: 107.

Creation of — in threefold darkness.
39: 7.

— shall be tried in his possessions
and in his person. 2: 156—158; 3:
187.

—'s possessions and children are a
trial. 8: 29; 24: 16.

—-'s complete submission to Allah is
most beneficial. 2: 132; 4: 126.

— is impatient. 70: 20—22.

— is most contentious. 18: 55.

— is prone to despair. 30: 37; 41: 50.

— loves wealth and is niggardly. 17:
101; 89: 21.

— is prone to transgress. 96: 7—8.

— is subject to loss without faith
and righteousness. 103: 3—4.

— is superior to other creation. 17:
71.

MARRIAGE (See under WOMEN)

MARTYRS
— live an eternal life. 3: 170.

MARY
Quran mentions true events of the
life of —. 3: 45; 19: 17.

—, her family and her birth. 3: 36, 37.

— was the ward of Zachariah. 3: 38.

— was provided for by Allah. 3: 38.

—, her piety, chastity and high
status. 21: 92; 66: 13.

— was truthful. 5: 76.

— was chosen of Allah. 3: 43.

Visit of angel in the form of a man
was a vision. 19: 18.

MECCA
— is called Mecca because of abundance of blessings. 3: 97.

— is also called Balad-al-Ameen i.e.
town of security. 95: 4.

Abraham's prayer for — and its
security. 2: 127; 14: 36.

— is made sacred. 27: 92.

Prophecy of return of Holy Prophet
to — after emigration. 17: 81; 28:
86; 90: 3.

Efforts necessary for the return to —.
2:151.

Prophecy of the security of —. 28: 58.

Prophecies relating to future of —.
3: 97.

Jewish objections met by the conquest of —. 2: 151.

Prophecy of the conquest of —. 13:
32.

MEEKNESS
Believers should cultivate —. 25: 64;
31: 19, 20.

MENSTRUATION
Purification from —. 2: 223.

MESSENGERS (See also under
PROPHETS)
All — dubbed sorcerers and mad-
men. 51: 53.
It is wrong to compare —. 23: 53.
Rejection of one Messenger is rejection of all —. 26: 106, 124, 142,
161, 177.
— shall be witnesses. 4: 42; 16: 85,
90; 33: 46.

MESSIAH
— was the servant of Allah. 4: 173.

MIDIAN
— and its dwellers. 7: 86; 9: 70; 11:
85.

MIGRATION IN THE CAUSE OF
ALLAH
One who emigrates in the cause of
Allah shall have plenty. 4: 101.

MIRA'J
Holy Prophet had the vision of —
twice. 53: 14.
No mistake in seeing the vision —.
53: 18.
— of Moses. 18: 61—63.
Prophet Muhammad went on a jour-
ney in a vision from Masjid-e-
Haram to Masjid-al-Aqsa. 17: 2.
The — was a clear vision. 17: 61.

MONASTICISM
— was not prescribed by Allah but
was self-imposed by the Christians.
57: 28.

MONTH OF HARAM
Sanctity of the —. 2: 218.

MONTHS, THE TWELVE
The number of —. 9: 36.
Sacred months. 2: 195; 9: 36.

MOON, THE
— and its stages. 36: 40, 41.
Lunar system in Islam. 2: 190.
— gets light from the sun. 71: 17.
Crescent —. 36: 40.
— has reference to the Reformers
who would follow the Holy Prophet (i.e. the sun) and would get
their light from him. 91: 3.
— signifies Arab power. 54: 2.
Reckoning time by the —. 2: 190.
Prophecy of eclipse of the sun and
— on the advent of Mehdi. 75: 10.

MORAL TEACHINGS
(See under DEEDS)

MOSES
Quran gives the true events of the
life of —. 19: 52.
Purpose of advent of — was to free
Israel from the cruelties and
bondage of Pharoah and to foster
their progress. 28: 6, 7.
—, birth of, and his being cast afloat
in the river in an ark. 20: 40;
28: 8.
Pharoah's daughter picks — out of
the river. 28: 9, 10.
— refused wet-nurses and was restored to his mother. 20: 41; 28:
13.
— was given wisdom and knowledge.
28: 15.
— smote Copt with his fist and caused his death. 20: 41; 28: 16.
— was repentant. 28: 16, 17.
Chiefs of Pharoah's people counselled
together to kill — and he was
warned. 28: 21.
— emigrates to Midian. 20: 41; 28: 23.
— helps two women to water their
flocks at the well of Midian. 28:
24, 25.
— receives offer of marriage on condition of staying in Midian for
eight years serving the family.
28: 28.
— returns from Midian with his
family. 28: 30.
— perceived fire near Mount Sinai.
20: 11; 27: 8; 28: 30.
— sees his rod as a serpent and is
frightened. 7: 108; 20: 21, 22; 27:
11; 28: 32.
— perceives his hand turned white
without any ill effects. 7: 109; 20:
23; 28: 33.
— had shown nine signs to Pharoah.
7: 134; 17: 102; 27: 13.
— prays Aaron be appointed to
assist him. 20: 30—36; 26: 14;
28: 35.
— and Aaron commanded to go to
Pharoah. 20: 43—45; 26: 16—18.
— and Aaron preached to Pharoah.
7: 105, 106; 10: 76—79; 17: 102,
103.
— had a debate with Pharoah. 20:
50—53; 26: 19—34.
Pharoah demanded Sign from —. 7:
107; 26: 32.
— showed his signs. 7: 108, 109; 79:
21.

-- possessed excellent moral qualities. 68: 5.

— is described as a lamp which gives bright light. 33: 47.

By following — one can win the love of Allah. 3: 32.

By following — one becomes heir to Allah's blessings and can achieve the highest spiritual status. 4: 70.

— did not know reading or writing. 29: 49.

— was sent after a break in the series of prophets. 5: 20.

Allah would not punish disbelievers of Mecca while — was among them. 8: 34.

Asra of — from Masjid-e-Haram to Masjid-e-Aqusa. 17: 2.

Mira'j of — 53: 9—14.

Allah and His angels send blessings on —. 33: 57.

Believers commanded to submit disputes to — for decision. 4: 66.

Spiritually dead resurrected through —. 8: 25.

Principal missions of —. 2: 130; 62: 2, 3.

Wives of — as mothers of believers. 33: 7.

People who malign — shall have severe punishment. 9: 61; 33: 58.

— was enjoined to be affectionate towards the believers. 26: 216.

Concern of — for his followers. 3: 160; 9: 128.

Enemies persecuted — and forbade him offering Prayers. 96: 10, 11.

Non-believers plotted to murder —. 8: 31.

Emigration of — to Medina. 9: 40.

Divine assurance given to — of his return to Mecca. 28: 86.

Hypocrites took objection to distribution of charity money by —. 9: 58.

Hypocrites objected that — listened to complaints against them. 9: 61.

— did not have the knowledge of the unknown. 6: 51.

— never demanded any reward from the people. 6: 91; 12: 105; 23: 73.

— wished only that people should turn to Allah. 25: 58.

— was enjoined to continue his worship of his Lord till his death. 15: 100.

— was enjoined to convey the revelation which he received to the people. 5: 68.

Accusation of unbelievers refuted that — was a lunatic. 68: 3—7.

Non-believers raised same objections against — as were raised against previous Prophets. 41: 44.

Non-believers asked — why Allah did not speak to them. 2: 119.

Non-believers demanded why — did not bring a Sign. 2: 119; 6: 38; 7: 204.

Objection that — was taught the Quran by someone else. 16: 104.

Objection that — had no treasures, gardens, or royal grandeur. 11: 13; 25: 9.

Demand for miracles from —. 17: 91—94.

— was told to endure steadfastly their mockery and persecution. 6: 35, 36; 15: 98, 99; 27: 71; 36: 77.

-- was commanded to be alert and ever ready for spreading the truth. 74: 2.

Success of — in the propagation of Islam. 110: 3.

— was thereupon commanded to seek Allah's protection and His blessings. 110: 4.

— was an excellent and perfect man. 20: 2.

Prophecy of treasures and palaces being given to —'s followers. 25: 11.

Commandments addressed to — are the commandments to his people as well. 10: 95; 17: 24, 25; 30: 39; 65: 2.

Prophecy for the advent of a witness to testify to the truth of —. 11: 18.

Pure life of — before his claim to prophethood. 10: 17.

—'s message was universal. 7: 159; 10: 58; 22: 50; 34: 29.

— was excellent exemplar for mankind. 33: 22.

— was favoured with abundance of good. 108: 2.

MUHAMMAD'S COMPANIONS

Higher spiritual status of —. 2: 116.

Emigrants and Helpers and their sacrifices. 9: 117.

Helpers' love for the Emigrants. 59: 10.

Love of — for each other. 48: 30.

Allah pleased with Emigrants and Helpers. 9: 100.

Allah pleased with pledge of believers at Hudoubiyyah. 48: 19.

High spirit of sacrifice of — despite their poverty. 9: 92.

Believers enjoined to remember sacrifices of —. 18: 29.
Prayer of the Holy Prophet for companions who were ready for any
sacrifice. 17: 81.
Efforts of — for the cause of Islam.
37: 2—4; 79: 2—6; 100: 2—6.
— were the offerers of prayers. 26:
220

MUHAMMAD, WIVES OF
— are as mothers of Muslims. 33: 7.
Marrying any of — is unlawful. 33: 54.
Status and deportment of —. 33:
31—34.
— called upon to choose between
worldly life and devotion to faith.
33: 29, 30.
Holy Prophet confided a secret to one
of his wives and she failed to
keep it. 66: 4.
Holy Prophet gave up eating honey
to please his wives. 66: 2.
Hypocrites malign Ayesha. 24: 12.
Ayesha cleared of accusation. 24: 17.
Marriage of Holy Prophet with Zainab
was enjoined by Allah. 33: 38.

MURDER
— forbidden. 17: 34; 25: 69.
Law of retaliation —. 2: 179.

MUSLIMS
To outstrip each other in doing good
is the goal of —. 2: 149.
— were averse to fighting. 2: 217.
— are the best people for they are
raised for the good of mankind. 3:
111.
— forbidden to fight in Sacred Month
but may defend themselves against
aggression. 2: 218.
Restriction on fraternisation of —
with disbelievers. 3: 29.

NATIONS
Doom of — at the end of their assigned term of rise. 7: 35.
— are destroyed when they transgress. 17: 17.
— cannot rise until they amend
themselves. 13: 12.

NATURAL RELIGION
Right religion is the —. 30: 31.

NATURE, DIVERSITY OF
Signs in the —. 13: 4, 5.

NATURE, HARMONY IN
No incongruity of flaw in universe.
67: 4, 5.

NEEDY & THE POOR
Duty of looking after the —. 51: 20;
90: 15—17.
End of those who do not care for —.
107: 4.

NICKNAMES
Calling one another by — is forbidden. 49: 12.

NIGGARDLINESS
— is forbidden. 3: 181; 4: 38.

NOAH (PROPHET NUH)
Prophecy about the Holy Prophet in
the events of the life of —. 11: 50.
— chosen as a Prophet by Allah.
3: 34.
— preaches to his people. 7: 60; 10:
72; 11: 26, 27; 23: 24; 71: 2—21.
—'s people reject him. 7: 65; 10: 74;
11: 28; 23: 25; 54: 10.
—'s people demand punishment. 11:
33.
— builds the Ark and his people
mock at him. 11: 38, 39.
Flood came as punishment on his
people and — is told to take the
needed animals in the Ark with
him. 11: 41, 42; 23: 28.
—'s son refuses to go into Ark and is
drowned. 11: 43, 44.
—'s Ark was fully laden. 26: 120.
— makes his supplication to Allah
on behalf of his son. 11: 46, 47.
—'s Ark settles on Mount Judi. 11: 45.
—'s flood is a Sign for people. 54: 16.
Prophethood in —'s progeny. 57: 27.
—'s rejection is the rejection of all
prophets. 26: 106.

OATHS
Allah will not call you to account
for vain —. 2: 226.
Guarding of —. 5: 90.
Expiation of —. 5: 90; 66: 3.
— should not be broken. 16: 92.
— should not be made means of
deceit. 16: 93, 95.
Vowing abstinence from wives. 2:
227, 228.

OBEDIENCE & SUBMISSION
Allah enjoins on you — to Him and
His Messenger. 3: 133, 173.
— to Allah and His Prophet leads to
the highest spiritual upliftment.
4: 70.
— to Allah and His Messenger leads
to success. 24: 53.

Obedience of Messenger is obedience
of Allah. 4: 81.
Obedience of those in authority is
enjoined. 4: 60.
Messengers are sent to be obeyed. 4:
65.
Those who love Allah are enjoined to
follow the Holy Prophet. 3: 32.

OCEANS
Prophecy of joining the —. 55: 20, 21.
Prophecy of huge ships sailing on —.
55: 25.

ORBS
Movement of — in their spheres.
21: 34.

ORPHANS
— not to be oppressed. 93: 10.
Feeding of —. 90: 16.
Care of —. 2: 221.
Property of — should be safeguarded.
4: 3; 6: 153; 17: 35.
Penalty for misappropriation of pro-
perty of —. 4: 11.
Proper upbringing of —. 4: 7.
Equitable treatment of —. 4: 128.

PARABLES OR SIMILITUDE OF
— person kindling fire. 2: 18.
— heavy rain and lightning. 2: 20, 21.
— a gnat. 2: 27.
— birds obeying call. 2: 261.
— grain of corn growing seven ears.
2: 262.
— seeds sown on stones. 2: 265.
— garden on elevated ground. 2: 266.
— garden smitten by a fiery whirlwind. 2: 267.
— one bewildered. 6: 72.
— one who rejects Divine Signs. 7:
176, 177.
— thirsty dog. 7: 177.
— flood of rainwater bearing foam.
13: 18.
— good tree. 14: 25, 26.
— evil tree. 14: 27.
— pure and pleasant milk. 16: 67.
— liquor and wholesome food. 16: 68.
— bee. 16: 69, 70.
— slave and free man. 16: 76.
— dumb man and of one who enjoins
justice. 16: 77.
— one who breaks her strong yarn to
pieces. 16: 93.
— secure and peaceful city which
neglected the favours of Allah.
16: 113.

— arrogant rich man and humble
poor man. 18: 33—45.
— vanity of life of this world. 18: 46.
— one who associates anything with
Allah. 22: 32.
— helplessness of those who are called
upon beside Allah. 22: 74.
— Light of heavens and earth. 24: 36.
— mirage in the desert. 24: 40.
— thick darkness in a vast and deep
sea. 24: 41.
— spider who makes a house. 29: 42.
— master and slave cannot be partners. 30: 29.
— slave belonging to several people.
39: 30.
— ass carrying a load of books. 62: 6.
— arrogant owners of a garden.
68: 18—34.

PARADISE
Life in —; Fruits of 2: 26.
—; Extent of 3: 134; 57: 22.
Fulfilment of all desires of soul in —.
41: 32, 33.
— after death and — in this world.
19: 62; 55: 47.
Earthly —. 2: 36.
Dwellers of — shall not be driven out
of it. 15: 49.
Description of — symbolical. 13: 36;
47: 16; 57: 13.
No one can conceive reality of —.
32: 18.
Believers will be led towards —.
39: 74.
High status of dwellers in —. 83:
19—21.
Believers shall enjoy — in this world
as well. 55: 47.

PARADISE (DESCRIPTION)
Dwellers of — shall suffer neither heat
nor cold. 76: 14.
No vain talk in —. 19: 63.
No death nor punishment in —. 37:
59, 60; 44: 57.
Dwellers in — will be vouchsafed
sight of Allah. 75: 23, 24.
Pleasure of Allah will be greatest
reward in —. 9: 72.

PARADISE (THE DISTINGUISH-
ING FEATURES)
Fruits and shade of — shall be
everlasting. 13: 36.
Greatest favour of — will be the
attainment of Allah's pleasure.
3: 16; 9: 72.

Delightful dwelling places in —. 9: 72.
Lofty mansions in —. 25: 76; 39: 21.
Abundance of water, milk, wine, and honey in — will never lose their taste. 47: 16.
Gardens and rivers of —. 3: 16, 196, 199; 4: 14, 58, 123; 5: 13, 86; 7: 44; 9: 72, 89, 100; 10: 10; 13: 36; 22: 15, 24; 25: 11; 47: 16; 58: 23; 61: 13; 64: 10.
Thrones in —. 15: 48.
Carpeted floors in —. 55: 55.
Carpets and cushions in —. 88: 16, 17.
Pure drink of —. 83: 26—29.
Wine of — will not induce levity or sin. 52: 24.
Fountains tempered with camphor in —. 76: 6, 7.
Fountains tempered with ginger in —. 76: 18.
Fountain called salsabil in —. 76: 19.
Fountains tempered with tasneem in —. 83: 28.
Sustenance in —. 19: 63.
Food and drink in —. 77: 43, 44.
Bananas and lote trees in —. 56: 29, 30.
Dates and pomegranates in —. 55: 69.
Grapes in —. 78: 33.
All kinds of fruits in —. 55: 53; 77: 43.
Fruits in — as rewards of good deeds. 37: 42—44.
Clustered fruits of —. 76: 15.
Meat of birds in —. 56: 22.
Shade of —. 13: 36.
Green garments of fine silk in —. 18: 32.
Bracelets of gold in —. 18: 32; 35: 34.
Gold and silver cups in —. 43: 72.
Vessels of polished silver in —. 76: 16, 17.
Pure spouses in —. 3: 16; 4: 58.
Chaste women with restrained looks and large eyes in —. 37: 49, 50.
Youths waiting on dwellers of —. 52: 25; 56: 18; 76: 20.
Angels shall greet dwellers of —. 13: 24, 25.

PARADISE, PEOPLE ENTERING
Believers who act righteously. 2: 26.
Righteous who are mindful of their duty to Allah to the utmost. 3: 134—137.
The steadfast. 13: 23.
Those who are foremost in obedience to Allah. 56: 11.
Those of the right hand. 56: 28.
— will be brought near to the righteous. 50: 32.

PARENTS
Treating — kindly is enjoined. 17: 24; 29: 9; 31: 15.
Prayer for — is enjoined. 17: 25.
Obeying — in all matters excepting *shirk* is enjoined. 29: 9.

PEACE
Suing for — through weakness is forbidden. 47: 36.
When enemy is inclined towards — so should you be. 8: 62.

PEOPLE, THE (THE TRIBES)
1..— of *A'd.* 7: 66; 11: 51.
   Punishment of destructive wind on —. 46: 25, 26.
2. — of *Thamud.* 7: 74; 11: 62.
   Sign of a she-camel for —. 11: 65.
   — hamstrung the she-camel and according to the warning were punished. 11: 68.
   Earthquake seized —. 7: 79.
   — lay prostrate when the punishment came. 7: 79.
3. Dwellers of the *Wood* (Asaha'bul Aika)
   People of Shoaib were called —. 15: 79.
   — and their place. 15: 79; 50: 15.
4. — of *Tubba*
   — and their destruction. 44: 38; 50: 15.
5. — of *Well* (Asaha'bul Ras)
   — were a section of the tribe of Thamud. 25: 39.
6. — of the *Elephant*. (Asaha'bul Fiel)
   — were Abraha, Abyssinian king's Governor in Yamen, and his army. 105: 2.
   Design of — against Baitullah and their destruction. 105: 3.
7. Sabians 5: 70.
8. — of Cave (Asaha'bul Kahf)
   Situation of the Cave. 18: 18.
   Number of —. 18: 23.
   Length of period — lived in the Cave. 18: 26.
   Dog of —. 18: 19.

PHARAOH
Quran affirms body of — was preserved. 10: 93.
Curse on —'s people in this world and in the Hereafter. 11: 100; 28: 43.

PILGRIMAGE (See WORSHIP)

PLAGUE
Eruption of — during latter days for

not believing in Allah's signs.
27: 83.

PLEDGE
-- with possession. 2: 284.

POET
Muhammad was not a —. 36: 70;
69: 42.
Characteristics of —s. 26: 226—228.

POLYGAMY
Permission for —. 4: 4.
Equality between wives. 4: 4.
Neglect of one wife and preference of
another not permitted. 4: 130.

POLYTHEISM
— is gravest sin. 4: 49; 4: 117.
— is devoid of basis. 30: 36.

POOR
Care for the —. 69: 35; 90: 12—17;
107: 2—4.

PRAYER (SALA'T, FASTING, HAJJ
AND ZAKAAT, see under WOR-
SHIP)
Need for —. 25: 78.
Unto Allah alone is the —. 7: 195;
13: 15; 46: 6.
— of the distressed person is heard.
27: 63.
Allah's promise to answer — of His
people. 2: 187; 40: 61.
Even if the deed is good — should be
continued for it. 2: 124.
— taught by Allah absorbs His
blessings more effectively. 2: 38.
Supplicant should seek good in both
worlds. 2: 201, 202; 4: 135.
Offer — to God and be steadfast in it.
19: 66; 20: 15.
Neglect of — leads to destruction.
19: 60.

PRAYERS OF THE HOLY QURAN
FOR
Guidance along straight path. 1: 2—7.
— peace and provision. 2: 127.
(Abraham's Prayer).
— for the acceptance of prayers and
for being taught the method of
worship. 2: 128—130. (Abraham's
and Ishmael's prayer).
— seeking good here and Hereafter.
2: 202.
— help against disbelievers. 2: 251.
(Talut's prayer).
— imploring Allah's forgiveness. 2:
286. (Prayer of Believers).

— being saved from punishment and
for Allah's help. 2: 287. (Believers
prayer).
Prayer that our hearts might not
become perverse after guidance.
3: 9. (Believers' prayer).
-- forgiveness of sins. 3: 17.
— grace and help. 3: 27, 28.
— Divine favour. 3: 54. (Prayer of
the disciples of Jesus).
— steadfastness. 3: 148.
— being saved from the Fire. 3: 192.
— forgiveness of sins and removal of
ills. 3: 194, 195.
— seeking refuge from oppressors.
4: 76.
— distinction between the faithful
and the disobedient. 5: 26. (Prayer
of Moses).
— being counted among the righteous.
5: 84, 85.
— prosperity. 5: 115. (Prayer of
Jesus for his people).
— forgiveness of error. 7: 24. (Prayer
of Adam and his wife).
— truimph of truth over falsehood.
7: 90.
— steadfastness. 7: 127.
— Allah's mercy. 7: 150, 152, 156.
— good here and Hereafter. 7: 157.
— deliverance from evil of enemies.
10: 86, 87.
— destruction of oppressors. 10: 89.
— security in a boat or vessel. 11: 42.
— security while riding or driving.
43: 14, 15.
— being joined to the righteous. 12:
102. (Prayer of Joseph).
— self and progeny. 14: 36—42.
(Prayer of Abraham).
— parents. 17: 25.
— entering or coming out of a place
or building. 17: 81.
— mercy and guidance. 18: 11.
— righteous offspring. 19: 5—7; 21:
90. (Prayer of Zachariah).
— success in the propagation of
truth. 20: 26—36. (Prayer of
Moses).
— increase of knowledge. 20: 115.
— deliverance from distress. 21: 84.
(Prayer of Job).
— security against consequences of
default. 21: 88. (Prayer of Jonas).
— Allah's help and His judgement.
21: 113.
— victory over those who reject the
truth. 23: 27. (Noah's prayer).
— a safe landing. 23: 30. (Noah's
prayer).

— not being counted with the wrong-doers. 23: 94, 95.
— seeking refuge from incitements of evil ones. 23: 98—99.
— forgiveness of sins and mercy. 23: 110.
— forgiveness and mercy. 23: 119.
— being saved from the punishment of hell. 25: 66, 67.
— family and children. 25: 75.
— wisdom and being counted among the righteous. 26: 84—90. (Prayer of Abraham).
— victory of truth. 26: 118, 119.
— deliverance from the torment of the enemy. 26: 170.
— being grateful and being among the righteous. 27: 20. (Prayer of Solomon).
— peace on the righteous. 27: 60.
— forgiveness. 28: 17. (Prayer of Moses).
— deliverance from unjust people. 28: 22. (Prayer of Moses).
— seeking good from Allah. 28: 25. (Prayer of Moses).
— help against wicked people. 29: 31. (Prayer of Lot).
— for a righteous son. 37: 101. (Prayer of Abraham).
— for forgiveness and grant of vast kingdom. 38: 36. (Prayer of Solomon).
— deliverance from hell and all evil. 40: 8—10.
— appreciation of Allah's favours. 46: 16.
— help from Allah when overcome. 54: 11. (Prayer of Noah).
— deliverance from rancour. 59: 11.
— seeking protection against the non-believers. 60: 5, 6. (Prayer of Abraham's people).
— perfection of Allah's blessings. 66: 9.
— deliverance from Pharoah and wrongdoers. 66: 12. (Prayer of Pharoah's wife).
— forgiveness of all believers. 71: 29. (Prayer of Noah).
— protection against all evil. 113: 2—6; 114: 2—5.

PRAYER, DAILY (Salaat; see under WORSHIP)

PREDESTINATION (Taqdeer i.e. determining the measure of everything)
Meaning of —. 7: 35; 57: 23, 24.
Allah has determined the measure of everything. 25: 3; 54: 50; 65: 4.

Good or evil befalls as result of Divine law. 4: 79, 80.
Man is free to act as he chooses but must face the consequences thereof. 74: 39.
Believers and non-believers are both helped. 17: 21.

PRISONERS OF WAR
(See under WAR)

PRIVACY
Personal —. 24: 59, 60.

PROPERTY
— is a means of transport. 4: 6.
— should not be acquired unlawfully or unjustly. 2: 189; 4: 30.

PROPHECIES, GENERAL
— either contain glad news or give warning. 18: 57.
Fulfilment of — which warn can be put off by repentance. 10: 99; 43: 50, 51; 44: 16.
Fulfilment of — bearing glad tidings can be postponed by failure to comply with conditions. 5: 27.
Prophet is justified if some of his — are fulfilled during his lifetime. 13: 41; 40: 29.

PROPHECIES OF THE HOLY QURAN (See under QURAN)

PROPHETS
Allah revealed some of His secrets to —. 3: 180; 72: 27, 28.
— are innocent and are safeguarded from error. 6: 163; 53: 4, 5.
Prophet and Messenger are synonymous. 19: 52—55.
Purpose of —. 20: 135; 28: 48.
— were sent to all people. 10: 48; 13: 8; 16: 37.
Superiority of some prophets over others. 2: 254; 17: 56.
Two kinds of —, the law-bearing and non-law-bearing. 2: 254; 5: 45; 36: 15.
Quran makes mention of a few — only. 4: 165; 40: 79.
Same objections raised against all —. 41: 44; 51: 53, 54.
Disbelieving one prophet is disbelieving all —. 4: 151.
— submit themselves to the will of Allah. 10: 73.
Only men are raised as —. 12: 110.
Allah chooses the — Himself. 6: 125; 16: 3.

665

Purpose of — is to purify people and to guide them to their Lord. 79: 18—20.

— cannot act unfaithfully. 3: 162.

Sinlessness of —. 21: 28.

False — do not prosper. 69: 45—48.

— are the rope of Allah which should be held fast. 3: 104

All — are opposed and mocked at. 6: 113; 21: 42; 25: 32; 36: 8, 31; 43: 8.

Followers of — are succoured. 2: 215.

Satan puts obstacles in the way ot what the — seek after but always fails. 22: 53.

— were accused of being bribed for acting as agents of others. 26: 154.

— were accused of madness or of being magicians. 34: 44; 51: 53.

— were charged with falsehood. 3: 185; 34: 46.

— are helped by Allah in this world as well as in the Hereafter. 37: 172, 173; 40: 52.

— are human beings. 14: 12; 18: 111; 19: 59; 21: 8, 9.

— marry and have children. 13: 39.

— eat food. 21: 9; 25: 8, 21.

— do not fear anyone except Allah. 33: 40.

— receive revelation in the language of their people. 14: 5.

— convey message of Allah to the people. 5: 100; 33: 40.

—' duty is to warn people and to give them glad tidings. 6: 49.

— do not ask for any reward from the people. 11: 30, 52.

— and their followers always prevail over others. 40: 52; 58: 22.

Attempts of people to kill their —. 2: 62; 3: 113; 4: 156.

Not all — were given the Book separately. 2: 214.

All — have a common mission of establishing unity of Allah. 23: 53.

Reason why — and believers suffer from afflictions. 2: 156, 215.

Unreasonable demands of the opponents of —. 2: 119.

PUNISHMENT

— is inflicted for disregarding the warnings of Allah's Messengers. 6: 132; 17: 16; 42: 22.

Allah does not inflict — unjustly. 11: 118; 29: 22.

Purpose of — is to reform. 23. 77: 78.

Allah is slow in sending —. 22: 48—52.

— follows upon transgression and injustice. 4: 31.

— for theft. 5: 39.

Delay in —. 6: 19; 10: 12; 11: 9.

— for adultery. 24: 3.

— for calumniating chaste woman. 24: 5.

— is warded off by seeking forgiveness. 8: 34.

— serves as an example and lesson. 2: 67.

Repentance and amendment avert —. 5: 40.

— averted from the people of Jonah. 10: 99.

Allah's mercy averts —. 7: 157.

PURDAH (Veil, for Women)

Directions about —. 24: 31—32, 61; 33: 60.

Old women exemption for —. 24: 61.

Privacy, periods of 24: 59.

QURAISH

— safeguarded against Abraha's design. 106: 2—5.

QURAN, THE HOLY

Purpose of gradual revelation of —. 17: 107; 25: 33, 34.

Seeking refuge with Allah before recitation of —. 16: 99.

Recitation of — should be listened to with attention. 7: 205.

Abrogation of previous commandments. 2: 107.

— also called the Book. 15: 2.

— called pure scriptures comprising everlasting commandments. 98: 3, 4.

Divine promise to guard —. 15: 10; 56: 78—81.

— gives good tidings and warns. 19: 98.

— is an Exhortation for those who fear Allah. 20: 3, 4.

— is a revelation from the Creator of heavens and earth. 20: 5.

— is a well-preserved Book. 56: 79.

— discriminates between truth and untruth. 25: 2.

— was mentioned in scriptures of previous prophets. 26: 197, 198.

— is healing and mercy for believers. 17: 83.

— speaks at every level. 18: 55; 39: 28; 59: 22.

— repeatedly exhorts observation, reflection, exercises of reason, and understanding. ¡2: 270.

constantly exhorts towards remembrance of Allah through:
- (i) observation, 5: 22; 43: 52;
- (ii) reflection, 2: 220, 267; 7: 185; 34: 47;
- (iii) meditation, 4: 83; 47: 25;
- (iv) exercise of reason and understanding, 6: 152; 16: 13; 23: 81; 28: 61;
- (v) seeking of knowledge, 20: 115; 29: 44; 35: 29;
- (vi) pondering over intellectual problems, 9: 122; 17: 45;
- (vii) fostering of spiritual vision, 7: 199; 11: 21; 28: 73;
- (viii) gratitude to Allah, 14: 8; 16: 15; 23: 79; 56: 71.

Objection why — was not revealed all at once. 25: 33.

Objection why a written book was not sent directly from heaven. 17: 94.

Objection why — was not revealed through a great man. 43: 32.

— contains verses with decisive meanings and verses susceptible of different interpretations. 3: 8; 39: 24.

— yields new truths and fresh guidance in every age and at all levels. 18: 110.

Companions of the Holy Prophet were exalted by —. 80: 17.

— is a widely read Book. 27: 2.

— is a Light and clear Book guiding along the paths of peace. 5: 16, 17.

Falsehood shall never approach —. 41: 43.

Every one desiring to go straight can benefit from —. 81: 29.

— is a Book honoured and well guarded. 85: 22, 23.

— is decisive and definite. 86: 14, 15.

— comprises all basic commandments. 98: 3, 4.

— is Divinely safeguarded. 15: 10.

— discourages seeking regulation of everything by Divine command. 5: 102.

— is free from all doubt. 2: 3.

— is a guide for the righteous. 2: 3.

— is healing. 10: 58; 17: 83; 41: 45.

— expounds all that is needed by mankind for complete fulfilment of life and furnishes guidance and is a mercy for those who submit. 10: 58; 16: 90.

— enjoins worship of Allah. 2: 22.

The wisdom comprehended in — is inexhaustible. 18: 110; 31: 28.

— is the most effective instrument for propagating the truth. 25: 53.

— is peerless and cannot be matched. 2: 24; 10: 39; 11: 14, 15; 17: 89; 52: 35.

— was revealed on a blessed night. 44: 4; 97: 2—6.

— is free from discrepancies. 4: 83.

Seeking refuge with Allah against evil promptings before recitation of —. 16: 99.

QURAN, PROPHECIES IN THE HOLY

Holy Prophet's emigration from Mecca and his return to it. 17: 81; 28: 86.

Battle of Badr and victory for Muslims. 30: 6; 79: 7.

Battle of Ahzab. 38: 12; 54: 46; 79: 8.

Arab nations accepting Islam. 56: 4.

Byzantines overpowering the Persians and then being overpowered by Muslims. 30: 3—4.

Jews occupying Palestine. 17: 105.

Muslims reoccupying Palestine. 21: 106—107.

Appearance of Gog and Magog and events thereafter. 21: 97—105.

Opening of Suez and Panama canals. 55: 20, 21; 82: 4.

Huge ships floating on seas. 55: 25.

Jews, abasement of 3: 113; 7: 168.

People of the Book accepting Islam. 3: 200.

Transportation, development of means of 16: 9; 36: 43; 81: 5.

Blasting off of mountains i.e. great kingdoms. 79: 10; 77: 11.

Cosmic rays and nuclear bombs. 44: 11; 55: 36.

Animals being gathered in zoological gardens. 81: 6.

Peoples and nations coming together. 81: 8.

Criminal justice, administration of 81: 9.

Books, increase in publication of 81: 11.

Geology, minerology and astronomy, progress of 81: 12; 84: 5.

Earth, reaching out of to other planets. 84: 4.

Tombs being laid open. 82: 5.

Sin, increase of 81: 13.

Atheism, spread of 82: 7—9; 114: 5, 6.

Islam, rise of after decline 32: 6; 81: 19.

Wars and earthquakes. 99: 2.

Earth revealing its treasures. 99: 3.

Latter Days, signs of 81: 3—17.

Discovery of new countries and continents. 84: 4.
Earth yielding up its hidden treasures. 84: 5.
Safeguarding of Quran by Allah. 15: 10.
Spread of Islam after emigration. 17: 81, 82.
World wars and nations being gathered together. 18: 100.
Destruction of atomic powers. 55: 32; 111: 2.

RECORDING ANGELS
— know all actions of man. 82: 11—13.

REPENTANCE
— wins Allah's forgiveness and mercy. 2: 161.
— is possible at all times. 3: 90.
Seeking forgiveness of Allah along with —. 11: 4.
Allah forgives all sins. 39: 54.
— should be sincere. 66: 9.
Allah accepts true —. 9: 104; 42: 26.
— converts evil propensities into good ones. 25: 71.
Doing good after — is true —. 25: 72.
Whose — is accepted. 4: 18; 16: 120.
Whose — is not accepted. 4: 19.

RESURRECTION DAY (QUIY'AMAT)
There is no doubt about —. 4: 88.
— also designated the Hour. 20: 16.
— of each individual. 19: 96.
— also signifies day of downfall or ruin. 17: 52; 40: 60; 54: 2; 70: 43—45.

RESURRECTION AFTER DEATH
— is a certainty. 2: 49; 22: 8; 23: 116; 58: 19.
Spiritual resurrection. 2: 57, 74, 261; 6: 37; 8: 25; 30: 51; 41: 40.

RESURRECTION OF THE DEAD
Physically dead cannot be brought back to life on earth. 21: 96; 23: 101; 36: 32; 39: 43.
— also signifies revival of a people. 7: 58.
Prophets revive the spiritually dead and not the physically dead. 6: 37; 8: 25.
Jesus gave life to the spiritually dead. 5: 111.

RETALIATION, LAW OF (QUAS'AS)
— safeguards human life. 2: 179, 180.

REVELATION
— vouchsafed to Prophets as well as others. 4: 164, 165; 5: 112; 20: 39; 28: 8.
— is a universal experience. 4: 165; 10: 48; 35: 25; 40: 79.
— is received in the language of the recipient. 14: 5.
—, forms of 42: 52.
— descends upon the heart. 2: 98; 26: 193—195; 53: 11, 12.
— furnishes guidance and promotes righteousness. 2: 39; 7: 36; 14: 2; 17: 83; 41: 45; 47: 3.
No spiritual life without —. 21: 31.
— is received by chosen servants of Allah. 16: 3.
— stimulates reflection. 16: 45.
— also signifies inspiration. 16: 69.

REWARDS AND PUNISHMENTS
Basis of —. 4: 41, 79, 80; 6: 161.

RIBA (INTEREST)
— is forbidden. 2: 276, 277, 279— 281; 3: 131; 30: 40.
Prohibition of —. 2: 276, 277, 279; 3: 131.
— does not promote true prosperity. 30: 40.
Warning of evil consequences of taking —. 2: 280.

RIGHTEOUSNESS (TAQWA)
—, attainment of, through worship of Allah. 2: 22.
—, what constitutes. 2: 178.
Killing of evil desires by piety and —. 2: 55.

RIGHTS OF MANKIND
— and obligations in respect thereof. 4: 37—41; 17: 24—40; 25: 64—73.

ROCK, DWELLERS OF THE
Punishment of —. 15: 81—85.

SABA, PEOPLE OF
Sign for the —. 34: 16—22.

SABA, QUEEN OF
— and Solomon. 27: 23—45.

SABBATH
Observance and violation of — by the Jews. 2: 66, 67; 4: 48, 155; 7: 164; 16: 125.

SACRIFICE
—, rites of, appointed for every people. 22: 35.
— should be offered to Allah alone. 22: 35.
Flesh or blood of sacrificed animal does not reach Allah but it is the spirit inspiring the sacrifice that reaches Him. 22: 38.

SAFA AND MARWA
— are the Signs of Allah. 2: 159.

SALA'T (See under WORSHIP)

SALIH, PROPHET
— was sent to the people of Thamud. 7: 74; 11: 62; 27: 46.
Name of —'s people was Asaha'bul Hijir. 15: 81.
— admonished his people to ask forgiveness of Allah. 11: 62.
Nine mischief-mongers in —'s town. 27: 49.
Plan to kill — at night. 27: 50.
Sign of she-camel for the people of —. 7: 74; 11: 65; 26: 156.
People of — hamstrung the she-camel. 7: 78; 26: 158.
People of — punished for their transgression. 7: 79, 80; 11: 68.
—'s people accused him of being bewitched, or working on behalf of someone else. 26: 154.
Disbelieving in — was to reject all prophets. 26: 142; 54: 24.

SALVATION
Promise of — for the righteous. 2: 6; 19: 73.
Person receiving — is loved by Allah and is at peace. 3: 32; 89: 30, 31.
— through prayer. 2: 187.
— from evil. 8: 30.
— through purification of soul. 91: 10.
— through seeking forgiveness and following guidance. 3: 136; 39: 54—56.
— is everlasting. 11: 109; 18: 109; 95: 7.
Belief in all revealed Books is necessary for —. 2:5.

SAMIRI
— produced a calf for worship when Moses had gone to the Mount. 20: 89.
Moses questioned — about his conduct. 20: 96.

— had turned away from obedience. 20: 97.
Punishment of —. 20: 98.

SATAN
— has no power over those who believe and put their trust in Allah. 16: 100.
— has power only over those who make friends with him and set up equals to Allah. 15: 43; 16: 101.
— had no connection with creation of universe. 18: 52.
— watches man but man does not perceive him. 7: 28.
— is the declared enemy of man. 17: 54; 25: 30; 35: 7; 36: 61; 43: 63.
— caused Adam to slip. 2: 37; 7: 21—23.
— has a fiery temperament. 7: 13.
— is an evil companion. 4: 39.
— was granted respite. 7: 15, 16.
— was abased. 7: 14.
— lies in wait for people to persuade them to abuse Divine bounties. 7: 17, 18.
— prompts people to evil practices. 4: 120, 121.
— makes false promises. 14: 23.
— incites unbelievers to disobedience. 19: 84.
— misleads his friends through inspiring them with fear. 3: 176.
— places obstacles in the way of Prophets. 22: 53, 54.
— is prototype of all wicked persons. 2: 103; 38: 42; 43: 37.
— should be shunned. 2: 169.
— has recourse to futile devices. 4: 77.
How to guard oneself against —. 7: 201, 202.
— has no power of his own but takes advantage of people's weaknesses. 14: 23; 15: 43.
— was rejected and cast away by Allah. 15: 35, 36.
Whoever makes friends with — is bound to be led astray. 22: 5.

SAUL (KING TALUT)
— appointed king. 2: 248.
Companions of — were put to test by means of the river. 2: 250.

SCANDAL MONGERING
Prohibition of —. 24: 24—27.

SEAS; THE CONFLUENCE OF TWO
— means the end of Mosaic dis-

pensation and the beginning of
Islamic dispensation. 18: 61.

SERVANTS OF GRACIOUS ALLAH
— walk on earth in dignified manner.
25: 64.
— say 'peace' when addressed by
the ignorant. 25: 64.
— pass their nights in worship of
Allah. 25: 65.
— beseech Allah to avert the punishment. 25: 66.
— are neither niggardly nor extravagant but are moderate in spending. 25: 66.
— do not associate partners with
Allah nor kill any person unlawfully nor commit adultery or
fornication. 25: 69.
— do not bear false witness. 25: 73.
Reward of —. 25: 76, 77.

SHU'AIB, PROPHET
— was sent to Midian tribes. 7: 86;
11: 85; 29: 37.
— admonished his people to give full
measure and full weight. 7: 86;
11: 85, 86.
—'s people threatened to expel him
from his town. 7: 89.
—'s people seized by earthquake. 7:
92; 11: 95, 96.

SLANDER
Prohibition of —. 24: 5, 24—27;
104: 2.

SLAVES
—, procuring freedom of, is highly
meritorious. 2: 178; 4: 93; 5: 90;
9: 61; 90: 14.

SOLOMON (PROPHET SULAIMAN)
— was heir of David. 27: 17.
— was favoured with special knowledge by Allah. 21: 80; 27: 16.
— was bestowed everything by Allah.
27: 17.
Propaganda of rebels against —. 2:
103.
Winds were subjected to — (i.e. his
people carried on trade in sailing
boats). 21: 82; 34: 13; 38: 37.
Deep-water divers in —'s service.
21: 83.
Jinn (i.e. gentile artisans) made
palaces, statues, large cooking
vessels, and reservoirs for —. 34:
13, 14.

Jinn (i.e. expert workmen, builders
and divers) owed allegiance to —.
27: 40; 38: 38.
Satans (i.e. giants and slaves) who
worked for him were in fetters.
38: 38, 39.
—'s factories manufactured articles
from molten copper. 34: 13.
Three divisions of —'s army, (gentiles,
Jews and saintly people). 27: 18.
— was taught the language of the
sacred scriptures. 27: 17.
—'s army moved to the valley of
Naml. 27: 19.
— invited Queen of Saba to submit.
27: 29—32.
Queen of Saba sent gifts to —. 27: 36.
— orders a throne better than that
of Queen of Saba. 27: 39—42.
Queen of Saba goes to — and believes
in Allah. 27: 43—45.
—'s love for noble steeds. 38: 32—34.
— saw in a vision an incapable son
as his successor. 38: 35.
—'s death and decline of his power
at the hands of his incapable
successor. 34: 15.
— was diligent in turning to Allah.
38: 31.
— was bestowed a high rank in the
eyes of Allah. 38: 41.

SONSHIP OF GOD
Doctrine of — condemned. 2: 117;
6: 101, 102; 10: 69; 18: 5, 6; 19:
36; 19: 91—93; 23: 92; 37: 150—
160; 39: 5; 112: 2—4.

SOUL-HUMAN (RUH)
— is Allah's creation. 17: 86.
—, purification of, is salvation. 91: 10.

SPIRIT
— means mercy from Allah. 4: 172.
Ruh means angel. 19: 18.
Faithful —. 26: 194.
— at rest. 89: 28—31.
Self-accusing —. 75: 3.
God breathes His spirit into man i.e.
man can receive the revelation.
15: 30; 21: 92; 32: 10; 38: 73.

STATE
International relations. 16: 93, 95;
60: 9, 10.
Government by consultation. 3: 160;
42: 39.
Best fitted persons to be placed in
authority. 4: 59.

Justice as basis of rule. 4: 59, 106—
108, 136; 5: 9; 16: 91; 38: 27;
42: 16.
Obedience to authority. 4: 60.
War, obligatory or permissible 2:
191—194; 4: 76; 8: 40; 22: 40—42.
Peace. 8: 56—64; 9: 1—4.

STEADFASTNESS
— in seeking help of Allah enjoined
on believers. 2: 154.
Allah is with those who show —. 2:
154.
Trials of fear, hunger and loss of
wealth and lives and fruits but
good news for the patient. 2: 156.
Truly patient persons. 2: 157.

STRAIGHT PATH
Prayer for —. 1: 6.
Prophet Muhammad followed the —.
6: 162; 36: 5; 43: 44.
Prophet Muhammad guides to the —.
14: 2, 3; 23: 74, 75; 42: 53.
Quran guides to the — 5: 17.

SUN, THE
— radiates light and the moon
reflects lustre and each has stages
determined for it. 10: 6; 25: 62.
— and moon are made subservient
and glide along their respective
orbits. 7: 55; 21: 34.
Harmony of spheres illumined by —
and moon. 71: 16.
Eclipse of — and moon, significance
of. 75: 8, 10.
— determining shadow, significance
of. 25: 46, 47.
—, no object of worship. 41: 38.

SWINE, FLESH OF
Unlawful to eat —. 2: 174; 5: 4; 6:
146; 16: 116.

TABLET, WELL-PRESERVED
Holy Quran contained in —. 85: 23.

TABLETS OF MOSES
— contained directions on all matters. 7: 146.
— thrown aside by Moses in his
wrath and picked up by him
when his wrath subsided. 7: 151,
155.

TABUK; THE EXPEDITION TO
Muslims enjoined to march forth
to —. 9: 41.
Length of the journey to —. 9: 42.

TAGHOUT
— are transgressors who exceed all
bounds and must be shunned. 2:
257, 258; 4: 52, 61, 77; 5: 61; 16:
37; 39: 18.

TAYAMMUM (Symbolic Ablution)
—, when permissible. 4: 44; 5: 7.

THEFT
Punishment for —. 5: 39.

TORAH
— was revealed to Moses, containing
guidance and light and all necessary instructions for Beni Israel.
3: 4; 5: 45; 6: 155; 23: 50; 28: 44;
37: 118.
Mosaic prophets decided according
to —. 5: 45.
Prophecies concerning the Holy Prophet of Islam in —. 7: 158; 48: 30.
Those who profess belief in — but
do not carry out its commandments. 62: 6.
Promise of ample provision to believers in — if they had believed in
Quran. 5: 67.
People of — invited to believe in the
Holy Prophet. 5: 16, 17, 20.
Perversion of —. 2: 80; 3: 79; 5: 14,
16.

TOWNS; MOTHER OF
(UMMAL QURA'A)
Mecca as —. 6: 93.

TRADE
— is lawful. 2: 276; 4: 30.
— should not divert attention from
Prayer or remembrance of Allah.
9: 24; 24: 38; 62: 12.
— which is most profitable. 61: 11—
14; 35: 30, 31.
Taking error in exchange for guidance
is wasteful —. 2: 17.

TREATIES 9: 4, 7, 12, 13.

TRINITY
—, condemnation of. 4: 172; 5: 74.

TRUMPET
Blowing of —. 6: 74; 18: 100; 20:
103; 23: 102; 27: 88; 36: 52; 39:
69; 50: 21; 69: 14; 78: 19.

UHAD
Battle of —. 3: 122, 123.
Enemy returned to Mecca frustrated.
3: 128.

— forbidden during period of pilgrimage. 2: 198.
—, object of. 2: 224.

(v) WAITING PERIOD (IDDAT) BEFORE REMARRIAGE
—, observance of. 65: 2.
— for widow. 2: 235.
— for a divorced woman. 2: 229.
— for a pregnant woman. 65: 5.
— for women who do not menstruate. 65: 5.

(vi) DIVORCE
Procedure for —. 2: 230, 231.
Revocable —. 2: 232.
Irrevocable —; 2: 231.
Arrangements concerning children after —. 2: 234.

(vii) PERIOD OF GIVING SUCK
— is two years. 2: 234.

(viii) VOWING ABSTINENCE FROM WIVES, (ILLA)
Maximum period of — is four months after which there must be reconciliation or divorce. 2: 227, 228.

WORM OF THE EARTH (DABBATUL ARZ)
— meaning one following low desires. 34: 15.
— meaning germs of plague. 27: 83.

WORSHIP
Object of —. 1: 5; 2: 22.

(i) SALAT; (NIMAZ OR OBLIGATORY PRAYER)
Obligatory —. 4: 104; 24: 57.
Ablution for —. 5: 7.
Prohibition against offering — when not in full control of senses or in state of impurity. 4: 44.
Postures of —. 22: 27.
Times of —. 2: 239; 4: 104; 11: 115; 17: 79; 30: 18, 19.
Observance of —. 2: 44, 111, 278; 5: 56; 8: 4; 9: 71; 27: 4; 31: 5.

Watching over —. 2: 239.
—, when it may be shortened. 4: 102.
—, form of, in face of the enemy. 4: 103.
Friday —. 62: 10—12.
Tahajjud (prayer before dawn). 5: 16—19; 17: 80; 32: 17; 73: 2—9.
— safeguards against misconduct. 29: 46.
—, constancy in. 70: 24.
—, neglect of, condemned. 107: 5—7.
Exhorting others to performance of —. 20: 133.
Offering — in congregation. 2: 44.
Offering — with propriety and in a state of purity. 4: 44; 7: 32.
Allah provides for those who are constant in —. 20: 133.

(ii) FASTING
— prescribed during month of Ramadhan. 2: 184—186.
Exemption from —. 2: 186.
Expiation for —. 2: 185.

(iii) PILGRIMAGE (HAJJ)
— is obligatory upon every Muslim who can afford the journey. 3: 98.
Directions concerning —. 2: 197—204; 5: 2, 3.
Punishment for those who hinder people from the Sacred Mosque. 22: 26.
Abraham was commanded to proclaim — unto mankind. 22: 28.
Object of —. 22: 29—34.

(iv) ZAKAT (CAPITAL LEVY)
— prescribed. 2: 111; 22: 79; 24: 57; 73: 21.
—, objects of. 9: 60.
—, disbursement of. 9: 60.

ZACHARIAH
Allah's favour bestowed upon —. 3: 39—42; 19: 3—12.

ZAKAT — SEE UNDER "WORSHIP"

673